LONGMAN BIOGRAPHICAL DIRECTORY OF DECISION-MAKERS IN RUSSIA AND THE SUCCESSOR STATES

LONGMAN BIOGRAPHICAL DIRECTORY OF DECISION-MAKERS IN RUSSIA AND THE SUCCESSOR STATES

Edited by
Martin McCauley

LONGMAN BIOGRAPHICAL DIRECTORY OF DECISION-MAKERS
IN RUSSIA AND THE SUCCESSOR STATES

Published by Longman Group UK Limited, Westgate House,
The High, Harlow, Essex CM20 1YR, United Kingdom

Distributed exclusively in the United States and Canada
By Gale Research Inc., 835 Penobscot Building, Detroit,
Michigan 48226, USA

ISBN 0–582–20999–4

DPA
DIRECTORY PUBLISHERS
ASSOCIATION

A catalogue record for this publication is available from the British Library

Typesetting by The Midlands Book Typesetting Company, Loughborough
Printed in Great Britain by BPCC Wheatons Ltd, Exeter.

CONTENTS

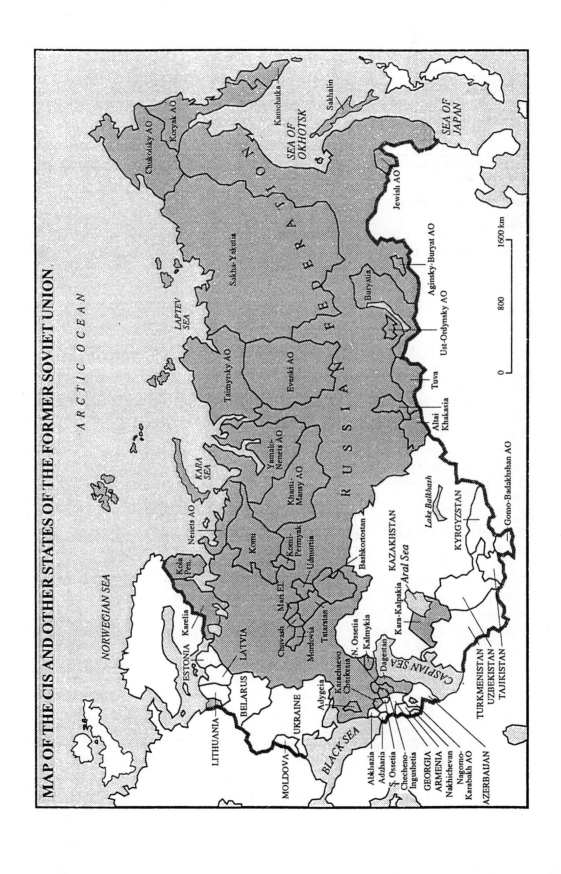

MAP OF THE CIS AND OTHER STATES OF THE FORMER SOVIET UNION

ARCTIC OCEAN

NORWEGIAN SEA

LAPTEV SEA

KARA SEA

SEA OF OKHOTSK

SEA OF JAPAN

RUSSIAN FEDERATION

Chukotsky AO
Koryak AO
Kamchatka
Sakhalin
Jewish AO
Sakha-Yakutia
Taimyrsky AO
Evenki AO
Buryatia
Aginsky-Buryat AO
Ust-Ordynsky AO
Tuva
Altai
Khakasia
Yamalo-Nenets AO
Khanti-Mansy AO
Nenets AO
Komi
Komi-Permyak
Udmurtia
Bashkortostan
Kola Pen.
Karelia
Chuvash
Mari El
Mordovia
Tatarstan
N. Ossetia
Kalmykia
Dagestan
Adygeia
Karachaevo Cherkesia

ESTONIA
LATVIA
LITHUANIA
BELARUS
UKRAINE
MOLDOVA

BLACK SEA
CASPIAN SEA
Aral Sea
Lake Balkhash

KAZAKHSTAN
Kara-Kalpakia
KYRGYZSTAN
Gorno-Badakhshan AO
TURKMENISTAN
UZBEKISTAN
TAJIKISTAN

Abkhazia
Adzharia
S. Ossetia
Checheno-Ingushetia
GEORGIA
ARMENIA
Nakhichevan
Nagorno-Karabakh AO
AZERBAIJAN

0   800   1600 km

INTRODUCTION

This biographical directory concentrates on the new decision-making élites in Russia and the other successor states to the Soviet Union, with a particular focus on Russia, Ukraine and Belarus. The principle of selection was to cover as far as possible the main political élites, government, the economy, military and security, media, political parties and movements and religion. A detailed listing of the entries under their relevant heading is provided in the pages immediately following. This is not a conventional *Who's Who*. It provides assessments of most of the entries and some of the judgements may be controversial. They are value judgements and the editor would welcome corrections and additions for the second edition. His fax number is 081 445 2236. In some cases candidates for inclusion have been excluded because of lack of reliable and balanced information. Those included are viewed as members of the new élites, and many of those who were prominent under communist rule have been omitted. Almost all the information was collected on the spot, for which thanks are due to Aleksandr Barsenkov, Valery Koretsky and Aleksandr Ostapenko. Andrew Wilson is to be thanked for his efforts in Ukraine, Charles King in Moldova and Vera Rich in Belarus.

A quick glance through the biographies will reveal how well the old nomenclature is faring. The sad fate of the Popular Front in Azerbaijan is testimony to the failure of the new political élite to consolidate itself in power. Its task was formidable. It set out to replace the old élites with its own nominees, many of whom had no experience of administration, as a conscious attempt to bring in "socially marginal" individuals and weld a new élite out of them. The Popular Front collapsed and the old nomenclature, through the person of Geidar (also Heidar) Aliev, recaptured power. However the personality of Colonel Suret Guseinov (also Huseinov) is difficult to gauge and he may not permit the old guard to slip comfortably back into their old seats.

The other state in which the former communists have swept back to power is, astonishingly, Lithuania. Algirdas Brazauskas and his Lithuanian Democratic Labour Party (the ex-Communist Party) scored startling gains in the democratic elections in late 1992, and later he was elected President by a handsome margin. The voters of Lithuania thereby rejected the man who had symbolized the independence struggle, Vytautas Landsbergis, and *Sajudis*, the movement which effected independence. On the other hand, Estonian voters failed to return even one ex-communist to parliament in their democratic elections, and Latvia is somewhere in the middle. Hence the new élites in the Baltic States do not conform to a uniform pattern.

In Kazakhstan and Central Asia the old élite is the new élite. This is especially so in Tajikistan where a bloody civil war has been raging between ex-communists and Islamic forces. Helped by the Russian army the old guard has been winning but the long-term outlook is cloudy. The most skilful politician in the region is President Nursultan Nazarbaev who has to perform a balancing act between Kazakhs and non-Kazakhs in the country and between Russia, the east and the west. In Uzbekistan, President Karimov rules with renewed vigour, ever mindful of the potential threat of Islamic radicalism. In Kyrgyzstan, President Akaev provides brave, courageous leadership while trying to retain Russians and other Europeans who are so valuable to the future development of his country. In Turkmenistan a Turkish face has been given to the old ex-communist élite. Oil and gas has made it possible to subsidize enterprises and prevent the rise of social tension.

Political tension is high in Ukraine and Belarus with the old élites proving very resilient. In Russia the most striking new élite are the pro-market economists around President Yeltsin. There is a network which stretches back to the Andropov years now dominating in Moscow, and another group which is new to the seat of power are the presidential advisers and the members of the presidential Council. Yeltsin's apparatus is, not surprisingly, from the old élites, with a striking number from Ekaterinburg, and the media provide new faces. Something which is also striking is the failure of the new political parties and movements to gel and develop into parties in the Western sense, but this is partly due to the fact that there have been no democratic elections in Russia since the failed coup of August 1991. Arguably only democratic elections can forge coalitions which give birth to Western-style political parties. Russian politics, indeed politics in all the states of the former Soviet Union, is personal politics with a dominant leader and, normally, a small number of followers. There is as yet no sense of collective responsibility, indeed personal responsibility, in politics. The way up is not through a party or movement but through new ideas and garnering personal supporters. Democracy is still a tender plant.

Russia in some ways is at the back of the queue. It is the only state which has not had elections since August 1991 and the consequences of this have been dire. Lack of understanding of institutional politics allowed a window of opportunity to fashion a new constitutional parliament, the constitutional Court, to close. The constitutional conflict between parliament and the President rages through these pages. The membership of the Constitutional Court is conservative, with radical, democratic lawyers elsewhere in the apparatus. Only a minority of the Russian governors are in favour of privatization, the market and democracy, and the percentage of Presidents, Prime Ministers and Speakers of parliament in the republics within Russia is even lower.

Looking at the élites in this book one may divide them into three groups: the old (communist) élite; the new communist élite (those who were in the middle reaches of the communist apparatus in 1991); and the new élite, those who have suddenly risen to positions of influence. President Yeltsin is a member of the old communist élite, and was a major political actor under communism. An example of the new communist élite would be Sergei Shakhrai. Egor Gaidar and Boris Fedorov, both leading economists, are representatives of the new élite which, according to the above, is in favour of democracy and a market economy.

However, the political odyssey of Ruslan Imranovich Khasbulatov, the Speaker of the Russian parliament, gives food for thought. He is clearly a member of the new élite, but is very hostile to the goals of the Yeltsin administration and has forged coalitions with conservatives, communists and nationalists. As an outsider, a Chechen and a Muslim, he might have been expected to stay with Yeltsin after the defeat of the coup in August 1991, and this suggests a different way of viewing the élites in this directory. They may be divided into conservative communists, neo-conservatives, centrists, radicals and far left radicals. The conservative communists are the old élite. The neo-conservatives, into which framework Khasbulatov fits, consist of the old communist and new communist élites and the Russian nationalists. The centrists are mostly industrialists, trying to manage the market to benefit themselves. These pages reveal the many who appeared from 1989 to 1990 to be radicals but who have ended up as neo-conservatives, of which Vladimir Isakov, the organizing mind behind the Russian Unity bloc, in the Russian Congress of People's Deputies, is just one example.

A note on orthography is needed. Until August 1991 all names and locations in the Soviet Union were transliterated from the Russian spelling, but now the new states have reverted to their own languages and hence the orthography is often quite different. Azerbaidzhan has become Azerbaijan after the adoption of Turkish as the official language; Tadzhikistan is now Tajikistan; Kirgizia is Kyrgyzstan; Moldavia is Russian and Moldova is Romanian, hence the name has not changed; and Belorussia is now Belarus. Before August 1991 all republics, except the RSFSR, were Soviet Socialist Republics (SSR). Hence the full title of Ukraine, for instance, was Ukrainian SSR; Georgia, Georgian SSR; etc. In Russian, "e" is preceded by a phonetic "y". Names which begin in Russian with E have been transliterated without the phonetic Y, hence Egor, Erin, Efimov and Eromenko. There is one exception to this, Yeltsin. This has been adopted because it is widely used in the English-speaking world.

The adjectives denoting these new states are as follows: Tajik; Azeri for the citizen and Azerbaijani for the state; Kyrgyz for the state, the citizen, language; Moldovan for the state, the citizen, language (or Romanian); Belarusian for the state, language, citizens (previously Belorussian or Byelorussian). In the Russian Federation, the new names of the republics have been used: e.g. Sakha (Yakutia). Primorsky *krai*, on the Pacific with its capital Vladivostok, appears as Maritime *krai*. In June 1993 it declared itself a republic within Russia, as has Sverdlovsk (Ekaterinburg) *oblast*. The Chukotka (Chukchi) autonomous *okrug* declared itself an *oblast* and separated from Magadan *oblast* and this was judged constitutional by the Russian Constitutional Court in June 1993. This last change has not been included, nor have the claims to republican status by the other two.

The official name of the successor state to the RSFSR is Russia-Russian Federation and these terms have been used interchangeably in the directory. The goal for the information in the biographies was the spring of 1993, but in some cases it has proved possible to add additional information up to July 1993.

Over 200 more biographies of Russian MPs will be found in Martin McCauley (ed.), *Directory of Russian MPs: People's Deputies of the Supreme Soviet of Russia-Russian Federation* (Longman 1992).

Martin McCauley
July 1993

NATIONAL TERRITORIAL SUB-DIVISIONS
OF RUSSIA-RUSSIAN FEDERATION

Until December 1990 the national territorial sub-divisions of the Russian Federation consisted of 16 autonomous republics (ASSR), five autonomous *oblasts* and 10 autonomous *okrugs*. As a result of the declarations of sovereignty of the autonomous territories (referred to on occasion as the "parade of sovereignty"), the formal status of all the autonomous republics and four of the autonomous *oblasts* changed. Most of the autonomous republics and *oblasts* changed their names, reverting to their own language. Amendments were made to the Constitution of the RSFSR on December 15, 1990, deleting the word "autonomous" before "republic". Hence the 16 autonomous republics (ASSR) of the Russian Federation simply became "republics forming part of the Russian Federation".

On July 3, 1991 the Russian Supreme Soviet passed decrees constituting republics of four of the five autonomous *oblasts* (Adygei, Gorno-Altai, Karachai-Cherkess and Khakas), thus freeing them from the jurisdiction of the *krais* on whose territory they had previously been. This increased the number of republics within the Russian Federation to 20, which rose further to 21 on June 4, 1992 when the Russian Supreme Soviet promulgated a law dividing the Chechen-Ingush republic into separate Chechen and Ingush republics. The only autonomous *oblast* whose status has not changed is the Jewish AO. The position of the autonomous *okrugs* has not so far changed constitutionally. However, in June 1993 the Russian Constitutional Court acknowledged the legality of the declaration of the Chukotka (Chukchi) autonomous *okrug*'s withdrawal from Magadan *oblast*. The new entity became known as the Chukotka (Chukchi) *oblast*.

Official titles of the republics
Republic of Adygea or Adygea
Republic of Altai
Republic of Bashkortostan or Bashkortostan
Republic of Buryatia
Chechen Republic or Chechnia or Chechnya
Chuvash Republic
Republic of Dagestan
Ingush Republic or Ingushetia
Kabardino-Balkar Republic
Republic of Kalmykia or Khalmg Tangch
Karachai-Cherkess Republic
Republic of Karelia
Republic of Khakasia
Republic of Komi

Mari Republic or Republic of Mari El
Mordovian Republic
North Ossetian Republic
Republic of Sakha (Yakutia)
Republic of Tatar or Tatarstan
Republic of Tuva
Udmurt Republic

Russian oblasts *which have been renamed*
(*old name on left, new name on right*)

Gorky	Nizhny Novgorod
Kalinin	Tver
Kuibyshev	Samara

Those in process of being renamed

| Kirov | Vyatka |

Cities which have been renamed

Gorky	Nizhny Novgorod
Kalinin	Tver
Kuibyshev	Samara
Leningrad	St Petersburg
Ordzhonikidze	Vladikavkaz
Sverdlovsk	Ekaterinburg

Kyrgyzstan

| Frunze | Bishkek |

GLOSSARY

AO	Autonomous *Oblast*.
ASSR	Autonomous Soviet Socialist Republic; an administrative unit of a republic which was populated by a nationality other than the titular nationality: e.g. the Tatars made up the Tatar ASSR in the RSFSR. Although they had their own government they were ruled from the titular nationality's capital; in the Tatars' case, from Moscow. Hence autonomous here did not mean independent.
collective farm	members farm the land as a co-operative, but in reality have little say over what was produced as this was laid down in the annual state plan. A basic guaranteed wage was only introduced in 1966. Operatives were technically not workers but co-operative members.
congress	most important meeting of Party, soviet, trade union or other organization; at a congress the Party reviewed its past record and laid down goals for the future; a new Central Committee was elected and it in turn elected a new secretariat and Politburo.
CPSU	Communist Party of the Soviet Union; founded in 1898 as Russian Social Democratic Labour Party; split into Bolsheviks and Mensheviks in 1903; renamed all-Russian Communist Party (Bolsheviks) in 1918; the all-Union Communist Party (Bolsheviks) in 1925; and the Communist Party of the Soviet Union in 1952.
Gosplan	state planning commission of the USSR Council of Ministers; was responsible for drafting economic plans and checking their implementation.
khozraschet	economic or regional self accounting; administrative body (*oblast*, etc.) which acquired limited right to regulate economic activity on its territory; more taxes paid into its budget; it gained more control over all-Union (USSR-wide) and republican enterprises.
Komsomol	communist union of youth; CPSU youth movement.

krai	administrative sub-division of a republic; differs from an *oblast* in that it contains on its territory another nationality, e.g. Krasnodar *krai* contains the Adygei autonomous *oblast*.
national state formation	autonomous *oblast*, *raion*, *okrug*.
national territorial district	Soviet of Nationalities constituency.
nomenclature or *nomenklatura*	list of top state and Party posts filled by Party nominees; those who occupied the posts, in essence the élite of the USSR. As a rule all were members of the CPSU.
obkom	*oblast* Party committee.
oblast	administrative sub-division of a republic.
okrug	administrative sub-division of an *oblast*; less significant than a *raion*. Always inhabited by a small nation.
party	party other than the Communist Party of the Soviet Union (CPSU).
Party	Communist Party of the Soviet Union (CPSU); upper case always refers to it. Each republic, except the RSFSR until 1990, had its own Communist Party. However, these were not independent but fused into the CPSU. The instrument for effecting this was democratic centralism. Members of, for example, the Communist Party of Ukraine, were simultaneously members of the Communist Party of the Soviet Union.
Party Central Committee or CPSU Central Committee	this organization acted in the name of the Party congress when the latter was not in session; it consisted of all the important Party officials, government ministers, leading armed forces' personnel, key ambassadors, etc.
raion	administrative sub-division of an *oblast* or a city.
RSFSR	Russian Soviet Federated Socialist Republic; constitution adopted July 1918. When the USSR was formed in December 1922 the RSFSR became the largest republic and dominated the USSR. Its capital was Moscow and it formed its own Communist Party in 1990.
Russian parliament	consists of a super parliament, the Congress of People's Deputies, with nominally 1,068 members; and a standing parliament, the Supreme Soviet, composed of two houses, each nominally with 126 members, the Council (Soviet) of the Republic and the Council (Soviet) of Nationalities.

small nation	group of people inhabiting an autonomous *raion* or *okrug*, or may have no defined territory.
soviet	council, as in local government.
state farm	originally set up where there were few or no peasants and treated as a factory in the countryside. Operatives were classified as workers, paid better on average and received more social benefits.
Supreme Soviet	set up by the 1936 constitution, the USSR Supreme Soviet was bicameral, consisting of the Soviet of the Union and the Soviet of Nationalities. The number of deputies of the former was based on the adult (18-years-old) population, while the number of the latter was fixed; the houses were of equal status and often met in joint session. A parliament only in name, the key decisions were taken by the government and the Party, and the chairman of the Presidium of the USSR Supreme Soviet was often referred to as the president of the country although this word did not appear in the constitution. Each republic and ASSR had its own Supreme Soviet.
territorial district	constituency of the Council of the Republic.
USSR	Union of Soviet Socialist Republics.

LISTING OF ENTRIES BY STATE/TOPIC AREA

Law

DIRECTORY OF
DECISION-MAKERS IN RUSSIA
AND THE SUCCESSOR STATES

Abalkin, Leonid Ivanovich

Director of the Institute of Economics, Russian Academy of Sciences.

Born on May 5, 1930 in Moscow; Russian. He was a member of the CPSU from 1956 to 1991 (he was elected a member of the Party Central Committee in July 1990). In 1952 he graduated from the G. V. Plekhanov Institute of the National Economy, Moscow, and from 1952 he was assigned to the agricultural technical college in Gusev, Kaliningrad *oblast* as a lecturer and later deputy director. From 1958 to 1961 he was a postgraduate student at the Moscow State Institute of Economics and in 1962 successfully presented his candidate dissertation in economics on "The law of the planned proportionate development in the world socialist economic system" (PhD (Econ)).

In 1961 he was appointed an assistant, then senior lecturer, assistant professor (*dotsent*), and in 1966 head of department of the G. V. Plekhanov Institute of the National Economy, Moscow. In 1971 he successfully presented his doctoral dissertation in economics on "The role of the socialist state in the planned regulation of social production" (DSc (Econ)). In 1976 he was appointed professor, deputy head, and head of the department, Academy of Social Sciences, Party Central Committee. He was elected a member of the USSR Academy of Sciences.

He was an active supporter of *perestroika* from its inception. In 1986 he became director of the Institute of Economics, USSR Academy of Social Sciences and from 1988 to 1990 a member of the Presidium of the Academy. From June 1989 to December 1990 he was deputy chairman of the USSR Council of Ministers (Nikolai Ryzhkov was chairman) and chairman of the USSR state commission on economic reform. He resigned along with Ryzhkov to make way for Valentin Pavlov, and Abalkin is at present director of the Institute of Economics of the Russian Academy of Sciences.

His main publications are: *Political Economy and Economic Policy* (1970); *The Economic Laws of Socialism* (1971); *The Economic Mechanism of Developed Socialist Society* (1973); *Managerial Strategy* (1975); *The Foundations of the Economics of a Developed Socialist Society* (1975); and *The Dialectics of Socialist Economics* (1981). He has also published a volume of memoirs on his experiences in the Ryzhkov government, *A Lost Opportunity* (1991). Abalkin was never as radical as Shatalin, Yavlinsky and Gaidar in espousing the market mechanism. He lives in Moscow.

Abdulatipov, Ramazan Gadzhimuradovich

Speaker of the Council of Nationalities of the Supreme Soviet of the Russian Federation.

Born on August 4, 1946 in Dagestan ASSR into a large Avar family, whose father was a soldier during the Great Fatherland War (1941-45). He graduated from a medical institute and then from the faculty of history, Dagestan State

University. He was a member of the CPSU until August 1991 and was assigned to work in the *Komsomol* and Party agencies in Tyalatinsky *raion*.

In 1975 he became a postgraduate student in the faculty of philosophy, Leningrad State University, and in 1978 he successfully presented his candidate dissertation in philosophy on "Personality and national relations in developed socialist society" (PhD). He returned to Makhachkala and became a senior lecturer in a pedagogical institute, later becoming head of a sociological laboratory in Murmansk. In 1985 he successfully presented his doctoral dissertation in philosophy on "Nationality relations in developed socialist society" (spiritual and moral problems of their practice and development) (DLitt). In 1987 he returned to Dagestan as head of the philosophy department of a pedagogical institute. He took part in the founding of a centre for the study of public opinion of the Council of ministers, Dagestan ASSR, and was one of the founders of the Dagestan management school.

He was invited to work in the Party Central Committee, Moscow, and in December 1989, he became head of the sector of analysis and forecasting of the department of nationality relations, Party Central Committee and remained there until June 1990. In January 1990 he was nominated for election as an RSFSR people's deputy in the No. 93 Buinaksky national territorial district, Dagestan ASSR, by the collective of the Tsumilyukhsky state farm in Tlyaratinsky *raion* and won in the second round, polling 59.2% of the votes. His main opponent was M. O. Tolboev, who received 37.9% of the votes. Abdulatipov was elected a member of the RSFSR Supreme Soviet at the I Congress of People's Deputies (618 voted for, 305 against).

During the election campaign he advocated that a special economic strategy for Dagestan be developed and based on local climatic conditions, the development of traditional branches of the economy, the use of hydrotechnical and other resources. He believed that the food processing sector of agriculture should be developed to provide more employment, and that several new laws should be promulgated including the prohibition of territorial claims within the country, the free development of the traditions of each nationality and the dissolution of organizations and groups which propagate national enmity. He said at the I Congress that the attempt to solve all the problems of society at one stroke was the main defect of *perestroika*. He was elected Speaker of the Council of Nationalities, and was one of the six leaders who signed a letter expressing distrust of the policies of Boris Yeltsin when he was Speaker of the RSFSR Supreme Soviet. When Yeltsin became President Abdulatipov revealed his conservative side and opposed the rapid move to the market. He became an ally of Ruslan Khasbulatov when the latter succeeded Yeltsin as Speaker of the Supreme Soviet. He belonged to the centre right bloc in congress and parliament which attempted to impeach the President in March 1993, and in June 1993 he made some attempts to mediate between the Supreme Soviet and President and his supporters who were attempting to draft a constitution which would downgrade parliament.

Address: 103274 Moscow, Krasnopresnenskaya nab., d. 2, Dom Sovetov; *telephone*: Moscow 205 61 71; 205 44 21.

Aboimov, Ivan Petrovich

Russian Ambassador to Hungary.

Born on November 6, 1936 in the village of Zarechnoe, Tashla *raion*, Orenburg *oblast*. Russian. He was a member of the CPSU until August 1991. He graduated from the Lipeja, Latvian SSR, State Pedagogical Institute in 1959, and was then appointed head of the propaganda department of the Lipeja city *Komsomol* committee. Later in 1959 he became a student on a training course of the Baltic Naval Air Force. From 1960 to 1963 he was again a *Komsomol* functionary, then he moved into Party work and from 1963 to 1969 was instructor in the ideology department, head of foreign policy, propaganda and foreign relations department, and deputy head of the propaganda department of the Central Committee, Communist Party of Latvia.

From 1969 to 1972 he attended the Higher Diplomatic School of the USSR Ministry of Foreign Affairs, and from 1972 to 1979 he was first secretary and counsellor of the USSR embassy in Budapest, Hungary. In 1979 he was appointed counsellor, and between 1979 and 1983 he was head of the fifth European department, USSR Ministry of Affairs, Moscow. From 1983 to 1984 he was assistant to Andrei Gromyko, USSR Minister of Foreign Affairs.

From 1984 to 1986 he was minister counsellor in the USSR embassy in Budapest, then in 1986 he returned to Moscow as chief of the personnel department of the USSR Ministry of Foreign Affairs and a member of the collegium of the ministry. From 1986 to 1988 he was head of the personnel and educational establishments department in the ministry, and in 1988 was appointed deputy USSR Minister of Foreign Affairs responsible for the socialist countries of eastern Europe. From 1989 to 1990 he was general secretary of the political consultative committee, Warsaw Treaty Organization. He was appointed USSR ambassador to Hungary in 1990 and in January 1992 he became ambassador of the Russian Federation to Hungary.

He was awarded the order of the Red Banner of Labour, the Hungarian order of Peace and Friendship, the honorary diploma of the Presidium of the Latvian Supreme Soviet, and three medals. He speaks Hungarian, English and German. He is married.

Address: Russian Embassy, Budapest VI, Bajza utca, 35; *telephone*: Budapest 132 0911; 134 2718; 131 8985.

Abramov, Sergei Aleksandrovich

Editor-in-chief of the newspaper *Semya* (Family).

Born on April 10, 1944 in Moscow; Russian. He was a member of the CPSU until August 1991. He graduated from the Institute for Highway Construction, Moscow, in 1966. From 1969 to 1972 he was senior editor of the department of literary life, *Literaturnaya gazeta*, and then was head of the department of science and technology, *Smena* magazine (1972-77), special correspondent of the department of literature and arts, *Pravda* (1977-86), and deputy editor-in-chief of the *Teatr* magazine (1986-87). He was appointed editor-in-chief of the weekly *Semya* in November 1987.

He is a prolific author and has published over 20 books, including *The Wall*. He speaks English and enjoys cycling. He is married with a son.

Address: 103803 Moscow, ul Chekhova, d. 3 kv. 10; *telephone*: Moscow 209 0651 (office); 264 1629 (home).

Achalov, Vladislav Alekseevich

Military Adviser of the Speaker of the Supreme Soviet of the Russian Federation. Head of the Centre for Analysis of the Supreme Soviet of the Russian Federation. Colonel-General since 1988.

Born on November 13, 1945 in the village of Atamysh, Arsk *raion*, Tatar ASSR (now Tatarstan), into a collective farmer's family. Russian. He graduated from the Kazan tank officers' technical school in 1966; the Military Academy of the Armoured Forces in 1973; the Military Academy of the General Staff in 1984. He received a higher military education and was a member of the CPSU from 1965 to August 1991.

After completing technical school he served in the Soviet forces in Germany (in the German Democratic Republic) as a tank platoon commander, then as a tank company commander. He was noticeable among young officers for his ambition, careerism and servility to superior officers. His professional knowledge and instructor's skills were good. He actively participated in the work of the Party organizations and he had close ties with political agencies. During his study at the academy, according to contemporaries, he deserted his family to further his career and married the daughter of the deputy head of the academy, the latter being an intimate front-line friend of the then deputy Minister of Defence, General of the Army Sergei Sokolov. The General, according to Achalov's colleagues, was present at the wedding reception and later always favoured Achalov. This fact became widely known in military circles and many officers disapproved of it. After graduating from the academy of armoured forces in 1973 Achalov was directed to the airborne troops where he was rapidly promoted to deputy commander and commander of a tank regiment, then deputy commander and commander of an airborne division.

He took part in military operations in Afghanistan against the *mujahidin* and the civilian population. Afterwards he often emphasized that he was proud to have participated in that destructive war and prided himself on belonging to the "Afghan fraternity". Gen. Achalov's record as an officer revealed him as possessing a sound operational-tactical and military-technical training. His further military career was in land forces, rather untypical for the Soviet army, and testifying to the young General's close ties with top military leaders. From

1984 to 1987 he was the first deputy commander, and commander of an army in the German Democratic Republic. In 1987 he was appointed Chief of Staff, first deputy commander of the Leningrad military district. In 1989 Lieut.-Gen. (later Col.-Gen.) Achalov was appointed commander of airborne troops. He was directly involved in planning and supervising the use of paratroops in domestic and inter-ethnic conflicts in the USSR. He was tough and resolute and did not flinch from adopting severe measures. His reaction to democratic movements and reformers in the army was extremely negative. He demonstrated communist convictions and participated in the work of the XXVIII Congress of the CPSU, where he was elected a member of the Party Central Committee in July 1990.

He was also elected a RSFSR people's deputy in March 1990 in the No. 708 Efremovsky territorial district, Tula *oblast*, and sided with the conservative bloc of communists and national patriots at congresses. He is a member of the deputies' group, *Otchizna* (native land). He is a member of the Supreme Soviet committee on inter-republican relations, regional policy and co-operation. At the end of 1990 he was appointed head of the Supreme Soviet analytical group on the forecasting and study of the situation in the regions of the Russian Federation.

On December 26, 1990 Gen. Achalov was promoted to the newly created post of deputy Minister of Defence of the USSR for states of emergency. He was directly responsible for the use of the army against the civilian population. He was one of the organizers and leaders of the bloody clashes in the Baltic. During the anti-constitutional putsch in August 1991 Gen. Achalov was a leading executor of the Emergency Committee's plans, took part in top sessions with the plotters, and supervised the movement and operations of troops in Moscow and other strategic regions of the country. He personally took part in planning the storming of the Russian White House. This aspect of his activities was brought to light in the press, including the military newspaper, *Krasnaya Zvezda*. He was dismissed from his post immediately after the failure of the coup, something which was warmly welcomed by many officers, including paratroops, among whom Achalov had never been popular.

The public prosecutor of the Russian Federation attempted to call Achalov to account for his activities in August 1991. People's deputies of the Russian Federation, who may have been unwilling to set a precedent, refused, by a majority, to lift Achalov's parliamentary immunity so as to permit him to be investigated. Achalov was transferred to the reserve in November 1991 by Order No. 01396 of the USSR Ministry of Defence.

In the summer of 1992 Ruslan Khasbulatov, the speaker of the Russian Supreme Soviet, appointed the dismissed General his personal military adviser, a move viewed by democrats as an indication of the growing intimacy between extremely conservative forces and the ambitious chairman of the Supreme Soviet. Achalov has proved himself capable of adapting to any new powerful authority and making a successful career out of it. On February 20, 1993 the Russian Union of Officers, a conservative grouping of officers in the Russian armed forces, held a conference in Moscow and called on the Russian Defence Minister, Gen. Pavel Grachev, to resign. Achalov was their nominee as the new Russian Defence Minister. At the conference Grachev was accused of "precipitating the collapse of the armed forces" and Marshal Evgeny Shaposhnikov, Commander-in-Chief of the Unified CIS Armed Forces was held responsible for the breakup of the Soviet Union. Achalov was thereby identified as a supporter of a strong, centralized Russian state and the bringing into being of a successor state to the Soviet Union which would be dominated by Russia.

In his spare time Achalov engages in very competitive hobbies which are in vogue. He does not speak any foreign language and has not been abroad as a member of an official delegation. He is married. He has been awarded three orders and nine medals.

Office address: Moscow, Supreme Soviet of the Russian Federation.

Adamishin, Anatoly Leonidovich

First deputy Minister of Foreign Affairs of the Russian Federation.

Born on October 11, 1934 in Kiev; Russian. He was a member of the CPSU until August 1991. In his first year at secondary school he was in the same class as Savely Kramarov and Igor Netto. He graduated from the Moscow State Institute of International Relations of the USSR Ministry of Foreign Affairs in 1957 and was one of the new appointments to the central apparatus of the Ministry in the first post-Molotov wave. In 1959 he was attaché, then third and second secretary in the USSR embassy in Italy until 1965. Then he was appointed second, then first secretary, counsellor and adviser in the first European department, USSR Ministry of Foreign Affairs until 1971. He was senior counsellor, head of the administration for the planning of foreign policy measures (1973-78), and then acquired one of the plum jobs, head of the first European department (1978-86).

During *perestroika* Adamishin was head of the USSR commission on UNESCO and became a deputy Foreign Minister under Eduard Shevardnadze in May 1986. In 1990 he was appointed ambassador extraordinary and plenipotentiary of the USSR in Italy, and was there during the attempted August state coup in Moscow and the signing of the treaty which established the CIS. His whole career has been devoted to European affairs, and he speaks Italian and English. He was appointed first deputy Minister of Foreign Affairs by decree of the President of the Russian Federation on October 16, 1992. He lives in Moscow.

Adrov, Aleksei Nikolaevich

Chairman of the commission of the Council of the Republic of the Russian Supreme Soviet on transport, communications, information sciences and space.

Born on November 19, 1946 in Uryupinsk, Volgograd *oblast*; Russian. He was a member of the CPSU until August 1991. He graduated from the Moscow

Aviation Institute, and began his career in 1963 as a fitter in the Tushino machine building enterprise; he was a senior laboratory assistant in the Moscow Aviation Institute (1967-68); an engineer, senior engineer, head of a group, head of sector, and head of department, Energiya scientific production association (1969-90). In 1990 he was elected a member of the RSFSR Congress of People's Deputies and also a member of the Council of the Republic, RSFSR Supreme Soviet. From July to December 1991 he was head of the publication department of the Presidium of the RSFSR Supreme Soviet and in December 1991 he was elected chairman of the commission of the Council of the Republic of the Russian Supreme Soviet on transport, communications, information sciences and space. He is married with a son and a daughter, and loves playing chess.

Address: 103274 Moscow, K 274, Krasnopresnenskaya nab., d. 2, Dom Sovetov.

Advadze, Valerian Sergeevich

Chairman of the State Committee for the Administration of State Property of Georgia; Deputy of the Parliament of Georgia.

Born in 1930 in Akhalkalaki, Georgian SSR; a Georgian whose parents were peasants. His brother was a teacher and is now a pensioner and his sister is a peasant. He was a member of the CPSU until August 1991 and graduated in economics. He successfully presented his candidate dissertation in economics (PhD Econ) and his doctoral dissertation in economics (DSc Econ), and is a professor. In 1978 he became deputy director of the Scientific Research Institute of Economics, Planning and Management of the Economy of Gosplan, Georgian SSR, and in 1988 was appointed director.

In 1989 he was elected a USSR people's deputy for the Tbilisi Oktyabrsky national territorial district. He was elected to the USSR Supreme Soviet. He was a member of the Soviet of Nationalities and a member of its commission on the social and economic development of the Union and autonomous republics, autonomous *oblasts* and *okrugs*.

In 1990 he was elected chairman of the Union of National Accord and Renaissance of Georgia; in 1992 he became a member of the State Council of Georgia and in October 1992 a member of the parliament of the Republic of Georgia. He was nominated for election to parliament by the Union of National Accord and Renaissance of Georgia and has published widely on economic matters.

Advadze is married. His wife, Ketevan Vasilevna, née Kopaleishvili, is a graduate economist, a candidate in economic sciences (PhD Econ) and an assistant professor at Tbilisi State University. They have a daughter who is 30 years of age and is a doctor, and a son who is 24 years old and a postgraduate student. Advadze loves poetry and likes to listen to classical music.

Home address: Tbilisi, pr. Vazhi Pshaveli 4, kvartal 17, korpus, kv. 18; *telephone*: Tbilisi 31 15 20.

Afanasev, Yury Nikolaevich

Leader of the group Independent Civil Initiative; Russian Federation People's Deputy.

Born on September 5, 1934 in the settlement of Maina, Ulyanovsk *oblast*; Russian. He was a member of the CPSU from 1961 to April 1990. In 1957 he graduated from the faculty of history, Moscow State University, and from then until 1968 he worked in the *Komsomol* organizations in Krasnoyarsk *krai* and in the *Komsomol* Central Committee. From 1968 to 1971 he was a postgraduate student in the Academy of Social Sciences, Party Central Committee. In 1971 he successfully presented his candidate dissertation in history on "Contemporary French bourgeois historiography of the Great October Socialist Revolution" (PhD).

From September 1971 he lectured in history, was secretary of the Party committee, then pro-rector of the Higher *Komsomol* School of the *Komsomol* Central Committee. In 1980 he successfully presented his doctoral dissertation in history on "The French historical school, Annales, in contemporary bourgeois historiography 1929-1979 (a critical analysis of the evolution of its theoretical methodological foundations)" (DLitt). In 1982 he moved to the institute of general history, USSR Academy of Sciences, where he was senior scientific assistant and was head of the sector on the history of culture.

From September 1983 to 1986 he was a member of the editorial board and editor of the department of history of the Party journal, *Kommunist*. In December 1986 he was appointed rector of the Moscow State Archival Institute. He published widely, concentrating on the history of Soviet society and the reformation of public consciousness. He edited the collection of articles, *Inogo he dano* (there is nothing else), and was elected a delegate to the XIX Party conference. He was a member of the club of the Moscow intelligentsia, *Moskovskaya tribuna*, and was behind the creation and for a time co-chairman of the all-Union historical cultural society, Memorial.

In early 1989 he was nominated for election as a USSR people's deputy in the No. 36 Nogin territorial district, Moscow *oblast*. During the election campaign he stated that it was important to have an understanding of the very essence of *perestroika*, the society in which one lived. Russian society should have its past returned to it. No one had a monopoly and he was opposed to bans, the elimination of certain material, the internal censor in all of us, the closure of archives, and the modernized form of half-truths. He advocated looking at the past with all its variations and the contradictoriness of its spiritual experiences. He proposed the extirpation of Stalinism from everyday life and the elimination of bureaucratic rights over the archives, and believed that the archives should become national property. He opposed the party monopoly of truth.

He called for Soviet society to be provided with advanced humanitarian education, for an end to the low priority given to its financing and to alter the very content of higher education. Other strands of thought and cultural experience, besides the revolutionary democratic tradition, should be made accessible. He advocated the reformation of the USSR, based on the Leninist principles of nationality policy, full sovereignty, autonomy, independence and federalism and was against the centralized nature of the USSR with weakly developed national autonomous regions. He opposed the total étatization of society. He called for the development of the co-operative movement, democratization, genuine sovereignty, the discovery of the dignity of the individual and the full development of public independent movements.

There were three candidates. Afanasev won in the first round, polling 72.09% of the votes. His main opponent was V. N. Gladkovskaya, an operator of winding machines in the Akimov Kupavinsky fine cloth factory, who received 12.29% of the votes. In the USSR parliament Afanasev was elected co-chairman of the interregional group of deputies. He opposed the premature involvement of democratic leaders in the structures of power. In October 1991 he was elected co-chairman of the co-ordinating council of the Democratic Russia (DemRossiya) movement.

He did not believe that representative authorities were well structured. The activity and reality were well in advance of the deputies who often prevented the implementation of necessary measures. He believed that executive power should be strong, capable and effective, and advocated land reform and genuine privatization. He criticized the contradictions in the Russian leadership and the gulf between it and the democratic forces. He thought that the fall in output only affected the state sector while the private, co-operative and the shadow economy experienced growth. The strict vertical lines of communication in the Soviet economy had been giving way to horizontal links over the last 20 years. The economy had been surviving and working out its own solutions, and there was no need to attempt to reform everything, merely to make some amendments which had already become reality and make legal and more effective horizontal links. There was a need to come to terms with the shadow economy since it was functioning successfully.

Afanasev is one of the most prominent first wave democrats and an academician of the Russian Academy of Social Sciences. In early 1991 he renamed the historical archival institute the Russian humanitarian university. In 1991 he was elected an RSFSR people's deputy, and on January 23, 1992 he suspended his participation in Democratic Russia because of dubious behaviour, the settling of personal accounts in the leadership and the discrediting of the very concept of democracy. He founded and led the public group, "independent civil initiative".

He saw the VII Congress of People's Deputies as communist and traditional and as aiming at levelling society, collectivism and supremacy. A powerful bloc of communists and anti-communists who favoured a strong state had formed at the congress to oppose the course of the reforms. Economic reform needed a democratic way of satisfying the interests of the majority, and the mistakes of the Gaidar government were the underestimation of the resources needed and the postponement of privatization for a year. The main democratic idea is not social equality but the provision of equal opportunities in the beginning, and he believed that this is a general human value which should be put into effect. He favoured the deepening of reform in all spheres, the dissolution of the Congress of People's Deputies, the convention of a constituent assembly and the adoption by it of a new constitution. He is married with two children and lives in Moscow.

Afanasevsky, Nikolai Nikolaevich

Russian Ambassador to Belgium.

Born on October 1, 1940 in Moscow; Russian. He was a member of the CPSU until August 1991. He graduated from the State Institute of International Relations, Moscow, in 1962. From 1962 to 1963 he was an assistant in the USSR embassy in Paris; in 1964 assistant in the second African department of the USSR Ministry of Foreign Affairs; from 1964 to 1965 acted as interpreter at the USSR embassy in the Cameroon and from 1965 to 1966 was attaché there. From 1966 to 1970 he was an attaché, third secretary, and second secretary in the translation department, USSR Ministry of Foreign Affairs.

From 1970 to 1976 he was second secretary, first secretary, and counsellor of the first European department, USSR Ministry of Foreign affairs and then he was first secretary (1976-77), counsellor (1977-79), and minister counsellor (1979-83), in the Soviet embassy in Paris. From 1983 to 1990 he was head of department of the first European department, USSR Ministry of Foreign Affairs. In 1990 he was appointed USSR ambassador to Belgium and in January 1992 became Russian ambassador to Belgium. He speaks French and English and is married.

Address: Russian Embassy, 1180 Brussels, 66 avenue de Fré; *telephone*: Brussels 374 6886; 374 3406.

Agafonov, Valentin Alekseevich

Deputy Speaker of the Russian Supreme Soviet; chairman of the Russian Supreme Soviet committee on the social development of rural areas, agricultural questions and food.

Born on August 24, 1935 in the village of Vypolzovo, Poretsky *oblast*; Russian. He was a member of the CPSU until August 1991. He started work in 1954. He graduated from the Chuvash Agricultural Institute in 1962 and the Academy of Social Sciences of the Party Central Committee. After graduating from the institute he worked as a senior research assistant in the department of propaganda and implementation of advanced techniques at the Chuvash agricultural experimental station, Tsivilsk. He moved into Party work and was an instructor in the department for organization, Vurnarsky Party *raion* committee (1962-63); inspector and Party organizer of the party committee of the Vurnarsky agricultural production administration (1963-64);

deputy secretary and head of the organizational department of the Party committee of the Vurnarsky production administration (1964-65); head of the Vurnarsky *raion* agricultural production administration (1965-71); head of the administration of agriculture and deputy chairman of the executive committee of the Vurnarsky *raion* soviet of people's deputies (1970-71); director of the Chuvash Skotoprom trust, Cheboksary (1971-72); first deputy Minister of Agriculture of the Chuvash ASSR (1972-75); and Minister of Agriculture of the Chuvash ASSR (1975-79). In 1979 he was appointed first deputy chairman of the Council of Ministers, Chuvash ASSR and in 1982 also chairman of the council of the agro-industrial association of the republic. In 1985 he became chairman of the state agro-industrial committee of the republic as well as deputy Prime Minister.

He was nominated as a candidate for election as an RSFSR people's deputy in the No. 890 Alatyrsky territorial district, Chuvash ASSR. During the election campaign he advocated equal distribution of consumer goods in the republic, improvement in the agricultural infrastructure and expansion of the building materials sector to permit more house construction. Eight candidates stood for election, and he won in the second round, polling 46.9% of the votes. He was elected a member of the RSFSR Supreme Soviet at the I Congress of People's Deputies (533 voted for, 389 voted against), and as a deputy he voted with the communist and conservative factions.

He a member of the Chuvash Party *obkom*; and a deputy of the Chuvash Supreme Soviet. In 1990 he was appointed chairman of the committee of the Russian Supreme Soviet on the social development of rural areas, agricultural questions and food, and in 1992 he was elected deputy Speaker of the Russian Supreme Soviet. He is married with two daughters, and loves hunting.

Address: 103274 Moscow, K 274, Krasnopresnenskaya nab., d. 2., Dom Sovetov; *telephone*: Moscow 205 65 15.

Aganbegyan, Abel Gezevich

Rector of the Academy of the National Economy.

Born on October 8, 1932 in Tbilisi, Georgian SSR; Armenian. He was a member of the CPSU from 1956 to August 1991. He graduated from the State Institute of Economics, Moscow, in 1955, became a postgraduate student and successfully presented his candidate dissertation in economics (PhD (Econ) and later his doctoral dissertation in economics (DSc (Econ). He is a Professor.

From 1955 to 1961 he was an economist, head of sector and deputy head of the general economics department, USSR state committee for labour and social problems, USSR Council of Ministers. He was head of laboratory, Institute of Economics and Organization of Industrial Production, Siberian branch of the USSR Academy of Sciences (1961-67) and was also (1964-67) scientific head of a production association, USSR Ministry of Instrument Making, Automation

Equipment and Control Systems, Novosibirsk. From 1964 to 1974 he was a corresponding member, economics department, USSR Academy of Sciences.

From 1967 to 1985 he was director of the Institute of Economics and Organization of Industrial Production, Siberian branch, USSR Academy of Sciences; head of the scientific council for the construction of the Baikal-Amur railway (BAM), USSR Academy of Sciences; and professor of economics, Novosibirsk State University. From 1967 to 1988 he was editor-in-chief of *Eko*, the journal of the Siberian branch, USSR Academy of Sciences and one of the most innovative, especially in economics, in the Soviet Union. In 1974 he was elected a member of the sub-department on foreign relations, Siberian branch, USSR Academy of Sciences and also a full member of the Academy, economics department.

From 1987 to 1989 he was academic secretary of the economics department, USSR Academy of Sciences and in 1989 he was appointed rector of the Academy of the National Economy. In December 1991 he was elected a member of the Russian Academy of Sciences. He was a major influence on the evolution of the thinking of Mikhail Gorbachev on the economy, and Gorbachev attended various seminars led by Aganbegyan, Tatyana Zaslavskaya and other radical thinkers before he became general secretary of the CPSU in 1985.

Aganbegyan has published widely on economic themes, such as labour productivity, wages, living standards and mathematical models of long-term planning. His books include: *The Challenge: The Economics of Perestroika* (1987); *Inside Perestroika: The Future of the Soviet Economy* (1989). He was one of the prime movers behind the policy of acceleration in 1985 but it proved incapable of solving the deep structural problems of the USSR economy. As the crisis deepened other more radical economists, such as Shatalin and Yavlinsky, came to the fore, advocating market solutions.

Aganbegyan was awarded the order of Lenin (1967), two orders of the Red Banner of Labour (1975 and 1982) and medals. He received honorary doctorates from Lodz university, Poland, in 1975 and the University of Alicante, Spain, in 1989. He was a founding member of the Soviet econometrics society in 1974. He is a member of the Bulgarian (1986) and the Hungarian (1987) Academies of Science, and a corresponding fellow of the British Academy (1988). He speaks English, and is married with two children.

Address: Moscow, Prospekt Vernadskogo 82; *telephone*: Moscow 434 8389.

Akaev, Askar Akaevich

President of Kyrgyzstan.

Born in 1944 in the village of Kyzyl-Bairak, Keminsky *raion*, Kirgiz SSR; Kyrgyz. He was a member of the CPSU until August 1991. He completed secondary school with a gold medal, and then graduated from the Institute of Precision Engineering and Optics, Leningrad, specializing in the use of computers in engineering. He became a postgraduate student immediately and successfully presented his candidate dissertation in technical sciences (PhD (Eng)). In 1980 he successfully presented his doctoral dissertation on the "Theory and calculation of the principles and methods of information storage and the transformation of holographic systems" at the Institute of Physics and Engineering, Moscow (DSc (Eng)). He then became a lecturer, assistant professor, head of department, and professor at the Frunze Polytechnical Institute and in 1982 he founded a chair of computer technology and became its first holder. He supervised 12 candidate dissertations and five of his students won Kirgiz *Komsomol* prizes.

In 1984 he was elected a corresponding member and, in 1987, a full member of the Kyrgyz Academy of Sciences. In 1986 he was elected a member of the Central Committee, Communist Party of Kirgizia, and was also elected a peoples deputy of the Supreme Soviet, Kirgiz SSR. In March 1989 he was elected president of the Academy of Sciences of Kyrgyzstan, and also in 1989 he was elected a USSR people's deputy, a member of the USSR Supreme Soviet Council of Nationalities and a member of the committee on economic reform of the Supreme Soviet. He was elected a member of the Party Central Committee at the XXVIII congress in July 1990.

On October 12, 1990 he was elected the first President of Kyrgyzstan. He was a strong supporter of *perestroika* and the maintenance of the Soviet Union, as his republic is small and needs close relations with Russia as well as Kazakhstan. Akaev advocated privatization and private ownership of land, but rising Kyrgyz nationalism ensured that only Kyrgyz could acquire land. Many Russians left the republic and Akaev saw this as a grave disadvantage to a young state fighting to modernize its government and economy. He appealed to Russians and others to stay and build up Kyrgyzstan. The republic is not as richly blessed with raw materials as its Muslim neighbours Kazakhstan and Uzbekistan, and so Akaev is keen to maintain the CIS and to form closer economic and political links with Russia.

All his academic publications are on physics. He is married with two daughters and two sons. His wife, Mairamkul Duishenovna, successfully presented her candidate dissertation in technical sciences (PhD (Eng)) and is head of the Kyrgyz State University.

Address: The Residence of the President, 720003 Bishkek, Kyrgyzstan; *telephone*: Bishkek (83312) 21 2466.

Akhmadov, Khusein Saidaminovich

Speaker of the Parliament of the Chechen Republic, Russian Federation.

Born in 1950; a Chechen; he was never a member of the CPSU. He graduated from the faculty of history of the Chechen-Ingush State University and then became a postgraduate student at Moscow State University. From 1978 to 1987 he worked in the Chechen-Ingush scientific research institute of economics, sociology and philosophy, and afterwards taught history in the village of Dzhalka, Gudermessky *raion*, Chechen-Ingush ASSR.

In March 1990 he was elected a deputy of the Supreme Soviet of the Chechen-Ingush ASSR. He was one of the most radical deputies in the parliament, finding himself always in the minority and often in isolation. In November 1990, in connection with the All-National Congress of the Chechen People (ACCP), which was ignored by the Supreme Soviet, he proposed its dissolution. In March 1991 he became a member of the extraordinary commission on food and goods of the Supreme Soviet of the Chechen-Ingush Republic, and was elected deputy chairman of the executive committee of the ACCP.

On August 21, 1991 he spoke at a meeting of the Supreme Soviet of the Chechen-Ingush Republic and opposed the neutral position of the leadership towards the Extraordinary Committee. At an extraordinary session of the Supreme Soviet he proposed the removal of the Speaker. On September 1 he participated in the opening and work of the congress of the Chechen people and was elected chairman of the Provisional Supreme Council of the Chechen-Ingush Republic, established on the initiative of the Speaker of the RSFSR Supreme Soviet, Ruslan Khasbulatov, himself a Chechen.

On assuming office he stated that the most important function of the Provisional Supreme Council was to adopt draft proposals and organize and conduct elections for the President of the republic. He thought that the peoples of the autonomous republics lived in colonies and that they should now decide their own historical fate and political orientation. He appealed for the sovereignty of the republic to be made real and not to permit the infringement of the rights of other peoples.

In October 1991 Akhmadov was removed from the leadership of the Provisional Supreme Council by the opponents of D. Dudaev, who declared the results of the election for President illegal. Akhmedov was proposed by the committee for the defence of human rights for election as a deputy of the new parliament. On October 27, 1991 he was elected a deputy and on November 2, Speaker of the parliament.

On assuming office he advocated that parliament be independent of party structures and policy, the replacement of the old executive power, and the elimination of bureaucratism as the second stage of the August revolution. He proposed collaboration with President D. Dudaev and the executive committee of the ACCP and the most rapid drafting of a constitution for the Chechen Republic. He was in favour of all forms of ownership and freedom of trade. He lives in Grozny.

Akhmedov, Khan

Deputy chairman of the Council of Ministers of Turkmenistan.

Born in 1936 in the village of Parau, Kyzyl-Arvat *raion*, Krasnovodsk *oblast*, Turkmenistan SSR; Turkmen. He was a member of the CPSU from 1963 to August 1991. He graduated from the Institute of Railway Transport, Tashkent, in 1959 and then began working on the Ashkhabad railway, Turkmenistan SSR. Later he moved into Party work and in 1980 was head of a department of the Central Committee, Communist Party of Turkmenistan. In 1985 he was elected first secretary of the Ashkhabad city Party committee, in 1988 was appointed first deputy chairman and in 1989 chairman of the Council of Ministers of Turkmenistan.

He was elected a member of the Party Central Control Commission at the XXVIII congress in July 1990 and on November 13, 1991 he was appointed deputy chairman of the Council of Ministers of Turkmenistan. He is responsible for the railway network. Turkmenistan has rapidly developed its natural gas and to a certain extent its oil resources since independence, in collaboration with Western companies. This has provided hard currency to cushion the transition to a market environment and the government's policy is a slow, regulated move to the market. Subsidies are provided to enterprises to ensure that they remain operating. The government has reverted to Turkish administrative terminology and a multi-party system exists in theory. However, no party which advocates Islamic solutions is permitted.

The old communist nomenclature, of which Akhmedov is a member, has effected an almost effortless transition to being a secular Muslim state. Good relations are maintained with Iran and economic links, especially transport, are developing quite well. Turkmenistan has also fostered relations with Ukraine, and has entered various agreements which cement links between the former Soviet Central Asian states. It is cool towards the CIS, apparently feeling that it is economically viable on its own. Akhmedov is married with four children.

Address: 744014 Ashkhabad, ul. Karla Marksa 24; *telephone*: Ashkhabad 25 4534.

Akhmedov, Rustam Urmanovich

Minister of Defence of the Republic of Uzbekistan.

Born on November 10, 1943 in Bagdadsky *raion*, Fergana *oblast*, Uzbek SSR; Uzbek. He was a member of the CPSU until August 1991. In 1961 he graduated from the Technical College for Mechanization and Electrification of Agriculture, Kokand, in 1965 from the Kokand Tank School and in 1985 from the Military Academy of Armoured Troops. His military career began in 1962 and in 1965 he became a tank platoon commander, and was then secretary of the *Komsomol* committee of an artillery regiment. In 1969 he was appointed assistant to the head of the *Komsomol* political department of a motor rifle division and from 1969 to 1970 of a tank division.

From 1970 to 1972 he was deputy commander for political affairs of a tank battalion and from 1972 to 1974 of a tank battalion at Samarkand Higher Tank Command School. From 1974 to 1976 he was deputy commander of a battalion for political affairs at the command school and of a training battalion at the command school (1976-78). From 1978 to 1982 he was deputy commander for political affairs and from 1982 to 1986 commander of a training battalion at the Tashkent Higher Command School. He was Chief of Staff, and deputy head of civil defence, Tashkent *oblast* (1986-91), was appointed Minister for Defence Affairs and commander of the national guard of the Republic of Uzbekistan (1991-92). In July 1992 he was appointed Minister of Defence of the Republic of Uzbekistan. He is a major-general.

He is married with a son and three daughters.

Akhmetaliev, Amangeldy Akhmetolimovich

Director of the Kazakh Telegraph Agency (KazTAG).

Born in 1937 in Stepnyak, Kokchetav *oblast*, Kazakh SSR; Kazakh. He was a member of the CPSU until August 1991. He graduated in 1960 from the faculty of journalism, Kazakh State University, Alma Ata, and became head of a department in the *oblast* newspaper *Ortalyk*, Kazakhstan. He entered Party work, became an instructor in the Karaganda Party *obkom* and later press chief of the Central Committee, Communist Party of Kazakhstan. He was appointed director of the Kazakh Telegraph Agency in July 1987.

The agency has to be sensitive to the ethnic mix of Kazakhstan. Just over half the population is Slav with the Russians as the largest group and some Russians, especially Cossacks, would prefer to break away from Kazakhstan and join the Russian Federation. Under the astute leadership of Nursultan Nazarbaev the Kazakhs have occupied most of the top positions while assuring non-Kazakhs that they have a future in the new state. Kazakhs are becoming culturally more assertive and Russians, especially, complain that they are not able to develop their language and traditions as they would like. Other Muslim groups, especially Tatars, find this much easier. Akhmetaliev's task is to present the acceptable face of Kazakh tradition to the outside world, but also to develop good relations with the foreign business community to encourage a flow of investment and know-how to the republic.

Akhmetaliev speaks English and is married with two sons.

Address: 480091 Alma Ata, Prospekt Ablai Khana 75; *telephone*: Alma Ata 62 5037 (office); 63 4335 (home).

Aksyuchits, Viktor Vladimirovich

Chairman of the Russian Christian Democratic movement (RKhDD), chairman of the sub-committee on links with foreign organizations of the Russian Supreme Soviet committee on freedom of conscience, religion, mercy and charity.

Born on August 28, 1949 in a west Belarusian village. Belarusian. He spent his childhood in Riga, Latvia. His father was a stevedore in the port of Riga and his mother was a caretaker. Aksyuchits attended the marine technical college in Riga from 1965 to 1969. He served in the Soviet Navy in the Baltic from 1969 to 1973 and joined the CPSU in 1971. Later he maintained that his goal at that time was to become General Secretary of the CPSU in order to "reform the Party and the country and save it from dogmatism and bureaucratism". In 1972 he joined the preparatory course (*rabfak*) of the faculty of philosophy, Moscow State University, and on completing this course in 1973 he became a full-time student of the faculty. He graduated in 1978 and immediately began postgraduate studies in the faculty of foreign philosophy. He was elected secretary of the bureau of the student and then postgraduate Party organization. His thesis was on Western Protestantism.

In 1979 he was arrested by the KGB for reading and distributing religious and political literature. During the search of his flat the KGB found a library of *samizdat* (illegal material printed in the Soviet Union and abroad). He was expelled from the Party and his postgraduate studies and until 1986 he was obliged to take seasonal work (construction work and *shabashnik* or contract work) as a brigade leader in collective and state farms in Siberia, Kazakhstan, in the Soviet Far East, in central Russia, Ukraine and the North Caucasus. During this time he wrote theological, religious-philosophical and other articles which were published in the Russian émigré press.

In 1987 he and Gleb Anishchenko began to publish the illegal Christian religious-philosophical and literary journal, *Vybor* (choice). In 1988/89 he participated in the work of the initiative group, Church and *Perestroika*, which had been set up on the suggestion of Father Gleb Yakunin. From 1988 to 1991 he was a "hidden member" (i.e. he had the right to conceal his membership) of the People's Labour Union (NTS), an anti-communist but overwhelmingly émigré organization whose headquarters were in Frankfurt-am-Main, Germany. From 1989 to 1991 he was a member of the "ruling circle" of the NTS but in 1991 refused to become an "open member" and as a result was removed from the "ruling circle". In 1988 he joined the board of the *Perspektiva* scientific-technical co-operative which had been set up by members of a public movement. This latter was simultaneously a commercial undertaking and a legal cover for the activities of the informal political movements of various shades, ranging from liberals to anarcho-syndicalists.

One of Aksyuchits's first successful commercial deals for *Perspektiva* was the sale of a ship for scrap in Klaipeda, Lithuania, to a Spanish company. The proceeds were used to buy computers which were sold in Russia at a profit. There were press reports that this deal made Aksyuchits his first million. In 1989 he was involved in setting up Puico, a Soviet-Panamanian joint venture. He became a member of the board and chairman of the publishing department.

A quite lucrative undertaking by Puico was the publication and huge sale in the Soviet Union of the *God's Commandments. The Ten Commandments. The Sermon on the Mount of our Lord Jesus Christ. Vybor.* Puico claimed copyright of the biblical quotations in the text and this caused, understandably, some amusement in the press.

During the election campaign to the RSFSR Congress of People's Deputies in early 1990 Aksyuchits joined the Democratic Russia (DemRossiya) democratic block of candidates. He stood in the No. 45 Profsoyuzny territorial district, Moscow. During the election campaign he advocated the annulment of Article 6 of the USSR constitution (on the leading role of the CPSU), the creation in Russia of a multi-party political system, radical economic reform, genuine implementation of freedom of conscience, other rights and freedoms for the citizens of Russia, the sovereignty of Russia within the USSR, the resolution of political and inter-ethnic conflicts by peaceful means. Support in the election campaign came mostly from the members of the democratic faction of the Moscow People's Front, many of whose members had gained electoral experience in the spring of 1989 during the election of Sergei Stankevich to the USSR congress of people's deputies. Aksyuchits was a candidate in the same electoral district of Moscow as Stankevich.

There were nine candidates. Aksyuchits polled 39.5% of the votes in the first round and won in the second round, polling 49.7% of the votes. His main opponent was D. V. Beskishkov, who received 15.9% of the votes in the first round and 41.2% in the second. At the I Congress of People's Deputies Aksyuchits nominated himself for speaker of the RSFSR Supreme Soviet, but withdrew before the voting began. He was elected chairman of the sub-committee of the Supreme Soviet committee on the freedom of conscience, religion, mercy and charity.

At this time Aksyuchits was also preparing the founding conference of the Russian Christian Democratic Movement (RKhDD), which took place on April 8/9, 1990. At the conference Aksyuchits, Vyacheslav Polosin and Gleb Anishchenko were elected co-chairmen. Aksyuchits became chairman of the political council of the People's Party of the RKhDD (later Party of the RKhDD), the structure of which was much tighter than that of the RKhDD movement. In early October 1990 Aksyuchits became a member of the organizational committee of the Democratic Russia Movement which had been set up during the summer of 1990. At the founding conference of the movement on October 20/21, 1990, he opposed personal and collective membership, arguing that DemRossiya should be a coalition of parties, but was defeated. He joined the DemRossiya group of deputies in parliament.

In December 1990 Mikhail Astafev and he were the driving forces behind the establishment of the Russian Union deputies' group. This was the term used by Aleksandr Solzhenitsyn to describe the proposed state of the eastern Slavs. Aksyuchits was elected chairman of the sub-committee of the Russian Supreme Soviet committee on freedom of conscience, religion, mercy and charity. From December 1990 to November 1991, as a co-chairman of RKhDD, he was a member of the co-ordinating council of the DemRossiya movement. In this movement, Aksyuchits, together with Nikolai Travkin (Democratic

Party of Russia) and Mikhail Astafev (Constitutional-Democratic Party—Party of People's Freedom), headed the so-called "democratic-supremacy of the state" wing which opposed the leadership core of the movement on the issue of the future of the Soviet Union after the collapse of the communist regime. The "state supremacists" regarded as undesirable the division of the Soviet Union into independent republics and did not approve of DemRossiya's alliance with the "national-separatists" in the republics within the framework of the Democratic Congress, which had been set up in Kharkov, Ukraine, in January 1990.

Aksyuchits and the others spoke out in support of the South Ossetians in their struggle to leave Georgia and unite with the North Ossetians in Russia, and Pridnestrovie in its battle to establish its own autonomy within Moldova or even to leave Moldova. In April 1991 the parties of Aksyuchits, Travkin and Astafev signed an agreement to establish, within the framework of the DemRossiya movement, "Popular Accord", a constitutional-democratic bloc. Opponents of Popular Accord referred to it as a "union of the elephant, the pug-dog and the cockroach", an allusion to the relative sizes of the three parties. Aksyuchits's RKhDD was seen as the pug. The task of Popular Accord was to save the single Union from the wreckage of the communist regime, at least in those areas where the population had voted for a "renewed Union" in the referendum of March 17, 1991. Personally Aksyuchits opposed "separatism" quite vigorously, even considering that the Baltic States could get by without independence. This promoted a split between Aksyuchits and other democratic leaders and led to Father Gleb Yakunin leaving the RKhDD in August 1991 and his accusing Aksyuchits of chauvinism.

The failed coup of August 1991, during which Aksyuchits was one of the most active defenders of the Russian White House, slowed down for a time the fragmentation of the Democratic Russia Movement. However, differences surfaced again in the autumn of 1991 with renewed vigour. At the II congress of the Democratic Russia Movement in November 1991 Aksyuchits, Travkin and Astafev again tried in vain to ban individual membership of the movement and to transform it into a coalition of parties and other collective groups, affording every collective group the right of veto over the most important decisions. The Civil Accord Party, after being defeated, resigned from the Democratic Russia Movement. Soon after the establishment of the CIS in December 1991 and the liquidation of the USSR, Aksyuchits announced that the RKhDD was joining the opposition to the government of President Boris Yeltsin and attempted to rally the Civil Accord Party, the People's Party of Free Russia (Rutskoi's party) and the non-communist wing of the national-patriot grouping, around the concept of "enlightened patriotism". To achieve this a "congress of civil patriotic forces" was convened on Aksyuchits's initiative in February 1992 and at it the establishment of the Russian People's Assembly (RPA) was proclaimed. However the parties of Rutskoi and Travkin did not join the RPA and the latter in reality became a coalition of national-patriotic and post-communist organizations. Aksyuchits was elected a member of the central council, the presidium of the central council and chairman of the board of the RPA. In June 1992 he ceded the post of chairman to Ilya Konstantinov.

In April 1992 he took part in the establishment of Russian Unity, a parliamentary coalition of communists and anti-communist-state supremacists, the goal of which was to force the Yeltsin-Gaidar government to resign. As successor to Egor Gaidar as Prime Minister, Aksyuchits proposed Valentin Fedorov, the Governor of Sakhalin. The alliance between Aksyuchits and Konstantinov and the communists and national patriots resulted in a split in the Civil Accord bloc, with Travkin's party quitting, and an internal crisis in the RKhDD. Aksyuchits expelled his fiercest critics from the party and promised the others that the RKhDD, apart from the Russian Unity parliamentary coalition, would not enter into any permanent alliance with communists within the so-called "unified opposition". At the RKhDD congress on June 20, 1992 Aksyuchits was unanimously elected chairman of the RKhDD party and was proposed as a candidate for the post of Russian President.

During the spring and summer of 1992 Aksyuchits took part in the formation of the so-called "unified left-right opposition" but in October 1992 when this process had led to the setting up of the National Salvation Front, Aksyuchits declined to become a member of its organization committee and left the Front. Nevertheless, at the VII Russian Congress of People's Deputies, in April 1992, he proposed Vice-President Aleksandr Rutskoi as successor to Egor Gaidar as Prime Minister. Aksyuchits favours a constitutional monarchy, at least in theory, but believes that the restoration of the monarchy in Russia will not take place in the near future. For him it is important to re-establish a federal government on the territory of the former Russian Empire—USSR. In case this does not occur then all territory inhabited by Russians should come under the jurisdiction of Russia. He genuinely believes in the existence of "Russophobia", a particular anti-Russian ideology which finds expression in the works of Igor Shafarevich and often includes pathologically negative attitudes to Russia or the Russian people.

Aksyuchits supports the views of Vladimir Korsetov, a member of the political council of the RKhDD, on the principles which should underlie the privatization of industrial enterprises: "it should be based on administrative personnel who truly represent the future middle class and these should be given a controlling package of shares and preferential credit... and not less than 20% of enterprise shares should be handed over to honest workers and officials to ensure the participation of ordinary people". Family farms have a future in Russia but Aksyuchits sees the move to family farming taking 10-15 years. In the meantime he proposes that "collective farms should be reorganized by giving the majority of shares to their management". In an interview in early 1993 Aksyuchits stated that the "most totalitarian government was preferable after all to chaos" and that "only a national dictatorship could save Russia". He means by this a "powerful legal authority, defending the national and state interests of Russia".

He is a Russian Orthodox Christian. He speaks English and likes philosophy and classical music. He is married to his second wife and has five children and a grandson.

Alekseev, Anatoly Alekseevich

Deputy head of the inter-departmental commission on social problems of military men and members of their families of the government of the Russian Federation; Captain, 3rd class.

Born on January 1, 1950; Russian. He graduated from F. E. Dzerzhinsky Higher Naval Engineer Technical School in 1972, having received a higher technical education. He was a member of the CPSU from 1971 to August 1991.

After graduating from technical school he served in the Pacific Fleet as head of physical training and sport of a guided-missile ship, mechanical engineer of a large torpedo-boat, teacher and senior teacher in a training submarine detachment. In 1984 he was transferred to Leningrad naval base to fill the post of assistant to the head of the school for training and drill of a training submarine detachment, and from 1987 he taught electro-mechanics at the school for technicians and midshipmen in Kronstadt.

Alekseev's record was that of an officer with insufficient specialist and naval training, an inadequate knowledge of the subjects he taught, a passive role in developing new materials for training and writing new manuals on methods. At the same time he was known for his activity in defending the interests of military men, and he contributed to the military press and was recommended to serve as a military journalist. In 1978, Senior Lieut. Alekseev was expelled from the CPSU by the Party organization of his unit for the attempted theft of gold jewellery from a woman he had happened to meet. However, the Party commission of the political department did not confirm the decision and limited itself to recording a severe reprimand in his personal file (one of the most severe punishments for a CPSU member). This badly damaged Alekseev's reputation among naval officers.

At the end of the 1980s Alekseev went into politics, co-operating with democratic forces in Leningrad. In the spring of 1990 he was elected an RSFSR people's deputy in Kronstadt territorial district. At the congresses and sessions of the RSFSR Supreme Soviet he adopted a radical anti-communist stance and supported all the proposals of the Democratic Russia bloc. In his parliamentary work he focused on defending the political, civil and social rights of the military and the democratization of the armed forces. In 1990 he was elected chairman of the RSFSR Supreme Soviet commission for the investigation of the reasons for the death, traumas and violations of the legal rights of military men and military construction troops in peacetime. He became a senior organizer of the all-Union movement of parents of perished servicemen, and initiated proceedings in a number of cases into the death or taunting of soldiers and sailors.

In August 1991 Captain 3rd class Alekseev was one of the organizers and leaders of the defence of the Russian White House, and he himself was one of the front-line defenders and participated in capturing eight armoured personnel carriers from the rebels. By the USSR Minister of Defence order of September 7, 1991 he was promoted ahead of his time to Captain 1st class, something which caused dissatisfaction in the officer corps.

By the USSR President M. Gorbachev's order of September 26, 1991 Alekseev was appointed chairman of the Committee of the USSR President on military men and members of their families. In October 1991 he organized the all-Union congress of parents of military men. Alekseev's activities were opposed by the Shield, the rival union of the military men, and its chairman, Russian people's deputy V. Urazhtsev.

From January 1992 he headed the Committee of the RSFSR President on military men and members of their families. Due to a resolute stand taken by the Committee in investigating accidents, injuries and unregulated relations in the armed forces, Alekseev was in constant conflict with top military officers. The Russian Minister of Defence and the Commander-in-Chief of the unified armed forces of the CIS managed to have the committee dissolved in May 1992. However, the intervention of democratic organizations and campaigns by public organizations and the mass media forced them to reinstate the committee on military men and members of their families, as an agency of the Russian Federation government.

On May 5, 1992, because of objections by the public prosecutor, Commander-in-Chief of the unified armed forces of the CIS cancelled the order promoting A. Alekseev to captain 1st class as it constituted "a violation of the current law".

The agencies under Alekseev pursued a policy of clarifying and analysing the reasons for accidents involving military and special equipment, the violation of law in the army and navy, the promotion of the democratization of all spheres of military life and the social protection of personnel. According to experts from *Nezavisimaya Gazeta*, Alekseev is one of the most influential figures in Russian politics. After the reorganization of the top executive agencies in October 1992 and the dissolution of the Committee, Captain 3rd class Alekseev was appointed deputy head of the inter-departmental commission for the social problems of military men and their families. Politically he is a convinced advocate of democratic reform and is actively involved in parliamentary and public work. He appears in the press, radio and TV.

He is fond of literature and theatre, and is a sportsman. He does not have a good command of foreign languages, and has not been abroad as a member of an official delegation. He has been awarded six medals; he has been married twice.

Office address: Moscow, ulitsa Schepkina, 42.

Alekseev, Sergei Sergeevich

Member of the Presidential Council of the President of the Russian Federation.

Born in 1924; Russian; member of the CPSU until August 1991. He successfully presented his candidate dissertation in law (LLM) and his doctoral dissertation (LLD). He was a corresponding member of the USSR Academy of

Sciences, then of the Russian Academy of Sciences, and is now director of the institute of philosophy and law of the Urals section of the Russian Academy of Sciences. His father was a victim of the Stalin terror.

In 1989 Alekseev was elected a USSR people's deputy as one of the nominees of the USSR Academy of Sciences. He was elected a member of the USSR Supreme Soviet at the I Congress of People's Deputies and was chairman of the USSR Supreme Soviet committee on legislation, law and order. In the spring of 1990 he was appointed chairman of the USSR constitutional review committee. According to him the committee was to fit into the general structure of semi-democratic institutions, which were not to undermine the authoritarian nomenclature power of the Party apparatus or the whole bureaucratic system which was founded on the state monopoly of property. As soon as the committee touched the foundations of authoritarian power, it encountered an information blockade.

The committee took decisions in connection with the following matters: the bloody events in Lithuania in January 1991 and the introduction of joint military patrols, and on the inadmissibility of deploying the armed forces in political affairs; on the revocation of the decrees on military regulations which permitted Party agencies to issue direct orders to military units; on the invalidity of all unpublished normative documents affecting the rights, freedoms and duties of citizens; on the abolition of the prohibitive nature of internal passports and their transformation into mere registration.

In early 1992 Alekseev became chairman of the council of the Research Centre on Private Law, an independent firm set up on his initiative. In his view the law which had developed during the Soviet era was anti-legal, a severe state legal system based on the legal justification of administrative omnipotence, the dominance of an authoritarian regime over society and the lack of rights of the individual. The present Russian legal system is also not prepared to bring into being a *Rechtsstaat*, a law governed state. The law is state based and essentially based on public law. It is not enough just to have a series of good laws but rather a system which expresses the spirit and essence of the laws. The present system is based on overcoming the state property monopoly and the "omnipotence" of soviets, but what is needed is a decisive change in the very essence of the legal system. This involves the privatization of law, its transformation from public to private law, in which priority is afforded the will and interests of the person. Private law should be re-created and a leading, authoritative position afforded it in the legal system and, by generally recognized rights and freedoms of the individual, which form the significance of this determining link, the centre of a democratic legal system should be established. Alekseev advocates a greatly enhanced role for the courts in the life of society. The Constitutional Court is not the third power but the whole system of law and all its parts should become so.

Alekseev advised the President of Kyrgyzstan in the drafting of that state's constitution. He is the author of a draft Russian constitution, together with Anatoly Sobchak and Gavriil Popov. It includes the concept of a "secular" state, one in which the constitution is above all political machinations. It is based on the individual and his or her right to private property, freedom of development and creativity. Its view is that it is worthless to create laws for a society which is developing autonomously. The ideal constitution is one in which there is limited power, which does not hold back but promotes human life, and it is necessary to establish a legal system which protects the individual. Many ideas which originated with Academician Andrei Sakharov have been included in the draft constitution. Alekseev supports the privatization of enterprises through handing them over to workers' collectives and opposes a purely ideological understanding of capitalism and socialism. Capitalist societies enjoy more freedom but they only embrace one side of the coin, money/goods exchange, and need to develop further. Private ownership of land should be accompanied by a whole range of institutes defending the rights to own land, including its selling, leasing and using it as collateral. He does not regard the slogan "all power to the soviets" and the idea of people's power as adequate. Democracy involves the division of three powers, the legislative, executive and judicial. Division does not merely imply the breaking up of power but the equality of all three branches.

It is important precisely to delineate the functions of the central and local authorities, otherwise they will block one another, pushing society towards the dangerous situation of anarchy. The country needs strong executive power. The independence of the law and the courts should be the guarantee that strong presidential power does not turn into absolute power. In order for the presidential regime to be effective it needs to wield quite a lot of power throughout the country. Presidential decrees should be effective and capable of implementation, and at the *oblast* level, prefects or governors, representatives of the President, are necessary. Local soviets appear to be effective but have not yet proved themselves in practice. The power structure needs to be reformed so as to establish a clear hierarchy and a clear definition of the division of powers. Alekseev became a member of the presidential Council in February 1993.

He is a well-known legal specialist and is the author of the books: *The Content of Soviet Socialist Civil Law* (1959); *General Theoretical Problems in Soviet Law* (1961); *The XXII CPSU Congress and Questions of State and Law* (1962); *Civil Law During the Period of the Rapid Construction of Communism* (1962); *General Theory of Socialist Law* (1963); *The Mechanism for the Regulation of Law in a Socialist State* (1966); *Socialist Legal Values in Soviet Society* (1971); *Law in Our Life* (1975); *Introduction to Specialization in Law* (1976); *Law and Our Life* (1978); *General Theory of Law* (2 vols, 1981); *A Rechtsstaat, the Fate of Socialism* (1988); *Historical Types of State and Law* (1986); *Property, Law, Socialism: Polemical Notes* (1989); *Soviet Legislation: The Way to Restructure* (1989); *What is Permitted and What is Forbidden in General in Soviet Law* (1989); *Before the Elections. Renewal or Catastrophe?* (1990); *Before the Elections: The Socialist Ideal: Present and Future* (1990).

Alekseev is married with two daughters who live in St Petersburg, one of whom is a doctor and the other a philologist. He loves nature, tourism and paddling his kayak. He lives in Ekaterinburg, and has turned down moving into a larger apartment and permanent residence in Moscow.

Aleksi II, Patriarch

Head of the Russian Orthodox Church.

Aleksi Mikhailovich Ridiger (Aleksi is his monastic name: the Russian tradition is to choose a Christian name and officially drop one's surname when taking the tonsure) was born in Tallinn, Estonia, on February 23, 1929. Ridiger is not an Estonian name but derives from the German landowning aristocracy which dominated the region for so long. His patronymic Mikhailovich points to some Russification and this was on his mother's side. He was brought up bilingually in Russian and Estonian.

His grandmother gave him a copy of the Gospels when he was six and he began attending church at the same age. He was baptized in Tallinn and was already thinking of becoming a priest. His parents were devout and the two pilgrimages he made as a child to the Valaam Monastery on Lake Ladoga had a lasting impact on his spiritual journey.

The outbreak of the Second World War was a disaster. In 1940, when Aleksi was 10 years old, the Red Army occupied Estonia and incorporated it into the USSR. Estonia had been apportioned to Stalin by Hitler in the Nazi-Soviet Pact of August 23, 1939. Stalin's policy was to crush and deport all independent-minded individuals in the Baltic States. The invasion of the German *Wehrmacht* in the summer of 1941 halted this process, but it resumed after the region was recaptured by the Red Army. These were formative years for Aleksi and he suffered along with the rest. He retained his Christian faith and in 1947 began applying to the Leningrad Theological Seminary. He was considered too young but remarkably he was able to study and graduated in 1949, at the age of 20 years, having completed four years' study in two. A year later he returned to Tallinn and pastoral responsibility.

The next 40 years were spent functioning as a believer, propagating a religion, in an officially atheist state. He was a model priest, bending with the winds of change in state and society. He is not on record as having opposed the state. In Estonia he witnessed the growing dominance of the Russian language and Russian ways and did his best to protect the Orthodox Church, its buildings and monasteries. Culturally he belonged to the Russian minority in Estonia and was Orthodox, whereas most Estonian believers were Lutheran. Nikita Khrushchev savagely oppressed churches and believers in the late 1950s, when tens of thousands of believers of all faiths were imprisoned and about 13,000 out of 20,000 Orthodox churches closed, were handed over to the secular authorities or destroyed. Most of these had been reopened during and after the Great Fatherland War (1941–45).

It was during this period of persecution that permission was given by the Soviet communist authorities for the Russian Orthodox Church to join the World Council of Churches, at its New Delhi meeting, in 1961. The Kremlin had presumably come to the conclusion that the Orthodox Church could be used as a vehicle for propagating Soviet views and values throughout the world. This was a time of great communist self-confidence after Yury Gagarin's flight and various other firsts in space. Khrushchev was convinced that communism would prevail soon over capitalism and that Moscow would "bury the USA".

The confrontation almost led to nuclear war over Cuba in October 1962 and henceforth the Church was to be a faithful propagator of the view that the Soviet Union wanted peace and disarmament.

Aleksi became Bishop of Tallinn at the very young age of 32 years, also in 1961. This meant that the KGB could not fault his commitment to the Soviet state and that he revealed no glimmerings of Estonian nationalism. Remarkably, he was nominated by the Orthodox Church and became a member of the Central Committee of the World Council of Churches. In his contacts with western churchmen he did not reveal the true state of the faith and the persecution at home. Had he done so his career would doubtless have been at an end.

He was elected Archbishop in 1964 and Metropolitan in 1968. He became a member of the Holy Synod, the governing body of the Church. He moved to Leningrad in 1986 to become Metropolitan and number two in the Church. He retained responsibility for Estonia, being the only bishop who spoke the language. Internationally he flourished in the World Council of Churches and the Conference of European Churches in Geneva. He became president of the latter in 1972 and chairman in 1987, a more responsible post, which he has retained to the present day. He garnered much experience in committees and gained widespread knowledge of European Churches, except the Roman Catholic, which was not a member.

He was always under close scrutiny by the KGB and, since he had access to hard currency, in Geneva, was a member of a small Soviet élite. He had to report to the KGB and there were those in his entourage who did the same about his activities and views. He was a good administrator in Estonia and gained respect for his serving of the liturgy. He was chairman of the education committee, but no Christian teaching could be conducted in secular society. He was also chairman of the pensions committee at a time when no charitable work was permitted by the state. He was made deputy chairman of the committee preparing for the millennium celebrations of the Orthodox Church in 1988.

The advent of President Mikhail Gorbachev resulted in breath-taking changes in Church life. He summoned the leaders to the Kremlin in April 1988 and promised them a new deal if they supported *glasnost* and *perestroika*. Gorbachev was no stranger to the Orthodox tradition, having being baptized as a child and whose mother was a believer. He spoke of a common cause between religion and communism, a strange combination for Marxists-Leninists, and invited the Church to become deeply involved in charitable work. He had been impressed on his travels by the role of the Church in western societies and always made a point of finding out more wherever he went. He became the first Soviet leader to enter churches without embarrassment. He promised the Church a more liberal law which would remove some of the suffocating restrictions of Lenin (a passionate atheist and great enemy of the Church) and Stalin, a failed Georgian Orthodox seminarian. The millennium was celebrated shortly after the historic Kremlin meeting and a *Sobor*, or council, presaged a new era.

Patriarch Pimen, head of the Church for nearly 20 years, died in May 1990. For the first time since the October Revolution the Church was able to choose its own head, without having to accept the state's choice. Aleksi was swiftly elected and took the name of Pimen's predecessor, becoming Aleksi II. He has his detractors who are critical of his complacent attitude to the communist state. His training and experience have made him a man of compromise and consensus, who is not given to bold initiatives or rash actions. His German and Estonian background have influenced him and he retains the calm and balance of his compatriots. His task is immensely difficult, since the end of the communist era and the renaissance of the Russian state have placed enormous responsibilities on his shoulders. President Yeltsin sees the Church as a symbol of Russian nationhood and statehood and attends many important occasions. When he was sworn in as Russian President in 1991 the Church was present and gave its blessing.

Internally the Orthodox Church is riven with dissent as one would expect after so many years when priests could not express themselves in direct language or participate openly in the development of state and society. There are those, like Father Gleb Yakunin, who confronted the Soviet authorities and paid a heavy price for their dissent. Yakunin is now a member of the Russian Parliament. The archives have revealed that many high Church dignatories collaborated, some beyond the call of duty, with the KGB. No incriminating evidence has come to life about Aleksi's activities. The Ukrainian Autocephalous Orthodox Church has split from Moscow and the Ukrainian (Greek) Catholic Church has re-emerged triumphant from the underground and forced fusion with the Russian Orthodox Church, reclaiming thousands of its churches and properties. Other parishes have joined the Russian Orthodox Church in Exile.

The attempted August 1991 coup was a severe test for Aleksi. On August 19, the first morning of the coup, he was due to celebrate the liturgy in the Cathedral of the Dormition in the Kremlin, which only recently had been restored to the Church for worship during major festivals. He called for the voice of President Mikhail Gorbachev to be heard so that people could be directly informed about the momentous events under way. In the early hours of the next morning he wrote an appeal which declared that the Church "did not and could not bless illegal, violent or bloody acts. I beg all of you, dear people, to do all you can to put out the flame of civil war. Stop!". This was a message for everyone, since it did not take sides and did not refer to the unconstitutionality of the attempted coup. President Yeltsin looked to the Church for moral support and it did play a leading role during the official burial of the three young men killed during the attempted coup. One of them was given a Jewish burial.

The old animosity between the Russian Orthodox Church and the Roman Catholic Church surfaced at Lambeth Palace in November 1991 when Aleksi used the occasion, as chairman of the Conference of European Churches, to attack the Catholics for their "illegitimate" missionary activity in Siberia. The Catholic Church has seen a renaissance in Russia in many regions, such as Nizhny Novgorod and Siberia, where there have been prominent converts. Roman Catholic bishops have been appointed to new Russian sees. The Orthodox Church, theologically, lacks the skill to counter many thrusts from other Christian churches.

Aliev, Geidar Alirza Ogly

Chairman of the *Milli Mejlis* (Soviet) of the Republic of Azerbaijan; Acting President of the Republic of Azerbaijan.

Born on May 10, 1923 into an Azeri worker's family in the city of Nakhichevan and a member of the CPSU from 1945 to August 1991. Hasan, his brother, is an academician, Academy of Sciences of Azerbaijan, who from the 1960s to 1980s was director of the institute of geography of the Academy of Sciences of Azerbaijan. Agil, another brother, is a professor and Doctor of Economic Sciences. Djalal, another brother, is a biologist and an academician, Academy of Sciences of Azerbaijan. His wife, Zarifa Aziz Kyzy, died in 1984 and is buried in Moscow. She was the daughter of A. Aliev, who during the 1940s and 1950s was Minister of Health of the Azerbaijan Soviet Socialist Republic and chairman of the Council of Ministers of the Dagestan Autonomous Soviet Socialist Republic (ASSR). She was an ophthalmologist and a corresponding member of the Academy of Sciences of Azerbaijan. There are two children. The daughter Sevil graduated in the 1970s from the faculty of oriental studies, Kirov Azerbaijan State University. She is a candidate of sciences (PhD), and her dissertation was supervised by Evgeny Primakov. The son Ilkham graduated in 1982 from the Moscow State Institute of International Relations. Both children live in Moscow.

Aliev studied at a teachers' college from 1941 to 1949. After graduation he performed various functions in the agencies of state security and the Council of Ministers of the Nakhichevan ASSR and furthered his education from 1949 to 1950. From 1950 Aliev was in Baku and worked in the apparatus of the Ministry of State Security, Ministry of Internal Affairs and KGB of Azerbaijan. He received his further education in the 1950s in the extra-mural department of the department of history, Azerbaijan Kirov State University. From 1964 to 1967 he was deputy chairman of the KGB in Azerbaijan at a time when the chairman was Semon Tsvigun. From 1967 to 1969 Aliev was chairman of the KGB in Azerbaijan. From 1969 to 1982 he was first secretary of the Communist Party of Azerbaijan. In 1976, at the XXV Party Congress, he was elected a candidate member of the Politburo, CPSU. In the autumn of 1982 Aliev was promoted to full membership of the Politburo, CPSU, and was also made first deputy chairman of the USSR Council of Ministers. After precisely five years he retired from the Politburo and took his pension "for health reasons". He was not a member of Gorbachev's inner group. Aliev returned to politics in January 1990.

He was one of the first to condemn the actions of the Soviet Army in Baku on January 20, 1990 which resulted in several hundred fatalities. During the autumn of 1990 he moved from Moscow to Baku and a month later to Nakhichevan. Also during the autumn of 1990 he was elected a deputy of the Supreme Soviets of the Azerbaijan SSR and Nakhichevan ASSR. In 1990 he became president of the parliament of the Nakhichevan Republic.

Azerbaijani politics were transformed in the spring of 1993. The decline in living standards, the continual military defeats in Nagorno-Karabakh and the internal wrangling among Poular Front members seriously weakened the

Elchibey administration. On June 1, 1993, the Russian garrison in Gyanja suddenly departed, leaving its food and equipment. Suret Guseinov, a young Azeri officer at the head of a group of soldiers, seized control of the garrison. Attempts by the pro-Elchibey forces to disarm them resulted in over 50 deaths. Guseinov and his men then marched on Baku. President Elchibey fled to Nakhichevan after the military informed him it would not fight the Guseinov's forces. Aliev then returned to Baku and was elected speaker of the *Milli Mejlis* on June 15, 1993 and thereby acting President. The constitution provided for this. The speaker resigned, as did Prime Minister Panakh Guseinov. Eventually Aliev had to compromise with Suret Guseinov who took control of the security forces and police; and became Prime Minister.

Alimpy, Head of the Russian Orthodox Old Believers' Church

Born on July 31, 1929 as Aleksandr Kapitonovich Gusev in Gorky (Nizhny Novgorod) into a large Old Believers' family; Russian. He only completed four years of schooling and began work as a buoy keeper in Lyskovo (1946-48); then as a fireman in the Lyskovo fire brigade (1949-50). He served in the Soviet army (1950-53); then was again a fireman until 1960; he was a painter in the Lyskovo repair and construction administration (1960-63); a stoker in the Old Believers' church in Gorky (1966-67); in February 1967 he became a deacon and served as a deacon in the same church until 1986. In the assembly in 1986 he was made archbishop of Moscow and All Russia. At a jubilee assembly commemorating the millennium of the conversion of Rus to Christianity, in 1988, he was unanimously elected the first Old Believers' metropolitan of Moscow and All Russia.

Alin, Oleksandr Serhiiovych

Leader of United Social Democratic Party of Ukraine.

Born in 1951 in Vinnytsia *oblast* in central Ukraine. He studied, like many social democratic intellectuals, in the faculty of law, Kiev State University. Thereafter he worked as a lawyer in Makarivskyi *raion*, Kiev *oblast*, but in 1982 he was removed from his job and placed in a psychiatric hospital for engaging in unofficial political activity. After his release in 1983 he worked on a collective farm, and after 1988 was unemployed. He was therefore active in the various social democratic groups that sprang up around Kiev in the late 1980s.

After the social democratic movement split at its founding congress in May 1990, Alin led the more left-wing faction, which named itself the United Social Democratic Party of Ukraine (USDPU). Alin's USDPU, which claims 1,000 members (mostly leftist intellectuals) and one people's deputy (Volodymyr Moskovska), sees itself as closer to the social democracy of the Second International than to the social democracy of the present-day German SPD, which the SDPU supports. Nevertheless Alin steered the USDPU into membership of the centrist *New Ukraine* movement in 1992, and by the time of the third USDPU congress in December 1992 was clearly headed towards reunion with the SDPU.

Telephone: Kiev 546 9722.

Ali-Zade, Zardusht Mamed-Mubariz Ogly

Editor-in-chief of *Istigal*, the newspaper of the Social Democratic Party of Azerbaijan.

Born on February 2, 1946 into an Azeri family in Baku. His father is Mamed Mubariz Ali-Zade, a well known philologist, specialist in Farsi, professor and Doctor of Philology. His mother is Zinnyat Ali-Zade, a well-known philologist, specialist in the Azeri language, professor and Doctor of Philology. Both parents teach at Baku State University. He has two sisters and a brother. His brother Araz is chairman of the Social Democratic party of Azerbaijan and a deputy of the parliament of Azerbaijan. His wife is Niyal Barkhalova, a candidate of mathematical physics (PhD), and a lecturer in the physics faculty of Baku State University. They have two sons. The elder one is a student in the faculty of oriental studies at Baku State University. The younger one is still at school.

Ali-Zade graduated in oriental studies from the Baku State University in 1967. From 1967 to 1970 he was a military translator in Egypt. On his return to Baku he became a junior scientific assistant in the institute of oriental studies, Academy of Sciences of Azerbaijan. He worked in the People's Democratic Republic of Yemen (1973-74). From 1974 he was again a junior scientific assistant and from 1987 a scientific assistant in the institute of oriental studies, Academy of Sciences of Azerbaijan. In 1985 he successfully presented a dissertation on contemporary Arab literature (PhD). He has published many articles on Arab literature.

Together with A. Ali-Zade and L. Yunusova, he was one of the founders of the social democratic movement and then of the Social Democratic Party of Azerbaijan. In January 1990 he resigned from the CPSU. In 1991 he stood for President of the Azerbaijan Republic. However a week before the election he withdrew his candidature, which left A. Mutalibov as the sole candidate.

Alksnis, Viktor Imantovich

Military politician.

Born in 1950 in Tashtagol, Kemerovo *oblast*; Latvian. He was a member of the CPSU until August 1991. He graduated from the Alksnis (named after his grandfather) Higher Aeronautical Engineering College, Riga, Latvian SSR, and was a radio electronics engineer in a unit in the Moscow military district, later in a unit in the Baltic military district. In 1988 he was appointed senior engineer inspector of the combat training department of the Baltic military district air force.

He became notorious during *perestroika* for his eloquent attacks on *glasnost* which he saw as a mechanism for attacking the CPSU and the Soviet military. He joined with others, such as Col-Gen. Albert Makashov, in attacking *perestroika* and calling for a return to Party discipline. Although a Balt and a Latvian he spoke as an assimilated Russian, and he encouraged Russians living in the Baltic republics to organize and resist the rising tide of nationalism. Alksnis was a vociferous opponent of the breakup of the Soviet Union and the movement for Baltic independence. He was a USSR people's deputy, a member of the Soyuz parliamentary faction (a conservative communist faction) and a member of the Latvian Supreme Soviet.

He supported the Extraordinary Committee during the attempted coup of August 1991 and gave interviews to Western TV companies. His star waned after the defeat of the coup, the collapse of the Soviet Union and the rise of President Yeltsin's Russia, as he was an archetypal Soviet military man who did not fit into the post-communist Russian armed forces or the new Latvia. He resigned his commission and devoted himself to political matters, where his views were in accord with those of the National Salvation Front. He is married with a son and a daughter.

Ambartsumov, Evgeny Arshakovich

Member of the Council of the President of the Russian Federation.

Born on August 19, 1929. Armenian. He was a member of the CPSU until 1991. He graduated from the Moscow State Institute of International Relations, USSR Ministry of Foreign Affairs, having successfully presented his candidate dissertation in history (PhD). When elected a people's deputy he was head of department, institute of economics of the world socialist system, USSR Academy of Sciences.

In early 1989 he was nominated for election as an RSFSR people's deputy by the collective of his institute in No. 53 Tushinsky territorial district, Moscow. During the election campaign he signed the platform of the Democratic Russia (DemRossiya) electoral bloc. Ambartsumov advocated the acquisition by Russia of the status of a sovereign state within the framework of the USSR and the immediate establishment of treaty relations with the other republics of the Soviet

Union and foreign states, and RSFSR representation in the United Nations. He regarded the primary task of Russian deputies to be the adoption of laws on property, land, state enterprises and co-operatives, which would guarantee equality before the law and many different forms of property ownership. He proposed the adoption of a temporary RSFSR constitution during the transition period before the coming into being of a new RSFSR constitution and the signing of a new Union treaty. He regarded it as necessary to afford the various types of autonomous entities (*republic, oblast, okrug*) equal status in the RSFSR.

There were four candidates. Ambartsumov polled 31.8% of the votes in the first round and won in the second round, polling 46.7% of the votes. His main opponent was A. V. Arkhipov, who received 33.2% of the votes in the first round and 43.5% of the votes in the second round. He was elected a member of the RSFSR Supreme Soviet at the I Congress of People's Deputies. He is a member of the Supreme Soviet Council of the Republic, chairman of the Supreme Soviet committee on foreign affairs and foreign economic links, and a member of the Constitutional Commission.

He is a member of the parliamentary faction, *Rodina* (motherland). Previously he was a member of the Russian Supreme Soviet committee on inter-republican relations, regional policy and co-operation, a member of the deputies' groups, united parliamentary faction of social democratic and republican parties of the Russian Federation, Russian Union, ethics group and Moscow deputies. The resolutions adopted by his Supreme Soviet committee on foreign policy were generally critical of the Yeltsin government's foreign policy. The committee was especially critical of Andrei Kozyrev and did not regard him as defending Russian national interests in the successor states or abroad with sufficient vigour. The committee tended to adopt a Eurasian approach as opposed to the Western orientation of much of Yeltsin's administration. Ambartsumov was invited to participate in arms negotiations between Russia and the US and this was regarded as a shrewd tactical move by the Yeltsin government. Ambartsumov became a member of the presidential Council in February 1993 and hence participates in top policy-making debates on foreign affairs and other matters. He is the recipient of various state awards, and lives in Moscow.

Ametistov, Earnest Mikhailovich

Member of the Constitutional Court of the Russian Federation.

Born on May 17, 1935 in Leningrad into a Russian family, he was a member of the CPSU until August 1991. He graduated from the law faculty of Moscow State University in 1958, and then worked as an editor on *Yuridicheskaya literatura* (law literature) and *Mezhdunarodnye otnosheniya* (international relations). In 1966 he began to research in the institute of the international workers' movement, USSR Academy of Sciences, then in the all-Union scientific research institute for Soviet state formation and law, and in 1971 successfully presented his candidate dissertation on "International labour law and the working class" (LLM). In 1983 he successfully presented his doctoral dissertation on "The factors for the implementation of the norms of international law (for example, norms of international labour law)" (LLD).

He was regarded as the leading specialist in the USSR on international law and human rights law, and is the author of over 100 publications, including eight monographs on international law, the activities of international organizations, the defence of human rights, the legal regulation of foreign economic relations and many articles devoted to politics and law. He participated in the drafting of the law on international treaties, and on situations of emergency. From 1990 to 1991 he was an expert on the constitutional commission of the Russian Federation.

In 1991 the USSR Ministry of Foreign Affairs sent him to the European Community and the Council of Europe to work on the provision of humanitarian aid to the USSR. Just before he was elected a member of the Constitutional Court he was a senior scientific assistant in the all-Union scientific research institute of Soviet state formation and law, and is a professor. He was one of the founders of the public organization, Memorial, a member of the Moscow Helsinki group and a participant in many international conferences and seminars on the problems of defending human rights.

In early 1990 he was nominated as a candidate for election as an RSFSR people's deputy in the No. 22 Krasnopresnensky territorial district, Moscow. In the election campaign he advocated the legal strengthening of human rights and freedom of the citizens of Russia as the main condition for overcoming the economic and political crisis in the country. There were 13 candidates, and Ametistov polled 11.2% of the votes in the first round but lost the second round, receiving 34.8% of the votes. The victor was O. M. Poptsov, editor in chief of *Selskaya Molodezh* (rural youth), the newspaper of the Central Committee of the *Komsomol*, who polled 26.87% of the votes in the first round and 57.7% in the second round.

The parliamentary group of the united faction of social democratic and republican parties of the Russian Federation, nominated him as a candidate for the Constitutional Court. During the hearings in the various Supreme Soviet committees and commissions Ametistov received the highest number of votes and he was elected a member of the Constitutional Court at the V Congress of People's Deputies on October 29, 1991 in the first round of voting, receiving 635 votes for and 237 against.

Ametistov advocates restricting administrative interference in the legal sphere and the elimination of extra-legal instructions. Russia needs a new constitution as quickly as possible, the goal of which is to strengthen the regulation by law of all questions affecting the rights, freedoms and duties of the citizens of Russia. He regards it as incumbent on the government, in introducing the market economy, to provide state funds to ensure basic human rights, the right to leave and return to the country, freedom of the press and so on. He regards it as important that authorities realize that the non-implementation of the decisions of the Constitutional Court means that the implementation of their own decisions becomes virtually impossible.

He has often expressed his concern about the conflict between the three branches of power, the legislature, the executive and the judiciary, seeing the basis of the conflict in the personal ambitions of some politicians. All agencies of power need to be consolidated in order to ensure the success of economic reform. The failure of economic reform would lead inevitably to the breakup of Russia. He did not support the ruling of the Constitutional Court that several of the decisions of President Yeltsin, during his address to the Russian people on March 20, 1993, on introducing special rule, were unconstitutional. He lives in Moscow.

Anchevsky, Igor Georgievich

President of the Sagan joint stock company, Alma Ata.

Born on December 18, 1957 in Tkibuli; Jewish. He graduated in 1979 from the faculty of history, North Ossetian State University, and became an industrial psychologist. In 1983 he became editor (psychology) of the state Kazakh advertising agency, and in 1985 he was appointed head of the advertising department, Ministry of Trade of the Kazakh SSR. In 1989 he became an editor and commentator on Kazakh state TV. From 1988 to 1990 he was head of the advertising department of the Kazakh state television and radio company (Gosteleradio) and in 1990 was appointed its director of marketing. In December 1991 he became the major shareholder (40%) and president of the Sagan joint stock company.

He is married with a son and speaks English and French. His hobbies include hunting, using his video camera and driving his car.

Address: Alma-Ata, ul. M. Makataeva 47; *telephone*: Alma Ata 30 44 14; 30 6156 (office).

Andreeva, Nina Aleksandrovna

General Secretary of the all-Union Communist Party of Bolsheviks (ACPB).

Born in 1938. Russian. She was a lecturer in chemistry in the Leningrad Technology Institute, but in 1993 she did not enter the competition for reappointment as she was too busy with Party work and was of pensionable age. She is a candidate of technical sciences (PhD).

She became a member of the CPSU in 1966. She became famous as a result of her letter in the newspaper *Sovetskaya Rossiya* on March 13, 1988, which appeared under the heading "I can't forego my principles". It was an attack on *perestroika* and *glasnost* from a conservative Party position, and also had anti-Semitic overtones. She had submitted the original letter some time before, but it was reworked and published when President Mikhail Gorbachev was out of the country. Many observers regarded Egor Ligachev, the moderate reformer, as her patron, but he always denied any connection with the publication.

In May 1989 she was elected chairwoman of the political executive committee of the all-Union society, "Unity: for Leninism and communist ideals". She played an active part in establishing the all-Union communist party of Bolsheviks. At the founding congress in November 1991 she was elected general secretary of the Central Committee, which consisted of 15 persons. At that time the Party claimed a membership of about 35,000. The basic goals of the Party are the re-establishment of the USSR and the restoration of "Marxist-Leninist norms and principles" in everyday life.

She is very hostile towards the Russian government and its domestic and foreign policies. Foreign leaders and ex-leaders she has most sympathy for include Dolores Ibarruri, Fidel Castro, Alvaro Cunhal and Erich Honecker. Politically she is closest to the leaders of the Russian communist workers' party. She loves to sew and eat tasty food. She lives in St Petersburg.

Anikiev, Anatoly Vasilevich

Deputy Speaker of the Council of Nationalities, Russian Supreme Soviet.

Born on May 29, 1939 in Belomorsk, Karelian ASSR where his father was a worker; Russian. He was a member of the CPSU until August 1991. He graduated from the Rybinsk River Navigation Technical College, and Air Force Institute. He qualified as a radio engineer, and successfully presented his candidate dissertation in economics (PhD (Econ)). He worked in *Komsomol* organizations for 13 years, and participated in the war in Afghanistan. From 1977 he was head of chief directorates; head of the administration for cadres; and head of the political administration, USSR Ministry of Internal Affairs (MVD). In 1990 he was appointed first deputy RSFSR Minister of Internal Affairs. He is a Lieutenant-general of the MVD.

He was nominated for election as an RSFSR people's deputy in the No. 107 Segezhsky national territorial district by 12 collectives of workers in the Belomorsky, Loukhsky and Kemsky *raions*. During the election campaign he advocated increasing the economic independence of the republics and simplifying administration, but avoiding regional isolationism. There should be various approaches deployed to raise agricultural production and every person afforded the right to contribute creatively to society. A major concern was the protection of society against crime, and another was how Russia was to find the resources to implement a legal system which guaranteed civil and human rights and brought about stability in civil and legal relations. At the I Congress of People's Deputies he spoke of the need for the government to take urgent short-term economic measures and to reorient the economy rapidly to meet the needs of the people. He opposed a rapid transition to the market which could be a tragedy for many people, and believed that there should be a law protecting citizens against losses during the transition period to the market. There was an urgent need to promulgate a law on the protection of the environment and natural resources of the RSFSR.

There were seven candidates. In the first round Anikiev polled 20,794 votes and he won the second round, polling 43,256 votes. His main opponent was V. S. Posnov, general director of the Karellesprom trade and industrial association, who received 10,909 votes in the first round and 23,913 votes in the second round. Anikiev was elected a member of the Council of Nationalities, RSFSR Supreme Soviet, at the I Congress of People's Deputies (669 voted for, 254 voted against). He is a member of the Sever (north) parliamentary group. In 1992 he was elected chairman of the commission of the Council of Nationalities, Russian Supreme Soviet, on oppressed and deported peoples; and later elected deputy Speaker of the Council of Nationalities, Russian Supreme Soviet. He is married with a son, and enjoys basketball, football and skiing.

Address: 103274 Moscow, K 274, Krasnopresnenskaya nab., d. 2, Dom Sovetov.

Anisimov, Stanislav Vasilevich

Minister of Trade and Material Resources of the Russian Federation.

Born in 1940 in the village of Suvorovo-Telegulo, Berezansky *raion*, Nikolaev (Mykolaiv in Ukrainian) *oblast*, Ukraine. From 1957 to 1962 he was a repair mechanic and production worker in the Mykolaiv southern pipe factory. In 1967 he graduated from the Moscow Institute of Steel and Alloys, specializing in metallurgy and pressed metals, and between 1967 and 1970 he was a senior engineer in the labour organizational bureau and head of a section in the Mykolaiv southern pipe factory. Between 1970 and 1978 he worked in the Ukrainian and USSR state committees of supply (Gossnab); from 1978 to 1982 he was an instructor in the department of planning and financial agencies of the economic department in Ukraine and the USSR.

In 1983 he graduated from the Academy of Social Sciences of the Central Committee, CPSU. Between 1988 and 1991 he was deputy chairman of USSR Gossnab. In 1990 he was appointed first deputy chairman of USSR Gossnab and in 1991 USSR Minister of Material Resources. Ella Pamfilova, the chairwoman of the USSR Supreme Soviet commission on privileges and later Russian Minister of Social Security, opposed his nomination maintaining that he used his official position for personal gain, although it was unclear how this actually was done. In November 1991 he became Minister of Trade and Material Resources in the new Russian government. During the difficult winter months Anisimov headed a special governmental commission (the so-called winter commission) which was responsible for providing electrical power supply and resources, of vital importance to the functioning of the economy, during a period of economic dislocation and confusion. Egor Gaidar stated that this commission had been granted "very wide powers" to carry out its work.

As early as the beginning of August 1991 Anisimov had declared that the Gossnab system had completely outlived its usefulness and had transformed itself into a brake on the development of the national economy. According to him, the Ministry of Material Resources was a totally new type of government agency for a market economy which provided economic stimuli and a legal framework. He stated that economic links between enterprises should be market based and that goods and raw materials exchanges promote the development of an intermediary infrastructure. He was in favour of the simultaneous privatization of wholesale and retail trade, and believed that current high prices were the consequence of the large number of monopolies in the economy and the "collusion of whole regions".

He has been awarded the order of the badge of honour and the medal for exemplary work in commemoration of the centenary of the birth of V. I. Lenin. He is married with two children.

Anpilov, Viktor Ivanovich

Leader of the Russian Communist Workers Party; leader of the Moscow Workers Movement.

Born in 1945 in Krasnodar *krai*; Russian. He was a member of the CPSU until August 1991. After school he entered a college and learnt a trade; and then worked in the Taganrog combine enterprise. He served in the Soviet army, and after demobilization, on the recommendation of his unit, he entered the faculty of journalism, Moscow State University. After graduating he was a commentator for USSR Gosteleradio, writing and delivering contributions in Spanish for Latin America.

In 1990 he was nominated as a RSFSR people's deputy in the No. 3 Nizhegorodsky national territorial district, Moscow. During the election campaign he advocated an economy that served the people and not one which served to enrich a small circle of individuals, and equal initial opportunities for all. He opposed a policy which led to social differentiation, a rise in crime and ethnic conflict, the dismemberment of the RSFSR and the trading of its resources. He was in favour of the state sovereignty of the RSFSR and the state monopoly of foreign trade.

There were 10 candidates. V. Mukusev, head of the TV programme *Vzglyad* (view), polled 34.7% of the votes in the first round and won in the second round, polling 59.1%. The runner up was V. Korelev, a turner in the Ordzhonikidze enterprise who had resigned from the CPSU in 1989, who received 16.1% of the votes in the first round.

Anpilov is at present leader of the Russian Communist Workers' Party and also leader of the opposition movement, Moscow Workers. In August 1992 President Yeltsin announced in Omsk the beginning of criminal proceedings against Anpilov for incitement to overthrow the legitimate state authorities by force. However, neither the Ministry of Internal Affairs nor the Ministry of Justice confirmed this statement and stated that they lacked information on the affair.

Anpilov played a leading role in organizing the demonstrations in Moscow on May 1, 1993 which resulted in clashes between the demonstrators and the Moscow militia and OMON. Several hundred demonstrators and many members of the militia and OMON were injured, and an OMON member later died from his injuries. During the demonstration on May 9, 1993, the anniversary of the Soviet victory over Nazi Germany in 1945, Anpilov was abducted and savagely beaten up, and a warrant was issued for the arrest of his attackers. He lives in Moscow.

Antonov, Guryan Vasilevich

Old Believers' Archbishop of Novozybkov, Moscow and All Russia.

Born on March 15, 1903 in the village of Bokla, Bashkiria (Bashkortostan); Russian. He completed secondary school and was trained by the old believers. From 1958 to 1979 he was deacon of the Buguruslan, then of the Ufa old believers' community and was appointed head of the old believers' Orthodox archdiocese and archbishop of Novozybkov, Moscow and All Russia. The collapse of communism provided a new lease of life for the old believers who can now develop their communities. Prior to the October Revolution many of the traders and industrialists were old believers.

Address: Novozybkov, Bryansk *oblast*, ul. Nekrasova 28; *telephone*: Bryansk 3 1910.

Antonov, Viktor Ivanovych

Minister for Heavy Industry, Ukraine.

Born into a Russian family in 1935 in the town of Batayska. He graduated from Taganrog radiotechnical institute in the south-west of Russia and on the border with Ukraine in 1958, and then worked in the Kiev *Mayak* factory from 1966 to 1986, first as an engineer and then rising to the post of director by 1974. In 1986 he was transferred to the Kiev Gosplan as its deputy head, and became its temporary head in November 1990.

In May 1991 he was appointed Minister for Machine Building, the Military-Industrial Complex and Conversion. As someone who has spent his entire career in the military-industrial complex, Antonov is widely perceived as a spokesman for its interests, especially after he was appointed to Kravchuk's Defence Council in 1992. He has a brusque manner, and a more conservative reputation compared to other industrialists such as Kuchma and Evtukhov.

If the latter represent those industrialists who see no alternative to market reforms and privatization, Antonov has always urged a gradualist approach and the importance of maintaining links with Russia (his industries in particular being anything but self-sufficient). Under increasing pressure from nationalists who would like to develop a strong domestic arms industry, and state managers in military factories bereft of orders, Antonov has made it clear that he has an open mind on questions of arms sales. In 1993, he has attempted to recapture many former Soviet arms markets, and Ukraine has been reported as supplying weapons to both Serbia and Iran.

Official (Ministry) address: 252008 Kiev, Vul. M. Hrushevskoho 12/2; *telephone*: Kiev 293 7442.

Apryska, Ales (Alaksandravic)

Chairman of the Social Democratic Party of Belarus.

Born on August 27, 1941 in Dzierdicy, Buda-Isasalouski *raion*, Homiel (Gomel) *oblast*. His parents are Alaksandr Michailevic and Nadzieja Prakonauna, and the family is Belarusian. He graduated from the Construction Engineering Institute, Leningrad, and is a civil design engineer. He is chief inspector of design in the Inkaprajekt Design Institute, Minsk. He was elected chairman of the Social Democratic Party of Belarus, and supports the renaissance and national independence of Belarus. He is married and his wife is Hanna. They have two sons, Siarhiej and Viktar.

Address: 2200085 Minsk, pr. Rakasouskaha, d. 109, kv. 16; *telephone*: Minsk (0172) 48 25 73.

Arabiej, Lidzija (Lvouna)

Belarusian writer.

Born on June 27, 1925 in Nizok, Minsk *oblast*; Belarusian. Her parents are Leu Kackouski and Marija Machnac. She graduated in philology and successfully presented her candidate dissertation in philology (PhD), and worked at the Belarus publishing house and was on the editorial board of the monthly journal, *Polymia*. She is a member of the union of writers of Belarus. She has never been a member of a political party and regards herself as a democrat. Her novels include *Iskry u Papianisce* (Sparks in the Ashes), *Suzorie Vialikaj Miazvredzicy* (The Constellation of the Great Bear), numerous novellas and short stories. She is married to Jauhien Markavic Hankin.

Address: 220029 Minsk, vul. Naturalistau, dom 6, kv. 19; *telephone*: Minsk (0172) 64 28 60.

Arbatov, Georgy Arkadevich

Director of the Institute for the Study of the USA and Canada, Russian Academy of Sciences.

Born in Kherson, Ukraine, in 1923; Russian (although some commentators claim that he was previously Jewish). He was a member of the CPSU from 1943 to August 1991. From 1941 to 1944 he served in the Soviet army during the Great Fatherland War (1941-45), and at the age of 18 was commanding a battery of Katyusha rockets. He graduated from the Moscow State Institute of International Relations of the USSR Ministry of Foreign Affairs, and in 1949 he became a journalist and was editor and later senior editor of *Voprosy filosofii*, *Novoe Vremya* and *Kommunist*. He was a columnist on *Problemy mira i sotsializma* (1960-62), and in 1955 successfully presented his candidate dissertation in juridical sciences on "The role of the imperialist state in the ideological oppression of the popular masses" (LLM).

In 1962 he was appointed head of sector in the Institute of World Economics and International Relations, USSR Academy of Sciences, and in 1964 moved into the apparatus of the Party Central Committee. In 1965 he successfully presented his doctoral dissertation in history on "The ideological struggle in contemporary international relations" (DLitt). He was appointed director of the institute for the Study of the USA and Canada, USSR Academy of Sciences in 1967, and from 1971 to 1976 he was a member of the Central Party Revision Commission. From 1976 to 1981 he was a candidate member and from 1981 to July 1990 a member of the Party Central Committee. He was also a deputy of the USSR Supreme Soviet, a delegate to the XIX Party conference, and was an adviser on foreign policy (especially American) to Presidents Gorbachev and Yeltsin. He accompanied Gorbachev to his summit meetings with US Presidents Reagan and Bush. He was avidly sought as a commentator on Soviet and world affairs by the Western TV media, especially the US.

He was a member of the main editorial commission of the multitome history of the Great Fatherland War. He opposed military intervention in Angola, but was not able to express his opposition to the invasion of Afghanistan in December 1979. He learned about the Soviet military action from the newspapers, but as early as spring 1980 he tabled a question to the leadership about the earliest possible withdrawal. He was against the stationing of medium range missiles in Europe and took part in the first negotiations about their removal. From the second half of the 1960s onwards he advocated more radical reforms. He and Academician Inozemtsev prepared material for a plenum of the Party Central Committee which posed the question of more rapid scientific-technical progress and economic reform. He is a professor, an Academician of the Russian Academy of Sciences and a member of its Presidium.

In 1989 Arbatov was elected a USSR people's deputy as a nominee of the USSR Academy of Sciences. He was a member of the Supreme Soviet committee on international affairs, and from 1991 to 1992 he was a member of the consultative council of the President of the Russian Federation. Arbatov is strongly in favour of economic and political reform, and the market, but a modern one, not the wild kind, which existed in the West in the 19th century.

The first sacrifices of such a market are science, education and health care, and without these Russia will be transformed into a poorly developed country. The intellectual potential of the country is being valued less and less and there is a real danger of a scientific brain drain abroad.

There are few firms at present which are honest and look to the future, and most are concerned with gain or survival. It is not appropriate to demand that fundamental science pays it way and switching over to commercial contracts would be the end for science. He criticized the Gaidar government for its utopian policies, the adoption of International Monetary Fund (IMF) models appropriate for countries in the Third World whose goal is to extort debts from them, and believes there are other alternatives. He advocates breaking up monopolies by using force, enforcing the introduction of competition and a fundamental agrarian reform. It is quite inappropriate to base policy on the free interplay of prices and the spontaneous market. A well thought out industrial, agrarian and social policy is necessary.

He criticized the liquidation of the private accumulation of the population, and thought that large-scale privatization needed the denationalization of whole branches of the economy. At present ministries and authorities possess the level of uncontrollable monopoly. He was against the shock therapy and called it absurd, senseless and incredibly severe towards one's own people. It was not necessary to suffer in order to achieve something.

He regards Egor Gaidar as an able young scientific assistant and personally an honest man but a fanatical neophyte, with his head engrossed in conservative Western economic theory and without practical experience. Arbatov is critical of the lack of discipline and lack of professionalism of the administrative apparatus and the huge extent of corruption. He feels that priority should be afforded to the construction of housing, roads and the demilitarization of the economy. The search for foreign enemies by extremists he regards as political primitivism as their goal is to compromise the democrats. The US is not now trying to achieve world hegemony.

He is sceptical about Western aid; the US$24 billion promised in 1992 and never disbursed is a drop in the ocean to a country which will not be dictated to. Russia has everything to become one of the most advanced countries of the world, including natural resources and huge intellectual potential. All that needs to be done is to utilize them rationally. Reforms are not formally democratic, but they are elaborated in secret, in association with Western experts, who prefer their own specialists. There is a danger of massive support for extremism among the population because of shock therapy. He points out the danger of political apathy which is a symptom of lack of faith in the authorities and inability to influence the course of events.

Arbatov advocates fundamental change in economic policy, believing in a modern socially-oriented market economy. He is opposed to the Latin Americanization of Russia. The country needs a goal-oriented policy for the development of democratic institutions and institutes, the creation of a *Rechtsstaat* (law-governed state), a humane society, the effective defence of human rights, of national minorities and the reform of the instruments of coercion of the state. He is married, and his son, a doctor of sciences, is at present working in the Institute of World Economics and International Relations. Arbatov speaks English and lives in Moscow.

Arbuzov, Valery Petrovich

Head of the Administration of Kostroma *oblast*, Russian Federation.

Born in 1939 in the village of Bykovo, Sharinsky *raion*, Kostroma *oblast* into a peasant family; Russian; member of the CPSU from 1966 to August 1991. In 1969 he graduated from the Kirov Agricultural Institute and was chief veterinary surgeon and director of the inter-*raion* veterinary laboratory, Kostroma *oblast*. In 1970 he transferred to Party work as first secretary of the Sharinsky city Party committee and Susaninsky Party *raion* committee. He graduated from the academy of social sciences of the Party Central Committee. In 1987 he was elected first deputy chairman of the Kostroma *oblast* soviet executive committee and chairman of the *oblast* agro-industrial committee. In 1988 he became secretary of the Kostroma Party *obkom*. He has received state awards.

In 1990 he was elected a deputy of the Kostroma *oblast* soviet. At its first session, in April 1990, he was appointed chairman of the soviet executive committee in a contested election, when he received 77 votes for and 67 votes against. His main opponent was A. E. Eremin, ex-chairman of the *oblast* soviet executive committee, who received 51 votes for and 93 votes against. In May 1990 he was elected a member of the Kirov Party *obkom*.

In August 1991 Kostroma *oblast* soviet executive committee supported the actions of the President of the RSFSR in re-establishing constitutional order. On September 12, 1991 Arbuzov was elected chairman of the Kostroma *oblast* soviet and resigned as chairman of the *oblast* soviet executive committee. Then, after two rounds of voting, Arbuzov was chosen from six candidates for nomination by the President as head of the administration of Kirov *oblast*. In the second round of voting he received 93 votes for and 50 votes against. On December 14, 1991 he was appointed head of the administration of Kostroma *oblast* by presidential decree.

On assuming office he assured everyone that he would take decisive measures to promote radical economic and political reform, and appealed for the consolidation of all political and public movements to make the reforms a success. It was also necessary to ensure the social security of the poor strata of the population during the transition to a market economy. In December 1992 he did not comment on the activities of the Congress of People's Deputies. He is married with a daughter and lives in Kostroma.

Ardzinba, Vladislav

Speaker of the Supreme Soviet of Abkhazia, Georgia.

Born in 1945; Abkhaz. He graduated from the Sukhumi Pedagogical Institute where he specialized in the history and culture of the peoples of Asia Minor. He then became a postgraduate student in the Institute of Oriental Studies, USSR Academy of Sciences, and successfully presented his candidate dissertation in history (PhD). He was employed in the institute until 1989 and became head of a cultural section.

From 1988 to 1989 he was a people's deputy and chairman of the USSR Supreme Soviet Council of Nationalities commission on the autonomous republics, *oblasts* and *okrugs*. In 1989 he was elected a USSR people's deputy and a member of the Supreme Soviet Council of Nationalities. He was also a member of the Council of Nationalities commission on the national state system and inter-ethnic relations. In 1989 he was appointed director of the Dmitri Gulia Abkhaz Institute of Language, Literature and history, Sukhumi. In 1991 he was elected speaker (chairman) of the Supreme Soviet of the Autonomous Republic of Abkhazia.

The advent of Georgian independence led to attempts by the south Ossetians and Abkhazians to secede and rejoin the Russian Federation, and in both areas a bitter civil war broke out between the locals and the Georgian forces. In Abkhazia Tbilisi accused Moscow of intervening on the Abkhaz side, but the Russian Ministry of Defence denied this. However, Pavel Grachev went on record stating that Russian forces should stay in Abkhazia since if they left Russia would lose its key position on the Black Sea. President Yeltsin and Eduard Shevardnadze, Georgian head of state, attempted many times to broker a settlement but without success. Abkhazians only account for about a sixth of the republic's population due to waves of Georgian in-migration.

Arinin, Aleksandr Nikolaevich

Co-Chairman of the People's Party Free Russia; Chairman of the *Duma* of the Rus Public Association, Ufa, Republic of Bashkortostan, Russian Federation.

Born in 1955 in Ufa. A Russian, whose parents live in Ufa. His father was an engineer in the oil pipeline construction trust and his mother was a teacher. His sister, Natalya Nikolaevna Arinina, graduated from the faculty of history, Bashkir State University, and is a chief librarian. He was a member of the CPSU until August 1991.

He graduated from the faculty of history, Bashkir State University, in 1979, and is a qualified historian. In 1980 he became a postgraduate student at the A. A. Zhdanov State University, Leningrad. In 1983 he successfully presented his candidate dissertation in history on industrial workers in Bashkiria during the 9th Five-Year Plan (1971–75) (PhD). In 1983 he became an assistant in the faculty of history of the USSR during the Soviet period, Bashkir State

University. From 1985 to 1987 he was secretary of the *Komsomol* committee at the university and in 1987 he was appointed senior lecturer, then in 1988 head, of the faculty of USSR history of the Soviet period.

In 1989 he became a lecturer in the ideology department, Bashkir Party *obkom*. In 1990 he was deputy head of the ideology department and head of the sector on nationality relations and international links of the Party *obkom*. Since June 1991 he has been head of the faculty of political history of the Ufa branch of the Moscow Institute of Technology.

He was one of the organizers of the Party, the Movement for Democratic Reform, then the People's Party of Free Russia, and became co-chairman of the latter. In March 1992 he participated in the constituent assembly of the Rus Public Association and was elected chairman of its *Duma*. He is also an active member of the Congress of Democratic Forces of Bashkiria and is a member of the council of representatives of the Congress. He advocates that Bashkortostan remain within the Russian Federation. He published widely in the republican press on the public and political life of the republic. He is married with a daughter who is still at school, and lives in Ufa.

Arutyunyan, Gagik Garushevich

Vice-President of Armenia; acting Prime Minister of Armenia, November 1991 to August 1992.

Born in 1948 in the village of Gekhashen, Abovyansky *raion*, Armenian SSR; Armenian. He was a member of the CPSU until August 1991. He graduated in 1970 from the faculty of economics, Erevan State University, and from 1975 to 1977 he was a lecturer at the Institute of the National Economy, Erevan. From 1977 to 1978 he was a postgraduate student at the universities of Belgrade and Skopje, Yugoslavia, where he researched the development of the economy under self-management and successfully presented his candidate dissertation in economics (PhD (Econ)).

From 1982 to 1988 he lectured in the Central Committee apparatus of the Communist Party of Armenia. In 1988 to 1989 he was head of the department of economics, then head of the economic and social department of the Central Committee (1989-90) and deputy Speaker (chairman) of the Armenian Supreme Soviet (1990-91). In October 1991 he was appointed Vice-President of the republic of Armenia and from November 1991 acting Prime Minister of the republic.

Arutyunyan had a difficult task as Armenia was reduced to penury by the war in Nagorno-Karabakh and the Azerbaijani blockade. Most industry came to a halt and heating and fuel were in desperately short supply. Armenia clung to the CIS, hoping it would provide a lifeline.

Arutyunyan, Khosrov

Prime Minister of the Republic of Armenia.

Born in 1946; Armenian. He graduated from the polytechnical institute, Erevan, as a mechanical engineer, and afterwards worked in industry. He became director of a knitted garments factory, then chairman of the city soviet executive committee. In 1990 he was elected a people's deputy of the Armenian Supreme Soviet. In 1991 he was elected chairman of the Armenian Supreme Soviet standing commission on self-government.

He was nominated several times for Speaker (chairman) and deputy Speaker of the Armenian Supreme Soviet, and was active in searching for a solution to the Nagorno-Karabakh conflict which flared up between Armenia and Azerbaijan in June 1988. He was appointed Prime Minister of the Republic of Armenia in August 1992. He is viewed as a centrist and does not belong to any parliamentary faction. His burden as Prime Minister was heavy given the catastrophic economic situation and the debilitating war over Nagorno-Karabakh.

The Azerbaijani blockade almost strangled the Armenian economy and industry all but shut down due to lack of fuel, energy and inputs. Armenia proved adept at tapping the Armenian diaspora in the West for funds and resources to prosecute the war. By June 1993 Armenia had spread its control beyond Nagorno-Karabakh in Azerbaijan, but this in turn led to disaffection with the administration of President Elchibey in Azerbaijan who was overthrown by a military rebellion in June 1993. Arutyunyan is married with two children.

Asanbaev, Erik Magzutovich

Vice-President of the Republic of Kazakhstan.

Born in 1936 in the village of Baigabul, Amangeldinsky *raion*, Turgai *oblast*, Kazakh SSR; Kazakh. He was a member of the CPSU until August 1991. He graduated from the faculty of economics, Kazakh State University, Alma Ata, in 1958 and from the Institute of Finance, Moscow, in 1963. From 1958 to 1959 he was an economist in the department for the industrial finance, Ministry of Finance, Kazakh SSR, and from 1959 to 1960 was a lecturer in economics at the Kazakh State University. Then he entered the Institute of Finance, Moscow, as a postgraduate student and successfully presented his candidate dissertation in economics (PhD (Econ)).

From 1963 to 1967 he was head of department, scientific research institute of economics, and from 1967 to 1973 head of department, Gosplan, Kazakhstan. He was deputy Minister of Finance (1975-79); head of department in the administrative affairs department, and deputy head of the administrative affairs department, Council of Ministers, Kazakhstan (1975-79). In 1979 he moved into Party work as head of the trade and the municipal services department, Central Committee (CC), Communist Party of Kazakhstan (CPKaz). From 1983 to 1986 he was deputy head of administration, Council of Ministers, Kazakhstan and from 1986 to 1988 was head of the science and education department, CC, CPKaz.

He was deputy chairman of the Council of Ministers, Kazakhstan (1988-89), secretary of the CC, CPKaz (1989-90) and Speaker (chairman) of the Supreme Soviet, Kazakhstan (1990-91). He was elected a member of the CPSU CC in July 1990 at the XXVIII congress. In 1991 he became a USSR people's deputy, and in October 1991 he was elected Vice-President of the Republic of Kazakhstan on the same ticket as Nursultan Nazarbaev. There were no other candidates for either post. Asanbaev is also a deputy in the Supreme Soviet of the republic.

Asanbaev belongs to the ex-communist nomenclature and under Nazarbaev's skilful leadership the republic is making the transition to a Muslim secular state. The President's approach is corporatist and he is much taken by the South Korean model of economic development. The ethnic mix of Kazakhstan in which native Kazakhs are still just under half requires sensitive handling as some in the large Russian minority favour joining Russia. Asanbaev's experience in finance is a valuable asset to the young state as it negotiates with foreign oil, gas and other companies on the development of Kazakhstan's rich natural resources. He is married with two children, and his wife is a schoolteacher.

Address: 480091 Alma Ata, pl. Respubliki 4; *telephone*: Alma Ata 62 0630; 62 3016.

Askalonov, Artur Aleksandrovich

Chairman of the Russian Supreme Soviet committee on health, social security and physical culture.

Born on November 4, 1940 in the village of Kurakino, Serdobsky *raion*, Penza *oblast*; Russian. He was a member of the CPSU from 1963 to August 1991. In 1964 he graduated from the Altai State Medical Institute, and after graduation he worked in the *raion* department of health, Barnaul (1965-66); was head doctor of the medical centre, Barnaul tyre works (1967-72); doctor and surgeon in the first aid hospital, Barnaul (1972-77); head doctor of the clinic and assistant in the department of traumatology and orthopaedics, Altai State Medical Institute (1977-81); and head of the department of health of the Altai *krai* soviet executive committee, Barnaul (1981-90). In 1974 he successfully presented his candidate dissertation in medical sciences (MD) and in 1989 his doctoral dissertation in medical sciences. He is a professor, was elected a deputy of the Altai *krai* soviet of people's deputies, and in 1981 was made an honoured doctor of the RSFSR. He is engaged in many scientific activities and is the author of over 85 publications on medical topics.

He was nominated for election as an RSFSR people's deputy in the No. 153 Blagoveshchensky territorial district, Altai *krai*, by collectives of five hospitals, four *raion* epidemiological stations, two chemists' shops, two Farmatsiya local departments and a medical school, located in five *raions* of the *krai*, as well as the plenum of the Suetsky Party *raion* committee. During the election campaign he advocated quality medical care for the residents of villages; providing rural medical establishments with competent specialists; retaining all graduates of the *krai* medical institute in the *krai*; attracting finance, including hard currency, from enterprises in the *krai* to procure the most urgently needed medicines; the establishment of a centre of eastern medicine with the participation of Chinese doctors in the *krai*; the closing down of the nuclear testing range at Semipalatinsk, Kazakhstan; legal responsibility for violating labour legislation and the environment; and children up to the age of three years to be cared for by their mothers on full pay from their workplace. Priests should be afforded the opportunity of preaching moral values. He underlined the need to fight for the rights of all nationalities, the development of national languages, literatures and customs.

There were three candidates. Askalonov polled 61.6% in the first round and was therefore elected. His main opponent was V. D. Chernyaev, first secretary of Kluchevsky Party *raion* committee, Altai *krai*, who received 15.4% of the votes. Askalonov was elected a member of the RSFSR Supreme Soviet at the I Congress of People's Deputies (548 voted for, 386 voted against). He is a member of the Council of the Republic, the Presidium of the Supreme Soviet, and on August 16, 1990 he was elected chairman of the Supreme Soviet committee on health, social security and physical culture. He was awarded the order of the Red Banner of Labour. He is married with a daughter, and is fond of hunting.

Address: 103274 Moscow, K 274, Krasnopresnenskaya nab., d. 2, Dom Sovetov; *telephone*: Moscow 205 50 54.

Aslakhanov, Aslanbek Akhmedovich

Chairman of the Russian Supreme Soviet committee on legality, public order and the struggle against crime.

Born on March 11, 1942 into a Chechen family in the village of Novye Atagi, Shalinsky *raion*, Chechen-Ingush ASSR. From 1959 to 1961 he was a worker, asphalt layer and brigade leader in Argun, then from 1961 to 1962 he was a student in the Grozny Pedagogical Institute and served in the armed forces from 1962 to 1965. He continued his studies as an external student and graduated in 1965 from the Grozny Pedagogical Institute, in 1971 from the Institute of Law, Grozny, in 1975 from the Institute of Economics, Grozny, and in 1981 from the Academy of the USSR Ministry of the Interior. He successfully presented his candidate dissertation in law (LLM).

In 1965 he was appointed a lecturer in the Institute of Mining and in 1967 joined the Ministry of Interior, Chechen-Ingush ASSR, as an operational officer, later promoted to senior officer and chief of service for the struggle against economic crime within the Ministry of Interior in Grozny. From 1975 to 1979 he was deputy chairman of the Dinamo *oblast* soviet executive committee, chief of the police department, and deputy head of the criminal investigation department of the USSR Ministry of Interior administration on the Baikal-Amur railway (BAM). From 1979 to 1981 he studied at the Academy of the USSR Ministry of the Interior.

From 1981 to 1989 he was a senior inspector, deputy head of department, head of department, and chief inspector of the USSR Ministry of the Interior in Moscow. He is a colonel-general of the militia and has received nine government awards. In June 1989 he was awarded the order of the Red Star for overcoming terrorists who had seized an aircraft with 54 passengers on board. In January 1990 he was nominated for election as an RSFSR people's deputy in the No. 138 Gudermes national territorial district, Chechen-Ingush ASSR. Seventeen candidates stood for election, and Aslakhanov polled 22.4% of the votes in the first round and won the second round, polling 50.1% of the votes. His main opponent was R. A. Bisultanov who received 36.8% of the votes in the second round. He was elected a deputy of the Supreme Soviet Council of Nationalities at the I Congress of People's Deputies (748 voted for, 175 voted against).

During the election campaign he advocated the use of preventive measures to ensure that juveniles do not break the law, effective measures to promote personal security and the property of citizens, the stimulation of citizens' involvement and initiative in ensuring peace and order in the locality, the stepping up of the struggle against bribery, theft and speculation, misuse of power in trade and services, and crimes against the person. He promised to take all these issues up if elected a deputy.

He was elected chairman of the Supreme Soviet committee on legality, public order and the struggle against crime. He was also a member of the Extraordinary Committee on food supply. He is a member of the sovereignty and equality faction, and as such he belongs to the centrist and conservative opposition to the Yeltsin administration. He favours a slow, regulated transition to the market and sees little advantage in privatization since it passes the wealth of the country to a minority, many of whom acquired their wealth by dubious means. He is a member of the ex-communist nomenclature who has found it difficult to come to terms with post-communist Russia with its "wild Western capitalism", lawlessness and corruption. He enjoys sport, and is married with two children.

Address: 103274 Moscow, Krasnopresnenskaya nab. 2., d. 2., Dom Sovetov; *telephone*: Moscow 205 9448 (office); 415 9869 (home).

Astafev, Mikhail Georgevich

Chairman of the Central Committee of the Constitutional Democratic Party — Party of Popular Freedom.

Born in 1946 in Moscow into a Russian family. He was never a member of the CPSU. He graduated in physics from Moscow State University in 1970 and worked afterwards in the institute of physical chemistry, USSR Academy of Sciences, as a scientific assistant.

In February 1989, during the election campaign to the USSR Congress of People's Deputies, he joined the Moscow popular front and became one of the leaders of its non-socialist democratic faction. From August 1, 1989 he was deputy chairman of the council of the Moscow popular front, and in January 1990 was one of the founding members of the election bloc, Democratic Russia. Its name was proposed by Astafev and he succeeded in having the former name, Elections 90, changed.

He was elected to the RSFSR Congress of People's Deputies in March 1990 for the No. 11 Dzerzhinsky territorial district, Moscow. During the election campaign he advocated a realistic approach to the problem of finding a way out of the crisis, the establishment of a coalition government consisting of the representatives of all constructive, creative attitudes. He favoured the municipalization of property and, based on it, the establishment of about ten competitive corporations, the agreement of general programmes and co-operation during the election campaign.

There were 13 candidates. Astafev polled 36.72% of the votes in the first round and won in the second round, polling 61.7% of the votes. His main opponent was Stanislav Kunyaev, editor-in-chief of the journal *Nash Sovremennik* (our contemporary), which published many Russian nationalist articles, who received 13.74% of the votes in the first round and 29.6% in the second. He is a member of the Supreme Soviet committee on the freedom of conscience, religion, mercy and charity.

During the autumn of 1989 he had joined the Union of Constitutional Democrats, and in May 1990 he participated in the constituent congresses of the Party of Constitutional Democrats, led by V. Zolotarev, and the Democratic Party of Russia, headed by Nikolai Travkin. He was also a member of the Moscow organizational committee of the Free Democratic Party of Russia but did not became a member of any of these parties. In the summer of 1990 he took part in the unsuccessful attempts to unite the Kadet (constitutional democrats) and the organizations connected with the Kadets (Kadet Party — Party of Constitutional Democrats — PKD, the Small Constitutional Democratic Party — Party of Popular Freedom — KDP-PNS, young Russia and so on).

In August 1990 he joined the KDP-PNS and became chairman of its central committee. In September 1990 he became a member of the organizational committee of the liberal forum movement. During the summer of 1990 he was elected to the organizational committee of the Democratic Russia movement (DemRossiya) and in December 1990 became a member of its co-ordinating committee as a representative of the KDP-PNS. In December 1990, at the RSFSR Congress of People's Deputies, he joined the parliamentary group

Russian union, set up by Viktor Aksyuchits (Russian Christian Democratic Movement, the KDP-PNS, part of the Democratic Party of Russia, and so on). During the autumn of 1991 he, Aksyuchits and Travkin left DemRossiya.

At the beginning of 1992 he and Aksyuchits helped to found the Russian popular assembly movement (RNS) which led to their breaking away from the democratic camp and forming a close bloc with the national-patriots, and Astafev became co-chairman of the RNS. He played an active part in the setting up of Russian unity, a parliamentary opposition bloc of conservative communists and, on April 5, 1992 he was elected to its co-ordinating council. On the instigation of Astafev and Aksyuchits the RNS did not join the united opposition, an extra-parliamentary opposition group, which had been founded by ex-communists. Unlike many of those who share his views, Astafev has a sense of humour. During one of the meetings of the council of DemRossiya in 1991, which was discussing the savage attacks by Saddam Hussein on the Kurds, he proposed two amendments: replace Saddam Hussein by Zviad Gamsakhurdia (the Georgian leader) and Kurds by the inhabitants of South Ossetia.

He is a national patriot, a westerner and a liberal, placing greatest store in the freedom of the individual, the defence of human rights within their national context and tries to stress pre-revolutionary traditions. His party is in opposition to the government since January 1992 when Astafev spoke out against Gaidar's reforms which favoured not the producer but the trader and would lead to a fall in production. In his view, Gaidar was a technocrat whose policy of a balanced budget had collapsed. He had excessive freedom and his economic policy should be curbed by the authority above him. Astafev viewed the freeing of prices in an absolute monopoly as senseless. The course being conducted by the government was leading to huge losses for the country in the political, military and economic spheres. The government consisted of temporary ministers and it would be no surprise to him if they emigrated.

He was opposed to the left radical, destructive forces which were deliberately causing Russia harm, and advocated genuine multi-party politics, with the parties agreeing with the government on the appointment of ministers. Astafev leans to the right of centre and favours the evolutionary path of development. He does not play the liberal as the "whining intelligentsia" does, is drawn to traditional conservative values and is banking on Russian entrepreneurs.

He accepts as unconstitutional the dissolution of the USSR and the founding of the CIS and supports the unification of South Ossetia, Pridnestrovie and the Crimea with Russia. He advocates the re-establishment of the USSR, the convention of a constituent assembly of the citizens of the USSR and the creation of a new federation, preferably consisting of four republics, Russia, Ukraine, Belarus and Kazakhstan. He is opposed to a confederation, or commonwealth, which underlines the collapse of the state. He believes that it is not necessary to use military force and shed blood in order to unite the country, but he regards it as his duty to proclaim the goal of unification. He is against accepting aid from the West, as he thinks its credits are only being extended to break up Russian high technology branches. He recognizes the right to private property but simultaneously criticizes it, believing that only by means of this can national patriotic interests be defended. However, the creation of a situation as in 1917 when the differences between the very rich, the rich and the poor had reached dangerous proportions should be guarded against. He favours the promotion of a powerful middle class, the drafting of economic programmes by parties and the formation of a shadow cabinet. Tactically he regards Ruslan Khasbulatov as an ally, and supports an early general election and co-operation with the centre. He is against the convention of a constituent assembly.

He is one of the co-chairmen of the National Salvation Front. His party decided to join the Front but local organizations decide for themselves if they wish to join. He was nominated as a candidate for the post of mayor of Moscow at the session of the Moscow city council (Mossovet) which announced the election on February 28, 1993, and in his election campaign argued in favour of dropping the terms mayor and Moscow government, referring to it as a town council (*uprava*) and placing it under the control of representative authorities. He promised to put an end to the war between the administration and Mossovet. He opposed privatization, and advocated a coalition government consisting of representatives of all political organizations belonging to the National Salvation Front.

He favoured the openness of the apparatus to control by the deputies and the fusing of the executive and representative powers. The market should not be a goal in itself and the introduction of the market should not lead to poverty. He called the policies of Popov and Luzhkov (the former mayor and vice mayor) a diversion and promised to take administrative measures to ensure the collection of taxes, to continue the struggle against the mafia and to provide credits and advantages to producers. The chief task of the political forces in Moscow was the removal of those in power in the Kremlin. He is a member of the editorial board of the newspaper, *Den* (day). He lives in Moscow.

Aushev, Ruslan Sultanovich

President of the Ingush Republic, Russian Federation.

Born in 1954 in the village of Volodarskoe, Kokchetav *oblast*, Kazakhstan, into a civil servant's family. He was born in exile in Kazakhstan since his parents and the rest of the Ingush nation had been deported there in 1944 by Stalin, due to their alleged collaboration with the German *Wehrmacht*. They returned to the Chechen-Ingush Autonomous Soviet Socialist Republic in the late 1950s after Khrushchev had quashed the accusations. He is Ingush. He graduated from the Ordzonikidze (now Vladikavkaz) Higher General Army Command Technical College and in 1985 from the M. V. Frunze Military Academy.

He fought in Afghanistan, commanding a motorized rifle battalion, and was made a hero of the Soviet Union. In 1989 he was commander of a motorized rifle regiment in the Far East military district, and was also elected a USSR people's deputy in 1989. He ended his service in the Far East as deputy head of a department of the military preparation army.

Maj.-Gen. Aushev is head of the committee for Afghan war veterans in the CIS. On February 28, 1993 he was elected the first President of the Ingush Republic. He is married with two children and lives in Nazran.

Aven, Petr Olegovich

Minister of Foreign Economic Relations of the Russian Federation, February to December 1992.

Born on March 16, 1955 in Moscow into a Latvian family. In 1977 he graduated from the economics faculty of Moscow state university, began postgraduate work and in 1980 successfully presented his candidate dissertation in economics (PhD Econ). From 1981-88 he was a junior, then senior scientific assistant of the All-Union scientific research institute of systems analysis, USSR Academy of Sciences. From 1989 to 1991 he was an adviser of the USSR Ministry of Foreign Affairs and simultaneously worked under contract for the International Institute of Applied Systems Analysis, Vienna. During the autumn of 1991 he became a member of the "reform government" as chairman of the committee of foreign economic relations and first deputy Russian Minister of Foreign Affairs. Aven's committee operated within the ministry and he acted as a minister of the Russian government.

In February 1992, Aven was appointed minister of the newly formed Ministry of Foreign Economic Relations. He was optimistic about the potential of Russia to export, believing that the ruble would be fully convertible in the near future. The main functions of his ministry were the sale of quotas and licences for the export of goods and the supervision of their implementation. He accompanied President Boris Yeltsin to Madrid and Paris and took part in discussions with politicians and businessmen in Spain and France. Agreement was reached to provide large credits which were essential for the import of food by Russia. He was targeted by the industrial lobby as it gained in influence. Civic Union in parliament accused him of incompetence and failure to defend the interests of Russia. He was regarded as an academic and a theoretician without "hands-on" experience of industry.

When Yeltsin's authority declined in the autumn of 1992, he was forced to make concessions. At the December 1992 Congress of People's Deputies the President was obliged to choose his Prime Minister from among three candidates proposed by the Congress. When Egor Gaidar came bottom of the poll, Yeltsin appointed Viktor Chernomyrdin Prime Minister. He represented the industrial lobby and there was speculation that all the reform-minded ministers might have to go. However, in the end, only Aven departed. He was a member of the group of ministers who favoured "shock therapy" for the Russian economy, starting from January 1992. He favoured the integration of Russia into the world market economy as quickly as possible, huge foreign investment in the Russian economy and full convertibility of the ruble. Poland's shock therapy had been accompanied by a freeing of external trade, but Russia rejected this policy, preferring industry to concentrate on the domestic market. The result was that much was exported, especially oil, without authority, due to the lack of adequate checks at frontiers. The Russian government also lost much revenue as companies opened accounts abroad and left earnings there. The failure of the Russian parliament to pass the corporate law necessary to establish a market economy meant that Aven's hopes for a rapid integration of Russia into the world economy were dashed.

Averbakh, Yury Lvovich

International Grand Master; first deputy chairman, Russian Chess Federation.

Born in Kaluga in 1922. He graduated in 1945 from the Higher Technical College, Moscow, and from 1945 to 1950 he was a junior scientific assistant in the scientific research institute, USSR Ministry of Aviation. From 1950 to 1962 he was chess coach to the Zenit sports society, and in 1962 was appointed editor-in-chief of the magazine, *Shakhmatny Vestnik* (Chess news). He was deputy chairman (1962-72), then chairman (1972-77), USSR chess federation, and in 1977 became first deputy chairman. He was a member of the commission for the media and information and a Soviet delegate to FIDE (the world chess federation).

He has published over 40 books on chess and is an honoured master of sport (chess). His hobbies are swimming and numismatics. He speaks English and German and is married with a grown-up daughter.

Address: 121019 Moscow, Bul. Gogoevskogo 19a, kv. 45; *telephone*: Moscow 245 5697.

Babenko, Vladimir Dmitrievich

Head of the Administration of Tambov *oblast*, Russian Federation.

Born January 20, 1931. He spent his childhood and youth in Ryazan *oblast* in a family of a collective farm worker. He is Russian, and was a member of the CPSU until 1991. In 1965 he graduated from Ryazan Medical Institute and was a surgeon for three years in the Mordvin Autonomous Soviet Socialist Republic. In 1968 he moved to Tambov and began working in the *oblast* hospital. In 1971 he was appointed head of the urological department of the second city hospital, Tambov, and acquired the title of surgeon urologist because of his high professional qualifications. In 1977 he became chief doctor of the *oblast* hospital. Under his direction, the reconstruction of the *oblast* began, a new specialized department was opened and the hospital was equipped with up-to-date diagnostic equipment. He became an honoured doctor of the USSR and received the order of the Friendship of Peoples.

In March 1990 he was nominated for election as an RSFSR people's deputy in the No. 688 Leninsky territorial district, Tambov. During the election campaign he declared that he viewed Russia as a free autonomous republic which should enjoy wide-ranging political and economic rights. The wasteful attitude towards the wealth of Russia should cease, there should be a reorientation of the industrial potential and those economic programmes which ignore Russian interests should be terminated. More investment in culture, science and health was needed and the main reason for the poor state of the country was that investment in these areas had low priority.

There were eight candidates. In the first round Babenko polled 27.8% of the votes and won the second round, polling 55.5% of the votes. His main opponent was Yu. N. Blokhin, second secretary of the Tambov Party *obkom*, who received 15.3% of the votes in the first round and 24.2% in the second round. At the same time Babenko was elected a deputy to the Tambov *oblast* soviet of people's deputies. He was a member of the Supreme Soviet Council of the republic commission on the budget, plans, taxes and prices, a member of the Supreme Soviet committee on health, social security and physical culture, and also a member of the medical workers' group and the coalition of reforms bloc of deputies. He had previously been a member of the communists for democracy faction.

In August 1991 at an extraordinary session of the Tambov *oblast* soviet he condemned the position of the *oblast* soviets which were slow to evaluate the political situation after August 19. He was appointed head of the administration of Tambov *oblast* on December 23, 1992 by presidential decree. Previously he had been acting head of the administration. He lives in Tambov.

Badretdinov, Nil Karamovich

Director of the Altynai Fund for the Development of Tatar Culture, Republic of Bashkortostan, Russian Federation.

Born in 1936 in the village of Urazbakhtino, Chishminsky *raion*, Bashkir ASSR. Tatar. His parents were ordinary rural dwellers and are both dead. His brother is Flyur Badretdinov. He graduated from the Institute of Communications, Kuibyshev, as an electrical engineer. From 1960 to 1962 he worked as an electrical engineer in Ufa and from 1970 to 1976 as head of the communications service. In 1976 he was elected chairman of the *oblast* committee of the trade union of workers in communications, Bashkir ASSR. He held this post until 1983. In March 1988 he proposed the establishment of a Tatar culture and art appreciation society. At the first *kurultai* (congress) of the Tatar Public Centre (TPC) he was elected to the *Gali Mejlis* (leading organization), Bashkir ASSR. He is an active member of the TPC and the Ufa club for Tatar culture. In February 1992, under the aegis of the TPC, the Altynai fund for the development of Tatar culture was established and Badretdinov was elected its director.

He was a member of the TPC of Bashkiria delegation which presented President Boris Yeltsin with documents proposing the establishment of a Ufa Republic (*oblast*) within the Russian Federation if the national problems of the Tatar people in the Bashkir ASSR could not be resolved. Badretdinov advocates that the Republic of Bashkortostan remain a subject of the Russian Federation.

He is married to Roza Galievna Badretdinova, who is a teacher and the daughter of teachers. They have two children; a son, Ildar, and a daughter who is still at school; and they live in Ufa.

Home address: Russia, Republic of Bashkortostan, Ufa, ul. Krasina, Dom 13, kv. 19.

Badzio, Yurii Vasylovych

Leader of the Democratic Party of Ukraine until December 1992.

Born into a large Ukrainian peasant family, with nine brothers and sisters, in 1936. After finishing philology studies at Uzhhorod State University in Transcarpathia, he worked until 1965 in the Ukrainian Academy of Sciences, where he prepared his candidate dissertation on theories of literature. At the same time he took an active part in the developing 1960s "informal" movement, including the Club of Working Youth, and as a result was forced to leave the Academy of Sciences in autumn 1965. He was prevented from working in his discipline and remained effectively unemployed from 1965 to 1979.

He remained a Eurocommunist, but wrote many critical letters to the authorities on the school system and on the decline of the Ukrainian language, culminating in the 2,000-page long *Pravo zhyty* (right to live) in 1979. This led to his arrest and sentence to seven years' severe regime in the Mordovian camps, plus five years' exile. He was freed with most other Ukrainian political prisoners in December 1988, and immediately returned to opposition activity.

In 1989 he drafted a political programme for a political party that *Rukh* leaders such as Ivan Drach and Dmytro Pavlychko hoped to create on the basis of the movement, which would still retain a strongly social democratic stance. After the failure to so transform *Rukh* at the meeting of the movement's Grand Council in Khust in March 1990, Badzio organized the formation of what became the Democratic Party of Ukraine (DPU) in December 1990. It claimed the support of 2,800 members and 23 people's deputies, and Badzio was elected leader with 413 votes in favour and 74 against. If the URP was dominated mainly by former political prisoners, the DPU was above all the party of the Ukrainian cultural intelligentsia.

The programme of the DPU was based on Badzio's slogan during his unsuccessful campaign in the March 1990 elections "Amongst all human values, HUMANISM stands in first place". The party regarded itself as centrist, and Badzio saw to it that its economic programme remained broadly social democratic. The party, and Badzio, however, are strongly nationalist. Badzio organized an alliance with the URP in summer 1992, and the two parties then formed the Congress of National-Democratic Forces in August 1992. Badzio sits on the Congress' Council.

However, Badzio became frustrated with the difficulties of organizing his unruly colleagues in the DPU, and at the party's second congress in December 1992 stepped down in favour of Volodymyr Yavorivsky (although he remained a member of the party's Grand Council). He is married with two children.

Address: 252006 Kiev, Vul. Chervonoarmiiska 93, kv. 14; *telephone*: Kiev 269 7697 (home) or Kiev 268 5743 (work).

Bagrov, Mykola Vasylovych

Head of the Crimean Republic.

Born into a Russian family in 1937. He graduated from the Crimean State Pedagogical Institute in 1959, and thereafter worked as a geography and biology lecturer. He joined the Communist Party of Ukraine (CPU) in 1962 and worked his way up the *apparat*. After various positions and a spell in Moscow from 1988 to 1989 he returned to his native Crimea as first secretary of the local CPU *oblast* committee in 1989. After the local elections in March 1990 he also took over the post of leader of the local soviet. At the same time he was elected people's deputy for the Nyzhnogirskii *raion* in the Crimea (in the first round) to the Kiev Supreme Soviet, where he is a member of the committee on state sovereignty and international and inter-republican relations.

Since the first stirrings of the national movement in Kiev, Bagrov has sought to preserve his position by distancing the peninsula from Kiev. In November 1990 the Crimean Supreme Soviet condemned the 1954 transfer of the peninsula from the RSFSR to Ukraine, and in January 1991 Bagrov organized a referendum to give the Crimea the status of an Autonomous Soviet Socialist Republic, which secured 93% support on an 80% turnout. The Declaration of Ukrainian Independence in August 1991 placed Bagrov in a more difficult position, however.

Since then he has sought to play off Ukrainian and Russian support to secure the best deal for himself and the local élite he represents. In September 1991 he declared Crimean sovereignty, but promises made by Kravchuk during a visit to the Crimea that October to allow the local élite to remain in power disarmed the separatist impulse for the time, and the Crimea voted 54% (on a relatively low turnout) for Ukrainian independence on December 1, 1991.

However, the conflict over the Black Sea Fleet and growing interference by Russian politicians, plus the campaign for a separatist referendum by the Republican Movement of the Crimea, forced Bagrov to adopt a harder line in early 1992, culminating in a Declaration of Crimean Independence in May 1992. Bagrov survived calls for his arrest in the Ukrainian Supreme Soviet, and a compromise emerged whereby Bagrov withdrew the Declaration in return for a favourable division of powers between Kiev and the peninsula.

Bagrov was soon threatening to disrupt the fragile consensus, however, by his hardline attitude to the Crimean Tatars (he called for their main organization, the *Majlis*, to be banned in October 1992) and by a controversial visit to Moscow seeking economic support in November 1992. Bagrov remains an unprincipled opportunist, but one in an exceptionally favourable position so long as both Moscow and Kiev are competing for his favour. Moscow so far has not chosen to support the demands of the ethnic Russian majority in the Crimea in their conflict with Kiev. This could be used by the Russians to put pressure on the Ukrainian government to make concessions to their northern neighbour. President Boris Yeltsin is content not to raise this hornet's nest but his obstreperous Vice-President, Aleksandr Rutskoi, has called for the Crimea to be returned to Russia. This puts Bagrov is quite a strong position but a cloud on his horizon is the demand by the Tatars, deported by Stalin in 1944 for allegedly collaborating with the German *Wehrmacht* (charges dropped by Khrushchev), for the return of their property. They have so far been confined to the less hospitable north of the peninsula but covet the richer south.

Official address (Crimean Supreme Soviet): 333005 Simferopol, Vul. Karla Marksa 18; *telephone*: Simferopol (0652) 25 6404.

Bakatin, Vadim Viktorovich

Former chairman of the USSR KGB.

Born on November 6, 1937 in Kiselevsk, Kemerovo *oblast*, Siberia; Russian. He was a member of the CPSU from 1964 to 1991 (he was a member of the Party Central Committee, 1986-91). In 1960 he graduated from the Novosibirsk construction engineering institute, and then began working in the Kemerovo chemical construction trust first as a foreman, then works superintendent, head of a section, chief engineer, and head of the construction board of the trust. In 1971 he became chief engineer of the house-building combine, Kemerovo. In 1973 he moved into Party work when he was elected second secretary of the Kemerovo city Party committee. In 1975 he became head of department, and in 1977 secretary of the Kemerovo Party *obkom*. In 1983 he was appointed an inspector of the Party Central Committee, and in 1985 he graduated from the Academy of Social Sciences of the Party Central Committee.

The same year he became first secretary of the Kirov Party *obkom*, and in 1987 he became first secretary of Kemerovo Party *obkom*. In 1988 he was appointed USSR Minister of Internal Affairs, and then in March 1990, at the III USSR Congress of People's Deputies he was nominated for the post of USSR President by the Soyuz parliamentary group of deputies but withdrew. In March 1990 he was appointed to the USSR presidential Council. In June 1990 he was nominated for the post of first secretary of the Russian Communist

Party but again withdrew, and in December 1990 he was dismissed as USSR Minister of Internal Affairs. Some commentators saw him as a sacrifice to the rising tide of conservative influence around Gorbachev. Bakatin was not regarded by conservatives as sufficiently willing to use force to secure the continued dominance of the CPSU, especially against nationalist opposition in non-Russian republics. His successor General Boris Pugo was one of the conspirators during the attempted August 1991 coup.

In February 1991 Bakatin became a member of the USSR security council. In 1991 he was nominated by various work collectives in Kirov *oblast* as a candidate for the post of President of the RSFSR. In his election campaign he advocated the setting up of a round table of the basic public political forces of Russia so as to get agreement on how to surmount the political and economic crisis, the immediate signing of a new Union treaty and the drafting of a Russian federal treaty which would expand the rights of local self-government and avert the collapse of the RSFSR.

Economically he proposed measures to stabilize and gain greater Russian control over the Russian economy: reform the taxation system, liberalize prices, and implement gradual privatization beginning on a small scale. In agriculture he favoured collective forms of economy, proposing instead of private ownership of land the establishment of leasing and confirmation of the right to use of the land for ever. He supported the provision of social guarantees to the population during the transition to the market economy. On June 12, 1991 Bakatin polled 3.42% of the votes and hence was bottom of the poll of six candidates. Boris Yeltsin was elected President of the RSFSR.

On August 19, 1991 Bakatin forwarded to Gennady Yanaev a declaration about his inability to carry out his duties as a member of the USSR security council. V. M. Primakov and he signed the declaration of the members of the USSR security council which stated that they regarded the activities of the Extraordinary Committee as illegal and demanded the return of President Mikhail Gorbachev to his duties as USSR President. On August 21, 1991 Bakatin spoke at the session of the RSFSR Supreme Soviet and proposed himself as head of the operation to bring President Mikhail Gorbachev back to Moscow. He took part in the operation the same day, and on August 22-23, as a member of the security council, he conducted an investigation into the activities of the Alpha group on August 19-21, 1991.

On August 23, 1991 he was appointed chairman of the USSR KGB, renamed the Inter-republican Security Service (ISS), following the arrest of KGB chief Vladimir Kryuchkov and the suicide of Boris Pugo. Bakatin was charged with liquidating the former KGB, and divided it up into three independent branches; law and order, intelligence, and counter-intelligence. He gave an interview in his office in the Lubyanka and appeared in a TV discussion with Vladimir Bukovsky, a famous former dissident. Bakatin was opposed to immediate free public access to KGB files but stated that the greater part of them should be transferred to national archives. This has not so far happened.

In January 1992, after the collapse of the USSR and the liquidation of the ISS, he ceased to be head of the ISS. He is married with grown-up children, and his son worked in the USSR KGB and was dismissed on August 23, 1991.

Bakatin likes to play tennis. He built his own dacha and paints. He lives in Moscow.

Baklanov, Oleg Dmitrevich

Member of the Extraordinary Committee.

Born on March 17, 1932 in Kharkov (Kharkiv), Ukraine. Ukrainian. He was a member of the CPSU from 1953 to August 1991. He began work in 1950 as a fitter in a Kharkov factory, then as a tuner, a foreman, head of a section, deputy head and head of a shop and deputy chief engineer of the enterprise. In 1958 he graduated from the all-Union extra-mural institute of energy. In 1969 he successfully presented his candidate dissertation in technical sciences (PhD). From 1963 to 1976 he was chief engineer, director of a factory and general director of a production association. In 1976 he became deputy, in 1981 first deputy and in 1983 USSR Minister of General Machine Building (the ministry responsible for the production of nuclear weapons).

In 1986 he was elected a member of the Party Central Committee and in 1988 became a secretary of the Party Central Committee responsible for the military industrial complex. He was a delegate to the XXVI and XXVII Party congresses and XIX Party conference. He was elected a USSR people's deputy in 1986, and in March 1989 he was nominated as a USSR people's deputy by the CPSU and was elected. He was made a hero of socialist labour in 1976 and awarded the orders of Lenin, the October Revolution, two orders of the Red Banner of Labour, badge of honour and medals. He received the Lenin prize in 1982.

He was a member of the Extraordinary Committee in August 1991 and was arrested on August 22, 1991. During the investigation he was held in the *Matrosskaya tishina* isolator. He and other members of the Committee were later released.

He is married and his wife, Liliya Fedorovna, is a radio engineer. Their son, Dmitry, is an economist and their granddaughter, Liliya, is 11 years old. He lives in Moscow.

Balakshin, Pavel Nikolaevich

Head of the Administration of Arkhangelsk *oblast*, Russian Federation.

Born in 1936 in the village of Dementevo, Kotlassky *raion*, Arkhangelsk *oblast*; Russian; member of the CPSU from 1964 to August 1991. He graduated in 1965 from the Sokolsky Pulp and Paper Technical College and in 1972 from the Arkhangelsk Timber Technical College, as an extra-mural student. He began his working life as a fitter in the construction section on the Pechora railway line, then served in the Soviet Army, and from 1959 to 1985 worked in the Kotlassky pulp and paper combine, where he began as a worker and ended as chief engineer. He was director of the Aldinsky pulp and paper factory in Ioshkar-Ola for two years while it was being built and then became chief engineer of the *Soyuztsellyuloza* all-Union association. In 1987 he was appointed general director of the production association, *Arkhangelsky tsellyulozno-bumazhny kombinat*. He is the recipient of the orders of the October Revolution and the Red Banner of Labour, and medals.

In 1990 he was elected a people's deputy of Arkhangelsk *oblast* soviet. On April 7, 1990, at the first session of the *oblast* soviet, he was elected chairman of the *oblast* soviet executive committee. On August 20, 1991 he sent a telegram to the chairmen of the *raion* soviet executive committees and the managers of enterprises, stating that power in the *oblast* belonged to the legally elected soviets and their executive committees, implementing the RSFSR constitution and the decrees of the RSFSR President. No extraordinary committees have been set up in the *oblast*, cities and *raions* and there is no need to set them up. At 13.15 he sent a telegram to Gennady Yanaev, Vice-President of the USSR and one of the coup leaders, President Boris Yeltsin and V. A. Makharadze, declaring his subordination to the constitution, laws and President of the RSFSR.

The Presidium of the Arkhangelsk *oblast* soviet proposed Balakshin for the post of head of the administration of Arkhangelsk *oblast* and on September 19, 1991 he was appointed head of the administration by presidential decree. On assuming office he appealed for the creation of a fund to support small and medium size businesses, the most rapid transition to a market economy, improvements in the structure of the administration, more power and autonomy for the *oblast*, and the drafting of the budget at the local level. He participated in the drafting of the government decrees on the social and economic development of the *oblast*.

In December 1992, during the VII Congress of People's Deputies, he supported President Yeltsin and proposed Egor Gaidar as Prime Minister. However, he did not agree with the threatening tone of the declaration of the governors of Russia, opposed the confrontation with the Supreme Soviet and appealed for the situation to be overcome. He thought that the executive power should not act as a political force and that there would be no coup during the congress. He lives in Novodvinsk, Arkhangelsk *oblast*.

Baltin, Eduard Dmitrievich

Commander-in-Chief of the Black Sea Fleet; Vice-Admiral.

Born on December 21, 1936 in Smolensk into a civil servant's family, Russian. He graduated from the Caspian S. M. Kirov Higher Naval Technical School, mine-torpedo department in 1958; the Naval Academy in 1975; the Military Academy of the General Staff in 1980. His higher military education was specializing in naval operational-tactics. He was a member of the CPSU from 1959 till August 1991.

He began his career as an officer on surface vessels of the Black Sea Fleet as a commander of a mine-torpedo section. He was a good professional seaman and interested in his service and military profession. He was actively involved in Party-political work, was elected to *Komsomol* agencies, and was eager to gain support from commanders and political agencies to ensure promotion. Soon he volunteered to serve in a submarine formation of the Black Sea Fleet. Here he was a section commander, assistant and senior assistant commander and commander of a submarine. He took part in long voyages, including the first voyages by Soviet ships into the Mediterranean. The crew under him gained distinction and repeatedly attained high results in special combat training.

After graduating from the higher special classes he was appointed senior assistant commander of a nuclear submarine in the Northern fleet in 1969, and from 1971 he was commander of a nuclear submarine. He often did his military service at sea, making long voyages and ensuring a high level of combat readiness of his submarine, and his work was approved by commanders and political agencies. After graduating from the Naval Academy he was Chief of Staff and later commander of a nuclear submarine division.

On October 9, 1981, Captain Eduard Baltin was made Hero of the Soviet Union for courage and prowess in carrying out important tasks and for mastering new strategic weapons.

In 1983 he was appointed commander of a nuclear submarine flotilla in the Pacific Fleet; in 1987 the first deputy Commander-in-Chief of the Pacific Fleet. He was personally in charge of combat and special training of heterogeneous naval forces in the Pacific Ocean, and he himself took part in ocean voyages. He proved to be a highly qualified military professional. His record was that of an officer with a sound operational-tactical and military-technical training, capable of a creative approach and comprehensive appraisal of the situation when making decisions. He proved to be an orthodox communist, strictly adhering to ideological dogmas. He was elected to leading Party agencies of the fleet and in Kamchatka *oblast*. He reacted extremely negatively to democratic forces; in 1990 the mass media brought to light Vice-Admiral Baltin's conflict with democratic organizations and the "greens" over the setting up of a base to make use of obsolete nuclear submarines near inhabited areas of Maritime *krai*.

In 1990 Vice-Admiral Eduard Baltin was appointed head of the department of operational art of the navy at the Military Academy of the General Staff in Moscow. He played his part in the planning and deployment of the Navy and in the training of top commanders. Politically he advocated conservative views and a strong state. After August 1991, like most conformist Soviet generals and admirals, he renounced communist ideology and the idea of retaining the USSR and expressed his support for the new authorities.

He avoids contacts with the press, and does not broadcast his views on political and social-economic problems. He claims to be a military professional who strictly obeys the command that the army should not be involved in politics.

In January 1993, as a result of the agreement reached in the course of the Russian-Ukrainian summit, he was appointed Commander-in-Chief of the

Black Sea Fleet. On January 19, 1993 in an interview with *Krasnaya Zvezda* he outlined his main tasks: avert a confrontation on the fate of the fleet, take into consideration political realities while adhering to international law, observe the laws and international agreements of all states in the Black Sea region.

He has been awarded an order of Lenin, an order "for service to the motherland in the armed forces of the USSR", 3rd class, and 10 medals.

He is not indifferent to literature, especially to history on military and patriotic subjects and to art. He is interested in the history of Russia and the Navy. He does not speak any foreign language. He has not been abroad as a member of an official delegation but has visited foreign ports when his ship docked there. He is married, but there is no information about any children.

Barabanov, Vladimir Aleksandrovich

Head of the Administration of Bryansk *oblast*, Russian Federation.

Born on August 1, 1951 in Navlinsky *raion*, Bryansk *oblast* into a peasant family; Russian; member of the CPSU until August 1991. He attended the Zharovsky secondary school and graduated from the all-Union institute of agriculture. In 1990 he was elected a deputy of Navlinsky *raion* soviet and then deputy chairman of the executive committee.

In early 1990 he was nominated by the work collectives of Navlinsky *raion* for election as a RSFSR people's deputy in the No. 296 Navlinsky territorial district, Bryansk *oblast*. During the election campaign he advocated sovereignty for Russia within the USSR based on the conclusion of inter-republican treaties and low contributions to the Soviet budget of all-Union enterprises in Russia. He opposed economic autonomy for the regions, and proposed that the role of the soviets be increased and they be afforded real power, adopting a law on the status of people's deputies. He devoted a great deal of attention to the problems of social justice and how to overcome the Chernobyl disaster.

There were four candidates. He polled 37% of the votes in the first round and won the second, polling 50% of the votes. His main opponent was V. M. Eslikov, first deputy chairman of Bryansk *oblast* soviet executive committee, who received 31% of the votes in the first round and 41% in the second. Barabanov is a member of the Supreme Soviet committee on the soviets and development of self-government, a member of the non-party deputies' faction and the Chernobyl and soviets and local self-government groups of deputies.

In October 1991 he was appointed the President's representative in Bryansk *oblast*. On December 14, 1991 he was appointed acting head of the administration of Bryansk *oblast* by presidential decree and on January 22, 1992 head of the administration. On assuming office he stated that among the most pressing duties was speeding up the transition to a market economy, the provision of social security guarantees to the population, the implementation of the law on land reform and the law on enterprise, and overcoming the consequences of the Chernobyl disaster.

In December 1992 he expressed his support for the reforms being carried out by the government of Egor Gaidar. He judged the declaration of the President at the congress to be necessary and the result of the anti-reform stance of the majority of deputies, and took part in the meeting in the Granovitaya palace after the President's address to the Russian people. He lives in Navlya, Bryansk *oblast*.

Barannikov, Viktor Pavlovich

Minister of State Security of the Russian Federation until July 1993; General of the Army since 1992.

Born in 1940 in the settlement of Fedosevka, Pozharsky *raion*, Maritime *krai*, into a working-class family. Russian. He began work in 1957 as a turner at a plant in Tatarstan and became active in the *Komsomol*. After national service in the army he began his career in the internal forces. He graduated from Elabug secondary special police school in 1963 and the Sverdlovsk department of the Moscow higher school of the USSR Ministry of Internal Affairs (MVD) in 1969. His higher education was in law and he was a member of the CPSU until August 1991.

He was a district police officer, worked in the criminal investigation department and was head of an *oblast* MVD department. He worked in Chelyabinsk-65, previously a closed city engaged in nuclear research and development (1963-69), in Kaliningrad (Tver) (1973-83) and Moscow from 1983. He proved himself a highly qualified professional, carried out dozens of criminal investigations and participated personally in the arrest of criminals who put up armed resistance. He also worked in Party organizations. He did not participate in corrupt activities.

In 1985 he was head of the main department of the struggle against theft of socialist property in the central apparatus of the USSR MVD. Boris Yeltsin, when he was first Party secretary in Moscow, encouraged Barannikov to combat corruption and the mafia in Moscow. In 1988, after Yeltsin's dismissal as Moscow first Party secretary, Barannikov was appointed first deputy Minister of Internal Affairs of Azerbaijan. The practice of appointing Moscow representatives as deputy ministers to ensure control from the centre was typical of the Soviet period. Gen. Barannikov's role in the events in Baku in January 1990 still remains unclear. However, top MVD officials could not have avoided being drawn into the conflict which resulted, in January 1990, in troops being brought into Baku and the deaths of numerous victims.

It is unclear how Barannikov came into contact with Boris Yeltsin, but they may have established close ties when they worked together in Sverdlovsk (Ekaterinburg). Yeltsin was involved in the General's promotion to the post of RSFSR Minister of Internal Affairs after Yeltsin became speaker of the Russian Supreme Soviet. Barannikov proved his loyalty to the Russian authorities and the republic's sovereignty, which caused dissatisfaction on the part of the USSR

MVD authorities and led to conflict between them and Barannikov. During the anti-constitutional putsch of August 1991 Barannikov remained solidly behind the legitimate authorities. He was one of the organizers of the defence of the Russian White House and ensured the arrival of internal sub-units and students of the MVD schools in Moscow. He personally took part in the arrest of the members of the Emergency Committee. On August 23, 1991 he was appointed Minister of Internal Affairs of the USSR and on September 5, 1991 he was promoted to Colonel-General. Barannikov was personally responsible for the reorganization of the MVD apparatus, the defining of priority spheres of its activities and its relationship with republican ministries. He ended all Party and political activity in the agencies of the Ministry.

According to Barannikov's personal statement, law-enforcing agencies were to be guided by law and only by law. He opposed the deployment of MVD troops and personnel in domestic political conflicts and took all possible steps to end this practice. By President Boris Yeltsin's decree, Gen. Barannikov was appointed head of the Ministry of State Security and Internal Affairs of the RSFSR when it was set up on October 19, 1991. This appointment revealed the closeness of his relationship with the President and the latter's confidence in him. However the creation of a unified "punitive agency" caused grave concern among the public, politicians and the law enforcing agencies themselves and was seen as a throw-back to the Bolshevik past, reminiscent of Stalin's People's Commissariat of Internal Affairs (NKVD). State security officers were quoted in the press as stating that one of first measures of the new leaders of the ministry was the destruction of KGB files on corrupt MVD officials who had worked closely with Barannikov. The President's decree was the subject of an appeal to the Constitutional Court which ruled that it was illegal. As a result, Barannikov became head only of the Ministry of State Security of the Russian Federation.

As head of this governmental body he is responsible for state security, counter-intelligence (including military), the struggle against organized crime, corruption among top officials, drugs trafficking and terrorism. He advocates close co-operation with Western special services in the struggle against the international drug mafia, terrorism and control over nuclear weapons pro-liferation. He met the director of the CIA during the latter's visit to Moscow in October 1992. He has added fresh impetus to work on the exoneration of the victims of the communist security services. His struggles against violations of the law and waste of state property have received wide press coverage.

By his own personal order, a special commission looked into the legality of the distribution of flats and dachas among generals. This resulted in about 20 top officials being dismissed, including Gen. Oleinik, the first deputy Minister of State Security. In July 1992 Barannikov was promoted to General of the Army, which made him equal in rank to the Minister of Defence, Pavel Grachev. Barannikov is a member of the security council of the Russian President. He is regarded as one of President Yeltsin's closest top officials, an adviser on domestic and foreign policy. According to experts on *Nezavisimiya Gazeta* he was one of the most influential persons in Russian politics. He was regarded as enjoying close relations with Yury Skokov, secretary of the Russian Security

Council. However, he was dismissed in July 1993 and accused of corruption and professional incompetence after the death of 25 Russian border guards on the Tajik-Afghan border.

He is fond of literature and sport as a recreation. He often spends his holidays with President Yeltsin. He does not speak any foreign language and has not been abroad as a member of an official delegation. He has been awarded an order, seven medals and the badge of an honorary internal affairs officer. He is married.

Barchuk, Vasily Vasilevich

Russian Minister of Finance, December 1992-March 1993.

Born on March 11, 1941 in Komsomolsk-on-Amur, Siberia, into a Russian family, and was a member of the CPSU until August 1991. From 1958 he was employed in the financial inspectorate in Komsomolsk-on-Amur and simultaneously enrolled in the all-Union institute of finance and economics in Moscow as an external student from which he graduated in 1966. He remained in the financial inspectorate until 1972, and then was invited to work in the USSR Ministry of Finance. In 1984 he graduated from the Academy of the National Economy of the USSR Council of Ministers and in 1986 he became deputy head, and later head, of the budgetary administration of the USSR Ministry of Finance. In April 1991 Barchuk was appointed deputy RSFSR Minister of Finance, and later first deputy Russian Minister of Economics and Finance when Egor Gaidar was minister.

In December 1992 Barchuk became Russian Minister of Finance. He was a supporter of a policy of keeping the budget deficit down as low as possible, and thought it necessary to cut governmental expenditure drastically with particular attention being paid to the defence sector. He stated that he had arrived at a working relationship with the young economists who had entered the government with Gaidar, despite his own *apparat* background. He was dismissed as Minister of Finance immediately after the VIII Congress of People's Deputies in March 1993.

Bashashkin, Anatoly Vasilevich

Russian footballer.

Born on February 24, 1924; Russian. He is an Honoured Master of Sport (1955). His position was central defender or half back, and he began his playing career in Reutov, Moscow *oblast*, in the youth team of Moscow Spartak in 1941. He played in the officers' team, Tbilisi, Georgia (1945-46); the Central Club of the Red Army (1947-53 and 1954-58); and for Moscow Spartak (1953). He played 183 matches and scored one goal; 171 games for the Central Club and one goal; and 12 games for Spartak. He was a member of the Central Club team which won the USSR championship in 1948, 1950 and 1951 and with Spartak in 1953; and of the Central Club team which won the USSR cup in 1948, 1951 and 1955.

He played in the USSR team in the Olympic Games in Helsinki, Finland, in 1948, and played 24 times for the Soviet Union between 1952 and 1956. He was a member of the winning team in the Spartakiad of the Peoples of the USSR, and in 1956 in Melbourne was a member of the USSR team which won the gold medal. He was captain of the Central Club and the Soviet Union.

Bashmakov, Lev Polievktovich

Head of the Administration of Ryazan *oblast*, Russian Federation.

Born in 1938 in Shue, Ivanovo *oblast*; Russian; member of the CPSU from 1967 to August 1991. He began working in 1961, after graduating from the Krasnoyarsk Polytechnical Institute, as an engineer technologist, foreman, senior engineer technologist, senior foreman, head of a bureau, and deputy head of a shop of an enterprise in Krasnoyarsk. From 1966 to 1980 he worked in the Khmelnitsky radiotechnical enterprise. He was senior engineer technologist, senior foreman, deputy head of a shop, and deputy head of production.

He spent eight years as secretary of the Party committee in the enterprise, and then from 1980 to 1983 he managed a mechanical engineering enterprise in Rovno. From 1983 to 1988 he was general director of the Krasnoe Znamya production association, Ryazan and from December 1988 to March 1990 he was chairman of Ryazan soviet executive committee. In March 1990 he became director of marketing of the Internaut joint venture. He was a member of the bureau of the Ryazan Party *obkom*, a deputy of the Ryazan *oblast* and city soviets. He is the recipient of the orders of the Red Banner of Labour and the badge of honour.

In early 1990 he was nominated for election as an RSFSR people's deputy in the No. 624 Moscow territorial district, Ryazan *oblast*. During the election campaign he advocated raising the legal status and autonomy of local soviets at all levels and the drafting of the budget at the local level, based on the economic activities of local enterprises. He proposed guarantees of autonomy and independence for enterprises, the delineation of the rights and duties of soviets at all levels. He favoured support for the producers of goods by affording them tax breaks; was in favour of the co-operative movement and for the reform of prices but with the maximum compensation for the population. He advocated co-operating with the Green Movement in the *oblast*.

There were four candidates. Bashmakov polled 21.9% of the votes in the first round but lost the second round, polling 41.6% of the votes. A. A. Gvardilov, head engineer of the Spektr special construction bureau, Ryazan Polytechnical Institute, was elected the deputy, receiving 40.7% of the votes in the first round and 50.6% in the second. Bashmakov was elected a deputy of the *oblast* soviet. At the first session of the *oblast* soviet, in March 1990, he was a candidate for the post of chairman of the executive committee but he was defeated by V. V. Kalashnikov, secretary of the Party *obkom*.

On August 21, 1991 Bashmakov criticized the leadership at an extraordinary session of the *oblast* soviet. At the next session, on August 28, 1991, he was proposed for the post of chairman of the *oblast* soviet but refused to stand. On September 25, 1991 he was appointed head of the main administration of Ryazan *oblast* by presidential decree. On assuming office he advocated change in production relations and many forms of property ownership: private, collection and joint stock. He favoured the introduction of market relations, the need to agitate for them, the privatization of trade and support of private farming. He wanted to see changes in the structure of the administration and opposed the command-administrative system. He appealed for the creation of conditions which favoured economic growth. He advocated the conversion of the military economy, the transforming of large agricultural complexes into joint stock companies, the development of free enterprise and autonomy for regions. In December 1992, during the VII Congress of People's Deputies, he supported Egor Gaidar as candidate for Prime Minister. In his spare time he likes gardening, joinery, fishing and reading economic and artistic literature. He lives in Ryazan.

Basin, Efim Vladimirovich

Chairman of the Russian State Committee on Architecture and Construction.

Born on January 3, 1940 in the settlement of Khislovichi, Rzhaksinsky *raion*, Tambov *oblast* into a Russian family, and was a member of the CPSU from 1967 to August 1991. He is a qualified engineer, having graduated from the Belarusian Institute of Railway Transport, Gomel, in 1962, and from the Academy of the National Economy of the USSR Council of Ministers in 1980. In 1980 he successfully presented his candidate dissertation in economics on "Managing the social development of labour collectives in the far North" (PhD (Econ)).

After graduating from the institute of railway transport he was sent to Yaroslavl where he worked until 1969 as a norm setter, foreman, head of No. 302 section, chief engineer and head of the construction administration of the *Sevtransstroi* trust. From 1969 to 1972 he was deputy head, and later chief engineer of the *Gortranstroi* trust in Gorky (now Nizhny Novgorod). From 1972 to 1978 he was head of the *Pechorstroi* administration, Komi autonomous republic. Between 1978 and 1980 he was a member of the first group of students at the Academy of the National Economy of the USSR Council of Ministers and in 1980 began work on the Baikal-Amur main railway line. In 1986 he was appointed head of *Glavbamstroi* and deputy USSR Minister of Transport Construction and in May 1988 he became head of *Bamtransstro*.

He was elected a deputy of the Supreme Soviet of the Komi autonomous republic, a deputy of the Amur *oblast* soviet of people's deputies. He was also a member of various *raion* and city Party committees (*raikoms* and *gorkoms*), Amur *oblast* Party committee (*obkom*) and a delegate to the XIX Party conference in 1988. He was also a member of the railway trade union of BAM construction workers.

In January 1990 he was nominated as a candidate for election as an RSFSR people's deputy in the No. 90 Pribaikalsky national territorial district, Buryat autonomous republic. In his election programme he proposed that BAM's economic potential should be used to transform Buryatia: the development of its agriculture, the strengthening of its social infrastructure and the resolution of its ecological and housing problems. He advocated solving the food problem by promoting economic self-accounting (*khozraschet*) and the leasing and private farming of land. There were 11 candidates.

In the first round Basin polled 16.9% of the votes but won the second round on March 18, 1990, polling 48.7% of the votes. His main opponent was V. B. Saganov, a former Prime Minister of Buryatia, who had been sent in 1987 to the People's Republic of China as a diplomat. He polled 24.2% of the votes in the first round and 40.2% in the second round. Basin was elected a member of the RSFSR Supreme Soviet at the I Congress of People's Deputies on June 11, 1990. From September 1, 1990 he was chairman of the Supreme Soviet committee on construction, architecture and municipal housing. He was a member of the Soviet of Nationalities, the presidium of the Russian Supreme Soviet, of the left centre parliamentary faction and of the *Rossiya* (Russia) and *Sever* (north) parliamentary groups. On September 6, 1991 he was co-opted to the Russian Supreme Soviet presidium commission on the distribution and use of the former buildings and property of the CPSU. In December 1992 he was appointed chairman of the Russian state committee on architecture and construction.

By decree of the USSR President of August 10, 1990 he was made a hero of the Soviet Union for his great contribution to the construction of the Baikal-Amur main line (BAM), ensuring the constant use of the whole railway line. He was awarded the orders of Lenin, Friendship of the Peoples, badge of honour and the medal for outstanding labour, and on the occasion of the 100th anniversary of the birth of V. I. Lenin, for building BAM, the hammer and sickle gold medal. He has also been awarded the badge of honoured transport worker.

His wife, Lyudmila Nikolaevna, is chief engineer of the production department of the Bamstroimekhanizatsiya trust. Their son Oleg works as a shift engineer and their daughter Svetlana is a student. Basin lives in Moscow.

Batagaev, Aleksei Nikolaevich

Head of the Administration of the Ust-Ordinsky Buryat Autonomous *okrug*, Russian Federation.

Born in 1950 in Ust-Ordinsky Buryat autonomous *okrug*. Buryat; member of the CPSU until August 1991. He is a graduate, and until March 1990 he was chairman of the Bokhan *raion* soviet, Ust-Ordinsky Buryat autonomous *okrug*. In March 1990 he was elected a deputy of the Ust-Ordinsky *okrug* soviet of people's deputies, and at the first session in March 1990 he was elected chairman of the *okrug* soviet executive committee.

On December 26, 1991 he was appointed head of the administration of Ust-Ordinsky Buryat autonomous *okrug* by presidential decree. On assuming office he stated that his main task was not to get involved in "big" politics but to do real work. He supported the transformation of collective and state farms into production co-operatives; he advocated extensive inter-regional and foreign links and the conclusion of many different types of barter deals; and supported entrepreneurs who invested in the material sphere and the commercialization of trade. There was a need for measures to be taken concerning relations with monopoly enterprises since the future belonged to small- and medium-scale production units. The latter would find it much easier to adjust to the conditions of a market economy which depend on the level of demand for their products.

In November 1992 he expressed publicly his agreement in principle with the policy of the President and the conduct of economic reform. He lives in the *raion* village of Bokhan.

Bayandin, Lev Sergeevich

Head of the Administration of Yamalo-Nenets Autonomous *okrug*, Russian Federation.

Born in 1942, he is a graduate and was a member of the CPSU until August 1991. In March 1990 he was chairman of the Yamalo-Nenets *okrug* soviet executive committee, was elected deputy for No. 111 electoral district of the Yamalo-Nenets autonomous *okrug*, Tyumen *oblast*, soviet. At the first session of the *okrug* soviet of people's deputies, in May 1990, he was elected chairman of the *okrug* executive committee.

During the attempted coup of August 1991 the Yamalo-Nenets *okrug* executive committee decided to implement existing legislation, the decrees and instructions of the President and government of the RSFSR, but not to permit the formation of state authorities which were not included in the USSR constitution. Strong support was voiced for the constitutional state authorities and the legally elected Presidents of the USSR and RSFSR. No document supporting the Extraordinary Committee was adopted.

In October 1991 Bayandin was appointed head of the administration of the Yamalo-Nenets autonomous *okrug* by presidential decree. On assuming office he reiterated his support of the government of the RSFSR and the economic reforms adopted by it. He called himself a supporter of the development of market relations and he saw a regulated market as the future of the RSFSR. He advocated economic and political autonomy for the republics and autonomous *okrugs*, the rapid expansion of horizontal relations between them and the possible attraction of foreign capital in the economic development of the northern and eastern regions of the RSFSR. These resources should be invested in the extractive industries and there should be joint venture co-operation in the discovery of natural resources.

In December 1992 he stated that in the present difficult economic and political situation, there was no need for a Congress of People's Deputies, as the most important questions were on the agenda of the congress. However, a concrete programme of action which addressed the demands of the present day, was absent. Despite the fact that some ministers were more favoured than others, there was no point in changing the government, and this included the acting Prime Minister, Egor Gaidar, at present. Economic reform should be carried through by those ministers who had begun it. He lives in Salekhard, Yamalo-Nenets autonomous *okrug*.

Beisenov, Sayat Dyusenbaievich

Minister of Labour, Republic of Kazakhstan.

Born in 1940 in the village of Kondratevka, Karaganda *oblast* Kazakh SSR; Kazakh. He was a member of CPSU until August 1991. He began work after secondary school as an electrician in the municipal electrical system, Karaganda, and then served in the Soviet army. After demobilization he entered the Lenin Institute of Power Engineering, Ivanovo, and after graduation was employed in the Temirtau enterprise as a foreman, engineer and later was head of municipal services, Temirtau. Then he was elected deputy chairman, and later chairman of the soviet executive committee.

He then transferred to the apparatus of the Council of Ministers, Kazakh SSR, and in 1985 he was appointed Kazakh Minister of Consumer Services. In 1991 he was appointed Minister of Labour, Republic of Kazakhstan. He is faced with a difficult task as he attempts to increase the skill and labour productivity of the republic's workforce. The skilled industrial labour force is predominantly Slav, especially Russian, and is concentrated in the centre and north of the state. In order to vitiate thoughts of secession to Russia Beisenov needs to ensure that living and working conditions in Kazakhstan are equal to or better than in Russia, and in this he is helped by the fact that Kazakhstan is rich in natural resources, especially fuel and hydrocarbons. Foreign companies are to help in the development of these resources. Privatization will make little headway in Kazakhstan as it would be ethnically divisive, as the political élite favours a corporatist approach.

He is married with a son and two daughters.

Address: 480091 Alma Ata, Prospekt Ablai Khana 93-95; *telephone*: Alma Ata (8 33272) 62 1168.

Belanov, Igor Ivanovich

Russian footballer.

Born on September 25, 1960; Russian. He is an Honoured Master of Sport, (1986), and his position was a forward. He began playing for Chernomorets Odessa in the premier league (1981); moved to Dinamo Kiev in 1985 and remained until 1989 when he signed for Borussia Mönchengladbach, in the West German Bundesliga. He then moved to Eintracht Braunschweig, in the same league. He played 237 matches and scored 65 goals in the USSR championship; 221 matches and 39 goals for Dinamo Kiev and 116 games and 26 goals for Chernomorets Odessa.

He was a member of the Dinamo Kiev championship winning teams of 1985 and 1986; and the USSR cup winning teams in 1985 and 1987. He also played in their team which won the cup of cups in 1986. He played 33 times and scored eight goals for the USSR international team. He played in the World Cup in 1986 and was in the team that was defeated in the final of the European championship in 1988. He was voted European footballer of the year in 1986.

Belyaev, Evgeny Nikolaevich

Chairman of the state committee on sanitary epidemiological inspection and chief medical officer of the Russian Federation; Minister.

Born on October 22, 1937 in the settlement of Peskovka, Kirov *oblast*; Russian. He was a member of the CPSU until August 1991. He graduated in 1961 from the Perm State Institute of Medicine, and worked as a medical officer for work hygiene, Perm sanitary epidemiological station (1961-65); head of the sanitary hygiene department and deputy chief doctor, Perm station (1965-69); chief medical officer of the Perm city station and chief medical officer, Perm (1969-71); instructor in the department of administrative agencies, Perm Party *obkom* (1971-75); chief medical officer of the Perm *oblast* station and chief medical officer of Perm *oblast* (1975-86); deputy RSFSR Minister of Health and chief medical officer of the RSFSR (1990-91).

In 1991 he was appointed chairman of the RSFSR state committee on sanitary epidemiological inspection, and from December 1991 to May 1992 he was chairman of the state committee on sanitary epidemiological inspection of the President of the Russian Federation and chief medical officer of the Russian

Federation. In May 1992 he became chairman of the state committee on sanitary epidemiological inspection of the Russian Federation and chief medical officer of the Russian Federation. He was awarded the order of the badge of honour. He is married with a daughter, and lives in Moscow.

Belyakov, Aleksandr Semenovich

Head of the Administration of Leningrad *oblast*, Russian Federation.

Born on May 20, 1945 in Sortavala, Karelian Autonomous Soviet Socialist Republic, into a working-class family. His father was killed in action in 1945. He was a member of the CPSU until August 1991. He began working in 1963 in the Petrozavodsk locomotive depot as a fitter and assistant to a steam train mechanic, after finishing at the Petrozavodsk Railway Technical College. He served in the Soviet Army from 1964 to 1967, and then from 1968 to 1978 he worked in the Voiskovitsy chicken factory, Leningrad *oblast* as a fitter, engineer and chief engineer. In 1979 he graduated from the Leningrad Agricultural Institute, as an external student, then as an engineer. In 1978 he was assigned to the construction of the Sinyavinsky chicken complex, the largest chicken factory in Europe, as chief engineer. After it began operating in 1980 he became director of the Zavodskaya chicken factory, and in 1984 he was appointed director of the 50th anniversary of the USSR chicken factory, in the village of Pervomaisky, Vyborg *raion*, Leningrad *oblast*. He was elected a deputy of the Vyborg *raion* soviet.

In early 1990 he was nominated by the work collective of the 50th anniversary of the USSR chicken factory for election as an RSFSR people's deputy in the No. 138 Vyborg territorial district, Leningrad *oblast*. During the election campaign he advocated equality for all forms of ownership and the transfer of the means of production to work collectives, the adoption of laws on property, taxes, land and entrepreneurial activity. He appealed for economics to be placed ahead of politics. He supported the implementation of the separation of powers, the transfer of power to the soviets and the establishment of a multi-party system. He proposed that Leningrad *oblast* be afforded the rights of a republic, that Leningrad *oblast* soviet and Leningrad city soviet should be joined and Vyborg transformed into a free enterprise zone.

There were nine candidates. Belyakov lost in the first round and V. I. Gerasimov, chief doctor in Vyborg, was elected people's deputy for the district. In 1990 Belyakov was elected a deputy of the Leningrad *oblast* soviet and its deputy chairman, in a contested election. In October 1991 he was appointed head of the administration of Leningrad *oblast* by presidential decree. He is a member of the board of the union of governors of Russia. He is married and his home is in the village of Roshchino, Vyborg *raion*, Leningrad *oblast*. His son is an officer in the CIS armed forces and his daughter is a graduate of the Leningrad Agricultural Institute.

Belykh, Yury Vasilevich

Head of the Administration of Saratov *oblast*, Russian Federation.

Born in 1941 in the village of Nikolaevka, Ivanteevsky *raion*, Saratov *oblast*, into a civil servant's family; Russian. After secondary school he entered the No. 1 Technical College, Saratov, and qualified as a metal turner. He worked in the No. 122 P/Ya organization. In 1961 he entered the Vavilov Agricultural Institute, Saratov, in the extra-mural department and went to work in the Kuibyshev state farm, Ivanteevsky *raion*, Saratov *oblast*. He began as a mechanizer, then became a mechanic in a repair garage. After graduating from the institute Belykh worked in the administration of agriculture, Ivanteevsky *raion*. In 1965 he was assigned to work in the Bartenevsky state farm as chief agronomist. After two years he was sent to Tatishchevsky *raion* and made chief agronomist of the *raion* administration of agriculture.

In 1973 he was elected chairman of the N. K. Krupskaya collective farm, Tatishchevsky *raion*; in 1974 he became director of the Lesnoi state farm and in 1983 head of the board of the state farm in Tatishchevsky *raion*. From September 1985 to February 1992 he was director of the Dubkovsky chicken factory, Saratov *raion*. He was a member of the CPSU until August 1991, and has received state awards.

In March 1990 he was nominated for election as an RSFSR people's deputy in the No. 646 Saratov rural territorial district. During the election campaign he declared that for him and all those who worked in agriculture, the main problems were agrarian. A land reform was needed and it should be returned to its rightful owner. Legal and economic guarantees of just payment for agricultural labour were necessary and the producers of agricultural products should themselves decide and name the prices. The labour of a peasant should be paid the same as a worker in industry.

There were four candidates. Belykh polled 19.36% of the votes in the first round and won the second round, polling 54.38% of the votes. His main opponent was P. S. Sadovoi, head of department of the Higher Military Aviation Technical School for pilots, Saratov, who received 36.67% of the votes in the second round.

Belykh was appointed head of the administration of Saratov *oblast* by presidential decree on February 25, 1992. When he took up his post he stated that there were a few things which should be changed: monopoly in production, the rule of the mafia in distribution, the incompetence of the representative agencies and the complete degradation of executive power. He again stressed the need for private ownership of land but on condition that every farmer would be guaranteed real support. However, the complete elimination of collective forms of ownership would be inopportune. Privatization should be orderly and well regulated, and observe the principles of social justice and the elimination of monopolies. The market is necessary but it has to be a civilized market. The activities of businessmen should concentrate on the material sphere and it should be advantageous to them as entrepreneurs to invest their capital in material production.

In December 1992, during the VII Russian Congress of People's Deputies,

Belykh stated that he supported the reforms of the Russian government and that he regarded Egor Gaidar as the only logical and correct Prime Minister of the country. Criticism of the government was quite acceptable, according to him, but it had to be constructive criticism and not degenerate into criticism for its own sake. He lives in Tatishchevo, Saratov *raion*.

Berestovoi, Vladimir Ivanovich

Head of the Administration of Belgorod *oblast*, Russian Federation.

Born on May 9, 1948 in the village of Garbuzovo, Alekseevsky *raion*, Belgorod *oblast* into a family of collective farm workers. His mother was a milkmaid and animal specialist and his father was head of a part of the collective farm. Both are now pensioners. He is Russian, and was a member of the CPSU from July 1976 to August 24, 1991. He attended the eight year school and then entered the Novooskolsky Technical College for the mechanization of agriculture. After completing the course he became head of a station for the technical servicing of the vehicles of *Rakitnyansky Selkhoztekhnika*, and after six months entered Voronezh Agricultural Institute and graduated in 1972. He began postgraduate studies at the institute and was secretary of the *Komsomol* organization. He served in the Soviet Army (1972-73), and then worked as chief engineer, secretary of the Party committee and chairman of various collective farms in Alekseevsky *raion*, Belgorod *oblast*. He was then appointed chairman of the *raion* agro-industrial association, later secretary, and then in 1988 second secretary of the Belgorod Party *obkom*. He graduated from the Rostov Higher Party School. He was a delegate to the XXVIII Party congress, and has received state awards.

In early 1990 he was nominated by the work collectives of the Olminsky, Rodina and Leninsky collective farms, Belgorod *oblast*, for election as an RSFSR people's deputy in the No. 283 Alekseevsky territorial district. During the election campaign he advocated greater economic and legal sovereignty for Russia within the USSR and relations with other republics based on equal rights and a partnership. He devoted much attention to the future development of the Black Earth region (*chernozem*), the renewal of the CPSU on the basis of *glasnost* and democratization. His most important task was to solve the food problem by introducing leasing in the countryside and the development of private and subsidiary plots. Priority should be afforded to moral and spiritual values and to the problems of the environment.

He was the only candidate and won in the first round with over half the votes. He is a member of the Supreme Soviet committee on the soviets and development of self-government, and was previously a member of the communists of Russia group of deputies. In 1990 he was elected a deputy of Belgorod *oblast* soviet, and was a member of the mandate commission and the commission on ethics of the *oblast* soviet. On July 18, 1991 he was elected chairman of the Belgorod *oblast* soviet, defeating the only other candidate.

On August 19, 1991, being in Moscow, he sent an order to Belgorod forbidding the implementation of the orders of the Extraordinary Committee, and on August 24 he resigned from the CPSU because the central agencies had usurped the Party's power. In December 1991 he was appointed head of the administration of Belgorod *oblast* by presidential decree.

In December 1992, during the VII Congress of People's Deputies, he was critical of the President's appeal to the people but conceded that in the tense situation, besides the President and the government, the congress was to blame since it was attempting to limit the powers of the executive. The congress, in his view, was a defective body and was unnecessary in the future, although at the present time it was playing a stabilizing role. He is married with two sons. His favourite form of relaxation is to analyse articles in the newspapers and journals, and to read the Russian classics and historical literature.

Bessonov, Vladimir Vasilevich

Russian footballer.

Born on March 5, 1958; Russian. He is an Honoured Master of Sport (1986). and played defender or half back. He began his career playing in the Metallist, then Dinamo Kiev youth team (1976-80), and played 277 games and scored 27 goals, all for Dinamo Kiev. He was a member of their championship winning teams in 1977, 1980, 1981, 1985, 1986 and 1990; their winning USSR cup teams of 1978, 1982, 1985, 1987 and 1990; and the team that won the cup of cups in 1986. He played 85 times for the USSR team and scored five goals.

He was a member of the winning team in the 1976 UEFA youth tournament and the 1977 junior world championship, and won a bronze medal with the USSR team at the 1980 Olympics. He played in the World Cup in 1982, 1986 and 1990, and was in the team which was beaten in the final of the European championship of 1988. In 1990 he was transferred to Maccabi, Tel Aviv, Israel, and in 1991 he returned home and is now the manager (trainer) of Dinamo Kiev.

Bicheldei, Kaadur-Ool Alekseevich

Speaker of the Supreme Soviet of the Republic of Tuva, Russian Federation.

Born on January 2, 1950 in the Tuva ASSR; a Tuvinian; member of the CPSU from 1982 to August 1991. In 1973 he graduated from the Mongolian State University in philology and in 1985 he successfully presented his candidate dissertation on "Vocalism in the modern Tuvinian language" (PhD). When elected a deputy he was a senior scientific worker in the sector of language, literature and the arts of the Tuvinian scientific research institute of language, history and literature. His research concentrated on the philological problems of the Tuvinian language and he is the author of several scientific articles. On February 26, 1991 he was appointed head of the consulting group on drafting the Culture of Russia information programme.

In January 1990 he was nominated by the plenum of the Dzun-Khemchiksky *raion* Party, Tuva ASSR, for election as an RSFSR people's deputy in the No. 132 Shagonarsky national territorial district, Tuva ASSR. During the election campaign he advocated the transition of power to the soviets, economic and social development of the Tuva ASSR based on greater independence within the RSFSR. He supported policies which would result in more products remaining within the republic and the development of local industry, and the construction of enterprises but under very strict environmental control. The spiritual health of society and the renaissance of the national culture, customs and traditions of Tuvinians were of great importance to him.

There were three candidates. He polled 52% of the votes in the first round and was declared elected. His main opponent was D. K. Oorzhak, chairman of the Ulug-Khemsky *raion* soviet executive committee, who received 18.7% of the votes. Bicheldei was elected a member of the Supreme Soviet at the I Congress of People's Deputies (696 voted for, 235 against). He is a member of the Council of Nationalities, a member of the Council of Nationalities commission on culture, language, national traditions and protection of the national heritage of the peoples of the Russian Federation. He participated in the work of the *glasnost* group of deputies and is a member of the sovereignty and equality parliamentary faction.

In 1990 he was elected a deputy of the Supreme Soviet of the Tuva ASS. In April 1990, at the first session, he was a candidate for the post of Speaker. There were three candidates and Bicheldei received nine out of 116 votes, and Ch.-D. B. Ondar was elected Speaker. After Ondar's resignation as a result of his activities during the attempted state coup of August 1991 Bicheldei was nominated for Speaker and on October 2, 1991 he was elected Speaker. The only other candidate was Sh. D. Oorazhak, the present President and Prime Minister of Republic of Tuva. Bicheldei is married with children and lives in Kyzyl.

Biembiel, Aleh Andrejevic (pseudonym Znic)

Member of the Francisak Skaryna National Scientific Educational Centre, Minsk, Belarus.

Born on December 16, 1939 in Minsk. His parents are Andrej Anufryjevic Biembiel and Volha Anatoleuna, née Dziadok, and he is Belarusian. He graduated in 1969 from the Belarusian State Conservatory (classical pianoforte) and in 1974 became a postgraduate student at the Institute of Philosophy and Law, Belarusian Academy of Sciences, researching the history of philosophy. He is a member of the board of the Belarusian Christian Democratic Union, and advocates an Orthodox constitutional monarchy for Belarus and a free Christian Belarus in the Christian community of nations.

He is a writer, poet and publicist. His publications include: (as Znic) *Recha Malitvy* (echoes of prayer), poems (New York 1988); *Sakala Rostani* (falcons of distance), poems (Bialystok 1988); and *Malitvy za Belarus* (prayers for Belarus), poems (Minsk 1989): (as Aleh Biembiel) *Rodnaje slova: maralna-estetyeny prahres* (the native work and moral aesthetic progress) (London 1985); *Pravaslaunaja Bielarus* (Orthodox Belarus), poems, in *Carkounaja Slova*, No. 3 (1993); *Sviaty Pokpyu nad Bielarussiu*, poems, in *Chram i Viers* (shame and poetry) (Bialystok 1993); *Chryscijanskaja Bielarus u Chryscijanskaj Sadruzkasci nacyj* (Christian Belarus in the Christian community of nations), in *Kultura*, 1/ix (1992); *Urodzinoe u Metahistoryju Bielarusi* (introduction to the metahistory of Belarus), *Kultura* (November 9, 1992): (as Oleg Bembel, in Russian): *N. G. Chernyshevsky i problema natsionalnogo v dukhovnoi kulture* (N. G. Chernyshevsky and the problem of the national in spiritual culture), in the collection *N. G. Chernyshevsky i ego nasledie* (Novosibirsk 1980).

He is divorced with two daughters, Tatiana and Irena. He has a fluent knowledge of Russian, a reading knowledge of Ukrainian and Polish, and, with a dictionary, English.

Address: 220013 Minsk 13, vul. Jakuba Kolasa, 29a; *telephone*: Minsk (0172) 32 03 01.

Biryukov, Nikolai Vasilevich

Speaker of the Supreme Soviet of the Republic of Tuva, Russian Federation.

Born in 1944 in the village of Mordovskoe Kolomasovo, Bovylkinsky *raion*, Mordovian ASSR, where his father was a collective farm worker. He is a Mordovian and was a member of the CPSU until August 1991. He graduated in economics and began his career in 1964 as a teacher of mathematics in his home village. He served three years in the Soviet armed forces, and was involved in political and state affairs. He progressed from being deputy chairman of a collective farm to secretary for the agro-industrial complex of the Party *obkom*.

He was elected a deputy of the Supreme Soviet of the Mordovian ASSR, and in April 1990 he was elected deputy Speaker and in December 1990 Speaker. There were four candidates. During the attempted state coup of August 1991 he signed the declaration of the Presidium of the Supreme Soviet and Council of Ministers of the Mordovian Soviet Socialist Republic to the population of the republic stating that it was not opportune to introduce a state of emergency in the republic. He is married with two sons and lives in Saransk.

Biryukov, Vladimir Afanasevich

Head of the Administration of Kamchatka *oblast*, Russian Federation.

Born in 1933 in Astrakhan, and graduated from the Astrakhan Institute of the Fish Industry and Economy. In 1956 he moved to Kamchatka and has lived there ever since, working in the Kikhchiksky, Oktyabrsky and Ozernovsky fish combines. He was then appointed director of the Kamchatka fish industry. In 1972 he was elected second secretary of the Kamchatka Party *obkom* and in 1977 chairman of the Kamchatka *oblast* soviet executive committee. In 1980 he was dismissed after an inquiry by the public prosecutor's office for "malfeasance during his time as general director of the Kamchatka fish industry". He was expelled from the CPSU and the Party control committee began criminal proceedings against him, but the investigation by the public prosecutor's offices of the RSFSR and USSR was abandoned after seven years. During this time Biryukov worked in a fish research institute. In 1987 he was offered the post of deputy chairman of the agro-industrial committee on processing, and then became general director of the Kamchatka fish industry association. In 1987 he was readmitted to the CPSU and remained within its ranks until August 1991.

In April 1990, at the first session of the *oblast* soviet of people's deputies, he was elected chairman of the executive committee. On August 20, 1991 it was decided at a meeting of the Presidium and executive committee of the Kamchatka soviet not to introduce a state of emergency in Kamchatka and only to recognize the constitutionally elected state authorities.

In November 1991 Biryukov was appointed head of the administration of Kamchatka *oblast* by presidential decree. On assuming office he stated that he supported the concept of the political and economic autonomy of Russia and the other republics, and intended to devote most attention to the development of agriculture. The key to agricultural development was the complete autonomy of the producers, state and collective farms, lessees and individual peasant farms. He advocated the expansion of a network of state, leased, co-operative and individual enterprises.

In December 1992 Biryukov declared complete support for the economic reforms which were being implemented by the Russian government, but at the VII Congress of People's Deputies he thought it too early to judge the reforms. He is married with two children, and lives in Petropavlovsk Kamchatsky. His wife and daughter work in the fish industry and his son is a student.

Blinnikov, Sergei Petrovich

Chairman of the Council of Ministers of the Republic of Karelia, Russian Federation.

Born in 1945. Russian. Member of the CPSU until August 1991. He is a graduate. He began his career in 1964 as a road foreman of the Petrozavodsk No. 166 motorway section, then was an engineer in the design department, northern administration of motorways, foreman, chief engineer, director of the combine of the production enterprises of the city repair and construction trust, deputy, then chairman of the executive committee of the Leninsky *raion* soviet of the city of Petrozavodsk. In 1985 he was Minister of Housing and Municipal Services, Karelian Autonomous Soviet Socialist Republic, and in 1988 he was appointed general director of the housing and municipal services association. He was a deputy of the Supreme Soviet of the Karelian ASSR and a member of the revision commission of the *oblast* Party organization. At the XV extraordinary session of the Supreme Soviet of the Karelian ASSR he was appointed Chairman of the Council of Ministers of the Karelian ASSR.

In 1990 he was elected a deputy of the Supreme Soviet of the Karelian ASSR. At the XLIV conference of the Petrozavodsk city Party organization he was nominated as a delegate to the XXVIII Party congress by the work collectives of the territorial production association of housing and municipal services, the Karelian building materials production association, the Keramik and Rosorgtekhstroi co-operatives, the building materials enterprise, the Karelian grain production association, the executive committee of the city soviet, the Council of Ministers of the Karelian ASSR and the Nos. 4, 6, 8 and 9 micro *raions*. He was elected a delegate in the second round of voting.

At the first session of the supreme Soviet of the Karelian ASSR, in April 1990, he was elected Chairman of the Council of Ministers of the Karelian ASSR. On assuming office he advocated the autonomy of the republic in planning and in the taking of administrative decisions in regional economic policy; the satisfaction of the demand for consumer goods and services; more radical economic reforms; the restructuring of the national economy; and the creation of effective mechanisms for the management of the economy, administration and the regulated market. He proposed the simplification of mutual links with the centre, the reduction of unnecessary links of the administration, the transition of enterprises to leasing, their associations into joint stock companies, and the development of small and collective enterprises and co-operatives. He considered it necessary to move to free prices accompanied by social support for the population, the redistribution and retraining of cadres, the development of foreign economic links and the attracting of foreign capital. He advocated equality for all types of farms, support of private farmers, small co-operatives and a reduction in the construction of enterprises.

On August 20, 1991, at a meeting of the Council of Ministers of the Karelian Soviet Socialist Republic, Blinnikov stated that there was no reason for introducing a state of emergency in Petrozavodsk and the republic and appealed for the maintainance of a quiet work rhythm. In December 1992 he stated that there was no point in carrying through a monetary reform since this would result in the impoverishment of the population. He advocated serious changes to the course of the reform by combining the government programme, the programmes of Civic Union and leading economists in the country. He wanted a solid exchange rate for the ruble, reasonable combination of market self-regulation and governmental regulation, the production of competitive goods, demonopolization and privatization.

He is married and his wife is the manager of an artistic salon. Their daughter is studying in a pedagogical institute and their son in a transport technical college. They live in Petrozavodsk.

Blokhin, Oleg Vladimirovich

Ukrainian footballer.

Born on November 5, 1952; Ukrainian. He is an Honoured Master of Sport (1975). Forward. He is a product of the Dinamo Kiev team, joining in 1962, and was a member of its great teams from 1969 to 1987. He played 432 times and scored 211 goals in the USSR championship. He holds the records for the number of games played (112) and the goals scored (42). He was a member of the Dinamo Kiev USSR championship winning teams of 1974, 1975, 1977, 1980, 1981, 1985 and 1986; their USSR cup winning teams of 1974, 1978, 1982, 1985 and 1987; and their cup of cups winning team of 1975 and 1976.

He won a bronze medal at the Olympic Games of 1972 and 1976. He played in the USSR team during the qualifying matches in 1977 for the World Cup and in the World Cup in 1982 and 1986. He was voted USSR footballer of the year in 1973, 1974 and 1975. He was top scorer in the USSR championship in 1972, 1973, 1974, 1975 and 1977, and was European footballer of the year in 1975. He holds the Soviet record for playing in most matches, 79, and scoring most goals, 26, in European cup club games. He won the European super cup in 1975. He signed for Vörwarts Steier, Austria, in 1987 and remained until 1988. In 1989 he moved to Aris Limassol, Cyprus, until 1990, and then became manager (trainer) of Olympiacos Athens, Greece.

Bochin, Leonid Arnoldovich

Chairman of the State Committee of the Russian Federation on anti-monopoly policy and support of new economic structures; Minister.

Born on July 11, 1949 in Korosten, Zhitomir (Zhytomyr) *oblast*, Ukrainian SSR. He was a member of the CPSU until August 1991. He graduated from Novosibirsk State University, became a postgraduate and successfully presented his candidate dissertation in economics (PhD Econ). He is a mathematical economist, and after graduating from university he worked in a scientific research institute, Novosibirsk (1971-73); was senior engineer in the North Caucasian branch of the all-Union state technology design institute, USSR Central Statistical Administration, Krasnodar (1974-77); senior engineer in the centre for scientific organization of labour, RSFSR Ministry of Agriculture (1977-79); leading scientific assistant, all-Union scientific research institute for the study of the market and demand, USSR Ministry of Trade (1979-89); general director of the Razvitie company (1989-90); and deputy chairman of the state committee of the Russian Federation on anti-monopoly policy and support of new economic structures (1990-92). In July 1992 he was appointed the committee's chairman with the rank of minister. He is married with a daughter and lives in Moscow.

Boldin, Valery Ivanovich

Member of the Extraordinary Committee.

Born on September 7, 1935 in Tutaevo, Yaroslavl *oblast*. Russian. He was a member of the CPSU from 1960 to August 1991. He began working in 1950 as a signalman on the Moscow Ryazan railway line. In 1960 he became a literary assistant on the editorial board of *Pravda*, and in 1961 he graduated from the faculty of economics of K. A. Timiryazev Agricultural Academy, Moscow. From 1961 to 1965 he was an official in the apparatus of the Party Central Committee. Then he was a student at the academy of social sciences of the Party Central Committee and graduated in 1969, having successfully presented his candidate dissertation in economics (PhD (Econ)).

In 1969 he became an economic observer, then an editor of the agricultural department of *Pravda* and joined the editorial board of the newspaper. He also lectured in the advanced economic courses of USSR Gosplan. In 1981 he became an assistant of the CC secretary for agriculture, Mikhail Gorbachev, and in 1985 he became an assistant to Gorbachev when he became General Secretary of the Party. In 1987 he was appointed head of the general department of the Party Central Committee. Between 1986 and 1988 he was a candidate member of the Party Central Committee and in 1988 he became a full member. In 1989 he was nominated as a USSR people's deputy by the CPSU and was elected. In March 1990 he was appointed to the USSR presidential Council.

In August 1991 he was a member of the Extraordinary Committee and was a member of the delegation which visited President Mikhail Gorbachev at his dacha in Foros, in the Crimea, on the evening of August 18, 1991. Gorbachev refused to resign and the delegation returned to Moscow. The conspirators had no contingency plan in the event of the President refusing to step down, which has led some observers to conclude that the President had given the impression that he would acquiesce in a lurch to the right. Boldin was arrested on August 22, 1991 and during the initial investigation was confined to the *Matrosskaya tishina* isolator. He and other members of the Committee were later released. He lives in Moscow.

Boldyrev, Yury Yurevich

Chief State Inspector of the Russian Federation, February 1992 to March 4, 1993.

Born in 1960 in Leningrad; Russian. He was a member of the CPSU from 1987 to August 1991. He graduated from the V. I. Ulyanov-Lenin Electrical Engineering Institute, Leningrad, and the N. A. Voznesensky Institute of Finance and Economics, Leningrad. He was a senior engineer in the Central scientific research institute of electrical engineering for the shipbuilding industry, Leningrad. In 1986 he was elected secretary of the committee of the *Komsomol* of the institute, then a member of the council of the work collective.

In 1989 he was nominated by the work collective of the Central scientific research institute for election as a USSR people's deputy in the No. 54 Moskovsky territorial district, Leningrad. During the election campaign he spoke of the impossibility of solving separately the problems of housing, food and transport with a fundamental reform of the economy and which legislators should provide. He advocated many types of economic activity with all being treated equally, limits on price rises but equal provision of goods, the stimulation of competition, the encouragement of leasing and co-operatives, first and foremost where there were no shortages or grounds for speculation. He favoured the provision of guarantees to defend enterprises from the arbitrary interference of state authorities and ministries losing their right to command.

He advanced an anti-inflationary programme: cutting back investment on construction projects of the century, independent groups of experts assessing large state projects, and anti-monopoly legislation. He appealed for the drafting of a state programme to help the aged poor, invalids and mothers, to provide youth with credits, and to abolish all privileges and advantages linked to one's job. Pensions and student grants should be indexed in line with inflation, society should have the right to information about the ecology and independent ecological advisers, criminal responsibility for ecological crimes should be introduced and projects which affect the population should be put to referendum.

He believes that the deployment of the military abroad should only be possible after permission by the Congress of People's Deputies. As long as the monopoly on power remains, the interests of the people will always be infringed, always in the interests of the state. Fundamental political reforms are needed, as well as real self-government at all levels, independent courts, the separation of executive and legislative power, independent public control and the right of citizens to establish independent public and political organizations, providing their activities are not anti-constitutional. He advocated a review of the law on elections to local soviets, the abolition of reserved resources for public organizations and nominations without going through electoral commissions.

The CPSU should not enjoy a monopoly on socialism, opposition structures should have the right to exist, providing they do not appeal for the violent alteration of the existing state structure, or for nationalism, war or racial discrimination. Parties should not be obliged to struggle for power, they may simply defend the interests of their members by campaigning for representation in the highest state authorities. Collegial rule is necessary, preferably as a parliamentary republic. Domestic legislation should be brought into accord with international law, there should be constitutional and administrative courts and the administrative obligation to work should be abolished.

There were two candidates and Boldyrev won in the first round, polling 74.3% of the votes. His opponent was A. N. Gerasimov, first secretary of the Leningrad city Party committee, who received 19.7% of the votes. In 1989 Boldyrev was also elected a delegate to the XXVIII Party congress, at which he asked a question about Party property. He was a member of the USSR Supreme Soviet committee on the work of the soviets of people's deputies, the development of administration and self-government. In 1990 he was appointed a member of the higher co-ordinating consultative council of the Speaker of the RSFSR Supreme Soviet and later of the RSFSR President. He was a member of the interregional group of deputies and the Democratic Russia movement, but he resigned from it in early 1992.

After the dissolution of the USSR Supreme Soviet he was unemployed from January 2 to February 20, 1992. Anatoly Sobchak (mayor of St Petersburg) offered him the post of head of the committee on the extraordinary situation in the Leningrad soviet (Lensovet), but Boldyrev declined because he did not have the same views in policy and working methods. Boldyrev was preparing himself to work on privatization in the state property committee, but on February 20, 1992 he was appointed a governmental adviser and a week later head of the state inspection of the Russian Federation and head of the main control board of the administration of the President of the Russian Federation.

While he was head of the main control board the heads of administration (governors) of Krasnodar *krai*, Voronezh and Pskov *oblasts*, the chairman of the committee on trade of the Ministry of Trade and Material Resources, two of his deputies, the first deputy Minister of Agriculture and the first deputy chairman of the Russian committee on Chernobyl, were all dismissed from office. On the evidence of the chief state inspector the deputy heads of administration of Arkhangelsk, Belgorod and Tomsk *oblasts* were relieved of office. One hundred and sixteen orders were dispatched to the regions, ministries and authorities to correct infringements of the law. An enquiry was carried out in the western group of forces and in the central apparatus of the Ministry of Defence of the Russian Federation.

On March 4, 1993, by presidential decree, Boldyrev was relieved of his functions as chief state inspector of the Russian Federation as a result of the elimination of this post and the introduction of new presidential administrative structures. The reason for his removal is thought to be his refusal to subordinate himself to day-to-day political policy and his attempts to transform the main control board into a non-political agency, ignoring the division between supporters and opponents of the Yeltsin administration. He did not believe that there should be closed areas for investigation and he was forced against his will to suspend investigations into the affairs of the Moscow authorities. He is opposed to the most radical circle around the President who are wont to regard all blunders as the intrigues of enemies and who are wedded to confrontation. The government did not implement the order of the President on the system of declaration of income of state officials and it sabotaged the establishment of an inspection of hard currency control.

He is critical of the illegal preferences, licences, advantages, and the absence of elementary order in the country, beginning at the top. He does not regard the partocrats, perched in their offices, as responsible for interference in the reform process, but some democrats. Sometimes there is naked violation of the law, and he believes that corruption is the result of the conditions and the unpolitical and human qualities of the leaders. He is opposed to a witch-hunt which can be used to settle personal scores and against the view that there is no other way from a totalitarian to a civilized society than through a wild period of the primitive accumulation of capital. This would lead to a refusal to combat negative tendencies.

He advocates ensuring the independence of various control structures from local and central interests, putting in place a mechanism for the removal of officials and compensation for those relieved of their duties due to their inability to compete on the labour market. The small chamber of the Moscow city council (Mossovet) offered Boldyrev the post of chairman of the Moscow control chamber. He is married with two children and lives in St Petersburg.

Bondarev, Yury Vasilevich

First Secretary of the Board of the Union of Writers of Russia.

Born on March 15, 1924 in Orsk, Orenburg *oblast*. His father was an office worker. Then the family moved to Moscow. He passed his childhood and youth in Zamoskvoreche, loved books, football, skating and volleyball. He is Russian and was a member of the CPSU from 1944 to August 1991. His interest in writing arose during his schoolboy years and he criticized the mechanistic, superficial teaching of literature in the senior classes. He finished secondary school in June 1941. He and his class mates helped to build defences outside Smolensk, but he was encircled, broke out and returned to Moscow. After a few months he volunteered for the front. He graduated from an artillery college, was an anti-tank artillery soldier, sergeant, lieutenant and commander of an artillery piece of ordnance. His war began in the winter of 1942 at Kotelnikovo in the second guards' army, then he fought at the Kursk salient, crossed the Dnieper river, liberated Zhitomir, Kamenets-Podolsk, fought in the Carpathians near Prague and finished the war in Czechoslovakia. He was wounded twice, the second time a few months before the end of the war.

After the war he studied at the pre-entry department, Moscow aviation and technical institute, then trained as a chauffeur, and attempted to enter the department of scenery, all-Union state institute of cinematography. However, after his wartime tales had been positively received he became a student of the Gorky institute of literature and was in the seminar of K. Paustovsky and F. Gladkov. He graduated in 1951. His first story, *En Route*, appeared in the *Smena* journal and in 1953 his collection of stories, *On the Large River*, appeared. He also wrote the novellas *The Youth of a Commander* (1956); *The Battalions Request Fire* (1957); *Last Salvos* (1959); *Two* (1963), the novel *Quietness* (1962), the novella *Relatives* (1969), the novel *Burning Snow* (1970). Then he wrote the novels *Choice, Game, Shore, Wind, Temptation, Moscow Time, Neutral Zone* and the autobiographical book *A Flash*. O. Mikhailov published a study of his works, *Yury Bondarev*, in 1976.

He worked in Mosfilm as chief editor of the sixth creative association and helped film the adaptations of *Last Salvos* and *Quietness*, and wrote the film script of *49 Days* and the film epic *Liberation*. He was awarded the Lenin prize in 1972, the USSR state prize in 1976, and the Brothers Vasilev RSFSR prize for film art. He was elected a people's deputy for Volgograd in the RSFSR Supreme Soviet in 1982. In March 1984 he became a hero of socialist labour. In 1988 he was elected deputy chairman of the board of the RSFSR Union of Writers.

In 1974 Bondarev participated in the persecution of Aleksandr Solzhenitsyn for his article *Envy Devours Truth*. The *Word to the People*, signed by Bondarev, Rasputin and Prokhanov, was judged by the secretariat of the board of the USSR Union of Writers on August 23, 1991 as providing the ideas to ensure an anti-state conspiracy. After August 1991 Bondarev was head of the Union of Writers of Russia and left the USSR writers' union. Bondarev regards himself as a patriot and condemns western mass culture and rock music. He regards the people as having been robbed and deceived and the country occupied by pseudo-democrats whose goal is to lead the country to destruction and slavery.

He opposes the spontaneous market, the "pitiable IMF credits which subject the country to crucifixion", global unemployment, the sale of land to foreigners for next to nothing, and full and one-sided disarmament of the whole army. He regards the army as the only serious force which can defend people from the present slavery. *Glasnost* is the distortion of truth, the destruction of the biography of the country. All are led not by love, but cynicism and naked physiological naturalism and the fancy of the day. He neither believes in the cunning theorizing of Dmitry Likhachev nor the political historiography of Gen. Dmitry Volkogonov. Culture should interact and cannot be separate and remote, but Russia only knows the confirmation of a foreign culture. He appeals for the saving of tradition and history, and all that is spiritual, unique and great which was created by the Russian people.

He is in favour of national roots, originality and non-repetition. He believes that all European culture derives from Russian 19th-century literature. His favourite authors are Anton Chekhov and Ivan Turgenev. He is married and has a daughter and lives in Moscow.

Bonner, Elena Georgievna

Human rights campaigner.

Born on February 15, 1922 in Mary, Turkmenistan; an Armenian. She was never a member of the CPSU, and is at present a pensioner. Her father, Gevork Alikhanov, was head of department in the Communist International (Comintern), a member of the Bolshevik Party from 1917, arrested in May 1937 as a traitor to the motherland and was posthumously rehabilitated in 1954. Her mother, Ruf (Ruth) Grigorievna Bonner, daughter of a Jewish revolutionary, was a member of the CPSU from 1924, was also arrested in 1937, as a member of the family of a traitor to the motherland, rehabilitated in 1954 and was made an honoured Union pensioner. Elena Bonner completed seven years of secondary school in Moscow and after the arrest of her parents she and her younger brother accompanied their relatives to Leningrad. She completed secondary school in 1940 and while there worked as a charwoman in a home and during the summer holidays after the eight and ninth classes she was an archivist in the Ernst Thälmann factory, Moscow.

In 1940 she entered the evening department of the faculty of Russian language and literature, A. I. Gertsen Pedagogical Institute, Leningrad, while being a Young Pioneer leader in a school. After the outbreak of war she volunteered for the army and completed the courses of the Russian Society of the Red Cross and became a nurse. On October 26, 1941 she was seriously wounded and shell shocked near Valya station, Volkhovsky front and was in hospital in Vologda and Sverdlovsk. At the end of 1941 she reported to the evacuation point in Sverdlovsk and from there dispatched as a nurse to the military medical train No. 122. In 1942 she became a senior nurse and she was appointed a junior lieutenant of the medical services. In 1945 she was promoted to lieutenant of the medical services.

In May 1945 she was assigned to Belomorsky military district as deputy head of the medical unit of the separate sapper battalion and was demobilized from there in August 1945 as an invalid, second class, with almost complete loss of sight in the right eye and progressive blindness in the left eye. After a course of treatment in the first Leningrad medical institute for eye diseases and the institute for eye diseases in Odessa (Odesa) her condition stabilized. In 1970 she was recognized as an invalid, second class, of the Great Fatherland War for life.

In 1947 she entered the No. 1 Leningrad medical institute and completed the six-year training in 1953, graduating as a paediatrician. She worked until pensionable age with the exception of 1961-62 when her son was seriously ill and completed 32 years of service. She was paediatrician in a maternity home, a lecturer in a medical college and from 1959 to 1960 was assigned to work in Iraq by the USSR Ministry of Health.

While working she engaged in literary pursuits and published articles in the journals *Neva* and *Yunost*, wrote for all-Union radio, articles in *Literaturnaya gazeta*, the newspaper, *Medrabotnik* and contributed to the book *Actors who Died at the Front during the Great Fatherland War*. She was one of the authors of the book by V. Bagritsky, *Diaries, Letters, Poems*, which was awarded the prize of the Leninist *Komsomol*. She collaborated as an unofficial literary consultant in the literary consultations of the Union of Writers, was an editor in the Leningrad department of the state medical publishing house. She was made an excellent worker of USSR health. In 1938 she became a member of the *Komsomol*, and all the time she served in the army she was a *Komsomol* organizer, while in the institute she was a union organizer of her year.

She did not believe she could enter the CPSU since her parents were classified as enemies of the people. After the XX and XXI Party Congresses she decided to apply for Party membership and in 1965 she became a Party member. After the invasion of Czechoslovakia in August 1968 she realized that she had made a mistake and in 1972 resigned from the Party.

Her first husband was Ivan Vasilevich Semenov who was a fellow student at the No. 1 Leningrad Medical Institute and still works there. They divorced in 1965. Their daughter Tatyana was born in 1950 and graduated from Moscow State University with distinction, but she was sent down between 1972 and 1974 for demonstrating outside the Lebanese embassy at the murder of the Israeli sportsmen by terrorists at the Munich Olympics. Their son, Aleksei, was born in 1955 and was a brilliant student in the faculty of mathematics, V. I. Lenin Pedagogical Institute, Moscow, but was barred from the final year because of his refusal to do military service. In 1977 the children emigrated to Israel and then to the US.

Elena Bonner first met Andrei Sakharov in 1970, when she actively participated in the defence of human rights. She spoke in Moscow and abroad about human rights problems, and she contributed to the book *The Concluding Document on the Conference in Belgrade* on the failure of the USSR to fulfil its human rights obligations. This was regarded as an infringement of the democratic rights and freedoms of citizens by the state. It was stated that in the USSR there was persecution for political, ethical or religious beliefs and psychiatric persecution for political purposes. She believes that she influenced Sakharov in these matters and that he, through theorizing about human rights, arrived at an understanding of people's fate.

In the mid-1970s she underwent treatment for her eyes in Italy and in 1975 received the Nobel Prize for her husband. After Sakharov's exile to Gorky in January 1980 she maintained links between him and the world outside (Gorky was closed to foreigners). In 1984 she was condemned according to article 190-1 of the RSFSR code for false fabrications, damaging to the Soviet state and public order, to five years' exile in Gorky. She was amnestied on December 17, 1986 on the direct intervention of Mikhail Gorbachev who wanted to win over the intelligentsia to *perestroika*.

She is a great lover of the music of Mozart, Chopin and Schumann and contemporary American jazz, and regards her library and record collection as her most prized possessions. She has been driving for 15 years and her favourite dish is fried potatoes. Her book of memoirs about her childhood and youth, *Dochki-materi*, was published in the US; *Postskriptum*, in Paris in 1988 and Moscow in 1990; *The Bell is Tolling. . . a Year without A. Sakharov* (1991); and she compiled the book by Andrei Sakharov *Anxiety and Hope* in 1990.

She believes that the young sovereign states should develop without infringing human rights and base themselves on two principles: the rights of the personality, expressed in the universal declaration of human rights and the right of a nation to self-determination. The republics should live separately. At present there is no question of integration but economic links remain. She regarded the VII Congress of People's Deputies, in December 1992, as undemocratic and anti-Sakharov and the constitutional crisis as unresolved, merely postponed. She would like to see the convening of a constitutional assembly which would adopt a new constitution. She believes a personal dictatorship is possible, but also a collective one with the congress, the Supreme Soviet and its Speaker, and she regards a referendum on the constitution as a dead end. She called on the President not to make any concessions to or make any deals with the Speaker, Ruslan Khasbulatov, and the congress.

The constitutional assembly should decide what is to become of Russia. She supported the Gaidar government, because its members had not lied and promised to make everyone participants in reform. She is an active supporter of President Yeltsin and spoke at a meeting on the Vasilevsky slope on March 28, 1993. She lives in Moscow.

Borodin, Oleg Petrovich

Co-chairman of the Bureau of the Political Council of the People's Party of Russia (PPR).

He was a member of the CPSU until 1990 and stated that he had no wish to join any other party. He was a member of the democratic platform in the CPSU and helped to found the Democratic Party of Russia. He opposed Nikolai Travkin's aspirations to become leader and as a result ceased his activities in the Party. In January 1991, after the storming of the Vilnius TV tower by security forces resulting in loss of life, he thought it necessary to oppose the brutality of the state structures which were under the control of the nomenklatura mafia. This led to the formation of an initiative group to set up the People's Party of Russia.

Borodin was elected co-chairman at its founding congress on May 19, 1991 in Zelenograd, near Moscow. He regards the PPR as a liberal democratic party based on the state for the people, and not the people for the state, as the basic foundation of the future Russian society. The splintering of democratic forces after the collapse of the CPSU is a basic law of the world political process. It is stimulated by opposition to parties of a totalitarian, fascist orientation and a move towards to a more civilized division of parties along social democratic and liberal democratic lines. Governments everywhere in civilized states are liberal democratic, and history has condemned the view that the world is an arena in which there are endless battles for the happiness of a humanity lacking consciousness. He opposed the values of socialism, which he considers divides everything into rich and poor. He maintains that in a poor country social democracy inevitably leads to bolshevism. The most important thing of all is the sovereignty of the individual and respect for all people, not only workers.

The main tasks of liberal democracy are not to take power but to distribute it so that no one can rule on his or her own and everyone must learn to work in conditions where there is strong opposition. True democracy is not a goal but a means for creating a democratic space where the interests of all strata of society and each person can be realized. The PPR does not favour entering any coalition government to save the country. However, it does take practical measures at present as its members stand as candidates for election to the agencies of power. Being active during the election campaign is more important than being constantly active politically.

Borodin does not believe that any strong party or any person can save the country from its present woes. One should believe in the talent of each person, his or her common sense and spiritual strength. Morality is and should be the foundation of politics, and general human values should be higher than party values and should not be goals which justify criminal means to implement them. He would like to see a renaissance of society through love for endeavour, desire to do things well for the individual's own good and the good of others, all based on the love of men and women who understand the value of a tightly-knit family based on the love of children, grandchildren, parents and older members for one another. All this should be founded on love for one's native land, the cradle of the best human feelings and the support and basis of the development of each person.

Borovoi, Konstantin Natanovich

Co-Chairman of the Party of Economic Freedom of the Russian Federation.

Born on June 30, 1948 in Moscow. His father was a doctor of technical sciences (DSc (Eng)) and his mother a Party worker; his grandfather was a victim of Stalin's purges. He graduated from the Moscow Institute of Railway Engineers and then from the faculty of mechanics and mathematics, Moscow State University, specializing in applied mathematics. During his studies he spent some time working on the Virgin Lands programme, initiated by Khrushchev in 1954, mainly in northern Kazakhstan and west Siberia. In 1982 he successfully presented his candidate dissertation in technical sciences at Moscow State University on research into the "Dynamics of the underground train traffic using computers as a management aid" (PhD (Eng)). He then became a lecturer in various Moscow technical colleges, and in 1987 became an assistant professor in the technical college of the Likhachev car plant, Moscow.

In 1987 in the youth centre of scientific-technical invention he established a co-operative to service computer technology, and in 1988 he abandoned teaching. On April 2, 1989 the Russian raw materials commodity exchange, set up by Borovoi, began trading in the polytechnic museum. It was the first institution of its kind in the Soviet Union, and the first period of trading lasted three hours. Borovoi's initial investment in the exchange was 60,000 rubles, which had grown to 12 million rubles by the summer of 1992. By then the exchange accounted for 12% of the Russian economy and its daily turnover was about 40 million rubles. Borovoi also participated in the establishment of the Russian national commercial bank, the Rossiya international trading house, the agency of economic news, the Rinako company, the institute of commercial engineering and the convention of entrepreneurs and about 50 other businesses.

From August 20, 1991, led by Borovoi, all employees of the Russian raw materials commodity exchange took part in the defence of the Russian White House. In May 1992 he retired from business and became one of the founders and then co-chairman of the Party of Economic Freedom (PEF) which was registered on June 22, 1992. In Borovoi's view the PEF should become a parliamentary-type party, promoting the interests of those in the new market economy. He advocated the establishment of a free democratic society, based on priority being given to human rights. The basic principles which the PEF should defend are economic freedom for the citizen, the transfer to him or her of state property, an effective economy and social security for the population. The social base of the party consists of the 40 million persons who are interested in a free economy, fair privatization, social stability and national harmony. Businesses which supported the PEF in May 1992 contributed 150 million rubles to a fund to help with the organization and promotion of the party.

In May-June 1992 Borovoi negotiated with the central TV authority to alter the principles on which financing was based and to establish an economically independent TV centre. In October 1992 Borovoi declared his intention to stand for election as a people's deputy in the No. 17 national-territorial district district, Krasnodar, in place of V. F. Shumeiko who had given up his mandate after becoming first deputy Russian Prime Minister. Others who had earlier declared their candidature were Oleg Kalugin, a former KGB general, T. Podlipentsev, Cossack ataman of the district, and N. Kondratenko, former second secretary of the Krasnodar *oblast* Party committee.

In December 1992 the PEF nominated Borovoi for election as mayor of Moscow. At the first congress of the PEF Borovoi, S. N. Fedorov and V. B. Zolotarev, former chairman of the Party of Constitutional Democrats of the Russian Federation, were elected co-chairmen. I. Khamanada became secretary general.

During 1992 Borovoi repeatedly spoke out in support of the policies of the Gaidar government, pointing out that the government contained world class specialists but that they needed good practices. In February 1993 he opposed the dropping or the postponement of the referendum, and supported the adoption of a new Russian constitution by a constitutional or constituent assembly. The new constitution, in Borovoi's view, should establish a mixed state system, including elements of a presidential as well as a parliamentary republic and a bicameral legislative system.

He is married and lives in Moscow. His wife, Tamara, was a lecturer in technical colleges in Moscow, and he has two daughters from the first and second marriages. He loves tennis, and when younger engaged in free-style wrestling and achieved the level of a candidate for master of sport in it. He took up karate for three years and also was involved in volleyball, boxing, water polo, diving and shooting. He is a collector of books: dictionaries, literary mementos and Japanese prose and poetry, and his favourite author is Thomas Mann. He has two cars, a Mercedes Benz and a Soviet.

Bragin, Vyacheslav Ivanovich

Chairman of the Ostankino Television and Radio Company.

Born in 1939 in Bezhetsko, Tver *oblast*. Russian. A member of the CPSU until January 1990, he began his working life as a fitter. He graduated from the history faculty of Moscow State University and the Academy of Social Sciences of the Central Committee, CPSU, from which he successfully presented his candidate dissertation in history (PhD). Until 1980 he worked in Tver *oblast* on a *raion* newspaper where he began as a correspondent and finished as editor. In 1980 he entered the Party apparatus and was elected secretary, then first secretary of the Party central *raion* committee in Tver. He has received state awards.

In early 1990 he was nominated as a candidate for election as a people's deputy in the No. 406 Zavolzhsky territorial district, Tver *oblast*, was supported by the democrats and defeated a candidate put forward by the Party *oblast* committee. On January 15, 1990 he resigned from the CPSU in protest against the events in Vilnius when Soviet forces stormed the TV station, resulting in loss of life. During the presidential elections in the RSFSR in June 1991 he headed the campaign in Tver in support of Boris Yeltsin, and after the attempted coup in August 1991 he was appointed President Yeltsin's representative in Tver.

As a people's deputy he joined the coalition for reform of the parliamentary bloc and began working in the RSFSR Supreme Soviet committee on the mass media, links with public organizations of mass movements and the study of public opinion. He took part in the drafting of the RSFSR law on the mass media. In November 1991 he was elected chairman of the committee on the mass media and became a member of the Supreme Soviet Presidium. He is a strong supporter of the freedom of expression and the press and in early 1993 was appointed chairman of the Ostankino TV and radio company. He supports free and honest journalism and the most daring and creative programmes and has declared himself willing to enter into dialogue with all sides of the political spectrum. He has played an important role in ensuring that TV vigorously supports the Yeltsin administration. He lives in Moscow.

Brazauskas, Algirdas Mykolas

President of Lithuania.

Born on September 22, 1932 in Roniskis, the independent Republic of Lithuania; Lithuanian. He was a member of the Communist Party of Lithuania (1959-90). He graduated in 1956 from Kaunas Technical University in civil engineering and successfully presented his candidate dissertation in economics (PhD(Econ)) in 1974. He was first deputy chairman of the Lithuanian Gosplan (state planning committee) (1966-77), and then became a secretary of the Central Committee, Communist Party of Lithuania until 1989. In 1989 he was elected first secretary of the Central Committee, Communist Party of Lithuania and was chairman of the Presidium of the Supreme Soviet, Lithuanian SSR (1989-90). In December 1990 Brazauskas and other pro-reform and pro-independence communists declared the Communist Party of Lithuania renamed Lithuanian Democratic Labour Party independent of the Communist Party of the Soviet Union, and so the pro-Moscow communists set up their own party. He was deputy Prime Minister of the Republic of Lithuania, 1990-91.

After independence Brazauskas and other like-minded communists transformed the Communist Party of Lithuania into the Lithuanian Democratic Labour Party, but it was never viewed as a serious threat to *Sajudis*, the nationalist party. However, the state of the economy and the poor leadership of Vytautas Landsbergis led to astonishing gains for the LDLP in the first democratic elections after independence, in September 1992. Quite unexpectedly, especially to Brazauskas and his supporters, the LDPD emerged from the first round of voting as the strongest party, polling 44.7% of the votes. They swept the board in the second round of the elections, in November 1992, and emerged with a majority in parliament. Had the LDLP put up more candidates they would have secured even more parliamentary seats. The election results did not tally with opinion polls and it emerged that 12% of voters had stated they had voted for *Sajudis*, whereas in reality they had voted for the LDLP.

Brazauskas became the dominant figure in Lithuanian politics and became acting President. His standing was confirmed in February 1993 when he won the presidential election by polling 60.1% of the votes. He took on a heavy task as the Lithuanian economy, heavily dependent on the Russian economy, especially for fuel and energy, had little room for manoeuvre. Brazauskas's approach was reminiscent of that of the industrial lobby in Russia, Civic Union. He is married with two daughters.

Address: The Residence of the President, Gedimino pr. 53, Vilnius 232026; *telephone*: Vilnius 628 986.

Bugdaev, Ilya Erdnievich

Speaker of the Supreme Soviet of the Republic of Kalmykia, Russian Federation.

Born in 1938 in the village of Maly Derbety, Maloderbetovsky *raion*, Kalmykia Autonomous Soviet Socialist Republic (ASSR) into a shepherd's family. He is Kalmyk, and was a member of the CPSU until August 1991. After graduating from the Achinsk Agricultural Technical College he served in 1958 as an officer in the Baltic Fleet. He graduated with distinction from the Volgograd Agricultural Institute as a qualified animal specialist and successfully presented his candidate dissertation in agricultural science (PhD). After graduating from the institute he was chief animal specialist in the Put k kommunizmy collective farm, Maloderbetovsky *raion*, and in 1968 was appointed director of the M. I. Kalinin animal breeding state farm, Tselinny *raion*. Under his direction the farm became the centre for the breeding of Kalmyk fatstock and won various gold and silver medals at the Exhibition of Economic Achievements, Moscow, and other awards.

In 1975 he was appointed head of the department of animal husbandry and deputy head of the republican association of state farms, Priozerny *raion* Party committee. In 1982 he became minister of agriculture of the Kalmyk ASSR and in 1986 first deputy chairman of the state agro-industrial committee of the Kalmyk ASSR. In October 1989 he was elected chairman of the union of agro-industrial enterprises (*Kalmagropromsoyuz*) while remaining minister of agriculture. He has been awarded the orders of the Friendship of the Peoples, the badge of honour and the medal for exemplary work. On the centenary of the birth of V. I. Lenin the title of honoured animal specialist of the RSFSR was created and he was one of the recipients.

In 1990 he was elected a people's deputy of the Supreme Soviet of the Kalmyk ASSR. At its first session, in April 1990, he was nominated for the post of Speaker (chairman) but did not obtain the requisite number of votes. In November 1992, at the XVI session of the Supreme Soviet of the Republic of Kalmykia, he was elected Speaker of the Supreme Soviet. On assuming office he declared that it was essential to understand the present situation well, that if Russia fell into a difficult position then it would be impossible for a part of it, for example Kalmykia, to flourish. The leadership of all the republics should unite their efforts to bring the country out of crisis.

He advocated full autonomy for collective farms or enterprises but also for joint stock companies or private farms. The problem about who was the master of the land and agricultural production should have been resolved long ago, since most of the economic problems in the country derived from the failure to answer this question. He stated that the question of private farming had long since concerned him, as it was not enough to give peasants land. The whole process had to be put on a sound footing with methods worked out about how the state should support private farming in the early stages and strictly supervise its implementation.

Bugdaev stated that introducing the post of President in the Republic of Kalmykia was inopportune, but considered that a final answer to the question of whether there should be a President should be resolved by the people through a referendum. He enjoys reading and devotes much of his time to self-education. He lives in Elist.

Bukreev, Yury Dmitrievich

Chief of the Main Headquarters of the Land Forces of the Russian Federation. Colonel-General since 1991.

Born in 1941. Russian. He graduated from the Tashkent Tank Technical School in 1962; the Military Academy of Armoured Forces and the Military Academy of the General Staff. He received a higher military education and was a member of the CPSU till August 1991.

He began his career as officer as a tank platoon commander, then as a tank company commander in the Turkestan military district. He immediately demonstrated sound tactical and specialist training and the ability to organize and conduct a combat. He was notable among young officers for his eagerness to study and for the use of advanced methods of training and education of soldiers and sergeants under his command. He actively participated in the CPSU organizations, together with various undertakings of the Party-political agencies. He was ambitious and enjoyed the support of superior commanders.

After graduating from the Academy he was assigned to the group of Soviet troops in Germany as a deputy commander of a tank regiment. He demonstrated a sound operational-tactical and military-technical training, awareness of the requirements of modern-day army combat and was good at organizing the co-ordinated action of tank and motorized-rifle sub-units. He was promoted to Chief of Staff of a motorized-rifle division, where he mastered the planning and control of combat and special training of various types of land forces.

For three years he was a commander of a motorized-rifle division in Kiev military district, after which, as a promising military leader, he was sent to study at the Academy of the General Staff.

Later he served in the Far East military district as a deputy army commander and an army commander for two and a half years. Then he became Chief of Staff of the Turkestan military district. At the time of the anti-constitutional putsch in August 1991 he was not very active, meticulously fulfilling all instructions coming from the General Staff. However, he is known to have expressed support for the ideas and actions of the Emergency Committee.

In November 1991 Lieut.-Gen. Yu. Bukreev became Chief of the Main Headquarters of the Land Forces of the Soviet army and was soon promoted to Colonel-General. From February 1992 he was Chief of Staff of the land forces of the Unified Armed Forces of the CIS. He participated in the work of the State Commission from April 4, 1992 on setting up the Ministry of Defence, Army and Navy of the Russian Federation.

By President B. Yeltsin's decree on August 21, 1992, he was appointed chief of Main Headquarters of the land forces of Russia.

A highly qualified military professional, he proved capable of conceiving and assessing new forms and methods of troop training and their combat use. In the sphere of military construction he favours the creation of highly mobile land forces equipped with up-to-date weapons, capable of acting in different regions and theatres of operations. He expressed his ideas in the article "I am for land forces" ("*Krasnaya Zvezda*", November 28, 1991). He favours military reform to meet contemporary demands but is against abolishing the traditional forms of recruitment and training of personnel. He has close ties with the leaders of the Russian Ministry of Defence.

He does not normally express his political views. He advocates the idea of strong state power and of Russia regaining its position as a great power. His attitude towards the democratic public organizations of officers is negative.

There is no information about his hobbies. He does not speak any foreign language. He has been awarded several orders and medals and is married with a son (who is 25, an officer and company commander in the Far East), and an 11-year old daughter, who is still at school.

Office address: 103175, Moscow, K-175.

Bulgak, Vladimir Borisovich

Minister of Communications of the Russian Federation.

Born on May 9, 1941 in Moscow into a Russian family. In 1963 he graduated from the Moscow electrical institute of communications, specializing in radio communications. He left the CPSU in August 1991. In 1972 he graduated from the institute of the management of the national economy. He was a candidate of technical sciences (PhD). In 1963 he began work as a mechanic in the faculty of radio systems and equipment of the Moscow electrical institute of communications. Also in 1963, he became an instructor in the Moscow city *Komsomol* organization. From 1963 to 1968 he was deputy secretary, then secretary of the department of communications enterprises and organizations of the *Komsomol*. From 1968 to 1970 he was chief engineer of the fifth radio broadcasting channel of the Moscow network. From 1969 to 1970 he worked as the chief engineer responsible for foreign broadcasts of the Moscow city radio broadcasting network. From 1970 to 1972 he was deputy head of the board of the Moscow city radio broadcasting network.

Between 1983 and 1988, Bulgak was head of the main planning and finance administration of the USSR Ministry of Communications. From 1988 to 1989 he was head of the main economic administration of the USSR Ministry of Communications and in 1990 head of the main administration of the economics of management of the ministry. In July 1991 he was appointed RSFSR Minister of Communications, Information and Space in the government of Ivan Silaev and in November 1991 he became Minister of Communications in the "reform government". Under him the ministry began work on constructing a radio-telephone system covering the Russian Federation and linking it to a global network, and the building of new international automatic telephone exchanges in Moscow and St Petersburg. The whole project is based on foreign companies providing the necessary investment. Considerable progress was made in providing new satellite telephone lines to the outside world from Moscow. The declining authority of the centre made the ministry's task more difficult as regions sought to promote their own communications links. An ambitious project to lay fibre-optic cable from Moscow to Vladivostok could not be implemented. However, fibre-optic cable links were under way from Denmark via Poland.

In late December 1991 the ministry decided to raise the price of delivering periodicals to the public. As a result of this many publications were threatened with closure, and in January 1992 the ministry postponed the increases until the end of the year.

Bulgak was awarded the orders of the Red Banner of Labour, the Friendship of Peoples and the badge of honour, and was awarded the prize of the USSR Council of Ministers.

Bunich, Pavel Grigorevich

Member of the Council of the President of the Russian Federation.

Born on December 25, 1925 in Moscow; Russian. He was a member of the CPSU from 1956 to August 1991 and was elected a member of the Central Committee in July 1990. In 1952 he graduated from the faculty of economics, Moscow State University and then became a postgraduate student. In 1955 he successfully presented his candidate dissertation in economics on "Branch co-operation in the USSR and its role in raising further the production of consumer goods in the 5th Five Year Plan" (PhD (Econ)). From 1955 he became a senior scientific assistant, head of section, and deputy director of the scientific research institute of finance, USSR Ministry of Finance. In 1961 in the G. V. Plekhanov Institute of the National Economy, Moscow, he successfully presented his doctoral dissertation in economics on "Basic funds in socialist industry" (DSc (Econ)).

In 1971 he was elected a member of the Presidium of the Far East scientific centre, USSR Academy of Sciences, in 1975 he became a professor at Moscow State University, and in 1976 was head of department in the S. Ordzhonikidze Institute of Management, Moscow. In 1989 he was elected a USSR people's deputy as one of the nominees of the USSR Academy of Sciences and was a member of the USSR Supreme Soviet committee on economic reform. In 1990 he was appointed pro-rector for scientific work of the academy of the national economy of the USSR Council of Ministers, and was also elected president of the USSR union of lease holders and entrepreneurs. In 1991 he became rector of the academy of the national economy of the USSR Council of Ministers.

He is a corresponding member of the Russian Academy of Sciences. His most important publications are: *Problems of Economic Cost Accounting and*

Finance Reform (1970); *Economic Cost Accounting and the Effectiveness of Production*, (1974); *Management, Economic Levers, Economic Cost Accounting* (1976); *The Economy of the World Ocean* (1977); *The Economic Mechanism of Developed Socialism* (1982); and *The Problems of the Stabilization of the Market Economy in the USSR* (1991). In 1990 he was appointed a member of the higher consultative co-ordinating council of the Speaker of the RSFSR Supreme Soviet and then, in June 1991, of the RSFSR President. On August 19, 1991, as rector of the academy of the national economy, he ordered the implementation of the decrees of the President of the RSFSR. He was a appointed a member of the Council of the President in 1992.

He is a supporter of the introduction in Russia of private property in land and the most rapid implementation of privatization (first type) which provides work collectives with 20% of the shares of their enterprise free of charge. He opposes other types of privatization which, in his view, would leave most Russians without any property. He opposes extreme measures in pushing through economic reform, favours the regulation of the prices of certain goods and the careful use of the law of bankruptcy. He advised agreeing reasonable compromises with the constructive opposition, especially with Civic Union, but criticized the latter for its commitment to the Chinese model of economic reform.

In early 1993 he criticized the government of Viktor Chernomyrdin for attempts to introduce regulated prices, and to rehabilitate state planning and moves away from reform. He was opposed to holding a referendum, seeing it as promoting divisions in society. His preferred option was to achieve a compromise between the various branches of power through negotiations. He lives in Moscow.

Burbulis, Gennady Eduardovich

Former State Secretary and Head of the Presidential Advisory Council.

Born on August 4, 1945 in Pervouralsk, Sverdlovsk (Ekaterinburg) *oblast*. He served in the rocket forces in the army. In 1969 he worked as pipe layer fitter in the mechanization trust of the municipal housing administration, Sverdlovsk. The same year he enrolled in the philosophy department of the Urals State University and graduated in 1974. From 1974 to 1975 he was assistant in the faculty of philosophy of the S. M. Kirov Urals Polytechnical Institute where he successfully presented his candidate dissertation (PhD) in 1978. He came into contact with Boris Yeltsin who was first Party secretary in Sverdlovsk *oblast*. From 1978 to 1983 he taught Marxism-Leninism at the latter institute, where he was first assistant professor and then professor. He successfully presented his doctoral dissertation in 1981 on "knowledge and conviction as integral phenomena of consciousness" (DLitt).

From 1983 to 1989 he was head of the faculty of social sciences, deputy director for science and methodology in the all-Union institute for improving the qualifications of specialists in the Ministry of Non-Ferrous Metallurgy in Sverdlovsk. In May 1987, on the initiative of the Sverdlovsk city Party organization, the Tribune for Discussion, a political club, was set up as an alternative to the Fatherland patriotic organization run by Yury Lipatnikov. The Tribune for Discussion became the basis of the Sverdlovsk association of public organizations. Burbulis was a founding figure and "father" of the new club and chaired its monthly meetings. According to some sources it was Burbulis who changed the club into a tribune for city radicals and created a powerful mechanism for the democratization of public life in Sverdlovsk. According to other sources, being a reform communist, he tried to exclude the radicals.

In May 1988 Burbulis emerged as one of the organizers of the association of public organizations and in September 1988 of the Sverdlovsk branch of the Memorial society. The sessions of the Tribune for Discussion appeared to be out of control on occasions and Burbulis gave the radicals their heads at times. This did not meet with the approval of the leadership of the city Party committee and several sessions were almost banned, but in the end the Tribune for Discussion managed to get a good report from the Party committee. The desire of the Tribune for Democracy to become actively involved in politics led to its council setting up the movement for democratic elections during the elections to the USSR Congress of People's Deputies in the spring of 1989.

The movement supported many democratic candidates including Burbulis himself, L. Kudrin, V. Volkov and V. Isakov. It is of interest that Vladimir Isakov, who later moved over to the conservative camp, was regarded by many observers at the time as a more convinced democrat than Burbulis. Unexpectedly in the Lenin electoral district, Sverdlovsk, there were three democrats left on the ballot slip: Yeltsin, Burbulis and A. Epp. Yeltsin withdrew, and most informal groups supported Burbulis. The leader of Fatherland, the influential patriotic organization, Yury Lipatnikov, proposed that voters should strike out Burbulis and Epp together, thus ensuring that if Yeltsin failed in Moscow he could come back to Sverdlovsk. This was in line with the views of the conservatives in Sverdlovsk, but in the end Burbulis just won (114,530 votes and 91,309 for Epp).

After Burbulis's election as a USSR people's deputy the Tribune for Democracy folded and this led to his being criticized by the informal groups. Burbulis joined the interregional group of deputies when it was set up at the I Congress of People's Deputies and was elected a member of its co-ordinating council. Many of the members favoured Burbulis becoming one of the five leaders of the group and he was placed on the same list as Yeltsin, Afanasev, Popov and Palm, but due to the unexpected nomination of Andrei Sakharov at the constituent conference he was not elected a co-chairman.

At this point the close collaboration between Burbulis and Yeltsin began. In May 1989, at the I USSR Congress of People's Deputies, he nominated Yeltsin as speaker of the USSR Supreme Soviet as an alternative to Mikhail Gorbachev. However, Yeltsin withdrew, and in December 1989 Burbulis was among the deputies who moved over to the opposition. In September 1989 Burbulis took part in convening the constituent congress of the RSFSR united front of workers in Sverdlovsk. He helped the organizers to book a hall, but due to the negative attitude of several members of the interregional group, including Academician Sakharov, to the united front of workers, Burbulis withdrew his support. He was a member of the CPSU from 1971 to 1990. According to him he was a "convinced communist" during these years.

From January 1990 for a few months he was a member of the Democratic Platform in the CPSU. He became one of the most prominent leaders of the Democratic Party of Russia, "Travkin's party" and at the constituent congress he was elected a deputy chairman, but did not play an active part in the affairs of the party. He became a member of the State Council and left the party. Nikolai Travkin explained Burbulis's departure from the party by the fact that he was now occupying official posts and Burbulis repeated this explanation at the II Party Congress in May 1991, but the real reason may have been that the party was incapable of uniting all democrats around it. From 1989 to 1990 Burbulis was chairman of the sub-committee of the USSR Supreme Soviet committee on the work of the soviets of people's deputies, the development of administration and self-administration.

During the autumn of 1990 he was Yeltsin's agent during elections to the Russian Congress of People's Deputies and as such the main organizer of his electoral campaign. From January to July 1990 Burbulis was leader of the working group of the co-ordination consultative council of the RSFSR Supreme Soviet. He was called Yeltsin's *eminence grise* and was rated the main intellectual force behind Boris Nikolaevich. He was head of the staff running Yeltsin's campaign for President and played a key role during the attempted coup in August 1991, acting as liaison and food distribution point for Muscovites. From July to November 1991 he headed the State Council of the President of the RSFSR and was made a state secretary.

He was influential in the selection of ministers. Egor Gaidar and Aleksandr Shokhin are regarded as Burbulis men. Ruslan Khasbulatov and he played a key role in "engineering" the resignation of Ivan Silaev as Russian Prime Minister. Then began the battle between Burbulis and Khasbulatov for primacy in Yeltsin's closest circle. They traded insults: Khasbulatov referred to Burbulis as a "boy in the affairs of state"; Burbulis riposted: "I feel for him". Burbulis has many detractors besides Khasbulatov, including Vice-President Aleksandr Rutskoi whom Burbulis tried to get dismissed for disloyalty to the President during Rutskoi's tour around the country in November 1991. Burbulis managed to reduce some of Rutskoi's power.

Viktor Barannikov, Minister of State Security, is another adversary. Another is Sergei Stankevich, presidential counsellor for political affairs, and Yury Petrov, until December 1992, head of the administration of the President, who is also critical. Burbulis is the link man between Yeltsin and the rest of the administration when the President is on holiday. He is regarded as the organizer of the "conspiratorial" meeting on December 8, 1991 at Viskulyi, near Brest in Belarus, between Yeltsin, Leonid Kravchuk, the Ukrainian leader, and Stanislau Shushkevich, the Belarusian leader, which established the CIS.

Burbulis was a leading figure in the battle against the monopoly of the State Bank (Gosbank) and the Foreign Trade Bank (Vneshekombank) in transactions at home and abroad, and was influential in the take-over by Yeltsin's Russia of the Soviet financial institutions. From March 1992 Burbulis, in consequence of the decree of the President, became the overseer of the political ministries (state-legal administration, the Ministry of the Press and Media Information and the Ministry of Foreign Affairs). Burbulis cultivates the air of an intellectual and loves Berdyaev, the Russian pre-1917 philosopher, and Freud, and was a great admirer of Academician Sakharov, but he is not an orator. He is married with one child and the family lives in Yekaterinburg.

He regards himself as Russian. His grandfather, a gunsmith, emigrated to the Urals from Lithuania in 1915, but his father did not speak Lithuanian and his mother was Russian. There are rumours that his grandfather was not a Lithuanian but a Latvian and, moreover, one of the Latvian sharpshooters who defended the Bolsheviks in the early days.

After being made deputy Prime Minister of Russia, in December 1991, it was stated on television that the stress on his name is on the first syllable. He loses no opportunity to underline his loyalty to Yeltsin and refers to himself as "Yeltsin's closest ally". The most memorable event for him was the raising of the Russian flag over the Kremlin on December 25, 1991, which to Burbulis completed a long episode in the history of Russia. In February 1992 he spoke of the need to set up a "ruling party" to support President Yeltsin and the government in seeing through economic reform at a time when democratic forces were weakening and there was danger from the right. At the VI Congress of People's Deputies in April 1992, as one of the concessions made by Yeltsin to the conservative majority in the congress, Burbulis was relieved of his duties as deputy Prime Minister. He remained a state secretary and lost none of his influence. In October 1992, together with Andrei Kozyrev, Mikhail Poltoranin and Aleksandr Shokhin, he signed an open letter about the danger to reform in Russia, including the sources of danger from amongst the people's deputies. In November 1992 under pressure from the Civic Union Yeltsin removed Burbulis as a state secretary but made him head of a presidential advisory council. At the VII Congress of People's Deputies in December 1992 some observers criticized Burbulis for the tactical mistakes made by the President and he had to give up his post as head of the presidential advisory council.

He has been a frequent visitor abroad and speaks German. He was awarded the 20th anniversary of the victory in the Great Fatherland War medal. He likes sport, including boxing, weightlifting, running, football (he has played for the Russian government team) and tennis. His wife, Natalyia, graduated from the philosophy faculty of the Urals State University and is involved in the study of culture and aesthetics, and their son, Andrei, is 12 years old. He lives in Moscow.

Burkov, Valery Anatolevich

Adviser of the President of the Russian Federation on invalids.

Born on April 26, 1957 in Shadrinsk, Kurgan *oblast*; Russian. He was a member of the CPSU until August 1991. He graduated from the Higher Military Aviation Technical College, Chelyabinsk, as a navigator and the Yu. A. Gagarin Military Aviation Academy. He is a colonel, and served in the air defence forces in the Far East (1978-83) and in the centre of administration of air movement, Chelyabinsk, in 1983. He saw active service in Afghanistan and he was severely wounded twice (1983-84). After graduating from the Gagarin academy he served in the main staff of the air defence forces (1988-91). He was appointed chairman of the co-ordinating committee on invalids of the President of the RSFSR and also adviser of the RSFSR President on invalids (1991-92). In September 1992 he was appointed adviser of the President of the Russian Federation on invalids. He is a hero of the Soviet Union and was awarded the order of the Red Flag. He is married with a son and lives in Moscow.

Buryak, Leonid Iosifovich

Ukrainian footballer.

Born on July 10, 1953; Ukrainian. He is an Honoured Master of Sport (1975) and played half back. He began his career with Chernomorets Odessa (Odesa), then with Dinamo Kiev (1973-84); Torpedo Moscow (1985-86), Metallist Kharkov (Kharkiv) (1987-88); and Vantaan Pallo, Helsinki (1990). He played in the USSR championship winning sides of 1974, 1975, 1977, 1980 and 1981; also the USSR cup winning teams of 1974, 1978 and 1982, all with Dinamo Kiev, and with Metallist Kharkov in 1988. He was also a member of the victorious team in the cup of cups and supercup in 1975. He played 50 times for the USSR team and scored eight goals between 1974 and 1983. He also played in the Soviet team during the qualifying matches of the World Cup in 1977 and 1981.

Buzgalin, Aleksandr Vladimirovich

Co-Chairman of the Marxist Platform Public Political Movement.

Born on July 19, 1954 in Moscow; Russian. In 1976 he graduated from the faculty of economics of Moscow State University. He then became a postgraduate student there and in 1979 successfully presented his candidate dissertation in economics (PhD (Econ)). Then he was appointed to the staff of the faculty of economics in the same university, first as a junior scientific assistant, later as a senior scientific assistant, senior lecturer, and assistant professor.

He was a member of the CPSU from 1987 to August 1991 and was elected a member of the Party Central Committee in July 1990. V. F. Isaichikov and he were elected co-chairmen of the Marxist Platform movement which was registered on January 9, 1992.

The movement's main aims are: support for the socialist development of society, the bringing together of people who share the idea of social equality and justice, provision of help to the poor, ensuring the democratic development of Russia as a unified federal state of free peoples and the renaissance of the soviets as agencies of popular power. At present Buzgalin is the co-ordinator of the consultative council of the congress of left democratic forces. He opposed the declaration of President Boris Yeltsin on March 20, 1993, about the introduction of a special regime in the country. In his view "Yeltsin impeached himself". Buzgalin lives in Moscow.

Certan, Sergiu

Minister for the Economy, Republic of Moldova.

Born in 1952 in Chişinău. An ethnic Moldovan, who completed Moldovan middle school No. 1 and then graduated from the Faculty of Economics at the Polytechnic Institute in Chişinău. He gained his doctorate in economics (DSc Econ) from the Central Economics/Mathematics Institute of the USSR Academy of Sciences, Moscow (1976). He worked for 17 years as researcher at the Planning Institute and then at the Ministry of National Economy. He also worked as director of the Institute for Economic Research of the Moldovan Academy of Sciences and as director of the Study Centre on Problems of the Market.

Chaptynov, Valery Ivanovich

Speaker of the Supreme Soviet of the Republic of Gorny Altai, Russian Federation.

Born on June 11, 1945 in the village of Verkh-Anshuyakhta, Shebalinsky *raion*, Gorno-Altai autonomous *oblast* into a peasant family. He is an Altai, and was a member of the CPSU until August 1991. In 1967 he graduated from the Altai institute of agriculture. He was director of the Ust Koksinsky inter-*raion*, state breeding station. In 1969 he was secretary, later deputy chairman of the *raion* soviet executive committee, and head of the *raion* administration of agriculture of Ust Koksinsky. From 1972 to 1976 he worked in the *Komsomol* organization as secretary, second secretary, first secretary of the Gorno-Altai *Komsomol obkom*. He was a delegate to the XVII *Komsomol* congress.

In 1978 he graduated from the Academy of Social Sciences of the Party Central Committee. In the same year he was an instructor of the Party *obkom*, then first secretary of the Kosh-Agachsky *raion* Party committee. In 1983 he was secretary, and in 1984 second secretary of the Gorno-Altai Party *obkom*. In November 1988 he was appointed chairman of the soviet executive committee of the Gorno-Altai autonomous *oblast*, and was elected a member of the bureau of the party *obkom*, a deputy of the Altai *krai* and Gorno-Altai *oblast* soviets. He was awarded the orders of the Red Banner of Labour and the badge of honour and three medals.

In early 1990 he was nominated by the work collectives of the Maiminsk enterprise (a butter and cheese combine), the Yabogansky state farm, the Altai geophysical expedition, the plenums of the city and *oblast* soviet of veterans and the meeting of the electors of the village of Turachak for election as a RSFSR people's deputy in the No. 162 Gorno-Altaisky territorial district. During the election campaign he advocated the sovereignty and independence of the RSFSR within the USSR, the setting up of the region's own system of administration and political and social structures. He favoured the raising of the legal status of local education, the secession of the Gorno-Altai autonomous *oblast* from Altai *krai* and its direct subordination to the RSFSR, and the retention and development of the language, cultural and other characteristics of the native peoples. He appealed for the raising of rural living standards by going over to economic cost accounting, self-financing, self-administration and the transfer of the levers of administration to the local state authorities. He advocated the reform of health and education and social guarantees to be given to the poor strata of the population. He proposed the strengthening of the Soviet Army and the law enforcing agencies and opposed those who were trying to promote the ideas of national capitalism, unlimited democracy and non-party *glasnost* among Soviet people.

He was the only candidate and won in the first round, polling 71.3% of the votes. He is a member of the constitutional commission and was a member of the Communists of Russia group of deputies and the parliamentary faction, "sovereignty and equality".

In 1990 he was elected a deputy of the *oblast* soviet. On March 27, 1990 he was elected unopposed Speaker of the Gorno-Altai *oblast* soviet. From July 3, 1990 after the establishment of the Republic of Gorny Altai, he became the Speaker of the Supreme Soviet of the Republic of Gorny Altai. On April 28, 1990 he was elected first secretary of the Gorno-Altai Party *obkom*. He was a delegate to the XXVIII Party congress. He was nominated for election to the Party Central Committee by the *oblast* Party conference.

On August 20, 1991 he declared on republican radio, in the name of the soviet and executive committee of the Republic of Gorno-Altai, that all constitutional authorities and the RSFSR constitution were functioning and appealed for calm and restraint. At the same time he sent a telegram to the local state authorities ordering them to organize clarification of the work and support for the Extraordinary Committee. In September 1991 several deputies of the republican soviet brought up the question of his resignation but the majority of deputies did not agree with them. He lives in Gorno-Altaisk.

Chepurnyi, Anatolii Grygorovych

Chairman of the Ukrainian Supreme Soviet Committee on the Agro-Industrial Complex.

Born into a Ukrainian family in 1941. After studying at the Kharkiv Institute of Agricultural Economics, he worked as an agronomist. In March 1990 he was elected people's deputy for Kupyanskyi *raion*, Kharkiv *oblast*. Once in the Supreme Soviet he put himself forward as the spokesman of Ukraine's highly conservative collective farm lobby, and secured the chairmanship of the influential agro-industrial committee, and is therefore an *ex officio* member of the Presidium of the Supreme Soviet.

Like most conservative communists, he remained a member of the Communist Party right up until August 24, 1991, when Ukraine declared its independence. Chepurnyi has continued to use his position to block significant agricultural reform. In spring 1993 he claimed the credit for a massive boost to agricultural subsidies of more than one trillion coupons, which kept many collective farms afloat, but undermined the government's reformist credentials. Moreover, he openly boasted that it was pressure from his committee that brought about the resignation of First Vice-Premier Yukhnovskyi in March 1993.

Official address: Kiev, Vul. M. Hrushevskoho 5; *telephone*: Kiev 252 019.

Cherkesov, Georgy Mashtaevich

Chairman of the Council of Ministers of the Kabardino-Balkar Republic, Russian Federation.

Born in 1938; member of the CPSU until August 1991. In 1990 he was general director of the Kabardino-Balkarskoe territorial poultry production association, and early that year he was nominated by the work collective of the Kabardino-Balkarskoe association for election as a RSFSR people's deputy in the No. 819 Oktyabrsky territorial district. During the election he advocated acceleration of economic reform, preference for the market economy over the planned economy, full autonomy for enterprises and the bridging of the gulf between democratic and economic development. He regarded the primary task of deputies to be the resolution of the food problem.

He supported the removal of the CPSU from the leadership of the economy, the annulment of article 6 of the constitution of the USSR (on the leading role of the Party), political pluralism and the concentration of power in the local soviets. One of the key questions was improving inter-ethnic relations in the region. He favoured a new federal treaty which the Kabardino-Balkar ASSR would sign as a Union republic.

There were five candidates. Cherkesov polled 20.3% of the votes in the first round and lost in the second round, polling 37% of the votes. F. A. Kharaev was elected people's deputy and received 31.5% of the votes in the first round and 56.2% in the second. On September 28, 1991 Cherkesov was nominated as the only candidate for the post of Chairman of the Council of Ministers of the Kabardino-Balkar Republic and was confirmed at a session of the Supreme Soviet. On assuming office he stated that the main tasks of the new government had to be improvements in the availability of consumer goods, the resolution of the food problem and the provision of social guarantees to the population during the transition to the market. He lives in Nalchik.

Chernavin, Vladimir Nikolaevich

Commander of the Navy; deputy Commander-in-Chief of the unified armed forces of the Commonwealth of Independent States (CIS); Admiral of the Fleet since 1983.

Born on April 22, 1928 in Mykolaiv (Nikolaev in Russian), Ukraine, into a working-class family. Russian. He graduated from the Baku Naval preparatory technical school and completed two years at the engineering technical school in Ulyanovsk (Simbirsk), Russia. His service career began in 1947. He graduated from the M. V. Frunze higher naval technical school in 1951, the Naval Academy in 1965 and the Military Academy of the General Staff in 1969, and in his higher military education he specialized in naval operations and tactics. He was a member of the Communist Party of the Soviet Union (CPSU), from 1949 to August 1991.

He began his career as an officer as a commander of an artillery and mine-torpedo section (*chast*) of a diesel submarine of the Northern Fleet in 1951. He immediately demonstrated exceptional command and naval abilities and was a qualified specialist. He was appointed aide to the commander of a submarine in 1953 and after completing the higher classes for officers with the rank of senior lieutenant in 1954 he became the youngest senior aide of a commander of submarines of the Northern Fleet. He took part in long voyages in the Atlantic and the northern Arctic and in the testing of new military equipment and armaments systems. He was held in respect by commanders and crew.

In 1956 he was appointed commander of an atomic submarine under construction. He saw the submarine completed and a year later joined the Northern Fleet. He was a commander for five years, completed many missions at sea and participated in patrolling and shadowing NATO fleets. He studied at the St Petersburg Naval Academy from 1962 to 1965. After graduating he was appointed chief of staff and commander of a division of submarines of the Northern Fleet where he achieved a high level of military preparedness of the unit. He actively sought personally to take part in long distance voyages, including those to areas near the North Pole. He imposed strong discipline and strict order in the units under his command. After study in the Military Academy of the General Staff he returned to the Northern Fleet where he was commander of a division of submarines, 1969–72; chief of staff and deputy commander of a flotilla of submarines, 1972–73; commander of a flotilla of submarines, 1973–74. His units played their part in solving complex naval tasks in the North Sea, central Atlantic and northern Arctic and patrolled the US coast. Chernavin repeatedly served in atomic submarines in distant waters.

In 1974 he was appointed chief of staff and first deputy commander of the Northern Fleet and from 1977 to 1981 he was commander of the Northern Fleet, where he was respected and popular. From 1981 he served in Moscow as Chief of the General Staff and first deputy Commander-in-Chief of the Navy. He skilfully developed good personal relations with the then Commander-in-Chief, Admiral of the Fleet of the Soviet Union Sergei Gorshkov, who was close to and an old friend of Leonid Brezhnev, President of the Soviet Union and General Secretary of the CPSU.

Chernavin supported those who advocated the construction of a powerful, ocean-going fleet, the development of atomic submarines armed with rockets and torpedoes, aircraft carriers and a balanced mix of types and classes of surface ships, capable of equalling the naval power of the US and NATO countries. He actively supported the concept of the permanent naval presence of the Soviet fleet in the world's oceans and naval bases in friendly countries. He championed the fleet. From 1985 he was Commander-in-Chief of the Navy and deputy USSR Minister of Defence.

A convinced communist, he was elected a candidate member of the Central Committee (CC), CPSU, in 1981 and a member of the CC, CPSU, from 1986 to 1990. He was a deputy of the USSR Supreme Soviet, 1981–90. He was a delegate to CPSU Congresses. In 1989 he was elected a USSR people's deputy by the Lenkoransky territorial district (constituency), Azerbaijan, and belonged to the group of the most convinced supporters of the retention of CPSU power and the inviolability of the territory of the USSR. He spoke as one of the authors of a series of declarations opposed to the democratic forces of Russia and the sovereignty of the republic. He was subject to great pressure from the top circle of military and communist leaders, especially the chief of the Political Administration of the Navy, Admiral V. I. Panin, a former leading official of the CC, CPSU.

He was on leave during the attempted coup of August 1991 and only returned to Moscow during the evening of August 19. Doubtless he was informed about the real course of events and he issued a series of decrees to the fleet, all geared towards raising their battle preparedness. In his absence, but doubtless with Chernavin's knowledge, Admiral Panin put out a declaration of support of the Extraordinary Committee, the coup leaders. On the whole during the days of the attempted coup the Navy did not participate in any anti-constitutional activities. However some naval officers and ratings who supported the Russian leadership were severely punished.

During the morning of August 21, 1991, in the collegium of the USSR Ministry of Defence, Chernavin opposed the further use of the armed forces in domestic political affairs. He was one of the initiators of the decision of the collegium to withdraw the troops from Moscow. Afterwards he maintained constant contact with President Boris Yeltsin and worked on raising the blockade of the presidential dacha at Foros, in the Crimea, by ships of the Black Sea fleet and arranged for the landing of the aircraft carrying the representatives of the Russian leadership at the airports in the Crimea. President Boris Yeltsin, at the extraordinary session of the RSFSR Supreme Soviet after the collapse of the putsch, referred positively to Chernavin's role. Soon afterwards *Morskoi Sbornik* (no. 8, 1991, pp. 3–5) published an interview with Chernavin entitled: "The sailors remained with the people." Chernavin, besides giving a detailed and quite reliable elucidation of the events, tried to whitewash the activities of his immediate subordinates, the commanders of the fleets, stating that they only issued decrees aimed at raising the battle preparedness of the naval forces. He claimed this in spite of the fact that the decrees of the commanders of the Black Sea and Baltic fleets and the Kamchatka flotilla, on measures supporting the activities of the Extraordinary Committee and also the activities of the political agencies and organizations of the CPSU, were public knowledge.

During the investigations, anti-constitutional actions by the Navy came to light, but Chernavin attempted to absolve the top naval leadership of blame. Admiral Panin enjoyed special support from Chernavin and after the dissolution of the political agencies in the Navy he became head of the all-Russian fund for naval exhibits and traditions (*Morskoe Kumpanstvo*). In February 1992 Chernavin was appointed Commander of the Navy and deputy Commander-in-Chief of the unified forces of the CIS. He supports the retention of a strong, unified fleet, capable of action in the oceans of the world. He opposes the break-up of the fleet.

He has expressed his views on military policy in a number of articles in *Morskoi Sbornik*: "On Naval Theory" (no. 1, 1982, pp. 20–24); "The Navy: Problems of Contraction and Development" (no. 11, 1991, pp. 3–13), etc. He is writing a book, *The Battle for Communications: Lessons of War and the Contemporary Scene*, parts of which have been published in *Morskoi Sbornik*, nos. 1–2, 1990. His opinions are conservative and he supports the views of the "statists", who favour the retention of the former Soviet Union but attempt to refrain from expressing political views. During the communist meeting and the illegal Congress of USSR people's deputies on March 17, 1992, Chernavin, without his knowledge, was named as a member of the possible leadership of a reconstituted unified state. This resulted in a cooling of relations with Boris Yeltsin for a while, but relations were soon back to normal. The democratic forces and progressives in the military react negatively to Chernavin.

Among his distinctions are: hero of the Soviet Union (February 18, 1981); two orders of Lenin; orders of the red banner of labour, the October revolution, Red Star and 12 medals. He enjoys historical and naval literature and is not indifferent to the theatre. He does not speak any foreign languages. He has been abroad often, including a trip to the US and Cuba during the autumn of 1991. He is participating actively in preparations for the celebrations marking the 300th anniversary of the Russian fleet. He was appointed honorary president of the collegium of the Russian state and social naval historical and cultural centre.

Service address: 103175 Moscow K-175; *Service telephone number of the secretariat*: Moscow 204 30 87.

Cherniak, Volodymyr Kurylovych

Rukh Economist.

Born into a Ukrainian peasant family in the village of Manshin in what is now Rivne *oblast* in western Ukraine during the German occupation in 1941. He went to medical school in Dubno in Rivne *oblast* and then worked as a medical assistant for two years before doing his national service from 1960 to 1963 in a rocket division near Leningrad. He then changed course by studying in the faculty of political economy at Kiev State University (1964-69).

After graduation he worked in the Kiev Institute of Economics, rising to become departmental director. He successfully presented his dissertation in economics (PhD (Econ)) and his doctoral dissertation (DSc (Econ)), and he is a member of the Ukrainian Academy of Sciences. In the elections to the USSR Congress of People's Deputies in March 1989 he stood for the Kiev city national-territorial district. He defeated the then first secretary of the Kiev Communist Party, Konstiantyn Masyk, in the first round, and then triumphed over 33 others in the second. He was a member of the USSR Supreme Soviet committee on economic reform, participating in the elaboration of the Shatalin and Yavlinsky plans.

He publicly quarrelled with President Mikhail Gorbachev at the IV Congress of the USSR People's Deputies over the latter's swing to the right in December 1990, and over the choice of Gennady Yanaev as Vice-President. He was one of the founders of *Rukh*; co-wrote the first *Rukh* programme, and was elected Deputy Head of the movement and a member of its Grand Council at its first congress in September 1989.

Cherniak was the co-author of the *Rukh* economic programme adopted at the movement's IV congress in December 1992, which committed *Rukh* to a more pro-market stance. He also has good official links, and in April 1992 was appointed by President Kravchuk as a member of the Economic Section of the President's advisory council or *Duma*. In October 1992 he was *Rukh's* candidate for Prime Minister, but his radical pro-free market views were too much for some.

Nevertheless, new Premier Kuchma invited him and other non-government economists to participate in drafting a new programme of reform. Under pressure from Cherniak and others, the Kuchma government gradually began to edge towards a serious programme of market reforms, including the first privatizations of small Ukrainian enterprises in early 1993.

Address (home): Kiev 207, Vul. Terensyvska 3, kv. 43; *telephone*: (home) Kiev 266 3140, (work) Kiev 290 1859.

Chernichenko, Yury Dmitrievich

Chairman of the Peasants' Party of Russia.

Born in 1929 in Moscow; Ukrainian; member of the CPSU to July 1990. He graduated from the faculty of philology, Kishenev State University, Moldova, and was assigned to work in the Altai *krai* as a journalist in the agricultural department of the *krai* newspaper, *Altaiskaya pravda*. Then he moved to Moscow and was a journalist on the newspaper *Sovetskaya Rossiya* and, from the mid-1960s, on *Pravda*. In 1974, after a row with V. I. Boldin, the editor of the agricultural department of *Pravda*, he was obliged to leave the newspaper. In 1976 he became a commentator on Central TV for one of the leading programmes, *Selsky chas* (rural hour).

He was a member of the USSR Union of Writers and author of the collections of documentary prose: *The Riches of the Virgin Lands for the People* (1960); *The Needle of the Compass* (1965); *At Home* (1967); *Known Equation* (1974); *Spring Crop Area* (1975); *Russian Chernozem* (1978); *Potatoes* (1982); *The Smith, Ploughman and Miller* (1982); *The Ability to Run a Home* (1984); *Russian Wheat* (1987); *Long Journeys* (1988); *Russian Grain* (1988); *Grain*, (1988); *Land and Will* (1991); the tales *Virgin Lands* (1973) and *One's Own Bread* (1972); the scripts of the documentary films: *The Plan and the Milkmaid Vera*, *The Collective Farm of Collective Farms, Uprooting, My Grandson's Allotment*, *The Tree of Life, The Price of Water*, and co-author of the script of the film *Hope and Support* (1982). He was secretary of the USSR Union of Writers until March 1991.

In early 1990 he was nominated for election as an RSFSR people's deputy in the No. 7 Gagarin territorial district, Moscow. There were 12 candidates, including D. A. Volkogonov, E. A. Ryazanov and A. A. Leonov. Chernichenko polled 38.75% of the votes in the first round and won the second round, polling 67.73% of the votes. In the election programme he stated his primary function as a people's deputy, if elected, would be making it possible for the population to feed itself and for the Soviet Union to cease importing agricultural produce. The best way to achieve this was the development of the leasing system in the countryside. Urban help for the countryside was needed but should consist not only of extra labour but also of scientific, technical and cultural assistance to ensure agricultural production. Chernichenko joined the interregional group of deputies.

He was one of the prime movers behind the establishment of the *Aprel* all-Union association of writers in 1990 and the Moscow fund for a clean city in 1989, and was elected chairman of the latter. On August 19, 1991 he broadcast a declaration about the unconstitutional state coup, instigated by the Extraordinary Committee, on radio *Svoboda*. In the autumn of 1991 he was one of the organizers of the declaration by 800 Moscow writers which expressed their unwillingness to be members of the same union as the "chauvinists who were disgracing Russian letters". In March 1992 a non-ideological creative union was established.

In February 1991 he issued a declaration about the setting up of a new party, an alternative to the peasants' union, formed by Egor Ligachev and headed by V. Starodubtsev. The founding congress of the Peasants' Party of Russia (PPR) took place on March 16-18, 1991 and Chernichenko was elected chairman. The programme of the PPR includes private ownership of land, free competition among the various forms of agriculture, the development of the market economy and agricultural co-operatives. He views the collective farm as the only full and complete entity brought into being by the Bolsheviks. The only alternative to the collective farm is peasant farming, founded on the private ownership of land. However, without the peasantry being represented in the state it cannot become a powerful force in the social struggle. The PPR should become the representative of the peasantry in the country. He lives in Moscow.

Chernomyrdin, Viktor Stepanovich

Prime Minister of Russia, December 1992-

Born on April 9, 1938 in the Cossack village of Cherny Otrog, Saraktashsky *raion*, Orenburg *oblast*, into a large Russian family. His father was head of a motor tractor station (MTS). He joined the CPSU in 1961 and resigned in 1991. He began work in 1957 as a fitter and mechanic at the Orsk oil refinery, Orenburg *oblast*. After national service he returned to the factory. From 1962 to 1966 he studied at the V. V. Kuibyshev polytechnical institute, Kuibyshev, and became an engineer technologist. After graduation he became head of a technological section of the Orsk oil refinery. From 1967 to 1969 he was an instructor in the Orsk city Party committee (*gorkom*); until 1973 deputy head, then head of the industry and transport department of the Orsk Party *gorkom*.

In 1972 he graduated from the All-Union extra-mural polytechnic institute as an engineer-economist. In 1973 he became deputy chief engineer of the Orenburg gas refinery, then until 1978 director of the enterprise. From 1978 to 1982 he was an instructor in the department of heavy industry of the Party Central Committee. Here he came into contact with Boris Yeltsin and Arkady Volsky. In 1982 he was made deputy USSR Minister of the Gas Industry. In 1983, while still retaining his ministerial portfolio, he became head of the All-Union industrial association for the extraction of gas in Tyumen *oblast* (*Tyumengazprom*). From 1985 to 1989 he was USSR Minister of the Gas Industry. During this time he clashed with Egor Gaidar. The latter was on the editorial staff of *Kommunist*, the Party's theoretical journal. Gaidar criticized sharply plans to begin construction of five multi-billion ruble gas projects and, despite a fierce defence by six ministers on the same issue, Chernomyrdin's project in Tyumen *oblast* did not go ahead.

In 1989 the ministry was transformed into the State Gas Concern (Gasprom) and Chernomyrdin became chairman of the board of the concern. It quickly established itself and was soon providing about a third of the country's hard currency earnings. At present the concern controls nine exchanges (*birzha*), eight joint ventures, seven commercial banks and one foreign, and two offshore companies in Liechtenstein. Its sister concern, Rosshelf, won the contract to exploit the Shtokman gas reserves. The concern sells gas directly to foreign companies and has two European trading houses. It competes successfully with the German company Ruhrgas and owns a third of the natural gas pipelines in east Germany. Chernomyrdin's experience convinced him that the way forward for Soviet industry was to establish huge vertically integrated trusts which controlled everything from raw materials to banking. He has no faith in the privatization of part or all of the gas industry.

He is committed to a state corporatist approach and views the attempts of Anatoly Chubais, in charge of privatization, as ill-advised. His experience with natural gas, which is abundantly available and which finds a ready foreign market, may mislead him into believing that the gas industry is typical of Russian industry. He was a USSR people's deputy from 1981. In March 1990 he stood as a candidate for election to the RSFSR Congress of People's Deputies in the No. 60 Orenburg national territorial district. During the election campaign he advocated reform of the economy by adopting a more flexible approach based on human values and including different types of property ownership, full economic cost-accounting (*khozraschet*), Russian sovereignty over raw materials, all power to the soviets, and the implementation of the ideals of social justice. He was defeated in the second round of voting by Gen. Dmitry Volkogonov, who received 46.09% of the votes to Chernomyrdin's 42.38%.

Chernomyrdin is a candidate of technical sciences (PhD). He is an academician of the Academy of Engineering. According to specialists, he unites the experience of an industrial organizer of the communist period with the practice of a present-day businessman. In the West he is rated one of the small number of managers of world class among top Russian leaders. He demonstrated his lobbying skills in 1992 when Vladimir Lopukhin was Russian Minister of Fuel and Energy. The minister attempted to break up the energy monopolies, but Chernomyrdin and his fellow monopolists lobbied strongly against the plans of the minister. Gasprom and Rosneftegas, strongly supported by Civic Union, the parliamentary industrial lobby, eventually wore down President Yeltsin and he sacked Lopukhin in June 1992. Chernomyrdin became deputy Russian Prime Minister for fuel and energy.

One of Chernomyrdin's first acts was to award the rights to develop the huge Shtokman natural gas deposits in the Barents Sea to Rosshelf, a subsidiary of Gasprom. The Scandinavians, especially, were bitterly disappointed at this decision. At the VII Congress of People's Deputies, in December 1992, Chernomyrdin was elected Prime Minister of Russia. The congress had obliged President Yeltsin to select the Prime Minister from among three candidates proposed by the congress. This followed Egor Gaidar's failure to be confirmed as Prime Minister by the congress. Chernomyrdin came second to Yury Skokov, head of the Russian Security Council, with Gaidar third. Yeltsin then sacked Gaidar and proposed Chernomyrdin, arguing that Skokov could not be relieved of his important functions.

There were fears among the reformers that Chernomyrdin would choose a cabinet of conservatives, but in the eventuality almost all the pro-market ministers retained their portfolio. Chernomyrdin accepted Boris Fedorov as deputy Prime Minister responsible for macroeconomic policy and finance and he became the guiding spirit behind economic reform. Chernomyrdin was a quick learner and soon picked up the difference between nominal and real rates of interest. During the tumultuous months after the VII Congress he was guarded in his public utterances, neither opposing nor coming down unequivocally on the side of the President. He revealed that he was no puppet of Civic Union. He made an impressive speech at the IX Congress of People's Deputies in March 1993, calling for compromise between the legislative, the parliament; and executive, the President and the government. However, his words went unheeded, since the Congress had no desire to compromise with the President, only to remove him. The Congress refused to approve the budget for 1993. Chernomyrdin made little impact on the IX Congress, also in March 1993, as deputies were concerned to provoke conflict with the President.

Chernomyrdin has been awarded the order of the October Revolution, the order of the Red Banner of Labour and the badge of honour. He is more skilled in inter-personal relations and small groups than in making speeches to large audiences. He is married with two sons, one of whom works in the gas industry. His hobby now is playing the harmonica. He lives in Moscow.

Chikin, Valentin Vasilevich

Editor-in-chief of the newspaper *Sovetskaya Rossiya*.

Born on January 25, 1932 in Moscow; Russian. He was a member of the CPSU from 1956 to August 1991. He was a candidate member (1986-90) and a member of the Party Central Committee from 1990 to 1991, and was also a member of the Russian bureau of the party Central Committee. In 1951 he was a literary assistant on the newspaper *Moskovsky komsomolets*, and in 1958 graduated from the faculty of journalism, Moscow State University. Then he rejoined *Moskovsky komsomolets* as a literary assistant, becoming in turn deputy editor, editor of a department and deputy editor-in-chief. In 1958 in *Komsomolskaya pravda* B. D. Pankin, G. Oganov and Chikin published an article attacking statements made by Evgeny Evtushenko while on visits abroad. Together with B. A. Grushin, he organized in *Komsomolskaya pravda* an institute of public opinion, and some of the results of the polling were published in the books *In the Name of the Happiness of the People* (1960); *The Face of the Generation* (1961); and *Confession of a Generation* (1962), all co-edited with B. A. Grushin.

In 1971 he was appointed deputy, then first deputy editor-in-chief of the newspaper *Sovetskaya Rossiya*. In 1984 he became first deputy chairman of the USSR state committee on publishing, printing and the book trade, and in 1986 he became editor-in-chief of *Sovetskaya Rossiya*. He was elected a deputy of the RSFSR Supreme Soviet (1981-85), and has received state awards. He has published books on the life and career of V. I. Lenin: *One Hundred Winter Days* (1968); *So and So* (1977), *Circle on the Large Circle* (1979); and on Karl Marx, *Confession* (1978).

In 1990 he was nominated for election as an RSFSR people's deputy in the No. 96 Khasbyurtovsky national territorial district, Dagestan ASSR. During the election campaign he advocated the establishment of a legal basis for the sovereignty of Russia and the concept for the evolution of a Russian economy. Experienced practical deputies should be elected to the Russian parliament who were capable of guaranteeing order and discipline in the country. He appealed for greater efforts to combat crime and defend morality, and he advocated the consolidation of all constructive forces of Russia to overcome the inter-ethnic contradictions. He also devoted considerable attention to the problem of saving the Caspian Sea.

There were four candidates and Chikin won in the second round. In 1990 he became a member of the Russian bureau of the Party Central Committee and was then elected to the Politburo of the Central Committee of the Russian Communist Party.

Chikvaidze, Aleksandr Davidovich

Foreign Minister of the Republic of Georgia to August 1993.

Born in 1932 in Tbilisi, Georgian SSR; Georgian. He was a member of the CPSU until August 1991. In 1955 he graduated from Moscow State University and Pedagogical Institute of Foreign Languages, Tbilisi, in 1966 from the academy of social sciences of the Party Central Committee, and in 1977 from the diplomatic academy of the USSR Ministry of Foreign Affairs.

He made his career from 1956 to 1964 in the *Komsomol* as secretary of the *Komsomol* organization of an aviation enterprise; then deputy secretary of the *Komsomol* committee of the Georgian institute of agriculture; later he was head of department, second, and first secretary of the *Komsomol* organization in Ordzhonikidze *raion*, Tbilisi; and second, then first secretary of the Tbilisi *Komsomol* committee. Then he moved into Party work as an inspector of the Central Committee, Communist Party of Georgia. From 1967 to 1969 he was head of department of the union of Soviet friendship societies and cultural links with foreign countries in Bombay, India, and from 1969 to 1972 performed the same function in Great Britain. From 1972 to 1977 he was a Party functionary: head of the department of administrative and financial agencies, Tbilisi Party city committee; first secretary of the Ordzhonikidze *raion* committee, Tbilisi. In 1977 and 1978 he was chairman of the state committee for publishing, printing and the book trade, Georgian Council of Ministers.

From 1979 to 1983 he was USSR consul general in San Francisco, USA; from 1983 to 1985 Soviet ambassador to Kenya and also USSR permanent representative to international organizations in Nairobi; between 1985 and 1988 he was head of section of a department, Party Central Committee, Moscow. From 1988 to January 1992 he was USSR ambassador to the Netherlands and then Russian ambassador to the Netherlands. In February of the same year he left the Russian diplomatic corps and became Minister of Foreign Affairs of the Republic of Georgia.

Chizhov, Lyudvig Aleksandrovich

Russian Ambassador to Japan.

Born in 1936 in Radomyshl, Zhitomir *oblast*, Ukrainian SSR; Russian. He was a member of the CPSU until August 1991. He graduated from the Moscow State Institute of International Relations of the USSR Ministry of Foreign Affairs and from the diplomatic academy of the ministry. From 1960 to 1962 he was an assistant in the USSR embassy, Tokyo, and from 1962 to 1965 was an interpreter and attaché in the embassy. From 1965 to 1968 he was an attaché and third secretary, and then from 1968 to 1971, second and first secretary in the Far East department, USSR Ministry of Foreign Affairs, Moscow.

From 1971 to 1976 he was first secretary, and from 1976 to 1977, counsellor, in the Soviet embassy in Tokyo. In 1977 he was counsellor, then deputy head of department, of the second Far East department, USSR Ministry of Foreign Affairs (1979-80). From 1980 to 1986 he was minister counsellor in the Soviet embassy in Tokyo, then was head of the department of Pacific countries, USSR Ministry of Foreign Affairs (1986-87) and later was head of the department of Pacific and south-east Asian countries (1987-90), in the ministry. In 1990 he was appointed USSR ambassador to Japan and in January 1992 ambassador of the Russian Federation to Japan.

He has received several awards, including the order of the badge of honour and the honorary diploma of the Presidium of the Supreme Soviet of the Russian Federation. He is married and speaks Japanese and English.

Address: Russian Embassy, Tokyo 106, 1-1 Azabudai, 2-chome, Minato-ku; *telephone*: Tokyo (10 81 3) 583 4224; 583 5982; 583 4297; 583 4445.

Chkheidze, Revaz Davidovich

President of the Georgia Film Company; Head of the Faculty of Film, Tbilisi Institute of Film, Theatre and Cinema; Member of Parliament of the Republic of Georgia.

Born on December 8, 1926 in Kutaisi, Georgian SSR; a Georgian. His father was a writer who was a victim of Stalin's purges in 1937 and his mother is a pensioner. He is a graduate of the faculty of production, all-Union State

Institute of Cinematography, Moscow. His best known films are *Father of a Soldier*, *Your Son Earth* and *Don Quixote*. He was elected a member of parliament, representing the Ertoba block.

He is married and his wife, Tinatin, née Gambashvili, is a teacher of voice in a film school. They have three children. Their son, Bidzina, is a film producer; their daughter Tamara is an historian and a member of parliament of the Republic of Georgia, and their daughter Khatuna is a specialist on art history. Chkheidze enjoys watching parliamentary debates on television.

Home address: Tbilisi, ul. Larskaya, Dom 5, kv. 3; *telephone*: Tbilisi 23 38 84.

Chkheidze, Tamara Revazovna

Politician; Member of Parliament of the Republic of Georgia; historian.

Born on February 11, 1960 in Tbilisi, Georgian SSR. She is a Georgian. Her father, Revaz Davidovich, is a film producer. Her mother, Tinatin, née Gambashvili, is a teacher of voice in a film school. Her brother, Bidzina, is also a film producer and her sister Khatuna is a specialist in the history of art.

She completed secondary school in 1976 and was a student in the faculty of history, Tbilisi State University from 1976 to 1981. From 1981 to 1983 she was a junior scientific assistant in the David Garedzhi museum, and from 1983 to 1985 she was a political prisoner. In 1985 she was appointed a junior scientific assistant in the state archive of the history of Georgia. In 1992 she was elected a member of parliament of the Republic of Georgia for the Ili Chavchavadze society. Besides politics she is interested in history, philosophy and religion. She has published many articles on these matters. In her free time she loves walking in the country, visiting and studying historical monuments and sights.

Home address: Tbilisi, ul. Larskaya Dom 5, kv. 3; *telephone*: Tbilisi 23 38 82.

Chochaev, Sharabuddin

Mufti; chairman of the Muslim religious administration of the Kabardino-Balkar Republic.

Born on January 9, 1960 in the settlement of Gundelen, Baksan *raion*, Kabardino-Balkar ASSR; Balkar. He graduated in 1987 from the Al Buhari Islamic Institute, Tashkent, Uzbekistan, and from 1987 to 1990 he was *imam-haty* of the Gundelen mosque, Gundelen. In 1990 he was appointed chairman of the Muslim religious administration of the Kabardino-Balkar republic. He is married with a daughter.

Address: Nalchik, ul. Sovetskaya 43.

Chornovil, Viacheslav Maksymovych

Leader of *Rukh*.

Born into a Ukrainian family in 1938 in Erki in Cherkasy *oblast*, central Ukraine, where both of his parents were village teachers. He graduated from the faculty of journalism, Kiev State University in 1960, and worked in TV in Lviv and in Kiev and on newspapers such as *Moloda hvardiia*. His application to become a postgraduate student to work on a candidate dissertation on the history of Ukrainian literature was blocked in 1963 as he was already associated with the dissident cultural intelligentsia circles that were increasingly prominent in 1960s Kiev.

When many of his friends were arrested between 1965 and 1966 Chornovil's account of their trial, published in English as *The Chornovil Papers*, earned him his first spell in prison from 1967 to 1970. On his return he moved to Lviv and began to edit the main *samizdat* journal of the period, the *Ukrainian Herald*, six issues of which appeared between 1970 and 1972. The *Herald* focused on human rights issues in the dry legalistic style common to many dissident groups of the period. In January 1972 Chornovil was again arrested and, after 15 months' isolation, received another six-year sentence, followed by exile in Yakutia, where he was again arrested in 1980 and received another five-year sentence for attempting to make contact with the Ukrainian Helsinki Group (UHG) back in Ukraine.

He only returned to Lviv in 1985. Chornovil's Open Letter to M. Gorbachev in 1987 marked the rebirth of Ukrainian dissent, and was soon followed by the relaunch of the *Ukrainian Herald* and the UHG, renamed the Ukrainian Helsinki Union (UHU) in 1988. Chornovil soon quarrelled with other members of the UHU, however, especially after the return of Levko Lukianenko as leader in January 1989. He attacked his old colleagues at the founding congress of the Ukrainian Republican Party in April 1990, accusing them of "creating a strongly centralized organization of the bolshevik-fascist type".

In the March 1990 elections he was elected both as people's deputy for Shevchenskyi *raion* in Lviv (on the first round with 69% of the vote), and as a local deputy. As the opposition had swept the board in Lviv *oblast*, Chornovil resigned from the UHU and became leader of the *oblast* soviet. However, after an initial wave of euphoria in which the soviet was able to make several popular low-cost moves, such as the restoration of national symbols and the property of the Greek Catholic Church, his tenure as leader of the Lviv soviet was not always a happy one, as he faced growing opposition from local nationalists and rising public disillusion, especially once his inability to control the local economy, or deliver "capitalism in one region" became clear.

Chornovil was always a charismatic speaker and effective populist politician, however, especially in the Supreme Soviet, where he also served as a member of the committee on *glasnost* and the mass media and the committee on the constitution set up after the student hunger strikes in October 1990. On September 1, 1991 he was chosen by the Grand Council of *Rukh* as the movement's official candidate for President of Ukraine, although many of *Rukh's* leading members, such as Ivan Drach and Mykhailo Horyn campaigned for Levko Lukianenko. Chornovil's programme "The Route to Freedom" placed much greater emphasis on anti-communism and on forthright opposition to Kravchuk than the other *Rukh* leaders desired.

Nevertheless, Chornovil's energetic campaign earned him second place to Kravchuk on December 1, 1991 with 7,420,727 votes, or 23.27% of the total. After Kravchuk's triumph, Chornovil attempted to switch his power base from Lviv to Kiev by taking over *Rukh*. In the run-up to the movement's third congress in February-March 1992 Chornovil pressed for a radical change in *Rukh's* orientation, by "departicizing" its leading organs (i.e. removing people such as Horyn) and becoming the *de facto* opposition to Kravchuk. Drach and Horyn on the other hand wanted *Rukh* to become a support movement for the President.

Chornovil was backed by a majority of the rank and file delegates, although an attempt by Drach to split the movement resulted in the temporary solution of a joint leadership between Drach, Horyn and Chornovil. Drach, however, soon retired from active politics, and Horyn was squeezed out when he became leader of the URP in May 1992. By the time of *Rukh's* fourth congress in December 1992, Chornovil's supremacy was unquestioned (he had left his position in Lviv *oblast* in March 1992). The congress formally turned *Rukh* into a political party with a reregistered membership of 50,000. Chornovil continued to be the main thorn in President Kravchuk's side, launching a campaign in July 1992 (A New Parliament for a New Ukraine) to collect the three million signatures necessary to force a referendum on the dissolution of the Supreme Soviet (although this particular campaign rather had the wind taken out of its sails by the formation of the new Kuchma government in October 1992: only 1,175,068 signatures, or 2.9% of the total electorate, were eventually collected). Kravchuk, seemingly rattled, launched an intemperate attack on Chornovil at the Congress of World Ukrainians in Kiev in August 1992.

Official address (*Rukh* office in Kiev): 252032 Kiev, Bulvar Tarasa Shevchenka 37/122; *telephone*: Kiev 224 9151.

Chub, Vladimir Fedorovich

Head of the Administration of Rostov *oblast*, Russian Federation.

Born in 1948 in Pinsk, Brest *oblast*, Belarus. His father is a Belorussian (Belarusian) and his mother a Cossack from the upper Don. He was a member of the CPSU. After completing the 11 year school he entered the Institute of Marine Engineers, Leningrad. After graduation in 1971 he worked as a foreman in the Krasny Flot repair base, Rostov-on-Don, and also worked there as the head of a shop, production and as chief engineer. Between 1980 and 1983 he was first secretary of the Proletarsky *raion* Party committee, Rostov-on-Don. In 1983 he was assigned as chief engineer to the Volga-Don river steamship company. In 1985 he was elected first secretary of the Proletarsky *raion* Party committee and was also elected a deputy of the city and *raion* soviets. In 1989 he was elected chairman of the Rostov city executive committee in a contested election, and in 1990 he graduated from the Academy of the National Economy.

In early 1990 he was nominated by various work collectives in Rostov-on-Don for election as an RSFSR people's deputy in the No. 601 Proletarsky territorial district, Rostov *oblast*. During the election campaign he advocated the development of various forms of collective ownership, leased, co-operative and individual activity and the adoption of laws on local self-government, and he opposed the low priority afforded investment in the activities of the city.

There were ten candidates. Chub polled 28% of the votes in the first round but lost the second round, polling 42.8% of the votes. His main opponent was Yu. S. Sidrenko, director of the Rostov oncological centre who received 12% of the votes in the first round and won the second round with 45% of the votes.

In 1990 Chub was elected a deputy of the Rostov city soviet and then its chairman. On April 22, 1990, during the second round of voting, he was elected a deputy of the *oblast* soviet, then a member of the Rostov soviet executive committee. He was a delegate to the XXVIII Party congress.

On August 20, 1991 the Presidium of the Rostov city soviet, headed by Chub, declared its support of the legally elected USSR and RSFSR Supreme Soviets and declared that only the decrees of the RSFSR President and government were valid on the territory of Rostov-on-Don. Chub resigned from the CPSU in August 1991 and made a declaration in the People's Party, Free Russia.

In September 1991, at a session of the *oblast* soviet, Chub was proposed as chairman but withdrew. The same session proposed to the Russian President V. F. Chub and A. I. Bely, first deputy chairman of the *oblast* soviet executive committee, as candidates for the post of head of the administration of Rostov *oblast*, and Chub was appointed by presidential decree. On assuming office Chub declared his primary objectives to be the drafting of an *oblast* budget, the protection of entrepreneurs, the solution of the food problem, the rebirth of the Don Cossacks and the promotion of good economic relations between the *oblast* and the *raions*.

In December 1992, during the VII Congress of People's Deputies, he criticized the policies of the Gaidar government and blamed it for the fall in production and the impoverishment of the population. The main defect of Gaidar's cabinet was the deployment of theory to the detriment of practical solutions, and Chub appealed for the ending of tension between the various branches of power. He is married with a daughter who is a student, and lives in Rostov-on-Don.

Chubais, Anatoly Borisovich

Deputy Prime Minister of the Russian Federation and Chairman of the State Committee on the Administration of State Property.

Born in 1955 in Borisov, Belarus, into a military family. Russian. He was a member of the CPSU until August 1991. He graduated in 1977 from the Palmiro Togliatti Leningrad Engineering and Economics Institute, and after graduating worked in the same institute as an assistant, then as an assistant professor, then as a senior research worker. In 1983 he successfully presented his candidate dissertation in economics on "research and elaboration of methods of planning improvements in the management of branches of scientific-technical organizations" (PhD (Econ)).

In 1984 he and other economics graduates of the Leningrad Institute engaged in a study of the economic policy of various periods of Soviet history, economic reforms in West European states and also a critical analysis of the contemporary state of the Soviet economy. Later he found out about the existence of a similar group in Moscow, headed by Egor Gaidar, and began to collaborate with it. In 1985 he was part of the democratic movement in Leningrad, and in 1986 a group for the study of the social sciences in the Leningrad palace of youth developed out of the discussion club of young economists from the Leningrad Institute and in 1987 became known as *Sintez* (synthesis). Chubais was one of the organizers of the Leningrad *Perestroika* club in 1987. Whereas *Sintez* was intellectual and appealed to a minority, *Perestroika* attempted to promote democratic ideas among wider groups of the intelligentsia.

At its peak *Perestroika* had about 100 members and many of them became people's deputies at various levels and leaders of political parties and movements in and after 1989. Chubais consistently refused to be elected to any committee or post in *Perestroika* and this led to suggestions that he wished to avoid conflict with the CPSU. He was also accused of being committed to Gorbachev. Chubais's elder brother, Igor, was a leading light in the Moscow *Perestroika* club, based on the Leningrad club and eventually to become better known. Unlike his brother, Igor Chubais was always a radical and when the Moscow *Perestroika* club split at the end of 1987 into Democratic *Perestroika*, the moderate wing, and *Perestroika*-88, the radical wing, Igor Chubais was more or less the leader of the latter. After the breakup of *Perestroika*-88 Igor Chubais became the founding father of the Democratic platform in the CPSU. Afterwards he joined the Republican Party, but only stayed a short time and then became a member of the bureau of the People's Party of Russia, headed by Telman Gdlyan.

In 1989 Anatoly Chubais became a member of the economics and agriculture section of the Elections-89 group, set up by Leningrad informal associations. In 1989 he was a candidate for the post of director of the Leningrad Institute of Socio-economic Problems but was unsuccessful. As a member of the CPSU he supported the Democratic platform set up by his elder brother. Nevertheless, Anatoly Chubais did not play a prominent role in the Leningrad organization of the Democratic platform and neither joined the Republican Party which emerged from it, nor any of the other parties which sprang up after the collapse of the Soviet Union. In 1990 Petr Filippov, a leading figure among democrats in the election campaign of 1990 invited Chubais on several occasions to accept nomination as a people's deputy of Russia or to Leningrad city council. Chubais always declined, stating that he did not wish to pursue a political career.

However, in 1990, at the suggestion of A. Shchelkanov, the chairman of the Leningrad soviet executive committee (Lensovet) and supported by the democratic majority on Lensovet, Anatoly Chubais became deputy, then first deputy chairman of the Leningrad city soviet executive committee. He became known as Len-gor-Abalkin (Leningrad city's Abalkin), a reference to the role played in the Soviet government by Academician Leonid Abalkin. In 1991 he became the senior economic aide of Anatoly Sobchak, the mayor of St Petersburg, and also supported the latter's policies. Chubais was a strong supporter of the creation of a free economic zone in St Petersburg to attract heavy foreign investment to establish a market infrastructure. This led to a cooling of relations with his former associates on *Perestroika*, the majority of whom went over to the opposition soon after Sobchak's election as chairman of Lensovet and later mayor of St Petersburg.

A conflict arose between Chubais and Filippov, an RSFSR people's deputy who was also on Lensovet, with the latter leading the campaign against the setting up of a free economic zone. In November 1991 Egor Gaidar appointed him chairman of the state committee of the RSFSR administration of state property. He has developed a policy for the privatization of large, medium and small enterprises and shops in Russia. During 1993 it is planned to turn about 700 large and medium size enterprises, from all sectors of the economy, into joint stock companies. Chubais regards this as vital to the struggle to reduce inflation and the state budget deficit, and it will also force these enterprises to begin to restructure and become more competitive. He opposes handing over most shares to employees free of charge. All Russian citizens were given free of charge privatization vouchers worth 10,000 rubles, beginning in December 1992, but they had to be redeemed for shares in companies being privatized by the end of 1993. Foreigners could buy vouchers and acquire company shares. Chubais has come under vigorous attack over his privatization policy from those who believe that all enterprises should be returned to the people free of charge, especially Larisa Piyasheva and communist-oriented economists. Nevertheless, Chubais is convinced that making a person a present of shares does not give him or her the feeling of being an owner.

Chubais enjoys water sports. He is married with two children and he and his family live in Moscow.

Churanov, Vladimir Timofeevich

Head of Rear Services of the Armed Forces of the Russian Federation; Major-General.

Born on October 22, 1945 in Nevinnomysk, Stavropol *krai*; Russian. The social status of his parents is unknown.

He received a higher military education and graduated from Volga Military Rear Technical School in 1966, the Military Rear and Transport Academy in Leningrad in 1979, and the Military Academy of the General Staff in 1987. He was a member of the CPSU until August 1991.

He did his military service, holding posts as a rear officer: head of material support services of a unit, deputy divisional commander for rear services, chief of staff of an army rear, and deputy Commander-in-Chief of a military district for rear services. He proved to be an experienced specialist in providing material support, with a sound operational-tactical and special training. He actively participated in Party-political agencies, which was crucial for a successful career in the Soviet army, and by President B. Yeltsin's decree on August 21, 1992 he was appointed head of rear services of the armed forces of the Russian Federation.

Gen. V. Churanov has had to tackle the problems involved in the army and navy adapting to the market economy, ensuring the all-round material support of the armed forces during a period of economic crisis and the reform of the economy.

He favours the supremacy of the state and Russia regaining its status as a great power. He does not express his political views in public, and like other generals with a Soviet communist education he is a conformist in his relations with authorities.

His views on the reorganization of the work of his department were expressed in an interview, "The rear under reform", published in *Krasnaya Zvezda* on August 26, 1992.

There is no information about his hobbies. He does not speak any foreign language and has not been abroad as a member of an official delegation. He has been awarded two orders and several medals. He is married with two children.

Office address: 103175, Moscow K-175.

Churkin, Vitaly Ivanovich

Deputy Minister of Foreign Affairs of the Russian Federation.

Born in 1952. He was a member of the CPSU until August 1991. He graduated from the Moscow State Institute of International Relations of the USSR Ministry of Foreign Affairs; and began his career in the Soviet embassy in Washington DC as an assistant. He became famous for his address to the US Congress during the hearings on the Chernobyl nuclear disaster, and amazed the Americans with his fluent command of English and ability to answer difficult questions. This was partly due to the fact that he had grown up in the US and received part of his education there. After returning to Moscow he was invited to work in the international department of the Party Central Committee, and in 1980 he successfully presented his candidate dissertation in history on "China and Japan in the foreign policy strategy of the US 1969-80" (PhD).

In 1989 he returned to the USSR Ministry of Foreign Affairs and became the press secretary of Eduard Shevardnadze. He replaced Gennady Gerasimov as press spokesman for President Mikhail Gorbachev and gave the press briefings. In November 1990 Shevardnadze made him head of the administration of information of the Ministry, and he campaigned for Shevardnadze's return after the latter's resignation in December 1990. Churkin remained in the Ministry until August 24, 1991, when the collapse of the Soviet Union led to his having to go to Chile as Russian ambassador. However, on the initiative of Andrei Kozyrev, Russian foreign minister, Churkin was recalled and appointed deputy minister, responsible for European affairs.

In March 1993 Churkin, as a special representative of the President of the Russian Federation, participated in negotiations on Bosnia. He did not believe that Russia should be the mouthpiece of one of the delegations and should not accept responsibility for the activities of Serbia, but should make use of open lines of communication with Belgrade for a more frank discussion of the problems which had arisen during the negotiations. He believes that the majority of Russian deputies are concerned and wish to cope honestly with the problems. He would like to see co-operation with them and the search for a common language.

The positions of the Foreign Ministry and the Supreme Soviet have come closer together of late, but there are those in the opposition who have no real interest in the former Yugoslavia and who wish to use this issue as a means for stoking up political passions. He speaks English and lives in Moscow.

Chyngyshev, Tursunbek

Prime Minister of the Republic of Kyrgyzstan.

Born in 1942 in Tyan-Shan *raion*, Narym *oblast*, Kirgiz SSR (Kyrgyzstan); Kyrgyz. He was a member of the CPSU until August 1991. He graduated in 1975 from the Kirgiz State University, Frunze (Bishkek) and, in 1987, from the academy of social sciences of the Party Central Committee, Moscow.

In 1963 he was a foreman in a road maintenance administration, and then from 1963 to 1966 he served in the Soviet army. From 1966 to 1969 he was *Komsomol* secretary in the Avtozapas enterprise, Kaliningrad, Kaliningrad *oblast*, RSFSR, and was then head of department of the *Komsomol* in Pervomaisky *raion*, Frunze (1969-70). From 1977 to 1980 he was first secretary of the Kara Kul city committee, Communist Party of Kirgizia (CPKir), and from 1980 to 1989 he was deputy head of the industrial department of the Central Committee, CPKir.

In 1989 he was appointed head of the social and economic department of the Central Committee, CPKir, from 1989 to 1991 he was first secretary of the Tokmak city committee, CPKir, and in April 1991 he was appointed state secretary of the Republic of Kyrgyzstan, then deputy Prime Minister. In February 1992 he became Prime Minister of the Republic of Kyrgyzstan. He is faced with an onerous task as he seeks to steer Kyrgyzstan towards a market economy while ensuring ethnic stability in the state. The skilled industrial labour force is predominantly Russian or Ukrainian and there has been tension between them and the Kyrgyz. The Kyrgyz regime is very keen to keep its European labour force as the republic has only a small indigenous skilled labour force. The state also has to come to terms with the breakup of the Soviet Union and the need to establish a modern state governmental and economic machine. Kyrgyz policy has been to cleave close to the CIS and Russia, and Russian, German and English have been declared official state languages. Chyngyshev is married with two children.

Dabravolski, Alaksandr Alhiertavic

Chairman of the United Democratic Party of Belarus.

Born on November 23, 1958 in Sula, Minsk *oblast*. His parents are Alhiert and Alaksandra, and the family is Belarusian. He graduated in 1982 from the faculty of electronics, Belarusian State University, Minsk, and then from 1982 to 1991 he was a design engineer in the bureau of the electronic precision machine building, Minsk. In 1989 he was elected a USSR people's deputy for Minsk, in 1991 he was elected deputy chairman of the USSR Supreme Soviet committee on human rights and freedoms, and in 1992 he became executive director of the independent Institute of Social Economic and Political Research, Minsk. He was elected chairman of the United Democratic Party of Belarus and regards himself as a liberal democrat. His hobby is music. He is married, his wife is Natalla and they have a son, Ales and a daughter, Volha. Dabravolski speaks English.

Address: 220101 Minsk, vul. Plachanava, 93-160; *telephone*: Minsk (0172) 49 99 64; 29 08 34 (Party).

Danilov-Danilyan, Viktor Ivanovich

Minister of Ecology and Natural Resources of the Russian Federation.

Born on May 9, 1938 in Moscow into a Russian family. In 1960 he graduated in mathematics from Moscow state university. He was a member of the CPSU until August 1991. Between 1960 and 1964 he was a junior assistant, engineer, senior engineer in the computer centre at the university. From 1964 to 1976 he was junior scientific assistant, senior engineer, head of the laboratory of the Central Institute of Econometrics of the USSR Academy of Sciences. (Director of the Institute was Academician Petrakov, while Boris Saltykov, later Russian Minister of Science and Technology, also worked in the institute at that time.) In 1966 he successfully presented his candidate dissertation in economics on "questions of current optimal planning of economic complexes" (PhD (Econ)). In 1973 he successfully presented his doctoral dissertation in economics on "problems of optimal perspective planning of the national economy" (DSc (Econ)). He was a professor.

From 1976 to 1980 Danilov-Danilyan was head of the laboratory of the All-Union scientific research institute for systems analysis of the state committee for science and technology and the USSR Academy of Sciences. (Director of the institute was N. Fedorov and a colleague of Danilov-Danilyan at that time was Vladimir Lopukhin, Russian Minister of Fuel and Energy until December 1992.) Between 1980 and 1991 he was head of the laboratory, afterwards head of faculty of the Academy of the National Economy of the USSR Council of Ministers. He attended meetings of the Leningrad club *Perestroika*. An active member of the club was Anatoly Chubais, later Russian deputy Prime Minister for privatization. In February 1989 Danilov-Danilyan was elected to the presidium of the co-ordinating council of the Green Movement, together with Egor Gaidar. In 1991 he became deputy RSFSR Minister of Ecology and Natural Resources, the Minister being N. N. Vorontsov. On November 15, 1991 he became RSFSR Minister of Ecology and Natural Resources and on November 27, 1991 Minister of Ecology and Natural Resources of the Russian Federation in the first reform government.

He is a leading specialist in the field of automated systems for the planning of the economy and the rational use of natural resources and has written several books on these subjects. He was on the editorial board of the publishing arm of the Academy of the National Economy. He was an active member of the *Znanie* (Knowledge) society. His ministry, in collaboration with the Ministry of Science, Higher Education and Technology, has been developing a programme on Russian ecology. It is characterized by its emphasis on the human element and the interests of society. He was influential in the drafting of the Russian law on the protection of nature, the Russian forest code, the Russian law on resources, the Russian law on the atomic industry and protection against radiation, and the state programme for the rehabilitation of *raions* suffering from radiation pollution. He regards it as very important that a market for ecological services should be created in Russia and this would include the monitoring of environmental change. The financing of the protection of the environment should come from charges for the use of natural resources, fines on enterprises, state hard currency allocations and public ecological funds. He speaks English and is married.

Deinekin, Petr Stepanovich

Commander-in-Chief of the Air Forces; Air Force Colonel-General.

Born on December 14, 1937 in Morozovsk, Rostov *oblast* into a military pilot's family; Russian. He graduated from the Balashov Military Aviation Technical School for pilots in 1957, the Air Force Academy in 1969 and the Military Academy of the General Staff with a gold medal in 1982, having received a higher military education. He was a member of the CPSU until August 1991.

After graduating from technical school he served in long-range aviation, flying in strategic bombers and missile-armed aircraft. He was a right-wing pilot, and then became a plane commander (of the crew of a plane).

He loved flying, had a good knowledge of complex aviation technology and good skills as a combat tactician. In accordance with the conditions of service in the Soviet armed forces, he was active in Party-political work in the CPSU regimental organization and enjoyed the support of his superior officers, political agencies and authority among his colleagues. After graduating from the Academy he was rapidly promoted, from 1971 he was deputy commander of an air regiment, from 1973 air regimental commander, and from 1977 commander of divisions of long-range bombers and missile-armed aircraft.

In 1982 he was appointed deputy commander of an air army for combat training and from 1985 a commander. Air units under Gen. Deinekin prepared for operations against strategic objects deep in the rear of a possible enemy. In 1988 Air Force Lieut.-Gen. Petr Deinekin was appointed commander of long-range aviation, deputy Commander-in-Chief of the Air Forces, and headed strategic aviation forces which were one of the major strike groups capable of using nuclear weapons and rockets against key objects in contemporary war.

Due to his convictions and advanced specialist training Deinekin was a military professional and criticized the excessive emphasis on ideology in the armed forces of the USSR. He worked in close contact with Gen. Evgeny Shaposhnikov, who chose Deinekin as his first deputy when the former was appointed Commander-in-Chief of the Air Forces.

At the time of the anti-constitutional putsch in August 1991 Deinekin fully supported E. Shaposhnikov's actions, ensured high combat readiness of the air forces and the non-involvement of airmen in operations against the legitimate authorities. He left the CPSU of his own free will.

On August 31, 1991 he was appointed Commander-in-Chief of the Air Forces and deputy Minister of Defence of the USSR. From February 1992 he was commander of the air forces of the unified armed forces of the CIS; from

August 21, 1992, by President Yeltsin's decree, he was appointed Commander-in-Chief of the Air Forces of the Russian Federation.

He advocates a thorough-going reform of the armed forces, the creation of an army, air force and navy to meet the demands of contemporary war, equipped with high-precision and high-technology weapons and the latest aviation technology. He is against political intrigues at the expense of the armed forces and strongly supports the elimination of party-political activity in the military. An excellent and highly qualified professional, he mastered ten types of combat planes, including the most recent strategic bomber TU-160, and has clocked up almost 5,000 flying hours. He pursues a firm policy aimed at equipping the air forces with up-to-date aviation *matériel*. He has managed to overcome the latent resistance of the leaders of the military-industrial complex and to solve problems associated with the rapid building of new types of aircraft. According to air force officers, Gen. Deinekin has a passion for aviation and flying.

When the division of the former USSR air forces began, he argued vigorously for the retention of integral long-range aviation as part of the strategic forces. He repeatedly visited airfields in Ukraine and tried to influence those officers and the personnel of units who have taken an oath of loyalty to Ukraine. As a result his relations with Ukraine's leaders and military personnel degenerated into hostility.

In May 1992 he visited the USA. While there, as a crew commander he flew an American B1-B Lancer strategic bomber with in-flight refuelling, and his flying skills won the admiration of the Americans.

He has appeared in the press several times on the development and combat use of aviation, and a long interview with him was published in *Krasnaya Zvezda* on October 26, 1991.

He has been awarded two orders "For service to the motherland in the armed forces of the USSR" and ten medals. He is a merited military pilot of the USSR.

There is no information about his hobbies. He does not speak any foreign language. He is married with three children.

Office address: Moscow, Ulitsa Bolshaya Pirogovskaya, 23.

Derkach, Ihor Stepanovych

Ukrainian Youth Movement Leader.

An up-and-coming young Ukrainian politician born in 1963. He was educated at Lviv Polytechnic Institute and, after graduation worked as an engineer, but quickly became involved in Lviv opposition politics. He joined the Ukrainian Helsinki Union, and was active in the youth movements that developed initially under its wing. Derkach organized the founding of the Union of Independent Youth (in Ukrainian, SNUM), in May 1990, although his commitment to democratic nationalism and peaceful means of struggle soon led to arguments with the Union's radical wing, led by Oleh Vitovych and Dmytro Korchynskyi, who split away to form the Ukrainian Nationalist Union in November 1990.

Derkach was left in charge of SNUM, renamed the Union of Ukrainian Youth in the autumn of 1991. It claims 800 members, and Derkach has insisted on its general support for the new independent Ukrainian state. Derkach also organized the Congress of Ukrainian Youth Groups, held in Kiev in August 1991, that attempted to unite Ukraine's many rival youth organizations. In March 1990, Derkach was elected people's deputy for the town of Sambir in Lviv *oblast* in the first round. In the Supreme Soviet he is a leading member of the committee on defence and state security, where he has long advocated the idea of an independent Ukrainian nuclear deterrent.

Official address: Kiev, Vul. M. Hrushevskoho 5; *telephone*: Kiev 252 019 or Kiev 291 5659 (work).

Deryagin, Aleksandr Vasilevich

Head of the Administration of Kaluga *oblast*, Russian Federation.

Born on February 19, 1941 in Arkhangelsk *oblast* into a peasant family; Russian. He was never a member of the CPSU. He graduated from the Urals State University, and in 1971 successfully presented his candidate dissertation in physical and mathematical sciences on "The magnetic characteristics and the blast furnace structure of manganese gallium alloy" (PhD). In 1982 he successfully presented his doctoral dissertation (DSc). He is a USSR state prize winner in science and technology, and is a corresponding member of the Russian Academy of Sciences. In 1990 he was head of department of the all-Union scientific research institute for electronics materials and head of the department of general physics and chemistry in the Kaluga branch of the N. E. Bauman Higher Technical College, Moscow.

In early 1990 he was nominated for election as an RSFSR people's deputy in the No. 417 Leninsky territorial district, Kaluga *oblast*. During the election campaign he advocated the establishment of a *Rechtsstaat* (law-governed state), full sovereignty for Russia, the transfer of power from the CPSU to the soviets, the constitutional underpinning of a multi-party system and direct contested elections for President. He supported equality for all forms of ownership, including private ownership of land and means of production and market socialism.

There were 11 candidates. He polled 17.7% of the votes in the first round and won the second round, polling 51.6% of the votes. His main opponent was A. I. Panarin, pro-rector of the Kaluga Pedagogical Institute, who received 11.1% of the votes in the first round and 35.7% in the second. Deryagin is a member of the Supreme Soviet committee on science and education and a member of the coalition of reforms bloc of deputies. Previously he was a member of the education, science and culture, Chernobyl and Russian union groups of deputies and the faction of non-party deputies.

He was appointed head of the administration of Kaluga *oblast* on September 27, 1991 by presidential decree. On assuming office he stated that he supported the economic reforms of the government of Egor Gaidar, but underlined the lack of social security of the population, the unexpectedly fast rise of prices and the lack of competence of the banking sector. He advocated the liberalization of prices after privatization and favoured private ownership of land and the right to buy and sell it. He opposed the convocation of the VII Congress of People's Deputies in December 1992, proposing that it be postponed until March or April 1993 when results of some of the reforms would be visible. He lives in Kaluga.

Desyatnikov, Valery Alekseevich

Head of the Main Administration of Kirov *oblast*, Russian Federation.

Born on January 14, 1942 in the village of Berezovka, Tamalinsky *raion*, Penza *oblast*; Russian; member of the CPSU from 1971 to August 1991. He graduated from the Construction Engineering Institute, Perm, in 1964, and then worked as a foreman in the *Promstroi* trust, Perm, then in the construction administration of the *Glavprivolzhskstroi* trust, Saratov, as a foreman, works superintendent, head of the production department and head of the construction administration. From 1980 to 1982 he was secretary of the Party committee and then manager of the *Glavprivolzhskstroi* trust, and from 1984 to 1985 he was head of the department of construction of the Saratov Party *obkom*. In 1985 he graduated from the Higher Party School, Saratov, and from 1985 to 1987 was secretary of the Kirov Party *obkom*. In 1987 he was elected chairman of the Kirov *oblast* soviet executive committee. He was a delegate to the XXVIII Party congress, and has been awarded medals. He was a deputy of the RSFSR Supreme Soviet.

In early 1990 he was nominated by the work collective of the *Za kommunizm* state farm, Kotelnichsky *raion*, Kirov *oblast* and the *Kotelnichsky* repair enterprise for election as an RSFSR people's deputy in the No. 452 Kotelnichsky territorial district. During the election campaign he advocated sovereignty for Russia within the USSR, the reorientation of administration and planning in favour of the local state authorities and the delineation of the functions of the legislative, executive, Party and state agencies.

There were three candidates. Desyatnikov polled 45% of the votes in the first round and won the second round, polling 52.2% of the votes. His main opponent was S. V. Forsov, a military officer, who received 25% of the votes in the first round and 38.9% in the second. Desyatnikov is a member of the Council of the Republic commission on the budget, plans and taxes. He was previously a member of the communists of Russia group of deputies.

In 1990 he was elected a deputy of the Kirov *oblast* soviet and in April 1990 at the session of the *oblast* soviet he was elected chairman of the Kirov *oblast* executive committee. He was the only candidate and received 207 votes for and 16 votes against. On August 20, 1991 the executive committee of the Kirov *oblast* soviet declared that on the territory of Kirov *oblast* only the decisions and decrees of the President, the Supreme Soviet and the government of the RSFSR were valid. He pointed out that it was impermissible to establish power structures other than the soviets and demanded that the Extraordinary Committee provide Kirov *oblast* with lines of communication to Russian state agencies.

In November 1991 he was appointed head of the administration of Kirov *oblast* by presidential decree. In December 1992 he stated that the Congress of People's Deputies was incapable of finding a way out of the present critical situation and that its political ambitions were above its station. He viewed the government of Egor Gaidar as full of first-class theorists at a time when Russia needed a government of first-class practical ministers. He lives in Kirov.

Dneprov, Eduard Dmitrievich

Adviser of the President of the Russian Federation on Education and Humanitarian Reforms; Minister of Education of the Russian Federation, November 1991 to December 1992.

Born on January 1, 1936 in Moscow into a Russian family and attended Nakhimov Naval Technical College in Leningrad (1948-54). In 1958 graduated from the Frunze Higher Naval Technical College as submarine navigator. From 1958 to 1971 he served in the navy, in the Northern and Baltic Fleets and in the Leningrad naval base. In 1961 as an external student he graduated from the philology faculty of Leningrad State University as a qualified philologist and journalist. He resigned from the navy. In 1967 he successfully presented his candidate dissertation in history (PhD). He joined the CPSU in 1970. Between 1971 and 1974 he worked as a senior scientific assistant of the scientific research institute for general pedagogy of the USSR Academy of Pedagogical Sciences. In 1974/75 he was head of the editorial group of the Pedagogika publishing house, which produced material on research into teaching. In 1975/76 he was editor-in-chief of the Pedagogika publishing house, and from 1976 to 1978 he was head of the department of pedagogical information of the scientific research institute of the USSR Academy of Pedagogical Sciences.

Between 1978 and 1988 he was head of the laboratory of school history and pedagogy in pre-revolutionary Russia in the same institute. From 1984 he actively opposed the so-called school reforms, drafted by the leadership of the USSR Academy of Pedagogical Sciences and the Ministry of Education. As a result, he was branded an opponent of Soviet schools and pedagogy and someone who opposed the decisions of the CPSU and the Soviet government. Over the years 1984-88 he was closely associated with V. F. Matveev, the editor-in-chief of *Uchitelskaya gazeta* (Teachers' newspaper), and also with Simon Soloveichik, the well-known journalist and writer. In 1988 Dneprov became head of *Shkola* (school), the All-Union scientific research committee which, over a period of 18 months, prepared a series of documents proposing radical educational reforms.

Between 1988 and 1990 he was director of the Centre of Innovation of the USSR Academy of Pedagogical Sciences and was a candidate of historical sciences (PhD). He was RSFSR Minister of Education in the government headed by Ivan Silaev from 1990. E. Saburov was his deputy Minister of Education until August 1991 when he became RSFSR Minister of the Economy. After Dneprov's appointment as Minister, criticism of him by conservatives continued. It was led by L. I. Ruvinsky, head of the Soviet association of research teachers and its journal *Pedagogichesky vestnik* (pedagogical bulletin).

Dneprov supported the introduction of theology into intermediate schools, on a purely voluntary basis, based on a course of lectures given by Fr Aleksandr Men (a well-known Orthodox priest who was later found murdered). As a Minister Dneprov was accused of corruption. In early 1992 five of his six deputy Ministers forwarded a letter to President Yeltsin requesting that the Minister be sacked. An investigation into the running of the Ministry led to a decree of the Presidium of the Supreme Soviet on October 26, 1992 which questioned the suitability of Dneprov for the post of Minister. On November 3, 1992, by decree of the President of the Russian Federation, Dneprov was appointed adviser to the President on education and humanitarian reforms. The dismissal of Egor Gaidar as acting Prime Minister in December 1992 led also to Dneprov's removal as Minister. He was replaced by Evgeny Tkachenko.

Dneprov is married with two children and lives in Moscow.

Dovhan, Serhii Vasylovych

Leader of the Peasants' Party of Ukraine.

He is an ethnic Ukrainian, who was the director of the state farm *Kosmos* in Bereslavskyi *raion*, Kherson *oblast*. In January 1992 he was elected head of the newly-formed Peasants' Party of Ukraine (PPU), which represents the largely conservative interests of collective farm chairmen and leaders of the agro-industrial complex. A major concern was to delay the process of privatization of the state and collective farms since this would eventually bring to the top a new generation of owner managers in the countryside. One tactic adopted was to transform farms into closed joint stock companies, whereby the shares could only be sold with the permission of the majority shareholders. The sorry state of Ukrainian agriculture presaged a difficult future for the agrarian sector which lacked infrastructure and capital investment. There was also reluctance to enter into joint ventures with foreign companies, especially in the food processing industry.

Drach, Ivan Fedorovych

Leader of *Rukh* 1989-92.

Born into a Ukrainian family in 1936 at Telezhentsy, near Kiev. He studied philology at Kiev State University, and took a stage director course at Moscow State University. He joined the Communist Party of Ukraine (CPU) in 1959, and in the 1960s he was one of the leading figures in the *Shestydesiatnyky* (sixty) generation of new Ukrainian poets and writers that rose to prominence promoting a Ukrainian cultural renaissance.

Among his most famous works are *Soniashnyk* published in 1962 and *The Kiev Sky* in 1976. Nearly all his best work was done in the 1960s, before the political climate became more oppressive in the 1970s. He is first secretary of the Kiev branch of the Writers' Union of Ukraine and, in 1991 he was appointed head of the cultural society *Ukraïna*. After the abortive attempt to establish a Ukrainian Popular Front (*Rukh*) under the leadership of the Ukrainian Helsinki Union and other informal groups in the summer of 1988, leadership passed to the Union of Writers in the winter of 1988-89.

Drach took a prominent part in organizing the movement, heading the committee of twenty writers that drew up the draft *Rukh* programme that finally appeared in February 1989. He was elected leader at *Rukh's* first congress in September 1989, a position he retained at the second congress in October 1990. In March 1990 Drach was elected as people's deputy for Artemivskyi *raion*, Lviv *oblast* (on the first round) and he left the CPU in the same month. In the Supreme Soviet he is a member of the committee on foreign affairs. Although nominally a member of the Democratic Party of Ukraine, founded in December 1990, he had never taken much part in its leadership.

After August 1991 and the election of Kravchuk in December 1991, Drach became a keen supporter of the new President as, although a humanist, Drach is also an emotional nationalist. At the same time, however, Drach grew increasingly tired of mainstream politics and he was never particularly concerned with organizational minutiae, and was therefore unable to deliver *Rukh* to Kravchuk at the movement's third congress in February-March 1992. In April 1992, however, he was appointed a member of the President's advisory *Duma* on humanitarian affairs and he remained close to Kravchuk. Despite nominally remaining as co-leader of *Rukh*, Drach no longer took any active part in its proceedings, not even bothering to attend its fourth congress in December 1992. In February 1993, however, he was persuaded to make something of a political comeback when he became chairman of the newly-created Anti-Imperial Anti-Communist Front, that united most nationalist parties in opposition to the growing threat of a neo-communist *revanche*.

Home address: 252005 Kiev, Vul. Gorkoho 18/7; *telephone*: (home) Kiev 227 2401.

Dubynin, Viktor Petrovich

Chief of the General Staff of the Armed Forces; first deputy Minister of Defence of the Russian Federation until November 22, 1992. General of the Army 1992.

Born on February 1, 1943 in Kamensk-Uralsk, Sverdlovsk (Ekaterinburg) *oblast*, into a working-class family. Russian. Died on November 22, 1992.

He graduated with distinction from the Far East Tank Officers' Technical School, Blagoveshchensk, in 1964; with distinction from the Military Academy of the Armoured Troops in 1978; with distinction from the Military Academy of the General Staff in 1984. He received a higher military education and was a member of the CPSU from 1970 to August 1991.

He began his career as an officer as a tank platoon commander in 1964. He was immediately recognized as a promising commander due to his talent for organization, military skills and his high level of professional training. He was respected by superior officers and Party political agencies. He was actively involved in the work of the Party organization and proved himself a convinced communist, something which contributed to his rapid promotion. Despite his lack of an advanced academic education he was appointed a company commander, then a battalion and regimental commander (it was a rule in the Soviet army that regimental commanders had to have advanced education). He was quite popular with his subordinates and the officer corps. After graduating from the Academy of the Armoured Troops in 1978 he was immediately appointed a deputy divisional commander and later a tank divisional commander in the Belarusian military district. The units and sub-units under Dubynin demonstrated a high level of combat readiness and successfully carried out their training tasks. Immediately after graduating from the Military Academy of the General Staff in 1984 Maj.-Gen. Dubynin became the first deputy army commander of the 40th Army in Afghanistan, thereby jumping over several ranks. From 1986 he was commander of the 40th army in Afghanistan and supervised the planning of military operations against the *mujahidin* and the civilian population. He had quite close ties with the top military officials of the USSR and this later helped in his promotion. He had a sound operational-tactical and military-technical training and a talent for organization, paying special attention to military theory. His level of culture was quite acceptable. Like other generals in the Soviet army he was a conformist, supporting the CPSU and USSR government policy in domestic and foreign affairs. He was never known to express his own political views in public.

From 1987 he was tank army commander of the Belarusian military district, which was one of the most advanced districts as it bordered on states in the west European strategic direction. The district was always held to be one of the best as regards combat readiness, versatile training and opportunities for promotion. In 1988 Lieut.-Gen. Dubynin was appointed Chief of Staff and the first deputy army commander of the Kiev military district, a traditionally prestigious district in the eyes of the Moscow and Kiev leadership. In 1989 he became commander of the Northern group of troops in Poland and the senior Soviet military official in Poland. He proved himself a good diplomat who firmly defended the interests of the USSR and Soviet troops in a foreign state where the domestic political situation was unstable. He organized the withdrawal of matériel and personnel from Poland, ensured a high level of discipline and order and arrived at a mutual understanding and close co-operation with the Polish authorities.

In early 1990 Dubynin was nominated as a candidate for election as a people's deputy of the Supreme Soviet of Belarusia in the No. 307 Khotim electoral district, Mogilev *oblast* by a collective farm in Mogilev *oblast* and five military units. He won in the first round on March 4, 1990. On June 10, 1992 he was appointed Chief of the General Staff of the Armed Forces and first deputy Minister of Defence of the Russian Federation. He was directly involved in the elaboration of military doctrine. He was notable among top generals for his grasp of theory and capacity for imaginative work. He did not reveal his political views in public but remained a supporter of a strong state domestically. He advocated the creation of up-to-date armed forces to protect Russia's status as a great power. Democrats in the military were watchful, seeing him as a protégé of conservative circles which influenced Russian President Boris Yeltsin on military issues. His interviews on the withdrawal of Soviet troops from Poland appeared in *Krasnaya Zvezda, Pravda, Izvestiya, Moskovskie novosti* and *Kommunist vooruzhennykh sil*.

He was fond of reading, interested in military theory and the problems of military history and was not indifferent to art. He engaged in sporting activities. He was awarded five orders and many medals, including two orders of the Red Banner and one order of the Red Star. He was married with a daughter.

Official address: 103175 Moscow, the General Staff of the Armed Forces of the Russian Federation.

Dudaev, Dzhokhar

President and Chairman of the Government of the Chechen Republic, Russian Federation.

Born in 1944; a Chechen. He and his family were deported by Stalin, along with the rest of his nation, in 1944, for alleged collaboration with the German *Wehrmacht*, to Kazakhstan. The family returned from Kazakhstan in the late 1950s after Khrushchev had declared that the grounds for the deportation could not be substantiated. He completed secondary school and the professional technical college in Grozny. He was a student for a short time in the faculty of mathematics, North Ossetian State University, but broke off his studies and entered the Tambov pilots' technical college. After graduating he entered the N. I. Zhukovsky Military Aviation Academy, and then entered the air force, progressed to major-general and commanded a squadron of bombers in the strategic air forces. He began his political activities under pressure from the All-National Congress of the Chechen people (ACCP), a national movement whose goal was to establish the sovereignty of the Chechen state. He agreed to become its leader and in March 1991 voluntarily resigned from the post of head of the garrison in Tartu.

On September 1, 1991 Dudaev, as chairman of the executive committee of the ACCP, spoke at a congress of the Chechen people. He proposed the resignation of the chairman (Speaker) of the Supreme Soviet of the Chechen-Ingush Republic and his deputies, the confirmation of the rights of deputies and the creation of a provisional government. He characterized the attempted state coup as a most serious crime against the peoples of the Soviet union. The goal of the executive committee of the ACCP, he declared, was the democratic transformation of the republic, peacefully and constitutionally. On September 6, under pressure from the ACCP, the chairman of the Supreme Soviet resigned. Dudaev referred to the Supreme Soviet as having the rights enjoyed by a colony, and on September 15, the IX extraordinary session of the Supreme Soviet of the Chechen-Ingush Republic formally confirmed the dissolution of the parliament and the resignation of its Speaker.

On October 27, 1991 Dudaev was elected President of the Chechen Republic in national elections which were boycotted by a significant part of the electorate. The RSFSR Supreme Soviet declared the election illegal and on November 8, 1991, by decree of the President of the RSFSR, a state of emergency was declared on the territory of the Chechen-Ingush Republic. In response Dudaev declared martial law and the national guard of Chechnia took over the roads, communications and the airport. A unit of the OMON (the black berets and special troops of the Ministry of Internal Affairs) was blockaded in the airport and then expelled to Russia. The Chechen Republic has still not been recognized by the President and Supreme Soviet of the Russian Federation.

In 1992 Dudaev sharply criticized the "imperialist" policy of Russia and its leadership. He appealed for an end to the colonial status of Chechnia, and for its economy to be developed on the basis of local raw materials, and he criticized the Russian blockade of the Chechen economy and the financial and transport systems of the republic. An especially sharp declaration was issued in December 1992 when Russian troops were moved into the Ingush Republic to prevent an Ossetian-Ingush conflict. Later, Dudaev toned down his utterances but has demanded that Chechen citizens should be allowed to participate in the privatization of Russian property, created by all the peoples of the Russian Federation. He advocates the development of mutually beneficial economic relations with Russia and the re-establishment of the former economic ties. He is married with three children and lives in Grozny.

Dudnik, Vladimir Mikhailovich

Member of the co-ordinating council of the "Movement for Democracy" and the Moscow regional organization "Democratic Russia". Political scientist. Military analyst on *Moscow News*. Candidate of pedagogical sciences (PhD), Assistant Professor. Major-General since 1977.

Born on January 28, 1933 in Orenburg into a military pilot's family. Russian. His career in the military began at the age of 10. He graduated from the Stalingrad (Volgograd) Suvorov Military Technical School in 1950; the 1st Leningrad S. M. Kirov Land Technical School in 1952; the Military Faculty of the V. I. Lenin Military Political Academy in 1964; and completed a postgraduate course with a degree in military pedagogy and psychology in 1970. He received a higher military and political education and was a member of the CPSU from 1956 to August 1991.

After completing technical school he served, from 1952 to 1955, in the Baltic and Leningrad military districts as commander of a motorized-rifle platoon and company. He was actively involved in Party political work, contributed to the military press, and was notable among young officers for his intellectual pursuits and profound interest in political science. He was elected to the *Komsomol* agencies of his units. In 1955 he was transferred to political posts and worked as secretary of a *Komsomol* committee and as a political department officer for four years.

When studying at the Academy he became a member of the USSR union of journalists in 1963. From 1964 he worked in Party political agencies in the Moscow military district. He was senior instructor of a tank divisional political department, deputy political commander of a training tank regiment, deputy head of the political department of a training division, and head of the political department of a tank division and an army corps. As a combat officer he researched and successfully presented his candidate dissertation (PhD) in 1973 on the system of training of junior specialists in the land forces, in which he used data gained from his own career experience.

In 1979 Gen. Dudnik was appointed deputy head of the political department of the Carpathian military district. He had to take part in planning the intended invasion of Poland, where, in 1980, there arose conflicts between the communist authorities and the independent trade union, Solidarity. His record was that of an experienced political commander with a sound operational-tactical training, highly intelligent and able to react adequately to the new realities of the international situation. From 1984 he was deputy head of the political department of the headquarters of the Western direction, in Legnice, Poland. He was an immediate subordinate of the military leaders Marshal of the USSR Nikolai Ogarkov and political commander Col.-Gen. B. Utkin, who had fallen out of favour. In 1987 Dudnik was chosen personally by the then head of the political administration of the Soviet army and navy, General of the Army, A. Lizichev, to fill the post of head of the department of Party political work in the Soviet armed forces at the V. I. Lenin Military Political Academy.

As early as the mid 1980s Gen. Dudnik tried to introduce far-reaching *perestroika* and democratization into the army. In April 1986, at the Party meeting of staffs and administrations of the general headquarters of the Western direction, he presented a report on the results of the work of the XXVII Party Congress, expressing his own views on democratization and reform in the armed forces. Dudnik's report *"Perestroika* in the armed forces: theory, practice, concepts" (later published as a booklet), and delivered at a conference in the military political academy in 1988, attracted a great deal of attention, since it included an analysis of the CPSU's loss of authority and position in the Soviet political system. The conclusions reached in his report and the author's conviction that fundamental reform was necessary in the military and political spheres were sharply criticized by the leadership of the chief political administration and the academy. As a consequence, Gen. Dudnik was forced to stop researching his doctoral dissertation on the activity of commanders, staffs and political agencies of strategic formations devoted to achieving moral superiority over the enemy. Because of his public adherence to democratic views and support of reform in the army, he was dismissed from the post of head of the department in August 1989 and transferred to the reserve in March 1990.

Dudnik was one of the organizers of the "Movement for Democracy". He also participated actively in the "Democratic Russia" movement. He took part in independent military and public expert discussions of draft reforms of the armed forces and in elaborating concepts of national security in a completely new international environment. In January 1990 he participated in an "independent public expert analysis of the existence or otherwise of a military threat and the activities of the USSR armed forces". He often appeared in the mass media and at various congresses and conferences on the problems of democratization of the army and on the drafting of completely new approaches to military planning. He was the first author to tackle the subject of the army and religion in an article published in 1990 in the newspaper *Tserkovny Vestnik*. Dudnik's analytical articles were included in the collection entitled *Glasnost* (Moscow 1989) and in *Armiya i Obshchestvo* (Moscow 1990). The General remained in the Party, hoping that it would reform itself. His article on reform in the Party was published in *Kommunist* on the eve of the XXVIII Party Congress.

His predictions about the evolution of the situation in the USSR were often highly accurate. For instance, on August 15, 1991, at the X international convention of the END (for nuclear disarmament in Europe), he warned of the danger of an anti-constitutional putsch and named its organizers as Vladimir Kryuchkov (KGB), Marshal Dmitry Yazov (army) and Boris Pugo (MVD). During the attempted coup on August 19-21, 1991 Dudnik was a military adviser of the Moscow soviet (city council) emergency group and directly supervised the collection, co-ordination and analysis of material on the situation and reported to the leaders in the Russian White House. He went himself to see the plotters' troops (including the 103rd airborne division) and to hold talks with commanding officers so as to explain the situation.

In 1991/92 Gen. Dudnik was actively involved in political, scholarly and journalistic work. He headed independent expert groups examining the problems involved in elaborating concepts of national security, military reform and military planning. He advocates fundamental reform in the army and the creation of armed forces for a democratic country, under strict parliamentary and civil control. He often appears in the press and TV. He does not agree with the imperial ambitions of the national patriots and advocates a strong state; vigorously opposes the ideas of the "Afghan Generals" and is resolutely against those who supported the plotters rising to power in the army. He attended the Helsinki Congress of the CSCE and the XI Congress of END as a member of the Russian delegation. He is respected among political scientists, journalists and the military and has close ties with colleagues in the West, the ecumenical movement and NATO specialists. He is interested in art, theatre, imaginative writing and historical research. He has over 38,000 volumes in his personal library. While working on historical archives, he discovered and revived the works of the founder of Russian military psychology, G. Shumkov, and of the orientalist, Lieut.-Gen. A. Snesarev. His recreations are fishing and sport. He has several military scholarly publications to his credit but they are still classified. He does not have a good command of foreign languages. He has been awarded the orders of the Red Banner, and "For service to the motherland in the armed forces of the USSR", 3rd class, two orders of the Red Star, 22 Soviet, Mongolian, GDR and Czechoslovak medals, including "For valour during the extinguishing of fires". He is married with two daughters, whose husbands are officers, and has three grandchildren.

Home address: 115541 Moscow, ul. Luganskaya, d. 8, kv. 8; *telephone*: Moscow 322 10 22.

Durdynets, Vasyl Vasylovych

First Deputy Chairman of the Ukrainian Supreme Soviet.

Born into a Ukrainian family in 1937. He was educated at Lviv State University, after which he worked as a lawyer before taking up *Komsomol* work in 1960 and moving on to Party employment in 1970. In 1978 he was appointed a deputy Minister of Internal Affairs (MVD), and first deputy Minister in 1982. In 1990 he was elected a people's deputy for Bobrynetskyi *raion*, Kirovohrad *oblast*, in central Ukraine on the first round. In February 1991 he became head of the Supreme Soviet's committee on defence and state security, and is therefore an *ex officio* member of the Supreme Soviet's Presidium, where he was soon identified with the growing nationalist communist trend.

After Kravchuk's elevation to the Presidency, and Pliushch's election to his place as Speaker of the Supreme Soviet, Durdynets became Pliushch's First Deputy in January 1992, leapfrogging over Pliushch's long-time deputy, Vladimir Griniov. At the same time he relinquished his position on the defence committee, although he remains a member of Kravchuk's Defence Council. More urbane and diplomatic than Pliushch, Durdynets has tended to be the leading figure in negotiations between the Ukrainian Supreme Soviet and other states or parliamentary delegations. In particular, he was in charge of the difficult negotiations in 1992 with Russia over the Black Sea Fleet and other issues.

Official address: Kiev, Vul. M. Hrushevskoho 5; *telephone*: Kiev 252 019.

Dzharimov, Aslan Alievich

President and Chairman of the Council of Ministers of the Republic of Adygeia, Russian Federation.

Born in 1939 in the village of Egerukhai, Koshekhablsky *raion*, Adygeia autonomous *oblast* into a peasant family; member of the CPSU until August 1991. He began his working life on the local Put k Kommunizmy collective farm. He graduated in 1964 from the Kuban Agricultural Institute and then was an agronomist and senior economist of the Koshekhablsky *raion* agricultural administration. From 1967 to 1968 he was a postgraduate student in the faculty of agricultural economics, Kuban Agricultural Institute. He successfully presented his candidate dissertation in economics in 1975 on "The economic effectiveness of mineral fertilizers in the collective farms of the Adygeia autonomous *oblast*" (PhD (Econ)). From 1968 to 1975 he was head of the agricultural economics department of the agricultural administration of the *oblast* soviet executive committee, deputy head of the agricultural department of the Adygeia Party *obkom*, and director of the Adygeia *oblast* agricultural experimental station.

From 1975 to 1984 he was head of the agricultural department and secretary for agriculture in the Adygeia Party *obkom*. He was head of the department of agriculture and food industry, Krasnodar Party *kraikom* from 1984 to 1987, and in 1985 graduated from the Academy of Social Sciences of the Party Central Committee. He was secretary for the agro-industrial complex in the Krasnodar Party (1987–89) and, in January 1989 he was elected first secretary of the Adygeia Party *obkom*. He was a deputy of the USSR Supreme Soviet.

In 1990 he was elected a deputy of the Adygeia *oblast* soviet of people's deputies and at its first session, in March 1990, he was elected its chairman. Dzharimov stated that in order to create an effective economy, economic cost accounting, leasing and the transition of the *oblast* to economic autonomy were necessary. He was a strong supporter of various types of ownership.

In August 1991 the Presidium and the executive committee of the *oblast* soviet addressed the population and called on them, without commenting on the attempted state coup, to implement strictly the laws and the constitutions of the USSR and RSFSR and to concentrate on the most important task, which was bringing in the harvest.

In December 1991 there were elections to the Supreme Soviet and the election of the head of the executive of Adygeia republic. There were five candidates for President and in the second round of voting, in March 1991, Dzharimov won, polling 69.4% of the votes. On assuming office he stated that in the present situation the most important thing was to establish political stability since without it a normal transition to economic reform would be impossible. It was important to halt the fall in production and protect the population during the transition to a market economy. The key to the implementation of economic reform was the privatization of state property, but priority during this process should be afforded work collectives. He stated that the basic producer of agricultural products for a long time yet would be the collective farms and hence dissolving them would be harmful. At the same time, however, greater attention should be paid to the promotion of private farming and the development of the private farms which were already functioning than to the distribution of land. There should be no talk of decollectivization in the countryside, since the combination of various forms of land ownership could help to maintain a stable situation.

In December 1992 he stated that it was clear that during the VII Congress of People's Deputies deep and dramatic contradictions had developed in society and a serious political crisis could erupt if government leaders did not pluck up the courage to make concessions and arrive at an agreed correct policy. He is married with two children and lives in Maikop.

Dziuba, Ivan

Former Dissident and Minister of Culture of Ukraine since November 1992.

Born into a Ukrainian peasant family in 1931 in the Donbas mining region in eastern Ukraine. In 1949 he entered the faculty of philology of Donetsk (at the time known as Stalino) Pedagogical Institute. After graduation he worked as a literary researcher in the Ukrainian Academy of Sciences' institute of literature. His first published work was the essay collection *The Ordinary Man*, in 1959. He grew notorious, however, as a leading member of the *Shestydesiatnyky* (sixty) movement of literary and cultural dissidents, and was expelled from his editorial post on the journal *Vitchyzna* (fatherland) in 1963.

In 1965 he wrote a seminal critique of Soviet nationalities policy, published in the West as *Internationalism or Russification?*, in which he attacked various "deviations" from the correct path of Leninist nationalities policy, since his death in 1924, arguing that formulae concerning the "friendship" and eventual "drawing closer" of the nations of the Soviet Union were a hypocritical cover for the destruction of non-Russian cultures and outright Russian chauvinism. Significantly, the book continued to circulate semi-officially and Dziuba was not publicly denounced.

Reportedly he enjoyed the protection of Petro Shelest, first secretary of the Communist Party of Ukraine (CPU) from 1963 to 1972. When the power of Shelest began to weaken, however, a campaign against Dziuba began in 1969. In 1972 he was expelled from the Writers' Union, and in 1973 sentenced to five years' imprisonment. He was soon released, however, after publishing a humiliating self-criticism in *Literaturna Ukraïna*, on November 9, 1973. Thereafter he lived somewhat in limbo, until his rehabilitation in the late 1980s.

Since then he has become the father figure of Ukrainian literature, heading the International Association of Ukrainian Studies in Kiev and editing the journal *Suchasnist* (modern times) after its transfer to Kiev from Munich, Germany, where it had originally been founded as a diaspora journal. In April 1992 he was appointed a member of the President's advisory *Duma* on humanitarian affairs. In November 1992 his rehabilitation was completed when he was appointed Minister of Culture in the new Kuchma government to replace the ineffectual Larysa Khorolets.

Official (Ministry) address: 252030 Kiev, Vul. Ivana Franka 19; *telephone*: Kiev 224 4911.

Ebzeev, Boris Safarovich

Member of the Constitutional Court of the Russian Federation.

Born on February 25, 1950 in the village of Djangi-Djer, Kyzyl-Askersky *raion*, Frunze *oblast*, Kirgizia (Kyrgyzstan), into a Karachai family. His family had been deported to Central Asia by Stalin in November 1943 for allegedly collaborating with the Germans. The Karachai were rehabilitated by Khrushchev in 1956 and Ebzeev returned to the Karachaevo-Cherkess Autonomous Soviet Socialist Republic (ASSR). In 1968 he entered the D. I. Kursky Institute of Law, Saratov, graduating in 1972 and immediately beginning postgraduate studies in the same institute. In 1975 he successfully presented his candidate dissertation on "The constitutional foundations of the freedom of the personality of Soviet citizens" (LLM) and in 1989 his doctoral dissertation on "The constitutional problems of the rights and duties of the individual in Soviet society" (LLD). From 1975 to 1976 he served in the Soviet Army, and then joined the staff of the institute as a lecturer and was promoted to senior lecturer, assistant professor and professor. He is the author of three monographs. His main research interests are in constitutional law, power, sovereignty, freedom of the individual and the problems of the rights and duties of Soviet citizens. He is a co-author of the draft constitution (basic law) of the Russian Federation. The draft was prepared by a group of specialists at the Institute of Law, Saratov and they were awarded an honorary certificate by the Presidium of the Supreme Soviet of the Russian Federation for their work. He took part in drafting the RSFSR law on the Constitutional Court.

He was proposed as a member of the Constitutional Court by the autonomous republics in the Russian Federation. On October 29, 1991, at the V Congress of People's Deputies, he was elected in the first round of voting with 657 votes for and 227 votes against. He regards the maintenance of the unity of Russia to be one of the key tasks of the Constitutional Court since, according to him, regional sovereignty mainly signifies its transformation into the personal fiefdom of local rulers. The Constitutional Court should be a guarantor of the rights not only of peoples but of the individual person. The main danger facing the Constitutional Court is that it may be transformed into the servant of politics and some politicians, despite the fact that the chief task of the Court is strictly to serve only the law.

Efimov, Vitaly Borisovich

Minister of Transport of the Russian Federation.

Born on April 4, 1940 in the *Krasnaya zarya* (red sunrise) state farm, Malinsky *raion*, Moscow *oblast*, into a Russian family. He was a member of the CPSU until August 1991. From 1957 to 1959 he worked as a fitter in a technical repair centre in Sergach, Gorky (Nizhny Novgorod) *oblast*. In 1964 he graduated from the Gorky agricultural institute as an agricultural mechanic. Later he successfully defended his candidate dissertation and became a candidate of technical sciences (PhD (Eng)). From 1964 to 1968 he was a repair engineer in the Novinka training farm of the Gorky agricultural institute. From 1968 to 1973 he was chief engineer of a transport column of the Volgo-Vyatsky territorial transport administration of the RSFSR Ministry of Automobile Transport. From 1973 to 1983 he worked as chief engineer at the No. 8 production association of heavy goods transport and then as chief engineer of the Volgo-Vyatsky territorial transport administration. Between 1983 and 1986 he was head of the Gorky territorial transport association, *Gorkiiavtotrans*, of the USSR Ministry of Automobile Transport. From 1986 to 1990 he was deputy RSFSR Minister of Automobile Transport. He is an academician of the RSFSR Academy of Transport. In September 1991 he was confirmed by the RSFSR Supreme Soviet as RSFSR Minister of Transport and in November 1991 he was appointed Minister of Transport of the Russian Federation by presidential decree, and was therefore a member of the "government of reform".

He emphasized several times that he finds the economic policy of the Russian government attractive and the fact that the President has committed himself to the government's reforms augurs well for their success. He regards the duties of the Ministry to be primarily promoting legislation and implementing current laws. He was one of those responsible for drafting the laws "on transport in the RSFSR" (the main principles of which were maintaining a united transport network, equality of various forms of property ownership and the mutual rights and responsibilities of transport and the authorities), "on the security of the transport and road network", "on ecological responsibility in the USSR", and the "law on compulsory insurance of the citizens' responsibilities". He played a part in the creation of a transport inspectorate in Russia. Among the new state projects under way are "Terminal", the establishment of loading and unloading networks where railway and road transport intersect; "Avtobus" and "Passenger services". He feels it is important to establish a transport system which benefits first and foremost the passenger, client and society, and then the authorities, and not the other way round.

As Minister, he has been confronted with extremely difficult problems. Under-investment in transport during the last two decades of Soviet power has left a legacy which will require heavy investment in the near future. Efimov's problems are compounded by the fragmentation of the Russian Federation as central power weakens and each region attempts to solve its problems in its own way. A Russia-wide transport policy is extremely difficult to implement. He has also to integrate Russia and the other successor states of the Soviet Union. Moving goods from one republic to another is a taxing problem.

He is married with one child. He was awarded the order of the Red Banner of Labour and lives in Moscow.

Egorov, Nikolai Dmitrievich

Head of the Administration of Krasnodar *krai*, Russian Federation.

Born in 1951 into a Cossack family in the village of Zassovskoi, Labinsky *raion*, Krasnodar *krai*, he was a member of the CPSU until August 1991. He attended the local secondary school, then studied in the Military Political Aviation College, and graduated from the Stavropol Agricultural Institute and the Higher Party School. At various times he was secretary of a Party committee, chairman of a collective farm in Krasnodar *krai*, chairman of the Labinsky *raion* soviet executive committee, Krasnodar *krai*, first deputy chairman of the economics department of the Krasnodar *krai* agro-industrial committee, and was head of the department of agriculture of the Krasnodar *krai* government.

In March 1990 he was elected the deputy for electoral district No. 160 in the Krasnodar *krai* soviet of people's deputies. On December 30, 1992 he was appointed head of the administration of Krasnodar *krai* by presidential decree. On assuming office he stated that his most important task was to re-establish economic links in the structures of the administration to acquire expertise in how a market functioned, and to resolve the problem of price formation. He viewed the market as a precise regulatory mechanism.

In December 1992 he stated that the results of the VII Congress of People's Deputies gave him hope for the future. He viewed them as a new stage of the political development of Russia where passions had cooled and the politicians had become more sober and far-sighted. Ideology for him at present meant a policy of social reconciliation and common sense. He is married and his wife is a musician. There are two children; their daughter is a student at the polytechnical institute and their son is still at school. He lives in Labinsk, Krasnodar *krai*.

Egorov, Vladimir Grigorevich

Commander-in-Chief of the Red Banner Baltic Fleet. Admiral since 1992.

Born on November 26, 1938 in Moscow. Russian. He worked as a turner for a year at one of the plants in Leningrad, and graduated from the M. V. Frunze Higher Naval Technical school with a gold medal in 1962; the Naval Academy in 1985; took an external degree at the Military Academy of the General Staff in 1990.

He is a submariner. He began his naval career as a commander of a submarine section and was then promoted to senior assistant commander and commander of a huge anti-submarine vessel. He proved to be a qualified officer and an excellent sailor, demonstrating exceptional command abilities. He took part in many long voyages and saw service at sea. He successfully fulfilled the tasks of tactical search, tracking and attacking the submarine strength of a possible enemy. The high command promoted him to divisional chief of staff, and later he became commander of anti-submarine surface forces. He was politically active only to the extent necessary for his career.

After graduating from the Academy he was appointed a commander of a naval base, successfully fulfilling the tasks of fleet support and keeping the coastal forces prepared for action. In 1986 he became a flotilla commander; his formation displayed a high level of training. From 1988 he was the first deputy Commander-in-Chief of the Red Banner Baltic fleet. While at this post, Admiral V. Egorov, together with Commander-in-Chief V. Ivanov, took part in decisions about the use of the coastal units of the Baltic fleet against the national-democratic forces of the Baltic republics. He did not express his political views in public.

There is no reliable information about V. Egorov's activity during the anti-constitutional putsch in August 1991. After V. Ivanov had been dismissed and transferred to the Naval Academy, Vice-Adml Vladimir Egorov filled the post of Commander-in-Chief of the fleet.

At present he has under his command the naval forces stationed in the sovereign Baltic states and in Kaliningrad *oblast* of Russia. The Admiral has to deal with important diplomatic problems to ensure the rights of Russian citizens.

In his every-day activity he seeks to carry out meticulously any instructions coming from Moscow and to restrain extremist sentiments of his subordinates. He does not express his political views in public and wants to be regarded as a military professional not involved in politics.

On October 12, 1991 he published an article in *Krasnaya Zvezda* on the problems of the Baltic fleet.

He was awarded two orders "for service to the motherland in the armed forces of the USSR", and many medals. He does not speak any foreign language.

Adml Vladimir Egorov's headquarters are in Baltiisk, Kaliningrad *oblast*.

Elagin, Vladimir Vasilevich

Head of the Administration of Orenburg *oblast*, Russian Federation.

Born in 1955 in the village of Dobrinka, Aleksandrovsky *raion*, Orenburg *oblast*; Russian. His father was a school teacher and his mother worked in a laboratory. He was a member of the CPSU until August 1991. After secondary school he entered the faculty of industrial and civil construction of the Polytechnical Institute, Orenburg, and after graduation he was foreman of the construction administration of the Orenburg oil and gas construction trust. He served a year and a half in the Soviet Army, and after being demobbed he returned to Aleksandrovsky *raion* of the agricultural construction administration. Then he moved into *Komsomol* work. Initially he was deputy, then head of the *oblast Komsomol* construction brigade, and was for five years first secretary of the Orenburg *Komsomol obkom*. In 1990 he was elected first secretary of the *Komsomol* Central Committee of the RSFSR.

In early 1990 he was nominated for election as an RSFSR people's deputy in the No. 549 Tsentralny territorial district, Orenburg *oblast*. During the election campaign he advocated the equality of the RSFSR as a republic, a full-blown federation in Russia and the autonomy of the autonomous republics and *oblasts*. He called for land to be given to those who would work it, make workers co-owners of the means of production and personally interest them in the results of their labour. He proposed radical economic reform, the elimination of unnecessary links in the bureaucratic apparatus and criticized the state bureaucratic machine.

There were seven candidates. Elagin lost in the first round, polling 7.3% of the votes, and the winner was M. N. Zilist, first secretary of the Orenburg Party *raion* committee, who received 17.3% of the votes in the first round and 46.3% in the second. Elagin was elected a deputy of the Orenburg *oblast* soviet.

On October 24, 1991 he was appointed head of the administration of Orenburg *oblast* by presidential decree. On assuming office he appealed for a solution to the problem of bringing urban and rural areas closer together in the new economic circumstances, and stated that priority should be afforded collective and private farms and loss-making collective farms should be dissolved. There should be foreign trade agencies which would have access to foreign markets and advanced technology should be acquired and local demand and competitiveness studied. He advocated the adoption of a market economy, with priority being given to economics but with social factors being taken into account.

In December 1992 he stated that he expected nothing useful from the VII Congress of People's Deputies. It was a huge forum which was incapable of thinking in a balanced manner or displaying expertise in any aspect of economic and social reform. The congress was dominated by emotion and party and factional infighting and its effectiveness as a working institution was low. Nevertheless he stated that shock economic therapy had been initiated with an evaluation of the situation in Russia, without serious analyses and forecasts of the likely effects. A strict system was necessary but not the present one. He expressed his disagreement with the activities of the President and those in government, and called Egor Gaidar a poor organizer. The appointment of Viktor Chernomyrdin was not a disaster and he needed to choose a good government team as reform could not be reversed. He is married with two sons and lives in Orenburg.

Elchibey (Aliev), Abulfaz Gadirgulu Ogly

President of the Republic of Azerbaijan until June 1993; chairman of the Popular Front of Azerbaijan.

Born on June 7, 1938 in the village of Keleki, Ordubansky *raion*, Nakhichevan ASSR, into a peasants family; an Azeri. His father did not return from the front during the Great Fatherland War (1941-45).

In 1957 he became a student of the department of Arab philology, faculty of oriental studies, S. M. Kirov Azerbaijani State University, and after graduating he worked as a translator in the Arab Republic of Egypt. In 1965 he became a postgraduate student in the faculty of oriental studies, Azerbaijani State University, and in 1969 successfully presented his dissertation in history on "The state of the Tulunids in the 9th century" (PhD). From 1969 to 1975 he taught in the faculty of oriental studies in the university. In 1975 he was arrested and sentenced for "slandering the Soviet state", and was also banned from teaching. He was in prison for two years. In 1977 he was released and found a position in the department of manuscripts, Academy of Sciences of Azerbaijan, where he rose to become a senior scientific assistant.

He is one of the founders of the People's Front of Azerbaijan. In 1989, at the founding conference, he was elected its chairman, and in July 1991 he was re-elected chairman. He is the author of over 50 articles on oriental philosophy, history, literature and religion. He was elected a member of the *Milli Mejlis* (National Council or parliament).

Dissatisfaction within the military over continuing defeats at the hands of the Armenians in the war over Nagorno-Karabakh, popular discontent and economic difficulties led to military rebellion in June 1993. The rebel forces, led by Col. Suret Guseinov, marched on Baku and demanded the resignation and impeachment of the President. Elchibey fled to Nakhichevan after being informed that the military would not shoot at Guseinov's forces. A compromise was negotiated by President Elchibey and his Popular Front supporters and the opposition, consisting of former communists and disgruntled former Popular Front supporters, and the chief beneficiary turned out to be Geidar Aliev, the former Communist Party leader of Azerbaijan. On June 15, 1993 the President had to watch the *Milli Mejlis* elect Aliev speaker or chairman. The President now took a back seat while the old nomenclature reasserted itself, and Surat Guseinov took over the military, the security forces and the militia.

Elchibey is married with two children. His daughter Chilenai is still at school and son Turgut is six years old. He lives in Baku.

Emelianov, Oleksandr Sergeiovych

Chairman of the President of Ukraine's Economic Commission.

Born into a Russian family in Kharkiv in eastern Ukraine in 1932. He graduated from the Kharkiv engineering and economics institute in 1955, and then worked in the same sphere until 1971, when he joined the economic institute of the Ukrainian branch of Gosplan. He then worked his way up within its ranks to the position of deputy head by 1990, having spent a stint in Moscow as the director of the institute of material resources after 1987.

Emelianov successfully presented his candidate dissertation in economics (PhD (Econ)) and his doctoral dissertation in economics (DSc (Econ)). He is a professor of economics and a corresponding member of the Ukrainian Academy of Sciences: his theoretical work concentrated mainly on the development of econometric models. In March 1990 he was elected people's deputy for Sosnovskyi *raion*, Cherkasy *oblast* in central Ukraine (on the second round), and is a member of the Supreme Soviet committee on questions of economic reform and regulation. He remained in the CPU until August 24, 1991, the day of Ukraine's Declaration of Independence. His close ties with Kravchuk and Fokin led to his appointment as head of the economic section of the presidential Council of Advisers (*Duma*) in March 1992.

His blunt manner did not go down well on trips abroad, however. The more urbane and liberal Volodymyr Lanovyi was used to front relations with the West until the latter's dismissal in July 1992, although the more populist Emelianov continued to enjoy better personal access to Kravchuk. He was made a leading member of the Co-ordinating Council on Economic Reform, created by Kravchuk in July 1992, to oversee the process of economic reform. Emelianov was responsible for the controversial March 1992 economic programme, which proposed the rapid introduction of a Ukrainian currency and the severance of economic links with Russia.

However, this was quickly dropped after protests from western financial institutions and governments. Despite pressure from Kravchuk to include him in the new Kuchma government, formed in October 1992, his populism now seemed out of fashion, and he had to content himself with the position of head of the President's economic commission, after Kravchuk agreed to dissolve both the *Duma*, and the Co-ordinating Council on Economic Reform.

Official address: 252005 Kiev, Bankivska Boulevard 7; *telephone*: Kiev 226 2442.

Emelyanov, Aleksei Mikhailovich

Member of the Council of the President of the Russian Federation.

Born in 1935 in the village of Vydrankom, Smolensk *oblast* into a collective farm peasant's family. Russian. He was a member of the CPSU from 1959 to August 1991. After finishing secondary school he entered Moscow State

University, and in 1957 he graduated from the economics faculty and then began postgraduate studies. In 1961 he successfully defended his candidate dissertation in economics on cost accounting (*khozraschet*) and profitability of collective farms (theory and methodology) (PhD (Econ)).

He was on the staff of the faculty of political economy in natural sciences faculties and in 1971 became head of the faculty of agricultural economics of the economics faculty. He successfully presented his doctoral dissertation in economics there and became a professor. Many of Emelyanov's propositions went unrecognized for a long time. In the autumn of 1985 he was elected a corresponding member and in June 1988 an Academician of the V. I. Lenin all-Union academy of agricultural sciences. He is one of the leading agronomists in the country and has published over 190 books and articles. In 1985 he was awarded a Lomonosov prize by the council of Moscow State University for his scientific work.

In early 1989 Emelyanov was nominated as a candidate for election as an RSFSR people's deputy by Moscow State University in No. 1 Leninsky territorial district, Moscow. During the election campaign he advocated the need to subject all production to the interests of the people, the democratization of economic and social life, the structural *perestroika* of the agrarian sector so as to improve the provision of food to the population, a rational balance between large- and small-scale production, a variety of socio-economic forms of production and ownership and the all-round development of co-operatives. He proposed the reorganization of the administration. He opposed the forcible dissolution of collective and state farms and advocated their transformation into unions (co-operatives) of collectives, which had leased land and worked on a contractual basis. He supported the democratization of the political system, the overcoming of the monopoly of Party agencies over all social structures, the liquidation of the monopolistic position of the Party state apparatus, the restriction of the functions of the Party and soviet economic agencies, regular change of leaders and a new law on elections, envisaging direct and equal elections. The state budget deficit should be eliminated by ceasing huge construction projects and lowering expenditure on the apparatus and defence.

There were two candidates. Emelyanov defeated his opponent, V. M. Savitsky, head of the department of the institute of state and law of the USSR Academy of Sciences. Elemyanov was elected a member of the USSR Supreme Soviet at the I Congress of People's Deputies, and was a member of the USSR Supreme Soviet committee on agrarian questions and food. In 1992 Emelyanov stood for election as rector of Moscow State University but lost to V. N. Sadovnich.

Emelyanov advocated guaranteeing land to peasants. He thought that everyone should have the right to leave the collective or state farm and receive free of charge sufficient land to farm economically. However, he warned that not many would take up private farming because of the lack of machinery and finance, but the most important factor holding back private agriculture was the social psychological unpreparedness of village-dwellers to take risks. There were very few genuine peasants left in the villages, according to

Emelyanov; the majority had been transformed into a rural lumpen-proletariat, or day labourers, unprepared to take up private farming.

It was necessary to develop the peasant's private plot as one way of re-organizing the collective and state farms from within to prepare them for private farming. In the near future private farmers were only capable of producing 4-7% of agricultural produce at most, but the traditional private plot already produces 25-27% of global agricultural output. Land should be distributed up to 1-1.5 ha to everyone who wants it and city-dwellers should be able to acquire land for market gardening. Though Emelyanov supports private ownership of land, he opposes the statement in the referendum about land which speaks of unconditional ownership and its purchase and sale. Inheritance of land should only occur with the permission of a competent commission taking into account the way the land was worked. Purchase and sale of land should be restricted (sale due to old age or to moving away, and not only for agricultural production). Freedom of purchase and sale would lead to a great rise in the price of land which would make it beyond the means of the majority of the population. He advocates the distribution of land free of charge, and that businesslike solutions should be found to solve agrarian problems without politicizing them.

He is married and lives in Moscow. His wife is an engineer and their son is a lecturer in political economy in the Moscow Institute of Fine Chemical Technology. Emelyanov became a member of the presidential Council during the autumn of 1991.

Emets, Oleksandr Ivanovych

Adviser to the President of Ukraine.

Born into a Ukrainian family in Khmelnytskyi *oblast* in west-central Ukraine in 1959. He was educated as a psychologist at Kiev State University, and at Kiev Higher Military School. After finishing his studies, he worked as a teacher of young offenders. In the late 1980s he entered opposition politics, becoming involved in the attempts to create an opposition Popular Front in Kiev in 1988. In 1990 he joined the Democratic Platform of the CPU. After leaving the CPU in July 1990 with other members of the Democratic Platform, he was one of the main organizers of the centrist Party of Democratic Revival of Ukraine (PDRU) formed in December 1990, when he became one its original seven co-leaders.

In March 1990, he was elected people's deputy for No. 21 Central Region in Kiev city (on the second round). He was Chairman of the Committee on Human Rights, and therefore a member of the Supreme Soviet's Presidium, until March 1992, when he was appointed by Kravchuk to head the section on legal issues in the presidential *Duma* (his place on the Human Rights Committee was taken by Serhii Batiushko). A highly active deputy, Emets has specialized in security issues and legal questions (he was proposed as a candidate to head the new

Security Service of Ukraine in Autumn 1991). Despite his relative youth, he has become one of the key bridges between Kravchuk and the former opposition.

He has remained active in the PDRU, and in the *New Ukraine* coalition it initiated in January 1992. At the founding congress of *New Ukraine*, in June 1992, he was elected to its secretariat in fourth place with 206 votes. He has, however, tried to move both the PDRU and *New Ukraine* closer to Kravchuk, arguing that the PDRU should drop its commitment to federalism and support a more centralized state. He was therefore rewarded by Kravchuk by being retained as a presidential adviser, even after the dissolution of the *Duma* in October 1992.

Official address: 252005 Kiev, Bankivska Boulevard 7; *telephone*: Kiev 291 6248 or 291 5223.

Eremin, Alvin Evstafevich

Chairman of the Russian Supreme Soviet committee on industry and energy.

Born on May 4, 1932 into a peasant family in Kunikovo village, Kostroma *raion*, Kostroma *oblast*. He was a member of the CPSU from 1956 to August 1991. He graduated from the Kostroma Textile Technical College, the Kostroma Institute of Technology and the Higher Party School of the Party Central Committee (1971-73). In 1948 he began working as a turner in the Rabochy Metallist factory, and after service in the Soviet Army he worked as a turner in the Tekstilmash enterprise, Kostroma (1955-57); an engineer in the bureau of rationalization and invention in the same enterprise (1957-59); secretary of the Party organization in the same enterprise (1959-60); instructor in the department of industry and transport, Kostroma city Party committee (1960-63); head of the same Party department (1963-67); deputy chairman of the executive committee of the Kostroma city soviet of people's deputies (1967-71); head of the department of industry and transport, Kostroma Party *obkom* (1973-80); deputy chairman (1980-82), and first deputy chairman (1982-84), of the executive committee of the Kostroma *oblast* soviet of people's deputies; second secretary of the Kostroma Party *obkom*; and chairman of the executive committee of the Kostroma *oblast* soviet of people's deputies (1984-90).

He was nominated as a candidate for election as an RSFSR people's deputy in the No. 460 Sharinsky territorial district, Kostroma *oblast*, by the collectives of the Shortyugsky timber enterprise, the Zvezda, Kirov, Sverdlov, Erasny Putilovets and Krasny Sokol collective farms, Manturovsky *raion*, six collectives of Pyshugsky *raion*, the Luch and Troitskoe collective farms, Sharinsky *raions*, eight work collectives in Pevlinsky *raion* and the plenum of the *raion* Party committee of the trade union of workers in the agro-industrial complex. During the election campaign he devoted most attention to the transition of Russia to self-management and self-financing, and supported the introduction of the most recent price reforms in order to ensure economic equality among the different branches of the economy. He advocated the transfer of real power and resources to the soviets; more rapid construction of housing and improvement of the infrastructure of the health service and education; the solution of the food problem by reducing state procurements of animal products by all-Union and republican agencies and the transfer of the *oblast* to self-financing and self-government; and the cessation of work on the Kostroma atomic power station.

He won the election and was elected a member of the RSFSR Supreme Soviet at the I Congress of People's Deputies. He was elected chairman of the sub-committee of the Supreme Soviet committee on industry and energy (1990) and in 1991 chairman of the Supreme Soviet committee on industry and energy. He is a member of the Council of the Republic, and has been awarded the order of the badge of honour and two medals. He is married with two daughters.

Address: 103274 Moscow, K 274, Krasnopresnenskaya nab., d. 2, Dom Sovetov; *telephone*: Moscow 205 43 75.

Erin, Viktor Fedorovich

Minister of Internal Affairs of the Russian Federation.

Born in 1944 in Kazan, Tatarstan into a Russian family. He was a member of the CPSU until July 1991. He entered the service of the agencies of internal affairs in 1964 as a militia man in Kazan. In 1967 he moved to the criminal investigation department of the Ministry of Internal Affairs, Tatar ASSR, and participated in investigating dangerous crimes. In 1973 he graduated from the higher school of the militia, USSR Ministry of Internal Affairs. During 1980 to 1981 he worked in Afghanistan. From 1983 to 1988 he was head of a department of the main administration, USSR Ministry of Internal Affairs. From 1988 to 1990 he was first deputy Minister of Internal Affairs of Armenia. From 1990 he was deputy (head of criminal militia with the rank of general-major) and from February 28, 1991 first deputy Minister of Internal Affairs of the RSFSR.

Erin played a leading role in the suppression of the attempted August coup and was personally involved in the arrests of Boris Pugo, USSR Minister of Internal Affairs, Valentin Pavlov, USSR Prime Minister, and V. Ivanenko, chairman of the RSFSR KGB. In early September 1991, Erin was appointed first deputy Minister of Internal Affairs of the USSR (at that time the USSR and RSFSR Minister of Internal Affairs was Viktor Barannikov). During the autumn of 1991 Erin was involved in a head-on conflict with Gen. A. Gurev, head of the administration for combating organized crime in the USSR Ministry of Internal Affairs, which resulted in Gurev being forced out of the Ministry.

In mid-December 1991 Erin became the first deputy of Viktor Barannikov in the newly constituted Ministry of Security and Internal Affairs of the Russian Federation. He was one of the most active supporters of the unification of the agencies of security and internal affairs, which corresponded with his concept of strong and strict agencies to protect law and order. He was one of the main initiators and drafters of President Yeltsin's decree on the formation of the Russian Ministry of Security and Internal Affairs. However, this decree was greeted with dismay by democrats, who regarded it as a throwback to Stalinist times. It did not pass unnoticed that the last incumbent of the joint ministry was Lavrenty Beria. Opponents regarded the unified ministry as concentrating too much power, during the volatile post-coup period in Russia, in one ministry. The matter was referred to the Constitutional Court and it ruled in January 1992 that the joint ministry was unconstitutional. On January 15, 1992 Erin was appointed Russian Minister of Internal Affairs by presidential decree, with the rank of General-Colonel of internal forces. Erin had been a keen supporter of the exclusion of the CPSU and its organizations from the law-enforcing agencies. He was among the first of the top leadership to quit the CPSU in mid-1991. He enjoys a reputation as a highly skilled professional, with vast experience in the workings of the Russian Ministry of Internal Affairs, and is a specialist in dealing with organized crime. He had promoted new methods for keeping public order and fighting crime, concentrating on crime prevention.

Erin's appointment as Minister was not welcomed by many middle- and lower-ranking officers who supported the outgoing Minister A. Dunaev. When Erin took over he built up a team consisting only of skilled professionals who had long experience in the agencies of the USSR and RSFSR Ministries of Internal Affairs. He remains an optimist concerning the ability of his ministry to cope with the present crime wave and considers that the most important aspects of police work are the protection of the individual and the maintenance of law and order during the period of economic reform. Under his direction a programme for combating crime during 1992 to 1993 was drawn up and presented for discussion to the Russian Supreme Soviet. The goal of the programme was to guarantee within two years the security of the person and property. Most deputies were sceptical of this and regarded the programme as an attempt to extract large resources from the state budget. Erin strongly opposed the transfer of the Ministry's internal troops to a national guard. At the VII Congress of People's Deputies, in December 1992, he spoke after President Yeltsin and stressed that the activities of the law-enforcing agencies were based on the constitution and the laws of Russia. He retained his post under the new Prime Minister, Viktor Chernomyrdin. His fellow officers stress that he is a total professional, without any trace of ideological bias. However, he is regarded as succumbing at times to pedantry and sometimes seeks to carry out orders irrespective of the cost.

He was awarded the order of the Red Star and medals for his work in investigating very dangerous crimes. He lives in Moscow.

Ermolenko, Vitaly Petrovich

Director of the federal centre for land and agroindustrial reform, Russian Federation; Minister.

Born in 1942 in the settlement of Kondratevka, Gorlovsky *raion*, Donets *oblast*, Ukrainian SSR; Ukrainian. He was a member of the CPSU until August 1991. He graduated from the Donetsk Institute of Agriculture, and later successfully presented his candidate dissertation in agricultural sciences (PhD) and his doctoral dissertation in agricultural sciences (DSc). He is a corresponding member of the Russian Academy of Agricultural Sciences. He began his career as an agronomist, then senior agronomist on a collective farm, and later on a state farm (1953-70). He was elected chairman of a collective farm, Aksaisky *raion*, Rostov *oblast* (1970-77). In 1978 he was a appointed director of the Don Scientific Research Institute of Agriculture, Rostov-on-Don; became deputy head of administration of Rostov *oblast* for agrarian problems in 1992; and also in 1992 he became director of the federal centre for land and agroindustrial reform of Russia, with the rank of minister. He lives in Rostov-on-Don and Moscow.

Erofeev, Oleg Aleksandrovich

Commander-in-Chief of the Red Banner Northern Fleet. Admiral since 1992.

Born on July 10, 1949 in Petropavlovsk-Kamchatsky into an air-force officer's family. Russian. He graduated from the S. M. Kirov Caspian Higher Naval Technical school in Baku in 1961 with a navigator's degree; the Naval Academy in 1976; the Military Academy of the General Staff in 1987. He received a higher military education, and became a candidate of military sciences (PhD). He was a member of the CPSU until August 1991.

He began his career as an officer as a commander of a rudder group of a diesel medium submarine. He was notable among other young officers for his devotion to naval service and the sea. He took part in several important combat voyages. In 1963 he was appointed a group commander of a nuclear submarine, and later became commander of a navigation sector there. He participated in long voyages and efficiently carried out complicated tasks of tracking the US and NATO navies. An officer who had demonstrated exceptional command and naval abilities and an experienced submariner, he was sent to continue his education at the Higher Classes for Officers. Later he was an assistant, senior assistant commander and commander of a strategic nuclear submarine. The submarine he commanded frequently carried out its military service patrolling at sea.

After graduating from the Naval Academy he was Chief of Staff and a multi-purpose diesel submarine divisional commander of the Northern Fleet. Oleg Erofeev had a record as one of the most experienced naval commanders who ensured a high level of combat readiness of the troops under his command.

During the period of the communist totalitarian regime he was involved in political activity only to the extent necessary for his career. He was promoted to Chief of Staff of a submarine flotilla of the Pacific fleet and became commander of a submarine flotilla of the Northern Fleet after graduating from the Academy of the General Staff. He mastered the control of six types of nuclear submarines. Under his immediate command were shock nuclear forces of the Northern Fleet, fulfilling strategic tasks. Admiral Erofeev personally participated in long sea and ocean voyages. However, two nuclear submarines under his command were lost.

In 1990 he was appointed Chief of Staff, first deputy Commander-in-Chief of the Northern Fleet. In April 1992, with the rank of Vice-Admiral, he became Commander-in-Chief of the fleet. Under his command are the largest naval alignments of the CIS and Russia in the European theatres of operations and Atlantic direction. He published an article "Here is the basis of Russia's naval strength" in *Krasnaya Zvezda* on June 3, 1992, where he suggested that the main bulk of Russia's navy should be concentrated in the North.

There is no information available on Admiral Erofeev's political views and hobbies. He is married with a daughter, and has been awarded orders and several medals.

Adml Erofeev's headquarters are in Severomorsk.

Evtukhov, Vasyl Ivanovych

Deputy Prime Minister of Ukraine, Head of Industrialists' Faction in the Supreme Soviet and Chairman of the President's Council of Industrialists.

Born into a Ukrainian family in 1948 and educated at Kryvyi Rih Mining Institute. He then worked as an engineer, before rising to become the director of the Kryvyi Rih mining equipment factory, *Kommunist*. He remained a member of the Communist Party until August 24, 1991, but was always something of a technocrat. In March 1990 he was elected on the second round as people's deputy for the Central-City *raion* in the east Ukrainian city of Dnipropetrovsk, not far from Kryvyi Rih.

In the Supreme Soviet he heads the committee on the development of heavy industry, and is therefore an *ex officio* member of the Presidium. He is also head of the so-called industrialists' faction in the Supreme Soviet who consist mainly of managers of state industry, which has the support of 67 deputies. In 1991 these deputies provided key support to the national communist group led by Leonid Kravchuk, whilst Evtukhov himself acted as one of the crucial bridges between Kravchuk's group and the former opposition, particularly on the Presidium.

After the Ukrainian Declaration of Independence in August 1991, Evtukhov founded the Union of Manufacturers and Industrialists in autumn 1991. Although this group supported Kravchuk's election campaign, it was one of the founder members of the *New Ukraine* movement in January 1992, with

Evtukhov being a signatory to its founding declaration calling for a speedy path to a market economy. Evtukhov was elected to the *New Ukraine* secretariat (in ninth place, with 169 votes) at the movement's founding congress in June 1992. He kept a foot in both camps, however.

In May 1992 he was appointed by Kravchuk to head a presidential Council of Industrialists and Businessmen that would advise him on economic and industrial policy. He was instrumental in pushing the candidature of Leonid Kuchma as Ukraine's new Prime Minister in October 1992, and in the new government received the position of Deputy Premier with special responsibility for industry and development. In April 1993 he was appointed to head the commission for the deported nations of the Crimea.

Official address: Kiev, Vul. M. Hrushevskoho 5; *telephone*: Kiev 252 019.

Fadeev, Gennady Matveevich

Russian Minister of Railways.

Born on April 10, 1937 in Shimanovska, Amur *oblast* into a Russian family. He was a member of the CPSU until August 1991. He graduated from the Khabarovsk Institute for Railway Engineers and in 1961 he became an assistant station master in Taishet on the east Siberian railway. During the following two years he was a transport controller, assistant station-master, senior assistant station-master and chief engineer at Taishet.

In 1963 he was appointed deputy head, and later head of the traffic department of the Nizhneudinsky section of the east Siberian railway. During the next ten years he headed the railway collectives of the Nizhneudinsky (Taishet) and Krasnoyarsk section of the east Siberian railway. In 1977 he became first deputy head and from 1979 to 1984 head of the Krasnoyarsk railway, and from 1984-87 he was head of the collective of the Oktyabrsky railway. From 1987 he worked in the central apparatus of the USSR Ministry of Railways. He became a deputy USSR Minister and head of the main administration for the transport of goods in the ministry.

He was elected a deputy of the RSFSR Supreme Soviet in 1984, of the Krasnoyarsk *krai* soviet of people's deputies between 1975 and 1984, a member of the bureau of the Krasnoyarsk Party *krai* committee (*kraikom*) between 1981 and 1984 and a delegate to the XXVI Party Congress by the Krasnoyarsk *krai* Party organization. In early 1990 he was nominated for election as an RSFSR people's deputy in the No. 19 national territorial district, Krasnoyarsk *krai* by five work collectives in the area. During the election campaign he advocated the transfer of all power to the soviets, the strengthening of the state sovereignty of Russia, legal and social protection of citizens, the introduction of republican and regional cost accounting (*khozraschet*), the amelioration of the economy by technical re-equipping and modernization of the railways, the full satisfaction of the demand for railway places by the population and each enterprise to meet its contractual obligations for the delivery of raw materials and equipment on time.

There were 11 candidates. Fadeev polled 18.6% of the votes in the first round and won the second round with 48.7% of the votes. His main opponent was N. A. Adamsky, a captain of the Eneseilesoeksport floating timber concern. He received 7.1% of the votes in the first round and 35.6% in the second. Fadeev was elected to the Russian Supreme Soviet at the I Congress of People's Deputies on June 11, 1990. He became a member of the Supreme Soviet of Nationalities commission on the economic and social development of the autonomous republics, autonomous *oblasts*, autonomous *okrugs* and small nations. In December 1990 he joined the Extraordinary Commission on food.

In January 1992 he was appointed Russian Minister of Railways. Among the main tasks of the ministry he highlights the social security of railway workers, improving the railway tracks so that they can take more traffic, and the building of a fast line from Moscow to St Petersburg. The future belongs to such new lines.

He has been awarded the orders of the October Revolution, the Red Banner of Labour, the badge of honour and many medals, and was awarded the badge of honoured railwayman twice. His wife is a teacher and they have two grown-up daughters, one of whom is a doctor and the other a railway worker. There are two granddaughters. Fadeev lives in Moscow.

Fadeev, Nikolai Sergeevich

Russian Orthodox metropolitan of Tula and Belev (Serapion).

Born on May 27, 1933 in Moscow, where his father was an office worker; Russian. He graduated in 1966 from the ecclesiastical academy, Moscow, and then became a postgraduate student until 1969. From 1969 to 1971 he was a specialist in the department for external church relations, Moscow Patriarchate, and was then the representative of the Russian Orthodox Church in the Antioch Patriarchate, Syria (1971-74). In 1975 he was appointed bishop and administrator of the Irkutsk diocese, and in 1982 was elevated to archbishop and administrator of the Vladimir diocese. In 1990 he became metropolitan and administrator of the Tula and Belev diocese.

Address: Tula, ul. Zhukovskogo 61; *telephone*: Moscow 235 0454; 230 2118; 230 2431.

Fateev, Valery Petrovich

Head of the Administration of Smolensk *oblast*, Russian Federation.

Born in 1946 in Pavlovo, Gorky (Nizhny Novgorod) *oblast*, into a civil servant's family. After completing secondary school in 1964 he entered the faculty of physics, N. I. Lobachevsky State University, Gorky. In 1969 he began working in the experimental factory of the Sapfir Scientific Research Institute, Bolkhov, Orlov *oblast*, first as an engineer, then as head of a shop and head of the planned production department. In 1976 he entered the faculty of economics at the all-Union extra-mural Institute of Finance and Economics. From 1976 to 1989 was deputy chief engineer in the Vyazemsky branch of the Moscow projector factory. In 1988 he successfully presented his candidate dissertation in economics on "Improving the the use of labour in small series production" (for example, in the enterprises of the electrical engineering industry) (PhD (Econ)).

In early 1989 Fateev was nominated for election as a USSR people's deputy but the district electoral commission refused to accept him as a candidate after he had received only 150 votes out of 431 in the district assembly of electors. In April 1989 he was appointed director of the Vyazma linen combine. He was a member of the CPSU until August 1991 and was a member of the Party bureau, deputy chairman of the council of the work collective, Vyazma linen combine, head of the school of propagandists and chairman of the soviet of the Leninsky microraion, Vyazma.

In early 1990 he was nominated for election as an RSFSR people's deputy in the No. 684 Vyazma territorial district, Smolensk *oblast*, by the work collective of the Vyazma linen combine. The district electoral commission only accepted Fateev as a candidate under pressure from the work collective who threatened to strike if he were not accepted. During the election campaign he advocated full cost accounting for enterprises and regions, the establishment of firm norms for contributions into the all-Union budget, and the introduction of leasing in the various branches of the economy. He called for the establishment of a *Rechtsstaat* (rule of law) in Russia, based on political pluralism and the adoption of laws on land, property, local self-government, enterprises, the economic autonomy of Russia and the press.

There were five candidates. Fateev polled 29.8% of the votes in the first round but lost the second round, polling 40.9% of the votes. His main opponent was A. I. Orlov, chairman of the Smolensk *oblast* soviet executive committee who received 26.3% of the votes in the first round and won the second round, receiving 49.77% of the votes.

In November 1991 Fateev was appointed head of the administration of Smolensk *oblast* by presidential decree, and is deputy chairman of the union of governors of Russia. In December 1992 he viewed the results of the VII Congress of People's Deputies as a defeat for the supporters of reform. The removal of Gaidar revealed the weakness of the President and the influence over him of certain political circles. He regretted the resignation from the government of experienced professionals and feared for the fate of reform after the statements by Viktor Chernomyrdin, the new Prime Minister, at the congress. However, he declared his willingness to work on the basis of reasonable compromises with any government. He lives in Smolensk.

Fedorov, Boris Grigorevich

Deputy Prime Minister of the Russian Federation.

Born in 1958 in Moscow into a Russian family, and was a member of the CPSU until August 1991. According to him he became a member of the Party to further his career and was never committed to its ideology; he estimated that about 20% of Party members were convinced supporters. He graduated from the Moscow finance institute and then joined the main department for currency and economy of the USSR Central Bank as an economist. He later became chief economist and while there, in 1985, successfully presented his candidate dissertation in economics on the "organization and economic role of present day short term exchange trading in developed capitalist countries" (PhD (Econ)). From 1987 to 1990 he was a senior research member of the institute of world economy and international relations of the USSR Academy of Sciences.

In 1990 he successfully presented his doctoral dissertation in economics on the "loan capital market in the economies of developed capitalism" (DSc (Econ)). He also acted as consultant to the socio-economic department of the Party Central Committee. He became a member of the group around Academicians Shatalin and Petrakov and Grigory Yavlinsky who drafted the 500-day economic programme in the summer of 1990. This programme envisaged a transition in the Soviet Union from a planned to a market economy in 500 days. President Mikhail Gorbachev declined to endorse it in the autumn of 1990. In July 1990 Fedorov became RSFSR Minister of Finance in the government headed by Ivan Silaev. However, he resigned in December 1990 because of the lack of commitment of the Silaev government to market reform. In 1991 he became Russian representative in the European Bank for Reconstruction and Development (EBRD) in London and played an important role in framing the bank's policy towards Russia and the successor states of the Soviet Union. He gained valuable experience at the EBRD in macroeconomic policy and financial services. Russians liked to refer to him as "their man in the City". He turned down the opportunity to become chairman of the Russian Central Bank, believing that as it was subordinate to the Russian parliament his room for manoeuvre would be limited. He also acted as executive director of the Russian Federation in the International Bank of Reconstruction and Development in Washington. He is a fluent English speaker, partly gained from his postgraduate studies at the University of London.

He is the author of a Russian-English dictionary of currency and credit terminology. An able economist, he supports the concept of "shock therapy" so as to move Russia to a market economy as quickly as possible. After the failure of Egor Gaidar to be confirmed as Prime Minister at the VII Congress of People's Deputies in December 1992, the road was open for a pro-reform economist to enter the government to oversee the reform process. Viktor Chernomyrdin, the new Prime Minister, accepted Fedorov as his deputy responsible for macroeconomic reform and finance, and this was a great boost for the economic reform lobby. Fedorov quickly established himself as the main decision-maker on economic affairs and proposed economic reforms in March 1993 which were severe but offered some concessions to the population and the regions. In March 1993 Fedorov was also appointed Russian Minister of Finance, succeeding Vasily Barchuk. A battle developed between him and Viktor Gerashchenko, head of the Russian Central Bank, over monetary policy. Fedorov was determined to bring the bank under government control. The Democratic Russia (DemRossiya) Movement warmly welcomed Fedorov's appointment and offered its support. Fedorov regards the battle against inflation as a major priority and envisages new currency mechanisms and monetary policy based on a freely convertible currency. Enterprise should be free to enter foreign markets and to trade without hindrance. He lives in Moscow.

Fedorov, Nikolai Vasilevich

Russian Minister of Justice.

Born on May 9, 1958 in the village of Chedino, Marinsko-Posadsky *raion*, Chuvash republic into a peasant family. Chuvash. He was a member of the CPSU until August 1991. In 1980 he graduated from the faculty of law of the Chuvash State University, and then joined the faculty as an assistant. He began postgraduate studies at the USSR Institute of State and Law in 1982 and in 1985 he successfully presented his candidate dissertation on the "legal policy of the Soviet government (questions of history, theory and practice)", and became a candidate of juridical sciences (LLM). From 1985 to 1989 he was first lecturer, then senior lecturer in the faculty of scientific communism at the Chuvash State University, where he began work on his doctoral dissertation. In March 1989 he was elected to the USSR Congress of People's Deputies for the Moscow national-territorial district, Cheboksary, Chuvash republic.

He was elected a member of the USSR Supreme Soviet, the standing parliament, and joined the interregional group of deputies. He chaired one of the sub-committees of the USSR Supreme Soviet committee on legislation, law and order. At the II USSR Congress of People's Deputies he voted against the programme of the government headed by Nikolai Ryzhkov and against the amendment of part 2 of article 95 of the USSR constitution which permitted the election of some deputies from among public organizations. He also did not vote for the amendment, proposed by N. Reshetova, to restrict the suffrage of certain groups of persons, but he did vote for the removal of article 6 from the USSR Constitution which guaranteed the CPSU the leading role in society.

At the IV USSR Congress of People's Deputies he voted against the retention of the name of Soviet government and against the decree on the referendum about private ownership of land which had been proposed so as to hold up agricultural reform. He did not support the draft congress decree for a moratorium on strikes in 1991. During 1989 to 1990 Fedorov took part in the drafting of many democratic laws, including the law on the press. His decisive interventions helped to overcome the opposition of the higher levels of the Party *nomenklatura* which was using every means to halt the draft law. Fedorov was summoned to the Party Central Committee where attempts were made to put pressure on him. He also helped to draft the law on the rights and duties of the internal forces of the USSR Ministry of Internal Affairs.

In 1990 Fedorov declined an invitation by President Mikhail Gorbachev to become a member of the USSR Supreme Soviet commission to revise the USSR constitution, declaring that he wished to "concern himself with real politics". In July 1990 Fedorov was appointed RSFSR Minister of Justice in the government being formed by Ivan Silaev, and then called on the Supreme Soviet to agree a "real division of powers, freedom for the judicial and investigative agencies and the complete elimination of bureaucratic barriers". He left the CPSU just before the attempted putsch of August 1991. When the putsch occurred he was in his constituency in Cheboksary and immediately addressed city-dwellers and attacked the Extraordinary Committee. In September 1991 he took part in the campaign to remove Ivan Silaev as Russian Prime Minister.

In November 1991 he was made Minister of Justice in the Russian "reform government", when he declared he was going to fight and referred to the new government as the "Kamikaze government". As the minister responsible he always insisted on the forced repatriation of Erich Honecker, the former GDR leader, to face charges in a Berlin court. He was deeply involved in the drafting of the new Russian criminal code which was presented to the Russian Supreme Soviet in January 1992. The main features of the code were the introduction of international legal norms in human rights, the use of the death penalty and the introduction of new articles about the introduction of a market economy. Fedorov became a member of the state council of the Russian President.

He called the newly established state-political administration of Russia, headed by Sergei Shakhrai, "an unusual phenomenon in a system of state power" and criticized the administration's first draft law "on criminal responsibility for deliberately failing to implement RSFSR laws" as wild, and thought that the activities of the administration could lead to a "paralysis of power". The transfer of several departments of the Ministry of Justice, responsible for drafting laws, to the administration led to sharp conflict between Fedorov and Shakhrai, and Fedorov threatened to resign over the issue. Fedorov regards the creation of a strong independent judiciary as a major task, but this involves more resources from the budget permitting training of new and better qualified judges.

New legislation is of crucial importance. He has completed some and is working on other items of draft legislation on citizenship, taxation and combating crime. The judicial system is being reformed and he was the driving force behind the transfer of Party buildings to the courts after August 1991. The position of lawyers and notaries public is being reformed. In January 1992 he opposed the decree of the Russian President creating a joint Ministry of Security and Internal Affairs and protested to the Constitutional Court. The latter ruled the new ministry unconstitutional.

Fedorov is married with two children, and lives in Moscow. He speaks German and Chuvash. He likes the theatre and classical music, and used to like popular music. He loves sport, was previously a professional boxer and still enjoys karate and chess.

Fedorov, Svyatoslav Nikolaevich

Co-Chairman of the Party of Economic Freedom of the Russian Federation.

Born on August 8, 1927 in Leningrad (St Petersburg). His father was a former worker in the Putilov factory and became a commander during the Civil War (1918-21). He is Russian and was a member of the CPSU until August 1991. His father was arrested in 1938 and sentenced to 17 years in a labour camp. At the age of 17 Fedorov lost a leg which led him to think about studying medicine, and he graduated from a medical institute. Until 1960 he worked in Cheboksary, in a branch of the Gelmgolts State Institute of Eye Diseases, and successfully presented his candidate dissertation in medicine (MD). In 1960 he performed the first experimental operation to implant an artificial crystal into the human eye which had never been tried before in the Soviet Union or abroad. The local newspaper reported the extraordinary operation and this was reprinted in several central newspapers. In the article Fedorov was incorrectly identified as the director of the Cheboksary branch and this led to a conflict with the actual director, F. I. Purshev. Fedorov was sent off on a long trip and on his return was sacked from the institute. His laboratory was closed down and his research declared unscientific. Thanks to the intervention of the newspaper *Izvestiya* and its author, the well-known journalist A. Agranovsky, Fedorov was reinstated in the Cheboksary branch. However, the same year he applied for the vacant post of head of department of eye diseases in the Arkhangelsk Medical Institute, and became an assistant professor there.

Fedorov continued his experiments on implanting artificial plastic crystals and then silicon crystals, and by 1965 he had performed 62 such operations. He encountered quite a lot of opposition from the leading members of medical science and especially critical of his experiments was V. N. Arkhangelsky, the then chairman of the USSR opthamological society, the chief oculist of the USSR Ministry of Health, editor-in-chief of the journal *Vestnik oftalmologii*, and corresponding member of the USSR Academy of Sciences.

In the specialized literature Fedorov's method was dismissed as mechanical, anti-physiological and anti-Pavlovian. However, due to the support of the Arkhangelsky Medical Institute, the *oblast* Party committee and Arkhangelsk soviet executive committee his laboratory continued functioning. In February 1965 Fedorov's research was approved by the council on the co-ordination of scientific research work of the USSR Ministry of Health and was included in the plan of one of the scientific research institutes. It was possible for

Fedorov to open a special laboratory devoted to these problems, first of all in Arkhangelsk and then in Moscow in one of the opthamological departments of one of the city hospitals. In 1975, in Beskudnikovo *raion*, Moscow, Fedorov was apportioned a piece of land on which to build a special clinic. In 1980, the centre of microsurgery of the eye was established in this clinic. In 1986 Fedorov met Nikolai Ryzhkov, the Soviet Prime Minister, and made a great impression on him. With Ryzhkov's support, in 1988, by a joint decree of the Party Central Committee and the USSR Council of Ministers, the centre was transformed into an inter-branch scientific research complex for eye microsurgery and Fedorov became its director. The complex included two factories, optical and experimental equipment, a clinic with 600 beds and branches in Khabarovsk, Irkutsk, Novosibirsk, Ekaterinburg, Orenburg, Volgograd, Tambov, Kaluga, Krasnodar, St Petersburg, and a foreign trade firm, an agricultural complex, a hotel and a commercial bank with foundation capital of 25 million (1991) rubles. A clinic was also opened in the United Arab Emirates and a diagnostic centre in Italy. In June 1992 the annual income of the institute was 120 million rubles. The staff of the Moscow clinic participated in the profits and Fedorov's share was 0.6%.

He is an academician of the Russian Academy of Medical Sciences and a hero of socialist labour. From 1988 to 1990 he was chairman of the all-Union fund of mercy and health. In March 1989 he was elected a USSR people's deputy, as a nominee of the CPSU, and at the I Congress of People's Deputies a member of the USSR Supreme Soviet. On June 14, 1990, at the I RSFSR congress of the union of lessees and entrepreneurs, Fedorov was elected president. In August 1991, during the attempted anti-constitutional coup, Fedorov ordered mobile medical equipment and cars of food to be sent to the Russian White House. During the autumn of 1991 Fedorov was regarded as a candidate for the post of RSFSR Prime Minister.

In the spring of 1992 he was one of the founders of the Party of Economic Freedom of the Russian Federation (PEF) and in May 1992 became its co-chairman. In August 1992 the consultative council of the PEF nominated him for election as the mayor of Moscow but he withdrew before voting took place. In December 1992, at the I congress of the PEF, K. N. Borovoi, V. B. Zolotarev and he were elected co-chairmen.

He is married and lives in Moscow. As a young man he loved the novels of Maupassant, Balzac, Dumas and Dreiser. He skied, swam and attained the first rank in chess.

Fedorov, Valentin Petrovich

Head of the Administration of Sakhalin *oblast* or Governor (*gubernator*) of Sakhalin.

Born September 6, 1939 in Yakutsk, where his father worked on the waterways. Russian. He grew up in Sakha-Yakutia, and was a member of the CPSU until August 1991. In 1957 he completed secondary school in the village of Zhatai and received a gold medal. He graduated from Moscow Plekhanov Institute of the National Economy in 1962, and then began working in Gosplan in the Yakut autonomous republic. Later he began postgraduate studies and in 1968 successfully presented his candidate dissertation in economics in the Institute of World Economics and International Relations, USSR Academy of Sciences, on the socio-economic structure of personal consumption in the Federal Republic of Germany (PhD (Econ)). He was on the staff of the Institute until 1985.

In 1977 he successfully presented his doctoral dissertation in economics on the problems of the production of national capital in the present world economy (based on the Federal Republic of Germany) (DSc (Econ)). While still on the staff of the Institute of World Economics and International Relations he worked in the Federal Republic of Germany (1978-84). In 1985 he moved to the G. V. Plekhanov institute of the national economy, Moscow, where he was pro-rector and head of the department of political economy, and also professor. He has been a corresponding member of the RSFSR Academy of Social Sciences since 1990, and doctor of business of Loyola Jesuit University, Los Angeles, 1991. He is the author of six books on the market economy which provide an incisive analysis of "rotting" capitalism and its future demise.

In April 1991 he was elected chairman of the executive committee of the Sakhalin *oblast* soviet of people's deputies. On October 8, 1991 RSFSR President Yeltsin appointed him head of the administration of the *oblast*. On October 14, 1991 by decree No. 1 he proclaimed himself governor of the *oblast* and by instruction No. 1 appointed seven vice-governors.

On February 15, 1992 he was elected co-chairman of the *Duma* of the Russian national assembly. He was a member of the USSR Union of Journalists, and in March 1990 he was nominated for election to the RSFSR Congress of People's Deputies in the No. 71 Sakhalin territorial district. During the election programme he advocated a territorial economic experiment in Sakhalin which involved all enterprises and individuals being granted freedom of economic activity. The goal of the exercise was to raise the standard of living of those living in Sakhalin. He is a vigorous supporter of the market economy.

There were 10 candidates. In the first round Fedorov polled 12.7% of the votes and won the second round, polling 47.78% of the votes. His main opponent was Bok Zi Koi, head of the department of philosophy and political economy at the South Sakhalin State Pedagogical Institute, who received 17.65% of the votes in the first round and 39.07% of the votes in the second. Fedorov is a member of the Russian Supreme Soviet committee on inter-republican relations, regional policy and co-operation. He is a member of the *Otchizna* (Motherland) deputies' group, the co-ordinator of which is General Boris Tarasov.

Despite the decree of the I RSFSR Congress of People's Deputies on the mechanism of people's power and two decrees of the Presidium of the RSFSR Supreme Soviet (January and March 1991), Fedorov became a member of the leadership of the Sakhalin CPSU *oblast* committee and remained until the suppression of the attempted coup. Fedorov's rise began in 1988 when he first visited Sakhalin and saw it as a launch pad for a career in Moscow.

Circumstances favoured him as there was a political vacuum in Sakhalin due to *perestroika*, the population was discontented with the local leadership and there was no dominant Party politician in the vicinity.

In the *oblast* there was only one centre of higher education (a pedagogical institute), one newspaper and a very thin layer of the intelligentsia. The locals were in awe of his expertise in economics, an unknown discipline there, and his qualifications, but a disadvantage was his lack of contacts in the local bureaucracy. His concept of a zone of free enterprise was seductive and promised economic and administrative changes and an improvement in living standards. During the election Fedorov was supported by the popular front and the democratic union. The democratic elections club (similar to Democratic Russia) in the beginning remained neutral, but during elections for chairman of the soviet executive committee in April 1990 it proposed and supported Fedorov's candidacy. Politically he is on the side of the winners: "If there is a military coup and a totalitarian regime, I shall keep my position"; "If martial law is introduced, I shall not be satisfied with the rank of colonel, I shall be a general" (*Nezavisimaya gazeta*, March 7, 1991).

On August 19, 1991 he issued a declaration stating that a power struggle was going on in Moscow and that those in Sakhalin should look after their own affairs. He played a double game. He forecast that after the coup the democrats would change their colours, and then to balance this he gave an interview in Khabarovsk condemning the activities of the Extraordinary Committee. He sent a telegram to the soviet executive committee following the instructions of the Extraordinary Committee. On August 21, 1991 he called on all citizens in Sakhalin to support the legally elected President, Supreme Soviet and Council of Ministers of the RSFSR. He was the first leader in the Far East region who condemned the Extraordinary Committee and supported all the decrees of President Yeltsin.

He takes a very independent line towards federal authorities. When he proclaimed himself governor he added, "Soviet power has ended". Politically he is very ambitious and, on March 7, 1991 in *Nezavisimaya gazeta*, regarded himself as number three after Gorbachev and Yeltsin: "I am not 100% for Gorbachev. I am 100% for Fedorov". He published his economic proposals in *Rabochaya Tribuna* on March 20, 1991. The first principle was to establish a parallel economic structure: new forms, new firms and new farms. The second was the very careful dismantling of the old economic structures, which would take 10 years, not 500 days. The third principle was that development should originate with domestic producers and not with foreign firms.

At present Fedorov's concepts add up to the economic programme of the Russian national assembly, and since assuming power in the spring of 1991 Fedorov has not come up with any concrete plan for change. Cosmetic change is the order of the day. In January 1991 the trade administration was abolished and replaced in November by the budgetary commercial department of the administration of the *oblast* with almost the same functions. He is in conflict with Moscow over the results of the tenders to develop the continental shelf around Sakhalin. The Russian government favoured the Japanese company Mitsui, but Fedorov preferred the South Korean-US enterprise Palimco, which has nine employees and trades in coal and rice. He has control of a fund which disburses financial aid to companies in Sakhalin, and he personally regulates the foreign visits of all businessmen, irrespective of the type of property. This is even more severe than the regulations of 1989 imposed by Nikolai Ryzhkov, the Soviet Prime Minister.

He is a gifted propagandist and addresses the people of Sakhalin weekly by radio. He normally gives at least one interview a day, and when he is away from Sakhalin recorded interviews are recycled. On the Kurile islands he has developed a reputation as the strongest opponent of their transfer to Japan. However, he has also said that it is conceivable that the islands of Habomai and Shikotan could be returned. In November 1992, on the eve of the VII Russian Congress of People's Deputies, he appealed to those people's deputies who supported President Yeltsin to come to his aid and to boycott the Congress in December 1992.

He is short of stature, bald, decisive in movement and deeds. He has an excellent memory and is a gifted speaker, being especially good at monologues. He has the reputation of being vindictive: "It is difficult with me in control but worse without me". He is married with two children. The family continues to live in Moscow, while he lives in Yuzhno-Sakhalinsk.

Fedotov, Mikhail Aleksandrovich

Russian Minister of the Press and Information.

Born in 1949 in Moscow into a Russian family. He was a member of the CPSU until August 1991. He graduated from the law faculty of Moscow State University and after graduation began postgraduate studies, successfully presenting his candidate dissertation on the freedom of the press, the constitutional right of Soviet citizens (LLM) in 1976. In 1984 he successfully presented his doctoral dissertation on the mass media as an institution of socialist democracy (state legal problems) (LLD). Until September 1990 he taught in the Moscow Law Institute and was a professor.

In 1989 he was a member of groups preparing a new legislative basis for the activities of the press and other parts of the media and was one of the authors of the USSR law on the press and mass media, on public associations, and the Russian Federation law on the media. In the autumn of 1990 he was appointed deputy RSFSR Minister of the Press and Information when Mikhail Poltoranin was minister. He later became head of the Russian agency for intellectual property. In December 1992 he was appointed Russian Minister of Press and Information in the new Chernomyrdin government. His predecessor, Poltoranin, had been one of the principal targets for criticism of the opposition in parliament as he had adopted an abrasive style and President Yeltsin was obliged to sacrifice him.

The main tasks of Fedotov's ministry now are to move from the battle for *glasnost* and freedom of expression to guaranteeing the further existence of the press. The government needs to support the press, irrespective of its political orientation, so as not to limit its freedom. He believes that the press should reflect all views in society. He is married with two children and lives in Moscow.

Filaret, Metropolitan

Leader of the Ukrainian Orthodox Church (Kievan Patriarchy).

Filaret was born Mikhail Denisenko in 1929 in the village of Blahodatnoye in Donetsk *oblast*. He received his religious training first at the Odesa seminary and then at Moscow Religious Academy before taking up his orders in 1950. He first worked as a teacher at the Academy, before being appointed inspector of the Saratov seminary in 1956 and of the Kiev seminary in 1957. In 1960 he was promoted to the position of Chief of Staff of the Ukrainian exarchate. After a spell as head of a Russian Orthodox Church (ROC) mission to Egypt from 1961 to 1962 he was appointed firstly Bishop of Luga and then of Dmitrov, before returning to Ukraine as Archbishop of Kiev and Galicia in 1966.

Two years later he received the title of Metropolitan and a permanent seat on the Holy Synod. In the late 1980s the dominance of the ROC in Ukraine began to be challenged by the revival of both the Uniate Catholic Church, forcibly incorporated into the ROC in 1946, and the Ukrainian Autocephalous (Independent) Orthodox Church (UAOC) suppressed in 1930. The ROC hierarchy was particularly worried by the challenge of the UAOC, and in 1990 Filaret was made Exarch of all Ukraine, and certain cosmetic steps were taken towards the Ukrainianization of the Church.

Filaret was in a poor position to lead such a transformation, however. Like most senior ROC bishops he had been compromised by the KGB. Filaret has two daughters and a son by his supposedly secret marriage to Evgeniya Rodionova, and, as a loyal servant of Moscow, has long been distrusted. He desperately wanted to succeed the ROC's Patriarch Pimen in 1990, but in retrospect his failure to do so forced him to begin the process of reorienting himself away from Moscow. By spring 1992, although the old ROC retained 5,500 churches in Ukraine, it was under increasing pressure from the Uniates in west Ukraine with 2,700 churches, and the UAOC with 1,500.

Filaret came under increasing pressure from President Kravchuk and Ukraine's other national communist rulers to make the same leap they had done and establish a truly national church. The turning-point came in March-April 1992 when the Moscow Synod tried to force Filaret's resignation, forcing him finally to jump ship. In June 1992 Filaret accepted a merger with the UAOC led by the exiled Patriarch Mstyslav to create a new Ukrainian Orthodox Church (Kievan Patriarchy). Mstyslav became head, and Filaret his deputy. After the initial euphoria however, it became clear that Filaret could not deliver all of the old Ukrainian ROC's churches, priests and resources to the UAOC.

Kiev's Pechersk monastery in particular refused to join. Many in the UAOC continued to be alienated by his high-handed behaviour, and his willingness to allow his religious ceremonies to be guarded by the Ukrainian nationalist paramilitary group, UNSO. In November 1992 Mstyslav was publicly critical of Filaret, and the possibility remains that he might be removed in favour of Metropolitan Volodymyr.

Official address: Kiev, Sv. Sofia, Ploshcha Bohdana Khmelnytskoho.

Filatov, Sergei Aleksandrovich

Chief of Staff, Head of the Administration of the Russian President.

Born on July 10. 1936 in Moscow; Russian; Member of the CPSU until 1991. He started work in 1955 after leaving the Metallurgical Technical Secondary School, Moscow, in the Hammer and Sickle plant, first as an apprentice electrician in a rolling shop, then as a designer in the design department. He was secretary of the *Komsomol* committee in the factory. He entered the Institute of Energy, Moscow, in 1959 and graduated in 1964. He was a power generation specialist at the José Marti metallurgical plant in Cuba (1966-68). In 1969 he began working in the A. I. Tselikov all-Union scientific research and project design institute of metallurgical machine building, where he was an engineer and head of a department. In 1984 he successfully presented his candidate dissertation in technical sciences (PhD (Eng)), and in 1986 he became head of a new department of management using machines and processes of continuous casting. He is a state prize winner in technology and is the author of over 50 scientific articles.

In January 1990 he was nominated for election as an RSFSR people's deputy in the No. 24 Kuzminsky territorial district, Volgogradsky *raion*, Moscow. Two candidates stood for election and Filatov won in the first round, polling 51.64% of the votes. His opponent was V. K. Belyaninov, secretary of the Moscow Party city committee (*gorkom*), who received 28.39% of the votes. During the elections Filatov was supported by the Democratic Russia 90 bloc. Immediately after his election he played an active part in convening the I Congress of People's Deputies and became a member of various conciliation commissions bringing together the various blocs of deputies. He was a staunch supporter of Boris Yeltsin.

At the I Congress of People's Deputies he was elected to the RSFSR Supreme Soviet. In January 1991 he became secretary of the Presidium of the Supreme Soviet and there headed the staff preparing the Russian presidential elections.

In August 1991 he co-ordinated the activity of the groups of deputies, organizing work in the military units, the agencies of power, established contacts with parties and movements, provided groups of deputies with transport and communications and led the construction of barricades. He was chief of staff of the deputies. At the V Congress of People's Deputies in November 1991 he was elected first deputy Speaker and Ruslan Khasbulatov was the Speaker. Filatov was a member of the council of security and a representative of Democratic Russia (DemRossiya).

Filatov's differences of opinion with Khasbulatov began after the VI Congress of People's Deputies when he took upon himself the task of mediator between parliament and government. In the conflict between the Speaker and the newspaper *Izvestiya* when parliament attempted to take it over, Filatov supported *Izvestiya*. In August 1992 he was effectively removed from his position in violation of the parliamentary regulations. On January 19, 1993 he was appointed chief of staff of the President.

Filatov regards the primary task of the parliament to be the adoption of a new constitution, as the present constitution prevents radical initiatives. In his speeches he stresses that in the present economic crisis those forces which are responsible for the present poor state of the economy are uniting. The *nomenklatura* is combining and fusing from two directions: through penetrating the government apparatus and through setting up various political parties based on the CPSU. Only national accord can overcome the present difficult position. The people should be asked to freeze all political struggle for five years, otherwise reforms will not be implemented and there will be no way of avoiding human sacrifices. He advocates that representative and executive powers be delineated and that their relationship should be laid down in the constitution.

In December 1992 he stated that Russian people's deputies had changed their colours. They were not prepared to engage in constructive work and those deputies who did most to prevent legislation became well known, not the drafters of the laws. The VI and VII congresses were aggressively against the government and the course of the reforms. Whereas there was a desire by the Presidium of the Supreme Soviet to achieve a compromise, this was not evident at the VII congress. Nevertheless a Prime Minister was confirmed and a referendum became possible.

As head of the administration of the President, Filatov does not regard himself merely as a bureaucrat but as someone who supports the political stance of the President by providing effective programmes, scientific concepts and full and valuable information. He is opposed to a purge of the apparatus as experienced bureaucrats with high professional qualifications and good business skills are needed. Nevertheless in some posts there should be officials whose political views coincide with those of the President, and this is especially true of his advisers and those who are involved in shaping presidential policy. Analytical centres on general policy, socio-economic policy and special presidential programmes should be established. He advocates that more intellectual talent be attracted, the apparatus should be pruned, links established with authoritative scientific centres and an information service on current developments set up. He lives in Moscow.

Filenko, Volodymyr Pylypovych

Leader of the Party of Democratic Revival of Ukraine and Chairman of *New Ukraine* Secretariat.

Born into a Ukrainian family in Kharkiv *oblast* in 1955. His mother was a collective farm worker, and his father worked in a factory in Kharkiv. He graduated from the faculty of history, Kharkiv State University, in 1977, and then worked for two years as a history teacher in a secondary school. After 1979 he worked in the *Komsomol*, and in the army as a political worker, and then for five years as a Communist Party of Ukraine (CPU) secretary on a state farm. However, from 1989 to 1990 he gravitated towards the Democratic Platform of the CPU.

In March 1990 he was elected people's deputy for Hotvaldivskyi *raion*, Kharkiv *oblast* (on the second round), and in the Supreme Soviet from April 1990 he served as head of the (originally 43-strong) faction of the Democratic Platform, which after December 1990 became the Party of Democratic Revival of Ukraine (PDRU). He also served as Deputy Head of the People's Council opposition faction until its *de facto* collapse in December 1991. He is also Secretary of the Supreme Soviet's Committee on Human Rights.

He left the CPU in July 1990. In December 1990 he was elected one of the co-leaders of the PDRU, a position which he retained at the PDRU's second and third congresses in June 1991 and May 1992. He was one of the key driving forces behind the creation of the *New Ukraine* coalition, serving as the chairman of its parliamentary faction of 52 from February 1992, and as head of the *New Ukraine* secretariat, a position confirmed at the movement's first congress in June 1992.

Filenko is an excellent party organizer, and his diligent work in building up the *New Ukraine* group into the best-organized faction in the Supreme Soviet was rewarded in October 1992, when so many of its members joined the new Kuchma government (Filenko saw himself as still too young to be a minister). Filenko supports that wing of the PDRU and *New Ukraine* that favours a radical line on economic reform, but at the same time strongly supports Ukrainian independence. On the other hand he strongly favours the maintenance of friendly links with Russia and opposes radical nationalists like Stepan Khmara.

Filenko grew increasingly disgruntled with those of his colleagues, such as Vladimir Griniov and Volodymyr Lanovyi, whom he considered to be excessively critical of the new Kuchma government, and in March 1993 he resigned as chairman of the *New Ukraine* movement to concentrate on his work in the Supreme Soviet (he was replaced by Griniov).

Home telephone: Kiev 293 8202.

Filipenko, Aleksandr Vasilevich

Head of the Administration of Khanty Mansy Autonomous *okrug*, Russian Federation.

Born in 1950 in Karaganda, Kazakhstan; member of the CPSU until August 1991. He began his working career as a tuner of radio equipment in the Kirov enterprise, Petropavlovsk, north Kazakhstan *oblast*. He is a qualified bridge building engineer and is also a graduate in the humanities. He was foreman construction engineer, engineer, senior engineer in the No. 442 bridge production association, Surgut, west Siberia, and afterwards was an instructor, head of department of construction, Khanty Mansy *okrug* Party committee.

He began working in the Khanty Mansy *okrug* soviet executive committee in 1982 as first deputy chairman, then he was elected first secretary of the Berezovsky *raion* Party committee and later second secretary of the *okrug* Party committee. In March 1989 he became chairman of Khanty Mansy *okrug* soviet executive committee. He has lived in the *okrug* for about 20 years.

In March 1990 he was elected a deputy of the Tyumen *oblast* soviet of people's deputies for the town of Khanty Mansiisk. In May 1990 at the first session of the Khanty Mansy *okrug* soviet of people's deputies he was elected chairman of the executive committee. On August 20, 1991 the *okrug* executive committee of Khanty Mansy autonomous *okrug* declared that it viewed the activities of the Extraordinary Committee as illegal and amounting to an attempt at an anti-constitutional coup. All *okrug* and city authorities were in accord and were implementing the decrees of the President of the Russian Federation and the laws of the constitution of the Russian Federation.

On December 18, 1991 Filipenko was appointed head of the administration of Khanty Mansy autonomous *okrug* by presidential decree. On assuming office he stated that it was important to establish a new system of relations, to make greater use and apply the new economic conditions to the rich northern territories. He regarded the government economic programme as something very difficult to implement but nevertheless it was necessary in order for the country to find a way out of the economic crisis. The transition to the market economy should be gradual, with many stages and an effective policy of social security should be conducted in parallel. He underlined that he supported small businesses and saw in them the foundation of a market economy and that he, as head of the administration, would attempt to create a favourable climate for the useful activities of businessmen.

At the end of November 1992 he stated that he saw no need to convene the VII Congress of People's Deputies in December 1992, as he did not regard putting more pressure on the President in the present difficult circumstances as in any way necessary. The congress's first task was to find a way out of the present situation and not pose the question about confidence or lack of confidence in the President. Filipenko is married with three children and lives in Khanty Mansiisk.

Filippov, Petr Sergeevich

Head of the Analytical Centre on Socio-Economic Policy of the Russian President.

Born in 1945; member of the CPSU until August 1991. He graduated from the Institute of Machine Tools, Leningrad, and several years after graduating attempted to present his candidate dissertation. It was ready but at the last moment the subject, on the introduction of mathematical economics methods into industry, was judged inopportune for the beginning of the 1970s. Fifteen years later the economist with liberal views was in a position to put his theories into practice. High quality tulips were grown at his father-in-law's dacha and sold wholesale from time to time on the Leningrad market. In this way Filippov financed the discussion club, Informals, which he had set up in 1989 and which was the first of the democratic organizations in Leningrad.

He worked at that time as a scientific editor, head of a department of the journal *Ekho* (echo), a radical economics publication. He stood for election as a USSR people's deputy in the 1989 elections but was unsuccessful. Afterwards he published a semi-underground newspaper, *Nevsky kurer*, which had a print run of several tens of thousands and was printed in Latvia and Lithuania. His campaign to enter the Russian parliament and the Leningrad city soviet were both mainly financed by his tulips.

In early 1990 he was nominated for election as an RSFSR people's deputy in the No. 116 Moskovsky territorial district, Leningrad. During the election campaign he stated that he supported the views of the Leningrad popular front, the CPSU democratic platform and the group of journalist candidates. He was supported during the elections by the Democratic Elections 90 platform. He advocated freedom to set up new political parties, a new constitution and guarantees for the rights of all citizens. He proposed new laws on the press, conscience, assembly, meetings, demonstrations, strikes, referendum and defence of the dignity of citizens. He appealed for the setting up of a constitutional court, for trial by jury, for all power to the soviets, for the right to land and natural resources, and direct elections to the Supreme Soviet. He supported the concept of state sovereignty and economic autonomy for the Russian Federation. The various national territorial formations in the Russian Federation should all have equal rights and every nation should have the right to national cultural autonomy. He advocated the introduction of radical economic reform, was opposed to state monopoly and favoured equality for all types of property, including private property. Loss-making collective farms should be dissolved, peasants should be permitted to leave collective farms with land and equipment. Ecological problems should have the highest priority when deciding national economic goals. There should be legal responsibility for violations of the environment and no new atomic energy stations should be built. He supported those journalists who were calling for the setting up of Supreme Soviet commissions on *glasnost*, and the ending of the Party monopoly of the media.

There were eight candidates. Filippov polled 44.41% of the votes in the first round and won the second round, polling 69.23% of the votes. His main opponent was N. N. Lysenko, who received 22.41% of the votes in the first round and 11.44% in the second round. In March 1990 Filippov was elected a deputy in the Leningrad city soviet and was nominated for the post of chairman of the Leningrad city soviet executive.

He was chairman of the sub-committee on privatization of the Supreme Soviet committee on economic reform and property. He was a member of the radical democrats parliamentary faction, co-chairman of the Republican Party of the Russian Federation, and one of the leaders of the Democratic Russia (DemRossiya) movement. He is friends with Anatoly Chubais and Egor Gaidar but an opponent of Ruslan Khasbulatov, and is the acknowledged leader of the St Petersburg democrats. Among those in the presidential Council he is not the only one with a solid record of having "opposed totalitarianism", especially in the most recent period.

As a supporter of liberal economic reforms and the widest possible privatization Filippov is inclined to criticize President Yeltsin for being insufficiently radical. His DemRossiya colleagues confirm that the President invited him to join his council not only as an economist but also as an "engine" with limitless organizational abilities. An example of this was the activity of the St Petersburg DemRossiya movement during the collection of signatures for a referendum on land. Filippov is a candidate for high posts in the President's administration.

The official task of the centre for socio-economic policy, headed by Filippov, is to analyse the socio-economic situation in Russia and prepare expert situation papers and proposals. He is married and lives in St Petersburg.

Fokin, Vitold Pavlovych

Prime Minister of Ukraine to October 1992.

Born into a Russian family in 1932 in Novonikolaïvskyi *raion*, Zaporizhzhia *oblast*, although he speaks Ukrainian better than most. After education at Dnipropetrovsk mining institute, he worked as a mining engineer from 1954 to 1971 in the Donbas. From 1971 to 1990 he worked in the Ukrainian Gosplan, rising to head the organization after 1989, and from 1987 he was also a deputy Chairman of the Council of Ministers. In the republican elections of March 1990, he was elected to represent Darnytskyi *raion* in Kiev city.

He added membership of the Central Committee of the CPSU to that of the CPU in July 1990. During 1990 he was fortunate in rising to prominence as the joint sponsor of the republic's first Economic Stabilization Plan with the more overtly democratic Volodymyr Pylypchuk, endorsed by the Supreme Soviet on October 1, 1990. Therefore, when Masol, the unpopular conservative Chairman of the Council of Ministers, was forced out of office by the student demonstrations of that October, Fokin was well placed to succeed him as a compromise candidate, receiving 332 votes for and only 11 against.

His post was renamed Prime Minister in June 1991. He was also an *ex officio* member of the Defence Council, and the Deputy Head of the State *Duma* (advisory council to the President) created in spring 1992. As PM, however, Fokin was quickly overtaken by the march of events, so that by late 1991 he seemed a hangover from another era (that of Gorbachev's Prime Minister, Nikolai Ryzhkov and the Shatalin plan), whose Gosplan background left him ill-equipped to propose real market reform. The reformist promises made to the students in 1990 were never kept, and in retrospect, Fokin's early reputation for radicalism was due not so much for his sympathy with the opposition, but to his support for measures to empower the republican *apparat*, which had been obstructed by his predecessor Masol.

Therefore, he backed the June 1991 decisions establishing a National Bank on the platform of introducing a national currency, claiming jurisdiction over all-Union enterprises on Ukrainian territory, and asserting the sole right of the Ukrainian government to levy taxes within Ukraine. Internally, however, his most significant innovation was the system of coupon payment with salaries, designed to protect Ukrainian consumer goods from foreign, i.e. Russian, purchase. This scheme was soon discredited, as the coupon lost value even against the ruble. The events of August 1991 left him increasingly isolated, however. Already rumoured to be keener on Gorbachev's proposed Union Treaty than Kravchuk, he was widely credited with bouncing his reluctant colleagues into initialling the last-ditch treaty on Economic Union in Moscow on November 6, 1991, although it was soon transcended by the December 1 votes.

His government's failure to prepare an adequate response to Russia's January 1992 price reforms, and foot-dragging on the introduction of a Ukrainian currency that nationalists argued would have protected the country against deepening economic misfortune, brought demands for his resignation to a crescendo. Although his continued survival rather ritualized such demands, it is not clear why Kravchuk allowed such an obvious lame duck to continue in office for so long, having threatened "three-quarters" of his government with dismissal as early as January 1992. The most popular theory is that Kravchuk was horrified by Yeltsin's rashness in becoming his own Prime Minister, and kept Fokin as a lightning conductor for public protest. Alternatively, Kravchuk simply found it harder to distance himself from his old allies in the *apparat* than many realized, especially as neither the nationalist nor liberal oppositions were then large enough to provide an alternative power base on their own.

A weak Prime Minister did not threaten his own power. Fokin survived an attempt by the Supreme Soviet to dismiss him on the last day of the parliamentary session in July 1992, but at the same time a motion was passed requiring Kravchuk to "re-examine" the composition of the government by the time the Supreme Soviet did so in September. By then Fokin had lost the crucial support of other power-brokers, especially the Chairman of the Supreme Soviet, Ivan Pliushch, and Fokin was forced to resign on September 30, 1992. Despite an initial period of silent self-restraint, he was sniping at the new government from the sidelines by early 1993.

Official address: 252008 Kiev, Vul. M. Hrushevskoho 12/2; *telephone*: Kiev 293 7442.

Fuzhenko, Ivan Vasilevich

Chief of Rear Services, first deputy Commander-in-Chief of the Unified Armed Forces of the CIS. Colonel-General.

Born on June 5, 1937 in the village of Subbotsy, Znamensky *raion*, Kirovograd *oblast*, into a collective farmer's family. Ukrainian. He graduated from the Odessa Military Technical School in 1957; the M. V. Frunze Military Academy in 1970; the Military Academy of the General Staff in 1978. He received a higher military education and was a member of the CPSU until August 1991.

He began his career as an officer as a rifle platoon commander, then as a company commander, deputy commander and commander of a battalion. His units were often among the best. He enjoyed the respect of his superior officers and the support of Party political agencies. Immediately after the Military Academy he became a motorized rifle regimental commander. He was regarded as an officer with sound operational tactical and military technical training, capable of comprehending and implementing the instructions of modern-day military combat. He was soon promoted to the position of motorized rifle divisional commander. In 1978, after completing higher military education, he became deputy Chief of Staff of the Baltic military district, which represented rapid promotion. He proved to be a good staff officer, capable of drawing up plans for training and the use of combat troops. Later, he held the posts of first deputy Chief of Staff of the Leningrad military district, an army commander, first deputy Comander-in-Chief of the group of Soviet forces in Germany (German Democratic Republic), first deputy Commander-in-Chief of the Turkestan military district. In 1989 he was appointed Commander-in-Chief of the same district. He arrived at a mutual understanding and established close ties with the communist authorities in Central Asia. The troops under Col.-Gen. Fuzhenko were often deployed to put an end to armed ethnic conflicts and to counteract national democratic movements.

In March 1989 he was elected a USSR people's deputy in Termez territorial district, Surkhadarynsk *oblast*, Uzbekistan. He adopted a clear pro-communist position, supported right-wing conservative groups in parliament, but rarely participating in debates. During the anti-constitutional putsch of August 1991, Gen. Fuzhenko carried out without demur all instructions issued by Marshal Dmitry Yazov, the USSR Minister of Defence, and the General Staff, and ordered his troops on to a state of high combat readiness. According to democratic organizations and the investigations of the parliamentary commission, Fuzhenko expressed his disapproval of President Mikhail Gorbachev and Russian leaders. However, the documents compromising the commanders of the Turkestan military district, including those signed by Fuzhenko, were partly destroyed. On December 7, 1991, by the decree of the USSR President, Gen. Fuzhenko was appointed Chief of Rear Services of the Armed Forces and deputy Minister of Defence of the USSR. Democrats in the military and society reacted negatively to this promotion. They criticized it as an example of poor personnel policy, resulting in the substitution of conservative generals who had kept their heads down during the attempted coup by those who had been directly involved with the plotters.

Fuzhenko does not express his political views in public, confining himself to professional subjects at conferences and in his publications. He is regarded as a typically conservative General, a conformist, prepared to obey any well-established regime. He supports the concept of a strong state domestically and Russia as a great power externally. An interview by him, "Rear face to face with the market", was published in *Krasnaya Zvezda* on January 23, 1992. He was appointed Chief of Rear Services and deputy Commander-in-Chief of the unified armed forces of the CIS in February 1992. He was a member of the state commission for the establishment of the Ministry of Defence, Army and Navy of the Russian Federation.

He does not speak any foreign language and has not been abroad as a member of an official delegation. He has been awarded two orders of the Red Star, orders of the Red Banner and "for service to the motherland in the armed forces of the USSR", 3rd class, and medals. He is married with two children.

Official address: 103160 Moscow K–160.

Gadzhiev, Gadis Abdullaevich

Member of the Constitutional Court of the Russian Federation.

Born on August 27, 1953 in the village of Shovkra, Laksky *raion*, Dagestan Autonomous Soviet Socialist Republic (ASSR). After graduating in 1975 from the faculty of law, Moscow State University, he was a lecturer in the department of civil law, faculty of law, Dagestan State University. In 1979 at Moscow State University he successfully presented his candidate dissertation in law on "Civil legal questions in the specialization and concentration of agricultural production during agro-industrial integration" (LLM). From 1979, besides his academic activities, he acted as a legal adviser (*yuriskonsult*) to the Presidium of the Supreme Soviet of the Dagestan ASSR and from 1982 to May 1990 was head of the legal department of the *chef de cabinet*, Council of Ministers of the Dagestan ASSR. He is an assistant professor.

In 1990 he was elected a people's deputy of the Dagestan ASSR. In April 1990, at the I Congress of People's Deputies of the Dagestan ASSR, he was elected a member of the Dagestan Supreme Soviet, and in May of the same year he was elected chairman of the permanent commission on legislation, law and order of the Dagestan Supreme Soviet. In 1991 he studied in Moscow at the academy of law. He is researching his doctoral dissertation on the problems of taking into consideration regional problems when passing legislation.

On October 30, 1991, at the V Congress of RSFSR People's Deputies, he was elected a member of the RSFSR Constitutional Court in the third round of voting, receiving 635 for and 211 against. He had not participated in the first round of voting but received 438 votes for in the second round and 324 against. The minimum number of votes necessary was 529.

Gadzhiev is a specialist on the law of the republics and autonomous regions in the Russian Federation. A major task for the Constitutional Court, in his eyes, is to clarify Russian legal norms in the legislation of the republics and autonomous regions. He believes that members of the Constitutional Court should not reach decisions as representatives of republics or parties but should be outside politics, except in a private capacity. The Constitutional Court must not be against anyone; it is an arbiter. The conflict between the legislature and the executive is a natural conflict which the Constitutional Court should guide into legal channels and create the possibility of resolving it in a civilized manner, according to Gadzhiev. He lives in Moscow.

Gaidar, Egor Timurovich

Acting Prime Minister of Russia, June to December 1992. Member of the Presidential Council.

Born on March 19, 1956 in Moscow into a Russian family. He was a member of the CPSU until August 1991. His father is a retired rear-admiral and a military journalist, who is special correspondent of *Pravda* in Cuba and Yugoslavia, and also of *Krasnaya Zvezda*. In the 1980s he wrote in *Izvestiya* and *Moscow News* and supported reform of the armed forces. His grandfather was Arkady Gaidar, a Red commissar and author of children's books. His maternal grandfather was P. P. Bazhov, the author of *Uralskie skazki* (Stories from the Urals). Gaidar's mother, A. P. Gaidar, is a doctor of historical sciences (DLitt) and a specialist on the 18th century. She is on the staff of the Institute of National History. Gaidar left secondary school (part of it spent in Yugoslavia where his father was working) with a gold medal. He entered the economics faculty of Moscow State University in 1973, despite having ostensibly failed the entrance examination to the university. He graduated in 1979 in economics with a distinction and then began postgraduate studies. He successfully presented his candidate dissertation in economics in 1981 (PhD(Econ)), on value indicators in economic accounting of production associations (enterprises). His supervisor was Academician Stanislav Shatalin. Gaidar successfully presented his doctoral dissertation in economics in 1988 (DSc(Econ)).

Between 1981 and 1987 he was a scientific assistant in the faculty of economics, Moscow State University; senior research analyst in the All-Union scientific research institute of systems studies; leading research analyst, institute of economics and forecasting of scientific-technical progress, USSR Academy of Sciences. He concerned himself with econometrics. In 1984 V. I. Koshkin and he published the book *Economic Accounting and the Development of Economic Autonomy of Enterprises*. After the splitting of the All-Union scientific research institute of systems studies in 1985 into the central mathematical economics institute (whose director was A. Petrakov) and the institute of economics and forecasting of scientific technical progress (whose head was S. Shatalin), Gaidar remained with Shatalin. Shatalin and Gaidar published the book *Economic*

Reforms: Reasons, Directions, Problems, in 1989. In 1990 Gaidar published a monograph on *Economic Reforms and Hierarchical Structures*.

From 1983 to 1985 Gaidar, as an expert, took part in the work of a government commission, set up by Yury Andropov, studying the possibility of economic reform in a socialist economy. There he worked with many of his future colleagues: A. Golovkov, future head of the administration of the Russian government; P. Aven, future Russian Minister of Foreign Economic Links; and A. Chubais, future head of the Russian state committee of property. These contacts led to the holding of the first conference of economists who supported reform at Zmeinaya Gorka, near Leningrad. Gaidar was acknowledged as leader. From 1985 Gaidar maintained close contact with economists at Harvard and Yale Universities and the London School of Economics, especially Jeffrey Sachs and Peter Layard, who later acted as advisers to the Russian government.

In 1987, at the invitation of Aleksandr Yakovlev, he became editor of articles on political economy and economic policy in *Kommunist*, the theoretical journal of the CPSU, where Otto Latsis was editor-in-chief; and a member of the editorial board of *Kommunist*. In 1990 he was appointed editor of the section on economic policy of *Pravda* and a member of the editorial board of that newspaper.

In the autumn of 1990 he was appointed director of the institute of economic policy, USSR Academy of the National Economy; a body which was set up on his initiative, aided by Abel Aganbegyan. The deputy directors were A. Nechaev, a future Russian Minister of Economics, and V. Mashits, at present chairman of the Russian state committee on economic co-operation with CIS states.

He participated in the drawing up of the 500-day programme which sketched out a rapid route to the market. It was rejected by Gorbachev in the autumn of 1990. Gaidar soon associated with Yeltsin and contributed to the drafting of pro-market proposals. He was staunchly pro-Yeltsin during the attempted coup in August 1991.

After the defeat of the coup there were two main schools of economic thought competing for ascendancy around President Yeltsin: the Yavlinsky and the Gaidar schools. Grigory Yavlinsky had been closely associated with Stanislav Shatalin and Nikolai Petrakov during the drafting of the 500-day programme. Yavlinsky favoured co-ordinating the moves of all USSR successor states towards the implementation of a market economy and a common currency. An agreement proposing this was signed in October 1991. Gaidar, on the other hand, proposed that Russia set the pace in economic reform and should if necessary go it alone. This implied putting Russia's economic interests first. Gaidar and his team won the battle for Yeltsin's ear and by the end of 1991 dominated economic decision-making. However, the struggle between the two economic approaches had cost valuable time and an opportunity was lost to implement a radical political programme immediately after the failure of the coup when the communists were in disarray.

Gaidar became deputy Prime Minister for economic policy and Minister of Economics in early November 1991, and his reforms were launched in

January 1992. They were based on liberalization and stabilization. The former freed prices and resulted in rapid inflation and price rises. Stabilization implied a tight monetary policy—tight control of money supply and credit. Structural changes would come through privatization, but this would only affect shops. Large-scale privatization would take at least two years. Gaidar's "shock therapy" was deeply unpopular with the industrial lobby and agriculture.

At the VI RSFSR Congress of People's Deputies, in April 1992, President Yeltsin was obliged to step down as Prime Minister. Gaidar was not acceptable to the conservative Congress, but Yeltsin imposed him as his choice and Gaidar was given the title of acting Prime Minister on June 15, 1992, the day when Yeltsin was setting off for the USA in search of credits. He remained Minister of Finance and continued to dominate economic policy. A major weakness of Gaidar's policy was that he had little influence over the Russian Central Bank. Constitutionally, this institution was subordinate to the parliament, and not to the government or the President. This resulted in the Bank, under the direction of Viktor Gerashchenko, formerly the chairman of the USSR State Bank, conducting an inflationary policy by extending huge credits to ailing enterprises. The government, therefore, only had limited influence over industry.

When the Civic Union came into being in June 1992, it co-ordinated opposition to Gaidar's rush to the market. Among the parties which joined Civic Union was the People's Party for a Free Russia, headed by Vice-President Aleksandr Rutskoi. Civic Union gave parliamentary voice to the industrialists' lobby and also the agrarian lobby, which represented the views of agricultural managers hostile to privatization. Inflation declined until the summer but then Gerashchenko became chairman of the Central Bank and a flood of credit was extended to enterprises. This demonstrated the influence of the industrial lobby.

Inflation climbed rapidly and there was little that Gaidar and his government could do to stem the tide. His government issued vouchers, nominally worth 10,000 rubles, to every citizen, which were to be used to buy shares when the privatization of medium and large-scale enterprises got under way in 1993. This move was prompted by the desire to make the process of privatization irreversible and hence make the market economy a reality. Gaidar clung on until the VII Congress of People's Deputies in December 1992. The main reason for his tenure in office was the unflinching support he enjoyed from President Yeltsin. At the Congress, Yeltsin made several concessions to the conservative majority (only 15% of deputies supported Gaidar and Yeltsin's policies), but this failed to win the acceptance of Gaidar as Prime Minister.

Tactical errors by Yeltsin led to his having to accept the Congress's nominations for Prime Minister. Three were proposed but Gaidar received fewest votes. The President bowed to the inevitable and appointed Viktor Chernomyrdin as his Prime Minister. There were widespread rumours (which led to Yeltsin's early return from a visit to China) that Chernomyrdin was restructuring the government so as to remove Gaidar's pro-market associates. In the event only one was sacked but this was counterbalanced by the appointment of Boris Fedorov, a former RSFSR Minister of Finance and the Russian director of the European Bank for Reconstruction and Development in London, becoming deputy Prime Minister responsible for macroeconomic policy and finance. Gaidar returned to the institute for economic policy but was soon appointed economic adviser to President Yeltsin. He also became a member of the Presidential council. Under him about 40,000 businesses were privatized and about 1,000 enterprises turned into joint-stock companies. Output from the private sector, using this term in its most elastic sense, in 1992, amounted to 30% of global output.

Gaidar is director of the Institute of the Economics of the Transition Period, is an economic counsellor of the President and a member of the Presidential Council. An able economist, he speaks English, Spanish and Serbo-Croat, and is in great demand as a speaker at international gatherings. He enjoyed boxing and football and is keen on chess. He is married with three children and lives in Moscow.

Gailitis, Karlis

Chairman of Consistory of the Evangelical Lutheran Church of Latvia.

Born on March 3, 1936 in Riga, Latvia; Latvian. He graduated in 1963 from the Latvian agricultural academy. From 1981 to 1987 he was secretary of the consistory of the Evangelical Lutheran Church of Latvia, and in 1987 was appointed chairman of the consistory of the church. He is a bishop, and is married with two children.

Address: 1 Saules Street, Riga, Latvia; *telephone*: Riga 33 4194.

Gaji-Zade, Khikmet Abdul-Ragim Ogly

Plenipotentiary of the Republic of Azerbaijan in Moscow, Russian Federation, until June 1993.

Born on November 11, 1954 in Baku into an Azeri family. His father, A. Gaji-Zade, a professor, was head of the department of economic geography, faculty of geography, Azerbaijani State University. He has a brother, Orkhan, who was born in 1958 and is a geographer.

In 1977 Gaji-Zade graduated from the faculty of physics, Azerbaijani State University. He became a member of the institute of botany, Academy of Sciences of Azerbaijan, and remained until 1979. He then became a post-graduate student in the institute of biophysics, USSR Academy of Sciences, in Pushchino na Oka, Moscow *oblast*. In 1983 he successfully presented his candidate dissertation in mathematics and physical sciences on "Ionic transport across a channel formed by Amphobericine B in a non-flaky lipid membrane" (PhD). He returned to Baku and joined the department of biophysics, Institute of Botany, Academy of Sciences of Azerbaijan as a junior research assistant, then scientific assistant and senior scientific assistant. In January 1992 he also became editor in chief of *Svoboda* (freedom), the Russian language newspaper of the Popular Front of Azerbaijan.

He was appointed plenipotentiary of Azerbaijan in Moscow on May 25, 1992. He was one of the founding members of the Popular Front and one of the authors of its programme. He is married. His wife, Bakhar Rashid-Kyzy, works in the institute of botany, Academy of Sciences of Azerbaijan, and their son Adnan is 12 years old. Gaji-Zade has published 12 scientific papers on biophysics and dozens of articles on public and political matters. He loves to play the guitar and at present lives in Moscow.

Galazov, Akhsarbek Khadzhimurzaevich

Speaker of the Supreme Soviet of the North Ossetian Soviet Socialist Republic, Russian Federation.

Born on October 15, 1929 in the village of Khumalag, Pravoberezhny *raion*, North Ossetian ASSR; an Ossetian; member of the CPSU from 1959 to August 1991. In 1952 he graduated from the North Ossetian State Pedagogical Institute and since then has worked in the North Ossetian ASSR as a teacher, head of studies, Khumalag secondary school, Pravoberezhny *raion*, (1952); in 1958 as an inspector of schools, director of the institute of further education of teachers of the Ministry of Education of the republic; in 1960 as instructor of the party *obkom*; and in 1961 as minister of education of the republic.

In 1974, in the scientific research institute of general pedagogy of the Academy of Pedagogical Sciences of the USSR, Moscow, he successfully presented his candidate dissertation on "The organizational and pedagogical problems of teaching general secondary education in the national republics (based on the example of the North Ossetian ASSR)" (PhD). In 1975 he was appointed deputy Chairman of the Council of Ministers of the North Ossetian ASSR. In 1976 he became rector of the K. Khetagurov North Ossetian State University and was made a professor. On February 24, 1990 he was elected first secretary of the North Ossetian Party *obkom* in a contested election. He has received state awards.

In early 1990 he was nominated by several work collectives for election as an RSFSR people's deputy in the No. 845 Leninsky territorial district. During the election campaign he advocated the separation of the functions of the soviet and Party organizations, the development of the social sphere, the improvement of inter-ethnic relations in the region through the revival of national languages, cultures and historical traditions of the peoples of the North Caucasus. He proposed reform of the system of education, and was opposed to the blackening of national history. He was only in favour of co-operation with those informal organizations which were committed to socialism.

There were four candidates. Galazov polled 46% of the votes in the first round and won in the second round, polling 53% of the votes. His main opponent was V. I. Kopylov, chief specialist of the Caucasian Institute of

Non-ferrous Metals, who received 15% of the votes in the first round and 28% in the second round.

In 1990 he was elected a deputy of the Supreme Soviet of the North Ossetian ASSR. On March 21, 1990 the plenum of the North Ossetian Party *obkom* nominated him for the post of Speaker of the Supreme Soviet and the same day the Supreme Soviet elected him Speaker with a large majority unopposed. He was a delegate to the XXVIII Party Congress and a member of the Party Central Committee from July 1990.

In August 1991 Galazov stated that a state of emergency had already been declared in several *raions* of the North Ossetian Soviet Socialist Republic in December 1990 and in April 1991 and that the emergency committee of the Supreme Soviet of the North Ossetian SSR had contributed much to the stabilization of the situation in the region.

In December 1992 he was one of the prime movers behind the signing of the declaration on the principles of inter-ethnic relations in the North Caucasus which included the equality of peoples, respect for and development of national characteristics, the retention of the territorial integrity of national state formations, rejection of the use of force to change frontiers, the banning of illegal military formations, the guaranteeing of the rights of national minorities, the resolution of inter-ethnic problems through negotiations only, economic and political co-operation, the development of local traditions, self-government and the resolution of agrarian problems and the strengthening of law and order. He lives in Vladikavkaz.

Gambarov, Isa Yusif Ogly

Speaker of the *Milli Mejlis* (National Council), Republic of Azerbaijan until June 1993; acting head of state until June 1992; deputy chairman of the Popular Front of Azerbaijan.

Born in 1957 in Baku into an Azeri family. His father is a chemist and biologist and a doctor of sciences (DSc), and Gambarov has two brothers and a sister.

In 1979 he graduated from the faculty of history, Azerbaijani State University, and was assigned to Nakhichevan where he taught history. In 1986 he joined the Institute of Oriental Studies, Academy of Sciences of Azerbaijan, as a junior scientific assistant. He is a specialist on the history of Iran and has published articles on this subject.

He became a member of the leadership of the Popular Front of Azerbaijan at its inception. In 1990 he became head of the department of organization of the Front and in 1991was elected deputy chairman. In the autumn of 1990 he was elected a deputy of the Supreme Soviet of Azerbaijan and on May 18, 1992 he was elected Speaker of the parliament (*Milli Mejlis*) of the Republic of Azerbaijan. From then until elections for President on June 7, 1992 he was also acting President of the republic.

On June 15, 1993 he was replaced as Speaker of the *Milli Mejlis* by Geidar Aliev, the former Communist Party leader of Azerbaijan. This followed the military rebellion, led by Col. Suret Guseinov, which had resulted from dissatisfaction within the military at the string of defeats suffered in the war against Armenia over Nagorno-Karabakh, popular discontent and economic difficulties. Guseinov's forces were from Gyanja where the Russian garrison had abandoned its food and equipment on June 1, 1993. Elchibey's forces had tried to disarm the rebels but had failed, leaving over 50 dead. A compromise was negotiated between the President and his Popular Front supporters and the opposition, consisting of former communists and disgruntled former Popular Front supporters. This resulted in Aliev being elected Speaker of the *Milli Mejlis* on June 15, 1993, and becoming in effect the ruler of Azerbaijan.

He is married. His wife, Aida, is a candidate of sciences (PhD), and is a scientific assistant in the Institute of Oriental Studies, Academy of Sciences of Azerbaijan. They have two sons, the elder one is at secondary school and the younger one is not yet at school. He lives in Baku.

Gamidov, Iskander Mejid Ogly

Minister of Internal Affairs, Republic of Azerbaijan until June 1993; Lieutenant-General.

Born on April 10, 1948 in the village of Baglypei, Kelbajarsky *raion*, Azerbaijani SSR, into an Azeri family. His father was in the militia; he has a brother and two sisters and another, the youngest, died. His brother, Sardar, is the chairman of the soviet executive committee of the Tertersky *raion*, Azerbaijan. He was a member of the CPSU until January 1990.

From 1965 to 1967 he was a teacher in a secondary school in Kalbajarsky *raion*, and then from 1967 to 1969 he served in the Soviet Army. He was an ordinary militaman in Kirovabad (now Gyanja) (1970-71); and was then head of a division of night-time militia of the administration of Internal Affairs, Kirovabad (1971-72). From 1972 to 1974 he studied at a militia school, then he was inspector of the department of services, administration of Internal Affairs (1974-78), and inspector, then senior inspector, Baku city soviet executive committee (1978-83). In 1974 he graduated from the N. K. Rizaev Special Militia School, Baku, and in 1981 from the academy of the USSR Ministry of Internal Affairs.

From 1983 to 1988 he was inspector, then head of the militia, Ordzhonikidze *raion*, Baku, and from 1988 to 1992 he was senior head of the administration of Internal Affairs, central apparatus of the Ministry of Internal Affairs, Azerbaijan. From January to May 1992 he was head of the department for the struggle against corruption, administration of Internal Affairs, Ministry of Internal Affairs, Azerbaijan, and in May 1992 he was appointed Minister of Internal Affairs of the Republic of Azerbaijan. On June 1, 1993 the Russians abandoned their garrison in Gyanja, leaving all their food and equipment, and Col. Suret Guseinov and his men took over the garrison. The President's forces tried in vain to disarm them and they then began their march on Baku. Elchibey fled to Nakhichevan after being informed by his forces that they would resist Guseinov's advance. On June 15, 1993 Geidar Aliev was elected Speaker of the *Milli Mejlis* and acting head of state. Guseinov took over the military, security forces and the militia.

Gamidov is known for his radical speeches among members of the Popular Front, and is the organizer and leader of the *Boz gurd* (grey wolves) movement. However, the events of June 1993 broke up the Popular Front. He is married and has two sons of school age. He lives in Baku.

Gamsakhurdia, Zviad Konstantinovich

Former President of the Republic of Georgia.

Born in 1939 in Tbilisi; Georgian. He is the son of Konstantin Gamsakhurdia, a leading Georgian literary figure and Miranda (née Palavandishvili), and is of old princely stock. He graduated from the faculty of west European languages, Tbilisi State University, and successfully presented his candidate dissertation in philology (PhD). In 1991 he was made a doctor of philology *honoris causa* by the academic council (literature) of the Shota Rustaveli Institute of Georgian Literature, Georgian Academy of Sciences, for his book *The Language of the Forms of the Knight in a Lordly Skin*.

He became active politically in the 1950s and was arrested, but continued his political activities in the 1960s, 1970s and 1980s and became the editor of the first *samizdat* newspapers and journals. He was imprisoned between 1977 and 1979 in prisons in Tbilisi, Moscow and the Caspian region, and afterwards was a senior scientific assistant, Shota Rustaveli Institute of Georgian Literature. His interests include Georgian culture, theology, anthropology, foreign literature and mythology.

He was Speaker of the Supreme Soviet of Georgia (1990-91), and in April 1991 he was elected the first President of the Republic of Georgia in national elections. Unfortunately there was constant friction between him and the parliament, partly due to his authoritarian manner, and this eventually led to armed conflict and considerable damage to the centre of Tbilisi, but there was fighting in other parts of the country as well. His greatest support base was in the west of Georgia among the Mingrelians. Another source of conflict was Gamsakhurdia's view that Georgia was the republic of the Georgians. The attempts by the South Ossetians to rejoin their compatriots in North Ossetia, in Russia, and the desire of the Abkhazians to rejoin Russia were rejected and led to a bloody conflict. Georgia often accused Russia of intervening on the secessionists side, so as to weaken Georgia, and Gamsakhurdia was removed as President in January 1992 by the military council of the Republic of Georgia. He left Georgia and took refuge in the north Caucasus where he continued his struggle to return to Georgia as President. The presidency was abolished and Eduard Shevardnadze became head of state.

He is the author of monographs and articles, is a translator of American, British and French writers and has published a collection of poems and fairy tales. He speaks English, French and German. He is married with three sons.

Gasymov, Tofig Masim Ogly

Chairman of the commission of state formation of the *Milli Mejlis* (National Council) of the Republic of Azerbaijan to June 1993; Minister of Foreign Affairs May 1992-June 1993.

Born on April 10, 1938 in the village of Lyaki, Agdashsky *raion*, Azerbaijani SSR into an Azeri family. His father was a railway worker.

From 1955 to 1960 he was a student in the faculty of physics, Azerbaijani State University. He held a Stalin scholarship and was secretary of the *Komsomol* organization of the faculty, but in his last year as a student he resigned from the *Komsomol*. After graduating he joined the Institute of Physics, Academy of Sciences of Azerbaijan, as a senior laboratory assistant, and in November 1960 he became a postgraduate student in the Ioffe Institute of Physics and Technology, USSR Academy of Sciences, Leningrad.

After graduating in 1963 he remained in the Leningrad institute until 1970. In 1969 he successfully presented his candidate dissertation in mathematics and physical sciences on "Warming phonons in semi-conductors and their influence on electro-conductivity"(PhD). He returned in 1970 to Baku to the institute of physics, Academy of Sciences, Azerbaijan, and remained a senior scientific assistant until 1990. From 1990 to 1991 he was chief scientific assistant in the laboratory of semi-conductor theory.

In October 1990 he was elected to the Supreme Soviet (later the *Milli Mejlis*) of Azerbaijan and in December 1991 chairman of the commission on state formation. He is one of the founders of the Popular Front of Azerbaijan and a co-author of its programme, and at the first conference of the Popular Front he was elected to the board. At the first congress, in the autumn of 1991, he was elected deputy chairman and remained so until he became chairman of the parliamentary commission. His views are those of a liberal democrat.

He is the author of over 100 scientific articles: about 30 have been published in Azerbaijan, about 50 in the central Soviet media and about 20 abroad, on physics and semi-conductors. He has supervised three doctoral students. In May 1992 he was appointed Minister of Foreign Affairs, but the events of June 1993 brought an end to the Popular Front dominance of Azerbaijan. On June 1, 1993 the Russian garrison in Gyanja abandoned its food and equipment and Col. Suret Guseinov and his forces took over. The President's forces tried to disarm Guseinov's men but failed, and the latter then marched on Baku. On June 15, 1993 Geidar Aliev was elected Speaker of the *Milli Mejlis* and acting head of state.

He is married, and his wife, Firuza Mamedali Kyzy Gashim-Zade, is an assistant professor in the department of physics, Polytechnical University. They have two daughters, the elder of whom, Narmina, born in 1971, is a medical student at the university and the younger one, Nushaba, born in 1975, is still at school. Gasymov loves to play chess. He lives in Baku.

Home address: Baku, prospekt Matbuat, dom 2, kv. 10; *home telephone*: Baku 38 33 72.

Gavrilov, Yury Vasilevich

Russian footballer.

Born on May 3, 1953; Russian. He was a forward, and is an Honoured Master of Sport (1988). He began his career with Dinamo Moscow (1974-76); then moved to Spartak Moscow (1977-85); Dnepr Dnepropetrovsk (Dnipropetrovsk) (1986); Lokomotov Moscow (1987); TPS Turku, Finland (1988-90); and Amaral Moscow (1991). In the USSR championship, in the top league, he played 308 games and scored 91 goals; of which 216 games and 77 goals were for Spartak Moscow; 67 games and 11 goals were for Dinamo Moscow; and 25 games and three goals were for Dnepr Dnepropetrovsk. He played 51 times for the USSR national team and scored 13 goals between 1978 and 1985. He won a bronze medal with the USSR team in the Olympic Games of 1980, played in the World Cup finals in 1982, and was a member of the USSR championship winning side in 1979.

Gazabaev, Chakhit

Chairman of the Muslim Religious Board (MRB) of Chechen-Ingush ASSR, 1990-91; Mufti.

Born on October 1, 1949 in the settlement of Shubar Kuduk, Aktyubinsk *oblast*, Kazakh SSR; Chechen. He graduated in 1988 from the Islamic Institute, Tashkent, Uzbek SSR. From 1983 to 1985 he was *imam-hatyb* at the mosque in the village of Prigorodskoe, Grozny *oblast*, Chechen Ingush ASSR. He was the representative of the MRB of the North Caucasus in the Chechen Ingush ASSR (1985-90) and later was the chairman of the MRB in the Chechen Ingush ASSR (1990-91).

Address: Grozny, ul. Figurnaya 29, Chechnya.

Gdlyan, Telman Khorenovich

Co-chairman of the People's Party of Russia.

Born in December 1940 into a peasant family and grew up in Sukhumi, Georgia. He was the fifth child in the family and has seven brothers. Armenian; member of the CPSU until 1990. He completed five classes in school before he joined the Soviet Army. In the army he received a certificate of secondary education and after being demobbed he became a student in the Saratov Institute of Law. At the end of the 1960s he was assigned to work in Ulyanovsk *oblast*. In 1974 he became senior investigator in the *oblast* Procurator's Office. He stayed in this post 13 years and over half the time he was away from home. He was a member of the group of investigators in Smolensk, Moscow and northern Caucasus. In 1981 he was appointed investigator for especially important cases in the USSR General Procurator's Office. Soon afterwards he was appointed to head a group of investigators in Uzbekistan.

In 1989 Gdlyan was nominated for election as a USSR people's deputy in the No. 25 Tushinsky territorial district, Moscow. In his election programme he advocated the revolutionary renewal of society, the creation of a *Rechtsstaat* (law-governed state) in which the law is above the power of officials and not power above the law. He regarded his principal task in the supreme agency of power to be the struggle for the implementation of promulgated laws. He proposed the genuine equality of all before the law, the "high and mighty" to be responsible to the people, irrespective of position or knowledge. He called for the drafting of a state programme to combat crime, first and foremost organized crime, and to change and improve the structure of the law-enforcing agencies. He advocated the establishment of a USSR committee of investigation, the placing under the strictest control of the Supreme Soviet, the activities of the KGB, the public prosecutor's office, the militia and the investigative agencies and the removal of the secrecy around the figures for crime in the country. He called for the provision of legal guarantees for the new economic policy, for a guaranteed standard of living for citizens, the removal of all "caste" privileges, including those of the deputies of the Supreme Soviet, the stepping up of the struggle against non-earned income and the ending of egalitarianism. He wanted the CPSU to abandon its leadership role and for soviets to be given real power, with the banning of leading officials at various levels and ranks from functions for which they are not qualified. Trade unions should be independent and their task is to defend the genuine interests of the workers. He favoured a professional parliament whose work would be under public scrutiny.

There were five candidates. Gdlyan won in the first round, polling 86.8% of the votes. His main opponent was A. N. Napolnov, who polled 3.26% of the votes. In March 1990 Gdlyan was elected a people's deputy of the Supreme Soviet of Armenia but refused to take up a leading post and did not become a member of any committee or commission.

During the course of the investigation into the corruption of the "Uzbek case" an anti-Gdlyan campaign developed in the press. It maintained that although he was battling against corruption, it was not really the Uzbek case he had in mind but the corruption in the Kremlin. In 1990 a special group from the Union Procurator's Office was sent to Ulyanovsk to check the past cases which Gdlyan investigated. Many commissions were established to review the work of the group of investigators, by the Party Central Committee, the Presidium of the Supreme Soviet and finally the commission of the USSR Congress of People's Deputies, headed by Roi Medvedev. Gdlyan believed that the accusations against him about the illegal methods of investigation had no substance in fact because he was always very scrupulous in establishing factual evidence and never went beyond the limits of the law. He demanded that an independent international legal commission be established and that he should be given the opportunity to appear on TV to present the proof of his accusations, but this was denied him. In 1991 Gdlyan was dismissed from the USSR public prosecutor's office and a request was forwarded to the USSR Supreme Soviet to remove him as a people's deputy. On July 12, 1991 the USSR General Procurator forwarded a letter to President Mikhail Gorbachev which stated that the investigation had amassed enough proof to accuse Gdlyan of exceeding his legal authority.

On August 19, 1991 Gdlyan was arrested. However, on August 31, 1991, after the collapse of the attempted state coup, the criminal case against Gdlyan was withdrawn for lack of evidence of criminal activity on his part. The USSR Supreme Soviet, before its dissolution, annulled the illegal decree removing Gdlyan from the Procurator's Office and demanded that he be reinstated.

On May 19, 1991, Gdlyan, at the constituent congress of the People's Party of Russia (PPR), was elected co-chairman. He called on everyone not to permit a return to the past, or to any variety of totalitarianism, and to create genuine democracy and the rule of law and order. Weak power and a weak state are not capable of resolving the burning economic and social problems facing society. He advocated strong executive power, the primacy of law and legality, the strengthening of the state not to oppress the individual but to defend the interests of each person in the name of free development. The PPR joined the political bloc, People's Russia, consisting of six parties whose goal is to establish a democratic society and *Rechtsstaat* from a liberal democratic position. He supports taking into consideration the interests of entrepreneurs and producers, but this should also be accompanied by the state guaranteeing state support for the poorest strata of society. He thinks that the three branches of power should be balanced and believes that when political forces are equal, society stabilizes. The predominance of one form of power inevitably leads to a totalitarian form of government. Representative institutions are not carrying out their functions and deputies are not taking into account the balance of forces in society and the interests of electors. All representative institutions need to be reformed from top to bottom by holding elections with only candidates from political parties standing. However, there is no point in dissolving parliament at present. Gdlyan criticized the policy of Gaidar's government which regarded the liberalization of prices as its cornerstone while neglecting other important economic reforms such as demonopolization, privatization and satiation of the market with goods. Tax policy has been irrational and many enterprises put out of business. Vouchers are very necessary but their value has dropped and there is no precise method for making use of them.

GEFTER, MIKHAIL YAKOVLEVICH

In his own political programme Gdlyan advocates complete freedom for all types of ownership of land. All producers should work in the countryside, from private farmers to collective and state farms which are capable of competing in the market. He believes that the levers of command in all structures are still in the hands of the Party and economic *nomenklatura*; the democratic parties are deprived of support and they have not been afforded the chance of growing stronger. Together with E. Yu. Dodolev he published the book *Pyramid 1*, he participated in the establishment of an all-Russian fund of progress, defence of human rights and mercy. He is married and has a son and a daughter. He lives in Moscow.

Gedeon, Russian Orthodox Metropolitan of Stavropol and Baku

Born on December 18, 1929 as Aleksandr Nikolaevich Dokukin in the Cossack village of Novo-Pavlovskaya, Krasnodar *krai* into a peasant family. He graduated from the Stavropol Theological Academy and the Leningrad (St Petersburg) Theological Academy. He successfully presented his candidate dissertation in theology (PhD).

He was abbot of Pokrov church, Mineralnye Vody, Stavropol *krai* (1962-65); priest of the Krestovozdvizhensky cathedral, Petrozavodsk (1965); he took his vows as a monk in 1966, and became an archimandrite; was bishop of Smolensk and Vyazma (1967-72); bishop of Novosibirsk and Barnaul (1972-77); he became an archbishop in 1977, and was archbishop of Novosibirsk and Barnaul (1977-87); he became a metropolitan in 1987; metropolitan of Novosibirsk and Barnaul (1987-90); in 1990 he was appointed metropolitan of Stavropol and Baku.

Gefter, Mikhail Yakovlevich

Member of the Council of the President of the Russian Federation.

Born on August 24, 1918 in Simferopol. He graduated from the faculty of history, Moscow State University. He went to the front in 1941 as a volunteer, and served in the Krasnaya Presen detached pursuit batallion and the 8th regiment of Moscow workers of the 5th Moscow communist division. He took part in the battle around Riga and was awarded the order of glory. After the war ended in 1945 he worked in the institute of history, USSR Academy of Sciences, and was a member of the Party but resigned from it in 1982.

In 1953 he successfully presented his candidate dissertation in history on "Tsarism and monopolies in the Russian fuel industry on the eve of the First World War" (PhD). He specializes in the history of Russia under capitalism.

He has written studies of the development of capitalism in Russia at the beginning of the 20th century, Stolypin's agrarian reform, the creation of metallurgical trusts, the emergence of large investments in the oil industry and the Tsarist agrarian policy in Azerbaijan, monopoly capitalism in Russia, the emergence of sugar syndicates, the arrival of US capital in Russia before the First World War, foreign capital in the mining industry of the Urals and Siberia, on the problems of varied strata in capitalist Russia, the legal regulation of the activities and trusts, monopoly capitalism in the metallurgical industry in southern Russia, and the coal monopoly. These were published in the journals *Istoricheskie zapiski*, *Vestnik akademii nauk SSSR*, *Voprosy istorii*, *Istorichesky arkhiv* and *Voprosy istorii estestvoznaniya i tekhniki*.

In the 1960s Gefter was a member of the new wave of historians struggling to overcome the narrow framework of formal theory and historical materialism. In 1964 he headed the sector of methodology within the institute of history, USSR Academy of Sciences. In collaboration with philosophers the first tasks tackled were cultural problems, and collective essays on *History and Sociology* (1964) and *Historical Science and Some Contemporary Problems* (1969) were published. They conducted research into the methods of research of social problems, the asiatic mode of production, the relationship between world history and the history of separate countries, knowledge of natural science and humanities, logic and historicism of Marxist theory, and archaeological culture.

In 1965 Gefter considered problems connected with the cult of the personality (Stalinism), voluntarism, censorship, *glasnost* and democracy and historical research. At that time he was closely linked to the journal *Novy mir*, under the editorship of A. T. Tvardovsky. After the splitting of the institute in 1968, his sector became part of the department of general problems of the world historical process of the institute of general history, USSR Academy of Sciences. In 1969, under pressure from above, the sector ceased to exist and became an unofficial scientific community. In 1970 the department was abolished, but nevertheless in the succeeding years its work was carried on in the collections *The Laws of History and the Concrete Forms of the World Historical Process. Problems in the History of Pre-Capitalist Societies* (1968) and *The Study of Sources: Theoretical and Methodological Problems* (1970). *Lenin and Problems of the History of Classes and Class Struggle* and *Historical Science and Some Contemporary Problems. Articles and Discussions*, were never published. Gefter then joined the sector of modern and contemporary history (of the West) and left in 1974. Much of his work in the 1970s and 1980s was unpublished.

The advent of *perestroika* made it possible for him to publish once again. Many of his articles on the fate of Marxism and the phenomenon of Stalinism were published in the journals *Rabochy klass i sovremenny mir* and *Svobodnaya mysl*. Gefter believes that the centre of the contemporary world crisis is Russia. Russia has not become Eurasia and it is condemned to exist as a geopolitical area, but distinctions will emerge if the politics of force can be avoided. Sovereign states must live together with their adversaries and eventually they will co-operate on the basis of the international division of labour. We are now going through hard times and the failure of *perestroika* has led to the adherence to certain views, excluding others. The slogan of moving from socialism to capitalism is too simple. Gefter advocates the free market but is not in favour of a rapid transition to it and all alternatives should be considered, as the road to harmony is through conflict, which is normal. He is opposed to the enforced dissolution of collective and state farms.

He became a member of the presidential Council in February 1993. He lives in Moscow.

Gekht, Yury Grigorevich

Leader of the Russian parliamentary faction, Industrial Union.

Born on July 23, 1943 in Krasnovershersk, Perm *oblast*; Russian. He was a member of the CPSU until August 1991. He graduated from the S. M. Kirov Academy of Timber Technology, Leningrad (St Petersburg), and is an industrial economist. After graduation he worked as head of a department, then head of production, Arkhangelsk paper combine, Novodvinsk (1975-79); head of production and acting director of the Soyuz production association of technical paper, Moscow (1979-80); deputy general director of the same association (1980-82); deputy general director for production of the Voskhod scientific production association (1982-85); deputy general director for supply and sales of the Bratsky LPK production association, USSR Ministry of the Timber Industry, Bratsk (1985-87); and director of the Serpukhov paper factory, Moscow *oblast* (1987-90). In 1990 he became general director of the Sokolniki joint stock company and in 1990 he was elected an RSFSR people's deputy.

In the second half of 1991 Gekht joined the parliamentary faction, Industrial Union and became one of its leaders, although until then he had not participated in any political grouping. Under his leadership, Industrial Union (previously known as organizers of the national economy) changed from being a conservative communist faction into one of the factions of the parliamentary centre. One of the goals of Industrial Union was to secure priority for work collectives when the enterprises were privatized. At the VI Congress of People's Deputies, in April 1992, Gekht was one of the organizers of the "constructive opposition" coalition, Creative Forces. Gekht was cool towards Arkady Volsky, a key leader of Civic Union, and his attempts to establish a party of directors around his Russian union of industrialists and entrepreneurs. Gekht is married and has a daughter.

Address: 103274 Moscow, K 274, Krasnopresnenskaya nab., d. 2, Dom Sovetov.

Gen, Nikolai Leonidovich

Chairman of the commission of the Council of Nationalities, Russian Supreme Soviet, on nation state system and inter-ethnic relations.

Born on April 29, 1958; Russian. His father worked in the Storozhevsky timber production enterprise. He was a member of the CPSU from 1986 to August 1991. After secondary school he entered the faculty of law, Perm State University. He is a lawyer, and in 1981 he was appointed to the Komi ASSR public prosecutor's office. In 1990 he was an examining magistrate on the most important cases in the Syktyvkar public prosecutor's office, and specialized in economic crimes by public officials, the taking of bribes, rapes and murders. He was a member of the informal political associations: initiative; Democratic Elections 1990; *Komi kotyr* (Komi lights).

He was nominated for election as an RSFSR people's deputy in the No. 109 Syktyvkar national territorial district, Komi ASSR, by the city *Komsomol* organization. During the election campaign he advocated the creation of a *Rechtsstaat* (law-governed state); priority to be afforded human rights, and separation of powers; removal of the CPSU apparatus from the agencies of state power; the adoption of laws to prevent the armed forces and agencies of state security being deployed against the nation; and defence of citizens' social rights. He supported the establishment of strong economic, political and legislative mechanism to combat the shadow economy and corruption, and intensification of the struggle against crime. Relations between the Komi ASSR and the centre should be laid down in law. He favoured all power to the soviets; effective social policies to solve the food problem; and supplying the market with an adequate amount of consumer goods. An end should be made to the senseless waste of national resources.

There were eight candidates. Gen polled 27,603 votes in the first round, and won the second round, polling 55,144 votes. His main opponent was G. A. Yushkov, chairman of the board of the union of writers of the Komi ASSR, who received 19,422 votes in the first round and 51,030 votes in the second round. Gen was elected a member of the RSFSR Supreme Soviet at the I Congress of People's Deputies (878 voted for, 45 voted against), and he is also a member of the Council of Nationalities. He was secretary of the Supreme Soviet committee on legislation and on youth, and was elected deputy chairman of the commission of the Council of Nationalities, Russian Supreme Soviet, on the national state system and inter-ethnic relations; later he became chairman of the commission. He is a member of the Smena (new policy) parliamentary faction. He is married with three children.

Address: 103274 Moscow, K 274, Krasnopresnenskaya nab., d. 2, Dom Sovetov; *telephone*: Moscow 205 52 40.

Gerashchenko, Viktor Vladimirovich

Chairman of the Russian Central Bank.

Born on December 21, 1937 in Leningrad into a civil servant's family. His father was chairman of the administration of the USSR State Bank. He was a member of the CPSU from 1963 to 1991 and was a member of the Party Central Committee from July 1990. He graduated from the Moscow institute of finance in 1960 and then became a bookkeeper in the USSR State Bank. In 1961 he moved to the USSR Bank for Foreign Trade (Vneshtorgbank) as a bookkeeper, inspector, specialist and head of a section and in 1965 he was appointed director of the Moscow Narodny Bank in London, England. In 1967 he became deputy manager and then manager of the Moscow Narodny Bank in Beirut, Lebanon.

In 1972 he was appointed deputy head, then head of the board of the USSR Bank for Foreign Trade; in 1974 he became chairman of the board of the Soviet Bank in West Germany; and in 1977 he became manager of the Moscow Narodny Bank in Singapore. In 1982 he became the head of the administration, then deputy deputy chairman of the board and then first deputy chairman of the board of the USSR Bank for Foreign Trade. In 1985 he was appointed first deputy chairman of the board of the USSR Bank of Foreign Economic Affairs and between 1989 and 1991 he was chairman of the board of the USSR State Bank.

In August 1992 he was appointed acting chairman of the Russian Central Bank and at the V session of the Russian Supreme Soviet he was confirmed in office. His appointment was a victory for the industrial lobby which had severely criticized his predecessor for his tight monetary policy. Gerashchenko began to expand credit to enterprises very rapidly in order that they could pay inter-enterprise debt, but this increase in the money supply fuelled inflation. When Boris Fedorov joined the Chernomyrdin government and became responsible for state finances in March 1993 a battle developed between him and Gerashchenko. Fedorov appeared at times to have convinced Gerashchenko to restrict credit but the Central Bank in the end was subordinate to parliament and not the government. He lives in Moscow.

Gerasimov, Gennady Ivanovich

Russian ambassador to Portugal.

Born in 1930 in Elabug, Elabuzhsky *raion*, Tatar ASSR; Russian. He was a member of the CPSU until August 1991. He graduated from the faculty of international law, Moscow State Institute of International Relations. He has the rank of an ambassador extraordinary and plenipotentiary. He worked on *Novoe Vremya* (new times) and *Trud* (1960-67); then he was a political observer for Novosti (1967-83); he worked in the US; he was on the editorial board of the international communist journal, *Problems of Peace and Socialism*, Prague; editor-in-chief of *Moscow News*, and deputy chairman of the board of Novosti (1983-86); and head of the administration of information, USSR Ministry of Foreign Affairs (1986-90). He was then appointed USSR ambassador to Portugal and in December 1992 Russian ambassador to Portugal. He was co-chairman of the Soviet-US charitable fund, *Perestroika*: Washington-Moscow. He was awarded the prize "communicator of the year", by the national association of government spokesmen.

He became internationally famous during the *perestroika* years as the voice of *glasnost*. His fluent control of English and his quick mind and wit produced some memorable quotes, one of which was the Sinatra doctrine, borrowed from the well-known song: "I'll do it my way". He was a constant companion of President Mikhail Gorbachev and Eduard Shevardnadze at summits and other trips and he did much to bring Russian wit and humour back into international politics. He was moved to Portugal at a time when conservative communists were gaining in influence, as they did not take easily to his style and originality. He was succeeded by a fluent English-speaking spokesman who took no liberties with his brief.

Address: Embassy of the Russian Federation, Lisbon, Portugal.

Gerasimov, Valentin Pavlovich

Head of the Administration of Kurgan *oblast*, Russian Federation.

Born on May 28, 1940 in Shumikho, Shumikhinsky *raion*, Kurgan *oblast* into a worker's family; Russian; member of the CPSU until August 1991. He graduated from the Military Aviation Technical College, Kharkov (Kharkiv), Ukraine, and then entered the Institute of Machine Building, Kurgan. After graduation he worked as as an experimental engineer at a bus enterprise and later became chief engineer. He worked for 15 years in the bus enterprise, and then in 1979 transferred to Party and soviet work. He graduated from the academy of social sciences of the Party Central Committee as an external student, and in 1988 was elected chairman of the Kurgan *oblast* soviet executive committee. He has received state awards.

In March 1990 he was nominated as a candidate for election as an RSFSR people's deputy in the No. 485 Shumikhinsky territorial district. During the election campaign he stated that he supported the introduction of the post of President and democratic development, but opposed anarchy and voluntarism. The country needed order based on the strict observance of the law. He was in favour of market relations and economic cost accounting, and stated that in the near future equivalent exchange between urban industry and rural agriculture should be introduced.

In the first round Gerasimov polled 46.67% of the votes and his only opponent, A. B. Sokolov, chief engineer of the A. S. Pushkin collective farm, Shumikhinsky *raion*, 37.9% of the votes. Since neither candidate had secured over half the votes there had to be a second round of voting. However, both candidates declined to run a second time. In April 1990 Gerasimov was again nominated for election as an RSFSR people's deputy in the Shumikhinsky territorial district by the conference of the Shumikhinsky machine building enterprise, the assembly of the Zavety Ilicha collective farm and the conference of the Shumikhinsky *raion* union of consumers, and this time there were three candidates. In April Gerasimov won in the second round, polling 67.5% of the votes.

At the first session of the Kurgan *oblast* soviet of people's deputies, in April 1990, he was elected chairman of the executive committee. Previously Gerasimov was a member of the communists of Russia parliamentary group of deputies.

On August 21, 1991 Gerasimov spoke on Kurgan *oblast* radio on behalf of the soviet executive committee, and appealed to the population of Kurgan *oblast* to be calm, to observe law and order, and work honestly. He stated that on the territory of the *oblast* the laws of the Russian Federation and the previously adopted laws of the USSR would be observed.

In November 1991 he was appointed head of the administration of Kurgan *oblast* by presidential decree. On assuming office he again underlined his commitment to economic reform, supported the concept of economic cost accounting for the regions, the transition to the principle of self-financing and self-government. The economic programme was to bring benefits to the population soon and not in the distant future.

In December 1992 he opposed the holding of a referendum. However, he believed that the VII Congress of People's Deputies had not done its duty, since finding solutions to the economic problems had been pushed further down the agenda. Instead a political struggle had developed which benefited no one. He declared at the congress that he supported the President and in the future would continue to support his reforms. He is married with a daughter and lives in Kurgan.

Gidaspov, Boris Veniaminovich

Former first secretary of the Leningrad Party *obkom*.

Born on April 19, 1933 in Kuibyshev, where his father was an office worker. He is Russian, and was a member of the CPSU from 1962 to August 1991. In 1955 he graduated from the V. V. Kuibyshev Industrial Institute, Kuibyshev, and was immediately appointed an assistant lecturer. In 1959 he became a postgraduate student, then senior engineer in a design laboratory, and then junior scientific assistant, assistant, senior lecturer, assistant professor (*dotsent*) and in 1965 dean and professor of the institute. He successfully presented both his candidate dissertation (PhD) and his doctoral dissertation in chemistry

(DSc). From 1969 he was head of department, Lensovet technological institute, Leningrad, and from 1971 chief instructor of the Tekhnolog special construction and technology bureau.

In 1977 he was appointed director of the State Institute of Applied Chemistry and in 1985 general director of the scientific research association of the same institute. In 1988 he became chairman of the board of the inter-branch state association, Tekhnokhim, Leningrad, and was elected a corresponding member of the USSR Academy of Sciences. In 1989 he became first secretary of the Leningrad Party *obkom*, and in the same year was elected a USSR people's deputy for Petrogradsky territorial district, Leningrad. He became a member of the Party Central Committee and a secretary of the Party Central Committee in July 1990. He was a delegate to the XXVII, and XXVIII Party congresses and the XIX Party conference.

Gidaspov was on the conservative wing of the party and was critical of Gorbachev's handling of many issues. The Baltic republics were of special concern to him and he would have liked to have more decisive action by the USSR President to contain nationalism. He was swept aside by Anatoly Sobchak during the attempted state coup of August 1991.

He received several orders of Lenin, the October Revolution, the Red Banner of Labour and medals, and is a Lenin and state prize-winner. He is married, and his wife, Zinaida Ivanovna, successfully presented her candidate dissertation in chemistry (PhD) but is now a pensioner. Their son, Dmitry, works for the Tekhnolog special construction and technology bureau in St Petersburg. Gidaspov lives in St Petersburg.

Glazev, Sergei Yurevich

Russian Minister of Foreign Economic Relations.

Born on January 1, 1961 in Zaporozhe, Ukraine, he graduated from the economics faculty of Moscow State University, specializing in economics and cybernetics. He speaks English. From 1983 to 1986 he was a postgraduate student in the Central mathematical economics institute of the USSR Academy of Sciences and successfully presented his candidate dissertation (PhD (Econ)). From 1986 he headed a laboratory in the mathematical economics institute, and in 1989 he successfully presented his doctoral dissertation (DSc (Econ)) and thereby became one of the youngest doctors of economic sciences.

In 1991 he accepted an invitation to work in the International Institute of Applied Economics and Systems Analysis in Vienna, but declined at the last moment after having being invited by Petr Aven, the Russian Minister of Foreign Economic Relations, to become his first deputy minister. He was responsible for creating a normative basis for foreign economic activity, but this led to extreme conflict between importers and exporters. Glazev initiated the auctions of export quotas for goods and devised a list of principal normative acts, establishing the necessary legal minimum for normal foreign economic activity.

Petr Aven regarded Glazev as a very capable, responsible and highly educated person, but who could be excessively straightforward. Glazev's name sometimes came up as a desirable person for the government in the opinion of various factions and politicians. However, he does not regard himself as linked to any faction or movement.

In December 1992 he was appointed Russian Minister of External Economic Relations in the government headed by Viktor Chernomyrdin. Aven was one of the ministers sacrificed by President Yeltsin in a vain attempt to reach a compromise with the Congress of People's Deputies. As minister Glazev regards it as advisable to continue the policies of his predecessor since he believes that the stability of the rules of the game is just as important as trying to improve them. According to some specialists, Glazev is more inclined than Aven towards state intervention in foreign economic activity. Among the new minister's main tasks are support for the export drive and the discovery of markets for Russian products abroad, and better economic relations with the states of the former USSR. He is also responsible for Russia's negotiations with GATT (General Agreement on Tariffs and Trade). He is married with a son and lives in Moscow.

Golembiovsky, Igor Nestorovich

Editor-in-chief of the newspaper *Izvestiya*.

Born in 1936 in Tbilisi, Georgian SSR into a Russian-Georgian family. He graduated from Tbilisi State University, and then worked as a correspondent on one of the Georgian youth newspapers. Later he was invited to work in the Central Committee of the *Komsomol* where he wrote speeches and provided reviews of the press for the first secretary of the *Komsomol* Central Committee, V. Pavlov. However, due to divergences in the evaluation of some newspapers, especially *Yunost*, Golembiovsky was forced to leave the *Komsomol* Central Committee in 1966.

The same year he began to work on *Izvestiya*, in the department of letters. In the 1970s he was a special correspondent of *Izvestiya* and its special correspondent in several Latin American countries. In the early 1980s he was its secretary and from 1986 first deputy editor-in-chief. He was a member of the USSR union of journalists. From 1990 to 1991 there was conflict between the editor-in-chief of *Izvestiya*, N. I. Efimov, supported by the chairman of the USSR Supreme Soviet, Anatoly Lukyanov, and the collective of the newspaper, as regards its position and the material which was published in it. The work collective of *Izvestiya* expressed their lack of trust in the editor and proposed Golembiovsky as his replacement. N. I. Efimov decided to send Golembiovsky as special correspondent of the newspaper to Spain, but the work collective insisted that Golembiovsky remain first deputy editor-in-chief.

On August 22, 1991 the work collective of the newspaper decided that N. I. Efimov be removed as editor-in-chief because during the attempted state coup he had carried out all decisions of the Extraordinary Committee, and on August 23, 1991 Golembiovsky was elected editor in chief of *Izvestiya*. In September 1992 the newspaper publishing complex, *Izvestiya*, was established by decree of the chairman of the state committee on property of the Russian Federation, Anatoly Chubais, and Golembiovsky was appointed general director of the complex. He is married and his son lives in Tbilisi. He speaks Spanish and lives in Moscow.

Golikov, Vyacheslav Mikhailovich

Chairman of the council of workers' committee of the Kuzbass.

Born in 1952 in Komsomolsk-on-Amur, Siberia. His father had been designated a kulak and deported to the region during collectivization in the early 1930s. In 1953 the family moved to the Kuzbass, to the town of Berezovsky, and after secondary school he began work in the Pervomaiskaya coal mine where his father worked. He worked there until July 1989 (except for service in the Soviet army) as an electrical fitter repairing underground equipment. He graduated from the mining technical college as an external student.

In June 1989, on the second day of the miners strike, Golikov was elected chairman of the city strike committee in Berezovsky and in early 1991 he was one of the organizers and leaders of the all-Union miners' political strike. In 1992 by decision of the workers' committees of the Kuzbass he negotiated with Egor Gaidar and other members of the Russian government on the provision of guarantees for the social protection of miners and the enterprise board of the coal mining sector of the economy.

In 1990 he was elected a deputy of the Kemerovo *oblast* and city soviets. He was the only worker (in the spring and autumn of 1991) who was appointed to the consultative co-ordinating council of the Speaker of the RSFSR Supreme Soviet and the consultative council of the President of Russia.

At present he does not work as a miner but heads the council of the workers' committees of the Kuzbass. In early 1992 he was badly beaten and spent six months in hospital recovering. He has advocated that workers be afforded the right to participate in reform, privatization and freedom to dispose of their own produce, and he supports the creation in the Kuzbass of a free economic zone. In 1992 he repeatedly opposed a general strike and criticized the official trade unions for calling for one. In his view, such initiatives were only intended by the leadership of the federation of free trade unions of Russia to bring down the Gaidar government.

As an alternative to the official trade unions he proposes really independent unions which would guarantee the professional and human rights of working people. He accused the leadership of the federation of independent trade unions and the chairman of the Kemerovo *oblast* soviet, A. G. Tuleev, of conducting a policy aimed at blocking reform.

He is married and his daughter has just left school. He loves music, studied in a school of music and plays the accordion. He prefers light music and jazz, and is a great admirer of the Beatles. He lives in Berezovsky, Kemerovo *oblast*.

Golovnev, Anatoly Andreevich

Head of Chief Combat Training Administration, deputy Commander-in-Chief of land forces of the Russian Federation; Lieutenant-General.

Born in 1942 in the village of Medvedovka, Smolensk *oblast* into a collective farmer's family; Russian. He received a higher military education and graduated from the RSFSR Supreme Soviet Moscow Higher Military Officers' Technical school in 1963, from the M. V. Frunze Military Academy in 1973 and the Military Academy of the General Staff in 1980. He was a member of the CPSU until August 1991.

He began his career as an officer in the Far East as a motorized-rifle platoon commander, where he was noted for his sound professional training and a talent for organization and teaching. An enthusiastic member of the *Komsomol* and the Party, he enjoyed the respect and support of superior officers and Party-political agencies. He filled all officer and staff posts at battalion, regimental, divisional and army levels. Gen. A. Golovnev had the record of an officer with a sound operational-tactical and military-technical training, able to plan operations of heterogeneous land forces, devoted to communist ideology and strongly supporting the political line of the Soviet state. Golovnev served in Ukraine and in the group of Soviet troops in Germany.

In 1989 he was appointed the first deputy commander of Moscow military district, one of the most prestigious and promising places of service. Gen. A. Golovnev was directly in charge of organizing the combat training of troops, of keeping units and formations in high fighting trim.

During the anti-constitutional putsch in August 1991, together with the commander, Col.-Gen. Kalinin, he brought the troops into Moscow and ensured the state of emergency. He fully supported and obeyed without demur all instructions of the Emergency Committee and Minister of Defence Marshal D. Yazov. He is undoubtedly to blame for the use of the army against its own people. However, when the situation changed, as early as August 21, 1991 he supervised the withdrawal of troops and *matériel* from the city. Later his activity came under scrutiny but with no deleterious effects on his career.

He does not express his political views in public, but appeared in the press, justifying the actions of soldiers when they stormed the barricades which resulted in the death of three defenders of the White House. He is eager to have the image of a military professional who is above politics and advocates raising the army's authority, creating Russian armed forces to meet current demands. In his attitude towards state power he is a conformist who easily renounced his former convictions and views, and democratic forces in the army are suspicious of him. He enjoys the support of Minister of Defence P. Grachev.

He is interested in literature, art and sport as a recreation. He does not speak any foreign language and has not been abroad as a member of an official delegation.

In August 1992 he was appointed head of Chief Combat Training Administration and deputy Commander-in-Chief of land forces for combat training. He presented his programme in an interview with *Krasnaya Zvezda* on September 8, 1992, "Conscription, contract, and combat training". He has been awarded two orders and medals. He is married.

Office address: 103175 Moscow K-175.

Gorbachev, Mikhail Sergeevich

Former President of the USSR and General Secretary of the CPSU. President of the M. S. Gorbachev fund.

Born on March 2, 1931 in the village of Privolnoe, Krasnogvardeisky *raion*, Stavropol *krai*, into a Russian family during collectivization which caused great damage to the rich Cossack farmland. His father was Sergei Andreevich, a Stavropol peasant, who worked as a machine operator for 40 years. During the Great Fatherland War (1941-45) he was a sapper and was seriously wounded. Mikhail Sergeevich's mother is Maria Panteleevna, also a Stavropol peasant.

He is married to Raisa Maksimovna (née Titorenko) who was born in 1932 in Biisk, Altai *krai*. She studied in the sociology department of the philosophy faculty in Moscow State University. She met Mikhail Sergeevich at university and they married in 1953. She taught for over 20 years in further education institutions and successfully presented her candidate dissertation on the living standards of collective farm peasants in Stavropol *krai* in the philosophy department of Moscow State University (PhD). In 1987 she became a member of the board of the Lenin children's fund. After her husband became General Secretary of the CPSU in 1985 she accompanied him on visits at home and abroad. She became very popular abroad but caused great jealousy at home. This was partly due to male concern about her influence over her husband and female dislike of her extensive wardrobe and access to the good things of life. The Gorbachevs have a daughter, Irina, who is a doctor in Moscow. Her husband, Anatoly, is also a doctor, and they have two daughters, Xenia and Anastasia.

Gorbachev is a qualified lawyer and economist. He studied law at Moscow State University and graduated in 1955. Zdenek Mlynar, a Czech fellow student and later a leading figure in the Prague Spring of 1968, remembers him as possessing an independent mind, but others are not so generous, seeing him as a dedicated *Komsomol* activist and stern disciplinarian. He received his economics training as an external student of the economics faculty of Stavropol Agricultural Institute and graduated in 1967.

He has no advanced degrees, except honorary ones awarded when he was Soviet leader. He began work in 1944 (his region was under German occupation from August 1942 to January 1943 and the family appear to have remained there during that time) in a collective farm (*kolkhoz*) and in 1946 became an assistant to a combine harvester driver in a Machine Tractor Station. While still a teenager he was awarded the Red Banner of Labour, a high Soviet decoration, for good farm results. This was his passport to higher things and he was sent by the local Party organization to Moscow State University in 1950. He either chose or was advised to read law, which did not have a high status but it did include courses on the history of European law and training in rhetoric. He later remarked that mathematics was a great interest, but presumably he was not qualified to enter the prestigious mathematics faculty. On entering university he immediately became involved in the *Komsomol* and was a member of the faculty committee, worked in the instruction section of the faculty committee and became its deputy head.

He joined the CPSU in 1952 and quickly became the secretary of the *Komsomol* organization of the law faculty. On graduation in 1955 he either did not attempt to become a postgraduate or failed to become one. Instead he and his wife made for Stavropol *krai* where he worked for a short time as a lawyer before becoming deputy head of the department of agitation and propaganda of Stavropol Party *krai* committee (*kraikom*). In 1956 he was elected first secretary of Stavropol city *Komsomol* committee. In 1958 he became second secretary of Stavropol *Komsomol kraikom* and in 1960 first secretary. In March 1962 he made the transition to CPSU work when he was appointed a Party organizer of the territorial state and collective farm production administration of the Stavropol Party *kraikom*.

In December 1964 he was deputy head of Party agencies of the Stavropol agricultural Party *kraikom*. (In 1962 Nikita Khrushchev, the CPSU first secretary, divided Party organizations into industrial and agricultural wings according to the dominant economic activity of the region.) In September 1966 Gorbachev was elected first secretary of Stavropol city Party committee (*gorkom*). Then in August 1968 he moved upwards to become second secretary of Stavropol Party *kraikom* and in April 1970 was elected first secretary. He climbed the ladder of Party work quickly and could not have done so without powerful patrons. Among them were Fedor Kulakov, his predecessor as first secretary of Stavropol Party *kraikom*, and Mikhail Suslov, chief ideologist of the CPSU and closely linked to Stavropol *krai*. Gorbachev was fortunate that there are many spas and holiday resorts in the *krai* and this brought him into contact with many of the leading lights of Soviet life, since as Party leader it fell to him to welcome them when they descended on the region.

In July 1978 he again succeeded Kulakov who had died suddenly either from natural causes or by his own hand. This time it was in Moscow as Central Committee (CC) secretary for agriculture. He was confirmed in this post on November 27, 1978. On December 4, 1978 he was relieved of his duties as first secretary of Stavropol Party *kraikom*. On November 27, 1979 he was elected a candidate (non-voting) member of the Politburo of the CC, CPSU and on October 21, 1980 became a full member. The peasant's son from Stavropol who spoke with a southern accent had arrived at the summit of power. There was only one further step, to leader of the Party, and he was well qualified for the job, being a CC secretary and a full member of the Politburo. The Politburo he found himself in was staffed with geriatrics and Leonid Brezhnev was in physical and mental decline from the later 1970s. He was the youngest man there by over a decade. The fact that he was so rapidly promoted despite his modest success in charge of agriculture reveals that he had powerful patrons, and this, in turn, was due to Gorbachev's great interpersonal skills and his oral charm and fluency.

In May 1982 his agricultural production programme was adopted at a plenum of the Party CC, but it did not halt the decline of Soviet agriculture. From the mid-1970s the Soviet Union began to import more and more grain from North America despite being potentially one of the richest agricultural countries in the world. Brezhnev was succeeded by Yury Andropov as Party leader but he became mortally ill soon after assuming office. Gorbachev became his deputy and it was Andropov's wish that Gorbachev succeed him, but the old men in the Politburo ensured that this did not occur. Instead Konstantin Chernenko succeeded but was physically incapable of carrying out his full duties because of emphysema. Gorbachev again was his deputy and he probably chaired more Politburo meetings than Chernenko during the latter's reign at the top.

Gorbachev took the opportunity to travel; he had previously been in Italy, and when in Canada met the Soviet ambassador, Aleksandr Yakovlev, who had been banished there under Brezhnev for being too critically minded. The two took to one another instantly. In London, in December 1984, Gorbachev worked his magic with Margaret Thatcher who declared that he was a man she "could do business with". The British Prime Minister was always enormously supportive of Gorbachev's efforts to regenerate the Soviet Union and afforded him useful service. In December 1984 he had had to cut his visit short because of the death of Marshal Dmitry Ustinov, the Minister of Defence, who was followed soon after by Chernenko to the grave.

Gorbachev's election as General Secretary of the CC, CPSU, in March 1985 was a close run thing. Two conservatives, Vladimir Shcherbitsky, who was in the US, and Dinmukhamed Kunaev, Party boss in Kazakhstan, missed the meeting which was called by the sudden death of Chernenko, as Alma Ata was five hours by plane from Moscow. Gorbachev was proposed by Andrei Gromyko, the Soviet foreign minister, and Egor Ligachev. The decision of the Politburo was passed to the CC which was also hastily convened. One report states that about a third of the members were not present and Gorbachev was pushed through without a vote being taken.

It transpired later that Gorbachev was not the master in his own house. Gorbachev became General Secretary but Egor Ligachev was appointed head of the CC secretariat. The latter agency is the brain of the Party, receiving and processing reports from Party officials everywhere. It also controlled appointments. Gorbachev's two main opponents for the top spot, Grigory Romanov, the Leningrad boss, and Viktor Grishin, the Moscow boss, were quickly swept from the political stage, the former being accused of alcoholism and womanizing and the latter of corruption, being popularly known as the godfather. Some astute horsetrading by Gorbachev got some of his associates, including Yakovlev, into the Politburo.

Gorbachev was unaware of the systemic weakness of socialism when he took over. He later ruefully admitted that the first two years were wasted economically because he was oblivious to the crisis the country was in. There is an element here of being wise after the event since radical economists had pointed out the looming danger, but he complained that no one had the full picture and that much was kept secret. If we are to take him at his word the Soviet Union was being led by men who were unaware of the real state of the country. A less generous interpretation would be that Gorbachev did not bother himself unduly with economic policy.

Before he became leader he had attended many seminars by thinkers such as the economist Abel Aganbegyan and the sociologist Tatyana Zaslavskaya. Both regarded the communist system as sound in principle, all that was needed was to root out corruption and get people to work. Zaslavskaya regarded the party *nomenklatura* as parasitical and a brake on economic advance and believed that the solution was to remove its members from the levers of economic power. Gorbachev's early economic policies accepted that the system was basically sound, and he prescribed acceleration (*uskorenie*) (at least 4% annually) and an improvement of the whole mechanism. He devoted more attention to foreign affairs, as he was convinced by the argument that the defence burden was crippling the Soviet Union and hence a *rapprochement* with the US and NATO was necessary.

On his initiative President Ronald Reagan and he met in Geneva in November 1985 and their relationship blossomed. They agreed to speed up arms talks. Gorbachev was determined to demonstrate that he was a different type of Soviet leader, someone whose "new political thinking" represented a sea change in policy. One aspect of this new thinking was that the world was interdependent and that no country could achieve security if it made other states insecure. Gorbachev's new approach was a far cry from the foreign policy of Andrei Gromyko, known as "Grim Grom" and Mr "Nyet" or Mr No for always replying in the negative. Gorbachev showed scant regard for one of his patrons when, in July 1985, he moved Gromyko upwards to become Soviet President and made Eduard Shevardnadze, a former Georgian Party leader, foreign minister.

Disaster struck on April 26, 1986 at 01.23 am when the worst nuclear accident in history occurred at Chernobyl, in Ukraine. Gorbachev and the leadership appear to have been unaware of the dimension of the tragedy, possibly due to faulty reporting from Ukraine. The Politburo only met on May 2 after allowing May Day parades to take place in Kiev and other areas affected by fall-out. A hesitant Gorbachev waited until May 14 before addressing the nation on TV. A generous interpretation of this behaviour would be that he waited until the matter was under control before he spoke. However, the delay affected his credibility and the new policy of *glasnost* or openness was introduced. Glavlit, the official political censor, was deprived of its powers in the summer of 1986, and this was due to the efforts of Gorbachev and Aleksandr Yakovlev who championed the critics of conservative socialism.

The fiercest critic of openness was Egor Ligachev who saw it as undermining the authority of the Party and sowing ethnic distrust and conflict. Since Gorbachev wanted the intelligentsia on the side of his reforms, he found it useful to give Yakovlev some licence. Gorbachev does not appear to have perceived the danger of *glasnost* polarizing society. He arranged for the return of Academician Andrei Sakharov from exile in Gorky (Nizhny Novgorod) in December 1986 and this was followed by most dissidents being released from labour camps and prisons in 1987.

His bold attempt to strike a deal with President Reagan failed at Reykjavik in October 1986, but they narrowed their differences on an Intermediate Range Nuclear Forces (INF) treaty. Gorbachev's bid to eliminate ballistic missiles misfired because the Americans were determined to go ahead with the "Star Wars" programme. In Washington in December 1987 Gorbachev and Reagan signed the INF treaty abolishing land-based medium range missiles and made progress on a Strategic Arms Reduction Treaty (START).

A major step forward was the withdrawal of Soviet troops from Afghanistan in February 1989. In May-June 1989 the two presidents exchanged instruments of ratification for the INF treaty, but failed to make substantial progress on the START treaty. They signed agreements on ballistic missile testing, nuclear test monitoring, space research and cultural exchanges. In December 1988 at the UN in New York Gorbachev promised significant cuts in Soviet armed forces and President Reagan promised that existing US policies would continue under the incoming President George Bush, who attended the meeting. In December 1989 in Malta, Presidents Bush and Gorbachev agreed to activate START talks in time for the summit meeting in June in the US. They agreed not to interfere in the revolutions which were sweeping through eastern Europe, and the US promised to promote USSR participation in the Western market economy.

In May-June 1990 in Washington Gorbachev and Bush agreed to end production of chemical weapons and halve existing stocks by 2,000. They signed a START treaty which envisaged a 30% reduction in long range nuclear missiles. They were to have closer trade links but no agreement was reached on the security arrangements for a future united Germany. In July 1991 in Moscow, Gorbachev, in what was to prove his final flourish in foreign affairs, and Bush signed the START treaty. This was an historic agreement since it was the first to reduce and destroy existing nuclear weapons.

Gorbachev was by instinct a centrist, a man who always wanted to compromise, but the crisis now facing the country led to more radical solutions being offered. Political reform had to accompany economic reform, otherwise the latter would fail. Reformers can be divided into two groups: the moderates and the radicals. The moderates, led by Ligachev, preferred slow, controlled reform, based on the leading role of the Party. The radicals, led by Yeltsin, favoured breaking with the past. Gorbachev was not willing to back Yeltsin when the latter pilloried the privileges of the Party and Yeltsin was thrown to the wolves in October 1987 and dismissed as Moscow Party leader. However, Yeltsin was not banished from Moscow and was given a state post with the rank of minister.

Opposition to *perestroika* was becoming stronger and in March 1988 a vitriolic attack was published by Nina Andreeva, a Leningrad chemistry teacher, while Gorbachev was away from Moscow. Ligachev always denied that he was involved, but he was the spiritual father. Gorbachev was always in search of an institution to implement *perestroika*, but the obvious choice, the Party secretariat, was under the influence of Ligachev and most Party officials were conservatives. Gorbachev decided to cut the Gordian knot and to emasculate the secretariat. This he did at the XIX Party Congress in June 1988. The Party was withdrawn from involvement in the economy and the secretariat lost its control over soviets and its dominance of Party affairs. Gorbachev hoped that local soviets would take over the co-ordinating role which the Party had played but this was not to be. The Soviet Union began to unravel. Secretariat influence was reduced at a time of rising ethnic and nationalist tension and declining living standards. The conference also approved elections to the new USSR Congress of People's Deputies.

However, Gorbachev wanted to ensure a solid communist majority in the congress. He therefore proposed that there should be 2,250 deputies of whom 750 would be nominated by the CPSU and other bodies, and the others would be directly elected by the population. During his travels he had always taken a keen interest in the moral and social role of the churches and the millennium of Orthodox Christianity was celebrated in 1988 with much pomp and ceremony. Gorbachev had been baptized into the church and his mother was a believer, and his use of biblical allusions testified to his mother's influence. On one occasion he told his audience that *perestroika* was not like manna coming down from heaven and on another that he was not Jesus Christ nor was he a saviour.

Ill-equipped to comprehend ethnic nationalism, Gorbachev was shocked by the riots in Alma Ata and elsewhere in Kazakhstan after the dismissal of the Kazakh Party leader, Kunaev, and his replacement by a Russian, Kolbin. The conflict in Nagorno-Karabakh flared up in early 1988 and proved insoluble. Other ethnic bloodletting occurred in Uzbekistan, Kazakhstan, Azerbaijan (Sumgait and other towns), Georgia and the Baltic republics. Gorbachev decided that the old guard had had its day and he removed Gromyko and took on the presidency himself on October 1, 1988 as well as clearing the gerontocrats from the Politburo and Central Committee. Ligachev was moved from ideology to agriculture, a thankless task.

The anti-alcohol campaign, inherited from the Andropov era, finally ran out of steam and was abandoned. The General Secretary was dismissively referred to as comrade mineral water secretary. Gorbachev was the last of a long line of Soviet leaders who treated alcoholism as an economic problem: reduce output and raise the price was his only solution to this age-old Russian vice. Alcoholism is a medical problem and this aspect was not addressed. Sadly for Gorbachev the anti-alcohol campaign had unfortunate side-effects. It gave a powerful stimulus to the production of *samogon* or hooch and became a money spinner for the nascent mafia. Alcohol sales had previously contributed huge amounts to the Soviet treasury, but no one thought to compensate by imposing other taxes or cutting state spending. The result was inflation which began to accelerate from 1988. The other stimulus to inflation was the law on the state enterprise which became effective from January 1988 and permitted enterprises to set their own wage funds. They all seized this opportunity to pay themselves much more and the centre lost control of wages.

The first moderately democratic elections since November 1917 took place in March 1989 and resulted in many communist officials being defeated. Among those elected were Yeltsin and Sakharov. The first session, in May 1989, opened with a minute's silence for the victims of the Tbilisi massacre in April 1989 when 20 civilian demonstrators had been killed by the military. An official opposition was forming. Gorbachev soon tired of the congress and found it unwieldy and increasingly willing to challenge his authority.

He had come to the conclusion that the regimes in eastern Europe were anachronistic and needed their own brand of *perestroika*, so he encouraged radicals to challenge entrenched leaders but assumed that the result would be beneficial to the Soviet Union. Instead it revealed that communism in eastern Europe had little legitimacy and had no reserves to call on. He intrigued against Erich Honecker, the GDR leader, and assumed that Egon Krenz, his successor, would pilot the GDR forward towards democratic socialism. He is to be commended for allowing the revolutions (or perhaps change of ruling generation) to take their course, expressly ruling out Soviet military intervention to keep old leaders in power. In the GDR he was lulled into believing that the citizens there wanted democratic socialism and to remain within their own state. Instead communism collapsed almost overnight after the opening of the Berlin wall in November 1989 and the citizenry pressed for unification with West Germany.

Gorbachev struck the best deal he could, and traded land for money. A united Germany, friendly towards the Soviet Union, was not a bad bargain. The collapse of the Soviet empire in eastern Europe and indeed worldwide earned Gorbachev and Shevardnadze the undying hostility of many military and civilians. Gorbachev was greatly attracted to the concept of an executive presidency and decided that he would like to introduce it in the Soviet Union. He eventually chose a mixture of the US and French presidencies. How was he to be elected? Directly by the people or indirectly by the congress? Aleksandr Yakovlev regards Gorbachev's decision to be elected by congress as a fatal blunder. Had he been elected by the people he would have enjoyed considerable legitimacy. Even though he was the sole candidate he only polled 59% of the votes. He was sworn in as the Soviet Union's first President in March 1990.

He was referred to as *president* in Russian and he decided he needed a Vice-President, but unfortunately he chose Gennady Yanaev as his *vitse-president*. The *vitse* was borrowed from German but there is no Vice-President in Germany. The government became the cabinet of ministers (*kabinet ministrov*), from the French. The prime minister (*premer ministr*), again from French, was subordinate to him. Despite the new titles, things remained as they were and *perestroika* could not be successfully implemented. Indeed as time passed the economic situation got worse and the state faced disintegration. Article 6 of the Soviet constitution, which guaranteed the CPSU a monopoly of power, was removed by the congress in March 1990.

This made constitutional the multi-party system which was emerging, and popular fronts formed in the Baltic republics, expressly geared towards independence. Gorbachev's solution was a new Soviet Union, a federation of democratic sovereign republics. The rising star of Soviet politics was Boris Yeltsin. Since he had burnt his boats with the Communist Party his way forward was simple: resolutely oppose all communist positions. Elected speaker of the

RSFSR Congress of People's Deputies in May 1989, he used the Russian legislature as a platform to promote Russian over Soviet interests and to castigate Gorbachev and the CPSU for privilege and corruption. Yeltsin was elected President of Russia, by direct vote, in June 1991 and became an even greater threat to Gorbachev. Gorbachev's Nobel peace prize availed him nothing. Increasingly popular abroad, he signed arms treaties but gradually became more and more unpopular at home. The country was polarizing: the right wanted a strong President and an end to chaos and uncertainty; the radicals wanted democracy and change.

Gorbachev could not make up his mind which side to choose and always chose the middle ground. In the autumn of 1990 he declined to support the radical economists around Shatalin and Petrakov who had come up with a 500-day programme which envisaged a rapid transition to a market economy. His tragedy was that after giving in to threats from the industrial lobby he was bereft of an economic policy. The country drifted aimlessly downwards. At the end of 1990 he lost Eduard Shevardnadze who resigned and in an emotional speech warned of the danger of a coup. Nikolai Ryzhkov, his Prime Minister, was also out of office after a heart attack.

The killing of civilians in Vilnius and elsewhere in the Baltic in January 1991 increased tension, but Gorbachev did not condemn the actions of local commanders whom he claimed had overreacted. It appeared that he was under the influence of conservative forces. A new union treaty was at last agreed and was due for signing on August 20, 1991, but the attempted coup of August 19-21 was the death knell for Gorbachev and the Soviet Union. Led by Gorbachev's close associates, KGB leader Vladimir Kryuchkov, Minister of Defence Marshal Dmitry Yazov and Minister of the Interior Boris Pugo, backed up by Anatoly Lukyanov, speaker of the USSR parliament and fronted by Gennady Yanaev, all Gorbachev appointees, it collapsed ignominiously,leaving Russia and Yeltsin the real victors.

Imprisoned at Foros in his Crimean dacha Gorbachev did not sense the sea change the coup had engineered on his return. When he spoke of working with democratic elements within the CPSU he was talking about the past, not the present or the future. Yeltsin banned the CPSU in his presence and humiliated him. He struggled on and some former ministers returned to their posts, such as Shevardnadze. He tried in vain to form a new union but Russia for one did not want a centre and without one there was no role for Gorbachev.

Yeltsin struck a deal with Leonid Kravchuk, the Ukrainian leader, and Stanislau Shushkevich of Belarus, to destroy the Soviet Union. On December 8, 1991 they met near Brest, in Belarus, and formally committed the USSR to the grave. The three Slav powers claimed that they had the authority to do so since they had brought the USSR into being in 1922. Later in December, in Alma Ata, others joined what became known as the CIS. Gorbachev was now without a home and he formally resigned on Soviet television on December 25, 1991. The Soviet Union ceased to exist on December 31, 1991.

Gorbachev established his own foundation as many politicians had done in the West. He acquired a villa in Finland and was always a welcome guest there. He will go down as one of the most influential politicians of the 20th century with his greatest successes being in foreign affairs, and for these he deserves to be called a statesman. However, he failed domestically, partly because he never proved capable of presenting an intellectually coherent view of *perestroika*, and also because he failed to bring into being institutions which could implement his reforms. He set out to resurrect the Soviet Union but ended up burying it. Gorbachev had a limited grasp of ethnic nationalism and the deep resentments which many nationalities harboured towards Moscow. He was unfortunate in that he presided over the country at a time of economic decline when the latter was inevitable, but he accelerated it with unskilful economic policies. He must carry much of the blame for the poor monetary and fiscal policies. The putsch leaders always maintain that he was privy to the coup and if this is so, then some of the responsibility must rest with Gorbachev. He did not make his position sufficiently clear and allowed them to presume that he would accede to their wishes.

Beginning in 1986 Gorbachev wrote a series of books, a number of which were translated into many languages and enjoyed enormous popularity. Among his hobbies are reading literature, visiting the theatre, music, the cinema and walking. He and his wife live in Kutuzovsky prospekt, dom 26, Moscow.

Gorbunovs, Anatolijs

President of the Republic of Latvia.

Born in 1942. Latvian. He was a member of the Communist Party of Latvia from 1966. He graduated from the Riga Polytechnical Institute as a civil engineer in 1970, and then worked in the *Komsomol* and Party apparatus. He was secretary of the Central Committee, Communist Party of Latvia (1985-88), and was chairman of the Presidium of the Supreme Soviet of the Latvian SSR (October 1988-90). He was elected chairman of the Supreme Council of the Republic of Latvia in 1990, and became the first President of the Republic of Latvia after independence.

Address: Jekaba 11, Riga 226811; *telephone*: Riga 322 938.

Goryachev, Yury Frolovich

Head of the Administration of Ulyanovsk *oblast*, Russian Federation.

Born on November 11, 1938 in the village of Novo-Osorgino, Kamyshlinsky *raion*, Kuibyshev *oblast*, into a peasant's family; Russian; member of the CPSU until August 1991. His father was killed in action during the Great Fatherland War (1941-45) and his mother died in 1945, and so he was brought up by his elder sisters. After primary school he entered the Ulyanovsk Agricultural

Institute, from which he graduated in 1961 and was then appointed head of the veterinary bacteriological laboratory, Ulyanovsk *oblast*. After serving in the Soviet Army he was elected first secretary of the Novospassky *raion Komsomol* committee, *Komsomol* organizer of the Novospassky territorial collective and state farm administration, second secretary of the rural *oblast Komsomol* committee and second secretary of the Kuzovatovsky Party *raion* committee, Ulyanovsk *oblast*. In 1965 he was elected first secretary of the Ulyanovsk *oblast Komsomol* committee and in 1973 first secretary of Ulyanovsk *raion* Party committee. In 1974 he graduated from the Higher Party School of the Party Central Committee, and in 1987 he became chairman of Ulyanovsk *oblast* soviet executive committee and a member of the Party *obkom*. He has received state awards.

In 1990 he was nominated by 19 work collectives and social organizations in Ulyanovsk *oblast* for election as an RSFSR people's deputy in the No. 80 Ulyanovsky national territorial district. During the election campaign he advocated radical economic reform, many forms of ownership, gradual introduction of the market, political reform to achieve a redistribution and delineation of the functions of the various branches of state power and the establishment of a multi-party system. He believed that industry needed to reorient its priorities in favour of the output of consumer goods.

There were three candidates, and Goryachev won in the first round, polling 59.4% of the votes. His main opponent was A. S. Sergeev, a lecturer in the department of Marxism-Leninism, B. Khmelnitsky Higher Military Technical College, Ulyanovsk, who obtained 15.8% of the votes in the first round. In 1990 Goryachev was elected a deputy of the Ulyanovsk *oblast* soviet, and in April that year he was elected chairman of the Ulyanovsk *oblast* soviet (he was the only candidate and received 150 yes votes and 3 no votes) and first secretary of the Ulyanovsk Party *obkom*. He was a delegate to the XVIII Party congress, and was elected a member of the Party Central Committee in July 1990.

During the attempted coup of August 19-21, 1991 he did not comment on the activities of the Extraordinary Committee. The session of the Ulyanovsk *oblast* soviet in August acknowledged the activities of the Presidium of the soviet to be well founded and appropriate to the situation. Goryachev survived a vote of confidence in him by 153 votes for, 5 against and 6 abstentions.

In September 1991 the Ulyanovsk *oblast* soviet proposed Goryachev to the President as a candidate for the post of head of the administration of the *oblast*, but on October 24, 1991 V. V. Malafeev was appointed head of the administration of the *oblast*. This resulted in many protests to the President that he had rejected their nomination and in January 1992 Goryachev was appointed head of the administration of the *oblast* by presidential decree.

In December 1992, during the VII Congress of People's Deputies, he expressed his concern at the speech of President Yeltsin and called for agreement between the various branches of state power. He opposed the holding of a referendum in January 1993. He is married and lives in Ulyanovsk. His wife is a pensioner and they have two sons and a grandson. His favourite pastime is to visit the bathhouse on Sundays.

Grachev, Pavel Sergeevich

Minister of Defence of the Russian Federation. General of the Army since May 7, 1992.

Born on January 1, 1948 in the village of Rvy, Leninsky *raion*, Tula *oblast*, into a Russian working-class family. His father served in the Great Fatherland War (1941-45). He was a member of the CPSU until August 1991. He became a fitter at the Kosogorsky metallurgical enterprise, Tula; also a cowman.

He graduated with distinction from the Ryazan higher airborne officers' Technical School in 1969; with distinction from the M. V. Frunze Military Academy in 1981; with distinction from the Military Academy of the General Staff in 1990. He received a higher military education and was a member of the CPSU from 1972 to August 1991.

Grachev began his career as an officer as a platoon commander, then commander of the student company of his Ryazan technical school. Later he held posts in the airborne troops as a combat officer as battalion commander, deputy commander and commander of a detached guards regiment, deputy commander and commander of a guards division. He commanded a reconnaissance unit in Kaunas, Lithuania and a training parachute battalion in Lithuania. He took part in military operations in Afghanistan (1981-83). He then became head of staff of the 7th division in Kaunas. From 1985 he commanded the 103rd Vitebsk airborne division in Afghanistan. In 1986 he was promoted Major-General. A highly qualified professional, he proved a strong-willed and tough commander, and an experienced expert in the combat use of airborne troops with a talent for organizing operations under the conditions of present-day warfare. His personal courage, his excellent military, sporting and parachute training and concern for personnel gained him authority among the troops. The regiment and division under his command took part in a number of campaigns against the *mujahidin* and to pacify the civilian population of Afghanistan.

On May 5, 1988, Maj.-Gen. Grachev was made a hero of the Soviet Union for his efficient leadership and courage. After returning from Afghanistan he was appointed deputy commander, and on December 26, 1990, commander of airborne troops. He supervised the organization of combat training of troops and the deployment of airborne units in ethnic conflicts in the USSR. According to some sources, Grachev opposed the large-scale use of troops in order to resolve domestic political problems because it had a negative effect on their combat training and combat readiness. Grachev, although popular among airborne troops, was not widely known in the army or to the public since he avoided becoming involved in politics. He did not appear in the mass media, nor did he take part in discussions on military reform. He restricted himself to carrying out the instructions and orders of his superior officers. The name of Maj.-Gen. Grachev first became widely known when a series of articles appeared claiming that he had refused to participate in punitive operations in Lithuania in January 1991. Later he contradicted these claims (*Izvestiya*, October 14, 1991) by pointing out that he was not in the Baltic republics at the time, but confirming that he was vehemently opposed to the deployment of paratroops in domestic political conflicts.

During the anti-constitutional putsch of August 19-21, 1991 Lieut.-Gen. Grachev pursued a dual policy. Whilst carrying out all the instructions of Marshal Dmitry Yazov, USSR Minister of Defence, he established contact with Russian leaders. He promised to order the military not to use weapons. On his orders, during the evening of August 19, 1991, a paratroop battalion under the command of Gen. Aleksandr Lebed was sent to the Russian White House. A number of sources close to parliamentary and government circles claimed later that the task of the battalion was to attack the rear of the defences of the White House during its possible storming rather than the defence of the Russian seat of government. On the morning of August 20, Grachev ordered the battalion to withdraw. He is also reported to have been involved in working out tactics for the storming of the White House. At the same time he was one of the top military leaders insisting on the withdrawal of troops from Moscow. Despite being distrusted by some politicians, on August 23, 1991, President Mikhail Gorbachev, on the initiative of President Boris Yeltsin, appointed Grachev chairman of the RSFSR state committee on defence and security. He also became first deputy Minister of Defence of the USSR and was promoted to Colonel-General. While in these posts, however, Grachev did not play an active part in attempts to reform the army and did not attend the sessions of the state committee. On April 3, 1992 he was appointed first deputy Minister of Defence of the Russian Federation. On May 18, 1992 he became Minister of Defence with the rank of General of the Army. In July 1992 he and Viktor Barannikov were promoted Marshal, but Grachev later decided not to make use of this rank.

Democrats in the military and society reacted negatively to Grachev's appointment as Minister, seeing it as an indication of the growing influence on Yeltsin of the advocates of the use of force by top members of the military and the military industrial complex, and an indication of a weakening of resolve to create armed forces for a law-governed society. Disappointment was the more keenly felt, given that Andrei Kokoshin, a civilian and political scientist, who had been actively involved in elaborating proposals for military reform, was expected to get the post. Grachev's first steps were to appoint "Afghan Generals" to top posts, strengthen discipline and order in the army, restrict the rights of democratic agencies and organizations in the military, and cancel decisive measures aimed at reducing the size of the army and its conversion. At conferences and in the mass media Grachev confirmed that he was in favour of banning political parties in the military, its non-interference in domestic political problems, the creation of strong, highly mobile armed forces with up-to-date weapons, structured to meet the needs of a completely new Russia and the changed theatres of possible military operations. Grachev's programme was most clearly articulated in his speech on June 1, 1992 at the international conference on the democratization of society and military security at the Military Academy of the General Staff. He favours a tough policy to ensure the rights of Russian troops and the Russian-speaking population in the successor states of the Soviet Union. This policy enjoys considerable support within military and national patriotic circles and has contributed to the growth of Grachev's authority. Democrats in the military and society are critical and suspicious of the fundamentals of Russia's defence policy as elaborated by the Ministry of Defence.

Grachev has undertaken the reorganization of the administration of the army and has created rapid reaction forces from volunteers for deployment in flashpoints. He regards his major problems to be the withdrawal of troops from the former Warsaw Pact countries and Soviet republics coping with flashpoints in Russia, the social welfare of military men (mainly providing them with housing and money) and the call-up (he regards it necessary for all males to serve in the armed forces, but beginning at the age of 21 years). He is a strong opponent of the commercialization of the army but accepts that surplus weapons can be sold off to boost the military budget. During the VII Congress of People's Deputies, in December, speaking after the Presidential address, he underlined that the military would obey the constitution and laws of Russia. He has been awarded two orders of Lenin, two orders of the Red Banner, three orders of the Red Star, "for service to the motherland in the armed forces of the USSR", 1st and 3rd class, and many medals. He goes in for sport, has achieved various sporting grades, and likes literature on military patriotic subjects. He does not speak a foreign language. His first visit to the West was to Great Britain in July 1992. He appears regularly in the mass media on defence issues. He is married with three children and his wife, Lyubov Alekseevna, is from Ryazan. His elder son is an officer in the airborne troops and like his father graduated from the Ryazan higher airborne officers' technical school. He is a lieutenant in the Transcaucasian military district. The younger son is at the Suvorov cadet technical school. When younger he was a keen skier and is a master of sport in skiing, and wanted to become a coach. In his free time he plays tennis and volleyball and swims. He plays striker in the Russian government football team.

Postal address: 103175 Moscow K-160, Ministry of Defence of the Russian Federation.

Granberg, Aleksandr Grigorevich

Adviser of the President of the Russian Federation on Economic and Social Questions in the Commonwealth of Independent States (CIS).

Born in 1936; member of the CPSU until August 1991. He received his higher education in Novosibirsk, and after graduating from the institute in 1960 he became an economist in a computer centre. In 1963 he successfully presented his candidate dissertation in economics in Novosibirsk on "The problems of planning inter-branch balances in natural terms" (PhD (Econ)). In 1963 he became a lecturer and head of a department at Novosibirsk University. In 1969 he successfully presented his doctoral dissertation in economics on "The analysis and planning of inter-branch links" (mathematical economic research) (DSc (Econ)). Granberg was deputy director of the Institute of Economics and organization of industrial production of the Siberian branch of the USSR Academy of Sciences and later its director.

In early 1990 Granberg was nominated for election as an RSFSR people's deputy in the No. 526 Tsentralny territorial district, Novosibirsk *oblast*. During the election campaign he advocated fundamental economic change, economic autonomy for the republics, *oblasts* and for Siberia. He favoured the establishment of multi-branch complexes, groups of inter-linked branches, cost accounting links, territorial economic organizations, the all-round development of the eastern and northern areas of the country. Regions should have greater autonomy in the use of their resources. He regarded the economic programme, adopted at the II USSR Congress of People's Deputies, as not radical enough. He advocated a new approach to investment, the creation of effective mechanisms to oppose inflation, including the money which was in circulation but for which goods could not be provided, and for a reform of wholesale prices.

There were 24 candidates. Granberg polled 7.36% of the votes in the first round and won the second round, polling 48.7% of the votes. His main opponent was L. N. Shvets, head of the department of finance and credit in the New Institute of the National Economy, Novosibirsk, who received 6.7% of the votes in the first round and 37.7% of the votes in the second.

In 1991 Granberg became a state adviser of the RSFSR for economic and social questions in the CIS. Economic reform should always take into consideration regional differences and the real contradictions between pan-Russian regional interests. Regionalization and integration are not mutually exclusive, and these two necessary sides of economic federalism have to be integrated correctly. Regionalization, in Granberg's view, signifies, firstly, an assessment of the specifics of the region during the promotion of pan-Russian financial, investment, social and foreign trade policies; secondly, its autonomy when taking decisions about small enterprises, the social sphere, the protection of nature and the economic activities of enterprises of various types of ownership; and thirdly, the need to draft special programmes of reform for the regions. This does not presuppose separatism but, on the contrary, mutually advantageous interaction of all economic subjects. He advocates the development of a pan-Russian division of labour, a single economic area and overcoming the collapse of interregional links. In order to achieve this he proposes the strengthening of the federal monetary system which cements economic links, developing a general infrastructure of transport, communications and the energy system, retaining the multi-canal tax system as the basis of the federal budget and the state regulation of foreign trade.

He favours territorial associations, interregional economic integration which presupposes the unification of productive resources and the scientific-technical potential of regions, and the creation of federal regional funds to finance support for regions which will lead to their growth. This, in turn, will promote economic development. Granberg lives in Novosibirsk.

Griniov, Vladimir Borisovych

Deputy Speaker of the Ukrainian Supreme Soviet and Presidential Candidate.

One of the highest ranking ethnic Russians in Ukraine. He was born in 1945 in Belgorod *oblast* in the RSFSR and he was brought up by his Ukrainian mother, a village schoolteacher, without a father. He was educated at Kharkiv Polytechnic Institute, and is an engineer by profession. From 1974 he was a lecturer at the same institute. In other words, he is a typical representative of the Russian-speaking technical intelligentsia that is so numerous in Left Bank Ukraine.

In the late 1980s, he had links with both the Communist Party and the embryonic opposition movement *Rukh*. He quarrelled with the latter, after the influence of Galician nationalism began to rise in 1990 to 1991 and sponsored a *Rukh* breakaway in Kharkiv. He was a delegate to both the CPU and CPSU congresses in 1990, where he represented the pragmatic, technocratic wing of the Democratic Platform of the CPU. He therefore became a leading member of the Party of Democratic Revival of Ukraine (PDRU) which grew out of the Democratic Platform, leaving the Communist Party along with most of the Democratic Platform in July 1990.

At the PDRU's first congress in December 1990, he was elected fourth of seven co-leaders with 293 votes, a post he relinquished when the PDRU slimmed its number of co-leaders to three at its second congress in June 1991. He was elected people's deputy for Industrialnyi *raion* in Kharkiv city on the second round in March 1990. In the Supreme Soviet he became Deputy Speaker, and an *ex officio* member of the Presidium. A special vote was required to allow him to conduct official business in Russian. He has also headed the influential Commission of the Presidium for the preparation of legislative proposals, created by the amalgamation of various other commissions in January 1992 to improve legislative efficiency.

In the Supreme Soviet he has championed the cause of Russians living in Ukraine (although he has begun to speak in Ukrainian when necessary), whilst at the same time acting as an outspoken critic of old style *apparatchiki*. Such a position earned him many enemies amongst both nationalists and national communists and it was no surprise when Durdynets was promoted over his head in January 1992, although it was much resented by Griniov. Although the PDRU officially supported Ihor Yukhnovskyi in the December 1991 presidential elections, the maverick Griniov also stood on a platform of economic reform, respect for the rights of Ukraine's 11.4 million ethnic Russians and a federalized Ukraine.

He came fourth, beating Yukhnovskyi, with 1,329,758 votes, or 4.17% of the total. He did even better in areas of concentrated local Russian population, winning 10.9% of the vote in his adopted town of Kharkiv, 11% in Donetsk, and 9.4% in the Crimea. He was a founder member of the centrist *New Ukraine* movement founded in January 1992, and was elected in third place to its secretariat with 213 votes at *New Ukraine's* founding congress in June 1992. After its second congress in March 1993 he replaced Filenko as Chairman, demonstrating the rising power of Russophone feeling in Ukraine. Griniov is married with a son and daughter. His wife works as a teacher in Kharkiv's engineering and building institute.

Official address: Kiev, Vul. M. Hrushevskoho 5; *telephone*: Kiev 252 019.

Gromov, Boris Vsevolodovich

Deputy Minister of Defence of the Russian Federation. Colonel-General.

Born on November 7, 1943 in Saratov into a working-class family. Russian. Gromov graduated from the Kalinin (Tver) Suvorov Military School in 1963; the Leningrad Higher Military Officers' School in 1965; M. V. Frunze Military Academy with distinction in 1972; the Military Academy of the General Staff with distinction and a gold medal in 1984. He received a military education, and was a member of the CPSU from 1966 to August 1991.

He began his career as an officer as a commander of a motorized rifle platoon and was a company commander until 1968. After graduating from the Military Academy he was a battalion commander, Chief of Staff and a motorized-rifle platoon divisional commander. He proved himself a strong-willed and tough commanding officer and an excellent military specialist. He was promoted early to major, lieutenant-colonel, and colonel, something which seldom occurred in the Soviet army. From February 1980 to August 1982 Gromov's division, part of the 40th Army, was in Afghanistan. Gromov participated in a number of operations against the *mujahidin* and to pacify the civilian population and favoured severe measures against the Afghans. After graduating from the Military Academy of the General Staff he was appointed deputy army commander and served in Afghanistan again from March 1985 to April 1986. After that he was the army commander of the Belarusian military district. From 1987 to 1989 Gromov was commander of the 40th army and the senior Soviet military officer in Afghanistan. He was in charge of final military operations which were conducted with considerable severity and organized the withdrawal of Soviet troops. First ostentatiously, on an armoured troop carrier under a waving banner, and then on foot, he was the last Soviet soldier to cross the frontier between Afghanistan and the USSR. In 1989/90 he was commander of the Kiev military district.

An experienced military leader, a convinced communist and a supporter of the continued existence of the USSR, he enjoyed great authority and popularity in army circles, with top Party and government leaders and with the public at large. Rumour had it that he was to be appointed USSR Minister of Defence. In March 1989 he was elected a USSR people's deputy in the Priluksky territorial district, Chernigov *oblast*, Ukraine. He belonged to a group of deputies who vigorously opposed the democratic forces in Russia and the national liberation movements in the republics. He joined a group of orthodox communists and national patriots who, in a number of political appeals and letters, demanded the toughening of domestic and foreign policy, and the denial of sovereignty to the republics. In December 1990 Gromov was appointed first deputy Minister of Internal Affairs of the USSR but remained in the army. He advocated the strengthening of discipline in the militia and the interior forces. He was directly involved in ordering internal forces to act against democrats in Russia and the Baltic in January to March, 1991. According to the evidence of the commission investigating the reasons and circumstances of the attempted coup of August 1991, Boris Gromov played an active part in the actions of the Emergency Committee and in the planning of the seizure of the Russian White House. On August 20 he issued an order to the commander of KGB troops to block the passage to the White House. It was he who ordered the distribution of steel helmets, rubber batons, bullet-proof vests and ammunition. He is known, however, to have established contact with Russian leaders during the putsch.

Gromov returned to the army on September 5, 1991 and was appointed first deputy Commander-in-Chief of land forces. On June 29, 1992 he became deputy Minister of Defence of the Russian Federation. He supports the concept of a strong, highly mobile army with up-to-date arms, favours coercive methods to solve political problems and the defence of the Russian-speaking population in other ex-USSR states. He does not often express his views in the mass media. Democrats and progressive military officers reacted negatively to Gromov's promotion because he is opposed to radical reform of the army. On March 3, 1988 Gromov was made Hero of the Soviet Union for his endeavours in Afghanistan. Awarded an order of Lenin, two orders of the Red Banner, order of the Red Star, order "for service to the motherland in the armed forces of the USSR", 3rd class, and medals. He engages in sport, likes reading, especially books on history and military patriotism, and is fond of modern music. He does not speak any foreign languages. He is twice married with a son. His first wife was killed in an air crash.

Official address: 103160 Moscow K–160, Ministry of Defence of the Russian Federation.

Gromov, Feliks Nikolaevich

Commander-in-Chief of the Navy of the Russian Federation. Admiral since 1988.

Born on August 29, 1937 in Vladivostok into a military family. Russian. He graduated from the S. O. Makarov Pacific Higher Naval Technical School in 1959; the advanced training courses for officers in 1977; completed an extra-mural course at the Naval Academy in 1983; the higher academic classes at the Military Academy of the General Staff in 1986; took an external degree at the Military Academy of the General Staff in 1991. He was a member of the CPSU from 1958 to August 1991.

He began his career as an officer and gunner on surface ships in 1959, as a deputy commander of the main calibre gun battery of a destroyer. Then he became commander of a control group of the main calibre guns of an artillery cruiser and from 1965 as commander of an artillery section. Between 1967 and 1976 he served in the Pacific Fleet, became senior assistant and commander of a destroyer. He proved himself a qualified specialist in the combat use of ships' weapons and an experienced sailor. He demonstrated exceptional command abilities. In 1970 he was promoted to senior assistant of a commander of a cruiser, then became commander of a light cruiser, and control cruiser. He participated in long ocean voyages. He was sent to continue his studies in 1976 as a promising officer capable of becoming a senior commander. After graduating from these courses he was appointed Chief of Staff of a training division of vessels in the Leningrad naval base. From 1981 to 1984 he was Chief of Staff and an operational squadron commander. He was commander of the USSR navy in the Mediterranean and Atlantic which came face-to-face with the US and NATO navies. He proved capable of defending firmly the interests of the Soviet state in the complicated and changing circumstances of the military and political situations, of reacting independently to new conditions and taking good decisions. He was not politically active under the communist regime, doing only what was necessary for a successful career.

After graduating from the Naval Academy in 1984, Gromov was appointed first deputy Commander-in-Chief of the Red Banner Northern Fleet, and from 1988 Commander-in-Chief of the Northern strategic formation. Adml Gromov had under his command the largest Soviet naval alignment deployed in the European theatre of operations, the Arctic ocean and the northern and central Atlantic. However it was under his command that the *Komsomolets*, a nuclear submarine, was lost in April 1989. He was nominated as candidate for election as a USSR people's deputy in the Murmansk electoral district in March 1989 but was defeated by a representative of the democratic forces. Many naval officers voted against him. During the anti-constitutional putsch in August 1991 he was not very active but ordered troops under his command on to a state of high combat readiness. According to knowledgeable sources, he declared, "we should act in accordance with our officers' honour and conscience", but in his inner circle expressed support for the plotters. He enjoys the support of Adml of the Fleet Vladimir Chernavin. In the opinion of many officers, Gromov is conceited and ambitious, but short of knowledge, skill and ability. In March 1992 he was appointed first deputy Commander-in-Chief of the navy of the CIS; in April 1992 first deputy Commander-in-Chief of the Navy of Russia. On August 21, 1992 he became Commander–in–Chief of the Navy of Russia. He is chairman of the naval commission for the preparation of the celebrations marking the 300th anniversary of the founding of he Russian Navy. He is head of the departmental commission on the future of the Black Sea Fleet at the regular meetings of Russian and Ukrainian representatives. He does not express his political views in the mass media. He supports the concept of a powerful and balanced fleet for Russia. There is no information available about his hobbies. He is married with a daughter and a son, and has been awarded several orders and medals.

Official address: 103175 Moscow K-175; *telephone of Secretariat*: Moscow 204 30 87.

Grushin, Boris Andreevich

Member of the Council of the President of the Russian Federation.

He is a well-known Russian sociologist, who graduated from the faculty of philosophy of Moscow State University. In 1957 he successfully presented his candidate dissertation on methods and means in the reproduction of thought in the historical processes of development (PhD) and in 1967 he successfully presented his doctoral dissertation on the problems of the methodology of researching public opinion (DLitt). He is a Doctor of Philosophy and Professor. He was a member of the Soviet sociological association, worked in the institute of concrete social research, USSR Academy of Social Sciences, was a member of *Znanie* (knowledge) society and the USSR philosophical society. He was one of the organizers and leaders of the institute of public opinion in the 1960s and at present is the leader of the independent service for the study of public opinion, Vox Populi.

He is the author of the following books: *In the Name of the Happiness of Humanity* (1960); *The Results of the Third Survey of the Institute of Public Opinion* (1961); *Confessions of a Generation* (1962); *Notes on the Logic of Historical Research: Process of Development and Problems of its Scientific Reproduction* (1961); *Opinions about the World and the World of Opinion. Problems of the Methodology of Research of Public Opinion* (1967); *Free Time. Present Day Problems* (1967); *The Efficiency of Mass Information and Propaganda: Understanding and Problems of Measurement* (1979); *Mass Information in the Contemporary Industrial City: The Experience of Sociological Research* (1980); *Mass Consciousness: The Experience of Determining it and Problems of Research* (1987).

Grushin is concerned with the problems of the structure and content of public consciousness, the socialist form of life, general and specific, in the models of world development, the form of life of the urban population, methods of historical research, information and public consciousness, the mass as subjects of historical and social activity, logical principles of research of public consciousness, the structures of sociological activity, possibilities and perspectives of freedom, the creative potential of free time, the problems of social upheavals, social development and changes of civilization.

His articles appeared in the journals *Svobodnaya mysl*, *Problemy mira i sotsialisma*, *Kommunist*, *Voprosy filosofii*, *Rabochy klass i sovremenny mir*, *Sotsiologicheskie issledovaniya* and *Politika*. He became a member of the presidential Council in February 1993. He lives in Moscow.

Guslyannikov, Vasily Dmitrievich

President of the Mordovian Republic, Russian Federation.

Born in 1949 in the village of Peski, Borisoglebsky *raion*, Voronezh *oblast*; Russian. He graduated from the faculty of physics, Mordovian State University and began his career in the faculty of atomic magnetism of the Mordovian State University as an engineer. From 1972 to 1973 he served in the Soviet Army and after being demobbed returned to the faculty. A year later he moved to the Saratov semiconductor enterprise where he was an engineer and engineer technologist. In 1975 he moved to the Elektrovypryamitel scientific research institute production association as chief engineer, then as senior scientific assistant of the scientific production association of power electronics. He has published about 20 scientific articles.

He was one of the founders of the democratic movement in Mordovia, and headed the Mordovian republican regional branch of the Democratic Russia (DemRossiya) movement. In March 1990 he was elected a people's deputy of the Supreme Soviet of the Mordovian ASSR and participated in the work of the commission on legislation, law and order.

On December 22, 1991 he was elected the first President of the Mordovian Soviet Socialist Republic and on December 26, at the IX session of the Supreme Soviet of the Mordovian SSR, he took the presidential oath. He is married with two daughters, and his wife is an engineer who works in the scientific production association of power electronics. They live in Saransk.

Guzhvin, Anatoly Petrovich

Head of the Administration of Astrakhan *oblast*, Russian Federation.

Born on March 25, 1946; Russian; member of the CPSU until August 1991. He graduated from the Astrakhan Technical Institute for the Fish Industry and Economy and the Saratov Higher Party School. In 1990 he was chairman of the Astrakhan *oblast* soviet executive committee, and he is the recipient of state awards.

In early 1990 he was nominated by the work collectives of the Zelenginsky state farm, Volodarsky *raion*, the Semibugorinsky and Kommunar state farms and the Bolshevik collective farm, Kamyzyaksky *raion*, the Bolshevik, Leninsky put and V. I. Lenin collective farms and Limansky *raion* for election as an RSFSR people's deputy in the No. 279 Ikryaninsky territorial district, Astrakhan *oblast*. During the election campaign he advocated state sovereignty for Russia within the USSR, the social and economic renaissance of Russia, improvements in the provision of food to the population and solutions to ecological problems.

There were two candidates and he won in the first round, polling 57.1% of the votes. His opponent was I. F. Romantsov, head of the Astrakhan administration for boring, who received 30.2% of the votes. Guzhvin was previously in the communists of Russia group of deputies. In 1990 he was elected a deputy of the Astrakhan *oblast* soviet and at the first session, in April 1990, he was elected, being the only candidate, chairman of the Astrakhan *oblast* soviet executive committee. In his election programme he suggested measures to guarantee the economic and political sovereignty of the *oblast*, the development of the social sphere and solutions to ecological problems.

On August 21, 1991 the Presidium and executive committee of the Astrakhan soviet declared that the situation in the *oblast* was stable and did not require the introduction of a state of emergency, and demanded from the USSR Supreme Soviet the official medical report on the state of health of the USSR President and the publication of all official documents of the state agencies of the RSFSR. The soviet and executive committee did not judge the holding of any meetings or demonstrations opportune at that time.

On August 28, 1991 Guzhvin was appointed head of the administration of Astrakhan *oblast* by presidential decree, and on assuming office he stated that he intended to form an apparatus, composed of those who were capable of acting democratically. He advocated land reform and privatization, reform of national education, health and culture. Stabilization of the national economy was a prerequisite of successful reform.

In December 1992, during the VII Congress of People's Deputies, he stated that it was opportune and necessary to convene the congress. He advocated the continuation of the reforms of the Gaidar government, although he conceded that the implementation of the reforms had revealed that certain corrections had to be made. From this point of view the best candidate for the post of Prime Minister was Viktor Chernomyrdin, who had the practical experience which Gaidar lacked. The President's speech at the congress was unjustified, not constructive and destabilizing, in his view. Nevertheless he joined the meeting in the Granovitaya Palace after the President's declaration. He lives in Astrakhan.

Hadîrcă, Ion Dumitru

Resigned as first deputy president of the *Sfatul Ţării* (parliament) of the Republic of Moldova on January 29, 1993.

Born in 1949 in the village of Singerenii Vechi, Lazo *raion*, Moldovan SSR, to a family of farmers. He is an ethnic Moldovan who holds higher degrees. He was a deputy in the USSR Supreme Soviet and began work as copy editor at a *raion* newspaper. In 1974 he graduated from the "Ion Creangă" Pedagogical Institute in Chişinău, after which he worked at the Moldovan Academy of Sciences' Institute of Language and Literature and completed his doctorate. Between 1977 and 1982 he worked as an editor and then as editor-in-chief at the "Literatură Artistică" publishing house. In 1987 he was elected secretary of the board of the Moldovan Union of Writers. He was elected president of the council of the Popular Front of Moldova. On May 11, 1990 he was elected first deputy President of the Moldovan Supreme Soviet (the present *Sfatul Ţării*).

Harecki, Radzim Havrilavic

Vice-President of the Belarusian Academy of Sciences.

Born on December 7, 1928 in Minsk. His parents are Havriil Ivanavic and Larysa Vosipauna Harecki, and the family is Belarusian. He graduated in 1952 from the Moscow oil institute as a geologist, and from 1952 was a research assistant in the Institute of Geology, USSR Academy of Sciences, Moscow. In 1971 he was appointed head of the laboratory of geotectonics, Institute of Geochemistry and Geophysics, Belarusian Academy of Sciences, and between 1977 and 1992 he was its director. In 1992 he became vice-president of the Belarusian Academy of Sciences.

He is a member of the association of Belarusians throughout the world, and he views himself as a social democrat. His hobby is reading, and he speaks Russian, English and German (with a dictionary). His wife is Halina Ryhorauna Hareckaja and they have a daughter, Volha Radzimauna Hareckaja. He was awarded a USSR state prize, the state prize of the Belorussian Soviet Socialist Republic and the M. S. Shatskii prize of the USSR Academy of Sciences.

Address: 220072 Minsk, pr. Fr. Skaryna; *telephone:* Minsk (0172) 32 12 80; 64 85 02; *fax:* Minsk (0172) 39 31 63.

Hetman, Vadym Petrovych

Former Head of the National Bank of Ukraine.

Born into a Ukrainian family in 1935. He was educated at Kiev's Institute of Finance and Economics, and is an economist by profession. His first banking job was in an agricultural bank in Zaporizhzhia, and then in 1975 he was transferred to Kiev to become first deputy head of the state committee on prices. He rose to prominence as the head of the Ukrainian republican agro-industrial bank *Ukraïna*, a former state bank with close connections to the state *apparat* that had struck out on its own in the late 1980s.

In 1990 he was elected a people's deputy (on the second round) for Umanskyi region in Cherkasy *oblast* in central Ukraine, and is a member of the Supreme Soviet's committee on the plan, budget, finances and prices. The National Bank of Ukraine was established in June 1991 on a platform of introducing a national currency for Ukraine. Its original head, Volodymyr Matvienko, was soon enmeshed in scandal concerning the contracts for printing a new currency, and Hetman took over as head in April 1992.

He is also deputy chairman of the State Commission for Monetary Reform, established in November 1992, and a member of the Council of National Security set up in July 1992. However, Hetman has found it difficult to counter political pressure to maintain the supply of credit to troubled Ukrainian enterprises and, although he was reappointed by Kuchma in October 1992, the new Prime Minister criticized the past performance of the Bank with respect to monetary control and began a campaign to subordinate the Bank directly to the Cabinet of Ministers. In November 1992 Hetman was dismissed and replaced by B. Markov as acting Chairman. In January 1993, Hetman also lost his place on the National Security Council.

Official (Bank) address: 252007 Kiev, Vul. Zhovtnevoï revoliutsi, 9; *telephone*: Kiev 226 2914.

Holovatyi, Serhii Petrovych

Leading Nationalist Deputy and Chairman of the Association of Ukrainian Lawyers.

Born into a Ukrainian family in Odesa in 1954. After studying international law at Kiev State University's faculty of international relations and international law, he worked in the Ukrainian Academy of Sciences' institute for the study of the socio-economic problems of foreign countries, where he developed many foreign contacts and a fluent command of several languages, especially English. He successfully presented his candidate dissertation on international maritime law in 1980 (LIM).

Holovatyi was initially a *Komsomol* activist, but in the late 1980s rose to prominence in opposition movements such as the Taras Shevchenko Ukrainian language society, and *Rukh*, where he was first a member of *Rukh's* Grand Council and then head of its organization in Kiev. He left the Communist Party in March 1990. In the same month he was elected people's deputy for Syretskyi *raion* in Kiev city on the second round.

In the Supreme Soviet he made his name as one of the most active and able deputies, often dominating debate from the floor, and is one of the few Ukrainian deputies with a good understanding of constitutional law. Although a nationalist, Holovatyi has remained formally non-party. He supported the centrist Ihor Yukhnovskyi in the autumn 1991 presidential campaign, and is sympathetic to Viacheslav Chornovil's combination of nationalism and anti-communism.

He has maintained a high foreign profile, particularly in countries like Canada with a large Ukrainian diaspora (he is a member of the Supreme Soviet's committee of foreign affairs), and is often spoken of as a future presidential candidate. In spring 1992, however, he refused Kravchuk's offer to become Ukrainian ambassador to the United Kingdom. He has been Chairman of the Association of Ukrainian Lawyers since its foundation in May 1991.

Official address: Kiev, Vul. M. Hrushevskoho 5; *telephone*: Kiev 252 019 or Kiev 488 9266 (home).

Horyn, Mykhailo Mykhailovych

Head of Ukrainian Republican Party and Chairman of the Congress of National-Democratic Forces.

Born into a Ukrainian family in 1930 in a village in Zhydachivskyi *raion* in what is now Lviv *oblast*. His family were politically active peasants. His grandfather had served in the West Ukrainian People's Republic, and his father had been an OUN activist in the 1930s, arrested several times by the Polish government. His father had even been sentenced to death in 1939, but escaped from his prison during a bombardment. The whole family was deported to Siberia by the new Soviet authorities in 1944, but Mykhailo escaped on the way. From 1949 to 1954 he was a student in the department of logic and psychology, Lviv State University, where he was nearly expelled for refusing to join the *Komsomol*.

After university he worked as a teacher, first in Drogobytskii *oblast*, and after 1961 again in his native Lviv. In 1965 he received his first six-year sentence for political activity. He served his sentence in the camps with other Ukrainians such as Levko Lukianenko and Ivan Kandyba, and continued to earn the authorities' wrath by circulating *samizdat* and using hunger strikes to campaign for political prisoner status. After his release he was refused employment in his discipline, and was prevented from returning to Lviv.

He was forced to work as a stoker, but continued political activity by publishing the *Bulletin of the Ukrainian Helsinki Group*, Nos 4-7. Consequently, he was rearrested in 1981 and sentenced to ten years' severe regime and five years' exile. He was freed in President Mikhail Gorbachev's general amnesty of political prisoners in 1987. He immediately joined the editorial board of Viacheslav Chornovil's *Ukrainian Herald*, and headed the Ukrainian Helsinki Union's (UHU) committee for the defence of political prisoners.

His talent for organization meant that his hand was behind nearly all the opposition initiatives of the late 1980s. He was elected head of the *Rukh* secretariat at the movement's first congress in September 1989, and Deputy Head of *Rukh* and head of its political council at *Rukh's* second congress in October 1990. He organized most of *Rukh's* successful collective action, such as the human chain demonstration organized from Kiev to Lviv in January 1990, but he also earned many enemies who accused him of organizing such events primarily to benefit the UHU (later the Ukrainian Republican Party, or URP).

He was elected people's deputy for Zaliznychnyi *raion*, Lviv *oblast*, in 1990, receiving 70% of the vote on the first round. In the Supreme Soviet he is a member of the committees on the security service and international relations, and is head of the sub-committee for relations with Ukrainians beyond Ukraine. He has long advocated a nuclear Ukraine, and a posture of vigorous national defence and opposition to Russian interference in Ukrainian affairs. In January 1992 he became leader of the *Rukh* faction in the Supreme Soviet, or more precisely that proportion of *Rukh* that favoured close co-operation with President Kravchuk, such as Ivan Drach and Dmytro Pavlychko. At the third *Rukh* congress in February-March 1992, however, he failed in his attempt to be elected leader on a platform of support for President Kravchuk, having to settle for the position of co-leader with Drach and Viacheslav Chornovil. However, he was slowly forced out of *Rukh* by Chornovil's growing ascendancy, and he jumped ship to become leader of the URP at the party's third congress in May 1992.

On the basis of the URP and Democratic Party of Ukraine, Horyn then organized the formation of the Congress of National-Democratic Forces in August 1992, on a nationalist platform of conditional support for Kravchuk, in so far as he took resolute state-building measures. At the URP's fourth congress in May 1993, Horyn was unanimously re-elected leader.

Address: 252034 Kiev, Vul. Prorizna 27; *telephone*: Kiev 228 0772.

Ignatev, Kirill

Member of the Council of the President of the Russian Federation.

Born in 1966. He graduated from the Moscow State Institute of International Relations and at present he is preparing his candidate dissertation on the problems of organizing the election campaign in Germany. He is a member of the co-ordinating council of the movement Democratic Russia (DemRossiya) and deputy chairman of the political council of DemRossiya.

When appointed to the presidential Council in February 1993 Ignatev gave up his post as organizing secretary of Democratic Elections. Although not a people's deputy, he was an active member of the Supreme Soviet committee on the mass media where he was noticed by V. I. Bragin, and he participated in the drafting of the law on TV and radio, rejected by parliament. He was appointed head of the administration of Ostankino TV station. Shortly before the latter institution became official, Ignatev was engaged on acquiring his official status and technical equipment and he regards his new post as affording him the chance of putting into practice the programme of DemRossiya.

Recently he has been engaged on the draft law on banning certain groups from public life. He regards it as imperative to consider the experience of other countries, for instance Japan, but especially Germany where these measures were adopted after the war towards former Nazis and then to the communist party. The law will embrace secretaries of the CPSU, from the *raion* level upwards, to communists who did not leave the CPSU before August 1991, and full time and part time officials of the fifth administration of the KGB. His hobby is politics and he lives in Moscow.

Ilyumzhinov, Kirsan Nikolaevich

President of the Republic of Kalmykia-Khalmg Tangch.

Born on April 5, 1962 in Elista; Kalmyk. He was a member of the CPSU until August 1991. His father is an engineer and his mother a veterinary surgeon. After completing school in Elista he worked as a fitter in a factory, and in 1989 he graduated from the Institute of International Relations, Moscow. He was appointed manager of the Soviet-Japanese firm, Liko-Raduga, and in 1991 he became president of the San corporation. In 1992 he was elected president of the chamber of entrepreneurs of the Russian Federation.

In 1990 he was elected an RSFSR people's deputy for the No. 821 Manychsky territorial district, Kalmyk ASSR. He is a member of the Supreme Soviet committee on international relations and foreign economic links and a member of the mandate commission. He is a member of the *Smena* (change) parliamentary faction.

In 1993 he was nominated by the work collectives of the Zvezda enterprise and the Alachinsky state farm, the Cossack circle of Kalmykia and the congress of the entrepreneurs of the republic as a candidate for the post of President of Kalmykia. During the election campaign he advocated the creation of the organizational and legal prerequisites for the development of private property and entrepreneurship with equal legal protection for all types of ownership. Private property, in his view, is the "age-old motor" of civilization and functions successfully in market economies. However, in order to ensure the development and deepening of economic reform a reallocation of political power is necessary, since the Supreme Soviet of the republic and the local soviets in their present state have become a brake on forward movement. A small professional parliament is necessary and the present legislative organ dissolved and the government reshuffled.

He favours a reduction in the number of ministers and the administrative apparatus as a whole. The head of the administration should be subordinate to the President and the latter would be the only one to appoint him. Various newspapers should be closed down, meetings and demonstrations banned and a six-day working week introduced. These measures, in his view, should lead to the implementation of the main goal, the renewal of Kalmykia in a single, democratic Russian Federation. Kalmykia should not wait for someone to feed it, it should learn how to earn its living and measure its appetite by its purse. Requests for habitual subventions from the centre signify the continuing backwardness of the republic and the encouragement of parasitism.

An offshore (*offshornaya*) zone will be set up in Kalmykia, which will be guided by three fundamental principles: the dictatorship of economics, presidential rule and the transformation of Kalmykia into a centre of Buddhism. During the election campaign Ilyumzhinov repeatedly spoke out in support of President Boris Yeltsin in his conflict with the Russian parliament.

During the presidential election campaign from February 13 to March 11, 1993 Ilyumzhinov, out of his own pocket, provided funds to cut the price of bread and milk by 50%, presented the militia with a Mercedes Benz, gave the abbot of the Orthodox Church a Zhiguli car, donated 20,000 rubles to the

Ministry of Internal Affairs of the republic and 5,000 rubles to the Orthodox Church. He stated that he was capable of paying each Kalmyk family $100 from his own resources. Information about the sale of several million dollars, destined for the republic, began appearing in the local press and in the sessions of parliament. This information was linked to the name of Ilyumzhinov but it was never proven. Some observers saw him as buying the republic and it becoming his fiefdom.

There were three candidates during the election on April 11, 1993. He polled over 65% of the votes in the first round in an 82% voter turnout and thereby became President of the Republic of Kalmykia. His opponents, V. Bambaev, chairman of the association of farmers of Kalmykia and a former secretary of the Party *obkom*, and Major General V. Ochirov, first deputy commander of the air force of the ground forces of the Russian Federation, received 1.6% and 30% of the votes respectively.

Ilyumzhinov is married with a son and lives in Elista. He drives a Lincoln car. He bought the crown, with 1,022 diamonds, of the champion of the World Chess Championships from Gary Kasparov.

Ilyushin, Viktor Vasilevich

First Assistant of the President, Head of the Secretariat of the President of the Russian Federation.

Born in 1948 in Nizhny Tagil, where his father was a metallurgist; member of the CPSU until August 1991. He began his career in the Nizhny Tagil metallurgical combine where he worked six years as a fitter, and at the same time graduated from the evening department of the Urals Polytechnical Institute as a qualified electrical engineer. He graduated also from the Academy of Social Sciences of the Party Central Committee. He was active in political life and was transferred to *Komsomol* work. He was elected first secretary of the Sverdlovsk city *Komsomol* committee, then the *oblast* committee, then first secretary of the Party *raion* committee (*raikom*). He was then appointed deputy head of the organizational department of the Sverdlovsk *oblast* Party committee (*obkom*). It was there that he first met Boris Yeltsin who was *obkom* first secretary and was his assistant for 12 years. Then he became Yeltsin's assistant when he was Moscow city Party first secretary, and in the Party Central Committee. Ilyushin was sent to Afghanistan as an adviser. After Yeltsin's dismissal from his top Party posts Ilyushin also lost his job and did not acquire any responsible position.

In 1990 Ilyushin was appointed head of the secretariat of the speaker of the RSFSR Supreme Soviet and in July 1991 he was made head of the secretariat of the RSFSR President. He resigned from the Party immediately after the attempted coup since he could no longer remain in a party which called on its members to oppose the people.

For Ilyushin the secretariat is not merely an agency for transacting business but is in close contact with the Supreme Soviet and the government. The secretariat guarantees the transmission of documents but its head has the right to express his opinion and make proposals to the President. He has the opportunity of saying what he thinks. He is a skilled organizer, is precise and orderly in his work. He has three aides, one for international affairs, one for domestic Russian contacts and another for links with the parliament. He believes that the role of an assistant is different from that of an adviser in that an assistant has to construct a model of how parliament functions and plan its development.

Assistants should be loyal to the President, convinced of the correctness of their actions and be highly professional. Ilyushin attempts to shield the President from incompetent projects, checks on the effectiveness and quality of the work of the executives, keeps a very precise record of the meetings and measures adopted by the President. Ilyushin sees a danger that the CPSU could be reborn in its present form but there is no point in dismissing professional officials just because they once worked in the apparatus of the Party Central Committee. There were many first-rate specialists there and they were good people. He hopes for an improvement in the economy soon. Ilyushin is a master of the art of sounding people out and if he lobbies someone, his detractors never find out about it. He is married with a son and a daughter who are students and he has a granddaughter. He prefers vegetarian food and enjoys playing high-class tennis. He lives in Moscow.

Isabekov, Dulat Isabekovich

Director-general of Kazakh TV; deputy chairman of the committee for TV and radio broadcasting of the Republic of Kazakhstan.

Born in 1942 in Chimkent; Kazakh. He graduated in 1966 from the faculty of philology, Kazakh State University. He was a radio correspondent, then assistant for literature on the *Zhuldyz* magazine, and then director, and editor-in-chief of the Zhalyn and Zaman publishing house. In December 1991 he was appointed director-general of Kazakh TV. He is married with a son and two daughters.

Address: Alma-Ata, ul. Mira 175a; *telephone*: Alma Ata 63 6369 (office); 20 1214 (home).

Isaev, Boris Mikhailovich

Head of the social and economic department of the Presidium of the Russian Supreme Soviet.

Born on June 18, 1935 in Mikhailovka, Ryazan *oblast* in a family of five children; Russian. His father was a worker, and he was a member of the CPSU from 1964 to August 1991. He began work in 1956 as a combine harvester operator during harvest in Akmolinsk (Tselinograd) and Karaganda *oblasts*, Kazakh SSR. He graduated from the Ryazan Agricultural Institute in 1959, and after graduation taught in the school of the mechanization of agriculture, Mikhailov; he was foreman and mechanic of No. 21 column, Tsentrelektrosetstroi (1959-61); engineer, Mikhailov inter-*raion* association, Selkhoztekhnika (1961-62); senior engineer, inspector, and head of department of the Tatar association, Selkhoztekhnika, Kazan (1962-65); instructor of the Tatar Party *obkom*; first secretary of the Aksubaevsky Party *raion* committee, Aksubaevo (1965-73); deputy and first deputy chairman, Council of Ministers of the Tatar ASSR (1973-85); first deputy RSFSR Minister of Procurements (1985-86); first deputy RSFSR Minister of Grain Products (1986-88); chairman of Chelyabinsk *oblast* soviet executive committee; and chairman of Chelyabinsk *oblast* soviet of people's deputies (1988-90). The *zdorove* (health), *zabota* (care) and *zile* (housing) social programmes were carried out under his supervision. From the end of 1988 he was involved in introducing regional cost accounting (*khozraschet*) in Chelyabinsk *oblast*, and this was completed in 1989. In 1989 also he was nominated for election as a USSR people's deputy in the No. 336 Kartlinsky territorial district, Kratilinsky, Chelyabinsk *oblast*, but was defeated in the second round.

In January 1990 he was nominated for election as an RSFSR people's deputy by the collectives of six territorial *raions* of Chelyabinsk *oblast*, but he chose nomination in the No. 748 Ashinsky territorial district. During the election campaign he advocated full power for the soviets so that they could examine any question which affected the population of their area, and to achieve this it was necessary to enshrine these rights in law, to create a solid material and financial base for the soviets and to adopt a law on compulsory general education. He emphasized the need to delineate precisely between the functions of the Party and state agencies. A people's deputy should be independent of the local agencies of state administration; deputies should have greater power to intervene when social justice and public order were violated. He devoted great attention to the agro-industrial complex. He advocated the establishment of co-operatives, family and leased concerns on collective and state farms, the development of subsidiary farms by enterprises, personal holdings by the population, gardening and market gardening. In order to solve the food problem all food in excess of the plan should remain in the *oblast*. Measures to reduce the emission of hazardous substances and water pollution should be introduced, and greater control over the use of herbicides and pesticides was an urgent necessity.

There were three candidates. Isaev polled 42% of the votes in the first round and won the second round, polling 62.5% of the votes. His main opponent was

V. M. Melikhova, a design engineer in the Ust Katavsky coach works, who received 24.7% of the votes in the first round and 30.5% in the second round. Isaev was elected a member of the Russian Supreme Soviet at the VI Congress of People's Deputies in April 1992. He is a member of the Council of the Republic, and was deputy Speaker of the RSFSR Supreme Soviet (1990-91). In 1992 he was elected head of the social and economic development department of the Presidium of the Russian Supreme Soviet. He was awarded the order of the Red Banner of Labour, three medals and the diploma of honour of the Presidium of the Russian Supreme Soviet, and the Tatar ASSR. He is married with two sons and enjoys hunting.

Address: 103274 Moscow, K 274, Krasnopresnenskaya nab., d. 2, Dom Sovetov; *telephone*: Moscow 205 43 02.

Isakov, Vladimir Borisovich

Co-ordinator of the Russian Unity opposition bloc in the Russian Congress of People's Deputies; co-chairman of the Front of National Salvation.

Born on March 17, 1950 into a Russian family. He graduated from the R. A. Rudenko Institute of Law, Sverdlovsk (Ekaterinburg), having successfully presented his candidate dissertation in law (LLM) and his doctoral dissertation, in 1985, on the "theory of evidence" (LLD). He is a professor, and was a member of the CPSU. Until his election as an RSFSR people's deputy he was a professor in the Institute of Law, Sverdlovsk (Ekaterinburg). He campaigned as a member of the CPSU.

He was nominated as a candidate for election as an RSFSR people's deputy in the No. 655 Kirov territorial district, Sverdlovsk *oblast*. During the election campaign he stressed the necessity for strong local government, and he considered that an economic policy which stressed personal initiative had to be based on different forms of property ownership. He believes that Russia needs a leader whom the people can trust.

There were eight candidates and Isakov won in the first round, polling a total of 50.5% of the votes. His opponents were S. B. Vozdvizhensky, first deputy chairman of the Sverdlovsk *oblast* soviet executive committee; G. S. Zaikin, rector of the Sverdlovsk Institute of Architecture; O. V. Putilov, head of sector, Institute of Economics, Urals branch of the USSR Academy of Sciences; A. M. Chernyaev, director of the Urals Scientific Research Institute for the Use of Natural Resources; A. I. Sokolov, director of the centre of the all-Russian society of inventors and rationalizers; A. L. Strakhov, first deputy head of the territorial administration of USSR Gossnab; and A. I. Tatarkin, deputy director of the Institute of Economics, Urals branch of the USSR Academy of Sciences. Isakov was elected a member of the RSFSR Supreme Soviet at the I Congress of People's Deputies (649 voted for, 285 against).

He is a member of the Council of the republic and a member of the constitutional commission. At the I Congress he was elected Speaker (chairman) of the Council of the republic, and in February 1991 he signed the political declaration which condemned the leadership and the policies of President Yeltsin. On October 2, 1991 he resigned as Speaker of the Council of the Republic in protest against the course the reforms were taking. He was annoyed at the shock therapy of Egor Gaidar and moved to the right. At the VI Congress of People's Deputies, in April 1992, he was very critical of the Yeltsin administration, opposing the rapid introduction of the market economy, the pro-Western policies of the government and the plans for privatization. He joined forces with Civic Union, founded in the summer of 1992 and primarily the industrialists' lobby, and the former communists and nationalists.

These formed the Russian Unity bloc in the Congress of People's Deputies and demonstrated their power and influence at the VII Congress in December 1992 when they forced President Yeltsin to drop Egor Gaidar as Prime Minister and appoint Viktor Chernomyrdin, a former industrialist. Isakov became the co-ordinator of the bloc and worked closely with Ruslan Khasbulatov, the Speaker, on parliamentary tactics. Some observers regarded Isakov as the brains of the bloc. It chose confrontational tactics to bring down the President, either by rendering him impotent or causing him to resign or impeaching him. Isakov's bloc did not offer an alternative economic strategy but devoted its energies to disparaging the record of the government. At the congress Isakov, as befits a skilled lawyer, engaged in sharp-tongued criticism of the President and his proposal to hold a referendum. He stated that no one feared a referendum, the question was merely what form it should take. The President's referendum, as it stood, was unconstitutional.

The Russian Unity bloc enjoyed its greatest influence from December 1992 to April 1993. Khasbulatov and Isakov made a formidable combination and its destructive approach undermined the confidence of the President. At the VIII and IX Congresses, in March 1993, he appeared at times to be on the verge of conceding defeat. The congress countered Yeltsin's announcement of a referendum on April 11, 1993 with one of its own on April 25. Eventually the latter was held and a majority of the voters approved of the President and, somewhat surprisingly, of his economic and social policies. Tactically the initiative passed to the President and he convened a constitutional assembly on June 5, 1993 to draft a new Russian constitution which envisaged a French-US style presidential system. The Parliament produced its own version which foresaw a German style parliamentary system with the President as a figurehead.

Some parliamentary deputies changed sides and this weakened the parliamentary opposition to Yeltsin and so Khasbulatov's influence waned and with it that of Isakov. Isakov's home is in Ekaterinburg.

Ishaev, Viktor Ivanovich

Head of the Administration of Khabarovsk *krai*, Russian Federation.

Born in 1948; Russian; member of the CPSU until August 1991. He is a graduate, and was director of the aluminium construction enterprise, Khabarovsk. In 1990 he became a deputy of Khabarovsk city soviet in a contested election, and on May 12, 1990 he was confirmed as first deputy chairman of Khabarovsk *krai* soviet executive committee and head of the main economic planning administration.

In August 1991 the leadership of the *krai* soviet executive committee supported the decision of the Presidium of the *krai* soviet not to introduce a state of emergency and stated that all power rested with the soviets which were subordinate to the RSFSR and USSR constitutions, RSFSR laws and the decrees of the President of the RSFSR. It appealed to the public for discipline and to refrain from demonstrations and strikes.

Ishaev was proposed as head of the administration of Khabarovsk *krai* by the *krai* soviet who chose him from four candidates. On October 24, 1991 he was appointed chief of the administration of Khabarovsk *krai* by presidential decree. On assuming office he advocated strong executive power and promised to follow the policies of the President of the RSFSR, relying on the support of all the public and political forces of the *krai*. He appealed for the development of market relations and foreign economic links, a smooth and painless transition to the market, different levels of taxes and the economy to be run with expertise.

In December 1992 he stated that he had never seen anything more senseless than the VII Congress of People's Deputies. It did not debate the course of the reforms but engaged in a struggle over power. He viewed the President's speech as weak and that of the Speaker, Ruslan Khasbulatov, as of an extremely low order. The only notable speech was that of Egor Gaidar who displayed intelligence and competence in economic affairs, and although he conceded that Gaidar could be criticized for many things Ishaev nevertheless opposed his removal. The people's deputies had presented no alternative programme of reform, were merely concerned with evaluations and control, and did not wish to accept responsibility themselves. The President's address to the nation was not unconstitutional but he viewed the concept of a referendum as potentially dangerous. Since those who supported and those who opposed the President were about equal, a referendum would lead to a split in society and he appealed for the search for compromise to continue. He lives in Khabarovsk.

Ismailov, Ilyas Abbas Ogly

Minister of Justice, Republic of Azerbaijan to June 1993.

Born on March 20, 1938 in the *raion* centre, Tauz, Azerbaijani SSR, into an Azeri family. The same year his father, a member of the agencies of the Ministry of Internal Affairs, was killed by bandits. His three sisters died when young, and his brother Idris, born in 1930, was chairman of the Tauz *raion* soviet executive committee, during the 1980s. He was a member of the CPSU from his student days until August 1991.

Ismailov began his career in Tauz where he was a worker from 1956 to 1957. He graduated from the faculty of law, Azerbaijani State University, in 1962 and from 1962 to 1963 he worked in the Institute of Philosophy and law, Academy of Sciences, Azerbaijan, as a junior scientific assistant. In 1963 he became a postgraduate student in the faculty of law, A. A. Zhdanov Leningrad State University and successfully presented his candidate dissertation in 1966 in law on "The deliberae infliction of gross bodily harm" (LLM).

He returned to Baku to the Institute of Philosophy and Law, Academy of Sciences, as a senior scientific assistant until 1970. He also lectured on Soviet law at the Azerbaijani State University and on philosophy in the Institute of the National Economy. From 1970 to 1972 he was an assistant of the Procurator of the Azerbaijani SSR, and from 1972 to 1978 he worked in the Central Committee, Communist Party of Azerbaijan, as an instructor in the department of administrative agencies. In 1978 he returned to the Procurator's office as deputy procurator for cadres and remained until 1985, and then between 1985 and 1990 he was Procurator of Azerbaijan. In 1990, in the faculty of law, Leningrad State University, he successfully presented his doctoral dissertation in law on crime and criminal policy (LLD).

He is the author of dozens of articles on criminal law and criminology. From August 1990 to December 1991 he was head of the department supervising the laws in labour corrective institutions of the USSR Procurator's Office. He was appointed Minister of Justice, Republic of Azerbaijan, in April 1992 and in September 1990 he was elected to the Supreme Soviet (later *Milli Mejlis*) of Azerbaijan for Tauz *raion*, but the election result was annulled by A. Mutalibov. The commission of the USSR Procurator's office decided that this action was illegal but its enquiries remained unanswered. In the autumn of 1991 he became chairman of the movement for democratic reforms and the defence of human rights in Azerbaijan. He stood for President in the elections of June 7, 1992. He is a state counsellor in law, second class. On June 1, 1993 the Russians abandoned their garrison in Gyanja and Col. Suret Guseinov and his forces took over. The President's forces tried to disarm them but failed. Guseinov then marched on Baku. Elchibey fled to Nakhichevan after being informed that his military would not resist Guseinov's men and on June 15, 1993 Geidar Aliev was elected Speaker of the *Milli Mejlis* and acting head of state.

Ismailov is married. His wife, Zakiia Djabrail Kyzy, graduated from the Institute of Chemistry and Pharmacology, Leningrad, and successfully presented her candidate dissertation (PhD) and doctoral dissertation (DSc) and is head of the department of pharmacology of the Azerbaijani Medical University. They have two sons. The elder one, Etimad, born in 1969, graduated from the faculty of law, University of St Petersburg, in 1992 and the younger son, Matin, born in 1970, graduated from the faculty of law, Moscow State University, in 1992. Ismailov is a keen fisherman. He lives in Baku.

Ispravnikov, Vladimir Olegovich

Deputy Speaker of the Russian Supreme Soviet.

Born on October 14, 1948 in Omsk, where his father was an office worker; Russian. He was a member of the CPSU until August 1991. He graduated from the Omsk Polytechnical Institute with distinction in 1972 and then began working in one of the machine building plants in Omsk. He was a postgraduate student in the faculty of economics, Moscow State University (1975-79), and successfully presented his candidate dissertation in economics on "the Scientific and technical revolution as a factor in the development of production relations" (PhD (Econ)). E. M. Emelyanov and G. Kh. Popov were among his teachers. Afterwards he worked in the V. V. Kuibyshev Siberian road transport institute, Omsk. When elected an RSFSR people's deputy he was head of a department of the institute, and his research interests included devising ways of improving the regional economic mechanism and research into the social and economic problems of Omsk *oblast*.

In January 1990 he was nominated for election as an RSFSR people's deputy in the No. 538 Pervomaisky territorial district, Omsk *oblast*. During the election campaign he devoted much attention to political and economic reform, ecology, social security and the development of science. He advocated the adoption of a new Russian constitution based on the universal declaration of human rights, granting republics sovereignty and the legal standing of a state, the signing of a new mutually beneficial Union treaty, the fundamental renewal of the CPSU along the democratic lines and its transformation into a parliamentary party, the right freely to establish social organizations and trade unions, all power to the soviets elected by the people, the division of the functions and financial resources of the Party and soviet organizations. In his view the separation of powers would eliminate the environment which fostered corruption, and he favoured the election of the Russian President by direct popular vote. Most hard currency revenues earned by enterprises should be retained by them.

In 1990 he was elected secretary of the higher economic council of the RSFSR; in 1991 chairman of the commission of the Council of the Republic of the USSR Supreme Soviet of economic co-operation, and on October 2, 1991 he was elected deputy chairman of the commission for monitoring banking legislation. Ispravnikov became a member of the temporary committee of the Russian Supreme Soviet Presidium, established to administer the higher economic council of the Russian Federation after the resignation of its chairman, on September 30, 1991. On November 11, 1991 he was appointed chairman of the higher economic council of the Russian Federation, and also a member of the Supreme Soviet committee on economic reform and property and a member of the committee on science and national education (1990-91).

He is the author of 36 scientific publications and a prize-winner in the all-Union competition in economic theory for young specialists. He has published several articles on property and is the editor of the book *Reform Without Shock Therapy*. He is married with a daughter. Tennis is his main relaxation and he is a former Omsk tennis champion. He is regarded as more moderate than other members of the leadership of the Russian Supreme Soviet.

Address: 103274 Moscow, K 274, Krasnopresnenskaya nab., d. 2, Dom Sovetov; *telephone*: Moscow 205 99 58.

Ivanov (Skuratov), Anatoly Mikhailovich

Member of Russian National Patriotic Movement.

Born April 2, 1935 into a Russian family in Moscow, where his parents were teachers of Russian language and literature. In 1955 he entered the history faculty of Moscow State University but at the end of 1957 was expelled because of "political unreliability". At that time there was a witch-hunt in the history faculty after the arrest of the "Krasnopevtsev group", an underground group of students and postgraduates interested in the Yugoslav model of socialism. Ivanov engaged in frank political discussions with other students and never became a member of the *Komsomol*. In December 1958 a search began for Ivanov and on December 31, 1959 he and S. I. Avdeev were arrested.

Ivanov met Avdeev after being expelled from university and the latter asked him to write something about the Krasnopevtsev affair. Although Ivanov knew practically nothing about the activities of the group he wrote an article entitled "waiting" and signed it with his pseudonym Manuilov. The Krasnopevtsev group merely engaged in debate and never intended to put their ideas into practice. Avdeev took the article to Stalinsk-Kuznetsky (now Novokuznetsk) and on December 5, 1958 he was arrested. During a search the manuscript with the signature Manuilov was found. After Ivanov's arrest an article was found: "The workers' opposition and the dictatorship of the proletariat", about two currents in socialism: the "correct" one, beginning with Bakunin, and the "incorrect" one, from Marx to Lenin. Ivanov has read this article at meetings of the circle to which some of his friends, including Vladimir Osipov, went.

Some of this circle also participated in poetry readings on Mayakovsky Square. Ivanov was examined in the Serbsky institute (notorious for the role it played in diagnosing dissidents as schizophrenic or suffering from other disorders) where he was diagnosed as mentally not responsible for his actions. The trial took place in May 1959, and Avdeev was given six years but Ivanov was placed in the Leningrad special psychiatric hospital for compulsory treatment. Avdeev served his full sentence but Ivanov was released in August 1960. Afterwards he began to play an active part in the *Mayak* (lighthouse) group and got to know many of its leading members, including Yury Galanskov, Vladimir Bukovsky, Viktor Khaustov and Eduard Kuznetsov.

On October 6, 1961 Ivanov, Osipov, and Kuznetsov were arrested and accused of preparing to assassinate Nikita Khrushchev, first secretary of the CPSU and Prime Minister of the USSR. (There may have been some discussion about an attempted assassination among some of the *Mayak* members but the KGB was not able to prove anything conclusive.) Osipov, Kuznetsov and Ilya Bokstein were sentenced to a term in the camps under article 70 of the criminal code (anti-Soviet activity) and Ivanov to more treatment in the Kazan special psychiatric hospital where he remained until 1964. After his release he learned from Avdeev, back from the camps, that some of the political prisoners, including Osipov and Galanskov, were attracted to Slavophilism and Ivanov fell immediately under their influence. In the extra-mural department of the history faculty of Moscow State University, where he rehabilitated himself, Ivanov wrote a study on the teachings of the Slavophiles.

From 1964 Ivanov worked as a translator in the Poligrafmash scientific production association. He is fluent in German and reads English, French, Spanish, Italian, Polish and Serbian. From 1965 to 1968 he was connected with the so-called Fetisov group or the society for the study of systems theory, which was a political club which tried to marry orthodox Stalinism and Russian nationalism. In 1968 the four most active members of the club, Fetisov, V. Bykov, O. Smirnov and M. Antonov, were arrested and sentenced to varying periods in psychiatric hospitals. Fetisov is now dead but Mikhail Antonov often appears in the pages of *Nash sovremennik* (our contemporary) and is chairman of the union for the spiritual renaissance of the fatherland.

In 1970 Ivanov published and distributed a document called *Slovo natsii* (the word of our nation), a reply to the manifesto of the Democratic Movement of the Soviet Union, penned by Sergei Soldatov. While writing *Slovo natsii* Ivanov took into account the views of nationalist opposition groups, including Vladimir Osipov and his circle, former members of the Fetisov circle and other former political prisoners. This document became quite well known and was often reprinted in the West as documentary proof of the existence of Russian fascism. In 1971 Vladimir Osipov began to publish the journal *Veche* (popular assembly in medieval Russia) in which Russian nationalists of various shades published articles, from the national Bolsheviks to the Orthodox anti-communists. Nine numbers of the journal appeared under Osipov's editorship.

Articles by Ivanov, either anonymous or under the pseudonym of Skuratov, his grandmother's name, always made up a significant part of each number. The editorial board split after the ninth number, and Ivanov sided with the opponents of Osipov, Svetlana Melnikova and Ovchinnikov. It would appear at that time that Osipov was in favour of an alliance with the pro-Western dissidents and against the communists but that his colleagues took the opposite point of view. Osipov left and began to publish the journal *Zemlya* (earth) and was sentenced to eight years for it. Melnikova and Ovchinnikov managed to publish only one more number of *Veche*. At the end of the 1970s Ivanov was on close terms with Leonid Borodin, Ilya Glazunov and Dmitry Vasilev and they all met regularly at Glazunov's.

In August 1981 Ivanov was arrested for the third time because of his association with the almanac *Moskovsky sbornik* (Moscow handbook), edited by Leonid Borodin, and which contained an article by Ivanov. In 1982 he was sent again to a psychiatric hospital and the previous diagnosis about mentally not being fully responsible for his actions was overruled and he was sentenced, according to article 70 of the criminal code, to one year in a labour camp and five years exile, less than the legal minimum. Borodin got 10 years for possessing and distributing anti-Soviet literature. Ivanov's testimony was viewed, in print, by many critics as the reason for the guilty verdict against Borodin. Ivanov also disputed this view.

He spent two and a half years in exile and was freed in 1985. From 1989 he began to publish his articles in the official press (*Molodaya gvardiya* "young guard", *Literaturnaya gazeta* "literary newspaper", and so on). Since 1990 he has been a regular contributor and a member of the editorial board of the radical national-patriotic weekly *Russky vestnik* (Russian herald). From 1987 to 1988 Ivanov began to associate closely with the *Pamyat* (memory) group of Dmitry Vasilev and has often defended Vasilev. Supporters of the pagan current in *Pamyat*, (the Yemelyanov group) now distribute the article *Khristianskaya chuma* (the Christian plague), written by Ivanov in 1978, and revere him as one of their intellectual leaders. Ivanov does not regard himself as belonging to any of the groups within *Pamyat*; nor does he see his religious-philosophical views as pagan and whimsically calls them Zoroastrian. Orthodox monarchist views, widely held in *Pamyat*, are alien to him.

Ivanov, Boris Petrovich

Head of the Administration of Chita *oblast*, Russian Federation.

Born in 1941. He is a graduate, was a member of the CPSU until August 1991, and until April 1990 was head of the main economic department of Chita soviet executive committee. In March 1990 he was elected the deputy for No. 8 Balyabinsky territorial district, Chita *oblast* soviet of people's deputies. At the first session of the *oblast* soviet he was elected first deputy chairman of the executive committee, and at the sixth extraordinary session of the *oblast* soviet he was elected chairman of the executive committee.

On August 19, 1991 an extraordinary session of the Chita *oblast* soviet executive committee took place and it was decided that there were no grounds for introducing a state of emergency on the territory of the *oblast*. However, it was stated that in the decrees of the Extraordinary Committee there were many points which addressed the aspirations of the population, for instance, the restoration of order, the struggle against economic chaos and the shadow economy. At the seventh extraordinary session of the *oblast* soviet in August 1991, however, it was decided to note that the executive committee had guaranteed the normal functioning of the economy and had acted strictly in accordance with the constitution and laws of the USSR and RSFSR.

On November 30, 1991 Ivanov was appointed head of the administration of Chita *oblast* by presidential decree. On assuming office he stated that he would always promote the development of a free democratic society in which the will, aspirations and creative potential of each person would be realized. The most important point of his activities would be a complete review of the programmes for the agricultural development of the *oblast* which, under the new conditions, could not expect to be financed from the centre. The main prerequisite for the expansion of agricultural production was the promotion of various types of rural economy and support for collective as well as individual farming.

In November 1992 the administration of Chita *oblast* officially stated that there was no reason to convene the VII Congress of People's Deputies because of the deepening economic and political instability. It expressed its concern that such a situation could lead to a reversal of reform and chaos in the administration of the state and declared its support for reform and the efforts of the President and government. It was hoped that the Supreme Soviet would postpone the convocation of the VII Congress of People's Deputies to the spring of 1993, since it would be more sensible to concentrate then on debating the draft constitution of the Russian Federation. Ivanov lives in Chita.

Ivanov, Kliment Egorovich

Speaker of the Supreme Soviet of the Republic of Sakha (Yakutia), Russian Federation.

Born in 1936 in the village of Elgyai, Suntarsky *raion*; a Yakut; member of the CPSU until August 1991. After graduating from the Vilyuisky Pedagogical College he was a teacher and worked in the *Komsomol*. He was elected first secretary of the Suntarsky *raion Komsomol* committee, *Komsomol* organizer in the Vilyuisky production association, and first secretary of the Ordzhonikidze *raion Komsomol* committee. After graduating from the Khabarovsk Higher Party School in 1968 he was elected second, then first secretary of the Abyisky *raion* Party committee, and from 1975 to 1983 he was chairman of the executive committee of the Suntarsky *raion* soviet of people's deputies. In 1983 he was elected first secretary of the Verkhnevilyuisky, then in 1984 first secretary of the Olekminsky *raion* Party committee. In 1986 he was appointed first deputy chairman of the state agro-industrial committee and Minister of Agriculture of the Yakut ASSR. From 1988 to 1989 he was general director of the Yakut Sever agro-industrial combine.

In 1989 he was elected a people's deputy of the USSR, a member of the USSR Supreme Soviet and a member of the planning, budget and finance commission of the USSR Supreme Soviet. He was elected several times a people's deputy of the Yakut-Sakha Soviet Socialist Republic. He was awarded the orders of the Red Banner of Labour and the badge of honour and medals.

On December 29, 1990, at the IV session of the Supreme Soviet of the Yakut-Sakha SSR, he was elected Speaker in a contested election. On August 20, 1991 Ivanov signed the declaration of the Presidium of the Supreme Soviet and the Council of Ministers of the Yakut-Sakha SSR, which reiterated its support for the leaders of the republic according to the "principles of the declaration on the state sovereignty of the Yakut-Sakha SSR" and also underlined the absence of "objective reasons for the introduction of a state of emergency and the establishment of extraordinary committees or other agencies of the USSR Extraordinary Committee". He lives in Yakutsk.

Ivanov, Vitaly Pavlovich

Head of the Admiral N. G. Kuznetsov Naval Academy, St Petersburg. Admiral since 1987.

Born on August 12, 1935 in Poltava, Ukraine, into a civil servant's family. Russian. Ivanov graduated from the Saratov Naval Preparatory Technical School; Lenin Komsomol Higher Naval Submarine Technical School in Leningrad in 1957; the Naval Academy in 1974; the Military Academy of the General Staff with a gold medal in 1979. He received a higher military education, specializing in strategic and tactical naval affairs. He was a member of the CPSU from 1957 to August 1991.

He began his career as an officer in the Northern fleet as a commander of a section of a nuclear submarine, and was soon promoted senior assistant of the captain of the submarine. He served in the North until 1965, participated in campaigns in the north Atlantic, tracking US and NATO naval forces. From 1966 to 1972 he served in the Pacific fleet as a senior assistant and captain of a nuclear submarine. The crew under his command carried out a number of complex tasks in the Pacific ocean in areas of considerable navigational and military political difficulties. He proved himself a strong-willed and tough commander as well as an experienced specialist and sailor. After graduating from the Naval Academy he was appointed, in 1974, deputy commander of a submarine formation of the Northern Fleet and later became a commander. He graduated from the Military Academy of the General Staff, was appointed deputy head of the operational administration of the main headquarters of the navy and was then promoted to head this administration. He supervised plans for the construction and combat use of new equipment for the navy and often visited strategic units as an inspector and in order to supervise combat readiness.

In December 1985 Adml Ivanov was appointed commander of the Red Banner Baltic Fleet. His service there coincided with the national liberation struggle of the republics to secede from the USSR and end communist influence. Under these circumstances he proved to be a hard-line defender of the totalitarian regime and of the retention of the Soviet Union, and was a convinced communist. He repeatedly used the forces under his control, especially the marines, against the Baltic national democratic forces and in support of the communist authorities. He expressed publicly his conservative views and demanded that the leaders in Moscow take more severe measures against democrats, including those in Russia. He was elected a delegate to the XXVII Party congress and XIX Party conference, a deputy of the Kaliningrad *oblast* soviet of people's deputies and a member of the bureau of the Kaliningrad *oblast* Party committee.

In March 1989 he was elected a USSR people's deputy for the Kaliningrad rural territorial district of the RSFSR (the city of Kaliningrad). According to information from progressively-minded sailors in the Baltic fleet, he was elected despite some violations of the electoral law. He became a member of the USSR Supreme Soviet committee on defence and security. He repeatedly expressed his conservative views at the USSR Congress of People's Deputies and at USSR Supreme Soviet sessions. He sharply criticized allegedly insufficiently drastic measures being taken to counteract democratic forces and movements struggling for the sovereignty of the Baltic republics. He opposed plans to reorganize the army and navy and make them subordinate to the law and draft military reforms proposed by democratic military deputies. In 1990/91 he approved the use of the marines in the Baltic.

During the anti-constitutional putsch in August 1991, he ordered the forces under his command on to a state of high combat readiness and expressed his support for the plans of the Emergency Committee. Ivanov escaped censure for his behaviour during the attempted coup largely due to the support he received from Adml of the Fleet Vladimir Chernavin, Commander-in-Chief of the Navy. However, as a result of the extremely negative attitude towards him in the Baltic he was transferred from the navy to the post of head of the Naval Academy in St Petersburg. He has not expressed his political views recently in the mass media. He still, however, favours the construction of a strong navy, balanced as regards structure and types of forces, and capable of acting in various regions of the world's oceans. He retains his conservative views on politics, economic reform and the possibility of reforms in the armed forces. The attitude of democrats and progressives in the military to him is negative. He has been awarded orders "for service to the motherland in the armed forces of the USSR", 2nd and 3rd class and medals. He is fond of books on the history of the navy, literature on national and patriotic subjects and partakes in sporting activites.

Official address: 197045 St Petersburg, The Naval Academy, Vyborgskaya naberezhnaya, Dom 73/1.

Ivanov, Vladimir Aleksandrovich

Chairman of the Russian Party of National Renewal; co-chairman of the Front of National Salvation.

Born in 1947; Russian. He was a member of the CPSU until August 1991. He graduated from the Buryat Institute of Agriculture and the Academy of Social Sciences of the Party Central Committee, and worked in the economy and in the Party apparatus. In 1991 he was first secretary of the Dzhidinsky *raion* Party committee.

He was nominated for election as an RSFSR people's deputy in the No. 89 Seliginsky national territorial district. During the election campaign he advocated that all power should pass to the soviets, a *Rechtsstaat* (law-governed state) should be brought into being, local soviets should have the authority to control their financial and material resources, and a law on local self-government was needed. He stressed that local soviets should have control over land. In multi-ethnic areas the CPSU platform on national and inter-ethnic relations should be strictly implemented. The command economy should be extirpated by economic methods by affording republics and *raions* economic autonomy, in other words enterprises, collective farms, and so on should have the right to manage themselves.

The volume of new and uncompleted construction projects should be cut back and the freed resources devoted to solving social problems. He believed that budgetary allocations for health, education and culture should rise, and that greater attention should be paid to the social protection of women, military men and youth. As regards ecology he spoke of the need for a code of laws for the protection of Lake Baikal. He won in the second round, polling 50.52% of the votes, and his opponent, Ts. D. Tsybikzhapov, received 46.83% of the votes. Ivanov lives in the village of Petropavlovka.

Ivanov, Vladimir Leontevich

Head of Space Weapons of the Strategic Forces of the Unified Armed Forces of the CIS. Colonel-General.

Born in 1936 in Kamenka-Dneprovskaya, Zaporozhskaya *oblast*, Ukraine. Russian. He graduated from the S. M. Kirov Caspian Higher Naval Technical School in Baku in 1958; the F. E. Dzerzhinsky Military Academy in 1971.

After graduating from the technical school he was assigned to the strategic rocket forces. He played a part in the mastering of qualitatively new specimens of rocket space technology and weapons and participated in the launching of ballistic missiles.

He has filled all the posts from a team commander to deputy commander of a rocket army. He took an active part in Party-political work, and was a member of the CPSU till August 1991. He was elected to Party agencies.

From 1979 to 1984 he was head of the space test range Plesetsk in Arkhangelsk *oblast*. He supervised the launching of earth satellites and other orbital space vehicles destined for civil and mixed (military-civil) use. In 1984 he was appointed to high posts in the chief administration of space units. From 1989 he was head of space units of the USSR Ministry of Defence.

Gen. Ivanov is a supervisor of space weapons and combat vehicles and of test ranges in Baikonur and Plesetsk. These forces are under the immediate command of the Commander-in-Chief of the Unified Armed Forces of the CIS, Air Force Marshal E. Shaposhnikov; Gen. Ivanov being one of his top aides.

He is an experienced military professional with a sound operational-tactical, military-technical and engineer training. He engages in scientific research, has the degree of doctor of military sciences (DSc (Eng)). He participates directly in designing, testing and approving new rocket space technology. He is a technocrat. He is head of the State Commission for flight tests of the orbital station "Mir".

He advocates a tough state policy and does not approve of social organizations in the army and navy. He does not reveal his political views in public, confining himself to specialist military-technical and scientific problems in his contacts with the mass media. After the unauthorised publication of interviews with several officers from the press centre of the space troops, he took the decision to break up this sub-unit and to fire the employees.

During the anti-constitutional putsch in August 1991 he was not active, confining himself to ordering the units and establishments under his command on to high combat readiness. There is no information to prove that Gen. Ivanov expressed support for the Emergency Committee.

At present he supports the authorities of Russia, advocating the re-emergence of the former state-territorial divisions and united armed forces.

He is interested in literature, art, scientific and technological problems. He has a good command of English and has never been abroad as a member of an official delegation. He has close business and personal ties with top officials of the military-industrial complex and research institutes of the defence industry. He has been awarded two orders and a number of medals, and is married.

Office address: 103160, Moscow, K-160.

Kadagishvili, Amiran

President of the Caucasian Exchange; Vice-President of the Congress of Exchanges.

Born in 1949 in the Georgian SSR; Georgian. He graduated in 1972 from the faculty of physics, Tbilisi State University, where he specialized in quantum radiophysics. After graduation he was appointed to an academic institute and remained there ten years; he then worked in the department of computers. In 1986 he became head of the alternative economics enterprise and became a member of the Russian mercantile exchange. He founded the regional Caucasian exchange; later became President of the Caucasian Exchange and Vice-President of the Congress of Exchanges. He likes reading science fiction and is married with two sons.

Address: 38 0020 Tbilisi, Pr. Ketevan Tsambeuli 71; *telephone*: (8 832) 74 4299; 74 3549; 74 6266.

Kadannikov, Vladimir Vasilevich

Member of the Council of the President of the Russian Federation.

Born on September 3, 1941 in Gorky (Nizhny Novgorod). Russian. His father was killed during the Great Fatherland War and he was brought up by his grandmother. From the age of 16 he was an apprentice fitter in the Gorky automobile works, and later served in the Soviet Army. In 1965 he graduated from a polytechnical institute. From 1967 and from the beginning of the construction of the Volzhsky automobile works in Tolyatti he was a deputy head of the shop of heavy stamping equipment. He was a member of the CPSU until August 1991, and was Party secretary of the enterprise for a time. At present he is general director of the Volzhsky automobile works and also head of the council on industrial policy of the Russian government.

In early 1989 Kadannikov was nominated for election as a USSR people's deputy in Tolyatti and elected. At the I Congress of USSR People's Deputies he was elected a member of the USSR Supreme Soviet. He was a member of the Soviet of the Union commission on labour, prices and social policy.

His active co-operation with Boris Yeltsin began in the autumn of 1992 when he came out in support of Egor Gaidar, the Russian Prime Minister, and his reforms. In November 1992 Yeltsin considered replacing Gaidar with Kadannikov, but the latter only discovered that he was being considered as Prime Minister at the VII Congress of People's Deputies in December 1992. He became a member of the presidential Council in February 1993. He thinks that the leaders of large industrial enterprises, and not the government, carry the responsibility of economic reform on their shoulders and their task also includes the social security of the people. Enterprise directors have formed the council on industrial policy in order to exert influence on government policy. He has stated that it is necessary to limit increases in the price of raw materials, otherwise all other prices will rise out of all proportion. He favours state subsidies for enterprises, cheap credits and tax advantages. He lives in Tolyatti.

Kagalovsky, Konstantin Grigorevich

Director of the International Monetary Fund for the Russian Federation.

Born in 1957; Russian. He graduated from the Institute of Finance, Moscow, and in 1980 was appointed to the scientific research institutes of USSR Gosplan and the USSR Academy of Sciences. In 1989 he founded and headed the international centre for research into economic reform. He then became the representative of the Russian Federation for liaison with the IMF and World Bank (1990-91); representative of the government of the Russian Federation for liaison with international financial institutions, and adviser on economic affairs of the government of the Russian Federation (January-September 1992); and representative of the Russian Federation, with the rank of ambassador, on the IMF board (September-October 1992). In October 1992 he was appointed executive director of the IMF, representing the Russian Federation, and is also an unofficial adviser of the President of the Russian Federation. He speaks English.

Kalnins, Haralds

Head of German Lutheran Church; Bishop.

Born on July 22, 1911 in St Petersburg; Latvian. He graduated in 1937 from the Institute of Theology, Basel, Switzerland, and from 1946 to 1974 he was pastor of various Lutheran parishes in Latvia. In 1975 he was appointed head of the German Lutheran Church, and a bishop. He is married and speaks German.

Address: 8 Remines Street, Riga.

Kalugin, Oleg Danilovich

Former KGB Major-General.

Born in Leningrad in 1934 into a military family. He graduated from the faculty of journalism, Leningrad State University and Columbia University, New York, where he was among the first students in the exchange, headed by Aleksandr Yakovlev (1958-59). He was Moscow radio correspondent in the US (1960-65), and joined the USSR KGB in 1958 and worked in the intelligence and counter-intelligence agencies. He regards as one of his greatest coups the recruitment of agent Vodka which saved the Soviet Union about a million dollars. He recruited a naval communications officer who had access to the codes for planning and communications of the US Navy. From 1965 to 1970 Kalugin was first secretary of the Soviet embassy in Washington DC, and had been head of Soviet espionage in the US for 12 years.

When he returned to the Soviet Union he became head of the counter-espionage department of the KGB and later first deputy chief of the Leningrad KGB. In 1990 he was obliged to take early retirement from the KGB and is a major-general (1974) in the reserve. In 1990 he caused a sensation by publicly criticizing the role of the KGB in Soviet society, accusing it of being a bastion of Stalinism while engaging in lip-service to *perestroika* and revealing some of its activities. He was deprived of his military rank, awards and pension by decree of the President of the USSR, which overnight made him extremely popular and a major celebrity. General Vladimir Kryuchkov referred to him as an incompetent troublemaker, but Kalugin continued his campaign and revealed that the KGB had suffered numerous defections to the West.

In 1990 on a wave of popularity he was elected a USSR people's deputy in Krasnodar *krai* national territorial district. He was the author of the Soviet bestseller *View from the Lubyanka* (1990). He was an adviser to Boris Yeltsin on security matters from 1990, and revealed details of KGB operations in the West which led to the death of the Bulgarian journalist, Georgy Markov, working for the BBC in London (killed by a poisoned umbrella dart), and the activity of KGB agents in Radio Liberty in Munich. He was completely rehabilitated in 1991 after the attempted coup and criminal proceedings against him were dropped.

He was active on the radical wing of the democratic movement, and was a member of the co-ordinating council, "military for democracy", the union of journalists of Russia and chairman of the branch of the charitable Russian-British fund for Russian orphans. He has 22 governmental and other awards. In October 1992 he stood for election as an RSFSR people's deputy in the No. 17 national territorial district, Krasnodar. During the election campaign he advocated that the opposition of the former Party nomenclature, occupying several echelons of power, be overcome so as to accelerate reform; the tactical course of the government be altered by dropping the concentration on purely financial levers; the creation of actual conditions for the functioning of market mechanisms; private land ownership; the establishment of a state programme of social protection; the retention of the Soviet system of power; and support for Cossack autonomy and traditions.

There were 19 candidates. Among the leading opponents were: N. I. Kondratev, former chairman of Krasnodar *krai* soviet executive committee (he had been dismissed from the position because of his behaviour during the coup, rehabilitated but not reinstated in office); A. M. Zhdanovsky, chairman of the Krasnodar city soviet; S. G. Alimov, chairman of a collective farm and member of the Democratic Party of Russia; G. N. Len, independent (representing democratic tendency); I. V. Kasatonov, admiral, former commander of the Black Sea Fleet. The election was declared void, as there were 1,707,012 voters on the register but only 636,003 (37.26%) cast their votes. Kalugin polled 22,420 yes votes and 587,193 no votes (92.32%). Kondratev received the largest number of yes votes, 64.43%.

Kalugin speaks English and lives in Moscow.

Kalvanas, Jonas

Chairman of consistory of the Evangelical Lutheran Church of Lithuania; Bishop.

Born on April 24, 1914 in the village of Ruobezu, Birzai district, Lithuania; Lithuanian. He graduated in 1939 from the faculty of theology, Latvian University, Riga. From 1940 to 1955 he was pastor of the Taurage Lutheran church, and then from 1955 to 1970 he was a member of the consistory of the Evangelical Lutheran Church of Lithuania. In 1970 he was appointed chairman of consistory, then bishop, of the church. He is married with six children.

Address: Taurage, ul. Gagarina 68; *telephone*: Taurage 3 2310.

Kamarouskaja, Zinaida Mikalauna

Director of the Jakub Kolas Literary Museum, Minsk.

Born on July 21, 1952 in Sidoubey, Minsk *oblast*. She is Belarusian, and her parents were Mikalaj Navaravic Salaujou and Lidzija Kanstancinauna Salaujova. She graduated from the faculty of philology, Belarusian State University, Minsk. From 1975 to 1986 she worked in the Janka Kupala Literary Museum, Minsk and in 1986 was appointed director of the Jakub Kolas Literary Museum. She is apolitical and her hobbies are literature and the theatre. She is married and her husband is Viktar Michailavic Kamarouski. They have two daughters, Ludmila and Sviaclana. She speaks Polish, Russian and English.

Address: Minsk, vul. Asanalieva 7, 35; *telephone*: Minsk (0172) 39 45 84 (office); 79 37 55 (home).

Kanapacki, Ibrahim Barysavic

Vice-President of the Belarusian Al Kitab Association of Tatar Muslims.

Born on February 28, 1949 in Smilovicy, Cervienski *Raion*, Minsk *oblast*. His father is Barys, and the family is Belarusian. He graduated from the faculty of history and geography, Minsk Pedagogical Institute, and in 1975 successfully presented his candidate dissertation in history (PhD). Since 1970 he has been a teacher and lecturer, first at a village school in Kamienny Barok, Bieiezinski *raion*. He is the author of over 100 articles on Belarusian history, and is now working on the revival of the Belarusian Tatars, their national consciousness and the revival of Islam. He is the co-author of the *Belarusian Tatars: Their Past and Present* (1993). He is now preparing for publication the *Al Kitab* (a medieval Belarusian text of the Koran in Arabic script), and is also working on an encyclopaedic directory *The Tatars of Belarus, Lithuania and Poland*.

He supports and participates in the meetings of all democratic movements and campaigns in Belarus, and is in favour of the "independent and democratic flowering of the land of our fathers". He is married and his wife is Hanna Fiodarauna and they have a son, Zachar, and a daughter, Zorina. He speaks Russian, Polish, German and Arabic. He was awarded the honorary diploma for pedagogic work of the Ministry of Education and Culture of Belarus.

Address: 220000 Minsk, vul. Saveckaja 18, department of history, Minsk pedagogical institute (work); 220131 Minsk, ul. Mirasnicenki d. 51, kv. 312 (home); *telephone*: Minsk (0172) 26 40 22 (work); 61 34 93 (home).

Kapitanets, Ivan Matveevich

First deputy Commander of the Navy of the Unified Armed Forces of the CIS until April 1992. Admiral of the Fleet since 1988.

Born on January 10, 1928 on the *khutor* (farm) Nekludovka, Kosharsky *raion*, Rostov *oblast*, into a peasant family. Ukrainian. Kapitanets graduated from the S. M. Kirov Caspian Higher Naval Technical School in Baku in 1950; higher classes for officers in 1957; the Naval Academy in 1964; the Military Academy of the General Staff in 1970. He received a higher military education and was a member of the CPSU from 1952 to August 1991.

He began his career as an officer in 1950 as a commander of a ship's section. He was an officer with a sound professional training who loved the sea and the fleet and was eager to gain more specialist knowledge. He was actively involved in the work of *Komsomol* and Party organizations and was elected to Party agencies. He enjoyed the support of superior officers and Party political agencies. He was rapidly promoted and became senior assistant commander of a ship and took part in long sea voyages. In 1957 he was appointed a commander of a destroyer and his crew were awarded a distinction. Between 1964 and 1973 he was Chief of Staff, commander of a destroyer formation of the Northern Fleet, deputy commander of a mixed formation of the surface ships. He supervised groups of ships carrying out military duties in the oceans. In 1973 he became commander of a flotilla of the Pacific Fleet. The ships of the formation under Adml Kapitanets were involved in military duties whose aim was to ensure favourable operational conditions in the Sea of Okhotsk and the Sea of Japan, off the coast of Kamchatka. In 1978 Kapitanets was appointed first deputy commander of the Red Banner Baltic Fleet. In 1981 he became a commander. He supervised successfully the training of the fleet's forces in the closed sea theatre, ensured a high level of combat readiness, established close ties with the Party and Soviet leaders of the Baltic republics of the USSR and knew how to acquire a good reputation with the top military commanders in Moscow. He used tough measures to strengthen discipline and order among the sailors, engendering fear and hostility on their part.

In 1985 Adml Kapitanets was promoted to commander of the Northern Fleet which is traditionally considered by naval officers to be a major success. He demonstrated the ability to ensure the fulfilment of major tasks by naval forces in one of the most important strategic directions — the northern theatre of operations. The largest Soviet fleet, under his command, had a high level of combat readiness, and carried out its military duties in the Atlantic Ocean, in the regions of the Far North and in the Mediterranean. His activities during the anti-alcohol campaign in the USSR (1984-86) caused hostility because officers and midshipmen were dismissed even for minor offences. During Mikhail Gorbachev's visit to Murmansk and the fleet in 1987, Kapitanets organized a hearty reception for the distinguished guest. He did his best to impress the General Secretary of the CPSU and his wife. Later this contributed to the Admiral's promotion. In 1988 Kapitanets was appointed first deputy Commander-in-Chief of the Navy. On November 4, 1988 he was promoted to the highest rank in the navy, Admiral of the Fleet. In this post he headed and supervised the multi-faceted training of all naval forces.

Politically Kapitanets was a convinced communist. He was elected to the Party *oblast* committees in Kaliningrad and Murmansk *oblasts*. From 1986 to 1990 he was a candidate member of the Party Central Committee. His attitude towards democratic reform in the country was negative and, being a conformist by nature, he publicly expressed his support for the policies of the top Party and government leaders. He supported the reform of the armed forces so as to enable them to meet the demands of present-day warfare. He favoured a gradual transition to a professional navy. During the anti-constitutional putsch in August 1991 he acted as Commander-in-Chief in place of Adml Chernavin, who was on holiday. Kapitanets took part in the meeting of the collegium of the USSR Ministry of Defence on August 19, where, according to Marshal Evgeny Shaposhnikov, he remained passive. Later he played a waiting game. In February 1992 he became first deputy Commander of the Navy of the Unified Armed Forces of the CIS. In April/May 1992 he was a member of the state commission for the establishment of the Ministry of Defence, Army and Navy of the Russian Federation. Until summer 1992 he headed the preparations for the celebrations marking the 300th anniversary of the Russian Fleet and was chairman of the naval anniversary commission. He has published several articles, including one entitled "Problems of ensuring the stability of vessels", in *Morskoi sbornik*, No. 4, 1991, and "On stability", also in *Morskoi sbornik*, Nos. 8-9, 1992. He is interested in literature on military, historical and patriotic subjects. He has visited foreign countries in an official capacity during visits by vessels of the USSR navy, but does not speak any foreign language. He has been awarded orders of the Red Banner, of Lenin, "for service to the motherland in the armed forces of the USSR", 3rd class, and 11 medals. He is married.

Official address: 103175 Moscow K–175.

Kapshtyk, Ivan Markovych

Prefect of the President of Ukraine in Kiev *Oblast*.

Born into a Ukrainian peasant family in 1939 in Kharkiv *oblast*. He was educated at the Kiev Academy of Agricultural Economics and worked in various branches of the agro-industrial economy, including the *Kyïvska* poultry factory. He was expelled from the Communist Party of Ukraine for his unorthodox views in 1978, rejoined it under *perestroika*, and then left it voluntarily in 1990. He has been a member of the Supreme Soviet since 1990, where he enhanced his reputation as a democrat. Hence his appointment as prefect in Kiev *oblast* in March 1992 was widely seen as providing a counterweight to the more conservative Ivan Salii in Kiev city. Kapshtyk is married with two children.

Karaev, Tamerlan Elmar Ogly

First deputy Speaker of the *Milli Mejlis* (National Council), Republic of Azerbaijan, until June 1993.

Born on January 30, 1952 in the village of Kasymly, Agdamsky *raion*, Azerbaijan SSR, into an Azeri family. His father, Elmar, was Procurator of Baku transport authority in the 1970s but in 1982 was expelled from the CPSU and retired for "serious deficiencies in his work". Karaev has two sisters. He was a member of the CPSU from 1976 to January 20, 1990.

In 1973 he graduated from the faculty of law, Azerbaijani State University, and from 1977 to 1980 he was a postgraduate student in the extra-mural department, Institute of Philosophy and Law, Academy of Sciences, Azerbaijan. He successfully defended his candidate dissertation in law in 1981 on recidivism (LLM), and after graduating from the faculty of law he was assigned to the procurator's office in Leninsky *raion*, Baku, as a probationer. After six months he became an assistant to the Procurator of Nasiminsky *raion*, Baku, and from 1977 to 1978 he was Procurator in the department of investigation, Procurator's Office, Baku.

In 1978 he moved to the Azerbaijani State University. Between 1978 and 1986 he was a lecturer in the department of criminal law, faculty of law; in 1986 he became an assistant professor (*dotsent*), and in 1988 he was elected deputy dean of the faculty of law. He was elected a deputy to the Supreme Soviet, Azerbaijani SSR, in March 1990 and at its first session he was elected deputy Speaker. In May 1992 he became first deputy Speaker of the parliament. In the spring of 1992 he was nominated to stand for President of the republic in the elections of June 7, 1992.

In 1989 he became a member of the university organization of the popular Front of Azerbaijan and a member of its *Mejlis* (council), and sees himself as a politician who adopts a moderate centrist position in the leadership of the National Front. On June 1, 1993 Russian forces abandoned their garrison with all their food and equipment in Gyanja and Col. Suret Guseinov and his forces took over. The President's military tried to disarm them but failed, and they then began to march on Baku. President Elchibey fled to Nakhichevan on learning that his military would not resist the advance of Guseinov's forces, and on June 15, 1993 Geidar Aliev was elected Speaker of the *Milli Mejlis* and acting head of state. Guseinov took over the military, security forces and the militia.

Karaev is the author of over 20 articles and four books, published in Baku, Moscow, Saratov and Havana, Cuba, on criminal law. He is married. His wife is Farid Abas Kyzy and they have three children. His daughter, A. Zamanovva, was a procurator in the Azerbaijani SSR from 1976 to 1985. The elder son, Farman was born in 1977 and the younger, Ruslan, in 1982. He lives in Baku.

Karaganov, Sergei Aleksandrovich

Member of the Council of the President of the Russian Federation.

Political scientist and deputy director of the institute of Europe, Russian Academy of Sciences. In 1979 he successfully presented his candidate dissertation in history on "Transnational corporations and the foreign policy of the USA" (PhD), and is the author of the books, *USA: Transnational Corporations and Foreign Policy*, (1984); *USA: Dictator of NATO* (1985); *Militarism and Contemporary Society* (1987); *Reasonable Sufficiency and New Political Thinking* (1989); *The Common European Home: What Do We Think About It?* (1991).

Karaganov is engaged on problems of US domestic and foreign policy, and on European integration. He has published articles about the US cinema industry, the disposition of US nuclear rockets in Europe, problems of disarmament, security of western Europe, the "Star Wars" programme, the common European home from the military point of view, support in western Europe for nuclear weapons, problems of the European policy of the USSR, on military and nuclear strategy of the USA, which have been published in the journals *SShA: Ekonomika, politika, ideologiya*, *Mirovaya ekonomika i mezhdunarodnie otnosheniya*, *Novoe Vremya*, *Kommunist*, and *Mezhdunarodnaya zhizn*. He lives in Moscow.

Karaman, Aleksandr Akimovich

Vice-President of the "Moldovan Transnistrian Republic".

Born in 1956 in the city of Slobozia, Slobozia *raion*, Moldovan SSR. His parents were teachers and he is an ethnic Moldovan. He graduated from the Chişinău Institute of Medicine in 1978 specializing in surgery and began his career as a surgeon at Chişinău's city hospital No. 4. From 1980 to 1982 he served in the military, after which he worked as a surgeon in the *raion* hospital in Slobozia. From 1986 to 1989, he worked as the principal physician in Slobozia *raion*. He was elected in 1989 secretary of the Slobozia party committee. In March 1990 he was elected deputy to the Soviet of People's Deputies in Slobozia. From November 1990 he was a deputy in the Supreme Soviet of the "Moldovan Transnistrian Republic", where he was named president of the Soviet of Nationalities. At the beginning of 1991, he was elected deputy president of the Executive Committee of the Slobozia Soviet of People's Deputies. He is married with two children.

Karamanov, Uzakbai Karamanovich

State adviser, Republic of Kazakhstan.

Born in 1937 in the village of Uyala, Kzyl-Orda *oblast*; Kazakh. He was a member of the CPSU until August 1991. He graduated from the Institute of Construction Engineering, Kuibyshev (Samara), and the advanced engineering courses of the USSR Academy of Architecture and Construction, and then began work in 1959 as a works' superintendent in Aktyubinsk. He worked in Kzyl-Orda, Aralsk, Alma Ata on construction sites and enterprises of the building industry, and from 1967 to 1980 worked on construction projects and with the main administration of the Ministry of Construction of Heavy Industry Enterprises, Kazakhstan. From 1980 to 1986 he was deputy Minister of Light Industry, Kazakhstan, and first deputy Minister of Construction, Kazakhstan. In April 1987 he was appointed chairman of the Kazakh state committee for materials and technical supplies, and in November 1990 he was appointed chairman of the Cabinet of Ministers, Kazakhstan. He was also a people's deputy of Kazakhstan. In November 1991 he became a state adviser, Republic of Kazakhstan. He is married with three children.

Address: Government House, 480091 Alma Ata; *telephone*: Alma Ata 62 3097

Karimov, Islam Abduganievich

President of the Republic of Uzbekistan.

Born on January 30, 1938 in Samarkand, Uzbek SSR; Uzbek. He was a member of the CPSU from 1964 to August 1991. He graduated in 1960 in machine building, from the Central Asian Polytechnic, Tashkent, and in 1967 from the Institute of the National Economy, Tashkent, where he successfully presented his candidate dissertation in economics (PhD (Econ)). After graduation in 1960 he began working as an assistant foreman, and then later a foreman and technologist at the Tashkent agricultural machinery enterprise (Tashselmash). From 1961 he was a design engineer, then chief engineer of the Chkalov aircraft production association, Tashkent. From 1966 to 1983 he was a specialist in a department, assistant to the chairman of the state planning committee (Gosplan) of the Uzbek SSR, chief expert in a department, assistant to the chairman, head of department, head of a directorate, and first deputy chairman of Gosplan, Uzbek SSR.

In 1983 he was appointed Minister of Finance of the republic. In 1986 he became deputy chairman of the Council of Ministers of Uzbekistan; then chairman of the republic's Gosplan. In December 1986 he was elected first secretary of the Kashkadarya *oblast* committee of the Communist Party of Uzbekistan (CPUzbek), and in 1989 was elected first secretary of the Central Committee, CPUzbek. In July 1990, at the XXVIII CPSU Congress, he was elected a member of the Central Committee and the Politburo. He was also a USSR people's deputy.

In March 1990 he was elected President of the Uzbek SSR at a session of the Supreme Soviet of the republic, having been the only candidate. On December 29, 1991 he was elected the first President of the Republic of Uzbekistan in national elections, and again he was the only candidate. At his inauguration he deemed it politic to swear the oath of loyalty to the republic with one hand on the Koran and the other on the republican constitution.

In October 1991 he joined the People's Democratic Party of Uzbekistan, which was the successor party to the CPUzbek after it was banned. Uzbekistan was the last Central Asian republic to be recognized diplomatically by the United States, and this was because of doubts over the civil rights record of the young state. This was embarrassing for Karimov, but the President of the US was concerned about the stability of the republic, although in fact the former communist nomenclature made the transition to a democratic, secular Muslim state effortlessly.

Nascent Islamic fundamentalism is a threat and Muslim moves in Namangan *oblast* have been countered. Uzbekistan is potentially rich, with gold, oil, natural gas and minerals to offer the foreign investor, but it has been slow to sign agreements with Western concerns due to lack of expertise in assessing the various bids on offer. Karimov runs a tight ship and there are opposition parties but they appear to be officially sanctioned. The republic maintains good relations with Russia and is a keen supporter of the CIS. Karimov and his regime have entered into several agreements with the other ex-Soviet Muslim republics to set up an embryonic common market, common media policy and so on, but these are, at present, more an expression of the aspirations of the region than concrete reality.

He was awarded the order of the Red Banner of Labour, the order of the Friendship of the Peoples (1988), and medals. He is married with two daughters.

Address: 170163 Tashkent, Uzbekistansky prospekt 43; *telephone*: Tashkent 39 5456; 39 5300 (office).

Karmokov, Khachim Mukhamedovich

Speaker of the Supreme Soviet of the Kabardino-Balkar Republic, Russian Federation.

Born in 1941 in the village of Zayukovo, Baksansky *raion*, Kabardino-Balkar ASSR. He grew up in a large family with four brothers and three sisters, and his father was the chairman of a collective farm. He was a member of the CPSU until August 1991. He graduated from the Kabardino-Balkar State University, and began his career in 1963 as a foreman of the No. 5 construction administration, No. 15 Bryanskstroi construction trust, and later was head of the MSO–3 production technical department of the council of the Kabardino-Balkar inter-collective farm construction trust. From 1964 to 1966 he was an architect in the Tyrnyauzsky city soviet executive committee, and senior work superintendent of the construction administration of No. 3 North Caucasian co-operative construction trust. From 1966 to 1967 he was a lecturer at Kabardino-Balkar State University.

In 1967 he became a postgraduate student at the S. Ordzhonikidze institute of engineering and economics, Moscow, and in 1971 successfully presented his candidate dissertation in Economics (PhD (Econ)). From 1971 to 1978 he was a lecturer at Kabardino-Balkar State University, then assistant, senior lecturer and assistant professor. He was head of the construction administration, Kabardino-Balkar motorway construction trust (1978–81), and from 1981 to 1983 he was an assistant professor in the faculty of economics of the national economy, Kabardino-Balkar State University. From 1983 to 1990 he was deputy manager for economics of the Kabardino-Balkar industrial construction trust and in 1990, after the reorganization of the trust, he was appointed commercial director of the Kabardino-Balkar construction design company.

In 1990 he was elected a deputy of the Supreme Soviet of the Kabardino-Balkar ASSR, and at the first session he was elected a member of the commission on the plan and the budget, finance, labour, prices and social policy. In August 1990 he was appointed deputy Chairman of the Council of Ministers of the Kabardino-Balkar Soviet Socialist Republic, and chairman of the commission on economic reform of the republic. In May 1991 he was elected deputy Speaker of the Supreme Soviet of the republic.

Despite the fact that the Supreme Soviet of the Kabardino-Balkar SSR in August 1991 judged the activities of the Presidium of the Supreme Soviet during the anti-constitutional state coup to be correct and the state authorities functioned normally, Karmokov and other members of the Presidium, under pressure from some deputies and public movements, resigned. In September 1991 Karmokov's resignation was not accepted. He stood for Speaker of the Supreme Soviet of the Kabardino-Balkar SSR and was elected in the second round of voting. There were four candidates.

From October to December 1991 he was a candidate for the post of President of the Kabardino-Balkar Republic. During the election campaign he advocated the implementation in the republic of the separation of powers. He regarded the transition to a market economy as inevitable and the only choice, and proposed the following measures as necessary to ensure the transition: privatization, elimination of state administrative interference in the economy, and active foreign economic activity. The indexation of the incomes of the population was necessary, as were budgetary transfers to the social sphere. He opposed the introduction of the private ownership of land and proposed that the sale of land be prohibited. He also considered that the activities of nationalist groups should be restricted and he acknowledged the right of the Balkar people to create their own statehood.

There were four candidates. Karmokov lost in the first round as V. M. Kokov was elected President of the Kabardino-Balkar Republic.

Karmokov is married with a daughter and lives in Nalchik.

Karpenko, Vitalii Opasnovych

Ukrainian People's Deputy and Editor of the *Vechirnii Kyïv* newspaper.

Born into a Ukrainian family in 1941. He was educated at Kiev State University, and is a journalist by profession. Although a member of the Communist Party of Ukraine (CPU), under his editorship the main Kiev evening paper *Vechirnii Kyïv*, published in both Ukrainian and Russian, became a beacon for *glasnost* in the late 1980s. At a time when the CPU retained its monopoly control over almost all other sections of the mass media, Karpenko tried to provide both balanced reporting and a news outlet for the burgeoning informal organizations, raising his paper's circulation to 534,645 by March 1991.

Even during the attempted coup in August 1991 he published *Rukh's* call for a general strike (on Tuesday August 20). Karpenko himself is close to the centrist Party of Democratic Revival of Ukraine. During 1991 to 1992, *Vechirnii Kyïv* was often starved of paper, and was outflanked by other, more radical, papers. In March 1990 he was elected on the first round as people's deputy for Pryrichnyi *raion* in Kiev city, and in the Supreme Soviet he is a member of the committee on *glasnost* and the mass media.

Address (of *Vechirnii Kyïv*): 254136 Kiev, Vul. Marshala Grechka 13; *telephone*: Kiev 434 6109.

Karpinsky, Len Vyacheslavovich

Editor-in-chief of the newspaper *Moskovskie Novosti*.

Born in 1932. His father was an Old Bolshevik (had joined the Party before the October Revolution), a comrade-in-arms of Lenin and named his son to honour Lenin. Len Vyacheslavovich was evacuated with his family from Moscow to the Urals during the Great Fatherland War (1941-45). He later taught Marxism-Leninism in Gorky (Nizhny Novgorod). He graduated from the faculty of philosophy, Moscow State University and was in the same year as Raisa Maksimovna Gorbacheva. He was Editor-in-chief of *Molodoi kommunist* (1959), and was secretary of the Gorky *Komsomol oblast* committee, then secretary of the *Komsomol* Central Committee for ideology (1959-62). He made his career under Vladimir Semichastny. In 1962 he began working on *Pravda*, was a member of the editorial board, editor of the department of propaganda, then editor of the department of culture and life. He had close contact with Aleksandr Yakovlev and Egor Yakovlev.

In 1967 he and Fedor Burlatsky published the article *On the way to the première*, targeted at the state censorship in the newspaper *Komsomolskaya pravda*. Despite the fact that the article had been approved by the editorial board of *Komsomolskaya pravda* and *Pravda*, Karpinsky was sacked from the editorial board of *Pravda*. He became a political columnist on *Izvestiya* (1967), but parted company with the government newspaper in 1968 and joined the institute for sociological studies, headed by Fedor Burlatsky, in 1968. Karpinsky was head of the editorial board for scientific communism and the experience of socialist construction of the publishing house Progress (1973-75). In 1969 he wrote the book *The Word is also Action*, in which he demonstrated that a process was developing in the USSR which could lead to a second Prague Spring (the events in Czechoslovakia in 1968). The book only existed in manuscript and he passed it to Roi Medvedev to read but it was seized by the KGB during a search of Medvedev's flat. In the first half of the 1970s Karpinsky organized the circle "free, pure Marxism" and among those who participated were Otto Latsis, I. Klyamkin and V. Glotov. A special collection was prepared by the circle which was intended for distribution by *samizdat*, but in June 1975 Karpinsky was summoned by the KGB for a discussion and after his case was reviewed in the committee of Party control of the Party Central Committee, he was expelled from the CPSU on the orders of Mikhail Suslov. From 1975 to 1985 he did not engage in journalism.

In 1987 he appealed to the committee of Party control for reinstatement in the CPSU but was turned down. However, after a letter from 12 well-known members to the XIX Party conference in June 1988, the committee of Party control reviewed his case and reinstated him as a Party member. In 1987 he began writing in *Moskovskie novosti* and became famous for an article on *perestroika*. Later he became first deputy editor-in-chief, while Egor Yakovlev was editor. In January 1991 he resigned from the CPSU in connection with the events in the Baltic republics, and in September of the same year he was elected editor-in-chief of *Moskovskie novosti*. He lives in Moscow.

Karpov, Anatoly Evgenevich

Former world chess champion.

Born on May 23, 1951 in Zlatoust, Chelyabinsk *oblast*; Russian. He graduated in 1978 from the faculty of economics, Leningrad State University, and was a member of the CPSU until August 1991. In 1966 he was awarded the title of chess master and in 1970 became an international grand master. He won the world youth tournament in 1969 and became world chess champion in 1975. He defended his title successfully against Viktor Korchnoi, the former Soviet grand master, in 1978 and 1981, and was USSR chess champion in 1976 and 1983. In 1985 he lost his world title to Gary Kasparov in an epic contest. Karpov was supported by the Soviet government and regarded as the establishment candidate, whereas Kasparov, an Azerbaijani Jew, symbolized the outsider and the non-Russian.

Karpov was president of the international association of grand masters until 1990, and was also editor-in-chief of the *64 Chess Review* magazine. He was also a USSR people's deputy, and was president of the Soviet peace foundation until 1991. In March 1992 he was elected president of the international association of peace funds. He is chairman of the council of trustees of the international humanitarian non-governmental organization, Aid for Chernobyl; and chairman of the council of trustees of the new names charity programme.

He has published books and many articles on chess. He is married with a son and speaks English. He became a USSR master of sport in 1974; has won the Oscar chess prize nine times, the order of Lenin in 1981; and the order of the Red Banner of Labour. He won the international chess tournaments in Moscow in 1971; Hastings in 1971 and 1972; San Antonio in 1972; Madrid in 1973; Amsterdam in 1985; Brussels in 1986; and Tilburg in 1988, among others.

Address: 119889 Moscow, ul. Prechistenka 10; *telephone*: Moscow 202 4171.

Karyakin, Yury Fedorovich

Member of the Council of the President of the Russian Federation.

Born in 1930, Russian; was a member of the CPSU. He is a university graduate and writer and publicist who was a senior scientific assistant in the institute of the international working class movement, USSR Academy of Sciences. In early 1989 he was elected a USSR people's deputy as one of the nominees of the USSR Academy of Sciences. He was one of the first to begin the process of "amnesting" and later "rehabilitating" Fedor Dostoevsky. He is author of the books: *Mister Cohen Researches the "Russian Soul"* (1961); *Forbidden Thought Acquires Freedom. 175 Year Struggle Over the Ideas and Legacy of Radishchev* (1966); *The Self-Delusion of Raskolnikov. F. M. Dostoevsky's Novel "Crime and Punishment"* (1976); *Chernyshevsky or Nechaev? On Genuine and Transient Revolutionary Thought in the Liberation Movement in Russia in the 1850s and 1860s* (1976); *Dostoevsky. Essays* (1984); *Dostoevsky and the Threshold of the 21st Century* (1989).

Karyakin believes that the written word can influence the reader. In order to remove evil from the world, it needs to be removed from the individual, from his own heart. He regards international frontiers as a transient phenomenon and quite accidental and advocates the return of the Kurile islands to Japan, maintaining that this does not amount to selling parts of the motherland but merely historical generosity. He underlines the fact that Russia is now in no state to have an empire, and it is late in developing because of its enormous area. He sees no external threat to the state but acknowledges that general ecological misfortune does exist. He believes that all the troubles of Russian society derive from atheism, hence people need to turn to religion. One should remember death without which there is no morality.

He supports private property and the concepts of labour, democracy and law, the rebirth of national feelings and cultures. He maintains that conscience and consciousness determine being and that democracy originated in Christianity. He opposes the chauvinistic slogans of the Russian "patriots", arguing that they only express hatred and that there is no generosity or aesthetic feeling in them. He concedes that it is difficult to restructure consciousness but that all present leaders have gone through this process. He thinks that President Mikhail Gorbachev was very innovative in foreign policy, but domestically had to come to terms with reality and was blinkered by Marxism-Leninism. Karyakin believes that the whole generation of his contemporaries should engage in confession and repentance and be merciless towards themselves, as the wall of unbelief and lack of trust towards this generation on the part of the young has to be broken down. Karyakin took part in the defence of the Russian White House in August 1991 and regards it as a good sign that there were many young people there. He opposed the appointment of Yury Petrov as head of the administration of President Yeltsin. Karyakin became a member of the presidential Council in February 1993.

Kasatonov, Igor Vladimirovich

First deputy Commander-in-Chief of the navy. Admiral since 1992.

Born on February 10, 1939 in Vladivostok into a naval officer's family. (His father was an Admiral of the Fleet and first deputy Commander-in-Chief of the Navy.) Russian. Kasatonov graduated from the Black Sea P. S. Nakhimov Higher Naval Technical School in Sevastopol in 1960; the Naval Academy in 1975; the Military Academy of the General Staff in 1979. He received a higher military education and was a member of the CPSU until August 1991.

He served on surface vessels of the navy. He owes his successful career not only to his powerful father's influence but also to his own personal qualities as a highly qualified specialist and experienced sailor with a sound operational tactical training. He was respected by his subordinates and superior officers. He was a battery officer, combat section commander, senior assistant commander, and commander of the Provorny and Ochakov, large anti-submarine vessels. He participated in many long voyages at sea. The ship under Kasatonov's command often fulfilled difficult missions when it came into direct contact with the US and NATO navies.

From 1975 Kasatonov was Chief of Staff of a surface ship division; from 1980 to 1982 he was an anti-submarine divisional commander; from 1982 commander of the Kola flotilla. He ensured a high level of combat readiness of the forces under his command. Besides his professional abilities, Kasatonov weas notable for his high level of culture. He was not politically active and participated in Party work only to the extent necessary to further his career. In 1988 he was appointed first deputy Commander-in-Chief of the Red Banner Northern Fleet. He was responsible for the organization of combat training of the largest part of the Soviet navy in the European theatre of operations. During the anti-constitutional putsch in August 1991 there were no reports of Kasatonov's involvement in political activities. He concentrated on his immediate duties and did not express his political views in public.

In August 1991 Kasatonov was appointed Commander-in-Chief of the Red Banner Black Sea Fleet, replacing Adml M. N. Khronopulo, who had been dismissed for supporting the plotters. Kasatonov had an important political role to play in the Black Sea. He succeeded in manoeuvring between different groups to preserve a unified navy and defend the interests of Russia in the south-western strategic direction. In these circumstances, Kasatonov became, according to knowledgeable sources, a hostage of the top political leaders of Russia and Ukraine and his fate was decided when the two Presidents reached an agreement on the Black Sea Fleet during their meetings at Dagomys and Yalta. At first, Kasatonov was not opposed to the idea of Ukraine creating its own naval forces and personnel taking an oath of loyalty to Ukraine. Later, however, instructions from Moscow, the details of which are not known to the public at large, obliged him to take a firm stand *vis-à-vis* Ukraine. Presumably the sailors who had taken an oath of loyalty to Ukraine were disciplined against the wishes of Kasatonov.

The Admiral enjoyed great support among national patriotic groups and servicemen as a symbol of the Russian Fleet and Russia's interests in the Crimea and the Black Sea. He is undoubtedly popular with the majority of top leaders and the Russian public at large. He was elected a member of the Public Council for the preparation of the celebrations of the 300th anniversary of the Russian navy and a member of the collegium of the Russian naval historical and cultural centre. He is a convinced believer in Russia and the navy. Politically he supports the national patriotic movements. He favours the retention of a strong state possessing considerable military and economic strength. He often appears in the mass media where he concentrates on patriotic subjects. He published an article, "There will be no Russia without the navy and there can be no navy without Russia", in *Krasnaya Zvezda*, on September 27, 1992. In early October 1992 he was appointed first deputy Commander-in-Chief of the Navy, in Moscow. He is interested in the history of the Russian state and navy. He engages in sport and likes literature and art. He has been awarded orders of the Red Star, two orders "for service to the motherland in the armed forces of the USSR", and 12 medals. He is married with three children.

Official address: 103175 Moscow K-175.

Kasparov (Vainshtein), Gary Kinovich

World chess champion.

Born April 13, 1963 in Baku into a Jewish family, and was known by his father's name of Vainshtein until the age of 13. He became keenly interested in mathematics when four years old and at the age of 18 became a Soviet grand master. He won the youth tournament in Dortmund, West Germany in 1981. He won gold medals in Malta (1980) and in Lucerne (1982). He met Anatoly Karpov, also of the Soviet Union, in late 1984 for the world title. Karpov had taken the world title in 1975 by default, the only world champion ever to do so. Bobby Fischer, United States, won a celebrated contest in Reykjavik, Iceland, in 1972 and three years later he put forward his proposals for a new championship, but Fide, the ruling international body and dominated by the Soviet Union, brushed them aside. Fischer abdicated and Karpov was declared world champion.

In the Karpov-Kasparov contest, the world champion swept into an early lead and appeared to be near victory. However, Kasparov fought back and gradually began to catch up. On February 15, 1985, after 46 games and many months of play in Moscow Kasparov was beginning to look the eventual winner. The Fide president, Florencio Campomanes of the Philippines, then flew into Moscow and declared the game over, but there would be another match later in the year. Kasparov had already made himself unpopular with Fide by criticizing Campomanes. Kasparov and the world of chess were outraged and the match made the headlines in many world newspapers. There was a widely-held belief that Kasparov had been cheated of the title, and from then onwards Kasparov was the sworn enemy of Fide and Campomanes and vowed to destroy both. Kasparov exacted his revenge and on November 9, 1985 Kasparov became world champion at the age of 22. The match was given extra spice in that Karpov, a Russian, was seen as the embodiment of Soviet communism, and Kasparov, a Jew and outsider, was viewed by many non-Russians and political activists as their champion.

Now with the moral authority of the world title around him Kasparov could take on Fide and Campomanes, but Fide was still dominated by the Soviets and their Third World allies. With their world collapsing around their ears the Soviets clung on to Fide like grim death. Kasparov became very popular in the West for his brilliant play, panache, handsome good looks and fluency in English. He also participated in the democratic movement and played a political role but soon left the active political arena. The massacre in Sumgait, Azerbaijan, of Armenians and other non-Azeris and the murder of civilians by the Soviet military in Baku in January 1990 convinced Kasparov that his future lay elsewhere and he and his family moved to Moscow. Kasparov defeated Karpov again in 1989 to retain his title, playing brilliantly to do so.

In February 1993 Nigel Short of Great Britain won the right to challenge Kasparov for the world title. Fide decreed that the event should take place in Manchester, England, because it judged the financial arrangements to be the most advantageous. Campomanes took the decision without consulting either player, something he was required to do by the federation's rules, but Short was angered by this peremptory behaviour and was determined to strengthen the position of the players. He contacted Dominic Lawson, son of Lord Lawson, Chancellor of the Exchequer under Margaret Thatcher and editor of the journal *Spectator*, and together with Kasparov decided to break away from the world federation, set up a new professional association and invite the world's players to join them. Kasparov's fluent command of English was of considerable value.

Kazannik, Aleksei Ivanovich

Member of the Council of the President of the Russian Federation.

Born in 1941 in the village of Perepis, Chernigov (Chernihiv) *oblast*, Ukraine, into a large peasant family. Ukrainian. He was not a member of the CPSU. His father and two elder brothers were killed in action during the Great Fatherland War, but his mother and three children survived the German occupation. In 1959, after completing school, he went to work in Kazakhstan as a carpenter and then served in the Soviet Army in the engineering troops. After being demobbed he enrolled in the law faculty of Irkutsk State University and graduated as a lawyer.

His most formative years were during the Khrushchev "thaw" during the late 1950s and early 1960s. He was engaged on Soviet state law and in 1970 successfully presented his candidate dissertation on the co-ordinating function of local soviets of workers' deputies at present (based on eastern Siberia) (LLM) where he for the first time studied the interrelationship between local soviets and enterprises, institutions, organizations which were not subordinate to, but on the territory of, the local soviets. In 1975 he became an assistant professor in the department of labour, economic and agricultural law, Omsk State University.

He came to the conclusion that in the 1970s state law had been reduced to the level of a "servant" of the dominant ideology and that specialists were left only with the task of producing commentaries on quotations from the Marxist-Leninist classics and leading contemporary figures. He therefore gave up state law and devoted himself to ecology. He regarded it as a purely humanitarian, non-politicized area of endeavour where it was possible to reach decisions without the intervention of law. In 1979, shortly after the Soviet invasion of Afghanistan, he made negative comments about this policy. In 1991 he successfully presented his doctoral dissertation in law on regional problems on the legal protection of the environment in the USSR (LLD), and was also appointed head of the department of state law, administration and Soviet construction, Omsk State University. He has taken part in drafting practically all Russian legislation on ecology. He is also interested in the scientific organization of administrative work and business correspondence in state institutions. He gives lectures for the *Znanie* (knowledge) society.

In early 1989 he was nominated as a candidate for election as a USSR people's deputy in the No. 22 Omsk national territorial district and in the election programme he appealed for a return to common sense in agrarian policy, to stop pressurizing peasants and telling them what, how and when to do everything. He argued that investment in the rural sector should be effected differently, via a relaxation of tax policy, the creation of a system of benefits, long-term credits and the promotion of various types of leasing. He advocated the construction of modern enterprises to store and process agricultural produce in the countryside, the construction of roads and housing by the Ministry of Water Transport and the carrying out of improvement work at the request of the collective and state farms.

He called for the establishment of a constitutional mechanism which would remove high state officials from office for unconstitutional acts or misuse of their official position, and bring about the sharp reduction of their physical and psychological well-being and thereby protect the country from the remnants of the Stalin and Brezhnev eras. In his judgement it was necessary for a Supreme Soviet commission to supervise all ministries and for the people's congress and Supreme Soviet to have the right to pass a vote of no confidence in the government and individual ministers. The supremacy of the USSR constitution should be assured and all legislation which contradicts this should be annulled.

There should be a regular review of wages in the light of inflation and genuine regional cost accounting. Expensive projects such as the Baikal Amur railway, redirecting northern flowing rivers to the south and the construction of huge hydroelectric stations, should cease. Expenditure on some space programmes, defence, land improvement and the maintenance of the administrative apparatus should be cut back. The armed forces should be reduced in size but firm social security guarantees should be provided for those going into the reserve. There should be legislation to protect the environment, payment for the use of nature and ecological education for all.

There were two candidates: Kazannik won, polling 55.61% of the votes, and his opponent was I. I. Yanovsky who received 40.26% of the votes. Kazannik was elected to the USSR Supreme Soviet at the I Congress of People's Deputies. However he proposed that Boris Yeltsin take over his place and President Gorbachev could find no legal reason to block this move, so in this way Yeltsin became a member of the Supreme Soviet and was provided with a national platform for his views for the first time. Kazannik worked in the USSR Supreme Soviet committee on ecology and the rational use of natural resources.

He was active politically, stating that since society had been politicized, he, as a people's deputy, could not remain outside politics. He stated that he harboured no feelings of pathological hatred of the CPSU, but produced a draft law on the legal responsibility of political parties and mass movements which have committed crimes against their own people, the world and humanity. He regarded the Party as the main part of the state structure, depending on the KGB, the army and other coercive agencies for its effectiveness.

In Kazannik's view, the Party had committed crimes against the world: the war against Finland and the Baltic states in 1940, the interventions in 1956 in Hungary, 1968 in Czechoslovakia and 1979 in Afghanistan. The mass repression of the Stalin era on class, religious and national grounds amounted to a crime against humanity. Pointing out that about one third of the country suffered from ecological damage, he stated that decisions which had resulted in this situation were taken at the level of the Party Politburo. This was a crime against the environment. The Party should be held legally responsible for all these actions.

At the V Congress of RSFSR People's Deputies in October 1991 Kazannik stood for election to the Constitutional Court but was not successful. He found the organization and the arrangement of the work of the Court interesting as he regarded its main function was to engage in all the main branches of law since the terms of reference of the Court are extremely wide and it has no parallel in any other country. He advocated the establishment of a highly qualified legal consultative council without the right of recall of its members for the setting up of a secretariat, chancellery and library. The Constitutional Court needed a specialist on state law and constitutional supervision in bourgeois states. He became a member of the presidential Council in February 1993. He is married with two sons, one 17 years old and the other 13, and lives in Omsk.

Kerestedzhiyants, Leonid Vladimirovich

Russian ambassador to Croatia.

Born on July 11, 1931 in Melitopol, Zaporozhe (Zaporizhzhia) *oblast*, Ukraine; Armenian. He graduated in 1955 from the Leningrad Institute of Shipbuilding, and from 1955 to 1956 he was an engineer in a Leningrad enterprise. Then he became a *Komsomol* official, first in Leningrad and then in Moscow until 1963. From 1963 to 1969 he was chairman of the Sputnik international youth tourist agency, Moscow; in 1970 he became a diplomat and was appointed first secretary in the USSR Embassy in Yugoslavia and in 1973 was promoted counsellor for cultural affairs in the embassy. In 1975 he returned to Moscow to the USSR Ministry of Foreign Affairs as head of section, department for cultural ties with foreign countries. From 1978 to 1986 he was counsellor for cultural affairs, attaché for cultural affairs, counsellor, and minister counsellor in the USSR embassy in Bulgaria.

In 1986 he was made deputy head of the personnel department in the USSR Ministry of Foreign Affairs, Moscow, and was then first deputy head of department, the main administration for personnel and educational establishments in the ministry (1986-87). He was appointed deputy chairman of the USSR state committee for foreign tourism, Moscow (1987), and in 1989 became chairman of the main production and commercial administration for services, Moscow. In 1992 he was appointed ambassador extraordinary and plenipotentiary of the Russian Federation to the Republic of Croatia. He is married and speaks Serbian, Croatian and Bulgarian.

Address: Embassy of the Russian Federation, Zagreb.

Khaindrava, Ivlian Levanovich

Editor-in-chief of the newspaper *New Gazette*; Member of Parliament of the Republic of Georgia.

Born on April 8, 1951 in Tbilisi, Georgian SSR. A Georgian, whose father, Levan Ivlianovich, is a writer. His brother, Georgy (Goga), is a film operator and a winner of international film awards. He is well-known for his film on the events of April 9, 1989 in Tbilisi when demonstrators were killed by the military. He was arrested in October 1991 when Zviad Gamsakhurdia was President of Georgia and was released in December 1991. In September 1992 he was appointed State Minister for Abkhazian Affairs.

He is a graduate in chemistry and is also a qualified translator and besides Georgian is fluent in Russian and English. From 1974 to 1988 he worked in a scientific research institute as a laboratory assistant, scientific assistant, and senior scientific assistant. From 1988 to 1992 he was engaged in the Unifilm joint venture, then became head of department, and in 1992 editor-in-chief of the newspaper *New Gazette*. He has published many articles on public and political matters in the Georgian press. In 1992 he was also appointed a member of the State Council and in October 1992 a member of parliament of the Republic of Georgia. He represents the 11 October block in parliament.

Khaindrava is married and his wife, Elena Grigorevna, is a ballet dancer. They have two daughters, Shorena, 11 years old, and Nino, 10 years old who are both at school. He loves sport and sometimes watches it on television. He likes chess, especially high speed chess.

Home address: Tbilisi, ul. S. Chikovani, Dom 22, kv. 38; *telephone*: Tbilisi 30 41 34.

Khakamada, Irina

General Secretary of the Party of Economic Freedom of the Russian Federation.

Born in 1956 in Moscow; her father was a Japanese who had emigrated to the Soviet Union for political reasons as an orthodox communist; member of the CPSU (1984-89). She graduated from the faculty of foreign economics of Patrice Lumumba University, Moscow, and successfully presented her candidate dissertation in economics (PhD). She was on the staff of the scientific research institute of USSR Gosplan, then a lecturer in the technical college of the Likhachev car plant, and in 1986 she became an assistant professor. In 1988 she began working in the co-operative for the servicing of computer technology which was headed by K. N. Borovoi. She and he helped run the first auctions in the Russian raw materials commodity exchange in 1989. She then abandoned teaching and became head of the scientific information centre of the exchange and the leading specialist of the Russian commodity exchange.

She was a founding member of the PEF in May 1992. At its first congress in December 1992 she was elected general secretary of the party. She has been married three times. Her present husband, Dmitry, is a leading specialist in the Russian raw materials commodity exchange and the Rinako company. Her son, Daniil, is from her first marriage. She lives in Moscow.

Khasbulatov, Ruslan Imranovich

Speaker of the Russian Supreme Soviet.

Born on November 22, 1942 in Grozny, Chechen-Ingush ASSR; Chechen. He was a member of the CPSU from 1966 to August 1991. His early years were traumatic, as his family and his nation, the Chechens, and the Ingushi, were deported to the arid steppes of northern Kazakhstan on Red Army day, February 23, 1944. Stalin accused them of collaborating with the German *Wehrmacht*. Many other non-Russian nationalities suffered the same fate, but Khrushchev later conceded that the accusation was baseless and allowed them to begin returning to their homeland in the mid-1950s. Khasbulatov's father died almost immediately, never reaching the Kazakh steppes, and perhaps a third of the nation died en route and just after arrival, which made many Chechens very bitter and they sought revenge. However, Khasbulatov decided to make a career in the Soviet system and in his memoirs he recalls how he was encouraged at school and was not treated as an enemy of the people. He became acquainted from a young age with hard farm work, as his mother was a milkmaid on a collective farm. He decided not to accompany his mother and family back to the Chechen-Ingush ASSR.

He began working at the age of 14 years and by dint of effort managed to enter the faculty of law, Kazakh State University, Alma Ata, in 1960 and, even more remarkable, the faculty of law, Moscow State University, in 1962. He graduated in 1965 and immediately became a postgraduate student in the faculty of economics. This was something which Mikhail Gorbachev had failed to do when he graduated from the same faculty of law. Khasbulatov turned his attention to Canada, a capitalist, federal state, as the subject for his dissertation. He was more concerned with economic law than pure economics, and in 1970 he successfully presented his candidate dissertation in economics on "The management of the state sector in the Canadian economy" (PhD(Econ)). Such a brilliant career for an outsider, a deportee, a Chechen and a Muslim, was only possible with the help of and loyalty to the Communist Party. He was active in the *Komsomol* movement and was elected secretary of the *Komsomol* organization at Moscow State University (1965-67).

In 1970 he moved into the apparatus of the *Komsomol* Central Committee, and in 1972 he managed to obtain an appointment in the prestigious G. V. Plekhanov Institute of the National Economy, Moscow. He began work on his doctoral dissertation on "State monopoly capitalism in Canada" and successfully presented his dissertation in 1980 (DSc(Econ)). This research took him to

Canada where he did not display an aptitude for the English language and failed to acknowledge Western students who had known him in Moscow during his *Komsomol* days. He is a professor, and was academic secretary of the science council, USSR Academy of Sciences, on the economic problems of the scientific-technical revolution; head of the sector of the scientific research institute of public opinion; head of the sector of the scientific-research institute on the problems of high schools, USSR Ministry of Higher and Secondary Education; and head of department, G. V. Plekhanov Institute of the National Economy. He was elected a corresponding member of the Russian Academy of Sciences in 1991.

Given his *Komsomol* background he could have chosen a career in the Communist Party, like Gorbachev. However, he appears to have decided that, as an outsider and Muslim, Party advancement might be difficult, although his political gifts, especially his skill at intrigue and coalition building, might have carried him far. He was active politically from the inception of *perestroika*. In *Pravda* and *Komsomolskaya pravda* he published several articles strongly opposing increases in food prices, on leasing and regional cost accounting, and much greater authority for enterprises and work collectives, and his articles provoked a nationwide debate on prices. He played an active role in the drafting of the USSR law on leasing.

In 1990 he was nominated for election as an RSFSR people's deputy in Grozny and was elected. During the election campaign he advocated a united Russia with considerable autonomy; a union of equal sovereign states; the construction of democratic power in Russia; local soviets be able to legislate, own and manage their own municipal economy and receive considerable tax revenue to resolve social problems; not less than 50% of enterprise profits should pass to the soviet; leasing; and that work collectives should participate in the distribution of their products.

At the I Congress of Peoples Deputies Boris Yeltsin nominated him as deputy Speaker of the Supreme Soviet and on June 5, 1990 he received 604 votes (531 were necessary for election). On July 10, 1991 Yeltsin stepped down as Speaker of the Supreme Soviet after being elected RSFSR President and Khasbulatov was put forward, with President Yeltsin's support, for the post of Speaker, but he could not obtain the required number of votes, despite several rounds of voting, as many delegates were not confident that he would act democratically. He remained acting Speaker until October 29, 1991, at the V Congress of People's Deputies, when he eventually obtained enough votes (559) to secure election. Sergei Filatov was elected first deputy Speaker and it was this combination which finally secured a majority of votes.

The break with Yeltsin came early. By December 1991 Khasbulatov was criticizing the shock therapy of Egor Gaidar and the gulf widened until it became a rift at the VI Congress of People's Deputies, in April 1992. The communists by then had rallied and their self-confidence had begun to return and to the dismay of Yeltsin Khasbulatov became the organizer of opposition to the President in parliament. Khasbulatov took as his military adviser General Achalov who had sided with the Extraordinary Committee in August 1991. Gradually the legislation necessary for the implementation of a market economy dried up. Under Khasbulatov's direction parliament would not pass it and began amending the constitution (the parliamentary opposition could normally muster the two thirds majority necessary) to restrict the President's room for manoeuvre.

Many observers were astonished by the verbal dexterity, tactical skill and ruthlessness which Khasbulatov displayed. By the VII Congress of People's Deputies, in December 1992, Khasbulatov and the conservatives were ready to fight Yeltsin. The President threatened congress with dissolution but his confrontational tactics misfired, the tactical initiative passed to parliament and Egor Gaidar had to go in favour of parliament's choice as Prime Minister, Viktor Chernomyrdin. Between December 1992 and March 1993 the President was on the ropes and visibly losing self-confidence. Khasbulatov scored time and again and the decision was taken to force the President to resign or have him impeached. The Constitutional Court, under Valery Zorkin, began finding in favour of the parliament in constitutional disputes.

Khasbulatov reached the zenith of his influence at the VIII and IX Congresses of People's Deputies in March 1993. The IX congress had been called after President Yeltsin's television address to the Russian people on March 20, 1993 and his declared intention of introducing a "special regime". However, the wily President dropped his idea of a special regime and the Constitutional Court ruled that his actions were not grave enough to constitute grounds for impeachment. This was a defeat for Khasbulatov and he even tried to broker a deal with the President envisaging parliamentary and presidential elections in late 1993, but congress savaged Khasbulatov for having the temerity to negotiate over its head. Yeltsin's supporters were appalled that the President would seriously consider cutting a deal with a man such as Ruslan Imranovich.

Khasbulatov's behaviour as Speaker outraged many and it lowered the standing of the Russian parliament. He was openly contemptuous of the President, using the most sarcastic and abusive language. He was more than a Speaker, he was the ringmaster and even instructed deputies how to vote. His marvellous fluency in Russian wore down many but it eventually took its toll on his health. A highly emotional man, he had to draw on immense reserves to keep going, and some saw him as unbalanced, others as neurotic, others as a power hungry politician who would eventually devour himself.

Yeltsin's unexpectedly good showing in the April 25, 1993 referendum was a body blow to Khasbulatov. The Chechen had no popular following in the country and could never contemplate running for President, but some thought his goal was to become the *éminence grise*, the kingmaker, but never to become king. His passionate dislike of the President and his associates, almost exclusively Russian, rubs salt in the wounds of his being an outsider. Khasbulatov was left with little else than to dismiss the referendum result as an irrelevance and to declare parliament as sovereign. The President went on the offensive after the referendum and put forward a draft constitution, envisaging a presidential republic. Khasbulatov and parliament offered their own, sketching out a parliamentary republic, and various attempts were made to reach a compromise at a constitutional assembly. The key question was over how much authority the republics, *oblasts* and *krais* would be accorded.

Khasbulatov's attempt to allow parliament to decide was being forced to face the reality of the weakness of the centre and the gathering strength of the regions.

Khasbulatov is married with a son and a daughter. His mother still lives in Grozny but he has been declared *persona non grata* by his homeland. He speaks English, and has been awarded USSR medals. He has published widely and his biography, *The Struggle for Power*, appeared in May 1993.

Address: 103274 Moscow, K 274, Krasnopresnenskaya nab., d. 2, Dom Sovetov; *telephone*: Moscow 205 48 39

Khetagurov, Sergei Valentinovich

Chairman of the Council of Ministers of the North Ossetian Soviet Socialist Republic, Russian Federation.

Born on January 19, 1942; Ossetian; member of the CPSU until August 1991. He began his career as a worker in a machine building-enterprise in Ordzhonikidze (Vladikavkaz), and graduated from the N. E. Bauman Higher Technical College, Moscow. Afterwards he was a chief engineer, then director of the Ordzhonikidze enterprise of automobile transport equipment, first secretary of the Leninsky *raion* Party committee, Ordzhonikidze, and instructor of the department for organizational Party work of the Party Central Committee until 1988.

On October 9, 1988 he was elected a member of the Supreme Soviet: 99.5% of the registered votes participated and he received 99.9% of their votes. On October 22, 1988 he was elected a member of the North Ossetian Party *obkom* and recommended by the *obkom* plenum as Chairman of the Council of Ministers of the North Ossetian ASSR. He was confirmed unanimously as Chairman the same day at a session of the Supreme Soviet, and was a delegate to the XXVIII Party congress. In January 1990 he was nominated as first secretary of the North Ossetian Party *obkom* but withdrew. He is the recipient of state awards.

In early 1990 he was nominated as a candidate for election as an RSFSR people's deputy in the No. 123 Sovetsky territorial district. There were two candidates, and Khetagurov won with 56% of the votes in the first round. His opponent was G. M. Alborov, an engineer, who received 32.5% of the votes. Khetagurov is a member of the Supreme Soviet Council of Nationalities commission on social and economic development of the republics with the Russian Federation, the autonomous *oblasts*, autonomous *okrugs* and small nations. He was a member of the communists of Russia group of deputies.

In 1990 he was elected a deputy of the Supreme Soviet of the North Ossetian ASSR. On March 21, 1990, on the recommendation of the plenum of the Party *obkom*, the session of the Supreme Soviet confirmed him unopposed as Chairman of the Council of Ministers of the republic. On assuming office he stated that he supported the transfer of leading functions from the Party to the soviets, economic reform based on economic cost accounting and leasing, contracts, and various forms of ownership. The goal of economic reform should be the creation of a market economy but the transition to the market should be gradual with central planning retained for a specific period. He advocated land reform based on leasing, contracts and private farming in agriculture. He proposed to transform the republic into a major tourist and medical spa centre. He lives in Vladikavkaz.

Khizha, Georgy Stepanovich

Deputy Prime Minister of Russia.

Born on May 2, 1938 in Ashkhabad, Turkmenistan. Russian. He was a member of CPSU until August 1991. He graduated from the Leningrad Polytechnical Institute as an engineer and began work as a senior engineer in 1961 in the F. Engels Leningrad engineering works, subsequently the leading enterprise in the Svetlana experimental production association of the electronics industry. He was a leading engineer, head of the security section, deputy chief engineer and head of the special security department.

In 1986 he graduated from the Academy of the National Economy of the USSR Council of Ministers. He successfully presented his candidate dissertation (PhD (Eng)) and his doctoral dissertation (DSc (Eng)) on engineering subjects which are still on the secret list. He is a professor, and is the author of 20 inventions and 66 scientific works, including co-authoring two monographs. From February 1988 to 1991 he was general director of the Svetlana scientific research association. He was president of the Leningrad association of state enterprises, and participated in economics conferences, convened by President Mikhail Gorbachev, where he advocated stringent financial policies to combat inflation in the country. In 1991 he was appointed deputy mayor of St Petersburg under Anatoly Sobchak, the mayor. He was the chairman of the collegium of the mayoral administration of St Petersburg and was chairman of the commission for the economic development of the city.

He and Anatoly Chubais attempted to organize the Lengosfund (the Leningrad state fund) to carry out privatization in the city. In July 1991 he signed a declaration supporting the "movement of democratic reforms". In November 1991 he was invited by Egor Gaidar to transfer to governmental work, probably under Anatoly Chubais, but declined, stating he wished to complete his work in St Petersburg. In May 1992 he was appointed deputy Prime Minister in the Russian government and became responsible for the military-industrial complex and problems associated with its conversion to civil use.

In July 1992 he became head of the commission on export control in the government, taking over from Egor Gaidar. After the beginning of the Ossetian-Ingush conflict he was appointed head of the provisional administration responsible for the North Ossetian Soviet socialist republic and the Ingush republic, but was replaced by Sergei Shakhrai after stating that the Russian army had to overcome its "Tbilisi syndrome". (This referred to the massacre of civilians by the military in Tbilisi in April 1989.) In December 1992 he was appointed deputy chairman of the Council of Ministers-government of the Russian Federation responsible for military conversion and the organization of the work of the branches of industry, transport and communications.

He oversees the Ministry of Industry, Railways, Transport, Communications, the state committee on standardization, metrology and certification, the Russian space agency and the state commission on the use of space and administration of air traffic. He was a firm supporter of the policies of Egor Gaidar, especially his stringent financial and credit policies, but as a practical politician is ready to revise some of the abstract models advanced by theoreticians. He likes to play tennis. He is married with two daughters, one of whom is a sports enthusiast and Leningrad ladies' tennis champion. She is trained by her father and is at present playing in the US. Khizha lives in Moscow.

Khlystun, Viktor Nikolaevich

Russian Minister of Agriculture and Food.

Born on March 19, 1946 in the village of Dmitrievka, Shchuchinsky *raion*, Kokchetav *oblast*, Kazakhstan into a Russian peasant family. He was a member of the CPSU until August 1991. From 1963 to 1965 he worked as an assistant to an excavator driver and electrical welder in the Sokolovsko-Sarbaisky ore enriching combine, Kazakhstan. Then he worked in agriculture and graduated from the Moscow Institute of Agricultural Engineers in 1970. After graduating he became an assistant in the faculty of land use in the institute and began postgraduate research in 1971. In 1974 he was an assistant, senior lecturer, assistant professor, deputy dean and dean of the faculty of land use in the institute. He successfully presented his candidate dissertation (PhD (Econ)) and doctoral dissertation (DSc (Econ)), and is a professor. He is a corresponding member of the Russian Academy of Agricultural Sciences, specializing in agrarian relations and land use.

From 1977 to 1980 he was secretary of the Party bureau of the institute. From 1980 to 1990 he was pro-rector for scientific research in the institute and in 1990 was appointed chairman of the RSFSR state committee on agrarian reform, then of the RSFSR state committee on agrarian reform and support of the peasant economy (family farming). In November 1991 he was appointed RSFSR Minister of Agriculture. He is also chairman of the Russian government commission on the social development of villages.

Khlystun is in favour of promoting commercial agriculture as rapidly as possible. The government should not run agriculture but create the conditions for farmers to use their own initiative. To this end he supports the coming into being of a wide network of family farms, believing that collective farms are not efficient. It is necessary to work out a system of insurance, the provision of credit and services for agriculture and to expand its social infrastructure. "When I see long queues for food I want to close my car window. It is very embarrassing for me and my industry. Our predecessors have left us a difficult legacy, but nevertheless their debts are my debts", the minister once stated.

He is a member of groups drafting legislation on tax law, the establishment of agricultural banks and the elaboration of republican programmes (for example, the potato programme), providing benefits to those involved. He is in favour of the state agreeing contracts for deliveries of agricultural produce and is against *goszakazy* (compulsory state orders). Some adjustments should be made to agrarian reform but not in favour of returning to the state dominated system.

He believes that all peasants should have an equal chance to acquire the basic means of production, being permitted to choose which form of property relations they wish (co-operative, family, etc.). The main emphasis of land reform should be transferred to the local level with the state favouring the most productive form of economy. Town-dwellers should be given land as quickly as possible to pursue market gardening as this would rapidly ease the tight food situation and reduce prices in agricultural markets. The minister himself is a keen market gardener on his private plot in Shchelkovsky *raion*, Moscow *oblast*. He is married with two daughters who at present are both students. He is keen on volleyball, and is improving his knowledge of English all the time. He lives in Moscow.

Khmara, Stepan Ilkovych

Leader of the Conservative Republican Party of Ukraine.

Born into a Ukrainian family in 1937 in what is now Lviv *oblast* in western Ukraine. His parents were collective farm workers, and he was educated at Lviv Medical Institute and then worked as a doctor. He was soon involved in underground dissident politics, in particular the journal *Ukrainian Herald*, founded by Viacheslav Chornovil in 1970. After Chornovil's arrest in 1972 Khmara edited the next two issues (Nos. 7-9). They were considerably more radical in tone than any of Chornovil's issues (when Chornovil refounded the *Herald* in 1987 he started at No. 7, explicitly repudiating Khmara's issues).

In 1980 Khmara was arrested for his activity and sentenced to seven years under a severe labour regime, and five years' exile. He was only released after President Mikhail Gorbachev announced a general amnesty for political prisoners in 1987. Khmara immediately recommenced his opposition activity, joining the reformed Ukrainian Helsinki Union (UHU) in 1988. He consistently promoted a radical course, overseeing the formation of strike committees in Lviv during the winter of 1988-89, and organizing hunger strikes by Ukrainian Catholic militants in the centre of Moscow in May 1989.

Khmara's high public profile earned him election to the Supreme Soviet on the first round (with 64% of the vote) in Industrialnyi *raion*, Lviv *oblast*, in March 1990. At the UHU's founding congress in April 1990, when it became the Ukrainian Republican Party (URP), Khmara was elected Deputy Leader. In the Supreme Soviet he served on the committee for state sovereignty, inter-republican and international relations, whilst in the chamber he quickly earned a reputation as one of the most uncompromisingly radical deputies. In October 1990 he proposed a provocative bill to ban the Communist Party of Ukraine, and nationalize its property.

He also began to argue that all opposition groups should withdraw from the Supreme Soviet. It was therefore perhaps no surprise when he was singled out for provocation by the KGB in November 1990 on trumped-up charges of assault, stripped of his parliamentary immunity and arrested. The campaign to free him became something of a *cause célèbre*, although his release was only finally secured after the failed August 1991 coup in Moscow.

He was, however, temporarily released in order to disrupt the second URP congress in June 1991. Although his radical supporters were in a minority, the URP leadership felt compelled by his notoriety to allow his reelection as Deputy Leader. They came to regret the decision deeply, however, as Khmara thereafter ignored all notions of collective responsibility, and pursued a course far to the URP's right, continuing to attack President Kravchuk when the rest of the URP wished to support his state-building efforts. He was therefore forced out of the URP at its third congress in May 1992.

His dissident faction then formed the Conservative Republican Party of Ukraine, a populist, anti-communist and extreme nationalist party, in June 1992, and Khmara was elected leader. In the Supreme Soviet Khmara's ultra-radical motions can still command the support of 20-30 deputies, and Khmara maintains his high profile as the parliamentary spokesman for both the radical independent trade union movement *VOST*, and the Union of Officers of Ukraine. Khmara is a fervent supporter of the idea of Ukrainian nuclear defence, and has called on the Ukrainian government to work for the dissolution of the Russian Federation.

Official address: Kiev, Vul. M. Hrushevskoho 5; *telephone*: Kiev 252 019 or Kiev 229 3056 (hotel).

Khmelko, Valentyn

Co-Leader of the Party of Democratic Revival of Ukraine.

Born into a Ukrainian family in 1939. He was a student in the faculty of physics, Kiev State University, until 1962, followed by study in the faculty of philosophy until 1971. From 1975 to 1990 he worked in the faculty of scientific communism in the institute of history of the Central Committee of the Communist Party of Ukraine (CPU). He joined the CPU in 1971, and remained a member until July 1990. He successfully presented his candidate dissertation (PhD) and in 1988 his doctoral dissertation on "Methodological and other problems in sociological research on the influence of scientific-technical work on the management of the individual worker in industry" (DSc).

In 1990 he transferred to the Sociological Association of Ukraine becoming in turn its first vice-president, director and then head of research department. He has pioneered the application of western sociological methods in Ukraine since 1990, in particular in public opinion polling, for both the Academy of Sciences and foreign organizations. From 1989 to 1990 he was a supporter of the Democratic Platform of the CPU, along with many other members of the Kiev academic establishment.

At the first congress of the PDRU in December 1990 he was elected one of seven co-heads, becoming one of three co-heads at the PDRU's second congress in June 1991. Khmelko was one of the key figures in organizing the Democratic Congress of opposition parties from all over the Soviet Union in Kiev in January 1991, and he drew up the PDRU's draft programme for a Commonwealth of Sovereign States that the PDRU like to claim was adopted as the basis of the Commonwealth of Independent States (CIS) in December 1991. Khmelko represents the more liberal wing of the PDRU. An active member of *New Ukraine*, he was elected to the movement's secretariat (in 19th place) in June 1992.

Home telephone: Kiev 263 3568.

Khomenko, Mykola Grygoryovych

Head of the Ukrainian Presidential *Apparat*.

Born into a Ukrainian family in 1934. He was educated as an electrical engineer at Zaochnyi polytechnic institute and at the Academy of Social Sciences of the CPSU Central Committee. He was elected a people's deputy for Konotopskyi *raion*, Sumy *oblast*, in March 1990 (on the second round), and is a member of the Supreme Soviet's committee on mandates and deputies' ethics. As a long-standing colleague of Kravchuk's from the *apparat*, he has been secretary of the presidential staff since Kravchuk became the first holder of the new office of executive President in December 1991.

He functions as the nearest equivalent to a White House Chief of Staff, organizing the President's diary and overseeing the presidential *apparat*. (His equivalent in Russia is Sergei Filatov.) He also acts as *de facto* spokesman for Kravchuk, particularly on foreign trips, and has the power to sign *ukaz* (decrees) on the President's behalf. Hence he has often been accused of exercising power without responsibility, and of screening access to the President.

Official address: 252005 Kiev, Bankivska Boulevard 7; *telephone*: Kiev 226 2442.

Khorolets, Larysa Ivanivna

Former Minister of Culture, Ukraine.

Born into a Ukrainian family in 1948. She graduated from Kiev Institute of Theatrical Arts in 1970, and then worked both as an artist and a dramatist and as one of Ukraine's most famous actresses. From 1970 to 1973 she worked in the Writers' Union theatre in Kiev, and then in the Ivan Franko theatre. She is both a people's artist of Ukraine, and, since 1977, a member of the USSR Writers' Union.

She has had many of her works on Ukrainian TV, radio and film, and in her last film in spring 1991 she appeared with her then eight-year-old son, Olesyk. In June 1991 she was appointed Minister of Culture, where she defined her priorities as raising the profile of Ukrainian culture abroad and promoting a cultural revival at home. She also campaigned for the return of Ukrainian cultural artefacts from abroad. She was, however, much criticized for lacking the administrative drive to overcome the conservatism of the old guard *apparat* who continued to dominate the department, and in November 1992 she was replaced by the famous 1960s dissident Ivan Dziuba.

Official(Ministry) address: 252030 Kiev, Vul. Ivana Franka 19; *telephone*: Kiev 224 4911.

Khubiev, Vladimir Islamovich

Chairman of the Council of Ministers of the Karachaevo-Cherkess Republic, Russian Federation.

Born on March 26, 1932 in the village of Arkhyz, Zelenchuksky *raion*, Karachaevo-Cherkess autonomous *oblast*; a Karachai; member of the CPSU from 1959 to August 1991. He began his career in 1954 as a land technician in Kirgizia (Kyrgyzstan) after graduating from the hydro-amelioration Technical College, Frunze (Bishkek), Kirgizia. From 1956 to 1962 he was an agricultural engineer, and manager of a section of the Storozhevsky state farm, and from 1962 to 1967 he was an instructor, deputy head of the department of agriculture of the Karachaevo-Cherkess Party *obkom*, and deputy chairman of the *oblast* committee of state control. In 1967 he was elected chairman of the Prikubansky *raion* soviet executive committee and in 1971 first secretary of the Karachaevsky *raion* Party committee committee. In 1969 he graduated from the Stavropol Institute of Agriculture as an external student.

In March 1979 he was elected chairman of the executive committee of the soviet of people's deputies of the Karachaevo-Cherkess autonomous *oblast*. He was a deputy of the Supreme Soviet of the RSFSR, deputy chairman of the commission on legal proposals, member of the *krai* Party committee, bureau of the Party *obkom*, a delegate to the XXVI, XXVII Party congresses and XIX Party conference. He is the recipient of the orders of the Red Banner of Labour, the Friendship of Peoples, medals and diploma of the Presidium of the USSR Supreme Soviet.

In early 1990 he was nominated by the work collectives of the Eltarkach and Pregradnensky state farms, the Zelenchukskoe and Karachaevskoe repair technical enterprises, the Malokarachaevsky *raion* industrial combine and the Karachaevo-Cherkess hydro-amelioration association for election as an RSFSR people's deputy in the No. 156 Ust Dzhegutinsky national territorial district. During the election campaign he promised to play an active part in the legislative process. His solution to the food problem concentrated on developing the processing industry, the removal of the disproportionate prices paid for agricultural produce and technical equipment and the full-scale introduction of new economic relations in the countryside.

He advocated the rapid expansion of state, co-operative and individual construction and the development of the building materials industry as ways of solving the housing shortage. He also proposed raising the status of the autonomous *oblasts*, an increase in their economic, political and cultural prerogatives and the accelerated adoption of laws on the rehabilitation of nationalities which had been oppressed under Stalin.

There were three candidates. Khubiev polled 35.5% of the votes in the first round and won in the second round, polling 49.2% of the votes. His main opponent was A. A. Katchiev, head of the Karachaevo-Cherkesskstroi trust, who received 29.6% of the votes in the first round and 40.9% in the second round. He was elected to the RSFSR Supreme Soviet at the I congress of people's deputies. He is a member of the constitutional commission, the legislation committee of the Supreme Soviet, and the sovereignty and equality parliamentary faction, and he has been a member of the Communists of Russia group of deputies. In 1990 he was elected a deputy of the *oblast* soviet and at its first session, on March 22, 1990, he was elected its chairman. In August 1991, when he was in Moscow, he supported the President and the Supreme Soviet of the RSFSR and played an active role in eliminating the remnants of the attempted state coup.

He was appointed acting head of the administration of Karachaevo-Cherkess Soviet Socialist Republic on January 13, 1992 by presidential decree. The most important aspects of policy for him were economic reform, the liberalization of prices, the privatization of state and municipal property and the drafting of new tax legislation. He regarded his main tasks as halting the fall in output, the introduction of tax breaks and to attract those who were capable to become producers of goods. In the social sphere he set up a republican fund for the social security of the population and the provision of rapid social aid. He issued a statement on how to prevent the collapse of Karachaevo-Cherkessia.

In December 1992, at the VII Congress of People's Deputies, he supported the views of the Supreme Soviet, its Speaker and the Vice-President and viewed the policy of the government negatively. In January 1993 he was elected Chairman of the Council of Ministers of the Karachaevo-Cherkess Republic. He lives in Cherkessk.

Khudyaev, Vyacheslav Ivanovich

Chairman of the Council of Ministers of the Komi Republic, Russian Federation.

Born in 1946 in Syktyvkar, where his father was a fireman and his mother was an office cleaner; a Komi; member of the CPSU from 1972 to August 1991. He graduated from the Leningrad Construction Engineering Institute and the Academy of Social Sciences of the Party Central Committee. He began his career in 1969 as a senior engineer technologist of the No. 1 shop, Ukhtin enterprise of reinforced concrete units of the main Komi oil and gas construction trust, and in 1971 he became head of a shop in the enterprise. From 1973 to 1976 he was chief engineer, director of the concrete units and ceramics section of the Ukhtin housing trust combine, head of the construction department of the construction industry, and director of the combine of production enterprises of the main Komi oil and gas construction trust.

In 1976 he was deputy head of the construction section of the Komi Party *obkom*, and in 1980 he was elected second secretary of the Syktyvkar city Party committee. From 1982 to 1983 he was a student at the Academy of Social Sciences of the Party Central Committee. From 1983 to 1987 he was second, then first secretary of the Syktyvkar city Party committee, and was a member of the bureau of the Komi Party *obkom* and a deputy of the Supreme Soviet of the Komi ASSR. In 1987 he was elected Chairman of the Council of Ministers of the Komi ASSR. He is the recipient of the order of the badge of honour.

In March 1990 he was a candidate in the No. 843 Syktyvkar territorial district for election as an RSFSR people's deputy. There were three candidates, and he polled 36.9% of the votes in the first round but lost in the second round, polling 38.75% of the votes. The winner was A. V. Misharin, director of the 50th anniversary of the USSR state farm who won in the second round, obtaining 51.96% of the votes.

Khudyaev was elected a deputy of the Supreme Soviet of the Komi ASSR and at the first session, in April 1990, he became Chairman of the Council of Ministers of the Komi ASSR. On assuming office he advocated freedom, economic and political autonomy of the autonomous republics, transition to economic cost accounting and self-financing. The republics, in his view, should themselves decide all questions concerning the administration of the territory and the state development of language and culture. He criticized the command administrative style of the leadership, and favoured the working out of a new mechanism of mutual relations between representative and executive power. He advocated the establishment of a new model of administration and the employment of highly skilled specialists.

On August 20, 1991 the Council of Ministers and Presidium of the Supreme Soviet of the Komi ASSR addressed the population of the republic stating that the future of the country was in danger since the state had become ungovernable. The question of state power should only be resolved on the basis of the USSR constitution. The Council of Ministers and the Supreme Soviet stated that they would strictly adhere to the constitutional laws and decrees of the USSR and RSFSR.

In November 1992 Khudyaev stated that under market conditions it was necessary to keep a close watch on the economic situation and not allow spontaneity to take over. In agrarian affairs equal opportunities should be afforded collective and state farms and also individual concerns. It was not possible to proceed without regulation and support of agriculture by the state. Collective farms should be transformed into sub-units, driven by the market, and privatization should first of all affect the processing and service enterprises.

Khudyaev is married and his wife is the director of a choral school. They have two sons and live in Syktyvkar.

Khvatov, Gennady Aleksandrovich

Commander-in-Chief of the Red Banner Pacific Fleet. Admiral since 1987.

Born on May 3, 1934 in Myshkono, Yaroslavl *oblast*. Russian. His navy career began in 1952. He graduated from the higher naval technical school in 1956; the Naval Academy in 1973; the Naval Academy of the General Staff in 1976. He received a higher military education, and was a member of the CPSU from 1958 to August 1991.

He began his service career in the submarine forces of the Pacific Fleet. From 1957 to 1961 he was commander of a section and an assistant commander of a submarine. Then from 1962 he was senior assistant of a submarine commander and from 1969 commander of a submarine. He took part in long voyages in the Pacific Ocean, including the region near the coasts of the USA and its allies. He was regarded as a highly qualified specialist and an experienced sailor with a talent for organization. He was quite active in his Party organizations, which is seen as essential for a successful career in the armed forces. After graduating from the Naval Academy in 1973, he was appointed Chief of Staff of a submarine division, and then a submarine divisional commander. He proved to be good at organizing combat control and the training of troops and mastered the essence of contemporary operations in sea and ocean theatres. He was regarded as an officer with sound operational tactical and military technical training, able to carry out any order from the communist leaders of the USSR, and an active supporter of the domestic and foreign policy of the CPSU. He proved himself a convinced communist.

From 1978 to 1983 Adml Khvatov was Chief of Staff and later commander of a submarine flotilla. In 1983 he was appointed Chief of Staff and first deputy Commander-in-Chief of the Pacific Fleet. In 1986 he was promoted to Commander-in-Chief of the fleet.

He heads a large Russian naval force in the Pacific theatre of operations. He has under his command considerable surface, submarine and aviation troops of the fleet, mobile formations and coastal troops. Before the collapse of the communist regime, he co-operated actively with the local Party and soviet authorities and was elected a member of the bureau of the Maritime *krai* Party committee. He was elected a member of the Party Central Committee in

July 1990. His attitude towards democratic organizations was extremely negative and he was also in conflict with those who advocated the ecological purity of the Maritime *krai* and the withdrawal of nuclear submarines from the territory. He encouraged the persecution of progressive naval officers, including those who had participated in Boris Yeltsin's election campaign.

During the anti-constitutional putsch in August 1991 Adml Khvatov obeyed all orders and instructions of the General Staff of the Navy and the General Staff without demur, ordered the troops under his command on to a state of high combat readiness and, in his inner circle, approved of the actions of the Emergency Committee. It was he who ordered that measures be taken to force the crew of the *Tallinn*, a large anti-submarine vessel, and that of a submarine to obey the communist authorities when the former supported the elected Presidents of the USSR and the RSFSR.

After the collapse of communist power and the disintegration of the USSR, Adml Khvatov proved himself a skilled conformist and adjusted quickly, changing his political complexion and expressing support for President Boris Yeltsin. He does not express his political views in the mass media and prefers the role of a non-party military professional. He supports the concept of a strong state domestically and of a Great Russia, and vehemently opposes any territorial concessions. In early 1989 Khvatov, on the recommendation of the higher military political agencies, was nominated as a candidate for election as a USSR people's deputy but was defeated by a civilian, a representative of the democratic forces. There is no information available on his hobbies. He has been awarded several orders and medals. He is married.

Adml Khvatov's headquarters are in Vladivostok.

Kiebic, Viaceslau Francjevic

Prime Minister of the Republic of Belarus.

Born on June 10, 1936 in the village of Konyushevshchina, Volozhinsky *raion*, Minsk *oblast*. His father worked on a collective farm, and the family is Belarusian. He was a member of the CPSU from 1962 to August 1991, and a member of the Party Central Committee (1990-91). He graduated from the Belarusian Polytechnical Institute and the Minsk Higher Party school. After graduating from the institute he worked as an engineer, senior engineer, head of a section, head of a shop, deputy head engineer, Minsk enterprise of automated processes; then chief engineer, and director of the S. M. Kirov machine tool enterprise, Minsk (1973-78); and general director of the S. M. Kirov production association for the manufacture of machine tools, Minsk (1978-80).

He then moved into the party apparatus. He was elected second secretary of the Minsk city Party committee and was head of department, Central Committee, Communist Party of Belorussia, and second secretary of the Minsk Party *obkom* (1980-85); deputy Chairman of the Council of Ministers, Belorussian SSR, and chairman of the republican Gosplan (1985-90). In 1990 he was appointed of the Council of Ministers, Belorussian SSR, and in 1992 became chairman of the anti-crisis committee of the Republic of Belarus (Prime Minister). He is faced with formidable economic problems as Belarus attempts to conduct an autonomous economic policy. The state is heavily dependent on Russia for energy and industrial inputs, and the electronics industry is finding it difficult to compete on the international market. Kiebic is more conservative than Stanislau Suskevic, the acting head of state, and there have been many conflicts between them with Kiebic favouring a conservative approach to the market, slow privatization and caution about foreign investment. He favours closer association with Russia and in July 1993 Russia, Ukraine and Belarus agreed to form a common economic area. Inevitably this will mean that Belarus's room for manoeuvre will be restricted by Moscow's policies. Suskevic is more amenable to closer links with central and western Europe than Kiebic.

Kiebic is a corresponding member of the International Academy of Engineering (economics section). He was awarded the state prize of the Belorussian SSR, the honorary title of merited mechanical engineer of the Belorussian SSR, two orders of the Red Banner of Labour and the order of the badge of honour. He is married with a son and a daughter.

Kirpichnikov, Yury Aleksandrovich

Editor-in-chief of the newspaper *Delovoi Mir*.

Born in 1939 in Barnaul, Siberia; Russian. He was a member of the CPSU until August 1991. He grew up in an orphanage and began his working career there in 1956. Later in 1956 he became a miner in the Aktashsky ore dressing combine and remained there until 1963. In 1968 he was assigned to Guinea and Congo, Africa, as a Russian-French interpreter and remained until 1971. After he graduated from the faculty of journalism, Moscow State University in 1973, he was appointed editor of the weekly magazine *Za Rubezhom* (abroad). In 1980 he became head of the international department of the Gudok *Siren* newspaper, and in 1982 was an editor and consultant of the *World Marxist Review* magazine in Prague. In 1986 he became editor and consultant of the CPSU theoretical journal *Kommunist*.

In 1987 he was appointed a member of the collegium and editor of the international department of the newspaper *Sotsialisticheskaya industriya*. In 1990 he became editor-in-chief of the newspaper *Delovoi mir* (business world). He is a member of the international congress of industrialists and entrepreneurs; a member of the foundation for economic and social reform; and a member of the foundation for guaranteeing foreign investment in the Russian economy.

His hobbies are work and literature; his favourite authors being Pasternak, Mandelstam and Brodsky; and he is fond of cats and dogs. He is married with two children and speaks French.

Address: 121170 Moscow, Prospekt Kutuzovsky 39; *telephone*: Moscow 249 9864.

Kiselev, Evgeny

Author and presenter of the weekly analytical television programme, *Itogi*.

Born in June 1956; Russian. His parents were ordinary workers in public metallurgy and expected their son to follow in their footsteps. However, as a boy Kiselev dreamed of working abroad and therefore entered the institute for the study of the countries of Asia and Africa, Moscow State University, where he was an excellent student and specialized in Persian affairs. After graduation he was sent to Tass and then assigned to Afghanistan as an interpreter of military advisers. He spent two years in Afghanistan and, after returning he found it difficult to readjust to work, but then taught Persian in the higher KGB school to future military advisers. Then he worked in foreign language broadcasting and eventually joined television in 1987 and worked in the international department of the news programme, *Vremya*. In 1990 he attempted to be nominated for election as a people's deputy to Moscow city council (Mossovet) but failed.

In 1990 he was working on *Vremya* but after disagreements with the leadership he moved to the programme *Utro*, and then to Russian television, together with his friend, Oleg Dobrodeev. He was one of the originators of the news programme, *Vesti*. In 1992 he returned to Ostankino to Egor Yakovlev. Kiselev believes that political journalism influences public opinion. He respects Mikhail Gorbachev but regards him as out of date and unlikely to raise his political standing. He is keen to invite on to his programme former politicians who held high office since this increases his programmes popularity.

He writes the material for each programme himself and loves working on live television. His main criteria in selecting interviewees are their professionalism, the ability to cope with TV cameras and express themselves concisely. He is his own editor, decides the themes to be discussed, instructs journalists and agrees their material. He regards himself as reserved and serious and does not like familiarity. He lives for television; it is his passion and he does not leave his room for two or three days when he is preparing a programme. There is no conflict with the management. The *Itogi* programme has 22 staff and this includes journalists from the information TV agency.

He advocates an objective style in presenting news. He is a quiet conservative but on June 21, 1992 became angry and reacted negatively to the picketing of Ostankino by patriotic circles. He is opposed to renting a crowd from a liberal centrist point of view, and is afraid that television and the first channel may be transformed into an arena of competing political forces. He believes that television channels should reflect varying points of view: the first is the President's, the second could belong to parliament which could appoint its own staff. Kiselev does not favour dividing news into contentious and non-contentious categories; he advocates that all types of news should be presented together and believes censorship to be impermissible.

He regards the popular, oppositional programme, "600 seconds", presented by A. G. V. Nevzorov on St Petersburg TV, as propaganda, not news. He is married and his son was born in 1981. He lives in Moscow.

Kislyuk, Mikhail Borisovich

Head of the Administration of Kemerovo *oblast*, Russian Federation.

Born in 1951; Jewish; member of the CPSU until August 1991. His father was a mining foreman, and he spent his childhood in the villages of Bachaty and Kedrovka, Kemerovo *oblast*. He graduated from the Kuzbass Polytechnical Institute. He was a mining foreman, deputy head and head of a section, chief technologist and chief economist at various open cast coal mines in the Kuzbass, and deputy head of the economic planning department of the Kemerovo coal association. He lectured on economics in the Kuzbass Polytechnical Institute. In 1986 he was appointed as chief economist of the Chernigorsky open cast mine, took part in turning it into a leased enterprise and in drafting the minutes of the meetings between the regional strike committees of the Kuzbass and the government commission. He is a member of the council of workers' committees of the Kuzbass and one of the authors of the statutes and programme of the workers of the Kuzbass. He has a permanent commission to draft and implement economic reforms in the *oblast*.

In early 1990 he was nominated by the workers' committees of the Kuzbass for election as an RSFSR people's deputy in the No. 45 Kemerovo national territorial district. His election campaign was entitled: "The well-being of the people is the highest law!" He advocated social justice, the establishment of a *Rechtsstaat* (law-governed state), the transfer of power to the soviets, the renaissance of Russia, the adoption of a new Union treaty and the right of each republic to establish its statehood. He stated that he supported the views of Academician Andrei Sakharov and the platform of the interregional group of deputies. He was in favour of the most rapid reform of prices, defence of the interests of citizens as consumers, the gradual introduction of a market economy and complete economic autonomy for enterprises and regions. He believed it was necessary to limit the authority of ministries and authorities.

There were nine candidates and Kislyuk won in the second round, polling 45.1% of the votes. His main opponent was V. V. Shlykov, senior lecturer at the Kemerovo *oblast Komsomol* school, who received 38.1% of the votes in the second round. Kislyuk is a member of the workers' union of Russia parliamentary faction and the group of deputies "coalition for reforms".

On August 27, 1991 Kislyuk was appointed head of the administration of Kemerovo *oblast* by presidential decree. On assuming office he appealed for a struggle with the administrative command system and he advocated decisive support for market reform, free competition, private property, the concept of a social market economy and the creation of democratic structures in the administration. The solution to economic problems lay in raising labour productivity. He opposed localism and was in favour of attracting foreign capital and new technology and the setting up of new commercial banks. A free economic zone for the Kuzbass, on whose drafting he had participated, was accepted.

In December 1992 he stated that in the highly politicized and personalized situation in Russia it was not important who was Prime Minister. He underlined that as a result of the compromises reached after the VII Congress of People's

Deputies the President was again in charge and did not need his supporters. He is married with two daughters and lives in Kemerovo.

Kivelidi, Ivan Kharlampievich

Director-general of the *Vneshekonomkooperatsiya* Association; Vice-President of the Union of Co-operatives and Entrepreneurs of Russia.

Born in 1949 in Sukhumi, Abkhazia, Georgian SSR; Greek. He graduated in 1966 from the Petrochemical Institute, Moscow, and until 1986 he did various jobs including that of an engineer and later became manager of a café. In 1989 he became director general of *Interagro* association, and in 1990 was appointed director-general of the *Vneshekonomkooperatsiya* (foreign economic co-operation) association and Vice-President of the union of co-operatives and entrepreneurs of Russia. In 1991 he was also appointed a member of the council on entrepreneurship of the President of the USSR. He is divorced with two children and speaks English.

Address: Moscow, pereulok Tokmakova 14; *telephone*: Moscow 267 8548 (office); 261 2276 (union).

Klimov, Fedor Matveevich

Chairman of the Board of the Orbita Commercial Bank.

Born in 1935 in Mogilev *oblast*, Belarus; Russian. He graduated from the Belarusian State Institute of the National Economy, specializing in accounting and economics, and after graduation began working as an accountant in a clothes-making factory in Kaluga. Later he was appointed chief accountant of the Kalugapribor enterprise; then head of the administration, USSR Ministry of Transport. In January 1991 he became head of the Orbita commercial bank. He is married with a son and a grandson.

Address: Moscow, Vtoroi Pereulok Spasonalivkovsky 6; *telephone*: Moscow 238 8720.

Klimov, Oleg Aleksandrovich

President of Exportkhleb foreign economic joint stock company.

Born in 1936 in Moscow; Russian. He graduated in 1958 from the Institute of Foreign Trade, Moscow, and from 1964 to 1967 he was on the staff of the all-Union Exportkhleb association and then a member of the trade mission to Kuwait. From 1974 to 1978 he was deputy head of department, and later head of department, main administration of the USSR Ministry of Foreign Trade; then on the staff of the trade mission to Sweden; director of the Soyuzpromexport company; and deputy director-general of the Exportkhleb association. In July 1987 he was appointed director-general of the all-Union Exportkhleb association, and in December 1991 he became president of Exportkhleb foreign economic joint stock company. He is married with three children and speaks English.

Address: Moscow, pl. Smolenskaya Sennaya 32-34; *telephone*: Moscow 244 4701.

Klochkov, Igor Evgenevich

Chairman of the Federation of Independent Trade Unions of Russia.

Born on July 30, 1939 in Rostov-on-Don into a military family. He is Russian, and a member of the CPSU until August 1991. He completed secondary school on Kamchatka where his parents were living, and in 1956 he entered the Odessa (Odesa) hydrotechnical (now construction engineering) institute, graduating in 1961. He was assigned to Moscow *oblast* as a foreman of construction train No. 181 of the Moscow heavy electrical construction trust, and was then a senior engineer in the Gidromontazh trust of USSR Ministry of Medium Building. He was secretary of the Party committee of the trust, and then moved into *Komsomol*, Party and soviet work: he was secretary of the Naro-Fominsky city *Komsomol* committee, chairman of the executive committee of the Naro-Fominsky city soviet, first secretary of the Naro-Fominsky city Party committee and secretary of the Moscow Party *obkom*. From 1986 to September 1989 he was secretary of the all-Union central soviet of trade unions.

In 1990 he was nominated by various work collectives in Moscow *oblast* for election as a RSFSR people's deputy in the No. 7 Istrinsky national territorial district, Moscow *oblast*. During the election campaign he advocated the strengthening of the sovereignty of Russia within the USSR, the ending of the non-equivalent exchange between the RSFSR and the other Union republics, the resurrection of the national spirit, language and culture and freedom of religion. He supported the consolidation of all socialist forces and organizations in the struggle for the *perestroika* of society.

The reason for his participation in the elections was to ensure the establishment of a group of deputies from the trade unions in the RSFSR Supreme

Soviet to defend the interests of the workers. He proposed the creation of conditions making it possible to reduce manual labour considerably and to eliminate heavy and monotonous work, to establish funds to help the poor, raise pensions and allowances, defend work collectives against the dictates of the central and local authorities and expand the autonomy of enterprises. He devoted special attention to measures to ensure the development of the Non Black Earth zone of central Russia.

There were six candidates. Klochkov lost in the first round, polling 11.17% of the votes, and V. M. Prilukov, head of the USSR KGB in Moscow and Moscow *oblast*, was elected the deputy for the district. In February-March 1990 Klochkov was chairman of the organizational committee for the preparation of the constituent congress of the Russian trades unions, which took place on March 21-23. At the congress Klochkov was elected chairman of the Federation of Independent Trade Unions of the RSFSR from three candidates. In March 1990 the federation consisted of four organizations, and by July 1991, there were 54 *krai* and *oblast*, 12 branch republican organizations and total membership had reached 45 million persons. The federation is openly critical of the economic policies of the Yeltsin administration and is not in favour of the privatization of enterprises. He is married with two daughters and lives in Moscow.

Klyuchnikov, Igor Konstantinovich

Chairman of the St Petersburg Stock Exchange.

Born in 1949 in Chernovtsy (Chernivtsi), Ukrainian SSR; Russian. He graduated in 1970 from the Leningrad Institute of Finance and Economics, then became a postgraduate student and successfully presented his candidate dissertation in economics (PhD (Econ)) and doctoral dissertation in economics (DSc (Econ)). After graduation he was appointed an economist, later senior economist, head of department, and head of the Leningrad branch of the USSR State Bank. In 1977 he was appointed a lecturer and later an assistant professor in the Leningrad Institute of Shipbuilding.

In 1981 he became an assistant professor in the Leningrad Institute of Engineering and Economics, and in 1983 he was academic secretary of the economics section, Leningrad branch of the USSR Academy of Sciences. In 1986 he was appointed professor of management at Leningrad State University and in 1991 of St Petersburg State University. In February 1990 he was elected chairman of the board of the Leningrad, then the St Petersburg stock exchange. He is married with a child and speaks English.

Address: 190107 St Petersburg, ul. Plekhanova 36; *telephone*: St Petersburg (8 812) 312 7993.

Kobets, Konstantin Ivanovich

Chief military inspector of the armed forces of the Russian Federation; chairman of the military legislative commission of the Russian Ministry of Defence. General of the Army.

Born on July 16, 1939 in Kiev. Russian. Kobets graduated from the Kiev Military Communications Technical School in 1959; the Military Academy of Communications in 1967; the Military Academy of the General Staff in 1978. He received a higher military education and was a member of the CPSU until August 1991.

After completing technical school he began his career as officer as a communications platoon commander. He was later appointed a company commander and became an expert on communications services. He was a promising young officer with a sound professional training. He actively participated in the work of Party organizations. From 1967 he was a communications battalion commander, a communications regimental commander, head of communications of an all-arms army. He was notable for his high level of operational tactical and military technical expertise, together with his ability to analyse and improve communications organizations and technical services. Kobets had a good reputation among officers as someone with organizational talent. He was fair in his contacts with his colleagues and personnel.

After graduating from the Academy of the General Staff he was appointed head of communications troops of the Far East military district, then was promoted to deputy Chief of Staff of the Far East military district. He supervised the communications systems and the automatic troop control of several military districts and the fleet in the Far East strategic direction. From 1986, Gen. Kobets was first deputy head of communications of the USSR Armed Forces; in 1987 he became head of communications of the armed forces and deputy Chief of the General Staff.

Towards the end of the 1980s he became acquainted with Boris Yeltsin who was out of political favour at the time. Kobets, however, supported him and became an adviser on military issues. Kobets's close contacts with representatives of democratic movements caused an extremely negative reaction among top USSR military leaders and resulted in his gradually being deprived of any real influence in the army. When pressed on a number of occasions to stop co-operating with Boris Yeltsin, he flatly refused. He was very popular among democratically-inclined officers. In 1990 he was assigned to the RSFSR Supreme Soviet at Boris Yeltsin's personal request. He was appointed chairman of the RSFSR state committee on defence issues, state adviser on defence and, simultaneously, presidential adviser.

During the anti-constitutional putsch in August 1991 Gen. Kobets was on the first list of people to be arrested by the KGB. Marshal Dmitry Yazov, USSR Minister of Defence, threatened him over the telephone with the internment of his family. On August 19 Gen. Kobets was in charge of the defence of the Russian White House. On August 20, by President Boris Yeltsin's decree, he was appointed RSFSR Minister of Defence with all armed forces in Russia under his command. His firm and resolute position and his personal appeals to the personnel of the army, navy, KGB and the MVD contributed to the demoralization of the plotters' troops and the solidarity of the democratically-inclined military, and also influenced many military commanders who ceased to support the Emergency Committee. As early as August 21, many Generals who had appraised the situation correctly were trying to get an appointment with Kobets in the White House. His behaviour during the attempted coup resulted in his promotion to General of the Army in late August 1991.

On September 21, 1991 he headed the committee, set up by decree of the USSR President, for the preparation and implementation of military reform. Kobets supervised the drafting of the fundamentals of a radical restructuring of the army and navy and of transforming them into the up-to-date depoliticized armed forces of a law-governed state. However, Kobets's activities did not bear tangible fruit because of opposition in conservative circles by top military leaders. As a result, the work of the committee was blocked. At the same time his insufficient determination to reform the army and dismiss conservative Generals led to criticism by democratic military organizations and a gradual decline in mutual contacts and co-operation. Some experts also pointed to a certain coolness on the part of President Yeltsin who had to react tactfully to the mood of the Generals, since the latter were suspicious of Kobets whom they regarded as a traitor to the army and the Party leadership. By decree of the Russian President, the agencies for the preparation of military reform under Kobets were dissolved in the spring of 1992. The General himself was out of office but remained officially a presidential adviser.

In April 1992 Kobets returned to the inner circle of the President as a result of sophisticated political manoeuvring in the corridors of power in the Kremlin. He was appointed deputy chairman of the state commission for the establishment of the Ministry of Defence, Army and Navy of the Russian Federation. On September 16, 1991, by presidential decree, he became chief military inspector of the armed forces of the Russian Federation. Simultaneously, he was made chairman of the military legislative commission of the Ministry of Defence. The chief military inspector is in charge of maintaining mutual contacts with the civil authorities, supervising the implementation of presidential decrees and Supreme Soviet resolutions on the armed forces. As chairman of the military legislative commission, Gen. Kobets supervises the drafting of laws on military planning, national security and the fundamentals of military service to be considered by the Supreme Soviet of the Russian Federation. He appears frequently in the mass media, commenting on military problems. He advocates the fundamental restructuring of the army and navy, the creation of armed forces to cope with the demands of present-day war and the new realities of the international situation. He participated in the drafting of the plan for national security. He has actively worked on the problems of military planning and lectures in higher military educational establishments. He is a doctor of military sciences (DSc) and professor. He has published a number of articles but they are still classified. He is a member of the International Russian Club, an élite liberal democratic organization, established in September 1992.

He likes history, art, literature and the theatre. He is interested in science and technical problems. He partakes in hunting and sport. He does not have a good command of foreign languages. He was awarded orders of the Red Star, "for service to the motherland in the armed forces of the USSR", order of the badge of honour, and medals. He is married.

Official address: 103175 Moscow K-175, Ministry of Defence of the Russian Federation.

Kogan, Evgeny Vladimirovich

Russian political activist in Estonia.

Born in 1954 in Vladivostok into a military family; Russian. He was a member of the CPSU from 1984 to August 1991. He moved to Tallinn, Estonian SSR in 1974 and in 1977 graduated from Tallinn Polytechnical Institute. He worked as a motor mechanic in the Estonian merchant fleet, then moved to the *Estrybprom* production association, was head of laboratory for the protection of labour of the association, and head of a thermal laboratory. He devotes his spare time to economic problems, having studied in the evening department of the Tallinn Polytechnical Institute.

In 1989 he was nominated for election as a USSR peoples deputy in the No. 450 Tallinn-Kalinin national territorial district, Estonian SSR. During the election campaign he advocated that the factories should be handed over to the workers and the land to the peasants; full economic cost accounting (*khozraschet*), especially at the place of work, in sections, brigades and in enterprises; all power for the soviets; that branch ministries should only be left with co-ordinating functions; free market for the means of production, raw and other materials, equal rights for and competition among all sectors of the socialist economy; and the establishment of an association of free producers on a voluntary basis. He favoured the provision of legal guarantees for a *Rechtsstaat* (law-governed state), elections to the Supreme Soviet by direct elections and the creation of a bicameral parliament.

He called for the universal declaration of human rights to be adopted, and the elimination of the privileges of those in the service and public spheres. There should be genuine bilingualism in the national republics. He called for the destruction of the bureaucratic system; workers' jobs should not be abolished before they had been retrained and the right to a job ensured. He advocated socialist principles when distributing material goods; pensions to be raised to the level of subsistence; the upper limits on the earnings of pensioners should be abolished; and freedom to choose one's place of residence. As regards the environment, specialists were needed and all enterprises and farms should use environmentally safe technology. He called for advanced professional training of officers and non-commissioned officers; a reduction in the length of national service; and believes that higher quality of training of ordinary soldiers was necessary. There should be strict military discipline; a reasonable defence budget; the creation of a nuclear free zone in the Baltic depending on the resolution of the question in northern Europe.

He advocated resistance to the decree of Tallinn city council about residence permits. He favoured the deliniation of functions between all-Union and republican authorities; the establishment in the USSR Supreme Soviet of a commission on control of the activities of the Ministry of Defence and law-enforcing agencies; the introduction of a special form of regime on the territory of the USSR only if approved exclusively by the USSR Supreme Soviet in cases of natural disasters and social conflicts which lead to violence.

He advocated the promulgation of a law on language; the harmonization of mutual relations between republics; and the individual as the most valuable aspect of a democratic society. He supported the slogan: "strong republics – a strong centre", but thought that sovereignty should not bring into question the very existence and power of the USSR. He wanted legal guarantees and the possibility of a normal existence for the Russian-speaking population and opposed the putting into effect of the concept of national segregation. The law on language of the Estonian SSR violates the rights of the non-autochthonous population. Kogan called for equal rights to choose one's language and was against dividing peoples into different sorts. He was one of the founders of the international movement of workers of the Estonian SSR, the first congress of which convened on March 4, 1989. He began his electoral campaign in hospital where he was taken after a serious car accident.

There were six candidates. Kogan polled 48.8% of the votes in the first round and won the second round, polling 63.22% of the votes. His main opponent was R. A. Veideman, editor-in-chief of the journal *Vikerkaar* (rainbow), who received 21.46% of the votes in the first round and 34.8% in the second round. Kogan was one of the prominent representatives and one of the leaders of the Soyuz deputies group. He insisted on the representatives of Abkhazia, South Ossetia, Pridnestrovie, Gagauzia (Moldova), Shalchininsky *raion*, Latvia, and the interregional council of Estonia being permitted to sign the federal treaty. In 1991 he advocated the introduction of direct presidential rule in South Ossetia and the declaration of a state of emergency throughout the whole country. He called for the removal of President Gorbachev by impeachment at the Congress of People's Deputies and favoured Valentin for the post. He criticized President Gorbachev for his half measures and warned against too personal contacts with the West.

In December 1991 Kogan announced plans to found the Party of renewal. He regarded himself as an internationalist, someone who paid little attention to the new state frontiers and as guided by the *rapprochement* of national minorities in the former Union and autonomous republics. He engaged in a propagandistic tour of the north Caucasus, Pridnestrovie and Gagauzia, and did not recognize the legality of the new state formations on the territory of the former USSR and opposed Russia taking over Union structures. He regarded the sole source of legitimacy to be the USSR constitution. He called for a hard struggle and he was ready to go to prison or even perish, and he did not exclude the emergence somewhere of a new Northern Ireland. He is married and lives in Tallinn.

Kogatko, Grigory Iosifovich

Head of the Chief Railway Administration of the Ministry of Architecture and Construction of the Russian Federation (head of railway troops); Lieutenant-General.

Born in 1944 in the village of Bolshaya Aleksandrovka, Novobug *raion*, Nikolaev *oblast*, Ukraine, into a collective farmer's family; Ukrainian. He received a higher special military education, and graduated from the Railway Transport Technical School, Courses for Officers, and the Military Rear and Transport Academy. He was a member of the CPSU until August 1991.

He began his military career as a soldier in the railway forces, and in 1963 became an officer. Later he was a commander of a platoon, company, battalion, brigade, corps, and took part in the construction of railway units and lines in different regions of the USSR under unfavourable climatic conditions. He directly supervised construction work at the Eastern section of the Baikal-Amur main line. He proved to be an able commander who organized engineering and prospecting expeditions, and he enjoyed the support of his superior officers. G. Kogatko was made a Hero of Socialist Labour for his participation in the construction of the Baikal–Amur main line. He was often elected to local Party agencies and had close ties with civil authorities.

For a long time Gen. Kogatko was head of Leningrad M. V. Frunze Higher Military Technical School of railway troops and military communications, and then he was head of the Central Road-Transport Administration of the USSR Ministry of Defence which was responsible for building communications in the distant regions of Central Russia and the North.

At the beginning of 1992 he was appointed head of railway troops of the unified armed forces of the CIS, which were later subordinated to the Ministry of Architecture, Construction, Housing and Communal Services. The establishments, enterprises and military units under Gen. Kogatko are building communications in Russia, especially in remote and difficult regions, co-operating with the Ministry of communications and the state corporation Transstroi. In some regions the troops are the prime users of the railways, especially in those where there are large military formations or where civil railway workers cannot work because of the unfavourable conditions.

He is not active politically and rarely appears in the press. Like most generals with a Soviet education, he is known for his conformism and ability to adapt to any state power. He enjoys authority as a professional; he takes part in technical expert assessments of construction designs. His interview with *Krasnaya Zvezda* was published on May 23, 1992.

He has no known hobbies. He does not speak any foreign languages, and has not been abroad as a member of an official delegation. He has been awarded the star of the Hero of Socialist Labour, three orders and 13 medals. He is married with two children. Gen. G. Kogatko's headquarters are in Moscow.

Kokoshin, Andrei Afanasevich

First Deputy Minister of Defence of the Russian Federation. Corresponding member of the Russian Academy of Sciences.

Born on October 26, 1945 in Moscow into an officer's family. Russian. He graduated from Moscow Bauman Higher Technical School in 1969; took a postgraduate course at the Institute of the USA of the USSR Academy of Sciences. He received a higher engineering education and was a member of the CPSU from 1969 to August 1991.

He worked at the Institute of the USA (renamed the Institute of the USA and Canada) of the USSR Academy of Sciences and was a junior research assistant, head of department, head of section, deputy director of the institute. He was a lecturer at Moscow State University and at the Institute of International Relations, specializing in military and political issues and problems of international and national security. After completing a postgraduate course in 1973 he successfully presented his dissertation on the "developments in forecasting of international relations in the USA (methodology, organization and the use of forecasts in the making of US foreign policy)" and became a candidate of historical sciences (PhD).

He actively engaged in scientific research and was enlisted to tackle problems set by top Party and government leaders and to draft practical proposals in international economic relations, the domestic policy of the USSR and national security. Kokoshin's major scholarly works deal with the domestic and foreign policy of the USA, the theory of international relations, arms reductions and disarmament. His best known works are: *The USA: Behind the Facade of Global Politics (the Domestic Factors Influencing the Foreign Policy of American Imperialism on the Eve of the 1980s)* (Moscow 1981); *The USA: the Crisis of Political Power* (Moscow 1982); *The USA in the System of International Relations in the 1980s: Hegemony and Washington's Foreign Policy* (Moscow 1984); joint author, *The USA: Information and Foreign Policy* (Moscow 1979); joint author, *The Kennedy Brothers* (Moscow 1985); joint author, *The US Congress and Problems of Domestic and Foreign Policy* (Moscow 1989), and others.

Both in his scholarly work and in lectures he advocated the necessity of gaining strategic parity with the USA and NATO and demonstrated theoretically the essence of the USSR's "peaceful policy", basing his views on realism and denying the irreversibility of the arms race. He often took part in international conferences and bilateral and multilateral negotiations on the problems of easing international tension and disarmament as a member of the Soviet delegation. On December 23, 1987, at the annual general meeting of the USSR Academy of Sciences, he was elected a corresponding member in the department of world economy and international relations. At the age of 42 he became one of the youngest corresponding members of the Academy in social sciences. He is well known in academic and military intellectual circles and has worked closely with the top figures of the army and military-industrial complex, diplomats and statesmen. He enjoys a considerable reputation at home and abroad.

With the adoption of the "new thinking" in the foreign policy of the USSR in the second half of the 1980s he became one of the most active and closest academic advisers of the top leaders. He owed his promotion primarily to Academician Georgy Arbatov and General of the Army Vladimir Lobov. When Kokoshin published his article on "Military Doctrine in the Service of Peace", in *Kommunist*, No. 15, 1990, a thorough analysis of the problems of national security and the development of the military during détente, it became very popular in academic, intellectual and political circles.

He actively co-operated with officers involved in the Military for Democracy, the military democratic movement, and the union, Shield, who were advocating fundamental reform of the armed forces. He was head of the centre for the study of the problems of conversion and privatization at the USSR Academy of Sciences (later Russian Academy of Sciences). He participated in discussions on military reform and in the development of a concept of national security. He was considered one of the front runners for the post of USSR Minister of Defence, then of Russia, providing a civilian took over the ministry, as is common in democratic, law-governed states.

On April 3, 1992, by decree of Russian President Boris Yeltsin, Andrei Kokoshin was appointed first Deputy Minister of Defence of the Russian Federation. He also became deputy chairman of the state commission for the establishment of the Ministry of Defence, Army and Navy of the Russian Federation. He supervises the work of the chief armaments administration, the chief international military co-operation administration, the international and treaty administration and the drafting of programmes on Russian industrial policy. He is in charge of state defence procurement. He has established working relations with the leaders of the military-industrial complex, he visits design bureaux, plants and test ranges and oversees the testing of new weapons.

On March 17, 1992, in *Krasnaya Zvezda*, he published his programme: "One should create an army when one knows what it is for". Politically he is a liberal, favouring centrist solutions, and is a convinced advocate of the need to restore Russia's great power status and peaceful co-operation with Western countries. He is the first civilian military leader in the history of Russia who has remained a civilian after assuming office. He has a broad palate of interests and has a good command of English. He has often been abroad where he has a wide circle of acquaintances, and he belongs to the intellectual élite of Russia. He has been awarded medals. He is married with two children.

Official address: 103160 Moscow K-160, Ministry of Defence of the Russian Federation.

Kokov, Valery Mukhamedovich

President of the Kabardino-Balkar Republic, Russian Federation.

Born on October 18, 1941 in Tyrnyauz, Kabardino-Balkar Autonomous Soviet Socialist Republic (ASSR). He is Kabardin, and was a member of the CPSU from 1966 to August 1991. In 1964 he graduated from the Kabardino-Balkar State University and in 1978 from the Rostov Higher Party School. In 1964 he was chief agronomist of the Trudovoi Gorets collective farm, Baksansky *raion*. In 1966 he became a postgraduate student at the all-Union scientific research institute of agriculture and successfully presented his candidate dissertation in economics (PhD (Econ)). In 1970 he was chief economist, head of a department of the Ministry of Agriculture of the republic, and director of the Leskensky state farm, Urvansky *raion*.

In 1974 he was appointed first secretary of the Urvansky *raion* Party committee and in 1983 chairman of the state committee of the republic for the technical provisioning of agriculture. In 1985 he was secretary, from 1988 second secretary, and from February to September 1990 first secretary of the Kabardino-Balkar republican Party committee (until July 1990 it was the Party *obkom*). He was a member of the Party Central Committee from July 1990, and has been awarded the orders of the October Revolution, the Red Banner of Labour and the badge of honour.

In early 1990 he was nominated by several work collectives for election as an RSFSR people's deputy in the No. 818 Baksansky territorial district, Kabardino-Balkar ASSR. During the election campaign he advocated a unified and indivisible Kabardino-Balkaria within a renewed Russian Federation, the provision of guarantees about the defence of human rights and the freedom of every citizen of the republic, independent of nationality and religion. He favoured radical economic reform.

He was unopposed and won in the first round, polling 89.7% of the votes. He is a member of the constitutional commission and the sovereignty and equality group of deputies and in 1990 he was elected a deputy of the Supreme Soviet of the Kabardino-Balkar ASSR. The plenum of the Kabardino-Balkar Party *obkom* nominated him as Speaker of the Supreme Soviet and on March 30, 1990 he was elected by a majority of votes unopposed. On assuming office he stated that he regarded his basic duties to be the acceleration of economic reform, the promotion of a new agrarian policy, based primarily on the development of public production and private plots, and the social reorganization of the countryside. He advocated the adoption of rapid measures to satiate the market with consumer goods and strengthen inter-ethnic relations in the region.

On August 24, 1991 a session of the Supreme Soviet of the Kabardino-Balkar ASSR judged the conduct of Kokov during the attempted state coup to be correct and he ensured the functioning of the constitutional, state authorities and the national economic complex. However, under pressure from some deputies and public movements he resigned on September 9, 1991 as Speaker of the Supreme Soviet. This was accepted on September 17, 1991 after two votes, one open and the other secret.

In October 1991 he was nominated for President of the Kabardino-Balkar

Republic. There were four candidates and Kokov won in the second round, on January 5, 1992, polling 88.86% of the votes (56.8% of the registered voters participated). His main opponent, F. A. Kharaev, general director of the Kabardino-Balkar automobile transport territorial production association, withdrew from the second round. On January 9, 1992, after taking the presidential oath, Kokov stated that, in his new post, he would concentrate on strengthening inter-ethnic relations and providing social guarantees to the population during the transition to a market economy.

In December 1992 he supported those reforms which do not result in a lowering of the standard of living of the population. He advocated privatization but nevertheless thought that the state should retain control over enterprises on which depended the well-being of the republic, but other enterprises should be privatized giving priority to the work collectives. He declared his support for entrepreneurs whose activities were associated with the creation of new jobs in the republic.

The main task of the state authorities of the republic was the promotion of measures to raise the social security of the population, first and foremost by creating jobs, maintaining wages at the level of the cost of living, and the state financing of education, science and culture. One of the main problems, in his view, was the struggle with organized crime. He considered that a combination of a presidential and parliamentary form of administration was the most acceptable for the Russian Federation. He stated that only the wisdom and restraint of the VII Congress of People's Deputies, in December 1992, could provide a way out of the constitutional crisis. He lives in Nalchik.

Kokunko, Georgy Valentinovich

Acting ataman of the Moscow Society of Cossacks; deputy Chief of Staff of the Cossack Troops of the Union of Russia.

Born in 1961 in Moscow; Russian Cossack. He graduated in 1983 from the Institute for Geological Prospecting, Moscow, and then began working in the Russian society for the preservation of historical and cultural monuments, Moscow. From 1985 to 1987 he worked in the historical restoration club of the Preobrazhensky Old Believers' foundation, Moscow. In 1987 he returned to the Russian society for the preservation of historical and cultural monuments, Moscow, as chairman of the restoration group. In 1989 he was appointed a member of the staff of the propaganda and social initiative centre of the society, and in 1991 he was elected acting ataman of the society of Cossacks, Moscow, and deputy chief of staff of the Cossack troops of the Union of Russia.

The Cossacks are re-forming in Russia and in other successor states of the Soviet Union. They were originally formed to protect Russia's frontiers, especially in the south against Tatars and Turks. They belong to the nationalist wing of Russian politics and place great emphasis on patriotic education and the role of the Russian Orthodox Church as the bearer of Russian culture.

Kokunko's hobbies are the study of Russian history, journalism, folklore and the restoration of the monuments of Russia's past. He is married but has no children.

Address: Moscow, ul. Varvarka 8 b; *telephone*: Moscow 298 5602 (office).

Kolesnikov, Mikhail Petrovich

Chief of the General Staff of the Armed Forces of the Russian Federation. Colonel-General.

Born on June 30, 1939 in Eysk, Krasnodar *krai*. The social status of his parents is unknown. Russian. His career in the military began in 1956. He graduated from the Omsk Tank Technical School in 1959; the Military Academy of Armoured Troops in 1975 and the Military Academy of the General Staff in 1983. He received a higher military education and was a member of the CPSU till August 1991.

He began his career as an officer as a maintenance platoon commander. Later he became a combat officer. He was a tank company and battalion commander. The units under him demonstrated a high level of training and were awarded a distinction. His reputation with superior officers and Party-political agencies was good and he was considered a promising officer. He was politically active in his unit's CPSU organization to the extent necessary for a successful career.

After graduating from the Academy he became a tank regiment commander, which distinguished him from other graduates who would be later appointed Chiefs of Staff or deputy regiment commanders. Kolesnikov achieved good results in the combat and political training of the regiment. As early as 1977 he was appointed Chief of Staff, deputy tank divisional commander; from 1979 he was a divisional commander. He was in Afghanistan for a short period, and participated in planning operations against the *mujahidin*.

From 1983, as a graduate of the Military Academy of the General Staff, Gen. M. Kolesnikov was appointed a corps commander, and was then promoted to army commander of the Transcaucasian military district. He demonstrated a talent for organization, a sound operational-tactical and military-technical training, and knew how to develop a good reputation with Party-political agencies and local authorities. He was a convinced communist, supporting the domestic and foreign policy of the top Party and government leaders of the USSR. Like all Soviet generals, he was a conformist, adapting to the changing political scene.

In 1987 he occupied the post of Chief of Staff, first deputy commander of the Siberian military district, one of the least significant in the Soviet army in numbers and tasks. Having gained experience in commanding large army formations, Lieut.-Gen. M. Kolesnikov was a year later, in 1988, appointed Chief of Staff, first deputy army commander of the Southern direction. He supervised the planning of combat use and training of land troops and aviation at one of the most important strategic directions, including Transcaucasia and Central Asia. He was involved in the events in Afghanistan.

From 1990 he became chief of the main headquarters and first deputy Commander-in-Chief of land forces. From 1991 he was deputy chief of the General Staff of the Armed Forces of the USSR and head of the Chief Organization and Mobilization Administration.

He was an immediate subordinate of General of the Army M. Moiseev, and, according to democratic officer sources, Gen. Kolesnikov was undoubtedly aware of the plans for the use of the army against the forces opposing the communists. At the time of the anti-constitutional putsch in August 1991 he was not active and fulfilled obediently all the instructions of the Minister of Defence and the chief of the General Staff. He did not question the legitimacy of the Emergency Committee's activity.

He is intimately acquainted with the Commander-in-Chief of the Armed Forces of the CIS, Air Force Marshal Shaposhnikov, and the Minister of Defence of Russia, General of the Army P. Grachev, and works closely with them. When the General Staff was put under Russia's jurisdiction he was left in the same post.

He was a member of the state committee for the establishment of a Ministry of Defence, Army and Navy of the Russian Federation. In June 1992 he was appointed first deputy chief of the General Staff of the Armed Forces of the Russian Federation.

He does not express his political views in public, remains a supporter of the ideas of the supremacy of the state and of a powerful up-to-date army and navy. He does not recognize the existing democratic organizations in the armed forces. He was awarded three orders and ten medals. He is married.

Office address: 103175, Moscow, Ministry of Defence of the Russian Federation.

Komarov, Evgeny Borisovich

Head of the Administration of Murmansk *oblast*, Russian Federation.

Born in 1942; Russian; member of the CPSU until August 1991. He worked in Murmansk *oblast*, and was chairman of Kovdorsky *raion* soviet executive committee, deputy chairman of Murmansk *oblast* soviet executive committee and secretary of the Murmansk Party *obkom*. Until recently he was head of the RSFSR state committee on the social and economic development of the north.

In early 1990 he was nominated for election as an RSFSR people's deputy in the No. 511 Kolsky territorial district. There were 13 candidates, and Komarov was defeated in the first round. R. Z. Chebotarevsky, a naval officer and commander of a large formation of submarines, was elected deputy. He polled 12.21% of the votes in the first round and 45.98% in the second.

Komarov was elected a deputy of Murmansk *oblast* soviet, and at its first session in May 1990 he was one of the candidates for chairman but was not elected. On November 8, 1991 he was appointed head of the administration of Murmansk *oblast* by presidential decree. On assuming office he advocated the development of small and medium entrepreneurs, the scaling down and even the closing of loss-making enterprises and basic branches of the economy, greater economic activity of the population, greater investment in health and education, the attraction of foreign investors and the establishment of a hard currency fund. He called for the local budget to receive part of the profits of local enterprises, the restructuring of the economy, enlarging the range of products from local industry and the establishment of direct horizontal links with the territories and providers of agricultural products. There should be a considerable extension of the rights of regions which would then rely on themselves and not on Moscow.

In April 1992 he was elected to the board of the union of governors of Russia. In February 1993, he was one of the group of eight heads of administration and ten chairmen of soviet executive committees who proposed that the referendum of April 11, 1993 be postponed and that an extraordinary VIII Congress of People's Deputies should be convened. Its agenda should include bringing order to the constitution of the Russian Federation and strengthening the separation of powers. He regarded it as inopportune to conduct a referendum since it involved the expenditure of considerable resources from the state budget at a time when the political activity of the population was zero. The question posed by a referendum would not introduce anything new and the congress and the President should reach a compromise. He opposed the concept of a constituent assembly. He lives in Murmansk.

Komarovsky, Yury Vladimirovich

Head of the Administration of the Nenets Autonomous *okrug*, Russian Federation.

Born on May 18, 1952 in Obluche, Khabarovsk *krai* into a worker's family; Russian. After secondary school he entered the Khabarovsk Institute of Railway Engineers and graduated in 1974 as an engineer electrical mechanic. From 1974 to 1976 he served in the Soviet Army, and in 1976 he was appointed an engineer in the Naryan-Mar aviation enterprise. From 1979 to 1982 he was senior engineer for the servicing of aviation and radioelectronic equipment, then became head of the political section of the enterprise. From 1988 to 1989 he was a senior design engineer for flight safety and from 1989 to 1990 again deputy head of the political section of the enterprise.

In March 1990 he was elected a deputy of the Nenets *okrug* soviet of people's deputies, and in May 1990 at the first session of the Naryan-Marsky city soviet he was elected first deputy chairman of the soviet executive committee. In September 1991 at an extraordinary session of the Nenets *okrug* soviet of people's deputies Komarovsky was nominated for the post of head of the administration of the autonomous *okrug*.

On November 30, 1991 he was appointed head of the administration of the Nenets autonomous *okrug* by presidential decree. On assuming office he stated that at present the most important policies were now at the local level and in this he saw the future of Russia. The main approach of his administration to resolving the problems connected to the transition to the market would be to utilize the natural resources of the *okrug* for the welfare of the population, to acquire advanced foreign technology and to retrain cadres abroad. The most important task was to develop local oil potential, but the *okrug* soviet did not support him in this endeavour and in fact opposed his activities.

In November 1992 he stated that, irrespective of the decisions of the VII Congress of People's Deputies, he would remain a supporter of the economic reform programme of the government. He hoped that the President and his team, even during the present sharp political conflict, would retain true to their convictions. He lives in Naryan-Mar.

Komendant, Grigory Ivanovich

Chairman of the Union of Evangelical Christian Baptists.

Born on January 8, 1946 in the village of Stavishche, Dunaevtsy *raion*, Khmelnitsky (Khmelnytyskyi) *oblast*, Ukrainian SSR; Ukrainian. He graduated in 1975 from the theological seminary in Hamburg, Federal Republic of Germany, and from 1975 to 1978 he was a deacon of the Dunaevtsy community of Evangelical Christian Baptists. From 1979 to 1980 he was senior deacon of the church for the Kiev region and, since 1981, has been deputy senior deacon of the Union of Evangelical Christian Baptists in Ukraine. In 1990 he was elected chairman of the union. He is married with three children.

Address: Moscow, Maly Vuzovsky Pereulok 3 *telephone*: Moscow 297-363; 297 8164; 297 6700; 227 8947.

Kondratev, Aleksandr Andreevich

Head of the Administration of Penza *oblast*, Russian Federation.

Born in 1947 in Penza; Russian; member of the CPSU until August 1991. He began working in 1962 as a turner in the Penzmash enterprise, Penza. After graduating from the Polytechnical Institute, Penza, he served in the Soviet Army, and after being demobbed he was a foreman, then an engineer in the instrument making factory, Penza. In August 1972 he was appointed head of the production technology department of the Penza *oblast* consumer goods repair association. In 1974 he became head of the department of local industry and consumer services of the population, Penza *oblast* soviet executive committee.

In November 1979 he was appointed director of the Penza *oblast* consumer goods repair association. In late 1986 he became head of the department of consumer services of the population, Penza soviet executive committee, then general director of the territorial production association for consumer services and in 1990 chairman of the Penzbyt association of enterprises and organizations concerned with providing consumer services to the population. In 1986 he was awarded the title of honoured worker of consumer services in the RSFSR.

In 1990 he was elected a deputy of the Penza *oblast* soviet and on October 24, 1991 he was appointed head of the administration of Penza *oblast* by presidential decree. On assuming office he stated that the most important aspects of economic reform were the liberalization of prices, the restructuring of the economy, the conversion of defence industry, land reform, demonopolization, support for small and medium businesses and the creation of a class of property owners in Russia. He advocated the rapid introduction of the market economy, fast privatization, the development of private farming, and the construction of private housing financed by bank loans at low rates of interest.

He proposed sovereignty for entrepreneurs, free economic activity for the individual and a strong state. He appealed for the promotion of various types of economic activity by means of tax breaks, the attraction of foreign investment, the re-education and retraining of officials to cope with the market. The reforms should be carried out if possible without social sacrifices. They were necessary, and the majority of the population should readjust psychologically and associate themselves with the market economy. He was sharply critical of the economy which was based on orders by the ruling Party, and the pillage of Russia and its people by the military industrial complex.

In December 1992 Kondratev pointed out the attempt of the majority of people's deputies to alter the relationship between the branches of power in favour of the legislature and to the disadvantage of the executive. He supported the President and his appeal to the people and did not see in it any attempt to depart from representative institutions. He advocated a referendum which should put everything in place and remove the barriers on the road to economic reform and a *Rechtsstaat* (law-governed state). He saw the referendum as normalizing the situation in the country. The appointment of a new Prime Minister could not alter the substance of government policy since the previous team was still in place. He saw Viktor Chernomyrdin as an excellent manager and industrialist who had contacts with the west but, of course, he had his own views on reform. Kondratev appealed for the consolidation of all state authorities. He is married with two children and a granddaughter, and lives in Penza.

Kondratev, Aleksei Aleksandrovich

Chairman of the Ufa Club of Chuvash Culture, Republic of Bashkortostan, Russian Federation.

Born on May 18, 1930 in the village of Dyurtbli, Sharansky *raion*, Bashkir ASSR. He is Chuvash, and his father, Aleksandr Semonovich Kondratev and his mother, Mariya Tikhonovna Kondrateva, both worked on the collective farm. He has four brothers and three sisters.

He graduated from the oil institute, Ufa, in 1953. He remained in the institute as an assistant, senior lecturer, and assistant professor in the faculty of oil chemistry and technology. He successfully presented his candidate dissertation in technical sciences (PhD), then in 1974 his doctoral dissertation on the "elaboration of new systems of rectification and methods of calculating complex columns for the fractionation of oil and the products of its refining" (DSc). For over 20 years he was a professor and head of faculty.

During *perestroika* Kondratev was one of the first in Bashkortostan to advocate the renaissance of the national culture of the Chuvash people in the republic. He was one of the organizers in Ufa of the appreciation society of Chuvash culture. He is now the chairman of the Ufa club of Chuvash culture and also participates in the activities of the Druzhba city centre of national culture. He is married, and his wife, Tatyana Ilinichna, is the daughter of ordinary rural dwellers. They have two adult sons and a daughter. Kondratev lives in Ufa.

Kondratev, Georgy Grigorevich

Deputy Minister of Defence of the Russian Federation; Colonel-General since 1992.

Born on November 17, 1944 in Klintsy, Bryansk *oblast*. The social status of his parents is unknown; Russian. He graduated from the Khartov Guards Tank Officers' Technical School with distinction in 1965, the Military Academy of armoured troops with distinction in 1973 and the Military Academy of the General Staff with distinction and a gold medal in 1985, having received a higher military education. He was a member of the CPSU until August 1991.

He began his career as an officer as a commander of a tank platoon, became a company commander and held other combat posts. After graduating from the Academy he was appointed Chief of Staff of a tank regiment, and the next year, in 1974, he became a regimental commander. He served in interior military districts and groups of troops, and proved to be an experienced commander of armoured troops, aware of the essence of present-day army combat. The units under Kondratev's command frequently showed good results in training and were awarded a distinction.

In 1978 he was appointed a deputy divisional commander and soon became a divisional commander. He ensured a high level of combat readiness and participated in military operations in Afghanistan. He was politically active to the extent necessary for a successful career in the Soviet army, and was convinced of the need for the CPSU to play a leading role in the USSR, the implementation of harsh domestic and foreign policies, the building up of military strength, and the use of force in solving the domestic problems of the Soviet Union. He had a good reputation among superior commanders and was respected by his subordinates.

After graduating from the Military Academy of the General Staff he was appointed first deputy army commander of the Turkestan military district, and became an army commander in 1987. From 1989 he was the first deputy commander of the Turkestan military district, and was directly involved in the use of troops in resolving ethnic conflicts in Central Asia and ensuring the security of the civil population. During the anti-constitutional putsch in August 1991 he was not very active, and performed his usual duties, keeping the troops of the district in fighting trim.

On December 7, 1991, after his predecessor's promotion to a higher post at the USSR Ministry of Defence, Lieut.-Gen. Kondratev was appointed commander of the Turkestan military district (with headquarters in Tashkent). He was soon promoted to colonel-general. While Gen. Kondratev was in this post, there was an outbreak of acute inter-ethnic and religious tension in Central Asia and different national forces became especially active. As commander of the district, the general succeeded in preventing the army from becoming involved in internal conflicts and ensured sufficient order and discipline.

In June 1992 Col.-Gen. Kondratev was appointed deputy Minister of Defence of the Russian Federation. According to knowledgeable democratic military sources, this appointment was personally organized by the Minister of Defence, P. S. Grachev, who was building up his team with veterans of the Afghan war whom he knew well. Gen. Kondratev supervises Russian troops on the territories of the independent states of the CIS and other regions of the former USSR. He has made it a rule to be present in regions where there are armed conflicts or tense situations, where he organizes political and military measures to ensure the safety of Russian subjects. He skilfully carries out Russia's policy in the former Soviet republics; he prefers a peaceful settlement of conflicts, but is not averse to demonstrating strength in certain situations, for example in South Ossetia.

He does not express his political views in the mass media. He supports the idea of creating up-to-date armed forces, capable of guaranteeing Russia the status of a great power, and is against the idea of having any political organizations in the army and the navy.

He has been awarded orders of the Red Banner, two orders of the Red Star and "For service to the motherland in the armed forces of the USSR", 2nd and 3rd classes, and 10 medals.

There is no information about his hobbies. He is married with two children.

Office address: 103175 Moscow K-105, Ministry of Defence of the Russian Federation.

Kononov, Anatoly Leonidovich

Member of the Constitutional Court of the Russian Federation.

Born on June 28, 1947 in Moscow. Russian. He was a member of the CPSU until August 1991. He began his career in 1965 as an aviation mechanic, and then from 1966 to 1971 he was secretary and bailiff in people's courts in Zhdanov and Volgograd *raions*, Moscow. He graduated from the law faculty of Moscow State University in 1973, and regards Valery Zorkin as having a formative influence on him. He has spent over 25 years as a practising lawyer and in legal research. From 1971 to 1979 he was investigator, then senior investigator in the Procurator's Office, Kirov *raion*, Moscow, and from 1979 to 1981 he was senior legal assistant of the USSR Ministry of Machine Building for the Light and Food Industries. He then became a postgraduate student. From 1981 he worked in the all-Union institute for the problems of strengthening law and order where, in 1986, he successfully presented his candidate dissertation in law on "the problems of criminology" (LLM). In 1991 he became a senior scientific assistant of the institute.

His main legal interests are the sociology of crime, research into the reasons for contemporary crime, problems connected with the development of a legal culture, the history of law and procuratorial supervision. He is a specialist on economic law, criminal law and criminal procedure and is the author of over 20 academic articles. From 1979 to 1990 he taught a course on Soviet law at the institute for instrument making, Moscow. In early 1990 he was nominated for election as an RSFSR people's deputy in the No. 31 Lyublinsky territorial district, Moscow. There were seven candidates, and Kononov polled 34.32% of the votes in the first round and won the second round, polling 60.4% of the votes. His main opponent was K. V. Fedyunin, who received 11.63% of the votes in the first round and 25.5% in the second.

Kononov was a member of the RSFSR Supreme Soviet committee on human rights, deputy chairman of the RSFSR Supreme Soviet presidium commission on granting pardons and a member of the mandate commission. He was a member of the Democratic Russia parliamentary faction and the Moscow deputies' group. He helped to draft the RSFSR law on the rehabilitation of the victims of political repression.

He was nominated as a member of the Constitutional Court by the RSFSR Supreme Soviet committee on human rights. He was elected on October 30, 1991, at the V Congress of People's Deputies, in the third round of voting when he received 535 votes for and 314 against. In the first round he got 507 votes for and 384 against and in the second 470 votes for and 355 against, with 529 votes necessary for election. On the same day he surrendered his role as a people's deputy. He lives in Moscow.

Kononov, Vitalii Mykolayovych

Leader of the Green Party of Ukraine.

Born into a Ukrainian family in 1956 in the town of Kobulet in the Georgian SSR. His father was in the Soviet Army and his mother was a doctor. Vitalii graduated from Kiev Polytechnic Institute in 1974, having studied chemical engineering, and worked as an engineer thereafter, including a stint in the industrial trust *Orkhim*. An early ecological activist, he joined the *Zelenyi svit* association, and in 1990 the newly formed Green Party of Ukraine (GPU).

In 1990 he was elected to the Kiev city soviet, where he was one of the key initiators of the decision to declare Kiev city a victim of the Chernobyl accident. He is also a member of the town soviet's cultural commission. In March 1992 he stood unsuccessfully as the GPU's candidate in a by-election to the Supreme Soviet in Zaliznychnyi *raion* in Kiev city. In 1991 he became the speaker of the GPU's Political Council and therefore the main public spokesman for the party. He also became a deputy director of the ecological business company *Chervona ruta*. In October 1992, the GPU, which had suffered from its decentralized structure and multiplicity of public spokesmen, elected Kononov as its sole leader at the party's third congress.

He faces a difficult task in remoulding the GPU into an organization strong enough to capitalize on its still broad public support. Kononov speaks Russian, Polish and German, and has a great interest in philately and literature. He is married, with a daughter Maria, born in 1979.

Address: 252070 Kiev, Kontraktova ploshcha 4; *telephone*: (work) Kiev 417 0283 or (home) Kiev 294 6248.

Kopekov, Danatar

Minister of Defence of the Republic of Turkmenistan.

Born in 1933 in Ashkhabad, Turkmen SSR; Turkmen. He was a member of the CPSU until August 1991. He graduated in 1954 from the Chardju State Pedagogical Institute, and in 1961 from KGB School of the Turkmen SSR. From 1954 to 1959 he was a teacher, and later director of studies in a secondary school; inspector in the Kum Dag *raion* department of education, and a secondary school teacher in Ashkhabad. From 1959 to 1961 he was a student at the KGB School of the Turkmen SSR, and then made a successful career within the KGB of the Turkmen SSR (1961-84). In 1984 he was appointed deputy chairman, KGB of the Turkmen SSR, for personnel and later for operational activities.

From 1990 to 1991 he was first deputy chairman, KGB of the republic, and in 1991 he became chairman of the republic's KGB. In January 1992 he was appointed Minister of Defence Affairs of the Republic of Turkmenistan and in July 1992 Minister of Defence of the Republic of Turkmenistan.

His main concern is to build up the Turkmen armed forces and to secure the frontier with Iran. The republic has only modest military resources and relies to a large extent on the Russian military (under the heading of CIS forces), and so it collaborates with the Russians to ensure the security of its frontiers. Turkmenistan has been developing closer relations with Iran, but this does not include any tolerance of Islamic activity. There are political parties but open opposition to the ruling ex-communist nomenclature is not encouraged. Turkmenistan is fortunate in that it has reserves of gas and oil which are being developed in collaboration with Western companies. Income is being used to subsidize enterprises and farms and hence the republic in the former Soviet Union where living standards have not dropped since the collapse of the USSR in December 1991.

Address: Ministry of Defence, Ashkhabad.

Kopsov, Anatoly Yakovlevich

Chairman of the Council of Ministers of the Republic of Bashkortostan, Russian Federation.

Born in 1942 in the settlement of Krasnousolsky, Gafuriisky *raion*, Bashkir Autonomous Soviet Soviet Republic (ASSR); Russian. In 1965 he graduated from the Ivanovo Institute of Energy as an engineer, specializing in automation, and began his working life as a electrical fitter in the Kaliningrad hydroelectric station in Svetly, Kaliningrad *oblast*. After graduating from the institute he returned to the Kaliningrad hydroelectric station as an engineer and foreman of a shop. In 1968 he returned to Bashkiria and worked as a foreman, deputy head of a shop, and head of a shop, Karmanovo hydroelectric station. In 1976 he was sent to the People's Republic of Bangladesh to provide specialist help to the Gorozal thermal electrical plant. He returned to Bashkiria in 1978 and again became head of a shop in Karmanovo hydroelectric station.

In 1978 he was elected secretary of the Party committee of the station and from 1983 to 1988 he was director of the station. In September 1988 he was appointed general director of the Bashkirenergo production association of energy and electrification (now the Bashkirenergo joint stock company). At the XIV extraordinary session of the Supreme Soviet of the Bashkir ASSR in 1989 he was elected Chairman of the Council of Ministers.

He is an honoured energy specialist of the Republic of Bashkortostan and has received the badge of excellent worker in energy and electrification of the USSR. He believes that his work at the head of the government should be based on the fact that Bashkortostan is a sovereign state. The Council of Ministers should be active in promoting draft legislation, and place before the Supreme Soviet new draft laws on economic questions for discussion. Enterprises should be autonomous, and should develop links throughout the territory of the republic and abroad. For this reason the whole state administration of the territory should be unified under government direction.

In December 1992 Kopsov stated that the course of events at the VII Congress of People's Deputies should not lead to a worsening of the political situation in the country. Whatever the outcome, the government of the Republic of Bashkortostan would be guided by the constitution of the Russian Federation and the constitution of the Republic of Bashkortostan. He looked forward to the same response to the events in Moscow from the representatives of all political parties and organizations, and believed that a successful resolution of the economic problems was possible only if there was political stability and a consolidation of all social forces. He lives in Ufa.

Koptev, Yury Nikolaevich

Director-General, Russia's Space Agency.

Born in 1941; Russian. He was a member of the CPSU until August 1991. He graduated from the Bauman Higher Technical School, Moscow, and began his career as an engineer in the Lavochkin research and development association. He later progressed to deputy USSR Minister of General Machine Building, and has spent his whole career in the Soviet military industrial complex. In early 1992 he was appointed director-general of Russia's space agency.

Kopysov, Viktor Andreevich

Commander of the Siberian Military District; Colonel-General since 1991.

Born on November 7, 1940 in the settlement of Zavitaya, Amursk *oblast* into a working-class family; Russian. He graduated from the Kharkov Guards Tank Officers Technical School in 1962, the Military Academy of Armoured Troops in 1970 and the Military Academy of the General Staff in 1979, having received a higher military education. He was a member of the CPSU until August 1991.

He began his career as an officer as a tank platoon commander in 1962. He demonstrated good professional knowledge, a talent for organization, command and teaching abilities in personnel training and soon became a company commander. He actively participated in the work of the Party organizations and this brought him to the attention of superior officers and the political agencies. After graduating from the Academy he became a tank battalion commander, which was not typical of a graduate of a higher military educational establishment because it was a low-ranking post. Due to good operational-tactical and military-technical training he was rapidly promoted: a tank regimental chief of staff, a regimental commander, and deputy commander of a tank division. He served in interior military districts and groups of troops abroad. After graduating from the Academy of the General Staff in 1979 he became a tank divisional commander and his formation was awarded a distinction. From 1983 to 1985 he was Chief of Staff and first deputy army commander, and from 1985 to 1988 an army commander. In 1988 he became first deputy commander of the Central Asian military district. As one of the best-qualified generals, he was sent abroad and was the senior military adviser in African countries between 1988 and 1991. He was responsible for personnel training, for *matériel* and military equipment maintenance and the direct deployment of the Soviet military in operations.

After he returned from his military mission in August 1991 he was appointed commander of the Siberian military district and his appointment was confirmed by President Yeltsin's decree in October 1992. He was soon promoted to colonel-general.

Gen. Kopysov is head of one of the most undermanned and under-equipped military districts, its main task being to train junior officers and to store military equipment and weapons.

Kopysov is not widely known in the army and does not express his political views in public. A military professional, not active in politics, he favours the non-involvement of the army in non-military issues.

He has not revealed his hobbies, but does not speak any foreign language. He is married. He has been awarded two orders "For service to the motherland in the armed forces of the USSR" and 12 medals.

Gen. Kopysov's headquarters are in Novosibirsk.

Kornilova, Zoya Afanasevna

Chairwoman of the commission of the Council of Nationalities, Russian Supreme Soviet, on the social and economic development of the republics within Russia, autonomous *oblasts*, autonomous *okrugs* and small nations.

Born on May 22, 1939 in the village of Kyyllaakh, Yakut ASSR; Yakut. She was a member of the CPSU from 1968 to August 1991. Her father worked on a collective farm. In 1966 she graduated from the Novosibirsk Institute of Soviet Co-operative Trade, and in 1971 successfully presented her candidate dissertation in economics on "Ways of raising the profitability of consumer co-operatives under socialism" (PhD (Econ)). The main theme of her research is the standard of living of the peoples of the North and she has published widely on this theme. She is at present working on her doctoral dissertation. On June, 24, 1991 she was made an honoured economist of the Russian Federation. She worked on the draft of the self-government and self-financing proposal of the Yakut ASSR which was presented to Moscow at the end of 1989. When elected a people's deputy she was head of sector at the Institute of the Economy for the Development of the Natural Resources of the North.

In January 1990 she was nominated for election as an RSFSR people's deputy in the No. 145 Yakut national territorial district, Yakut ASSR. During the election campaign she advocated the transition of the republic to self-accounting and cost accounting, and devoted considerable attention to ways of reforming economic and financial policy. Many of the problems confronting the Yakut

ASSR could be solved by transferring jurisdiction over Union and RSFSR republican property to the Yakut ASSR.

There were 13 candidates. In the first round Kornilova polled 21.1% of the votes and won the second round, polling 63.5% of the votes. Her main opponent was T. S. Shamshurina, editor of the *Molodezh Yakutii* (youth of Yakutia) newspaper, who received 11% of the votes in the first round and 25.3% in the second round. Kornilova was elected a member of the RSFSR Supreme Soviet at the I Congress of People's Deputies (729 voted for, 194 voted against), and on October 1, 1990 she was elected chairwoman of the Council of Nationalities commission on the social and economic development of republics within the Russian Federation, autonomous *oblasts*, autonomous *okrugs* and small nations.

On March 5, 1991 she was elected to the working group on the preparation of draft documents on the Union treaty, and on October 14, 1991 she became a member of the group of deputies preparing for ratification the treaty on the economic commonwealth. On November 25, 1991 she was elected a member of the commission on the implementation of the decrees of the President. She is a member of the Sever (north) parliamentary group and the communists of Russia group. She is married with a son, Vladislav, a daughter, Aisena and a grandson, Dima. Her husband, Dmitry, successfully presented his candidate dissertation in geography (PhD).

Address: 103274 Moscow, K 274, Krasnopresnenskaya nab., d. 2, Dom Sovetov; *telephone*: Moscow 205 43 84.

Kornukov, Anatoly Mikhailovich

Air Defence Commander-in-Chief of Moscow district. Colonel-General of Air Forces.

Born on January 10, 1942 in Stakhanov, Lugansk *oblast*, Ukraine, into a working-class family. Russian. He graduated from Chernigov Higher Military Aviation Technical School of Pilots in 1964; the G. K. Zhukov Military Officers' Academy of Air Defence in 1980; the Military Academy of the General Staff in 1988. He received a higher military education and was a member of the CPSU till August 1991.

After graduating from technical school he served in air defence aviation, his first post being that of senior pilot. He was on alert and flew several types of interceptor-fighter. He was notable for his sound knowledge of aviation technology and tactical methods of conducting aerial combat. He was actively involved in the work of *Komsomol* and Party organizations. He enjoyed the support of superior officers and Party-political agencies.

His promotion was rapid; at the age of 32 he became commander of a fighter-plane regiment. His unit held a distinction in combat and political training. He was elected to the Party committee.

After the Academy, from 1980, he was a fighter air division and corps commander. A. Kornukov's record was that of an officer with excellent operational-technical training and high-flying professional skills. He was not actively involved politically, except as a member of the CPSU, which was essential for promotion.

From 1988 Gen. Kornukov was the first deputy commander of fighter aviation of the air defence troops of the USSR, the first deputy air defence formation commander. In 1989 he was appointed air defence corps commander, the corps including all types of air cover forces: aviation, anti-aircraft missile and radio-technical troops. He successfully commanded different types of troops and ensured high combat readiness.

At the time of the anti-constitutional putsch in August 1991 he was not active but fulfilled unquestioningly all orders and instructions from the General Staff and main air defence headquarters of the country, and the working bodies of the Emergency Committee. He ordered his units on to high combat readiness and ensured the air cover of important strategic objects against possible attacks.

On August 31, 1991 Air Force Col.-Gen. A. Kornukov was appointed Air Defence Commander-in-Chief of Moscow district, replacing Gen. Viktor Prudnikov, who had been promoted to Commander-in-Chief.

The troops under Gen. Kornukov's command provide air cover for the Moscow region and the capital of Russia and are constantly on alert. The General is an immediate subordinate of the Air Defence Commander-in-Chief and Moscow authorities.

He does not express his political convictions in public. He advocates a strong state; the reform of the armed forces to meet the demands of present-day war, and possession of the latest matériel and weapons.

A highly qualified military professional, with a talent for organization, sound operational-tactical and military-technical knowledge, Gen. Kornukov was awarded the title of military pilot, 1st class. He was also awarded two orders and several medals.

There is no information about his hobbies. He does not speak any foreign language and has not been abroad as a member of an official delegation. He is married with children.

Office address: Moscow, ul. Myasnitskaya.

Korolev, Vladimir Mikhailovich

Director-general of the second watch-making enterprise manufacturing association.

Born in 1947 in Uglich; Russian. He was a Member of the CPSU until August 1991. He graduated in 1970 from the radiotechnical institute, Ryazan, began working as an engineer in the Uglich watch-making enterprise in 1972 and by 1985 had become deputy director. In 1985 he was appointed chief engineer of the USSR Ministry of Instrument Making, and in 1987 he became director-general of the second watch-making enterprise manufacturing association. He has published articles on technical subjects and is the author of a number of inventions. His main hobby is finding ways to improve production efficiency. He is married with two children.

Address: 125040 Moscow, Leningradsky Prospekt 8; *telephone*: Moscow 251 2937.

Korotich, Vitaly Alekseevich

Former editor-in-chief of *Ogonek*; US correspondent of the newspaper *Vzglyadi drugie*.

Born on May 26, 1936 in Kiev; Ukrainian. He was amember of the CPSU until August 1991. He graduated in 1959 from the Kiev Medical Institute, and after graduation worked as a doctor in Kiev. His first article was published in 1954, and in 1961 he joined the USSR union of writers. He continued to work as a doctor in Kiev and successfully presented his candidate dissertation in medicine (MD). He edited several Ukrainian journals and newspapers in the 1960s, and in 1966 he ceased practising medicine and became secretary of the Ukrainian union of writers, remaining until 1969. He became a member of the CPSU in 1967, but had no fixed position until 1978. During this period he translated English language poets and writers and Russian writers into Ukrainian, and also wrote some poetry and lectured at several US universities. In 1978 he was appointed editor of the journal *Inostrannaya literatura* (foreign literature).

From 1981 to 1991 he was secretary of the USSR union of writers. In 1986 he was appointed editor-in-chief of the magazine *Ogonek* and co-chairman of the all-Union Aprel association of writers, and in December 1991 he was elected a member of the Russian union of writers. He transformed *Ogonek* into the flagship of *perestroika* and *glasnost* and he often stated that he had a direct line to President Gorbachev. Encouraged by Aleksandr Yakovlev, Korotich published many sensational articles and the magazine jumped from a readership of 300,000, publishing mainly reproductions of socialist realist art, to over 5 million. A special target was Stalin and his crimes. Korotich and Egor Yakovlev, editor-in-chief of *Moskovskie novosti*, became the most famous Soviet journalists, and Korotich was much sought after by the foreign media, especially television, for his comments on Soviet politics.

He did not stay in Moscow during the attempted coup of August 1991 but travelled to the US. He declined to return afterwards and resigned as editor-in-chief of *Ogonek*, which disappointed many who hoped that he would continue to fight for democratic views in Russia. He began lecturing at US universities and in January 1992 became the US correspondent of *Vzglyadi drugie*. He is married with two sons and speaks English.

Among his major published works are: collections of poems: *Golden Hands*, *Odour of the Heavens*, *Cornflower Street*, *Diary*; short stories and essays: *Oh, Canada!*, *Stars and Stripes*, *Man at Home*, *Perpendicular Spoon* (together with Imant Ziedonis), *Cubic Capacity*, *Reflections on a Visit to America*; novels: *Evil*

Memory, and *The Tenth of May*. He was awarded the Nikolai Ostrovsky prize of the Ukrainian *Komsomol* for his poems *Possibility* (1971-72).

Korovnikov, Aleksandr Venediktovich

Chairman of the Russian Supreme Soviet committee on invalids, war and labour veterans, social protection of the military and their families.

Born on April 30, 1955 in Gryazi, Lipetsk *oblast*, into a military family; Russian. He was a member of the CPSU from 1976 to August 1991. He graduated from the Higher Political Technical College, USSR Ministry of Internal Affairs (MVD), and the V. I. Lenin Military Political Academy in 1986. He is a lieutenant-colonel. In 1976 he became deputy commander for political affairs of a regiment; then deputy head for political affairs of a sergeants' school (1979-81); deputy commander for political affairs of a battalion (1981-83); deputy commander for political affairs of a military unit (1986-88); and head of political affairs of a military unit (1988-90).

He was elected an RSFSR people's deputy in March 1990 and is a member of the Council of the Republic. He was elected deputy chairman of the Russian Supreme Soviet committee on invalids, war and labour veterans and the social protection of the military and their families in 1990, and in 1991 was elected its chairman. He is a member of the Presidium of the Russian Supreme Soviet. He is married and his wife, Natalya Vladimirovna, is an industrial economist. They have a daughter.

Address: 103274 Moscow, K 274, Krasnopresnenskaya nab., d. 2, Dom Sovetov.

Korovyakov, Igor

Chairman of the Party of Free Labour.

Born in 1947. He graduated from the faculty of philosophy, Moscow State University, and after graduation worked in the Institute of Technical Aesthetics. From 1979 to 1988 he was a metalworker in the Moscow city repair technical enterprise and in 1988 he became chairman of the *Posrednik* co-operative.

The Party of Free Labour was founded in January 1991. It unites those involved in free labour: those working in co-operatives, lease holders and those in the creative professions working on patents. Its main task is to campaign for the rights of entrepreneurs and support this new stratum in society. The composition of the stratum who are entrepreneurs has no significance, in his view, except that it would consist of former Party officials and mafiosi. There is no distinction between those who produce public goods, but nevertheless these representatives often do not know how to work within a competitive market and do not last, on average, more than six to seven months. He is married with two children and lives in Moscow.

Kosolapov, Richard Ivanovich

Co-leader of the Russian Communist Workers' Party.

Born in 1930 in Volgograd *oblast*, he is a Russian of Cossack lineage. He was a member of the CPSU until August 1991. In 1962 he successfully presented his candidate dissertation in philosophy on "Communism and the liberation of the working person" (PhD) and graduated from the department of philosophy, Academy of Social Sciences of the Party Central Committee. In 1970 he successfully presented his doctoral dissertation in philosophy on "Socialism and the problems of the liberation of labour" (DLitt). He was editor-in-chief of the Party journal, *Kommunist*, professor and head of the department of historical materialism, faculty of philosophy, Moscow State University, and devoted many years to research, journalism and political work. He was a delegate to three Party congresses, was elected twice a member of the Party Central Committee and USSR Supreme Soviet. He was awarded three orders.

He is the author of over 200 publications, including the following books: *On the Question of the Dialectic of Goods under Socialism* (1961); *Communism and Freedom: The Problem of the Liberation of Labour* (1965); *Communist Labour: Nature and Stimulus* (1968); *In the Shadow of Utopia. Socialism: Questions of Theory* (1971); *The XXIV Party Congress on the Social and Political Development of Soviet Society* (1972); *Socialism. On Questions of Theory* (1975); *Socialist Society. Social and Philosophical Problems of Contemporary Society* (1975); *Developed Socialism: Problems of Theory and Practice* (1979); *Freedom and Responsibility* (1969); *The Origin of Personality* (1979); *On the Most Important. Ten Years of Varied Work* (1983); and *Leading Communist Construction* (1983).

In early 1990 he was nominated by the work collective of the Klimovsky mechanical punch factory for election as an RSFSR people's deputy in the No. 9 Podolsky national territorial district, Moscow *oblast*. During the election campaign he advocated honest, principled relations with electors and preference for those living on wages, pensions and student grants. He called for the avoidance of budget deficits and believed that the national economy should be subordinate to the real needs of the person and the working family. Workers in state enterprises should be afforded the chance of earning as much as those in co-operatives. Labour should be valued not according to expenditure and profits but by the quantity and quality of production.

He advocated reducing prices in line with the increase of labour productivity, and that co-operative prices should fall to the level of state prices, public output should be subordinate to the needs of the environment, the level of technology should be raised and inventions should be made use of in Russia. He was in favour of freedom for intellectual creativity, freedom of speech, meetings, joining together to form public organizations and free access to the mass media. He called for more ordinary workers to be elected to state authorities and for the renaissance of the national dignity of the Russians and those who live in Russia. Full sovereignty, in his view, was one of the prerequisites for the saving of the Union. He was in favour of the Russian Communist Party of Labour being integrated in the CPSU.

He was against the concealment of shadow capital and its alliance with the bureaucracy, the sale of national riches and territories, the insulting and discrediting of the USSR armed forces and the replacement of general democracy by élite power groups. There were 11 candidates and Kosolapov lost in the first round, polling 3.27% of the votes. V. P. Lukin, co-ordinator of the group for analysis and forecasting of the USSR Supreme Soviet, was elected people's deputy. He received 12.26% of the votes in the first round and 46.57% of the votes in the second.

Kosolapov is well known for consistently arguing in favour of the priority of the interests of the working class, intelligentsia and co-operative peasantry, for an alliance of labour, science and democracy and against corruption, and he actively supported the cleansing and renewal of Soviet society. From the 1960s he demonstrated that Soviet society had not passed beyond the stage of the transition from capitalism to socialism, and concluded that the programme of Nikita Khrushchev, launched in 1961, to achieve communism, beginning in 1980, was utopian.

He supported restructuring based on socialist, democratic and patriotic principles and argued in favour of more precise economic, social and political goals which were closer to the working masses. The Russian Communist Party of Labour emerged from the movement for a communist initiative, and after August 1991 the movement decided to found a new communist party to replace the dissolved CPSU. Kosolapov spoke at the constituent congress of the new party on November 24, 1991 in Ekaterinburg and was elected to the leading bodies of the party. He is in favour of socialism and is opposed to the private ownership of the means of production, and exploitation. He advocates power for the working people, members of the intelligentsia and peasants, and opposes the consumer "paradise" of the West and the authoritarian system of the "iron fist".

He does not believe that the models of development should be out of step with history. It is necessary to take into account the particularities of the country, the way of life and the psychology of the average worker. Decisions should be taken by the working class and the industrial intelligentsia and not by career advisers from academic and diplomatic milieux. He is opposed to full economic cost accounting, taxes on the wage fund and higher prices. He is regarded as the leader of the moderate, intellectual wing of the Russian Communist Party of Labour. He is married and lives in Moscow. His wife works in the Russian Academy of Sciences, and he has two children from his first marriage.

Kostikov, Vyacheslav Vasilevich

Head of the Press Office of the President of the Russian Federation.

Born in 1940; Russian; member of the CPSU until August 1991. Both his father and mother were from Ryazan peasant stock and moved to Moscow in the 1920s, escaping from poverty and hunger. His father worked as a news vendor. Kostikov had great difficulty with mathematics at school but loved history, Russian language and literature. He also loved to draw and sang in the choir in the palace of pioneers. After completing school he entered a technical secondary school and worked two years as a turner in a factory. Then he entered the faculty of journalism, Moscow State University, and during his practical experience went to the Virgin Lands (the rapid expansion of the sown area, predominantly in northern Kazakhstan and western Siberia, launched by Khrushchev in 1954). During his last years as a student his reports were published by Novosti. When he graduated in 1967 he joined Novosti, and after the founding of the Russian information agency he joined as a columnist. He was sent to London on an exchange between Novosti and the *Daily Mirror* and studied for three months at the University of Sheffield.

He graduated from the faculty of international economics in the Academy of Foreign Trade, at the end of the 1960s, and in 1972 joined the secretariat of UNESCO in Paris. He spent about ten years in France, and speaks French and English well. In France he began writing detective novels, many of which were published in various journals. He regards Yulian Semenov as having the greatest formative influence on him, and he wrote philosophically ironic prose. He has written *Brilliance and Poverty of the Nomenclature* (1989); *Mistral (Political Novels* (1988); *Bridges on the Left Bank: Tales* (1988); *Heir; a Novel* (1985); *We Shall Not Damn Banishment . . . Roads and Fates of the Russian Emigration* (1990); *Vernisage: Tales* (1990); *Glimmers of Freedom: Extracts* (1991). Among his recent books is the novel *Dissonance of the Siren* which is about the Russian intelligentsia and culture.

Kostikov has published many articles which have made him well known in Russia and abroad, and among his colleagues he was rated a first-class journalist. He published regularly in *Izvestiya*, *Ogonek*, and other periodicals and in recent years has been a regular columnist on the *Times of India*.

In May 1992, by decree of the President of the Russian Federation, he was appointed head of the press office of the President. He was recommended for the post by Mikhail Poltoranin, a former colleague on Novosti. Kostikov believes that he is a member of the presidential apparatus because he is a convinced democrat and a person who is not an extremist. To work effectively one has to be politically involved and to be able to work in a team. It is pointless in politics to talk about everything since there are too many contradictions and nationality problems. If a particular type of information is fed to journalists and the public it can have serious consequences.

After leaving the Party he decided never again to become a member of any association or group. He wishes to be an independent journalist and person. His relations with the opposition are various: he has no contact with the extremists, but with the rational, moderate opposition, for example, Civic

Union, he maintains normal working relations. Kostikov decided in these difficult times when the country is going through a political and economic quagmire to work for the President and his team. If the President goes he is prepared to go as well.

He is married and his wife is a journalist who is concerned with sociology of the media. His daughter graduated from the faculty of journalism, Moscow State University, and works for the radio.The family keeps up the old tradition of reading aloud to one another. His favourite authors are Nikolai Gogol, Anton Chekhov, Fedor Dostoevsky and Mikhail Bulgakov. He loves meat and home cooked dishes. He lives in Moscow.

Kotelnikov, Vladimir Aleksandrovich

Chairman of the council for international co-operation in the exploration and use of outer space (Intercosmos).

Born on August 24, 1908 in Kazan; Russian. He was a member of the CPSU 1948 to August 1991. He graduated in 1931 from the Institute of Power Engineering, Moscow, and was then appointed a lecturer in the institute. He successfully presented his candidate dissertation (PhD (Eng)) and his doctoral dissertation (DSc (Eng)), and became a professor of the institute in 1947. In 1953 he was elected an Academician of the USSR Academy of Sciences, and in 1954 was appointed director of the institute of radio engineering and electronics, USSR Academy of Sciences. In 1970 he became Vice-President of the USSR Academy of Sciences, and from 1973 to 1980 he was Speaker (chairman) of the RSFSR Supreme Soviet.

In 1980 he was appointed chairman of the Intercosmos council of the USSR Academy of Sciences, and in December of the same year he was elected an Academician of the Russian Academy of Sciences. He is the author of many scientific articles on the development of radio reception, overcoming radio interference, potential interference proof theory, and on radio location of Mars, Venus and Mercury. Many of his articles remain classified.

He is the recipient of many awards including: hero of socialist labour (1969 and 1978); the USSR state prize (1943 and 1946); the Lenin prize (1965); six orders of Lenin; the Popov gold medal (1974); the Keldysh gold medal; and the Lomonosov gold medal of the USSR Academy of Sciences (1982). He was elected an honorary member of the American Institute of Electronics and Radioelectronics in 1964; a foreign member of the Czechoslovak Academy of Sciences in 1965; an honorary doctor of technology of the Higher Technical School, Prague in 1967; a foreign member of the Polish Academy of Sciences; a foreign member of the Mongolian Academy of Sciences in 1983; and a foreign member of the Bulgarian Academy of Sciences. His hobby is skiing. He is married with a child.

Address: 117901 Moscow V-71, GSP-1, Prospekt Lenina 14; *telephone*: Moscow 954 3006.

Kotenkov, Aleksandr Alekseevich

Head of the state and legal administration of the President of the Russian Federation. Major-General.

Born in 1952 into a working-class family. Russian. He graduated from the agricultural machine-building institute in Rostov-on-Don in 1974; completed an extramural course at the V. I. Lenin Military Political Academy with distinction in 1988. He received a higher political education and was a member of the CPSU from 1977 to August 1991.

After graduating from the institute he worked as a production engineer in the Rubin plant, Rostov-on-Don. In June 1975 he joined the Soviet army. For three years he was a tank platoon commander in the Trans-Baikal military district. He was very active politically, and had the reputation of being a careerist, focusing mainly on his work in Party organizations. In 1978 on the Party committee's recommendation he was transferred to Party political posts, which, in the military, ensured more rapid promotion. For 10 years Kotenkov was a political commander of a tank battalion and a tank regiment in the Trans-Baikal military district; from 1980 in the north Caucasian and from 1986 in the far East military districts. He implemented CPSU policy and proved himself a convinced communist who did not question Marxist-Leninist dogma. He was highly regarded by his superior officers. From 1988 he was deputy head of the political department of the military garrison in Birobijan. The advent of *perestroika* and the revival of political and social life in the USSR saw him express unusual views about the history of the CPSU and current events in the country.

In early 1990 Kotenkov was nominated for election as a RSFSR people's deputy in the No. 257 Birobidzhan territorial district. During the election campaign he advocated all power to the soviets, freed from the *diktat* of other agencies. He held that the functions of soviet and Party agencies should be delineated, as well as legislative and executive power. He favoured the introduction of various types of ownership of land and freedom for enterprises to set their own budget. Regional groups of deputies should be set up to maintain constant links with electors. All draft legislation should be frankly discussed and referenda held on particularly important laws. All forms of ownership should be equal before the law and every work collective free to decide its own form of ownership. The agencies of state and political administration in the USSR and RSFSR should be delineated, each Union republic should have real economic and political sovereignty within the USSR, national territories should have economic autonomy and self-government and national cultures should be promoted. The armed forces need fundamentally restructuring.

There were three candidates. Kotenkov polled 34.2% of the votes in the first round and won the second round, polling 50.4% of the votes. His main opponent was B. L. Korsunsky, first secretary of the Birobidzhan Party *obkom*, who received 28.4% of the votes in the first round and 36.5% in the second.

During the anti-constitutional putsch in August 1991 Kotenkov was one of the organizers and leaders of the defence of the Russian White House. He participated in talks with military commanders. After the defeat of the coup he was elected deputy chairman of the Russian Supreme Soviet committee on defence and security and was simultaneously chairman of the Soviet of the Republic commission of the USSR Supreme Soviet on defence and security. He was promoted to Colonel and became one of the closest associates of President Boris Yeltsin on military affairs. He was concerned with the reform of the armed forces, the banning of the CPSU and democratization in the military. He participated in the investigations into the involvement of the military leadership in the attempted coup. When, late in 1991, the presidential state and legal administration was set up, he became head of the law-enforcement agencies and problems of defence and security department, and deputy head of the department. Its chairman was Sergei Shakhrai.

Kotenkov is not popular among democratic military men. He is disliked for his careerism and for his rapid promotion to Major-General. Many democrats in the military are suspicious of his active communist past and his quick renunciation of former convictions and ideals. In May 1992, he was appointed head of the state and legal administration and thus became one of the main associates of the President on the reorganization of the armed forces, on state security, the law-enforcement agencies and the constitutionality of legislation. He does not regard the state legal administration as a state administration but as fundamentally an agency of the President. The administration is responsible for vetting all normative acts which emanate from the President and government, but the administration itself does not have the right to issue its own acts. In Kotenkov's view, the President was correct to set up consultative and co-ordinating structures; the legal administration is his agency which guarantees the legal side of the President's activities. It co-ordinates all the activity involved in setting norms and investigates the consequences of government decrees for the decisions being made by the President.

One of the most important functions of the legal administration is to provide a legal information service which makes known to the public the activities of the government and the President. The legal administration, Kotenkov points out, is the only agency of the government and President which does not have any relations with former Party structures. This is a new agency which does not contain anyone from the Party Central Committee apparatus. Kotenkov was one of the President's main representatives during the case brought by the CPSU in the constitutional court of the Russian Federation, which challenged the legality of the banning of the Party in August 1991. He supervised the preparation and analysis of archival documents presented to the court. He was very active in court and succeeded in proving convincingly the unconstitutional character and criminal essence of the Communist Party.

He is influential politically and is one of the organizers and ideologists of the national patriotic party, and a member of the coalition of movements which support the reform policy of the Russian leadership. He does not reveal much about his interests and hobbies. He does not have a good command of foreign languages and has not been abroad as a member of an official delegation. He values the privileges which the new Russian élite has inherited from the former communist system. He has been awarded five medals. He often appears in the press on social and political issues. For instance, his article, "We should set up a ministry of military reform" on military planning, appeared in *Krasnaya Zvezda* on April 14, 1992. He is married.

Official address: 103132 Moscow, ul. Ilyunka, Dom 10.

Kotsiuba, Oleksandr Pavlovych

Chairman of the Ukrainian Supreme Soviet Committee on Legislation and Legality.

Born into a Ukrainian family in 1939. He studied at Kiev State University and then worked as a lawyer. He successfully presented his candidate dissertation on "The legal regulation of the citizen who works on the land in 1984" (LIM). A long-standing Communist Party member (until August 1991), he was elected people's deputy for the Radianskyi *raion* in Kiev city in 1990 (on the second round).

In the Supreme Soviet he heads the committee on legislation and legality, a rough equivalent of the US house rules committee, although it does not have the same clearing committee powers. It shares some of its functions with the committee for draft legislation, headed by Vladimir Griniov, of which Kotsiuba is also Deputy Head. He is an *ex officio* member of the influential Supreme Soviet Presidium. Although Kotsiuba had the reputation of a typical *apparatchik*, he soon showed a certain independence of mind in his position.

At the time of his election in 1990 he was thought to be associated with the opposition, but he soon defected to the conservative camp, voting for the arrest of the radical deputy Stepan Khmara in November 1990. *Rukh* therefore organized an unsuccessful campaign to cancel his deputies' mandate in early 1992. Kotsiuba campaigned against Kravchuk's creation of a State *Duma*, or council of presidential advisers, in February 1992, arguing that it was unconstitutional and that it usurped the powers of the government and the Supreme Soviet.

He also attacked the draft new Ukrainian Constitution, published in July 1992, as authoritarian, and concentrating too much power in the hands of the President. He was not alone in this opinion, and Kravchuk was forced in October 1992 to concede the abolition of the *Duma* and the transfer of emergency powers to the Cabinet of Ministers, as the price for the creation of the new Kuchma government. In December 1992 Kotsiuba caused a storm following the Russian Supreme Court's lifting of President Yeltsin's ban on local branches of the Communist Party by suggesting that the decision to ban the Communist Party in Ukraine was similarly unconstitutional.

Official address: Kiev, Vul. M. Hrushevskoho 5; *telephone*: Kiev 252 019.

Kovalev, Aleksandr Yakovlevich

Head of the Administration of Voronezh *oblast*, Russian Federation.

Born on September 30, 1942; Russian; member of the CPSU until August 1991. He began his working life as an assistant to a machinist, and then received secondary specialized education, graduating from the Railway Transport Technical College, Voronezh. In 1987 he was appointed deputy general director of the production association for heavy mechanical presses and in 1988 became general director.

In March 1990 he was nominated for election as an RSFSR people's deputy in the No. 335 Comintern territorial district, Voronezh *oblast*. During the election campaign he advocated the restoration of the moral, cultural and religious values of Russia, and stated that Russia should remain within the USSR but have autonomy and equal legal relations with other republics. The way out of the economic crisis was to grant autonomy to all enterprises and they should decide themselves how they were going to operate.

There were seven candidates. Kovalev polled 25.9% of the votes in the first round and won the second round, polling 63.9% of the votes. His main opponent was V. I. Yudin, head of department of radiotechnical systems, Voronezh Polytechnical Institute, who received 26.4% of the votes in the second round. Kovalev was also elected a deputy of the Voronezh city soviet of people's deputies, and was a member of the parliamentary faction "communists for democracy".

In August 1991, at the VII session of the city soviet, Kovalev was elected chairman of the Voronezh city executive committee. On April 11, 1992 he was appointed head of the main administration of Voronezh *oblast* by presidential decree, and regarded his main task as solving agricultural problems and establishing a contractual relationship between the countryside and the towns for the sale of agricultural and other products.

In December 1992 he stated he was not in favour of the convocation of the VII Congress of People's Deputies because the majority of deputies were not capable of solving the complicated economic and political problems. He regarded the President's speech at the congress as not well thought out and blamed those around him for this. Kovalev is married with a son and lives in Voronezh.

Kovalev, Sergei Adamovich

Member of the Council of the President of the Russian Republic; member of the Russian Supreme Soviet Council of Nationalities.

Born on March 2, 1930. Russian. He graduated from the faculty of biology of Moscow State University, and in 1964 he successfully presented his candidate dissertation in biological sciences on the "Electric characteristics of the mio-cardinal fibres of the frog's heart" (PhD). He was never a member of the

CPSU. When elected a people's deputy he was an engineer in the institute for the problems of the transmission of information, USSR Academy of Sciences. He is well known for his defence of law, and for this he spent more than 10 years in prison and exile.

He was nominated for election as an RSFSR people's deputy in January 1990 in the No. 58 Chertanovsky territorial district, Moscow. In the election programme he advocated the transformation of the soviets into the only source of power within the country, the state and economic sovereignty of Russia, the rejection of Marxism-Leninism as the official state ideology, the annulment of clause 6 of the USSR constitution (on the leading role of the Party in society), the ending of the KGB's right to conduct political searches, freedom of activity for all public organizations, including political parties and independent trade unions, freedom of conscience, speech and the press.

The state's economic monopoly should be terminated, there should be equal rights for state, collective and private property, an opportunity for everyone to obtain land which can be passed on to their heirs. He appealed for the revival of the dignity and culture of all peoples living in the Russian Federation. Economic problems could not be resolved without taking into account the ecological situation in the region. The Army and military expenditure should be reduced and the savings allocated to social needs. The privileges of the *nomenklatura* should be abolished.

There were four candidates. Kovalev polled 53.7% of the votes in the first round and was proclaimed the winner. His main opponent was T. E. Khokhlova, deputy head of the No. 45 department of the militia, who polled 18.2% of the votes in the first round. During the election campaign Kovalev was supported by the Democratic Russia bloc and the Moscow Memorial society. He was elected a member of the Russian Supreme Soviet at the I Congress of People's Deputies.

He is a member of the Council of Nationalities, chairman of the Supreme Soviet committee on human rights and member of the constitutional commission. He participated in the activities of the parliamentary faction, Democratic Russia (DemRossiya), and coalition for reform of the deputies' group, bloc of the federation of independent trade unions, Moscow deputies, group on ethics and member of the faction, "accord for progress".

At the IX Congress of People's Deputies he opposed the premature terminating of the special powers of the President and voted in support of the President's TV address on March 20, 1993 on the introduction of a special regime in the country. Kovalev lives in Moscow.

Kovlyagin, Anatoly Fedorovich

Head of Administration of Penza *oblast*, Russian Federation.

Born in 1938 in the village of Blokhino, Bessonovsky *raion*, Penza *oblast*, into a large peasant family. He became acquainted with hard peasant work at a young age; Russian. He was a member of the CPSU from 1962 to August 1991.

In 1956 he entered Penza Agricultural Institute and graduated in 1961 as an agronomist. He wrote his diploma essay in his fourth year while working on one of the collective farms of the *oblast*. After graduating he was appointed instructor of the *oblast Komsomol* committee, head of department and first secretary of the Gorodishchensky *raion Komsomol* committee. In 1964 he became an agronomist in the Gorodishchensky agricultural production adminis-tration, then director of the Boyarovsky state farm, Kameshkirsky *raion*, and head of the Kameshkirsky *raion* agricultural production administration. In 1967 he moved into Party work.

He was first secretary of the Kolshleisky *raion* Party committee and achieved high marks in this post, especially in the social sphere. In 1974 he was confirmed as head of department of organizational Party work, Penza Party *obkom*. In 1979 he became a postgraduate student at the Academy of Social Sciences of the Party Central Committee. In 1982 he successfully presented his dissertation in economics on "Improving the management of the reproduction of the labour force in socialist agriculture" (PhD (Econ)).

After completing his postgraduate studies in 1982 he worked in the apparatus of the Party Central Committee as an instructor, then assistant to the head of department of organizational Party work. In 1986 he was assigned to the Penza *oblast* Party organization where he was elected second secretary and a member of the bureau of the Party *obkom*. On October 10, 1989 at a session of the *oblast* soviet, he was elected chairman of the soviet executive committee.

In 1990 he was nominated by the inhabitants of Serdobsk and the work collective of the Serdobsk electric lamp factory for election as a RSFSR people's deputy in the No. 573 Serdobsky territorial district. During the election campaign he advocated the election of a qualified group of deputies, calling on deputies not to deal in slogans and promises but to get down to practical details. He was in favour of strict labour and production discipline, raising the quality of output, the struggle against absenteeism and was opposed to the inefficient use of equipment in enterprises.

He outlined three priorities: finding a solution to the food problem, the housing problem and the ecological problem. He advocated the most rapid satisfaction of consumer demand, satiating the market with the most necessary goods, especially food products. He was standing unopposed since there had been no permission for other candidates to contest the election. He was elected on the first round unopposed with 82.5% of the vote, and was also elected a deputy of the Penza *oblast* soviet.

On August 20, 1991 he spoke at a meeting of the Presidium of the penza *oblast* soviet. He noted that the enterprises and organizations of the *oblast* were functioning normally, the situation was under the control of the executive and representative authorities, and all forms of state authority and administration were working normally on the territory of the *oblast*. The Presidium address called for the population to remain calm and confident and to devote all their energies towards solving the economic tasks. It appealed for the consolidation of all political parties and movements, for the stabilization of the economy and the re-establishment of law and order.

He was elected head of the administration of Penza *oblast* on April 11, 1993. He was awarded the order of Lenin, the badge of honour and medals. He is married and lives in Penza.

Kozyrev, Andrei Vladimirovich

Minister of Foreign Affairs of the Russian Federation.

Born on January 1, 1952 in Brussels, Belgium into a Russian family. His father was an engineer. He was a member of the CPSU until 1991. In 1968/69 he worked as a fitter in the Kommunar machine building enterprise in Moscow. In 1974 he graduated from the Moscow state institute of international relations of the USSR Ministry of Foreign Affairs. From 1974 to 1979 he was adviser, then senior adviser in the department of international organizations, USSR Ministry of Foreign Affairs. In 1977 he successfully presented his dissertation on the "role of the UN in the development of détente" in the institute of international relations. He was a candidate of historical sciences (PhD). From 1979 to 1980 he was attaché in the department of international organizations, USSR Ministry of Foreign Affairs. Between 1980 and 1986 he was third, second and first secretary of the department of international organizations. From 1986 to 1988 he was counsellor and head of department of the administration of international organizations. From 1988 to 1989 he was deputy head and from 1989 to 1990 head of the administration of international organizations. He was a member of the Soviet delegation at the UN. He never served in a permanent capacity abroad. He was one of the key advisers of Eduard Shevardnadze when he was Soviet Foreign Minister. In October 1990 Ivan Silaev, RSFSR Prime Minister, invited Kozyrev to leave the USSR Ministry of Foreign Affairs and take over the RSFSR Ministry of Foreign Affairs. He had the diplomatic rank of ambassador extraordinary and plenipotentiary.

Kozyrev quickly established himself as a supporter of Russian sovereignty. On August 20, 1991 he was sent by the Russian government to Paris and during the autumn of 1991 he helped to prepare the agreement between the governments of Russia, Ukraine and Belarus, which led to the formation of the Commonwealth of Independent States. In November 1991 he became Minister of Foreign Affairs of the Russian Federation. He is the author of several books on armaments control and the arms trade such as *No to the Trade in Death!*, Moscow 1980; *Arms Trade and Imperialist Politics*, Moscow 1985; *The Firepower Business (Arms Trade in Imperialist States)*, Moscow 1985; *We and the World in the Mirror of the UN*, Moscow 1991; *The UN: Structure and*

Activities, Moscow 1991. Kozyrev has played an important part in presenting the views of the Yeltsin administration to the outside world and attracting support for them. He always underlines his support of President Yeltsin. The chief tasks of Russian diplomacy, as far as he is concerned, include a radical reduction in the number of nuclear weapons, the eventual goal of which is the elimination of nuclear arsenals, and the ending of the arms race. He advocated Russia's membership of the International Monetary Fund (IMF) as a way of integrating Russia into the world market economy. To him the developed Western countries are Russia's natural allies. This has brought him into conflict with conservatives and nationalists who oppose the pro-Western slant of his foreign policy. They have accused him of kowtowing to the West in order to get aid and investment. He is the target of vitriolic attacks in the Congress of People's Deputies and the Supreme Soviet. His views, which can be labelled Atlanticist, are counterposed by those who regard Russia as both in Europe and Asia and therefore must conduct a policy which reflects this. They have been called the Eurasians. During 1992, Kozyrev's pro-Western foreign policy was balanced by Yeltsin's visits to China, South Korea and India. Kozyrev worked closely with the USA in the UN security council and supported sanctions against Serbia and Iraq. A close working relationship developed between the Russian ambassador to the UN and the USA and the UK. Russia also provided troops for UN peace-keeping operations in the former Yugoslavia and offered to help with the air drops to Muslims in Bosnia in February and March 1993.

Kozyrev has committed some diplomatic *faux pas*. One was in Stockholm in December 1992 at the meeting of the Council for Security and Co-operation in Europe, when he made a speech in which he warned of a complete reversal of Russia's foreign policy with Russia becoming a national, aggressive state. This backfired and he afterwards made a totally different speech. He made the spoof speech during the VII Congress of People's Deputies, and many observers expected him to lose his post; however, he survived.

In office he has lobbied hard for Western aid and investment in Russia, but only after the arrival of President Bill Clinton in office did his words begin to bear fruit. Germany had always been a close ally but could not rally enough financial support for Russia. Japan remained cool due to the inability of the two sides to resolve the dispute over the Kurile islands. Kozyrev was a keen supporter of Gaidar's economic package, including private ownership of land and property.

He speaks English, French, Spanish and Portuguese and is married with a 14-year-old daughter. He is fond of philosophy and painting. His favourite authors are Vladimir Nabokov and N. Gumilev. He lives in Moscow.

Kraiko, Aleksandr Nikolaevich

Russian scientist and politician.

Born in 1934 in Moscow. His father was an engineer who was killed at the front during the Great Fatherland War (1941-45), and his mother was a machine operator. He is Russian, and after completing school he entered the Institute of Physics and Technology, Moscow. After the revelations at the XX Party congress he decided on principle not to join the CPSU. In 1958 he began working in the P. I. Baranov Tsentralny Institute of Aviation Engine Construction, first as a technologist, then as an engineer, and from 1970 as head of the department of a division. In 1968 he successfully presented his candidate dissertation in physics and mathematics (PhD), and in 1972 successfully presented his doctoral dissertation in physics and mathematics on "Some variational tasks of gas dynamics" (DSc).

He was a member of the national committee of the USSR on theoretical and applied mechanics, and a member of the editorial council of the Mir publishing house. He is the author of articles, monographs and brochures, and he has six inventions to his name. In 1968 he began teaching at the Institute of Physics and Mathematics, Moscow, part-time, and in 1978 he was promoted to professor. In 1979 he bought a co-operative apartment. He was awarded the USSR state prize and the N. E. Zhukovsky prize, and is the founder of his own scientific school.

In 1989 he was nominated for election as a USSR people's deputy in the No. 3 Bauman territorial district. During the election campaign he outlined many obstacles to *perestroika*, and stated that changes could not take place painlessly. He advised that the work of the USSR Supreme Soviet should cease to be a ritual and become a creative process for drafting laws and the responsibility of all members. He advocated the transition of the national economy to a system of economic management; and the introduction of the market with a small surplus of consumer goods, especially food products. He maintained that the food problem could be resolved in three to four years if land were handed over to the peasants and their associations, for example, on a long lease. He favoured price control and social security payments to poor families; the modernization of industry; the development of medicine, education, housing and the protection of the environment. The resources should come from cutting back military and space expenditure, huge industrial projects (such as the project of the century of the USSR Ministry of the Water Economy to reverse the flow of some Siberian rivers) and the introduction of progressive taxation of co-operatives.

However, defence and space savings should not lead to the decline of design and scientific organizations. State orders were necessary, as were national programmes for the development and preparation of these organizations to compete in the international market of ideas, and he advocated their participation in large projects in association with Western companies. Only the Communist Party could overcome the forces of disunity, destabilization and totalitarian tendencies which were manifesting themselves.

There were two candidates and Kraiko won in the first round, polling 64% of the votes. His opponent, E. O. Adamov, director of the Institute of Energy

Technology and a member of the Sokolniki Party *raion* committee, received 27.52% of the votes. At the USSR Congress of People's Deputies Kraiko became a member of the interregional group of deputies. He was a member of the USSR Supreme Soviet committee on science, education, culture and training.

However, he soon left the interregional group of deputies. In 1991 he proposed that the Supreme Soviet should examine the possibility of depriving those deputies who were provoking the miners' strike of their parliamentary immunity. He referred to Democratic Russia and the interregional group as Bolshevik-type structures with strict discipline, based on democratic centralism, with no respect for the individual. During the autumn of 1990 he demonstrated that he was a passionate conservative, criticized the 500-day programme, the democrats and Boris Yeltsin, who were wrecking the country. He was one of the co-chairmen of the group for constructive interaction, which called for the neutralization of opposition intrigues, and he refused to appear in the TV programme *Vzglyad*, because he thought that there should be various points of view in a programme. He appealed for co-operation with the reformed CPSU and opposed calls by deputies for anti-democratic measures which are not adopted in any civilized country. He is married for the second time and has three daughters. He lives in Moscow.

Krasikov, Anatoly Andreevich

Head of the Press Office of the President of the Russian Federation.

Born in 1931; member of the CPSU until August 1991. He graduated from Moscow State Institute of International Relations and the Academy of Social Sciences of the Party Central Committee, and was a postgraduate student in the department of international relations and foreign policy. He successfully presented his candidate dissertation on "Spain in the military policy strategy of the West in the post-Franco period (1976-86)" (PhD), and in 1990 he successfully presented his doctoral dissertation in the department of world politics and international relations on "Spain in international relations 1945-89 (Evolution of its foreign policy orientation)" (DLitt). Krasikov worked for thirty years in TASS as a journalist, editor, correspondent, political columnist and head of the agency in Italy and France.

He was head of a group of political columnists, on the main editorial board for news from abroad, and from 1978 to 1992 was deputy general director of TASS. During the summer of 1991 he openly opposed the then information policy of the agency and was informed that he was to be demoted, but after the collapse of the attempted coup he remained in his post. After the attempted coup the staff made him general director of TASS, although he never took up the post. Afterwards he was head of the department of international affairs of *Nezavisimaya gazeta* (independent newspaper). He was also official representative of the USSR in the international programme for the development of communications, UNESCO, for ten years and also lectured in the faculty of journalism, Moscow State University.

He is a leading specialist on the Vatican, and on Spain. He has written the books *Reporting Spain* (1981); *Spain after Franco* (1982) which was about the experience of Spain during the transition from dictatorship to democracy; *Spain and World Politics: Half a Century of Diplomatic History* (1989); *Reporting the Vatican* (1990); *Vatican: History and the Present Day* (1991). He recently wrote a review of the book by the French journalist, Bernard Le Comte, *Truth Must Prevail Over Lies. How the Pope Defeated Communism*.

Krasikov was appointed head of the press office of the President of the Russian Federation by presidential decree of August 6, 1992. He is respected by democratically minded journalists, although those on *Nezavisimiya gazeta* always retain their scepticism of him. Among world newspapers Krasikov singles out *The Washington Post*, *The Times* (London), *Le Monde* and *El Pais* (Spain), as papers which are distinguished by their wide general coverage of news and their respect for their readers. They are not didactic in presentation but allow readers to judge for themselves, and he believes that the Russian media should also not instruct but inform Russians. Among novels he has recently read are *The Dissonance of the Siren* by Vyacheslav Kostikov and *Nineteen Eighty Four* by George Orwell, and he selects Cervantes as one of the writers whom he finds most illuminating. He speaks Spanish, French, Italian and English. Krasikov lives in Moscow.

Krasnoyarov, Evgeny Alekseevich

Head of Administration of Sakhalin *oblast*, Russian Federation.

Born on November 24, 1939 in the village of Kholbon, Shilkinsky *raion*, Chita *oblast*. His forbears were trans-Baikal Cossacks. In 1957 he entered the Dalnevostochnoe Naval college, Nakhodka, and after graduation he was a sailor: third, second and first mate of the captain of the Korsokovsky base of ocean-going fishing vessels. A few months later he had moved into *Komsomol* work but again went to sea. He graduated as an external student from the Far East fish technical college.

He was captain and director of a large fishing trawler for many years, but, at the end of 1980 he was assigned to the apparatus of the Sakhalin fish industry, becoming deputy general director of an association. His main concerns were foreign economic links and the safety of the fishing vessels. In 1988 he was general director of the Russian-Japanese joint venture, Pilenga Godo, which specialized in the cultivation of strains of salmon and has survived despite the economic crisis. He worked for over 30 years in the fish industry and did not get involved in politics.

At present Krasnoyarov is completing his studies in the school of business, University of Portland, Oregon, and is sitting an examination in the Khabarovsk branch of the US university. He speaks English and is preparing his diploma project.

He was nominated for the post of head of the administration to the President of the Russian Federation as one of eight candidates. On March 31, 1993 he was nominated to the President as a possible candidate for the post of head of administration at a session of the *oblast* soviet. On April 2, 1993 the *oblast* soviet confirmed his nomination and on April 13, 1993 he was appointed head of administration of Sakhalin *oblast* by presidential decree.

Krasnoyarov intends to continue the changes introduced by his predecessor Valentin Fedorov, but with some corrections. He believes that serious business should not only take into account present-day interests but also long-term goals and work towards them. For Sakhalin *oblast* fishing offers the best prospects for the future. Considerable attention now should be paid to the ecology, otherwise correcting mistakes will cost ten times as much. The federal authorities and the entrepreneurs should conduct a single policy, as economic separatism, in his view, is a transient illness. Only the central authorities have the means to create great energy and financial resources, and private business is not capable of doing this. There is a way out of the economic crisis and he is against returning to the system which failed. He is convinced of the value of the market, believing that absolute equality is not possible, the individual has to fight for his survival, mutual relations between people should be regulated by the market and people are equal only in the sense that they have the right to improve their lives.

Nevertheless Russia should not enter the market in one leap and he views the 500-day programme as being politically and economically absurd. It is necessary to work for 20 years, 15 hours a day, in order to raise Russia to the level of a modern economy. Bankruptcy should be introduced and enterprises closed down, and then when the economy is stronger they can be reopened and modernized. The main barrier to the introduction of the market is the psychology of social levelling in which Soviet people have been indoctrinated for 70 years. It will therefore need a long transition period in order to overcome it.

This will require deliberate centralization, the regulation of economic activities which ensure the economic freedom of the citizens and the free development of the territory. Separatism arises from the desire of the centre to acquire for itself greater administrative control than is necessary, and Krasnoyarov advocates the adoption of a new constitution, based on market principles, in the near future. Since the Congress of People's Deputies will never accept it the only solution is to convene a constituent assembly (constitutional assembly). Russia needs a presidential republic with a bi-cameral parliament.

All developed countries have by one route or another ended up with the same variant of a liberal democratic state which is the optimal variant for social development. President Yeltsin should be afforded what he needs since his political intuition is to seek to bring peace to society. All-Russian elections are needed with the representatives of political parties and movements participating. The President made a mistake in not founding his own party; he has to make compromises with parliament since plebiscites promote a new round of political conflict which, in turn, is dangerous for the territorial integrity of Russia. He also proposed that elections for the head of administration should be postponed for a year to allow leaders to appear and form support groups.

He was awarded the orders of the Red Banner of Labour and the October Revolution and the silver medal of the Exhibition of Economic Achievements, Moscow. He is married with two children and three grandsons, and lives in Yuzhno-Sakhalinsk.

Kravchuk, Leonid Makarovych

President of Ukraine.

Born into a Ukrainian peasant family in 1934 in the village of Velykyi Zhyttyn in what is now Rivne *oblast* in the traditionally nationalist region of western Ukraine. In Kravchuk's youth, the area was a stronghold of the Ukrainian nationalist army, the UPA, which maintained its armed struggle against the Red Army into the late 1940s. After Kravchuk's election as President of Ukraine in 1991, myths began to circulate to the effect that he had collected money for the UPA in his teens, and even that his father had been killed by the Red Army, but such rumours say more about the politics of the 1990s than about the probable facts of the 1940s.

Like many bright peasants' sons of his generation, Kravchuk soon benefited from rapid upward social mobility. After education at Kiev State University, he worked as a lecturer in economics from 1958 to 1960 at the financial technical college in Chernivtsi *oblast*, before transferring to full-time Party work in 1960 in the Chernivtsi *obkom* department of agitation and propaganda. He successfully defended his candidate dissertation in Moscow in 1970 on "The essence of profits under socialism, and their role in collective farm production" (PhD). He was promoted to work in the *apparat* of the Central Committee of the Communist Party of Ukraine (CPU), firstly in the department preparing cadres for Party work, then from 1980 in the propaganda and agitation department, and from 1988 to 1990 in the ideological department, rising to the position of secretary for ideology in 1989, and achieving membership of the Ukrainian Politburo and the position of second secretary in the CPU in June 1990.

After July 1990, he was a member of the CPSU Central Committee in Moscow. During this period, Kravchuk developed close relationships with the Ukrainian cultural intelligentsia, as the *de facto* supervisor of their work. In the TV debates that led up to the first congress of the opposition movement *Rukh*, in September 1989, it was Kravchuk who was chosen to front the case for the CPU against *Rukh* spokesmen such as the philosopher Myroslav Popovych. He acquitted himself well, although he earned much hostility for his broken promise to the first *Rukh* congress that the organization would be officially registered in time to participate in the March 1990 republican elections. In the new Supreme Soviet elected in March 1990 Kravchuk was chosen as Chairman, when Volodymyr Ivashko departed to Moscow in July, partly because of his supposed ability to come across well on TV. As yet, there was still little to mark him out from his colleagues, and his election was in fact boycotted by the opposition.

However, over the winter of 1990-91 the CPU began to split under the twin pressures of Ukraine's push for sovereignty and the turn to the right in Moscow. Kravchuk was well placed to lead the emergent "national communist" faction, as the CPU in the Supreme Soviet was more inclined to co-operate with the opposition than the CPU *apparat*, now led by Stanislav Hurenko. The split was formalized in January 1991, when the Presidium of the Ukrainian Supreme Soviet broke with the official CPU line by condemning the events in the Baltic. Thereafter, the political initiative passed to Kravchuk, who manoeuvred skilfully to maximize Ukrainian sovereignty in the weeks leading up to the attempted August 1991 state coup. Kravchuk revealed the cautious side of his nature during the coup itself, declining to condemn the plotters until it was clear who would emerge victorious.

Thereafter, however, Kravchuk, partly because of his equivocal behaviour in August, embraced the national communist cause with enthusiasm. He campaigned hard for the new post of Executive President (with the right to govern by decree) on the slogan "statehood, democracy, prosperity, spirituality and trust", placing most emphasis on the likely economic benefits of independence, and trust in his position as the only candidate able to unite the different regions and interests of the fragile young state.

He triumphed on December 1, 1991, with 19,643,481 votes, or 61.59% of the total. He won support across the board, but fared best in rural and small town areas, and in the east and south. Kravchuk quickly amassed other powers: he declared himself Commander-in-Chief of the new Ukrainian armed forces on December 12, 1991, and since July 1992 has headed a Council of National Security. He also strengthened the institution of the presidency by creating a *Duma* (Council) of presidential advisers in February 1992, although its members frequently quarrelled with the Council of Ministers and it was replaced by a series of "Presidential Commissions" in October 1992.

Kravchuk also imposed a system of directly appointed prefects to enforce presidential rule in Ukraine's regions in March 1992. The draft of the new Ukrainian constitution published in July also promised to increase his powers. Despite accumulating considerable theoretical authority, Kravchuk has used it cautiously. Like the early Gorbachev, he has tried to maintain his position as the indispensable centrist, courting both left and right. From 1990 to 1992 this was a popular course, as so many centrifugal forces threatened Ukraine, and his support in public opinion polls held up around the 50% level throughout 1992. However, as the economic crisis deepened, there were increasing calls for him to take a firmer hand, particularly as he had made little use of the emergency economic powers granted him in the spring. Kravchuk came out of the October 1992 government crisis with his powers and reputation somewhat diminished. He lost Premier Vitold Fokin, and was unable to impose Valentyn Symonenko as his first choice as successor.

New Premier Leonid Kuchma forced Kravchuk to dissolve the *Duma* and the Co-ordinating Council for Economic Reform set up in July 1992, and sanction the transfer of emergency economic powers to the government for six months from November 1992. Hence Kravchuk was forced back into his reserved domain of foreign and defence policy, but may have been happy to see others take responsibility for economic reform at a time of deepening crisis. In May 1993 Kravchuk provoked a political crisis by asking the Supreme Soviet to restore his powers, appoint him as head of the Council of Ministers and create the new position of Vice-President to oversee the government. However, the Supreme Soviet voted instead to restore the *status quo ante* in November 1992, which seemed likely merely to prolong the constitutional struggle among the various branches of state.

Official address (of the President's *apparat*): 252005 Kiev, Bankivska Boulevard 7; *telephone*: Kiev 226 2442.

Kress, Viktor Melkhiorovich

Head of the Administration of Tomsk *oblast*, Russian Federation.

Born in 1948; he is a graduate and was a member of the CPSU until August 1991. He has been living in Tomsk *oblast* since 1971. He began his career as an agronomist in the Kornilovsky state farm, then was director of the Rodina state farm, Tomsk *oblast*, and has devoted many years of his life to agriculture. Until April 1990 he was first secretary of the Pervomaisky *raion* Party committee.

In March 1990 he was elected a deputy of the Tomsk *oblast* soviet of people's deputies and at its first session, in April 1990, he was elected chairman of the soviet executive committee. On August 23, 1991 at the plenum of the Tomsk Party *obkom*, Kress declared that he was resigning from the Party *obkom* because of the unprincipled position adopted by the first secretary of the Party *obkom*. However at the fifth extraordinary session of the Tomsk *oblast* soviet it was noted that in his commitment to the President of the RSFSR and his new course, Kress had nevertheless had adopted a wait and see policy of neutrality. He stated that he had acted consciously and deliberately since he had not wished to provoke any passions.

In October 1991 he was appointed head of the administration of Tomsk *oblast* by presidential decree, and on assuming office he as before supported the policy of economic reform of the Russian government. He would attempt to increase the economic autonomy of the *oblast*, expand contacts with other regions and utilize the economic and scientific potential of the *oblast* more fully. He favoured the establishment of international links and the attraction of foreign capital. As someone who had previously worked in agriculture he viewed the measure of economic success to be first and foremost greater agricultural production, and this was not possible without the introduction of differing types of economic activity with priority being afforded lessees and private farming.

On January 12, 1992 an election was announced to the RSFSR Congress of People's Deputies, in the No. 698 territorial district, because the deputy,

N. T. Vedernikov, had been elected to the Constitutional Court of the Russian Federation. Kress was nominated by the collectives of the Stepanovsky, Chernorechensky and Tomsk state farms. However, a week before the election he withdrew as a candidate stating that this was because of the instability of the *oblast* and lack of time to campaign. He declared that he preferred to work rather than to waste his time on politics. He lives in the village of Pervomaiskoe, Tomsk *oblast*.

Krivchenko, Albert Arkadevich

Head of the Administration of Amur *oblast*, Russian Federation.

Born on December 22, 1935 in Komsomolsk, Amur *oblast*, where his parents were the builders of the city. He is Russian, and was never a member of the CPSU. In 1951 the family moved to Blagoveshchensk, and after finishing school he worked as a fitter, and chauffeur in the motor column No. 275. He graduated from the faculty of journalism, Urals State University and was on the staff of the newspapers, *Amur pravda* and *Bloknot agitatora*. He was special correspondent of TASS in Amur *oblast*, is the author of seven books and has received state awards.

In March 1990 he was nominated for election to the RSFSR Congress of People's Deputies in the No. 24 Amur national territorial district. During the election campaign he advocated the development of the collective and state farms on a par with lessees and individual peasant farms. He declared that the soviets of people's deputies should be the only state authorities in the republics and the Soviet Union.

There were seven candidates. Krivchenko polled 17.6% of the votes in the first round and won the second round, polling 52.2% of the votes. His main opponent was V. N. Shilov who received 45.9% of the votes in the second round. He was a member of the Supreme Soviet committee on the media, links with public organizations and mass citizen movements and the study of public opinion, and had previously been deputy chairman of this committee. He belonged to the parliamentary faction "non-party deputies", and the bloc of deputies "coalition for reform", and was previously a member of the *glasnost* group of deputies.

On October 8, 1991 he was appointed head of the administration of Amur *oblast* by presidential decree, and on assuming office he stated that he was completely in agreement with the policy of the government on agriculture. Equal opportunities should be afforded all forms of ownership and all types of economic activity, and entrepreneurship should be taken seriously, especially small-scale, since, in Krivchenko's view, it was the only thing that could save Russia in the near future. The export of raw materials should cease and the most advanced technology should be acquired and used. Russia now needed to move to a civilized market economy and the policy of economic reform would be very harsh and rigorous.

In December 1992 he viewed the VII Congress of People's Deputies as conservative, reactionary and in no way expressing the views of the people. It was distancing itself not only from the government but from reform as well. He is married with two daughters and and a granddaughter.

Kruglov, Anatoly Sergeevich

Chairman of the state customs committee of the Russian Federation; Minister.

Born on March 25, 1951 in the village of Ulyanki, Moscow *oblast*; Russian. He was a member of the CPSU until August 1991. He graduated from the Lobnin Industrial Technical College and the all-Union Extra-mural Institute of Law. In 1973 he was appointed inspector, later senior inspector, head of department, and deputy head of the customs at Sheremetevo airport; head of the Chkalov customs, Moscow *oblast* (1984-87); head of department, and deputy head of administration, chief administration of the state customs control, USSR Council of Ministers (1987-90); and head of customs at Sheremetevo airport (1990-91). In December 1991 he was appointed chairman of the state customs committee of the Russian Federation. He is married with two daughters and lives in Moscow.

Kryuchkov, Vladimir Aleksandrovich

Member of the Extraordinary Committee.

Born on February 29, 1924 in Volgograd into a working-class family; Russian; member of the CPSU from 1944 to August 1991. In 1941 he began working as a marker in factories in Volgograd and Gorky (Nizhny Novgorod). In 1943 in Volgograd he was the *Komsomol* organizer on the building site, and later became secretary of the Barrikadny *raion* committee (*raikom*), then second secretary of the city *Komsomol* committee. In 1946 he entered the Procurator's office in Volgograd *oblast*. He was a people's investigator of the Procurator's office in Traktorozavodsky *raion*, Procurator of the investigative department of the Procurator's office and Procurator in Kirov *raion*, Volgograd.

In 1949 he graduated from the all-Union extra-mural institute of law and in 1954 from the Higher Diplomatic School, USSR Ministry of Internal Affairs. In 1954 he became third secretary of a department, USSR Ministry of Internal Affairs, and in 1955 he was appointed third secretary in the Soviet embassy, Budapest, Hungary. In 1959 he became an official in the apparatus of the Party Central Committee: he was a reviewer, head of sector of the Party Central Committee department for liaison with communist and workers' parties of socialist countries. In 1965 he became an assistant of a secretary of the Party Central Committee; from 1967 he occupied leading posts in the USSR KGB; in

1978 he was appointed its deputy chairman and in 1988, chairman of the USSR KGB. In March 1990 he became a member of the USSR presidential Council. He was a delegate to the XXV, XXVI, XXVII Party congresses and the XIX Party conference.

He was a member of the Party Central Committee from 1986 and from September 1989 to July 1990 a member of the Party Politburo. He was elected a member of the USSR Supreme Soviet in 1986, and in 1988 he was promoted to the rank of general of the Army. He is the recipient of two orders of Lenin, the order of the October Revolution, the Red Banner, two orders of the Red Banner of Labour, the order badge of honour and medals.

He was a member of the Extraordinary Committee in August 1991 and many observers see him as the organizing brain behind the failed coup. He was arrested on August 21, 1991 and dismissed as chairman of the USSR KGB on August 22, 1991. During the investigation he was incarcerated in the *Matrosskaya tishina* isolator. He and the other conspirators were later released and their trial began in April 1993. After his release Kryuchkov was actively involved in the opposition to President Yeltsin and participated in many demonstrations organized by the national Salvation Front, including that on May 2, 1993 which resulted in about 150 police and civilians being injured. It was the worst violence in Moscow since the failed coup.

Kryuchkov is married and his wife Ekaterina Pavlovna is a teacher of Russian language and literature. They have two children and live in Moscow.

Kryzhanivskyi, Volodymyr Petrovych

Ukrainian Ambassador to Russia.

Born into a Ukrainian family in 1940 in Vinnytsia *oblast* in central Ukraine. He was educated at Kiev Institute of Engineering and Building Science, and from 1963 to 1990 worked as an engineer. He joined the opposition movement *Rukh* at an early stage, and was associated with its liberal centrist wing. After 1990 he was close to the Party of Democratic Revival of Ukraine (PDRU). In March 1990 he was elected a people's deputy (on the second round) for the Left Bank district in Kiev city, and was the head of the Supreme Soviet sub-committee on the agreement of Ukrainian law with international standards of human rights.

In August 1991 he was appointed Ukraine's first "Permanent Representative" in the RSFSR. As a centrist, he helped to cement Kravchuk's growing alliance with the old opposition, whereas a radical nationalist would have offended Russia. Kryzhanivskyi, on the other hand, was close to the PDRU, which had long favoured the maintenance of friendly relations with Russia. His post was upgraded to Ambassadorial status in 1992.

Kubarev, Eduard Alekseevich

Speaker of the Supreme Soviet of the Chuvash Republic, Russian Republic.

Born in 1939 in the village of Kozlovka, Kozlovsky *raion*, Chuvash ASSR; a Chuvash. In 1962 he graduated from the construction engineering institute, Kazan, and in 1976 from the Higher Party School of the Party Central Committee. He began his career in 1962 as a foreman work superintendent of the SU-2 trust No. 16, USSR Ministry of Construction, in Rybinsk, Yaroslavl *oblast*, and then he became chief engineer, and head of the construction administration. From 1972 to 1974 he was deputy chairman of the executive committee of the Proletarsky *raion* soviet of people's deputies, Rybinsk and in 1974 he moved to Cheboksary where he was head of the PMK-137 Chuvash rural construction trust, and deputy manager of the trust. From 1986 to 1990 he was manager of the *Spetsstroi* construction design trust of the Chuvash agro-industrial association.

He was elected a deputy of the Supreme Soviet of the Chuvash ASSR and in 1990 he was elected first deputy Speaker of the Supreme Soviet of the Chuvash ASSR. The VI extraordinary session of the Supreme Soviet condemned the role of the Speaker, A. M. Leontev, during the attempted state coup of August 1991. On August 29, 1991, at the VI extraordinary session of the Supreme Soviet, Kubarev was elected Speaker of the parliament.

He took a negative view of the proceedings of the VII Congress of People's Deputies in December 1992 and underlined the fact that "in the country in reality an anti-nomenclature revolution had taken place but the main legislative agency had not undergone any changes". He supported the government of Egor Gaidar, seeing it as "consistently implementing a policy of raising the sovereignty of the republic and the autonomy of the regions". He is married with two sons and two daughters, and lives in Cheboksary.

Kuchma, Leonid Danylovych

Prime Minister of Ukraine.

Born into a Ukrainian family in 1938, Chernihiv *oblast* in central Ukraine. He studied mechanical engineering at Dnipropetrovsk State University, and straight after graduating in 1960 began his 32-year career at the massive *Pivmash* (short for *Pivdennyi mashynobudivnyi zavod* or "Southern Machine-building Factory") missile-building complex near Dnipropetrovsk. The plant employs somc 50,000 workers and produced the USSR's Scud, SS-4, SS-5 and SS-18 nuclear missiles, However, it has also always produced tractors, and since Mikhail Gorbachev's conversion drive of the late 1980s has switched some of its production to trolleybuses.

Kuchma worked his way up in the factory as engineer, senior engineer, senior designer, and then deputy chief designer. From 1975 to 1982 he was the secretary of the communist party committee at the plant, and from 1982 to 1986 deputy general designer. In 1986 he was appointed general manager of the plant. In March 1990 Kuchma was elected a people's deputy for Dnipropetrovsk. In the Supreme Soviet Kuchma kept something of a low profile, but made good political alliances with both Vasyl Evtukhov, leader of the industrialists' faction, and (not surprisingly, given his background) with Viktor Antonov, the Minister for Heavy Industry. By 1991 Kuchma was identified as a national communist supporter of Leonid Kravchuk, and hence began to develop good contacts with the former opposition.

In April 1992 he was appointed to the President's advisory *Duma* on economic affairs, and in May 1992 to the newly-formed President's advisory Council of Businessmen and Industrialists. When former Premier Vitold Fokin resigned on September 30, 1991 Kuchma was the candidate pushed by both the industrialists' lobby and by *New Ukraine*. Kuchma's appointment as Premier was ratified by the Supreme Soviet by 316 votes to 23 on October 13. In a separate vote, the Supreme Soviet also gave him the power to appoint his ministers for parliamentary ratification *en bloc*. Although three-quarters of ministers from the Fokin government were reappointed, all the Vice-Premiers were replaced in the new administration and most economic portfolios were given to pragmatists or representatives of the industrial lobby.

Kuchma also strengthened his position by forcing Kravchuk to dissolve the state *Duma* and the Co-ordinating Council on Economic Reform, which had functioned as rival power centres to the government. Moreover, the special powers granted to the presidency in spring 1992 to govern the economy by decree were transferred to the government for six months beginning in November 1992. On November 9 Kuchma further strengthened his powers when he was appointed as the head of the new State Commission for Monetary Reform, empowered to oversee monetary reform and the possible introduction of a new Ukrainian currency. Although Kuchma was initially inclined to support a partial restoration of central planning, a series of meetings with the then Russian Prime Minister Egor Gaidar in autumn 1992 convinced Kuchma that this was impossible (Ukraine could not restore a centralized economy on its own). Thereafter Kuchma's approach was pragmatic.

Some of his measures were designed to recentralize the economy, others to quicken the pace of economic reform. He also pledged to clamp down on corruption, and restore economic links with Russia. At the same time he promised to keep an open door to radical outsiders, such as Volodymyr Cherniak, the *Rukh* economist, and Volodymyr Lanovyi, although the latter were openly critical of the new government's crab-like approach by spring 1993. Kuchma found it difficult to push through the radical reforms he had promised, and in May 1993 asked the Supreme Soviet to accept a prolongation of his special powers, and grant him control over both the National Bank of Ukraine and the State Property Fund in charge of privatization. When it refused, Kuchma resigned on May 20. The Supreme Soviet, however, voted by 212 votes to 90 to refuse to accept his resignation, whilst at the same time also rejecting President Kravchuk's alternative proposal to head the government himself. A period of prolonged constitutional instability seemed likely to follow.

Official address (Council of Ministers): 252008 Kiev, Vul. M. Hrushevskoho 12/2; *telephone*: Kiev 293 7442.

Kudryavtsev, Gennady Georgievich

Chairman of the council of directors of the Intertelecom joint stock company.

Born in 1941 in the village of Slavinka, Maritime *krai*, RSFSR; Russian. He was a member of the CPSU until August 1991. He graduated in 1974 from the all-Union institute of electrical engineering. From 1958 to 1959 he was a diesel operator in an urban power station, and from 1959 to 1969 he was a student, then electrician and served in the Soviet army. From 1969 to 1970 he was a senior engineer; between 1970 and 1974, head of department; and then deputy head of the main administration of linear cable and radio relay communication facilities, USSR Ministry of Communications (1979-80). In 1980 he was appointed first deputy USSR Minister of Communications, and in 1991 he became USSR Minister of Communications. In November 1991 he was appointed chairman of the council of directors of the Intertelecom joint stock company.

He was awarded the orders of the October Revolution, and of the badge of honour. He is married with two children.

Address: Moscow, ul. Tverskaya 7, 103 GSP; *telephone*: Moscow 292 5691.

Kukharets, Volodymyr Oleksiiovych

Head of the National Guard of Ukraine.

Born in 1938 into a working class Ukrainian family in the town of Okhtyrka in the north Ukrainian *oblast* of Sumy. He worked in a Kharkiv factory before doing his national service and was then educated at the M. V. Frunze Military Academy, after which he served in the internal guards, eventually becoming first a battalion commander in Dnipropetrovsk, and finally a colonel.

As part of Ukraine's state-building measures in the wake of the Declaration of Independence in August 1991, a 6,000-strong National Guard was created in November 1991 drawn from Ministry of Internal Affairs (MVD) troops already stationed in Ukraine. Kukharets was appointed its first head, and declared his intention of building up its future strength to around 30,000 men. Kukharets was also made responsible for providing guards for ceremonial occasions and for the protection of Ukrainian and visiting dignitaries. He is also an *ex officio* member of Ukraine's Defence Council. He is less keen on the Ukrainianization of the Armed Forces than Morozov or the nationalist Union of Officers of Ukraine.

Telephone: Kiev 226 2252.

Kulakov, Mikhail Petrovich

Chairman of the council of the Seventh Day Adventists of the CIS; President of the Europe and Asia department of the general confederation of the Seventh Day Adventists.

Born on March 29, 1927 in Leningrad; Russian. He graduated in theology in the US and is a doctor of theology. From 1962 to 1976 he was pastor of communities of Seventh Day Adventists in Alma Ata and Chimkent, Kazakh SSR, and then from 1976 to 1990 he was senior preacher of the communities in the Russian Federation. In 1990 he was elected chairman of the Seventh Day Adventists council, in 1991 he was elected chairman of the all-Union council of the Seventh Day Adventists, and in 1992 of the council in the CIS and president of the Europe and Asia department of the general confederation of the Seventh Day Adventists. He is married with six children and speaks English.

Address: Tula, ul. Furmanova 26; *telephone*: Moscow 476 5348 (home); Tula 25 4966.

Kuliev, Avdy

Foreign Minister of the Republic of Turkmenistan.

Born in 1936 in Ashkhabad; Turkmen. He was a member of the CPSU until August 1991. He graduated in 1960 from the Maxim Gorky Turkmen State University and in 1976 from the Academy of the USSR Ministry of Foreign Affairs, where he successfully presented his candidate dissertation in philology (PhD). From 1960 to 1971 he was a scientific assistant, Institute of Language and Literature, Turkmen Academy of Sciences, then junior scientific assistant, Institute of Asia, Turkmen Academy of Sciences, and later was appointed head of the Russian language training courses in the Soviet cultural centre, Aden, Yemen People's Democratic Republic.

In 1971 he transferred to diplomatic work. From 1971 to 1987 he held various diplomatic posts in USSR embassies in Arab countries, and from 1987 to 1989 he was chargé d'affaires in the Soviet embassy in Oman, Qatar. Then he was appointed to the USSR Ministry of Foreign Affairs, Moscow, where Eduard Shevardnadze was Foreign Minister, as counsellor in the department of the Middle East and north Africa.

In 1990 he was appointed Minister of Foreign Affairs of the Turkmen SSR, and later the same year became Minister of Foreign Affairs and Foreign Economic Relations of the Turkmen SSR. In December 1991 he became Minister of Foreign Affairs of the Republic of Turkmenistan, and was also appointed a member of the presidential Council of the republic.

Address: Ministry of Foreign Affairs, Ashkhabad.

Kulsharipov, Marat Makhmutovich

Chairman of the Bashkir National Centre, Ural, Republic of Bashkortostan, Russian Federation.

Born on January 7, 1941 in the village of Zerikli, Kugarchinsky *raion*, Bashkir ASSR. His father, who had worked on a collective farm, was killed in action during the Great Fatherland War (1941–45). His mother is now a pensioner and worked previously on a collective farm.

He graduated from the faculty of history, Bashkir State University, and is a qualified historian. In 1971 he completed his postgraduate studies in the faculty of history, Moscow State University, and in 1973 successfully presented his candidate dissertation in history on Tsarist policy in Bashkiria (1775–1800) (PhD). In 1971 he joined the faculty of history, Bashkir State University. He is at present assistant professor in the faculty of history of Bashkiria at the university.

In February 1991, at the V all-Bashkir congress, he was elected chairman of the Bashkir national centre, Ural. He is one of the most active ideologists of the Bashkir national movement. He advocates full independence of the Republic of Bashkortostan from the Russian Federation. He opposed the initialling and signing by the leadership of the republic of the Federal treaty with the Russian federation. He proposes that the Bashkir language be recognized as a state language. In his view all the troubles of the Bashkir people are due to Russian and Tatar expansion. He has published over 20 articles in the republican press during the last two years on national sovereignty, culture and language.

He is married. His wife, Fauzika is the daughter of ordinary rural dwellers. They have two adult daughters who are graduates. His hobby is reading.

Address: Ufa, ul. Rabkorov, Dom 5, kv. 36.

Kuptsov, Valentin Aleksandrovich

Secretary of the Central Committee of the Russian Communist Party.

Born on December 4, 1937 in the village of Mindyukino, Cherepovetsky *raion*, Vologda *oblast*, into a peasant family; Russian. He was a member of the CPSU until August 1991. He began his career as a collective farm worker in 1955, then became head of a reading room in Ulomsky *raion*, Vologda *oblast*, and from 1956 to 1958 he served in the Soviet army. In 1958 he began working in Cherepovets as a sheetmetal worker, as foreman of presses, and in 1966 he graduated as an external student from the North West Polytechnical Institute as a metallurgical engineer. He was elected secretary of the Party committee of the shop, and deputy secretary of the Party committee of the enterprise.

In 1974 he became second, then first secretary of the Cherepovets Party city committee and in 1984 was elected second secretary of the Vologda Party *obkom*. In 1985 he became an inspector of the Party Central Committee, and also in 1985 he was appointed first secretary of the Vologda Party *obkom*. In 1986 he was elected a member of the Party Central Committee, and in 1988 he graduated from the Higher Party School, Leningrad.

In 1989 he was elected a USSR people's deputy for Velikoustyugsky territorial district, Vologda *oblast*. From December 1989 to June 1990 he was a member of the Russian bureau, Party Central Committee, and in March 1990 he was elected chairman of the Vologda *oblast* soviet of people's deputies. In April 1990 he became head of the department for social and political organization, Party Central Committee. In July 1990 he was elected a secretary of the Party Central Committee and was a delegate to the XXVI, XXVII, XXVIII Party congresses and the XIX Party conference.

In July 1991 he was elected first secretary of the Central Committee, Russian Communist Party. After Party activity was banned he was one of the initiators of the appeal to the Constitutional Court about the legality of the ban and was a witness during the hearing. He has been secretary of the Central Committee of the Russian Communist Party since February 1993.

He was awarded the order of Lenin, two orders of the Red Banner of Labour, the order of the badge of honour and medals. He is married and his wife, Lyudmila Alekseevna, was a metallurgical engineer, but is now a pensioner. They have two daughters; Natalya who is a teacher and Irina who graduated from Leningrad State University, and grandsons. He lives in Moscow.

Kuramin, Vladimir Petrovich

Chairman of the state committee for the social and economic development of the North, Russian Federation; Minister.

Born on January 7, 1937 in the village of Bakury, Bakursky *raion*, Saratov *oblast*; Russian. He was a member of the CPSU until August 1991. He graduated from the road transport institute, Saratov, then later became a postgraduate and successfully presented his candidate dissertation in technical sciences (PhD). After graduating from the institute he was a works superintendent, head of a department, and head of a section of the Tobolsk city construction administration, Tyumen *oblast* (1959-61); head of administration, and senior works superintendent, No. 23 administration of construction, Tyumen council of the national economy, Tobolsk, Tyumen *oblast* (1961-63); deputy head, then head of department of the Tyumenobstroi trust, USSR Ministry of Industrial Construction, Tyumen (1963-67); deputy manager of the Tyumenobstroi trust (1967-68); chief engineer of the Tyumengorstroi trust (1968-69); manager of the Tyumengorstroi trust, Tyumen (1969-70); head of the department of construction Tyumen Party *obkom* (1970-74); head of the main administration on the construction of enterprises of the oil and gas industry, USSR Ministry for the Construction of Enterprises of the Oil and Gas Industry (1974-81); and chairman of the inter-departmental territorial commission on the development of the north Siberian oil and gas complex and head of the department of

Gosplan, Tyumen (1981-83). In 1983 he was appointed deputy USSR Minister for the Construction of Enterprises for the Oil and Gas Industry, Moscow.

In 1986 he became deputy chairman of the bureau of the USSR Council of Ministers on the fuel and energy complex. In 1991 he was appointed first deputy Minister of Fuel and Energy of the Russian Federation, and in February 1992 he became chairman of the state committee of the Russian Federation on the social and economic development of the North with the rank of Minister of the Russian Federation. In April 1992 he was also appointed chairman of the state commission on the Arctic and Antarctic.

He was awarded the USSR state prize, the prize of the USSR Council of Ministers, the orders of the October Revolution, and Red Banner of Labour. He is married and his wife, Lyudmila Stefanovna, is a doctor. They have a son and two daughters.

Kuzmin, Anatoly Alekseevich

Deputy Commander-in-Chief of the navy for combat training; chief of combat training in the navy. Vice-Admiral since 1984.

Born on March 12, 1933 in Leningrad. Russian. Kuzmin graduated from the Higher Naval Technical School, with a degree in navigation, in 1955; the Higher Classes for Officers in 1966; the Naval Academy in 1971. He received a higher naval education, and was a member of the CPSU until August 1991.

He began his career as an officer as a commander of a navigation section of a base mine sweeper. A year later, in 1956, he became commander of a navigation section of the *Bunar*, a rescue vessel. He demonstrated exceptional naval abilities and a sound navigational and command training. He was actively involved in the work of the Party organization. He enjoyed a good reputation with superior officers and Party political agencies. He took part in a number of important rescue operations. Later, he requested a transfer to the submarine forces and, from 1960 to 1969, was commander of a group, of a navigational section, assistant commander, senior assistant commander and a submarine commander. He participated in many long voyages at sea, ensured the fulfilment of a number of important tasks and maintained the high level of the submarine's combat readiness. He repeatedly proved himself an experienced and resolute commander with an excellent naval, tactical and technical training, supporting the domestic and foreign policy of the CPSU. After graduating from the Academy in 1971 he was appointed Chief of Staff, deputy commander of a submarine sub-division of the Northern fleet; in 1974 a sub-division commander. He was regarded as a promising and experienced naval officer. Between 1978 and 1981 he was Chief of Staff, deputy commander of a submarine squadron of the Northern fleet; was an efficient commander of formations in the north Atlantic and Arctic oceans and was frequently at sea.

In 1981 Adml Kuzmin was promoted to commander of a submarine squadron of the Pacific Fleet and it did not take him long to master the demands of a completely new theatre, different in its military, political and geographic conditions. From 1984 to 1987 he was commander of an operational squadron of the Pacific Fleet which served in the Indian Ocean and came into direct contact with the US and allied navies. Kuzmin succeeded in defending the state interests of the USSR despite the political instability of the region. In 1987/88 he was first deputy Commander-in-Chief of the Red Banner Black Sea fleet, concentrating on versatile training and a high level of combat readiness. In 1988, Vice-Adml Kuzmin was appointed deputy Commander-in-Chief of the Navy for combat training. Due to the specific character of the post Kuzmin did not engage in politics, being responsible for the military and combat training of all forces and combat facilities of the navy. He frequently participated in operational formations, headed various inspection and test commissions, and took part in voyages, manoeuvres and exercises. He was a non-Party military professional. Like almost all members of the top military élite he is a conformist who recognizes any superior authority in a way which typically reflects the education and service in the Soviet armed forces. He supports the concept of a strong state, of Great Russia and the adoption of a hard line in relations with the former republics of the Soviet Union and foreign countries. He is interested in the history of the navy and Russia. He has been awarded several orders and medals. He is married.

Official address: 103175 Moscow K-175, Bolshoi Kozlovsky pereulok.

Kuznetsov, Boris Yurevich

Head of the Administration of Perm *oblast*, Russian Federation.

Born in 1935 in Kirov *oblast*; Russian; member of the CPSU until August 1991. He graduated from the Institute of Engineers of Marine Transport, Gorky (Nizhny Novgorod), as an engineer pilot. In 1954 he worked in the Kama river steamship company as third mate on the General Vatutin steamship, and later he was second, then first mate. He was a captain for several years and headed the safety service for navigation and pilotage of the Kama river steamship company. He was first deputy head and from 1985 head of the Kama marine steamship company.

In 1990 he was elected a deputy of the Perm *oblast* soviet of people's deputies and in April 1990, at the first session of the soviet, he was elected chairman of the permanent planning and budgetary commission of Perm *oblast* soviet. In November 1991 he was elected a member of the small soviet of Perm *oblast* soviet. Six candidates were nominated for the post of head of the administration of Perm *oblast* by the soviet and proposed to the President and 40 out of 145 deputies voted for Kuznetsov. The key role in selecting the head of the administration was played by V. Makharadze, chief government inspector of the RSFSR and head of the control administration, who interviewed all the candidates. Kuznetsov was recommended and confirmed by the soviet.

On December 12, 1991 Kuznetsov was appointed head of the administration of Perm *oblast* by presidential decree, and on assuming office Kuznetsov declared that he regarded his key duty to be the honest implementation of the reforms of President Yeltsin. The proposed liberalization of prices would be hard but unavoidable during the transition to the market.

In December 1992 he declared that he hoped the new government of Viktor Chernomyrdin would continue the reform course of the Gaidar government. Kuznetsov is married with a son and lives in Perm.

Kuznetsov, Evgeny Semenovich

Head of the Administration of Stavropol *krai*, Russian Federation.

Born in 1938; Russian; member of the CPSU from 1972 to August 1991. From 1983 to December 1989 he was general director of the Elektroavtomatika scientific production association, and in 1990 he was elected first secretary of the Oktyabrsky Party *raion* committee, Stavropol.

In 1990 he was elected a people's deputy of Stavropol city soviet and in April of that year, at the first session of the soviet, he was elected chairman. He advocated very rapid democratization, a transition to a market economy, based on competition between various types of ownership and an effective system of social security, the annulment of article 6 of the USSR constitution (on the leading role of the CPSU in society), the establishment of a *Rechtsstaat* (law-governed state) and the extension of the rights of local soviets.

In August 1991 he opposed the Extraordinary Committee and declared that only the decrees of the RSFSR President and decisions of the RSFSR Supreme Soviet were valid in Stavropol. On October 24, 1991 Kuznetsov was appointed head of the administration of Stavropol *krai* by presidential decree. When he became head of the administration he stressed that the most important aspects of economic reform were budgetary and tax policy, the programme of action connected with the liberalization of prices, the legal guaranteeing of the functioning of the national economy, questions of social security, privatization, land reform, changes in the system of executive power, depriving the apparatus of the ability to distribute resources and personal responsibility of officials.

He advocated the structural reorganization of the economy and the banking system, the development of interregional and foreign trade links, various forms of ownership in the countryside and the deployment by the Yeltsin administration of some aspects of the command-administrative system. In December 1992 he stated that the results of the VII Congress of People's Deputies signified the division and parity of power in the country. He proposed a presidential republic, but believed that parliament should act as a restraining force and a counterweight. He judged that the change of government would mean that the decisions of the executive would be more restrained. However, he had a high opinion of the work of Egor Gaidar in attempting to break quickly the old economic mechanisms, but in doing so incorrect policies were inevitable. He lives in Stavropol.

Kuznetsov, German Serapionovich

Deputy Prime Minister of Kyrgyzstan.

Born in 1948 in Ivanovo, Ivanovo *oblast*, RSFSR; Russian. He was a member of the CPSU from 1979 to August 1991. He graduated in 1971 from the Krasnoyarsk polytechnic, and in 1988 from the Academy of Social Sciences, CPSU Central Committee, where he successfully presented his candidate dissertation in economics (PhD (Econ)). He began his working career as an electrician in Saratov. He then served in the Soviet army. After demobilization he was an engineer, and deputy head of department of the television factory, Krasnoyarsk.

In 1972 he transferred to *Komsomol*, and in 1979 to Party work: he was deputy secretary of the Party committee in the factory; later he was a Party instructor, Krasnoyarsk *obkom*; secretary of the Party committee of the Krasnoyarsk combine building enterprise; and first secretary of the Divnogorsk city Party committee. In August 1987 he was elected secretary of the Bishkek city committee of the Communist Party of Kyrgyzstan, and was also elected a people's deputy of Kyrgyzstan.

In November 1990 he was appointed a member of the presidential Council of Kyrgyzstan. From January 22, 1991 to March 1992 he was Vice-President of Kyrgyzstan (Askar Akaev was President), and in March 1992 he was appointed deputy Prime Minister of the Republic of Kyrgyzstan. He is married with three children.

Address: Government House, 720003 Bishkek; *telephone*: Bishkek 218935.

Kuznetsov, Vladimir Sergeevich

Head of the Administration of Maritime *krai*, Russian Federation.

Born in 1954; Russian; member of the CPSU until August 1991. After graduating from the A. A. Andreev Railway Engineering Technical College, Moscow, he served in the Soviet Pacific Fleet, and after being demobbed he graduated from the Moscow State Institute of International Relations, USSR Ministry of Foreign Affairs. He then began postgraduate studies at the institute of the world economy and international relations, USSR Academy of Sciences, and successfully presented his candidate dissertation in economics on "The world economy and international economic relations" (PhD (Econ)). In 1983 he began working in the Far East department of the USSR Academy of Sciences, and became deputy director for scientific work in the institute of economics and the problems of utilizing the oceans, Far East department of the USSR Academy of Sciences.

His research concentrated on the problems of foreign trade and economic co-operation in the Asian Pacific region, especially integrating the development of the Soviet Far East into the international division of labour. He combined his academic work with practical participation in the development of business ties between organizations and enterprises in Maritime *krai* and firms and companies in the countries of the Asia Pacific region, the organization and running of international conferences, symposia and meetings on questions of economic co-operation. He was a member of the Far East department of the Soviet association of assistance to the UN, the *Znanie* (knowledge) society and other public organizations.

At the first session of the Maritime *krai* soviet in April 1990 he was elected chairman of the soviet executive committee from seven candidates. In August 1991 he set up a consultative group composed of representatives of the *krai* soviet executive committee, Vladivostok city soviet executive committee, the Pacific Fleet, the health authorities, work collectives and the border troops. A state of emergency was not introduced in the *krai*, and at an extraordinary session of the *krai* soviet the activities of the leadership of the *krai* soviet executive committee were judged correct.

On October 8, 1991 Kuznetsov was appointed head of the administration of Maritime *krai* by presidential decree. On assuming office he advocated the development of market relations but a balanced, sensible transition in all activities and a gradual, step by step approach to reform. In his view the appointment of the heads of administration by the President was not contrary to democratic practice. He is married with a daughter and lives in Maritime *krai*.

Kvasov, Vladimir Petrovich

Head of the Apparatus of the Government of the Russian Federation.

Born in 1936 in Shaturo, Moscow *oblast*; Russian; member of the CPSU until August 1991. He began his working life as a furnaceman in a metallurgical combine, but then graduated from the Institute of the Oil and Gas Industry, Moscow. He was head of the secretariat of L. Ryabev, deputy chairman of the USSR Council of Ministers, responsible for the fuel and energy complex, and was then appointed deputy head of the department of capital construction of the Gazprom concern, whose director was Viktor Chernomyrdin. He was appointed head of the apparatus of the Russian government in January 1993. He lives in Moscow.

Laar, Mart

Prime Minister of the Republic of Estonia.

Born on April 22, 1960 in the Estonian SSR; Estonian. He graduated in 1983 from the University of Tartu in history. An historian, he was a co-founder of the Estonian Heritage Society (1987), and has published several works on the Soviet take-over of Estonia and the crimes committed at that time. He was a founding member of the Estonian Christian Democratic Union (modelled on the German CDU) and was a strong and active proponent of Estonian independence from the USSR. He was a member of the Council of Estonia and a deputy of the Estonian Supreme Soviet (1990).

In the first democratic elections after independence, on September 20, 1992, Pro Patria (or Fatherland coalition of five conservative parties) won just over half the 101 seats in the *Riigikogu* (parliament). On October 5, 1992 the parliament elected Lennart Meri President of the Republic, although he had only polled 29.5% of the votes and been soundly defeated by Arnold Rüütel, an ex-communist, he received 59 extra votes mainly due to the majority enjoyed by the Pro Patria coalition. Rüütel did remarkably well in the presidential election, given that no communist was elected to parliament.

Meri nominated Laar as Prime Minister on October 8, 1992 and on October 21 he announced his government, consisting of three political groups which have a bare majority in the *Riigikogu*. In addition to Pro Patria, the administration included Moderates and members of the ENIP.

Address: Parnu mut 195-96, Tallinn 200016; *telephone*: Tallinn 510 845 .

Lakhova, Ekaterina Filippovna

Adviser of the President of the Russian Federation on the Family and the Protection of Mothers and Children.

Born in 1948; member of the CPSU until August 1991. She graduated from the Institute of Medicine, Sverdlovsk, and worked for many years as a divisional paediatrician. She was deputy head of the main administration of health of Sverdlovsk *oblast* soviet executive committee on the protection of mothers and children.

In early 1990 Lakhova was nominated for election as a RSFSR people's deputy in the No. 654 Zhelezhodorozhny territorial district, Sverdlovsk. During the election campaign she stated that the main concern of the state should be the health of its children. Up-to-date polyclinics and diagnostic centres should be built and the most modern technology should be available and great attention should be paid to handicapped children and expectant mothers. Pregnancy should not only be at the centre of medical attention but of society as a whole. The material resources for child health should be made available. She objected to the fact that parliament was dominated by economists and managers. Specialists, including medical ones, were needed in order to draft really effective laws.

There were nine candidates. Lakhova polled 14.43% of the votes in the first round and won the second round, polling 46.3% of the votes. Her main opponent was V. N. Borozdin, instructor fitter in the Sverdlovsk-Sortirovochny train depot, who received 14.16% of the votes in the first round and 40.6% of the votes in the second round.

In 1991 Lakhova was appointed an RSFSR state adviser on the family and the protection of mothers and children. By decree of the President of the Russian Federation of August 28, 1992, she was appointed adviser of the President on the family and protection of mothers and children.

Her interventions resulted in Supreme Soviet hearings on the demographic situation in the Russian Federation and possible ways of improving it. The hearings revealed the disastrous situation with the lowest birthrate and the highest mortality since 1945. The reasons for this state of affairs, in her view, are the long-term merciless exploitation of the family which is seen as a provider of human and labour resources for the state, the huge proportion of women in public production (95%) which has automatically led to a drop in the birth-rate and the absence of equal professional opportunities for women. In 1986, as one of the consequences of the war, there was a drop of 14% in the number of women of child-bearing age. The final reason is the present social and economic crisis.

Lakhova advocates finding ways to support children, irrespective of the economic crisis. The President of the Russian Federation signed the international declaration on the survival, development and protection of children which is a basis for protecting handicapped children and the children of Chernobyl. Lakhova is participating in the drafting of the children of Russia programme which envisages the establishment of centres of research of parents, the provision of modern equipment for maternity homes, ecologically pure children's food and first class pre-school, school and outside school institutions.

The decree of the President of the Russian Federation on social support for large families provides help for this group in society. The legislation envisages material support for them, financial and material concessions, the opportunity to engage in private agriculture and market gardening. State legislation on helping families and children is being drafted which includes providing new organizations such as shelters for mothers and children. Lakhova believes that not only the government should help but also non-governmental agencies and Russian private enterprise. She is closely involved in the drafting of the law on protecting families, mothers, paternity and childhood. The decree of the Supreme Soviet on immediate measures to improve the situation of mothers and families and the protection of mothers and children in the countryside has been adopted. Thus, she says, it is important to remember that without women there are no families, without families there are no villages and without villages Russia will not be reborn. She is married with a son and lives in Ekaterinburg.

Landsbergis, Vytautas

Former President of Lithuania.

Born on October 18, 1932 in Kaunas in the then independent Republic of Lithuania; Lithuanian. His father, Vytautas Landsbergis-Zemkalnis, was a famous architect and his mother came from a well-known literary family. He studied piano at the Conservatoire in Vilnius, but because of his small hands decided against becoming a concert pianist and instead embarked on a career as a piano teacher and musicologist at the Conservatoire, becoming a professor in 1978. Had he accepted an invitation to join the Communist Party of Lithuania he might have become director of the Conservatoire.

President Mikhail Gorbachev's policy of *glasnost* had unexpected side effects for the Soviet leader. The peoples of Lithuania, Latvia and Estonia grasped the opportunity to claim their autonomy and later independence which they had lost as a consequence of the Nazi-Soviet pact of August 1939. They had been incorporated into the Soviet Union in 1940, were occupied by the German *Wehrmacht* (1941-44) and supplied troops to the German war effort. The brutal deportation of the intelligentsia to Siberia and other unpleasant locations left deep scars.

Landsbergis came to symbolize the determination of Lithuania to break free from the USSR. Given the choice he would have preferred to be an academician but only in an independent Lithuania, and in order to achieve that goal he reluctantly became a politician. He was a retiring man but keen to see Lithuania live a quiet, peaceful existence as a European state. He was sharply critical of the US, Great Britain and other Western nations for their refusal to support self-determination for Lithuania. It was cold comfort to him that the West saw Mikhail Gorbachev as the leader who was bringing democracy to the Soviet Union. As far as Lithuania was concerned the USSR was an imperialist power and strengthening Gorbachev would only make it more difficult for Lithuania to break free. Landsbergis's task abroad, as when he visited London in November 1990 and held talks with Prime Minister Margaret Thatcher, was to counter the Western belief that Gorbachev was a democrat. Lithuania's experience of Gorbachev was an unhappy one.

A national organization, *Sajudis*, emerged in Lithuania and Landsbergis was elected its first chairman in November 1988, and when independence was declared in March 1990 Landsbergis was elected its first President. Moscow's response was to blockade the republic in an effort to bring it to its knees, but this was lifted in June after Vilnius suspended the declaration pending independence talks. The collapse of the Soviet Union and its demise in December 1991 brought world-wide recognition for Lithuania's independence.

However, Landsbergis's skills as a politician were found lacking after independence and his confrontational tactics towards Moscow gradually became self-defeating. Russia was of key importance to the Lithuanian economy with almost all energy and industrial inputs emanating from there. Forcible decollectivization was set in train but resisted by the peasants who were quite unprepared to farm on their own. The first democratic elections after independence, in September 1992, produced a shock result, when the Lithuanian

Democratic Labour Party (LDLP), led by Algirdas Brazauskas, topped the poll with 44.7% of the votes. The LDLP was the name adopted by the pro-reform and pro-independence Communist Party of Lithuania, which broke away from the pro-Moscow Party of the same name. *Sajudis* only received 19.8% of the votes. In the second round, in November 1992, the LDLP swept the board (it would have obtained more seats in parliament had it had more candidates) and obtained a majority in parliament. *Sajudis*, which had piloted the country to independence, was comprehensively rejected. Its leadership style, confrontational, nationalist, intellectual, but at times outstandingly brave and skilled, proved too much for the electors. It was also significant that many voters were unwilling to state that they had voted for the ex-communist. Analysis revealed that 12% of those who stated they had voted for *Sajudis* had in fact voted for the LDLP. Landsbergis was anything but gracious in defeat, blaming the electorate for being stupid.

A government was formed, headed by Algirdas Brazauskas, and he also became acting President. Presidential elections were held in February 1993 and Brazauskas polled 60.1% of the votes thereby becoming President. Landsbergis must bear some of the responsibility for the fact that nationalist Lithuania became the first post-Soviet state to elect the former communists to power. He has published eight monographs on the history of Lithuanian music. He lives in Vilnius.

Lanovyi, Volodymyr Tymofiyovych

Former Vice-Prime Minister of Ukraine and Minister for Economics.

Born into a Ukrainian family in 1952. After studying at Dnipropetrovsk Institute of Agricultural Economics until 1973, he served in the Soviet Army, and from 1975 worked as an engineer and economist in the *Krystal* factory in Kiev. In 1986 he joined the Ukrainian Academy of Sciences institute of economics, and by 1990 headed the department on the forms and methods of socialist management.

He joined the Communist Party surprisingly late, in the heady days of the early Gorbachev era in 1986, and only left it on August 24, 1991. In May 1991 he began to work in the state Ministry of Property and Industry. He gained a reputation as a reformist, and helped to formulate the Ukrainian plan for economic reform in December 1991 that was soon overtaken by Russia's price liberalization in January 1992. He was one of the founder members of the *New Ukraine* movement cstablished in January 1992, as an alliance of centrist political parties and reform-minded industrialists and government ministers. As a result of its pressure for more decisive moves towards a market economy, Lanovyi was made Minister for Economic Reform and Privatization, and Vice-Premier in March 1992. Lanovyi understood Kravchuk to have promised him sweeping powers to implement economic reform, but these were not forthcoming and he soon found himself isolated in what remained a basically conservative government. He became well known in the West, however, as the token economic liberal in the Ukrainian government and the man used to front negotiations with the West. His struggle with the more populist Emelianov to produce an economic plan acceptable to the West, and end Ukraine's credit isolation, led to the April 1992 "Programme of Economic Reforms and Politics of Ukraine", which secured provisional membership of the International Monetary Fund in May 1992.

However, the government was dragging its feet on economic reform, and Lanovyi's position became particularly difficult after the inaugural congress of *New Ukraine* in June 1992 (when his popularity won him first place in the elections to the movement's secretariat, with 247 out of 268 votes), declared itself in open opposition to the Fokin government's economic policy. On the other hand, his conservative critics accused him of failing to back up his free market rhetoric with solid administrative effort.

When Lanovyi ostentatiously refused to join a walk-out by the government from the Supreme Soviet chamber in protest at a threatened vote of no-confidence, Kravchuk's anger with him boiled over, and he was sacked for being "half in, half out" of the government in July 1992. He continued to be a popular figure in the *New Ukraine* movement, founding a Centre for the Promotion of Market Reforms in August 1992. Although *New Ukraine* contributed three Vice-Premiers to the new Kuchma government in October 1992, Lanovyi was not among them, presumably due to the legacy of his summer arguments with Kravchuk. In January 1993, however, he was consulted by Kuchma over the new government's plans for economic reform, and rumours of his return to office abounded, but Lanovyi's open criticism of the new government's less than fulsome commitment to market reforms made such a comeback unlikely.

Telephone: Kiev 291 5247, the *New Ukraine* office.

Laptev, Adolf Fedorovich

Head of the Administration of Ivanovo *oblast*, Russian Federation.

He is Russian, and was a member of the CPSU until August 1991. He is a graduate. He was deputy chairman of the *oblast* agro-industrial committee, and on April 6, 1987 he was elected first deputy chairman of the Ivanovo *oblast* soviet executive committee. On April 9, 1990, at the first session of the *oblast* soviet he was elected chairman of the executive committee.

On August 21, 1991 he stated that there was no state of emergency in the *oblast* and no prerequisites for introducing one, the constitutionally elected agencies of state power and administration were functioning and their task was to implement the laws of the RSFSR and the decrees of the RSFSR government which did not contravene the USSR constitution and Union laws. He appealed for calm and order, and to refrain from thoughtless activities which could lead to an increase in political and social confrontation.

He was proposed to the President by the soviet and people's deputies of Ivanovo *oblast* for confirmation as head of the administration and on December 24, 1991 he was appointed head of the administration of Ivanovo *oblast* by presidential decree. On assuming office he stated that he was convinced of the necessity to introduce fundamental economic reforms, develop interregional and international links, attract foreign investment and technology to Russian enterprises, and to reorient production towards the output of consumer goods. He advocated a mixed economy, the implementation of land reform and the gradual transition to a civilized market economy. He stated he supported cooperatives, entrepreneurs and joint ventures and called for Ivanovo goods to become competitive on the world market.

In December 1992, during the VII Congress of People's Deputies, he criticized the gulf between the laws and decrees of the Russian government and reality, the abstract nature of various branches of power and the abandonment of concrete economic policies and the failure to take into account the critical state of the economy and living standards of the population. In Laptev's view the population had been thrown into the market without the necessary psychological and economic preparation. It was opportune to convene the Congress of People's Deputies and its main task was to discuss the course of economic reform. The government should present a programme of escape from the economic crisis. Part of it should be replaced but most ministers should remain. He lives in Ivanovo.

Laptev, Ivan Dmitrievich

Director-general of the Izvestiya company.

Born in 1934; Russian. He graduated from the Siberian Institute of Road Transport and from the Aacademy of Social Sciences of the Party Central Committee, where he successfully presented his candidate dissertation (PhD). He began his working career in 1952 as a stoker, later as a crane operator and mechanic in the Omsk river port. After graduation in 1960 he was appointed a lecturer in the Siberian Institute of Road Transport, and later became an instructor in the Central Army sports club, Moscow. In 1964 he became a special correspondent on the *Sovetskaya Rossiya* newspaper and was also an adviser for the Party theoretical journal, *Kommunist*. In 1973 he was appointed a lecturer, then an adviser in the department of agitation and propaganda, Party Central Committee. In 1978 he was appointed editor, then deputy editor-in-chief of *Pravda*, and in 1984 he moved to *Izvestiya* as editor-in-chief and remained there until 1990. In February 1990 he was elected chairman of the board of the USSR union of journalists. At the XXVI Party congress, in 1986, he was elected a candidate member of the Party Central Committee, and he was also a people's deputy of the USSR Supreme Soviet.

From April 3, 1990 to October 1991 he was Speaker (chairman) of the USSR Supreme Soviet Soviet of the Union, and as such presided over the tumultuous events after the attempted state coup of August 19-21, 1991. Anatoly Lukyanov, the Speaker of the USSR Supreme Soviet, was one of the plotters and it fell to Laptev to chair sessions of the Supreme Soviet after the collapse of the coup. His task was extremely difficult since the RSFSR Supreme Soviet claimed precedence after the defeat of the coup. President Gorbachev's loss of authority was clear as well as was his misjudgement of the political mood. He spoke of working with democratic elements within the CPSU in order to regenerate the country. Laptev presided over the Soviet parliament in its dying days, until the resignation of President Mikhail Gorbachev on December 25, 1991 signalled the end of the Soviet Union and the USSR Supreme Soviet. In November 1991 Laptev was appointed director-general of the Izvestiya company. He lives in Moscow.

Latsis, Otto Rudolfovich

Member of the Council of the President of the Russian Federation.

Born on June 22, 1934 in Moscow; Latvian; member of the CPSU 1959 to August 1991. In 1956 he graduated from Moscow State University and became a literary assistant on the newspaper *Sovetsky Sakhalin*. In 1957 he successfully presented his candidate dissertation on the role of the profitability of enterprises based on the economic control of the management of production during various stages of development of socialist industry in the G. V. Plekhanov institute of the national economy, Moscow (PhD (Econ)). From 1960 he was a literary assistant, then senior consultant on *Ekonomicheskaya gazeta*, and from 1964 literary assistant, special correspondent and economic columnist of the economic department of the newspaper *Izvestiya*.

Already in the 1960s he had begun to defend the ideas of the economic reforms of that time. He was also employed on the journal *Novy mir*, where he worked closely with Aleksandr Tvardovsky. In 1971 he became consulting editor, then head of the editorial department of the journal *Problemy mira i sotsializma*, in Prague, Czechoslovakia.

The intervention in Czechoslovakia in August 1968 led to the collapse of economic reform, associated with Prime Minister Aleksei Kosygin, and Latsis's room for manoeuvre was restricted. In the mid-1970s he received a severe Party reprimand and was excluded from journalism for writing a study which traced the roots of Stalinism. Deprived of the ability to publish, he devoted himself to the study of economics and in 1975 became a senior scientific assistant and head of department of the institute of the economics of the world socialist system, USSR Academy of Sciences.

In 1980 he successfully presented his doctoral dissertation in economics on the problems of the development of national and international concentrations of production in Comecon countries in the form of associations (DSc (Econ)). From 1986 he was a political columnist and from 1987 deputy editor in chief of the revamped journal *Kommunist*, which, mainly due to his efforts, strongly supported *perestroika* and renewal.

Latsis is the author of the following books: *Conversations About Economic Reform* (1968); *Associations in Comecon Countries: Forms of National and International Concentration* (1978); *The Art of Addition: Essays on Economic Life* (1984); *Sun in the House* (1982); *A Tale in Prison Notebooks (About K. and E. Rosenberg)* (1983); *The Socio-Economic Development of Foreign Socialist States, 1981-85* (1987); *Economic Centralization and the Centralism of Management: Problems of Interdependence* (1987); *To Know One's Manoeuvre,* (1987); *To Escape from the Square: Notes of an Economist* (1989); *Turning Point: The Experience of Reading Non-Secret Documents* (1990).

In early 1990 Latsis was nominated for election as a USSR people's deputy in the No. 20 Leningrad village national territorial district. During the election campaign he advocated an increase in agricultural production and the re-emergence of social justice in the countryside. He stated that the country was in a financial and economic crisis, and it was necessary to halt inflation and to close the flow of unguaranteed money into the economy. He proposed one-off purchases of consumer goods abroad at the expense of cutting back investment goods imports. He demanded a parliamentary investigation into large foreign economic deals, opposed ecologically dangerous technologies and supported the battle against corruption. He demanded that order be introduced into the import of food and that import policy be examined and corrected. He believed that exceptional measures were needed but these could only be taken by the people's deputies.

Nineteen candidates stood for election. Latsis polled 15% of the votes in the first round but lost the second round, polling 45.7% of the votes. The victor was A. M. Obolensky, an engineer with the Polar geophysical institute, Kola scientific centre, USSR Academy of Sciences. At the XXVIII Party Congress in July 1990 Latsis was elected a member of the Party Central Committee.

Latsis believes that over the last 60 years an anti-market psychology has developed in the country with the state playing a debilitating role in the economy and this is the reason for the unreasonable demands which are made: provide more goods, lower prices and raise wages. However, an enormous change is taking place in public consciousness with people beginning to realize that a transition to the market is necessary. Strikes, meetings and political conflict are inevitable since without them there can be no move to the market. The older economic order ceased to function as long ago as the early 1970s, and hence the collapse of the economy was inevitable without *perestroika*. The transition to the market is a painful move which is accompanied by the necessary price rises and unemployment. He favours rapid privatization, the creation of new markets in housing, building materials, investment goods and investment funds. The run-down of the military industrial complex should be carried out carefully since it affects millions of people.

It is impossible to retain the present parliament, and the many congresses of people's deputies, meeting for a few days and incapable of decisive activity while lacking permanent personnel. The election of the Russian Supreme Soviet by the congress and not the people weakens the standing parliament which in order of precedence is subordinate to the popularly elected President. The Russian Supreme Soviet Presidium, the only one in the world, has the possibility of acquiring an uncontrolled concentration of power, similar to that of the former Party Politburo. Latsis favours the convocation of a constituent assembly since the congress is not capable of agreeing a new constitution which would end its existence. He does not believe that a presidential republic would develop into the rule of one person. Any state institution can claim some power and the slogan: "all power to the soviets" is very dangerous.

In Russia where the multi-party system has not yet emerged, the most legitimate and sound power may be a popularly elected president but accompanied by the division of powers and the counterbalance of the soviets. The Gaidar government's greatest achievement was that it brought into being a functioning ruble and its greatest mistake was in the summer of 1992 when it gave in to parliamentary pressure and enterprise directors and emitted a vast amount of money. It was important for Russia to become a member of the International Monetary Fund because as a result creditors' confidence in Russia grew. He believes that the Yeltsin-Gaidar government did more in a year than other governments in several decades. Its main failure was to move to the market too slowly. The VIII Congress of People's Deputies, in March 1993, made a very negative impression. Latsis does not think that a real analysis of the course of economic reform was attempted at the congress and the deputies abdicated any responsibility for their decisions and placed all the blame on the government. This is unjust since the economic situation cannot be improved immediately.

He became a member of the presidential Council in February 1993. Latsis lives in Moscow and is married with a son and a daughter. His son is a scientific assistant in an academic institute.

Lebed, Aleksandr Ivanovich

Commander of the 14th Guards Army, stationed in Moldova and Odessa *oblast*, Ukraine. Lieutenant-General since 1992.

Born in 1950, in Novocherkassk. Ukrainian. His military career began in 1969. He graduated from the Ryazan Higher Airborne Officers' Technical school in 1973 and the M. V. Frunze Military Academy in 1985. He received a higher military education and was a member of the CPSU from 1972 to August 1991.

He began his career as officer as a commander of a student platoon of the Ryazan Technical School (the company commander was the future Minister of Defence, P. S. Grachev). Then till 1981 A. Lebed was a student company commander. From 1981 to 1982 he was a commander of a paratroop battalion of the 40th Army in Afghanistan. He participated in many military operations against the *mujahidin* and civil population, often adopting severe measures. In 1982 he was awarded the order of the Red Banner for this activity.

He had a successful career after graduating from the Academy. He was a deputy commander and a commander of a paratroop regiment (1985-86), deputy commander (1986-88) and commander of an airborne division in Tula (1988-91). He was one of the youngest generals in the Soviet army.

He enjoyed great popularity with his subordinates, and had the following record: "Independent . . . well-balanced, firm, tough . . . has a sound operational-tactical and military-technical training, understands the essence of current combat . . . copes well with physical and psychological strains."

He was in command of the paratroop operations whose aim was the elimination of national democratic uprisings and ethnic conflicts in Transcaucasia and Central Asia. Lebed displayed toughness and resoluteness. He took part in the events in Baku in January 1990, though this fact is now denied by official sources.

He was a convinced communist and a supporter of the imperial ambitions of the top Party, government and military leaders of the USSR. His attitude towards democratic organizations and reformers in the CPSU was extremely negative. He took the floor at the XXVIII Congress of the Party in opposition to A. N. Yakovlev, and insulted him.

In February 1991, a protégé of P. S. Grachev, Lebed was appointed his deputy commander of airborne troops for training and education. He supervised the training of airborne units and command personnel.

During the anti-constitutional putsch of August 19-21, 1991 he carried out the personal instructions of Gen. P. Grachev. On the evening of August 19, leading a paratroop battalion with their matériel, he arrived at the Russian White House with the alleged purpose of defending the leaders of Russia. He was extremely rude to the representatives of the defence staff, stressing his immediate subordination to the commander of airborne troops and his readiness to carry out any order whatsoever. According to knowledgeable sources, Lebed's task was a rear attack of the White House during a possible storming rather than the defence of the legitimate authorities. On the morning of August 20, Lebed secretly left the White House.

Gen. A. Lebed's appointment as commander of the 14th Army was considered by democratic forces to be a serious concession by President Yeltsin to conservative national circles in the military and political leadership, and to advocates of the use of force in contacts with the former Soviet republics. Typically, Lebed arrived at the 14th Army headquarters (in Tiraspol) under the alleged name of "Colonel Gusev", long before his official appointment; actually the President of Russia only confirmed *de jure* the General's promotion which had been already put into effect by certain individuals in his own inner circle. Evidently expecting the backing of the top Russian leaders, Lebed, in his first public speeches, was highly critical of Moldova's and Russia's foreign policy, exceeding his brief as a commander. On the other hand, it was due to Lebed's resolute stand that the armed conflicts in Pridnestrovie were brought to a halt.

Gen. A. Lebed, as a combat officer, enjoys great popularity in neo-communist, national and aggressively patriotic circles of Russian society and the army. He makes no secret of his imperial ambitions; he is praised as a defender of the Russian-speaking population; he is a convinced advocate of the use of force in resolving ethnic, foreign and domestic conflicts. At the same time he emphasizes that he supports the banning of political parties in and depolitization of the armed forces. In the field of military planning, he favours the concept of up-to-date highly mobile armed forces, underlining Russia's prestige as a great power with considerable military strength.

Lebed is married with two sons and a daughter. His younger brother, Col. Aleksei Lebed, is a commander of a paratroop regiment stationed in Kishinev (the capital of Moldova).

Gen. Aleksandr Lebed has been awarded several orders and medals. There is no information available on his hobbies.

At present he is resident at the headquarters of the 14th Army in Tiraspol.

Leonov, Yury Yurevich

Member of the organizing committee of the Workers' Party.

Born in 1963 in Moscow. He graduated in 1985 from the faculty of journalism, Moscow State University, and then became a teacher in Russian language and literature in a secondary school. In 1987 he was appointed editor-in-chief of the factory newspaper of the Kalinin machine building enterprise in Moscow. He became active in politics in 1989 and was chairman of the organizing committee which founded the Marxist Workers' Party in March 1990. In February 1992 the party was renamed the Workers' Party. He is a member of editorial boards of the party's newspapers *Rabochaya Gazeta* and *Proletary* and of the journal *Marksist*.

He has published articles on economics in *samizdat* and abroad. The Workers' Party was bitterly critical of the policies of the CPSU under Gorbachev, as its members saw them as a betrayal of its socialist legacy. In the post-communist Russia they advocate a return to Marxist socialism and oppose the introduction of a market economy and privatization. Given the economic plight of the country they will be able to expand their influence if they acquire the requisite political and organizational skills. They need to form a coalition with other left wing parties in order to contest elections successfully and exert constructive influence on policy formation. Leonov is keen on chess and football. He is unmarried.

Address: 115380 Moscow, P. O. Box 48; *telephone*: Moscow 252 4415 (office); 255 0695 (home).

Leonty, Russian Orthodox Metropolitan of Kherson and the Tauride

Born in 1928 as Ivan Afanasevich Gudimov in the village of Novaya Sloboda, Putivlsky *raion*, Sumy *oblast*, Ukrainian SSR, into a peasant family. He was educated at the Odessa (Odesa) Theological Academy, and the Moscow Theological Academy, where he successfully presented his candidate dissertation in theology (PhD). In 1942 he entered the Glinskaya Pustin monastery, he took his vows as a monk in Izmail cathedral, Izmail, Odessa *oblast*, Ukrainian SSR (1948-51); in 1960 he became an archimandrite; then deputy of the Uspensky monastery, Odessa; aide to inspector, lecturer, and rector of Odessa theological seminary (1957-62); representative of the Moscow patriarchate in the Antioch patriarchate, Damascus, Syria (1962-65); bishop of Simferopol and the Crimea, and temporary administrator of the Dnipropetrovsk diocese (1965-67); and bishop of Kharkov and Bogodukhov (1967-68). He was made an archbishop; and became archbishop of Kharkov and Bogodukhov (1968-70); exarch of the Moscow patriarchate in Central Europe (1970-73); archbishop of Simferopol and the Crimea (1973-89); in 1989 he advanced to metropolitan and became metropolitan of Simferopol and the Crimea, 1989-90; in 1991 he was appointed metropolitan of Kherson and the Tauride.

Leonty, Russian Orthodox Metropolitan of Orenburg and Buzuluki

Born in 1913 as Leonid Faddeevich Bondar in the village of Merkino, Troksky *uezd*, Vilno (Vilnius) *guberniya*. He graduated from the Vilnius Theological Seminary, and the Russian Orthodox faculty, Warsaw University. He successfully presented his candidate dissertation in theology (PhD). He took his vows as a monk in 1943, and was subsequently rector of the courses in theology in Zhirovits monastery; acting rector of Minsk theological seminary (1946-47); priest in the village of Kholkho, Molodechnensky *raion*, the village of Yastrebl, Brest *oblast*, Belorusian SSR (Belarus) (1947-49); and lecturer and inspector in Minsk Theological Seminary (1949-53). In 1953 he was appointed an archimandrite; then deputy of Zhirovits monastery (1953-56); bishop of Bobrui (1956-60); temporary administrator of the Minsk diocese (1960-61); and bishop of Novosibirsk and Barnaul (1961-71). In 1971 he was made an archbishop and became archbishop of Orenburg and Buzuluki (1971-92); he was appointed metropolitan of Orenburg and Buzuluki in 1992.

Leushkin, Sergei Gennadevich

Head of the Administration of the Koryak Autonomous *okrug*, Russian Federation.

Born in 1950; Russian; member of the CPSU until August 1991. He graduated from the Institute of National Economy, Khabarovsk, as an engineer and economist, and became an engineer at the Tilichiki airport, later chairman of the Koryak village soviet, then chairman of the Korf village soviet and chairman of the Ólyutorsky *raion* soviet.

In May 1990 he was elected a deputy of the Koryak *okrug* soviet in the second round of voting, and at the third session of the *okrug* soviet in October 1990 he was elected chairman of the Koryak *okrug* executive committee. During the election campaign he stressed the necessity of agreeing to introduce key economic levers in agricultural production, to transfer part of the income of local enterprises to the *okrug* budget for the transformation of the *okrug* into a republic, for its autonomy as a subject of the federation, for the ending of the pillage of its natural riches and for legally equal economic relations with Kamchatka *oblast*.

On August 2, 1991 the Presidium and executive committee of the Koryak *okrug* soviet of people's deputies adopted a resolution expressing support for the decrees and statements of the President of the RSFSR, the government and Supreme Soviet of the RSFSR of August 19, and appealed for their implementation. It stated that on the territory of the *okrug* the USSR and RSFSR constitutions and laws of the RSFSR were being observed. The leadership of the Koryak autonomous *okrug* subordinated itself to the legally elected authorities, the President, the RSFSR Supreme Soviet and the chairman of the Council of Ministers of the RSFSR. No state of emergency would be introduced in the *okrug*.

On November 16, 1991 Leushkin was appointed head of the administration of the Koryak autonomous *okrug* by presidential decree, and on assuming office he advocated radical economic reform, strictly implemented. He appealed for relief from the tutelage of the central ministries and authorities, the right for the *okrug* to use its resources autonomously and overcome the reliance on raw materials of the local economy. He appealed for help from commercial bodies, the establishment of municipal trade, the development of foreign economic ties, for example, with north and south Korea. It was necessary to process local resources and to improve significantly the standard of living of the many nations of the north. He favoured retaining a stratum of the old administrative machinery and retaining stability in market relations, and was opposed to an uncontrolled market.

In December 1992, during the VII Congress of People's Deputies, he appealed for opposition to the attempts to resurrect totalitarianism and the command administrative system. He believed that Viktor Chernomyrdin would continue to support the reforms under way and observe the pre-eminence of economic policy. He lives in the village of Korf, Koryak autonomous *okrug*.

Likhachev, Dmitry Sergeevich

Russian Academician.

Born on November 26, 1906 in St Petersburg into an intelligentsia family, whose father was an electrical engineer. He is Russian; and was never a member of the CPSU. He attended the *gimnaziya* of the philanthropic society, then in 1915 entered the K. I Mai *gimnaziya* and real school. The grandson of Mechnikov and the son of the banker Rubinshtein attended the same school. Likhachev was very keen on drawing and working with his hands. He then moved to the Lentovskaya school (the theatrical entrepreneur), and was greatly influenced by the school excursions, in 1921, to Arkhangelsk, Murmansk and Kotlas, in the north of Russia. In 1924 he entered the faculty of social sciences, department of anthropology and linguistics, in the Romance-German and Slavonic-Russian section, Leningrad State University, although he was still not 18 years old. He visited the Philharmonic and greatly enjoyed the theatre. He graduated in 1928 and wrote two diploma works, one on Shakespeare in Russia in the late 18th and early 19th centuries, and one on the stories of the patriarch Nikon. He built up the library of the institute of phonetics of foreign languages, and studied English poetry under V. M. Zhirmunsky, logic under A. I. Vvedensky and attended the lectures of the historian, E. V. Tarle.

In 1928 he was arrested for giving a humorous lecture on the superiority of the old Russian orthography, composed in the style of the Old Believers' works of the 17th century for a student company calling itself the space academy of sciences. He spent the years from 1928 to 1932 in the Solovki special concentration camp and in 1931 participated in the construction of the White Sea-Baltic canal. This damaged his health and he suffered from stomach ulcers and bleeding. He was released on August 4, 1932 and given a red mark for his work on the White Sea-Baltic canal, which permitted him to live where he liked in the Soviet Union. During the autumn of 1932 he became an editor in the socialist encyclopedia publishing house, and was later a proof reader of foreign languages in the Komintern printing works. In 1934 he moved to the Leningrad publishing department, USSR Academy of Sciences. His closest friend at this time was M. I. Steblin-Kamensky. In 1938 he began working in the department of old Russian literature, Institute of Russian Literature, USSR Academy of Sciences (Pushkinsky dom). He edited and proof read *Review of Russian Manuscript Codes* by A. A. Shakhmatov, and wrote a chapter for volume two of the *History of the Culture of Kievan Rus*, for which he was awarded a state prize. On June 11, 1934 he successfully presented his candidate dissertation on the Novgorod chronicles of the 12th century (PhD). He was rejected for military service at the beginning of the Great Patriotic War (1941-45), but participated in the defence of Leningrad, helped to guard the tower of the Pushkinsky dom and lived in the institute. He survived the blockade of Leningrad (1941-44), when over half his relatives and acquaintances perished from hunger. He wrote the books *Defence of Old Russian Cities* (published in the autumn of 1942), *Great Novgorod. Outlines of its History from the 5th-17th Centuries*, and *National Consciousness in Early Rus*, which appeared in 1945. In 1947 he successfully presented his doctoral dissertation in philology on "An outline of the history of the form of chronicles of the 11th-16th centuries" (DLitt). Then followed books on the *Russian Chronicles* (1945); *Development of Russian Literature from the 10th-12th Centuries* (1946); *The Culture of Rus during the Formation of the Russian National State* (1946); *People in the Culture of Early Rus* (1958); *Textual Criticism of Russian Literature from the 5th-17th Centuries* (1962); and *Poetics in Old Russian Literature* (1967), for which he was awarded his second USSR state prize. He is now a professor, an Academician of the Russian Academy of Sciences, and head of the department of old Russian literature, Institute of Russian Literature, Russian Academy of Sciences. He edits the annual publication *Cultural Monuments. New Discoveries*, and his book, *Russian Art from Ancient Times to the Avantgarde*, will appear in 1993.

In 1989 Likhachev was elected a USSR people's deputy as a nominee of the Soviet cultural fund. He was elected a member of the USSR Supreme Soviet committee on science, education, culture and upbringing, and was a member of the commission on deputies' ethics. He thought of the establishment of the Soviet cultural fund and wanted Raisa Gorbacheva to head it, as in the West, but she insisted that he be its chairman. He headed the Soviet, international and then Russian cultural fund, but offered his resignation in February 1993 since he lived in St Petersburg and the board met in Moscow and it was difficult for him to assess its scientific and social work. He worked for the fund without being paid, he did not travel abroad at the expense of the fund and economized on its resources. His main tasks for the near future are to publish things that have not been published over the last 75 years; to research local affairs, raising the level of culture of small towns and rural areas; the development of the culture of the small nations of Russia, discovering and developing young talent, the return to the motherland of cultural treasures now abroad; and a programme for the maintenance and development of the Russian language in a bilingual east European context. The fund acquired the M. I. Tsvetaeva museum and the K. I. Chukovsky dacha.

Before the attempted state coup of August 1991 Likhachev called on the authorities, in an article in *Moskovskie novosti*, not to use force against its own people. On August 20, 1991 he was the only member of the USSR Academy of Sciences who spoke at a demonstration on Dvorets Square against his inclusion in the Presidium of the St Petersburg scientific centre of the Academy. He believes that the putsch failed not because it was poorly organized but that it encountered a different people to the one it expected, one which refused to accept a new dictatorship. He favours retaining cultural links with the former Soviet republics and their mutual openness. He is non-political in principle and regards non-intervention in politics as the cornerstone of his approach. He believes that people should be intellectually and civically free of pressure from the state, party, ideology, career views and external circumstances. Supreme power rests with conscience, strengthened by education and personal experience, and this is what being a member of the intelligentsia means, being a cultured person. Recently Likhachev spoke in the Institute of World Literature on the Russian language, as he believes that without it the development of culture on the territory of the former Soviet Union is impossible. He favours bilingualism, otherwise the region will descend to the level of a Third World country. It is senseless to dream of re-establishing the old territories by military force. The authority of a people is not defined by the number of tanks and the size of its territory but by its moral dignity and by its people's culture. The way out of the crisis of society is through the rebirth of culture, the development of Russian culture, which objectively occupies first place on the territory of the former Soviet Union, and being patient towards other peoples and other cultures. Concern about culture will help economic renewal, and he supports universalism and a world culture.

He believes that a situation of extreme crisis became evident after the VII Congress of People's Deputies, in December 1992. A frenzied, no-holds- barred struggle got under way, not for power but for political dominance. He favours the convocation of a constituent assembly, based on the principles enunciated by G. Kh. Popov, that only it can resolve the crisis of our statehood. He calls for the reforms, begun by Stolypin, to be carried through to a successful conclusion and for the reconstruction the Russian state on the basis of President, parliament and supreme court. He advocates the unification of the Russian intelligentsia, opposes Ruslan Khasbulatov and Sergei Baburin, and calls for the creation of democracy in Russia. There is no need to expand Moscow and St Petersburg, but what is needed are first class roads which will bring people closer to culture. The geography of agriculture should be altered with the assimilation of the North.

He was made a hero of socialist labour; he was awarded the order of Lenin and the gold hammer and sickle medal; the order of the Red Banner of Labour; and foreign awards. He has the order of Cyril and Methodius, first class; the order of Georgy Dimitrov; the Evfimy Tyrnovsky prize; the Cyril and Methodius prize; member of the Academy of Sciences of Bulgaria, Hungary, Italy, Serbia; a corresponding member of the Austrian, British Gvttingen, Germany, Academies; an honorary doctor of sciences of the University of Torun, Poland, and of Charles University, Prague, Czech Republic; honorary doctor of law, University of Oxford, England, and other foreign awards. He has over 1,500 publications to his name, including dozens of books and many of his works have been translated into foreign languages. He is married with a daughter and lives in St Petersburg.

Lipitsky, Vasily Semenovich

Chairman of the Board of the People's Party Free Russia; Chairman of the Executive Committee of Civic Union.

Born in 1947. He was a member of the CPSU until August 1991. He graduated from the faculty of history, Moscow State University, and then became head of the centre of sociology at the university and later was head of scientific research in the Institute of Marxism-Leninism of the Party Central Committee. In 1973 he successfully presented his candidate dissertation in philosophy on "Productive labour as a factor in the formation of the Soviet specialist" (based on the material of the "third semester" of student youth) (PhD) and in 1989 his doctoral dissertation in philosophy on "The problems of stimulating creative activity in people" (Marxist-Leninist methodology and the contemporary scene) (DLitt).

He began his involvement in politics in the late 1980s and, not being an RSFSR people's deputy, played an active role in the communist split and the appearance of Aleksandr Rutskoi's faction, communists for democracy. On August 6, 1991 he was expelled from the CPSU, as he was actively involved in the foundation of the People's Party of Free Russia. This party's faction is now one of the largest among Russian parliamentary deputies, with about 100 members. The party advocates a united, indivisible Russia but rejects the use of force to achieve this.

On June 21, 1992 Lipitsky was elected chairman of the executive committee of Civic Union. He regards Gaidar's economics as a liberal utopia, is opposed to a rush to the market and favours gradual reform under strict government control. The tactics of Civic Union should be the principles of evolutionary change and pragmatism, close to those of social democracy. He believes that Gaidar should have attracted to his team other well-known economists, taken into consideration the experience of China, granted concessions to foreign companies and sharply increased Russian exports.

He believes that the VII Congress of People's Deputies, in December 1992, completed the post-August stage of development. Until then the party had influenced the government through consultations in small groups, using personal contacts, but it is now going over gradually to opposition. The government of Viktor Chernomyrdin has only presented a programme to plug holes, intensive therapy is nowhere to be seen and is actively banning certain activities. Lipitsky believes that a political solution to the crisis cannot be found, given the present institutions of power.

Provisional agreements and compromises will not make the situation any easier. Early elections are needed to both branches of power, the legislature and the executive, and a referendum on the fundamentals of a new constitution, not about who is to rule. However, this is not now possible since it would hasten the disintegration of Russia. One of the positive steps of the VII Congress was to expand the powers of the government over the economy but, however, overall the congress exhausted all its possibilities. Constitutional reform is necessary, as is a new political system, and an election campaign can be run at the same time. He thinks the best time for elections would be the spring of 1994.

Lipitsky sharply criticized the TV address of the Russian President of April 3, 1993, and he regards the results of the IX Congress of People's Deputies, in March 1993, as positive since they articulated, within bounds, severe criticism of the infringement of the constitution by senior state officials. This is a great achievement for a society which is bogged down in anarchy, as is a move to early elections. However, the negative consequences of the IX Congress are greater. Confrontation has become more acute, regional élites have strengthened their power and influence and the federation is weaker. The future can only hold a sharpening of the conflict, and the only way to avoid this is to form a coalition government to stabilize the situation until the elections are held. He is married and lives in Moscow.

Lisitsyn, Anatoly Ivanovich

Acting Head of the Administration of Yaroslavl *oblast*, Russian Federation.

Born in 1947 in the village of Bolshie Smenki, Sonkovsky *raion*, Kalinin (Tver) *oblast*; member of the CPSU until August 1991. From 1963 to 1987 he worked in the Rybinsk furniture and wood processing combine, Svoboda, beginning as a joiner and eventually becoming director of the enterprise. He graduated from the Leningrad Timber Technical Academy, and in 1987 moved into work in the soviets. He was chairman of the Tsentralny *raion* soviet executive committee, Rybinsk, first deputy chairman of Rybinsk city soviet executive committee and in May 1990 was elected its chairman.

In March 1990 he was elected a deputy of Yaroslavl *oblast* soviet of people's deputies and a deputy of Rybinsk city soviet. At the first session of the Yaroslavl *oblast* soviet he was proposed as a candidate for the post of chairman of the *oblast* soviet executive committee but, instead, V. A. Kovalev was elected chairman and Lisitsyn first deputy chairman.

In December 1992 Lisitsyn was appointed acting head of the administration of Yaroslavl *oblast* by presidential decree. On taking office he stated that the highest priority for the *oblast* in the next few years was the development of agriculture and the adequate development of all forms of ownership, collective as well as individual. In his view if the successful collective, state and individual farms did not pass into the ownership of those who worked them, there was no hope for reform in the countryside. Cities should be united with agricultural regions. A single budgetary policy, the redistribution of resources in favour of the countryside, based on general interests, would stimulate the development of the countryside and quickly supply the cities with food. However, a strong government was needed to implement reforms. He also advocated the expansion of foreign economic links and stressed the need for foreign investment in Russian industry which was the key factor in the recovery of the Russian economy.

In December 1992, during the VII Congress of People's Deputies, he declared his support for the President in the extremely difficult situation and called Egor Gaidar the linchpin of the economy. He maintained that it was essential that he be confirmed as Prime Minister. Lisitsyn lives in Rybinsk.

Lobov, Oleg Ivanovich

Head of the Working Apparatus of the Council of Experts of the President of the Russian Federation.

Born on September 7, 1937 in Kiev, Ukraine; Russian. In 1960 he graduated from the Institute of Railway Engineers, Rostov-on-Don and successfully presented his candidate dissertation in technical sciences (PhD (Eng)). He was a member of the CPSU from 1971 to August 1991. He began working in Sverdlovsk in 1960: as an engineer, senior engineer, head of a group, senior design engineer, acting head of the construction department of the Urals chemical institute, chief design engineer of the construction department, head of a sector, chief engineer and deputy director of the Urals industrial and construction scientific research institute project. In 1972 he was appointed deputy head, in 1975 head of department of construction, Sverdlovsk Party *obkom*, and in 1976 he became head of the main territorial administration of construction of the main central Urals construction trust, USSR Ministry of Heavy Construction.

In 1982 he was appointed secretary, in 1983 second secretary of Sverdlovsk Party *obkom*, and in 1985 he became chairman of the Sverdlovsk *oblast* soviet executive committee. In 1987 he was appointed an inspector in the Party Central Committee and deputy chairman of the RSFSR Council of Ministers, and in 1989 he was elected second secretary of the Communist Party of Armenia. He was a member of the Party Central Committee from July 1990 to August 1991, and was a USSR people's deputy and an honoured constructor of the RSFSR.

In 1990 Lobov and Ivan Polozkov were competitors during the second round of voting at the constituent congress of the RSFSR Communist Party for the post of first secretary of the party, but Polozkov won the election. In June 1991 Lobov was appointed first deputy chairman of the RSFSR Council of Ministers, and in August 1991 he was head of the shadow Russian government which President Yeltsin sent underground. In November 1991 Lobov lost his position as first deputy chairman of the RSFSR government, but became head of the council of experts for the appraisal of radical socio-economic, scientific technical, investment and other programmes and proposals which the government was receiving. On September 2, 1993 it was transformed into the council of experts of the President of the Russian Federation and was to carry out appraisals of large programmes, projects and proposals which were being forwarded to the Russian President. Lobov became head of this new council.

Lobov favours strong government. Reforms were necessary since otherwise the whole system would have become unmanageable. Reforms are taking place at a time when there is no reproduction of goods and the whole sphere of material production is in state ownership and so consequently there is no limit to price increases. Privatization is proceeding slowly and by the end of 1993 only about 1% of all property will have been privatized, but this will not give rise to competition. A rapid rise in incomes is not necessary, only a basic minimum standard of living which keeps in step with inflation. A market economy need not be unplanned and government management should be retained. He is opposed to radicalism and the unfounded dreams of a free market which allegedly do everything and make everyone rich. He favours a transition from a revolutionary to an evolutionary course of development since if commercial structures link up with the authorities it could lead to even more extreme forms of monopoly. Government reshuffles are not necessary but reform tactics have to be refined. Russia should have its own currency system and move slowly towards the market. During this period the economy needs to be run with skill and professionalism and this involves the government putting together structures to manage state property until it has been privatized. He lives in Moscow.

Lobov, Vladimir Nikolaevich

Independent military expert and consultant. Chief of the General Staff of the Armed Forces of the USSR, first deputy Minister of Defence of the USSR in the autumn of 1991. General of the Army since 1989.

Born in 1935 into a civil servant's family. Russian. He graduated from a tank technical school in 1959; the M. V. Frunze Military Academy; the Academy of the General Staff in 1979. He received a higher military education. He became a doctor of military sciences (DSc), a candidate of sciences (history) (PhD) and a professor. He was a member of the CPSU from 1959 to August 1991.

He began his military career as a private in the Turkestan military district. After graduating from technical school he held officers' posts as a commander of a platoon, company, battalion and regiment. He was notable for his intellectual abilities, for his creative approach to official duties, for his excellent operational-tactical and military-technical training. He defended fearlessly his views when arguing with his superior officers. He took part in Party-political work only to the extent necessary for a successful career in the Soviet army. He was critical of many traditional tenets of military science and practice.

Having completed his higher military education, V. Lobov was a divisional commander, first deputy army commander and an army commander. In 1984 he was appointed commander of the Central Asian military district. Here he completed his research which he had been carrying out for several years and, in 1985, at Alma Ata university, he successfully presented his candidate dissertation "Military Cunning in the History of Wars (based on the History of World War II 1939-45)". For three years, Col.-Gen. V. Lobov was commander of the military district of one of the major strategic directions against China. He established official contacts with the Party and governmental leaders of Kazakhstan and was elected a deputy of the Supreme Soviet of Kazakhstan. From 1986 to 1989 he represented the interests of this republic in the USSR Supreme Soviet.

During the violence in Alma-Ata in December 1986, as commander of the military district, Lobov flatly refused to use army units against the civilian population without a written order from the Minister of Defence.

From 1987 Col.-Gen. Lobov was the first deputy Chief of the General Staff of the Armed Forces of the USSR. Under his immediate command were leading administrations of the General Staff (chief strategic administration and others), which carried out the analysis of the military and political situation and the state of the USSR defence potential, military planning and the preparation of the country for a sudden war. Gen. Lobov was one of the first among top military leaders who realized that military reform was necessary and inevitable. In the autumn of 1988 he invited a group of radical scientists and politely informed them about his views and ideas in this respect. The same year he successfully presented his doctoral dissertation on the problems of military planning (DSc). He had a good reputation as a teacher at the Military Academy of the General Staff and became a professor.

Lobov's reformist ideas and his articles in the press (*Pravda*, December 17, 1988, *Moskovskie Novosti*, December 18, 1988 and others) caused a highly negative reaction among the then military leaders, Marshals D. Yazov and Sergei Akhromeev. From 1989 Lobov was actually relieved of real power in the army and was appointed Chief of Staff, first deputy Commander-in-Chief of the Unified Armed Forces of the Warsaw Treaty countries, the post having become merely representative.

In March 1989 General of the Army V. Lobov was elected a USSR people's deputy in Ayaguzsky national-territorial district, Semipalatinsk *oblast*, Kazakhstan. There were no other candidates during the election since two others stepped down at the pre-election district meeting. Lobov polled 225,315 votes from an electoral roll of 238,702. His programme envisaged focusing on economic policy, the rejection of high-cost military expenditure and maintenance of the army, the democratization of the armed forces, and *glasnost* in the military policy of the country. Lobov was elected to the USSR Supreme Soviet at the I Congress of People's Deputies and became a member of the committee on international affairs. He was not very active at sessions and congresses, but on the whole he argued vigorously for the principles he presented in his own programme. A convinced reformer on military issues, he expressed moderately liberal political views.

After the dissolution of the military structures of the Warsaw Pact organization he was appointed head of the M. V. Frunze Military Academy. During the anti-constitutional putsch in August 1991 he did not take part in the events.

At the suggestion of democratic military organizations, by the USSR President Gorbachev's decree on August 23, 1991, General of the Army V. Lobov was appointed Chief of the General Staff of the Armed Forces of the USSR and first deputy USSR Minister of Defence. His first interview on September 7, 1991 with the newspaper *Krasnaya Zvezda*, "No Project Should be Rejected", dealt with the problems of far-reaching reforms in the army and the whole defence complex of the country. The principles of military planning suggested by Lobov included the following: the army is necessary not for promoting war but for preventing it, and the military strategy of the country should be altered accordingly; thus policy should be aimed at preventing war at any cost and by all possible means — political, economic, diplomatic, social and military. Lobov advocated the creation of a mobile professional army equipped with up-to-date matériel, which would prevent wars and conflicts and not be economically burdensome for the country. According to him, the Ministry of Defence should become a civil institution in charge of military industry, building, social policy, and rear services. Direct troop control should be transferred to the General Staff. The Minister of Defence and Chief of the General Staff, in his opinion, should be immediate subordinates of the President, being his advisers on military-political issues. These principles were actively opposed by Marshal E. Shaposhnikov, who managed to persuade M. Gorbachev to remove Lobov. The decree of December 6, 1991, dismissing him from the post of Chief of the General Staff, came as a surprise both to the General himself and to the military community, which rightly regarded it as a result of intrigue. The day before the decree, V. Lobov had returned from his official visit to the UK where he had established contacts with military officials and politicians.

At present retired, General of the Army Lobov continues his active work; he acts as an expert and consultant for liberal public organizations and the Russian Supreme Soviet on military issues. He enjoys considerable popularity among the military intelligentsia, political scientists and the academic community.

Lobov has a wide range of interests in the field of literature, art, military and political science. He does not have a good command of foreign languages, and he has been abroad several times as a member of official delegations.

He is the author of a number of classified works on military planning: a book *Military Cunning in the History of Warfare* (Moscow 1988); articles as follows: "Military reform: aims, principles, content", *Kommunist* No. 13, 1990; "Politics, doctrine and strategy in a changing world", *Krasnaya Zvezda*, October 23, 1991; "The armed forces of the motherland today and tomorrow", *Krasnaya Zvezda*, November 29, 1991; "We need an army to prevent war", *Pravda*, May 5, 1992, and others. He is co-author of the book *The Warsaw Treaty Organization: History and the Contemporary Scene* (Moscow 1990); chief editor of the book *On Military Duty and Honour in the Russian Army: A Collection of Materials, Documents and Articles* (Moscow 1990).

He was awarded orders of the Red Banner, of Kutuzov, 2nd class, two orders "For service to the motherland in the armed forces of the USSR", and 10 medals. He is married with two children and lives in Moscow.

According to experts on *Nezavisimiya Gazeta*, Gen. Lobov is one of the most influential people in Russian politics.

Lopatin, Vladimir Nikolaevich

Deputy chairman of the co-ordinating council of the "Movement for Democracy". First deputy chairman of the Russian Federation state committee on defence issues until July 1992. Major.

Born on March 17, 1960 in the village of Fomka, Krasnoyarsk *krai*, into a collective farmer's family. Russian. He began to work while at secondary school, aged 12, and organized one of the first forest reserves in the *krai*. He graduated from Achinsk Construction Technical School in 1977; Kurgan Higher Military-Political Aviation Technical School with a gold medal in 1981. He received a higher military-political education and was a member of the CPSU from January 1980 to July 1990. He left the Party for political reasons of his own free will. He saw military service in naval aviation, in the Red Banner Northern Fleet as a political commander of a ground support sub-unit, as a propagandist in an air regiment, and as head of the university of Marxism-Leninism of Kipelevo garrison. He stood out because of his professional and scientific knowledge, ability to establish contact with personnel, honesty, and eagerness to reform the outdated military rules. He was interested in political science, psychology and pedagogy. He wrote a booklet on military psychology. He was elected a member of the Party bureau and headed the people's control group. He often achieved excellent results in military and political training. Very soon, however, he found himself in disfavour with superior officers and political agencies as a result of denouncing the illegal activities of the garrison commanders and unregulated relations in the army.

In early 1989 Lopatin was nominated as a candidate for election as a USSR people's deputy by his military collective and local community in the No. 145 Vologda territorial district. His election programme proposed the reform of the social, economic and political infrastructure of the Soviet state and fundamental changes in defence policy. He won in the first round, polling 70.8% of the votes and easily defeating his opponent. He immediately took a resolute democratic stand at the congresses and sessions of the USSR Supreme Soviet. He became a member of the inter-regional group of deputies and one of the most active reformers.

At the beginning of 1990 he was appointed chairman of a special parliamentary commission to draft and implement military reform in the USSR. He was responsible for formulating the conceptual basis of a defence doctrine which included the radical restructuring of the very essence of military planning, operating within the rule of law and finding ways of maintaining an army in a democratic state. He strongly supported making use of international experience to ensure national security and to protect the various aspects of personal, state and public well-being. He opposed the dictates of the CPSU and favoured its banning, together with the depoliticization of the armed forces.

In December 1990, at the IV Congress of the USSR People's Deputies, he demanded that President Mikhail Gorbachev explain why proposals for declaring a state of emergency were being discussed. He was severely criticized and persecuted by superior officers and political agencies in the navy and the USSR Ministry of Defence for "being out of touch with the primary Party organization". Lopatin was supported by the democratic community and USSR people's deputies. He sent a letter to President Gorbachev in June 1990 including his programme. In order to try to halt the widespread political campaign, which had escaped the control of the Party agencies, the committee on Party control decided to reinstate Lopatin in the CPSU. However, Lopatin decided to leave the Party to underline his belief in the need to ban the CPSU in the military and the state.

With the creation of the RSFSR governmental agencies after the declaration of national sovereignty, in the summer of 1990, Maj. Lopatin was appointed deputy chairman of the state committee for social security and co-operation with the USSR Ministry of Defence and the USSR KGB. During the anti-constitutional putsch in August 1991, he was one of the organizers and leaders of the defence of the Russian White House. On September 7, 1991 he was promoted to colonel for his services to democracy. He became deputy chairman of the USSR Ministry of Defence commission for the dissolution of the military-political agencies, for setting up military training agencies and structures and for work with personnel in the armed forces of the USSR. He was appointed first deputy chairman of the RSFSR state committee on defence. He continued his active work in drafting plans for military reform and democratization in the army and this provoked a highly negative reaction on the part of top generals. Lopatin's early promotion was also criticized and he decided to reject the rank of colonel and revert to his former rank of major.

On May 5, 1992 the Commander-in-Chief of the Unified Armed Forces of the CIS cancelled the order promoting Lopatin to colonel as a result of the objections of the public prosecutor who claimed that the original order "violated current law". In July 1992, with the dissolution of the state committee on defence, Lopatin was transferred to the reserve. He continues his active political work as deputy chairman of the "Movement for Democracy", advocates fundamental reforms in the military sphere and appears in the mass media. Among his latest publications are the articles: "Will the Red Army defend the White House?" (*Izvestiya*, February 13, 1992); and "The President and a man with a rifle" (*Nezavisimaya Gazeta*, November 17, 1992).

Lopatin still enjoys a certain authority among younger officers and the democratic public who regard him as a victim of conservative forces who are exacting revenge for the events of August 1991. He supports the demands for the drafting of a policy of national security which ensures the stability and state interests of Russia, establishes strict parliamentary and civil control over the military and sets up a political administration to tackle defence issues, professionalization and the social protection of the military. Experts on *Nezavisimaya Gazeta* name him among the most influential people in Russian politics. He is interested in literature, history, political science, art and sport. He has a good command of English. He often meets representatives of foreign political, parliamentary and military circles. He has been awarded two medals and is married.

Office address: Moscow, Novy Arbat 19.

Lopukhin, Vladimir Mikhailovich

Minister of Fuel and Energy of the Russian Federation, November 1991 to June 1992.

Born on May 23, 1952 in Moscow into a Russian family. In 1975 he graduated in economics from Moscow State University. From 1975 to 1977 he was a probationer in the institute of world economics and international relations of the USSR Academy of Sciences. Between 1977 and 1983 he was a junior scientific assistant in the All-Union scientific research institute of systems analysis of the USSR State Committee of Science and Technology and the Academy of Sciences. Viktor Danilov-Danilyan, later Russian Minister of Ecology and Natural Resources, worked in the institute at the same time. From 1983 to 1991 he was a senior scientific assistant, then head of the laboratory of natural resource potential of the national economy of the institute of national economic forecasting of the USSR Academy of Sciences. He worked on the problems of the development of the raw materials sectors and was involved in research into the basic problems of energetics, ecology and the use of natural resources.

In 1991 he was deputy RSFSR Minister of the Economy in the government of Ivan Silaev and in November of that year he was appointed Minister of Fuel and Energy of the Russian Federation. He said that he entered the Russian government with the intention of implementing his ideas of how to reform fuel and energy. He held that the key is the privatization of some of the fuel and energy enterprises, the reorganization of the existing structure, the creation of a competitive environment in this sector of the economy and the gradual removal of the system of licensing exports. It was necessary to determine the capacity and capabilities of the large, medium and small enterprises in this sector as international experience has demonstrated that the most efficient units are the large ones. Mikhail Khodorovsky, one of the founders and leaders of the international financial group, Menatep, became one of Lopukhin's deputy ministers.

Lopukhin is chairman of the board of the joint venture, Vespek, formed by the firms AVV of the USA, Neste of Finland and Tobolsk petrochemical combine. In fact, government ministers in Russia may not pursue outside business interests while in office, but Lopukhin got round this by handing his Vespek salary over to the No. 1 educational and training complex in Tobolsk.

Lopukhin's plans for the reorganization of the oil and gas industry were fiercly resisted by Viktor Chernomyrdin and others. Gasprom and Rosneftgas took particular umbrage at the efforts of Mikhail Khodorovsky to break down existing energy monopolies. They lobbied Yeltsin and their work bore fruit in June 1992 when Lopukhin was dismissed and Viktor Chernomyrdin was appointed deputy Prime Minister responsible for fuel and energy. This was a concession by the President to Civic Union, the industrial managers' lobby. It also spelled the end of the government's attempts to break up the powerful energy monopolies.

Lopukhin speaks English. He is married with a daughter who is a student, and a young son.

Lortkipanidze, Grigory Davidovich

Theatre and Cinema Producer; Chairman of the Union of Theatrical Workers of the Republic of Georgia; Member of Parliament of the Republic of Georgia.

Born on September 19, 1927 in Tbilisi, Georgian SSR. A Georgian, whose father, David, was an engineer and fell victim to Stalin's purges in 1938. His mother, Nina, was a housewife. His sister, Mariya Davidovna, is a corresponding member of the Academy of Sciences of Georgia and head of the department of the history of Georgia, Tbilisi State University.

He graduated from the department of production, Lunacharsky State Institute of Theatrical Art, Moscow. He was artistic director of the K. Mardzhanishvili theatre. From 1962 to 1967 he founded and directed the Rustaveli theatre, and was artistic director of the Griboedov theatre (1967–73). During his career he has written over 100 articles on the cinema and the theatre and made seven films. Among these are *The Sworn Record*, a documentary on the Georgievsky treaty which united Georgia and Russia in the early 19th century.

Lortkipanidze was made a people's artist of the USSR and of Georgia and is also a professor. He is a sports fan. He is married and his wife, Kitevan, is a theatrical and cinema actress and a people's actress of Georgia. They have three daughters. Nina is 32 years old and an actress, Nana is 30 years old, also an actress, and Maya is 19 years old and a student.

Home address: Tbilisi, ul. p. Yashvili, Dom 7; *telephone*: Tbilisi 99 75 95.

Lubenchenko, Konstantin Dmitrievich

Director of the Russian parliamentary Centre.

Born on October 27, 1945 in Zhukovsky, Moscow *oblast*; Russian. He was a member of the CPSU from 1972 to August 1991. His father was a colonel who was a member of the commission for the rehabilitation of the innocently condemned and tortured during the Stalin terror. He retired at the age of 43 years and died tragically in 1965. In 1957 Lubenchenko fell under a car and suffered a badly damaged hip which threatened to paralyse him, and so he took up yoga. He began his career as an electrician in 1964 in Zhukovsky, and in 1968 he entered the faculty of law, Moscow State University. In his third year he delivered a brilliant lecture on law and morality which drew attention to him and he joined the department of the theory of state and law, from which he graduated with distinction in 1973. He then became a postgraduate student and in 1978 successfully presented his candidate dissertation in law on "the problems of systemic-structural research into the law of developed socialist society" (LLM).

In 1976 he became an assistant, and in 1981 an assistant professor in the department of the theory of state and law, faculty of law, Moscow State University. He was a member of the specialized candidate state legal council of the university, and scientific secretary of the section on the history of the state and law, scientific methodological council of USSR institutes. He has published many legal articles and chapters in textbooks, and had almost completed research on his doctoral dissertation when he became active in public and political life. He was a permanent member of the Party bureau of the department, secretary of the Party bureau, member of the commission of the ideological department of the Party committee, Moscow State University, a lecturer at the University of Marxism-Leninism, and member of the *Znanie* society. He has university awards, and the badge of excellent militiaman. For a time he was a public assistant in the procurator's office in Zhukovsky.

In 1989 he was nominated by the work collectives of the Tsentralny hydro-dynamics institute, Zhukovsky electromechanical enterprise, and the Ramenskoe production design bureau for election as a USSR people's deputy in the No. 40 Ramenskoe territorial district, Moscow *oblast*. During the election campaign he advocated the elimination of the privileges of the nomenclature; a struggle against corruption, bribe taking and the mafia; the autonomy of state socialist enterprises; a struggle against the bureaucratic distortion of the law; the amendment of the taxation system; the establishment of strict financial supervision over all forms of income in the state; the publication of the salaries of public officials; a minimum wage and pension; in agriculture a move from leasing to large peasant enterprises; the soviets should be the sole economic centre and the sole representative of state ownership of land; the removal of all unnecessary bureaucratic links between the soviets and agricultural producers; raising the quality of the laws which should reflect the will of the whole people and not that of officials in the apparatus. He believes that most of the existing laws are bad resulting in illegality and injustice. He called for the institution of referenda and general consultations to resolve political problems, and for the illegal law on elections to be amended and democracy and *glasnost* expanded.

There were five candidates and Lubenchenko won in the first round, polling 51.8% of the votes. His main opponent was A. A. Eltsov, a teacher of physics in the No. 5 secondary school, Ramenskoe, who received 17.6% of the votes. In the USSR Supreme Soviet he became deputy chairman of the committee on legislation, law and order and was an opponent of Anatoly Lukyanov. In 1990 he was a candidate for Speaker (chairman) of the Supreme Soviet but then lost to Anatoly Lukyanov. Lubenchenko was elected Speaker of the USSR Supreme Soviet in October 1991, but only remained in office for two and a half months. He thought that the collapse of the Soviet Union was mainly due to the subjective factor, which was artificially provoked in order to undermine the power of President Gorbachev and the centre that he represented. He spoke out against the Minsk (Belovezhsky) agreement, believing that ways were available to reform the Union, even after August 1991. He regarded Anatoly Lukyanov as the most significant political figure during the attempted coup, as he held all the threads of power in his hands and introduced a strict administrative Party style of leadership in parliament.

In 1992 Lubenchenko became director of the Russian parliamentary centre. The concept of the centre belongs to him and it should become the brain, the intellect of the Supreme Soviet, including the library, the research service and the bank of deputies' ideas. He was invited to join the Russian governmental apparatus and was even proposed for the post of chairman of the Russian KGB. His candidature was vitiated by General Sterligov, then the main contender for the post. There was a proposal that the members of the Constitutional Court should vote on the matter, but Lubenchenko refused due to the fact that the job would be long term and he would have to leave politics. He opposes surgical methods for solving problems of power, and believes that the constituent assembly cannot be a purely democratic assembly. He opposes the immediate promulgation of a new constitution. First of all, a constitutional law should be adopted, amending the new agency of political power, then a law on elections should be agreed; they should be held, and only then should the new members of parliament adopt a new constitution. In 1992 he was also elected chairman of the council of the movement in support of parliament in Russia. He is married with a son and lives in Zhukovsky, Moscow *oblast*. He enjoys carving in wood and stone.

Luchin, Viktor Osipovich

Member of the Constitutional Court of the Russian Federation.

Born on March 26, 1939 in the Cossack village of Ladva-Vetka, Prionezhsky *raion*, Karelian ASSR; Russian; member of the CPSU until August 1991. In 1965 he graduated from the faculty of law, Voronezh State University. In 1966 he became a postgraduate student and in 1971 at Voronezh State University he successfully presented his candidate dissertation on "Procedural norms in Soviet state law" (LLM).

From 1971 to 1979 he was a senior lecturer, assistant professor, head of the department of the theory and history of the state and law, faculty of law, Kuibyshev State University, and from 1979 to 1989 he was senior scientific assistant, institute of state and law, USSR Academy of Sciences. In the early 1980s he prepared a doctoral dissertation on the relationship between constitutional law and public practice and the implementation of constitutional norms and principles, but he did not present it since his views were not in accord with official jurisprudence. From 1989 to 1991 he was an assistant professor in the department of state formation and legal policy, Russian social and political institute (the former Higher Party school of the Central Committee, CPSU). He gave lectures on constitutional and state law to members of the Party and state apparatus.

The main areas of his legal interests are constitutional and state law, the analysis of constitutional legislation and its use. He has published over 50 academic articles and books including the monographs *Procedural Norms in State Law* and *Sources of Soviet State Law*.

He was nominated for election to the Constitutional Court by the communists of Russia parliamentary group. He was elected a member on October 30,

1991, at the V Congress of People's Deputies, in the second round of voting, when he received 529 votes for and 301 votes against. In the first round he got 472 votes for and 421 against, and a candidate needed 529 votes to be elected.

He regards the key duties of the Constitutional Court to be the defence of constitutional rule in Russia in order to develop a law-governed state. He has appealed for the elimination of the legal nihilism and legal cynicism of Russian authorities and support only for those parties and public organizations which function within the constitution. The Constitutional Court docs not have the right, in his view, to shut its eyes to infractions of the constitution even though it is an old one. He lives in Moscow.

Lucinschii, Petru Chiril

Speaker of the *Sfatul Ţării* (parliament) of the Republic of Moldova.

Born in 1940 in the village of Radulenii Vechi, Floreşti *raion*, Moldova. He is an ethnic Moldovan, who was a candidate (PhD) of philosophy. He graduated from the State University in Chişinău and the Higher CPSU Party School in Moscow. For 10 years he was one of the leaders of the *Komsomol*: first secretary of the Bălţi *Komosomol* committee, and second, then first secretary of the Moldovan *Komsomol* central committee. From 1971 to 1976 he was a secretary of the Central Committee of the Communist Party of Moldova. From June 1978 he worked as the assistant head of the propaganda department of the CPSU Central Committee. From 1986 he was a secretary of the Central Committee of the Communist Party of Tajikistan. In November 1989 he was named first secretary of the Communist Party of Moldova, replacing Semion Grossu. He served as a deputy in the Moldovan Supreme Soviet (and of the present *Sfatul Ţării*). In 1992 he was named ambassador to the Russian Federation. On February 4, 1993 he was elected to replace Alexandru Moşanu as speaker of the *Sfatul Ţării*.

Lucko (Lutzko), Alaksandr Michajlavic

Rector, International Sakharov College of Radioecology, Minsk, Belarus.

Born on January 23, 1941 in Salihorsk, Minsk *oblast*. His parents are Michajl Lucko and Tatiana Kuznecova, and the family is Belarusian. He graduated in 1963 from the department of nuclear physics, Belarusian State University, Minsk, was a postgraduate student at the university from 1964 to 1968 and successfully presented his candidate dissertation in physics and mathematics (PhD). From 1963 to 1969 he was head of the laboratory of dosimetry, Institute of Cancer, Minsk, from 1969 to 1979 he was a lecturer in the department of nuclear physics, Belarusian State University, and from 1979 to 1987 he was head of the laboratory of radioactive isotopes and instrumentation methods, Far East Institute of Biorganic Chemistry, USSR Academy of Sciences, Vladivostok, Maritime *krai*, RSFSR. From 1987 to 1991 he was a lecturer in the department of nuclear physics, Belarusian State University, Minsk.

In 1992 he was appointed rector of the International Sakharov College of Radioecology, Minsk. He is a supporter of the declaration of human rights, and his hobbies are mountaineering, the arts and ethnography. He is married to Valeria Mamontova and they have a daughter, Tatiana Kushnir. He speaks English.

Address: The International Sakharov College of Radioecology, 220009 Minsk, Douhabrodskaja 23; 220082 Minsk, P. O. Box 180 (home); *telephone*: Minsk (0172) 306 998; Minsk (0172) 59 70 56 (home); *fax*: Minsk (0172) 366 897; *E-mail*: Lutsko %iscr.minsk.by@relay.ussr.eu.net.

Luhin, Jauhien Michajlavic

Chairman of the Central Council of the Belarusian Peasant Party (BSP).

Born on February 23, 1935 in the village of Barbarova, Hlusk *raion*, Mahilou *oblast*, whose parents are Michail and Adaria Luhin. He is Belarusian, and was a member of the CPSU until 1990. He was trained as a military construction engineer and later obtained a higher education and became a lecturer. In 1955 he began his military career and retired in 1986 as a lieutenant-colonel, and then from 1987 to 1991 he worked on his parents' private plot in a village. He was a member of the organizing committee which prepared the establishment of the Belarusian Peasant Party (1990-91), and on February 13, 1991 he was elected chairman of the Central Council of the BSP. He views himself as a liberal democrat, and his hobbies are philosophy and politics. His wife, Nela, was born in 1940 and they have two sons, Siarhiej, born in 1961, and Alaksandr, born in 1965. He speaks Russian, Polish and German (with a dictionary).

Address: 2200068 Minsk, ul. Haja 38, kv. 1; *telephone:* Minsk (0172) 34 38 35.

Lukianenko, Levko Grygorovych

Presidential Candidate; Ex-Leader of the Ukrainian Republican Party; Ukrainian Ambassador to Canada.

Born into a Ukrainian peasant family in 1927 in a village in Chernihiv *oblast* in central Ukraine. From 1944 to 1953 he served in the Soviet Army, firstly in occupied Austria, where he was impressed by the rapid recovery of its capitalist mixed economy, and then in Azerbaijan. From 1953 to 1958 he studied law at Moscow State University, at the same time as Mikhail Gorbachev, although the two never met. From 1958 to 1961 he worked as a lawyer in Lviv *oblast*, where he formed an underground nationalist group, the Ukrainian Workers' and Peasants' Union, committed to struggling for Ukrainian independence by peaceful means.

Lukianenko and six others were arrested in 1961, and Lukianenko was sentenced to death. After 70 days on death row his sentence was reduced to ten years in the camps, and five of exile. In autumn 1976 he was freed, and immediately resumed his activities, joining the Ukrainian Helsinki Group (UHG). He was rearrested at the end of 1977, and received the same sentence of fifteen years' prison and exile. When the UHG reformed itself as the Ukrainian Helsinki Union (UHU) in 1988, Lukianenko was asked to become its leader. At the time, in March 1988, he was still in exile, only returning to Ukraine under President Mikhail Gorbachev's general amnesty in January 1989, after a sentence totalling 27 years.

He led the UHU through its transformation in April 1990 into the Ukrainian Republican Party (URP), which became the main opposition party in Ukraine. In March 1990 he was elected people's deputy for Zaliznychnyi *raion*, Ivano-Frankivsk *oblast*, in western Ukraine, in the first round with 54% of the vote. In the Supreme Soviet he was a member of the committee on legislation and legality, and from the moment of his symbolic candidature for the post of Supreme Soviet chairman in May 1990 (the URP had only 11 deputies at the time) his weighty interventions as the elder statesman of the national movement were always listened to with respect.

He was also a member of the Political Councils of both *Rukh* and the People's Council. Lukianenko meanwhile presided over the growing influence of the URP. It had 9,000 members by its second congress in June 1991, making it the largest non-communist party in Ukraine. Lukianenko stood for the Ukrainian presidency in autumn 1991, and achieved the best result of any party figure, coming third behind Kravchuk and Chornovil with 1,432,556 votes, or 4.49% of the total. Although an ardent nationalist, Lukianenko consistently opposed Khmara's ultra-radical wing of the party, and organized their defeat at the URP's third congress in May 1992.

If Khmara wished to continue in opposition to President Kravchuk, Lukianenko argued that Ukraine's Declaration of Independence in August 1991 had changed the situation completely. From being a "semi-underground party" faced with an "occupation government", the URP should now become a "party of respectable conservatism" and support a vigorous state-building process. Lukianenko therefore became a strong supporter of Kravchuk, and accepted his offer to become the first Ukrainian ambassador to Canada in spring 1992 (where he would attempt to mobilize the support of the one million strong Ukrainian diaspora community for the young state). He therefore resigned his deputies' mandate, and his position as URP leader, although he remains its honorary Chairman.

Address: 252034 Kiev, Vul. Prorizna 27 *telephone*: Kiev 228 0772.

Lukin, Vladimir Petrovich

Russian Ambassador to the United States.

Born on July 13, 1937 in Omsk. His parents were Party workers and were arrested in 1937, but were freed after the "unmasking" of Nikolai Ezhov. Russian. Member of the CPSU from 1961 to August 1991. He graduated in 1959 from the history faculty of the V. I. Lenin Moscow State Pedagogical Institute and spent a year as a scientific assistant in the state historical museum, Moscow. Then he commenced postgraduate studies in the Institute of World Economics and International Relations, USSR Academy of Sciences. In 1964 he successfully presented his candidate dissertation on social democracy in south and south-east Asia (PhD). His book, *Trade Unions in South East Asia*, appeared in the same year.

From 1965 to 1968 he was on the editorial staff of the international communist journal, *Problems of Peace and Socialism*, in Prague, Czechoslovakia, where he struck up friendly relations with some of those around Alexander Dubček. As a result of his unhappiness with the Warsaw Pact intervention in Czechoslovakia in August 1968 he was sent back to Moscow. For the next 19 years he worked in the institute for the study of the US and Canada, USSR Academy of Sciences, specializing on US relations with Asia, and successfully presented a doctoral dissertation (DLitt). He is a professor and has an honorary doctorate from the Simón Bolívar University, Bogotá, Colombia. He was awarded various Soviet orders and medals.

He became one of the leading specialists in the Soviet Union on international relations and political science and was well known abroad. In 1983 his book, *The Centres of Power: Concepts and Reality*, was published in Moscow and in 1987 followed *The Place of China in Global US Policy*. In 1987 he joined the USSR Ministry of Foreign Affairs and stayed two years. From 1989 to 1990 he organized and headed the centre for the analysis and forecasting of the secretariat of the USSR Supreme Soviet where he was called upon to provide deputies with information and analyses. On January 16, 1991 he signed a declaration to the intelligentsia protesting against the events in Vilnius when Soviet forces had stormed the TV station.

In January 1990 he was nominated for election as an RSFSR people's deputy in the No. 9 Podolsk national territorial district, Moscow *oblast*. There were 11 candidates. Lukin polled 12.3% of the votes in the first round and won the second round, polling 46.6% of the votes. In his election campaign he advocated real and not cosmetic Russian state sovereignty, freedom to set up public organizations, the gradual elimination of the internal passport system, the establishment of a jury system, professional armed forces, economic independence for enterprises and regions, transfer of land to those who wanted to work it and the elimination of privilege.

He was elected a member of the Supreme Soviet, Soviet of Nationalities, the Presidium of the Supreme Soviet and was chairman of the RSFSR Supreme Soviet committee on international relations and foreign economic links. He was a member of the constitutional commission and a member of the coalition of reform parliamentary bloc. In July 1991 he stood for election as speaker of the RSFSR Supreme Soviet. During the attempted putsch in August 1991 he was in the building housing the RSFSR Supreme Soviet and RSFSR government and maintained contacts with foreign countries. On November 25, 1991 he became a member of the commission on the supervision of the implementation of the decrees of the President of Russia.

On January 24, 1992 he was appointed Russian ambassador to the United States and the title of ambassador extraordinary and plenipotentiary was conferred on him. He was the first post-communist Russian ambassador. In Washington he began by meeting Russian émigré representatives, including Aleksandr Solzhenitsyn, Vasily Aksenov, Mstislav Rostropovich, Ernst Neizvestny and N. Korzhavin. He quickly established good working relations with the Bush administration, but underlined that democracy by itself does not guarantee full mutual understanding although commonly held views, values and the same point of departure for analysis are extremely important. Clashes were inevitable but they would be resolved by different methods than in the past. Policy should be based on the defence of national interests, without extremes and risk taking, within the context of co-operation and with each side enjoying equal rights. He speaks English, French and Spanish. He is married and has a grown up son who is studying at the University of Oxford. He lives in Washington, DC.

Lukyanov, Anatoly Ivanovich

Member of the Emergency Committee.

Born on May 7, 1930 in Smolensk. Russian. Member of the CPSU from 1955 to August 1991. He began working in a military factory at the age of 13 years in 1943. In 1953 he graduated from the law faculty of Moscow State University, where he was a fellow student of Mikhail Gorbachev. Lukyanov then became a postgraduate student at Moscow State University and successfully presented his candidate dissertation in law (LLM). In 1979 he successfully presented his doctoral dissertation in law (LLD), and became a senior consultant in the legal commission of the USSR Council of Ministers.

From 1961 to 1976 he was a senior reviewer, then deputy head of department on the activities of the soviets in the Presidium of the USSR Supreme Soviet, and in 1976 he became a consultant in the department of the organization of

Party work in the Party Central Committee. From 1977 to 1983 he was head of the secretariat of the Presidium of the USSR Supreme Soviet and from 1981 to 1986 he was a member of the central revision commission of the Party. In 1983 he became first deputy head and in 1985 head of the general department of the Party Central Committee. In 1986 he was elected a member of the Party Central Committee and in 1987 he became a secretary and then head of the department of administrative agencies of the Committee.

In 1988 he became first deputy chairman of the Presidium of the USSR Supreme Soviet (this role was equivalent to that of deputy President). From September 1988 to July 1990 he was a candidate member of the Party Politburo. He was a delegate to the XXVI, XXVII Party congresses and the XIX Party conference. He was elected a USSR and RSFSR people's deputy in 1986. He was awarded the orders of the October Revolution, the Red Banner of Labour and medals.

In 1989 he was nominated for election as a USSR people's deputy by the CPSU and was elected. At the I Congress of People's Deputies he was elected to the USSR Supreme Soviet and became first deputy Speaker. In March 1990 he was elected Speaker of the USSR Supreme Soviet.

On August 19, 1991 he signed the decree of the USSR Supreme Soviet convoking an extraordinary session of the USSR Supreme Soviet and the declaration of the Speaker of the Supreme Soviet on the draft Union treaty. The declaration stated that the Union treaty did not express the results of the referendum of March 17, 1991 and does not create the circumstances for the renewal of the federation of equal, sovereign states, or a single economic area and banking system; does not contain guarantees against the "war of laws", and does not provide clear mechanisms for its implementation. Lukyanov regarded it as intending to create a confederation and not a federation of states. For this reason it could not be adopted in its present form and new deliberations were necessary.

Lukyanov was regarded by some observers as the master behind the intrigue but he vigorously denied that he had been involved in the organization of the putsch. On August 28, 1991 he resigned as Speaker of the USSR Supreme Soviet. On August 29, 1991 the session of the USSR Supreme Soviet agreed that Lukyanov should be held criminally responsible and arrested. From August 29, 1991 to December 1992 he was held during investigations in the *Matrosskaya tishina* isolator.

He is a poet and under the pseudonym of A. Osenev he published a book of verse and the collection of poems, *Poems from Prison*, under his real name in 1993. He is married and his wife is a corresponding member of the Academy of Medical Sciences. They have a daughter who is an assistant professor at Moscow State University. He lives in Moscow.

Lukyanov, Nikolai Nikolaevich

Chairman of the Moscow monarchist centre.

Born in 1965 in Moscow; Russian. He completed secondary school, and began his working career in 1982 as a cook, then as a docker. He did his national service from 1984 to 1986 in the internal troops of the USSR Ministry of the Interior. From 1986 to 1990 he served in the militia department responsible for guarding the USSR state planning committee (Gosplan) and the USSR Council of Ministers, and had the rank of a sergeant of the militia. In 1989 he established contacts with various Russian monarchist organizations, and early in 1990 he was appointed head of the Moscow detachment of the Russian people's guard. In December 1990 he was elected chairman of the order of the Russian Royal Union, Moscow branch. In April 1991 he was elected a member of the council of the all-Russia Monarchist Front and in November 1991, chairman of the Moscow monarchist centre. His hobby is stamp collecting and he is unmarried.

Address: 123181 Moscow, ul. Isakovskaya 2, d. 2. kv. 66; *telephone*: Moscow 944 3032 (home).

Luzhkov, Yury Mikhailovich

Head of the Administration, Mayor of Moscow.

Born on September 21, 1936 in Moscow into a carpenter's family; Russian; member of the CPSU from 1968 to August 1991. In 1958 he graduated from the I. M. Gubkin Oil Institute, Moscow, and during his studies he augmented his income by managing some flats and also worked in the Virgin Lands (initiated by Khrushchev in 1954 mainly in north Kazakhstan and west Siberia). After graduating he worked in the scientific research institute for plastics as a scientific assistant, head of a group, head of a laboratory and chief engineer. In 1964 he was appointed head of a department in the USSR Ministry of the Chemical Agro-Industry and in 1974 became head of the research bureau of the same ministry. From 1980 to 1986 he was general director of the scientific production association, Neftekhimavtomatika. In 1987 he moved into work in the soviets: as first deputy chairman of the soviet executive committee of the Moscow city soviet, then as chairman of the Moscow agro-industrial committee. From April 14, 1990 he acted as chairman of the Moscow city soviet executive committee.

In 1975 he was elected a deputy of the Babushkinsky *raion* soviet, was a deputy of Moscow city soviet (1977–90), and deputy of the RSFSR Supreme Soviet (1987–90). He was awarded the USSR state prize, the order of Lenin and the Red Banner of Labour and the medals for the assimilation of the Virgin Lands, a defender of a free Russia and others. He was an honoured chemist of the RSFSR and USSR.

On April 25, 1990 he was appointed chairman of the Moscow city soviet executive committee and in 1991 Gavriil Popov, chairman of Moscow city soviet, and Luzhkov, stood for the posts of mayor and vice-mayor of Moscow. Popov and Luzhkov won the election on June 12, 1991 in the first round, polling 65.32% of the votes. Their main opponents were V. T. Saikin, formerly chairman of the Moscow city soviet executive committee, and V. Kraiko, a USSR people's deputy, who received 16.35% of the votes. After the election Luzhkov was appointed Prime Minister of the government of Moscow.

In August 1991 the city soviet and government of Moscow played a major role in overcoming the consequences of the attempted state coup. In August 1991 Luzhkov was appointed a member of the committee for the day-to-day management of the Soviet economy, by decree of Mikhail Gorbachev, the USSR President. Luzhkov was made responsible for the agro-industrial complex, fuel, foreign economic links and the social sphere. He continued as Prime Minister of Moscow. On June 5, 1992, after the resignation of Gavriil Popov as mayor, Luzhkov assumed the functions of mayor and head of the administration of Moscow, and was then appointed head of the administration of Moscow by presidential decree.

In December 1992 Luzhkov denied the accusation that the President of the Russian Federation was organizing a constitutional coup and blamed the Congress of People's Deputies for the constitutional crisis. Luzhkov stated that the deputies were shifting responsibility for their decisions on to the government and that the congress was an example of collective madness. However, the mayor of Moscow criticized the Gaidar government which had acted unprofessionally and was enamoured of reform theory to the detriment of practice. Viktor Chernomyrdin, in becoming Prime Minister, now occupied the position he should have had long ago.

Luzhkov is married with two sons from his first marriage and a daughter from the second. He enjoys swimming in ice holes and football, and captains the Moscow government football team. He lives in Moscow.

Lyashenko, Vladimir Efimovich

First Deputy Chief of the main headquarters of the Navy. Vice-Admiral since 1990.

Born on July 4, 1937 in Moscow. The social status of his parents is unknown. Ukrainian. Lyashenko graduated from M. V. Frunze Higher Naval Technical school in Leningrad in 1958; the Higher Classes for Officers in 1967; the Naval Academy in 1975. He received a higher naval education and was a member of the CPSU till August 1991.

He became commander of a motor torpedo-boat and rocket boat in the Baltic Fleet from 1967 to 1970, Chief of Staff of a rocket boat flotilla of the same fleet in 1970/71, Chief of Staff of a rocket boat sub-division from 1971 to 1973. He proved to be a qualified officer and sailor, capable of planning and organizing the training of boat forces in the closed Baltic theatre of operation. He was respected by commanders and Party agencies and was actively involved in the work of local Party organization. He was no different from his colleagues either in professional or official interests, and expressed political views typical of military circles in support of the CPSU and the top leaders of the USSR.

After graduating from the Academy he was commander of a rocket ship sub-division from 1975 to 1982 and Chief of Staff of a naval base in the Baltic Fleet from 1982 to 1984. In 1984 he was appointed Chief of Staff of the Caspian flotilla and from 1988 he was a commander of the same Baku-based flotilla. He actively supported the communist leaders of Azerbaijan. The Caspian sailors took part in armed counter-activities against national democratic forces and in suppressing ethnic conflicts in Transcaucasia. On the orders of the high command, Lyashenko ordered the flotilla under his command to intervene in the events in Baku in January 1990, to ensure the evacuation of refugees by sea and to support the troops brought into the city.

In 1991 he was transferred to Moscow and appointed deputy chief of the main headquarters of the navy. He supervised naval units under central command. Since 1992 he has been the first deputy chief of the main headquarters of the navy, head of leading administrations (strategic and others). He is actively involved in preparations of the celebrations for the 300th anniversary of the Russian navy.

He has never expressed his political views in the mass media. According to knowledgeable sources he is eager to retain the image of a non-party military professional, while actually supporting state supremacy. Due to his political education in the army he is a typical Soviet military official of the conformist type who supports the existing state regime.

He is fond of reading books on the history of the navy, on historical and military subjects. He has been awarded orders and medals, and is married.

Office address: 103175, Moscow, K-175.

Magomedov, Magomed-Ali Magomedovich

Speaker of the Supreme Soviet of the Republic of Dagestan, Russian Federation.

Born in 1930 in the village of Levashi, Levashi *raion*, Dagestan Autonomous Soviet Socialist Republic (ASSR); member of the CPSU from 1954 to August 1991. He attended Levashi secondary school between 1938 and 1949, and from 1949 to 1950 he was a teacher and class leader in the same school. In 1950 he entered the Dagestan Pedagogical Institute and graduated in 1952. In 1968 he graduated from the extra-mural department of the Dagestan Agricultural Institute. From 1952 to 1957 he was director of the Levashi secondary school and head of the Levashi *raion* department of education. In 1957 he was elected chairman of the Komintern collective farm where he remained for nine years, and in 1966 was appointed head of the agricultural production administration of Levashi *raion*. In 1969 he was elected chairman of the *raion* soviet executive committee, in December 1970 he was elected first secretary of the Levashi *raion* Party committee, and in September 1975 head of the agricultural department of the Dagestan Party *obkom*. From January 1979 to May 1983 he was deputy, and from May 1983 Chairman of the Council of Ministers of the Dagestan ASSR. In August 1987 at the VI session of the Supreme Soviet he was elected chairman of the Presidium of the Supreme Soviet of Dagestan ASSR. He was awarded the orders of the October Revolution, Red Banner of Labour, badge of honour and medals.

In early 1990 he was nominated for election as an RSFSR people's deputy in the No. 813 Levashi territorial district. During the election campaign he advocated the restoration of the full powers of the soviets and criticized the bureaucratic approach to human problems. He supported the implementation of the programme, "Housing 2000", economic cost accounting and food and consumer goods for the population. He wanted the restructuring of defence enterprises to produce goods for the civilian population, the cleaning up of environmental problems and improvement in inter-regional relations.

Magomedov won in the second round, his main opponent being N.-I. S. Dzhidalaev. Magomedov was then re-elected a people's deputy of the Dagestan ASSR and was also elected a delegate to the XXVIII Party congress. At the first session of the people's deputies of Dagestan ASSR, on April 24, 1990, he was elected unopposed Speaker (Chairman) of the Supreme Soviet of the Dagestan ASSR. On assuming office he spoke out against the omnipotence and dictates of the central authorities, for an increase in the rights of the republics in all spheres of public life and for real sovereignty. He advocated moving to self-financing and self-government, the extension of the economic autonomy of the republic, the development of local industry, foreign economic links and the scaling down of new industrial investment.

On August 21, 1991 the decree of the Presidium of the Supreme Soviet of the Dagestan Soviet Socialist Republic stated that there were no grounds for introducing a state of emergency in the republic and appealed for social peace and no strikes. In 1992 a referendum was carried out in the republic in which the population voted against the introduction of the post of President and private ownership of land. Magomedov proposed his own regional programme of economic reform which would introduce correctives and some amendments to the all-Russian reforms. Reforms should be based on local sources of raw materials and traditional branches of industry. He advocated a social approach, based on various forms of ownership and equal rights for all forms of property and the development of market relations. He was for financial stability, the need to transform the agrarian sector by rapidly introducing leasing, the structural reform of the economy and guarantees of employment for the population. He advocated economic links and help from Russia and the co-ordination of the republic's policy with that of the basic tenets of all-Russian policy.

In December 1992 he expressed his concern and anxiety at the conflict between the legislative and executive branches of power, and criticized the incorrect, ambitious and sometimes insulting utterances of some members of the leadership of both the legislature and the executive. Such an atmosphere, in his view, does not nurture confidence and respect on the part of citizens towards the legislature and the government and their policies. The Supreme Soviet and the government should work together in an agreed manner and be in constant contact, based on the interests of the peoples of Russia and not on the personal bias and emotions of individual deputies. He lives in Makhachkala.

Maiorov, Leonid Sergeevich

Commander of the North-Western group of troops. Colonel-General.

Born on July 22, 1941 in Georgievsk, Stavropol *krai*, into a working-class family. Russian. He graduated from the Military Automobile Officers' Technical School in 1961; the Military Rear and Transport Academy in 1972; the Military Academy of the General Staff in 1986. He received a higher military education and was a member of the CPSU until August 1991.

He began his career as officer as an automobile platoon commander. Later, he held staff posts in sub-units and rear services of the land forces. He was notable among rear officers for his eagerness to improve his military and tactical training and for studying special instructions. After graduating from the academy with a degree in staff and rear work he was appointed head of the special service of a formation. He possessed a sound operational-tactical and military-technical training, understood military equipment and the essence of present-day combat in land forces. In 1976 he was appointed Chief of Staff, deputy commander of a motorized-rifle division, which was quite untypical for a rear officer in the Soviet army and indicated Gen. Maiorov's exceptional abilities. In 1979 he became a motorized-rifle divisional commander.

After graduating from the Academy of the General Staff in 1986 he was assigned to the Trans-Baikal military district. He was Chief of Staff of an army and then an army commander. Under his command were units stationed in Mongolia and he organized their withdrawal to the Soviet Union. From 1991 he was Chief of Staff and first deputy commander of the Volga-Urals military district. In July 1992 he became commander of the north-western group of troops in Lithuania, Latvia and Estonia. At the end of October 1992, by decree of President Boris Yeltsin, he was appointed the senior official of the Russian Federation in Lithuania, Latvia and Estonia responsible for the temporary stationing and withdrawal of troops and the navy from the region.

Gen. Maiorov is in charge of the preparations for the withdrawal of Russian troops from the Baltic states, keeping them on high combat readiness in circumstances restricted by various conditions imposed by the local authorities. He is a member of Russian Federation working group negotiating with the Baltic states. He has demonstrated diplomatic skill, tact and self-control in relations with local authorities and politicians, is a military professional and is not active in domestic Russian political affairs. His status as a Russian military leader on foreign territory makes it impossible for him to issue political declarations or express his personal views. His work is made all the more difficult by contact with unsophisticated groupings of the Russian-speaking population who are susceptible to views which promote Russia as a strong state domestically and as a great power internationally, and who are also uncertain about their future status in the Baltic. He is quite successful at promoting the interests of Russia in the region. He is interested in literature and the military history of his country. He does not speak any foreign language and has not been in the West as a member of an official delegation. He has been awarded two orders, and medals. He is married with children.

Gen. Maiorov's headquarters are in Riga.

Makarov, Andrei Mikhailovich

Russian lawyer.

Born in 1955; Russian. He graduated from the faculty of law, Moscow State University, and in 1979 he successfully presented his candidate dissertation in law on "The use of scientific and technical means by the courts during the investigation of criminal cases" (LLM). He is a member of the board of the Moscow collegium of lawyers, was one of the founders of the USSR union of lawyers, and is a member of the Moscow tribune club of the intelligentsia. He defended Yury Churbanov during the Uzbek corruption case and was invited by Academician Andrei Sakharov and Yury Afanasev to act in the case of the political strike at the Nogina newspaper, *Znamya kommunizma*.

In 1992 Makarov acted for the prosecution during the case against the CPSU in the Constitutional Court. From a legal point of view he regards the decision of the court as absurd and, from an historical point of view, criminal. He regards the decision (to decriminalize the CPSU) as the result of specific political motives and considered his main opponent during the hearing to be the Constitutional Court itself. He maintains that, nevertheless, he won the case but regrets that the state was not on the President's side, merely a group who shared his views.

He is opposed to the creation of extra-legal entities to fight professional crime and appeals for the struggle against crime to be separated from politics. It is necessary not to make statements about corruption, but in reality to fight it and not to make use of these slogans to introduce extraordinary measures which could open up a route to dictatorship. He is critical of the fact that there is no political, legal or public culture in Russia. The Constitutional Court should not be seen as the crown of the judiciary. The latter should include, besides the Constitutional Court, the court of arbitration and the whole judicial system. The decisions of the VII Congress of People's Deputies, in December 1992, were the crudest form of the violation of the constitution, and violation of the principle of the separation of powers and of all power resting with the people. Political reform should have been carried through immediately after the failed coup of August 1991 since the policy of compromise has proved a failure. He is critical of the President for dismissing Egor Gaidar and Gennady Burbulis whom he regards as the most committed reformers, and he advocated confiscating the property of the CPSU. The Party nomenclature has only conceded a small morsel of power to the democrats, that of the post of President and a more or less democratically elected parliament. At a time when reforms at the local level are being sabotaged by restoring the old system, democrats have no real levers of power.

There should be a wide-ranging campaign to explain to the population the goals of economic policy, especially how one is to use the vouchers during privatization. A new state mechanism to implement reforms is necessary since the existing system is in reality a barrier. First and foremost, political relations should be reformed and the Prime Minister should be a politician, the most acceptable person for this post being Sergei Shakhrai since he is one of the generation of new politicians. The establishment of the CIS was an illegal act which nevertheless confirms *de jure* the existing situation when there is no single state. He is critical of the populist decisions of the parliament, for example the raising of pensions, since this only stokes up inflation. He regards himself a patriot and does not want to leave the country but wishes that propitious conditions for life be created in Russia. He lives in Moscow.

Makarov, Konstantin Valentinovich

Chief of the main headquarters of the navy until September 1992. Admiral of the Fleet since 1989.

Born on June 18, 1931 in Tikhoretsk, Krasnodar *krai*. Russian. Makarov graduated from the 1st Higher Naval Submarine Technical School in 1953; the Higher Classes for Officers in 1960; completed an extra-mural course at the Naval Academy in 1967. He received a higher naval education and was a member of the CPSU from 1956 to August 1991.

He began his career as officer as a group commander on a submarine, then until 1959 he was a section commander, assistant commander of a submarine. He participated in several long voyages, was notable for his advanced special training and eagerness to gain more professional skills and knowledge. He actively participated in the work of the *Komsomol* and Party organizations and enjoyed the support of superior officers and Party agencies. After graduating from the classes for officers he was appointed senior assistant commander, and in 1963 commander of a nuclear submarine of the Northern Fleet. The submarine was often on duty at sea. Makarov graduated from the Academy without giving up his many duties. He was regarded as an officer with a sound operational technical, military technical and naval training and a tough commander. In 1971 he was appointed Chief of Staff of a submarine division and, a year later, a divisional commander. Between 1975 and 1980 he served in Moscow as deputy head of the strategic administration of the main headquarters of the navy. He was in charge of planning and drafting programmes for the construction and combat use of the navy. He was elected to the Party Central Committee. He was considered one of the most promising staff officers.

From 1981 to 1984 as Rear Admiral, then as Vice-Admiral, Makarov was Chief of Staff of the Red Banner Baltic Fleet. In 1985 he was appointed commander of the same fleet. He took part in the official visits of vessels to the German Democratic Republic and Poland. He was tough in maintaining discipline and firm in controlling naval forces in the closed Baltic theatre of operations. He maintained close ties with the leaders of the Baltic republics of the USSR and with the Party, state and military authorities of the GDR and Poland. From 1985 to September 1992 he was chief of the main headquarters of the navy. He supervised the work of the central agencies of the naval administration at a time of defence cuts, peaceful co-operation with the West and disarmament. He supported the policy of the CPSU and state leaders. His methods were tough and, as a consequence, he was not very popular with sailors. He was opposed to democratic movements and persecuted dissenting officers. During the anti-constitutional putsch in August 1991 he was not very active but in his inner circle approved of the actions of the Emergency Committee. In September 1992 he was dismissed from his post as a result of changes at the top of the navy and the replacement of the Commander-in-Chief. He is now head of the union of submarine officers which is influential among sailors and is conservative in its political orientation. He has been awarded orders and medals. There is no information available on his hobbies. He is interested in the history of the navy and the Russian state. He does not speak any foreign language and he is married.

Official address: 103175 Moscow K-175.

Makarov, Vladimir

Director of the Stroitelnaya Birzha (construction exchange), Irkutsk, Russian Federation.

Born in 1938; Russian. He graduated from the Irkutsk Institute of Agriculture as an agricultural engineer, and began working in the construction industry in 1965. He was director of the Stroidetal enterprise; director of a prefabricated house construction enterprise in Melnikovo; deputy head of the Irkutsk house construction enterprise; chief engineer of the Zhelezobeton (reinforced concrete) trust, and head of the administration of the Vostoksibstroi (east Siberian construction) association. In August 1991 he was appointed director of the Stroibirzha (construction exchange), Irkutsk branch. He enjoys driving his car and gardening. He is married with two children and a grandson.

Address: Stroibirzha, Irkutsk.

Makashov, Albert Mikhailovich

Member of the Central Committee, Russian Communist Workers' Party; Lieutenant-General.

Born on June 12, 1938 in the village of Levaya Rossosh, Voronezh *oblast*; Russian. He was a member of the CPSU until August 1991. His father was a soldier and his mother a nurse. In 1951 he entered the Suvorov Technical College, and later graduated with distinction from the Tashkent all-arms command technical college, from the M. V. Frunze Academy with a gold medal, and the Academy of the General Staff. He commanded a regiment, a division and an army, and served in the Transcaucasian (from 1977), Kiev and Urals military districts and the western group of forces. The Karabakh committee was arrested on his orders. From January to September 1989 he was commander of the Urals military district; and from September 1989 to September 1991 commander of the Volga-Urals military district.

In 1989, in a contested election, he was elected a USSR people's deputy for Irbitsky territorial district, Sverdlovsk (Ekaterinburg) *oblast*. During the election campaign he advocated the continued existence of the USSR with a non-standing army (the existing system involving national service). He opposed deferment for those in higher education until they had completed their studies because this would lead to armed forces consisting of workers and peasants. He was also against the withdrawal of Soviet forces from eastern Europe. He was a delegate to the XXVIII Party congress, and shocked President Gorbachev and the reformers at the congress by his outspoken attack on *perestroika* and *glasnost*. He called on the General Secretary of the Party to return to the principles of Lenin, and was loudly supported by other military and KGB delegates. He is a Lieutenant-General in the reserve.

In 1991 he was nominated as a candidate for the presidency of the RSFSR. During the election campaign he advocated a unified, indivisible Russia in the frontiers of 1945; the stabilization of the situation and inter-ethnic agreement; the legally equal development and existence of all forms of property ownership, including state, collective, labour and private; the closing down of speculative firms and co-operatives; the lowering of prices of consumer goods; aid to agriculture and an end to interference by the state in collective and state farm management; the establishment of normal conditions for the withdrawal of Soviet troops from eastern Europe; and the rebirth of the tradition of patriotism, Russian history and Cossackdom. He opposed the penetration of society by capitalism, unemployment and rising prices. On June 12, 1991 Makashov lost the RSFSR presidential election, polling 3.74% of the votes, and taking fifth place out of six candidates.

In August 1991 he was retired from the USSR armed forces for supporting the organizers of the anti-constitutional putsch. From 1990 to 1991 he was a member of the of the Central Committee, Russian Communist Party, and from February to March 1992 he took part in the conflict in Moldova on the side of the Pridnestrovie republic. In 1992 he was elected a member of the Central Committee, Russian Communist Workers' Party; he is head of the *Duma* of the national *veche* (assembly) and the Human of the Russian national assembly. He is one of the leaders of the National Salvation Front, and he also participated in the all-army (combined services) officers' assembly (1992-93). He supports the advent to power of the opposition but only by peaceful means, in other words via parliamentary elections. He has several awards.

He is married with three children and five grandchildren, and lives in Samara. He is a qualified translator from German, is an excellent dancer and enjoys hunting and driving a car.

Makharadze, Valery Antonovich

Deputy Prime Minister of the Russian Federation, March-December 1992.

Born in 1941. He was director of a glass factory in Kamyshino, Volgograd *oblast*. In March 1990 he was elected a people's deputy of the Volgograd *oblast* soviet of people's deputies and later chairman. Volgograd *oblast* soviet was one of the few in which Democratic Russia (DemRossiya) was victorious. From July to August 1991 Makharadze was a member of the organizational committee of the Movement for Democratic Reform. On August 26, 1991 he was appointed chief government inspector of the Russian Federation and head of the control board of the administration of the President of the Russian Federation. The main task of the administration was supervising the implementation of the presidential and governmental legislation on economic reform. He was a member of the State Council of the Russian Federation.

At the end of February 1992 President Yeltsin passed to the control board the task of combating the indiscipline and lack of activity of state officials and their involvement in the so-called *nomenklatura* privatization. This resulted in state officials acquiring state assets as private persons. Makharadze set out during the spring of 1992 to investigate 10 to 15 territories of the Russian Federation. By decree of the President of March 2, 1992 Makharadze was appointed deputy Prime Minister of the Russian Federation. He became responsible for the effective administration of the Russian economy. This Herculean task was beyond him and indeed would have been beyond any minister.

The refusal of the parliament to promulgate the legislation necessary for the introduction of a market economy made Makharadze's task almost hopeless and the weakening of the power of the centre meant that Moscow could not implement much of its legislation. Instead each region battled to keep control of its resources and output and to circumvent controls from Moscow. He became a victim of the VII Congress of People's Deputies in December 1992 when President Yeltsin was forced to accept Viktor Chernomyrdin as Prime Minister. He did not become a member of the Chernomyrdin government. He is married. In February 1992 his wife, Maisarat, was appointed deputy Minister of the Press and Media of the Russian Federation.

Makhkamov, Kakhar

President of Tajikistan, November 1990 to September 1991.

Born in April 16, 1932 in Leninabad (Khuzhand), Tajik SSR; Tajik. He was a member of the CPSU from 1957 to August 1991. He graduated in 1950 from the Dushanbe College of Industry, and in 1953 from the Leningrad Institute of Mining. From 1953 to 1957 he was head of the ventilation system in the No.1/5-6 mine, assistant to the chief engineer, head of a shop, chief engineer, and manager of a coal mine in Leninabad *oblast*, and then from 1957 to 1961 was manager of the Tajikugol state coal production enterprise.

In 1960 he was elected an alternative member of the Central Committee, Communist Party of Tajikistan (CPTajik) and in 1963 became a full member. In 1961 he was elected chairman of the Leninabad city soviet executive committee and chairman of state planning committee (Gosplan) of the Tajik SSR. In 1965 he was also appointed deputy chairman of the Council of Ministers of Tajikistan, then Speaker (chairman) of the Supreme Soviet of Tajikistan.

In 1985 he was elected first secretary of the Central Committee, CPTajik, and then in 1986, at the XXVI CPSU congress, he was elected a member of the Central Committee, CPSU. He was elected a USSR people's deputy and a member of the USSR Supreme Soviet (1989). In 1988 he became chairman of the commission for inter-ethnic relations of the Central Committee, CPTajik, and in 1989 became a member of the military council of the Turkestan military district. At the XXVIII CPSU congress, in July 1990, he was elected a member of the CPSU Politburo, and in November 1990 he was elected the first President of Tajikistan.

He was regarded by many deputies in the Supreme Soviet as a conservative communist and increasing parliamentary pressure and also demonstrations in the streets led to his resignation in September 1991. He remained a member of the ex-communist nomenclature after the collapse of the CPSU in December 1991 and the proclamation of the Republic of Tajikistan. The civil war which broke out between the supporters of President Nabiev and radicals, loosely grouped around the Islamic Revival Party, in May 1992, led to a chaotic situation. Eventually Niyazov's supporters succeeded in taking Dushanbe in December 1992 and consolidating their position, and in 1993 they were helped by the Russian military to fend off attacks from the rebels.

Makhkamov was awarded four orders of the Red Banner of Labour and the honorary certificate of the Supreme Soviet of the Tajik SSR. He is married.

Address: 734051 Dushanbe, Prospekt Lenina 42; *telephone*: Dushanbe 23 2343; 223821.

Maksimov, Yury Pavlovich

Commander of Strategic Forces of the Unified Armed Forces of the CIS. General of the Army since 1982.

Born on June 30, 1924 in the village of Kryukovka, Michurinsk *raion*, Tambov *oblast* into a peasant family. Russian. His military career began in August 1942. He graduated from the Moscow Machine-gun Military Technical school in 1943; the M. V. Frunze Military Academy in 1950 and the Military Academy of the General Staff in 1964. He received a higher military education and was a member of the CPSU from 1943 to August 1991.

He participated in battles during the Great Patriotic War (1941-45), and was a commander of sub-units in infantry units. He demonstrated courage, military skill and tactical knowledge in action and was respected by his soldiers. He joined the CPSU at the front. After the war he remained in the army as a knowledgeable and promising officer, where he had a good reputation with commanders and Party-political agencies. After graduating from the Academy, he held staff and command posts in the land forces. He was seen by his commanders as an officer with sound operational-tactical and military-technical training, aware of the requirements of present-day combat and able to predict the course of events. He was actively involved in the work of Party organizations and proved to be a convinced communist, supporting the CPSU and the USSR government policy at home and abroad.

In 1965 Col. Yu. Maksimov was appointed commander of a motorized-rifle division and was soon promoted to General. Then he occupied the post of first deputy commander of an army. He was quickly promoted. In 1973 he became the first deputy commander of the Turkmenistan military district and in 1979 he became commander of the same district. In 1984 he was transferred to an important top post in the central body of the USSR Ministry of Defence in Moscow. In 1985 he was appointed Commander-in-Chief of strategic missile troops and deputy Minister of Defence of the USSR. He lost no time in mastering the new high-tech type of arms and adapting himself to the new task. He studied in detail the organization and use of nuclear missile forces, duty rosters and armament systems.

As a commander of the Turkmenistan military district, Gen. Maksimov was directly involved in organizing the intervention of Soviet troops in Afghanistan and later in ensuring their activity and he often went there. He is a member of the group of "Afghan Generals" which is now in power. He was involved in social and political activity. He was a candidate member of the Party Central Committee from 1981 and member of the Central Committee between 1986 and 1990 and was a delegate at Party congresses. He was a member of the USSR Supreme Soviet of the 10th and 11th convocations. In March 1989 he was elected a USSR people's deputy in Krasnoyarsk *oblast*. He was not active at congresses, and voted to support the general line of the leaders.

During the anti-constitutional putsch in August 1991 Gen. of the Army Yu. Maksimov and missile troops under his command were loyal to the legitimate authorities of the USSR and the RSFSR. In a situation tantamount to anarchy he succeeded in establishing strict control over nuclear weapons and in preventing the possibility of unsanctioned use.

By the USSR President's decree on November 12, 1991, he was appointed head of a newly created type of armed forces — deterrent strategic forces. Under his command were strategic missile forces, missile attack warning systems, space control, anti-missile defence, administration of the head of space weapons, and also air and naval strategic nuclear forces.

Since February 1992 Gen. Maksimov has been commander of the strategic forces of the Unified Armed Forces of the CIS, Marshal E. Shaposhnikov's deputy Commander-in-Chief.

A typical Soviet General in his political convictions, he supports the idea of state supremacy and of strong power, and the retention of a unified defence space and nuclear missile control. He advocates the view: "the army is over and above parties and politics and only serves the motherland".

He was made a Hero of the Soviet Union on July 5, 1982 for the successful completion of government missions and displayed courage and heroism (for his military performance in Afghanistan). He was also awarded two orders of Lenin, three orders of the Red Banner, orders of the Red Star and "For service to the motherland in the armed forces of the USSR" 3rd class, and many medals.

There is no information available on his hobbies. He does not speak any foreign language and has not been abroad in an official capacity. He is married with children.

Official address: 103160 Moscow K-160.

Maldzis, Adam Vosipavic

Director of the Francisak Skaryna National Education Centre.

Born on August, 7, 1932 in Rasoly, Astravecaha *raion*, Hrodno (Grodno) *oblast*. His parents were Vosip and Maryja Maldzis. He is Belarusian, and was a member of the CPSU until August 1991. He graduated from the faculty of journalism, Belarusian State University, Minsk, and successfully presented his candidate dissertation in philology (PhD) and his doctoral dissertation in philology (DLitt). He is a professor, and is a member of the council (*sejm*) of the Belarusian Popular Front. He has published many articles and books, and his hobby is collecting books. He is married. He was awarded the Belarusian state prize and the Francisak Skaryna medal. He speaks Polish and Russian.

Address: 220068 Minsk, vul. Carvajakova d. 18 kv. 4; *telephone*: Minsk (0172) 69 05 30.

Malei, Mikhail Dmitrievich

Adviser of the President of the Russian Federation on Conversion.

Born in 1941; member of the CPSU until August 1991. He graduated from the Institute of Technology, Leningrad, successfully presenting his candidate dissertation (PhD), and began his career as an official of the chemical industry. He was an engineer, head of a laboratory, head of a department of a scientific research institute, and first deputy general director of the all-Union scientific production association, Potentsial. In 1986 he became an official in the Ministry of the Electrical Engineering Industry and in 1988 was appointed director of the all-Union scientific research institute, Informelektro.

In early 1990 he was nominated for election as an RSFSR people's deputy in the No. 41 Pervomaisky territorial district, Moscow. In the election campaign he appealed for the retention of historical and cultural monuments, for the restoration of the Izmailovsky cemetery and Pokrovsky cathedral. There were seven candidates. Malei polled 37% of the votes in the first round and won the second round, polling 58.9% of the votes. His main opponent was V. B. Popov, director of the experimental factory of the all-Union scientific research institute of electromechanics, who received 9.8% of the votes in the first round and 30.1% of the votes in the second.

Malei was elected to the RSFSR Supreme Soviet at the I Congress of People's Deputies in June 1990. In January 1991 he was appointed deputy RSFSR Prime Minister, and chairman of the RSFSR state committee on the management of state property. In 1991 he was made a RSFSR state adviser on conversion (switching military enterprises to the production of civilian goods). By the decree of the President of the Russian Federation of August 8, 1992, Malei was appointed adviser of the President of the Russian Federation on conversion. He believes that the headlong rush to conversion has seriously harmed the economy, especially the output of goods for the civilian sector, including technologically complex consumer goods. The law on conversion is not being implemented since there is no budgetary help for the enterprises. He thinks that investments should be channelled to certain enterprises and projects and not to the whole branch in general. He favours concentrating the management of conversion in one institution and advocates economic conversion, that is restructuring, self-financing, and not mere physical conversion which has resulted in complex production facilities producing the most elementary domestic goods. He does not believe that Russia should abandon the arms market and that new technology should be sold abroad and the Russian armed forces equipped with the newest technology. The money earned can be invested in civil production. New export firms should be set up, and an increase in the number of exporters of arms and defence plants should be registered. A market structure is necessary to service the military-industrial complex such as a Russian military industrial bank, insurance companies, an information agency with data on modern technology and to make scientific and commercial proposals. He regards the hopes that large investments would flow into the defence industry from private Russian sources as unfounded. He is concerned about the loss of scientific personnel and the possible decline of the intellectual and scientific level of the military industrial complex. He lives in Moscow.

Malyshev, Nikolai Grigorevich

Head of the Centre of Analysis of Special Presidential Programmes of the President of the Russian Federation.

Born in 1945, and began his career in 1964 as a technician. He graduated from the Radiotechnical Institute, Taganrog and then joined the staff, beginning as an assistant in a department and ending up as rector. He successfully presented his candidate dissertation (PhD) and then in 1979 his doctoral dissertation in technical sciences on "Research and elaboration of methods of forecasting normative algorithm models of productive systems" (DSc). He is a professor.

He was appointed deputy chairman of the RSFSR Council of Ministers and chairman of the RSFSR state committee on science and higher education by decree of the RSFSR Supreme Soviet, signed by Boris Yeltsin, as Speaker of the Supreme Soviet, on July 14, 1990. He resigned on July 10, 1991 when the first Russian government was formed. He was again appointed chairman of the RSFSR state committee on science and higher education by decree of the RSFSR President on August 12, 1991. Malyshev was later appointed an RSFSR state adviser for science and higher education.

He was appointed presidential adviser on science and higher education by decree of the President on August 8, 1992, and is at present head of the centre of analysis of presidential programmes. The main task of the centre is to draft proposals on science and technology, energy, ecology, transport, communications and other government programmes.

He regards it as inexcusable to neglect Russia's intellectual potential, and believes that there needs to be more humanities taught in high schools. The humanities and sociology, freed from dogma and ideological dictates, will create a true intelligentsia without which Russia cannot survive. Wide general education should be expanded by establishing new universities in old Russian cities such as Novgorod, Tula, Orel and so on. His home is in Taganrog.

Manukovsky, Andrei Borisovich

Director-general of the School of International Business; Vice-President of the Russian Association of Business Schools.

Born in 1960 in Moscow; Russian. He graduated in 1981 from the department of international economic relations, Moscow State Institute of International Relations (MGIMO) and afterwards was a postgraduate student, successfully presenting his candidate dissertation in economics (PhD (Econ)). He was appointed a lecturer at MGIMO, then from 1984 to 1989 he was deputy dean and senior lecturer of MGIMO, and in March 1989 he was appointed director-general of the International Business School at MGIMO. In 1991 he was a postgraduate student at the University of Virginia, USA. He is Vice-President of the Russian association of business schools; a member of the council of the European management development foundation, Brussels; and a member of the editorial board of the journal *Ekonomicheskiye Nauki* (economic sciences). He enjoys travelling, visiting the theatre, tennis, football and swimming. He is married with two children and speaks English and French.

Address: 117454 Moscow, Prospekt Vernadskogo 76; *telephone*: Moscow 434 9196.

Marakutsa, Grigory

Chairman of the Supreme Soviet of the "Moldovan Transnistrian Republic".

Born 15 October, 1942, to a peasant family in the village of Teia, Grigoriopol *raion*, Moldovan SSR. An ethnic Moldovan, who was a member of the CPSU from 1967 and completed his general education in Parcani, after which he worked as a collective-farm labourer. He graduated from the technical-professional school in Dubăsari in 1961 and worked for two years as a tractor driver in the region of Karaganda, Kazakhstan. He graduated from the Tselinograd Agricultural Institute, Kazakhstan in 1968, specializing in electrical engineering. From 1968 to 1969 he was secretary of the *Komsomol* committee of the Tselinograd Agricultural Institute. He served as chief engineer from 1969 to 1970 in the experimental farm at the Agricultural Institute, and from 1971 to 1973 he worked as the deputy head of the Camenca *raion* electrical facility, Moldova. From 1974 to 1975 he was the vice-president of the Camenca *raion* construction association and secretary of the party organization. From 1975 to 1981 he was the president of the *Dnestr* collective farm. After the restructuring of the latter he became the president of the "CPSU 25th Congress" Inter-Vineyard Enterprise in the village of Nemirovca. Between 1981 and 1990 he was the deputy president of the Camenca Soviet Executive Committee. He then became a member of the Central Committee of the Communist Party of Moldova. On August 2, 1990 he was elected first secretary of the Camenca party committee. At the 5th session of the "Moldovan Transnistrian Republic" Supreme Soviet, he was elected president of this organ.

Marakutsa is married, and his wife is the deputy president of the agro-industrial co-operative firm *Moldseverstroitrans*. They have two children.

Marchuk, Evhen Kyrylovych

Head of the Security Service of Ukraine.

Born into a Ukrainian family in 1941. He graduated from Kirovohrad State University in 1963, and by profession was a teacher of Ukrainian language and literature. However, he began to work for the KGB in Kirovohrad *oblast* in 1963, and by 1988 he was head of inspection for the KGB in Ukraine. From 1988 to 1990 he was appointed head of the KGB in Poltava *oblast*, before returning to Kiev in 1990 as first deputy head of the Ukrainian KGB.

In May 1991 he was appointed Minister for Defence, National Security and States of Emergency. In the aftermath of Ukraine's Declaration of Independence in August 1991, the old KGB apparatus in Ukraine was simply renamed the National Security Service of Ukraine (the word "national" was dropped in 1992) in September 1991, and Marchuk became its first head in November 1991. Although personnel for the new security service were vetted by two Supreme Soviet committees, there has been virtually no turnover of membership.

Like Kravchuk, Morozov and Vasylyshyn, however, Marchuk has successfully made the transition from *apparatchik* to national communist, although he has been criticized by some nationalists for failing to take resolute action against regional separatists in Ukraine, particularly in the Crimea, the Donbas and in Transcarpathia, despite the law of October 1991 criminalizing action aimed against "the territorial integrity of Ukraine". The radical Union of Officers of Ukraine specifically called for his reappointment in October 1992, and new Prime Minister Kuchma seemed happy to oblige. Marchuk is an *ex officio* member of the Defence and National Security Councils established in 1992.

Official (Ministry) address: 252003 Kiev, Vul. Volodymyrska 33; *telephone*: Kiev 291 9152.

Marchuk, Gury Ivanovich

Director of the Institute of Computing Mathematics, Russian Academy of Sciences.

Born on June 8, 1925 in the village of Petro-Khersonets, Grachev *raion*, Orenburg *oblast*; Ukrainian. He was a member of the CPSU from 1947 to August 1991. He graduated in 1949 from Leningrad State University, after having served in the Soviet army during the Great Fatherland War (1943-45). He became a postgraduate student in 1949, and successfully presented his candidate dissertation in mathematics and physics (PhD). In 1952 he became a junior scientific assistant at the Institute of Geophysics, USSR Academy of Sciences; then became head of department of the Institute of Physics and Power Engineering, Obninsk. In 1962 he was appointed deputy director of the Institute of Mathematics, Siberian branch; director of the computer centre; later deputy chairman and chairman of the Presidium of the USSR Academy of Sciences,

Siberian branch. He successfully presented his doctoral dissertation in physics and mathematics (DSc), and is a professor.

He was elected an Academician of the USSR Academy of Sciences in 1968, and in 1975 he became Vice-President of the USSR Academy of Sciences. In 1980 he was appointed deputy chairman of the USSR Council of Ministers, and chairman of the USSR state committee for science and technology. In 1976 he was elected a candidate member and, in 1981, a member, of the Party Central Committee. In 1980 he was appointed director of the Institute of Computing Mathematics, USSR Academy of Sciences, and was president of the USSR Academy of Sciences from 1986 to December 1991. In December 1991 he became an Academician of the Russian Academy of Sciences and director of the Institute of Computing Mathematics. He was elected a USSR people's deputy as a nominee of the USSR Academy of Sciences and became a member of the USSR Supreme Soviet.

He is one of the major mathematicians and computer specialists in Russia, and has published widely in computing and applied mathematics. He worked out algorithms for the computational solution to neutron transport equations which served as a basis for the computation of critical parameters for nuclear reactors. He is the author of several theoretical works on methods of computing short-term weather forecasts, the dynamics of the atmosphere and the ocean, and has worked out numerical methods for the computation of automated control systems.

Among his many awards are hero of socialist labour, (1975), the Lenin prize in 1961 and the USSR state prize in 1979. He enjoys fishing, and is married with three sons and six grandchildren.

Address: 117901 Moscow, Prospekt Lenina 32; *telephone*: Moscow 954 3506 (secretary); 938 6859 (office).

Martynov, Aleksandr Gavrilovich

Ataman of the union of Cossacks of Russia.

Born in 1945 in the Cossack village of Gnilovskaya, Rostov *oblast* into a Cossack family; Russian. He was a member of the CPSU until August 1991. After national service in the Soviet army he entered the Institute of the National Economy, Rostov-on-Don, then the Institute of Administration, Moscow, and successfully presented his candidate dissertation in economics (PhD (Econ)). He has recently been the director of a motor works. In 1990 he was elected ataman of the union of Cossacks of Russia and in Krasnodar, in 1991, the large Cossack circle confirmed his election. He participated in the drafting of legislation on the rebirth of Cossackdom in commissions of the Russian Supreme Soviet and the Russian council of security.

The task of the union of Cossacks is the rebirth of Cossackdom, bearing in mind Cossack traditions that in a unified, strong Russia Cossacks should be dependable defenders of the bases of Russian statehood. Cossack military service should be reintroduced and there should be Cossack units in the Russian army. The rebirth of Cossackdom implies the return of the land to its zealous owners and this in turn will serve to raise the level of the Russian economy. He is opposed to the politicization of and consequently presence of bitterness in society.

From February to March 1992 he participated as head of the Cossack unit in the conflict in the Pridnestrovie republic. In connection with this he declared that the union of Cossacks was not attempting to exacerbate the situation in Pridnestrovie, as participation in the fighting was purely voluntary for Cossacks and they were only there to aid their compatriots who were in trouble. He lives in Novocherkassk, Rostov *oblast*.

Martynov, Andrei Vladimirovich

Vice-President of the Interfax joint stock company.

Born in 1964 in Moscow; Russian. He graduated in 1986 from Moscow State University, and in the same year was appointed correspondent of the north European service of USSR state television and radio company (Gosteleradio). From 1988 to 1990 he was a commentator on USSR Gosteleradio, and from 1990 to 1991 was director of economics of the information department of the Interfax information agency. In 1991 he was appointed Vice-President of the Interfax joint stock company and director of economics of the information department.

He is divorced without children and speaks English and Hungarian. His hobbies are basketball, scuba diving and literature.

Address: Moscow, ul. Pervaya Tverskaya-Yamskaya 2; *telephone*: Moscow 250 9637.

Mashits, Vladimir Mikhailovich

Chairman of the Russian state committee on economic co-operation with states of the CIS.

Born in 1953 in Moscow. His father was a Belarusian and his mother a Russian. Member of the CPSU until August 1991. He graduated from the economics faculty of Moscow State University and after graduation began postgraduate research and successfully presented his candidate dissertation in economics (PhD (Econ)). His research supervisor was Academician Nikolai Petrakov. He worked in the Central mathematical economics institute and the institute of market economics and became deputy director of the institute of economic policy in Moscow. Andrei Nechaev, a former Russian Minister of the Economy, also held the same post. Mashits was a member of the group which drafted all the USSR and RSFSR economic programmes of the Gorbachev era, for example, the Ryzhkov programme and the 500-day programme.

In December 1991 Mashits was appointed chairman of the RSFSR state committee for economic co-operation with CIS states. He is committed to market economic reform and has close links with Egor Gaidar and other reform economists. He favours trade between CIS states being based on mutual advantage. In order for Russia to develop advantageous trade relations with other CIS states a single economic area using the ruble needs to be created, as well as the co-ordination of import and export policies, especially for hard currency goods; and information provided to the central bank about the state of finances in each state. If any state is not willing to go along with the above policies, Russia should go over to trading with them in hard currency and using world market prices. He lives in Moscow.

Maslennikov, Arkady Afrikanovich

Editor-in-chief of the newspaper *Birzhevye Vedomosti* (Stock Exchange Bulletin).

Born 1931 in Kostroma *oblast*; Russian. He was a member of the CPSU until August 1991. He graduated in 1954 from the faculty of economics, Moscow State University, and from 1954 to 1965 he was a junior scientific assistant, then senior scientific assistant, at the Institute of the World Economy and International Relations, USSR Academy of Sciences. He successfully presented his candidate dissertation in economics (PhD (Econ)). In 1965 he became *Pravda* correspondent in India, then in Pakistan and Great Britain; he was an editor, and member of the editorial board of *Pravda*. His commentaries in *Pravda* evoked great interest and served as a barometer for the course of *glasnost*. In 1989 he left *Pravda* and was appointed head of the press service of the USSR Supreme Soviet, and in 1991 he became editor-in-chief of the newspaper *Birzhevye Vedomosti*. He was also elected chairman of the supervisory council of the all-Russia exchange bank. He is a member of the confederation of journalist unions.

He is a merited worker of culture. He is married with a daughter and three grandchildren. He speaks English, Urdu and Hindi. He enjoys gardening.

Address: 113035 Moscow, ul. Bolshaya Ordynka 7, kv. 5; *telephone*: Moscow 188 2053; 233 3863 (office).

Masyk, Konstiantyn Ivanovych

Vice-Prime Minister of Ukraine to October 1992.

Born into a Ukrainian family in 1932. He was educated at the Gorky (now Nizhny Novgorod) Institute of Water Transport Engineering and at the Higher Party School, CPSU Central Committee. From 1960 to 1972 he worked in the *Komsomol*, followed by a post as an inspector of the Central Committee of the CPU from 1974.

From 1976 to 1981 he was second secretary, then secretary of the Odesa CPU committee. In 1981 he returned to Kiev for two stints as deputy Chairman of the Ukrainian Council of Ministers (1981-86 and 1989-90), punctuated by a period as head of Kiev city CPU committee, where he gained a reputation as a conservative. In January 1988 he became a candidate member of the Ukrainian Politburo. He was a deeply unpopular Party leader in Kiev, and in the March 1989 all-Union elections failed to secure his seat, despite being unopposed, with 62.8% voting against him.

Nevertheless Kravchuk appointed him Vice-Premier in May 1991, and he spent an undistinguished period in office as a typical old-style *apparatchik*. Although he was accused of collaboration with the Extraordinary Committee in Moscow in August 1991, neither Fokin nor Kravchuk tried to remove him from office. Few were surprised when the new Prime Minister, Leonid Kuchma, refused to sanction his reappointment in October 1992.

Official address: 252008 Kiev, Vul. M. Hrushevskoho 12/2; *telephone*: Kiev 293 7442.

Matochkin, Yury Semenovich

Head of the Administration of Kaliningrad *oblast*, Russian Federation.

Born on October 18, 1931; Russian; member of the CPSU until August 1991. In 1955 he graduated from the Leningrad Higher Naval Border Guards Technical College, USSR Ministry of Internal Affairs, and until 1960 he served in the border guards and was commander of a patrol boat. Then he became involved with fishing, beginning as fourth mate in the Tungus fish base and finished his 13-year career as a captain and director of the Priboi transport refrigerator ship. He was chairman of the large fishing collective, Za rodinu, for four years, and in 1977 was appointed rector of the all-Union institute for raising the qualifications of leading workers and specialists in the fishing industry and economy. In 1974, while still working, he successfully presented his candidate dissertation in economics on "the problems of improving the organization of labour and production on the mother ships of the fish industry" (PhD). Later he successfully presented his doctoral dissertation in economics (DSc). He is a professor, and was the recipient of state awards.

In March 1990 he was nominated for election as an RSFSR people's deputy in the No. 400 Baltiisky territorial district. During the election campaign he supported the concept of a free economic zone for Kaliningrad *oblast* and understood this as meaning priority for the expansion of foreign economic links. Sensible economic activity permitted the more efficient resolution of domestic economic problems.

There were six candidates. Matochkin polled 27.87% of the votes in the first round and won the second round, polling 51.45% of the votes. His main opponent was G. F. Trotsenko, brigadier of fitters of shop No. 3 in the Yantar enterprise, who received 13.01% of the votes in the first round and 32.77% in the second. Matochkin is a member of the constitutional commission, a member of the committee of the Supreme Soviet on inter-republican relations, regional policy and co-operation, a member of the higher economic council of the Presidium of the Supreme Soviet and a member of the free Russia parliamentary faction. Previously he was co-ordinator of the group of independent deputies, a member of the communists for democracy parliamentary faction and a member of the specialists in economics and management group of deputies.

On September 21, 1991 he was appointed head of the administration of Kaliningrad *oblast* by presidential decree. On assuming office he stated that his main tasks were ensuring that the move to the market was irreversible and the setting up of a free economic zone. Free entrepreneurship should be promoted, ways of aiding entrepreneurship worked out and a favourable milieu for small business developed. He advocated the adoption of laws on local self-government, on land and property and the extension of the rights of the regions to set their own budgets and use their own resources. He is married with two sons and lives in Kaliningrad.

Matusievic, Jan

Dean of Greek Rite (Uniate) Catholics in Belarus; rector of the parish of St Joseph, Minsk.

Born on June 21, 1948 in Minsk. His parents are Jan Matusievic and Anastasija, née Karpovic, and the family is Belarusian. He graduated from the Belarusian State Theatrical institute, Minsk, and Zagorsk (now Sergiev-Posad) Seminary, Russia. He served as a priest in various parishes, and in May 1991 was appointed priest of the Greek Catholic (Uniate) parish of St Joseph, Minsk. He views himself as a democrat. His hobby is collecting miniature books. He is unmarried, and speaks Polish, Russian, Ukrainian and some English.

Address: 220074 Minsk 74, vul. Adajeuskada, dom 25 kv. 40; *telephone*: Minsk (0172) 51 63 26 (home).

Matvienko, Anatolii Serhiiovych

Chairman of Union of Youth Organizations of Ukraine.

Born in 1953 into a Ukrainian worker's family in the town of Bershad. He was educated at the Lviv Institute of Agricultural Economics as an engineer and, after graduation, he worked his way up through the branches of the local *Komsomol*. In 1977 he became the first secretary of the Bershad *Komsomol*, and by 1985 was secretary of the Central Committee of the Ukrainian national organization of the movement.

In 1989 he became its first secretary, and the head of the Ukrainian section of the international fund of youth co-operation. In March 1990 he was elected people's deputy for Bershadskyi *raion*, Vinnytsia *oblast*, in central Ukraine (on the first round). In the Supreme Soviet he is Chairman of the Committee on Youth and Sport, and is therefore a member of the influential Presidium. In 1991 he gained a reputation as a national communist and supporter of Leonid Kravchuk's assertion of Ukrainian sovereignty.

However, he is very much his own man, as the ex-*Komsomol* gives him his own independent power base. He has had to "depoliticize" and modernize the *Komsomol* of course, under pressure from below. It lost a number of members between 1990 and 1992. The entire Lviv *oblast* organization, for example, split away to form the Democratic Union of Lviv Youth, but Matvienko has managed to preserve much of the *Komsomol's* membership and resources, especially after it was renamed the Union of Youth Organizations of Ukraine at its 27th congress on September 21, 1991.

Official address: Kiev, Vul. M. Hrushevskoho 5; *telephone*: Kiev 252 019.

Mazaev, Ivan Sergeevich

Chairman of the board of the Khimbank commercial bank of the chemical industry.

Born in 1933 in the village of Klepovka, Voronezh *oblast*; Russian. He was a member of the CPSU until August 1991. He graduated from the Moscow Institute of Finance, and then worked in the finance department of the Khimvolokno (chemical fibre) production association, Kursk; later he became deputy director-general for economics of the Khimvolokno production association, Klinsk; deputy head of the finance administration; head of the finance administration, and USSR Ministry of the Chemical Industry. On May 7, 1989 he was appointed head of the finance administration, USSR Ministry of the Medical Industry, and in 1991 he was appointed chairman of the board of the Khimbank commercial bank of the chemical industry. He is also an assistant professor of the Institute of the Chemical Industry, Moscow.

He has published articles on finance and the circulation of money. He is married with two children and three grandchildren. He enjoys chess and filming.

Address: 101851 Moscow, ul. Myasnitskaya 20; *telephone*: Moscow 928 4978 (office).

Mazaev, Vladimir Aleksandrovich

Chairman of the Prio-Vneshtorg Bank.

Born in 1961 in Ryazan; Russian. He graduated in 1983 from the Moscow Institute of Management, and from 1983 to 1989 he was an engineer, head of laboratory, and head of the finance department, Ryazan machine tool enterprise. He was chairman of the board of the Prio-Bank (1989-90), chairman of the board of the Agroprom Bank (1990-91), and in 1991 he was elected chairman of the board of the Prio-Vneshtorg Bank. He enjoys travelling and is married.

Address: 390006 Ryazan, ul. Griboedova 24; *telephone*: Moscow 459 7549; Ryazan (0912) 44 4720 (office).

Medvedev, Nikolai Pavlovich

Head of the federal and inter-ethnic relations department of the Presidium of the Russian Supreme Soviet.

Born on November 26, 1952 in the village of Anaevo, Zubovo-Polyansky *raion*, Mordovian ASSR; Mordovian. His father worked on a collective farm. He was a member of the CPSU until August 1991. He graduated in 1973 from the Mordovian Pedagogical Institute, and then worked in the Saransk State Professional Technical College. He was elected secretary of the *Komsomol* organization; he served in the border guards (1973-75); then became a *Komsomol* official; was secretary at the Saransk instrument factory, and first secretary of the Kovylkinsky city committee; head of a group of lecturers; and head of the Sputnik youth tourism department, Mordovian *Komsomol oblast* committee (1975-83). He graduated from the Higher *Komsomol* School of the *Komsomol* Central Committee in 1979. He became a Party official in 1983; and then instructor in the Saransk Party city committee and head of the department of Party organization, Oktyabrsky *raion* Party committee. He graduated from the Mordovian State University in 1987, and in January 1989 he was elected secretary of the Party committee in the Saransk instrument factory. He was a people's deputy of the Kovylkinsky and Oktyabrsky *raion* soviets.

He was nominated for election as an RSFSR people's deputy in the No. 117 Proletarsky national territorial district, Mordovian SSR. During the election campaign he advocated the transfer of all power to the soviets; the annulment of article 6 of the USSR constitution (on the leading role of the Party in society); the promulgation of a law on political parties; the creation in Russia of independent political institutions; the promulgation of a law on autonomous *oblasts* and *okrugs*, regulating their status; the state should play an active role in social policy; housing construction should be speeded up; and facilities in education, health and culture should be improved. All privileges of the nomenclature should be abolished.

There were seven candidates and Medvedev won the second round, polling 70.9% of the votes. His main opponent was A. S. Kupchin, a school director, who received 21.9% of the votes in the second round. Medvedev was elected to the RSFSR Supreme Soviet at the I Congress of People's Deputies (593 votes for, 330 voted against). He is a member of the Council of Nationalities. He was elected chairman of the Supreme Soviet committee on the national state system and inter-ethnic relations; later head of the federal and inter-ethnic relations department of the Presidium of the Russian Supreme Soviet. He is a member of the communists for democracy parliamentary faction. He is married with two children.

Address: 103274 Moscow, K 274, Krasnopresnenskaya nab., d. 2, Dom Sovetov; *telephone*: Moscow 205 44 28.

Medvedev, Roi Aleksandrovich

Chairman of the Socialist Workers' Party.

Born on November 14, 1925 in Tbilisi, Georgian SSR; Russian. He was a member of the CPSU from 1959 to August 1991. He graduated from the faculty of philosophy, Leningrad State University, in 1951, and successfully presented his candidate dissertation in pedagogical sciences (PhD). He fought in the great Fatherland War (1941-45) and worked in an artillery arsenal in Tbilisi in 1943.

In 1951 he was a teacher in a secondary school in Sverdlovsk (Ekaterinburg) *oblast*. In 1954 he was appointed director of a seven year school (for 7-14 year olds) in Leningrad *oblast*, and in 1957 he became a postgraduate student at the V. I. Lenin State Pedagogical Institute, Moscow. In 1958 he became an editor, then deputy editor-in-chief of the state pedagogical publishing house. In 1961 he was appointed senior scientific assistant, then head of sector, scientific research institute of production training, USSR Academy of Pedagogical Sciences.

In June 1990 he was elected a member of the Party Central Committee, and in 1989 he was elected a USSR people's deputy for Voroshilov territorial district, Moscow. He was elected a member of the Soviet of the Union, USSR Supreme Soviet, and a member of the USSR Supreme Soviet committee on legislation and law and order. He is a writer and historian, who is famous for his book *Let History Judge* which in the 1970s was published in 12 countries. It was the first Soviet attempt to come to terms with the phenomenon of Stalinism.

He is also the author of *Political Portraits: Historical Notes and Articles* (1990); N. S. Khrushchev: A Political Biography (1990); *Personality and the Epoch: A Political Portrait of L. I. Brezhnev* (1991); *The Retinue and Family of Stalin* (1991); and *The Links of Time* (1992).

Despite his experiences he remained within the ranks of the CPSU until the demise of the Party and objected to the term dissident since he saw himself as a Leninist attempting to reform the Party from within. He sees the Socialist Workers' Party as a neo-communist party which advocates the hegemony of the working class, state ownership of the means of production, the rejection of the market, private ownership and bourgeois democracy. His brother, Zhores Medvedev, left the Soviet Union and settled in England, where he has written many well-known biographies of Soviet leaders, such as Khrushchev, Andropov, Chernenko and Gorbachev. Roi Medvedev lives in Moscow.

Melikyan, Gennady Georgevich

Russian Minister of Labour.

Born in 1947. He graduated from the economics faculty of Moscow State University, and then began postgraduate studies in economics and successfully presented his candidate dissertation on the "final social product of social production" (PhD (Econ)). Worked in the USSR state committee on labour. He became a member of the commission on economic reform, headed by Leonid Abalkin, deputy chairman of the USSR Council of Ministers. The commission's task was to draft proposals for economic reform under Nikolai Ryzhkov, chairman of the USSR Council of Ministers. Ryzhkov was a moderate reformer and attempted to graft market principles on to the planned economy. He spoke of a regulated market economy.

In July 1991 Melikyan was appointed deputy chairman of the USSR state council on economic reform. In 1991 he became Vice-President of the inter- national fund of economic and social reform. The President of the fund was Academician Stanislav Shatalin. In June 1992 Melikyan was appointed Russian Minister of Labour. He was not a member of the CPSU and at present does not belong to any party, but he regards his views as close to those of the Party of Social Democrats. He is married with two children. His son completed middle school in 1991 and entered the Moscow economics and statistics institute, and his daughter is eight years old. Melikyan is fond of sport and as a young man was a professional footballer; in his spare time he now likes to play tennis. He lives in Moscow.

Melnikov, Igor Ivanovich

Director of the Omega Company.

Born in 1949 in Arkhangelsk; Russian. He graduated in 1971 from the Moscow Institute of Mining, and after graduation was appointed an engineer in the all-Union scientific research institute, USSR Academy of Sciences. He progressed to head of laboratory, specializing in radio-electronic software, and in 1981 he moved to the Institute of Social and Economic Problems, USSR Academy of Sciences, as head of the computer laboratory. In April 1991 he became director of the Omega company which specializes in consulting, software development, advising on accounting in small businesses and generating information data bases. He is married with a son and speaks English. He enjoys reading fiction and woodwork.

Address: 117335 Moscow, ul. Vlasova 19, d. 2, kv. 29, P. O. Box 104; *telephone*: Moscow 936 4237; 237 3880 (office); 128 4349 (home).

Mendrelyuk, Dmitry Evgenevich

President of the Computer Exchange.

Born in 1965 in Kostroma, Kostroma *oblast*; Russian. He graduated in 1990 from the Institute of Economics and Statistics, Moscow, and after graduation worked in the Novinka joint venture, part of the Mir business co-operation association. In December 1990 he was appointed president of the computer exchange. His hobby is business. He is married with a son and speaks English.

Address: 119517 Moscow, P. O. Box 9; *telephone*: Moscow 441 5635.

Meri, Lennart Georg

President of the Republic of Estonia.

Born in 1929 in the independent Republic of Estonia; Estonian. His father was in the Estonian diplomatic service and he went to school in Berlin on the eve of the Second World War. He graduated in 1953 from the University of Tartu in history. He worked in the studios of Tallinnfilm (1963-71 and 1976-78) and has published many travel stories, literary essays and made many films depicting the life and history of the Finno-Ugrian peoples and nations. He is an honorary PhD (Helsinki) and a corresponding member of the European Academy of Sciences and Arts.

He was appointed Minister of Foreign Affairs of the Republic of Estonia in 1990. On October 5, 1992 the *Riigikogu* (parliament) elected him President of the republic. In the presidential election of September 20, 1992 Meri had polled only 29.5% of the votes and Arnold Rüütel, an ex-communist, topped the poll with 41.8% of the votes. Since no candidate had secured at least 50% plus one vote it was left to parliament to decide who would become President. Parliamentary elections, also on September 20, 1992, resulted in the Pro Patria (or Fatherland coalition of five conservative parties) winning just over half the 101 seats. On October 8, 1992 Meri named Mart Laar, the 32-year-old chairman of Pro Patria, Prime Minister. A major concern for Meri has been the adoption of a new constitution and electoral law, as both have given rise to strong opposition from the Russian-speaking minority (about 40% of the population) who are concentrated in the north-east of the country. There has been conflict with Moscow over the withdrawal of Russian forces, but President Yeltsin has stated that the issue of the standing of Russian speakers in Estonia is relevant to the date of the withdrawal.

Address: Lossiplats 1a, Tallinn, Estonia; *telephone*: Tallinn 426 200; *fax*: Tallinn 436 389.

Meshcheryakov, Sergei Alekseevich

Ataman of the union of Cossacks of the *oblast* of the Don army; ataman of Cossackdom of southern Russia.

Born in 1953 in the Cossack village of Semirakorskaya, Rostov *oblast*; Russian; He was a member of the CPSU until the summer of 1990. After completing secondary school he served in the Soviet army in the air defence forces, and is now a senior lieutenant in the reserve. He graduated from the Don Institute of Agriculture, and he worked on the Sysatsky state farm in the department of agronomy, was senior agronomist and then for four years was elected Party secretary of the farm.

In October 1991 he was elected ataman of the union of Cossacks of the *oblast* of the Don army. In his decree No. 1 he declared martial law and the mobilization of all Cossacks with their own weapons, but later confirmed that the introduction of martial law was conditional due to the need to establish a national guard in the Don region. In 1992 he issued a decree to register all the indigenous population of the *oblast* of the Don army, to bring together all those interested in recreating Cossackdom. As regards the national service of the non-indigenous population of the *oblast*, Meshcheryakov believes that that should be decided by Cossacks after the *oblast* of the Don army becomes a subject of the Russian Federation.

He regards Cossackdom as consisting of five characteristics: i) land is the property of the army; communal *(obshchina)* ownership of land, including private ownership by individual families, and not collective or state farms, is the only way to ensure the transition from a wild market to a type of American farming; ii) a cheap mobile army; iii) Cossack self-government, founded on democracy; iv) tax privileges for Cossacks; and v) culture based on the Russian Orthodox Church. He favours the establishment of a Don republic-*oblast* of the

Don army as a subject of the Russian Federation. He is married and his wife runs a kindergarten in the Cossack village of Semikarakorskaya. They have two daughters of school age. He lives in Novocherkassk, Rostov *oblast.*

Migranyan, Andranik Movsevovich

Member of the Council of the President of the Russian Federation.

Born in 1949 in Erevan, Armenian SSR; Armenian. He is a graduate of the Moscow State Institute of International Relations, USSR Ministry of Foreign Affairs, and was on the staff of the institute of eastern Europe and the institute of economics of the world socialist system, USSR Academy of Sciences. In 1979 he successfully presented his candidate dissertation in history on the "US socialist party after the Second World War: ideology and practice" (PhD).

Migranyan believes that the transition from totalitarianism to democracy is only possible through authoritarian rule. First of all it is necessary to modernize the spiritual sphere, then the economic, by introducing various types of ownership, bringing into being a civil society and only then moving to changes in the political system, by, among other things, strengthening the representation of real interests. Authoritarian rule presupposes the concentration of all power in a few hands, does not permit division or even polarization of power and interests, but does not exclude elements of democracy such as elections and a parliamentary struggle. The "powerful hand" does not permit power being seized by various groups; it creates conditions for the harmonization of interests and democratic reforms.

A "good" dictatorship is needed so that the whole evolution of state and society can be guided, which will lead to the creation of stable democratic institutions in society. Migranyan advocates the modernization of the country by introducing the market economy and real democracy. He proposed a confederation or community of republics and is against a single federal government with great power at the centre. He is opposed to the Russian Congress of People's Deputies and advocates extraordinary powers for the President and a democratic dictatorship.

He believes that Russia is now in an extremely difficult position because of the collapse of the USSR as a great power, the breakdown of the effective system of a bipolar world and the formation of a multitude of independent states on the territory of the former Soviet Union. Russia needs to determine its true national state interests, based on what it is really possible for it to do and the relationship of forces in the world. In 1992 the Ministry of Foreign Affairs did not cope successfully with this task and needs to overcome the ideological nature of its foreign policy, but commitment to democratic policies does not involve following everything the West does.

The espousal of the values of liberal democracy, decidedly but in a simplified manner, does not involve the end of all struggle, conflicts and contradictions between Russia and the West. The geopolitical interests of Russia *vis-à-vis* the successor states of the Soviet Union (the "near abroad") and the fate of the 25 million Russians outside the Russian Federation should be taken into account. It was a mistake to recognize these states hastily without regulating with them the problems of citizenship and property rights. The West should recognize that Russia has special interests in the near abroad, especially the defence of the rights of the Russian-speaking population. He regards it as advisable that there should be a market in arms and for advanced technologies to secure a place in the market. He advocates finding a solution to the problem of collective security in the Commonwealth of Independent States, the laying down of frontiers and the effective organization of their defence. He became a member of the presidential Council in February 1993. He lives in Moscow.

Mikhailov, Viktor Grigorevich

Head of the Administration of Magadan *oblast*, Russian Federation.

He is Russian and was a member of the CPSU until August 1991. He graduated as a construction engineer and set up the construction base in Ol. In 1986 he was first deputy chairman of Magadan *oblast* soviet executive committee, and head of the main economic planning administration. He has received state awards.

On April 17, 1990, at the first session of the Magadan *oblast* soviet executive committee, he was elected chairman. On August 20, 1991 an extended meeting of the Magadan *oblast* soviet executive committee acknowledged that the laws of the RSFSR and the decrees of the President of the RSFSR were the only valid ones and had to be implemented in the *oblast*. The soviet committee also declared itself opposed to the calling of a general political strike. On August 22 the Presidium and executive committee of the *oblast* committee appealed to the citizens of Magadan *oblast* to support the legally elected state authorities of the republic and to be guided by the constitution and laws of the RSFSR.

On October 24, 1991 Mikhailov was appointed head of the administration of Magadan *oblast* by presidential decree. On assuming office he appealed for a transition to a market economy which would not adversely affect the population, for the creation of conditions for high labour productivity, for the expansion of the rights of the regions to use their natural resources, and for horizontal links in trade. He advocated the setting up of commodity exchanges, a reduction in the level of subventions to loss-making enterprises, the attraction of foreign investment, the limiting of the authority of central bodies and a reduction in the size of the bureaucracy. He opposed severe administrative measures and thought that a competitive milieu should be established, fashioned by anti-monopoly legislation. It was idle to expect reform to be successful very quickly and Russia would have to live through all the negative aspects of capitalism.

In December 1992, during the VII Congress of People's Deputies, he stated that Egor Gaidar did not understand the problems of the regions and that it was difficult for him to support the policies of President Yeltsin although he was obliged to do so. As a result of this Aleksandr Rutskoi and Nikolai Travkin called on him to support the Congress of People's Deputies, but he did not do so since he did not wish to engage in political games or to damage the country. He lives in Magadan.

Mikhailov, Viktor Nikitovich

Minister of Atomic Energy of the Russian Federation.

Born in 1934 in Moscow into a Russian family. In 1957 he graduated with first-class honours from the Moscow engineering and physics institute, specializing in theoretical and atomic physics. The same year he was invited by Academician Ya. B. Zeldovich to join the All-Union scientific research institute of experimental physics, the director of which was Academician Yu. Khariton, in the town of Arzamas 16, the leading scientific centre in the Soviet Union on the development of atomic weapons. In a competitive election he became head of a faculty in the institute of experimental physics. He worked with Academician Andrei Sakharov; hence Mikhailov is one of the fathers of Soviet nuclear weapons. Until 1990 he was not permitted to travel abroad. He became a doctor of technical sciences (DSc) and a professor and was awarded Lenin and state prizes.

In 1988 Mikhailov was appointed deputy minister and in 1989 first deputy USSR Minister of Medium Machine Building. Later this ministry became the USSR Ministry of Atomic Energy and Industry (*Minatomenergoprom*). He was responsible for the production of nuclear weapons. In December 1991, when the USSR Ministry of Atomic Energy and Industry was transformed into the Ministry of Atomic Energy of the Russian Federation, Mikhailov was still first deputy minister, responsible for nuclear weapons. President Yeltsin met Mikhailov during a visit to Arzamas 16 in February 1992, when he was acquainted with the problems of the conversion of the atomic industry. He was proposed as Russian Minister of Atomic Energy by the collective of the Arzamas 16 institute and was appointed to the post by presidential decree of March 3, 1992.

Mikhailov is keenly interested in making use of the intellectual potential of the defence sector for the national economy and attracting domestic and foreign investment in large scientific projects — lasers, use of extremely powerful magnetic fields, directed explosions, etc. Talk about the emigration of some Russian physicists and the possibility of a mass exit leading to the wide dispersal of knowledge about nuclear technology is the result, in his eyes, of attempts by those at home and abroad to sow distrust concerning Russia's nuclear weapons and energy sector. Nevertheless Mikhailov, in his speeches, underlines as a major task the prevention of the proliferation of nuclear weapons technology, the guarding of nuclear materials and the elimination of nuclear weapons. A Russian nuclear centre was set up to conduct research into the problems of conversion and advance new proposals about the use of nuclear energy. Mikhailov is concerned about the social problems of production staff in nuclear enterprises and especially those resident in closed cities. He is a keen supporter of the expansion of international atomic energy ties. In early March 1992 the Russian electro-chemical consortium (part of the Ministry of Atomic Energy group) and the US company Engelhard Corporation reported the signing in Ekaterinburg (formerly Sverdlovsk) of an agreement on the transfer of American technology and patents under licence for the production of catalyst converters for automobile exhaust gases. Production will take place at the Ekaterinburg electro-chemical factory, which is engaged in the enrichment of uranium for military purposes. This was the first such agreement in this sector of the economy. The Russian and US governments collaborated in an effort to find employment for Russian nuclear scientists in Russia.

Preventing the export of enriched uranium and other substances such as beryllium, vital for the production of nuclear weapons, was a major headache for the ministry. Given the confusion in the country it was likely that some of these substances found their way abroad.

Mikhailov is a keen gardener on his private plot and lives in Moscow.

Milyukov, Oleg Vadimovich

Editor-in-chief of the magazine *Business Contact*.

Born in 1936 in Moscow. He graduated in 1965 from the faculty of journalism, Moscow State University, and was a journalist on *Yuny Tekhnik* (young technician) and *Sovetsky eksport* (Soviet export) magazines. In 1991 he was appointed editor-in-chief of the magazine *Business Contact*. He is a merited cultural worker of the RSFSR, and is married with a daughter.

Address: 113461 Moscow, ul. Kakhovka 31, d. 2; *telephone*: Moscow 332 8344 (office).

Minakov, Yury Aleksandrovich

Speaker of the Supreme Soviet of the Republic of Mari El, Russian Federation.

Born on May 26, 1945 in the Cossack village of Kanevskaya, Krasnodar *krai*; Russian. He graduated from the Polytechnical Institute, Krasnodar, and successfully presented his candidate dissertation in technical sciences (PhD). He began his career in 1968 as foreman of the Mari industrial construction SMU-2 trust, Ioshkar Ola, and the same year he became a foreman, then work superintendent of the SMU-1 Mari territorial construction administration, Ioshkar Ola. From 1973 to 1975 he was chief engineer of the Ioshkar Ola construction SMU-1 trust, and was then chief engineer and manager of the Orgtekhstroi trust, Ioshkar Ola. From 1979 to 1987 he was chief engineer of the Mari territorial construction administration.

In November 1987 he was elected chairman of the executive committee of the Ioshkar Ola city soviet of people's deputies. He was awarded the order of the badge of honour and is a state prizewinner of the Mari ASSR. He is a people's deputy of the Mari ASSR and at the IX session of the Supreme Soviet of the Mari Soviet Socialist Republic, on December 24, 1991, he was elected Speaker. He lives in Ioshkar Ola.

Minin, Evgeny Georgievich

Editor-in-chief of the magazine *Joint Venture*.

Born in 1938 in Moscow; Russian. He graduated in 1962 from the Bauman Higher Technical School (now Technical University), Moscow, and worked as an engineer in a number of enterprises and research institutes in Moscow. He took up journalism in 1985 and was a reporter on the magazine *NTR: Problemy i Resheniya* (the scientific and technical revolution: problems and solution). In 1987 he was appointed press attaché of the Interquadro Soviet-French-Italian joint venture, and in 1990 he became editor-in-chief of the magazine *Joint Venture*, published by the association of joint venture enterprises and organizations. He is unmarried and speaks German. He enjoys motor racing.

Address: 125190 Moscow, P. O. Box 157; *telephone*: Moscow 940 0622 (office).

Mirgazyamov, Marat Parisovich

Chairman of the Council of Ministers, Republic of Bashkortostan, Russian Federation.

Born on February 26, 1942 in the village of Karaidel, Karaidelsky *raion*, Bashkir ASSR. He is Bashkir, and his father, Paris, and his mother, Kamilya, were ordinary rural dwellers. He has six brothers and two sisters. He was a member of the CPSU from 1969 to August 1991.

In 1961, on graduating from the No. 1 technical college, he began working as a operator in the XXII Party congress oil refinery, Ufa. In 1966 he graduated from the oil institute, Ufa as an electrical engineer. He worked as such in the oil refinery, was head of a section, then head of a shift. In 1973 he moved into Party work. He was an instructor of the Ufa city Party committee, then head of the department for the organization of Party work of the party city committee. In 1976 he was elected second secretary of the Ordzhonikidze *raion*

Party committee, Ufa. In 1980 he became deputy head of the department for the organization of Party work, Party *obkom*.

In 1982 he was elected first secretary of the Tuimazinsky *raion* Party committee, Bashkir ASSR. In 1984 he graduated from the academy of social sciences of the Party Central Committee as an external student. In 1986 he was appointed Chairman of the Council of Ministers, Bashkir ASSR. In 1989 he was elected a USSR people's deputy for the Birsky national territorial district, Bashkir ASSR. He is a people's deputy of the Bashkir ASSR. He was elected a delegate to the XXVII and XXVIII Party congresses.

In 1990 at the first session of the Supreme Soviet he was confirmed as Chairman of the Council of Ministers of the republic. In March 1992 he was a member of the delegation of the Republic of Bashkortostan which signed the federal treaty in Moscow. On November 5, 1992 the session of the Supreme Soviet of the republic expressed no confidence in the Council of Ministers, but a decision on the question was postponed to the next session of parliament.

Mirgazyamov is the author of many articles on public and political questions in the republican press and his hobbies are playing volleyball and tennis. He is married. His wife, Lyubov Aleksandrovna, was in the same year at the oil institute, Ufa. They have a daughter, Liliya, who lives in Kazan and a son, Vadim, who is a student in the faculty of economics, Bashkir State University. They live in Ufa.

Mironov, Nikolai Efimovich

Chairman of the Council of Ministers of the Udmurt Republic, Russian Federation.

Born on May 8, 1936 in the village of Stary Yatchi, Grakhovsky *raion*; Russian; member of the CPSU from 1960 to August 1991. In 1961 he graduated from the Izhevsk Mechanics Institute as an engineer and began working in the Izhevsk engineering enterprise in 1954. He was an electrician, foreman, senior foreman, and deputy head of a shop. In 1965 he transferred to work in the Udmurt Party *obkom*. In 1969 he was elected first secretary of the Industrialny *raion* Party committee, Izhevsk and in 1981 he was appointed director of the No. 13 state ballbearing plant, Izhevsk. He was awarded two orders of the Red Banner of Labour and two orders of the badge of honour.

He was elected a deputy of the Supreme Soviet of the Udmurt ASSR and on April 19, 1990, at the first session, he was appointed Chairman of the Council of Ministers of the Udmurt ASSR. He lives in Izhevsk.

Mironov, Valery Ivanovich

Deputy Minister of Defence of the Russian Federation; Colonel-General.

Born on December 19, 1943 in Moscow; the social status of his parents is unknown; Russian. He graduated from the Suvorov Military Technical school in 1961, the RSFSR Supreme Soviet Moscow Higher army officers' technical school in 1965, the M. V. Frunze Military Academy in 1973 and the Military Academy of the General Staff in 1984, having received a higher military education. He was a member of the CPSU until August 1991.

He began his career as an officer in the Turkestan military district as a commander of a motorized-rifle platoon and then became a company commander. He ensured a high level of combat readiness in units under his command, and had the record of a promising officer with a sound training. He was actively involved in the work of Party organizations, which was essential for a successful career in the Soviet army.

After graduating from the Academy in 1973 he was appointed Chief of Staff, and a deputy motorized-rifle regimental commander. He was a regimental commander from 1975, a deputy divisional commander from 1977 and a divisional commander from 1979. The units and the formation under his command were awarded a distinction; he ensured a high level of combat readiness and had a good reputation with superior officers. In 1979 his division was one of the first to invade Afghanistan, where, until 1982, Maj.-Gen. V. Mironov participated in operations against the *mujahidin* and the civilian population. In Afghanistan he became acquainted with other current top military officials in Russia, including B. Gromov and P. Grachev.

From 1984 he was the first deputy army commander, and in 1989 he was appointed the first deputy commander of the Leningrad military district. He was not active during the anti-constitutional putsch of August 19–21, 1991, concentrating on his immediate duties to keep the troops of the district in fighting trim. At the same time, according to democratically-minded military sources, he took no measures to block the movement of the plotters' troops to Leningrad.

In August 1991 he was appointed army commander of the Baltic military district (later the north-western group of troops). He proved his ability to take political steps to defend the interests of Russian servicemen and the Russian state *vis-à-vis* the authorities of the independent Baltic states, and social and political movements. He took part in diplomatic meetings and talks between the Russian Federation and Lithuania, Latvia and Estonia. His intellectual and cultural background helped him, to some extent, to find a common language with the leaders of the Baltic states and arrive at a mutual understanding on a number of burning issues.

In June 1992 Col.-Gen. V. Mironov became deputy Minister of Defence of the Russian Federation. He is a member of the "Afghan generals" group around the Minister of Defence, P. Grachev, to whom he owes his high post, according to democratic army sources. He heads the military administration which ensures the training and the appointment of personnel of different categories and is responsible for providing the social and legal security of military men and their families.

He does not express his political views in the mass media, and is a convinced supporter of creating an up-to-date and highly mobile Russian army. He advocates the idea of restoring Russia's statehood and its status as a great power.

He is interested in literature and art and has the reputation of being a commander of considerable intellectual ability. He has been awarded two orders "For service to the motherland in the armed forces of the USSR", order of the Red Banner and many medals.

He is married, with a son still at school and a daughter who is a student.

Office address: 103175 Moscow K-175, Ministry of Defence of the Russian Federation.

Mironov, Vladimir Nikolaevich

President of Inter-Bank Finance House.

Born in 1954 in Moscow; Russian. He was a member of the CPSU until August 1991. He graduated in 1976 from the Moscow State Institute of International Relations, and was then a postgraduate student and successfully presented his candidate dissertation in history (PhD). In 1977 he was appointed an attaché in the USSR embassy in Belgium. In 1980 he returned to Moscow and joined the staff of the department for general international problems, USSR Ministry of Foreign Affairs. From 1987 to 1989 he engaged in research in the institute of social sciences of the Party Central Committee, and from 1989 to 1990 he acted as a consultant to the Party's theoretical journal, *Kommunist*. From 1991 to 1992 he was deputy general director of *Vozrozhedenie* (resurrection), the foundation for the social development of Russia of the Supreme Soviet of the Russian Federation, and in March 1992 he was elected president of the Inter-Bank Finance House. He joined the People's Party of Free Russia.

He is the author of articles and chapters in books on the problems of *perestroika* in Russia and on international relations. He is unmarried and speaks English, French and Italian.

Address: 109383 Moscow, ul. Lunacharskogo, 10, kv.15; *telephone*: Moscow 241 8907.

Mirsaidov, Shukrullo Rakhmatovich

Representative of the international fund for the promotion of privatization and foreign investment in Uzbekistan.

Born in 1939 in Leninabad (Khuzhand), Tajik SSR. He graduated in 1959 from the Institute of Finance and Economics, Tashkent, and successfully presented his candidate dissertation in economics (PhD(Econ)) and also his doctoral dissertation in economics (DSc(Econ)). In 1959 he was appointed economist in the planning commission, and later became head of sector, Tashkent *oblast* committee, deputy chairman, and chairman of the planning commission, Tashkent city committee. From 1981 to 1983 he was deputy chairman of the state planning committee (Gosplan) of the Uzbek SSR, and was first deputy chairman of Gosplan, head of the central statistics board, and chairman of Tashkent city committee (1983-88).In 1988 he was appointed chairman of Gosplan in the republic.

In 1990 he became chairman of the Council of Ministers of the Uzbek SSR, and was until January 1992 Vice-President of the republic. In January 1992 he was appointed state secretary of the President of the Republic of Uzbekistan, but after only a few days in office he resigned. In February 1992 he became the representative of the international fund for the promotion of privatization and foreign investment in the Republic of Uzbekistan, and as such occupies a strategic position in the republic as it seeks to attract foreign know-how and investment. Privatization is unlikely to proceed in Uzbekistan as in Russia since there is a shortage of land in Uzbekistan, and industry is likely to stay in the state sector for the time being. He is married with two children.

Address: 109028 Moscow, ul. Solyanka 3, d. 3; *telephone*: Moscow 924 6061; Tashkent (8-3712) 45 8725.

Mirzabekov, Abdurazak Mardanovich

Chairman of the Council of Ministers of the Republic of Dagestan, Russian Federation.

Born in 1938 in Makhachkala; member of the CPSU until August 1990. He grew up and went to school in Khasavyurt. After graduating from the institute he worked in Kaspiisk in the Dagdizel enterprise as an engineer, then as head of a shop and deputy head of the production planning department. He was director of the Kizlyar electromechanical enterprise for 12 years and it became one of the best in its branch of activity. In 1984 he was appointed deputy and, in August 1987, chairman of the Council of Ministers of the Dagestan Autonomous Soviet Socialist Republic (ASSR). In 1987 he graduated from the Academy of Social Sciences of the Party Central Committee. He was awarded the orders of the Red Banner of Labour and the badge of honour and medals. He was a member of the bureau of the Party *obkom* and a deputy of the Supreme Soviet of the

Dagestan ASSR. He was a delegate to the XXVI and XXVIII Party congresses and the XIX Party conference.

On March 26, 1989 he was nominated for election as a USSR people's deputy in the No. 534 Khasavyurtovsky national territorial district by the work collective of the Khasavyurtsky state farm and many other collective and state farms, industrial enterprises and construction organizations. He was the only candidate and polled 95.99% of the votes in the first round. In 1990 he was elected a people's deputy of the Dagestan ASSR.

At the first session of the Supreme Soviet of the Dagestan ASSR, in April 1990, Mirzabekov was elected chairman of the Council of Ministers of the republic. On assuming office he advocated raising the status of the republic, increasing its economic autonomy, implementing local cost accounting and developing co-operatives.

In 1992 he judged his main task to be overcoming the budget deficit, something which he believed could not be achieved before 1995. He advocated the utilization of internal reserves and structural alterations to industry in favour of the production of consumer goods. He opposed the dictates of the central ministries and authorities, and favoured the creation of joint ventures and the development of foreign economic links. He appealed for the export potential of the republic to be grasped, for new oil and gas reserves to be tapped and processed on the spot, for traditional artisan activities to be revived and viticulture and tourism promoted. He advocated the freeing of countryside from taxation, the transformation of state farms into joint stock companies, many different forms of property ownership in rural areas and the restructuring of loss-making, but not the profitable collective and state farms, and the ending of the monopoly of the processing of agricultural products. He was opposed to parasitism, but favoured relentless, selfless labour and the retention, if it proved impossible to improve, of social security at its previous level. He lives in Makhachkala.

Mirzoev, Akbar

Prime Minister of the Republic of Tajikistan to September 24, 1992.

Born in 1939 in Nurek, Tajik SSR. He graduated in 1960 from the Tajik Institute of Agriculture, and is a qualified engineer and hydrologist. In 1960 he was a foreman in the department of construction in Kulyab, Tajik SSR, and then from 1961 to 1963 he served in the Soviet army. After demobilization in 1963 he worked as a foreman, head of section and chief engineer in the department of construction, Tajik Ministry of Land Amelioration and Hydrology. From 1969 to 1974 he was head of a mobile mechanized column of the ministry.

From 1974 to 1975 he was chief of Kulyab *oblast* irrigation management in the ministry, and later was manager of the Kulyab water construction trust (1975-84), and first deputy head of the main administration for irrigation and state farm construction of the Tajik SSR (1984-87). In 1987 he was elected chairman of the Kulyab *oblast* soviet executive committee; from 1988 to 1990 he was chairman of the soviet executive committee of Khatlansky *oblast*, and in 1990 he was reappointed chairman of Kulyab *oblast* soviet executive committee.

In January 1992 he was appointed Prime Minister of the Republic of Tajikistan. Civil war broke out in May 1992 between supporters of President Nabiev, the former communist, and more radical forces, grouped around the Islamic Revival Party. Nabiev was forced to resign on September 7, 1992 and Mirzoev also went later in the month. He was succeeded as acting Prime Minister by Abdumalek Abdulayanov, but these and other changes did not halt the fighting and forces loyal to Niyazov took Dushanbe in October for a time. In November presidential rule was abolished and Tajikistan was declared a parliamentary republic. The new government, controlled by ex-communists, took Dushanbe in December, but their power base was the Kulyab area, and they held on to power afterwards partly due to the aid extended by the Russian military. The civil war resulted in most Europeans, especially Russians and Germans, fleeing the republic, often with their equipment and belongings.

Address: Government House, Dushanbe.

Mitkova, Tatyana

Journalist, Ostankino television, Moscow.

Her family goes back to the court of Boris Godunov and another ancestor was a member of the Decembrists (uprising against Tsar Nicholas I in 1825). The soft sign (b) after the letter t was dropped during the Stalinist era to cover up the noble origin of the name. Her father was a military officer, fought at the front during the Great Fatherland War (1941-45), then worked in the agencies of state security. In her childhood she dreamt of becoming a pianist and studied in a school of music, but at the end of her studies she realized that she lacked the "divine spark" to become great and entered the school of young journalists at Moscow State University. She graduated from the television department, faculty of journalism, Moscow State University.

She began working at Ostankino in 1977 in the cutting room and eventually became editor of an international panorama programme. She regards Bovin, Kondrashov, Gerasimov and Ovsyannikov as her main teachers, and was a member of the bureau of the *Komsomol* organization of central television. She loves visiting the theatre and cinema, has a wide circle of friends, whom she meets often, and reads many books but has less time for periodicals. She drives her own Mercedes Benz and all the hard currency she earns abroad she spends on expensive cosmetics and elegant jackets.

She became a news reader on television in 1990. In the winter of 1990-91 she was one of the few who separated facts from the official point of view, was the first to show the tanks in Vilnius and was invited to leave television because of her lack of professionalism. She was out of work for ten months and in the autumn of 1991 a US organization to defend journalists awarded her a prize for the highly professional conduct of her work. She now presents *Novosti* (news), but not the 9 pm edition since she does not like having to make deals and it is easier to select the material herself, among her own group. She does not regard herself as prone to conflict or haughty. She opposes hidden advertising and is merciless about poor reporting by correspondents, although in her everyday life she is not strict. She gives priority to international conflicts and the vices of the world we live in, in order to convince people that they are senseless and should be ended. Propaganda and ideology were always dominant in Soviet television news programmes, whereas Mitkova concentrates on commenting on facts. However, pure facts have to be provided and Russian television is learning to do this, so she is now happier than before since there is no censorship of television and she does not fear being reprimanded by the boss.

She believes that there is more politically neutral news in *Novosti* than in *Vesti* (news) which adopts a clear position. She watches the television programmes *Until and After Midnight*, by V. Molchanov; *Matador*, by K. Ernst, the best programme on the cinema; *Portrait in the Foreground*, by L. Parfenov; *Beau Monde*, by Ganapolsky; and *Moment of Truth*, by Karaulov. She is not preparing to leave the country since there is no more interesting country in the world than present-day Russia. She is married, her husband also being a journalist, and lives in Moscow.

Mityukov, Mikhail Alekseevich

Chairman of the Russian Supreme Soviet committee on legislation.

Born on January 7, 1942 in the village of Ust Ude, Ust Udinsky *raion*, Irkutsk *oblast*, where his father worked on a collective farm. He is Russian, and was a member of the CPSU from 1967 to August 1991. He began work in 1959 as a navvy, then an electrician in the No. 16 mechanized column of the Krasnoyarsk Elektroseststroi trust. In 1961 he entered the faculty of law of Irkutsk State University, but then served in the Soviet army (1962-65). Afterwards he continued his law studies in the university (1965-68), and after graduating worked until 1979 as a member of the *oblast* court, Khakasia autonomous *oblast*. In 1979 he successfully presented his candidate dissertation in law on "Legislation on the autonomous *oblasts* (research on state law)" (LLM). He was deputy chairman of the *oblast* court of the Khakasia autonomous *oblast* (1979-87); simultaneously he was chairman of the court collegium on civil cases (1979-82), and on criminal cases (1982-87). In court he campaigned actively against corruption, bribe taking and the misuse of power by public officials. He was senior lecturer, head of the department of Soviet history and law, Abakan state pedagogical institute, 1987-90.

He was nominated for election as an RSFSR people's deputy in the No. 212 Altai territorial district, Khakasia autonomous *oblast*. During the election campaign he stated that a *Rechtsstaat* (law-governed state) could only be created if there was reform of the economy, democratization of political life, establishment of priority for social policy, transformation of the status of the non-Russian parts of the country, and the development and provision of real guarantees of rights and freedoms for Soviet citizens. He advocated the resolution of environmental problems, the fostering of good attitudes towards the historical heritage and the promotion of a healthy way of life. He showed how decentralization was necessary to bring about a legal democratic state and hence Khakasia should move to regional cost accounting (*khozraschet*), seceding from Krasnoyarsk *krai*. To achieve this, trade, local and light industry should be transformed into communal property, the Khakasia autonomous *oblast* soviet should have the exclusive right to the territory, local crafts and skills, pasture lands and forests, and set up nature zones. He supported the extension of the sovereignty of the Russian Federation, the creation of a complete state infrastructure in the RSFSR, including the establishment of an RSFSR committee on inter-ethnic relations. The privileges of the nomenclature should be abolished and a campaign waged against corruption. He advocated that everyone should be equal before the law, and should be entitled to the presumption of innocence until proved guilty and full *glasnost* in court cases.

There were six candidates. In the first round Mityukov polled 27.6% of the votes and won in the second round, polling 49.5% of the votes. His main opponent was V. N. Prelovsky, general director of the Abakanvagonmash industrial association, who received 19.9% of the votes in the first round and 38.6% of the votes in the second. Mityukov was elected a member of the RSFSR Supreme Soviet at the I Congress of People's Deputies (578 voted for, 344 voted against). He is a member of the Council of the Republic, a member of the Supreme Soviet Presidium, and on July 3, 1990 he was elected deputy chairman of the Supreme Soviet committee on legislation. On February 18, 1991 he became a member of the preparatory committee to establish a council for invalids in the Russian Federation. On November 20, 1991 he was elected a member of the working group for the preliminary drafting of the decrees of the Russian President. On November 21, 1991, he was elected chairman of the Supreme Soviet committee on legislation. He is a member of the communists for democracy parliamentary faction. He is married and his wife, Lyudmila Aleksandrovna, is a hydraulic engineer. They have two sons and a daughter.

Address: 103274 Moscow, K 274, Krasnopresnenskaya nab., d. 2, Dom Sovetov; *telephone*: Moscow 205 99 51.

Mochaikin, Aleksandr Gennadevich

Chairman of Co-ordinating Council of Officers' Assemblies; Chairman of the Committee on the rights of military men with the Commander-in-Chief of the Unified Armed Forces of the CIS; Rear-Admiral since October 1992.

Born on July 15, 1948 in the village of Pushkovo, Golovanevsky *raion*, Kirovograd *oblast*, Ukraine, into a civil servant's family; Ukrainian. He has had a military career since 1967. After national service in the army he entered Kiev Higher Military Naval Political School and graduated in 1973. He graduated from the V. I. Lenin Military-Political Academy (an extra-mural course) in 1981. He has received a higher military and higher political education, and was a member of the CPSU from 1969 to August 1991.

After graduating from naval school he held various political posts in nuclear submarines in the Northern Fleet: senior instructor for *Komsomol* work in the political department, assistant for *Komsomol* work to the head of the political department, political commander of a submarine, deputy head and head of political department of a nuclear submarine division and head of the military-political department of the same division. He proved to be a well-trained political commander and sailor with many special qualifications, good at organizing Party and political work with all categories of personnel. A convinced communist, he supported the CPSU policy in the military sphere, in international affairs and inside the country, and actively co-operated with local Party and security agencies when performing his official duties. He personally participated in many long sea voyages and served in the oceans. With the beginning of the democratization of Soviet society he actively opposed the spread of free thinking and anti-communist views among sailors, and negatively reacted to democratic and national-democratic movements.

He devoted much time to the issues of social welfare of military men and meeting their material and everyday needs, which helped him win authority among personnel. He was noted for his resoluteness and persistence in solving the problems of political training, defending the interests of personnel and imposing communist ideology among sailors.

During the anti-constitutional putsch in August 1991 he was not active and bided his time.

He was one of the organizers of officers' assemblies in the Navy, supporting this way of influencing officers' corps as a means of stabilizing the situation in military units. He was elected a delegate to the first all-army officers' assembly, took part in preparing it and worked there in January 1992. He participated in preparatory meetings with the USSR President M. Gorbachev and Minister of Defence Air Force Marshal Evgeny Shaposhnikov. At the assembly he was elected a member of the co-ordinating council of the officers' assemblies, and became its chairman in February 1992.

He actively organized officers' assemblies, defended the interests of military men, including the areas in which there was armed conflict. A convinced supporter of a strong state, he was in favour of retaining integral armed forces after the disintegration of the USSR. He personally went to conflict areas (Nagorno-Karabakh, Georgia, Pridnestrove, and so on). When dealing with the problems of social welfare he tenaciously defended his opinion at every level of authority, including top officials of the Ministries of Defence of Russia, Ukraine, the Caucasus and the Baltic. He took part in the talks with the states where Russian troops were stationed.

He does not broadcast his political views and is eager to maintain the image of a disinterested defender of the rights and interests of military men. He has close ties with military organizations of differing political persvasions (The Shield union, Officers' Union, "the movement of Officers for the Revival of the Motherland" and others) and with the independent trade union of military men. He participates in the drafting of agreements and laws defending the interests of military men and attends the sessions of the CIS council of ministers of defence and heads of governments; he is also in close contact with the personnel departments of ministries of defence of the CIS states.

Since the autumn of 1992 he has been chairman of the committee on the rights of military men of the Commander-in-Chief of the Unified Armed Forces of the CIS, retaining his post as Chairman of the Co-ordinating Council of Officers' Assemblies. In October 1992 Mochaikin was promoted to Rear-Admiral. He personally supervises the work on the issues of social welfare, personnel appointments and transfer of personnel in the Unified Armed Forces and national armies of the CIS states. He enjoys the support of national-patriotic forces and the political and military community, which advocates a strong state, and of Marshal Evgeny Shaposhnikov personally. Democratically-minded military men are suspicious of Rear-Admiral Mochaikin as a man with obviously pro-communist views. Neither does he enjoy the favour of the Minister of Defence of the Russian Federation, General of the Army Pavel Grachev, who is against the expansion of officers' assemblies and other public organizations in the army.

He is quite intelligent, being interested in literature and the theatre, and favouring the realist school in art. He does not speak any foreign language. He enjoys sport.

He often appears in the press on the problems of military planning and social welfare of military men. He has visited foreign countries where Russian troops are stationed, but has not been abroad as a member of representative delegations.

He was awarded the order "For the Service to the Motherland in the Armed Forces of the USSR", and has six medals. He is married with a daughter and a son who is a soldier in the interior forces of the MVD of Russia.

Office address: Moscow, Leningradsky prospekt, 41.

Moiseev, Mikhail Alekseevich

Chief of the General Staff of the USSR armed forces; first deputy Minister of Defence of the USSR; acting Minister of Defence on August 22–23, 1991; General of the Army.

Born on January 22, 1939 in the village of Maly Iver, Svobodnensk *raion*, Amur *oblast* into a working-class family; Russian. He graduated from the Far East Tank Technical school in Blagoveshchensk in 1962, the M. V. Frunze Military Academy in 1972, and from the Military Academy of the General Staff in 1982, receiving a higher military education. He was a member of the CPSU from 1962 to August 1991.

He began his career as an officer as a tank platoon commander and proved to be a promising leader with a sound professional knowledge and a great interest in his official duties. He actively participated in the work of the Party organizations. He enjoyed the respect and support of superior officers and political agencies and was promoted quite rapidly: tank company commander, deputy regimental commander, regimental chief of staff. After graduating from the Academy he was immediately appointed a tank regimental commander as one of the best graduates. His record was that of an officer with a sound operational-tactical and military-technical training, able to organize present-day combat, and to ensure high combat readiness and discipline. From 1976 to 1980 he was deputy commander and commander of a division, and in 1982 was appointed first deputy army commander and soon an army commander. When he was appointed a divisional commander in 1979 in the Far East he became acquainted with the future Minister of Defence, D. Yazov, and later enjoyed his support.

General M. Moiseev was a typical military professional, who advocated tough measures to strengthen further the Soviet military system and USSR policy. He enjoyed considerable authority in military circles for his professional skills as a true combat officer, and has served in 20 garrisons in the course of his military career.

In 1985 he was appointed Chief of Staff and first deputy commander of the Far East military district (with D. Yazov as commander), and then in 1987 he replaced Yazov in the post of commander of that district. On the initiative of his patron, who became the USSR Minister of Defence, he was appointed Chief of the General Staff in December 1988.

It was under General Mikhail Moiseev that military construction in the USSR was planned and executed during the period of *rapprochement* with Western countries, and defence expenditure cuts. He advocated the policy of reasonable sufficiency, favoured the retention of the considerable military potential of the country, and firmly defended the interests of the armed forces *vis-à-vis* state and Party leaders. He favoured a balanced development of all types of armed forces and their equipment with up-to-date high-precision weapons. He often paid official visits to the USA and Canada and participated in talks on the entire subject of strategic offensive and conventional arms reduction with the chairman of Chiefs-of-Staff Committee, General Collin Powell. He met President George Bush and Defence Secretary Robert Cheney.

He was elected a people's deputy of the Khabarovsk *krai* soviet, a USSR people's deputy (the CPSU candidate), and from July 1990 he was a member of the Party Central Committee. At the congresses of the USSR people's deputies he adhered to conservative views, opposed national-democratic movements in Union republics and democratic forces in Russia, and was a convinced advocate of the maintenance of the USSR. In December 1990, M. A. Moiseev signed an appeal to the USSR President demanding the introduction of a state of emergency. As a chief of the General Staff he was directly involved in the planning and use of troops in domestic conflicts.

In August 1991 he was on leave and was recalled by Yazov on August 19. He signed a number of instructions aimed at raising the combat readiness of the armed forces during the anti-constitutional putsch. On August 20 he suggested to Yazov that *matériel* should be withdrawn from the centre of Moscow, and in the collegium of the Ministry of Defence on August 21 managed to persuade the military leaders to withdraw all troops from Moscow.

By President Mikhail Gorbachev's decree on August 21, Moiseev was appointed Minister of Defence after he had presented a report on the state of affairs in the army and navy. But on August 23 he was dismissed from this post and that of Chief of the General Staff.

The prosecutor's investigation proved that Moiseev was not privy to the putsch and his activities at that time were judged to be no more than the exercise of his immediate functions as the officer responsible for state security and the combat readiness of the armed forces. Nevertheless, according to experts from the democratic military organizations, General Moiseev, because of his position, could not have failed to know of the preparations for the putsch and thus must bear responsibility for army involvement in the coup attempt. On November 6, 1991 he was transferred to the reserve at his own request.

At present he is a consultant to the Supreme Soviet Committee on the issues of interregional relations, regional policy and co-operation. In March 1992 he successfully presented his candidate dissertation (PhD) on the problems of the construction of the armed forces of Russia. He is a candidate of military sciences.

He enjoys considerable authority and influence in military circles. He is a convinced advocate of the creation of an up-to-date army and navy in Russia with modern combat *matériel*, of Russia retaining the status of a great power and its territorial integrity, and the defence of the interests of the Russian-speaking population in the former Soviet republics, by all possible means.

He is against the hasty withdrawal of troops from abroad, and is unhappy with the results of disarmament talks. He believes the latter mean that Russia will lose its most up to date rocket weapons and reasonable parity with the USA. He considers nuclear weapons to be a necessary political and psychological means of maintaining the prestige and strength of the country. He considers it his duty, while working in the Supreme Soviet, to warn the present political leaders of the country against rash actions which may drive the army into a hopeless situation which in turn may lead to a social explosion.

He is interested in literature, history, art and theatre, and tries to keep well informed about current events at home and abroad. He does not speak any foreign languages. He has been awarded two orders "For service to the motherland in the armed forces of the USSR", and more than 10 medals.

He is married and his wife, Galina Iosifovna, works on the committee for military men who served in Afghanistan. His son is an officer who is serving in Kamchatka; he has a daughter and two grandchildren. He now lives in a formerly official, now privatized, dacha in the prestigious area of Arkhangelskoe near Moscow.

Moiseev, Nikita Nikolaevich

Member of the Council of the President of the Russian Federation.

Born in 1917 into an intelligentsia family. His grandfather, a well-known railway engineer in the 1920s, refused to emigrate. Moiseev is a famous mathematician and specialist on information technology and cybernetics. He was on the staff of Rostov-on-Don State University, then worked in France and then in the computer centre, USSR Academy of Sciences. In 1955 he successfully presented his doctoral dissertation in physics and mathematics on "Research into solid bodies, containing liquid masses and having a free surface" (DSc). He was a state prize winner in 1977 and in 1987 was awarded the order of Lenin. He is a member of the V. I. Vernadsky centre for the problems of ecology and coevolution, USSR commission on UNESCO, the Soviet section of the international fund for the survival and development of humanity. He is an Academician of the Russian Academy of Sciences and an adviser of the board of directors of the computer centre, Russian Academy of Sciences.

Moiseev devoted much time to research into the fruitful fusion of natural science and the humanities. He has written the books: *On the Scientific-Technical Revolution* (1978); *The Person, the Environment, Society: Problems of Formalized Description* (1982); *People and Cybernetics* (1984); *Socialism and Information Technology* (1988); *The Ecology of Humanity Through the Eyes of a Mathematician: The Person, Nature and the Future of Civilization* (1988); *The Person and the Biosphere* (1990); *The Ideas of the Natural and Social Sciences* (1991); *Ways of Creation* (1992).

He believes that the average level of education in Russia is higher than in the West and that the greatest achievements have been in rocket, nuclear and computer technology. However, science has stagnated since 1985 and many talented people have left the country. The government does not comprehend that the real resources of Russia lie with its intelligentsia and it is important that the intelligentsia does not remain on the periphery of the reforms. It has no tradition or desire to fight for property. The greatest value of the intelligentsia is that it is capable of thinking and to be free. The future of the country depends on the national intellect, the ability to generate ideas and to turn them quickly and effectively into reality. The thinker and intellectual should be in the forefront of the reforms.

The maintenance and development of education, scientific creativity and the introduction of modern technology should be the cornerstone of reform. The intellectual should always be independent, always in opposition and have the right to his or her own opinion. The value of the intelligentsia, in Moiseev's eyes, is in the genetic variety of ideas without which the people and the nation cannot exist. The intelligentsia does not need posts and official positions. The intellectual élite is always linked to the people.

He regards the collapse of the Soviet Union as a step back for civilization. The main mistake of 1917 was to establish a federation of republics and not a federation of states in which members of various nationalities would live. In the world the nation is not dominant but the person, human rights and values common to all humanity. He believes that all states should have a very varied cultural and national base. He advocates a confederation of states and dual citizenship, and opposes the parading of national emotion and the breaking of all ties with and finally the destruction of the centre. One should only criticize one's own national leaders. He does not believe that any revolution can produce anything beneficial, but would only throw society backwards. Public consciousness by nature is very conservative and needs time to adjust to any change, and so he supports an evolutionary process of development. He became a member of the Presidential Council in 1992 and lives in Moscow.

Monakhov, Vladimir Georgievich

Director of the Sergo Ordzhonikidze machine tool enterprise, Moscow.

Born in 1947 in Moscow; Russian. He was a member of the CPSU until August 1991. From 1964 to 1965 he was a turner in an enterprise, and from 1966 worked in various engineer design bureaux. After graduating from the Machine Tool Engineering Institute, Moscow, he worked as an engineer in a Moscow production association, and then from 1978 to 1982 he was an engineer in the Stankoagregat enterprise, Moscow. In 1982 he was appointed deputy head of department, USSR state planning committee (Gosplan), and in 1988 became chief engineer in the *Stankostroitelny zavod* (machine building enterprise) production association, Moscow. In 1990 he was appointed director of the Sergo Ordzhonikidze machine tool enterprise. He is married with two daughters.

Address: 117908 Moscow, GSP, ul. Ordzhonikidze 11; *telephone*: Moscow 232 3828 (office).

Moroz, Oleksandr Oleksandrovych

Head of the Socialist Party of Ukraine, Former Leader of the Communist Majority in the Supreme Soviet.

Born into a Ukrainian peasant's family in Kiev *oblast* in 1944. He was educated at the Ukrainian Academy of Agricultural Economics and at the Communist Party of Ukraine's (CPU) Higher Party School in Kiev. By profession he is an engineer, but spent his working career in the *apparat* of the CPU, becoming the director of its agricultural division. He was elected people's deputy for the rural *raion* of Taraschanskyi, Kiev *oblast*, on the first round in March 1990.

In the Supreme Soviet he is the Secretary of the committee on the agro-industrial complex, but he rose to fame as the leader of the majority communist faction in the Supreme Soviet formed in June 1990 in opposition to the radical

People's Council, which referred to itself as being "For the Soviet Sovereignty of Ukraine", but was popularly known as the Group of 239. Moroz maintained a conservative course, even when his communist group began to split between supporters of Kravchuk and the hardline first secretary of the CPU, Stanislav Hurenko, in 1991.

In the debates on August 24, 1991 that preceded Ukraine's Declaration of Independence, Moroz declared his intention to sever the CPU's ties with Moscow, but this was too late to prevent the banning of the Party and the dissolution of its parliamentary group in August-September. Nevertheless, Moroz quickly formed an initiative committee for a revived and revamped communist party, which held its founding congress in Kiev as early as October 26, 1991, choosing the name Socialist Party of Ukraine (SPU).

It claimed to be the largest party in Ukraine, with 30,000 members and 38 supporters in the Supreme Soviet. The SPU was far from being a carbon copy of the old Communist Party, however. Moroz aimed to copy the success of the Polish communist party in reinventing itself as a party of populist opposition to market reforms. He therefore steered the party away from radical demands to oppose Ukrainian independence in the December 1, 1991 referendum and to put up an SPU candidate for President in opposition to Kravchuk.

The SPU then benefited from its forthright opposition to the price increases in Ukraine from January 1992 onwards and from its nostalgia for the lost certainties and centralized order of the past. By the summer it was topping some opinion polls in Kiev city. However, Moroz was under increasing pressure from his more radical deputies, including the academic Kyzyma, and the SPU's first all-Ukrainian conference held in June 1992 showed a marked swing to the left.

In June 1992 the SPU set up a committee for the annulment of the anti-constitutional decision to ban the Communist Party of Ukraine. After the decision by the Russian Supreme Court partially to rescind President Yeltsin's ban on the Communist Party in November 1992, pressure for a similar move in Ukraine began to increase, and a variety of openly revivalist neo-communist groups emerged. The SPU therefore began to lose its monopoly status on the Ukrainian left, but its second congress in November 1992 confirmed its status as the strongest left-wing group in Ukraine.

The SPU was the only group to vote against granting the new Kuchma government emergency economic powers in November 1992. Moroz's SPU, however, was increasingly criticized by newer left-wing groups, whose main spokesman in the Ukrainian Supreme Soviet was Borys Oliinyk. They tended to view Moroz as an *arriviste*, and were strongly critical of his accommodation towards Ukrainian independence, preferring instead to call openly for the restoration of the USSR.

Official address: Kiev, Vul. M. Hrushevskoho 5; *telephone*: Kiev 252 019 or (Kiev) 291 6063 (Socialist Party).

Morozov, Konstantin Petrovych

Minister of Defence of Ukraine.

An ethnic Russian, although his mother is Ukrainian and he began to learn Ukrainian after his appointment as Defence Minister in September 1991. He was born in 1944 in the town of Bryanka in the highly Russified Luhansk *oblast* in eastern Ukraine. A career officer, he was educated at the General Staff Academy and the military-aviation academy in Kharkiv. Thereafter he flew bombers, becoming the commander of a bomber division, and an Air Force Major General by the time of his appointment in September 1991 as the first Defence Minister of independent Ukraine in the wake of the failed August 1991 coup and Ukraine's Declaration of Independence.

At the time it was thought that an ethnic Russian would help smooth relations with Russia, and with the mainly Russian officer corps then stationed on Ukrainian territory. He then set about building up first his own department and then Ukrainian Armed Forces from scratch. Outside observers may have been surprised by the speed with which Ukraine moved towards this goal in autumn 1991 at the expense of other, notably economic, reforms, but it was axiomatic in Ukrainian circles that Ukraine had lost its independence during 1917 to 1920 because of the lack of military preparedness and there was a broad political consensus that it should not make the same mistake again, especially as tensions with Russia began to rise in autumn 1991.

In October, Morozov announced plans to build Ukrainian armed forces of 450,000 (later it was announced that the long-term target would be 220,000). This threatened to provide Ukraine with the second largest standing army in Europe, but was in fact based on the supposedly average figure of 0.8% of population. Morozov became Commander of the Armed Forces, when their formation was announced in December 1991 (answerable to Kravchuk as Commander-in-Chief), and a Member of the Defence and Security Councils established in 1992. Ukraine had rejected the Baltic strategy of seeking to expel ex-Soviet forces and form indigenous armed forces. Rather, it attempted to build its own forces on the basis of such ex-Soviet forces left on its territory.

Morozov was therefore placed in charge of the campaign that began in January 1992 to persuade ex-Soviet servicemen to take an oath of loyalty to Ukraine. This succeeded remarkably well, as only 10,000 refused to do so by summer 1992, primarily because Morozov resisted nationalist calls for a purge of the armed forces and made expensive promises concerning salaries and general living standards in an independent Ukraine. Morozov nevertheless had critics on both the right and the left.

By summer 1992 Morozov was faced with growing complaints concerning his cautious approach, particularly from the radical Union of Officers of Ukraine (UOU). They argued that he should now proceed to the Ukrainianization of the armed forces, replacing the materially-minded with the estimated 300,000 ethnic Ukrainian officers stranded elsewhere in the former USSR. Morozov therefore bent with the wind by proposing this formally to the CIS high command in May 1992, and by appointing four deputy defence ministers and a Chief of Staff in June 1992, all of whom were ethnic Ukrainians.

Despite his Russian origins, Morozov proved adept at playing the nationalist card, even letting it be known that he had opposed the agreement to establish joint control over the Black Sea Fleet for three years, reached between Kravchuk and Yeltsin in August 1992. Morozov also faced nationalist pressure to revise Ukraine's commitment to neutral and non-nuclear status. The draft defence doctrine that he twice presented to the Supreme Soviet in October 1992 and April 1993 was rejected for failing to move sufficiently in this direction.

By this stage, however, Morozov also faced potentially more serious criticism from the other direction, as 155 neo-socialist and Russophone deputies had signed a motion calling for the reversal of his policies and his possible removal by early 1993. Therefore, the nationalists closed ranks behind him in late 1992 and early 1993, securing his confirmation in his post by new Prime Minister Leonid Kuchma in October 1992.

Official (Ministry) address: 252005 Kiev, Vul. Bankivska 6; *telephone*: Kiev 291 5441.

Morozov, Yury Valentinovich

Co-chairman of anti-monopoly exchange conference; chairman of the auditing commission of the Russian union of private owners.

Born in 1955 in Moscow; Russian. He completed secondary school, then began his working career in 1972 as a worker in an enterprise, and in 1980 became an accountant. Since 1988 he has been chairman of a co-operative; co-chairman of the conference of anti-monopoly exchanges; and chairman of the auditing commission of the Russian union of private owners. He is a member of the exchange activity licence commission of the Russian state committee for anti-monopoly policy. He is married with two children.

Address: Moscow, Sushchevsky val 66; *telephone*: Moscow 971 6722.

Morshchakov, Fedor Mikhailovich

Head of the Main Social and Production Administration of the President of the Russian Federation.

Until he was over 70 years of age he was deputy chairman of the Sverdlovsk *oblast* soviet executive committee, and he is known for his accuracy, precision and incredible capacity for work. The democratically minded deputies of the Sverdlovsk *oblast* soviet were also pensioned off with Morshchakov, but he then joined President Yeltsin's apparatus in Moscow. His administration is responsible for providing all the economic needs of the President, the Vice-President and the government, but the status of this administration has declined significantly since originally it was directly subordinate to the President. Despite proposals to split it into economic and financial administrations, this eventually did not take place. He lives in Moscow.

Morshchakova, Tamara Georgievna

Member of the Constitutional Court of the Russian Federation.

Born on March 28, 1936 in Moscow; Russian; member of the CPSU until August 1991. In 1958 she graduated from the faculty of law, Moscow State University and from 1958 to 1971 she was a postgraduate student, junior scientific assistant, institute of state and law, USSR Academy of Sciences. The main areas of her legal interests are the sociology of justice, the judicial system and legal procedure in German-speaking countries, criminal procedure, the organization of the courts and the procurator's office. In 1966 in the institute of state and law, USSR Academy of Sciences, she successfully presented her candidate dissertation on "Criminal legal procedure in the German Democratic Republic" (LLM). From 1971 to 1991 she was a senior, head, chief scientific assistant in the all-Union scientific research institute of state formation and law, and in 1988 in the institute of law she was a member of a group of specialists working on problems of judicial reform in the USSR. In 1988 in the same institute she successfully presented her doctoral dissertation on "The theoretical bases of the evaluation of the quality and organization of justice in criminal cases (procedural, statistical and sociological aspects)" (LLD). For many years she has taught in the academy of law, USSR Ministry of Justice, and the institute of law, Moscow. She is a member of the scientific consultative council of the Supreme Court of the Russian Federation and the scientific council of the institute of law, Moscow. When elected a member of the Constitutional Court she was a senior scientific assistant in the all-Union scientific research institute of state formation and law. She is a co-author of the concept of judicial reform in the Russian Federation which was adopted by the Russian Supreme Soviet. She is an honoured lawyer of the Russian Federation.

She was nominated as a candidate for election to the Constitutional Court by the parliamentary group of non-party deputies. She was elected a member of the Constitutional Court on October 29, 1991, at the V Congress of People's Deputies, in the first round of voting when she received 699 votes for and 212 against.

She regards the Constitutional Court to be of key importance in the development and implementation of legal order in Russia. It should confine the legislature within a strict legal framework and promote the emergence of a new Russian constitution. She regards her main duties in the Constitutional Court to be the resolution of problems of legal procedure and the judicial system. She is favourably disposed towards the establishment in Russia of the jury system, not only as a guarantee of the rights of the citizen, but also as a means of educating people about the state. She lives in Moscow.

Moskovchenko, Nikolai Mikhailovich

Military expert of the coalition of democratic factions in the Supreme Soviet of the Russian Federation; chairman of Shield, the Russian Union for the social welfare of military men, men liable for call-up and members of their families; Major.

Born on July 22, 1954 in the village of Chernomin, Peschansky *raion*, Vinnitsa *oblast*, Ukraine, into a soldier's family; Ukrainian.

He graduated from Vasilkovskoe Military Aviation and Technical School in 1974 and then attended the Professor Zhukovsky Military Aviation Engineering Academy. Following this higher military special education, he became a mechanical engineer for aircraft and engines. He was a member of the CPSU from 1980 to 1990, but left it voluntarily for political motives and publicly burnt his membership card at an all-Moscow rally.

After graduating from technical school he served in a transport air regiment of long-range aviation as a flight technician. He flew long-haul routes to all parts of the USSR, and had the reputation of being a highly qualified specialist, expertly maintaining complex aviation systems. He was noted for his independent views on the problems of politics and military planning, and for the firm stand he took to defend the interests of his colleagues against commanders and political agencies. Young officers saw him as a person with unbiased views, capable of protesting against unjust decisions of commanders. He was under the secret surveillance of the Party-political apparatus and KGB officers.

After graduating from the Academy he left to serve in a research unit as a section head, and was then appointed a lecturer. He enjoyed authority among students for his high professional and moral qualities. With the beginning of *perestroika* in the USSR under Gorbachev and the democratization of social life he was one of the first in the Soviet army to advocate drastically reforming relations within the army, and to oppose the command of the political apparatus and Party organizations in the armed forces; he spoke at officers' and Party meetings in favour of improving the social welfare of military men and the right for non-communist social and political movements to have military men as members. He was in close contact with Academician Andrei Sakharov and his inner circle; he participated in the March 1989 election campaign for the election of USSR people's deputies. In March 1989, together with a group of democratically-minded officers, he set up the Shield, a union for the social welfare of military men, men liable for call-up and members of their families, one of the most active democratic organizations in the USSR. He took part in meetings and sessions to spread objective information about the illegal use of the army against the people in Tbilisi and Yerevan in 1989. He participated in drafting a plan for military reform in the group led by the USSR people's deputy, Major Vladimir Lopatin.

In the autumn of 1989 at officers' and Party meetings at Zhukovsky Academy he strongly opposed the illegal distribution of flats among top commanders and, personally, to the head of the political department. In December 1989 he actively participated in the organization of the funeral of the leader of the democratic forces, Academician Andrei Sakharov. After this conspicuous activity, commanders, the Party-political apparatus, and air force security agencies organized a campaign of vilification against Major Nikolai Moskovchenko, accusing him of unscrupulousness so as to turn the men against him. Provocative material was widely published in the army and the communist press. The democratic mass media defended the major but he fell into disgrace. Security agencies and the commandant's office used underhand methods against Moskovchenko. On January 4, 1990, Moskovchenko was discharged from the army in a manner which violated the current law.

Since the beginning of 1990 Moskovchenko has devoted himself to social-political activity. He was nominated as a candidate for election as people's deputy of Russia in Pervomaisky territorial district (Moscow), but failed to win enough votes and was defeated by his colleague from the "Democratic Russia" bloc, Professor Yury Afanasev. In summer 1990 he was elected to the Co-ordinating Council of "Democratic Russia" by the Shield union and other military organizations. He actively participated in the organization of rallies in Moscow, took the floor at rallies in Manezhnaya Square and in Luzhniki stadium and became popular with Muscovites and in some regions of the USSR.

As a military expert he went to inquire into the anti-constitutional actions of the Soviet army against the civil population in Baku in 1990, the Baltic in 1991 and near Moscow in 1990. As a member of an expert team of civil and military scientists he participated in drafting several variants of how to implement a national military reform and the priorities of military planning at the end of 1990 and the beginning of 1991, in order to submit them to the Supreme Soviet and the USSR President. As one of the Shield leaders he concerned himself with establishing official contacts with military professional organizations abroad, and in October 1990 he went to Spain to take part in the work of the pan-European union of military men. He was one of the organizers of the all-Union Council of Military Men's Parents, the organization which brought together the relatives of soldiers and officers who died during peacetime as a result of unlawful acts within the army. He led protests by parents of soldiers who had died while in the army to demand that the Minister of Defence, Dmitry Yazov, should initiate legal proceedings to inquire into the unlawful acts, corruption and irregular relations in the army and navy. Moskovchenko was reported to have slapped the military commandant of Moscow, General Smirnov, in the face for insulting mothers of soldiers killed in the army and to have summoned the General to court. Marshal Yazov publicly called Major Moskovchenko his personal enemy.

During the anti-constitutional putsch in August 1991 Moskovchenko headed one of the sectors of the internal defence of the Russian White House. In autumn 1991 he was one of the members of staff to set up the Russian national guard and took part in planning the armed forces of the Russian Federation. In April 1992, at the III Congress of the Shield union he was elected a co-chairman of the organization and has been its chairman since the autumn of 1992.

At present he is the military expert of the coalition of democratic factions in the Russian parliament and was accredited as a correspondent of several newspapers by the Supreme Soviet. As a member of the Co-ordinating Council of "Democratic Russia" he concerns himself with co-ordinating the actions of the military organizations. He headed commissions of independent military experts inquiring into the deployment of the army against the civil population in Pridnestrovie in 1992 and North Ossetia and Ingushetia in January 1993, which presented their conclusions to parliamentary hearings.

He often appears in the press on problems of military planning, social and legal welfare of military men, corruption among the top officials of the Ministry of Defence, the demilitarization of the capital of Russia and the regulation by law of the deployment of the army in the country. His latest article is "The Capital of the Military Industrial Complex?" in *Stolitsa*, No. 2 (112), 1993.

He is fond of literature, journalism, political and military history and technology. He goes in for sport and has achieved grades in parachute jumping and officers' combined events. He does not have a good command of foreign languages. He has been awarded four medals. He is divorced with two children.

Office address: Moscow, Bolshoi Cherkassky pereulok, house 4. Telephone: Moscow 921 28 58; 928 61 27.

Movchan, Pavlo Mykhailovych

Head of the Ukrainian Language Society *Prosvita*.

Born into a Ukrainian family in 1939. He studied at the Gorky Institute of Literature, Moscow, and took a two-year script-writing and stage directing course in the USSR Institute of State Cinema. Like many other members of the Kiev intelligentsia, he was prominent in the organization of *Rukh* over the winter of 1988-89. Movchan (together with Viktor Teren) in fact first proposed the idea of creating a Baltic-style Popular Front at a meeting in the Kiev Writers' Union building on November 1, 1988.

Movchan was also prominent in organizing the Taras Shevchenko Ukrainian language society in February 1989. The society, renamed *Prosvita* (which means "enlightenment" or "learning") in autumn 1991 when Movchan was already leader, aims to promote the revival of the Ukrainian language and increasingly the Ukrainianization of education and the state. He has radicalized *Prosvita* towards placing more emphasis on the latter goal and has argued for a strengthening of the relatively anodyne 1989 language law, causing disruption in its ranks and a split in the movement in 1992, and criticism from those who advocate a more conciliatory approach to Ukraine's massive (perhaps 40%) Russian-speaking population.

In March 1990 Movchan was elected people's deputy for Berezniakivskyi *raion* in Kiev city (on the second round). In the Supreme Soviet he is a member of the committee for the Chernobyl catastrophe, and head of its sub-committee for dealing with the problems of the 30-kilometre exclusion zone around Chernobyl.

Address (of *Prosvita*): 252001 Kiev, Muzenii provulok 8; *telephone*: Kiev 228 0229.

Mukha, Vitaly Petrovich

Head of the Administration of Novosibirsk *oblast*, Russian Federation.

Born on May 17, 1936 in Kharkov (Kharkiv), Ukraine; Ukrainian; member of the CPSU from 1963 to August 1991. In 1960 he graduated from the Kharkov Aviation Institute, and is a qualified engineer and assistant professor. After graduating he was a foreman, deputy head, and head of a shop in the V. P. Chkalov aviation enterprise, Novosibirsk. From 1966 he worked as head of a department, deputy chief engineer, chief engineer and from 1973 as director of the enterprise and general director of the *Sibelektroterm* association. From 1982 to 1988 he was general director of the Sibselmask production association. In 1988 he was elected second secretary and in 1989 first secretary of the Novosibirsk Party *obkom*. He is the recipient of various Soviet orders and medals. He was elected a member of the Party Central Committee in July 1990 and was a delegate to the XXVIII Party congress.

In early 1990 he was nominated for election as an RSFSR people's deputy in the No. 533 Chulymsky territorial district. During the election campaign he advocated the strengthening of the sovereignty of Russia within the USSR, the transfer of real economic and political power to the soviets, the development of democracy and *glasnost*, the establishment of conditions to implement local initiatives and real autonomy for enterprises and at the place of residence, and co-operation with informal groups which supported the renewal of socialism by legal means. He appealed for the renaissance of spiritual and moral values and co-operation with the creative intelligentsia.

There were three candidates. Mukha polled 41.9% of the votes in the first round and won the second round, polling 45.6% of the votes. His main opponent was N. G. Khmelev, editor of the Chulymsky *raion* newspaper, who received 25.3% of the votes in the first round and 44.2% in the second. In 1990 Mukha was elected a deputy of the Novosibirsk *oblast* soviet and in April 1990, at the first session of the soviet, he was elected chairman. Later he combined the posts of chairman of the *oblast* soviet, chairman of the *oblast* soviet executive and first secretary of the Party *obkom*.

On August 20, 1991 Mukha, in a statement, recommended the soviets to follow the provisions of the USSR and RSFSR constitutions. He did not support the call for an indefinite general political strike and appealed to the public to remain calm and restrained, not to permit illegal activities, and to decide all questions in a legal constitutional manner. He supported the legally elected RSFSR President and the state authorities.

On November 27, 1991 he was appointed head of the administration of Novosibirsk *oblast* by presidential decree. On assuming office he advocated the creation of a mechanism to implement the introduction of the market in the *oblast*. He expressed support for transforming enterprises into joint stock companies, the development of small businesses and the establishment of interregional and foreign trade links. The most important aspect of the reforms was raising the efficiency of production.

In February 1992 he was elected chairman of the council of the interregional association, *Siberian accord*. In December 1992, during the VII Congress of People's Deputies, he advocated the consolidation of legislative and executive power which bore a heavy responsibility to the people. He pointed out that the appeal of the governors of Russia to the congress had been a fiasco since it had attempted to put great pressure on the congress. He appealed to the congress not to enter into confrontation but to demonstrate that it was the supreme agency of the power of the people and not to search for scapegoats. The government should draft a programme to permit the country to escape from the economic crisis. The President should nominate the government, and he advocated the adoption of a new constitution as rapidly as possible. He lives in Novosibirsk.

Mukhamadiev, Rinat Safievich

Chairman of the commission on culture, language, national traditions and protection of the historical heritage, Council of Nationalities of the Russian Supreme Soviet.

Born on December 10, 1948 in the village of Malye Kirmeni, Mamadyshsky *raion*, Tatar ASSR; Tatar. He was a member of the CPSU until August 1991. He graduated from the faculty of philology, Kazan State University, and became an editor of children's and youth programmes on Kazan TV; then he worked on the editorial board of the *Kazan Utlaru* (Kazan lights) magazine. He became a postgraduate student at Moscow State University and in 1979 he successfully presented his candidate dissertation on "Problems of Tatar literary criticism, 1909-17" (PhD). He was director of the Tatar book publishing house, and in 1989 became head of the board of the union of writers, Tatar ASSR. After being elected a people's deputy he became a member of the *Federatsiya* (federation) magazine editorial board.

He was nominated for election as an RSFSR people's deputy in the No. 127 Leninogorsky national territorial district, Tatar ASSR. He devoted his election campaign to cultural problems, the preservation of the national Tatar language, the development of inter-ethnic relations, the protection and education of children and defence of the environment. Among the demands he articulated were that Tatarstan and other national state formations be afforded equal rights and that an end be put to the situation where Tatarstan was treated as a raw materials base for the rest of the country. At the II Congress of People's Deputies he twice criticized the Supreme Soviet's attitude towards the people of the Russian Federation, arguing that it contradicted the declaration on sovereignty. He supported the declarations of sovereignty by many republics and regions.

There were eight candidates and Mukhamadiev won the second round, polling 63.5% of the votes. His main opponent was I. G. Zhzhonov, chairman of the Tatar *oblast* committee of the trade union of workers in the oil and gas industries. Mukhamadiev was elected a member of the RSFSR Supreme Soviet at the I Congress of People's Deputies (695 voted for, 228 voted against), and is a member of the parliamentary sovereignty and equality faction; communists of Russia group. He is a member of the Council of Nationalities, Russian Supreme Soviet, and in 1991 he was elected chairman of the Council of Nationalities commission on culture, language, national traditions and protection of the historical heritage.

Address: 103274 Moscow, K 274, Krasnopresnensky nab., d. 2, Dom Sovetov; *telephone*: Moscow 205 43 95.

Mukhametshin, Farid Khairullovich

Speaker of the Supreme Soviet of the Republic of Tatarstan, Russian Federation.

Born in 1949 in Almetevsk; a Tatar; member of the CPSU from 1971 to August 1991. He is a graduate of the oil institute, Ufa, and the Saratov Higher Party School. He began his career in 1963 as a turner in the gas and petrol enterprise, Almetevsk. Then he was a chauffeur and fitter and served in the Soviet Army. After being demobbed he transferred to *Komsomol* work. In 1972 he was an instructor of the Almetevsk Party city committee, in 1978 deputy, and later first deputy chairman of Almetevsk city soviet executive committee. From 1985 to 1987 he was secretary, then second secretary of the Almetevsk city Party committee, and then was involved in economic and soviet work. In 1990 he was appointed Minister of Trade of the Tatar Soviet Socialist Republic, then first secretary of the Almetevsk city Party committee. In 1990 he was also appointed deputy Chairman of the Council of Ministers of the Tatar SSR.

In April 1990 he was elected a people's deputy of the Tatar SSR in the second round of voting and at the V extraordinary session of the supreme Soviet of the Tatar SSR, on July 5, 1991, he was elected Speaker. On assuming office he spoke of the republic finding its own route to economic development, but also advocated the retention of one economic and legal space and the intensification of economic links with other republics. He favoured the "soft" approach to market reform and the establishment of priorities for the social protection of the population. This was the state policy of Tatarstan. He opposed separatism and stated that in the declaration of the sovereignty of the Tatar SSR there was no intention to secede, only a desire to defend the legal rights and interests of the peoples of Tatarstan.

On August 22, 1991 a decree of the Presidium of the Supreme Soviet was adopted stating that a state of emergency would not be introduced in Tatarstan and appealing for greater control over the implementation of the existing legislation of the USSR and the Tatar SSR, and also that newspapers should refrain from publishing material which would destabilize the situation. It called on the population not to fall victim to provocations.

In December 1992 Mukhametshin spoke at the VII Congress of People's Deputies and pointed out that no agreed programme of action to resolve the economic crisis had been presented to congress. He lives in Kazan.

Mukhammad, Sodyk Mukhammad Yusuf

Chairman of the Muslim Religious Board of Central Asia (SADUM); Mufti.

Born on April 13, 1952 in the village of Bulak Pashi, Khozhiabad *raion*, Andizhan *oblast*, Uzbek SSR; Uzbek. He graduated in 1980 from the faculty of theology, University of Tripoli, Libya, and from 1980 to 1982, he was a specialist in the department of foreign relations, SADUM. From 1982 to 1989 he was vice-rector of the Islamic Institute, Tashkent. In 1989 he was elected chairman of SADUM, and was also elected a USSR people's deputy in the same year. He is married with three children and speaks Arabic.

Address: Tashkent, ul. Zarkainar 103; *telephone*: Moscow 248 4678; 248 6869; 247 1508.

Mukubenov, Maksim Bembeevich

Acting Chairman of the Council of Ministers of the Republic of Kalmykia, Russian Federation.

Born in 1940; he is Kalmyk and was orphaned early when his father was killed in the Great Fatherland War and his mother died in Siberia in 1947. He was a member of the CPSU until August 1991. He became acquainted with hard work and deprivation at an early age. After finishing school he worked in a tractor brigade, and in 1966 he graduated from the K. A. Timiryazev Agricultural Academy, Moscow, as an agronomist and economist. Then he worked as an agronomist and director of a state farm. He was also first secretary of the *raion* Party committee and secretary of the Kalmyk Party *obkom*. He was appointed first deputy chairman of the Council of Ministers of the Kalmyk Autonomous Soviet Socialist republic and chairman of the republican Gosplan. All his working life was connected with planning and the economy.

In early 1990 he was nominated for election as an RSFSR people's deputy in the No. 822 Stepny territorial district. During the election campaign he stated that his programme was based on the platform of the CPSU, and that land should be under the control of local soviets. The economy, with its various forms of ownership, could not function without some planning and so there should be a planned market economy. He advocated real autonomy and economic independence for republics and the Kalmyk language should become equal to Russian as state languages of the republic. His attitude to the new political parties was varied; he believed that only those which did not hold back the development of the country were necessary and he proposed the consolidation of society. The social programme should be based on the just distribution of the national income and the maximum concern for the interests of rural dwellers.

There were five candidates. Mukubenov polled 16.5% of the votes in the first round and won the second round, polling 48.8% of the votes. His opponent in the second round was Lidiya Davydovna Lebedeva, minister of social security of the Kalmyk ASSR, who received 22% of the votes in the first round and 39.4% in the second.

In April 1990 Mukubenov re-entered the government of the Kalmyk ASSR and at the XVI session of the Supreme Soviet of the Republic of Kalmykia he was elected acting Chairman of the Council of Ministers. On assuming office he underlined the following as having priority: the revival of production, first and foremost agricultural production, help for state and individual producers and implementation of the programme of social aid to the very needy strata of the population. He lives in Elist.

Muradov, Sakhat Nepesovich

Speaker (chairman) of the *Milli Mejlis* of the Republic of Turkmenistan.

Born on May 7, 1932 in Ivanovo, Ivanovo *oblast*, RSFSR; Turkmen. He was a member of the CPSU until August 1991. He graduated in 1956 from the Turkmen Institute of Agriculture and became a senior laboratory assistant, then assistant in the department of geodesy in the institute. From 1957 to 1960 he was a postgraduate student in the Institute of the Construction of Earthquake Resistant Structures, Ashkhabad, where he successfully presented his candidate dissertation in technical sciences (PhD(Eng)). In 1961 he became a junior scientific assistant in the institute.

From 1961 to 1964 he was a junior research assistant, then later head of department, Institute of Hydrotechnology and Land Amelioration, Ashkhabad. From 1964 to 1965 he was deputy chairman of the co-ordination council of the Turkmen Academy of Sciences, then he was deputy head, later of department, science and educational establishments, Central Committee, Communist Party of Turkmenistan (1965-70). From 1970 to 1979 he was rector of Turkmen State University, and successfully presented his doctoral dissertation in technical sciences (DSc (Eng)). In 1979 he was appointed Minister of Higher and

Secondary Specialized Education of the Turkmen SSR; and in 1985 became rector of the Turkmen polytechnical institute.

In 1990 he was elected first deputy Speaker (chairman) of the Supreme Soviet of the Turkmen SSR, in November of the same year he was appointed Speaker of the *Milli Mejlis* of the Turkmen SSR and in December of the Republic of Turkmenistan. He has published over 50 scientific articles and other academic literature. He was awarded two orders of the Red Banner of Labour, and medals. His main hobby is research. He is married with two sons and a daughter, and his wife, Sana, is a senior scientific assistant, institute of language and literature, Academy of Sciences of the Republic of Turkmenistan. She successfully presented her candidate dissertation in philology (PhD).

Address: *Milli Mejlis*, Ashkhabad.

Murtaza, Sherkhan

Editor-in-chief of the newspaper *Yesemendy Kazakhstan*, Republic of Kazakhstan.

Born on September 28, 1932 in the village of Myn-Bulak, Dzhambul *oblast*; Kazakh. He graduated in 1955 from faculty of journalism, Moscow State University, and he became a correspondent, then own correspondent of the newspaper, *Zhas Alash*; and subsequently editor, editor-in-chief of the magazine, *Zhuldyz*; second secretary of the board of the Kazakhstan writers' union; and editor-in-chief of the newspaper, *Kazakh Aidebioti*. In December 1989 he was appointed editor-in-chief of the newspaper, *Yegemendy Kazakhstan*. He is a member of the committee on national and cultural issues. He was awarded the Kazakhstan prize for literature. He is married with a son and a daughter.

Address: 480091 Alma Ata, ul. Gogolya 39; *telephone*: Alma Ata 62 3208 (office); 63 2546 (home).

Mutalov, Abdulkhashim

Prime Minister of the Republic of Uzbekistan.

Born in 1947 in the village of Telyau, Akhangaran *raion*, Tashkent *oblast*, Uzbek SSR; Uzbek. He was a member of the CPSU until August 1991. He graduated in 1976 from the all-Union institute of the food industry as an external student, and is also a qualified engineer. He began his career in 1965 as a worker in the Tashkent bakery products factory, and later held various management positions in grain products combines in Tashkent.

In 1979 he was appointed director of the Akhangaran grain products combine, Uzbek SSR, and from 1986 to 1987 he was deputy Minister, and from 1987 to 1991, Minister of Grain Products, Uzbek SSR. In 1991 and 1992 he was deputy chairman of the Cabinet of Ministers of the republic (subordinate to the President), and in January 1992 he was appointed Prime Minister of the Republic of Uzbekistan.

Mutalov is faced with many problems in effecting the transition from a centrally planned economy to a market economy. The industrial base of the republic is modest and is known mainly for its cotton, gold and hydrocarbons. The quality of the cotton has to be improved and during the Soviet period irresponsible use of irrigation water led to salination of large areas, and conservation of water is a major priority. The skilled industrial labour force is mainly Russian and Ukrainian and the government's policy has been to make it attractive for this valuable resource to remain in the republic.

Privatization has made little headway since the former communist nomenclature prefers a corporatist approach and regards the private ownership of land and resources as divisive. The population has increased rapidly and there is pressure on land and considerable unemployment. Various agreements have been signed with the former Muslim republics of the Soviet Union to establish a common market, common media policy and so on.

Relations with Iran are of considerable importance due to the possible rise of Islamic fundamentalism, which may never occur but it causes the regime to stifle any movement perceived to be inimical to the secular state. Uzbekistan has signed some agreements with foreign concerns to develop the rich potential of the state and this collaboration is likely to increase as oil and natural gas are prime areas of interest to international companies. Mutalov lives in Tashkent.

Nabiev, Rakhmon Nabievich

President of the Republic of Tajikistan to September 7, 1992.

Born in 1931 in the village of Shaiburkhan, Leninabad (Khuzhand) *oblast*; Tajik. He was a member of the CPSU until August 1991. He graduated from the Institute of Irrigation and Mechanization of Agriculture, Tashkent, Uzbek SSR, and began his working life in 1946 as a clerk on a collective farm. In 1954 he was appointed chief engineer of a machine tractor station (MTS), then was head of the main administration of the Ministry of Agriculture, Tajik SSR.

In 1961 he transferred to Party work. In 1971 he was appointed Minister of Agriculture of the republic and in 1973 became chairman of the Council of Ministers of the Tajik SSR. In 1982 he was elected first secretary of the Central Committee, Communist Party of Tajikistan (CPTajik), and in 1985 became chairman of the republican nature protection society. In 1990 he was elected Speaker (chairman) of the Supreme Soviet of the Tajik SSR, and in November 1991 he was elected the first President of the Tajik SSR, then the Republic of Tajikistan, and polled 58% of the votes.

Nabiev and the other members of the ex-communist nomenclature were challenged increasingly after the collapse of the Soviet Union and the establishment of the Republic of Tajikistan. Nabiev's support was centred in the Kulyab region and his opponents, loosely grouped around the Islamic Revival Party, had some support from Afghanistan and Iran. In April 1992, after almost a month of demonstrations in Dushanbe, some concessions were made, but the demonstrators demanded Nabiev's resignation, the dissolution of the Supreme Soviet, and multi-party elections and a new constitution. On May 11 an agreement was signed ushering in a government of national conciliation, but the next day fighting broke out once again.

Nabiev was forced to resign on September 7, 1992 and was succeeded by Akhbarshah Iskanderov. In October forces loyal to Nabiev captured Dushanbe for a while, and on November 20, the Supreme Soviet, meeting in the northern city of Khojand, away from the war-torn Kulyab region, replaced Iskanderov with Imomali Rakhmonov, a former communist from the Kulyab region. On November 27 presidential rule was abolished and Tajikistan declared a parliamentary republic. The new government, controlled by ex-communists, seized Dushanbe on December 10, 1992, but fighting continued. Nabiev and other ex-communists consolidated their position in early 1993, partly due to Russian military aid. He died on April 11, 1993.

Narolin, Mikhail Tikhonov

Head of the Administration of Lipetsk *oblast*, Russian Federation.

Born in 1933 in the village of Perlovka, Semiluksky *raion*, Voronezh *oblast*, into a peasant family. He began working in 1957 after graduating from Voronezh Agricultural Institute, as an engineer in the Vasilevsky Motor Tractor Station, Volovsky *raion*, Lipetsk *oblast*. After two years he was appointed chief engineer for technical servicing in the Volovsky repair technical station, and in 1960 became director of the station. From 1961 to 1962 he headed the Volovsky *raion Selkhoztekhnika* association. Then he became deputy chairman of the Lipetsk *oblast Selkhoztekhnika* association for the repair and use of technology.

In 1965 he was deputy head of the *oblast* administration of agriculture, and in 1969 head of the department of amelioration and water economy, Lipetsk *oblast* soviet executive committee. From 1975 to 1980 he headed the *oblast* administration of agriculture, in June 1980 he was elected deputy and in December 1980 first deputy chairman of the *oblast* soviet executive committee. In November 1991 he was appointed first deputy head of the administration of the *oblast*. When he was first deputy head of the administration he was responsible for greater capital investment effectiveness, improvements in the work of the municipal housing economy, transport, communications and other consumer services.

In March 1993 he was nominated by the work collectives of the Eletsky potato experimental station, the Lipetsk pipe factory, the Lipetsky meat combine, the open type joint stock company, *Galantereishchik*, and others (at 76 meetings) for the post of head of the administration of the *oblast*. He was elected on April 11, 1993. During the election campaign he stated that this was the only route to democracy which excluded the appearance behind the wheel of power of inconsequential, incompetent people. He regarded the appointment of a head of administration as a mistaken, faulty beginning and called for it to be ignored. He accepted that the old system had its faults, but there were also good sides to it and without knowing the old system it was impossible to construct a new one. This did not mean sweeping the old one away completely, and he regarded the implementation of economic reform as having thrown the country back decades. The government was full of ministers who were incapable of implementing reform. Narolin regarded them as pure theorists, without practical experience, who had not worked out a strategy of transformation.

The shock therapy of Egor Gaidar had been a mistake and the following regulation of prices had not been carried through to a conclusion. A move to the market was only possible when there was a plenitude of goods, and changes in property relations were also necessary in order to produce a different motivation among workers. He criticized the all-embracing privatization and the issuing of vouchers throughout the country, saying that the first stage should have been to prepare society for it. He opposed rapid reform since this had resulted in a 50% drop in production. The solution was to concentrate on production with workers becoming owners only when their enterprises were on a stable footing and making profits.

At present they are merely owners on paper. He favours the reorientation of production, concentrating on consumer goods, state aid for enterprises, financial, credit and tax advantages and the creation of new jobs in the enterprises which have switched to civilian production. A financial and credit system for the country should be set up. He opposes mass private family farming, favouring the retention of the collective and state farms, and believes that farmers should be afforded cheaper credit, machinery and help with setting up farms. Trade and consumer services had ceased to exist in the *oblast*. He opposes the wholesale commercialization of trade, but favours private and co-operative commercial firms competing with one another. Order needs to be restored in the country.

He was awarded the orders of the Red Banner of Labour, the badge of honour and the medal for exemplary labour and that commemorating the centenary of V. I. Lenin's birth. He lives in Lipetsk.

Navumcyk, Siarhiej Iosifavic

Member of Parliament; co-ordinator of the Belarusian Popular Front, Adradzennie; president of the Paviet independent information agency.

Born on December 15, 1961 in Pastavi, Vicieksk *oblast*. His parents are Iosif and Roza Navumcyk, and the family is Belarusian. He graduated in 1984 from the faculty of journalism, Belarusian State University, and then served in the Soviet army from 1984 to 1986. He was a correspondent of the *Vieciekski Rabocy* (1986-89); section editor of *Vozyk*, a Minsk satirical journal (1989–90);

and secretary of the commission on *glasnost*, mass media and human rights, Belarusian Supreme Soviet (1990-92). In 1993 he was a co-founder and elected president of the Paviet information agency.

He joined the Belarusian Popular Front in 1989 and is at present a member of its *Sejm* (council). He regards himself as a democrat, and his hobbies are literature, the theatre and art. His wife's name is Halina.

Address: 221025 Minsk, vul. Hintauta, d. 40, kv. 152; *telephone and fax:* Minsk (0172) 65 76 29.

Nazarbaev, Nursultan Abishevich

President of the Republic of Kazakhstan.

Born on July 6, 1940 in the village of Chemolgan, Alma Ata *oblast*; Kazakh. He was a member of the CPSU from 1962 to August 1991. He graduated in 1960 from the technical college in Dneprodzerzhinsk, Ukrainian SSR; in 1967 from the higher technical college of the Karaganda integrated steel enterprise; and in 1976 from the CPSU Central Committee's Higher Party School, Moscow, as an external student.

From 1960 to 1969 he worked in a construction administration, was a blast furnace operator, and engineer at the Karaganda steel enterprise. In 1969 he transferred to Party work in the Communist Party of Kazakhstan (CPKaz): he was appointed head of the department for industry and transport in the Temirtau city Party committee, Karaganda *oblast*. From 1969 to 1971 he was first secretary of Kazakh *Komsomol* Temirtau city committee; then was second secretary of the Temirtau city Party committee (1971-73), and secretary of the party committee at the Karaganda steel enterprise (1973-77). In 1977 he was elected secretary and, between 1977 and 1979, second secretary of Karaganda Party *obkom*. In 1979 he became secretary for industry, Central Committee (CC) of the Communist Party of Kazakhstan, and from 1980 to 1990 he was a people's deputy of the Kazakh Supreme Soviet.

From 1981 to 1986 he was a member of the CPSU central auditing commission, and was then a member of the CC, CPKaz, (1981-91), and a people's deputy of the Soviet of the Union of the USSR Supreme Soviet (1982-89). In 1984 he was appointed chairman of the Council of Ministers of Kazakhstan, and from 1986 to August 1991 he was a member of the CPSU Central Committee. In 1989 he was appointed by Mikhail Gorbachev as first secretary of the CC, CPKaz. Gennady Kolbin, a Russian, had been appointed first secretary after the removal of the long-term Kazakh Communist Party leader Dinmukhamed Kunaev, who had been for a long time a member of Brezhnev's Party Politburo. Kunaev was accused of corruption and nepotism and Moscow's control over the republic had slipped in the late Brezhnev era. The Kazakhs saw Kolbin as Moscow's man in Alma Ata and this led to riots in Alma Ata and other Kazakh cities. They were later admitted to have been inter-ethnic riots, the first serious outburst of the Gorbachev era.

Kolbin made little headway in Kazakhstan as the entrenched élites were too strong and eventually a Kazakh, Nazarbaev, was appointed to run the republic. Nazarbaev was a strong supporter of Gorbachev's policies and some *glasnost* and democratization occurred. Nazarbaev was a member of the military council of the Turkestan military district, and in 1989 he was elected a USSR people's deputy and a member of the USSR Supreme Soviet. In February 1990 he became the first President of Kazakhstan in an uncontested election, and when the Republic of Kazakhstan was set up in 1992 he became President of the Republic of Kazakhstan.

He is a member of the influential clans of southern Kazakhstan and has demonstrated considerable skill in steering the young state through the troubled post-communist waters. The republic is multi-ethnic with Slavs, predominantly Russians, making up just over half the population and forming an overwhelming majority of the skilled industrial labour forces. Nazarbaev has appealed to them to remain in Kazakhstan and help build a modern state. Kazakhstan is close to Russia and wishes the CIS to develop, although Nazarbaev supported Gorbachev to the end in an attempt to hold the Soviet Union together. When the CIS was founded in December 1991 Kazakhstan was not invited to be a founding member along with Russia, Ukraine and Belarus and understandably this caused some resentment in Alma Ata. However, at a followup meeting in Alma Ata other states joined the CIS. Kazakhstan is a nuclear power but has no ambitions to continue to be one. The republic has signed several large deals with Western companies to develop its rich natural resources, and the corporatist approach of South Korea is attractive as a model of economic development.

Nazarbaev was awarded the order of the Red Banner of Labour, the order of the Friendship of the Peoples (1988), and medals. He is married and has three daughters and a grandson.

Address: 480091 Alma Ata, pl. Respubliki 4; *telephone*: Alma Ata 62 0630; 62 3016 (press service).

Nazarkin, Yury Konstantinovich

Deputy secretary of the Security Council of the Russian Federation.

Born in 1932, Russian. He was a member of the CPSU until August 1991. He graduated from the Moscow State Institute of International Relations, and was a postgraduate, successfully presenting his candidate dissertation in history (PhD). He has the rank of an ambassador extraordinary and plenipotentiary, and joined the USSR Ministry of Foreign Affairs in 1956.

He has worked in the department of foreign political information; the first African department; then was in turn second, first secretary, counsellor, and expert of the department of international organizations (1966-78); counsellor of the secretariat of the inter-departmental commission of the USSR Ministry of Foreign Affairs on the non-proliferation of nuclear weapons (1978-86); head of the department on the peaceful uses of atomic energy and space of the ministry (1986-87); Soviet representative at the conference on disarmament, Geneva (1987-89); and head of the Soviet delegation in the Soviet-American negotiations on nuclear and space disarmament, Geneva (1989-91). In 1992 he was appointed director of the department of the Russian Ministry of Foreign Affairs on disarmament and control of military technology, and also deputy to Yury Skokov, the secretary of the Security Council of the Russian Federation. Nazarkin is married with a daughter and lives in Moscow. He speaks English.

Nazarov, Aleksandr Viktorovich

Head of the Administration of Chukotsk Autonomous *okrug*, Russian Federation.

Born in 1951 in Pavlodar *oblast*, Kazakhstan, into a collective farm worker's family; member of the CPSU until August 1991. After school he worked as an electrician in a machine building enterprise, and then he served in the Soviet Navy in submarines. Arkhangelsk *oblast Komsomol* committee assigned him to a *Komsomol* building site, the Bilibinsky atomic power station in Chukotka, where he was a carpenter and concrete layer, head of staff of the *Komsomol* central committee, foreman and works superintendent. He also worked on the construction of the Magadan, Arkagalinsky and Luchegorsky thermal electric plants.

In 1981 he was an official in the industrial and transport department, Bilibinsky Party *raion* committee, in 1983 he was elected deputy chairman of the Bilibinsky *raion* soviet executive committee, and in 1987 was elected deputy chairman of the Chukotsk *okrug* soviet executive committee. He graduated from the Makeevsky Construction Engineering Institute as an external student and the Khabarovsk Higher Party School.

In 1990 he was elected a deputy of the Chukotsk autonomous *okrug* soviet of people's deputies and the Magadan *oblast* soviet. During the election campaign he supported the basic tenets of the programme of the *raion* and *okrug* Party organizations but also parts of the programme of the Alternativa public organization. He advocated a strict professional approach to regional cost accounting, based on draft models drawn up in the G. V. Plekhanov Institute of the National Economy, Moscow. He worked on the drafting of a huge programme for the provision of thermal electrical power for the *okrug*. He defended the *okrug* against the attacks of the *oblast* and advocated autonomy for the RSFSR and the observation of the law on human rights.

On April 25, 1990 he was elected chairman of the Chukotsk *okrug* soviet executive committee at the first session of the soviet and was appointed head of the administration of Chukotsk autonomous *okrug* by presidential decree on November 11, 1991. On August 23, 1991 a declaration of the chairmen of the *okrug* soviet and the *okrug* soviet executive committee stated that a legal evaluation of the activities of the Extraordinary Committee should be presented at extraordinary sessions of the USSR and RSFSR Supreme Soviets, and it appealed for restraint and calm. Nazarov, who was in Moscow at the time, resigned from the CPSU and placed the blame for the attempted coup on the Party Politburo.

As head of the administration Nazarov advocated strong executive power and the total legal and economic responsibility of the heads of the administration *vis-à-vis* the President. He regarded the most important aspects of the development of Chukotka to be capital construction, municipal housing and the drafting of the budget. He advocated the paying of rent for the use of the natural resources of the *okrug*, tax policy to be decided at the local level, and the establishment of relations with Magadan *oblast* on a contractual basis and as equal partners. Village cultural and social buildings should pass to the local soviets, the administrations should consist of able, honest persons and administration put on a contractual basis. He proposed the establishment of commercial networks and the attracting of honest entrepreneurs and traders to establish market relations in the country. He raised the question of social security for all strata of the population and the transfer of resources to local budgets.

He viewed the VII Congress of People's Deputies, in December 1992, as a defeat for the reformers and retreat from the President but it was not so serious as to bring down the political system. Appropriate laws on property, land and entrepreneurship had not been adopted but nevertheless, he was convinced that despite the efforts of various "oppositions", the reforms would go forward. He is married with a daughter and lives in Anadyr.

Nazmetdinova, Minrauza Minikhazievna

Chairwoman of the Russian Supreme Soviet committee on women's affairs, the family and protection of the mother and child.

Born on December 29, 1940 in the village of Aksakovo, Belebeevsky *raion*, Tatar ASSR; Tatar. She was a member of the CPSU until August 1991. She graduated from the Belebei Medical School and later became head of a maternity centre in the village of Trubkino. Later she graduated from a medical institute, and is a qualified anaesthetist. She worked as a doctor in the republican children's hospital, where she was head of department and later a deputy chief doctor. In 1990 she was deputy Minister of Health of the Bashkir ASSR (Bashkortostan).

She was nominated for election as an RSFSR people's deputy in the No. 781 Kirov national territorial district, Bashkir ASSR. During the election campaign she advocated the adoption of a law on the rights of the child and the protection of the mother and child; the construction of a republican centre for diagnosis; more investment for the development of children's and maternity hospitals; larger social allowances for single mothers and large families and the period of leave on full pay to be increased to three years for single mothers.

There were nine candidates and Nazmetdinova won in the second round, polling 45.7% of the votes. Her main opponent was V. N. Polyakov, a factory worker, who received 42.2% of the votes in the second round. She was elected a member of the Russian Supreme Soviet at the V Congress of People's Deputies. She is a member of the Council of Nationalities; was elected a member of the Supreme Soviet committee on women's affairs, the family and protection of the mother and child; and later elected chairwoman of the committee. She is married with a son and daughter. Her husband teaches in the Bashkir Medical Institute.

Address: 103274 Moscow, K 274, Krasnopresnenskaya nab., d. 2, Dom Sovetov; *telephone*: Moscow 205 84 19.

Nechaev, Andrei Alekseevich

Minister of the Economy of the Russian Federation, February 1992 to March 1993.

Born in February 1953 in Moscow into a Russian family. He graduated in economics from Moscow State University and joined the CPSU in 1984. He began work in the institute of economics and forecasting of scientific-technical progress of the USSR Academy of Sciences. The director of the institute was Academician Stanislav Shatalin. He successfully presented his candidate dissertation on the acceleration of scientific-technical progress (PhD (Econ)). His supervisor was Professor Yaremenko, at present one of the leading economic policy makers of Civic Union. In 1988 he published a monograph entitled *International Analysis of the Structure of Economies*, in Moscow. He resigned from the institute as a result of disagreements with Professor Yaremenko. In 1990 he began work as deputy director of the institute of economic policy, the director of which was Egor Gaidar. He became a member of a group of economists preparing draft economic reforms. In 1990/91 he worked at the Sosna dacha for President Mikhail Gorbachev and Prime Minister Nikolai Ryzhkov and at Arkhangelskoe, near Moscow, on the "500-day programme". This group had close ties with Leszek Balcerowicz, the Polish deputy Prime Minister, who was pushing through his policy of "shock therapy" in Poland, and Professor Jeffrey Sachs, the American economist who propagated a programme of economic shock therapy for economies moving from a planned economy to the market. He began work on his doctoral dissertation (DSc (Econ)).

On August 19, 1991, the first day of the putsch, he and other members of the institute resigned from the CPSU. He was one of the authors of the document on the economic programme of the Extraordinary Committee, entitled *The Economic Policy of the Junta*, which contained severe criticism of the economic ideas of the Committee. In September and October 1991 he was a member of a group of economists, headed by Egor Gaidar, which drafted a new economic policy for the Russian government at dacha No. 15 in Arkhangelskoe.

In November 1991, as a result of Gaidar's proposal, Nechaev was appointed first deputy Minister of the Economy and Finance of the Russian Federation. He became Gaidar's right-hand man and was also a close friend. The presidential administration, headed by Yury Petrov, objected to this appointment. The decree appointing Nechaev, signed by Gennady Burbulis, was held up for three days in the White House administration and was referred back several times for "revisions". He was also chairman of the governmental commission on the analysis of the current economic situation. On February 19, 1992, by decree of President Boris Yéltsin, Nechaev was appointed Russian Minister of the Economy after Gaidar had decided to split the Ministry of the Economy and Finance into two separate ministries. He chaired 15 governmental commissions.

Nechaev is an adherent of the Chicago school of monetary economics of Milton Friedman. He was fully committed to Gaidar's policy of liberalization of prices, structural change through privatization and monetary reform to induce macroeconomic stabilization. He supports the concept of a balanced budget, but in present circumstances feels this is not feasible. He is viewed by economists as a realist and capable of standing his ground. Among his tasks was the prevention of a sharp decline in output which freed him to concentrate on the budget and finance, and on working out strategic guidelines for the economy. Ruslan Khasbulatov, Speaker of the Russian parliament, was a sharp critic of Gaidar's shock therapy. So too was Civic Union, the industrialists' lobby, in parliament. Nechaev defended the new economic policy and many observers expected him to be sacrificed by President Yeltsin in December 1992 at the VII Congress of People's Deputies when the President was searching for concessions in an attempt, vain as it turned out, to ensure parliament's acceptance of Gaidar as Prime Minister. He retained his office in the Chernomyrdin government. He was closely associated with Anatoly Chubais, deputy Prime Minister for privatization, and Boris Fedorov, deputy Prime Minister for macroeconomic policy and finance.

During the IX Congress of People's Deputies in March 1993 Nechaev was dropped by Yeltsin as Minister of the Economy. This was seen as a concession to the conservative majority in the Congress, which was implacably opposed to the President's views on economic reform. He moved to other work but remained a member of Yeltsin's team. His removal did not significantly weaken the economic reform package proposed by Boris Fedorov.

Nechaev speaks English. As a young man he was attracted to boxing and tourism. After acquiring a car he enjoyed travelling throughout the Soviet Union and Europe. He is married with a daughter, Kseniya (Xenia), who is 16 years old. They live in Moscow.

Nechaev, Eduard Aleksandrovich

Minister of Health of the Russian Federation; Colonel-General.

Born in 1934 in Smolensk into a Russian family. He received his medical training at the military medical faculty of Saratov Medical Institute. He began his medical career as a surgeon in the surgical department of a military hospital of the group of Soviet forces in Germany (GDR). After five years he became a postgraduate at the Military Medical Academy and graduated in 1959. His first research work was devoted to electro-stimulation of the heart and his doctoral dissertation to heart surgery. He is a Doctor of Medicine (MD). His training followed the teachings of Academicians P. Kupriyanov and A. Kolesov and he became a well-known surgeon. He taught in the Military Medical Academy and became a professor.

From 1976 to 1978 he was in Afghanistan, setting up hospitals, operating and training local doctors even before the invasion of Afghanistan. He became deputy head of clinical surgery of the Military Medical Academy and later chief surgeon of the group of Soviet forces in Germany. In 1989 he was appointed head of the Central military medical administration of the Soviet Army and later head of the medical services of the armed forces of the Russian Federation. He often helped to organize medical aid and set up military field hospitals for the victims of accidents and major incidents, as for example the railway explosion in Ufa and the earthquake in Armenia. He played a significant role in the establishment of faculties of emergency medicine in the leading medical schools of the country.

According to colleagues, Nechaev is a rather dry personality, is strong willed and loves discipline, but is a first-class professional and has a lively personality. He succeeded Andrei Vorobev as Minister of Health of the Russian Federation in December 1992 in the new government of Viktor Chernomyrdin. He regards strengthening the financial and material bases of medicine among the most important tasks facing him as minister. He believes that the most important role will be played by medical insurance, and he intends to promote its introduction. He will devote his attention to the problems of the medical services dealing with major incidents. He lives in Moscow.

Nechaev, Konstantin Vladimirovich (Pitirim)

Russian Orthodox Metropolitan of Volokolamsk and Yurev.

Born on January 13, 1926 in Michurinsk, Tambov *oblast*; Russian. He graduated in 1951 from the Moscow Theological Academy and later became a doctor of theology. From 1951 to 1962 he was a lecturer at the Moscow Theological Academy. From 1963 to 1968 he was co-ordinating editor of the *Journal of the Moscow Patriarchate*, and in 1968 was appointed chairman of the publishing department of the Moscow Patriarchate. In 1986 he became a metropolitan; and a member of the central council of the union of Soviet friendship societies. He was later appointed Metropolitan of Volokolamsk and Yurev, and was also elected a USSR people's deputy.

Address: Moscow, ul. Chasovaya 19, kv. 66; *telephone*: Moscow 235 0454; 230 2118; 230 2431.

Nedelin, Gennady Pavlovich

Head of the Administration of Taimir Dolgano-Nenets Autonomous *okrug*, Russian Federation.

Born in 1938 in the village of Klyuchi, Minusinsky *raion*, Krasnoyarsk *krai*; member of the CPSU until August 1991. After secondary school he served three years in the Soviet Army, then graduated from the Technical College for Mechanization, and then studied in the Agricultural Institute, Krasnoyarsk. In 1963 he was appointed secretary of the Minusinsk *raion Komsomol* committee, took part in bringing in the harvest and received the honoured title of master of harvesting. From 1971 to 1990 he was deputy chairman of the Dolgano-Nenets *okrug* soviet executive committee.

In March 1990 he was elected a deputy of the Krasnoyarsk *krai* soviet of people's deputies and at the first session of the Dolgano-Nenets *okrug* soviet executive committee, in April 1990, he was elected chairman. On August 19, 1991, on receiving the decree of the President of the Russian Republic, he immediately broadcast it on *okrug* radio and the Dudinka video channel. He viewed the activities of the Extraordinary Committee as preparations for the seizure of power in Russia. However he did not support the suggestion that there should be an indefinite political strike and on August 21-22 it was decided that only a warning strike should take place in the Dudinsk sea port. The executive committee underlined its determination to support only the legally elected President of the Russian Federation and unconditionally implement all the decrees and decisions of the government of the Russian Federation.

On December 18, 1991 Nedelin was appointed head of the administration of Taimyr Dolgano-Nenets autonomous *okrug*. On assuming office he stated the time for gradual reform and transformation was past, as inflation, the emission of money and the shortage of goods demanded decisive and rapid action and the transition of Russia to a market economy was the only correct policy. He advocated more rights for the autonomous regions, including the use of their natural resources, the economic autonomy of the autonomous regions and regional cost accounting. A programme for the stimulation of middle-scale businesses which would interest entrepreneurs should be drafted. He favoured the most rapid establishment of a democratic society in practice and not merely in theory, and co-operation with all political and public forces.

In November 1992 he stated that political conflict in the present circumstances was inappropriate and that only the consolidation of all forces in society would help the country to find a way out of the economic cul-de-sac. He is a bachelor and lives in Dudinka.

Nemtsov, Boris Efimovich

Head of the Administration of Nizhny Novgorod *oblast*, Russian Federation.

Born on October 9, 1959 in Sochi; Russian; he was never a member of the CPSU. In 1981 he graduated from the faculty of radio physics, N. Lobachevsky State University, Gorky (Nizhny Novgorod), and became a senior scientific assistant in the scientific research institute of radio physics, USSR Academy of Sciences. In 1985 he successfully presented his candidate dissertation in theoretical physics on "the coherent effects of the interaction of moving sources and radiation" (PhD). In 1986 he began to participate fully in the activities of the Gorky political club, Avangard. After the Chernobyl disaster, in April 1986, he, together with his mother, Dina Yakovlevna, and his sister, Yuliya Efimovna, actively collected signatures opposing the construction of the Gorky thermal nuclear plant, and he was one of the organizers of the voluntary society for atomic security. In early 1989 he was nominated by this society for election as a USSR people's deputy but was not accepted by the district electoral commission.

In early 1990 he was nominated for election as an RSFSR people's deputy by the collectives in the USSR Academy of Sciences in the No. 35 Gorky national territorial district. During the election campaign he signed the platform of the candidates for election at various levels, including the candidates for democracy, and organized various mass meetings in Gorky in support of democratically-inclined candidates. He advocated radical economic reform based on various types of ownership and the introduction of the market mechanism, political pluralism, the annulment of article 6 of the USSR constitution (on the leading role of the CPSU in society), the sovereignty of Russia within the USSR, the introduction of the post of President and limits to be placed on the power of agencies of state power.

There were 12 candidates. Nemtsov polled 22.8% of the votes in the first round and won the second round, polling 57.9% of the votes. His main opponent was G. N. Galkina, deputy chairwoman of the committee of Soviet women, who received 9% of the votes in the first round and 30.1% in the second. Nemtsov is a member of the Supreme Soviet committee on legislation and a member of the coalition of reforms bloc of deputies. He was previously a member of the *glasnost* and Russian union groups of deputies.

On August 27, 1991 he was appointed presidential representative in Nizhny Novgorod *oblast* by presidential decree and on November 28, 1991, simultaneously head of the administration of Nizhny Novgorod *oblast* by presidential decree. In collaboration with Grigory Yavlinsky's Epitsentr, the administration drafted a regional programme of economic and social measures, which included privatization, and the city and *oblast* became pioneers in this area.

In December 1992 he criticized the Gaidar government and the Congress of People's Deputies on numerous occasions, arguing that the President of the Russian Federation should distance himself from the government and the congress. He proposed the appointment of a new government which would include, among others, Grigory Yavlinsky and Arkady Volsky. He viewed the President's appeal to the population as destabilizing the situation and as head of the administration would not organize the collection of signatures for a referendum in Nizhny Novgorod. He was against the unconstitutional appeals to restrict the powers of the legislative and executive branches of government and announced that he might resign if any type of dictatorship appeared. He is married with an eight-year-old daughter, and lives in Nizhny Novgorod.

Nemtsov, Nikolai Fedorovich (Mefody)

Russian Orthodox Metropolitan of Voronezh and Lipetsk.

Born on February 16, 1949 in Rovenki, Lugansk *oblast*, Ukrainian SSR; Ukrainian. He graduated in 1976 from Leningrad Theological Academy, and from 1976 to 1979 he was an assistant and then deputy chairman of the department of external church relations, Moscow Patriarchate. From 1979 to 1980 he served as a priest in the Church of the Deposition of the Robe, Donskoi monastery, Moscow, and in 1980 was appointed bishop, then administrator of the Irkutsk diocese of the Russian Orthodox Church. In 1982 he was appointed administrator of the Voronezh diocese of the Russian Orthodox Church; in 1984 he became an archbishop and in 1987 Metropolitan of Voronezh and Lipetsk.

Address: Voronezh, ul. Osvobozhdeniya truda 6; *telephone*: Moscow 235 0454; 230 2118; 230 2431.

Neverov, Valery Ivanovich

Director-general of the Germes Scientific Technical Centre, Tyumen; president of the STC Germes joint stock company, Kaliningrad; chairman of the Tyumen-Moscow Exchange Germes, Moscow; chairman of the Germes Trading House.

Born in 1952 in the settlement of Golyshmanovo, Tyumen *oblast*, RSFSR; Russian. He graduated from the Urals State University, Sverdlovsk (Ekaterinburg), and then became a postgraduate student at the Institute of Metallurgy, Moscow, successfully presenting his candidate dissertation in physics and mathematics (PhD). He was a lecturer at the Udmurt and Tyumen State Universities. He became an entrepreneur in 1986, specializing in the commercialization of scientific projects in great demand by metal-working and oil-extracting enterprises of Tyumen *oblast*. In 1988 he resigned his post as head of the department of molecular physics to concentrate on writing a doctoral dissertation. In August 1990 he postponed the defence of his doctoral thesis and founded and registered the scientific technical centre (STC) Germes company with an authorized capital of 10,000 rubles. In early 1991 he was one of the founders of the Tyumen commodity and stock exchange. As a member of the council of the commodity exchange, he set up other exchanges covering the area from the Baltic republics to Siberia, and as a member of all the councils of the exchanges, he was elected president of Tyumen-Moscow Exchange Germes. In Tyumen he opened a technical park and an international scientific and technical centre, organized scores of Germes branches in the Kuzbass, Krasnodar *krai*, Kaliningrad and Rostov *oblasts* and in Ukraine. At the end of 1991 he founded the Tyumen Trading House and the Moscow Germes joint stock bank. By late 1992 he occupied 16 posts, among which are director-general of the STC Germes in Tyumen; president of STC Germes joint stock company, Kaliningrad; chairman of the board of directors of the Germes Tyumen-Moscow exchange, Moscow; chairman of the board of directors of the Germes Trading House.

He was awarded the order of the eagle, first class, in 1992. He is divorced with a daughter.

Address: 107174 Moscow, ul. Kalanchevskaya 2; *telephone*: Moscow 291 8070; 291 7343; 261 1590; 308 9667; *fax*: Moscow 291 2255.

Nevzorov, Aleksandr Glebovich

Journalist, St Petersburg television.

Born on August 3, 1958 in Leningrad (St Petersburg). He grew up without a father and his mother paid little attention to him. He was brought up by his grandfather, Georgy Vladimirovich Nevzorov, who was a high ranking officer in the USSR Ministry of State Security (MGB) and participated in the war against the "forest brothers" (nationalist opposition) in Latvia (1946-52). He was head of the department for the struggle against sabotage and banditry, Latvia (1946-53).

Nevzorov loved to read at four years of age, but objects to being called intelligent. His objection to this term was acquired from his grandfather, then from L. N. Gumilev, and to his mind it is a term of abuse, revealing a certain deformity of mind. He did not do well at school and does not regard anything he learnt there useful in later life. He was expelled from the pioneers and was not admitted to the *Komsomol*. At the age of 18 years he became a member of a church choir and was a bass in the choir of St Nicholas's cathedral. He fell in love, gave up thoughts of becoming a monk and married an actress. He served in the Soviet army, then afterwards worked as a porter, and for some time as a horseman in a film studio, in the A. S. Pushkin museum and as a nurse in a casualty ward. He broke in wild Dzhabe horses from Kazakhstan on a state farm in Leningrad *oblast*.

He became a student in the faculty of philology, Leningrad State University, but soon gave up. In 1983 he moved to Leningrad television as a script writer and reporter, and over the years about 150 programmes, films and shows, scripted by him, were shown on television. Among these were the scripts for the films *The St Petersburg Merchants' Court*, and *Twenty Years On*, directed by Evgeny Mravinsky. On December 23, 1987 the first edition of *600 Seconds*, a programme on political and social topics, in association with A. Borisoglebsky, was shown. It specialized on exposés of crime and corruption in and around Leningrad and he was much feared by Party bosses who had a lot to hide. He affected an arrogant stance, chain-smoked Marlboro cigarettes and was reported to receive over 100 fan letters a day from female admirers. He has a huge army of collaborators and three brigades, one involved in making set items, the second travels to collect material and the third is on stand-by to cover the other two. He is a strict editor and his only contact with the press is through his press secretary. On December 12, 1990 an attempt was made on his life.

He became politically famous after the programme, *Nashi* (ours), about the behaviour of the OMON (special forces) on January 13, 1991, in Vilnius, Lithuania, which attracted 47 million viewers. Afterwards he defended the actions of the OMON and immediately lost millions of viewers and the support of many colleagues. He was attending the Edinburgh festival during the attempted coup of August 1991. He also filmed the armed conflicts in Pridnestrovie, in Bosnia-Herzogovina and supported the proposal to picket Ostankino television station in the summer of 1992. He has been offered many posts, including the proposal by L. E. Kravchenko for him to be chairman of the St Petersburg committee for television and radio. He refused because he regards himself as a hooligan and a reporter. He is not going to write his memoirs but a book was published on them by the publishing house, Palei, in the series on the lives of outstanding Russians.

In December 1991 he was one of the organizers of the public movement, *Nashi* (ours) in St Petersburg. The task of the movement is to establish a single popular front against the anti-national policy of the authorities, to promote the concept of statehood and to set up a committee to supervise the activities of people's deputies. He advocates the rebirth of the USSR and the creation of a committee which could act in the case of the present leadership fleeing abroad. He became an Academician but regards himself as an academician of television. After the movement is victorious he wishes to remain in television and not to accept any ministerial post, and he believes that no other programme can rival his on television. The symbol of *600 Seconds* is an eagle, flapping its wings, and all seeing, and the programme is regarded as an important source of information.

He does not lean towards communist views but rubs shoulders with communists in a union since, according to him, they are better than those who are now in power and he believes that communists can support a USSR empire. He advocates Russian as the state language, and patriotism, but resolutely refuses to be labelled a Russian nationalist. He refers to those now in power as 50 representatives of the dregs of society who are ruining the country just like the communists before them. The best way to go is to die in battle for the motherland against those who are now occupying it, but he hopes it will be possible for a change of regime without the spilling of blood. On March 23, 1993 Nevzorov was temporarily suspended from the programme, apparently in response to a notice from the Procurator of St Petersburg concerning the impermissibility of airing topics which could be viewed as promoting violence to amend the constitutional order and the integrity of the state, the unleashing of national and social impatience and discord, lauding war and the establishment of illegal paramilitary formations. However, a few days later the city authorities, under the pressure of huge demonstrations, were forced to allow *600 Seconds* to resume transmission.

He is at present editor-in-chief of the independent TV company, NTK-600. He is an Academician of the international Slav Academy of Sciences; a member of the *Duma* of the Russian national assembly; a member of the *Duma* of the all-national *veche* (assembly); a member of the organization committee of the Front of National Salvation; and a member of the editorial board of the newspaper, *Den*, the Russian nationalist newspaper. He is married and his wife is a journalist, and they have a daughter. He lives in St Petersburg.

Nikolaev, Mikhail Efimovich

President of the Republic of Sakha (Yakutia), Russian Federation.

Born in 1937 in the village of Oktemtsy, Ordzhonikidze *raion*, into a peasant family. He is Yakut, and he was a member of the CPSU. He graduated from the veterinary institute, Omsk, and the Higher Party school of the Party Central Committee. He began his career in 1961 as a veterinary surgeon in Zhigansky *raion*, and was a *Komsomol* and Party worker for many years. In 1975 he was appointed deputy Chairman of the Council of Ministers, then headed the Ministry of Agriculture of the republic. From 1985 to 1989 he was secretary for the agro-industrial complex of the Yakut Party *obkom*.

In December 1989 he was elected chairman of the Presidium of the Supreme Soviet and, in April 1990, Speaker (Chairman) of the Supreme Soviet of the republic. He was also a people's deputy of Yakut-Sakha Soviet Socialist republic and the RSFSR. As a people's deputy of the RSFSR he was a member of the constitutional commission, deputy chairman of the *Sever* (north) group of deputies, a member of the Communists of Russia group and of the parliamentary faction "sovereignty and equality".

On August 20, 1991 Nikolaev signed the declaration of the Presidium of the Supreme Soviet and the Council of Ministers of the Yakut-Sakha Soviet Socialist Republic which confirmed the commitment of the leaders of the republic to the principles of the declarations on the state sovereignty of the Yakut-Sakha Soviet Socialist Republic and also underlined the absence of "objective conditions for the declaration of a state of emergency and the establishment of extraordinary committees or other agencies of the Extraordinary Committee of the USSR".

On December 20, 1991 Nikolaev was elected the first President of the Yakut-Sakha Soviet Socialist republic and on December 27, 1991, at an extraordinary session of the Supreme Soviet of the republic, he took the presidential oath. At the VII Congress of People's Deputies, in December 1992, he criticized the government of Egor Gaidar, stating that it was more oriented to the West and Gaidar's "gaze did not cover all parts of his motherland". He expressed concern about the lack of mechanisms for the implementation of the Federal treaty and placed the blame for this on the Supreme Soviet of the Russian Federation, since, in his view, there were "forces gathering which wished to recreate, reanimate the imperial policy of a unitary state. These forces do not permit this important document room and are doing everything to transform the Federal treaty into a purely formal act". In his speech he outlined the measures necessary to continue reform successfully.

First of all, he stated that "legal support for large investment capital should be provided"; and secondly, "during the transition to the market it is quite appropriate to speak of the Arctic economy" which "cannot be a copy of the economy of the more developed territories and regions of Russia". In his view "this economy should be seen as a parallel economy, that is, partly state and ethno-regional, under the protection of the state". Thirdly, he appealed for a strengthening of the regulatory role of the state, the expansion of its supervisory functions over the economy in place of the situation in which the state is the owner. Fourthly, he called for the immediate adoption of a mechanism to implement the provisions of the Federal treaty. Fifthly, he "judged it inopportune to continue the process of strengthening the executive power" and "proposed the extension of the special powers of the President of the Russian Federation in relation to the implementation of rapid economic reform and a limitation to the laws promulgated by parliament in this area". He is married with three children and lives in Yakutsk.

Niyazov, Saparmurad Ataevich

President of the Republic of Turkmenistan.

Born on February 19, 1940 in Ashkhabad, Turkmen SSR; Turkmen. He was a member of the CPSU from 1962 to August 1991. He grew up in a children's home. He graduated in 1967 from the Leningrad polytechnic, and in 1976 from the Higher Party School of the CPSU Central Committee as an external student. In 1959 he became an official in a geological prospecting trade union, and in 1965 he began working in an enterprise in Leningrad; in 1967 he moved to the Bezmeinsky power station, Ashkhabad *oblast*.

In 1970 he transferred to work in the Communist Party of Turkmenistan (CPTurk), and in 1980 he was appointed first secretary of the Ashkhabad city committee of the CPTurk. In 1984 he became an instructor in the department for the organization of Party work, CPSU Central Committee, and in 1985 was appointed chairman of the Council of Ministers of the Turkmen SSR. In December 1985 he was elected first secretary of the Central Committee of the CPTurk, and in January 1990 he was also elected Speaker (chairman) of the Supreme Soviet of the Turkmen SSR. He was elected a member of the Politburo of the Central Committee, CPSU at the XXVIII Party Congress in July 1990. He was also elected a USSR people's deputy and a member of the USSR Supreme Soviet.

On October 27, 1990 he became President of the Turkmen SSR and Prime Minister of the republic, and in June 1992 was elected the first President of the Republic of Turkmenistan in national elections. He was the only candidate and polled 99.5% of the votes. He is married with a son and a daughter.

He is a member of the ex-communist nomenclature which has made the transition from communism to a secular Islamic state with ease. Niyazov's main concern is to ensure that social unrest does not occur since this would provide a breeding ground for Islamic fundamentalism. Turkmenistan is a multi-party state but no party is permitted to advocate Islamic religious solutions to political, economic or social problems. The republic has reverted to Turkish terminology in government and administration and a conscious effort is being made to reclaim the Turkic past of the state.

Niyazov and the other members of the élite have shrewdly developed contacts with Western enterprises to develop the rich natural resources, especially oil and gas, of the republic. The wealth from these sources is being used to subsidize state enterprises and agriculture, and Turkmenistan is the only ex-Soviet republic where living standards have remained stable. In foreign affairs Niyazov has surprised many observers by cultivating close relations with Iran. There are increasing economic ties, and gas pipelines to Turkey and the West may be constructed through Iran. Air links between Ashkhabad and Tehran are being developed.

Address: 744014 Ashkhabad, ul. Karla Marksa 24; *telephone*: Ashkhabad 25 4534.

Novodvorskaya, Valeriya Ilinichna

Co-leader of the Democratic Union Party.

Born in 1950 in Moscow. Her great-grandfather was a social democrat and founded an underground printing press; her grandfather was born in Tobolsk jail. Her mother's forbears belonged to the nobility and those of her father were successful entrepreneurs. Her father was a scientist and worked in radio electronics, and her mother was a doctor and worked in the children's department, Moscow city medical department. Her parents were members of the CPSU and she grew up among adults, having no friends of her own age. According to her she preferred to wear jeans and dreamed of becoming a pirate, a spy and an intelligence officer.

At school she was a rank outsider, refused to perform all social duties, did not contribute to the *subbotniks* (unpaid social labour) and did not attend political lectures. She was a member of the *Komsomol* and asked to be sent to Vietnam to fight the American aggressors. Until she was 18 years old she remained completely within the law. After completing school she became a student at the Maurice Thores Institute of Foreign Languages, Moscow. When 19 years old she set up an underground student organization consisting of 12 members from her own institute, the State Institute of International Relations, Moscow and Moscow State University.

The minimal programme of the organization was proclaimed as the overthrow of the existing state order. The group was involved in *samizdat* (illegal self-publishing) and the distribution of leaflets. On December 5, 1969, on Soviet constitution day, she scattered 200 leaflets in the Kremlin Palace of Congresses during a performance of the opera, *Oktyabr* and tried to hold an improvised demonstration. She was sentenced under article 70 of the RSFSR criminal code for the distribution of anti-Soviet literature, anti-Soviet agitation and propaganda whose aim was the breakdown and weakening of the system. She was sentenced to two years' imprisonment which she served in Lefortovo prison and then in the Kazan psychiatric special prison.

After her release she acquired false documents and studied in the evening faculty of the institute of foreign languages, Moscow *oblast* Pedagogical Institute, becoming qualified as a translator and teacher. She regarded herself as primarily a journalist. She was sentenced for dissident activity in 1978, 1985 and 1986, spent three months in the closed sector of psychiatric hospital No. 15 where, according to her, she was tortured, mocked and her human dignity debased. During *perestroika* she was arrested 17 times for organizing unsanctioned demonstrations and each time she went on hunger strike.

She has been a leader of the Democratic Union since its establishment in May 1988 at its constituent assembly in Moscow. The last time she was arrested was on May 21, 1991 for the "letter of the 12" which sharply criticized President Mikhail Gorbachev's policy in Lithuania. She was accused of publicly slandering the honour and dignity of the USSR President and insulting the state flag of the USSR. On the first count the court decided it could not find her guilty since there were no uncensored expressions in her speeches. On the second charge she was found guilty and sentenced to two years of corrective labour and 20% of her wages to be deducted.

On August 19, 1991, hearing of a coup, she stated later that she prepared herself for execution. She slept in her clothes and handed over a leaflet and letter to Vladimir Kryuchkov, chairman of the USSR KGB and one of the coup leaders. She was released on August 23, 1991 and joined the Radical Party. At various times she translated artistic works, studied aesthetics, literature, the theatre and wrote articles on the cinema. She translated Camus, Sartre and Dumas père, and wrote two books, *The Absolute Albert Camus* and *The History of the Russian Intelligentsia, Related and Written by Anton Pavlovich Chekhov*, the manuscripts of which were seized by the KGB during her arrest in 1986. According to her own words these amounted to professional revolutionary activity.

She was the strategist of the Moscow organization of the Democratic Union and since January 1992 is a political columnist on the weekly *Khozyain* (owner) where she writes under her own rubric, *Bochka Degtya* (barrel of tar). She gives lectures on history and the history of religion at a private evening lycée.

She is critical of Gorbachev, Yeltsin, Popov, Sobchak, Shevardnadze and Yakovlev. She thinks the poison has moved from Yazov's tanks to Yeltsin's chambers, from the decrees of Yanaev to the orders of Rutskoi and, according to her, the present revolution is already well ahead. Its saints are honour, conscience, loyalty, happiness, courage, the barricades and revolution. She is against vengeance since she "does not wish to be the executioner of the executioners". Moral condemnation, in her view, is more important, and she supports the slogan,"let justice prevail even if the world is destroyed". She is opposed to Democratic Union demonstrations being broken up and sharply criticized President Yeltsin for the sentencing in 1992 of the anarchists Radionov and Kuznetsov.

She defends human rights and non-violent means of struggle. She thinks that the Russian government should have freed all political prisoners, reform the Gulag and end the death penalty. Jesus Christ, Mahatma Gandhi and Till Eulenspiegel are her heroes, her favourite writer is Aleksandr Solzhenitsyn and her favourite poet, Vladimir Vysotsky. She supports Zviad Gamsakhurdia, the former Georgian President, and General D. Dudaev, the Chechen leader. She reveres the memory of A. Marchenko.

She maintains that she loves beautiful clothes and good cosmetics but her mother buys them and that she cannot cook, except a fried egg. She prefers philosophical and magical prose and German, American and English literature but does not like French literature, except for the existentialists. Her favourite Russian writers are Chekhov, Bunin, Garshin, Dostoevsky and Turgenev. She detests Lev Tolstoy because of his "wretched moralizing". She advocates healthy individualism and capitalism as the society of "the most educated, clever, resourceful and talented". She is opposed to the absolute and uncontrolled power of the nomenclature. For her, politics is a dirty business. She regards herself as being involved in anti-fascist, anti-state activity, but this, however, is not politics but poetry, romanticism and art.

She is unmarried, and her family consists of her mother and grandmother. She avers that she is against sexual relations which debase and insult the individual. She lives in Moscow.

Nozhikov, Yury Abramovich

Head of the Administration of Irkutsk *oblast*, Russian Federation.

Born on February 17, 1934; Russian; member of the CPSU until August 1991. He graduated from the Institute of Energy, Ivanovo, and from 1958 to 1988 he worked in the Bratsk hydroelectric construction association, supervised the installation of boilers and aggregates and the construction of the hydroelectric station. He is a state prize winner of the USSR and has received other state awards. In 1988 he was appointed chairman of the Irkutsk *oblast* soviet executive committee, and was elected a deputy of the RSFSR Supreme Soviet.

In early 1990 he was nominated by various work collectives in Irkutsk *oblast* for election as an RSFSR people's deputy in the No. 386 Sverdlovsk territorial district, Irkutsk *oblast*. During the election campaign he signed the declaration of the inter-*raion* group of candidates to the electors. It stated that the conservative majority in the USSR Congress of People's Deputies was leading the country into a crisis and disaster. For this reason Russian electors should vote for democratically-inclined candidates who were proposing the annulment of article 6 of the Soviet constitution (on the leading role of the CPSU in society), the rejection of the principle of democratic centralism, the establishment in Russia of a multi-party system, the separation of powers and reform of the soviets, the election of the heads of the executive agencies of the region by all voters, the development of social programmes, and the introduction of genuine freedom of speech and the press in accordance with the universal declaration of human rights. The inter-*raion* group proposed the introduction of the local regulation of the economy in order to end the situation where Siberia was a colonial appendage of the all-Union economy.

There were four candidates and Nozhikov won in the first round, polling 79% of the votes. The other candidates received from 3 to 8% of the votes. He is a member of the Democratic Russia faction and the coalition for reforms bloc of deputies. In 1990 he was elected a deputy of the Irkutsk *oblast* soviet and at the first session, in April 1990, he was elected chairman.

On August 19, 1991 he declared, in the name of the *oblast* soviet executive committee, that the removal from office of the President of the USSR, Mikhail Gorbachev, was illegal, and that on the territory of Irkutsk *oblast* only the RSFSR constitution and the decrees of the RSFSR President were legally valid. However, he was opposed to strikes which could lead to loss of production and the harvest. He appealed to the population to support the President of the RSFSR. The Presidium of the Irkutsk *oblast* soviet decided that the activities of the Extraordinary Committee were anti-constitutional and the publication of their documents was banned.

In August 1991 a session of the Irkutsk *oblast* soviet proposed Nozhikov to the President for confirmation as head of the administration of the *oblast* and on August 19, 1991 he was appointed head of the administration of the *oblast* by presidential decree. On assuming office he stated that he intended to act within the law and on the basis of the strict separation of powers. In his view the *oblast* soviet was too large and should only consist of specialists, but he was prepared to co-operate with all political and public organizations of the *oblast*. Among the most pressing tasks during the transition to a market economy he included the privatization of some enterprises and the introduction of trading relations. He wanted the *oblast* to be a full and equal member of the Federation.

In December 1992 he stated that the Congress of People's Deputies and the President were equally responsible for the political crisis which had arisen and refused to take sides. He was opposed to a referendum. His favourite pastime is motoring, and he lives in Irkutsk.

Nurmagambetov, Sagadat Kozhakhmetovich

Minister of Defence of the Republic of Kazakhstan; Lieutenant-General (Ret.).

Born on May 25, 1924 in Alekseevsky *raion*, Tselinograd *oblast*, Kazakh SSR. He graduated in 1943 from the first Turkestan infantry school; in 1949 from the M. V. Frunze Military Academy; in 1970 and 1981 from the higher academic courses of the military academy of the USSR Armed Forces General Staff. From 1943 to 1945 he was platoon commander of a separate rifle brigade, then company commander of a rifle regiment, and from 1945 to 1951 was deputy battalion commander, commander of a rifle regiment, student at the Frunze Military Academy, and inspector in the department of military educational establishments. He was then senior officer in an operational section in the operational department, Turkestan military district (1951-54), commander of a regiment (1954-58), Chief of Staff of a motor-rifle division (1958-61), Chief of Staff of civil defence of the Kazakh SSR (1961-60), and deputy commander of the Central Asian military district and first deputy commander of the Southern group of forces (1969-89). In 1989 he was transferred to the reserve, and from 1989 to 1991 he was chairman of Kazakh republican council of war, labour and armed forces veterans. From 1991 to 1992 he was chairman of the state committee of defence of the Republic of Kazakhstan, and in May 1992 he was appointed Minister of Defence of the Republic of Kazakhstan.

He was awarded orders of Lenin, the order of the October Revolution, two orders of the Red Banner of Labour, the order of the Great Fatherland War (1st and 2nd class), and the order of the Red Star. He is married with a son and a daughter. His wife, Lira Sabirovna, was born in 1927 and is an engineer; their son, Talgat, was born in 1952, and is an army officer; and their daughter, Aislu, was born in 1956 and is a doctor.

Address: 480091 Alma Ata, pl. Respubliki 4.

Nysanbaev, Ratbek

Chairman of the religious board of the Muslims of Kazakhstan; Mufti.

Born on November 7, 1940 in the village of Muratbaev, Chimkent *oblast*, Kazakh SSR; Kazakh. He graduated in 1975 from the faculty of theology, University of Tripoli, Libya, and in the same year was appointed secretary of the representative and, from 1979, representative of the Central Asian Muslim religious board in Kazakhstan. In 1990 he was appointed chairman of the religious board of the Muslims of Kazakhstan. He is a people's deputy of the Republic of Kazakhstan. He is married with five children. He speaks Arabic.

Address: Alma Ata, ul. Dzarkentskaya 12.

Oboroc, Constantin Mihail

Presidential Counsellor, Republic of Moldova.

Born in 1950 in the village of Cozeşti, Teleneşti *raion*, Moldovan SSR, to a family of farmers. He is an ethnic Moldovan. He graduated from the Polytechnic Institute in Chişinău, specializing in engineering, and worked in Tiraspol and Nisporeni as an engineer in the planning bureau, chief engineer, and director-general of the *raion* food canning association. From 1988 to 1990, he served as president of the Executive Committee of the Nisporeni Soviet of People's Deputies. In 1990 he was elected second secretary of the Nisporeni party committee. On June 5, 1990, he was named first deputy president of the Moldovan SSR Council of Ministers.

Ogorodnikov, Aleksandr Ioilevich

Chairman of the Christian Democratic Union of Russia.

Born in 1950 in Chistopol, Tatarstan. He worked in the Chistopol watch factory, and headed the city *Komsomol druzhina* (voluntary militia). In 1970 he enrolled in the philosophy faculty of the Urals State University in Sverdlovsk (Ekaterinburg) but he was soon expelled from the *Komsomol* and the university. At university he and others held discussion evenings to mull over philosophy. The group's aim was to free the *Komsomol* from unnecessary bureaucratic tutelage, and Ogorodnikov was already a thorough-going anti-communist. They formed a discussion club but it did not last long. At that time *Molodoi kommunist* had named the Urals State University "the most Marxist further education institute in the Soviet Union". This was not surprising given the dominance of industry and the number of workers in the Urals. His fellow students viewed him as a "non-Soviet person".

He returned to Chistopol and the KGB conducted a search but only found material which was not then incriminating; Galich's songs, Khrushchev's secret speech, delivered at the XX Party congress in 1956, Sokolnikov's letter to Stalin and Solzhenitsyn's letter to the Union of Writers. He then moved to Moscow and covered up the fact that he had been expelled from the Urals State University. He continued his studies at the all-Union institute of cinematography but was expelled in 1973, in his third year, for attempting to make a film about the religious searchings of youth. After his expulsion he worked as a porter and guard and was baptised into the Orthodox faith.

In 1974 he organized a Christian seminar and, together with Vladimir Poresh, began to publish the *samizdat* (self-publishing, illegal in the Soviet Union) journal *Obshchina* (Commune). Between 1976 and 1977 he signed many letters in support of the Russian Orthodox Church and believers, and in 1978 he was arrested in Kalinin (Tver) *oblast*, accused of parasitism and was sentenced to a year's corrective labour which he served in a camp in the Far East.

On the day he was released he was arrested in connection with the distribution of the journal *Obshchina*. He was sentenced to seven years in a labour camp and five years' exile according to article 70 of the criminal code (anti-Soviet propaganda), and served this sentence in Perm zone No. 36. In 1985 in the camp he was given an extra three years, according to an "Andropov article", for insubordination by going on hunger strike (he had in fact demanded a Bible) and defending the rights of political prisoners. He was a prisoner of conscience from 1978 to 1987.

In 1987 Ogorodnikov was among the first to benefit from President Mikhail Gorbachev's amnesty, thanks to the extensive campaign in his defence in which Academician Andrei Sakharov and Margaret Thatcher took part. In the summer of 1987 Ogorodnikov began to publish the *samizdat Bulletin of the Christian Community*. From 1988 he was a regular visitor abroad and addressed the parliaments of the United Kingdom, France, the United States, Malta and Guatemala. He actively campaigned for the release from prison of the Karabakh committee in Armenia. In August 1989, based on the editorial board of the Bulletin, he organized the Christian Democratic Union of Russia and became its chairman. The statutes adopted afforded the chairman almost dictatorial power, but differences of opinion began to surface in the new party by the autumn. Ogorodnikov, without any explanation, removed V. Savitsky from his post as deputy chairman of the party for ideology, as he was dissatisfied with Savitsky's draft party which the latter had taken from the programme of the German Christian Democratic Union (CDU).

This was the first of many splits in the party which seriously weakened it. The more right wing Russian Christian Democratic Movement gained in influence and Viktor Aksyuchits, its leader, was elected to the Russian Congress of People's Deputies, representing a Moscow constituency, in March 1990, but he failed to win a seat on the Moscow city soviet (Mossovet). During the autumn of 1990 Ogorodnikov became involved in a political scandal over the so-called Programme of Action 90.

In the spring of 1990 the Russian Christian Democratic Union entered an alliance with the Russian National Front and founded, together with it and other small political groups, the Russian Democratic Forum. In August-September 1990, Valery Skurlatov, the leader of the Russian National Front, wrote, and without the knowledge of his associates, distributed in the name of the Russian Democratic Forum a Programme of Action 90. The communists tried to use this programme to discredit the whole democratic movement. After the RSFSR Supreme Soviet had identified the author of the programme, Ogorodnikov was under suspicion of being a possible "extremist" and his party was banned from participating in the constituent congress of Democratic Russia. After the *Bulletin of the Christian Community* ceased publication in 1990 Ogorodnikov became editor of the *Herald of Christian Democracy*.

In 1991 he discovered that the KGB had destroyed the file on him, opened in 1989, in July 1991 because of "lack of evidence". Ogorodnikov remains one of the most influential religious-political activists in Russia. He graduated as an external student from the Father Sergei Radonezhsky Orthodox Institute of Theology in Paris.

He has stated that he was moved to found a party as a result of a Christian's responsibility for this world. He regards his task as not to establish an organization to draw the church into politics but to draft its own political programme, based on the social teachings of the church and the Christian way out of the catastrophe. The party grew out of the dissident movement, criticized the church hierarchy for its co-operation with the authorities which in turn caused the church to be circumspect in its relations with them. He regards the view that compromise saved the church as ensnaring, since the church is not saved by people but by God. He is convinced that it is difficult to appeal to all to engage in asceticism and heroism, but bishops should be known for this. He calls for the renaissance of Russia through repentance, and he believes that the church hierarchy should serve as an example of this and take some of the responsibility on themselves and repent, as the Bulgarian synod and Romanian patriarch have done.

He has criticized Russian Orthodox appointments from the nomenclature entering the democratic establishment, since the church for them is just a form of ideology, and he condemns their religious lack of patience. He favours a strict separation of the church from the state, arguing that state guardianship of the church is a defeat for it and a limitation of its freedom. He is convinced that a proto-party period is now in existence, when there are practically no real parties and those that do exist are fighting for their survival. The multi-party era will dawn in 1996 when the values which they defend will be understood. Parliament does not represent the intellectual mood in society as it was elected for other reasons, in a different society, during the dominance of the CPSU. Aksyuchits's is not in the fullest sense a Christian Democratic Party and it is embarrassed by the open communist past of its leader.

He believes it is immoral to found a party if one is a deputy elected to parliament as a communist or an independent. He favours indirect influence on those in power and moral politics. His party has joined the New Russia bloc as an "anti-nomenclature and completely independent" party. He advocates the drafting of a law on anti-nomenclature privatization, for priority to be afforded human rights, the raising of the status of prisoners, reform in the armed forces and the rights of Russians in the Baltic States. His party is well known for its practical activities. It opened a welfare kitchen in Moscow, a charity centre which provides help for 8,000 persons a month, a refuge for soldiers who have deserted and a Christian refuge for girls in St Petersburg.

The party plans to open its own school of business and teach the Christian approach to business, found a Christian arts lycée and a boys' scout organization. Ogorodnikov advocates the unification of all the christian democratic countries of the CIS and eastern Europe in order to oppose post-communist nationalism, to renew in Russia Christian culture and morality, taking into consideration the democratic values of world civilization, parliamentarianism and the market economy. The fall in the standard of living, in his view, is not the result of the market but of muddled reforms.

The Christian Democratic Union constructively opposes the insufficiently professional government, the unpredictable President and parliament, who represent yesterday's men and values. Left wing radicalism, those who oppose the state and those on the right of centre are all alien to him. He supports freedom, justice, solidarity and the raising of people in love for one another. He would like to see a social market economy, an increase in the output of goods, the conversion of the military economy and the normalization of finance.

Land, property and the means of production should become goods which can be traded. There should be a Christian initiative in politics and he appeals for the re-establishment of the dignity of the human personality, the right to sovereignty of every nation and the creation of a commonwealth along the lines of the British Commonwealth of Nations. He lives in Moscow.

Oleinik, Vladimir Ivanovich

Member of the Constitutional Court of the Russian Federation.

Born on February 3, 1936 in the settlement of Dombarovka, Orenburg *oblast* into a working-class family; Russian; member of CPSU until August 1991. In 1959 he graduated from the faculty of law, Perm State University, and for 34 years has been involved with the law, mainly in the agencies of the Procurator's Office and in various functions (procurator of a *raion*, procurator for crime in Kirgizia (Kyrgyzstan) and Moscow *oblast*, senior investigator for especially important cases, the USSR and RSFSR Procurator's Offices).

At the beginning of the 1970s he was head of the investigative group into the affairs of Sokolov, the director of departmental store No. 1 in Moscow. The director was later executed for economic crimes. In 1986 by decree of the USSR Supreme Soviet Presidium he was awarded the order of the Red Banner for unearthing a series of extremely dangerous crimes against individuals. He was also awarded the medal for excellent service in maintaining public order and the honoured worker of the Procurator's Office medal.

Afterwards he was employed in the agencies of the Procurator's Office and was a member of the investigative group, headed by T. Kh. Gdlyan and N. V. Ivanov. This group had a wide-ranging brief to investigate corruption and devoted much attention to the long-standing Uzbek cotton scandal, whereby Uzbekistan was paid for fictitious deliveries of cotton to the Soviet state and which involved many leading Uzbek officials. At the end of 1989 and the beginning of 1990, for five months, Oleinik was head of the legal department of the V. I. Lenin Soviet children's fund. The areas of his legal interests, beginning with his degree essay, include the problems of legislative techniques, the rules for drafting laws, criminology and criminal law, criminal procedure, ecological law and the sociology of law. He has published articles on criminal law and procedure, environmental law, legal technique and the training of legal officials. He is a member of the association of ecology and peace and a participant in the ecological expeditions, Aral-88 and Aral-89. During the voting in the Congress of People's Deputies for membership of the Constitutional

Court Oleinik declared that he stood outside all parties and had little sympathy for them.

In early 1990 he was nominated as an RSFSR people's deputy in the No. 4 Ostankino national territorial district, Moscow. During the election campaign he advocated the establishment of a law-governed state (*Rechtsstaat*), a guarantee that all citizens were equal before the law, a battle with the command-administrative system, the creation of a multi-party political system and the legal equality of all public organizations. He maintained the priority of common humanitarian values, the right of peoples to self-determination, including the right to secede and establish their own national states. He supported freedom of the press, thought and information, the creation of an instrument to implement laws, the unity of all democratic forces and a decisive break with reactionaries. He proposed measures to deal with crime, and he supported the platform of the Democratic Russia bloc. Twenty candidates stood for election. Oleinik polled 35.28% of the votes in the first round and won the second round polling 65.1% of the votes. His main opponent was the artist, I. S. Glazunov, who polled 12.12% of the votes in the first round and 26% of the votes in the second round.

Oleinik was a member of the RSFSR Supreme Soviet committee on legislation, chairman of the sub-committee of the Supreme Soviet committee on the freedom of conscience, religion, mercy and charity, a member of the non-party parliamentary faction, the unified parliamentary faction of social democratic and republican parties of the Russian Federation, the Moscow deputies' group and the Russian union group.

He was nominated for election to the Constitutional Court by the RSFSR Supreme Soviet committee on freedom of conscience. He was elected to the Court on October 29, 1991, at the V Congress of People's Deputies, in the first round of voting. He received 637 votes for and 249 against. On October 30 he surrendered his mandate as a people's deputy. He lives in Moscow.

Oliinyk, Borys Illich

Writer and Head of Ukrainian Cultural Fund.

Born into a Ukrainian family in 1935. He was educated at Kiev State University, and after graduation worked on various newspapers as a journalist and literary critic, including *Molod Ukraïny* (Youth of Ukraine) (1958-62), and *Dnipro* and *Ranok* (morning) (1962-71). As a long-time stalwart of the Soviet Ukrainian cultural establishment he served from 1971 to 1973 as deputy head of the Writers' Union of Ukraine, and from 1976 as a departmental secretary in both the Ukrainian and USSR Writers' Unions.

He was regularly elected to the old-style Ukrainian Supreme Soviet, where he was head of the permanent committee on education and culture. In the early days of *glasnost* Oliinyk appeared as something of a radical. At the USSR Writers' Congress in July 1986 his speech covered hitherto taboo subjects such as Chernobyl, the status of the Ukrainian language, and blank spots in Ukrainian-Russian relations.

Although he therefore made an important contribution to initiating discussion of these questions, it became clear as the 1980s progressed that Oliinyk remained a strong supporter of the basics of the socialist system. In 1989 he became deputy head of the USSR Supreme Soviet Soviet of Nationalities, and later an adviser to President Mikhail Gorbachev (although in 1992 he published a bitter attack on his former patron as the man who had destroyed the Soviet Union), and in both capacities was often sharply critical of nationalists back in Kiev.

In May 1991, for example, he wrote a scathing attack on Dmytro Pavlychko in *Pravda*. In November 1992 Oliinyk won a by-election to the Ukrainian Supreme Soviet. Since his return to active political life in Ukraine he has, ironically for a member of the SPU, been sharply critical of the absence of *Realpolitik* in Ukrainian foreign policy, and in particular of Ukrainian unilateral disarmament, and has become the main standard bearer of those elements on the Ukrainian left who see Oleksandr Moroz's Socialist Party of Ukraine as too moderate.

Official address: Kiev, Vul. M. Hrushevskoho 5; *telephone*: Kiev 252 019.

Omelchenko, Hryhorii Omelianovych

Former Head of the Union of Officers of Ukraine.

Born in 1951 into a Ukrainian peasant's family in Poltava *oblast* in central Ukraine. After finishing school he worked on a state farm before entering the faculty of law, Kiev State University, from where he graduated in 1976. He then worked in the Ministry of Internal Affairs (MVD) and as a lecturer in the Ukrainian Academy of Internal Affairs (he is the author of over one hundred articles on politics and law). He took part in the drafting of the Ukrainian proposals concerning the prevention of crime amongst adolescents and youth at the VIII Congress of the UN at Helsinki in 1989.

After 1990 he worked as a consultant to the Supreme Soviet's committee on defence and state security, and after the Declaration of Ukrainian Independence in August 1991 took an active part in drafting the various laws enacted to create a Ukrainian National Army. He was an active member of the Union of Officers of Ukraine (UOU) since its inception in July 1991, becoming its leader in 1992.

In March 1992 he represented the UOU unsuccessfully in a by-election in Kiev city. The UOU represents mainly middle-ranking officers, and under Omelchenko's leadership has become firmly nationalistic. It has exerted strong pressure on Kravchuk and Morozov to Ukrainianize the Armed Forces and to organize the return of Ukrainian officers "stranded" in other republics of the former USSR, and to pursue a more aggressive foreign and defence policy.

Omelchenko has expressed doubts concerning Ukraine's non-nuclear policy and the UOU called the Yalta agreement on the Black Sea Fleet in August 1992

Ukraine's Munich. The agreement between Presidents Kravchuk and Yeltsin was that the Black Sea Fleet should be under joint Ukrainian and Russian command until 1995. On the contentious issue of which flag the ships should fly, it was agreed to retain the Soviet flag until an agreement could be reached. The UOU has a strong influence in the army's new social psychological service (i.e. national propaganda department) and in the Centre for Operational and Strategic Studies attached to the Ministry of Defence.

Omelchenko was appointed in autumn 1992 to head a special government department for the struggle against corruption and organized crime, where he increased his public profile by making accusations of corruption against many leading government officials, including those in the Ministries of Health and Interior. At the fourth congress of the UOU in April 1993, Omelchenko resigned his post to concentrate on his anti-corruption work. He was replaced by Maj.-Gen. Oleksandr Skypalskyi.

Official address: Kiev, Budynok ofitseriv, Vul. M. Hrushevskoho.

Oorazhak, Sherig-ool Dizizhikovich

President-Chairman of the Government of the Republic of Tuva, Russian Federation.

Born on June 24, 1942 in the village of Shekpeer Barun, Khemchinsky *raion*, Tuva Autonomous Soviet Socialist Republic (ASSR). He is a Tuvinian, and was a member of the CPSU until August 1991. He began his working career in 1962 as a carpenter in the Kyzyl-Mangalyksky Selstroi construction assembly administration. He served in the Soviet armed forces from 1962 to 1965. From 1965 to 1966 he was a carpenter and concrete layer in the Tuva asbestos construction administration, then was assigned by the *raion Komsomol* committee to the Ak-Dovuraksky No 2 secondary school as a physical education teacher.

In 1966 he entered the K. A. Timiryazev Agricultural Academy, Moscow, and graduated as an agronomist and economist. Between 1971 and 1976 he worked as an economist on the Shekpeer state farm, and from 1976 to 1980 as its director. In 1980 he was elected chairman of the Barun-Khemchinsky *raion* soviet executive committee, and in 1983 first secretary of the Ulug-Khemsky *raion* Party committee. In December 1986 he was appointed head of the agricultural department of the Tuva Party *obkom* and in April 1987 he was elected secretary for the agro-industrial complex of the Tuva Party *obkom*. He was elected a deputy of the Supreme Soviet of the Tuva ASSR three times. He is the recipient of state awards.

In 1990 he was nominated by the work collectives of the Pobeda, Shambalyg and Tere Khol state farms, Kyzyl *raion* and Churgui-oola Khomushku Tes-Khemsky *raion*, by the *Erzinskoe* automobile enterprise, for election as an

RSFSR people's deputy in the No. 870 Kyzyl territorial district. During the election campaign he advocated the renewal of the party, the acceleration of economic and political reform, and proposed the equalization of price and wage rises, the drafting of an all-Russian programme for the protection of motherhood and childhood and the adoption of a law on youth. He devoted special attention to the development of the social sphere in the countryside and the protection of the agro-industrial complex against the rise in prices of machinery and mineral fertilizers.

He supported the development of leasing, contracts, co-operation and peasant activities in the countryside. He proposed the transformation of the Tuva ASSR into a Union republic, the creation of the conditions to permit Tuva to move to regional cost accounting, the raising of the standard of living of the population of the republic to the all-Union level by allocating resources from the state budget. He touched on the environmental problems.

There were 21 candidates. Oorazhak polled 19.1% of the votes in the first round and won the second round, polling 49% of the votes. His main opponent was V. A. Vereshchagin, head of the department of traumatology of the republican hospital, who received 13.1% of the votes in the first round and 47.3% in the second round. In 1990 Oorazhak was elected a deputy of the Supreme Soviet of the Tuva ASSR and on April 28, 1990, at its first session, he was elected unopposed Chairman of the Council of Ministers of the Tuva ASSR, receiving 72 votes for and 44 votes against.

In 1992 he was a candidate for the post of President-Chairman of the Council of Ministers of the Republic of Tuva. During the election programme he advocated enhancing the state sovereignty of the republic within the Russian Federation, the most rapid implementation of economic reform, taking into consideration local conditions and the interests of the native peoples of Tuva, the establishment in the republic of a processing industry and energy system, and the transfer of property to the people by giving it to work collectives and not to the representatives of the new economics, mafiosi groups and the corrupt élite. He stood for the spiritual renaissance of society based on the development of democracy, the establishment of a *Rechtsstaat* (law-governed state) and the development of national science and culture. The Memorial society supported him during the election campaign and during sessions of the *raion* soviets. His only opponent was B. T. Sanchi, general director of the Tuvaposredkompaniya company and the Sayany commodity exchange. On March 15, 1992 Oorazhak won by a majority of votes and was elected President-Chairman of the government of the Republic of Tuva. He lives in Kyzyl.

Orlov, Aleksei Ivanovich

Chairman of the committee of the Russian Supreme Soviet on construction, architecture and municipal services.

Born on January 1, 1937 in Vyazma, Smolensk *oblast*; Russian. He was a member of the CPSU until August 1991. He began work after leaving school as a road worker, then became a section head of a road machine station in Vyazma. He graduated from the all-Union Extra-mural Institute of Finance, and then moved into Party work. He was an instructor in the department of construction and municipal services, Smolensk Party city committee; deputy chairman, Smolensk city soviet executive committee; and secretary, Smolensk Party *obkom* (1967-87). In 1987 he was elected chairman of the executive committee of the Smolensk *oblast* soviet of people's deputies. He was elected a member of the bureau of the Smolensk Party *obkom*; a people's deputy of the RSFSR Supreme Soviet for Vyazma electoral district in 1988, and was chairman of the RSFSR Supreme Soviet commission on the budget and plan (1988-90).

In January 1990 he was nominated for election as an RSFSR people's deputy in the No. 683 Vyazma territorial district, Smolensk *oblast*. During the election campaign he concentrated on social and economic questions. He regarded work as the most important concern for everyone and promised to implement eight *oblast* programmes involving the construction of roads and housing, health care, trade, the protection of socialist legality, the provision of food and, most important to him, the revival of the villages of Smolensk *oblast*. He demanded a slowdown in industrial development and the transfer of resources to the agrarian sector, which would help to expand the agrarian sector and provide more food for the population. Regional cost accounting (*khozraschet*) should be introduced in the *oblast* and co-operation rapidly developed. Soviets should be the real masters of the *oblast* but they would be faced with serious problems such as preventing the deterioration of the environment, combating the sharp rise in crime and raising the ideological and cultural level. There should be unquestioning respect for the military, and it should not be deployed against society. He was appalled by the unrestricted propagation of immorality, pornography and violence in the mass media, and felt there should be co-operation with the intelligentsia since it had the capacity to influence the population deeply.

There were four candidates. Orlov polled 26.3% of the votes in the first round and won the second round, polling 49.8% of the votes. His main opponent was V. P. Fateev, director of the Vyazemsky linen enterprise, who received 29.8% of the votes in the first round and 40.9% in the second round. Orlov was elected a member of the Russian Supreme Soviet at the V Congress of People's Deputies. He is a member of the Council of the Republic, and on July 3, 1990 he was elected a member of the Supreme Soviet committee on construction, architecture and municipal services; later he became its chairman. He was awarded the orders of the Red Banner of Labour, and the badge of honour.

Address: 103274 Moscow, K 274, Krasnopresnenskaya nab., d. 2, Dom Sovetov.

Ozerov, Mikhail Vitalevich

Literaturnaya Gazeta correspondent in the United Kingdom.

Born on August 15, 1944 in Moscow; Russian; son of Vitaly and Maria Ozerov. He graduated from the philological faculty of Moscow State University in 1967, specializing in west European languages and literatures. He joined TASS and was TASS correspondent in Sri Lanka (1971-73), and in London (1973-76); joined *Literaturnaya Gazeta* as political observer in 1976 and remained until 1979; then became a member of the editorial board of *Sovetskaya Rossiya*, until 1988. He became first deputy editor-in-chief of *Mezhdynarodnie otneshenie* (International Affairs), the monthly journal of the USSR Ministry of Internal Affairs (1988-90) and became London correspondent of *Literaturnaya Gazeta* in 1990.

As a leading member of the Soviet mass media he has travelled abroad extensively as head of various delegations and delivered speeches. When younger he played table tennis, became No. 3 in the Soviet Union and was a member of the Soviet team, and is now a keen tennis player. He is married to Margarita and they have twin daughters, Maria and Lyudmila. He speaks English and German. He has received state prizes for some of his books: e.g. Lenin *Komsomol* prize for *From Greenwich to the Equator* (in Russian) in 1982. Altogether he has published 15 books, including *Britain without Fog; Kampuchea; The First Year; From Greenwich to the Equator; This I Saw*, on US-Soviet and Russian summits, which he attended as a so-called Kremlin journalist.

Address: Flat 3, 51A Palace Court, London W2 4LF; telephone: 071 792 1573.

Pain, Emil Abramovich

Member of the Council of the President of the Russian Federation.

Born in 1948 in Kiev, Ukraine. He graduated in 1974 from Voronezh State University and in 1984 successfully presented his candidate dissertation in the institute of ethnography, USSR Academy of Sciences, Moscow, on "Ethno-social conditions of development of the rural population (based on Uzbekistan)" (PhD). His areas of research are regional sociology and ethnology, and problems of regional and national conflicts before they openly manifest themselves. He has published articles on the legacy of national architecture, for example, Georgian, on the problems of territorial commonality, the formation and reproduction of ethnocultural traditions during urbanization, on the traditional forms of settlement and life of the Uzbek rural population.

He has concentrated on the ethnographic study of rural life. His articles have been published in the journal *Sovetskaya ethnografiya* and he is the author of the book *Ethno-Cultural Processes: Methods of Historical and Synchronic Research* (1982). In 1990 he was invited to join the Eduard Shevardnadze foreign policy association as the head of the centre of ethnopolitical research. He was a specialist in the USSR Supreme Soviet commission on deported peoples and the state commission on the Crimean Tatars. He participated in the drafting of laws on nationality policy.

He believes the President genuinely wishes to receive new ideas and proposals. He regards conservative pragmatic ideas to be harmful to the present power of the President who intends to deploy his political experience to chart a clear course within the framework of a liberal pragmatic ideology. This, according to Pain, has not yet come to fruition since his liberal romantic ideas have still not been exhausted. The present situation is so bad that a referendum cannot do it any more damage. The social situation and inertia in society are such that they will undermine any compromise agreement reached by the various branches of power. He became a member of the presidential Council in February 1993 and lives in Moscow.

Pamfilova, Ella Aleksandrovna

Minister of Social Security of the Russian Federation.

Born on September 12, 1953 in Moscow into a Russian family. Member of the CPSU until July 1991. In 1976 she graduated from the Moscow Institute of Energy as an electronics engineer and from 1976 to 1989 she worked as an engineer and technologist concerned with the repair of electronic equipment in the Central repair mechanical enterprise of the *Mosenergo* production association. She was the chairwoman of the trade union committee of the enterprise. In March 1989 she was elected a USSR people's deputy, representing the trade unions. In her pre-election manifesto she stressed the importance of treating all workers equally and pointed out the lack of social justice in Soviet society. She proposed that the bureaucracy needed to be pruned back in order to resolve social problems. Officials should be subject to a "code of honour" which stressed moral issues. At the election meeting of the trade unions, 753 voted for her and only 57 against. She was a member of the credentials' commission of the I USSR Congress of People's Deputies and was a founding member of the interregional deputies' group, but left in October 1989.

In the summer of 1990 Pamfilova was elected to the USSR Supreme Soviet and was a member of its committee on ecology and the rational use of natural resources. She was also a member of the parliament's provisional committee for combating crime. In 1990 to 1991 she was secretary of the commission on privileges and benefits of the USSR Supreme Soviet, whose chairman was Evgeny Primakov. According to her it was a hopeless struggle just to obtain precise information about privileges, let alone trying to change the system of illegal benefits. Her last action on this commission was to organize an inspection of the financial and economic administration of the USSR Supreme Soviet. She was often a sharp critic of the privileges of the Party *nomenklatura*. It was then that she resigned from the CPSU and joined the opposition to the USSR leadership of the Supreme Soviet. Politically, she supported the democrats on

most issues. During the II USSR Congress of People's Deputies she voted
for the annulment of Article 6 of the USSR Constitution which afforded the
CPSU a monopoly of political power, and against the economic programme of
Nikolai Ryzhkov, the Prime Minister. At the IV Congress she voted against
the introduction of a moratorium on strikes and the placing on the agenda of
a motion of no confidence in the USSR President. She was a vigorous critic of
Telman Gdlyan in the congress commission on the Gdlyan and Ivanov affair.
(These two lawyers had investigated the great Uzbek cotton scandal which
had led to the fall of many leading political figures both in Uzbekistan and
also in Moscow. At the XIX Party conference in June 1988, Gdlyan accused
several of the delegates of corruption. He became enormously popular but
counter-accusations were made against him. His popularity fell sharply in 1992.)
During the election of a Speaker of the USSR Supreme Soviet Pamfilova
proposed the since deceased democrat V. Lubenchenko. Anatoly Lukyanov
was eventually elected.

In November 1991 Pamfilova was appointed Russian Minister of Social
Security. Her main concern was to establish a viable system of support for
the poor and to adopt measures to prevent an outburst of discontent. She
argued that all the Party social facilities should be handed over to services for
the people. She set up an administration to advise on the most efficient use of
social facilities.

Pamfilova decided to turn down all the benefits due to her as Minister
and continues to live in a flat in a five-story block built under Khrushchev
on the outskirts of Moscow. She succeeded in getting legislation adopted
which improved the position of the poor and held that if state resources are
inadequate then charitable organizations should be set up in the ministry and
at the local level. She enjoys the reputation of being untainted by corruption,
intrigue and scandal, and is highly respected. She is the only woman minister
in the government and is the least criticized by politicians, the media and the
population.

When Egor Gaidar was sacked as Russian Prime Minister by President Boris
Yeltsin in December 1992 as one of the concessions he was forced to make to
the VII Congress of People's Deputies, Pamfilova also lost her post. However,
she was invited to join the cabinet of Viktor Chernomyrdin in her old post.
She is married and has a daughter and lives with her mother on the outskirts
of Moscow in a three-room flat.

Panin, Vasily Ivanovich

President of the Naval Fraternity, the Russian Fund for Naval Exhibits and
Traditions. Former head of the military political administration of the Navy.
Admiral since 1989.

Born on September 15, 1934 in the village of Borovoe, Usmansky *raion*,
Lipetsk *oblast*, into an office worker's family. Russian. Panin graduated from

the Vyborg Technical School of Naval Marines in 1955; completed an extramural course at the V. I. Lenin Military Political Academy in 1966; took an external degree at the Military Academy of the General Staff in 1986. He received a higher military education and was a member of the CPSU from 1959 to August 1991.

After completing technical school he was appointed a platoon commander. He actively participated in Party political agencies and was a careerist. He sought to become a political worker, which, in the highly ideological climate of the armed forces of the USSR, ensured more rapid promotion without any personal responsibility for the situation in the units. In 1956 he was elected secretary of a *Komsomol* organization, then he became assistant to the head of the political department of the *Komsomol*. He preached communist fundamentalism enthusiastically to young sailors. He persecuted independent-minded young personnel, religious believers and those resisting barrack-room discipline. He was considered by superior officers to be a promising political commander who firmly adhered to Party discipline and policy.

After graduating from the Military Political Academy he became a political commander of a submarine. He participated in long sea voyages during his military service. He mastered the sophisticated combat matériel and equipment of a submarine and was granted the right to take independent decisions. From 1970 he was deputy head, then head of the political department of a detached submarine sub-division. In 1974 he was appointed head of one of the departments of the political administration of the Red Banner Pacific fleet. He was notable even among political commanders for communist phraseology and fundamentalism, which democratically-minded sources claim were deployed to conceal his hypocrisy and liking of personal accumulation. He was servile towards his superior officers and enjoyed their support.

In 1977 Captain (first class) Panin was appointed an instructor in the department of administrative agencies of the Party Central Committee where he was responsible for naval issues. He personally bears some responsibility for the arms race conducted by the navy and was a lobbyist for the naval command and military-industrial complex. He was responsible for the supervision exercised by the Party Central Committee over the construction and use of the navy and the discipline of personnel. His work in the Party Central Committee and the contacts he made there ensured further promotion.

In 1982 Panin was promoted to Rear Admiral and appointed a member of the military council and head of the political department of a flotilla of the Pacific Fleet. He was tough towards democratically-inclined sailors and is known to have organized several persecution campaigns of officers and midshipmen. At the same time he prevented commanding officers and their relatives from being called to account for military and criminal offences. His reputation in Moscow was good, due to the hard Party line he adopted. In 1985 he was appointed first deputy head of the political administration of the navy; from 1987 a member of the military council and head of the political administration of the navy; from 1990 head of the military political administration of the navy. In July 1990 he was elected a member of the Party Central Committee at the XXVIII Party congress. He pursued a policy of dismissing democratically-inclined officers and insisted on orthodox views. He supported right-wing circles in the Party, state and military leadership. He influenced Adml Vladimir Chernavin, Commander-in-Chief of the Navy, to the extent that the Admiral signed a number of letters and appeals demanding a toughening of the domestic policy in the USSR. During the anti-constitutional putsch in August 1991 he despatched telegrams to subordinate naval formations demanding support for the Emergency Committee. He personally co-ordinated activities aimed at the dissolution of democratic organizations. After the coup failed he was not called to account due to the protection of Admiral Chernavin and despite the demands of many naval officers.

With the dissolution of the military political agencies and the banning of the CPSU Panin lost his post but continued in service. For over a year, despite evident violations of the law, and personally subordinate to the Commander-in-Chief, he retained all his privileges and pay. According to democratic sources he used appropriated Party resources to establish the Naval Fraternity, the Russian fund for naval exhibits and traditions, under the cover of the preparations for the 300th anniversary of the Russian navy. The fund engages only in commercial transactions, in illegal oil exports and other frauds at home and abroad, according to a report in *Krasnaya Zvezda* on April 17, 1992. Panin has involved many admirals and officers in these activities, thus, in practice, exercising significant influence over the moral and political stance of the officials of the central apparatus of the navy. Democrats accuse him of corrupting naval leaders. He supports conservative political views, concealing them in patriotic phraseology. He is influential in top naval circles and, despite numerous demands by democratic military organizations, he has not been called to account because of the influence of powerful patrons. His critics make the accusation that, during his time of study at the Military Academy of the General Staff, he had his papers prepared by sub-units and the central apparatus of the navy. To democrats, Admiral Panin is the *éminence grise* of the naval command, conducting a policy of confrontation with the new Russian leadership.

There is no information available about his hobbies. He does not speak a foreign language, and visited Italy as president of his fund in early 1992. He has published articles in *Morskoi sbornik* and newspapers. He has been awarded two orders and many medals, and is married with two children.

Official address: 103175 Moscow K-175 Bolshoi Kozlovsky pereulok 4.

Pankin, Boris Dmitrievich

Russian ambassador to the United Kingdom.

Born on February 20, 1931 in Frunze (Bishkek), Kyrgyzstan, and was the grandson of a kulak or well-off peasant, exiled under Stalin; Russian. He was a member of the CPSU until August 1991. He graduated in 1953 from the faculty of journalism, Moscow State University, and he was a journalist from 1953 to

1973. He was elected a member of the USSR union of writers in 1970 and became a member of its board. He is at present engaged in writing a novel about Simonov. He became a member of the union as a result of a series of reports on miners (together with V. Chivilikhin) and reviews of readers letters to *Komsomolskaya pravda* (together with V. Chikin). On March 30, 1963, together with G. Oganov and V. Chikin, he published the article, "Where are the Khlestakov times leading" (from a character in Gogols *Government Inspector*) which served as the beginning of the persecution of Evgeny Evtushenko for his statements on Soviet society and history. Pankin became editor-in-chief of *Komsomolskaya pravda* in 1965. The all-Union copyright agency (VAAP) was established in 1973 and Pankin became the chairman of its board.

Vladimir Voinovich published an open letter to Pankin accusing him of acquiring publishing rights for VAAP. Pankin remained there until 1982, was then appointed USSR ambassador to Sweden and some maintain that he wrote daring reports from there, praising the Swedish model of social democracy. In 1990 he was appointed USSR ambassador to Czechoslovakia, and he was there during the attempted state coup in Moscow in August 1991, being one of the few officials to refuse to support the putsch. He expressed his support for the President of the RSFSR, Boris Yeltsin, and called for the release of the USSR President, Mikhail Gorbachev. The latter phoned him on August 28, 1991 and offered him the post of USSR Minister of Foreign Affairs, replacing Aleksandr Bessmertnikh because of the latter's lack of support of the constitutional order during the coup. The decision was taken during a meeting between President Gorbachev and Pankin, in the presence of Aleksandr Yakovlev.

During the campaign implicating the USSR Ministry of Foreign Affairs in the putsch Pankin did not refute press reports. He recalled disloyal ambassadors by bringing them back to Moscow for consultations, when they were offered the prospect of suggesting ways they could continue working under the new circumstances. They could either retire or be posted elsewhere. The collegium of the USSR Ministry of Foreign Affairs resigned when Pankin took over, officially, to permit him to reform it in line with his own plans. Pankin appointed V. F. Petrovsky his first deputy and immediately sacked Yury Kvitsinsky, without any explanation. V. P. Lukin, A. E. Sebentsov, O. O. Suleimenov and A. V. Yablokov also joined the new collegium. Pankin began setting up a council of the foreign ministers of some USSR republics (10-11 states took part) in order to replace the former Minsitry of Foreign Affairs, but its structure did not prove viable and many decisions were taken without its involvement. Then Andrei Kozyrev came into the council as minister, and Pankin carried out various official visits, to the UN general assembly, France and so on, during which he stated that the country would continue to be run from the centre by the President of the USSR. Then a conflict broke out between the USSR and the RSFSR Ministries of Foreign Affairs after Kozyrev had stated that Russia did not need such a huge institution as the USSR Minstry of Foreign Affairs.

Pankin declared the following to be the priorities of foreign policy: i) de-ideologization; ii) priority for economic relations; and iii) the human dimension. He demanded that intelligence officers should cease to be part of the diplomatic corps, and that the Baltic States should be recognized and diplomatic relations established with them. Diplomatic relations were re-established with Israel and, in line with the decision of the UN general assembly, Zionism ceased to be regarded as a form of racism. After the decision was taken that the USSR Ministry of Foreign Affairs was no longer needed and the USSR Ministry of Foreign Relations should be established instead, Pankin was appointed ambassador to the Court of St James. On November 19, 1991 Eduard Shevardnadze was appointed the first and last USSR Minister of Foreign Relations, and in January 1992 Pankin became Russian ambassador in London. He speaks English and German. He is married with a son and a daughter, and a grandson. He was awarded two orders of the Red Banner of Labour, and the order of the Friendship of Peoples, and medals.

Address: The Embassy of the Russian Federation, London W8.

Paton, Boris Evgenovich

President of the Ukrainian Academy of Sciences.

Born on November 27, 1918 into a Russian family. He was educated at Kiev Industrial Institute, and then worked as an engineer after 1941. From 1953 he was the director of an electrical welding institute. He is now a professor of technical sciences, and since 1961 has served as President of the Academy of Sciences of Ukraine. He joined the Communist Party of Ukraine (CPU) in 1952 and is a stalwart of the old guard establishment. He served as a people's deputy in the Kiev Supreme Soviet for seven sessions, and in the USSR Supreme Soviet for six (including in the Supreme Soviet elected in 1989).

From 1961 he served as a member of the Central Committees of both the CPU and the CPSU. He has accumulated the standard array of awards, including Hero of Socialist Labour twice, in 1969 and 1978. In April 1992 he was appointed a member of the President's advisory *Duma* on humanitarian affairs. Paton is a great survivor, but is an obvious conservative and it is unlikely that he can remain in charge of the Academy of Sciences for long.

Pavlov, Nikolai Aleksandrovich

Co-Chairman of the Front of National Salvation.

Born on June 30, 1951 in the village of Salkovo, Yaroslavl *oblast*; Russian. He was a member of the CPSU from 1990 to August 1991. He moved to Tyumen *oblast* in 1961, and after secondary school in 1968 entered the Tyumen Industrial Institute. Between 1970 and 1973 he worked as a carpenter on construction sites in the Tyumen north, in 1973 he entered the faculty of bio-chemistry, Tyumen State University, and graduated in 1978. He then became a postgraduate student in Leningrad and successfully presented, in 1983, his candidate dissertation in biological sciences on "Regulating brain haemorrhage in birds by modifying their blood pressure" (PhD). In 1983 he was appointed to the department of human and animal physiology, Tyumen State University as an assistant, then senior lecturer, and eventually assistant professor (*dotsent*). He began researching his doctoral dissertation there just before the election campaign.

In 1990 he was nominated by the collective of Tyumen State University, a machine tool factory, the plenum of the Tsentralny *Komsomol raion* committee, Tyumen, for election as an RSFSR people's deputy in the No. 79 Tyumen national territorial district, Tyumen *oblast*. During his election campaign he advocated real political and economic sovereignty for Russia, the exchange of goods between republics at world market prices, the raising of state prices for coal, oil, gas, timber and potatoes, the adoption of a special state plan for Tyumen *oblast* and, by applying economic cost accounting, an increase in the output of the building materials industry, processing industry and road construction, the building of social and cultural establishments and the provision of gas and electricity to villages.

He supported a debate in the Russian Supreme Soviet and a referendum on the advisability of constructing nuclear power stations and other environmentally harmful industries. He insisted on priority being given to the development of education and health. He proposed the drafting of a comprehensive programme on the family and argued strongly for a revision of the monopolistically high prices for agricultural machinery, building materials and fertilizers and the provision of services in the countryside. The Supreme Soviet should debate the results of the anti-alcohol decree of 1985 and submit to referendum future plans for regulating the production and sale of alcohol. He stressed the need to provide opportunities for the development of the national culture, language and traditions of all nations and nationalities living in Tyumen *oblast* and in the RSFSR in general.

He advocated the conferral of the title of juridical person on religious communities and the return by a single legislative act of all confiscated churches, mosques and synagogues to believers, simultaneously preserving them as publicly available cultural and historical monuments. He proposed the annulment of the anti-democratic articles of the constitution affecting the role of the Party and the *Komsomol* and to draft a law on parties. He insisted on the need to ensure equal rights for the development of all types of property which exclude the exploitation of any person and the promulgation of a law which would ensure that successful farmers cannot be moved. He proposed the drafting of legislation to improve the social protection of workers, including the promulgation of a law on unemployment.

Five candidates stood for election. Pavlov polled 23.8% of the votes in the first round and won in the second round, polling 52.7% of the votes. His main opponent was V. V. Kitaev who received 22.8% of the votes in the first round and 34.5% of the votes in the second round. He was elected a member of the RSFSR Supreme Soviet at the I Congress of People's Deputies (779 voted for, 114 against). He is a member of the Council of Nationalities and a member of the Council of Nationalities commission on the national state system and inter-ethnic relations. He was elected deputy chairman of the Supreme Soviet committee on women's affairs, protection of the family, maternity and childhood on August 8, 1990. He is a member of the parliamentary Russia faction. He is married and he and his wife are fostering two children. He lives in Moscow.

Pavlov, Valentin Sergeevich

Member of the Extraordinary Committee.

Born on September 26, 1937 in Moscow; Russian. In 1958 he graduated from the Moscow Institute of Finance, and successfully presented his candidate dissertation in economics (PhD (Econ)) and his doctoral dissertation in economics (DSc (Econ)). He was a member of the CPSU from 1962 to August 1991. In 1958 he became an inspector of state revenues in Kalinin *raion* financial department, Moscow, and in 1959 he was senior economist, later deputy head of a department, and deputy head of the board of the RSFSR Ministry of Finance.

In 1966 he was appointed deputy head of the board of the USSR Ministry of Finance; in 1979 he became head of the section of finance, cost and prices, USSR Gosplan and in 1981 a member of the collegium, member of USSR Gosplan. In 1986 he was appointed first deputy Minister of Finance of the USSR and later that year head of the USSR state committee on prices, and in 1989 became USSR Minister of Finance. He was a member of the Party Central Committee from July to August 1991.

In January 1991 he was appointed chairman of the Council of Ministers of the USSR (Prime Minister), in succession to Nikolai Ryzhkov. He was involved in various attempts to outmanoeuvre President Gorbachev and once claimed that foreign speculators were attempting to take over the country. He ordered the withdrawal of large denomination bank notes and only succeeded in penalizing the small saver.

He became a member of the Extraordinary Committee in August 1991 but the pressure was such that he fell ill, or claimed to be ill. On August 20, 1991 he resigned as USSR Prime Minister because of ill health. During the investigation he was incarcerated in the *Matrosskaya tishina* isolator, but he and other conspirators were later released. He was regarded by many foreign observers as a good economist. He was irreverently nicknamed "pig-hedgehog" due to his crew cut and corpulent appearance. He lives in Moscow.

Pavlychko, Dmytro Vasylovych

Chairman of The Ukrainian Foreign Affairs Committee and Leader of the Democratic Party in the Supreme Soviet.

Born into a Ukrainian peasant family in 1929 in the Hutsul region of the Carpathian mountains. He studied philology at Lviv State University, after which he was a poet, journalist and translator, and rose to fame as one of the celebrated *Shestydesiatnyky* (sixty) generation, the new wave of Ukrainian poets and writers of the 1960s. He was the chief editor of the literary journal *Vsesvit* from 1972 to 1979, and composed many prose and poetry collections, such as *Hranoslav* and *Pravda klyche*.

He was awarded the Shevchenko prize and was elected several times secretary of the Ukrainian Writers' Union. In other words, he was a leading member of the Ukrainian literary establishment in the 1970s and 1980s. He was, however, an early and enthusiastic convert to the oppositional movement that began to appear in the late 1980s. He was the first head of the Taras Shevchenko Ukrainian language society, founded in 1989 to promote the revival of the Ukrainian language.

In March 1990 he was elected a people's deputy in the first round for Zbarazkyi *raion*, Ternopil *oblast*, in western Ukraine. In the Supreme Soviet he was granted the chairmanship of the prestigious committee on foreign affairs (he often accompanies President Kravchuk and Foreign Minister Zlenko on trips abroad) in order to help improve Ukraine's image in the West. He is also an *ex officio* member of the Supreme Soviet Presidium.

In March 1990 Pavlychko and Ivan Drach unsuccessfully attempted to transform *Rukh* into a political party at a meeting of *Rukh's* Grand Council in Khust, after which both he and Drach left the Communist Party of Ukraine and announced their intention of forming what became, in December 1990, the Democratic Party of Ukraine (DPU). Pavlychko was one of its five deputy chairmen, and headed the DPU's faction of 23 deputies in the Supreme Soviet. Since autumn 1991 he has emerged as a strong supporter of President Kravchuk and his policy of building strong national defence, and pushed strongly for *Rukh* to adopt a formal position of support for Kravchuk at its third Congress in February-March 1992.

The attempt was defeated, and a formal breakaway by him and Drach was only narrowly avoided. Nevertheless, Pavlychko achieved his long-term goal by August 1992, when he was one of the prime movers behind the creation of the Congress of National-Democratic Forces, a nationalist alliance based on the Democratic and Republican Parties which backed President Kravchuk. Pavlychko in fact exerted strong backstage pressure to ensure that the Congress' final platform was more unequivocally supportive of the President than many others would have preferred. Pavlychko, an emotional man, was reportedly disappointed by Kravchuk's failure to appoint him as ambassador to Washington, a post he had long coveted, and there were small signs that he was becoming disillusioned with the President in autumn 1992.

Home address: 252001 Kiev, Vul. Khreshchatyk 13, kv. 42; *telephone*: (home): Kiev 228 7975.

Pecina, Ludmila Symonauna

Chairwoman of the Women's Christian Democratic Movement, Belarus.

Born on May 10, 1950 in Minsk. Her parents are Symon Saroka and Jefrasina, née Hrynkievic, and the family is Belarusian. She graduated in 1975 from the faculty of geography, Belarusian State University, Minsk. From 1975 to 1989 she was excursion leader in the Minskturist state tourist bureau; and from 1989 to 1993 was director of the Susviet-Tur private tourist company. She was elected chairwoman of the Women's Christian Democratic movement in 1993 and a member of council, Belrusian Popular Front. She supports the sovereignty of the Belarusian republic, a democratic society and a market economy, and is working for the renaissance of Belarusian culture and the moral and spiritual revival of society. She is divorced and has a son, Dzianis Pecin, born in 1976. She speaks Polish, Russian and English.

Address: 220022 Minsk, vul. Raduznaja 6-5; *telephone*: Minsk (0172) 235 172 (office); 503 168 (home); *fax*: Minsk (0172) 209 125.

Pekhota, Volodymyr Yuliyovych

State Secretary to the Ukrainian Council of Ministers.

Born into a Ukrainian family in Kharkiv in 1939. He was educated at the polytechnic institutes in Lviv and Kharkiv, and then at the Academy of Sciences of the CPSU Central Committee. Most of his career was spent in Galicia, including working at a chemical factory in Lviv from 1962, becoming the secretary of the factory's Communist Party cell in 1968. From 1980 to 1988 he served as the head of Lviv city soviet executive committee. Thereafter he became a functionary in the Ukrainian Council of Ministers, rising to the position of state secretary of the Cabinet of Ministers in May 1991.

In this position he wields considerable power over the workings of the government through his ability to control agendas, the flow of information, and so on. In the past he was seen as an old-style *apparatchik*, but a close ally of Kravchuk and Fokin.

Official address: 252008 Kiev, Vul. M. Hrushevskoho 12/2; *telephone*: Kiev 293 7442.

Petrov, Vladimir Ivanovich

Chairman of the Government of the Republic of Gorny Altai, Russian Federation.

Born on February 3, 1942 in the village of Yabogan, Ust-Kansky *raion*, Gorno-Altai autonomous *oblast* into a civil servant's family; Russian; member of the CPSU until August 1991. He began working after completing secondary school in 1958 as an instructor in the Ust-Kansky *raion Komsomol* committee. In 1960 he worked in the Yabogansky state farm, Ust-Kansky *raion*. In 1965 he graduated from the Altai Agricultural Institute as an engineer, and after graduating was head of the Yabogansky machine tractor repair state farm. From 1966 to 1967 he served in the Soviet Army.

Between 1967 and 1973 he was chief engineer on the Yabogansky state farm, and from 1973 to 1975 was an instructor in the agricultural department of the Gorno-Altai Party *obkom*. In 1975 he graduated from the Higher Party School. From 1975 to 1984 he was second, then first secretary of the Ust-Koksinsky *raion* Party committee, Gorno-Altai autonomous *oblast*. From 1984 to 1990 he was first deputy chairman of the Altai *oblast* soviet executive committee. When he was elected he was also director of the Gorny Altai agro-industrial complex. He was elected a deputy of the Ust-Koksinsky *raion*, Gorno-Altai *oblast* and Altai *krai* soviets of people's deputies. He is the recipient of two state medals.

In January 1990 he was nominated by the collectives of a state farm and secondary school for election as an RSFSR people's deputy in the No. 152 Chuisky national territorial district, Gorno-Altai autonomous *oblast*. During the election campaign he advocated the transfer of power to the soviets, the establishment of a *Rechtsstaat* (law-governed sate), the extension of the economic autonomy of the Russian Federation and the raising of the status of the Gorno-Altai autonomous *oblast*. He favoured many types of ownership and equality for all types.

In the social sphere he advocated the construction of well-built housing, kindergartens, schools and houses of culture, the provision by the government of real protection for the workers in animal husbandry, culture and health for those whose wages did not correspond to the quantity and quality of their work, and also protection for invalids, the aged and large families. He believed that the lowering of social tension in society would permit an improvement in the provision of consumer goods to the population and a change in the economy of the region towards the needs of the population. In general his election programme was based on the platform of the *oblast* Party organization.

There were five candidates. He polled 34% of the votes in the first round and won in the second round, polling 51.6% of the votes. His main opponent was G. P. Sumin, chairman of the Shebalinsky *raion* soviet executive committee, Gorno-Altai autonomous *oblast*, who received 20.38% of the votes in the first round and 42.17% in the second round. Petrov was elected a member of the Supreme Soviet Council of Nationalities at the I Congress of People's Deputies, receiving 632 votes for and 291 votes against. He is a member of the Supreme Soviet committee on international affairs and foreign economic links. He participated in the activities of the communists of Russia parliamentary faction and is also a member of the sovereignty and equality faction.

In 1990 he was elected a deputy of the *oblast* soviet. On March 27, 1990 he was elected unopposed chairman of the *oblast* executive committees, Gorno-Altai autonomous *oblast*. In July 1991, after the transformation of the Gorno-Altai autonomous *oblast* into the Gorno-Altai Soviet Socialist Republic, he was elected chairman of the government. On assuming office he stated that his primary tasks were to ensure priority for the development of the agro-industrial complex of the region, enhancing the status of Gorno-Altai in the RSFSR and establishing links between the region and other states. In August 1991, being in Moscow, he gave orders by telephone that the region was not to subordinate itself to the orders and decrees of the Extraordinary Committee and to act according to the constitution of the RSFSR and the decrees of the President of the RSFSR. He lives in Gorno-Altaisk.

Petrov, Yury Vladimirovich

Chairman of the Russian State Investment Corporation.

Born on January 18, 1939 in Nizhny Tagil, Sverdlovsk (Ekaterinburg) *oblast*; Russian. He was a member of the CPSU from 1962 to August 1991. He graduated from the Urals Polytechnical Institute in 1966 and the Sverdlovsk extra-mural Higher Party School, Party Central Committee in 1974. He began his working career in 1956 as a metal cutter in the Urals coach building enterprise, and served in the Soviet army (1959-62). After graduating from the polytechnical institute he worked as deputy head of a shop in a plastics enterprise, and in 1967 he was appointed to the city Party committee, Nizhny Tagil. In 1972 he became first secretary of the Nizhny Tagil city Party committee, and in 1977 he was elected secretary of the Sverdlovsk Party *obkom*. In 1982 he moved to Moscow to work in the department of organizational Party work, Party Central Committee.

In 1985 he returned to Sverdlovsk as first secretary of the Party *obkom*. During the summer of 1988 he was appointed USSR ambassador to Cuba, and struck up a good relationship with Fidel Castro. He was a member of the Central Committee, CPSU (1986-90) and a delegate to the XXVII Party congress at which he spoke on economic cost accounting. He was a deputy of the USSR Supreme Soviet until 1989, and regards himself as a recognized master of organizing conferences and filling in important documents. He has been friends with Boris Yeltsin for over 20 years.

In late July 1991 he was appointed head of administration of the President of the RSFSR, the apparatus of which consisted overwhelmingly of former officials of the Party Central Committee chosen for their professional expertise. After the collapse of the attempted state coup in August 1991, the Party Central Committee building was taken over on the orders of Petrov, and the commission of the Russian President on the listing and disposal of the property of the CPSU, after Party property had been identified, was dissolved by him. He regards his task as administrative and political, and he defined himself simultaneously as a democrat, a centrist and a pragmatic conservative. Democratic Russia and Civic Union were placed by him on the reform wing. He was sympathetic to the Cuban regime and its leaders and did not believe that the time had yet come to evaluate the tragic Soviet history of the communist period.

He offered his resignation in late April 1992 but the President did not accept it, but he retired from his post as head of administration in January 1993 and was replaced by Sergei Filatov. Petrov advocates compromise and the retention of the administrative élite and is against wholesale sackings. He supports the market economy, and is sharply critical of the impoverishment of the majority of the population, the depreciation of savings, the growth of crime, speculation, drug taking, drunkenness, the decline of morality and legal protection. He believes that reforms should be implemented in a more professional manner, and has sympathy for moderate leaders like Nikolai Travkin. He believes that Soviet citizens lived in a perverted, severe system but that there were also good sides to it. He advocates the retention of the moral and ethical values of society and conservative views which permit the retention and use of everything that is positive.

On February 5, 1993, by presidential decree, Petrov was appointed chairman of the Russian state investment corporation and he was given the task of establishing it. He favours the structural reform of the economy, which he feels should concentrate on meeting the needs of the public. Tax revenues should not be wasted and the market should be replete with goods and food. Referenda can be useful and other ways of reaching agreement among public and political forces should not be ruled out.

He has two orders of the Red Banner of Labour. He is a convinced teetotaller and loves fishing and mushroom picking. In summer he plays volleyball and in winter enjoys skiing. He has time to read the newspapers but not literature and the last book he read was on Parkinson's law. He is married with two sons and grandchildren; his wife was an engineer in a shop and taught in an institute but does not work at present. His son studied at the University of Havana, Cuba, then at Moscow State University. Petrov lives in Moscow.

Petrovsky, Vladimir Petrovich

First deputy Minister of Foreign Affairs of the Russian Federation; deputy UN Secretary General; director-general of the European Department of the UN.

Born on April 29, 1933 in Volgograd; Russian. He was a member of the CPSU from 1963 to August 1991. He graduated in 1957 from the Moscow State Institute of International Relations, USSR Ministry of Foreign Affairs, and then began his career in the ministry. Later he successfully presented his candidate dissertation in history (PhD) and his doctoral dissertation in history (DLitt), and also successfully presented his candidate dissertation in law (LLM). He was a member of the permanent Soviet delegation to the UN (1957-61); he worked in the department of international organizations, the secretariat of the

USSR Ministry of Foreign Affairs (1961-64); in the UN secretariat (1964-71); in the administration for the drafting of foreign political measures, USSR Ministry of Foreign Affairs (1971-78); then head of this department (1978-79); head of the department of international organizations in the ministry, (1979-86); deputy USSR Minister of Foreign Affairs (1986-August 1991); and first deputy USSR Minister of Foreign Affairs (September-December 1991). He was a key adviser on US affairs.

In 1992 he was appointed deputy Secretary General of the UN for political questions; and was also made head of the special working group for the preparation of the speeches of the UN Secretary General on raising the profile of the UN in the contemporary world. He was head of delegations at various international conferences, and was the Russian representative in the council of co-operation, NATO; was deputy head of the Russian delegation at the Moscow organizational conference for the regulation of the Middle East conflict; and a member of the council of directors of many Russian and international organizations.

He has published six books, including *Diplomacy of Downing Street*; *American Foreign Policy Thinking*; *The Doctrine of National Security and the Global Strategy of the USA*; *Security in the Nuclear Space Era*. He is one of the editors of the five-volume work on the *History of Diplomacy* and he has over 100 articles to his name. Some of his works have been published in the US, Mexico, Germany, Czechoslovakia, Hungary and Bulgaria. He has state awards. He speaks English and lives in Geneva.

Piatachenko, Hryhorii Oleksandrovych

Minister of Finance, Ukraine.

Born into a Ukrainian family in 1932. He graduated as an economist from Lviv Institute of Trade and Economics in 1956. He then worked as an accountant, joining the Ukrainian Ministry of Agriculture in 1966, and successfully presented his candidate dissertation in economics on "Questions of the control of losses in production in 1970" (PhD (Econ)). In 1984 he became head of the finance department in the Ukrainian SSR's Gosplan, in July 1991 deputy Minister of Finance, and in October 1991 Minister.

Piatachenko has long been in favour of introducing a Ukrainian currency, and he created a good early impression as a potential radical reformer by appointing two Ukrainian-Americans, Oleh Havrylyshyn and George Urchasin as his deputies. However Piatachenko's period in office has been beset by many practical difficulties, and by problems with establishing his department's competence in rivalry with the National Bank of Ukraine and the Ministry of Economics. Piatachenko was largely responsible for the introduction of the convertible coupon into the Ukrainian economy in January 1992, but was unable to control its rate of emission and prevent its subsequent loss of value (it was eventually worth less than the ruble).

Nevertheless he has good relations with nationalists such as Dmytro Pavlychko, which helped to smooth his reappointment in October 1992. In November 1992 he was appointed a member of the newly-formed State Commission for Monetary Reform, designed to guide Ukraine's departure out of the ruble zone after its formal withdrawal on November 7, 1992. He is married. His wife is a pensioner and they have two daughters, both of whom are industrial economists.

Official (Ministry) address: 252008 Kiev, Vul. M. Hrushevskoho 12/2; *telephone*: Kiev 226 2044.

Pilipovic, Uladzimir Antonavic

Director of the Institute of Electronics, Belarusian Academy of Sciences.

Born on January 5, 1931 in the village of Slabada, Mazyr *raion*, Homiel *oblast*. His parents are Anton and Lida Pilipovic, and the family is Belarusian. He graduated in 1957 from the Belarusian State University, Minsk, and from 1957 to 1971 he worked in the Institute of Physics, Belarusian Academy of Sciences. From 1971 to 1973 he was head of the electronics laboratory of the Academy, and since 1973 has been director of the Institute of Electronics of the Academy. From 1979 to 1985 he was chief academic secretary of the Presidium of the Academy.

He is currently not a member of any political party, but views himself as a democrat. His hobbies are literature and the visual arts, and he speaks English. His wife's name is Klarysa and they have two sons, Siarhiej and Ihar. He was awarded the Red Banner of Labour and is an "honoured scientific worker" of the Republic of Belarus.

Address: Minks, pr. Maserava 47, kv. 228; *telephone:* Minsk (0172) 65 61 51 (work); 23 08 91 (home).

Plachynda, Serhii Petrovych

Leader of the Ukrainian Peasants' Democratic Party.

Born into a Ukrainian family in 1928 in a hamlet in Kirovohrad *oblast* in central Ukraine. His father had received 10 hectares of land after the 1917 revolution and tried to make his way as a small farmer, but was arrested for resisting collectivization, and the young Serhii's earliest memories were of the Great Famine from 1932 to 1933. Nevertheless he secured a place in the faculty of philology at Kiev State University, graduating in 1953. He then began postgraduate studies and successfully presented his candidate dissertation (PhD), after which he worked in the editorial departments of the Kiev literary papers *Literaturna Ukraïna* and *Molod*. A member of the Writers' Union of Ukraine, he has over 500 publications to his name, including both poetry and prose.

He was a member of the Communist Party of Ukraine (CPU) until 1990, but combined his membership with opposition politics. He was the first chairman of the ecological movement *Zelenyi svit* from 1987 to 1988, and in June 1990 he became one of the co-leaders of the Ukrainian Peasants' Democratic Party (UPDP) at its founding congress, and its outright head in January 1991. The party campaigns for the revival of traditional Ukrainian village life, including small-scale private farming.

Although initially formed under the influence of moderate centrists such as Ihor Yukhnovskyi, the UPDP quickly fell under the influence of Plachynda's radical brand of nationalism. Plachynda has argued that national interests should be placed above civil rights, and has pressed for the Ukrainianization of the Ukrainian Armed forces and state. At the fourth *Rukh* congress in December 1992 he caused a storm by suggesting that Ukraine should sell its nuclear warheads to Iraq and Libya for hard currency. Plachynda's ultra-radicalism and fiery character has inhibited the growth of the UPDP, which remains largely confined to its peasant stronghold in Galicia.

The UPDP has pressed for the privatization of the land, but has found it extremely difficult to subvert the entrenched authority of the collective farm chairmen, who had successfully blocked significant agricultural reform in the Supreme Soviet up to 1992.

Address: 290061 Lviv, Vul. Volodymyr Velykoho 2; *telephone*: (Lviv) 35 3288.

Pliushch, Ivan Stepanovych

Speaker of the Supreme Soviet of Ukraine.

Like his close ally Kravchuk, Pliushch is a typical peasant product of post-war social mobility in Ukraine. He was born into a peasant family in Chernihiv in northern Ukraine, and retains a rough manner and even rougher Ukrainian accent. He was educated at the Ukrainian Agricultural Academy, and later at the Academy of Social Sciences of the CPSU Central Committee, Moscow. After initial work on collective farms, he graduated to Party work in 1975 in the agricultural department of the Kiev *oblast* Party *apparat*. By 1984 he was in charge of the Kiev *oblast* Party committee, and after the March 1990 local elections took over the leadership of the Kiev *oblast* soviet. However, in March 1990, he had also secured election (on the second round) to the Ukrainian Supreme Soviet as people's deputy for Makarivskyi *raion*, Kiev *oblast*. After being elected First Deputy Chairman of the Supreme Soviet in June 1990, Pliushch gave up his position on the *oblast* soviet.

After Leonid Kravchuk was elected Ukraine's first executive President on December 1, 1991, Pliushch was elected to replace him as Speaker of the

Supreme Soviet with 261 votes on December 5. He is an *ex officio* member of the Presidium of the Supreme Soviet and of the Defence Council. He was a member of the Communist Party of Ukraine right up to August 24, 1991 (the day of Ukraine's Declaration of Independence).

Firstly as Kravchuk's deputy, then Speaker himself of the Supreme Soviet, Pliushch has risen to a position of unquestioned pre-eminence in the legislature. Given that parliamentary factions are still relatively underdeveloped, he has been able to dominate proceedings through his brusque personality and his control of all questions of timetabling and procedure. The Supreme Soviet's Secretariat has been headed by a close ally of Pliushch's, Leonid Horovyi, since January 1992.

Pliushch's robust style often makes a mockery of formality, and has also meant that his more diplomatic deputy, Vasyl Durdynets, is more often used to front negotiations with foreign states and parliaments. Although initially a protégé of Kravchuk's, there were growing signs in autumn 1992 that Pliushch was beginning to build an independent base for himself in the Supreme Soviet. His public criticism of Prime Minister Fokin in September probably sealed the latter's fate, and in October he appeared to side with the Supreme Soviet against Kravchuk in its preference for Kuchma over Symonenko as Fokin's replacement as Prime Minister.

In a series of interviews he attacked President Kravchuk's unconstitutional accumulation of power, and in November 1992 emergency powers to run the economy were duly transferred from President to Premier. He has also begun to pose as the champion of the rights of local soviet administrations, under threat from the system of presidential prefects established in March 1992. In December 1992 Pliushch steered a compromise bill through the Supreme Soviet, which restored many of the powers of the local soviets at the prefects' expense. Kravchuk was predictably incensed and threatened to veto the bill.

Official address: Kiev, Vul. M. Hrushevskoho 5; *telephone*: Kiev 252 019.

Pochinok, Aleksandr Petrovich

Chairman of the commission of the Council of the Republic, Russian Supreme Soviet, on the budget, plans, taxes and prices.

Born on January 12, 1958 in Chelyabinsk; Russian. He was a member of the CPSU until August 1991. He graduated from Chelyabinsk Polytechnical Institute, then from the postgraduate school, Institute of Economics, USSR Academy of Sciences, and successfully presented his candidate dissertation in economics (PhD (Econ)). All his economic research concerns Chelyabinsk *oblast*. He was one of the authors of the concept of territorial cost accounting *(khozraschet)* in the *oblast*. In 1980 he became a senior scientific assistant in the Chelyabinsk branch of the Institute of Economics, Urals branch of the USSR Academy of Sciences.

He was nominated for election as an RSFSR people's deputy in the No. 81 Chelyabinsk territorial district by the collectives of the State Institute for the Design of Metallurgical Plants, the first Chelyabinsk assembly administration and the scientific research institute for measurement, Polet production association. During the election campaign he advocated real power to the soviets; full sovereignty for Russia and Russia to be afforded all the rights of a Union republic; the independence of enterprises and the transfer of land to farm workers; the indexation of incomes to take inflation into account; and banning the construction of environmentally harmful enterprises in Chelyabinsk *oblast*.

There were six candidates and Pochinok won in the second round, polling 57.6% of the votes. His main opponent was A. I. Krinitsyn, an electric welder, who received 32.7% of the votes in the second round. Pochinok was elected a member of the RSFSR Supreme Soviet at the I Congress of People's Deputies (623 voted for, 300 voted against). He was a member of the Supreme Soviet committee on inter-republican relations, regional policy and co-operation; deputy chairman of the Council of the Republic commission on the budget, plans, taxes and prices, and in 1992 he was elected chairman of the commission. He is married with a daughter, and is fond of the arts.

Address: 103274 Moscow, K 274, Krasnopresnenskaya nab., d. 2,. Dom Sovetov; *telephone*: Moscow 205 67 31.

Podgornov, Nikolai Mikhailovich

Head of the Administration of Vologda *oblast*, Russian Federation.

Born on May 15, 1949 in the village of Lezhdom, Gryazovetsky *raion*, Vologda *oblast* into a collective farmer's family; Russian; member of the CPSU until the end of 1990. In 1965 he graduated from the Velikoustyug Marine Technical School as a specialist in steam power plants, and was then a machinist, assistant to a mechanic on motor ships of the Kotlassky river steamship company, and a fitter on the Sidorovsky state farm, Gryazovetsky *raion*. In 1969 he was elected secretary of the *Komsomol* organization of the state farm. In 1971 he entered the Soviet Army and after being demobbed in 1973 he was chairman of the trade union committee and secretary of the *Komsomol* organization of the Zarya collective farm, Gryazovetsky *raion*. In 1976 he was appointed director of the Demyanovsky state farm and in 1979 director of the Avrora state farm, Gryazovetsky *raion*. Later the Avrora state farm was transformed into a collective share-owning farm. He completed three years at the all-Union institute of law as an external student. In 1988 he was elected a delegate to the XIX Party conference and member of the Vologda Party *obkom*. He was awarded the order of badge of honour.

In early 1990 he was nominated by the work collective of the Avrora state farm for election as an RSFSR people's deputy in the No. 332 Sokolsky territorial district, Vologda *oblast*. During the election campaign he advocated radical economic reform, the transfer of land to collectives or private ownership to those who wanted to work it. There were four candidates, and Podgornov polled 30.7% of the votes in the first round and won the second round, polling 49.3% of the votes. His main opponent was B. V. Zhdanov, director of the Totemsky state farm, who received 26.6% of the votes in the first round and 43.3% in the second. Podgornov was a member of the higher economic council of the Presidium of the Supreme Soviet.

In October 1991 at the session of the Vologda *oblast* soviet three candidates were proposed to the President for the post of head of the administration of the *oblast*: N. M. Podgornov, A. A. Titov, chairman of the *oblast* soviet executive committee, and V. I. Tarasov, first deputy chairman of the *oblast* soviet executive committee. In October 1991 Podgornov was appointed head of the administration of Vologda *oblast* by presidential decree. On assuming office he stated that he supported a free economy and the development of the social sphere based on a regional tax policy and the exploitation of local natural resources.

During the summer and in December 1992 Podgornov twice refused to become Minister of Agriculture of the Russian Federation. In December 1992, during the VII Congress of People's Deputies, he spoke out in support of the Gaidar government and hoped that the reforms would be continued under the new government of Viktor Chernomyrdin. He appealed for agreement between the various branches of state power in order to continue the economic and political reforms. He viewed the congress as full of good-for-nothings and supported the proposal of the President to conduct a referendum on confidence in various state authorities. He is married with two children and lives in the village of Braskoe, Gryazovetsky *raion*, Vologda *oblast*.

Podkolzin, Evgeny Nikolaevich

Commander of Airborne troops. Colonel-General.

Born on April 18, 1936 in the village of Lepsinsk, Andreevsky *raion*, Taldy-Kurgan *oblast*. Russian. He graduated from the Airborne Technical School in 1958; the M. V. Frunze Military Academy in 1973; the Military Academy of the General Staff in 1982. He received a higher military education and was a member of the CPSU till August 1991.

He began his career as an officer as a commander of an airborne platoon. Then he was a commander of a reconnaissance company of a guards airborne division and Chief of Staff of an airborne battalion. He proved himself a highly qualified commander, good at personnel training. He engaged in a number of important exercises in mass parachute jumping and planned operations in the enemy's rear. His unit took part in the intervention in Czechoslovakia in 1968. He actively participated in the work of the Party organization.

After the Academy in 1973 he was appointed commander of a guards airborne regiment, thereby outstripping many of his fellow graduates. After a year he was promoted to deputy commander of a guards airborne division. Col. E. Podkolzin was known as an officer with a sound operational-tactical and military-technical training, ready to carry out orders without demur. In 1976 he became a divisional commander. He served in the 40th army in Afghanistan for some time, and took part in military operations against the *mujahidin* and in pacifying the population. He was in close contact with many of the present military leaders of Russia who were participants in the Afghan war.

In 1982 he was appointed first deputy Chief of Staff of airborne troops and in 1986 Chief of Staff and first deputy commander of airborne troops. He himself supervised the planning and organization of airborne troops training and is responsible for their use in ethnic conflicts and operations against national-democratic movements in the republics of Russia and Russian democratic organizations. He fully supported the policy of the communist regime of the USSR both at home and abroad.

It was Gen. E. Podkolzin who organized the use of airborne units and formations in Transcaucasia and the Baltic during the anti-constitutional putsch in August 1991.

Podkolzin's behaviour during the putsch caused him to be regarded with some suspicion by the democratic military organizations. However, the support of Gen. Pavel Grachev helped him win the trust of the new leaders of Russia.

On August 31, 1991 Lieut.-Gen. E. Podkolzin was appointed commander of airborne troops. He was soon promoted to Colonel-General.

He enjoys the respect of the troops and is a well-trained military professional. He succeeds in training and ensuring the combat readiness of the airborne troops, which are at present one of the few types of armed forces to be well organized and capable of quick and decisive action. He does not normally express his political views in public, playing the role of a commander loyal to the state. He is against the use of troops inside the country, except in peace-enforcement missions and to support Russian armed forces in flash-points on the territory of the former USSR. In his relations with the present Russian authorities he is a conformist. He makes no secret of his favourable attitude towards national-patriotic movements and advocates the supremacy of the state. In the sphere of military construction he supports the ideas of reforming the armed forces to meet the demands of present-day warfare.

No information about his hobbies is available. He goes in for sport and enjoys parachute jumping. He does not speak any foreign language and has not been abroad as a member of an official delegation. He has been awarded orders "For service to the motherland in the armed forces of the USSR", 3rd class, the order of the Red Star, and more than 10 medals. He is married.

Office address: 103175, Moscow, K-175.

Podoprigora, Vladimir Nikolaevich

Deputy Head of the Administration of the President of the Russian Federation.

Born in 1954 in Mozhgo, Mozhginsky *raion*, Udmurt Autonomous Soviet Socialist Republic (ASSR); Russian; member of the CPSU until August 1991; received higher education. He was first deputy chairman, Mozhgo city soviet executive committee, responsible for services.

He withdrew as a candidate for election as a USSR people's deputy in 1989 because he was neither an Udmurt nor a country dweller, but in early 1990 he was nominated for election as an RSFSR people's deputy in the No. 135 Kamsky national territorial district, Udmurt ASSR. During the election campaign he advocated economic reform, a transition to territorial cost accounting and the restoration of social justice when distributing state funds. He suggested the transfer of financial and economic power to the soviets, the restoration of social justice with regard to women, the creation of good conditions for the bringing up of children, the adoption of a mechanism for the calculation of pensions and their indexing and for real autonomy for enterprises in the distribution of their profits. There should be legislation on the activities of local soviets, the levelling of the standard of living of urban and rural dwellers, and of inhabitants in small cities and capital cities.

He advocated the sovereignty of Russia in a renewed Union, and the establishment in it of Russia's own party, laws and capital. He opposed regional cost accounting in the form it was being proposed, believing this would merely create the councils of the national economy which had existed from 1957 to 1965. Ministries and authorities should be abolished, work collectives should have full autonomy and taxes should come down from 60-80% to 30-35%. He proposed a multi-party system and the elimination of specialist distributors. The family should be supported and he believed that giving economic support to the mother for three years was better than providing crèches. The group of deputies, "for a democratic Russia", supported him during the election campaign.

There were five candidates. He polled 17.1% of the votes in the first round and won the second round, polling 50.6% of the votes. His main opponent was E. S. Berdinsky, senior foreman of shop No. 5, Sarapulsky electrical generating production association, who received 16.8% of the votes in the first round and 34.9% in the second.

At the I Congress of RSFSR People's Deputies in June 1990 Podoprigora was elected a member of the RSFSR Supreme Soviet. He was deputy chairman of the Supreme Soviet committee on inter-republican relations, regional policy and co-operation.

He believes that the Supreme Soviet has yet to acquire a firm base which could be of assistance in the legislative process. A specialist parliamentary centre, including the parliamentary library, an information and research institute and a political institute, should be set up. He is a supporter of Democratic Russia and at the VII Congress of People's Deputies, in December 1992, there was a motion to remove him from office. In 1993 he moved to the apparatus of the President and became deputy head of the administration of the president. He is married and there are four persons in his family. His home is in Mozhgo, Udmurtia and he is living at present in Moscow.

Polenov, Fedor Dmitrievich

Chairman of the commission on culture, Council of the Republic, Russian Supreme Soviet.

Born on June 21, 1929 in Moscow; Russian. He was a member of the CPSU from 1958 to August 1991. He is the grandson of the famous Russian artist, V. D. Polenov, and lived with his parents in Polenovo until 1937 as his father was director of the museum there. He lived and studied in Moscow (1937-45), and during this time his father was a victim of the Stalinist terror. After finishing school in 1947 he entered the M. V. Frunze Naval Technical School and graduated in 1951. After graduation he served on several ships of the Soviet Navy and advanced to the rank of captain. In 1962 he became director of the state museum of the artist, V. F. Polenov, Zaoksky *raion*, Moscow *oblast*, and under his direction the museum became famous worldwide. In 1984, due to his efforts, the construction was halted of an experimental biochemical plant in Tarus, on the banks of the river Oka, which threatened to pollute the river. Over the years from 1962 to 1990 he prevented 18 attempts to build industrial enterprises in the nature reserves of the region. He is chairman of the committee for the defence of the river Oka and was a member of the USSR union of writers. He has published eight books and other publications about the museum, and is an honoured cultural worker of the RSFSR.

He was nominated for election as an RSFSR People's Deputy in the No. 706 Aleksinsky territorial district, Tula *oblast*. During the election campaign he advocated the establishment of a national park in the basin of the river Oka, its tributaries and all natural resources flowing into it, which was to serve as a model for those living in contiguous *raions* of central Russia. He believed that the Procurator's office should introduce an agency to supervise the environment, and that local soviets should be responsible for control over national parks. Russian Federation law should pay more attention to the environment, the construction of cultural establishments, the protection of society and the morality of the younger generation. Rivers, reservoirs and forests should have records kept of their use.

There were eight candidates. In the first round Polenov polled 38% of the votes and he won in the second round, polling 52.9% of the votes. His main opponent was A. Yu. Kuzmichev, director of the Zybino state stud farm, Yasnogorsky *raion*, Tula *oblast*, who received 21.7% of the votes in the first round and 35.6% in the second. Polenov was elected a member of the RSFSR Supreme Soviet at the I Congress of People's Deputies (727 voted for, 192 voted against), and was elected chairman of the Council of the Republic's commission on culture on July 3, 1990. He is also a member of the Supreme

Soviet committee on the freedom of conscience, religion, mercy and charity; a member of the Chernobyl group; and of the group on education, science and culture. On January 22, 1992 he was elected a member of the commission for awarding state prizes of the Russian Federation in literature and art. He is chairman of the central council of the all-Russian society for the maintenance of historical and cultural monuments. He was awarded five medals, including one for combat service. His wife, Natalya Nikolaevna (neé Gramolina), is director of the V. D. Polenov museum. They have children and grandchildren.

Address: 103274 Moscow, K 274, Krasnopresnenskaya nab., d. 2, Dom Sovetov; *telephone*: Moscow 205 42 88.

Polezhaev, Leonid Konstantinovich

Head of the Administration of Omsk *oblast*, Russian Federation.

Born in 1940 in Omsk; Russian; member of the CPSU from 1969 to August 1991. After school he worked as a blacksmith in the V. V. Kuibyshev factory, Petropavlovsk, Kazakhstan, and in 1956 he graduated from the Institute of Agriculture, Omsk and in 1986 from the Academy of Social Sciences of the Party Central Committee. After graduating from the Omsk institute he worked as a foreman and work superintendent in the *Tselinkraivodstroi* construction administration, chief engineer of the *oblast* administration of amelioration and water economy, deputy head of the *oblast* administration of agriculture, and manager of the *Irtyshsovkhozstroi* and *Pavlodarvodstroi* trusts, Kazakhstan. From 1976 to 1982 he was head of the administration of the *Irtyshkanalstroi* association, Karaganda, Kazakhstan. In 1982 he transferred to work in the soviets and from 1982 to 1987 he was first deputy chairman of Karaganda *oblast* soviet executive committee. From 1987 to 1989 he was head of the *Omskvodmelioratsiya* association for amelioration and the water economy and in 1989 was appointed head of the main economic planning department of Omsk *oblast* soviet executive committee, then acted as chairman of the committee. He is the recipient of orders of the Red Banner of Labour and the badge of honour, and medals.

In early 1990 he was nominated for election as an RSFSR people's deputy in the No. 536 Kuibyshev territorial district, Omsk *oblast*. In his election programme, entitled "No to an economy without ecology!", he advocated an economy for people and opposed the dictates of the branch authorities which threaten local interests. He was in favour of the sovereignty of Russia and the renaissance of its national honour. He supported the development of a multi-faceted economy. He worked on the project to reverse the flow of the northern rivers to the south, came to oppose it and was in conflict with the USSR Ministry of the Water Economy.

There were nine candidates. Polezhaev polled 12% of the votes in the first round but lost in the second round, polling 39.6% of the votes. The winner was O. G. Smolin, assistant professor at the State Pedagogical Institute, who received 12.5% of the votes in the first round and 46% in the second. Polezhaev was also elected a deputy of the Omsk *oblast* soviet in 1990, and at its first session on March 31, 1991 he was elected chairman of the *oblast* soviet executive committee.

On August 22, 1991 the declaration of the Presidium and *oblast* soviet executive committee stated that the legally elected state authorities were functioning in the *oblast*, a state of emergency would not be introduced and it appealed for calm and restraint, stating that the population should refrain from any illegal activities.

Polezhaev was appointed head of the administration of Omsk *oblast* on November 11, 1991 by presidential decree. On assuming office he advocated the development of interregional and foreign economic ties, the creation of a single economic space and co-operation with commercial structures. He appealed for co-operation with all political forces, and for Swedish socialism as the model for the economic and social development of the country. In December 1992, during the VII Congress of People's Deputies, he supported the strategic direction of reform and opposed unnecessary changes in the government. He lives in Omsk.

Polosin, Vyacheslav Sergeevich

Chairman of the Russian Supreme Soviet committee on freedom of conscience, religion, mercy and charity.

Born on June 26, 1956 in Moscow where his father was a worker; Russian. In 1973 he graduated from a school where he obtained an advanced knowledge of German, and in 1978 graduated from Moscow State University. After graduation he worked as a specialist in educational methods at the all-Union Institute of Cinematography. In 1980 he left the institute to serve in the Rozhdestvensky (Russian Orthodox) church in the village of Besedy, Leninsky *raion*, Moscow *oblast*, and he studied for two years at the Moscow theological seminary of the Russian Orthodox church in Sergiev Posad (Zagorsk). After graduating from the seminary in 1983 he served as a priest in churches in Tashkent, Uzbekistan, Frunze (Bishkek), Kyrgyzstan, and Dushanbe, Tajikistan. He also worked as an adviser in the publishing house of the Moscow Patriarchate, and in 1988 became a dean of the Russian Orthodox St Boris and St Gleb church, Obninsk, Kaluga *oblast*.

He was nominated for election as an RSFSR people's deputy in the No. 42 Kaluga national territorial district, Kaluga *oblast*. During the election campaign he advocated the spiritual purification and transformation of society, maintaining that these form the basis of all progressive social and economic changes. He spoke of the need to spread religious morality and to bring up children according to God's commandments, and on the foundation of the moral health of society. He proposed, on a voluntary basis, introducing the religious education of children and adults in schools, institutes and churches and to provide those who wished with a bible, the lives of the saints and other religious publications. It was desirable for the church to provide assistance to old people's homes, hospitals, prisons, children's homes and children's sections of police stations. He proposed the establishment of a republican institute of charity whose members would give free medical and spiritual assistance to the aged, lonely, sick and invalids. He advocated ideologically free laws, political pluralism and the holding of free elections. Land should be handed over to private ownership but only to those who work it.

He supported the existence of various types of economic activity, decentralization and the equality of different types of property ownership. The introduction of complete people's and workers' control was needed to counter the mafia, speculation, commercial and services crime and to gain control over the distribution of goods and products in short supply. He advocated the abolition of all the privileges of the nomenclature and for a sharp reduction in the size of the administrative apparatus at all levels. He demanded strict environmental control by the public and experts including the right of veto over the decisions of the authorities. There were 13 candidates. In the first round Polosin polled 23.6% of the votes and won the second round, polling 41.1% of the votes. His main opponent was V. A. Brukhnov, RSFSR Minister of Road Transport, who received 10.9% of the votes in the first round and 33% in the second. Polosin is a member of the Council of Nationalities and a member of the Presidium of the Supreme Soviet. On July 2, 1990 he was elected chairman of the Supreme Soviet committee on the freedom of conscience, religion, mercy and charity. He is married and speaks German.

Address: 103274 Moscow, K 274, Krasnopresnenskaya nab., d. 2, Dom Sovetov; *telephone*: Moscow 205 53 05.

Poltoranin, Mikhail Nikiforovich

Head of the Federal Information Centre, Office of the President of the Russian Federation.

Born on November 22, 1939 in Leninogorsk, east Kazakhstan *oblast* into a Russian family. There were four children and his father was killed in action during the Great Fatherland War (1941-45). His mother was illiterate. After school he worked as labourer on the construction of the Bratsk hydroelectric power station, and between 1958 and 1961 he served in the Soviet Army in the Soviet Far East. He was a member of the CPSU from 1961 to 1990.

In 1968 he graduated from the faculty of journalism of the Kazakh State University, Alma Ata. Between 1964 and 1968 he was a correspondent of the *Rudny Altai* and *Leninogorskaya pravda* newspapers, then their editor, then deputy editor-in-chief of the newspaper *Kazakhstanskaya pravda*, the official organ of the Communist Party of Kazakhstan. In 1970 he graduated from the

Higher Party School of the Central Committee, CPSU, after two years' study. From 1975 to 1978 he was *Pravda* correspondent in Kazakhstan, and between 1978 and 1986 was a special correspondent of *Pravda*. During the spring of 1986 he published a series of articles in *Pravda* on abuse of power by Party workers, police and KGB in Voroshilovgrad, Ukraine (now Lugansk), which produced a tremendous impression and made Poltoranin a household name.

In early January 1987 he became editor of the newspaper *Moskovskaya pravda* with the active support of Boris Yeltsin, at that time first secretary of the Moscow city Party organization. He was one of the few members of the Moscow Party organization who did not turn against Yeltsin after his removal from office in November 1987. Poltoranin was dismissed as editor-in-chief of *Moskovskaya pravda* in January 1988 as a result of the intervention of Lev Zaikov, a conservative member of the Party Politburo. The pretext was an article by L. Kolodny on the renaming of a number of Moscow streets bearing the names of close Stalin associates.

He began work as a *Novosti* political observer in the spring of 1988. In March 1989 he was elected a USSR people's deputy, representing the USSR Union of Journalists. He was elected a member of the USSR Supreme Soviet committee on the questions of *glasnost* and the rights and appeals of citizens, and during this period he defined Bolshevism as an extremist ideology which suppressed personality, destroyed national culture and placed the interests of one class above those of others. At the IV Congress of People's Deputies he voted for the concept of the introduction of private ownership of property. In July 1990 he was appointed Minister of the Press and Media of the Russian Federation.

After the abortive coup of August 1991 he supported the setting up of an RSFSR Supreme Soviet commission on the activities of the CPSU. He made quite clear that the main task of his ministry was to depoliticize the mass media, to provide the same opportunities for all parties and movements to express their views and to strengthen the financial base of local publishing houses (under the supervision of local soviets). He did not think the ministry should be responsible for the private media. Despite arguing in favour of treating all aspects of the media equally, Poltoranin quite clearly supported some large houses whose publications he regarded as beneficial. There were many disputes between him and Ivan Silaev, the Prime Minister, in September 1991, and eventually the government resigned. He was considered as a possible candidate for the post of Prime Minister.

In November 1991 when the new "reform government" took over he retained his post. He is a close confidante of President Boris Yeltsin and is influential in shaping the policy of the Russian government. At the end of February 1992 he was made deputy Prime Minister while retaining his ministerial post. He vigorously attacked the old *nomenklatura*, accusing them of engaging in secret and later open opposition in parliament and outside to the policies of President Yeltsin. He called on all democrats to unite to combat the old guard by making use of the radio, television and print media to propagate their views.

He was successful in keeping former communist leaders out of the media until the second half of 1992. Then as a consequence of the shifting balance of power they became more prominent, especially after those accused of involvement in the abortive August coup were released from detention, pending their trial. Poltoranin was a special target of the industrial lobby and all those to the right of Civic Union. Eventually Yeltsin was forced to compromise with his opponents and Poltoranin was dismissed in November 1992.

Poltoranin adopted a hardline position in the conflict with Chechnia and supported those who were attempting to remove President Dudaev. He also advocated prosecuting Russian national interests *vis-à-vis* Ukraine. President Yeltsin set up a federal information centre in January 1993, an agency attached to the President's office and headed by Poltoranin in order to keep him at the centre of politics. Poltoranin's brief was as before, to propagate the views of the President and government in such a way as to win support among the population for economic reform and democracy.

Poltoranin loves vodka and the Saturday evening parties with President Yeltsin and Gennady Burbulis at the presidential dacha have become notorious, leading to the three of them being dubbed the vodka troika. His favourite writers are Fedor Dostoevsky and Lev Tolstoy and he is especially attracted to their diaries. Poltoranin does not regard himself as an atheist, believing in a higher reason, and Immanuel Kant is his favourite philosopher. He is fond of sport and is a master of sport in Graeco-Roman wrestling. He is married with two sons and lives in Moscow.

Poluyanov, Nikolai Andreevich

Head of the Administration of Komi-Permyak Autonomous *oblast*, Russian Federation.

Born in 1952 in the village of Parfenovo Deminsky, Kudymkara *raion*, Komi-Permyak autonomous *oblast*; member of the CPSU until August 1991. After secondary school he attended the Perm Finance Technical College and then graduated from the faculty of economics, Perm State University. He worked for ten years in the financial organizations of Kudymkara *raion* and *okrug*, beginning as an inspector and ending as head of the financial department of the *okrug*. In 1983 he was nominated for the post of chairman of Yusvinsky *raion* soviet executive committee, but declined the offer. He was an instructor of the Kudymkara city Party committee. In 1986 he was appointed deputy chairman of the *okrug* economic agro-industrial committee, and in 1988 was elected chairman of the *raion* soviet executive committee of Kudymkara, Komi-Permyak autonomous *oblast*. He was also a member of the Kudymkara city Party bureau.

In March 1990 he was elected a deputy of the Perm *oblast* soviet of people's deputies and at the first session in Perm he was elected to the Presidium of the soviet. At the first session of the Kudymkara *raion* soviet he was elected chairman of the *raion* executive committee of the city of Kudymkara. On December 14, 1991 he was appointed head of the administration of the Komi-Permyak autonomous *oblast* by presidential decree.

On assuming office he stated that he was in favour of real economic reform and that his main task was to implement a social programme which would soften the blows of the market. He believed that economic transformation should not proceed spontaneously but gradually and logically. The local administration could co-operate with local enterprises, for example, in the construction of roads. Politically the most important thing was the extension of democracy; although he conceded that he was not yet a democrat, nevertheless he was attracted to the idea.

In December 1992, during the VII Congress of People's Deputies, he declared that the healthy elements in the congress should end their opposition to the government and President of Russia. He supported the President but saw the need for changes in the government while retaining a core of ministers. He is married with a son and lives in Kudymkara.

Popov, Gavriil Kharitonovich

Member of the Council of the President of the Russian Federation.

Born in 1936 in Moscow; Greek; member of the CPSU (1959-90). In 1959 he graduated with honours from the economics faculty, Moscow State University and is an economist and lecturer in political economy. In 1963 he successfully presented his candidate dissertation in economics on "The use of information-logical machines in the management of the economy" (PhD (Econ)). From 1960 to 1961 he was secretary of the *Komsomol* committee, Moscow State University, and after completing his candidate dissertation he joined the staff of the university. In 1970 he successfully presented his doctoral dissertation in economics on "Methodological problems of the theory of the management of socialist public production" (DSc (Econ)).

In 1971 he was head of one of the first departments of management, and from 1977 to 1980 he was dean of the faculty of economics, Moscow State University. From 1988 he was editor-in-chief of the journal *Voprosy ekonomiki*. He is a professor and the author of over 100 articles and many journalistic articles. He was awarded the Lomonosov prize in 1986 which he donated to the rebuilding of Solovetsky monastery. Popov has researched the Soviet economy and demonstrated the impossibility of creating a modern, effective economy within the framework of an administrative command system. He has analysed the problems of radical state economic and organizational reforms which attempt to bring into being a modern society.

In early 1989 Popov was nominated for election as a USSR people's deputy by the union of the USSR scientific and engineering societies and was elected. He was one of the leaders of the interregional group of deputies. At the I USSR Congress of People's Deputies he was elected to the USSR Supreme Soviet where he was a member of the sub-committee on the problems of the plans on the economic and social development of the Soviet Union, a member of the planning and budgetary commission of the Soviet of the Union, a member of the commission on the drafting of a new USSR constitution and of the commission on privileges enjoyed by certain categories of citizens.

In 1990 he was elected a people's deputy of the Moscow city soviet (Mossovet) and on April 20, 1990, at the I session of the Mossovet, he was elected the chairman. In 1991 he was nominated for the post of mayor of Moscow. In his election programme he proposed that people should be given the chance to work and earn, that state property should be privatized, that bureaucratic services and organizations be put on an entrepreneurial basis. He advocated the establishment of joint stock, leased and co-operative private enterprises. Housing, services, industry, city education, health, science and sport should be privatized, and people to be transformed from cogs in a machine, members of the workforce and labour reserves into bosses and owners. He stated that the following measures would ease the path to a market economy: anti-monopoly measures, the development of competition, the struggle with rising prices, economic help for the weak strata of city dwellers, a minimum wage related to the indexation of prices, the struggle against the shadow economy, speculation, crime, the defence of entrepreneurs and consumers, help for citizens to obtain additional jobs and extra income and help for the unemployed and the improvement of the living standards of families by providing them with plots of land.

He called for the scientific-technical potential of the city to be developed, to reduce old-fashioned military production and to transform it into civil production but at the same time turning out modern weapons. Moscow enterprises should become part of the world division of labour, the brain drain should be overcome, the construction of cottages and administrative buildings should be expanded and enterprises made ecologically clean. The administration of Moscow had to be reformed.

There were five candidates for mayor. Popov won on June 12, 1991, polling 65.32% of the votes. His main opponent was V. T. Saikin, first deputy chairman of the committee on machine building of the USSR Cabinet of Ministers, who received 16.35% of the votes.

On August 20, 1991 Popov addressed a meeting in front of Mossovet. He proclaimed that the anti-constitutional putsch to re-establish the power of the CPSU was doomed to failure since the people did not believe in the ability of the CPSU to run the country, the putschists had no plan to overcome the economic crisis and all their arguments were linked to tanks. He declared the Extraordinary Committee unconstitutional and its members to be criminally responsible as well as all those who carried out their orders. He stated that a state of emergency would not be introduced in Moscow. He designated all agencies which tried to administer Moscow, apart from those legally elected by Muscovites, self-styled and illegal. He banned all city, *raion* and other territorial organizations of the council of war and labour veterans which supported the attempted coup.

Popov was elected chairman of the board of the Russian movement of democratic reform at its constituent congress in Nizhny Novgorod on February 15, 1992. He stated that the movement supported the entrepreneur and the implementation of radical economic and political reform which would determine the fate of Russia. He not only advocated the economic transformation of society but also the establishment of a completely new social structure and political system.

He called for the most rapid drafting of a new constitution, believing that various important governmental correctives to the course of reform needed to be made, which were provoked by the continuing state monopoly of property. In this situation the state needed a mechanism to regulate the course of reform, including control over the setting of prices. It was necessary to restrict the functions of state officials and expand the sphere of the executive and to establish a strong administrative system, which would be counterbalanced by direct elections of the heads of administrations and supervision by deputies.

In June 1992 Popov resigned as mayor of Moscow. One of the reasons he gave for going was the inability of the mayor to carry through fundamental economic reforms, first and foremost privatization. He advocated the strengthening of the executive authority while retaining democratic principles. While mayor, Popov introduced the free privatization of housing in Moscow and fought for this for the whole of Russia. He advocated national privatization, the privatization of enterprise trade by workers' collectives, and opposed the monetary policies of Egor Gaidar.

Popov became a member of the higher consultative co-ordinating council of the Speaker of the RSFSR Supreme Soviet in 1990, then a member of the presidential consultative Council and is now a member of the presidential Council.

He regards parliamentary government as a cul-de-sac. It is impossible to carry out reforms by voting on every question, as the practical work of the parliament is paralysed. The crisis of the present concept of representative authority flows from its double structure, the number of deputies and the five-year term of office which is quite inappropriate in an era of change. A new constitution is needed, but not compromise at any price, which only deepens the contradictions. A Russian model of a long transition period should be fashioned which envisages the creation of private property and the impossibility of the bankruptcy of ineffective enterprises due to the fact that there are so many of them.

In place of financial stabilization he proposes the guaranteeing of food supplies, the distribution of plots of land to citizens free of charge, the continuation of the arms trade and the handing over of 10% of the land to private farmers. Reforms should be promoted by strengthening the executive power and according to the principle of the division of power. Popov regards the President as the best guarantee that reform will continue in Russia. He proposed that a constituent assembly should be called in 1993 and that it should adopt a new constitution not later than 1994. New elections should take place in 1995 when the writ of the present elected institutions runs out. He is married with two sons and lives in Moscow.

Poptsov, Oleg Maksimovich

Chairman of the Russian state television company.

Born in 1934 in Leningrad; Russian. He was a member of the CPSU until August 1991. He lived through the Leningrad blockade (1941-44), and later graduated from the S. M. Kirov Timber Technology Academy, Leningrad. He was first secretary of the Leningrad rural *oblast Komsomol* committee and an official of the Central *Komsomol* Committee, Moscow. From 1968 to 1990 he was editor-in-chief of *Selskaya molodezh* (rural youth), the journal of the Central *Komsomol* Committee, and was a member of the USSR union of writers. He is the author of the novels, *Nominative Case* (1975); *Prisoner of Power* (1986); the collection of stories *Orpheus Will Not Bring Happiness* (1978); *In Search of One's Own Alibi* (1984); and *Banal Subject* (1988).

In 1990 he was nominated for election as an RSFSR people's deputy in the No. 22 Krasnopresnensky territorial district, Moscow. During the election campaign he advocated autonomy for Russia within the USSR, and the establishment of equal exchange between the RSFSR and the other republics. He pointed out that the democratic process in Russia lagged behind that in other republics, and proposed the drafting of a new economic model for Russia which took into account national psychology, ways to overcome economic waste and corruption and the development of a labour morality. A Russian extraordinary council consisting of Soviet and Western specialists should be established, its goal being to draft a programme for the rebirth of Russia. He supported the democratic movement in the CPSU.

He put forward the idea of a round table of representatives of government, the Party leadership, parliament and democratic forces, and during the campaign he supported the platform of the Democratic Russia bloc. There were 13 candidates. Poptsov polled 26.87% of the votes in the first round and won the second round, polling 57.7% of the votes. His main opponent was E. M. Ametistov, at present a member of the Constitutional Court of the Russian Federation, who received 11.2% of the votes in the first round and 34.8% in the second round. Poptsov is a member of the Russian Supreme Soviet committee on the mass media, links with public organizations, mass movements and the analysis of public opinion. He is a member of the parliamentary faction, Democratic Russia, and the deputies' bloc "coalition for reform". In July 1990 he was appointed chairman of the Russian television company. He has awards, and lives in Moscow.

Porovskyi, Mykola Ivanovych

Leading Ukrainian Nationalist Deputy.

Born into a Ukrainian family in 1956, he was educated at the Ukrainian Institute of Water Engineering and is a construction engineer by profession. After flirting with the *Komsomol* in early life, Porovskyi threw himself into opposition activity in the late 1980s. As an extremely hard worker and skilled organizer, he rose within *Rukh* to become a member of its leadership and head of its co-ordinating council in 1990. This meant that he was in charge of the movement's central bureaucracy.

In March 1990 Porovskyi was elected people's deputy for Rovenskyi *raion*, Rivne *oblast*, in western Ukraine (on the second round), and he is a member of the Supreme Soviet's committee on the plan, budget, finances and prices. In the Supreme Soviet and in *Rukh*, Porovskyi demonstrated his passionate nationalism during 1990 to 1991, and his equally passionate support for President Kravchuk and the new Ukrainian state thereafter. He therefore sided strongly with Drach, Pavlychko and Skoryk's wing of *Rukh*, and against Viacheslav Chornovil, as the movement split in two in 1992. Consequently, in February 1992 he organized the formation of a (broadly) pro-presidential *Rukh* faction of 41 in the Ukrainian parliament after Chornovil's then ally Les Taniuk took over the leadership of the old People's Council in December 1991.

At the third congress of *Rukh*, in February-March 1992, an emotional Porovskyi almost quit the organization on the spot in protest at Chornovil's growing domination, and at the lack of recognition for his work. Although he was persuaded to stay on in the short term, he soon shifted his energies into organizing the rival Congress of National-Democratic Forces in August 1992, to create the kind of broadly pro-presidential movement that he and Ivan Drach had failed to secure in March.

Porovskyi is the classic back-room organizer. Although not a great public speaker, he exercises considerable influence behind the scenes. He was prominent in the campaign for a genuinely independent Ukrainian Orthodox Church, and was the organizer of the Crimea with Ukraine movement, established with government support (initially 30 million rubles) in response to the rising tide of Crimean separatism in 1992. It organized a Congress of Crimean Ukrainians in October 1992 as a counterweight to separatist and pro-Russian organizations such as the Republican Movement of the Crimea, and the leadership of the Crimean Republic, under Mykola Bagrov. In 1993 Porovskyi joined the Ukrainian Republican Party, and became one of its deputy leaders at the party's fourth congress in May 1993.

Official address: Kiev, Vul. M. Hrushevskoho 5; *telephone*: Kiev 252 019 or Kiev 229 2126 (home).

Potapov, Leonid Vasilevich

Speaker of the Supreme Soviet of the Republic of Buryatia, Russian Federation.

Born in 1935; Russian; member of the CPSU from 1964 to August 1991. He is a graduate, and was first secretary of the Buryat Party *obkom*. Then he became the deputy chairman (Speaker) of the supreme Soviet of Turkmenistan, and chairman of the executive committee of the Mary *oblast* soviet of Turkmenistan.

In January 1990 he was elected a people's deputy of Turkmenistan. In March 1990 the communists of the instrument-making production association, the Buryat energy administration, the Buryat scientific centre and other Party organizations, seeking a new first secretary of the republican Party committee of the Buryat ASSR, invited Potapov to return to the republic. In April 1990, at a plenum of the republican Party committee, he was elected first secretary of the republican Party committee of Buryatia.

In 1990 he was elected a deputy of the Supreme Soviet of the Buryat ASSR, and was also elected a delegate to the XXVIII Party congress and was a member of the Party Central Committee. In August 1991 he stated that the republican Party committee of the Buryat Soviet Socialist republic had not taken any decisions during the attempted state coup. He refused all interviews during this period and he regarded his caution to have been justified since "hasty" declarations could "excite passions".

After August 1991 he was acting chairman of the committee for the budget, finance and economic reform of the Supreme Soviet of the Buryat SSR. At the V session of the Supreme Soviet of the republic, in October 1991, he was elected Speaker of the Supreme Soviet of the republic. On assuming office he stated that he would "freeze" his membership of the CPSU, although in his heart he remained a communist. He described himself as a supporter of democratic methods in administration, and advocated the normalization of the consumer market, the restructuring of economic relations between urban and rural areas and the fair distribution of capital investment and material resources between the city and the countryside. He supported the transition from a strictly centralized planned economy to a planned market economy, self-administration and self-financing of the republic.

In November 1992 he stated that the President of the Russian Federation did not need an extension of his extraordinary powers in the present extremely difficult situation. He hoped that at the VII Congress of People's Deputies the legislative and executive branches would reach mutual understanding and consolidate the situation. He is a lover of literature and philosophy and subscribes to the journal *Voprosy filosofii*. He lives in Ulan Ude.

Potapov, Viktor Pavlovich

Commander of Naval Air Forces. Air Force Colonel-General since 1985.

Born on January 7, 1934 in the village of Muratovka, Makshansky *raion*, Penza *oblast*. Russian. His navy career began in 1951. He graduated from the Naval Torpedo Aviation Technical School in 1953; the Naval Academy with a gold medal in 1962; the Military Academy of the General Staff with distinction in 1980. He received a higher military education and was a member of the CPSU from 1956 to August 1991.

He served in the naval air forces of the Northern Fleet. He was a senior pilot, a detachment commander and an air squadron commander. He mastered all types of long-range aircraft, experienced all kinds of meteorological conditions when flying and all types of combat aircraft. He proved himself a dedicated pilot and an expert commander. His record included sound military tactical, flying and technical training. At the same time he was actively involved in Party work and was respected by the Party political agencies. He was sent to continue his education at the Naval Academy as a promising officer. While studying at the Academy he demonstrated considerable scientific ability and was recommended for a postgraduate course. However, he chose to remain in combat service and turned down the opportunity of further study to qualify for higher teaching posts. He returned to the Northern fleet as an air regimental commander. Then he was appointed a divisional commander and deputy air force commander of the fleet. He enjoyed the support of the former head of the air force, Col.-Gen. G. Kuznetsov, who later became Chief of Staff and chief of naval aviation. Through marriage he established many contacts in high Party circles. This, together with his profound operational and tactical knowledge and talent for organization and command, ensured his promotion.

Gen. Potapov successfully commanded air forces in the north Atlantic and northern hemisphere theatre of operations, ensured discipline, order and a high level of combat readiness of the air force of the Northern fleet. Between 1980 and 1986 he was air force commander of the Northern Fleet and deputy fleet commander of aviation. In 1986 he was appointed first deputy air force commander of the navy. He supervised the work of various organizations supplying naval aviation with advanced equipment and established close relations with the defence industry. He was elected to the Party agencies of Murmansk *oblast* and to the central agencies of the navy. In 1988 he was appointed commander of naval aviation and deputy Commander-in-Chief of the navy for aviation and a member of the military council of the navy. Politically, he is a hard-liner. He opposed democratic forces in the military and society and was a convinced communist.

During the anti-constitutional putsch in August 1991 he was not active but remained watchful. Then he displayed conformism and loyalty to the new authorities. He does not express his own political views in the mass media. He advocates a strong state and is attracted by imperial concepts. He supports the creation of a powerful army and navy, capable of defending the interests of the country by military means. He is a devoted air force enthusiast and he favours technical re-equipment at a time of declining military expenditure. He is fond of literature and art. A reserved man, he strictly observes the rules of seniority in his contacts. He is known to have used his subordinates for his own private purposes. He does not speak any foreign language. He has been abroad, for example to Cuba in 1991. His publications are prepared by his subordinate officers, and include "The wings get stronger in flight", which appeared in *Morskoi sbornik*, No. 8, 1991. He has been awarded orders and medals. He was an honoured military pilot of the USSR. He is married with two daughters.

Official address: 103175 Moscow K-175; *telephone*: Moscow 212 95 18.

Pravdenko, Serhii Makarovych

Ukrainian People's Deputy and Editor of the *Holos Ukraïny* newspaper.

Born into a Ukrainian family in 1949 in Dnipropetrovsk in eastern Ukraine. After studying at Kiev State University, he worked as a journalist on establishment papers such as *Robitnycha hazeta* (the Workers' Paper) and *Radianska Ukraïna* (Soviet Ukraine). He was elected people's deputy for Samarskyi *raion* in his local Dnipropetrovsk *oblast* in March 1990, and in the Supreme Soviet is a member of the committee on *glasnost* and the mass media, and sits on the influential Presidium, which governs the Supreme Soviet's affairs when the latter is not sitting.

Pravdenko has been the editor of *Holos Ukraïny* (the voice of Ukraine), the official paper of the Ukrainian Supreme Soviet, since its formation in early 1991. Although it was originally a lively forum for different opinions, it has increasingly become the official mouthpiece of the authorities. He is basically a national communist and is politically close to both Kravchuk and Pliushch. *Holos Ukraïny* has continued to be supplied with paper at a time when those newspapers less supportive of the authorities have been reduced to a single broadsheet.

Address (of *Holos Ukraïny*): 252047 Kiev, Vul. Nesterova 4; *telephone*: Kiev 441 8961 or (Kiev) 441 8946.

Primakov, Evgeny Maksimovich

Head of the Main Intelligence Administration (GRU) of the Russian Federation.

Born on October 29, 1929 in Kiev, Ukraine into a civil servant's family; Russian, although some regard him as partly Jewish; member of the CPSU from 1959 to August 1991. He graduated in 1953 from the Moscow Oriental Institute and began postgraduate studies at Moscow State University in 1956, later successfully presenting his candidate dissertation (PhD). He successfully presented his doctoral dissertation in 1969 (DLitt), and was elected an Academician of the USSR Academy of Sciences in 1979.

He began his journalistic career in 1956, becoming a correspondent of the main radio administration, then was an editor, deputy editor-in-chief, editor-in-chief and deputy chief editor of the main editorial board of the state committee for radio and television (Gosteleradio) of the USSR Council of Ministers. In 1962 he became a senior scientific assistant in the institute of the world economy and international relations, USSR Academy of Sciences. From 1962 to 1970 he was on the editorial staff of *Pravda*, where he was a columnist, then deputy editor of the department on Asia and Africa and special correspondent in the Arab world. Afterwards he worked in the USSR Academy of Sciences. In 1970 he was appointed deputy director of the institute of the world economy and international relations, USSR Academy of Sciences and in 1977 he became director of the Oriental Institute. In 1985 he was made director of the institute of the world economy and international relations.

From 1988 he was academic secretary of the section on the problems of the world economy and international relations, USSR Academy of Sciences and a member of the Presidium of the Academy. He was very active internationally and was elected chairman of the Soviet national committee on Asian-Pacific co-operation, a member of the UN University and of the Club of Rome. From 1986 to 1989 he was a candidate member of the Central Committee, CPSU, from April 1989 a member of the Party Central Committee and from September 1989 to July 1990 a candidate member of the Party Politburo. He was a delegate to the XXVII and XXVIII Party congresses and the XIX Party conference.

In 1989 he was elected a USSR people's deputy, being a nominee of the CPSU. He was elected to the USSR Supreme Soviet and its Presidium and from June 1989 to March 1990 he was chairman of the Soviet of the Union of the USSR Supreme Soviet and head of the USSR Supreme Soviet commission on privileges and benefits. In March 1990 he became a member of the USSR presidential Council. He was a frequent visitor to Iraq and the Middle East and some analysts believe that he had foreknowledge of the decision by Iraq to invade Kuwait. From December 1990 to January 1991 he travelled to Baghdad and negotiated with Saddam Hussein in an attempt to stave off the Gulf War. He also travelled to Baghdad during the war in order to attempt to broker a settlement which would not result in the total defeat of Iraq, and some Western observers regarded him as a Trojan horse at a time when President Gorbachev was supporting the UN campaign against the Iraqi leader. In January 1992 he was appointed head of the Main Intelligence Administration (GRU).

He has been awarded the orders of the Red Banner of Labour, Friendship of the Peoples, the badge of honour and medals, and gained a USSR state prize in 1980. He lives in Moscow.

Prokhanov, Aleksandr Andreevich

Editor-in-chief of the Russian newspaper, *Den*.

Born on February 26, 1938 in Tbilisi, Georgian SSR, and the family were members of the Molokane sect; Russian. He was never a member of the CPSU. In 1960 he graduated from the S. Ordzhonikidze Aviation Institute, Moscow, and he was an engineer and lumberjack in the Karelian ASSR and Moscow *oblast*. He was elected a member of the USSR union of writers in 1972. During the second half of the 1970s he wrote for *Literaturnaya gazeta* and was in Nicaragua, Afghanistan and Angola. He is the author of the novels *Wandering Rose* (1976); *Eternal City* (1981); *Lover of Islands* (1984); *And So the Wind Comes* (1985); *The Time Midday* (1986); *The Place of Activity* (1986); three novels on the war in Afghanistan: *The Tree in the Middle of Kabul* (1982); *Sketches of a War Artist* (1989); *600 Years After the Battle* (1990); the collection of documents *In Your Name* (1975); *Reflections of Mangazei* (1975); *Nuclear Defence* (1984); and others.

He is the author of the "collective word to the people", published in *Sovetskaya Rossiya* in June 1991, and the same year he was appointed editor-in-chief of the newspaper, *Den* (day), the organ of the "spiritual opposition". The main task of the newspaper is to bring together communist and anti-communist opposition to those in power at present, based on the concept of a strong Russian statehood. He supports an alliance of Russia and the Islamic states against the West, and is critical of the position of the Moscow Patriarchate and the Patriarch Aleksi II towards those in power in Russia.

He was awarded the Lenin *Komsomol* prize and the K. Fedin prize. He is married with three children and his passion is lepidoptery. He lives in Moscow.

Prudnikov, Viktor Alekseevich

Air Defence Commander-in-Chief of the Russian Federation. Air Force Colonel-General.

Born on February 4, 1939 in Rostov-on-Don into a civil servant's family. Russian. He graduated from the Armavir Military Aviation Technical School for Air Defence Pilots in 1959; the Military Air Force Academy in 1967; the Military Academy of the General Staff in 1981. He received a higher military education and was a member of the CPSU from 1960 to August 1991.

After graduating from technical school he was an instructor-pilot and senior instructor-pilot of a training fighter air regiment and took up flight training of students of the Armavir Technical School. He had the reputation of being a highly qualified professional with a passion for his work as a military pilot. He was actively involved in the work of *Komsomol* and CPSU organizations.

In 1967 he was appointed deputy commander and squadron navigator, and a year later an air squadron commander in a combat unit of air defence aviation. He himself took part in alert actions to defend the frontier. He was notable for his high level of flight and tactical skills and became a military pilot, first class. In 1970 he was appointed deputy commander of a fighter air regiment on flight training and in 1971 he became a regimental commander. From 1973 he was a deputy commander of an air defence division and from 1973 commander of the same formation which included all types of forces: aviation, anti-aircraft missile and radio-tactical troops. He was notable for his sound operational-tactical and military-technical training; he was politically active only to the extent necessary for a successful career.

In 1978 he was promoted to first deputy commander of a detached air defence army and from 1983 commander of the same army. In 1989 he became air defence Commander-in-Chief of Moscow district, the largest formation equipped with the latest weapons systems, which covers the Moscow region. He demonstrated a talent for organization and sound operational-tactical training, ensuring the constant readiness of his troops to fulfil the tasks set before them.

He himself continued to fly on various types of modern interceptors. From July 1990 he was a member of the Party Central Committee.

During the anti-constitutional putsch in August 1991 he was not active, concentrating on ensuring high combat readiness and the discipline of the troops.

By the USSR President's decree of August 31, 1991, he was appointed air defence Commander-in-Chief and deputy Minister of Defence, replacing Gen. I. M. Tretyak, dismissed for his involvement in the putsch. From February 1992 he was air defence commander of the Unified Armed Forces of the CIS. On August 21, 1992, by President Yeltsin's decree, he was appointed air defence Commander-in-Chief of Russia.

By conviction he is a military professional, eager to avoid being involved in politics. He supports the idea of Russia regaining the status of a great power. He advocates the supremacy of the state. He favours reforming the armed forces to ensure that they meet the demands of present-day war, developing high-precision weapons systems and qualitatively new aviation technology.

He has expressed his views in a number of publications, including "What Should Aerospace Defence Be Like?" (*Krasnaya Zvezda*, November 30, 1991); "We Need an Integrated System" (*Krasnaya Zvezda*, April 11, 1992).

He is interested in military-technical problems and the history and development of aviation. He enjoys sport and does not speak any foreign language. He has been awarded orders of the Red Banner "For service to the motherland in the armed forces of the USSR", 3rd class, and a number of medals. He is married with two children.

Office address: 103175, Moscow, K-175.

Prusak, Mikhail Mikhailovich

Head of the Administration of Novgorod *oblast*, Russian Federation.

Born in 1960 in Ivano-Frankovsk (Ivano-Frankivsk) *oblast*, Ukraine; member of the CPSU until August 1991. He completed the eight year school and in 1979 the Kolomyiskoe Pedagogical College. He was a teacher of an extended day class in a village school in Galich *raion*, Ivano-Frankovsk *oblast*. He served in the Soviet Army from 1980 to 1982, and after being demobbed he entered the faculty of history and communist education of the Higher *Komsomol* School of the *Komsomol* Central Committee. He graduated in November 1986 and was assigned to Novgorod *oblast* as second secretary and from May 1987 as first secretary of the *Komsomol* in Kholm *raion*. In December 1988 he was appointed director of the Trudovik state farm, Kholm *raion*, Novgorod *oblast*.

At the V plenum of the *Komsomol* Central Committee, in January 1989, he was nominated for election as a USSR people's deputy. During the election campaign he appealed for a solution to the food problem, the strengthening of the role of youth in the countryside, the development of leasing, the renaissance of the small villages and the raising of the economic and social standard of life in the countryside. He advocated the adoption of laws on youth, the establishment of a state committee on youth affairs and periodic alterations to legislation. In March 1989 he was elected a USSR people's deputy as one of the *Komsomol* nominees and then as a member of the USSR Supreme Soviet. He acted as agent for Boris Yeltsin.

On October 24, 1991 Prusak was appointed head of the administration of Novgorod *oblast* by presidential decree. On assuming office he advocated strengthening presidential power vertically and increasing the authority of the President. He supported the rapid adoption of strict measures to protect the economy from disintegrating, but the role of democratic institutions should not be restricted although they should observe economic laws. He supported strict observance of the laws, taxes and other economic mechanisms. Every citizen of Russia should have equal opportunities during privatization and social problems should be resolved. He declared he was not interested in politics but was not afraid of adopting unpopular measures.

In December 1992, during the VII Congress of People's Deputies, he supported the policies of the President and Egor Gaidar for the post of Russian Prime Minister. He is married with a son and a daughter and lives in Novgorod.

Pulatov, Timur Iskhakovich

First secretary of the International Association of Writers' Unions.

Born in 1939 in Bukhara, Uzbek SSR, where his father was a schoolteacher; Uzbek. He was never a member of the CPSU. His grandfather was a karakul wool trader, and after Soviet power was established in Bukhara he was executed on the basis of false evidence. His grandmother also suffered political oppression and his mother, at the age of 12 years, was left on her own after the confiscation of home and property. His father was persecuted as a helper of an enemy of the people. Pulatov was brought up on Muslim legends and traditions, related by his mother and old neighbours. His father was one of the first Bolsheviks in the city and took part in the struggle against the Bashmaki (Muslim opposition). He went to a Russian school, and at the age of 14 years he began working in a shoe factory, then in a brigade of geologists.

He graduated from the Bukhara Pedagogical Institute and taught in a village school. Later he studied in Moscow in the higher courses for script writers and began to publish in 1964. One of his first stories, *Call Me in the Forest*, appeared in the journal *Druzhba narodov*, in 1966. His main works are: *Rule*, *Guardian Towers*, *The Youth Choir*, *Sensitive Alisho*, *The Habitui*, and *Navigating Eurasia*. His books *The Tarazi Tortoise*, *The Passions of a Bukhara Home* and the short story *Sea Nomads*, lay in his writing table drawer for 15 years before being published. Pulatov's style is marked by its use of parable and he studies life abroad, childhood, old age and universal questions of existence.

In August 1991, at the extraordinary plenum of the USSR union of writers, he was elected first secretary of the board. He appealed against the persecution of writers for their political convictions, but regretted that many of them placed politics above literature. A writer can only be judged by his work and he praised the early prose of Belov, Rasputin and Bondarev but thought that their enthusiasm for politics had not enriched their artistic work. He called for a single literary, cultural and creative space to be retained, embracing the former USSR. The union of writers should not become a strict centralizing system but a small co-ordinating centre of the community of independent writers, based on democratic principles. It should be the mediator among the creative unions, not the higher state authorities, and apart from the Lenin prize, prizes should not be of two kinds.

He appealed for the creative intelligentsia to unite against violence and inter-ethnic discord. There were no great literary talents at present due to extreme politicization and all had launched themselves into publicistic work. He regards his own formative influences as being Turkish, Tajik-Persian and Russian literatures. In the past he was enthusiastic about Lev Tolstoi, then Fedor Dostoevsky, and in the Soviet era, firstly Konstantin Paustovsky, then Andrei Platonov and Mikhail Bulgakov.

In January 1992 Pulatov was appointed head of the executive committee of the association of unions of writers. In March 1992, the council of co-chairmen of the executive committee of the association of unions of writers and Moscow writers, headed by Yury Chernichenko, removed him from the post, criticizing him for three trips abroad for the union, his appointment without the consent of the co-ordinating council of Marina Kudimova and Igor Zolotussky, non-fulfilment of the decision of the executive committee about participation in the *Sovetsky pisatel* publishing house and, most serious of all, engaging in negotiations with the Russian Union, headed by Yury Bondarev. Nevertheless Pulatov continued with preparations for the IX congress of writers, planned for June 1992, and in June became the first secretary of the international association of unions of writers.

He is married. His home is in Tashkent, and in Moscow he lives in union of writers' accommodation. He has his own dacha.

Puşcaş, Victor Ştefan

Deputy president of the *Sfatul Tării* (parliament), Republic of Moldova.

Born in 1943 in the village of Adrioneşti, Donduşeni *raion*, Moldovan SSR. He was an ethnic Moldovan, who graduated from the M. V. Lomonosov State University in Moscow. He worked as farmer on the Kirov farm in Donduşeni *raion*. In 1961 he graduated from the professional school of agricultural mechanization and worked as a tractor driver on the Liubomirovsk *sovkhoz* in Tavricheskii *raion*, Omsk *oblast*. In 1971, when he graduated from university, he worked as senior consultant in the Moldovan SSR Ministry of Justice, and then as a judge. In 1976 he was elected president of the court in Rîbniţa. In 1977 he was elected to the Supreme Court of the Moldovan SSR, where he remained until 1985, when he was elected president of the Moldovan Supreme Soviet. In 1989 he became deputy president of the Moldovan Supreme Soviet. On May 11, 1990 he was elected deputy president of the new Moldovan Supreme Soviet (the present *Sfatul Ţării*).

Pyankov, Boris Evgenevich

Deputy commander-in-chief of the Unified Armed Forces of the CIS. Colonel-General since 1987.

Born in 1935 in Sverdlovsk (Ekaterinburg) into a working-class family. Russian. He began his military career as a soldier in 1954 and entered technical school two years later. He graduated from the Tank Officers' Technical School in 1959; the Military Academy of the Armoured Forces with a gold medal and the Military Academy of the General Staff with a gold medal. He received a higher military education and was a member of the CPSU from 1958 to August 1991.

After completing technical school he was appointed a tank platoon commander. He was noticeable among young officers for his professionalism, talent for organization and teaching, eagerness to gain more specialist knowledge and activity in Party political work. He held all officer posts at tank company, battalion, regimental and divisional levels. His record was that of an officer with sound operational-tactical and military-technical training. He participated in military operations in Afghanistan against the *mujahidin* and was awarded the order of the Red Star for his performance there. Later he was commander of a corps, first deputy commander of the Odessa military district. He personally took part in organizing the elimination of the consequences of the Chernobyl catastrophe and was awarded the order of the Red Star. From 1987 he was commander of the Siberian military district and responsible for a considerable number of educational establishments and units for the training of junior officers and specialists of various types of forces.

Pyankov proved himself a convinced communist who supported whole-heartedly all the measures adopted by Party leaders at home and abroad. He was elected a member of the Novosibirsk Party *obkom* and delegate to the I All-Army Party Conference in April 1991, where he took the floor. During the election campaign to the USSR Congress of People's Deputies, at the beginning of 1989, he was nominated in both a national (for Soviet of the Union) and a national-territorial (for Soviet of Nationalities) district. He enjoyed the support of part of the local electorate and was elected a people's deputy in the No. 231 Dzerzhinsky territorial district, Novosibirsk *oblast*. He adopted an extremely conservative stance at the Congress of People's Deputies, was not in favour of democratic movements, belonged to the group of the military-industrial and

Party leaders who continually opposed all the proposals of the democrats. He persecuted those with democratic views in his military district. On August 17, 1991, by the decree of President of the USSR Mikhail Gorbachev, he was appointed commander of air defences of the USSR and first deputy USSR Minister of Defence, but did not take up his posts.

During the anti-constitutional putsch of August 19-21, 1991, Col.-Gen. Pyankov was at his headquarters in Novosibirsk. He dutifully fulfilled all the instructions of the Emergency Committee, brought troops to a high state of combat readiness, was very active and expressed full support for the plotters. The parliamentary investigation established that he had issued coded telegrams expressing support for the Emergency Committee, demanding more decisive measures against the Russian population. Gen. Pyankov was, however, not called to account, due to the influence of his patrons among the top military and government officials.

From the autumn of 1991 he was deputy Minister of Defence of the USSR. He headed groups of military experts examining the problems involved in the withdrawal of troops from eastern and central Europe and the Baltic states, and the creation of the armed forces of the independent states after the disintegration of the Soviet Union. He was an adviser to the Ukrainian government on military planning. He went to Pridnestrovie, Moldova, to analyze the situation there. In January 1992 he was appointed deputy Commander-in-Chief of the Unified Armed Forces of the CIS and one of the closest advisers of Marshal Evgeny Shaposhnikov, the Commander-in-Chief.

A military professional with sound intelligence and general and technical knowledge, Pyankov enjoys great authority among his troops and tries to conceal his political views. He favours the restructuring of the armed forces to meet the demands of present-day war, the creation of a system of collective security in the CIS and strict control over unified strategic forces. He has proved himself a tough and resolute commander but a conformist in his attitude to the new state leaders, effortlessly renouncing his former convictions. He appears in the press on questions of military planning and national security. *Krasnaya Zvezda*, on October 15, 1992, published his article: "The collective forces of the CIS: reality and perspectives". He is interested in literature, art and sport. He does not possess a good knowledge of foreign languages and has not been abroad as a member of an official delegation, except on professional visits to the countries where CIS troops are stationed. He has been awarded three orders, and medals. He is married with a son who is an officer, and a daughter.

Office address: Moscow, Leningradsky prospekt 41.

Pylypchuk, Volodymyr Mefodiyovych

Chairman of The Ukrainian Supreme Soviet's Committee on Economic Reform.

Born into a Ukrainian family in Rivne *oblast* in western Ukraine in 1948. He was educated at the Kiev Institute for Light Industry, after which he worked as an engineer in the building industry in Rivne. In 1980 he became the director of a drainage pipe factory, before moving to Kiev to work as a lecturer at the Kiev Institute for Water Engineering from 1985 to 1990.

He was a member of the Communist Party of Ukraine from 1974 to June 1990, when he quit and joined the opposition movement *Rukh* amidst the disappointments of the XXVIII CPSU Congress. An energetic publicist and author of many articles on the transition to a free market, he had already been elected as an independent to the Supreme Soviet in March 1990 for Zhovtnevyi *raion*, Rivne *oblast* (on the second round). He made a big early impression as the chairman of the Supreme Soviet's committee on economic reform, and was the joint author with future Prime Minister Vitold Fokin of the plan of economic reforms unveiled in October 1990. However, Pylypchuk's star faded somewhat after most of the programme's radical proposals were blocked by the conservative majority in the Supreme Soviet. All that was left was the introduction of a coupon system to try and protect the Ukrainian consumer market, which was far from successful. Pylypchuk remained ambitious, however. He remains an *ex officio* member of the influential Supreme Soviet Presidium, and he was nominated by the main moderate nationalist party, the Democratic Party of Ukraine, as its candidate for President in the autumn 1991 race, although he himself did not formally belong to the party.

His campaign was lacklustre, however, and he was unable to collect the 100,000 signatures necessary to place his name on the final ballot. He then moved towards the political centre by joining the liberal *New Ukraine* movement in January 1992. He was elected on to its secretariat in June 1992 at the movement's founding congress (just, in the last of fifteen places, with 120 votes). In November 1992 he was appointed a member of the State Commission for Monetary Reform.

Official address: Kiev, Vul. M. Hrushevskoho 5; *telephone*: Kiev 252 019 or 291 5172 (work) and Kiev 291 5402 (home).

Pynzenyk, Viktor Mykhilovych

Vice-Prime Minister of Ukraine and Former Minister of Economics.

Born into a Ukrainian family in 1945. He is a professional economist, successfully presenting his candidate dissertation in economics (PhD (Econ)) and his doctoral dissertation (DSc (Econ)), who spent his working career in academia, rising to the position of head of the faculty of economics at Lviv State University, where he is also the head of the Lviv institute of management.

He was elected to the Ukrainian Supreme Soviet in a by-election in December 1991 to represent Radianskyi *raion*, Lviv city.

In 1992 Pynzenyk joined the centrist *New Ukraine* movement, whose official programme calls for the creation of a "socially-oriented market economy", although he is formally non-party. He has also cultivated good links with the old order through his appointment in April 1992 by President Kravchuk as a member of the economic section of the *Duma* or President's advisory council, where he established a good reputation as a non-partisan professional.

In October 1992 he was appointed Vice-Premier and Minister for Economic Reform in the new Kuchma government, replacing the more traditionalist Valentyn Symonenko. He immediately created a more pragmatic tone, stressing the importance of restoring links with Russia, and establishing good relations with international institutions such as the International Monetary Fund. He declared himself "in favour of economic reform, but not of adventurism". Ukraine withdrew in an orderly fashion from the ruble zone on November 7, and Pynzenyk negotiated two deals with Russia in November: promising to restore trading links, for Russia supposedly to take over Ukraine's share of the all-Union debt, and for Russia to supply a 227 billion ruble credit to Ukraine.

On December 1, 1992 an accelerated privatization programme was announced (25% of all small businesses within four months). On November 9, Pynzenyk was appointed deputy head of a new State Commission for Monetary Reform, empowered to oversee the introduction of a new Ukrainian currency. However, Pynzenyk's performance in government was strongly criticized both by the neo-socialist left and by those who regarded him as a better theoretician than administrator. The draft programme for economic reform that he presented to the Supreme Soviet in January 1993 was summarily rejected.

In April 1993 he lost his position as Minister of Economics, although he retained his position as Vice-Premier. He was replaced by Yuriy Bannikov, an industrialist from eastern Ukraine.

Official address: 252008 Kiev, Vul. M. Hrushevskoho 12/2; *telephone*: Kiev 293 7442.

Rahojsa, Viaceslau Piatrovic

Deputy director of the Francisak Skaryna National Educational Centre, Belarus.

Born on June 5, 1942 in the village of Rakau, Valozynski *raion*, Minsk *oblast*. His parents are Piotr and Valancina (née Kahanovic) Rahojsa, and the family is Belarusian. He graduated in 1963 from the faculty of philology, Belarusian State University, and in 1967 successfully presented his candidate dissertation on Belarusian literature (PhD). He is at present a professor at the university and is a literary critic, writer and translator, his research interests being the history of Belarusian literature, its international contacts, poetry and the theory, history and practice of literary translation.

He translates Polish and Ukrainian literature into Belarusian, and his translations from Ukrainian include M. Katsyubinskyy, *Shades Of Our Forgotten Forbears*, A. Honchar, Yu. Yavorivskyy, M. Shashkevich, Yu. Fedkarych, M. Rylskyy, I. Drach, etc. He has edited and published numerous works on literary criticism, poetics and the problems of translating closely related languages. He is not a member of any political party at the moment, but views himself as a national democrat. His hobby is agriculture; he and his wife, Tacciana, have three sons: Usievalad, Maksim and Piatrus. He speaks Russian, Ukrainian and Polish.

Address: 220002 Minsk, vul. Starazouskaja, d. 8, kv. 175; *telephone:* Minsk (0172) 20 51 57 (work); 33 64 51 (home).

Raifikesht, Vladimir Fedorovich

Head of the Administration of Altai *krai*, Russian Federation.

Born on April 15, 1951 in the village of Povalikha, Pervomaisky *raion*, Altai *krai*; German; member of the CPSU until the summer of 1990. From 1968 to 1973 he was a student at the faculty of agronomy, Altai Agricultural Institute, then served as an officer in the Soviet Army from 1973 to 1975. He was then an agronomist, brigadier, manager of a section, and secretary of the Party committee, and from 1981 director of the Logovskoi state farm, Pervomaisky *raion*, Altai *krai*.

In early 1990 he was nominated by the work collective of the Logovskoi state farm for election as an RSFSR people's deputy in the No. 156 Novoaltaisky territorial district, Altai *krai*. There were six candidates. He polled 24.5% of the votes in the first round and won the second round, polling 51.6% of the votes. His main opponent was I. T. Zelenin, director of the Ozersky state farm, Talmensky *raion*, Altai *krai*, who received 22.8% of the votes in the first round and 41.6% in the second. Raifikesht is a member of the coalition of reforms group of parliamentary deputies.

In 1990 he was elected a deputy of the *raion* soviet, and in 1991 he acted as Boris Yeltsin's agent in Altai *krai* during the presidential elections. In August 1991 the session of the Altai *krai* soviet proposed to the President two candidates for confirmation as head of the administration of Altai *krai*, Raifikesht and A. G. Nazarchuk, an RSFSR people's deputy, and on October 8, 1991 Raifikesht was appointed head of the administration of Altai *krai* by presidential decree.

On assuming office he stated that his main task was to promote economic reform and to take part in the creation of a *Rechtsstaat* (law-governed state) in Russia, based on the separation of legislative and executive power. In December 1992, during the Congress of People's Deputies, he called the congress archaic and incapable, and issued a declaration supporting the Gaidar government. The government of Viktor Chernomyrdin was doomed to continue the reforms and to share the fate of its predecessor. Raifikesht regarded the President's speech at the congress to be a mistake, based on incorrect information. Raifikesht lives in the village of Logovskoi, Pervomaisky *raion*, Altai *krai*.

Rakhimov, Murtaza Gubaidullovich

Speaker of the Supreme Soviet of the Republic of Bashkortostan, Russian Federation.

Born on February 7, 1934 in the village of Tavakanovo, Kugarchinsky *raion*, Bashkir ASSR. His father, Gubai Zufarovich, was a peasant as was his mother, Galima Abdullovna. He has two brothers, Garei who works on a collective farm and Rafik who works in a car factory. He is a Bashkir, and was a member of the CPSU from 1974 to August 1991. After graduating from the Oil Technical College, Ufa, in 1956, he was an operator in the Order of Lenin oil refinery, Ufa, then in the XXII Party congress oil refinery, Ufa, where he was head of the plant, chief chemist, chief engineer, and in 1986 director of the enterprise. In 1964 he graduated from the Oil Institute, Ufa, extra-mural department.

He was the technical head of the construction and starting of operations of the largest output of high heavy spirits and aromatic hydrocarbons, and organized the production of consumer goods at the enterprise. On his initiative the enterprise developed successful trading links with Finland and Sweden, through an exchange of goods of international quality for consumer goods and equipment for the processing branches of the agro-industrial complex. He was awarded the orders of the Red Banner of Labour, the badge of honour and the medal for exemplary work. He is an honoured "rationalizer" of the RSFSR and honoured oilman of the Bashkir ASSR. He was a people's deputy of the USSR and a member of the USSR Supreme Soviet.

In March 1990 he was elected a people's deputy of the Bashkir ASSR and at the first session of the Supreme Soviet of the Bashkir ASSR he was elected Speaker. During the attempted state coup in August 1991 Rakhimov issued a declaration to the citizens of the republic describing the course of events. He was in Moscow at that time and asked the leadership of the USSR and the RSFSR for clarification, being certain that the democratic processes and reform policy would continue under a new government. He regretted the fact that he found no mutual understanding nor desire to explain the essence of the events in the apparatus of the President of the Russian Federation.

As Speaker of the Supreme Soviet Rakhimov stated that his primary concern was to introduce market relations. He thought that the transition to a market economy could not be effected without the existence of a single economic area (including links with the other republics) and agreement on commercial ties. It was necessary to work out the legal basis of the market and the transition should be to a regulated market, as required by economic measures. The introduction of market relations to him was an attempt to "pour some new blood" into the economy, make it dynamic and oriented towards the interests of the individual person. He also advocated the development of small businesses, but not commerce or unimportant production, since the former are the most important constituent of a market infrastructure.

In November 1991 at a session of the Supreme Soviet of the Bashkir Soviet Socialist Republic he issued a statement whose aim was to postpone the election of a President of Bashkortostan. Parliament, as a consequence, postponed the election. However, this decision was condemned by several national movements and creative unions. In March 1992 Rakhimov was head of the delegation of the Republic of Bashkortostan which signed the Federal treaty in Moscow.

In December 1992 he expressed the hope that the VII Congress of People's Deputies would make the necessary amendments to the economic policy of the Russian government which would bring the fall in production to an end. He hoped that the conflict between the legislative and executive branches could be resolved and that this would permit the stabilization of the situation in Russia.

He is a regular contributor to the republican press on public and political matters, and about 30 articles and interviews on various problems in the republic have appeared. He was awarded the orders and medals of the Red Banner of Labour, the badge of honour, for exemplary work, on the centenary of the birth of V. I. Lenin. He received the honoured title of merited "rationalizer" of the RSFSR, and merited oil worker of the Bashkir ASSR. He is the author of over 40 proposals in oil chemistry for the rationalization of production and over 45 production innovations and inventions. His hobby is watching television, especially football and hockey. He is married, and he and his wife, Luiza Galimovna, live in Kazan. Their son graduated from the oil institute, Ufa, and continued his studies in the US in 1992.

Rakitov, Anatoly Ilich

Head of the Analytical Centre on General Policy of the President of the Russian Federation.

Born in 1928. He graduated from the faculty of philosophy, Moscow State University, and in 1956 he successfully presented his candidate dissertation in philosophy on "Some particularities of the influence of the Soviet state on socialist and production relations" (PhD) and in 1966 his doctoral dissertation on "A logical analysis of the systems of scientific knowledge" (DLitt). He was a chief scientific assistant in the institute of scientific information on the social sciences, USSR Academy of Sciences, was a member of the USSR Academy of Sciences and is now a member of the Russian Academy of Sciences. In 1991 he was chief consultant to the higher consultative co-ordinating council of the Speaker of the RSFSR Supreme Soviet. Then he was appointed head of the information and analytical centre of the RSFSR President.

Rakitov specialized in the problems of dialectical materialism and the philosophy of science, the provision of information to society, logic and methodology of science, dialectics and operational structure of knowledge, historical knowledge, the structure of historical research, the problems of the history of ancient Indian materialism, philosophical conceptualization of the problems of physics, and the analytical and semantic conceptualization of truth. He has written on Hegelian logic, the concepts of F. Schleiermacher, religious and Russian Orthodox morality, philosophical problems of probability and statistical methods, the theory of organization and the design of research systems and the philosophical ABC of business.

He has published articles in *Voprosy filosofii*, *Voprosy istorii*, *estestvoznaniya i tekhniki*, *Vestnik vyshei shkoly*, *Nauka i religiya* and *Novy mir*. He has published the following books: *Marxist Philosophy and Neo-Positivism* (1963); *Religious Morality and its Danger to Socialism* (1960); *The Anatomy of Scientific Knowledge (Popular Introduction to Logic and Scientific Method)* (1969); *The Principles of Scientific Thinking* (1975); *A Tract on Scientific Knowledge for Young, Inquisitive and Critical Minds* (1977); *Philosophical Problems of Science: The Systems Approach* (1977); *Philosophy. Basic Ideas and Principles. Popular Survey* (1985); *Historical Knowledge: A Systems and Gnosiological Approach* (1982); *Questions of Theory and Life* (1987); *A Critique of Non-Marxist Concepts of the Philosophy of Science* (1987); *Marxist-Leninist Philosophy* (1986); *The Computerization of Society and the Human Factor* (1988); *Information Technology and the Provision of Information in Modern Society* (1989); *Perspectives in the Provision of Information in Society* (1990); and *The Philosophy of the Computer Revolution* (1991).

In March 1993, by decree of the President of the Russian Federation, he was appointed head of the analytical centre on general policy of the President. Rakitov advocates genuine independence for Russia, the introduction of the market, return to Europe and a strong President. He favours the development of private farming and free entrepreneurship, and he approved of the activities of the Gaidar government although it committed many mistakes. To him the future holds only two alternatives, either reform or return to the prison camps. He lives in Moscow.

Ramazanov, Marat Davidovich

Chairman of the Tatar Public Centre; Chairman of the G. Ibragimov Club of Tatar Culture, Republic of Bashkortostan, Russian Federation.

Born on April 28, 1939 in Ufa. He is Bashkir. His father is Daut Gadeevich and his mother Fatima Magalimovna. His sister, Elza Davidovna, is a senior lecturer in the Bashkir state pedagogical institute.

He graduated from the faculty of physics and mathematics, Bashkir State University. From 1965 to 1971 he worked in Akademgorodok, near Novosibirsk. In 1970 his textbook *Equations in Mathematical Physics* was published. In 1974, in the institute of mathematics, Siberian branch of the USSR Academy of Sciences, he successfully presented his candidate dissertation in physical and mathematical sciences on volumetric formulae on specified lattices (PhD). Afterwards he was head of the department in the faculty of mathematics, Bashkir State University. Since 1989 he has been chief scientific assistant, institute of mathematics, Bashkir scientific centre of the Urals section of the Russian Academy of Sciences.

In 1988, at the first public meeting of the Tatar population of Ufa, he proposed the founding of an appreciation society of the Tatar culture, art and language. In 1989 at the constituent assembly of the Tatar Public Centre (TPC), he was elected chairman of the G. Ibragimov Club of Tatar Culture. Later he became chairman of the TPC of Bashkiria. In 1990, when the bureau of the Party *obkom* resigned, Ramazanov was elected a member of the provisional bureau of the Bashkir Party *obkom* and the 40th *oblast* Party conference was held.

He actively supports the setting up of classes and groups to learn the Tatar language and believes that it is necessary to accord the Tatar language the status of a state language in the Republic of Bashkortostan, along with Bashkir and Russian. He is married, and his wife is Saniya Sharafovna. They have three sons of school and pre-school age. He lives in Ufa.

Rodionov, Yury Nikolaevich

Deputy Commander-in-Chief of the Unified Armed Forces of the CIS for personnel; Colonel-General.

Born on March 12, 1938 in Taganrog, Rostov *oblast*; Russian. He graduated from Ryazan Artillery Technical School in 1958 and from F. E. Dzerzhinsky Military Academy in 1967, and received a higher military engineering education with a degree in electronic computers. He was a member of the CPSU until August 1991.

He began his career as an officer as an artillery platoon commander in the Carpathian military district, and after the Academy he conducted scientific research at one of the leading research institutes of the Ministry of Defence. In 1972 he became deputy head, and later head of the computer centre department at the Ministry of Defence. According to his long-time colleagues, Yu. Rodionov was ambitious, had a talent for organization and knew how to please superior officers. He enjoyed the support of superior officers and Party-political agencies. From 1976 he worked in the Chief Personnel Administration, holding various posts, and was promoted to major-general there.

In April 1991 he was assigned to the RSFSR Ministry of Defence and was soon appointed deputy chairman of the RSFSR State Committee on defence and security, and chairman of a sub-committee on defence. He was in close contact with the top leaders of Russia and enjoyed the respect of Gen. K. Kobets and B. Yeltsin. He co-operated with democratic forces in the army, avoiding, however, close ties with them for the fear of endangering his official status. In August 1991 he was one of the heads of defence of the Russian White House, actively taking security measures.

By a USSR President's decree in September 1991 he was appointed deputy Minister of Defence for personnel, becoming head of the Chief Personnel Administration of the USSR Ministry of Defence. The hopes of democratic forces in the army for a thorough personnel renewal in the armed forces proved unjustified, however, and Gen. Rodionov actually blocked the work aimed at dismissing compromised generals, admirals and officers from their posts in the army and navy. At the same time he offered no support to the military personnel being disciplined for their democratic convictions. Moreover, using his broad ties with top leaders he did his best to ensure his own promotion, and within two months (September–October 1991) he was promoted to Lieutenant-General and Colonel-General. Yu. Rodionov's activity caused strong protests from the public organizations, "The Military for Democracy" and the Shield union, and he does not enjoy respect in the armed forces.

Since February 1992 he has been deputy Commander-in-Chief of the united armed forces of the CIS for personnel. From April to May 1992 he was a member of the State Committee for establishing the Ministry of Defence, army and navy of the Russian Federation.

Gen. Rodionov has expressed his views in the press on personnel policy, and reorganization and improvement of training of the military men. His best-known publications are "I don't want to beat it to a pulp" (*Krasnaya Zvezda*, October 31, 1991), "Personnel: on training" (*Krasnaya Zvezda*, March 5, 1992), "Personnel training: on making it more humane" (*Krasnaya Zvezda*, March 13, 1992). He does not express his own political views or convictions in public.

He is fond of literature and the theatre, and is not indifferent to art. He is a sportsman, and is eager to gain the image of a military intellectual. He has never been abroad. He has been awarded several orders and medals, and is married with two children.

Office address: 103175, Moscow, K-175.

Roketsky, Leonid Yulianovich

Head of the Administration of Tyumen *oblast*, Russian Federation.

Born on March 15, 1942 in the village of Nosov Berezhansky *raion*, Ternopol *oblast* into a peasant family; member of the CPSU until August 1991. He was educated at the Zavalovsky secondary school and Lvov (Lviv) Cinematographical Technical College. After service in the Soviet Army, in 1965, he entered the Polytechnical Institute, Lvov, and graduated in 1970. During his studies he worked in a student construction brigade in Surgut, Siberia. After graduating he was assigned to the main Tyumen oil and gas trust and worked in construction organizations in Surgut performing various functions. In November 1981 he moved to work in the soviets and became deputy chairman and, in June 1988, chairman of the Surgut city soviet executive committee. He has received state awards.

On April 22, 1990, during the second round of voting, he was elected a deputy of the Tyumen *oblast* soviet, and in May 1990 he was a candidate for the post of chairman of the soviet. During the election campaign he stated that the most important tasks of the chairman of the soviet was the establishment in the *oblast* of a processing and oil refining industry, the development of local self-government and the drafting of an *oblast* budget, the development of the social sphere, satisfying the market with goods and solving the food problem. During the first round of voting he polled 52.8% of the votes of the deputies of the *oblast* soviet (there were five candidates) and was declared elected. In March 1990 he was elected a deputy to Surgut city soviet, and in May of the same year he was elected a member of the Tyumen Party *obkom*.

On August 20, 1991 Tyumen *oblast* soviet and *oblast* soviet executive committee declared the activities of the Extraordinary Committee to be anti-constitutional and decreed that the soviets were the only legal state authorities in Tyumen *oblast*. They appealed for only the implementation of the decrees of the President of the Russian Federation.

In October 1991 a session of the Tyumen *oblast* soviet proposed two candidates to the President as head of the Tyumen *oblast* administration: L. Yu. Roketsky and Yu. K. Shafranik, chairman of the *oblast* soviet. After Shafranik was appointed head of the administration by presidential decree in November 1991, Roketsky became first deputy head of the administration. On February 23, 1992, after Shafranik was appointed Russian minister of fuel and energy, Roketsky was appointed head of the administration of Tyumen *oblast* by presidential decree. He is married with two children and lives in Tyumen.

Romanov, Mikhail Alekseevich

Russian ambassador to Kyrgyzstan.

Born in 1936; Russian. He graduated in 1964 from the Moscow State Institute of International Relations. He was then appointed to the USSR embassy in Thailand, and then worked in the apparatus of the USSR Ministry of Foreign Affairs, Moscow. From 1971 to 1976 he was second secretary in the USSR embassy in Thailand. From 1976 to 1977 he studied in the diplomatic academy of the USSR Ministry of Foreign Affairs, and was first secretary, then counsellor in the department for south-east Asia in the ministry (1971-81).

From 1981 to 1987 he was counsellor in the USSR embassy in Nepal, and then was head of section and head of the department for south Asia of the USSR Ministry of Foreign Affairs (1987-92). From February 1992 to June 1992 he was senior counsellor in the department for west and south Asia in the ministry. In June 1992 he was appointed Russia's first ambassador to the Republic of Kyrgyzstan. He is ambassador extraordinary and plenipotentiary.

Address: Embassy of Russia in Kyrgyzstan, Bishkek; *telephone*: Moscow 244 1606 (Foreign Ministry enquiry office).

Rossel, Eduard Ergartovich

Head of the Administration of Ekaterinburg *oblast*, Russian Federation.

Born in 1937 in the village of Bor, Borsky *raion*, Gorky (Nizhny Novgorod) *oblast*; member of the CPSU until August 1991. In 1962 he graduated from the Institute of Mining, Sverdlovsk, as a specialist in the construction of mining enterprises, and in 1972 he successfully presented his candidate dissertation in technical sciences at the Urals Polytechnical Institute (PhD (Eng)). He began his career in 1962 as a junior scientific assistant in the Sverdlovsk Institute of Mining and in 1963 joined the Tagiltroi trust where he progressed from being a foreman to head of an administration. In October 1983 he was appointed deputy head of the Sreduralstroi territorial construction association and in January 1990 became the head of the association.

In 1990 Rossel was elected a deputy of the *oblast* soviet and at the first session of the soviet, on April 2, 1990, he was elected chairman of the *oblast* soviet executive committee. At the second session of the soviet on July 4, 1990 he was elected chairman of the *oblast* soviet as a result of the letter of the Speaker of the RSFSR Supreme Soviet (Boris Yeltsin) about introducing the experiment in Sverdlovsk *oblast* of appointing the same person as chairman of the *oblast* soviet and chairman of the executive committee.

On August 21, 1991 the *oblast*, soviet issued a declaration to those serving in the armed forces appealing to them not to fight against the people. At an extraordinary session of the *oblast* soviet support for the RSFSR President was voiced, the activities of the Extraordinary Committee were declared to amount to an anti-constitutional government coup and a pre-strike position was adopted in the *oblast*. A city strike committee was set up, as was a co-ordinating council of *oblast*, city and *raion* deputies to prepare for a possible appeal for a general political strike.

Rossel was appointed head of the administration of Sverdlovsk *oblast* on October 18, 1991 by presidential decree, and he is a member of the board of the union of governors of Russia. As head of the administration he advocated many different forms of ownership of land, the privatization of loss-making collective and state farms, not by order but according to the mature needs of the workers. His principal task was to support private farming, and he also advocated the free privatization of housing, the commercialization of the services sector, and the retention of a 60% tax on added value in the *oblast*. He favoured radical economic reform, opposed group egoism, and proposed the drawing up of territorial orders and plans for new production for the *oblast*.

In December 1992, during the VII Congress of People's Deputies, he stated that the government could no longer administer the country from Moscow. It should restrict itself merely to setting the general rules of the game and the actual course of the reforms should be left to the regions. A new Russian constitution was urgently needed and he considered that the VII congress would proceed "normally". He lives in Ekaterinburg.

Rudkin, Yury Dmitrievich

Secretary of the Constitutional Court of the Russian Federation.

Born on November 7, 1951 in the village of Burmakino, Nekrasovsky *raion*, Yaroslavl *oblast*; Russian; member of the CPSU from 1972 to August 1991. In 1972 he graduated from the higher anti-aircraft rocket forces technical school, and in 1973 enrolled in the law faculty of Yaroslavl State University and graduated in 1978 as a lawyer. He acted as a legal adviser during his undergraduate days. He became a lecturer at the Yaroslavl polytechnical institute where in 1990 he was an assistant professor. In 1984, in Kharkov (Kharkiv), Ukraine, he successfully presented his candidate dissertation on "natural sources of law (nature, structure and differences)" (LLM). He has published about 20 articles.

In early 1990 he was nominated for election as an RSFSR people's deputy in the No. 772 Krasnoperekopsky territorial district, Yaroslavl *oblast*, by the students of Yaroslavl polytechnic institute. During the election campaign he advocated greater activity for government agencies and public organizations in proposing legislation and overcoming the incompetence of legal agencies by electing legal professionals to parliament. He supported the immediate adoption of legislation on laws and property. He expressed his intention of adding important questions to referenda, questions about property, land and the role of the CPSU.

He was convinced that the concept of private property found little support among the mass of the population and that the introduction of private property would lead to social stratification. He was sure that society supported the collective ownership of property and its introduction would destroy the command-administrative system. There were eight candidates. Rudkin polled 12.66% of the votes in the first round and won the second round with 47.71% of the votes. His main opponent V. B. Valabuev, a grinder in the Yaroslavl diesel equipment factory who polled 12.52% of the votes in the first round.

Rudkin was deputy chairman of the RSFSR Supreme Soviet committee on legislation, a member of the Supreme Soviet of Nationalities' commission on the socio-economic development of the republics within the RSFSR, the autonomous *oblasts*, autonomous *okrugs* and small nations, a member of the Supreme Soviet Presidium commission on the problems of Soviet Germans, a member of the parliamentary Russia faction and the deputies' group of military men and a member of the constitutional commission. He is one of the co-authors of various draft laws, including the status of the RSFSR people's deputy, the rehabilitation of the nations which were victims of Stalinist oppression, on the permanent commissions of the chambers and committees of the RSFSR Supreme Soviet, on the sanitary and epidemiological well-being of the population, and the standing rules of the RSFSR Supreme Soviet.

He was nominated for election to the Constitutional Court by the Russia deputies' group. He was elected to the Constitutional Court on October 29, 1991, at the V Congress of People's Deputies, in the first round of voting, when he received 625 votes for and 264 against. On October 30 he surrendered his mandate as a people's deputy.

He regards the most important function of the Constitutional Court to be the establishment of a law-governed state (*Rechtsstaat*) in Russia, the prevention of the breakup of Russia and the defence of the constitutional order of the Russian Federation, but also the protection of the rights of the republics within the Federation.

The main obstacles to achieving these goals are economic and political instability and the absence of any sense of responsibility about the need to implement decisions of the Constitutional Court. He thinks that the present Russian constitution ties the hands and feet of the Constitutional Court and hopes that the Congress of People's Deputies will adopt a new constitution to replace the present one so as to cut down amendments and half-measures. However, he does not support other alternative draft constitutions, for example, the one proposed by Anatoly Sobchak, since there is much political trickery in them aimed at preventing the adoption of the draft constitution proposed by the Constitutional Court. He is married with a son and a daughter, and lives in Moscow.

Ryabov, Nikolai Timofeevich

Deputy Speaker of the Russian Parliament.

Born on December 9, 1946 in Salsk, Rostov *oblast*; Russian. He was a member of the CPSU from 1968 to August 1991. He graduated from the Salsk Agricultural Technical College and the faculty of law, Rostov State University. He began his career as a tractor driver on the Budenny stud farm, Salsk *raion*, Rostov *oblast*, and was later an engineer in the Salskselmash enterprise (1972-73); head of production training and military head of No. 78 school, in the settlement of Gigant, Rostov *oblast* (1973); lecturer and deputy director of the Salsk Agricultural Technical College (1973-90).

In January 1990 he was nominated for election as an RSFSR people's deputy in the No. 617 Salsk territorial district, Rostov *oblast*. During the election campaign he advocated sovereignty and full economic independence for Russia; separation of legislative, executive and judicial powers; all power to the soviets; the annulment of article 6 of the USSR constitution (on the leading role of the CPSU in society); the economic independence of enterprises and their right to dispose of their own income. He devoted considerable attention to increasing investment in rural areas and raising the status of agricultural labour.

There were four candidates and Ryabov won in the first round, polling over 50% of the votes. He was elected a member of the RSFSR Supreme Soviet at the I Congress of People's Deputies (629 voted for, 305 voted against), and he is a member of the Council of the Republic of the Supreme Soviet. He was elected chairman of the sub-committee of the committee on legislation of the RSFSR Supreme Soviet (1990-91); in October 1991 Speaker of the Council of the Republic of the Supreme Soviet of the Russian Federation; and in January 1992 chairman of the parliamentary group of the Supreme Soviet of the Russian

Federation. He is a member of the parliamentary faction, communists for democracy, and a member of the constitutional commission. In December 1992 he was elected deputy Speaker of the Supreme Soviet of the Russian Federation and second deputy chairman of the constitutional commission.

Ryabov shifted his position on the constitutional conflict between President Yeltsin and parliament on May 14, 1993. He appealed to parliament not to reject President Yeltsin's concept of holding a constitutional assembly to approve a new constitution and thereby broke with Ruslan Khasbulatov, the Speaker, who had declared the President's plan to be criminal.

Address: 103274 Moscow, K 274, Krasnopresnenskaya nab., d. 2, Dom Sovetov; *telephone*: Moscow 205 67 68.

Ryzhkov, Nikolai Ivanovich

Former chairman of the USSR Council of Ministers.

Born on September 28, 1929 in the village of Dyleevka, Dzerzhinsky *raion*, Donetsk *oblast* into a working-class family; Russian. He was a member of the CPSU from 1956 to August 1991. In 1950 he graduated from the Kramatorsk machine building technical college, Donetsk *oblast* and then worked in the Urals machine building enterprise, Sverdlovsk, as a shift foreman, head of a stage and from 1955 as head of a shop.

In 1959 he graduated from the Urals Polytechnical Institute and was then appointed head welder and deputy director of the enterprise. In 1965 he became chief engineer and then in 1970 director of the Urals machine building enterprise and in 1971 he was appointed general director of Uralmash, Sverdlovsk. In 1976 he became first deputy USSR Minister of Heavy and Transport Machine Building, and in 1979 first deputy chairman of USSR Gosplan. In 1981 he was elected a member of the party Central Committee, and in 1982 he became a Party Central Committee secretary and also head of the economic department of the party Central Committee. From April 1985 to December 1990 he was chairman of the USSR Council of Minsters (Prime Minister) and in 1989 was elected a USSR peoples deputy as a CPSU nominee. In March 1990 he became a member of the Council of the USSR President. He was awarded two USSR state prizes.

He belonged to the group of moderate reformers who rose to prominence under Gorbachev. His knowledge of the defence industry, heavy industry and the economy in general made him sceptical about the transition to a market economy as the solution to the Soviet Union's economic problems. A mild mannered, modest man, he was ill-suited to the hurly-burly of Soviet politics in the dying days of the empire. Technically competent, he was unable to devise a convincing alternative to the radical reformers, led by Yeltsin, and their desire for a rapid transition to the market. He was aware of the findings of the Shatalin report under Andropov about the structural imbalance of the economy. Shatalin rigorously demonstrated on paper the need for a market, but such a move proved politically impossible given the opposition of the moderate reformers, primarily Ligachev.

Ryzhkov appears to have been as unaware as Gorbachev of the systemic crisis facing the country from 1985. The policies of acceleration (*uskorenie*) and improvement (*usovershenstvovanie*), adopted during the first two years of the Gorbachev era, produced little. Then the law on the state enterprise and the law on co-operation allowed wages and prices to escape the control of the centre and Ryzhkov was ill-suited to the task of coping with rising inflation. He appears to have been a major influence in the autumn of 1990 when Gorbachev shied away from espousing the radical 500-day programme. Ryzhkov's health suffered and, after a heart attack, he gave way to Valentin Pavlov as Prime Minister on December 25, 1990. The latter had academic expertise but lacked industrial experience.

In 1991 Ryzhkov was nominated by work collectives for the post of President of the RSFSR. During the election campaign he advocated a socialist path for Russia, and favoured a transition to a regulated market but not at the expense of the people. He advocated the establishment of system of social protection of working people, the raising of wages in the key sectors of the economy and reduction of prices of the main consumer goods. He opposed privatization which he regarded as leading to a take-over of the economy by shadow businessmen. He did not support private ownership of land and opposed the enforced dissolution of state and collective farms. He did not want Western credits and capital to be accepted by Russia since this could lead to Western states enslaving Russia. He advocated that Russia remain part of the Soviet Union.

In the elections of June 12, 1991 Ryzhkov polled 16.85% of the votes and was second of six candidates, coming a long way behind Boris Yeltsin who was elected President. Ryzhkov was seen as the official communist candidate and had the approval of President Mikhail Gorbachev, which ensured that the anti-establishment vote mainly went to Yeltsin. Ryzhkov is the author of the book *Perestroika. The History of Treachery* (1992). He is now a pensioner and lives in Moscow.

Ryzhov, Yury Petrovich

Russian Ambassador to France and Member of the Council of the President of the Russian Federation.

Born on October 28, 1930 in Moscow; Russian. He was a student in the institute of physics and mathematics, Moscow (1948-54), then until 1958 he was an engineer in the N. E. Zhukovsky Central Aero-hydrodynamic Institute. From 1958 to 1960 he was senior engineer in the scientific research institute of thermal processes, and from 1960 to 1991 he was connected with the S. Ordzhonikidze Aviation Institute, Moscow, where he progressed from assistant professor to rector in 1986. The same year he met Boris Yeltsin who was first secretary of the Moscow city Party committee (*gorkom*). In 1968 he successfully presented his candidate dissertation in technical sciences on "Statistical sources of reactive force with artificial commutation of valves" (PhD (Eng)) and later his doctoral dissertation on a secret subject (DSc). In 1981 he was elected a corresponding member of the USSR Academy of Sciences and in 1987 an acting member. He is the recipient of various state awards.

In early 1989 he was nominated for election as a USSR people's deputy in the No. 14 Leningradsky territorial district, Moscow. During the election campaign he advocated radical changes in the structure of society. He believed that the reason for the failure to solve basic social problems in the country was not due to those in power but to the structure of society, and he supported the transfer of all power to local soviets at various levels though he pointed out that the administrative apparatus would not voluntarily give up their power. The future of parliament depended on deputies remaining true to their convictions and not bending to the political situation and the temptations of power, in other words moral problems.

There were three candidates. Ryzhov polled 46.53% of the votes in the first round and won the second round, polling 70.61% of the votes. He was elected to the USSR Supreme Soviet at the I Congress of People's Deputies. He became a member of its Presidium and headed the Supreme Soviet commission on science and education. He was a member of the interregional group of deputies.

In December 1990 he and Gennady Burbulis were appointed deputy chairmen of the higher consultative and co-ordinating Council of the RSFSR Supreme Soviet Speaker, Boris Yeltsin. In September 1991 he became a member of the political consultative Council of the USSR President, and in the autumn of the same year Ryzhov was one of those being considered for the post of RSFSR Prime Minister. In December 1992 he was proposed as Prime Minister, in which case Egor Gaidar would have remained in government, but he declined. He is a member of the presidential Council. On January 4, 1992 he was appointed Russian ambassador to France. He speaks English and French.

As a young man he was a professional cyclist. He is married and his wife is a graduate of the State Institute of International Relations, Moscow, and they have two daughters and grandsons. He lives in Paris.

Sabirov, Mukhammat Gallyamovich

Chairman of the Council of Ministers of the Republic of Tatarstan, Russian Federation.

Born in 1932 in the village of Novo-Kurmashevo, Kushnarenkovsky *raion*, Bashkir Autonomous Soviet Socialist Republic (ASSR); Tatar; member of the CPSU from 1958 to August 1991. He began working during the Great Fatherland War (1941-45) when he worked in the fields with grown-ups. After graduating from the Ufa Institute of Oil in 1955 he was an engineer, senior engineer, and deputy head of the production technical department of the Almetevsk oil boring trust, and in 1964 was elected secretary of its Party committee. In 1965 he was elected second secretary of the Almetevsk city Party committee and in 1968 was appointed manager of the *Vostokmontazhgaz* trust, Almetevsk. In 1984 he became deputy and in November 1989 Chairman of the Council of Ministers of the Tatar ASSR, and was also a deputy of the Supreme Soviet of the Tatar ASSR. He was awarded two orders of the Red Banner of Labour, the order of the badge of honour and medals.

In early 1990 Sabirov was nominated for election as an RSFSR people's deputy in the No. 869 Chistopolsky territorial district, Tatar ASSR. There were four candidates, and he won in the first round. He was also elected a people's deputy of the Tatar ASSR. He was confirmed as Prime Minister of Tatarstan by decree of the Speaker of the Supreme Soviet of the Tatar ASSR on July 5, 1991, and on assuming office he appealed for the republic to secure equal rights with the Union republics. The status of an autonomous republic, in his view, did not permit the satisfaction of the social, economic, national and cultural needs of the population of the republic. He advocated that the republic should independently provide the means to solve the problems associated with social and cultural development. He rejected the accusation that the republic's goal was political separatism, and insisted on the retention and development of historical, economic and cultural links with Russia, not on the basis of the Federal treaty but on separate inter-governmental equal treaties.

The fundamental way to reform the economy was to move to regulated market relations, the restructuring of the financial and credit policy, reform of price formation, anti-monopoly policies and measures to protect the population socially. He maintained that the primary task was to satisfy the demand of the population for food, goods and services, the protection of the environment and regional scientific technical progress. He advocated the conversion of the military economy for civil use, the development of foreign economic links and economic relations between branches and regions. He opposed the centralized distribution of resources and was for regional autonomy and self-financing. He appealed for greater social investment, for the construction of fewer new factories, for tax advantages to be given to consumer goods producers and the speeding up of privatization.

In August 1991, like all other leaders of the republic, he supported the Extraordinary Committee and met General Albert Makashov. He lives in Kazan.

Saenko, Gennady Vasilevich

Co-Chairman of the Front of National Salvation; co-ordinator of the Communists of Russia Parliamentary Faction.

Born on August 1, 1945 in the village of Malaya Kuznetsova, Zernogradsky *raion*, Rostov *oblast*, where his father was a collective farm worker. Russian. He was a member of the CPSU from 1967 to August 1991. After graduating in 1968 from the Azov-Chernomorsky Institute of Mechanization and Electrification, Rostov-on-Don, he worked as an engineer, then as deputy director of the motor repair plant. From 1970 to 1971 he worked in the apparatus of the Salsky Party city committee, Rostov *oblast*: first secretary of the Salsky *Komsomol* city committee, and then secretary of the Rostov *Komsomol* city committee (1971-77). He worked in the department for the organization of Party work of the Rostov Party *obkom*, first as an instructor, then as deputy chairman of the department (1977-81). In 1981 he graduated from the Rostov Higher Party School as an external student, and was an instructor in the department of the organization of Party work, Party Central Committee (1983-88). In December 1988 he was elected second secretary of the Kursk Party *obkom*, deputy of the Salsky city, Rostov and Kursk *oblast* soviets of people's deputies, member of the Salsky and Rostov city Party committees and the Kursk Party *obkom*.

In 1990 he successfully presented his candidate dissertation in history on "The activities of primary Party organizations in the formation of the political consciousness of working people during the revolutionary *perestroika* of Soviet society" (PhD). In January 1990 he was nominated as a candidate for election as an RSFSR people's deputy in the No. 493 Sovetsky national territorial district, Kursk *oblast*. During the election campaign he underlined that the most important thing was to ensure decisive changes in the social and economic sphere, including the radical reorienation of the economy, the rapid development of the infrastructure of society, the concentration of national economic resources to provide food and consumer goods, services and housing, together with faster development of the health service. He advocated the expansion of leasing throughout the economy and the inclusion of working people in the management of work collectives, the full economic independence of collective and state farms as regards the production and sale of their produce, an equal partnership between urban and rural areas, and the fusion of the advantages of rural life and urban comforts so as to attract labour to the collective and state farms.

There were three candidates. Saenko polled 45.9% of the votes in the first round and won the second round, polling 61.2% of the votes. His main opponent was V. S. Shatokhin, chairman of the *Komsomolets* collective farm, Chermisinovsky *raion*, Kursk *oblast*, who received 30.7% of the votes in the first round and 37% in the second round. Saenko was elected a member of the RSFSR Supreme Soviet at the VI Congress of People's Deputies.

In February 1990 he signed the declaration of 29 RSFSR people's deputies to the President and the Prime Minister of the USSR, demanding the banning of all marches, meetings and demonstrations during the III Congress of Russian People's Deputies in the environs of the Sadovoe Koltso in Moscow. On March 16, 1992 he became a member of the commission investigating the events of February 23, 1992 in Moscow.

He is a member of the Council of Nationalities and the commission of the Council of Nationalities on the social and economic development of the republics within the Russian Federation, autonomous *oblasts* and *okrugs* and small nations. He is a member of the communists of Russia group of deputies and co-leader of the Front of National Salvation. At the VII Congress of People's Deputies, in December 1992, he sharply criticized the policies of the government of Egor Gaidar, especially its economic record. Saenko was convinced of the need for a centralized management of the economy, subordinating the interests of production to the interests of the consumer.

He advocated the social orientation of the economy and believed the route to be taken should lead through state planning. He also posed the question of the need for the congress to decide about the formation of a special investigatory commission to review deputies' questions about the squandering of strategic raw materials, diamonds and gold. He moved a motion to set up a special congress commission on the mass media. At the VIII and IX Congresses, in March 1993, he continued his criticism of the Yeltsin administration. He and other communists vigorously opposed the economic policies of the new government and called for the impeachment of the President after his speech on television on March 20, 1993 intimating his intention of introducing a special regime in the country. The referendum result disappointed Saenko and his supporters but, led by Ruslan Khasbulatov, the parliamentary Speaker, the opponents of the President attempted to dismiss the result as an irrelevance. The convention of the constitutional assembly on June 5, 1993 added to the tension.

Saenko was awarded the order of the badge of honour and the medals for exemplary labour, also valiant labour and the centenary of the birth of V. I. Lenin. He is married to Lyudmila Semenovna and they have three children. His elder daughter graduated from the Moscow Medical Institute, his son is at medical school and his younger daughter, Anya, is at secondary school. His hobbies are reading, horse racing and fishing, and he lives in Kursk.

Safarov, Mars Gilyazevich

Leader of the Ecological Movement in the Republic of Bashkortostan, Russian Federation.

Born on April 18, 1937 in the village of Aidarali, Stellibashevsky *raion*, Bashkir ASSR. He is a Tatar whose father, Gilyazetdin Nizamutdinovich, was a teacher in a village school, as was his mother, Zifa Khamidullovna. He has a brother and a sister who are now both pensioners. He was a member of the CPSU until August 1991.

He graduated from the faculty of chemistry of the oil institute, Ufa, as a chemist and technologist. In 1960 he was appointed an assistant in the department in the oil institute, Ufa. In 1965, in the Gubkin institute of oil chemistry and the gas industry, Moscow, he successfully presented his candidate dissertation in chemistry on condensation of some unlimited hydrocarbons with formaldehyde in the presence of cations of KU–2 resin (PhD). In 1980 he successfully presented his doctoral dissertation in chemistry (DSc). In 1967 he was an assistant professor and in 1981 became head of the department of organic chemistry in the faculty of chemistry, Bashkir State University. He has over 100 scientific certificates and over 250 scientific publications. He was a member of the Party committee of the university for many years.

He is well known in the Republic of Bashkortostan as leader of the green movement and is referred to as the green professor. He advocates the cleaning up of the environment in the republic and in Ufa. In 1990 during the disaster in Ufa, when the city's water supply was poisoned by phenol, he became a member of the state expert commission for the inquiry into the reasons for the catastrophe.

In 1991, after the adoption by the Supreme Soviet of the Republic of a decree (later this decree was withdrawn) on the holding of elections for President of the Republic of the Bashkir Soviet Socialist Republic, Safarov was nominated as a candidate at a plenum of the representatives of the congress of democratic forces. Public opinion polls revealed him as a serious candidate. He believes that the republic should remain a subject of the Russian Federation.

He is married. His wife, Venera Gayazovna, is an assistant professor in the oil institute, Ufa. They have a son and a daughter and both have graduated from the faculty of chemistry, Bashkir State University. He lives in Ufa.

Saganov, Vladimir Bizyaevich

Chairman of the Council of Ministers of the Republic of Buryatia, Russian Federation.

Born in 1936 in the village of Kharbyaty, Tunkinsky *raion*, Buryat-Mongol Autonomous Soviet Socialist Republic (ASSR); Buryat; member of the CPSU until August 1991. He became acquainted with agricultural labour from an early age and this influenced his choice of career. He entered the faculty of veterinary science of the Buryat Agricultural Institute, from where he graduated with distinction and went back to his native village to work in the Sayansky state farm. After two years he was appointed chief veterinary surgeon, and later director of the state farm. In 1967 he was elected chairman of the executive committee of the Tuva *raion* soviet. Later he moved to top positions in the republic, first deputy, then Minister of Agriculture of the Buryat ASSR, and then first deputy Chairman of the Council of Ministers of the Buryat ASSR.

In 1977 he became a postgraduate student at the Academy of Social Sciences of the Party Central Committee. However, he was soon recalled from his studies to become Chairman of the Council of Ministers of the republic, and in June 1987 he became a diplomat and was envoy and counsellor on economic affairs in the Soviet embassy in the Korean People's Democratic Republic.

In early 1990 he was nominated for election as an RSFSR people's deputy in the No. 90 Pribaikalsky national territorial district. During the election campaign he stated that a people's deputy should first and foremost struggle for a sovereign, economically independent Russia. The future of the Soviet

Union was closely linked to a strong RSFSR. At the same time all territories and autonomous regions of Russia should possess all the necessary rights in the social and economic spheres. They should be able to resolve the food problem, adopt laws on property and on the use of land. The key question, according to Saganov, was the ownership of land. Land should remain the property of the state, otherwise it should be under the control of local soviets.

There were 11 candidates. In the first round he polled 24.19% of the votes but lost in the second round, polling 40.2% of the votes. The winner was Efim Vladimirovich Basin, head of Bamtransstroi trust, who received 16.94% of the votes in the first round and 48.7% in the second. Saganov was elected a people's deputy of the Buryat ASSR.

At the first session of the Supreme Soviet of the Buryat ASSR Saganov was elected Chairman of the Council of Ministers, and was also elected a delegate to the XXVIII Party congress. On August 27, 1991 he flew to Moscow and reported on republican radio that he was the plenipotentiary of the USSR Extraordinary Committee to head a similar committee in Buryatia. He set up this committee and information about it was broadcast on the radio. At an extraordinary session of the Supreme Soviet of Buryatia in late August 1991 he was recalled from his position as Speaker (Chairman) of the Supreme Soviet for his unprincipled position, adopted during the attempted August coup. However despite this the Supreme Soviet expressed its confidence in its head.

In 1992 he stated that he regarded his priorities, besides promoting new legislation, to be the resolution of the question of the social security of the population and the environmental clean up of the Lake Baikal Area. He lives in Ulan Ude.

Sale, Marina Evgenevna

Co-chairman of the North West Section of the Free Democratic Party of Russia.

Born in 1934. She was never a member of the CPSU. She graduated from the G. V. Plekhanov Mining Institute, Leningrad, and is a geologist with 33 years of experience. In 1963 she successfully presented her candidate dissertation on "Pegmatites in Chupinsky *raion* and the laws governing the place of deposition of muscovite in them" (north Karelia) (PhD). She did not present her doctoral dissertation, as in 1977 she unexpectedly received a negative review from the Central Mineralogical Institute. Despite having received 20 positive reviews, she decided to postpone her presentation and went off to Karelia to introduce her methods to find traces of "muscovite". She successfully presented her dissertation in 1985 on "Metallogenes in the regressive stage of regional metamorphism" (DSc). Until 1987 she was employed as senior scientific assistant of the institute of geology and pre-cambrian geochronology, USSR Academy of Sciences.

In 1987 she gave up her scientific work, set up a club of the friends of the journal *Ogonek*, participated in the meetings of the *Perestroika* club of the

Leningrad popular front and campaigned in the elections. In early 1989 she was nominated for election as a USSR people's deputy in the No. 19 Leningrad city national territorial district in the second round of elections. During the election campaign she argued that the only sure way of depriving the nomenclature of its power and privileges was the development of a massive popular movement for radical *perestroika*. She called for the implementation of genuine people's power, the creation of a multi-faceted economy and open democratic society. She advocated a multi-party system and the development of the market. Laws on leasing, elections and the press were needed. The command administrative system should be completely dismantled and a Leningrad democratic front established.

There were 28 candidates. Sale lost in the first round, polling 4.63% of the votes, and the winner was N. V. Ivanov, senior researcher on especially important cases in the USSR general Procurator's Office, polling 61.01% of the votes. In early 1990 Sale was nominated for election as a RSFSR people's deputy in the No. 107 Vasileostrovsky territorial district, Leningrad. In the election programme she proposed that the Congress of People's Deputies should adopt the decree on power of Academician Andrei Sakharov, take all power into its own hands and remove all Party agencies, irrespective of the level, from power. A new draft constitution should be drafted and debated by the population which guaranteed the state sovereignty of the Russian Federation, observed the principle of a multi-party system, rights and freedoms, proclaimed by the universal declaration on human rights, and the equality of all forms of property, including private property. The new regulations of the Leningrad city soviet should accept its temporary status and implement the slogan, "all power to the soviets", as regards its economic rights. The present Leningrad soviet executive committee should be dissolved and a new one elected, consisting of competent specialists and not nomenclature officials, and the maximum reduction of the apparatus attempted. A commission of deputies should be set up to conduct an inquiry into the present Leningrad city and Leningrad *oblast* soviets. They should be held responsible for building the dam in the Gulf of Finland, for the state of lake Ladoga and for the ugliness of the city. The nomenclature should be deprived of all privileges and the material and financial reserves should be devoted to the survivors of the wartime blockade, the poor and children. The congress should publish a list of nomenclature posts, introduce *glasnost* to all types of privilege, set up a commission of deputies to eliminate all privileges in soviets of all levels, review agreements with public organizations, CPSU, the *Komsomol*, the all-Union central council of trades unions, about leasing buildings and transfer the palaces of the apparatus to children and the poor. She advocated that new laws be promulgated on labour collectives, public organizations; there should be a thorough review of the activities of financial organizations and the banning of state donations and hidden subsidizing of public political organizations.

She was supported during the elections by the Democratic elections 90 platform and she supported the platform of the Green Party in its struggle to prevent further destruction of nature, for a clean environment and a healthy way of life. She supported universal human values, ecological wisdom, personal and public responsibility, respect for diversity, decentralization and lack of violence.

There were 11 candidates. Sale polled 32.5% of the votes in the first round and won the second round, polling 59.65% of the votes. Her main opponent was N. N. Korablev, first secretary of the Vasileostrovsky Party *raion* committee, who polled 9.45% of the votes in the first round and 28.65% in the second. In 1990 she was also elected a people's deputy of the Leningrad city soviet where she was chairwoman of the commission on food.

It was her idea to found the Democratic Party in the autumn of 1989, and the constituent congress of the party took place in Leningrad. However, Nikolai Travkin argued in favour of a vertical structure with a chairman at the top. There were former members of the CPSU Central Committee in the organizational committee and the majority of activists were ex-members of the Party democratic platform. The Leningrad delegation left the constituent congress and set up the Free Democratic Party of Russia.

Sale proposed the convocation of a constituent assembly for Russia. The Russian Democratic Movement should not only fight communists but struggle against communist ideology in the widest general meaning of the term, against a unitary state and the return of Russia to the course of development which was interrupted in 1917. She favoured a union with all democratic forces but opposed the seizure of power by force, rejecting the concept of armed struggle. In order for reforms to be implemented what was needed was a new constitution, expressing reform ideals, a new system of government based on the principle of the division of powers, a system of counterbalances, the constructive interaction of the branches of power which would prevent dictatorship. Cadres should come from among professionals and not those opposed to reform. New elections should not be run on a first past the post system but be proportional, based on Party lists. The present Congress of People's Deputies is incapable, in her view, of adopting a new constitution since it is made up of almost 80% of former communists to whom the concept of democracy is not only alien but dangerous. A situation in which all power rests with the congress, but the legislative power apportions the division of power, is absurd, and amounts to limitless power. However, immediate change in the way the state is administered should come about by peaceful means. She would like to see greater power to the courts and a strong government taking responsibility, strict observance of the laws, and equality of all three branches of power. The source of the latter is the people. She believes that President Yeltsin, immediately after the failed coup, should have convoked a constituent assembly and call on the world community to condemn the CPSU. She is divorced and has no children. She lives in St Petersburg.

Salii, Ivan Mykolaiovych

Former Prefect of the President of Ukraine in Kiev City.

Born into a Ukrainian family in 1943 in the village of Irzhavets in Chernihiv *oblast* in central Ukraine. He first studied at a food industry technical college, and then from 1961 to 1962 worked at various industrial jobs in Cherkasy and Kiev. After military service from 1962 to 1965 in the Baltic Fleet he studied at Kiev Polytechnic Institute and qualified as an engineer, and later at the Kiev Communist Party of Ukraine (CPU) Higher Party School. Thereafter he worked in various sugar refining factories, and at the *Lenin Forge* and *Kyïvtorgmash* factories in Kiev.

In 1976 he began to work in the industrial and transport division of the communist *apparat* in the Podil *raion* in Kiev city. By 1979 he was second secretary, and by 1983 first secretary of the Podilskyi *raion*, and chairman of the local soviet. As first secretary he was a somewhat ambiguous figure, meeting with members of the non-communist opposition while Shcherbytskyi was still first secretary of the CPU, but at the same time presiding over an administration that was notoriously corrupt.

In March 1990 he was also elected people's deputy for the Podilskyi *raion*, and in the Supreme Soviet he is a member of the committee on the plan, budget, finance and prices. He remained, like most national communists, a member of the Communist Party right up to the day that the Supreme Soviet declared Ukrainian independence on August 24, 1991. In March 1992 he was appointed President Kravchuk's prefect in Kiev city. The first signs were that the old guard side of his character was still dominant, as one of his first acts was to ban street traders from Transcaucasia peddling their wares in Kiev, and rumours of corruption amongst his circle began to circulate.

After failing to implement many of President Kravchuk's decrees, and perhaps unwisely installing his administration in a building destined for the Foreign Ministry, he was removed in April 1993 and was replaced by Ivan Dankevych. Salii retains his post as one of the directors of the Kiev Mohyla Academy. He is married with two sons.

Saltykov, Boris Georgevich

Russian Minister of Science and Technical Policy; Deputy Russian Prime Minister to March 1993.

Born on December 27, 1940 in Moscow; Russian; member of the CPSU until August 1991. He graduated from the Moscow Physics and Technology Institute in 1964 as an engineer and physicist. In 1967 he began postgraduate studies at the institute and in 1972 successfully presented his dissertation on the "Modelling of production structures and problems about the management of firms" as a candidate of economic sciences (PhD (Econ)). From 1967 he was a junior scientific officer, senior scientific officer, head of a laboratory and head of a department in the central mathematical economics institute, USSR Academy of Sciences. The director was Academician Nikolai Petrakov.

One of Saltykov's colleagues was Viktor Danilov-Danilyan, at present Russian Minister of Ecology and Natural Resources. From 1986 to 1991 Saltykov was head of department of the institute of economics and forecasting of scientific-technical progress, which became later the institute of economic forecasting, USSR Academy of Sciences. In 1991 he was appointed director of the analytical centre of the problems of socio-economic and scientific-technical progress. In November 1991 he became Russian Minister of Science and Technical Policy. On November 28, 1991 this ministry was renamed the Ministry of Science, Higher Education and Technical Policy. He heads the inter-departmental co-ordinating commission on scientific-technical progress of the Russian government.

Saltykov is a strong supporter of a market economy. He advocates the funding of basic research on the basis of commissions from enterprises, domestic and foreign funds and limited support from the state budget. To this end a joint Russian-US project was elaborated, the "programme of debt liquidation", which envisaged the Americans writing off that part of Russia's debt which was spent on scientific research with both sides sharing the results of the research. Saltykov made clear that he did not fear a brain drain to the West and young specialists are welcome to go since it was better for them to be there "than nowhere". He favours the university sector running its own affairs but with part funding from the centre, and believes that universities and research centres should co-operate fruitfully with their counterparts in all CIS states.

He is a major figure in the Russian fund for basic science. He promised the space industry that he would do everything in his power to ensure the completion of the research on Mars on schedule, including the launch of an automatic station in 1990. The financing of the latter had almost stopped in 1990 after the collapse of the Phobos programme. In March 1993, after the tumultuous events of the IX Congress of People's Deputies, Saltykov was deprived of his position as deputy Russian Prime Minister. His ministry lost its responsibility for higher education in February 1993, so he became Minister of Science and Technical Policy. He is a fluent speaker of English. He is married with two daughters, the younger of whom is a trainee teacher.

Samsonov, Viktor Nikolaevich

Chief of Staff; first deputy Commander-in-Chief of the Unified Armed Forces of the CIS; Colonel-General.

Born on November 10, 1941, on the Dukhovnitsky state farm, Dukhovnitsky *raion*, Smolensk *oblast* into a working-class family; Russian. He graduated from the Far East Higher Military Officers Technical School in Blagoveshchensk in 1964, the M. V. Frunze Military Academy in 1972 and the Military Academy of the General Staff in 1981, having received a higher military education. He was a member of the CPSU until August 1991.

After technical school he served in the marines of the Pacific Fleet as a platoon and company commander. He took part in sea voyages on landing craft, and was notable for his professional training and a considerable interest in his work. He was actively involved in the work of CPSU organizations and enjoyed the support of superior officers and Party-political agencies, which considered him to be a promising officer. After the Academy he did not return to the marines, since career opportunities were limited there due to the small number of this type of force. As early as 1972 he was appointed Chief of Staff of a motorized-rifle regiment, which immediately distinguished him from the vast majority of graduates who were usually given posts at battalion level. Soon he became a commander of the same regiment, then a Chief of Staff of a tank division. According to superior officers, V. Samsonov had a sound operational-tactical and military-technical training, was good at planning and conducting the versatile training of units and sub-units, and was aware of the essence of present-day combat for land forces.

In 1981 he was appointed a motorized-rifle divisional commander of the Transcaucasian military district, and later became Chief of Staff and army commander, Chief of Staff of the Transcaucasian district. During Gen. Samsonov's service in Transcaucasia, a national-democratic movement emerged there and, as a Chief of Staff, he directly participated in the planning and use of force against the opposition and the civil population. According to democratic sources he himself bears the blame for the bloodshed in Tbilisi on April 9, 1989, though he escaped publicity during the parliamentary investigation.

From 1990 Lieut.-Gen., then Col.-Gen. Viktor Samsonov was Commander-in-Chief of the Leningrad military district, one of the most prestigious in the Soviet army. At the time of the anti-constitutional putsch in August 1991 Samsonov became a member of the local Emergency Committee and took part in planning repressive operations. Due to the resolute actions of the St Petersburg mayor, Anatoly Sobchak, Gen. Samsonov soon stopped carrying out the orders of the Minister of Defence and kept his word not to use troops. He recognized the appointment of Vice-Admiral V. Shcherbakov as chief military commander in St Petersburg, prevented the bringing into the city of the plotters' units and stopped the movement of an armoured column of an airborne division.

According to knowledgeable sources, his further promotion is connected with the personal support of Anatoly Sobchak who rated Samsonov's activities during the putsch very highly.

On December 7, 1991 Col.-Gen. Viktor Samsonov was appointed Chief of the General Staff of the armed forces of the USSR. Experts regard this appointment as a poor substitute for General of the Army V. Lobov, known for his reform ideas and professionalism, who had been dismissed from the post. Democratic military organizations opposed Samsonov's appointment.

Gen. Samsonov is a typical military professional, indifferent to politics, not very keen on having serious reforms in the armed forces and preferring to carry out the instructions of his superior officers. Though possessing an excellent military training, he is not very broad-minded, limiting himself to official interests. Like most regular officers, he is a conformist, eager to adapt to any top authority, and by conviction is an advocate of a strong state domestically and internationally.

From February 1992 he was Chief of the General Staff, and then head of the main headquarters of the unified armed forces of the CIS. Since May 1992 he has been Chief of Staff of the unified armed forces of the CIS.

He is directly involved in drafting the documents on military issues and on the collective security of the independent states of the Commonwealth. He participates in working conferences and summits of top leaders and ministers of defence of the Commonwealth states. At the beginning of 1992 he undertook official visits to some European states.

He appears in the press, and his publications include two articles "Everybody suffers from the lack of laws—the army especially so" (*Krasnaya Zvezda*, March 18, 1992) and "The system of collective security is an objective necessity" (*Krasnaya Zvezda*, June 3, 1992), and an interview in the same newspaper on May 6, 1992. He has been awarded the order of the Red Banner, two orders "For service to the motherland in the armed forces of the USSR" and 10 medals. There is no information about his hobbies and interests, but it is known that he does not speak any foreign language. He is married with two children.

Office address: Moscow, Leningradsky prospekt, 41.

Sangheli, Andrei

Prime Minister of Moldova.

An ethnic Moldovan born in 1944, Sangheli is a trained agronomist and graduated from the Higher Party School in Kiev. From 1986 to 1992 he served concurrently as Moldovan first deputy Prime Minister and Minister of Agriculture. Until July 1990 he was a member of the Politburo of the Communist Party of Moldavia, when he became a member of the Central Committee of the Communist Party of the Soviet Union as a supporter of *perestroika*. At the Central Committee plenum of September 30, 1989, Sangheli issued a forceful statement calling for the resignation of first secretary Semion Grossu, who was in fact replaced just over a month later. From 1990 to early 1992, Sangheli chaired the conciliation commissions formed by the Moldovan parliament to negotiate with the separatists in Transnistria and Gagauzia. He thus has experience in dealing with the leadership of the two breakaway republics. More importantly, Sangheli (like President Snegur) enjoys strong support among the Agrarians in the *Sfatul Ţării* (the former Supreme Soviet), as well among ethnic Russian parliamentarians from outside Transnistria.

He was appointed Prime Minister in July 1992 and charged with forming a government of "national consensus", that is, a government which would include significant representation by the Transnistrian separatists. Sangheli is Moldova's third Prime Minister since the beginning of the independence movement in the late 1980s. The earlier governments of Mircea Druc and Valeriu Muravschi were composed largely of ethnic Moldovans bent on pursuing narrowly defined national goals. The strategy of the new Sangheli government, on the other hand, has been to seek to incorporate the more moderate elements among the Transnistrian and Gagauz separatists by reserving designated seats in the governement for representatives from these areas.

Satarov, Georgy Aleksandrovich

Member of the Council of the President of the Russian Federation.

Born in 1947 in Moscow. In 1972 he graduated from the faculty of mathematics of the V. I. Lenin State Pedagogical Institute, Moscow, and was on the staff there until 1990. In 1985 he successfully presented his candidate dissertation in technical sciences on "Dichotomous data on socio-economic systems" (PhD). In the 1970s he and Sergei Stankevich studied the US Congress by applying mathematical methods and models which permitted an analysis of the disposition of power based on congressional voting patterns. Stankevich and he wrote articles in *Sotsiologicheskie issledovaniya* on voting, the ideological divisions, a typological analysis and the dynamics of the distribution of power in the US Congress. Satarov is the author of the books *Computers Discover America*, (1989); and *Mathematical Methods and the IBM in Historical Typological Research* (1989).

In 1990 Satarov became one of the founders and directors of the centre for applied political research, Indem (information technology for democracy), a sub-department of the *Moscow News* newspaper. In February 1993 he became a member of the presidential Council. Whether or not the Council can escape from becoming purely decorative depends, according to Satarov, on the extent to which the intentions of the President about the Council are serious and how innovative and active the Council members are. At the meeting of the Council, before the referendum of April 25, 1993, Satarov stated that holding the referendum was dangerous. A plebiscite by a federal government on questions about the state could strengthen the divisions among the electors on views about the federal state. He lives in Moscow.

Savelev, Viktor Nikolaevich

Speaker of the Supreme Soviet of the Karachaevo-Cherkess Republic, Russian Federation.

Born on August 9, 1948 in Mineralny Vody, but his family then moved to Karachaevsk and later to Cherkessk. He was a member of the CPSU from 1974 to August 1991. After finishing secondary school he entered Novocherkassk Polytechnical Institute and graduated with an engineering diploma. He served in the Soviet Army, and after being demobbed was a work superintendent in the Peredvizhnaya mechanized column-755 of the Karachaevo-Cherkess rural construction trust (now the Karachaevo-Cherkess agro-industrial association), an instructor of the Party *obkom*, and head of the industrial and transport department of the Cherkess city Party committee. In March 1986 he was elected chairman of the executive committee of Cherkessk city soviet.

In March 1990 he was elected a deputy of the Karachaevo-Cherkess *oblast* soviet of people's deputies and on March 15, 1990 he was re-elected chairman of the executive committee of the Cherkessk city soviet. At the V session of the city soviet, on August 9, 1991, he was elected chairman of the Karachaevo-Cherkess *oblast* soviet. On assuming his post he appealed for the strengthening of peace and friendship among the peoples of Karachaevo-Cherkessia. He advocated autonomy, the realization of the principles of the equality of all peoples before the law, the transition to the market, the stabilization of the economy, privatization and the adoption of new economic relations.

On August 20, 1991 Savelev signed the resolution of the Presidium of the soviet on the social and political situation in the country. It stated that the setting up of the Extraordinary Committee without the appropriate decision of the Supreme Soviet of the USSR was illegal and unconstitutional. It confirmed that power, as previously, rested with the legally elected state authorities and administrations. He declared that a sharp turn towards the market and liberalization of prices were necessary, and criticized the government for its slow and irresolute conduct of reform, for the collapse of the union, the breakdown in economic ties and the damage done to financial and credit policy. The gradual restoration of economic ties between the regions and republics of the CIS and the establishment of joint ventures were needed in order to soften negative phenomena and hold down inflation.

In December 1992 he appealed for unconditional support for the legally elected state authorities and their leaders in all republics and in Russia as a whole. If there was a threat of their being overthrown by force there should be resolute action in accordance with the constitution of the Russian Federation and the constitutions of the republics and all legal means of defence should be deployed. He pointed out that there was still a lack of clarity about state structures, and confusion over certain functions among various levels and types of representative and executive power. He advocated a constructive search for decisions on the stabilization of the social and economic situation in Russia and the adoption of measures guaranteeing the defence of the rights and freedoms of the individual and the citizen and the peoples of Russia. He is married and his wife works in a pedagogical technical college. They have three children and live in Cherkessk.

Seleznev, Nikolai Vasilevich

Member of the Constitutional Court of the Russian Federation.

Born on May 2, 1945 in the village of M. Antibess, Mariinsky *raion*, Kemerovo *oblast*, Siberia; Russian; member of the CPSU until August 1991. He graduated from the No. 3 State Professional Technical College, Kemerovo, and began his working life as a worker in the Kuzbass, Siberia. He was assistant to a foreman in a creamery, then an electrician in a locomotive depot in the Mariinsk station, east Siberian railway. He served in the Soviet Army (1963-67), and after demobilization became a worker again. He graduated from the railway technical college, was an assistant engine driver of an electrical locomotive in the Mariinsk depot. In 1974 he graduated from the Novosibirsk faculty of the Sverdlovsk (Ekaterinburg) Institute of Law. He worked for over 20 years in the agencies of the Procurator's Office: from 1971 to 1983 he was an assistant Procurator, then deputy Procurator, and from 1983 to 1987 Procurator of the *raion* centre, Kemerovo *oblast*, and Procurator in Novokuznetsk, Kemerovo *oblast*.

He was the Procurator of Kemerovo *oblast* from 1987 to 1991. He has published various articles in the legal and local press on ways of improving the effectiveness of the Procurator's work and legal procedure, and is a specialist on civil law, and on civil and criminal cases. He was awarded the order of the badge of honour, the honoured certificate of the Presidium of the RSFSR Supreme Soviet and medals, for exemplary work, on the centenary of the birth of V. I. Lenin, 20th anniversary of victory in the Great Fatherland War (1941-45), veteran of labour and the badge of honoured official of the Procurator's Office.

He was proposed for election to the Constitutional Court in a contested election by the RSFSR Procurator's Office. He was elected to the Constitutional Court on October 29, 1991, at the V Congress of People's Deputies, in the first round of voting. He received 550 votes for and 328 votes against. As a member of the Court he has often revealed his opposition to a revision of the frontiers of the Russian Federation with former Soviet republics and also between republics and autonomous *oblasts* and *okrugs* within Russia. He lives in Moscow.

Selivanov, Valentin Egorovich

Chief of the main headquarters of the Navy; first deputy Commander-in-Chief of the navy. Admiral since 1992.

Born on March 17, 1936 in the village of Stanovaya, Stanovlyansky *raion*, Lipetsk *oblast*. The social status of his parents is unknown. Russian. His career in the navy began in 1954. He graduated from the M. V. Frunze Higher Naval Technical School in Leningrad in 1958; the Higher Classes for Officers in 1965; the Naval Academy in 1971. He received a higher military naval education and was a member of the CPSU until August 1991.

He served on surface ships of the navy. He began his career as officer as a commander of the anti-aircraft battery of a destroyer. As a young officer he was notable for his advanced specialist knowledge and naval qualifications and his ability to work well with his subordinates. He enjoyed a good reputation with superior officers and Party political agencies. He was actively involved in the work of the Party organizations, a *sine qua non* for a successful career. Then he became commander of an anti-submarine defence ship of the Pacific Fleet from 1962 to 1964, and a torpedo boat destroyer of the same fleet. The ships under his command were awarded a distinction. He sailed the oceans and helped to counter the US navy near the coast of Indo-China. He often fulfilled crucial tasks both by himself and as a part of naval groups and strategic formations. After graduating from the Naval Academy he was appointed Chief of Staff of an anti-vessel subdivision, then a commander of a subdivision of destroyers, from 1973 to 1975, and commander of a guided missile ship division of the Baltic Fleet, from 1975 to 1981. He ensured a high level of combat readiness, discipline and order in his formations. He established close ties with local authorities and engaged in Party political activities. He was regarded as a highly qualified military expert with profound training in operational tactical and military technical spheres, and as capable of conducting present-day combat in the marine theatre. From 1981 to 1985 he was commander of a strategic squadron in the Mediterranean. He ensured the fulfilment of the defence tasks of the Soviet Union under complex military and political circumstances and geographical conditions. The task of the forces under Adml Selivanov was to counter the US and NATO navies. From 1985 to 1989 he was Chief of Staff of the Black Sea Fleet. In 1989 he was appointed commander of the Leningrad naval base and commandant of the Kronstadt naval fortress. Under his command were the navy in the Gulf of Finland and on lakes Ladoga and Onega, the ships under construction in the Leningrad yards and naval educational establishments.

Selivanov actively co-operated with the Party and civil authorities of Leningrad and Leningrad *oblast*, and was elected a member of the bureau of Leningrad Party *obkom*. He proved himself a convinced communist, supporting CPSU policy at home and abroad. However, as a result of his career experience and training and like almost all Soviet admirals and generals, he was actually a conformist, prepared to support any legitimate regime in the USSR or Russia. During the anti-constitutional putsch of August 1991 he was not active but became a member of the Leningrad Emergency Committee and ordered forces under his command on to a state of high combat readiness. However, he did not dare use sailors against democratic forces without a definite order. After the appointment of Rear-Adml V. Shcherbakov as chief military commander by the vice-mayor of St Petersburg, in conformity with the decree of President Boris Yeltsin, Selivanov recognized his authority and undertook no further action.

Selivanov was not respected in democratic military circles. His ambiguous position led them to suspect him of sympathy for the plotters. However, due to the personal support of Adml of the Fleet Vladimir Chernavin, he retained his post. Politically, Selivanov is a supporter of a strong state domestically and of Russia regaining its position as a great power with powerful armed forces.

He does not express his political views in public, preferring the role of a non-party military professional. In September 1992 he was appointed chief of the main headquarters and first deputy Commander-in-Chief of the navy of Russia. He is interested in the history of the navy and likes literature and sport. He actively participates in the preparations of the celebrations marking the 300th anniversary of the Russian navy. He has been awarded three orders and 12 medals. He is married with a son.

Official address: 103175 Moscow K-175.

Semenov, Vladimir Magomedovich

Commander-in-Chief of Land Forces. Colonel-General.

Born on June 8, 1940, in the village of Khurzuk, Karachaevo *raion*, Karachaevo-Cherkess autonomous *oblast*, Stavropol *krai*. Karachai. The social status of his parents is unknown. He graduated from the Baku Higher Military Officers Technical School in 1962; the M. V. Frunze Military Academy in 1970; the Military Academy of the General Staff with distinction in 1979. He received a higher military education and was a member of the CPSU from 1963 till August 1991.

He began his career as an officer after technical school as a motorized-rifle platoon commander and from 1966 was a company commander. In 1970 he was appointed a motorized-rifle battalion commander, and after a year he became a regimental Chief of Staff. His reputation was that of an officer with high operational-tactical and military-technical training. He actively worked in the Party organizations of his sub-units. He enjoyed the support of political agencies and was considered to be a promising officer. At the age of 33, in 1973, he was promoted to regimental commander, and in two years he became Chief of Staff and deputy commander of a motorized-rifle division. The units under him were awarded a distinction for the high level of their combat training.

After graduating from the Academy of the General Staff he was a motorized-rifle divisional commander from 1979. In 1982 he was appointed commander of an army corps in one of the groups of Soviet troops abroad. From 1984 he was an army commander. He improved his professional skills during his short professional trip to Afghanistan.

In 1986 he became the first deputy Commander-in-Chief of the Baikal military district and from 1988 was commander of the same district, where there were traditionally large mobile groups of land and air forces of the Soviet army.

Under the difficult climatic conditions of Central and Eastern Siberia, the troops under Gen. Semenov acquired a high level of combat readiness which was often recognized by the military command. In March 1989 he was elected a USSR people's deputy in Kyakhtinsk national-territorial district, Buryat ASSR. He adopted a clear pro-communist stand and supported all the proposals of the conservative groups in parliament, but was not active at the sessions. From July 1990 he was a member of the Party Central Committee.

During the anti-constitutional putsch in August 1991, Semenov was not politically active, confining himself to fulfilling all instructions coming from the General Staff. However, according to democratically-minded military sources in the Trans-Baikal region, Gen. Semenov advocated tougher measures in the country and approved of the actions of the Emergency Committee.

On August 31, 1991, by the USSR President's decree, he was appointed Commander-in-Chief of Land Forces, deputy Minister of Defence, replacing General of the Army Varennikov who had been arrested because of his involvement in the putsch. Since February 1992 he has been Commander-in-Chief of Land Forces of the Unified Armed Forces of the CIS. By President B. Yeltsin's decree on August 21, 1992 he was appointed Commander-in-Chief of Land Forces of the Russian Federation.

A professional military man, Gen. Semenov is a convinced advocate of the supremacy of the state and of the creation of a strong and up-to-date army, capable of maintaining Russia's influence in the world. He does not express his political views in public, but judging by his education and the course of his successful career, he is a conformist, which is typical of Soviet generals, who support any power in the state which can ensure their social status and strong policies.

There is no information available on his hobbies. He does not speak any foreign language and has not been on any official visit abroad. He has been awarded two orders "For service to the motherland in the armed forces of the USSR", and medals. He is married with two children.

Office address: 103175, Moscow, K-175.

Sergeev, Anatoly Ipatovich

Commander of the Volga military district. Colonel-General since 1991.

Born on November 6, 1940 in the village of Ivanovka, Bolsherechinsky *raion*, Omsk *oblast*, into a working-class family. Russian. He graduated from the Far East Tank Technical School in Blagoveshchensk with distinction in 1963; the Military Academy of the Armoured Forces in 1973; the Military Academy of the General Staff in 1982. He received a higher military education and was a member of the CPSU until August 1991.

He began his career as officer as a tank platoon commander. He possessed a sound professional knowledge, with a talent for organization and the teaching of combat skills. He was soon promoted to student company commander, then became deputy commander of a student tank battalion. He trained a large number of sergeants and junior specialists in armoured warfare. His reputation with superior officers and political agencies was that of a promising officer and active communist. After graduating from the Academy of the Armoured Forces in 1973 he was appointed deputy commander of a tank regiment and became commander a year later. Having a sound operational-tactical and military-technical training, comprehending the essence of modern-day war, he ensured that his unit attained a high level of combat readiness and it was awarded a distinction. From 1978 he was a divisional commander.

After graduating from the Academy of the General Staff, Gen. Sergeev was appointed Chief of Staff and first deputy commander of the 40th Army, which was engaged in military operations against the *mujahidin* and civil population in Afghanistan. He served in Afghanistan until 1986. In 1986 he became a military army commander; in 1988 Chief of Staff and first deputy commander of Odessa military district. During the anti-constitutional putsch of August 1991 he was not particularly active. However, on his orders, democratically-minded officers were isolated. On the whole, he approved of the Emergency Committee's actions, ordered his troops on to a high state of combat readiness and dutifully fulfilled all instructions of the General Staff. His role during the putsch escaped close scrutiny. In August 1991 he was appointed commander of the Volga-Urals military district, replacing Gen. Albert Makashov who had been dismissed for supporting the plotters. In October 1992, by decree of President Boris Yeltsin, Col.-Gen. Sergeev was appointed commander of the Volga military district. He is a member of the "Afghan Generals" group which is closely associated with the Minister of Defence, Gen. Pavel Grachev.

Sergeev is a typical military professional, not very active in political life. He is not in favour of democratic movements, especially military ones. He advocates the supremacy of the state, the raising of the authority of the army by all possible means and the creation of up-to-date armed forces. He is an advocate of the use of force. He is a conformist in his attitude to state authorities. He is interested in sport as a recreation and in literature on military historical subjects. He does not have a good command of foreign languages and has not been abroad as a member of an official delegation. He has been awarded two orders of the Red Banner, the order "For service to the motherland in the armed forces of the USSR", and more than 10 medals, including foreign ones. He is married.

Gen. Sergeev's headquarters are in Samara.

Sergeev, Igor Dmitrievich

Commander-in-Chief of strategic missile troops of the Russian Federation. Colonel-General.

Born on April 20, 1938 in Verkhny, Voroshilovgrad *oblast*, Ukraine, into a miner's family. Russian. Sergeev graduated from the P. S. Nakhimov Black Sea Higher Naval Technical School in 1960 with a degree in rocketry; F. E. Dzerzhinsky Military Academy, officers' department with distinction in 1973: the Military Academy of the General Staff in 1980. He received a higher military education and was a member of the CPSU until August 1991.

He began his career in the rocket forces after graduating from the Naval Technical School. A specialist with a sound scientific, engineering, technical and military training, he was successful in climbing the career ladder. He enjoys a good reputation with superior officers and Party political agencies. He was actively involved in the work of Party organizations and proved himself a convinced communist. He held various command, engineering and staff posts in the field and central agencies of the administration for strategic missile troops. From 1971 he was Chief of Staff; from 1973 a regimental commander, from 1975 Chief of Staff and then a divisional commander. In 1980 he was appointed Chief of Staff, first deputy commander of a rocket army. From 1983 he was head of the operational administration, deputy chief of the main headquarters of the strategic missile troops. He was not politically active, becoming involved to the minimum extent required for a successful career. During the anti-constitutional putsch in August 1991, Gen. Sergeev and the whole of the command staff of the strategic missile troops remained loyal to the legitimate USSR and RSFSR authorities. From 1989 he was deputy Commander-in-Chief of strategic missile troops for combat training, for all types of combat and special training of units and formations. In February 1992 he became commander of strategic missile troops and deputy commander of strategic missile forces of the unified armed forces of the CIS. After the creation of the Ministry of Defence of the Armed Forces of Russia, Col.-Gen. Sergeev, by decree of the President of Russia, was appointed Commander-in-Chief of the strategic rocket troops of Russia on August 21, 1992. At the same time he retained his post as deputy commander of the strategic missile forces of the Unified Armed Forces of the CIS.

Sergeev is a true military professional, a member of a new technocratic élite, and is not involved in politics. He favours the creation of nuclear missile forces capable of meeting the demands of the latest achievements of science and technology and those of present-day war. He is responsible for missile troops, their combat readiness, their versatile training, controlling alert readiness and the guaranteed attainment of nuclear security. He is a convinced supporter of an integrated system of control and operation of strategic forces within the CIS and the guarantee of security of the successor states. An article of faith is that Russia is certain to have powerful and up-to-date armed forces in the future. He rarely appears in the mass media. His first interview was published in *Krasnaya Zvezda* on September 23, 1992. He does not express his political views in public or his views on the state of the country. There is no information available about his interests and hobbies. He does not have a good command of foreign languages, and has not been abroad as a member of an official delegation. He has been awarded two orders and 10 medals. He is married with a son who is an undergraduate.

Official address: 103175 Moscow K-175, Ministry of Defence of the Russian Federation.

Sevryugin, Nikolai Vasilevich

Head of the Administration of Tula *oblast*, Russian Federation.

Born in 1939; Russian; member of the CPSU until August 1991. He graduated from the agricultural institute, began working in 1962 as a brigadier and later became director of the Pravda state farm, Tula *oblast*. Then he was elected chairman of the Odoevsky *raion* soviet executive committee, first secretary of the Odoevsky Party *raion* committee, Tula *oblast*. In 1990 he was director of the Tulsky state farm in the village of Arkhangelsky, Leninsky *raion*.

In early 1990 he was nominated for election as an RSFSR people's deputy by the work collective of the Tulsky state farm in the No. 710 Kireevsky territorial district, Tula *oblast*. During the election campaign he devoted most attention to the problems of the social development of the countryside. There were five candidates, and he was eliminated in the first round, only polling 15.1% of the votes. A. A. Titkin, president of the Gefest joint stock company of the Tula production association, *Tyazhprodmash*, was elected the people's deputy for the district.

In 1990 Sevryugin was elected a people's deputy of the Tula *oblast* soviet and in April 1990, at the first session of the soviet, he was a candidate for the post of chairman. There were five candidates and Sevryugin withdrew after the first ballot. On October 20, 1991 he was appointed head of the administration of Tula *oblast* by presidential decree. He declared that the main functions of the *oblast* administration were: land reform and finding a solution to the food problem, providing a steady flow of fuel and smoothing out the problems of the municipal economy, creating a market system and privatization, conversion, the stabilization of the currency and combating crime.

In December 1992 he suggested that the most rapid way to implement economic reform was for the VII Congress of People's Deputies to extend the extraordinary powers, previously given only to the President. Sevryugin applauded the President's speech at the congress. He is married with two children and lives in Tula.

Shabunin, Ivan Petrovich

Head of the Administration of Volgograd *oblast*, Russian Federation.

Born on October 9, 1935 in Novoanninsky, Volgograd *oblast*; Russian; member of the CPSU until August 1991. After leaving school in 1953 he entered Volgograd Agricultural Institute, and then worked on the Rekonstruktsiya state farm as a livestock specialist and on the A. A. Zhdanov collective farm, Novoanninsky *raion*. He was a postgraduate student between 1960 and 1962 and successfully presented his candidate dissertation in economics on "The location and specialization of agricultural production in Volgograd *oblast* in 1970" (PhD (Econ)). After finishing postgraduate studies he was head of the economic planning department of the Uryupinsky *raion* agricultural production administration, and head of sector, agricultural economics department of the Party *obkom*.

From 1963 to 1971 he was head of the economic planning department of Volgograd *oblast* administration of agriculture and worked for some time as deputy director of the Volzhsky scientific research institute of agricultural irrigation. From 1972 to 1975 he was head of the production association of state farms, and from 1975 to 1985 was first deputy chairman of Volgograd *oblast* soviet executive committee. He was chairman of the *oblast* planning commission and director of the computer centre. In 1989 he was appointed director of the *oblast* state co-operative agro-industrial association. He was a member of the Party *obkom* bureau and received two orders of the Red Banner of Labour and three medals.

In early 1990 he was nominated for election to the RSFSR Congress of People's Deputies in the No. 322 Novoanninsky territorial district. During the election campaign he supported all power to the soviets, equality for all types of ownership, the sovereignty of Russia within the framework of the Soviet Union and economic autonomy for enterprises. There were four candidates. Shabunin polled 39.3% of the votes in the first round and won the second round, polling 60.5% of the votes. His main opponent was B. G. Butrin, chairman of the *oblast* union of consumers who received 31.6% of the votes in the first round and 20.5% in the second. Shabunin was a member of the RSFSR Supreme Soviet committee on economic reform and property, a member of the specialists in economics and management group of deputies.

In 1990 he was elected to the Volgograd *oblast* soviet and on April 5, 1990, at the first session, he was elected its chairman. On August 19, 1991 a decision was taken at a session of the Presidium and soviet executive committee to refrain from strikes, a state of emergency would not be introduced in the *oblast* and the activities of the soviets should be in accordance with the constitution and the laws of the RSFSR. At a session on August 20 it was decided to implement unconditionally the decrees of the RSFSR President. Shabunin spoke at the meeting.

On September 4, 1991 Shabunin was appointed head of the administration of Volgograd *oblast* by presidential decree, and on assuming office he declared that he supported the election of the head of the administration. He advocated co-operation with the soviets, the encouragement of the production of goods, the development of all forms of ownership in the countryside, support for private farming and the setting up of private farm associations. He was in favour of horizontal links and the political but not the economic sovereignty of the *oblast*, and he opposed localism and economic crudity.

In December 1992, during the VII Congress of People's Deputies, he stated that there was practically no support in Volgograd for the President and for his policy of confrontation with the congress. He judged that economic reform had not given rise to circumstances which promoted the emergence of a class of entrepreneurs. He lives in Volgograd.

Shafarevich, Igor Rostislavovich

Mathematician, academician, civil rights activist.

Born June 3, 1923 in Zhitomir, Ukraine. He entered Moscow State University in 1939 and graduated in mathematics in 1940 at the age of 17 years. He had completed the five-year course in one year. He later regretted losing four years because he missed out on a wide, general education. Brilliantly gifted, he successfully presented his candidate dissertation in mathematics in 1942, at the age of 19 (PhD). Soon after he presented successfully his doctorial dissertation (DSc). He was elected a corresponding member of the USSR Academy of Sciences in 1958. He was awarded a Lenin prize in 1959. He had to wait over 30 years to become an academician of the Russian Academy of Sciences. He was elected together with another Jew, Sinai, and several conservatives. There were two reasons for this delay: the internally complex academic politics and his direct, quarrelsome nature. He was feared as an examiner. In 1965, during an oral, which lasted four hours, he submitted the doctoral student to very sharp criticism. Her supervisor was an academician and his was the only dissenting voice. This was not the first occasion this had happened and ensured that Shafarevich had few friends among academicians. He was then working in the Steklov Institute of Mathematics and teaching algebra at Moscow State University. He was a brilliant if severe teacher.

A story circulated that he told his class that three students had come to him and said they could actually understand the course. One was called Kazhdan and the other two Bernshtein. (All three later became leading mathematicians.) In the mid-1960s Shafarevich was a member of the committee for the defence of human rights and worked closely with Andrei Sakharov and Aleksandr Solzhenitsyn (also a mathematician). He was dismissed from Moscow State University in 1974. He continued working in the Steklov Institute where he enjoyed the protection of academician Vinograd, the director. Shafarevich wrote a study of Soviet law on religion. A more ambitious study was a history of world socialism, *Socialism as a Phenomenon in World History*. It was published in France in 1977 and translated into several languages. It is a devasting critique of socialism which Shafarevich saw as humanity's death wish. His book, *Russophobia*, appeared in West Germany in 1988 and caused a scandal because of its anti-semitism. The Moscow mathematics community and others were appalled to discover Shafarevich among the "national patriots" and the most extreme anti-semites. *From Under the Block* contained some of the ideas which surfaced in *Russophobia*.

Shafranik, Yury Konstantinovich

Russian Minister of Fuel and Energy.

Born on February 27, 1952 in the village of Karasul, Ishimsky *raion*, Tyumen *oblast* into a peasant family; Ukrainian; member of the CPSU until August 1991. He graduated in 1974 from the Tyumen Industrial Institute as a mining engineer and began work in the *Nizhnevartovskneftegas* production association as a fitter and mechanic, and progressed until he became chief engineer of the enterprise. He worked on the exploitation of new oil deposits in a settlement and then in the town of Langepas. At the beginning of *perestroika* he was elected second secretary of the Langepas city Party committee (*gorkom*).

In 1987 he was appointed general director of *Langepasneftegas* production association and thereby became one of the youngest general directors in the oil and gas industry. In 1990 he was elected Speaker of the Tyumen *oblast* soviet of people's deputies. There were six candidates and Shafranik was one of the least known. In his election programme he demanded that relations between the region and Moscow should be on an equal basis, a single tax should be imposed on all industrial sectors by the centre and the money should feed into the central budget; a local oil refinery should be built, as should also a construction industry. He won in the first round, gaining 150 votes for and three against, with 34 votes to all the other candidates.

As speaker of the *oblast* soviet he became a member of the Party *oblast* committee (*obkom*) but refused election to the Party *obkom* bureau, stating that the tasks of the soviet were different from those of the Party committee. During the conflicts between the Tyumen oil workers and the Russian government he and the soviet strongly supported the demands of the labour collectives. In 1991 he was appointed head of the administration of Tyumen *oblast*. He took part in the drafting of the decree "on the development of Tyumen *oblast*" and the law on natural resources.

In 1992 he accompanied President Boris Yeltsin to England and had discussions with Jacques Attali, president of the European Bank for Reconstruction and Development (EBRD), which resulted in the signing of a memorandum of co-operation between Tyumen *oblast* and the EBRD. He devoted strenuous efforts to keeping together the Tyumen fuel and energy complex and there are today in Tyumen *oblast* three subjects of the Russian Federation, Tyumen *oblast* and two autonomous *okrugs*. He forcefully advocated the liberalization of Russian domestic energy prices because he believed that Tyumen *oblast* should get a fair rent for its resources. At the VI Congress of People's Deputies, in December 1992, he spoke of the correctness of the direction of reform but considered that the means of its implementation had not been sufficiently elaborated. In order for success to be achieved, political stability was necessary, the structure of power had to be well defined and changes introduced in the way reforms were implemented.

In February 1993 he was appointed Russian Minister of Fuel and Energy. He advocates the active participation of foreign oil companies and investment, the establishment of joint enterprises in the rehabilitation of existing oil wells and in the search for, exploitation and processing of raw materials. He is willing to co-operate with all enterprises, irrespective of the type of ownership, and favours partial privatization. He is in favour of free market prices for oil and gas.

A major problem is to address the chronic inefficiency of energy which rose by 38% per unit of industrial production over the period from 1990 to 1993. He is working on tax breaks for the industry where export taxes, royalties and other impositions can account for 55% of oil export revenue, before operating and transport costs are taken into consideration. Another headache is that 80% of the former Soviet Union's oilfield equipment capacity is in Azerbaijan and hence Russia needs to develop her own rapidly. He had warned that some of the coalmines in the Kuzbass, in western Siberia, are so inefficient that they will have to close. He supports stronger local government, acting in the interests of Russia, but without petty tutelage and taking into account regional conditions.

He is married with a son and a daughter, and lives in Moscow. He is a qualified stonemason and tractor driver and has several other skills. He has been awarded the order of the Friendship of Peoples.

Shaimiev, Mintimer Sharipovich

President of the Republic of Tatarstan, Russian Federation.

Born in 1937 in the village of Anyakovo, Aktanyshsky *raion*, Tatar Autonomous Soviet Socialist Republic (ASSR); Tatar; member of the CPSU from 1963 to August 1991. In 1959 he graduated from the Kazan Agricultural Institute and worked as an engineer, chief engineer of the *Muslyumovsky* repair technical station, and manager of the Menzelinsky *raion Selkhoztekhnika* association. In 1967 he was an instructor and deputy head of the agricultural department of the Tatar Party *obkom*. In 1969 he was appointed minister for amelioration and water economy of the Tatar ASSR. In 1983 he became first deputy Chairman of the Council of Ministers of the Tatar ASSR, was then elected secretary of the Tatar Party *obkom*, and then in 1985 he was elected Chairman of the Council of Ministers of the Tatar ASSR. In September 1989 he was appointed first secretary of the Tatar Party *obkom*. He was also a people's deputy of the USSR, the Tatar ASSR and a member of the bureau of the Party *obkom*. He was awarded the orders of Lenin, October Revolution, Red Banner of Labour and Friendship of Peoples.

In 1990 Shaimiev was elected a deputy of the Tatar ASSR. At the first session of the soviet of Tatarstan, in April 1990, he was elected Speaker of the Supreme Soviet. On August 31, 1990 the declaration on the sovereignty of Tatarstan was adopted. At the IV session of the Supreme Soviet, in April 1991, amendments were made to the constitution of the Tatar Soviet Socialist Republic, the statute on Tatarstan as a sovereign state and reform of the state structure of the Tatar Soviet Socialist Republic.

On June 12, 1991 Shaimiev was elected President of the Tatar SSR, in a national election and unopposed, polling 70.6% of the votes. After his election he advocated the sovereignty of Tatarstan, and the necessity for reform of the political and economic structures. He appealed for a solution to the critical decline of the economy and stabilization in the work of its leading branches. He favoured a gradual transition to the market, the rapid development of small and medium size businesses as the precondition for the growth of the economy, for an end to be put to the system of having enterprises which were monopolies, and the introduction of a extensive network of small mobile modern enterprises which would "embrace" the whole economy. In agriculture he appealed for protection against disintegration of the existing collective and state farms.

On August 20, 1991 he supported the position of A. I. Lukyanov on the non-acceptability of the Union treaty. He appealed for a halt to the collapse of the country, the overcoming of the economic crisis, an end to the destruction of one economic complex, and the stabilization of the political situation by extraordinary measures. He set up a special agency for the supervision of the activities of the mass media in the republic. The presidential declaration expressed support for the establishment of the Extraordinary Committee and its activities to prevent collapse and the stabilization of the situation in the country. He stated that on the territory of the republic the legally elected state authorities were functioning and reiterated his commitment to the USSR as a single state. Students trying to organize a meeting in Kazan were severely beaten.

In December 1992 he thought that in the present situation the legislative and executive branches of power should reach a compromise. The most important thing was to maintain social stability in Russia and not to allow a conflict to erupt, so that destabilization did not spread from the centre to the local level. He lives in Kazan.

Shakhlinsky, Ismail Gakhraman Ogly

Peoples writer of Azerbaijan; member of the *Milli Mejlis* (National Council).

Born on March 22, 1919 in the village of II Shikhly, Kazakhsky *raion*, Azerbaijan, into an Azeri family. His father was a teacher of the Russian language in a village school. He has a younger sister, Khabiba, who was a teacher of literature in a school in Kazakhsky *raion*, and is now a pensioner. He was a member of the CPSU from 1945 to January 1990.

From 1934 to 1936 he studied in the Kazakhsky Pedagogical College, and then graduated from the faculty of philology, V. I. Lenin Azerbaijani Pedagogical Institute. From 1941 to 1942 he taught literature in a secondary school in the village of Kosalar, Kazakhsky *raion*, and then from September 1942 to September 1945 he was a front line soldier during the Great Fatherland War (1941-45) and participated in military operations in the Caucasus, Crimea, Belarus and Kvnigsberg, East Prussia.

After demobilization he returned to teaching literature in the village of Kosalar. From 1946 to 1949 he was a postgraduate student at the V. I. Lenin Azerbaijani Pedagogical Institute, and in 1954 successfully presented his candidate dissertation in philology on "The life and works of Mekhti Gusein" (PhD). In 1949 he was elected a member of the Union of Writers of Azerbaijani SSR; he was a lecturer in the faculty of philology, Azerbaijani Pedagogical Institute (1949-65), and worked as secretary of the Union of Writers of the Azerbaijani SSR (1965-67). He was again a lecturer in the pedagogical institute from 1967-72, and from 1972 to 1977 he was head of the department of Russian and foreign literature at the institute. From 1977 to 1981 he was editor-in-chief of the journal, *Azerbaijan*, and from 1981 to 1987 he was first secretary of the Union of Writers of the Azerbaijani SSR. He retired in 1987.

In September 1990 he was elected a deputy of the *Milli Mejlis*, standing as an independent. He is the author of literary works and articles on philology. He is married, and his wife is a doctor who is now retired. They have two sons, the elder of whom, Elchin, was born in 1957, is a graduate of the Institute of Foreign Languages and is now deputy editor-in-chief of the *Aina* newspaper. The younger one, Farukh, born in 1962, is a graduate of the Institute of Art and works as a designer on the *Aina* newspaper. Shakhlinsky lives in Baku.

Shakhrai, Sergei Mikhailovich

Russian Deputy Prime Minister, Chairman of the State Committee on Nationality Policy.

Born on April 3, 1956 in Simferopol, Crimean *oblast*, Ukraine, into a military family; Russian; member of the CPSU from 1988 to August 1991. He went to a village school and left with a gold medal. In 1978 he graduated with distinction from the law faculty of Rostov-on-Don State University and began postgraduate studies in law at Moscow State University. He successfully presented his candidate dissertation in 1981 on the "Influence of the federal structure of Czechoslovakia on the organization and activities of the federal assembly". He was a candidate of legal sciences (LLM). From 1982 to 1984 he was assistant in the law faculty, Moscow State University, specializing in the activities of multi-national, federal states.

In 1986 he developed a new concept, the use of computers in the study of politics and law, and from 1987 he headed his own laboratory on legal information and cybernetics in the law faculty, Moscow State University. He acted as a consultant to the USSR Supreme Soviet on legislation, law and order and helped draft the rules of procedure of the Soviet parliament. He is the inventor of the electronic voting system used by the USSR Supreme Soviet. He was a member of the delegation of USSR people's deputies (others were K. D. Lubchenko, A. E. Sebentsov and N. V. Fedorov) who studied the workings of Congress in the US.

In January 1990 he was nominated a candidate for election as a people's deputy in the No. 10 Central national-territorial district, Moscow *oblast* by the collective of the Kaliningrad Strela construction production association, where Shakhrai had delivered lectures on law over a period of years. In his election programme he advocated an independent court, elected by the people, a clear division between the powers of the republics and the Union, a bicameral Supreme Soviet, a multi-party system, the annulment of article 6 of the Soviet constitution which guaranteed the CPSU the leading role in society, and the promulgation of a law on public organizations as the legal guarantee of the rights of the citizen, based on political convictions and the equality of all forms of ownership. He stated that land should belong to all the people, was owned by local soviets and they would divide up the land.

There were seven candidates. In the first round Shakhrai polled 29.2% of the votes and 51.9% in the second. His main opponent was Colonel-General V. V. Litvinov, first deputy Commander-in-Chief of air defence forces, who polled 13.6% in the first round and 34% in the second. Shakhrai was elected a member of the RSFSR Supreme Soviet at the I Congress. He was a member for a short time of the communists of Russia group in parliament. Its co-ordinator and one of the co-chairmen was I. Bratishchev, a doctor of law, who had been one of Shakhrai's teachers at Rostov-on-Don State University.

On the eve of the I Congress Shakhrai published an article in *Izvestiya* about his views on how the work of the congress should be organized. His active participation in assemblies to prepare deputies for their work in the congress gained him wide popularity, and in the autumn of 1990 he joined the *Smena* (change) group which brought together moderate democrats, including many former *Komsomol* workers. However, he left the group over disagreements with one of its leaders, A. Golovin.

On July 3, 1990 he was elected chairman of the Supreme Soviet committee on law. From July 4, 1990 to September 25, 1991 he was a member of the Soviet of Nationalities' commission on the national-state structure and inter-ethnic relations. On June 4, 1990 he was made a member of the commission on procedure in the Russian congress and Supreme Soviet. He was also a member of the Presidium of the Supreme Soviet. When Boris Yeltsin was speaker of the RSFSR Supreme Soviet he nominated Shakhrai on numerous occasions for election as deputy Speaker, but Shakhrai never received the requisite number of votes and Yeltsin then declared the post vacant.

He became one of the leaders of the left centre group of deputies and edited a number of amendments proposed by this group at the II Congress of People's Deputies. In July 1991 he was again a candidate for the post of Speaker (Yeltsin had by now become Russian President), but failed. He was then made RSFSR state counsellor on legal questions. He left the CPSU on August 20, 1991. On November 15, 1991 he offered his resignation as chairman of the Supreme Soviet committee on legislation. This was accepted, but he remained a member of the committee. On September 6, 1991 he became a member of the commission of deputies investigating the reasons and circumstances of the attempted state coup of August 1991. On October 14, 1991 he was elected a member of the working group preparing for ratification of the treaty on economic co-operation.

On December 6, 1991 he became a member of the working group on the drafting of proposals delineating the division of the functions of the agencies of power of the Russian Federation and its constituent parts. On December 9,

1991 he formed the commission to draft the law "on the rehabilitation of the Cossacks". On December 12, 1991 he was appointed deputy Prime Minister of the Russian Federation to supervise the Ministry of Justice, the agency of federal security, the Ministry of Internal Affairs and the state committee on nationality policy. He remained a Russian state counsellor. On December 27, 1991 Shakhrai was appointed head of the state legal administration. He was directly subordinate to the President and had the right to present draft laws to him, to see the texts of laws and decrees of the President and the Russian government which were to be promulgated, but before they were signed, with the right of a delaying veto.

His wide-ranging powers overlapped with many other authorities, for instance the Ministry of Justice. This led to conflict between him and Nikolai Fedorov, the minister, and Shakhrai gave up this post in May 1992. On January 14, 1992 Shakhrai represented the President in the Constitutional Court on the constitutionality of the President's decree setting up a unified Ministry of Security and Internal Affairs. (The court found against the President.) Shakhrai had been a strong advocate of a unified ministry, but told the court that its decision would be implemented. However, in an interview in *Rossiiskaya gazeta*, he declared that the disbanding of the unified ministry was not a juridical but a political decision. In May 1992 he resigned as deputy Prime Minister. From May to November 1992 he was the President's representative on the Constitutional Court on matters concerning the CPSU.

In November 1992 he was appointed chairman of the state committee on nationality policy, succeeding Valery Tishkov. He was also head of the provisional administration in the North Ossetian soviet socialist republic and the Ingush republic. In December 1992 Shakhrai was again appointed deputy Russian Prime Minister. While deputy Prime Minister Shakhrai remained a people's deputy, something which the rules ostensibly prohibited.

He is married with two young sons from his first marriage. His first wife was a graduate in philosophy but became a housewife. His second wife is ten years younger than he and is a student. His favourite pastime is bringing up his sons and enjoying a Russian bath. He lives in Moscow.

Shaposhnikov, Evgeny Ivanovich

Commander-in-Chief of the Unified Armed Forces of the CIS. Marshal of the Air Force since 1991.

Born on February 3, 1942 on the Bolshoi Log *khutor* (farm), Aksaisky *raion*, Rostov *oblast*, into a working-class family. Russian. He joined the military in 1959 after leaving secondary school, and graduated from the Kherson Higher Military Aviation Technical School for aviation pilots in 1963; the Air Force Academy in 1969; the Military Academy of the General Staff in 1984. He received a higher military education, and was a member of the CPSU from 1963, but left the Party for political reasons on August 23, 1991.

He began his career as an officer as a fighter pilot in 1963. He has held all posts in the air force: senior pilot, flight section commander, deputy squadron commander and squadron commander; from 1971 deputy regimental, then regimental commander. From 1975 he was a deputy commander, then commander of a fighter division; from 1979 deputy air force commander of the Carpathian military district; from 1984 air force commander of the Odessa military district; from 1987 air army commander of Soviet troops in Germany (the German Democratic Republic).

He developed a reputation as an ace pilot, qualified to fly in all weathers, experienced with all aspects of combat equipment and all types of fighter aircraft. He proved himself an experienced commander with a sound operational-tactical and military-technical training, aware of the essence of present-day combat. In 1988 Lieut.-Gen. Evgeny Shaposhnikov was appointed first deputy Commander-in-Chief of the air force; in June 1990 as a Colonel-General of the air force he became Commander-in-Chief of the air force and deputy Minister of Defence of the USSR. He was a qualified specialist, uninvolved in political intrigues and concerned only with raising the level of aircraft combat readiness and improving armament by integrating new aviation equipment. He enjoyed great authority among air force personnel. He was elected to the Party Central Committee at the XXVIII Party congress in July 1990. As early as August 19, 1991, at the meeting of the collegium of the USSR Ministry of Defence, he expressed doubts about the legitimacy of using the military to solve domestic political problems. He established contact with Russian leaders and refused to use the air force to implement the decisions of the Emergency Committee. It was then that rumours spread in the central agencies of the USSR Ministry of Defence that Shaposhnikov had been arrested. On August 21 he demanded that the legitimate constitutional government agencies be restored and threatened to launch an air-force strike against the Emergency Committee's residence. He gathered together officers of the main air-force headquarters, announced he was leaving the CPSU and was supported by the personnel. Shaposhnikov's resoluteness was of decisive importance in ensuring the defeat of the Emergency Committee.

On August 23, 1991 Shaposhnikov was appointed USSR Minister of Defence. In one of his first public speeches he declared he was taking all measures to counteract the use of the armed forces without the authority of top political leaders. He banned political agencies and communist structures in the army and navy and took decisive measures to democratize the armed forces. His first months in office were characterized by reshuffles in top echelons, the creation of officers' assemblies and other democratic structures, and the revitalization of work on the concept and practical measures for military reform. *Glasnost* was introduced into discussions about the problems of the army and navy. The military community and public at large were informed about current events in the military. It became customary to organize interviews with the press and conferences with representatives of political and social movements and soldiers' parents. The social security of military men received much attention, commercial structures were set up to sell stores in order to improve the material provisioning of personnel. As regards military planning, Shaposhnikov advocated a posture of "minimal sufficiency"; the smallest force which could defend the country, the elimination of superfluous military structures, and reorganization aimed at retaining a strong unified army over the entire territory of the USSR (with the creation of national territorial armies as a possibility). Since Shaposhnikov adhered to the traditional view on the organization of the central military agencies, he clashed with the Chief of the General Staff, General of the Army Lobov, who favoured a civil ministry. The conflict was resolved by the dismissal of Lobov by President Gorbachev's decree, but this lowered Shaposhnikov's standing among military democrats and progressives.

At the end of 1991 Marshal Shaposhnikov visited some Western countries and became the first Soviet military leader to appear at public meetings in mufti. At the end of 1991 and the beginning of 1992, with the disintegration of the USSR, he changed his policy and avoided close contacts with the democratic movement. He apparently wanted traditionalist military principles to survive intact and tried to preserve the old armed forces and those generals who shared that mentality. Gradually, officers expressing non-conformist views were retired and the drafting of military reforms underwent slight, but not significant changes. The mass media reported that Shaposhnikov was involved in illegal commercial transactions. At the same time he issued an instruction forbidding the involvement of the military in commercial activities. The forms and methods of military control became more severe. At the first all-army officers' conference, in January 1992, Shaposhnikov had to threaten to resign in order to overcome the conservative mood of the conference.

In February 1992, after the disintegration of the USSR, he was appointed Commander-in-Chief of the Unified Armed Forces of the CIS. At first, Shaposhnikov favoured the retention of unified armed forces which, in practice, placed them above the state during the transition period. Despite difficult conditions during the disintegration of the Soviet army, he succeeded in securing control over strategic and nuclear forces by relying on corps of top officers, first and foremost air-force generals, whom he knew well. He repeatedly expressed his commitment to democratic reforms in the country. Following the instructions of the political leadership, he ensured the transfer of matériel and property to the newly formed states. The result of the setting-up of the Ministry of Defence of the Russian Federation was that he found that only nuclear and strategic forces and a small administrative apparatus remained under his control.

Shaposhnikov often expresses his views in the mass media, particularly on TV, in *Izvestiya* and *Krasnaya Zvezda*. For example he wrote an article entitled "National and collective security in the CIS", in *Krasnaya Zvezda*, on September 30, 1992. There is no information available on his hobbies. He does not speak any foreign language, and has been awarded three orders and many medals. He is married with three children.

Official address: Moscow K-160, Leningradsky prospekt, Dom 41.

Shatalin, Stanislav Sergeevich

Co-chairman of the Movement of Democratic Reforms (International).

Born on August 24, 1934 in Pushkino, Leningrad *oblast*, into a family of Party workers. His father, S. N. Shatalin, was a commissar and secretary of the Kalinin Bolshevik Party *obkom*, and his uncle, N. N. Shatalin, was a member of the Party Central Committee, head of the Central Committee department of cadres and Central Committee secretary in the 1950s. Russian. He was a member of the CPSU from 1962 to January 1991. In 1958 he graduated from the faculty of economics, Moscow State University, and the department of mathematical methods of economic analysis. His teachers included Academician Kantorovich, a Nobel prize-winner in economics, V. S. Nemchinov and N. P. Fedorenko. In 1958 he was appointed economist in the scientific research institute of finance, USSR Ministry of Finance.

In 1959 he was a junior scientific assistant and later chief economist, and then from 1962, head of the sector of inter-branch balances, scientific research institute of USSR Gosplan. In 1964 he successfully presented his candidate dissertation in economics on "Problems in the theory of inter-branch balances and their utilization in plan calculations" (PhD (Econ)). In 1968 he was awarded a USSR state prize for participating in research on the elaboration of methods of analysis and planning of inter-branch links and branch structures in the national economy and the drawing up of plan and accounting inter-branch balances.

In 1965 he was appointed deputy director and head of the main theoretical department of the Central mathematical economics institute, USSR Academy of Sciences. The director was N. P. Fedorenko. In 1969, he and B. Mikhalevsky wrote and sent to Aleksei Kosygin, USSR Prime Minister, an analysis of the state of the Soviet economy, but he was almost expelled from the CPSU for his efforts. In May 1970 in conjunction with his work at the mathematical economics institute he became head of the department of mathematical methods for economic analysis, faculty of economics, Moscow State University. He headed the department for 14 years and lectured on the optimal functioning of a socialist economy, going beyond the bounds of official political economy.

In 1971 he successfully presented his doctoral dissertation in economics on "the problems of the theoretical analysis of proportionality in a socialist economy" (DSc (Econ)), and he was also made professor. During the 1970s he was a member of the commission of experts advising on annual and five-year plans for the development of the Soviet economy. He was also a member of the group on macroeconomic problems. In 1972 he and A. I. Anchishkin, later an Academician, worked on a complex programme of scientific technical progress and its social and economic consequences until 1990 and the theory of economic and social welfare.

Within the framework of the Franco-Soviet commission he headed a working group on mathematical economic modelling which extended over five Franco-Soviet seminars. In 1974, on the recommendation of the mathematical economics institute, he was elected a corresponding member of the USSR Academy of Sciences. From 1976 he was deputy director, head of laboratory, and leader of the scientific policy of the all-Union scientific research institute for systems research of the USSR state committee on science and technology and the USSR Academy of Sciences.

From then onwards he was organizer and leader of the seminar on systems modelling of social and economic processes. In 1978 he was sacked from his post as deputy director of the all-Union scientific research institute for systems research because too many of his assistants (24) had emigrated to Israel and the US. From 1978 to 1981 he worked closely with Hungarian economists, prepared a study for the re-establishment of the co-operative movement in the USSR and the development of individual labour activity.

In 1983 he became a member of the working group on improving the management of the national economy, set up by the Party Politburo on the initiative of Yury Andropov, general secretary of the Party Central Committee. He drew up three "uncensored" memoranda on the state of the Soviet economy and their contents found expression in Andropov's economic will on the need for a wide-ranging improvement in the management of the USSR national economy. In 1986 he became head of the laboratory of the institute of economics and forecasting of scientific technical progress, USSR Academy of Sciences.

In the same year at a conference on systems modelling of social and economic processes in Voronezh he delivered a paper which came to the conclusion that the social and economic system of the USSR should be changed. In 1987 he was elected a member of the USSR Academy of Sciences in mathematical economic research after two unsuccessful ballots. For about two years until the end of 1988 he did not do any research because of a serious illness.

In 1989 he became acquainted personally with President Mikhail Gorbachev at one of his meetings with leading Soviet economists. In the same year he withdrew from the elections to the USSR Congress of People's Deputies as a nominee of the USSR Academy of Sciences, irrespective of the fact that he achieved the second highest number of votes among the candidates. Academician Andrei Sakharov came top. During that summer he was appointed a member of the state commission on economic reform which was headed by Leonid Abalkin.

In February 1990, at a plenum of the Party Central Committee, he criticized the economic platform of the CPSU, prepared for the XXVIII Party congress, and then developed these ideas in an article in the Party theoretical journal, *Kommunist*. In March 1990 he became academic secretary of the department of economics, USSR Academy of Sciences, and a member of the Presidium of the USSR Academy of Sciences. He was also appointed to the USSR presidential Council. He was elected a delegate in a contested election to the XXVIII Party congress and the conference of the Russian Communist Party, and was elected a member of the CPSU Central Committee in July 1990.

During the summer of 1990 he headed the working group preparing the 500-day programme of economic reform. President Gorbachev personally took part in some of the deliberations and appeared to be convinced of the need to move from a planned to a market economy. However, during the autumn of 1990 he backtracked and attempted to broker a compromise between the Shatalin plan and the regulated market approach of Nikolai Ryzhkov, the Prime Minister. Shatalin was a possible candidate for the post of USSR Prime Minister, but neither the 500-day programme nor the President's compromise programme (drafted by Abel Aganbegyan on the basis of the 500-day programme) was ever put into effect.

After the tragic events in Vilnius in January 1991 Shatalin resigned from the CPSU. He acted as an agent for Boris Yeltsin during the RSFSR presidential campaign, and in June 1991 he became a member of the Democratic Party of Russia and worked in its consultative political council but left the party at the end of 1991. In July 1991 he became co-chairman of the Movement of Democratic Reforms (International). In September 1991 he was elected president of the fund of economic and social reform (reform fund) which had been set up in April 1990 on the initiative of the country's leading enterprises and organizations (Volga motor works, Likhachev motor works, Moscow, Kama motor works, Gosbank, Central trade union, Academy of Sciences, etc.) to draft a convention for an economic community of republics. In March 1993 a draft constitution, prepared by a group led by Shatalin, in collaboration with the reform fund, was published.

His main relaxation has always been football. In the early 1950s he played for the TsDKA club, Kalinin, and has supported the Moscow Spartak team for almost 50 years. He is its honorary president and the founder and president of the Brothers Starostin Spartak international fund. In the 1970s he was a member of the Presidium of the ice hockey federation and invented an automated system for the calculation of statistical data in the ice hockey championship. However, it was only used for a year since the resources to keep it going were lacking. He is married and has grown up children, and lives in Moscow.

Shatalin, Yury Vasilevich

Head of the provisional administration in the North Ossetian SSR and the Ingush Republic.

Born on December 26, 1934 in Dmitrovo, Moscow *oblast*; Russian. He was a member of the CPSU from 1958 to August 1991, and was elected a member of the Party Central Committee in July 1990. In 1957 he graduated from the Baku Military Technical College, and was commander of a platoon and deputy commander of a tank regiment in the Carpathian military district. In 1965 he graduated from the M. V. Frunze Military Academy and in 1976 from the military academy of the general staff of the USSR armed forces. He served in the Turkestan military district: as commander of a battalion, Chief of Staff, commander of a regiment and commander of a regiment in Kushka.

In December 1979 the division commanded by Shatalin was the first to enter Afghanistan as part of the limited Soviet contingent. In 1980 he was appointed Chief of Staff and in 1982 commander of the 7th army in the Trans-Caucasian military district. In 1984 he was made Chief of Staff and first deputy commander of the troops of the Moscow military district, in 1986 he was appointed commander of internal troops and from 1990 to August 1991, commander of internal troops and a member of the collegium of the USSR Ministry of Internal Affairs. He participated in the events in January 1990 in connection with the introduction of a state of emergency in Baku which resulted in many deaths and injuries.

In August 1991 he was relieved of his command. Three criminal charges were issued against Shatalin in connection with the events in Baku in January 1990, the Baltic republics in January 1991 and the isolation in August 1991 of President Mihhail Gorbachev in Foros in the Crimea, but all three were dropped for lack of evidence. In late 1991 Shatalin was appointed first deputy Commander-in-Chief of the border troops of the CIS. In January 1993 he became an adviser of the head of the provisional administration in the North Ossetian SSR and the Ingush Republic. In March 1993, by presidential decree, he was appointed head of the provisional administration in several regions of the North Ossetian SSR and Ingush Republic where there is a state of emergency.

Shatskikh, Viktor Mitrofanovich

Editor-in-chief of the business newspaper, *Aktsionerno-Birzhevoi Vestnik*, Alma Ata.

Born in 1959 in Novy, Donbas, Ukrainian SSR; Russian. He graduated in 1983 from the faculty of journalism, Kazakh State University, and was in turn a correspondent, and head of department of the *Ogni Alatau* newspaper; a correspondent of the Party newspaper *Kazakhstanskaya Pravda*; assistant to the deputy Speaker (chairman) of the Supreme Soviet of Kazakhstan; and head of department of *Kazakhstanskaya Pravda*. Then he became involved in the Alma Ata exchange. He was appointed deputy editor, then in March 1992 editor-in-chief, of the business newspaper, *Aksionerno-Birzhevoi Vestnik* (shareholder and exchange gazette). He speaks French and is divorced. He has a son and a daughter and enjoys travelling.

Address: 480091 Alma-Ata, ul. Tolibi 168; *telephone*: Alma Ata 69 4997.

Shavishvili, Revaz Leonidovich

Senior Scientific Assistant of the Institute of Geophysics, Academy of Sciences of Georgia; Chairman of the DAS-i (Democratic Elections in Georgia) Organization; Chairman of the Control Chamber.

Born in 1955 in Tbilisi, Georgian SSR. He is a Georgian whose father, Leonid Nikiforovich, is at present a pensioner. His mother, Aleksandra Alekseevna, is also a pensioner. His brother, Irakly Leonidovich, is an economist and his sister, Ketevan Leonidovna, is a musician.

Shavishvili graduated from the faculty of physics, Tbilisi State University, as a physicist and geophysicist. Then he became a postgraduate student in the institute of geophysics, Academy of Sciences of Georgia, and successfully presented his candidate dissertation in the physical and mathematical sciences (PhD). From 1978 to 1982 he was a senior laboratory assistant, then (1987–89) a scientific assistant and (1989–92) senior scientific assistant, institute of geophysics, Academy of Sciences of Georgia. He has published 17 scientific articles. From 1989 to 1992 he was chairman of the DAS-i organization and in 1992 he became a member of the State Council. In October 1992 he was elected a member of parliament of the Republic of Georgia for the October 11 block. In November 1992 his mandate as a member of parliament was suspended after his election as chairman of the control chamber.

He is married to Mariya Elizbarovna, née Tamazashvili.

Address: Tbilisi, tp. Vazhi Pshaveli 3, kv. 35; *telephone*: Tbilisi 39 83 64.

Shcherbak, Yurii Mykolayovych

Leader of Greens in Ukraine; Former Minister of Environment of Ukraine; Ambassador to Israel.

Born into a Ukrainian family in 1934. After graduating from Kiev Institute of Medicine in 1958, he worked as a doctor, practising at the Kiev Institute of Epidemology and Infectious Diseases until 1987. At the same time, he developed a parallel career as a well-known writer of prose and poetry (including nine novels and a controversial work on the 1932-33 Ukrainian famine), joining the Writers' Union of Ukraine in 1966.

He was one of the main leaders of the ecological protest movement that arose in response to the Chernobyl disaster in 1986, becoming president of the broad-based protest umbrella movement *Zelenyi svit* (Green World) at its second conference in January 1989, and leader of the Green Party of Ukraine at its founding congress in September 1990. In 1989 he was elected as one of Ukraine's people's deputies to the USSR Congress of People's Deputies as the surprise winner in Shevchenko territorial district in Kiev city.

Shcherbak maintained a moderate position as leader of both organizations, arguing against the spread of extreme nationalism, and in favour of co-operation with the authorities. Under his influence, the official ideology of *Zelenyi svit* was an ill-defined "eco-socialism". He was one of the officially approved writers allowed to meet President Mikhail Gorbachev on his visit to Kiev in February 1989. Thanks to his supposed moderation, and the high public profile he earned through his campaigning on the Chernobyl issue, he was made Minister of the Environment in June 1991.

However, he soon found that expensive ecological clean-ups were not high on the government's list of priorities. His budget was cut, and he was denied the powers necessary to push through a radical ecological programme. Nevertheless, and despite being a founder member of the centrist *New Ukraine* movement established in January 1992, he controversially sided with the Fokin government when the Supreme Soviet attempted to remove it by a vote of no-confidence in July 1992. He was appointed to Kravchuk's Council of National Security in the same month. He remained a popular figure, and was elected to the *New Ukraine* secretariat in 12th place in June 1992.

The Green Party meanwhile increasingly followed its own more radical path, Shcherbak having been little more than a figurehead since becoming Minister of the Environment, and Vitalii Kononov became its leader in September 1992. It was therefore with some relief that Shcherbak accepted the position of Ukrainian ambassador to Israel in November 1992.

Telephone (Ministry of the Environment): Kiev 226 2428.

Shengelaya, Georgy Nikolaevich

Film Producer, Republic of Georgia.

Born on May 11, 1937 in Tbilisi, Georgian SSR. A Georgian. His father, Nikolai Georgievich, is a film director and his mother, Nato Georgievna, née Vachnadze, is an actress. One brother, Tengiz Merabovich, is an engineer and the other, Eldar Nikolaevich, is a film producer.

Shengelaya graduated from the all-Union State Institute of Cinematography, Moscow. He was a producer, then director of the independent film studio, Luch. He is a national artist of Georgia and has received the Shota Rustaveli prize.

He is divorced. His son Nikolai is 32 years old and a film producer; Aleksandr is 26 years old and a student and Georgy is five years old. Shengelaya enjoys tennis and gardening.

Address: Tbilisi, ul. Kekelidze, Dom 16, kv. 12; *telephone*: Tbilisi 22 64 11.

Shenin, Oleg Semonovich

Chairman of the Union of Communist Parties — CPSU.

Born on July 22, 1937 in Vladimirskaya dock, Volgograd *oblast* into a civil servant's family; Russian; member of the CPSU from 1962 to August 1991. In 1955 he left the Krasnoyarsk Mining Technical School, began working in an enterprise in Krasnoyarsk and later became head of a department, chief engineer, and head of the construction administration of the *Krasnoyarskalyuminiistroi* trust. Afterwards he became head of the *Igarstroi* construction administration, and deputy manager and manager of the *Achinskalyuminiistroi* trust. From 1971 to 1976 he studied part-time in the Tomsk construction engineering institute.

In 1974 he switched to Party work and was elected first secretary of the Achinsk city Party committee (*gorkom*), and in 1977 second secretary of Khakass *oblast* Party committee (*obkom*), Krasnoyarsk *krai*. In 1982 he was elected secretary of Krasnoyarsk Party *krai* committee (*kraikom*), and in 1985 first secretary of Khakass Party *obkom*. In 1986 he graduated from the academy of social sciences of the Party Central Committee. In 1987 he was elected first secretary of the Krasnoyarsk Party *kraikom* and in March 1989 he was elected a USSR people's deputy in the Kansk territorial district, Krasnoyarsk *krai*.

In April 1990 he became the chairman of the Krasnoyarsk *krai* soviet of people's deputies (while retaining his Party post). He was a delegate to the XXVII, XXVIII Party congresses and the XIX Party conference. In July 1990 he was elected a member of the Party Central Committee, member of the Party Politburo and secretary of the Party Central Committee for cadre policy. From December 1989 to June 1990 he was a member of the Russian Bureau of the Party Central Committee and from June 1990 a member of the Central Committee of the RSFSR Communist Party.

He is the recipient of the orders of the October Revolution, the Red Banner of Labour, two orders of the badge of honour and medals as well as orders and medals of the republic of Afghanistan.

In August 1991 he was the organizer of the work of the secretariat of the Party Central Committee which aided the Extraordinary Committee. On August 18, 1991 he participated in the discussions between the coup organizers and President Mikhail Gorbachev at the latter's dacha at Foros, Crimea. Shenin was arrested on August 22, 1991 and was incarcerated in the *Matrosskaya tishina* isolator during the investigation. He and the other conspirators were later released and put on trial in April 1993. In March 1993 he attended the XXIX CPSU Congress and became chairman of the union of communist parties - CPSU.

He is married and his wife, Tamara Aleksandrovna, is a construction engineer. Their daughter Olga is also a construction engineer, daughter Angelina is a student and son Andrei is an officer and a military construction engineer. Grandchildren Vladislav and Kseniya are at school. Shenin lives in Moscow.

Shevardnadze, Eduard Amvrosevich

Chairman of the State Committee of the Republic of Georgia; Since October 1992 Speaker of Parliament; Head of State, Republic of Georgia.

Born on January 25, 1928 in the village of Mamati, Lanchkhutsky *raion*, Georgian Soviet Socialist Republic. A Georgian. His father, Amvrosy Georgevich, was a village school teacher and his mother, Sofiya Glakhunovna, a housewife. His brother Akaky Amvrosevich was killed defending the fortress of Brest in

June/July 1941. Another brother, Evgraf Amvrosevich, is a journalist and there is a third brother, Ippolit Amvrosevich. His sister, Venera Amvrosevich, is a housewife. He was a member of the CPSU from 1948 to 1991.

From 1946 to 1948 he was a student at Tbilisi medical college. In 1951 he completed the Party school of the Central Committee, Communist Party of Georgia (CPG) and in 1959 he graduated from the A. Tsulukidze state pedagogical institute, Kutaisi, as an historian. In 1946 he began working in the *Komsomol* (youth) organization. He was secretary of the *Komsomol* committee at the medical college, then instructor and head of a department of the Ordzhonikidze *raion Komsomol* committee, Tbilisi. He became instructor of the *Komsomol* republican organization, then secretary and second secretary of the Kutaisi *oblast Komsomol* committee. In 1953 he was an instructor in the Kutaisi city committee, CPG. Later that year he was elected first secretary of the Kutaisi city *Komsomol* committee, in 1956 second secretary, and from 1957 to 1961 first secretary of the Central Committee, *Komsomol* of Georgia. At the same time he was a member of the bureau of the *Komsomol* Central Committee.

In 1961 he moved into Party work. He was first secretary of Mtskhetsky *raion* CPG committee, then first secretary of the Pervomaisky *raion* CPG committee, Tbilisi. In 1964 he was first deputy Minister and in 1965 Minister of the Maintenance of Public Order, Georgian SSR. In 1968 he became Minister of Internal Affairs, Georgian SSR. In 1972 he was elected first secretary of the Tbilisi city CPG committee. From 1972 to 1985 he was first secretary of the Central Committee, CPG.

He was a member of the Gorbachev group of reformers, who knew the new General Secretary from their days in the *Komsomol* movement and were also familiar with Gorbachev's efforts to stimulate labour productivity in agriculture in Stavropol *krai*. Shevardnadze succeeded Andrei Gromyko as Soviet Minister of Foreign Affairs in July 1985. This caused considerable surprise, as Shevardnadze had a less than perfect command of Russian, no other western language, and no experience of world diplomacy. It was assumed that Gorbachev would be his own foreign minister, pushing through the new political thinking in world affairs. However, Shevardnadze soon proved himself a skilled propagator of the new thinking in the Kremlin and rendered Gorbachev invaluable assistance. Shevardnadze made a welcome change from "Grim Grom" and became a trusted interlocutor on the world stage. He contributed much to the credibility of the new Soviet foreign policy, especially in the USA and Germany. He took part in all the summit meetings and came in for violent criticism from the conservative, nationalist wing of the CPSU. There was a bitter wrangle over the "surrendering" of eastern Europe and the unification of Germany. He and Gorbachev were accused of giving away the fruits of victory in the Second World War.

Gorbachev's inability to adopt a consistent policy in 1990 and failure to pursue radical market-based economic reform lost the General Secretary many of his radical supporters. The right sensed that it was in the ascendancy during the autumn of 1990 and increased the volume of criticism directed at the Foreign Minister. Gorbachev's inability or unwillingness to defend Shevardnadze led the latter to resign his post in an emotional speech in December 1990. He warned of an impending attempted coup and thereafter joined in efforts to promote democratic reform within the CPSU. He was a member of Gorbachev's presidential council from March to December 1990.

Shevardnadze was a member of the CPSU Central Committee from 1976. He was a delegate to the XXI, XXV, XXVI, XXVII CPSU Congresses and XIX CPSU conference. In 1978 he was elected a candidate member of the CPSU Politburo. In July 1985, as Minister of Foreign Affairs, he was promoted to full membership of the Politburo and proved a valuable ally for Gorbachev in his battle with the moderate reformers around Egor Ligachev. Shevardnadze remained in the Politburo until July 1990 when all state office holders left the supreme Party body. He was elected a deputy of the USSR Supreme Soviet in 1974, 1979 and 1984 and a deputy of the Supreme Soviet of the Georgian SSR. He is a hero of socialist labour. He was awarded five orders of Lenin, orders of the October Revolution, the Red Banner of Labour and many medals. At the end of 1992 he converted to Orthodoxy and was received into the Georgian Orthodox Church with the given name of Georgy.

After burning his boats in Moscow he returned to Georgia to rebuild his political career there. Two factors destabilized Georgia after its independence following the collapse of the Soviet Union in December 1991. One was the mono-ethnic approach to politics and the other was the personality and policies of the first elected President, Zviad Gamsakhurdia. The desire of Tbilisi to regard Georgia as the state of the Georgians antagonized non-Georgians. Violence flared up in South Ossetia, where the local population wished to reunite with their compatriots in North Ossetia, which was part of the Russian Federation. Civil war also broke out in Abkhazia where the Abkhazians, only accounting for about one sixth of the local population due to inward Georgian migration, wished to rejoin the Russian Federation.

Gamsakhurdia's autocratic and erratic behaviour led to armed conflict and a bitter struggle among many rival factions. Eventually he was driven from the capital and took refuge just over the Russian border. In these unpropitious circumstances Shevardnadze was seen by many as more likely to broker a settlement than anyone else. His international standing was potentially of vital significance to Georgia. In due course he was elected head of state, the Georgians not willing to tempt fate and elect another President.

During 1992 and 1993 his efforts to bring the fighting in South Ossetia and Abkhazia appeared at times to be near success, but almost every agreement broke down. Shevardnadze met President Yeltsin many times, especially in pursuit of an Abkhazian solution. The two presidents had to acknowledge that neither was in complete control of his own military. An agreement was reached to withdraw Russian troops eventually from Abkhazia, but this was brought into doubt by the claim of Gen. Pavel Grachev, Russian Minister of Defence, that Russia could not leave, since if it did it would lose its influence over the eastern Black Sea area.

Shevardnadze is married. His wife, Nanuli Razhdenovna, née Tsagareishvili, is a journalist and until 1985 worked for a women's journal. They live in Tbilisi and also have an apartment in Moscow.

Shoigu, Sergei Kuzhugetovich

Chairman of the Russian State Committee on Civil Defence, Emergency Situations and Coping with the Consequences of Natural Disasters.

Born in Kyzyl, Tuva republic. His father was a Tuvinian, and was a journalist, who worked in the Party apparatus and the agencies of the Tuva soviet executive committee. His mother was Russian and worked as an economist on a state farm. He graduated as a construction engineer and after leaving the institute he went to work in Achinsk. There he began as an engineer and became the head of a trust. He was engaged on the construction of an alumina combine, an oil refinery and a fluoric aluminium enterprise in Armenia and on the Sayansk aluminium enterprise.

He was appointed deputy chairman of the Russian state committee on architecture and construction. However, he regarded helping people who had suffered disaster or any other extreme misfortune as his mission in life and together with others of like mind he set up rescue groups which went to disaster areas. He did this type of work in Armenia after the earthquake of 1988. In May 1991, together with Yu. Vorobev, his deputy, he proposed the creation of a corps of rescue workers. In August 1991 the President of Russia signed a decree establishing an RSFSR committee on emergency situations, which was then fused with the civil defence forces of Russia. Shoigu became head of this state committee.

Despite his government post he is always setting off for flashpoints and recently has been in Ingushetia and on the Russian-Georgian border. He is married with two daughters, one is 15 years old and the other almost two years old. He loves delicious food and good dry wine. However, he derives most pleasure from his work. He lives in Moscow.

Shokhin, Aleksandr Nikolaevich

Russian Deputy Prime Minister for Social Policy and Foreign Economic Issues.

Born in 1951 in the village of Savinskoe, Plesetsky *raion*, Arkhangelsk *oblast*; Russian; member of the CPSU until August 1991. From 1969 to 1970 he worked in the laboratory of the economics faculty of Moscow State University and in 1970 became a scientific-technical assistant in the central mathematical economics institute, USSR Academy of Sciences. In 1974 he graduated from Moscow State University in political economy, and from then until 1987 he was a scientific assistant in a number of branches and academic institutes, for example, the Gosplan scientific research institute of economics, the scientific research institute of labour and the USSR state committee on labour. Finally he was head of the laboratory of the institute of economics and forecasting of scientific-technical progress, USSR Academy of Sciences, where he worked with Egor Gaidar.

He was a member of the scientific council of the international centre for economic reform. The chairman of the council was Egor Gaidar and its director was K. Kagalovsky. He successfully presented his candidate dissertation in economics (PhD (Econ)), and his doctoral dissertation in economics (DSc (Econ)) in 1989. In 1987 Shokhin was appointed a counsellor in the Ministry of Foreign Affairs, an adviser of Eduard Shevardnadze. Shokhin was made head of the foreign economic administration of the USSR Ministry of Foreign Affairs. He was elected an Academician of the RSFSR Academy of Natural Sciences in 1991.

He was appointed RSFSR Minister of Labour on August 26, 1991 in the government headed by Ivan Silaev. By decree of the Russian President of November 6, 1991 he was appointed Minister of Labour and Employment of the Russian Population. He was proposed as minister by the Social Democratic Party of Russia, even though he was not a member. When offered the post by the social democrats he accepted, but informed them that he would not represent their interests in government since he wished to conduct himself as a non-party minister. Shokhin's deputy minister was P. Kudyukin, the well-known social democrat. Shokhin was appointed deputy Prime Minister and was also made responsible for social policy, but in July 1992 he stepped down as minister.

He remained deputy Prime Minister and now supervised the Ministry of Labour and Foreign Economic Relations, was responsible for economic links with CIS states and foreign economic activities and chaired the Russian agency of international co-operation and development. He supported the social democratic proposal for a system of coupons which guaranteed citizens a certain selection of products and monetary compensation so as to soften the blow of price rises. This never became policy.

In December 1992 Shokhin retained his post as deputy Russian Prime Minister concerned with foreign economic affairs. Besides this he has many other functions: chairman of the commission for the drafting of proposals to improve the system of state administration, chairman of the co-ordinating commission on religion, chairman of the economics and hard currency commission, head of the government commission on international investment co-operation and leader of the group for drafting a programme of measures to combat the present crisis.

He speaks English. His favourite pastime is playing football and he plays in the Russian government football team. His wife is a candidate of economic sciences (PhD (Econ)) and they have a son. He lives in Moscow.

Shorin, Vladimir Pavlovich

Chairman of the Russian Supreme Soviet committee on science and education.

Born on July 27, 1939 in Nizhny Lomov, Penza *oblast*, where his father was a worker; Russian. He was a member of the CPSU until August 1991. He graduated from the Academician S. P Korolev Kuibyshev (Samara) Air

Force Institute and joined the staff after graduation in 1966; he was assistant, senior lecturer, and assistant professor, department of construction and design of aircraft engines; head of department of automated systems of power plants (1982-88); and rector of the Kuibyshev Aviation Institute (1988-90). He successfully presented his candidate dissertation in technical sciences (PhD) and his doctoral dissertation in technical sciences (DSc) on aircraft engines. He is a professor, and a member of the Russian Academy of Sciences. He has worked on the automation of powerful lasers, and is an honoured scientist and technologist of the RSFSR. He has published 230 scientific papers, and has over 60 inventions, five monographs and six textbooks to his name.

He was nominated for election as an RSFSR people's deputy in the No. 465 Oktyabrsky territorial district, Kuibyshev *oblast*, by the collective of the Kuibyshev Air Force Institute. During the election campaign he advocated that Russia be treated equally with other Union republics; the adoption of a new Russian constitution ensuring the political and economic independence of Russia; equal rights for all types of economic activity; and introduction of strict control over the level and legality of incomes. He opposed private ownership of land but favoured leasing, and considered the main concern of local soviets should be finding solutions to problems of spiritual and national development. He devoted special attention to the development of higher education.

There were five candidates and Shorin won in the second round, polling 47.1% of the votes. His main opponent was A. I. Leushkin, a student, who received 41.6% of the votes in the second round. Shorin was elected a member of the RSFSR Supreme Soviet at the I Congress of People's Deputies (557 voted for, 365 voted against). He is a member of the Council of the Republic and chairman of the Russian Supreme Soviet committee on science and education, and is a member of the communists of Russia parliamentary faction. He is married with a daughter.

Address: 103274 Moscow, K 274, Krasnopresnenskaya nab., d. 2, Dom Sovetov; *telephone*: Moscow 205 43 24.

Shostakovsky, Vyacheslav Nikolaevich

Co-chairman of the Republican Party of the Russian Federation; chairman of the Political Council of the Party; Director of the centre of social knowledge of the international fund for social, economic and political research (Gorbachev fund).

Born on October 23, 1937 in the village of Stemas, Alatyrsky *raion*, Chuvash ASSR. Ukrainian. His father, Nikolai Mikhailovich, came from a family of office workers and was an agronomist, his mother, Olimpiada Zinovevna (née Giryavenko), is a housewife and his brother, Pavel Nikolaevich, is now a pensioner.

He graduated in 1960 from the faculty of pharmaceutical chemistry, Lvov (Lviv) Medical Institute as a pharmaceutical chemist, and from 1971 to 1973 he was a postgraduate student in the department of philosophy of the Academy of Social Sciences of the Party Central Committee. In the same year he successfully presented his candidate dissertation in philosophy on "The social function of higher education" (PhD). He is a professor and the author of over 50 publications.

From 1959 to 1960 he was head of the department of student youth, Lvov city *Komsomol* committee, and was then (1960-61) an instructor in the department of student youth, *Komsomol* Central Committee of Ukraine. From 1961 to 1962 he was an assistant in the department of pharmaceutical chemistry, Lvov Medical Institute, and then from 1962 to 1971 he was instructor, head of sector, deputy head, and head of the department of student youth on the all-Union *Komsomol* Central Committee. He was scientific secretary of the Academy of Social Sciences of the Party Central Committee (1973-78), from 1978 to 1986 was instructor in the sector for the training of cadres of the department for Party organizational work, Party Central Committee, and from 1986 to 1990 he was rector of the Moscow Higher Party School. From 1990 to 1992 he was director of the independent research information agency, Perpektiva, and in 1992 he became director of the centre of social knowledge of the international fund of social, economic and political research (Gorbachev fund).

He began to be politically active from the moment he joined the *Komsomol* and was elected to various functions. He was a candidate member of the all-Union *Komsomol* Central Committee, and from 1989 to 1990 he was a member of the Moscow Party city committee. In 1990 he was elected co-chairman of the Republican Party of the Russian Federation and at its III Congress chairman of its political council. He was a member of the plenum of the council of representatives of the movement Democratic Russia (1991-93), and was co-chairman of the international movement for democratic reform (1991-92). In 1990 he was a member of the council of the founding members of the newspaper, *Moskovskie novosti* (Moscow News). His hobby is going to the theatre. He is married, and his wife, Raisa Ivanovna (née Makretsova), born in 1942, is head of the board of the Ministry of Press and Information of the Russian Federation. He lives in Moscow.

Shtygashev, Vladimir Nikolaevich

Speaker of the Supreme Soviet of the Republic of Khakasia, Russian Federation.

Born in 1939 in the village of Tashtyp, Beisky *raion*, Khakasia autonomous *oblast*; member of the CPSU until August 1991. After the death of his father he and his brothers had to move to the Tashtyp children's home and he attended school there. After finishing school he worked in a geological expeditionary party in the Abazinsk iron ore mine and then in Tashtyp, in the agencies of internal affairs and the public prosecutor's office. At the same time he studied in the faculty of law, Tomsk State University, as an external student. He was first secretary of the Ust-Abakan *Komsomol raion* committee, then he was elected second and, in 1971, first secretary of the *oblast Komsomol* committee. He then worked in the Party apparatus and was head of department of the party *obkom* and first secretary of the *raion* Party committee. He was senior scientific assistant of the Khakasia scientific-research institute of language, literature and history for several years. In 1982 he was elected chairman of the Khakasia soviet executive committee.

In early 1990 he was nominated for election as an RSFSR people's deputy in the No. 213 Beisky territorial district. During the election campaign he stated that he intended to push for raising the status of the autonomous *oblast*, and its acquisition of political and economic autonomy within the framework of the RSFSR. He opposed the dictates of the central authorities, and in his view the autonomous *oblast* should itself dispose of its natural riches. It was essential to build a democratic society with the individual at the centre of attention. He devoted the greater part of his programme to ecological problems since the territory adjacent to Khakasia was being used as a nuclear testing ground.

There were three candidates. He polled 34.8% of the votes in the first round and won the second round, polling 52.2% of the votes. His main opponent was V. V. Lebedev, a doctor in the Sayanogorsk city hospital, who received 30.3% of the votes in the first round and 38.3% in the second. Shtygashev was also elected a people's deputy of the Khakasia autonomous *oblast*, and at its first session, in March 1990, he was elected chairman of the *oblast* soviet executive committee.

In August 1991 the Presidium and executive committee of the soviet of people's deputies of Khakasia autonomous *oblast* declared that it was necessary to implement strictly the demands of the legally elected state authorities of the RSFSR — the President, the Supreme Soviet and the Council of Ministers — and called on the citizens to observe restraint, be calm and orderly.

After the transformation of Khakasia into a republic, at the first session of the Supreme Soviet of the Khakasia Soviet Socialist Republic, in January 1992, Shtygashev was elected Speaker of the Supreme Soviet of the republic. He stated that the government of the republic would avoid all kinds of popularistic appeals, reforms and experiments so as not to destroy the economy and not precipitate the people into the abyss of uncertainty and chaos. He advocated the implementation of radical economic and political reform, privatization, land reform, anti-monopoly policy and the acceleration of the process of economic and social development.

However, he thought that the state should not abandon the levers of administration despite the development of market relations. The transition to the market had to be accompanied by compulsory protection of the population and the liberalization of prices had to be well thought through. Sovereignty to him meant a bicameral parliament for Khakasia, the introduction of a quota for those of Khakas nationality in the leadership of the republic, the compulsory teaching of the Khakas language in schools and the legal regulation of inward migration to Khakasia. Until 1991 he was a member of the Rossiya parliamentary faction but since then he does not belong to any faction or group. This is because as a deputy he expresses his position clearly.

In December 1992 the "Siberian agreement", forwarded to the VII Congress of People's Deputies, was signed by the Speaker of the Supreme Soviet and the Chairman of the Council of Ministers of the Republic of Khakasia. It stated that the reason for the crisis was not merely in the scale of the reforms but in the mistakes perpetrated during their implementation. Some of the legislation was classified as not well thought out. In Shtygashev's opinion the congress had saved the country from confrontation and had demonstrated character and wisdom. The course of events had demonstrated that economic stabilization could not be achieved in the near future. He viewed the decree on the stabilization of the constitutional order of the Russian Federation as something which had been adopted extremely hastily and in protest he had refused to vote on it. He is married with two children and lives in Abakan.

Shukhevych, Yurii Romanovych

Leader of the Ukrainian National Assembly.

He is the son of Roman Shukhevych, the famous wartime commander of the Ukrainian Insurgent Army from 1943 to 1950, killed by Soviet troops in 1950. Yurii was born in 1936, and his schooldays were interrupted by his forcible removal to a children's home in Donetsk after his mother's arrest in 1945. Upon his return to Galicia he was arrested in 1948 (at the age of twelve) and given twelve years' imprisonment, plus ten years' exile. In prison in 1958 his sentence was lengthened by another ten years, giving him the opportunity to train as an electrician.

He was freed in 1968, but not allowed to return to Ukraine. Consequently, he worked as an electrician in the north Caucasian city of Vladikavkaz. In 1972 he was arrested again, and received another ten-year sentence. Whilst imprisoned he lost his sight in 1981 and even after his release in 1983, therefore, he was confined to an invalids' hospital in Omsk *oblast*, where he remained until 1989, when he was finally allowed to return to Ukraine.

Understandably he was radicalized by his experiences and, as the son of a national hero, he was chosen to head the ultra-right Ukrainian Inter-party Assembly (after September 1991 the Ukrainian National Assembly or UNA) at its third congress in December 1990. Shukhevych led it further to the right, arguing for a total boycott of all Soviet institutions, and for extra-parliamentary struggle against the "occupying regime".

After August 1991, the UNA swung to the opposite extreme, giving unconditional support to national communists like President Kravchuk, and arguing that Ukraine should become a regional superpower leading a military alliance of all anti-Russian states. The UNA even founded its own paramilitary wing, the Ukrainian Self-Defence Forces (*UNSO*), which claimed to have 5,000 men in its ranks in 1992. In autumn 1991 Shukhevych became the first politician of substance to call on Ukraine to retain her nuclear weapons as defence against Russian "territorial pretensions". Shukhevych stood as the UNA's presidential candidate in autumn 1991, but failed to obtain the necessary signatures of 100,000 electors to allow his candidacy to proceed.

In 1992, however, increasing signs of dissatisfaction with Shukhevych's leadership emerged within the UNA as its younger leaders tried to develop a contemporary statist or corporatist-fascist ideology for the movement, as Shukhevych was felt to be out of touch after his long exile from Ukraine, and his language and ideology old-fashioned.

Address: 252001 Kiev, Muzeinyi provulok 8; *telephone*: Kiev 228 0130.

Shumeiko, Vladimir Filippovich

First deputy Russian Prime Minister.

Born on February 10, 1945 in Rostov-on-Don into a Russian military family; member of the CPSU until August 1991. In 1963 he completed basic training in the electrical measuring instruments factory in Krasnodar, fitter second grade, and entered the Rostov Polytechnical Institute the same year while still working in the enterprise. He then served in the Soviet Army, but after national service he resumed his work and studies. Then he moved to the all-Union scientific research institute for electrical measuring instruments where he progressed from engineer to head of a department. He completed postgraduate studies and successfully presented his candidate dissertation in technical sciences (PhD (Eng)). In 1985 he returned to the Krasnodar electrical measuring instruments factory, now a production association, as chief design engineer. In 1986 he became chief engineer and in January 1989 was elected general director. He was also a people's deputy of the Pervomaisky *raion* soviet of Krasnodar.

Shumeiko was nominated for election as an RSFSR people's deputy in the spring of 1990 in the No. 17 national territorial district, Krasnodar *krai*. During the election campaign he advocated that the slogan "all power to renewed soviets of people's deputies" be put into practice and that the political status and sovereignty of the RSFSR should be strengthened. He called for a resolute struggle against the command-administrative methods of managing industry and agriculture and the promotion of region cost accounting (*khozraschet*). He proposed the creation of inter-branch state association scientific-technical and production co-operatives but on a voluntary basis. He advocated a wide-ranging programme of social issues.

There were four candidates in the election. Shumeiko received 24.26% of the votes in the first round and won the second round with 45% of the vote. His most serious challenger was G. I. Vasilenko, head of the KGB in Krasnodar *krai* who polled 29.8% in the first round and 41% in the second. He was elected a deputy of the RSFSR Supreme Soviet of Nationalities at the I Congress. He became deputy chairman of the Supreme Soviet committee on economic reform and property. At the V Congress of People's Deputies he was elected deputy Speaker of the Supreme Soviet. He was active in the Communists of Russia faction. In February 1992 he headed the parliamentary group co-ordinating the decisions taken on economic and social questions, and he also became president of the confederation of the unions of entrepreneurs of Russia.

In June 1992 he was appointed first deputy Prime Minister of Russia. He was head of the commission on the stabilization of the economy and the co-ordinator of the commission for regulating relations between the trade unions, government and entrepreneurs. He retained his position under Viktor Chernomyrdin and is responsible for the activities of the cabinet, state support for small and medium sized enterprises, the collecting of information about reform and links with public and religious organizations. He is married and has two children and a grandson. He lives in Moscow.

Shumov, Vladimir Georgievich

Minister of the Interior of the Republic of Kazakhstan.

Born in 1941 in the village of Nizhny Mashad village, Sairamsky *raion*, Chimkent *oblast*. After secondary school he began working in 1958 in a Chimkent enterprise, and then served in the Soviet army from 1960 to 1963. From 1963 to 1965 he worked in the Chimkent electric apparatus enterprise, and then in 1965 became an officer in the criminal investigation department of the Karatau city militia, Dzhambul *oblast*; later he was appointed head of the Oitalsky village militia, and head of Zhanatassky city department of the interior. From 1979 to 1988 he was deputy head of Dzhambul *oblast*, Ministry of the Interior, and later deputy head of Semipalatinsk *oblast*, Ministry of the Interior, Kazakh SSR. In 1988 he was appointed head of Uralsky *oblast* department of the ministry, and in April 1992 he was appointed Minister of the Interior of the Republic of Kazakhstan.

Address: 480091 Alma Ata, pl. Respubliki 4.

Shurchkov, Igor Olegovich

Chairman of the state committee on industrial policy of the Russian Federation; Minister.

Born on November 11, 1950 in Armavir, Krasnodar *krai*; Russian. He was a member of the CPSU until August 1991. He graduated in 1973 from the Moscow Institute of Electronic Technology, and is a specialist on automated systems and electronics. He successfully presented his candidate dissertation in technical sciences (PhD) and his doctoral dissertation in technical sciences (DSc). After graduating he worked as an engineer, head of a section, deputy head, and head, of a shop in the Mikron enterprise of the scientific research institute of molecular electronics, Nauchny Tsentr scientific production association, USSR Ministry of the Electronics Industry, Moscow (1973-81); head of the scientific industrial complex and deputy chief engineer of the Nauchny Tsentr association (1981-86); deputy head of the main scientific technical administration of the USSR Ministry of Industry of the Means of Communications (1986-88); head of the main technical administration of the ministry (1986-88); and head of the main technical administration of the ministry (1988-89).

From January to May 1990 he was first deputy head of the main administration, scientific technical development of the USSR Ministry of Communications, and then head of the main administration of the ministry (May 1990-July 1991). From July to December 1991 he was a member of the board and head of the main administration of the Telekom scientific research association; and general director of the department of industry of the means of communications (1992). In July 1992 he was appointed adviser to the first deputy Prime Minister of the Russian Federation; and also chairman of the state committee on industrial policy. He was awarded the orders of the Red Banner of Labour and the order of the badge of honour. He lives in Moscow.

Shuteev, Vasily Ivanovich

Head of the Administration of Kursk *oblast*, Russian Federation.

Born on July 23, 1949 in the village of Alekseevka, Kromsky *raion*, Orlov *oblast*, into a peasant family. He graduated from the geological technical college, Novocherkassk, and was an assistant to a foreman borer during geological expeditions. Then he served in the Soviet Army, and after being demobbed entered Kursk Polytechnical Institute from which he graduated in 1970. Then he was an engineer, head design engineer and head of a special design bureau in the *Schetmash* enterprise. From 1977 he was deputy head of a shop, then head of S shop, and from 1980 to 1984 was chief engineer, then director of the enterprise, and then general director of the *Schetmash* production association. In 1988 he was appointed head of the main economic planning administration, and in 1989 was elected first deputy chairman of the Kursk *oblast* soviet executive committee.

In August 1991 he condemned the slowness and circumspection of the *oblast* soviet executive committee during the critical situation in the country after August 19. On September 25, 1991, at the VII session of the *oblast* soviet executive committee he was elected chairman, and on December 11, 1991 he was appointed head of the administration of Kursk *oblast* by presidential decree. As head of the administration he stated that he unreservedly supported the transition to a market economy. The existing economic mechanisms were of limited value and not capable of innovation. The transition would have to be implemented by skilled specialists who, taking important economic decisions, would bear in mind the problems of each citizen. It was important to develop various forms of economic activity. Laws which ensured equality between the collective and state farm sector and private ownership of land should be enacted.

In December 1992, during the VII Congress of People's Deputies, Shuteev came out strongly against the impeachment of the President and disagreed with the opponents of the right to sell land freely. He regarded it as opportune for the congress to meet since deputies had to agree a programme for resolving the present crisis and the Supreme Soviet had to create a solid legislative base, something which it had still not achieved. He lives in Kursk.

Shyshkin, Viktor Ivanovych

State Prosecutor of Ukraine.

An ethnic Russian born in 1952. He was educated at Odesa State University, and then worked as a lawyer; he successfully presented his candidate dissertation in juridicial science (LlM). In 1990 he became politically active as a member of the Party of Democratic Revival of Ukraine, a centrist group with many Russian members that grew out of the Democratic Platform of the Communist Party of Ukraine.

In March 1990 he was elected people's deputy for Kirovskyi *raion*, Kirovohrad *oblast*, in central Ukraine on the second ballot. He is Deputy Head of the Supreme Soviet committee on legislation and legality. In autumn 1991 he was appointed State Prosecutor, and therefore dropped his formal party affiliation. He inherited an institution with almost no independence from the state, discredited by its past involvement in blatantly political trials (such as the arrest and trial of people's deputy Stepan Khmara in November 1990).

It has proved difficult for Shyshkin to overcome the habits of the past, however. In August 1992 Kravchuk was threatening hostile journalists with prosecution, and unfriendly foreigners with deportation. On the other hand, Shyshkin has also been criticized by the authoritarian right for not prosecuting separatists in the Crimea and elsewhere. In spring 1993 he was also criticized by the far left for failing to clamp down on corruption in his office.

Official address: 252601 Kiev, MSP, Vul. Riznytska 13/ 15; *telephone*: Kiev 226 2027.

Sichko, Vasyl

Leader of the Ukrainian Christian Democratic Party.

Born into a Ukrainian family in Magadan in Siberia. His father Petro, a native of Galicia, had been deported as a long-standing member of both the OUN (Organization of Ukrainian Nationalists) and UPA (the wartime Ukrainian

Army). After completing their sentence, the family returned to Dolyna. Vasyl began to study journalism at Kiev State University in the early 1970s, but was expelled for publishing *samizdat* documents. In June 1979 he was arrested for organizing a meeting at the grave of Ukrainian national composer V. Ivasiuk (allegedly murdered by the KGB) in Lviv, and was sentenced to eight years imprisonment.

After his release in 1985 he joined the Ukrainian Helsinki Union at its foundation in 1988. In November 1988 father and son formed the Ukrainian Christian Democratic Front in Ivano-Frankivsk, which at its second congress in April 1990 became the Ukrainian Christian Democratic Party (UCDP), and Vasyl Sichko was elected leader. The UCDP is strongly nationalist. Although if professes an inter-confessional ideology, its support is in practice confined to the Uniate Catholic community in Galicia. Despite early promise, the UCDP was soon outflanked by the success of the Ukrainian Republican Party as the main *de facto* Christian Democratic Party in Ukraine, and debilitated by internal squabbles between Sichko, Mykhailo Boiko and others. The party split twice in 1992, but Sichko retained the largest faction of supporters, with 4,000 to 5,000 members. In August 1992 Sickho's UCDP supported the newly created Congress of National-Democratic Forces.

Telephone: Kiev 550 7372.

Sidarevic, Anatol Michailavic

Member of the Belarusian Popular Front.

Born on March 1, 1948. His parents are Michail and Maryja Sidarevic, and the family is Belarusian. He graduated from the faculty of philosophy, Belarusian State University, and was a journalist on the local newspaper and a teacher in village schools. He also worked for the journals *Litaratura i Mastactva* and *Krynica*. He now teaches at the Belarusian Lyceum of Humanities. He is a member of the Belarusian Popular Front and the Belarusian Social Democratic Hramada, and regards himself as a social democrat, while retaining independent views. He loves classical and folk music, and is unmarried. He speaks Polish, Ukrainian, Russian and German.

Address: Minsk, vul. Kalinouskaha 63–72; *telephone:* Minsk (0172) 65 54 56.

Sidorov, Evgeny Yurevich

Russian Minister of Culture.

Born in 1940 in Moscow into a Russian family; member of the CPSU from 1962 to August 1991. In 1962 he graduated from the law faculty of Moscow State University and afterwards became a journalist, beginning as a cinema critic and becoming a member of the USSR union of cinematographers. He was on the staff of the newspapers *Moskovskii Komsomolets*, *Literaturnaya Gazeta* and the magazine *Yunost* (youth). He graduated from the department of literary theory and criticism of the Academy of Social Sciences of the Central Committee, CPSU and taught there for five years.

In 1974 he successfully presented his candidate dissertation on the problems of the multi-faceted styles of contemporary Russian Soviet prose (1960s and 1970s) (PhD). He is the author of seven books and many articles on literary criticism on Russian literature at the beginning of the 20th century and the work of contemporary Russian and Soviet writers and poets. Among these publications are: *Time, the Writer and Style* (1978); *On the Way to a Synthesis: Articles, Portraits and Discussions* (1979); *In Search of the Truth: Articles and Discussions about Literature* (1983); *Evgeny Evtushenko: Personality and Creativity* (1987); *Currents of Poetry: Articles, Portraits and Discussions* (1988). In the late 1960s he wrote an epilogue to Vasily Aksenov's novel, *Surplussed Barrelware*, for which he was hauled over the coals at a meeting of the *raion* committee meeting of the CPSU. In 1975 he wrote a critical review of the novel *Shore* by Yury Bondarev, the secretary of the USSR Union of Writers.

In 1977 he defended A. Efros, the theatrical producer, against the "national patriots". In 1984, while the Siberian, Konstantin Chernenko, was General Secretary of the CPSU, he published an article casting doubts on the greatness of the "Siberian" novel. For many years before 1992 he taught at the Gorky Literary Institute in Moscow. He became a doctor of philological sciences (DLitt), professor, pro-rector and finally rector of the institute, and even as minister he still gives seminars on literary criticism. In February 1992 he was proposed as minister by some members of the creative intelligentsia, including D. Likhachev, M. Ulyanov and Yu. Karyakin, and was then confirmed as Minister of Culture. In March 1992 he was made Russian Minister of Culture and Tourism. He heads the state commission on the restoration of cultural values.

The main task of the ministry is the drafting of a state programme on culture, the analysis and forecasting of development trends, the defence of national cultural properties and the social protection of cultural workers. To achieve this a consultative council has been set up by the ministry and includes the major luminaries of Russian culture, at home and abroad, from Dmitry Likhachev to Ernst Neizvestny. Various programmes have been drawn up on the protection and use of the cultural heritage of Russia, the development of the national cultures of the peoples of Russia and the reform of cultural education.

Special concern has been devoted to programmes such as the "Russian provinces" and the "gifted young". The minister regards it as imperative that Russia joins international organizations for the protection of culture, including copyright. Sidorov took part in drafting the Russian law on culture and the presidential law on the defence of culture in a market economy. Since state provision for culture is small, other sources of funding have to be developed such as sponsorship and patronage with the state making such activities attractive from a tax point of view. Tourism, as in the West, can become a great potential source of income and the ministry should assume responsibility for granting licences in this area.

The minister regards a reasonable compromise with the Russian Orthodox Church on the question of the return of its cultural property as very necessary. In the autumn of 1992 he participated in the meeting in Paris of European Ministers of Culture and once again was struck by the interest in Russian culture and the possibility of earning hard currency by promoting it.

He is fond of poetry and classical music and graduated in music, spending all his free time when a student in the Moscow conservatory. Sundays are devoted to literature. His most recent articles have been devoted to the tales of Vasily Aksenov for a collection of his writings and on the semantics of the image of the butterfly in the work of Osip Mandelshtam and Joseph Brodsky. Sidorov loves to play chess and has an English bulldog as a pet. He has a rented a dacha from the literary fund in the writers' village of Peredelkino. He has been awarded the order of the Friendship of Peoples and the badge of honour for his literary criticism. He lives in Moscow.

Skokov, Yury Vladimirovich

Secretary of the Security Council of the Russian Federation until May 6, 1993.

Born in 1938 in Vladivostok, where his father was head of the USSR KGB in Krasnodar *krai*; Russian. He was a member of the CPSU until August 1991. He graduated from the Leningrad Institute of Electrical Engineering as a radio engineer and design technologist. In 1961 he began working in the No. 2 scientific research institute, USSR Ministry of Defence, Kalinin (Tver). He became a postgraduate student in the Leningrad institute in 1963 and in 1966 successfully presented his candidate dissertation in technical sciences on a classified subject (PhD).

In the No. 2 scientific research institute he was a junior research assistant and later a senior research assistant. In 1969 he was appointed head of sector in one of the departments of the third branch of the all-Union scientific research institute of the sources of current, Krasnodar. From 1970 to 1973 he was acting head of a department at the institute, and then was acting director of the institute's Saturn experimental enterprise, Krasnodar (1978-86). In 1986 he was appointed general director of the institute and chairman of the board of the Kvantemp inter-branch state association, Moscow, the first Soviet concern to link enterprises in 14 cities and five Union republics.

In 1989 he was elected a USSR people's deputy for the Dzerzhinsky territorial district, Moscow, but as a USSR people's deputy and later as a member of the

USSR Supreme Soviet he did not deliver a single speech. He was a member of the Supreme Soviet committee on economic reform and, in December 1989 he voted for Nikolai Ryzhkov's programme for the regeneration of the economy. In June 1990 he was appointed first deputy Chairman of the Council of Ministers of the RSFSR. According to Grigory Yavlinsky, who occupied a similar post, Skokov's first action in his new job was to transfer 10 million non-hard currency rubles to the account of the Kvantemp concern. In August 1991 he was a member of the shadow Russian government set up in the Urals.

After the resignation of the Ivan Silaev government, in the autumn of 1991, Skokov was appointed an RSFSR state adviser on security; secretary of the council on the affairs of the Federation and its territories of the RSFSR President; and secretary of the commission on the drafting of a statute and responsibilities of the RSFSR Council of Security. President Yeltsin's intention to make Skokov a member of the Russian government was opposed by the Democratic Russia movement.

On May 22, 1992 Skokov was confirmed as secretary of the Security Council of the Russian Federation, and in October of the same year he was appointed secretary of the heads of the republics of the Russian Federation. In the same month he was appointed head of the higher attestation commission of the President, and also in 1992 he was made head of the campaign to combat crime, the mafia and corruption. On March 20, 1993 Skokov refused to sign the draft decree of the President of the Russian Federation on the introduction of a "special regime". On March 21, in the Russian Supreme Soviet, he criticized the television address to the people by the President, delivered on March 20.

On May 6, 1993 Skokov was relieved of his duties as secretary of the Security Council by presidential decree. Sergei Filatov stated that the reasons for his dismissal was that Skokov did not support many of the policies of the President, and he was also accused of transforming the council of the heads of the republics into an anti-presidential forum. This was stretching a point since only a minority of the republican leaders were in favour of the President's policies. Skokov lives in Moscow.

Skoryk, Larysa Pavlivna

Leading Ukrainian Nationalist Deputy.

Born into a Ukrainian family in Liubech in 1939. Both of her parents were teachers. She was a student in the department of architecture, Lviv State University, and from 1972 worked in the Kiev Institute of Art. She was elected Vice-President of the Union of Ukrainian Architects at its ninth congress. Like many other members of the Kiev cultural intelligentsia, she was an early convert to the national movement that began to find its feet in the late 1980s.

She became a leading *Rukh* activist, and in March 1990 was elected on the second round as people's deputy for the Artemivskyi *raion* in Kiev city. At the time she was known for her strident nationalism. In the Supreme Soviet, she joined the radical nationalist *Nezalezhnist* (independence) faction, dominated by the Republican Party, and was also a member of the advisory board to the radical independent trade union movement *VOST*, set up in June 1991. Because of her specific interest in architecture, she has since 1990 chaired the Supreme Soviet's sub-committee on the renaissance of traditional national culture and architecture.

After the August 1991 Declaration of Ukrainian Independence, however, she sharply changed tack and became an increasingly vocal supporter of President Kravchuk. Like many nationalists, she placed heavy emphasis on the building of a strong national state and national defence, to which economic reform and de-communization should take second place. In April 1992 she was rewarded with appointment as a member of the President's advisory *Duma* on humanitarian affairs. Skoryk became increasingly critical of those of her former colleagues who chose to remain in opposition.

Her intemperate attack on Viacheslav Chornovil at *Rukh's* third congress in February-March 1992 led to uproar in the hall and almost caused a formal split in the movement. Although *Rukh* managed at the time to paper over the cracks between supporters of Kravchuk and Chornovil, Skoryk was one of the driving forces behind the subsequent creation of the Congress of National-Democratic Forces in August 1992, as a nationalist support group for President Kravchuk (she is a member of its Council). With Dmytro Pavlychko she exerted behind-the-scenes pressure to secure a pro-Kravchuk line.

Her political style remains somewhat extreme. In the summer of 1992 she caused a stir by calling for the use of the security forces against liberals and "pro-Russian chauvinists" in the *New Ukraine* movement.

Official address: Kiev, Vul. M. Hrushevskoho 5; *telephone*: Kiev 252 019.

Slepichev, Oleh Ivanovych

Vice-Prime Minister of Ukraine to October 1992.

Born into a Ukrainian family in 1949, Slepichev spent the early part of his career in the highly Russified eastern Ukraine. He finished his education at Luhansk technical college of Soviet trade in 1967, and then worked at various related jobs in Luhansk *oblast*, until taking further education at Donetsk institute of Soviet trade to 1976.

He then worked his way up through the Party *apparat*, becoming first Deputy Minister of Trade in 1987, and Minister of Trade in 1989. In June 1991 he became Vice-Premier with special responsibility for trade, whereafter he was closely associated with Premier Fokin's conservative approach to economic reform, and his attempt to maintain trading links with Russia. He became another victim of Leonid Kuchma's reported dislike of bureaucratic conservatives when he lost his job in October 1992.

Official address: 252008 Kiev, Vul. M. Hrushevskoho 12/2; *telephone*: Kiev 293 7442.

Sliva, Anatoly Yakovlevich

Deputy head of the state legal board of the administration of the Russian President; official representative of the President on legal matters in the Russian Supreme Soviet.

Born on February 10, 1940 in Propoisk (now Slavgorod), Mogilev *oblast*, Belorusian SSR (Belarus). He was a member of the CPSU from 1962 to August 1991. He graduated from the faculty of law, Moscow State University, and in 1970 he successfully presented his candidate dissertation in law on "The activity of the higher authorities of the Union republics and their leadership of local soviets" (LLM). In 1971 he joined the all-Union extra-mural Institute of Law: as a lecturer, assistant professor, and dean of the faculty of Soviet construction. He was then senior legal consultant and deputy head of department in the apparatus of the USSR Supreme Soviet (1988-91). He was appointed deputy head of the state legal board of the Russian presidential administration when it was established on December 27, 1991, and on the board he heads the section on links with the representative and executive authorities and national policy. He was appointed official representative of the President of the Russian Federation, by presidential decree, on July 27, 1992. He was a member of the governmental commission for the preparation of the Russian referendum of April 25, 1992.

He regards his task as facilitating contact between the President and the Supreme Soviet on legislation. He is not a representative for concrete draft legislation but a permanent representative, an ambassador for the President in parliament. The state legal board should be the "legal department of technical supervision" of the decisions of the executive power, be responsible for all legal matters and provide expert advice on all draft orders and decrees which the president receives. The instrument for ensuring legality should be a single legal service acting for the President, the government and the council of security, in which there can be no division of functions. He believes this agency should be independent, but not small, carrying out only the instructions of the leadership.

A law on state service is needed even though it is very difficult to achieve such a functioning law. However, he regards it as badly needed not only to combat corruption but to oblige the official to work within the law, providing him with a precise status, laws and responsibilities. State officials should be protected and should devote all their energies to the service. Sliva has the authority to participate fully in the deliberations of the Supreme Soviet, the two houses, the Presidium, the committees and commissions, to take part in the review of draft legislation, suggested legislation, orders and statements of the head of government and to represent the conclusions of the President on draft parliamentary legislation.

Sliva believes that the IX Congress of People's Deputies, in March 1993, limited its powers by handing over the decision about the basic contents of the new constitution to the people. From that moment, until the referendum and the results of the referendum became known, the people of Russia had the only legal right to decide the question about the basic contents of the constitution. Any other activity by the deputies, calling for the rescinding of the referendum, is unconstitutional. The struggle over the referendum is not a struggle against the President but a struggle against the right of the people to express its will. He is married and his wife, Regina Alekseevna, is a lawyer and editor of the law review of Moscow State University. They have a daughter. Sliva lives in Moscow.

Smirnov, Evgeny Aleksandrovich

Chairman of the Council of Ministers of the Republic of Khakasia, Russian Federation.

Born in 1936; member of the CPSU until August 1991. graduated from the V. I. Lenin Polytechnical Institute, Kharkov (Kharkiv), Ukraine, in 1960, as a qualified engineer. He was assigned to Kramatorsk and worked as an engineer on heavy iron pressing equipment. In 1961 he moved to Angara, and worked for three years as an engineer in the installation department of the Bratsk hydroelectric construction trust and in 1964 became foreman of the installation department of the specialized hydroelectric installation trust. From 1965 to 1976 he took part in the construction of the Krasnoyarsk hydroelectric station, lived in Divnogorsk, was head of a design group, deputy head, and head of the installation department of Krasnoyarsk hydroelectric construction trust. Then he became deputy chief engineer of the Krasnoyarsk hydroelectric construction trust during the construction of the Sayano-Shushensky hydroelectric station. In 1980 he was elected secretary of the Party committee of the Krasnoyarsk hydroelectric construction trust and in 1982 second secretary of the Sayanogorsk city Party committee. In 1985 he moved to Abakan and worked as head of the department of construction of the Khakasia Party *obkom*. From 1988 to 1990 he was first deputy head of the economic planning administration of the Khakasia *oblast* soviet executive committee.

At the first session of the Khakasia *oblast* soviet Smirnov was elected its deputy chairman and after Khakasia became a republic, he was elected chairman of the Council of Ministers of the Republic of Khakasia, in February 1992. On assuming office he stated that to develop economic relations it was necessary to concentrate on the enterprises, *raions* and cities. He advocated rapid privatization, the quickest solution to the problem of non-payment of debts, the development of interregional links and the establishment of a special non-budgetary fund.

In December 1992 the Chairman of the Council of Ministers and the Speaker of the Supreme Soviet of the Republic of Khakasia sent a telegram to President Yeltsin and the VII Congress of People's Deputies underlining their support of the legally elected state agencies of Russia, calling on them to display wisdom during the political crisis and to search for reasonable compromises, taking into consideration the interests of all of Russia. A "Siberian agreement" was adopted and forwarded to the VII Congress of People's Deputies stating that the crisis was not only the result of the reforms but also the mistakes committed during its implementation. It was necessary to rethink regional policy since the centre of gravity had now moved to the local level. Tax policy should be reviewed and the relations between the various types of ownership among subjects of the Russian federation should be laid down in law. The unity of Russia depended on the consistent implementation of the principle of federalism. Smirnov lives in Abakan.

Smirnov, Vladimir Sergeevich

Chairman of the co-ordinating council of the Military for Democracy Movement. Adviser on military issues to the government of the Russian Federation. Colonel.

Born on November 30, 1946 in Babaevo, Vologda *oblast*, into a working-class family. Russian. He graduated from Balashov Higher Military Aviation Technical School for Pilots in 1968; Moscow Aviation Institute in 1980. He received a higher technical education and was a member of the CPSU from 1969 to July 1990. He left the Party of his own free will after the XXVIII Congress.

After completing technical school he worked for seven years at Chelyabinsk Higher Military Aviation Technical School for Navigators as an instructor, crew commander and detachment commander. In 1975 he became a test pilot at the Red Banner state scientific and test institute of the air force. He mastered 30 types of aircraft and 25 types of long and front line bombers. He clocked up 3,500 hours of flying time. He was awarded the rank of military pilot, first class, and test pilot, first class. At the end of the 1980s he was deputy head of the test administration of the institute.

At the beginning of 1989 Col. Smirnov was nominated as a candidate for election as a USSR people's deputy by an initiative group of electors in Akhtubinsk territorial district, Astrakhan *oblast*. He supported the following views during the election campaign: the democratization of the army and its transformation into a professional military force; reduction in defence spending; more effective use of national resources; civil control of the armed forces by parliament; the establishment of a special agency of the Russian Supreme Soviet to exercise this control; full implementation in the country of the UN declaration on human rights; and the reduction of the power of the central apparatus. During the first round of voting on March 26, 1989, Smirnov polled

43,152 votes and came second out of four candidates. He won the second round on April 9 and was thereby elected a USSR people's deputy. He was a member of the inter-regional deputies' group and advocated fundamental changes in the military and the country. At the beginning of 1990 he participated in the drafting of proposals on military reform as a member of the commission of the USSR Supreme Soviet. He was an active member of the democratic platform in the CPSU, but left it together with other members of the movement after coming to the conclusion that it was impossible to reform the Party. He joined the Russian Republican Party.

Col. Smirnov made rousing and memorable speeches at demonstrations and rallies in Moscow. Politically he concentrated on reform of the army and raising its combat readiness, democratization of the military, and banning the use of troops in domestic political conflicts. He was a member of "Shield", the union of military men, from 1989 to December 1990. He left it during the II Congress because of the political intrigues and ambitious behaviour of some leaders who supported Vitaly Urazhtsev. In March 1991, at a meeting of military men in the Moscow Soviet, Smirnov founded The Military for Democracy Movement and was elected chairman at the first conference of the co-ordinating council. In 1991 he was head of the group of public observers of the situation in Nagorno-Karabakh which unearthed numerous violations of the law and the participation of Soviet troops in operations against the civilian population. During the anti-constitutional putsch in August 1991, he was in Nagorno-Karabakh where he was in constant danger of arrest and attack. From August 1991 to June 1992 he was head of the administration of the Russian state committee on defence issues.

Smirnov advocates thoroughgoing reforms in the army and navy, the creation of a system of civil parliamentary control over the evolution and use of the armed forces and the establishment of democratic principles and law within the military sphere. He participated in the drafting of principles and proposals for military planning in Russia and in the elaboration of the "fundamentals of the defence policy of the Russian Federation". In the autumn of 1992, he visited Brussels, and established professional contact with his colleagues in NATO as a member of a delegation which included academics, political scientists and military experts. He took part in the international conference in Riga on democratic institutions in the armed forces. In August 1992 he became an adviser of the Prime Minister of the Russian Federation.

He is fond of literature, technology, art and the theatre; prefers active recreation and hence goes in for sport. He does not have a good command of foreign languages. He has published articles in the press. He has been awarded the order of the Red Star and 10 medals, and is married with two children.

Telephone (*office*): Moscow 206 33 22; (*home*): Moscow 923 79 19.

Smirnov, Yuriy Kostiantinovich

Representative of the President of Ukraine in Donetsk; leading Russophone politician.

Born into a Russian family in 1939. He graduated in mechanical engineering from the Ukrainian Extra-mural Polytechnic Institute and after beginning a career in Party work later studied at the Academy of Social Sciences of the Central Committee of the Communist Party of Ukraine (CPU). In the 1980s he rose to the position of head of both the CPU organization and the local soviet in Donetsk *oblast*. In March 1990 he was elected people's deputy for Krasnolymanskyi *raion*, Donetsk *oblast*.

In the Supreme Soviet he is a member of the committee on the activities of local councils. Smirnov played an equivocal role during the attempted state coup in August 1991, and is widely seen as one of the main driving forces behind separatists movements in the volatile Donbas region, such as the United Society for the Protection of the Russian Language Population of the Donbas, formed in Mariupol in September 1991, and the Democratic Movement of the Donbas, set up in Luhansk in October 1991. In October 1991 a meeting of People's Deputies from local soviets throughout eastern and southern Ukraine met under Smirnov's auspices, and produced demands for a federalized Ukraine and special status for the Russian language.

Smirnov has campaigned for the Donbas to be given the status of a free economic zone, and has so far successfully lobbied for the maintenance of vast subsidies from Kiev to the industrial eastern Ukraine. Hence his appointment as Kravchuk's prefect in Donetsk *oblast* in March 1992 angered many Ukrainian nationalists, but reflected the importance to Kravchuk of conciliating key local élites, particularly in the strategically vital eastern Ukraine, where Kiev's long-term control of the region is far from certain. Smirnov is a typical example of Ukraine's new regional leaders, who are strongly rooted in traditional power networks, but are increasingly autonomous of Kiev.

Official Address (Donetsk soviet): 340105 Donetsk-105, Bulvar Pushkina 34; *telephone*: Donetsk (0622) 90 7121.

Snegur, Mircea Ion

President of Moldova.

Born in 1940 of ethnic Moldovan parents, Snegur graduated in 1961 from the Chişinau Agriculture Institute and joined the Communist Party of Moldavia three years later. In 1972 he received his candidate degree in natural sciences (PhD). As an agronomist, Snegur worked for a time as chairman of a collective farm in Moldova. In 1973 Snegur was appointed head of the Main Administration of the Moldovan Ministry of Agriculture, a post he held until 1978. The practical skills Snegur had developed on the collective farm were put to use from 1978 to 1981 when he served as Director-General of the *Selektsiya* scientific-production organization within the Ministry of Agriculture, a body which worked on developing more efficient methods of field cultivation. At this time, Snegur almost certainly had contact with the CPSU Central Committee secretary for agriculture, Mikhail Gorbachev (1978-85).

Snegur's career in the party hierarchy began in 1981 when he was appointed first secretary of the *raion* party committee (*raikom*) in Edineţ, a medium-sized town in northern Moldova. His assumption of the party post corresponded with the change of top leadership within the Moldavian Communist Party. In 1980 the Stalinist party first secretary, Ivan Ivanovich Bodiul, was promoted to the post of USSR deputy premier. His replacement, Semion Kuzmich Grossu, was at the time the youngest first secretary in all the union republics (and the last republican first secretary to be replaced under Brezhnev). Unlike Bodiul, Grossu was actually born in the Moldavian Soviet Socialist Republic. The new first secretary was only six years older than Snegur and also a trained agronomist who spent several years as head of a Moldovan collective farm. It is possible, then, that Snegur benefited from the advent of the younger, ethnic Moldovan Grossu to the top party post.

From his position in Edineţ, Snegur moved rapidly up through the party and state system. On May 31, 1985 he was made a secretary of the Central Committee of the Moldavian Communist Party, a position which he would hold until 1989. From November 1988, Snegur was in charge of the Central Committee's special commission for agro-industry. During this period he was also promoted to membership of the Politburo of the Communist Party of Moldavia and elected to the Moldovan Supreme Soviet.

On July 29, 1989 the Moldovan Supreme Soviet elected Snegur president of the Supreme Soviet presidium. The position had become open due to the promotion of the previous chairman, Alexandru Mocanu, to the position of deputy chairman of the Soviet of the Union of the USSR Supreme Soviet. The stenographic report from the Supreme Soviet session on July 29 revealed that all the other candidates publicly renounced their candidacies for the post, leaving Snegur as the sole candidate. As head of the Supreme Soviet, Snegur presided over the pivotal event in the Moldovan independence movement: the adoption of laws making Moldovan/Romanian, written in the Latin script, the state language of the republic (August 31, 1989). In addition, under Snegur's leadership, the Supreme Soviet declared its sovereignty within the USSR (June 23, 1990). By 1990 the power of the Communist party in Moldova had been eclipsed by the growing authority of the Supreme Soviet. Under Snegur, the Supreme Soviet ceased to be a rubber-stamp for Communist party directives and began to assert its own role as a properly functioning parliament. In late April 1990, Snegur was elected by the Supreme Soviet to a five-year term as President of the republic. Snegur's victory over the other candidate, republican first secretary Petru Lucinschi, put the final nail in the coffin in the Moldavian Communist party.

By September of the same year, the republican government was once again reformed by the Supreme Soviet and the post of popularly elected President was created to replace the indirectly elected presidency Snegur had occupied for only four months. The law establishing the presidential form of government provided for direct, popular elections, but Snegur was elected to the post by the Supreme Soviet on September 3, 1990 until popular elections could be held. In the event, the momentous events which took place at the republican and the all-union levels throughout the remainder of 1990 and 1991 forced the elections to be postponed until December 1991.

Elected to a five-year term as president of the Republic of Moldova on December 8, 1991, Snegur gained a reported 98.17% of the popular vote, with a total voter turnout of 88.88%. However, he was the only candidate in the presidential elections, his two potential opponents having been disqualified. Communist Party first secretary Gheorghe Eremei was not allowed to run since he had supported the August coup in Moscow, and Gheorghe Malarciuc, the candidate of the nascent Ecology Party, failed to collect the required number of signatures supporting his candidacy. Since taking up the presidential mantle, Snegur has struggled to maintain Moldova's territorial integrity and independence, despite pressures from Russian and Gagauz separatists and rumblings from Romania about Moldova's place in a reconstituted "Greater Romania".

Snegur's majority in Moldova's first direct presidential poll, as well as the single-candidate ticket, raised serious questions about the impartiality of the elections. Still, it is likely that Snegur, as the politician credited with leading Moldova out of the Soviet "prison house of nations", would have easily defeated any rival candidate.

Since December 1991, Snegur has continually insisted that the existence of "two Romanian states" is a political fact which precludes any talk of quick Romanian-Moldovan unification. His stance on the unification issue has won him the wrath of the Popular Front of Moldova, the most important informal organization during the independence movement. However, the Popular Front's waning support within Moldova and Snegur's strong base of support within *Sfatul Țării* (the former Supreme Soviet) mean that his future is relatively secure. His chief political support comes from the Agrarian Club within the parliament and from the leadership of the Democratic Agrarian Party. Both groups are composed largely of former collective farm administrators, many of whom Snegur must have known personally during his days in the Ministry of Agriculture. The groups are also strongly committed to maintaining Moldova's independence, a position on which Snegur himself has been unequivocal. Snegur's political fortune will depend in large part, though, on his handling of the Transnistrian conflict, an issue which continues to tax the political acumen and creativity of the entire Moldovan leadership.

Sobchak, Anatoly Aleksandrovich

Head of the Administration and Mayor of St Petersburg, Russian Federation.

Born in 1938 in Chita; Russian; member of the CPSU from 1988 to July 1990. He received his early education in Kokand and Tashkent, Uzbekistan, and then graduated with distinction from the faculty of law, A. A. Zhdanov Leningrad State University. He began as a lawyer in the Stavropol collegium of advocates, and a year later became head of the legal advice bureau and a member of the Stavropol collegium of advocates. In 1964 in Leningrad State University he successfully presented his candidate dissertation in law on "Civil-legal responsibility for causing damage to the functioning of sources of extreme danger" (LLM). Since 1965 he has been working and living in Leningrad as a lecturer in law at the Leningrad special school of the militia, USSR Ministry of Internal Affairs, and the Leningrad technological institute of the paper industry; later he joined the faculty of law of Leningrad State University and became a professor. In 1983 he successfully presented his doctoral dissertation in law on "Economic self accounting and civil-legal problems in improving the economic mechanism" (LLD).

In early 1989 he was nominated for election as a people's deputy by the collective of Leningrad State University in the No. 47 Vasileostrovsky territorial district, Leningrad. During the election campaign he advocated that soviets be made into agencies of real popular power and that they should be made more responsible to the electors. He supported the principle of the superiority of the law in all aspects of public life and activity. He opposed the election to the USSR Supreme Soviet of officials from the Party and state apparatus. He spoke of the need for the most rapid introduction of a new USSR constitution which would put an end to the monopoly of power of the Party and would place Party members and non-members on an equal footing. He devoted much attention to the organization and activities of the committee of constitutional supervision of the USSR.

There were six candidates, and Sobchak won the second round. In May 1989, at the I Congress of USSR People's Deputies, he was elected a member of the USSR Supreme Soviet, the Soviet of the Union, and also a member of the commission of the USSR Congress of People's Deputies to investigate the events in Tbilisi on April 9, 1989 when many civilians were killed by the military. At the first session of the commission Sobchak was elected chairman, and joined the interregional group of deputies. In December 1989, at the II Congress of USSR People's Deputies, he reported on the findings of the commission on the events in Tbilisi.

On May 13, 1990, during the second round of voting, he was elected a deputy of the Leningrad city soviet, and on May 23, in the Leningrad city soviet, he was elected chairman with 223 votes for, beating the other two candidates. On assuming his new functions he proclaimed the economic independence of the city, based on the development of industry and tourism and a multi-faceted economy. Among the most pressing duties were the protection of the poor strata of the population, increased struggle against crime and a solution to the ecological problems. He was a delegate to the XXVIII Party congress and at the end of it he resigned from the CPSU.

On June 12, 1991 he was elected mayor of Leningrad, after which he resigned as chairman of the Leningrad city soviet. During the summer of 1991 he was one of the founders of the movement for democratic reforms. On August 19, 1991 he declared that an anti-constitutional state coup was under way and appealed for support for all the legally elected state authorities. He declared that in Leningrad only the RSFSR constitution, RSFSR laws and decrees of the President of the RSFSR were recognized. On August 20 he managed to arrange for the troops to leave the city and declared that there was no state of emergency in the city. He addressed a meeting to oppose the Extraordinary Committee and to support the Russian President and parliament.

In August 1991, by presidential decree, he was appointed a member of the presidential Council and head of the USSR state delegation to negotiate with Estonia, and also headed a USSR Supreme Soviet delegation to Ukraine. In September 1991 Sobchak was appointed head of the administration of St Petersburg by presidential decree.

In December 1992 during the VII Congress of People's Deputies he spoke of the inertness of the people's deputies, 80% of whom were representatives of the old Party and Soviet *nomenklatura* and their inability to adopt a new Russian constitution. They should be removed either by referendum or by the decision of a new, specially created agency, elected by the people. Until then and during the political crisis a compromise should be reached between the present members of the legislature and the executive. However, this compromise should not affect the powers of the Russian President. Sobchak judged the most incisive speech at the congress to be that by Egor Gaidar, whose government should be rated very highly even though Gaidar and Chubais advocated universal privatization without taking into consideration the social consequences of the economic transformation. President Yeltsin's declaration at the congress was necessary and justified in view of the danger of the dictatorship of a conservative legislature becoming reality. Sobchak is married to his second wife and has a daughter from this marriage. He is fond of climbing and lives in St Petersburg.

Sokolov, Veniamin Sergeevich

Speaker of the Council of the Republic of the Russian Supreme Soviet.

Born on September 29, 1935 in Kostroma, Kostroma *oblast*; Russian. He was a member of the CPSU from 1964 to August 1991. In 1959 he graduated from the Institute of Physics and Technology, Moscow, and after graduating was assigned to the Novosibirsk Institute of the USSR Academy of Sciences where he worked until 1969. Then he moved into Party work, and was second secretary of the Sovetsky Party *raion* committee (1969-70). He then became head of a laboratory in the Institute of Theoretical and Applied Mechanics, Siberian branch of the USSR Academy of Sciences (1971-75). He was rector of Krasnoyarsk State University (April 1975-88), and successfully presented his candidate dissertation (PhD) and doctoral dissertation (DSc) on classified subjects in the scientific establishments of the Siberian branch of the USSR Academy of Sciences. He is a professor. He moved back into the Party apparatus in 1988 as secretary (1988-89), second secretary (February 1989-August 1990); and acting first secretary (August 1990) of the Krasnoyarsk Party *krai* committee. After the Krasnoyarsk *krai* Party conference, in August 1990, during which he was re-elected secretary of the *krai* committee, Sokolov concentrated on work in the Russian Supreme Soviet. He was elected a deputy of the Krasnoyarsk *krai* and city soviet of people's deputies.

He was nominated for election as an RSFSR people's deputy in the No. 216 Lesosibirsky territorial district, Krasnoyarsk *krai*. During the election campaign he advocated flooding the market with consumer goods by reducing the number of inefficient and capital intensive enterprises, the use of energy and resource saving technologies, the gradual introduction of the market economy and the harmonization of planning and market mechanisms to regulate production. Workers needed the opportunity to earn money, first and foremost in their enterprise. He opposed private property, but accepted various types of property ownership, and believed that bureaucratic control of the collective, state and private farms should cease. He strongly opposed the sale of national territory, natural resources and attempts to turn the Soviet Union into a raw materials colony of the more developed economies. The authority of the military, KGB and the militia should be strengthened and their links with the population enhanced.

There were six candidates. In the first round Sokolov polled 23.3% of the votes and he won the second round, polling 47.1% of the votes. His main opponent was A. N. Smirnov, editor of the *Kommunist zapolyarnaya* (communists of the Polar region) Igarsk city newspaper, who received 19.3% of the votes in the first round and 39.8% of the votes in the second round. Sokolov was elected a member of the Russian Supreme Soviet at the I Congress of People's Deputies during the second round of voting (748 votes for; 86 voted against). He is a member of the Council of the Republic of the Russian Supreme Soviet, and on September 24, 1990 he was elected chairman of the sub-committee of the committee on the budget, plans, taxes and prices of the Council of the Republic. He is a member of the Russia parliamentary faction, and at the congress he voted against banning the CPSU in the apparatus of the Supreme Soviet and against the law on the state sovereignty of the RSFSR.

Sokolov was elected Speaker of the Council of the Republic of the Russian Supreme Soviet on February 10 1993, replacing Nikolai Ryabov who later became deputy Speaker of the Russian Supreme Soviet after the resignation of Sergei Filatov. This appointment strengthened the position of Ruslan Khasbulatov, the Speaker of the Russian Supreme Soviet. Sokolov is a member of the Russian Unity faction which regards itself in implacable opposition to the President. He was one of the organizers of the Russian Unity faction and as such has close links with Sergei Baburin. The election underlined the move of the parliamentary centre to the right and the decline of the influence of the democrats over the office of speaker. Two of the parliamentary factions which backed Sokolov were *Rossiya* and communists of Russia.

Address: 103274 Moscow, K274, Krasnopresnenskaya nab., d. 2, Dom Sovetov; *telephone*: Moscow 205 52 96.

Solovev, Sergei Aleksandrovich

Chairman of the union of cinematographers of the Russian Federation.

Born on August 25, 1944 in Kem, northern RSFSR; Russian. He was never a member of the CPSU. He is a film producer and script writer. From 1960 to 1962 he worked in Leningrad television and studied at evening school, and then was a student from 1962 to 1969 at the all-Union State Institute of Cinematography, and in the classes of Mikhail Romm and A. B. Stolper. Romm was impressed with one of his projects and wrote to the Leningrad studio asking permission to turn it into a film. It appeared as the documentary film *Look at the Face*, in which a hidden camera filmed the reactions of visitors viewing Leonardo da Vinci's Madonna Litta, in the Hermitage. After graduating he joined Mosfilm, and his first film as producer, *Family Happiness*, appeared in 1970 and was based on two stories by Anton Chekhov. In 1971 he brought Maksim Gorky's play, *Egor Bulychov and Others*, to the screen and in 1972 made the television film, *Railway Spectator*, based on Aleksandr Pushkin. In 1975 came *One Hundred Days after Childhood* and at the XXV international film festival, in west Berlin, in 1976, he was awarded the silver white bear prize as best producer.

He was also awarded the Lenin *Komsomol* prize, the USSR state prize and the all-Union film festival prize. In 1980 he made the film *Rescuer*, and afterwards efforts were made to get him elected a people's artist of Russia but in vain. In 1976 he became a honorary (merited) artist of the RSFSR. In 1982 he made the film *Direct Heiress*, which completed the trilogy about the young heroes developing spirituality and an understanding of how complex life is. In 1977 he made *Melody of the White Night* with Japanese film makers, including K. Nazimura, and in 1983 *Selected* with film makers from Colombia. His film, *Strange, White and Pitted* won the special prize at the Venice film festival in 1987. His later films include *Assa* and *Black Rose, Symbol of Sorrow, Red Rose, Symbol of Love*. He is now working on *Anna Karenina*. He teaches in the institute of cinematography and in the higher classes for producers and script writers and has made Anton Chekhov's *Three Sisters* with the students. One of his latest films is *Home Under the Starry Sky* (1991).

In the union of cinematography he headed the commission for work with youth. He now has his own studio at Mosfilm, the association *Krug* (circle), and German, Dykhovichny, Lebeshev and Kaidanovsky are members of its council. The association plans to hire out its pictures and have its own cinema, but Solovev is against the commercialization of the cinema. He favours the entry of young talented producers and prefers the natural school of artistry as the way to train young actors and actresses, and advocates making films for young people. He regards the democratic declarations and reality of Russia as exact opposites. The market barons and the state democrats alike treat the artist with lordly neglect at present. Russia is living in a period characterized by a total lack of respect which has seen the end of the public honour and status of the creative artist. He believes that art and every artist need government protection, and support from the state intelligentsia. Russian spiritual life has collapsed, as has ethics, the personality and the family, and this, to him, is more important than the collapse of the economy. Solovev lives in Moscow.

Solovev, Vadim Pavlovich

Head of the Administration of Chelyabinsk *oblast*, Russian Federation.

Born in 1947; Russian; member of the CPSU until August 1991; and is a graduate. Until April 1990 he was first secretary of the Chelyabinsk city Party committee. In March 1990 he was nominated by the plenum of the Chelyabinsk city council of veterans for election as an RSFSR people's deputy in the No. 743 Kurchatovsky territorial district. During the election campaign he stated that Russia should follow the route of other civilized countries and develop a multi-faceted economy with regions and republics being autonomous.

There were six candidates. Solovev polled 18.2% of the votes in the first round and withdrew. I. I. Vishnyakov, head of the Chelyabinsk Higher Military Aviation Technical School for Navigators, was elected people's deputy. Solovev was elected a deputy of the Chelyabinsk city soviet of people's deputies and at the first session in April 1990 he was elected chairman.

On August 20, 1991, at an extraordinary session of the Presidium of the Chelyabinsk city soviet, the replacement of the USSR President was declared illegal and the actions of the Extraordinary Committee judged to be in contravention of the RSFSR and USSR constitutions. The city soviet appealed to the citizens of Chelyabinsk *oblast* to begin an indefinite strike. At a city meeting Solovev reaffirmed his commitment to the administration of President Yeltsin and declared that he did not recognize the newly established Extraordinary Committee of the USSR. The city was prepared to defend a free Russia.

The Democratic Russia movement proposed Solovev as head of the administration of the *oblast* despite the fact that the *oblast* soviet of people's deputies wanted their chairman in this post. On October 24, 1991 Solovev was appointed head of the administration of Chelyabinsk *oblast* by presidential decree. On assuming office he stated that he was a passionate supporter of market relations and reforms and an absolute supporter of the policies of President Yeltsin. During the transition to a market economy everyone should be afforded equal opportunities to display initiative and entrepreneurship. Small business, private farming and commodity exchanges should be supported and under no circumstances should state enterprises, collective and state farms be put at a disadvantage. They should be able to take part in honest competition, and his most important practical task was to promote the transition to the market as outlined by the President. However, during the period of decisive reform, strong executive power was needed at the local level. The policy being implemented by the head of the administration was at variance with that of the *oblast* soviet of people's deputies which had requested the President to review his decree appointing Solovev head of the administration. The small council of the *oblast* soviet in January 1993 announced elections for the post of head of the administration of the *oblast* on April 11. Solovev declared this decision to be illegal, which underlined the conflict between the representative and executive branches of power. Solovev is married and lives in Chelyabinsk.

Solzhenitsyn, Aleksandr Isaevich

Russian writer.

Born on December 11, 1918 in Kislovodsk, northern Caucasus; Russian. His grandfather, Semen Efimovich Solzhenitsyn, lived in the village of Sablinskoe, Aleksandrovsky *raion*, Stavropol *krai*. Until the revolution he was quite well off, owing about 2,000 desyatinas (1 desyatina = 1.09 ha), about 20,000 sheep and employed up to 50 land labourers. There were four sons: Isai, Vasily, Konstantin and Ilya and a daughter Mariya. Aleksandr's father, Isai Semenovich Solzhenitsyn, fought in the First World War and returned from the front as an officer and with a wife, but fatally wounded himself while out hunting in 1918. His mother, Taisiya Zakharovna, came from Kislovodsk, and died in 1944 in Georgievsk, Stavropol *krai*, from tuberculosis. She spoke French and English. Aleksandr's cousin, Kseniya Vasilevna, still lives in Sablinskoe. His uncle, Konstantin Semenovich, had five sons and a daughter, and in 1929 had his land confiscated and was dispatched with all his family to the Urals.

Solzhenitsyn completed secondary school in Rostov on Don. During the holidays he loved to cycle with friends through Rostov *oblast*, Transcaucasia and Ukraine. He visited the I. V. Stalin museum in Gori, Georgian SSR, and it was there that Solzhenitsyn's first doubts about the Stalin cult surfaced. These doubts were strengthened by the noisy show trials of Tukhachevsky, Uborevich and Blyukher. Solzhenitsyn was single-minded and well organized from his childhood years and in his fourth year at school headed an exercise book, *Complete Works*.

He graduated in 1941 from the faculty of mathematics and physics, Rostov State University, and had received no special literary education. He met his first wife, Natalya Alekseevna, née Reshetovskaya, at university where she was studying chemistry and they married in his third year. Literature became a passion during his student years, and he invented literary games and wrote his first stories, *River Keepers* and *Foreign Assignment*. In 1941 he was called up as a private into the Red Army, graduated in 1942 from the artillery technical college and as a mathematician, from the courses on acoustics; in May 1943 he became a commander of a battery at the front and fought in the third army of the Bryansk front. He was awarded two orders. In February 1945, as a captain, in east Prussia, he was arrested because his letters to a friend were viewed as critical of Stalin and was sentenced to eight years' imprisonment. While still at the front he wrote the stories together entitled *Lieutenant*, which received a positive review by B. Lavrenev and were recommended for publication in the journal, *Znamya*, but they were not published.

He was prisoner Shch-262 and he spent time in many prisons: Dubyanka, Butyrki, Lefortovo, and Krasnopresnenskaya transit prison. He worked in New Jerusalem, and worked on the construction of a building on Lenin Prospekt in Moscow where the shop Spartak is now situated. It all provided material for his play, *The Republic of Labour*. In 1946 in Butyrki prison he met Timofeev-Resovsky, delivered two lectures on acoustic intelligence gathering and the outlook for the nuclear age, at the prisoners' "scientific seminars". In 1948 he worked in Moscow in the classified scientific research institute in the acoustics laboratory where he studied the characteristics of sound during the transmission of a television and radio channel, and this provided the material for *The First Circle*. In May 1950 he was exiled to Kazakhstan. He lived in the village of Birlik, Chuisky *raion*, Dzhambul *oblast*, and taught mathematics, physics and astronomy in the senior classes of the secondary school and was at the same time an economist in a *raion* consumers' union. The pupils noted that he did not smoke, did not swear, and explained everything very clearly and treated the pupils with respect. He gave additional homework without payment. He was polite and correct, spoke Russian extremely well and demonstrated a tremendous knowledge of history and literature. The index finger of his right hand had been crushed while in prison. In the settlement of Kok Terek, southern Kazakhstan, in 1955, he began work on *The First Circle*. While in exile he contracted cancer but mainly through strength of will he achieved a complete cure, and *The Cancer Ward* describes this struggle. His experiences in Kazakhstan also provided background for *The Love Girl and the Innocent* and *One Day in the Life of Ivan Denisovich*. He was released after Stalin's death in 1953 but had to live in Kazakhstan or Central Asia.

He returned from exile on June 26, 1956. From 1956 to 1957 he lived n the village of Miltsevo, Vladimir *oblast* and was reunited with his wife Natalya, who during his absence had married another man and had had two children. In 1958 they moved to Ryazan where Natalya taught in the faculty of chemistry of the institute of agriculture. He taught mathematics, physics and astronomy in the No. 2 secondary school, Ryazan. He displayed great ingenuity in circumventing the KGB and the authorities (described in *The Calf and the Oak*). Solzhenitsyn's story, *One Day in the Life of Ivan Denisovich*, appeared in *Novy mir* in the autumn of 1962, thanks to the unremitting efforts of its editor-in-chief, Aleksandr Tvardovsky, after being approved by Nikita Khrushchev, head of the CPSU and the government, and his aide, V. S. Lebedev. It was an overnight sensation since it broke the taboo about the camps and described the tragedy of the Gulag. In 1963 the stories *Matrenin dvor* and the *Incident at the Krechetovka station* followed in *Novy Mir*. He became friends with Mstislav Rostropovich,

Galina Vishnevskaya, Kornei Chukovsky and Aleksandr Men, the charismatic Russian Orthodox priest. The well known campaigner for human rights, General Petr Grigorenko, came as Solzhenitsyn's guest to the village of Davydovo, near Ryazan. Solzhenitsyn attacked censorship, advocated religious freedom and a return to traditional Russian values, and these became well known in *samizdat* (unofficially published in the Soviet Union).

After the successful coup against Khrushchev in 1964 the persecution of Solzhenitsyn was stepped up. In 1965 his archive was seized and afterwards, during a search of his friends, the manuscript of *The First Circle* was discovered. The difficulties of the writer increased after his story, *The Feast of the Victors*, came to light and Petr Demichev, the USSR Minister of Culture, distributed the story to writers who began a campaign of persecution in the press. Fearing arrest, Solzhenitsyn did not live at home but with friends and at the dachas of Kornei Chukovsky and Mstislav Rostropovich at Peredelkino, near Moscow. Natalya published her diaries at the same time with Novosti. Solzhenitsyn called her a traitress for doing so and they divorced. He could no longer publish officially in the USSR and his published works were removed from libraries. At this time he also met Natalya Dmitrievna, a scientist, who was to become his second wife. She was a Muscovite, her grandfather had perished in the Gulag, many of her relatives had suffered oppression under Stalin and her maternal grandfather had been killed at the front.

The first discussion of his work in the USSR union of writers took place in late 1966 and the second in 1977 when he was urged to repent and refused. On November 4, 1969 he was expelled from the Ryazan branch of the USSR union of writers under pressure from N. S. Priezzhev, first Party secretary of the Ryazan *obkom*. In 1970 Solzhenitsyn was awarded the Nobel prize for literature. He declined the offer of the Swedish Academy that he receive it clandestinely and later accepted it in a grand ceremony in Stockholm when he was living in the West. By early 1970 he had completed *The Gulag Archipelago* and the KGB began a formal campaign against it. E. D. Voronyanskaya, one of the typists who had copied the novel, was arrested in Leningrad, on August 4, 1973. After torture and interrogation she revealed where one of the copies could be found and afterwards she hanged herself. After *The Gulag Archipelago* had fallen into the hands of the KGB, Solzhenitsyn gave permission for its publication abroad. On February 12, 1974, by decree of the Presidium of the USSR Supreme Soviet, he was deprived of his Soviet citizenship according to article 64 of the RSFSR criminal code and forcibly, under convoy and in handcuffs, put on a special plane to Cologne, guarded by the KGB. His wife and four children followed about six weeks later since his archive had to be transferred abroad. In 1974 he published the declaration: *Live and Do Not Lie*. He also forwarded *A Letter to the Leaders of the Soviet Union*, in which he called for a return of Russia to its European heartland and its traditional culture and religion, seeing its involvement in the Muslim republics of Central Asia and elsewhere as a millstone round its neck.

He stayed with the German novelist, Heinrich Böll, also a Nobel prizewinner for literature, then moved to Zürich where he completed work on *Lenin in Zürich*. In 1976 he moved to the US, near Cavendish in Vermont, and owns a farm with about 20 ha, a wood and a pond. He lives in a detached house, constructed like an archive and his library and study are there. He has four sons: Dmitry, an orientalist and university student; Ermolai, a professional musician, trained in London; Ignat, who graduated from Harvard University in June 1993; and Stepan, who is at college. All the sons, except the youngest, left home at 15-16 years of age, and his mother-in-law, 74 years old, lives with them, drives a car and does the shopping. When she was invited in 1974 to renounce Solzhenitsyn she placed her Party card on the table. He works from 6 am to late at night without a break, and on Sunday he goes to church with the family. There is no cult of food in the home, but they enjoy simple Russian fare of soup, chops, buckwheat porridge and borshch. He likes to listen to the news on the radio. It is a Christian family founded on love. He is working on his magnum opus *Red Wheel*, of which the central novel is *August 1917*. He believes that the present-day writer cannot be an anti-Semite. He enjoys good relations with the first wave of émigrés, but the majority of representatives of the third wave react negatively to him because he does not participate in their internecine wars and he does not comprehend what moral right those who have left the motherland have to act as teachers of the people they left behind. Solzhenitsyn published the article, "A poor understanding of Russia is a threat to America", in the journal *Russian American*, in 1984. He refused to attend receptions in the White House and criticized the American democratic system, accusing Americans of arrogance in regarding their society as the ideal one to be copied. In the late 1980s and early 1990s his works were published in the Soviet Union and his stature as the greatest living Russian literary figure was recognized. On September 18, 1990 *Komsomolskaya pravda* published his article on the future of Russia. Again he advocated its return to its heartland, breaking ties with the rest of the USSR, rebirth of local initiative along the lines of the *zemstvo* system (1864-1917) and a form of democracy based on consensus rather than the party politics of the West. *The Gulag Archipelago* was awarded a USSR state prize on December 11, 1990.

In August 1990 Ivan Silaev, RSFSR Prime Minister, sent him a letter inviting him to return to the motherland and Solzhenitsyn finally agreed to return with his family to Russia. His citizenship was restored by the USSR presidential decree of September 15, 1990 and the criminal case, begun against him for signs of being a traitor to the motherland was "ended due to lack of evidence". On the eve of the VIII Congress of People's Deputies, in March 1993, Solzhenitsyn forwarded several letters to Vladimir Lukin, the Russian ambassador in Washington, DC. He stated in the letters that what was transpiring in Russia was breaking his heart, and although there could be no return to the past, the future would be even more painful. The present breakup of the country began in 1930, and in 1985 the language was cured but the illness was not and merely tore the country further apart. At present some necessary reforms have been implemented but the people have been pitched into poverty and despair since January 1992. Sudden political revolutions are now a danger. Russia, given its size and variety, cannot exist without strong presidential power, not less than that in the US.

He is regarded as a towering man of letters but politically his impact is limited. His sharp attacks on Western democracy and lifestyle alienated many, although his espousal of topics such as the forced repatriation of Soviet prisoners of war forced a public debate and he was influential in moving the Russian Orthodox Church to lift its anathema on the Old Believers, thereby opening the way for the end of the schism.

Sorokin, Viktor

Commander of the Operative Group of the Armed Forces of the Russian Federation in Abkhazia, Georgia, to March 1993.

Born in 1948; Russian. He was a member of the CPSU until August 1991. From 1983 to 1985 he served as a deputy commander of the Soviet forces in Afghanistan, and later commander of a regiment as part of the 103rd airborne division. After returning from Afghanistan he served in various "hot spots" of the Soviet Union: in Gyanja, Azerbaijan and Tbilisi, Georgia. After the events of April 1989 in Tbilisi (when civilian demonstrators were killed by the military) he was the subject of an investigation for about 18 months, but the case was dropped in August 1990 and his orders were acknowledged as correct. From July to August 1992 he was in Pridnestrovie, Moldova, where he was responsible for separating the sides in Bendery.

He was head of the operative group of Russian forces in Abkhazia, Georgia (November 1992-March 1993), and participated in the defence of the Russian seismological observatory and the military hospital in Eshery. The Georgians accused him of issuing orders to Su 25 Russian aircraft to bomb Sukhumi. He supports severe measures in Georgia and strong-arm methods to resolve political conflicts.

Soshnikov, Igor Ivanovich

Co-chairman of the North West Section of the Free Democratic Party of Russia (FDPR).

Elected co-chairman of the FDPR at the constituent congress of the north-west section of the party on July 8, 1990. Nikolai Travkin advocated the establishment of the party along strict structural lines which would absorb many democratic movements and even parties. Soshnikov, on the contrary, proposed that each person should decide whether he or she wished to join the party. He favoured establishing the position of co-chairmen, priority being given to private property as the source of the wealth and freedom of society. He advocated a multi-party system, freedom for various associations, unions, religious and ethical associations, freedom of conscience, speech and press. He called for the rejection of state totalitarian structures, the legacy of Bolshevism. The future state structure of Russia can only be decided legally by the constituent assembly. It should be convened only once after elections, on a multi-party basis, to draft the principles of the formation of the state, and system of government. Then it should cease functioning.

Soshnikov favours a multi-faceted economy, free enterprise and market relations, rejects all forms of nationalism and chauvinism and is in favour of defending all strata of the population, but is opposed to "levelling down to poverty" and social parasitism. A radical redistribution of national income in favour of consumers is needed, by cutting back significantly state programmes, especially the military. He supports independent trade unions, strike committees and a state system of social security. He appeals for the constitution to be changed, and believes that the spiritual renaissance of Russia can only be achieved by taking a legal, parliamentary route and elections. He regards private property as sacred and inviolable and membership of the FDPR as incompatible with advocating violence, war and national, religious and class exclusivity. Earlier he had appealed for the consolidation of all democratic forces to remove the CPSU and the Russian Communist Party from power and to deideologize all aspects of life in society. He lives in St Petersburg.

Soskovets, Oleg Nikolaevich

First deputy Prime Minister of the Russian Federation.

Born on May 11, 1949 in Taldy Kurgan, Kazakh SSR into a working-class family; Russian. He was a member of the CPSU from 1972 to August 1991. He graduated from the technical college of the Karaganda metallurgical combine, and in 1985 successfully presented his candidate dissertation in technical sciences at the Moscow Institute of Steel and Alloys (PhD). He served in the Soviet army. He began his career in 1971 as an operator in a rolling mill in the Karaganda metallurgical combine, Kazakh SSR; as a foreman and head of a rolling mill department (1973-76); deputy head, then head of a rolled steel shop (1976-81); head of rolled steel shop No. 1 (1981-84); chief engineer and deputy director of the combine (1984-87); director (1987-88); general director of the combine (1988-91.

He was appointed USSR Minister of Metallurgy in 1991 and, in January 1992, president of the Roschermet (Russian ferrous metals) corporation; first deputy Prime Minister, and Minister of Industry, of the Republic of Kazakhstan; in September 1992 President of the Kazakhstan union of industrialists and entrepreneurs (with close links to the union in Russia whose co-leader is Arkady Volsky); and in October 1992 chairman of the committee of the Russian Federation on metallurgy.

He was a USSR people's deputy from 1989 to December 1991. As an industrialist he advocated greater autonomy for enterprises and opposed central state directives. His appointment as first deputy Prime Minister of the Russian

Federation, responsible for industry, on April 30, 1993, was seen as a compromise by President Yeltsin. The latter has sought to achieve a balance in his government between radical economic ministers without industrial experience and more conservative ministers who are competent technocrats from industry. Soskovets joined Vladimir Shumeiko and Oleg Lobov as first deputy Premiers. They are all senior to Boris Fedorov, deputy Prime Minister and Minister of Finance, the main driving force behind radical market reforms in Russia.

Soskovets is the author of over 100 articles on the metallurgical industry in Soviet journals. He is married and his wife, Evgeniya Valentinovna, is an economist, and they have a son and a daughter. He was awarded the order of the Red Banner of Labour. His hobbies are football and swimming.

Address: The Government of the Russian Federation, Moscow.

Spiridonov, Yury Alekseevich

Speaker of the Supreme Soviet of the Komi Republic, Russian Federation.

Born in 1938; Russian; member of the CPSU until August 1991. He graduated from the Sverdlovsk (Ekaterinburg) mining institute and the Higher Party School of the Party Central Committee. He successfully presented his candidate dissertation in technical sciences (PhD), and after graduating from the institute was an engineer in the Gorny mine, Magadan *oblast*. In 1969 he moved to the Yaregsky oil drilling administration, Komi ASSR, and worked as a mining foreman, head of a section, later as engineer, and head of the No. 2 Yaregsky oil shaft.

In 1975 he moved into Party work and was head of the industrial and transport department of the Ukhta city Party committee and first secretary of the Ukhta city Party committee. In January 1985 he was elected second secretary, and in August 1989 first secretary of the Komi Party *obkom*. He was elected a USSR people's deputy and a people's deputy of the Komi ASSR, and is an honoured worker in the economy of the Komi ASSR. He was awarded the order of the Red Banner of Labour and medals.

In March 1990 he was elected a people's deputy of the Supreme Soviet of the Komi ASSR and at the first session of the Supreme Soviet, in April 1990, he was elected Speaker. On assuming office he stated that his primary task was to resolve economic problems, to put the economy "on its feet". Those with entrepreneurial abilities should be afforded some room for manoeuvre. The rich potential of the republic should be tapped, production made effective so as to produce competitive goods and there should be no sparing of resources to acquire highly qualified specialists.

On August 20, 1991 the Speaker of the Supreme Soviet and the Chairman of the Council of Ministers of the Komi ASSR convened a large meeting which adopted a resolution to the people of the republic. It stated that there was a serious danger that the state would become ungovernable. The Supreme Soviet and the Council of Ministers of the republic declared that the resolution of the question of state power in the country should be based exclusively on the USSR constitution and that they would follow strictly the constitutional laws and acts of the USSR and RSFSR. They declared their intention of signing the treaty on the union of sovereign states and insisted on its being signed without delay.

In 1992 Spiridonov presented his programme of action and stated that he advocated the establishment, in a civilized, legal manner, of business contacts with other states. His administration was working with businessmen from Great Britain and were discussing a range of projects. He proposed the joint sinking of new coal mines with Western business interests, future co-operation in oil extraction and the exploitation of local reserves of bauxite. Spiridonov accompanied President Yeltsin during his official visit to Great Britain in November 1992.

In December 1992 he stated that the VII Congress of People's Deputies was keeping Russia together and that there were all the prerequisites for the continuation of reform. The election of a new head of government would permit changes in the policy of economic transformation and halt the fall of industrial output. He lives in Syktyvkar.

Spizhenko, Yurii Prokopvych

Minister of Health, Ukraine.

Born into a Ukrainian family in 1950. He is a qualified doctor, educated at Chernivtsi State Medical institute in south-west Ukraine, graduating in 1973. He then worked from 1973 to 1984 in various hospitals, before being appointed head of the health department in Zhytomyr *oblast* in central Ukraine in 1984. In 1986 he joined the Ministry of Health in Kiev as Deputy Minister, and became Minister in November 1989.

He replaced the deeply unpopular Anatolii Romanenko (reportedly the "most hated man in Ukraine" at the time) who as Minister of Health from 1975 to 1989 had been responsible for covering up the effects of the 1986 Chernobyl disaster, including delaying nine days after the accident before issuing a health warning. As a qualified doctor rather than an *apparatchik* (although he was widely seen as a protégé of President Kravchuk), Spizhenko promised a new broom, and greater honesty concerning health dangers. He also became famous internationally for campaigning for assistance in dealing with the consequences of the disaster, although, given Ukraine's severe energy generating problem, he has been unable to date to persuade the government to shut down Chernobyl completely.

In July 1992 he was made a member of the Council of National Security headed by President Kravchuk, and was reappointed Minister of Health in October 1992. In spring 1993 his reputation was badly tarnished by a series of scandals concerning foreign currency use and drug procurement in his ministry.

Official (Ministry) address: 252021 Kiev, Vul. M. Hrushevskoho 7; *telephone*: Kiev 226 2205.

Srybnykh, Vyacheslav Mikhailovich

Editor-in-chief of the newspaper *Kazakhstanskaya Pravda*.

Born in 1950 in Alma Ata, Kazakh SSR; Russian. He graduated in 1972 from the faculty of journalism, Kazakh State University, and then became a correspondent of the *Stepnoi Mayak* newspaper in Kokchetav, and deputy editor-in-chief of the magazine *Avtomobilist Kazakhstana*. He then moved into the apparatus of the Central Committee, Communist Party of Kazakhstan (CPKaz) as an instructor. In February 1992 he was appointed deputy editor-in-chief of the newspaper, *Kazakhstanskaya Pravda* (the organ of the CPKaz), and then editor-in-chief. He speaks English and is married with a son.

Address: 480044 Alma Ata, ul. Gogolya 39; *telephone*: Alma Ata 63 0398.

Stankevich, Sergei Borisovich

Adviser of the President of the Russian Federation on Political Affairs.

Born in 1953 in Moscow; member of the CPSU until August 1991. He graduated from the Moscow Pedagogical Institute in 1977, then began post-graduate studies and in 1984 successfully presented his candidate dissertation in history on "The struggle in the US Senate over social and economic questions (1971-74)" (PhD). He is the leading specialist on the US, and was a senior scientific assistant in the institute of general history, USSR Academy of Sciences.

In early 1989 Stankevich was nominated for election as a USSR people's deputy in the No. 26 Cheremushkinsky territorial district, Moscow. During the election campaign he advocated the *perestroika* of the political system, the removal of the obsolete administrative bureaucratic form of administrating the country and the establishment of mechanisms which would guarantee genuine people's power. He appealed for legislative power to be transferred completely to the soviets and for soviets to become complete masters of their territory and its material resources, based on local self-government. He favoured regular referenda, a review of the laws on elections, such as the nomination of candidates by collecting signatures and direct and equal elections to the Supreme Soviet. He demanded access for the public and the media to the meetings of the soviets, the publication of the minutes and results of voting and how each deputy had voted. He supported the introduction of petitions of no confidence in deputies and early elections. He called for full information to be provided to citizens on the state of the country, for the adoption of a law on setting up public organizations, for the freeing of journalists from censorship and guaranteeing them access to any non-classified document.

Stankevich polled 48.94% of the votes in the first round and won the second round, polling 56.86% of the votes. His main opponent was M. Ya. Lemeshev, head of the laboratory of ecological-economic problems of the commission on the study of productive forces and natural resources, USSR Academy of Sciences. He received 32.39% of the votes in the first round and 40.7% of the votes in the second.

In 1990 Stankevich was elected a people's deputy of Moscow city soviet (Mossovet). He became deputy mayor and provided the bulldozers and lorries for Muscovites to demolish some of the most hated symbols of Soviet power, for instance the statues of Dzerzhinsky, Sverdlov and Kalinin. They were dumped in a Moscow park and became the object of trophy hunters. When the crowd was trying to demolish Dzerzhinsky's statue Stankevich mounted the plinth and warned people of the physical danger of trying to bring it down. He promised equipment to do the job and the demonstrators followed his advice.

By decree of the President of the Russian Federation of September 2, 1992, Stankevich was appointed a presidential adviser on political affairs. He expressed his disagreement with certain aspects of government policy. He advocated strong and effective state power, the unity of democracy and patriotism and the gradual evolution of the reforms. He believed that a clear view about the goal of the Russian reforms, Russian history and the values of the past should be articulated. A strategy of development, not mere reactions to everyday problems, should be worked out. He called for the collapse of the country and the erosion of the economy within the present frontiers to be halted, and he defended evolutionary, humane reforms which guarantee at each stage maximum social support and a minimum of state intervention in the country. It is necessary not only to be concerned with macroeconomics but an attempt should be made to achieve stability in society and to make use of ideological values, such as patriotism, and state ideas. He advocated the self-government for the regions, their economic autonomy, the creation of a coalition government consisting of three forces: democrats, Civic Union and right wingers. He appealed for attention to be devoted to the problems of Russians in the "near abroad" (the successor states of the Soviet Union).

In December 1992 Stankevich believed that the most acceptable type of state system for Russia was a mixed one, including aspects of a presidential and parliamentary republic. The President should have the right to dissolve parliament and call early elections under certain conditions including the case if parliament proves incapable of adopting a budget, and within a time limit of confirming the government, proposed by the President, in office. Parliament, in its turn, should be able to impeach the President but only on condition that it can be demonstrated by an agreed procedure that the President consciously violated the constitution. Stankevich regards it as opportune to retain the Congress of People's Deputies in the new constitution. But as long as it exists it is quite inadmissible to speak about its dissolution. The wave of constitutional nihilism has to be held back, otherwise we are condemned to a long search for an acceptable state, hedged around by constitutional restrictions. Russia at present, without any shadow of doubt, needs a strong President since the implementation of reforms is inconceivable without a strong presidency. While some structures are breaking down and others emerging, only the President has the responsibility to guarantee Russia's territorial, legal and constitutional unity. The President must be the strategist and leader of reform and present it in a grand historical perspective. The prime minister and ministers may from time to time be replaced, but the guarantee that the reforms will continue and be prosecuted with due diligence finally rests with the President. There needs to be stabilization in three fundamental areas: agreement on an anti-crisis programme, the balance of power and the personnel of the government.

In early 1993 Stankevich prepared speeches on the position of the ethnic Russian population in the Baltic states, on the chances of forming new political blocs, and on the referendum of April 25, 1993. In Warsaw, in early 1993, he was reported to have told the Polish government that there was no point in building a large Polish embassy in Kiev since it would in the not too distant future be transformed into a consulate. This caused some concern among Ukrainians and strengthened their belief that Russia has still not accepted that Ukraine is an independent sovereign state. Stankevich is married with a daughter and lives in Moscow.

Starodubtsev, Vasily Aleksandrovich

Member of the Extraordinary Committee.

Born on December 25, 1931 in the village of Volovchik, Volovsky *raion*, Lipetsk *oblast*; Russian; member of the CPSU from 1960 to August 1991. He began working in 1947 on a collective farm as a mechanics and work brigadier, Lipetsk *oblast*. In 1949 he was a stevedore in Zhukovsky, Moscow *oblast*. He served in the Soviet Army (1951-55) and after being demobbed he was a miner in the No. 36 *Stalinogorskugol* trust in Novomoskovsk, Tula *oblast*. In 1964 he was made chairman of the Lenin collective farm, Tula *oblast*, and in 1966 he graduated from the all-Union extra-mural agricultural institute.

He successfully presented his candidate dissertation in agricultural science (PhD) and was elected a corresponding member of the all-Union Lenin Academy of Agricultural Sciences. In 1977 the collective farm was transformed into the Lenin stud farm and in 1984 into the agro-industrial association, *Novomoskovskoe*. In 1986 he was elected chairman of the all-Russian council of collective farms and from June 1990 chairman of the peasants' union of the USSR. He is a hero of socialist labour and a USSR state prize winner. He was a member of the Party Central Committee from July 1990 to August 1991, and in early 1989 he was nominated as a USSR people's deputy by the CPSU and elected.

In August 1991 he was a member of the Extraordinary Committee, and was arrested on August 22, 1991. During the investigation he was incarcerated in the *Matrosskaya tishina* isolator. Later he and the other conspirators were released. He lives in Tula *oblast*.

Starovoitova, Galina Vasilevna

Co-chairperson of the Democratic Russia Movement.

Born in 1946 in Leningrad; Russian. She was never a member of the CPSU. She completed three years in the military mechanical institute, then graduated from A. A. Zhdanov Leningrad State University with distinction. She worked as a sociologist in a factory, then devoted herself to research and in 1980 successfully presented her candidate dissertation in history on "The problems of ethno-sociology of outside ethnic groups in the contemporary city" (based on the Tatars in Leningrad) (PhD).

She worked in the Leningrad branch of the centre for the study of inter-ethnic relations of the Presidium, USSR Academy of Sciences, where she was a senior scientific assistant. In the early 1980s she participated in visits to Nagorno-Karabakh and was reponsible for part of the Soviet-American project on longevity. In 1987 she moved to Moscow to work in the centre for the study of inter-ethnic relations. She researched her doctoral dissertation on the ethnic composition and migration process in the largest cities of Russia and was preparing to present it in Moscow, but the election campaign intervened.

She believes that appearance plays the decisive role in the image of female political leaders. She recommends clothing in subdued pastel colours, opaque stones such as lapis lazuli, garnet and amber and five minutes a day spent on light make-up. She is a very poor housewife since she never has time, but she loves making herbal teas. She is a great admirer of poetry, especially that of Anna Akhmatova. Political leaders who impress her are Margaret Thatcher, Catherine the Great, Aleksandra Kollontai, Winston Churchill, Vaclav Havel and Tadeusz Mazowiecki. She regards politics as one of the hardest jobs in the world and admits that female politicians have to make great sacrifices in their family life. She loves to read but only has time now for newspapers. She has a sweet tooth.

Her political career began with her letter of sympathy to those in Armenia on the events in Nagorno-Karabakh. Unexpectedly she was nominated by the work collective of the Erevan scientific research institute of the technology of amino acids for election as a USSR people's deputy in the No. 393 Erevan Sovetsky national territorial district, Armenian SSR. During the election campaign she advocated democratization, internationalism, the unification of democratic forces and the priority of international law over domestic Soviet law. She appealed for recognition of the convention on genocide, signed by the USSR in 1951, and the rights of nations to self-determination.

She proposed amendments to the undemocratic electoral law and called for a struggle to disband the special forces and the removal of the decree on the order how to conduct meetings and demonstrations. She advocated supervision by the deputies of the activities of the Ministry of Defence, the Ministry of Internal Affairs and the KGB which should be accountable as regards their activities and financial affairs. She also wanted an independent enquiry into the events in Tbilisi on April 9, 1989 (when civilian demonstrators were killed by the military). She proposed that deputies decline their privileges, that the USSR constitution and the constitutons of the republics be amended so as to strengthen their sovereignty.

She spoke in favour of radical reform aimed at bringing into being a *Rechtsstaat* (law-governed state) and a market economy, improvements in Soviet federalism, equal development of languages, cultures and traditions and doing battle with any manifestation of Great Russian chauvinism. She proposed the creation of an ecological and seismological service in Armenia, the introduction of the right of veto on unfinished construction projects, the resurrection of the Armenian nation from the consequences of genocide and natural catastrophes, and the prevention of the assimilation of the Armenians living outside Armenia. She advocated the establishment of social and state help for young and large families, a just resolution of the Karabakh problem, based on the right of nations to national self-determination, and for the re-establishment of democratic political institutions in Nagorno-Karabakh.

There were five candidates. She won in the first round, polling 75.09% of the votes on May 14, 1989. In the all-Union parliament she was one of the leaders of the interregional group of deputies, an adviser of Academician Andrei Sakharov, a member of the informal inter-professional club of the Moscow intelligentsia, Moscow tribune, which was formed in the autumn of 1989. Together with Andrei Sakharov she took part in the struggle to free one of the leaders of the Krunk committee, A. Manycharov. In 1988 she travelled to Armenia and Azerbaijan with a draft proposal to solve the conflict.

In 1990 she was nominated by the residents of the Vyborg *raion*, the Leningrad writers' organization and the Leningrad institute of cytology, USSR Academy of Sciences, for election as a RSFSR people's deputy in the No. 12 Severny national territorial district, Leningrad. There were three candidates. Starovoitova won in the first round on June 14, 1990, polling 74.07% of the votes. Her main opponent was P. P. Glushchenkov. senior lecturer in the Grechko Naval Academy, who received 16.3% of the votes.

In 1991 she was elected a member of the co-ordinating council of the Democratic Russia Movement. In August 1991 she was on a visit to England and was on the list of people to be arrested first of all. She addressed the nation on the BBC World Service, pilloried the members of the Extraordinary Committee as state criminals and called on the West to impose an economic and diplomatic blockade on the conspirators. She founded, together with Margaret Thatcher, an international commission to monitor the state of health of President Mikhail Gorbachev.

In 1992 she was appointed adviser of the President of the Russian Federation on inter-ethnic problems. She was a candidate for the post of Russian Minister of Defence and was a member of the commission for the establishment of the Ministry of Defence, Army and Navy of the Russian Federation under the leadership of General Dmitry Volkogonov. She appealed against the use of force, and spoke of the possibility of commercial activity in the armed forces and favoured the military becoming deputies. She advocated the drafting of a strategy for the foreign policy of the CIS states, as she was concerned about the 25 million Russians in the "near abroad" (other states of the CIS) and those in the military. The victory of democracy, in her view, will be determined by changes in people's consciousness. The first step is to go through the stage of full sovereignty, which is an objective process, and then to proceed to a confederation. She is opposed to the reanimation of the USSR but favours Russia and the other CIS states joining NATO. She wants to write about her meetings with Mikhail Gorbachev and Andrei Sakharov.

In November 1992 Starovoitova was removed as adviser to the President on inter-ethnic relations. Those who wanted Russia to defend its own national interests more aggressively were critical of her attitude. In her view the VII Congress of People's Deputies, in December 1992, succeeded in severely limiting the power of the President, transformed the presidency into a purely cosmetic one and attempted to usurp power, and she believes that the President should not have conceded on the issue of governmental reform. She is now preparing a draft law on the struggle against the threat of fascism.

In March 1993 she was elected co-chairperson of the Democratic Russia Movement. She is critical of its lack of an independent political line but supports all the actions of the Russian government. She thinks that the Congress of People's Deputies has discredited itself but it should not be dissolved since this would threaten the stability of the country. She favours the convention of a constituent assembly and its adoption of a new constitution. She believes that 60% of the deputies should be elected by the peoples of Russia, 20% of the seats should be reserved for the present congress and the presidential apparatus and there should be a quota system for political parties and blocs. She speaks English. She is married with a son and lives in Moscow.

Stepankov, Valentin Georgevich

Procurator-General of the Russian Federation.

Born in 1951 in Perm into a working-class family; Russian; member of the CPSU from 1973 to August 1991. He began work in 1968 as an electrician in the Perm scientific research institute of vaccines and serums. At the same time he enrolled in the law faculty of Perm State University as an evening student and graduated in 1975 as a lawyer. He served in the Soviet Army between 1970 and 1972. In 1975 he became a researcher in the Procurator's Office in Sverdlovsk *raion*, Perm. In 1976 he was appointed Procurator in the department of general surveillance in the Procurator's Office in Perm *oblast*. From 1977 to 1981 he was the Procurator in the town of Gubakhi, Perm *oblast*, and between 1981 and 1983 he worked in the Party apparatus; he was an instructor in the department of administrative agencies of Perm *oblast* Party committee (*obkom*). He left after finding that the Party authorities were not always satisfied with his work.

From 1983 to 1987 he was Procurator of Perm. He was successful in carrying out his duties to his own satisfaction and he was proposed as Procurator of Perm *oblast*. However, the *oblast* authorities opposed this since they had found that Stepankov was not "accommodating" in a range of cases involving bribes, including one involving a friend of the *oblast* first secretary. As a result he was transferred to Moscow and from 1987 to 1988 was deputy head of the main investigative administration of the USSR Procurator-General's office. In

1988 he was appointed Procurator of Khabarovsk *krai*. Here he devoted much attention to the question of those who had suffered illegal repression (mainly for political reasons) and reviewed their cases. In 1990 he moved into the central apparatus of the RSFSR Procurator-General's Office and became first deputy RSFSR Procurator-General.

In January 1990 he was nominated as a candidate for election as an RSFSR people's deputy in No. 23 Khabarovsky national territorial district, Khabarovsk *krai*. There were 10 candidates. Stepankov polled 12.8% of the votes in the first round but won the second round, receiving 45.9% of the votes. During the election campaign he advocated the collection and listing of the key republican laws on the formation of public political organizations, on reform, on the freedom of conscience, on *glasnost*, on property, on the rights of small nations and others, on providing a legal basis to guarantee the effective development of the economy, the ending of the command administrative system of management, the transfer of real power to the soviets, the rapid bringing into line of Russian laws with the universal declaration of human rights and the drafting of republican and regional programmes to deal with crime.

He was elected to the RSFSR Supreme Soviet Council of Nationalities and became a member of the constitutional commission, a member of the Supreme Soviet committee on legality, order and the struggle against crime. In February 1991 he was appointed by the RSFSR Supreme Soviet and confirmed in April 1991 by the III Congress of RSFSR People's Deputies as RSFSR Procurator-General. In August 1991 he began the legal case against the members of the Extraordinary Commission, without waiting for the reaction of the USSR Procurator-General's office, and took part in the arrest of the plotters.

He regards his most important task to be the supervision of legal order within the country, including the courts and the guaranteeing of democracy and law and order, and advocates the depoliticization of the agencies of the Procurator-General's office. After President Yeltsin delivered his address to the nation on March 20, 1993 and introduced special rule Stepankov was called on to comment on whether the President was acting unconstitutionally and should be impeached. He kept a cool head and pointed out that he could not judge until the decree had been published. When it was published some days later the offending phrase had been removed. Stepankov revealed that he had a firmer grasp of law than Valery Zorkin, the chairman of the Constitutional Court, who unequivocally ruled the President's statement as unconstitutional before it had been published. Stepankov is married.

Stepanov, Viktor Nikolaevich

Speaker of the Supreme Soviet of the Republic of Karelia, Russian Federation.

Born in 1947; a Karelian; member of the CPSU from 1969 to August 1991. He was a postgraduate student at the Higher Political School of the Central Committee of the Communist Party of Czechoslovakia and successfully presented his candidate dissertation in philosophy in 1987. He began his career in 1962 as a joiner in the Ilinsk timber mill. In 1966 he moved into *Komsomol* work, and was head of the department of organizational work, second secretary, and first secretary of the Olonetsky *raion Komsomol* committee, and then instructor, head of department, and second secretary of the Karelian *Komsomol obkom*. After graduating from the Leningrad Higher Party School he moved into Party work in 1980. He was instructor of the Party *obkom*, instructor, head of the department of propaganda and agitation, and head of the department of Party organizational work, Karelian Party *obkom*. In 1988 he was instructor in the department of state and law, Party Central Committee. At the XV extraordinary session of the Supreme Soviet of the Karelian ASSR he was elected chairman of the Presidium of the Supreme Soviet.

In early 1990 he was nominated by the work collective of the Pryazhinsky wild animal breeding state farm for election as an RSFSR people's deputy in the No. 106 Pryazhinsky national territorial district, Karelian ASSR. During the election campaign he stated that the soviets should become complete masters of their territories on a solid economic and political base. He proposed the most rapid promulgation of laws on land, property, the local economy and local self-government. He advocated the introduction of modern technology in production, a change of emphasis to concentration on finished products, changes in tax policy to benefit producers of goods and the renaissance of the village through large state investments. Instead of constructing atomic power stations he recommended that the saving of energy resources and the setting up of joint ventures should be guided not only by economic benefits but also moral aspects.

There were four candidates. Stepanov polled 34.5% of the votes in the first round and won in the second round, polling 57.9% of the votes. His main opponent was V. N. Plekhanov, chairman of the *raion* committee of state control of Medvezhegorsky *raion*, who received 13.9% of the votes in the first round and 30% in the second round. Stepanov was also elected a deputy of the Supreme Soviet of the Karelian ASSR and in April 1990, at the first session of the Supreme Soviet of the Karelian ASSR, he was elected speaker.

In August 1991 he signed the decree of the Presidium of the Supreme Soviet of the Karelian ASSR on the political situation in the country which stated that the establishment of the Extraordinary Committee and the introduction of a state of emergency in various parts of the Soviet Union was illegal. It stated that all power in Karelia rested with the legally elected authorities, there were no grounds for the introduction of a state of emergency, the decrees of the acting President, Gennady Yanaev, and the decisions of the Extraordinary Committee on the territory of Karelia had no jurisdiction and would not be implemented. However, at an extraordinary session of the Supreme Soviet the tardiness of the Speaker of the Supreme Soviet was commented upon and the question of recalling deputy Stepanov was put on the agenda.

In December 1992 the declaration of the Presidium of the Supreme Soviet and Presidium of the Council of Ministers of the Republic of Karelia to the VII Congress of People's Deputies and the President of the Russian Federation expressed concern about the confrontation of the legislative and executive branches of power which was leading to a heightening of political tension. This state of affairs was rendering impossible the implementation of economic reform. It appealed to the deputies which had left the chamber to return and to the President to withdraw his appeal to the population. Stepanov advocated the retention of the constitutional order in Russia, based on popular power, federalism, republican form of government and the separation of powers. He proposed a compromise between the two branches of government and made proposals about altering the course of reform.

He is married and his wife is a teacher of chemistry and biology. They have one daughter and live in Petrozavodsk.

Stepashin, Sergei Vadimovich

Chairman of the Russian Supreme Soviet committee on defence and security.

Born on March 2, 1952; Russian. He was a member of the CPSU until August 19, 1991. He graduated from the Higher Political Technical College, USSR Ministry of Internal Affairs (MVD), and from the V. I. Lenin Military Political Academy, specializing in pedagogy. In 1986 he successfully presented his candidate dissertation in history on "Party leadership of fire prevention units" (PhD). He taught in the 50th anniversary of the *Komsomol* Higher Political Technical College, USSR MVD, Leningrad; in 1990 he was deputy chief of the department of political history of the technical college.

He was nominated for election as an RSFSR people's deputy in the No. 112 Krasnoselsky territorial district, Leningrad, and during the election campaign he was supported by the Democratic Election 90 bloc. There were six candidates. In the first round Stepashin polled 21.73% of the votes and he won the second round, polling 54.71% of the votes. His main opponent was A. N. Basov, a worker in the Vodtranspribor enterprise, who received 27.45% of the votes in the first round and 34.2% of the votes in the second round. Stepashin was elected a member of the RSFSR Supreme Soviet at the I Congress of People's Deputies (779 voted for, 12 voted against).

At the I Congress of People's Deputies he declared that he supported the position of the Democratic Russia and Communists of Russia blocs. At the II Congress he stressed that he supported the aspirations of the republics for autonomy but opposed the declarations of sovereignty since they could lead not only to the collapse of Russia but also the Soviet union. At the III Congress he was one of the authors of the amendment on observance of all laws on Russian territory by the military, internal troops, KGB and MVD forces and other military formations, and that they were not to undertake any action which infringed people's power and the sovereignty of Russia. He announced a joint declaration of four political groups (left centre, Smena or "new policy", united parliamentary faction of social democratic and republican parties, communists for democracy) directed against attempts to remove the President of the USSR. In his statement he said that existing contradictions between the President and these political groups had nothing to do with proposals to replace the existing agencies of power with emergency committees and that they would begin talks with all the parties concerned to form an inter-republican coalition government. At the extraordinary session of the Supreme Soviet on August 22, 1991 he proposed the recommendation of the nomination of the representative of the Russian Federation as USSR Minister of Defence. According to the decree by the President of the USSR, Stepashin was co-opted on to the state commission investigating the activities of the state security agencies.

He is a member of the Council of the Republic. He was elected chairman of the Supreme Soviet sub-committee of the committee on invalids, war and labour veterans, social protection of the military and their families, and in April 1991 he became chairman of the Supreme Soviet committee on defence and security. He is the co-ordinator of the left centre parliamentary faction; chairman of the state commission on investigating the activities of the agencies of state security; and is a lieutenant-general.

Address: 103274 Moscow, K 274, Krasnopresnensky nab., d. 2, Dom Sovetov; *telephone*: Moscow 205 42 76; 205 48 03.

Sterligov, Aleksandr Sergeevich

Co-Chairman of the *Duma* of the Russian National Assembly; General.

He is Russian. His father, Nikolai Ivanovich, was a sapper during the Great Fatherland War (1941-45), an engineer who worked on the south-eastern railway, while his mother, Aleksandra Ivanovna, worked as a printer in a printing press. There were four children in the family, and Sterligov began working on the railways at the age of 14 years.

He graduated from an institute and began his service in counter-intelligence. After 17 years on active duty he was one of the 150 KGB officers transferred on the orders of Yury Andropov to the USSR Ministry of Internal Affairs. He was head of the Moscow administration for the struggle against the theft of socialist property and speculation, and posed the question about the need to target the organizers of economic crimes rather than the small fry thieves. After three years he was obliged to step down from the post of head of the administration.

He was invited to work in the apparatus of the USSR Council of Ministers where he was appointed head of the sixth sector of the economic department. On Prime Minister Nikolai Ryzhkov's instructions the sector investigated the sale of uncut and cut diamonds and diamond jewellery on the domestic and foreign markets. The specialists of the sector were able to demonstrate that the situation in that branch did not fully reflect the economic interests of the USSR, and felt that it would be possible by introducing changes to raise the retail turnover to the state by 2 billion rubles. However, the proposals of the sector were not acted upon. Sterligov, proposed by Ryzhkov, was appointed head of the economic administration of the USSR Council of Ministers in charge of the most vital financial, material and domestic needs of the government. He attempted to reform the system of advantages and privileges.

Later Sterligov was invited to work in the RSFSR Council of Ministers. Ivan Silaev, chairman of the Council of Ministers, offered him the Ministry of Internal Affairs or to become Chief of Staff (*chef de cabinet*). Sterligov decided to become Minister of Internal Affairs, but Silaev insisted he become Chief of Staff and Sterligov believes that from that moment he lost the trust of the leadership of the USSR KGB. As Chief of Staff he regarded his function to be the drafting of government decrees by independent groups of experts in order to circumvent departmental lobbying, and he regretted that this did not become the practice of the Council of Ministers of the Russian Federation and that the role of the Chief of Staff was reduced to registering the decrees. This, he believed, led to many mistakes being committed. Lacking the opportunity to have any real influence over events, he offered his resignation and 53% of the Council of Ministers voted in favour.

The KGB leadership, where he had previously worked, offered him the post of deputy director of security of a defence enterprise but he declined the job and was soon invited to join the apparatus of the Vice-President. In August 1991 he flew as Rutskoi's assistant with the Vice-President to Foros, in the Crimea, to meet President Mikhail Gorbachev, who was being held there. In the apparatus of the Vice-President Sterligov worked on preparing the documents to establish the committee for the defence of the economic interests of the RSFSR.

After the collapse of the USSR he became an active participant in the Russian nationalist movement. He was one of the organizers of the Russian National Assembly, a "mass national patriotic movement", set up in Nizhny Novgorod in February 1991, and was elected chairman of the *Duma* of the Assembly. As a result of his speech the Assembly adopted the following resolutions: on the dismissal of B. N. Yeltsin as President of Russia; on Russians living outside the Russian Federation; on the south Kuriles; on the re-establishment of the traditional industrial financial centres of Russia. At the I Congress of the Russian National Assembly, in Moscow on June 12-13, 1992, Sterligov spoke on the situation in the country and the tasks of the national patriotic movement and sharply condemned the course of the reforms in the country. In November 1992 he issued a statement about possible co-operation with President Yeltsin and the formation, together with Civic Union, of a new Russian government.

Other leaders of the Assembly (V. Rasputin, G. Zyuganov and A. Makashov) saw this document as inappropriate and not in line with the letter and spirit of the programme documents of the congress. Sterligov presented his interpretation of the past and perspectives for the future in a booklet entitled *A Disgraced General Testifies*. In 1993 he was nominated for mayor of Moscow, and during the election campaign he stressed the need to introduce law and order and to combat crime. He lives in Moscow.

Stolyarov, Nikolai Sergeevich

Chairman of the committee for personnel of the general headquarters of the Unified Armed Forces of the CIS. Air Force Major-General since 1991. Adviser of Speaker of the Russian Supreme Soviet.

Born on January 3, 1947 in the village of Aleksandrovka, Kalinkovichesky *raion*, Gomel *oblast*, Belarus, into a working-class family. Belarusian. Stolyarov graduated from the Eisk Higher Military Aviation Technical School for pilots in 1969; the Military Air Force Academy in 1977; a postgraduate course at the academy in 1980. He received a higher military education. He was a candidate of philosophy (PhD), assistant professor, and was a member of the CPSU from 1968 to August 1991.

He began work, after receiving a secondary-school education, at the age of 16. After graduating from the technical school for pilots he served, from 1969 to 1974, in the air force of the Belarusian military district as aircraft controller of the control centre of an air regiment; assistant head of the operational department of the staff of an air division; deputy chief of staff of a regiment. He was notable for his advanced specialist and general knowledge, intelligence, thoughtfulness and analytical skills. He actively participated in the work of the Party organization and enjoyed considerable authority.

After graduating from the Academy in 1977 as one of the best graduates he was recommended for a postgraduate course on social and political subjects. From 1980 to 1990 he was a lecturer at the Air Force Academy. The lectures delivered by Col. Stolyarov were remarkable for their depth of analysis of the theoretical background and the current situation, and for their critical assessment of the CPSU and Soviet government. His analytical articles often appeared in the Party and social and political press, advocating reform in the CPSU to enable it to retain its leading role. He was elected a delegate to the XXVIII Party congress in July 1990, where he became a member of the Party Central Committee. In September 1990 he was elected chairman of the Central Control Committee of the RSFSR Party Central Committee. He adopted a reformist position and was elected head of the liberal wing of the Russian (RSFSR) Communist Party, whose first secretary was Ivan Polozkov. He argued vigorously against the use of force to counter national and democratic movements and against the deployment of the army in domestic political conflicts.

During the anti-constitutional putsch in August 1991 he opposed the plotters, went to the Russian White House and became one of the organizers of its defence. He took an active part in talks with the top plotters and tried to organize opposition in the top Party agencies. He himself participated in the arrest of the members of the Emergency Committee and in the investigation which followed. In late August 1991 he was appointed deputy chairman of the USSR KGB, supervising personnel policy. At that time Vadim Bakatin was chairman of the USSR KGB. Stolyarov was then promoted to Major-General of the air force. He was one of the heads of the commission which investigated KGB activity during the attempted coup and was personally involved in deciding personnel policy in the KGB. Regular KGB officers reacted extremely negatively to his work. On December 2, 1991, by the decree of the USSR President, he was appointed adviser of the deputy Minister of Defence of the USSR and chairman of the committee for personnel. Since February 1992 he has been chairman of the committee for personnel of the Unified Armed Forces of the CIS and in fact took over the role played by the chief military political administration.

Gen. Stolyarov supervises the education, culture and social security of military men. He has enlisted the co-operation of many former political workers who supported the attempted coup, and has gradually excluded democratic organizations in the army from any real influence on the course of military construction. He has been in conflict with the "Military for Democracy", "Shield" and "Live Ring" movements and other groups of democratic officers. In order to strengthen his influence in the army he organized and convened an all-army officers' assembly in January 1992, which revealed the dominance of conservative views in the military. According to some experts in social and political movements, Stolyarov's goal is to gain a top post under the existing authority. He successfully manoeuvred among the top leaders of the CPSU and the USSR and is now manoeuvring among the top leaders of Russia. At present he is in conflict with Marshal Evgeny Shaposhnikov and the leaders of the Russian Ministry of Defence and, as a result, his official standing has dropped. He may in the end be debarred from active work in the armed forces altogether.

He is interested in political science, philosophy, history, literature and is not indifferent to art and the theatre. He does not possess a good command of foreign languages. He has been awarded orders and eight medals. He is married with a son who is a student at Lugansk Higher Military Air Force Technical School for navigators and a daughter who is a student at Moscow State University.

Office address: 103160 Moscow K-160.

Stroev, Egor Semenovich

Head of the Administration of Orlov *oblast*, Russian Federation.

Born on February 25, 1937 in the village of Dudkino, Khotynetsky *raion*, Orlov *oblast*; Russian. His father was a collective farm worker, and was chairman of the collective farm and of the village soviet executive committee for many years. During the Great Fatherland War (1941-45) the *oblast* was occupied by the German *Wehrmacht* and the family helped the partisans. He was a member of the CPSU from 1958 to August 1991.

He began his career in 1955 working on the Progress collective farm, Khotynetsky *raion*, Orlov *oblast*. In 1957 he became a brigade leader and from 1958 an agronomist, head of a production section and was elected secretary of the Party bureau of the farm. In 1960 he graduated as an external student from the I. V. Michurin fruit and vegetable institute, Michurinsk. In 1963 he moved into Party and soviet work.

From 1963 he was deputy secretary and head of the ideology department of the Party committee of the Uritsky production collective-state farm administration, Orlov *oblast*. In 1965 he was elected secretary of the Khotynetsky *raion* Party committee, in 1969 second secretary of the Pokrovsky *raion* Party committee, in 1970 chairman of the executive committee of the Pokrovsky *raion* soviet, then first secretary of the Pokrovsky *raion* Party committee, Orlov *oblast*.

In 1973 he became secretary of the Orlov Party *obkom* responsible for agriculture, and in 1984 he was appointed an inspector of the Party Central Committee. In 1985 he was elected first secretary of the Orlov Party *obkom*, and was also a member of the Party Central Committee from 1986. In 1988 he graduated from the Higher Party School, Leningrad and was a delegate to the XXVII and XXVIII Party congresses and XIX Party conference.

At the July 1990 plenum of the Party Central Committee he was elected a member of the Party Politburo and Central Committee secretary for agriculture. In 1989 he was elected a USSR people's deputy for Livensky territorial district, Orlov *oblast*. During *perestroika* Stroev enjoyed the reputation of being a reformer, and under his guidance in Orlov *oblast*, leasing, contracts and considerable rural construction got under way. He paid special attention to the problem of migration, attracting new workers into agriculture and support of family farming. After becoming a Central Committee secretary he continued promoting many different types of ownership in agriculture.

He was appointed director of the scientific research institute for the selection and development of fruit, and in 1993 he was nominated for the post of head of administration of Orlov *oblast*. There were four candidates. During the election campaign he advocated priority for agriculture in the economic development of the *oblast* and opposed private ownership of land, and he came out against the economic policy of the Russian government. He proposed priority being afforded the social sphere and a guarantee of employment for the population. He was supported by the deputies of the Russian Unity bloc and also the Russian Communist Party, and on April 11, 1993 he was elected head of the administration, polling 53% of the votes in a 51% turnout. Most of his support came from rural voters.

He was awarded the orders of the October Revolution and the Red Banner of Labour and medals. He is married and lives in Orel. Both his wife, Nina Semenovna, and daughter Marina, are school teachers.

Sukhanov, Lev Evgenevich

Head of the Group of Advisers of the President of the Russian Federation.

Born in 1936 in Moscow; Russian; member of the CPSU until August 1991. He worked in Cuba renovating sugar refineries and afterwards, for almost ten years, he worked in the USSR state committee for construction (Gosstroi) as an assistant of various deputy chairmen until Boris Yeltsin took over Gosstroi in 1987. He became Yeltsin's assistant for economic questions, and then entered the political arena. He organized the "club of the supporters of Yeltsin" and maintained contacts with various electoral districts. His involvement in the election campaign resulted in democrats being elected, but he refused to stand for election himself so as not to leave Boris Yeltsin, and since then Sukhanov and he are inseparable. He was Yeltsin's assistant when the latter was Speaker of the RSFSR Supreme Soviet and then RSFSR President. He always accompanies the President on his trips at home and abroad and also when on holiday. In August 1991, armed with a revolver, he accompanied the President everywhere.

Sukhanov is regarded as closest to the President in the latter's whole entourage. He is, which is rare, an honest man in all circumstances and completely so with the President. He is preparing a book, *Notes of an Assistant*, about his three years with Yeltsin, beginning with his period in Moscow at Gosstroi. His chapter on why the state visit to Japan was postponed in 1992 caused some dissatisfaction in the land of the rising sun because it included negative comments on the Japanese Ministry of Foreign Affairs and Mitio Watanabe, the foreign minister.

Sukhanov is married with a son and together they have built the family a dacha. He lives in Krasnopresnensky *raion*, Moscow.

Suleimenov, Olzhas Omarovich

First secretary of the board of the Writers' Union of the Republic of Kazakhstan.

Born in 1936 in Alma Ata; Kazakh. He graduated in 1959 from the faculty of geology, Kazakh State University, and in 1961 from Gorky Institute of Literature. He became first secretary of the board of the union of cinematographers of Kazakhstan; and later chairman of the Kazakh state committee of cinematography. In 1983 he was elected first secretary of the board of the union of writers of Kazakhstan and the secretary of the USSR union of writers. He became chair of the Semipalatinsk-Nevada public movement for the prohibition of nuclear testing, which had considerable public success as nuclear fall-out in the Semipalatinsk area had led to birth defects and a degradation of the environment. The campaign was eventually successful.

He was elected a USSR people's deputy and a member of the USSR Supreme Soviet. He was a member of the USSR Supreme Soviet committee on legislation and also of the international Lenin prize committee. He is a prolific writer of poetry in Russian, and among his main poems are: *Bow to Man, Earth* (1961);

and a collection of poems *Over White Rivers* (1970). He has written the script for several films, including *The Land of Our Ancestors* (1966) and *Blue Route* (1968); and popular science films. He is married with two daughters.

Address: 480091 Alma Ata, Kommunistickesky Prospekt 105; *telephone*: Alma Ata 62 6295.

Suleimenov, Tuleutai Skakovich

Minister of Foreign Affairs of the Republic of Kazakhstan.

Born in 1941 in Semipalatinsk, Kazakh SSR; Kazakh. He was a member of the CPSU until August 1991. He graduated from the Karaganda polytechnical institute and the diplomatic academy of the USSR Ministry of Foreign Affairs. He began his career as a worker, then foreman of a shop in the Karaganda metallurgical enterprise, and then in 1969 he transferred to *Komsomol* and Communist Party of Kazakhstan work and acted as a functionary until 1979. In 1980 he was appointed to the USSR Ministry of Foreign Affairs, and then to the Democratic Republic of Afghanistan. From 1988 to 1991 he was a counsellor in the USSR Embassy in the Islamic Republic of Iran, and in December 1991 he was appointed Minister of Foreign Affairs of the Republic of Kazakhstan.

Relations with Russia, the other countries of Central Asia and the Near East are of great importance to Kazakhstan and Suleimenov's task has been to foster political and economic ties with the republic's neighbours. Kazakhstan is a close ally of Russia, partly because of the large Slav population but also due to economic dependency. This, however, will change as the rich natural resources of Kazakhstan are developed in collaboration with Western companies. Kazakhstan is also developing closer links with the other ex-Soviet Muslim republics and the intention is that a Central Asian common market will emerge. Relations with Iran are good, with the Iranian foreign minister visiting Alma Ata in 1992.

Some US specialists express concern about these links as Kazakhstan, a nuclear power, is a source of enriched uranium, but Kazakhstan has denied that there is any trade in this strategic product.

Address: 480091 Alma Ata, pl. Respubliki 4; *telephone*: Alma Ata 62 0630; 62 3016 (press service).

Suskevic, Stanislau Stanislaujevic

Chairman of the Supreme Soviet of Belarus; acting Head of State.

Born on December 15, 1934 in Minsk; Belarusian. His father was a famous Belorussian (Belarusian) poet who suffered oppression during the Stalin purges of the 1930s. He was a member of the CPSU until the beginning of 1991. He graduated from the V. I. Lenin Belarusian State University, Minsk, and then became a postgraduate student in the Institute of Physics, Belarusian Academy of Sciences. He successfully presented his candidate dissertation in technical sciences (PhD) and his doctoral dissertation in technical sciences (DSc). He is a professor, and a corresponding member of the Belarusian Academy of Sciences.

In 1959 he was appointed junior scientific assistant, Institute of Physics, Belarusian Academy of Sciences; senior engineer, SKB radio enterprise, Minsk (1960-61); senior engineer, chief engineer, head of a laboratory, Belarusian State University (1961-67); pro-rector for science, Minsk Radiotechnical Institute (1967-69); assistant professor, professor, and head of the department of nuclear physics, Belarusian State University (1969-86); pro-rector of the university (1986-90); and first deputy Speaker (chairman) of the Supreme Soviet of the Belorussian SSR. In September 1991 he was elected Speaker of the Supreme Soviet of the Republic of Belarus and since Belarus did not adopt a presidential system Suskevic became acting head of state. In 1989 he was elected a deputy of the USSR Congress of People's Deputies and the USSR Supreme Soviet.

He was awarded the state prize of the Belorussian SSR, the USSR Council of Ministers' prize, and was a merited worker in science and technology, Belorussian SSR. As a member of the CIS Belarus has attempted close security and economic relations with Russia. He is a democrat and supports the transition to the market economy, but the Belarusian parliament, elected in 1990, is conservative and replete with many ex-communists who side with the Russian Supreme Soviet against President Yeltsin which has led to many fraught exchanges between Suskevic and the Belarusian parliament. He is married with two children.

Suslov, Vladimir Antonovich

Head of the Administration of Tver *oblast*, Russian Federation.

Born in 1939 in Sverdlovsk (Ekatcrinburg) into a working-class family; member of the CPSU until August 1991. After completing the artisan technical school he began working in the Russkie Samotsvety factory and at the same time he studied at evening school, then at the Urals Polytechnical Institute as an engineer mechanic. After graduating from the institute, in 1963, he was assigned to Kimra, Kalinin (Tver) *oblast* and has spent almost thirty years there. He began as an engineer in a timber processing combine, then moved into

Komsomol work. He was elected first secretary of the Kalinin *oblast Komsomol* committee, was head of Kimra, then Kalinin *oblast Komsomol* committee and then moved into the Kalinin city Party organizations. He graduated from the Academy of Social Sciences of the Party Central Committee as an external student. In 1987 he was elected chairman of the Kalinin *oblast* soviet executive committee.

In March 1990 he was nominated for election as an RSFSR people's deputy in the No. 414 Nelidovsky territorial district, Kalinin *oblast*. He polled 48% of the votes in the first round and his only opponent, M. I. Migalov, a doctor in the Nelidovsky *raion* hospital, received 44% of the votes. Since neither candidate had obtained over half the votes, a second round of voting was announced, but Suslov withdrew.

Suslov was elected a deputy of the *oblast* soviet of people's deputies for the No. 123 electoral district, Kimra, and at the first session of the *oblast* soviet in April 1990 he was elected chairman of the soviet executive committee.

On August 21, 1991 the *oblast* soviet of people's deputies declared that it regarded bringing tanks on to the streets as a way of resolving political questions as hopeless and short-sighted. The declaration of a state of emergency could only be introduced by constitutional means. However, the decisions of the President and the government, based on the constitution, must be implemented by all government agencies. The *oblast* soviet appealed to the population of the *oblast* to support law and order.

Suslov was appointed head of the administration of Tver *oblast* on October 20, 1991 by presidential decree. As head of the administration he stated that he supported the concept of the economic independence of Russia and providing citizens with basic goods was his main priority. He was convinced that only the equal development of private and collective agriculture could ensure that the population of the country was fed. He supported commercializaton which opens the way to privatization, and was in favour of private enterprise and trade. However, state agencies should supervise the activities of all bodies and the market should not degenerate into anarchy.

In December 1992 he stated that he took, on balance, a positive view of the convocation of the VII Congress of People's Deputies and could not understand why many deputies were inclined to view it as high drama. He is married with two children and a granddaughter, and lives in Tver.

Symonenko, Valentyn Kostyantynovych

Vice-Prime Minister of Ukraine to October 1992.

Born into a Ukrainian worker's family in Odesa in 1940 (although his spoken Ukrainian is rusty). He graduated from the Odesa Institute of Engineering and Construction in 1962, and went to work firstly as an engineer in Odesa's film studio, and then in a reinforced concrete construction factory, where he eventually rose to become director. He joined the Communist Party of Ukraine

(CPU), and in 1973 was appointed second CPU secretary in Odesa city. By 1983 he was head of the city Party, and head of the local soviet after January 1991.

In March 1990 he was elected a people's deputy for Malnynovskyi *raion*, Odesa *oblast*. In the Supreme Soviet he is a member of the committee on foreign affairs. His blunt and forceful manner and his reputation for having skilfully redeveloped Odesa brought him to the attention of President Kravchuk, and in March 1992 he was appointed the President's representative in Odesa *oblast*, and a Vice-Premier in the Ukrainian government.

When the other Vice-Premier and Economics Minister Volodymyr Lanovyi was fired in July 1992, Symonenko was appointed to replace him (he then gave up his post as presidential representative). At the time Kravchuk envisaged retaining Fokin as Prime Minister, and therefore the forceful but undiplomatic Symonenko was appointed as his deputy. In July 1992 Symonenko was chosen to head the President's Co-ordinating Council on Economic Reform. However, the reform proposals that emerged from the Council in September disappointed many, and Symonenko discredited himself by calling in the press for a return to economic *dirigisme* and renewed central control (most industrial managers now preferred to keep their new-found freedom).

Therefore, although Kravchuk appointed Symonenko acting Prime Minister after Fokin's resignation on September 30, 1992, the President was unable to follow through his reported original intention of making Symonenko Prime Minister, and Kuchma received the position instead. In fact not only was there no place at all for Symonenko in the new Kuchma government, but Kuchma also forced Kravchuk to dissolve Symonenko's Co-ordinating Council for Economic Reform as Kuchma saw it as a potential rival power-base to the new government.

Symonenko was only left with the consolation post of chairman of a new "Socio-economic Council of the President" created by decree by Kravchuk on October 27, 1992, and with membership of the State Commission for Monetary Reform established on November 9.

Official address: 252008 Kiev, Vul. M. Hrushevskoho 12/2; *telephone*: Kiev 293 7442.

Syrovatko, Vitaly Grigorevich

Secretary of the Presidium of the Russian Supreme Soviet.

Born on April 2, 1940 in Kremenchug, Poltava *oblast*, Ukrainian SSR; Ukrainian. His father was a soldier. He was a member of the CPSU from 1960 to August 1991. In 1958, after graduating from the Armavir Machine Building Technical College, he began work at the Armavir experimental machine building enterprise as a milling machine operator and later was a shop foreman. He served in the Soviet army (1962-65), and then in 1967 he graduated from the Kuban agricultural institute as a qualified mechanical engineer. In 1977 he graduated from the extra-mural department of the Higher Party School of the Party Central Committee. He was a postgraduate student at the Academy of Social Sciences, Party Central Committee, and successfully presented his candidate dissertation on "The formation of a qualified workforce during the industrialization of agriculture (a case study of agricultural enterprises in Krasnodar *krai*)" (PhD). He was then elected first secretary of the Krasnodar *Komsomol* city committee; and then secretary, and first secretary of the Krasnodar *Komsomol krai* committee. He was elected a delegate to the XVI and XVII *Komsomol* congresses and was a member of the *Komsomol* Central Committee. In 1973 he was appointed first secretary of the Krasnodar *raion* Party committee, and in 1977 he became head of the department for organization of the Krasnodar *krai* Party committee. In 1981 he became an instructor in the agricultural and food industry department, Party Central Committee, Moscow. He was elected secretary of Bryansk Party *obkom* in 1988, and in February 1989 he was appointed chairman of the Bryansk *oblast* soviet executive committee. He was a delegate to the XXVI Party congress and the XV congress of the trade unions.

He was nominated for election as an RSFSR people's deputy in the No. 28 Bryansk national territorial district, Bryansk *oblast*. During the election campaign he advocated the creation of a powerful Russian state; Russia to be treated as an equal with the other Union republics; Russia to become self-governing; dynamic and all embracing social, economic and cultural development of the republic; and that local soviets should become agencies responsible for local administration. He was the only candidate since the other two candidates withdrew at the beginning of the election campaign. Syrovatko polled 63.2% of the votes in the first round and thereby became a people's deputy. He was elected a member of the RSFSR Supreme Soviet at the I Congress of People's Deputies (686 voted for, 237 voted against).

He is a member of the Council of Nationalities; he was elected deputy Speaker of the Council of Nationalities, and later was appointed secretary of the Presidium of the Russian Supreme Soviet. He is a member of the communists of Russia parliamentary group. He was awarded the order of the October Revolution, two orders of the Red Banner of Labour and six medals. He is married with two daughters.

Address: 103274 Moscow, K 274, Krasnopresnenskaya nab., d. 2, Dom Sovetov; *telephone*: Moscow 205 44 28.

Sytnyk, Viktor Petrovych

Vice-Prime Minister of Ukraine to October 1992.

Born into a Ukrainian family in Kharkiv *oblast* in 1939. After education at Dnipropetrovsk Institute of Agricultural Economics, he graduated in 1963 to work as an agronomist. From 1976 he worked in the government *apparat*, rising to manage the department of agricultural economy in 1978, and to become Minister of Agriculture in August 1991. He was appointed Vice-Premier with special responsibility for agriculture in February 1992.

He has served as people's deputy for Orzhytskyi *raion*, Poltava *oblast*, since 1990, and is secretary of the Supreme Soviet's committee on the agro-industrial complex. He gained a reputation as a supporter of Ukraine's conservative agricultural policy, in particular the government's reluctance to promote a law on private land ownership, and to maintain large agricultural subsidies to support the collective farm system. He lost his post as Vice-Premier in October 1992, but the power of the collective farm lobby in the Supreme Soviet made it difficult for the government to reverse his policies.

Official address: 252008 Kiev, Vul. M. Hrushevskoho 12/2; *telephone*: Kiev 293 7442.

Tabeev, Fikryat Akhmedzhanovich

Chairman of the Russian fund of federal property; Minister.

Born in 1928 in the village of Azeevo, Ryazan *oblast*; Tatar. He was a member of the CPSU from 1951 to August 1991. He graduated from Kazan State University, and was a postgraduate student who successfully presented his candidate dissertation in economics (PhD Econ). He began his career on the Verny Put collective farm, Ermishinsky *raion*, Ryazan *oblast* (1945-46); then after graduating from the university he was an assistant in the department of political economy in the university (1951-52); and later lecturer and assistant professor in the same department, (1952-57).

He then moved into Party work as head of departments, Tatar Party *obkom* (1957-59); secretary, then first secretary, of the Tatar Party *obkom* (1959-79); USSR ambassador in Afghanistan (1979-86); and first deputy chairman of the RSFSR Council of Ministers (1986-90). He retired on pension in 1990, and in 1992 he was appointed chairman of the Russian fund of federal property. He was elected a USSR people's deputy several times, was a member of the Presidium of the USSR Supreme Soviet; a member of the USSR parliamentary group and USSR people's deputy from 1989 to December 1991. He was awarded five orders of Lenin, the order of the October Revolution, the order of the Friendship of Peoples, and medals.

Taburianskyi, Leopold Ivanovych

Leader of the People's Party of Ukraine and Presidential Candidate.

Born into a Ukrainian family in 1940 in the industrial centre of Kryvyi Rih in east-central Ukraine. He was educated at Kryvyi Rih coalmining institute and the Kiev Institute of Economics. After graduation he worked first as an engineer, before rising to become head of the *Olimp* co-operative factory in Dnipropetrovsk, near Kryvyi Rih. In March 1990 Taburianskyi was elected people's deputy for his local Petrovskyi *raion* in Dnipropetrovsk (on the first ballot).

In the Supreme Soviet he is a member of the committee on the plan, budget, finance and prices. In September 1990, Taburianskyi founded the People's Party of Ukraine (PPU) in Dnipropetrovsk. The PPU is basically a centrist, pro-industry party, although it has accommodated itself to Ukrainian independence. At the time of its second congress in December 1990, 230 out of the party's 515 members worked at Taburianskyi's *Olimp* factory. Taburianskyi has, however, used the resources of his factory well. When he announced his surprise candidacy for the Ukrainian presidency in autumn 1991 no one expected his small party to be able to collect the 100,000 signatures necessary to place his name on the final ballot, but they succeeded, although he came seventh and last with only 182,713 votes (0.57% of the total). He obtained 1.85% in his native Dnipropetrovsk.

Official address: Kiev, Vul. M. Hrushevskoho 5; *telephone*: Kiev 252 019.

Taniuk, Les Stepanovich

Former Leader of People's Council Faction in the Ukrainian Parliament.

Born into a Ukrainian family in 1938. He was educated at Kiev State University of theatrical arts, and then worked as a stage director in Ukrainian theatre and cinema. Taniuk is the head of the Ukrainian union of theatrical workers. Like many members of the Kiev cultural intelligentsia he was an active and early member of many opposition groups from 1988 to 1990, including the Taras Shevchenko Ukrainian language society, *Memorial* (which Taniuk later headed) and *Rukh*.

In 1990 he was elected people's deputy for the Vatutynskyi *raion* in Kiev city (on the second round), and in the Supreme Soviet he secured the key position of chairman of the committee on culture and spiritual revival, responsible for promoting the revival of Ukrainian language and culture. He is therefore an *ex officio* member of the Presidium of the Supreme Soviet, and also sits on the influential Commission for the Preparation of Legislative Proposals, headed by Vladimir Griniov. Although formally non-party, he was traditionally a close supporter of Viacheslav Chornovil and therefore his election as head of the People's Council faction in the Supreme Soviet in December 1991 after the retirement of Ihor Yukhnovskyi was something of a surprise, and was largely a reflection of the splintering of the faction.

Taniuk, however, continued to lead a group of 40 or so Chornovil supporters until the group became a formal *Rukh* faction in September 1992. Like other nationalists, however, Taniuk slowly began to break ranks with Chornovil's strident anti-communism in 1992, and edge towards a position of support for President Kravchuk. In December 1992 he ceded his chairmanship of the People's Council faction to Ivan Zaiets.

Official address: Kiev, Vul. M. Hrushevskoho 5; *telephone*: Kiev 252 019.

Tazabekov, Marat Kasymbekovich

Chairman of the Board of the General Exchange Kyrgyzstan Joint Stock Company.

Born in 1958 in Osh *oblast*, Kyrgyzstan. Kyrgyz. He graduated in 1981 from the faculty of economics, Kyrgyz State University, and from 1981 to 1982 was a postgraduate student in the faculty of economics, Moscow State University. From 1982 to 1984 he was a junior scientific assistant in the institute of economics of the state planning committee (Gosplan) of Kyrgyzstan, and from 1984 to 1988 he was an economist and later chief specialist of the services department of the Kyrgyz state planning committee. From 1988 to 1990 he was head of the department for external economic relations of Kyrgyz Gosplan.

He was chairman of the board of the Nogra foreign economic company (1990-91). In April 1991 he became chairman of the board of the General Exchange Kyrgyzstan joint stock company. As such it was one of the first joint stock companies in the republic. He is married with two children and speaks English.

Address: 720000 Bishkek, Prospekt Chui 96; *telephone*: Bishkek (3312) 26 5322.

Tereshchenko, Sergei Aleksandrovich

Prime Minister of the Republic of Kazakhstan.

Born in 1951 in Lesozavodsk, Maritime *krai*. He graduated in 1973 from Kazakh Institute of Agriculture, and in 1986 from the Higher Party School, Alma Ata. From 1973 to 1981, he was chief engineer of a collective farm; first secretary of the *Komsomol raion* committee; head of department of the Tyulkubassky *raion*, Chimkent *oblast*, committee of the Communist Party of Kazakhstan (CPKaz). Between 1981 and 1983 he was second secretary of the Bugunsky *raion* CPKaz committee, Chimkent *oblast*, and from 1983 to 1985 he was first secretary of the Lengersky *raion* CPKaz committee, Chimkent *oblast*.

From 1985 to 1986 he was an inspector in the Central Committee apparatus, CPKaz, and secretary of Chimkent CPKaz *obkom*, and from 1986 to 1989 he was chairman of the Chimkent *oblast* soviet executive committee. In 1989 he was appointed deputy chairman, then in February 1990 first deputy chairman, of the Council of Ministers of the Kazakh SSR.

In May 1990 he was elected first secretary of the Chimkent CPKaz *obkom* and also chairman of the Chimkent *oblast* soviet of people's deputies. In October 1991 he was appointed Prime Minister of the Kazakh SSR and in January 1992 of the Republic of Kazakhstan. He was a people's deputy of the Kazakh SSR.

Tereshchenko, a Slav, is head of government while the President is a Kazakh. Kazakhstan has a multi-ethnic population with a small majority of Slavs, predominantly Russian, and the policy of the young state is to establish good relations with its neighbours, especially Russia. Kazakhstan is one of the strongest supporters of the CIS because of its Slav population and economic dependency on Russia. The skilled industrial labour force is mainly Russian and Ukrainian and the government needs to convince them that the republic has a bright future. Kazakhstan has been attracting back Kazakhs from Russia and Mongolia.

The government has negotiated several large contracts with Western firms which tap the rich natural reserves of the country. The state requires stability in order to realize its great potential, but much of the expertise necessary for the construction of a modern state is lacking so this will take time. Kazakhstan is attracted to the South Korean economic model with its emphasis on corporatism. Privatization in the republic will be limited because it could become a source of ethnic conflict.

Address: 480091 Alma Ata, pl. Respubliki 4.

Teterkin, Ivan Alekseevich

Chief arbitrator of the Republic of Kazakhstan.

He graduated from the faculty of law, Kazakh State University and began his career as a lawyer in Pavlodar *oblast*. He became an investigator in a prosecutor's office and was in turn a people's judge; a prosecutor in the investigation department, Pavlodar *oblast* prosecutor's office; and a senior legal consultant, department of propaganda, in the apparatus of the Communist Party of Kazakhstan. Later he was appointed first deputy Minister of Justice of the Kazakh SSR. In 1987 he became chief arbitrator of the Kazakh SSR and in January 1992 of the Republic of Kazakhstan. He lives in Alma Ata.

Tikhonov, Vladimir Aleksandrovich

Member of the Council of the President of the Russian Federation; President of the League of Co-operators and Entrepreneurs.

Born in 1928; Russian. In 1944, at the age of 16 years, he volunteered for the army and served until 1950. He graduated from the Urals State University in 1955, and was a member of the CPSU from 1951 to 1990. He resigned from the Party because of disagreements over the decision of the XXVIII Party congress and the constituent congress of the RSFSR Communist Party. He stated that he could not be a member of the same party as people like Ivan Polozkov, the first secretary of the RSFSR Communist Party. Tikhonov successfully presented his candidate dissertation on political economy (PhD (Econ)) and then in 1964 successfully presented his doctoral dissertation on the "Economic problems of using technology in agriculture at the present stage of communist construction" (DSc (Econ)).

In 1966 he was elected a corresponding member and in 1975 an Academician of the V. I. Lenin all-Union Academy of Agricultural Sciences. In 1972 he was appointed director of the all-Union scientific research institute of agricultural labour and management and in 1986 head of department, institute of economics, USSR Academy of Sciences. In 1989 he became a professor in the Academy of the National Economy of the USSR Council of Ministers and played an active role in drafting the USSR law on co-operation in the USSR.

In 1989 he was elected a USSR people's deputy, and in August of that year was elected president of the USSR union of united co-operators. On May 31, 1992, the league of co-operators and entrepreneurs was established as its legal successor and Tikhonov was also elected its president. He became a member of the presidential consultative and then presidential Council.

He advocates that in present-day Russia a stratum of civilized co-operators should be promoted. He favours the democratization of the whole economic system and public life and the creation of the most favourable conditions for the work of the co-operatives and co-operative unions, regional and branch. It is necessary to fight against high levels of taxation; money should not be invested in extracting raw materials but in processing industries which in Russia are still at the level of the 1930s. What is needed is not large-scale industry but the dominance of small trading and industrial enterprises. Co-operatives have been at a grave disadvantage since the beginning of the economic reforms, given the state monopoly of raw materials and technology. The number of construction co-operatives have dropped by a third and all production co-operatives have gone out of business.

One solution is a complete revision of tax policy and the introduction of changes to the privatization policy of state enterprises. Entrepreneurs should be afforded the chance of acquiring part of the production area and technical equipment. Funds for the support of small businesses should be available.

Gaidar's mistake was to adopt a purely Soviet approach which supposed that the taking of decisions would immediately solve all problems and transform everything. There is no single panacea which will permit Russia to escape all its economic troubles. Besides adjusting macroeconomic balances, local private projects should be carried out, privatization rapidly introduced, including enterprises in the military-industrial complex, and no new emissions of money should be permitted. Taxes should be reduced to 10-12%, the collective and state farms should not be dissolved but transformed into small peasant co-operatives with long land leases and eventually transferred to private ownership. The private ownership of land already exists, but land cannot be freely bought and sold and hence genuine private ownership of land is denied. Only genuine private ownership of land will permit the peasant to extend the amount of land he works and increase production. Tikhonov advocates the complete right of the owner to dispose of his land but only under one condition, land must not be taken out of agricultural production. He proposes the creation of a stratum of free entrepreneurs and the liquidation of the state monopoly.

He supports the dissolution of the Congress of People's Deputies and the introduction of presidential rule. He is opposed to dictatorship, but the state administrative system must function precisely and strictly in order to guarantee the social security of the population. He believes that the Russian parliament, elected in 1990, is not qualified to function in present-day circumstances since a significant number of the deputies are attracted to the old order. He is married with a daughter. His present duties are so heavy that he has been forced to give up temporarily his only form of relaxation, hunting. He lives in Moscow.

Timofeev, Lev Mikhailovich

Former political prisoner; writer; civil rights activist.

Born on September 8, 1936 in Leningrad into a Russian family. His father was a General and director of the transport depot of the Ministry of the Defence Industry. He graduated in 1958 from the faculty of commerce of the Moscow institute of foreign trade. Then he was a representative of Sovfrakht (Soviet freight company) in Novorossiisk, on the Black Sea, and Nakhodka, near Vladivostok on the Pacific. In 1961 he was a sailor on a trawler and in 1962 he was called up into the army and served as an officer in Ryazan. Since 1963 he has devoted himself wholly to writing, and has been published in the Soviet press: *Novy mir, Yunost* (youth), *Literaturnaya gazeta, Molodoi kommunist* (young communist), *V mire knig* (the world of books). In 1976 he became a candidate member of the CPSU, but at the end of his candidate period he was not accepted as a full member of the party. He was a member of the union of journalists and from 1980 member of the trade union "committee of writers" of the *Sovetskii pisatel* (Soviet writer) publishing house. He was expelled from both organizations after his arrest. Between 1973 and 1975 he participated in the *Solyaris* (solarium) group, which was founded by Len Karpinsky in association with the editorial board of *Molodoi kommunist*. Based on his own observations in the village of Zhelannoe, Kaluga *oblast*, where he lived for many years during the 1960s and 1970s, he wrote a series of socio-economic articles which were distributed by *samizdat* (unofficial self-publishing, strictly illegal in the Soviet

Union) and published abroad under his own name. The most important was "Technology of the black market or the peasants' art of starving". This is a bitter attack on the destruction of rural life and economy under communist rule. Timofeev had in 1978 already written a long piece which contained the basic ideas later developed in " Technology of the black market". This was the time when he lost his faith in the Soviet system. The *Druzhba narodov* (Friendship of Peoples) journal at first accepted it and then the newspaper *Komsomolskaya pravda* took a shortened version, but it was never published.

In the West, between 1980 and 1984, besides "Technology of the black market" he published "Lovushka, a novel in four letters", "Surviving the last hope: thoughts about Soviet reality" and "A prayer about a chalice". These works were read often on Radio Svoboda and the Voice of America. As a result of their publication abroad the KGB put together a case under article 70 of the criminal code of the Russian Federation (anti-Soviet propaganda). He was arrested on March 19, 1985. The KGB did not break Timofeev and on September 19, 1985 the collegium of the Moscow city court sentenced him to six years in a labour camp and five years of exile, almost the maximum sentence. He served his time in Perm political camp No. NVS 389/36. Like many other political prisoners, he was released at the beginning of February 1987.

After his release, Larisa Bogoraz, Sergei Grigoryants and he founded the *Glasnost* press club, which existed until 1989. The press club was the *de facto* successor to the Helsinki group and as such defended human rights. It joined the international Helsinki federation. In 1987 when the Soviet Union proposed a human rights conference in Moscow the *Glasnost* club debated for a whole week whether it would attempt to hold a genuine human rights conference in Moscow. The thinking behind this was that if the Soviet authorities banned it this would reveal to the world that the official conference was a sham. However, Academician Andrei Sakharov was against it. He opposed it on ethical grounds, for if the conference were held and attracted young people and they were arrested then the organizers would be responsible for this. The week-long discussions took place under the eyes of the KGB and debate ranged over many subjects, including how to bring down Soviet power. Among those who actively participated in *Glasnost* were L. Bogoraz, S. Kovalev, Fr Gleb Yakunin, Fr Grigory Edelshtein, Paruir Airikyan and Slava Chernovol. In 1989 it was transformed into the Moscow Helsinki group. Timofeev founded and headed the independent journal "Referendum" from December 1987 to late 1990. Thirty-eight numbers were published and it often appeared with *Russkaya mysl* (Russian thought). Its articles were often broadcast by Radio Svoboda, the BBC and Voice of America.

Timofeev is a member of the executive committee of the international Helsinki Federation, a member of the editorial board of the journals *Strannik* (wanderer), *Yunost*, and the Russian Pen Club. He is also in the group Civic Initiative, together with Yury Afanasev, Elena Bonner, Yury Burtin and L. Batkin. He is married.

Titov, Konstantin Alekseevich

Head of the Administration of Samara *oblast*, Russian Federation.

Born in 1944; Russian; member of the CPSU until August 1991. After leaving secondary school he began working as a milling machine operator in the aviation enterprise, Kuibyshev. In 1968 he graduated from the aviation institute, Kuibyshev, as a qualified engineer, and then worked as an aircraft mechanic in the aviation enterprise. He was elected deputy secretary of the enterprise *Komsomol* committee, and then became deputy head of the students' and pupils' department of the Kuibyshev *Komsomol* city committee and secretary of the *Komsomol* committee of a planning institute. There he began as a junior scientific assistant and later became head of the scientific economic research laboratory. In 1978 he successfully completed his postgraduate studies (PhD), and in April 1989 he became deputy director for economics in the Kuibyshev branch of the joint Soviet-Bulgarian enterprise, the Informatika scientific research centre.

In March 1990 he was elected a deputy to the Kuibyshev city soviet of people's deputies. At its first session, in April 1990, he was elected chairman. On August 21, 1991 he stated that he viewed the formation of the Extraordinary Committee as unconstitutional and all decisions of this body were illegal and had no validity on the territory of the city of Samara. He appealed to the city authorities to observe strictly all the decrees of the President of the RSFSR.

On August 31, 1991 he was appointed head of the administration of Samara *oblast*, and on assuming office he listed the main proposals of the administration to rescue the economy from crisis and effect a transition to a market economy. It was necessary to develop local autonomy, set up market mechanisms to run the economy, develop free enterprise and business activities of the population, denationalize and privatize property. Indices to permit measurement of changes in the standard of living of the population were price indices, indicators of accumulation of the means of production, savings, shares and securities. The privatization of state and municipal property together with the development of entrepreneurial activity constitutes the essence of the government's programme for the stabilization of the economy and the transition to the market. It was therefore necessary to speed up decisions about what property soviets at all levels possessed and, in addition, to set up a regional programme for the promotion of business and programmes for attracting foreign capital into priority sectors. In implementing anti-inflationary policies, draft extraordinary budgets should be drawn up which separated the current budget from the budget for development. A system of non-budgetary funds should be developed, a social security fund for the population set up, a fund to promote free enterprise and a fund for the development of private farming created.

In November 1992, addressing people's deputies of the Russian Federation in Samara, Titov appealed to them to afford general support to the government, and to vote against its removal, if such a question should come up at the VII Congress of People's Deputies, since the dismissal of the government and the formation of a new one would throw Russia into even greater chaos. He underlined that the government should not interfere in the activities of enterprises since its task was only to finance essential work. Even a government led by Arkady Volsky could not stop prices rising. The main task was to raise the incomes of the population, especially those of doctors and teachers. He lives in Samara.

Țîu, Nicolae

Minister of Foreign Affairs of the Republic of Moldova.

Born March 25, 1948 in the village of Andrușu-de-Jos, Cahul *raion*, Moldovan SSR. He was an ethnic Moldovan, who graduated from the Chișinău Agricultural Institute in 1970, and from the Academy of Social and Administrative Sciences (Sofia, Bulgaria) in 1983. He is a candidate of economic sciences (PhD (Econ)). From 1970 to 1979 he worked as an engineer, chief engineer, collective farm president, and president of the *Raion* Association for Mechanization in Ungheni. After receiving his degree in Bulgaria, he held several leading positions in republican agencies, including head of a city Soviet executive committee (1983-1990). In 1990 he became Minister of Foreign Affairs.

In addition to Romanian and Russian, Țîu also speaks French and Bulgarian. He is married with two children, a son aged 21 and a daughter aged 18.

Tiunov, Oleg Ivanovich

Member of the Constitutional Court of the Russian Federation.

Born on October 22, 1937 in Perm; Russian; member of the CPSU until August 1991. In 1959 he graduated from the law faculty of Perm State University, and then began work as an expert and criminologist. In 1965 in Moscow State University he successfully presented his candidate dissertation on "Neutrality in international law" (LLM) and in 1981 he also successfully presented his doctoral dissertation there on "The principle of honesty in the observation of international obligations" (LLD).

From 1966 to 1990 he was in the faculty of law, Perm State University, as a senior lecturer, assistant professor, head of the department of state law and dean of the faculty. He became a professor in 1979. He lectured on international law and state law in bourgeois states.

In early 1990 he was nominated for election as an RSFSR people's deputy by the collective of Perm State University in the No. 574 Dzerzhinsky territorial district, Perm *oblast*. In the election programme he advocated the removal of the command-administrative system, the development of self-administration as the basis of the work of local soviets, the introduction of a regulated market economy and changes in the way taxes were levied. He proposed not only greater power for the local soviets but also for the soviet executive committees, which should no longer be subject to superior agencies of state power but to corresponding soviets. The first task of Russian legislation should be to pass laws on property, land and taxation. There were seven candidates. Tiunov polled 23% of the votes in the first round and won the second round with 50.07% of the votes. His main opponent was N. A. Anikin, a blacksmith in the Mashinostroitelny zavod im. F. E. Dzerzhinskogo production association who polled 18% of the votes in the first round and 47% of the votes in the second.

In 1990 Tiunov was engaged full-time on RSFSR Supreme Soviet affairs. He was chairman of the sub-committee of the Supreme Soviet committee on international affairs and foreign economic links, a member of the parliamentary Russia faction, the communists of Russia deputies' group and the constitutional commission. He was chairman of the working group on drafting the declaration on the state sovereignty of the RSFSR and he participated in the drafting of the Russian laws on citizenship and on Russian international treaties. He submitted many opinions on a whole range of draft laws, debated by the Supreme Soviet.

He was nominated for election to the Constitutional Court by the deputies of the communists of Russia faction. On October 29, 1991, at the V Congress of the RSFSR People's Deputies, during the first round of voting, he was elected a member of the RSFSR Constitutional Court with 565 votes for and 333 against. On October 30 he surrendered his mandate as an RSFSR deputy.

In the Constitutional Court he is responsible for the legislation on international affairs and foreign economic links of the Russian federation. He advocates that the Constitutional Court should ensure the strict observance of the laws and constitutional norms of the Russian Federation. The Court should review annually the state of legality in Russia and remove lacunae in legislation for which the Court should make full use of its right to initiate legislation. The greatest weakness of the judiciary, in the eyes of Tiunov, is the absence in the present constitution of clear links between agencies of power and the determination of responsibility for non-implementation of decisions of the Constitutional Court. He has been awarded various state orders. He lives in Moscow.

Tkachenko, Evgeny Viktorovich

Russian Minister of Education.

Born in 1935 in Omsk into a large Russian family. His father died in 1936 and his mother was illiterate; he was a member of the CPSU until August 1991. He began work at the age of 14 years, but after completing his secondary education (with a silver medal) he entered the physics and technology faculty of the Urals Polytechnical Institute. Among his teachers were S. A. Voznesensky and pupils of S. Kurchatov. In 1957 he gained a diploma in the Mayak factory on eliminating the effects of radioactive contamination. He specialized as a chemist and ecologist on treating the emissions of atomic enterprises, and worked as a research engineer in the laboratory of S. A. Voznesensky. After completing postgraduate studies he successfully presented his candidate dissertation on metallurgical theory (PhD).

In 1969 he moved to Sverdlovsk University. He was an assistant professor, and later a professor in the department of inorganic chemistry in the faculty of chemistry. He and Professor V. Zhukovsky founded the school of the chemistry of solids. He successfully presented his doctoral dissertation (DSc), has published over 100 articles and supervised research students. He was deputy dean for five years, was elected chairman of the local committee of the university and secretary of the Party committee. In 1984 he was appointed rector of the Sverdlovsk engineering teachers' institute. Under his direction special units of instruction in various aspects of engineering were established which are now linked to over 100 teaching centres in former Soviet republics and abroad, and 15 methodology councils. The institute was the first in the Commonwealth of Independent States to have its diplomas recognized internationally.

He has 24 inventions to his credit and 270 published works, including two monographs. As a result he was awarded the badge of excellence in higher education. In the mid-1980s he participated as an expert in the activities of the discussion club organized by Gennady Burbulis. In November 1992 he was appointed first deputy Minister of Education under Eduard Dneprov, whom he had got to know when his Sverdlov institute had been placed under the jurisdiction of the Ministry of Education. In December Tkachenko succeeded Dneprov as Russian Minister of Education. He regards the main goal of educational reform to be the transformation of schools so as to prevent irreversible moral decline and is in agreement with the concept of reform initiated by Eduard Dneprov. Major priorities are to agree on the allocation of the educational budget, the parallel existence of free and non-state schools and standards in education.

His wife is a graduate of the Urals polytechnical institute and has taught communications for over 20 years in a technical secondary school. Their son is a surgeon, and their granddaughter is five years old. Tkachenko loves the theatre and classical music, especially Italian opera. He is a keen sportsman and has achieved grades in basketball, volleyball, athletics and chess. He normally spends his holidays walking the tourist routes in the Urals mountains and can cope with all domestic chores. He and his wife have a three-bedroom flat in Ekaterinburg and a modest dacha. He has never owned a car. He lives in Moscow.

Tkachuk, Vasyl Mykhailovych

Minister of Agriculture of Ukraine to October 1992.

Born into a Ukrainian family in western Ukraine in 1933. He was educated at the Ivano-Frankivsk oil and gas institute, and then worked for many years as the head of the Flag of Communism collective farm, also in Ivano-Frankivsk *oblast*. In the 1980s, based on it, he formed the agro-industrial firm *Prut*, which was given much publicity as a model new commercial enterprise.

In 1989 he was elected as a people's deputy for Ivano-Frankivsk to the USSR Congress of People's Deputies. In February 1992 he was chosen to replace the arch-conservative Oleksandr Tkachenko as Minister of Agriculture (who had entered the presidential race in autumn 1991 as the candidate of the old-style *apparat*, but then withdrew in favour of Kravchuk). However, despite his western Ukrainian background and reported support for private farming, he found it difficult to get radical measures past the powerful collective farm chairmen lobby in the Ukrainian Supreme Soviet, while at the same time was caught in a classic Soviet agricultural "scissors" crisis (the prices of agricultural inputs increasing much faster than agricultural products).

The old system of planning procurement had not been replaced by free market prices by 1992, when industrial, light industry and consumer goods prices began to explode, far outstripping still-controlled agricultural prices. Tkachuk therefore was powerless in the face of a rapid decline in agricultural production and delivery, and he was sacrificed in October 1992.

Official (Ministry) address: 252001 Kiev, Vul. Kreshchatyk 24; *telephone*: Kiev 226 3466.

Tleuzh, Adam Khuseinovich

Speaker of the Supreme Soviet of the Republic of Adygeia, Russian Federation.

Born in 1951; Adygeian; member of the CPSU until August 1991. Until 1991 he was second secretary of the Oktyabrsky *raion* Party committee. In March 1990 he was elected a deputy of the Adygei *oblast* soviet of people's deputies, and in December 1991 when temporarily unemployed and living in the village of Takhtamukai he was elected a deputy of the Supreme Soviet of the Adygei Soviet Socialist Republic.

On assuming office he stated that he viewed the main concern of the Supreme Soviet to be the social security of the population. He advocated the formation of a democratic republic in Adygeia which would guarantee equal rights for all nationalities and political stability, which would now allow conflict to emerge. If it did surface it should be resolved by peaceful means. He thought that fundamental changes in public life and in the form of the state should first be approved by an absolute majority of the population of the republic by referendum. He advocated precise implementation of economic, political and legal reforms, based on a professional approach. He proposed freedom for factions and groups whose work would be primarily directed towards resolving the problems of economic reform since, in his opinion, political reform was at present not of prime importance. He lives in the village of Oktyabrsky.

Toporov, Vladimir Mikhailovich

Deputy Minister of Defence of the Russian Federation. Colonel-General.

Born on February 7, 1946 in Baranovichi, Belarus. The social status of his parents is unknown. Russian. He graduated from the Odessa Artillery Officers' Technical School in 1968; the M. V. Frunze Military Academy in 1975; the Military Academy of the General Staff in 1984. He received a higher military education and was a member of the CPSU till August 1991.

After technical school he was assigned to airborne troops; was a platoon commander of an anti-tank battery; and a battery commander in an airborne regiment. His sub-units were awarded a distinction. He was actively involved in the work of the Party organization of his unit and conducted political seminars for soldiers and sergeants, which was crucial for a successful career in the Soviet army. He had a good reputation with superior officers, who decided to send the young officer Toporov to the Academy to continue his studies.

In 1975 he was appointed deputy regimental commander and in 1977 he became a regimental commander. He was deputy divisional commander from 1979. He proved to be an able and experienced military officer with a sound operational-tactical and military-technical training. He took part in military operations in Afghanistan.

After completing his studies at the Military Academy of the General Staff in 1984 he became a divisional commander. He ensured a high level of combat training in the formation, and succeeded in organizing versatile training for divisional units. According to democratic military sources, Gen. Toporov, as a divisional commander, repeatedly used equipment and personnel for private purposes, both his own and those of his superior officers. Such dealings in the Soviet army used to be essential for an officer or a General to be promoted. In 1987 Toporov was appointed first deputy commander and a year later, in 1988, a military army commander. In 1989 he filled the post of Chief of Staff, the first deputy army commander of the Far East military district which was traditionally considered to be a position necessary for further high posts in the central bodies of the military administration.

While in the Far East, Gen. V. Toporov demonstrated exceptional abilities in controlling the troops in a complicated military and political situation in a large theatre of operations under various military and geographical conditions. His record was that of an experienced military commander who ensured a high level of combat readiness of the troops under his command. He was not politically active at the time of the anti-constitutional putsch in August 1991.

In August 1991 he was assigned to one of the most prestigious posts in the Soviet army, that of the commander of the Moscow military district. He replaced Col.-Gen. Kalinin, dismissed for his involvement with the plotters. The head of the capital's military district has always enjoyed the favour of the top governmental officials and army command.

In June 1992 Col.-Gen. Toporov was appointed deputy Minister of Defence of the Russian Federation. He is a member of the "Afghan Generals" group, all of them protégés of Pavel Grachev. He does not enjoy the confidence of the democratically-minded military and is not well known in officers' circles. He does not express his political convictions in public. He supports the idea of a great Russia and the creation of powerful up-to-date armed forces.

He has been awarded four orders and five medals. He is fond of sport and has parachuted on numerous occasions. He is married.

Official address: 103175 Moscow K-160, Ministry of Defence of the Russian Federation.

Travkin, Nikolai Ilich

Leader of the Democratic Party of Russia (DPR).

Born in 1946 in the village of Novo-Nikolskoe, Moscow *oblast*. His father was a Party worker and his mother a teacher; Russian; member of the CPSU from 1970 to March 1990. He graduated from the Klin Construction Technical College and the extra-mural faculty of physics and mathematics, Kolomna State Pedagogical Institute. In 1969 he joined the main Moscow *oblast* construction trust as a brigadier, deputy head and manager, and was one of the initiators of the use of cost accounting (*khozraschet*) and self-management in the construction industry. In 1982 in the enterprise headed by Travkin the average monthly worker's wage was 700 rubles and the labour productivity was four times higher than the average for the industry. In 1986 he became a hero of socialist labour, and in 1987 he was appointed head of a construction association. Until 1987 he lived in the village of Shakhovskaya, Moscow *oblast*, afterwards in Moscow.

Between 1988 and 1989 he attended the Higher Party School of the Party Central Committee. He was a delegate to the XXVI and XXVII Party congress and the XIX Party conference. He is the recipient of state awards.

He has been active in politics since 1988. In 1989, during the second round of voting Travkin was nominated for election as a USSR people's deputy in the No. 45 Shchelkovsky territorial district, Moscow *oblast*. There were nine candidates. Travkin polled 29.28% of the votes in the first round and won the second round, polling 60.53% of the votes. At the I USSR Congress of People's Deputies he was elected to the USSR Supreme Soviet, then chairman of the sub-committee of the USSR Supreme Soviet committee on the soviets of people's deputies and the development of self-government. He joined the interregional group of deputies.

In early 1990 he was nominated for election as an RSFSR people's deputy in the No. 8 Veshnyakovsky territorial district, Moscow. There were seven candidates and Travkin won in the first round, polling 54.5% of the votes. In 1990 he stood three times for election to the RSFSR Supreme Soviet but was unsuccessful. From June to December 1990 he was chairman of the Supreme Soviet committee on the soviets of people's deputies and the development of self-government. He was a member of the coalition for reform bloc of deputies.

In early 1990 Travkin joined the Party Democratic platform. In March 1990 he declared that he was resigning from the CPSU and appealed for the founding of a democratic party, as an alternative to the CPSU, which would be organized on strictly vertical lines, based on strict discipline, with one leader and primary organizations in labour collectives, the armed forces and the Ministry of Internal Affairs. The task of the new party, deploying the same methods as the CPSU, would be to remove the latter from the political arena after defeating it in elections. In Travkin's view, it was necessary to set up a party which in size could compete with the CPSU. In May 1990 the constituent congress of the Democratic Party of Russia (DPR) took place and Travkin was elected chairman of its board. The DPR split in December 1990, at its first congress. A part of the membership, including the former deputy chairmen of the board Gary Kasparov, A. Murashev and Gennady Burbulis, left the congress in protest against the authoritarian methods of Travkin as party leader, and the re-establishment of neo-Bolshevik principles of party activity. Travkin was re-elected chairman of the board of the party.

In January 1991 he left the inter-republican democratic congress, accusing it of breaking up the USSR and neglecting the fate of Russians in the other sovereign republics. From January to April 1991 he repeatedly appealed for the maintenance of the USSR and called on citizens to vote for the retention of the Soviet Union in the referendum. In June 1991 he appealed for the founding of an alternative movement of democratic reform, a United Democratic Party, but he found no takers. In November 1991 the DPR left the Democratic Russia (DemRossiya) movement and together with the Russian Christian Democratic movement (V. V. Aksyuchits was the chairman of its duma), and the Constitutional Democratic Party (M. G. Astafev was the chairman of its central committee), set up the People's Accord bloc. However it disintegrated in February 1992 after the congress of civil and patriotic forces of Russia, at which the Russian People's Assembly was established. The DPR refused to join this organization.

At the end of December 1991 Travkin was appointed head of the administration of Shakhovsky *raion*, Moscow *oblast*. When taking over he stated that he regarded the *raion* as a testing ground for the introduction of economic reforms and the updating of many laws. His chief task was the introduction of privatization, raising the effectiveness of the economy and guaranteeing the population social security.

During the summer of 1992 the Civic Union bloc came into existence. It included the DPR, the People's Party, Free Russia (V. S. Lipitsky was chairman of the board), the all-Russian union, Renewal (co-chairmen were A. P. Vladislavlev and S. A. Polozkov) and the Russian Union of Industrialists and Entrepreneurs (A. I. Volsky was chairman). According to Travkin the motives behind the association were to achieve agreement on many aspects of the development of Russia, its indivisibility, the timing of the adoption of economic reform, which should lead to the market, but be gradual to ensure the stability of production and the living standards of the population.

During 1992 the USSR public prosecutor's office and the public prosecutor of Moscow *oblast* repeatedly warned Travkin since he held both party and state posts. At the IV congress of the DPR he resigned as chairman of the board. However, he acquired a specially created post, that of leader of the DPR, which afforded him a consultative voice but not access to the finances of the party and he received no material reward from the party.

Travkin is president of the fund for the support of peasant and private farm economies which was set up by the Germes joint stock company, the Germes Tyumen-Moscow commodity exchange and Grigory Yavlinsky's Epitsentr international food exchange. The basic capital was 10 million rubles.

Travkin is married and has two grown-up sons. He lives in the village of Shakhovskaya, Moscow *oblast*.

Tretyakov, Valery Stepanovich

Commander of the Baikal Military District; Colonel-General since 1991.

Born on December 24, 1941 in Syzran, Kuibyshev (Samara) *oblast*. The social status of his parents is unknown; Russian.

He graduated from the Tashkent Higher Military Officers Technical school in 1963, the M. V. Frunze Military Academy in 1972, and the Military Academy of the General Staff in 1985, having received a higher military education. He was a member of the CPSU until August 1991.

He began his career as an officer as a motorized-rifle platoon commander, where he demonstrated good professional skills, and a talent for organization and teaching. He actively participated in the work of *Komsomol* and Party organizations, enjoyed the support of superior officers and political agencies, and was quite rapidly promoted to company commander, and later to battalion Chief of Staff. After graduating from the Academy in 1972 he was appointed Chief of Staff of a motorized-rifle regiment. His record was that of an officer with a sound operational-tactical and military-technical training, aware of the essence of present-day military combat, and able to plan combat operations. From 1975 he was a regimental commander, from 1977 Chief of Staff, and from 1979 commander of a motorized-rifle division. For a certain period of time he was in Afghanistan where he gained combat experience.

After graduating from the Academy of the General Staff in 1985 he became the first deputy commander, and from 1987 an army commander. In 1988 he was appointed the first deputy commander of the Baikal military district.

During the anti-constitutional putsch in August 1991 he was not very active and concentrated on his immediate duties, ensuring high combat readiness.

In late August 1991 Lieut.-Gen. V. Tretyakov was appointed commander of the Baikal military district (his appointment was newly confirmed by President B. Yeltsin's decree in October 1992).

Under Col.-Gen. V. Tretyakov's command is one of the most powerful groups of land forces and front-line airborne divisions which covers a large region in Eastern Siberia. Gen. Tretyakov is a military professional, not active in political life, and like most ex-Soviet generals he advocates the supremacy of the state in domestic affairs and Russia as a great power externally. He is a conformist who has renounced orthodox communist views. He opposes democratic organizations and movements, and advocates strengthening law and order in the country.

There is no information about his hobbies. As is typical of military men, he is fond of hunting and sport as recreation. He does not speak any foreign language, and has not been abroad as a member of an official delegation. He has been awarded two orders and 11 medals, including foreign ones. He is married.

Gen. Tretyakov's headquarters are in Chita.

Tsedasheev, Gurodarma Tsedashievich

Head of the Administration of Aginsk Buryat Autonomous *okrug*, Russian Federation.

Born in 1948 in the village of Kunkur, Buryat autonomous *okrug*; Buryat; member of the CPSU until August 1991. In 1967 he completed secondary school and then began teaching physical education at Budalansk secondary school. From 1968 to 1970 he served in the Soviet Army. He graduated from the Buryat Pedagogical Institute in 1974 and was then appointed director of the *okrug* children's and youth sporting school in the village of Aginskoe. He was then appointed director of the Aginsk *raion* cinema board, chairman of the soviet executive committee of Aginskoe village soviet, deputy head of the cinema department of the *okrug* soviet executive committee. In 1986 he was elected deputy chairman of the Aginsk *raion* soviet executive committee, and from August 1988 to March 1990 he was chairman of the administration of Aginsk *raion*.

In March 1990 he was elected deputy for the No. 9 Lenin electoral district in the soviet of people's deputies of Aginsk Buryat autonomous *okrug*, and was also elected deputy for the Komsomolsk electoral district in the Aginsk *raion* soviet. At the first session of the Buryat *okrug* soviet of people's deputies in March 1990 he was elected chairman of the *okrug* executive committee.

In August 1991 the *okrug* executive committee of the Buryat soviet of people's deputies adopted a wait and see position during the attempted coup and appealed to the population of the autonomous *okrug* to be restrained and observe order until the outcome of events was clear. On December 26, 1991 Tsedasheev was appointed head of the administration of the Aginsk Buryat autonomous *okrug*, Chita *oblast*, by presidential decree. On assuming office he stated that he supported economic transformation, which implied the development of market relations and the most rapid privatization of state enterprises. He was in favour of a multi-faceted economy, especially agriculture, and believed that it was important to establish equal opportunities for the state sector, collective and state farms, and the lessees and private entrepreneurs. It was necessary to provide greater help to entrepreneurs and to attempt to interest them in investing their capital in material production.

In December 1992 he stated that the VII Congress of People's Deputies should not consider the question of confidence or lack of confidence in the government of the Russian Federation. Its main task was to make corrections to the work of the government and its policy of economic reform. He lives in the village of Aginskoe, Buryat autonomous *okrug*.

Tubylov, Valentin Kuzmich

Speaker of the Supreme Soviet of the Udmurt Republic, Russian Federation.

Born on November 13, 1935 in the village of Malaya Kibya, Mozhginsky *raion*, Udmurt ASSR; an Udmurt; member of the CPSU from 1964 to August 1991. He began his career as a carpenter in the Sarapulsky timber enterprise. After service in the Soviet Army he worked as a brigadier on the Iskra collective farm, Mozhginsky *raion*, and in 1959 became a student at the Sarapulski state farm college. After graduating in 1962 he worked as a brigadier, chief agronomist, and deputy chairman of the Molniya collective farm, Malopurginsky *raion*. He graduated from the agricultural institute, Izhevsk in 1969 as an agronomist. In 1970 he was elected second, and in 1977 first, secretary of the Malopurginsky *raion* Party committee. In 1986 he became chief agronomist of the Malopurginsky state farm and in 1988 was head of the Asanovsky state farm college.

He was elected a deputy of the Supreme Soviet of the Udmurt ASSR three times and was also a delegate to the XXVI Party congress. On April 14, 1990, at the first session of the Supreme Soviet of the Udmurt ASSR, he was elected Speaker. On August 19, 1991 Tubylov signed the decree of the Presidium of the Supreme Soviet of the Udmurt ASSR on current events which stated that the "state authorities and administration, elected in accordance with the constitution of the Udmurt ASSR, continue to function in the republic". There was "no need to adopt a range of measures to guarantee the stability of the political situation, the normal way of life of the population and the functioning of the economy, public security and law and order in the republic".

In connection with this the Presidium of the Supreme Soviet of the Udmurt ASSR has resolved to "take upon itself full responsibility for guaranteeing the stability of the situation in the republic" and also to "ban the establishment and activities of agencies and formations which have been formed illegally". The declaration of the Presidium of the Supreme Soviet of the Udmurt ASSR, signed by Tubylov, of August 21, 1991 underlined the fact that the "measures being undertaken by the Presidium of the Supreme Soviet made it possible to avoid having to introduce a state of emergency". He lives in Izhevsk.

Tuleev, Aman Gumirovich (Amangeldy Moldagazyevich)

Chairman of the Kemerovo *oblast* soviet of people's deputies.

Born on May 13, 1944 in Krasnovodsk, Turkmen SSR. His father, a Kazakh, was an office worker and his mother, a housewife, is a Tatar. He was a member of the CPSU until August 1991. He graduated from the Tikhoretsky Railway Technical College, Krasnodar *krai*, and became an assistant station master, Mundybash, Kemerovo railway line. After serving in the Soviet army he graduated as an external student from the Novosibirsk Institute of Railway Engineers, and was station master of the Mundybash and Mezhdurechensk stations. In 1978 he was appointed station master of the Novokuznetsk department of the Kemerovo railway line, and then he became head of the department of transport, Kemerovo Party *obkom*. He graduated as an external student from the Academy of Social Sciences, Party Central Committee. In 1990 he was head of the Kemerovo railway line, and was a member of the Kemerovo Party *obkom*.

In 1989 he was nominated for election as a USSR people's deputy but was defeated and Yu. Golik was elected instead. In 1990 he was nominated by several work collectives in Kemerovo *oblast* for election as an RSFSR people's deputy in the No. 46 Gorno-Shorsky national territorial district, and during the election campaign he advocated measures to improve the social situation of the workers of the Kuzbass. There were five candidates and Tuleev won in the second round, polling 75% of the votes. His main opponent was A. P. Shcheglokov, who received 18% of the votes in the second round. Tuleev was a member of the industrial union parliamentary group and is at present a member of the *Otchizna* (motherland) parliamentary faction.

In March 1990 he was elected a people's deputy of the Kemerovo *oblast* soviet, and in April 1991, at the first session of the *oblast* soviet, he was elected its chairman. He was supported by the Party *obkom* and work collectives in Kemerovo and Prokopevsk. He was also elected chairman of the executive committee of the Kemerovo *oblast* soviet. In April 1991 he was registered as a candidate for the post of RSFSR President, and was supported by 59 work collectives of Kemerovo *oblast* who collected 274,000 signatures of support. During the election campaign he advocated the democratization of the economy, the freedom to work, trade and to earn money within the law; the freezing of meetings and strikes so as to improve labour discipline; and priority in agriculture to be given to state and collective farms. From his point of view, the workers' movement was a destructive instrument of anti-socialist forces and the anti-crisis programme of the Russian government should be revised by taking into account regional conditions. The technology and expertise of the military industrial complex should be used in civilian production. The most important task of the RSFSR President was the struggle against crime and he expressed his lack of trust in the Speaker of the RSFSR Supreme Soviet, Boris Yeltsin. Tuleev polled 6.81% of the votes during the RSFSR presidential election on June 12, 1991 and was thereby fourth out of six candidates.

In August 1991 he was removed as chairman of the executive committee of the Kemerovo *oblast* soviet, and in early 1992 the parliamentary commission investigating the anti-constitutional state coup of August 1991 handed the Kemerovo *oblast* soviet documents confirming contacts between Tuleev and the Extraordinary Committee in August 1991 and his involvement in organizing measures to introduce a state of emergency. Tuleev offered his resignation as chairman of the Kemerovo *oblast* soviet of people's deputies because of the lack of attention by the central state authorities to the needs of the *oblast* and as a result the exacerbation of the food situation in the Kuzbass, but at the end of February 1992 he withdrew his resignation. At the IX Congress of People's Deputies on March 26-29, 1993 Tuleev assessed the television address of President Boris Yeltsin to the Russian people on March 20, 1993 as an attempt to establish an authoritarian regime in Russia. Tuleev is married with two sons and lives in Kemerovo.

Tumanov, Vladislav Nikolaevich

Head of the Administration of Pskov *oblast*, Russian Federation.

Born in 1958; Russian; he was never a member of the CPSU. He graduated in law and was head of the legal department of the Pskov mechanical gears factory. Then he became deputy director of the north-west centre of the all-Union legal firm, Kontrakt, of the USSR union of lawyers. In 1990 he was elected a deputy of the Pskov *oblast* soviet, and he was a member of the Democratic Russia group of deputies.

In August 1991 he addressed the extraordinary session of the *oblast* soviet. He stated that during the attempted coup the leadership of the Pskov *oblast* soviet had adopted a neutral position and he drew political lessons from this action, distancing himself from the position of the leadership of the soviet. On October 24, 1991 A. A. Dobryakov was appointed head of the administration of Pskov *oblast* by presidential decree, but he was relieved of his functions in May 1992.

In December 1991 Tumanov became first deputy head of the administration of the city of Pskov. After the departure of Dobryakov, the President of the Russian Federation proposed V. N. Tumanov as head of the administration of the *oblast* to the Pskov *oblast* soviet. On May 21 the *oblast* soviet agreed to the President's proposal, and on May 22, 1992 Tumanov was appointed head of the administration of Pskov *oblast* by presidential decree. On assuming office Tumanov advocated the expansion of interregional and foreign economic links, support for entrepreneurship, small and medium size businesses and the transfer of the centre of gravity of reform to the regions.

In December 1992 he declared that the Congress of People's Deputies had outlived its usefulness, and advocated the need to reform the Supreme Soviet whose work revealed incompetence. He opposed changing the Prime Minister. As regards President Yeltsin's address to the nation, he appealed to everyone not to begin searching behind the President's back for *eminences grises* on whom to place the blame. The President had acted decisively, although this has cost him many supporters. Tumanov lives in Pskov.

Tyazhlov, Anatoly Stepanovich

Head of the Administration of Moscow *oblast*, Russian Federation.

Born in 1942 in Kopeisk, Chelyabinsk *oblast*; Russian; member of the CPSU until August 1991. After school he worked as a bricklayer and reinforced concrete worker on construction sites in the Urals, and at the same time completed evening school and then graduated from an institute. He was a foreman, technician, head of a shop, head of a department and chief engineer of the enterprise which manufactured concrete reinforcement, Orenburg. In 1969 he began working on building sites in Moscow *oblast*. He was a senior engineer of the Orekhovo-Zuevo housing construction combine, chief engineer of the Egorevsky rural construction combine, the manager of a construction trust, first deputy chairman of the Moscow *oblast* construction committee and chairman of the state Moscow *oblast* building materials production association.

In December 1989 he was directly responsible for the work and social development of the building materials enterprises in Kolomno, Voskresensk, Zaraisk, Lukhovitsy, Kashir, Ozery, Pavlovy Posad and Orekhovo-Zuevo. He was a member of the executive committee of the Moscow *oblast* soviet and took part in the development of many innovations in developing contractual and leasing relations in production and other effective ways of increasing output. He was awarded the USSR Council of Ministers prize for heroism for work saving lives after the earthquake in Armenia and setting up a construction base there. He has also the order of the Friendship of Nations.

In early 1990 he was nominated for election as an RSFSR people's deputy in the No. 8 Kolomensky national territorial district, Moscow *oblast*. During the election campaign he advocated that the economic potential of the country be switched to meeting the needs of the population and providing social security. He proposed that laws on property and freedom of choice of economic activity be adopted and economically strong soviets at all levels be established. A dialogue with all public unions and associations should begin. The USSR should be retained and precise economic frontiers be established, as in a free economy strict state control of personal incomes and the realization of the principles of social justice were needed.

There were six candidates. He polled 13.06% of the votes in the first round and lost the second round, polling 25.06% of the votes. The deputy elected was A. N. Tikhomirov, political commentator of the USSR state committee for radio and television, who received 43.54% of the votes in the first round and 68.27% in the second round. At the first session of the Moscow *oblast* soviet in May 1990 Tyazhlov was elected chairman of the executive committee.

On assuming office he advocated the amalgamation of Moscow and the Moscow region (Podmoskove), a unified policy on prices, taxes and subsidies, the setting up of an association of all local branches of the economy and the direct fusion of management structures. He appealed for the most rapid introduction of Russian reforms, opposition to all efforts to slow them down and the retention of Russia as a whole and as a federal state. He participated in the drafting of the decrees of the President of the Russian Federation on various aspects of economic reform, made various proposals to the Supreme Soviet of the Russian Federation on improvement of legislation and advocated the establishment of a state agency for regional reform policy. He believed that there should be many different types of economic activity.

On April 8, 1992 he was elected president of the association of heads of the administration of *oblasts* and *krais* — union of the governors of Russia — and on November 17, 1992 he became a member of the government of the Russian Federation. In December 1992 he advocated, in the present circumstances, uniting the posts of President and head of the executive, and supported the current policy of the President and government.

On December 10, 1992 the heads of the executive and representatives of the President issued a statement condemning the attempts by some people's deputies to disturb the balance of power and to restrict the functions of the executive. It expressed complete support for the President as head of state, head of the executive and the constitution as the basic guarantee of law and order. It appealed for the strict observance of the constitution and the laws of the Russian Federation, the elimination of unconstitutional activities and unconstitutional state authorities and called for compromise. Tyazhlov was a member of the commission which sought to reach a compromise between the President and the Speaker of the Supreme Soviet, Ruslan Khasbulatov, and stated that a referendum was necessary to clarify the controversial questions about the new constitution. He is married and his wife is a construction engineer. They have two children, the son a student and the daughter still at school, and they live in Moscow.

Tyulkin, Viktor Arkadevich

Leader of the Russian Communist Workers' Party (RCWP).

Born in 1951. His grandfather was a revolutionary, one of the first chairmen of the soviets in Shlisselburg but was killed during the Civil War (1918-21); his father joined the Communist Party in 1919. Tyulkin was secretary of the Party committee of the Avangard scientific production association and was elected a member of its Central Committee of the RSFSR Communist Party in July 1991. He was leader of the movement for a communist initiative which was founded in later 1990. He was elected a leader of the party at its constituent congress on November 23-24, 1991, in Ekaterinburg.

Tyulkin is an active defender of the ideals of the October Revolution, an uncompromising opponent of opportunism in the CPSU, a participant in the work begun by Nina Andreeva, a comrade in arms of Ivan Polozkov, the former general secretary of the RSFSR Communist Party. Between 1990 and 1991 Tyulkin sharply criticized the CPSU leadership for lack of purpose and opportunism and lack of principle in the ideological struggle, and demanded that the USSR President implement the decisions of the XXVII CPSU congress which had confirmed "our socialist choice". He appealed for support for those types of economic activity which were not linked to the exploitation of man by man and opposed all measures designed to legitimize the shadow economy. He judged the CPSU to be in crisis with the openly anti-communist movement of Afanasev, Travkin and Sale emerging from its democratic left wing. The CPSU had adopted a non-communist position, was in fact a party faction and did not seek any advice from the masses. He believed that the ordinary rank and file communist should not have to suffer all the punishment for the 73 years of Soviet power and the collapse of *perestroika*. He advocated the establishment of communist initiative soviets in factories, collective and state farms and in military units.

Tyulkin was a candidate for the post of first secretary of the Kalininsky *raion* Party committee in Leningrad but was not elected. However, 147 of the 450 delegates at the Party conference voted for him. He says that the reason why he has parted ideologically with Nina Andreeva is due to her lack of a constructive position and her negative image. The introduction of the presidency was a contradiction of the fundamental principles of Soviet power, in his view. It is in the soviets that the power of the working people is expressed, although the present soviets in essence are comparable to a capitalist parliament. He laboured to set up workers' committees, military committees, and based on them, *raion*, city and republican soviets of workers. He expressed solidarity with the united front of workers, inter-movement and the united soviet of communist workers of the Baltic. He believed that they did not contravene the Soviet constitution and the Party rules but created parallel structures of power. A communist movement within a communist party is not possible. He warned of the danger of the decommunization of the CPSU which was being maintained with the Soyuz deputies' group in the USSR parliament. He advocated the unification of forces with the Marxist platform, the Soyuz group and the Marxist Workers' Party. One should not be a hard or softline communist, just a communist or nothing at all.

The goal of the RCWP ought to be the creation of a classless society, the liquidation of the exploitation of man by man in all its forms, the guaranteeing of prosperity and the free, all-round development of every person, the performing of labour in the common good as the only source of personal income, the provision of access to culture and creative activity for everyone, the elimination of social inequality and the retention of the unity of the motherland. He lives in St Petersburg.

Ubozhko, Lev Grigorevich

Chairman of the Conservative Party.

Born on March 12, 1933 in Kopeisk, Chelyabinsk *oblast* into a civil servant's family. In 1961 he graduated from the Engineering Physics Institute, Moscow. In the 1960s he was under investigation for criticizing the Soviet system and was dismissed from his job. In 1968 he began participating in the democratic movement, together with Petr Yakir, Aleksandr Solzhenitsyn and Andrei Sakharov, and on January 27, 1970 he was arrested under article 190 of the criminal code of the RSFSR for having a copy of Andrei Amalrik's book *Will the Soviet Union Survive until 1984?*. He was sentenced to three years' imprisonment. In the labour camp in Omsk he was additionally charged under article 70 of the criminal code (anti-Soviet agitation and propaganda) and removed to a special psychiatric hospital in Tashkent, Uzbekistan. He was then moved to a psychiatric hospital in Chelyabinsk from which he escaped, but he was arrested in Moscow and again placed in the special psychiatric hospital. Academician Andrei Sakharov, in his Nobel prize speech, included him in the list of prisoners who had been illegally sentenced.

He was freed on June 12, 1987. He was one of the first to suggest that the ideas of *perestroika* could be used to transform the civil rights movement into a mass opposition political party. During April and May 1988 he took part in the setting up of the Party of Democratic Union. V. Bogachev, R. Semenov and he were expelled from the party the same autumn for publishing in *Vechernyaya Moskva* extracts from a collective letter in which they accused the leaders of the party, V. Novodvorskaya and A. Lukashev, of intrigue, despotism and so on.

On January 13, 1989 Ubozhko announced the founding of the Democratic Party which was later renamed the Democratic Party of the Soviet Union (DPSU). At the constituent congress of the DPSU, on August 5-6, 1989, it was not Ubozhko who was elected chairman but R. Semenov. The congress took place in the latter's flat. During the autumn of 1989 Ubozhko set up yet another party, the Democratic Party (Ubozhko). At the II congress of the Democratic Party (Ubozhko), on October 6-7, 1990, he renamed his party the Conservative Party in order to avoid confusion. Some of the delegates opposed the renaming of the party and this in turn produced another split. In October 1990 the Conservative Party joined the centrist bloc of political parties and movements which was led by V. V. Voronin. However in December 1990, after a scandal, the Conservative Party left the bloc.

In the spring of 1991 Ubozhko declared himself the Conservative Party candidate for the post of Russian President. However, since the party had not yet been registered by the RSFSR Ministry of Justice his nomination was not recognized. In his election programme Ubozhko advocated a multi-party political system, the equality of all forms of property, the establishment of a standing army, the depoliticization of the armed forces, the Ministry of Internal Affairs, the legal agencies, etc., free exit and re-entry for all citizens, the division of powers and the creation of a law-governed state (*Rechtsstaat*).

Ubozhko states that he remains a candidate for the post of Russian President until the next elections. In May 1991 the Conservative Party had about 5,000 members. He lives in Moscow.

Valeev, Damir Zhavatovich

Co-Chairman of the Bashkir National Congress, Republic of Bashkortostan, Russian Federation.

Born in 1941 in Argayashsky *raion*, Chelyabinsk *oblast*. He is a Bashkir, whose parents were ordinary rural dwellers. He graduated from the faculty of law, M. Gorky Urals State University, Sverdlovsk (Ekaterinburg), in 1965. He then became a postgraduate student and in 1970 successfully presented his candidate dissertation in philosophical sciences on the problem of the imperative in ethics (PhD). In 1984 he successfully presented his doctoral dissertation in philosophical sciences (DLitt). He is at present head of the department of ethics, aesthetics and culture, Bashkir State University.

He is an active supporter of the Bashkir national centre, Ural, and is chairman of the commission on law and state formation of the Bashkir National Congress. He has published many articles in the republican press. In a series of articles he originally advocated affording Bashkiria the status of a Union republic, then for its complete independence. He also advocated the return to Bashkiria of Argayashsky and Kunashaksky *raions*, which were made part of the newly formed Chelyabinsk *oblast* by the decree of the all-Russian central executive committee of January 17, 1934. He is married. His wife, an historian, works in the central state archive of the Republic of Bashkortostan. They have no children and live in Ufa.

Varennikov, Valentin Ivanovich

Member of the Extraordinary Committee.

Born in 1923; Russian; member of CPSU from 1944 to August 1991. He was a candidate member of the Party Central Committee from 1986 to July 1990. He joined the Soviet Army in 1941 and participated in the Great Fatherland War, then after the war he graduated from the M. V. Frunze Military Academy and the Military Academy of the General Staff of the USSR Armed Forces. He occupied leading command posts: commander of a regiment, division, corps and an army. In 1971 he was appointed first deputy commander of the group of forces in Germany (German Democratic Republic).

In 1973 he was appointed commander of troops in the Sub-Carpathian military district, in 1979 he became first deputy head of the General Staff of the USSR Armed Forces and in 1989 he was appointed Commander-in-Chief of ground troops and deputy USSR Minister of Defence and was promoted to general of the Army. He is a hero of the Soviet Union. He was elected a member of the USSR Supreme Soviet in 1986 and in 1989 became a USSR people's deputy.

On August 18, 1991 he participated in the discussions between the plotters of the anti-constitutional putsch and President Mikhail Gorbachev, at the latter's dacha in Foros, Crimea. He played his role in the organization and implementation of the measures of the Extraordinary Committee. He was arrested on August 22, 1991 and dismissed from his military posts. During the investigation he was incarcerated in the *Matrosskaya tishina* isolator. He and the other conspirators were later released and Varennikov played an active part in the deliberations and demonstrations of the all-Russian officers' assembly. This was hostile to the Yeltsin administration and especially to General Pavel Grachev, Russian Minister of Defence. Varennikov lives in Moscow.

Vasilev, Dmitry Dmitrievich

Chairman of the National Patriotic Front, Pamyat.

Born in 1945 in Vyatka. His father died when he was very young, and Nikolai Petrovich Antsiferov, the writer, who had spent 27 years in Stalinist camps, was a very important influence when he was growing up. Vasilev served in the armed forces, and then completed a course of study on the theatre. He joined the Pamyat society in the late 1970s, at the very beginning of its existence, and was active in drafting the manifesto of the National Patriotic Front, Pamyat, which was adopted at an extended session of the society on January 12, 1989.

The preamble of the manifesto states that Pamyat is not a political organization and its programmatic demands are "based on the interests of the people and common sense". The manifesto speaks of the need to "withdraw the state from the ranks of the colonies and being the provider of raw materials to the world Zionist financial oligarchy". Among the main tasks of the organization are the "struggle against world Zionism", and the "strengthening of the armed forces, opposition to their reduction and their transformation into a hired band of professional killers".

The manifesto also demands economic "autonomy for all republics". Land reform should be implemented according to the slogan "land belongs to those who work it", and the financial strengthening of the family and a legislative struggle against the "exploitation of female and child labour" are also emphasized. The goals of Pamyat are to be realized by a series of measures to renew spirituality, based on the Orthodox Church and the implementation of the constitutional instrument on the feedom of religion for all faiths, "in the first place, for Orthodox christianity, which has suffered, on the whole, savage persecution". Those reponsible for the genocide of the Russian nation and other peoples of the country should be identified and the culprits publicly punished.

The document points out the need to struggle against "Russophobic protectionism". It is appropriate to establish Russia's own social and political structures and cultural centres and there should be "representation in leading authorities proportionate to the national composition" of the state. The manifesto also stresses the observance of the "legal right of every people to develop freely on its own age-old land in the given historical context". A stop should be put to the artifical assimilation and the mechanistic mixing of peoples. "True autonomy of the republics within a single, indivisible state" should be achieved, and an end should be put to the "predatory pillage of our resources, woods and water by international usurer Zionist capital". He lives in Moscow.

Vasylyshyn, Andrii Volodymyrovych

Minister of the Interior, Ukraine.

Born into a Ukrainian family in 1933. From 1952 to 1957 he served in the Soviet Army, and then spent two years as an officer cadet at the Ministry of Internal Affairs (MVD) school in Kiev. He then worked as an investigator, first for Kiev city soviet, and after 1964 for the MVD. Under their auspices, he studied law at Kiev State University until 1966 and by 1972 he had become a head of department in the MVD. In 1974 he moved to Chernivtsi *oblast* in south-west Ukraine to head its department of internal affairs, before returning to take up the same position in Kiev *oblast* in 1982.

By 1985 he had risen to the post of deputy Minister of Internal Affairs, and he became the Minister in 1990. As might be expected from someone with such a long career service in the MVD, Vasylyshyn has not rushed to make any radical changes in his department and its structures and personnel have remained largely intact from Soviet times. He has found it relatively easy to make common cause with the nationalists who since 1991 have stressed the importance of order and security in the young state.

However, he has often been criticized for insufficient action against those structures of corruption or local separatist forces whose links to the old order that Vasylyshyn represents are uncomfortably close. Leonid Kuchma, the new Prime Minister, nevertheless retained him in his post in October 1992. However, rumours concerning his protection of mafia structures began to circulate in early 1993, and the possibility of his resignation was therefore mooted.

Official (Ministry) address: 252024 Kiev, Vul. Bohomoltsia 10; *telephone*: Kiev 226 2004.

Vedernikov, Nikolai Trofimovich

Member of the Constitutional Court of the Russian Federation.

Born on December 17, 1934 in Anzhero-Sudzhensk, Kemerovo *oblast* into a Russian miner's family; member of the CPSU until August 1991. In 1953 he became a student in the faculty of law, Tomsk State University, and after graduation worked in local government, including being secretary of a soviet executive committee. He began teaching in 1959 as an assistant in the department of criminal law, procedure and criminology, faculty of law, Tomsk State University. In 1966, in Moscow State University, he successfully presented his candidate dissertation on "The study of the personality of the criminal during the investigation" (LLM).

In 1981, in Tomsk State University, he successfully presented his doctoral dissertation on "The personality of the accused in Soviet criminal procedure (concept, substance and methodology of study)" (LLD). He taught in the faculty of law, Tomsk State University and in 1990 was head of the department of criminal law. He has over 80 publications to his name, including two monographs.

In early 1990 he was nominated by the collective of Tomsk State University for election as an RSFSR people's deputy in the No. 698 Leninsky territorial district, Tomsk *oblast*. During the election campaign he signed the declaration to the electors of Tomsk *oblast* of a group of candidates seeking election to soviets at various levels. The declaration stated that the only way of overcoming the crisis was to put into effect genuine rule by the people through the local soviets. Economic reform was not possible without political democratization, which in turn was not possible until power passed to the people. Vedernikov was supported by the union of workers of the Kuzbass and the Anzhero-Sudzhen workers' committee. There were seven candidates. Vedernikov polled 14% of the votes in the first round and won the second round with 45% of the votes. His main opponent was A. A. Pomorov, secretary of the Tomsk *oblast* Party committee (*obkom*), who received 13% of the votes in the first round and 40% of the votes in the second.

From 1990 to 1991 he worked full-time in the RSFSR Supreme Soviet. He was chairman of the Supreme Soviet Presidium commission on granting pardons, a member of the Supreme Soviet committee on legislation, chairman of the sub-committee of the Supreme Soviet committee on legislation, order and the struggle against crime. He was a member of the parliamentary Russia faction, the deputies' group on education, science and culture and the constitutional commission.

He was nominated for election to the Constitutional Court by the Russia group of deputies and was elected a member of the Constitutional Court on October 29, 1991, at the V Congress of People's Deputies, in the first round of voting. He received 529 votes for and 303 votes against. Vedernikov's election was opposed by the Tomsk committee of electors, the Tomsk branch of Democratic Russia (DemRossiya) and the Tomsk people's movement because of the fact that Vedernikov's record of voting in the Supreme Soviet was at variance with his election programme. On October 30, 1991 he surrendered his mandate as a people's deputy.

In the Constitutional Court he advocated more resources for the legal system and not only the review of legislation by the Court but also its implementation, and he opposed dropping the death penalty. He has received various state awards. He lives in Moscow.

Vialacki, Ales Viktaravic

Director of the Maksim Bahdanovic Literary Museum, Minsk, Belarus.

Born on September 25, 1962 in Vartfilya, Karelian ASSR, and his parents are Viktar Uspinavic Vialacki and Nina Alaksandrauna Vialackaja. He is Belarusian. He graduated from Homiel Gomel State University and became a postgraduate student at the Belarusian Academy of Sciences. He is a member of the Belarusian Popular Front and the Belarusian Catholic Hramada, and also of the Minsk city council.

He is the author of various literary critical and historical works, including the book *Litaratura i nacyja* (literature and nation) (1991). He is co-editor of the journal *Chryscijanskaja Dumka*. His hobby is collecting postcards. He is married, his wife is Natalla and they have a son, Daminik.

Address: Minsk, vul. Varanianskaha dom 15, k. 3, kv. 70; *telephone*: Minsk (0172) 34 07 61.

Viktorov, Valeryan Nikolaevich

Chairman of the Council of Ministers of the Chuvash Republic, Russian Federation.

Born in 1951 in Kanash, Chuvash Autonomous Soviet Socialist republic (ASSR); Chuvash. He graduated from the physics and mathematics, and history faculties of the I. N. Ulyanov Chuvash State University, where he successfully presented his candidate dissertation in economics (PhD (Econ)). He began his career in 1973 as a junior scientific assistant in the scientific research sector of the State University, then from 1974 to 1976 he was a postgraduate student at the G. M. Krzhizhanovsky Institute of Energy, Moscow and after graduating was a scientific assistant at the Chuvash State University.

From 1978 to 1991 he was a junior scientific assistant, and head of the department of economics in the scientific research institute of language, literature, history and economics of the Council of Ministers of the Chuvash ASSR. In May 1991 he was appointed Minister for the Economy of the Chuvash Soviet Socialist Republic, and on February 12, 1992 at the IX session of the Supreme Soviet of the Chuvash SSR, Viktorov was appointed Chairman of the Council of Ministers. He lives in Cheboksary.

Vitruk, Nikolai Vasilevich

Deputy Chairman of the Constitutional Court of the Russian Federation.

Born on November 4, 1937 in the settlement of Zharovka, Pyshkino-Troitsky, Tomsk *oblast*, Siberia; Russian; member of the CPSU until August 1991. He graduated from the faculty of law, Tomsk State University, in 1959, and was head of the *raion* legal service in Molchanovsky *raion*, Tomsk *oblast* for a year. From 1960 to 1963 he taught in the faculty of law, Tomsk State University, as an assistant in the department of the theory and history of the state and law. In 1963 he enrolled as a postgraduate student at the T. G. Shevchenko Kiev State University where in 1966 he successfully presented his candidate dissertation on "Subjective views on law of Soviet citizens and their development during the construction of communist society" (LLM). In 1966 he returned to the department of the theory and the history of state and law, in Tomsk, as an assistant and was later promoted to senior lecturer and assistant professor.

He represented Ukraine in the UN commission on human rights. Afterwards, in a competitive election, he entered the institute of state and law, USSR Academy of Sciences, in Moscow, where he stayed ten years. It was there in 1979 that he successfully presented his doctoral dissertation on "The problems of the legal position of the individual in a developed socialist society" (LLD).

He participated in drafting the USSR constitution of 1977 and the RSFSR constitution of 1978 and the draft USSR law on the legal position of foreign citizens in the Soviet Union. After the establishment of the department of constitutional law in the Academy of the Ministry of the Internal Affairs of the USSR, he was invited to head it. Afterwards he set up his own department of state legal disciplines in the higher extra-mural school of law of the USSR Ministry of Internal Affairs and was its head and a professor from 1984 to October 1991. He helped draft the Russian law on citizenship. He is a specialist in the theory of law, constitutions and human rights and has over 250 publications to his name, including two monographs. He has acted as supervisor for 13 doctoral theses.

He was nominated as a member of the Constitutional Court by the parliamentary faction *Smena* (new policy) and was elected on October 29, 1991, at the V Congress of People's Deputies, in the first round of voting. He received 593 votes for and 289 votes against.

In his view the key concerns of the Constitutional Court are the guaranteeing of the functioning of constitutional norms, the dominance of the Russian constitution in the whole Russian legal system, the review by the Court of any legislation, including that of the Russian President, Russian Supreme Soviet and Congress of People's Deputies. The main obstacles to the above are political instability in Russia, unrestricted legal acts of the legal and executive branches of power and the low level of legal consciousness among Russian society. He was awarded the Veteran of Labour medal and the medal for exemplary service. He lives in Moscow.

Vladimir, Russian Orthodox Metropolitan of Kiev and All Ukraine

Born on November 23, 1935 as Viktor Markianovich Sabodan in Khmelnitsky (Khmelnytskyi) *oblast*, where his father worked on a collective farm. He graduated from the Odessa Theological Academy and was a postgraduate student at the Moscow Theological Academy. He successfully presented his master's dissertation in theology (ThM). In 1962 he was consecrated deacon, then priest and took his vows as a monk with the name of Vladimir. In 1966 he was appointed a bishop, then an archbishop, and in 1982 he became a metropolitan; he was a lecturer at the Odessa seminary, later became its rector; appointed deputy head of the Russian theological mission in Jerusalem (1966-68); bishop of Pereslav-Khmelnitsky, and bishop Patriarch Exarch of Ukraine (1968-73); archbishop of Dmitrov, and professor of the Moscow Theological Academy (1973-82). In 1982 he was appointed to the department of Rostov and Novocherkassk and also became metropolitan of Rostov and Novocherkassk, Patriarch exarch of western Europe (1986-87); metropolitan of Rostov and Novocherkassk, head of administration Moscow patriarchate and permanent member of the holy Synod (1987-92). In May 1992 he was appointed metropolitan of Kiev and all Ukraine. He was awarded the order of the Friendship of Peoples.

Vladimir, Russian Orthodox Metropolitan of Kishinev (Chisinau) and Moldova

Born on August 18, 1952 as Nikolai Vasilevich Kantaryan in the village of Klenkovtsa, Khotinsky *raion*, Chernovtsy (Chernivtsi) *oblast*, Ukrainian SSR, into a working-class family. He graduated from the Moscow Theological Seminary and the Moscow Theological Academy. He served in the Black Sea Fleet (1970-73); worked as a chauffeur for the Smolensk diocesan administration (1973-74); was deacon in the Uspensky cathedral, Smolensk; priest and steward (1976-81); priest in the Nicholas cathedral, Chernivtsi (1981-83); secretary of the Chernivtsi diocesan administration (1983-87); and in 1987 he became a monk. In 1988 he was appointed archimandrite; then archbishop of Kishinev and Moldova (1989); archbishop of Kishinev and Moldova (1990-92); and in December 1992 was appointed metropolitan of Kishinev and Moldova.

Vladimir, Russian Orthodox Metropolitan of Pskov and Veliky Luki

Born on May 2, 1929 as Vladimir Savvich Kotlyarov in Aktyubinsk, Kazakh SSR, where his father was an Orthodox deacon. He graduated from the Dzhambul Technical College for Statistics of the USSR Central Statistical Administration, Gosplan; from the Moscow Theological Academy and the Leningrad (St Petersburg) Theological Academy. He began teaching in the Leningrad Theological Seminary in 1959.

In 1962 he took his vows as a monk; he was then appointed deputy head of the Russian theological mission to Jerusalem and a archimandrite; representative of the Moscow patriarchate in the World Council of Churches; bishop of Zvenigorod (1962-64); bishop of Voronezh and Lipetsk (1964-65); bishop of Podolsk (1965-66); bishop of Kirov and Sloboda, (1966-67); bishop of Berlin and central Europe; exarch in Central Europe (1967-70); in 1967 became an archbishop, and was archbishop of Rostov and Novocherkassk (1970-73); archbishop of Irkutsk and Chita and temporary administrator of the Khabarovsk diocese (1973-75); archbishop of Vladimir and Suzdal (1975-80); archbishop of Krasnodar and Kuban (1980-87); archbishop of Pskov and Porkhov (1987-90); and archbishop of Pskov and Veliky Luki (1990-92). He was appointed a metropolitan in 1992 and became metropolitan of Pskov and Veliky Luki.

Vladislavlev, Aleksandr Pavlovich

Chairman of the all-Russian union of renewal.

Born in 1936; Russian; he was a member of the CPSU. He graduated from a technical institute, and he successfully presented his candidate dissertation (PhD) and his doctoral dissertation (DSc). He is a professor, and he was first secretary of the board of scientific and engineering societies of the USSR. In 1989 he was elected a USSR people's deputy as a nominee of the union of scientific and engineering societies. He was a member of the USSR Supreme Soviet committee on international affairs and a member of the committee on education, culture and training. In October 1990 he was elected chairman of the executive committee of the USSR scientific industrial union, and then became first Vice-President of the Russian union of industrialists and entrepreneurs. In May 1992 he played a leading role in the founding of the all-Russian union of renewal and was elected its chairman.

He played an active role in the drafting of the law on entrepreneurship in the USSR. He advocates support for business, the renaissance of the principles of industrial lobbying, protection of the interests of producers and the technological renewal of the country. He proposes the establishment of a public system of the management of scientific technical progress, autonomous economic cost accounting and self-financing of enterprises. He does not believe that the way out of the present crisis can be achieved by deploying only domestic resources.

The crisis in the country has not only touched the economic but also the political and social psychological spheres. He advocates democratization, privatization, the conversion of the defence industry and the acquisition of advanced technology. Foreign investment should not take the form of credits, debts and loans, but should consist of large investment programmes. Russia has not yet the capacity to work with hundreds of billions, hence appropriate legislation should be promulgated, the infrastructure set up and communications networks established. The government's economic reforms should be augmented by the programmes of entrepreneurs, heads of enterprises and directors. Commercial information should be broadcast and the business ignorance and incompetence of many new entrepreneurs overcome.

Vladislavlev adopts a left centrist position, and has criticized the indecisive transition to the market. He demands the re-establishment of the senselessly destroyed vertical lines of communication in the economy and the expansion of market structures. He is in favour of competence, pragmatism, order, common sense and decisiveness in reform policy, and believes that the state should protect entrepreneurs and create a level playing-field for all forms of property. Entrepreneurship has to be rehabilitated in the public mind and embedded in law, and this form of activity afforded high social standing. The population should be provided with social guarantees, such as the control of prices of basic goods during the transition period. All administrative superstructures concerned with redistribution should be dissolved, with enterprises and wholesale trade assuming these functions. He advocates creating conditions which ensure healthy competition among entrepreneurs, the demonopolization of the economy, the reform of finances and money circulation and a review of the rate of tax on enterprise profits and citizens' income.

Real power rests not with the party but with social forces and strata, in particular associations of people, representing a branch of production. He sharply criticized Egor Gaidar and his economic programme, and only complimented him for his courage and decisiveness in jumping into the morass of the economic crisis. A new political course for the conduct of economic reform is needed and its main support is production. In the agrarian sector Vladislavev advocates many different forms of land ownership, but he places his hopes on the state and collective farms. He lives in Moscow.

Vlasov, Yury Vasilevich

Head of the Administration of Vladimir *oblast*, Russian Federation.

Born in 1961; Russian; he was never a member of the CPSU. He graduated from the Institute of Administration, Moscow, and in 1988 successfully presented his candidate dissertation in economics on "The organization of administration in a scientific production association" (PhD (Econ)). He was appointed a junior scientific assistant in the all-Union scientific research institute for foot and mouth disease.

In 1990 he was elected a deputy of Vladimir *oblast* soviet, and at the first session of the soviet he was a candidate for the post of chairman of the permanent commission of the *oblast* soviet on economic reform, self-government and social policy. He was not elected chairman, but became a member of the commission. At the same session he and a group of deputies refused to take part in the voting for chairman of the soviet because there was only one candidate. He joined the renewal group of deputies.

In September 1991, at a session of the soviet, he criticized the behaviour of the soviet and administrative agencies of Vladimir *oblast* during the attempted coup of August 1991. Vlasov and A. P. Andreev, head of the laboratory of the Polimersintez scientific production association, were then proposed to the President as candidates for the post of head of the *oblast* administration and in September 1991 Vlasov was elected deputy chairman of the *oblast* soviet executive committee.

On September 25, 1991 he was appointed head of the administration of Vladimir *oblast* by presidential decree. On assuming office he stated that his main tasks were to promote economic reform and draft an investment programme for the *oblast*, to develop interregional ties to provision Vladimir *oblast* with food, to improve education, health and the development of culture and to set up an *oblast* committee on the use of the environment.

In December 1992 he supported President Yeltsin's proposal at the VII Congress of People's Deputies for a referendum in January 1993 which he regarded as the only correct, constitutional and civilized way of finding a way out of the political crisis. The Congress of People's Deputies had outlived its usefulness and did not display any wisdom in December 1992 when the President presented it with a reasonable compromise. It simply revealed inconsistency and slovenliness and its aim was merely to insult the President. Vlasov lives in the Yurevets workers' settlement, Vladimir *oblast*.

Voinov, Yury Nikolaevich

Russian footballer.

Born in 1931; Russian. He is an Honoured Master of Sport, (1959), and played half back. He began his career in Kaliningrad, Moscow *oblast*; played for Zenit Leningrad (1951-55); and Dinamo Kiev (1956-64). He played 271 games and scored 28 goals, of which 174 games and 22 goals were for Dinamo Kiev and 97 matches and six goals for Zenit Leningrad. He played in the USSR championship winning team in 1961. He played 26 times and scored five goals for the USSR national team between 1954 and 1960, was in the national team which won the European Cup in 1960, and played in the World Cup in 1958. He was manager (trainer) of Dinamo Kiev in 1964; of Chernomorets Odessa (1965-67); Sudostroitel Nikolaev (Mykolaiv) (1970-72), and other Ukrainian teams. He is the author of the book, *The Meridians of Football*.

Volkogonov, Dmitry Antonovich

Member of the Presidential Council of the Russian Federation; Member of the Soviet of Nationalities, Russian Supreme Soviet.

Born on March 21, 1928 in the village of Mangut, Kyrinsky *raion*, Chita *oblast* into an agronomist's family; Russian. He began his military career in the Army in 1949 and was a member of the CPSU from 1951 to 1991. In 1952 he graduated from the Orlovsky Tank College. After graduating he held various posts in the Army over many years. He served in units in the Privolzhsky and Kiev military districts and held various posts in the political administration, including that of the assistant head for *Komsomol* work. Between 1963 and 1966 he studied at the V. I. Lenin Military Political Academy; after graduating he joined the staff of the academy. In 1966 he successfully presented his candidate dissertation on the "Moral development of the personality of the Soviet soldier and the military-technical revolution" (PhD).

In 1971 he successfully presented his doctoral dissertation in philosophy on a "Sociological and gnosiological analysis of the problems of military-ethical theory" (DLitt) and became a professor. From 1969 to 1988 he worked in the main political administration of the Army and Navy as head of department, deputy head of the administration, and was General-Colonel in 1984. He was deputy head of the administration (1984-88) and in 1988 he was appointed head of the institute of military history of the USSR Ministry of Defence. In 1990 he successfully presented his doctoral dissertation in history (DLitt). Volkogonov has written over 20 books and 500 scientific and popular articles on current problems of policy, philosophy and history. A two-volume political biography of Stalin, *The Triumph and the Tragedy*, are among his latest publications.

He was elected a deputy of the RSFSR Supreme Soviet in 1985. He was elected to various Party agencies, delegate to the XXVII and XXVIII Party congresses and the XIX Party conference. He is a member of the board of the philosophical society *Znanie* (knowledge), member of the editorial board of the *Voenno-istorichesky zhurnal* (military historical journal) and the *Znamya* (banner) periodical, and is Vice-President of the international association of military historians. He has been awarded four Soviet and four foreign orders and several literary and scientific awards. His books have been published in many countries.

He was nominated as a candidate for election as an RSFSR people's deputy in the No. 60 Orenburg national territorial district, Orenburg *oblast*, by the collective of the Buguruslan administration for oil and gas boring. During the election campaign he supported the following views: an equivalent rate of exchange between republics; change the way the Union budget is drawn up by reducing the contribution of Russia, since Russia was the only republic whose whole national income was transferred into the state budget. He also supported the revival of Russian villages, especially in the Black Earth Zone. He advocated halting the flow of labour from the land and ensuring the reappearance of its true owner. He supported the transfer of the majority of Union enterprises on Russian territory to Russian jurisdiction, and the transition to cost accounting and self-financing in the republic. It was important to declare Russia a sovereign state within the USSR and to establish a Russian Academy of Sciences. He opposed the selling of land and enterprises to private owners.

The introduction of a free market economy was impossible without some state planning. He called for a struggle against the black economy, and supported the reform of the armed forces and the gradual transition to professional forces. It was important to set up an institute of demography in Russia. In resolving economic and social problems priority should be afforded to mothers, children, schools and the family.

There were nine candidates. In the first round Volkogonov polled 17.9% of the votes and won the second round, polling 46.1% of the votes. His main opponent was Viktor Chernomyrdin, who became Russian Prime Minister in December 1992, member of the Party Central Committee, chairman of the Gasprom state oil concern (called the USSR Ministry of the Gas Industry until the end of 1989), and who supported Nikolai Ryzhkov's (Gorbachev's Prime Minister) proposals for the introduction of a regulated market economy. Chernomyrdin polled 16.6% of the votes in the first round and 42.4% of the votes in the second. Volkogonov was elected a member of the RSFSR Supreme Soviet at the I Congress of People's Deputies (818 voted for and 105 against).

Volkogonov is a member of the Russian Supreme Soviet Soviet of Nationalities and of the Supreme Soviet committee on security, and he is an adviser to the Russian President on defence matters. He was a member of the Parliamentary faction, the "coalition for reform". He is co-chairman of the parliamentary faction, "left centre", the co-ordinator of the Russia deputies' group and is a member of the parliamentary faction, "left centre co-operation". He is married with two daughters, and lives in Moscow.

Volkov, Nikolai Mikhailovich

Head of the Administration of the Jewish Autonomous *oblast*, Russian Federation.

Born in 1951; Russian; member of the CPSU until August 1991. He is a graduate construction engineer, and has been working in the Jewish autonomous *oblast* since 1973. His last job was head of the Birobidzhan agro-industrial construction association.

In March 1990 he was elected a deputy of the Jewish *oblast* soviet of people's deputies unopposed. In August 1991 during the attempted state coup he adopted, in his own words, a democratic position. He was nominated for the post of head of the administration of the *oblast* by many work collectives, supported by the management of enterprises in Birobidzhan and *oblast* and by the majority of deputies in the *oblast* soviet.

On December 14, 1991 he was appointed head of the administration of the Jewish autonomous *oblast* by presidential decree. On assuming office he advocated the fundamental reform of social and economic relations, the most rapid transition to the market, the expansion of the output of goods and services, commercial trade, many different types of ownership in the countryside and development of foreign economic links. He underlined the need for a high sense of responsibility on the part of officials at all levels and the importance of those with economic expertise in administration. He thought that the *oblast*, being part of the republic, had acquired equal rights with other republics and had the opportunity to establish a free, civil society and the renewal of Jewish culture and spirituality.

Russia should be one economic space with unified laws and free producers and there was no point in breaking it up into small states. Basically the state should not concentrate on the rights of nations, which only leads to fascism, but on human rights, and he proposed that the status of the *oblast* be determined by a referendum. In December 1992, during the VII Congress of People's Deputies, Volkov supported President Yeltsin. He lives in Birobidzhan.

Volkov, Vyacheslav Vasilevich

Deputy Head of the Administration of the President of the Russian Federation.

Born in Murmansk; Russian; member of the CPSU from 1978 to August 1991. He completed secondary school and the No. 6 state technical college, where he was active in various groups and his talent for technical creativity, painting and music manifested itself. After graduating he worked as a fitter in sanitation engineering and later served in the Soviet Army. After being demobbed he entered the extra-mural faculty of the Institute of Architecture. He graduated with a diploma as a construction engineer which he obtained in 1976 in the faculty of architecture and production aesthetics. He was a foreman in a reinforced concrete shop, then senior engineer and technologist in the Stroikonstruktsiya combine. In 1980 he graduated from the University of Marxism-Leninism of the Murmansk Party *obkom*, and in 1990 was a member of the Party club, CPSU Democratic platform. He was head of a construction laboratory and until 1990 was head of the agency of inspection of housing and other public buildings.

In early 1990 Volkov was nominated for election as an RSFSR people's deputy in the No. 506 Leninsky territorial district, Murmansk *oblast*. During the election campaign he advocated the democratization and moral regeneration of society, universal human values, humanism and pluralism of views and social justice and respect for human beings. He supported full state sovereignty for the RSFSR, and political and economic sovereignty for all autonomous regions. He raised the question of abolishing residence permits and internal passports and permitting people to choose their place of residence. Other political organizations should be on an equal footing with the CPSU, there should be a standing army, every family should be provided with a flat or house, including individual homes and homes for pensioners in the far north and in central Russia. He advocated the setting up of public mass media, pan-Russian referenda, the amendment of the Russian constitution and the election of deputies who did not compromise themselves during the Stalin and Brezhnev eras.

He called for legislation to strengthen universal human values over class, group and national values. The rights of the individual should take precedence over those of the state and society; people should be the goal and not the means in economic activity. He proposed the adoption of laws on conscience, support for the Russian Orthodox Church, equality for all types of property, including private. He was in favour of regional cost accounting, the establishment of the bases of a market economy and the provision of a minimum level of subsistence for people. He appealed for RSFSR legislation to be reviewed and revised in the light of international treaties on human rights, to remove the political articles in criminal legislation and introduce the concept of environmental crime.

There were seven candidates. Volkov polled 14.67% of the votes in the first round and won the second round, polling 44.31% of the votes. His main opponent was S. L. Serokurov, second secretary of the Murmansk Party *obkom*, who received 18.67% of the votes in the first round and 40.7% in the second.

Volkov is the co-ordinator of the democratic factions in parliament. He worked in the committee on construction, architecture and municipal economy. He is a member of the co-ordinating council of the Democratic Russia parliamentary faction, is one of the founders and leaders of DemRossiya and was an opponent of Vice-President Aleksandr Rutskoi.

On February 1, 1993 Volkov was appointed deputy head of the administration of the President of the Russian Federation by presidential decree. Subordinate to him are the control administration, the department of letters and the centre of information. He advocates a new concept for the work of the apparatus; in addition to its usual functions a political aspect should be added and it should be a source of reliable information for the President. In order to achieve this the administration needs and will be provided with three centres of analysis: general policy, socio-economic questions, and special presidential programmes. He takes it for granted that these centres will have highly qualified specialists and that they will share the President's views on reform. The presidential Council, in Volkov's view, will not be transformed into a "village gathering" when the analytical centres are functioning. The centres will provide direct and interactive links with the presidential Council, influencing its opinions on programmes and proposals. Volkov is married and his home is in Murmansk.

Volsky, Arkady Ivanovich

President of the Russian Union of Industrialists and Entrepreneurs; Co-chairman of the Movement of Democratic Reforms (International).

Born on May 15, 1932 in Dobrusho, Gomel *oblast*; Russian. His father was a front line soldier during the Great Fatherland War (1941-45) and his mother was in a partisan detachment. He was a member of the CPSU from 1958 to August 1991. In 1955 he graduated from the Institute of Steel and Alloys, Moscow. He then became a foreman, senior foreman, head of a section, head of a shop and secretary of the Party committee in the I. A. Likhachev car factory, Moscow. In 1969 he was appointed director of the Kama automobile factory, but only stayed three days before being recalled to work in the Party Central Committee. He was head of the section of automobile machine building, deputy head, and first deputy head of the department of machine building, Party Central Committee.

He was an aide to Leonid Brezhnev when the latter was General Secretary of the CPSU. In 1983 he was an aide on economic questions to Yury Andropov when the latter was General Secretary of the CPSU. In 1985 he was appointed head of the department of machine building, Party Central Committee. In 1988 he became head of department, Party Central Committee, the representative of the Party Central Committee and the Presidium of the USSR Supreme Soviet in Nagorno-Karabakh autonomous *oblast*, Azerbaijan. In 1989 he was appointed chairman of the special regime committee, Nagorno-Karabakh *oblast*. He was a member of the Party Central Committee from 1986 to August 1991, a delegate to the XXVII and XXVIII Party congresses and XIX Party conference. He was the recipient of a USSR state prize and other state awards.

In early 1989 he was nominated for election to the USSR Congress of People's Deputies in the No. 682 Stepanakert (the capital of Nagorno-Karabakh) territorial district, Azerbaijan. He was the only candidate and won in the first round, polling 97% of the votes. In May 1990 he signed the letter by the 24 USSR people's deputies, and leaders of industrial enterprises, about the need to unify the economy at a time when the economic system was collapsing. This was the beginning of the formation of the USSR scientific industrial union. In June 1990 the constituent congress of the USSR scientific industrial union took place and Volsky was elected president. The goal of this new association, according to Volsky, was the defence of the interests of industrialists in a legal but also in a practical sense. When it was registered in September 1991 the union consisted of 1,500 large state enterprises and 39 associations based on various types of ownership. The union convened various meetings of industrialists between 1990 and 1991.

In July 1991 Volsky signed the declaration setting up the movement for democratic reforms, and he was elected co-chairman of the movement for democratic reforms (international). On August 21, 1991, Volsky, in the name of the USSR scientific industrial union, condemned the attempted coup by the Extraordinary Committee and distanced himself from the activities of Tizyakov, a member of the Committee and Volsky's deputy in the union. Volsky was appointed deputy chairman of the committee on the management of the Soviet economy.

In 1992 the USSR scientific industrial union was renamed the Russian union of industrialists and entrepreneurs (RUIE). From it emerged in June 1992 the all-Russian Renewal Party. Volsky's co-chairmen are A. P. Vladislavlev and S. A. Polozkov. In June 1992 the RUIE comprised 2,130 large state enterprises and 39 associations based on various types of ownership. Altogether they accounted for 65% of the industrial output of Russia. In June 1992 the RUIE, together with the Democratic Party of Russia, the all-Russian Renewal Party and the

People's Party, Free Russia, set up the Civic Union bloc. Volsky does not regard the RUIE as an opposition party but a party whose primary task is not to come to power. Its goal is to guarantee the smooth transition to a market economy without industrialists being disadvantaged and no drop in the level of production.

During 1992 Volsky often criticized the policies of the Gaidar government, but this criticism was not aimed at the strategy of the reforms but at the timing and tactics of specific actions and was not accompanied by demands for the resignation of the government. Despite the mass media and various politicians stating many times that the RUIE was after power, Volsky maintains that this is not the case. In September 1992 he was a witness in the case concerning the CPSU in the Constitutional Court of the Russian Federation. He lives in Moscow.

Vorfolomeev, Vladimir Petrovich

Chairman of the Russian Supreme Soviet committee on ecology and the rational use of natural resources.

Born on January 13, 1934 in the village of Stary Ertil, Voronezh *oblast* into a large family. He is Russian, and his father worked on a collective farm. During the Great Fatherland War (1941-45) he worked on a farm and was then evacuated. At the age of 16 he went to Leningrad and became a student at the G. V. Plekhanov Mining Institute; from where he graduated in 1955 and was assigned as a junior scientific assistant to the all-Union Scientific Research Mining Surveying Institute, Leningrad. He took part in sinking new mines in the Kuzbass and the Donbass, and was elected secretary of the *Komsomol* committee. In 1959 he transferred to work in the Leningrad *Komsomol* city committee as instructor in the department of organization; deputy head of a department (1959-61); and second secretary (1961-63), Leningrad *Komsomol* city committee. He was elected second secretary (1963-70); and first secretary (1970-74) of the Pushkino Party *raion* committee; head of the department of the light and food industries, Leningrad Party city committee (1974-76); head of the department of the light and food industries and trade, Leningrad Party city committee (1976); head of the department of the light and food industries, Leningrad Party *obkom* (1976-80); deputy chairman of the executive committee of Leningrad *oblast* soviet of people's deputies (1980-88); and secretary of the committee on the protection of the environment of Leningrad and Leningrad *oblast* (1988-90).

He was nominated for election as an RSFSR people's deputy in the No. 15 Leningrad national territorial district. During the election campaign he suggested that the food problem could be solved by stimulating the initiative of the peasants, ensuring republican and local support for the farms, improving rural supplies and regulating the use of chemical and biological fertilizers. He supported the use of local building materials and traditional methods of wooden construction as solutions to the housing problem. A law was needed to protect the environment and a national state system for the protection of nature should be implemented. All new building construction should be subject to environmental control and a wide-ranging programme of environmental education was needed. Among social problems he emphasized the problems associated with the revival of abandoned villages, health protection, cultural buildings and the restoration of monuments and he believed that education in the RSFSR should be reformed. He advocated political change without violence, the formation of a *Rechtsstaat* (law-governed state), transfer of all power to the soviets, the development of all nations and ethnic groups, and the transformation of Russia into an independent republic.

There were eight candidates. In the first round Vorfolomeev polled 15.3% of the votes and won the second round, polling 42.5% of the votes. His main opponent was Yu. V. Trusov, a Party member and director of the *Lenptitseprom* poultry farming production association, who received 16.3% of the votes in the first round and 40.5% of the votes in the second. Vorfolomeev was elected a member of the RSFSR Supreme Soviet at the I Congress of People's Deputies (731 voted for, 192 voted against). He is a member of the Council of Nationalities. In July 1990 he was elected chairman of a sub-committee and deputy chairman of the Supreme Soviet committee on ecology and the rational use of natural resources, and in 1991 he was elected chairman of the committee. He is a member of the Rossiya parliamentary faction. He is married. His son is a naval officer who has served in submarines and his daughter is a student at St Petersburg State University.

Address: 103274 Moscow, K 274, Krasnopresnenskaya nab., d. 2, Dom Sovetov; *telephone*: Moscow 205 69 48.

Vorobev, Andrei Ivanovich

Minister of Health of the Russian Federation, November 1991 to December 1992.

Born on November 1, 1928 in Moscow into a Russian family. His father, a professor in the No. 1 Institute of Medicine, Moscow, was arrested in 1937 and died in prison. His mother spent many years in exile in the Soviet Union. During the Great Fatherland War he worked as a painter in a special construction unit and as a laboratory assistant in the N. V. Sklifosovsky Institute, Moscow. In 1953 he graduated from the No. 1 Institute of Medicine, Moscow, and worked as a doctor in the *raion* hospital in Volokolamsk, Moscow *oblast*. Between 1956 and 1966 he was clinical assistant and an assistant professor in the faculty of therapeutics of the Central Institute for refresher courses for doctors of the USSR Ministry of Health. From 1966 to 1991 he was engaged in medical research in several scientific research institutes. He is a doctor of medicine (MD), professor and academician; he was a member of the USSR Academy of Medical Sciences. In 1991 he was appointed director of the All-Union Centre of Haematology of the USSR Ministry of Health, director of the Scientific Research Institute of Haematology and Blood Transfusion. In November 1991 he was appointed Minister of Health of the Russian Federation.

Vorobev is a world-class medical specialist and has elaborated an original classification of blood diseases. In 1973 he prepared a classification of leucoses and haemodyalisis of the blood. He made a major contribution to the treatment of radiation sickness, discovering a haematological mechanism in leukaemia and how radiation infects the intestine and stomach. In 1979 he was the first to develop a "biological dose metre" which measured the amount of radiation in the organism as a result of his research on blood and bone marrow, afterwards named the Vorobev system. He was the first in the Soviet Union to develop a method of treating advanced leucosis in children. This method of treatment was severely criticized and opposed by conservatives in the USSR Academy of Medical Sciences and the USSR Ministry of Health. In 1969 during a lecture at Moscow State University a Party scientist contemptuously referred to a well-known geologist called Maksimov as a renegade immigrant, someone who had betrayed the motherland. Vorobev, at that time an unknown scientist, sharply rebuked him by telling him not to speak in such a way about a person he was not qualified to judge.

Vorobev never joined the CPSU. In March 1989 he was elected a USSR people's deputy for the Academy of Medical Sciences and scientific medical societies. Soon after the I Congress he joined the interregional group of deputies but withdrew in October 1989. His political views emerge from his pattern of voting at the congresses. At the II Congress he voted against the election of certain of the deputies from public organizations and restricting the voting rights of particular categories of people. He abstained during the vote on the economic programme of Prime Minister Nikolai Ryzhkov. He voted for the annulment of Article 6 of the Soviet Constitution on the leading role of the CPSU. At the IV Congress he voted against the inclusion on the agenda of the vote of no confidence in the USSR President which had been proposed by the Union group of deputies, and against the retention of the name Soviet Union. He did not support the moratorium on strikes in 1991.

When he became Minister Vorobev did not present a draft proposal for the reform of the Soviet health system and was severely criticized for this by some Russian people's deputies. He took the view that the quickest way to resolve the problems confronting the health services, such as providing medicines and raising the wages of medical workers, was to move to a system of medical insurance, payment for services and greater autonomy for medical institutions. He was dismissed in December 1992 and the new Prime Minister, Viktor Chernomyrdin, chose Eduard Nechaev as his Minister of Health.

Vorobev speaks German and French. His wife is a doctor and they have two adult sons, one is a geologist and the other a doctor. They have grandchildren. Vorobev enjoys history, especially the history of the scientific academies. He was awarded the order of Lenin in 1986 and was a state prize winner in 1978.

Vorobev, Eduard Arkadevich

First deputy Commander-in-Chief of the Land Forces of the Russian Federation. Colonel-General since 1988.

Born in 1938 in Voronezh, into a civil servant's family. Russian. He graduated from the Baku Higher Military Officers' Technical school with a gold medal in 1961; the M. V. Frunze Military Academy in 1971; the Military Academy of the General Staff in 1981. He received a higher military education and was a member of the CPSU till August 1991.

He began his career as officer as a commander of a motorized-rifle platoon. He was known for his excellent professional skills and efforts to improve the methods used in his sub-unit's combat training. He was also politically active in Party and *Komsomol* organizations. Superior officers and political agencies regarded him as a promising officer and he was rapidly promoted. After graduating from the Academy, his record was that of an officer with advanced operational-tactical and military-technical training, aware of the essence of present-day combat and operations. He has held all staff and command posts during his career; at battalion, regimental and divisional level. He was a military army commander, first deputy commander of the Turkestan military district. In 1988 he was appointed commander of the Central group of troops stationed in Czechoslovakia and was responsible for the withdrawal of troops from there. He succeeded in establishing close working relations both with the former communist leaders and the new democratic leaders in Czechoslovakia who came to power in the wake of the "velvet" revolution of 1989. He demonstrated considerable skill in resolving the new political and military-economic problems which arose and revealed a talent for diplomacy. During the revolutionary events of November 1989 the Soviet troops, despite appeals from the orthodox wing of the communist leadership, observed neutrality and did not intervene in Czechoslovak domestic affairs.

From 1990 Col.-Gen. Vorobev was deputy Commander-in-Chief of Land Forces (combat training), head of the chief combat training administration. He was in charge of organizing, elaborating methods and inspecting the combat training of different types of troops and also of helping the KGB and the MVD forces in their study of military disciplines. He proved himself a true military professional, not interested in political issues. Like almost all Soviet generals he was not in favour of national and democratic movements and reformers among CPSU leaders, took a clear pro-communist stand and favoured the maintenance of the USSR. He was elected a USSR people's deputy in the Uzhgorod territorial electoral district, Trans-Carpathian *oblast*, Ukraine, in March 1989. He belonged to the group of military-industrial and Party-government conservatives who were in a majority in the congress.

During the anti-constitutional putsch in August 1991 he was not active and concentrated on his duties. However, in his inner circle he supported demands for the strengthening of law and order in the country. At the end of 1991 and the beginning of 1992 Gen. Vorobev was in charge of elaborating a concept to improve the combat training of general assignment forces during the restructuring of the armed forces. On January 31, 1992, *Krasnaya Zvezda* published an interview with him on "the army in the new conditions: the training process". He was a member of the state commission on the dissolution of the military political agencies, on setting up combat training agencies and structures to deal with personnel after the collapse of the attempted coup. In February 1992 he became deputy commander of the land forces (combat training) of the Unified Armed Forces of the CIS. In August 1992 he was made first deputy Commander-in-Chief of Land Forces.

He does not express his political views in public. He restricts himself to the role of a military professional. He is a convinced advocate of a strong state domestically and of Russia regaining its status as a great power, with an army and navy capable of coping with the demands of present-day war.

There is no information available about Gen. Vorobev's hobbies. He does not speak any foreign language and has not been abroad as a member of an official delegation. He is married with two children. He has been awarded two orders, and medals.

Office address: 103160 Moscow K-160.

Vorobev, Vasily Vasilevich

Head of the Chief Military Budget and Finance Administration of the Ministry of Defence of the Russian Federation. Lieutenant-General.

Born on May 11, 1946 in Gidrotorf, Balakninsk *raion*, Gorky (Nizhny Novgorod) *oblast* into a working-class family. Russian. He graduated from General of the Army A. V. Khrulev Yaroslavl Military Financial Technical School with distinction in 1966; the military faculty of the Moscow Finance Institute in 1974. He received a higher military education with a degree in finance and economics and was a member of the CPSU till August 1991.

He served in the Siberian and Far East military districts, holding the posts of head of financial services of a unit formation, and army. From 1982 he was deputy head of financial services of the Southern group of troops (Hungary); from 1986, head of financial services of the Urals military district and from 1987 of the Far East military district.

He proved to be a good specialist in providing financial means for military activities and had a sound economic training. He was actively involved in the work of CPSU organizations and was elected to Party agencies, which was a *sine qua non* for military commanders of the middle and high level. He enjoyed a good reputation among commanders and political agencies.

In November 1991 he was appointed head of the Central Finance Administration of the USSR Ministry of Defence and was soon promoted to lieutenant-general. His programme for the financial provision of the armed forces during the instability of the economy, budget deficits and devaluation of the ruble was presented in an interview to *Krasnaya Zvezda* on November 16, 1991, entitled "Money for the Army".

From February 1992 he was head of the Central Finance Administration of the United Armed Forces of the CIS. On April 4 he became a member of the State Commission for the establishment of the Ministry of Defence, Army and Navy of the Russian Federation.

According to experts in democratic military organizations, Gen. V. Vorobev is said to be involved in shady transactions such as the selling of stores, the illegal use of financial resources and the construction of country cottages. His name has been mentioned several times in the press in this connection.

In spite of the critical attitude of many democratic movements and organizations and due to the personal support of Marshal Shaposhnikov and the leaders of Russia's Ministry of Defence, Lieut.-Gen. Vasily Vorobev was appointed by President B. Yeltsin's decree, on August 21, 1992, head of the Chief Military Budget and Finance Administration.

He advocates a tough state policy and the transformation of Russia into a great power. He reacts negatively to the democratization of political and social life in the country and in the army. He does not publicize his convictions. He is a conformist in his contacts with top state leaders.

No information is available on his hobbies and interests. He does not speak any foreign language. He has been awarded several orders and medals and is married with two children.

Office address: 103175, Moscow, K-175.

Voronin, Yury Mikhailovich

First deputy Speaker of the Russian Supreme Soviet.

Born in 1939 in Kazan; Russian. He was a member of the CPSU until August 1991. He graduated from the Kazan Institute of Aviation, and successfully presented his candidate dissertation in economics (PhD (Econ)) and his doctoral dissertation in economics (DSc (Econ)). He is an Academician of the Russian Academy of Sciences, and worked in the military industrial complex in several aviation enterprises. He was elected deputy chairman of the Council of Ministers of the Tatar SSR in 1989; in 1990 he became chairman of the commission of the Council of the Republic of the RSFSR Supreme Soviet on the budget, plans, taxes and prices. He was elected an RSFSR people's deputy in March 1990, in November 1991 he was elected deputy speaker of the RSFSR Supreme Soviet and in January 1993 first deputy speaker of the Russian Supreme Soviet. He is also president of the league of the Russian Fatherland.

When Sergei Filatov resigned in January 1993 as first deputy Speaker of the Russian Supreme Soviet he criticized Ruslan Khasbulatov, the Speaker, for conducting a campaign of denigration. Filatov decided to accept the post of head of the presidential administration, and Voronin's election as replacement was regarded as strengthening the position of Khasbulatov in parliament.

Address: 103274 Moscow, K 274, Krasnopresnenskaya nab., d. 2, Dom Sovetov.

Vorontsov, Yuli Mikhailovich

Adviser of the President of the Russian Federation on Foreign Policy.

Born in 1929; member of the CPSU until August 1991, and member of the Party Central Committee from 1981. He graduated from the State Institute of International Relations, Moscow (MGIMO). He joined the USSR Ministry of Foreign Affairs in 1953 and also represented the Soviet Union in the United States. He began his diplomatic career as a reviewer, and then in 1970 was appointed counsellor at the Soviet embassy in Washington DC. In 1977 he became Soviet ambassador in India and in 1983 ambassador in Paris. In 1986 he was appointed first deputy USSR Minister of Foreign Affairs, with special responsibility for arms negotiations. From October 10, 1988 to September 1989 he was ambassador in Afghanistan, and in 1990 he became the permanent representative of the Soviet Union in the United Nations, having served there previously (1954-58 and 1963-65).

In January 1992 Vorontsov was appointed state adviser of the President of the Russian Federation on foreign affairs. By decree of the President of August 8, 1992 he became adviser of the President on foreign policy.

Vorontsov's whole professional life was devoted to the USSR Ministry of Foreign Affairs where he was known as a "diehard" diplomat. There are those who think that he would like to become the "shadow" head of Russian foreign policy and the fact that he joined the presidential apparatus to head Russian foreign policy has not surprised any observers. On the other hand Andrei Kozyrev, the Russian Minister of Foreign Affairs, strikes the President as a loyal politician but, in Yeltsin's view, he lacks the experience to conduct a carefully thought out policy in foreign economic issues. "We must strengthen Russian diplomacy by attracting real professionals", was Gennady Burbulis's comment when he heard of Vorontsov's promotion to presidential adviser. Vorontsov lives in Moscow.

Voznyak, Vasily Yakovlevich

Chairman of the state committee of the Russian Federation on the social protection of citizens and the rehabilitation of territory affected by Chernobyl and other radiation catastrophes; Minister.

Born on January 2, 1944 in the village of Vasilevka, Tyvrovsky *raion*, Vinnitsa (Vinnytsia) *oblast*, Ukrainian SSR, where his father was an officer worker. He was a member of the CPSU until August 1991. He graduated from the Nemirovo Construction Technical College, Vinnitsa *oblast* and the Lvov (Lviv) Polytechnical Institute, and he successfully presented his candidate dissertation in economics (PhD (Econ)). In 1961 he began working as a foreman, later as a technical leader of an inter-collective farm construction organization in the Mordovian ASSR; in 1967 he was appointed chief engineer, and head of the construction administration of the Shaimgazstroi trust, USSR Ministry of the Gas Industry, Khanty-Mansy autonomous *okrug*, Tyumen *oblast*.

In the following years he occupied various responsible posts in Tyumen *oblast* and in Moscow. He was head of the department responsible for eliminating the consequences of the Chernobyl nuclear accident, USSR Council of Ministers (1986-90); and first deputy chairman of the committee for eliminating the consequences of the Chernobyl nuclear accident of the USSR Cabinet of Ministers (1990-91). From January to June 1992 he was Vice-President of the Stroitransgaz joint stock company; and in July 1992 chairman of the state committee of the Russian Federation on the social protection of citizens and the rehabilitation of territory affected by Chernobyl and other catastrophes. He is married with two children, and lives in Moscow.

Vysotsky, Evgeny Vasilevich

Head of the Chief Administration for Personnel Training and Assignment of the Ministry of Defence of the Russian Federation. Lieutenant-General.

Born on April 4, 1947 in Belyov, Tula *oblast*, into a civil servant's family. Russian. He worked in the town of Termez, Surkhandarinskaya *oblast*, Uzbekistan. His military career began in 1966. He graduated from the Tashkent Higher Tank Officers Technical School in 1970; the M. V. Frunze Military Academy in 1978; the Military Academy of the General Staff in 1988. He received a higher military education and was a member of the CPSU from 1970 to August 1991.

After graduating from technical school he served in the Southern group of troops (Hungary) as a platoon, company commander, and Chief of Staff of a tank battalion. He demonstrated command abilities and a talent for organizing combat training of sub-units. He actively participated in the CPSU organizations. His reputation with superior officers and Party-political agencies was good.

From 1978 he was Chief of Staff, then a commander of a motorized-rifle regiment. Lieut.-Col. E. Vysotsky's record as an officer was that of one with sound operational-tactical and military-technical training and aware of the requirements of modern warfare.

He was in one of the first shock groups of the Soviet army to invade Afghanistan. The regiment under Vysotsky participated in combat operations against the *mujahidin* and in pacifying the civil population.

For his participation in the Afghan war he was made Hero of the Soviet Union on September 20, 1982. It was in Afghanistan that Vysotsky came to know well the present Russian military leaders, his name was often mentioned in the mass media and popularized in the army and public at large.

In the 1980s he held officer posts in land forces and headed formations. In 1990 he was appointed an army commander. From 1991 he was the first deputy

Commander-in-Chief of the Trans-Baikal military district. At the time of the anti-constitutional putsch in August 1991 he fulfilled his immediate duties, was not politically active and did not take sides.

By President B. Yeltsin's decree on August 21, 1991 he was appointed head of Chief Administration for Personnel Training and Assignment. According to experts among democratic military organizations, Vysotsky's promotion was due to the personal support of the Minister of Defence, Pavel Grachev, and his inner circle — all veterans of the Afghan war. Gen. E. Vysotsky is in charge of personnel policy in the army and navy, of the training of professional military men of various categories and of supervising military educational establishments.

Some experts fear that Vysotsky will adopt the policy of dismissing democratically-minded, independent-thinking officers from the armed forces.

By conviction he is a disciplined military professional, who tries to be above politics; he is a career man advocating the supremacy of the state. He is a conformist in his relations with those in power. He enjoys authority in military circles as a combat general with good professional skills. Like most Afghan war participants he is devoted to the veteran syndrome, sure of his superiority and experience over civil society. He has close personal ties with the present Russian military leaders who have been through the Afghan war.

He advocates the supremacy of the state, the creation of an up-to-date Russian army and Russia regaining its image of a great state.

He has expressed his views in an interview with *Krasnaya Zvezda* on September 15, 1991 in an article entitled "We Need a Strong Russia".

There is no information about his hobbies. He does not speak any foreign language and he has not been abroad on an official visit. He was awarded the Gold Star of the Hero of the Soviet Union, orders of Lenin, of the Red Star, "For Service to the motherland in the armed forces of the USSR", 3rd class, and medals. He is married with a son.

Office address: 103175, Moscow, K-175.

Yablokov, Aleksei Vladimirovich

Adviser of the President of the Russian Federation on Ecology and the Protection of Health.

Born in 1933; member of the CPSU until August 1991. He graduated from the faculty of biology, Moscow State University, then joined the N. K. Koltsov Institute of the Biology of Development, Moscow, in 1956 and became the chairman of the ichthyological commission of the USSR Ministry of the Fish Industry. In 1959 he successfully presented his candidate dissertation in biology on the "morphological peculiarities of the white whale, Delphinapterus leucas Pall" (PhD). In 1966 he successfully presented his doctoral dissertation in biology on "the experience of studying alterations in the structure of the organs of mammals" (DSc). He is an eminent biologist and ichthyologist.

In 1989 he was appointed deputy chairman of the USSR Supreme Soviet committee on ecology, and in 1991 he was made a state adviser of the RSFSR on ecology and health. On August 8, 1992, by decree of the President of the Russian Federation, Yablokov became adviser of the President on ecology and the protection of nature.

He regards his main tasks to be the drafting of proposals on the basics of policy in Russia on the protection of the environment, the health of the population and ecological security. It is necessary to agree ecological policy in Russia with that in other states, including the successor states of the Soviet Union, draft proposals on how to improve ecological legislation and raise the effectiveness of state administration in ecology, and use of nature and health. He is also responsible for drafting government programmes, decisions of the Russian President on ecology and health, arranging contacts and interaction between the President and the leaders of international organizations and foreign states on ecological security, the protection of the environment, the rational use of nature and the health of the population. He regards himself as the President's consultant, a supervisor of the implementation of his decrees and a proposer of the establishment of expert councils with domestic and foreign specialists. He lives in Moscow.

Yakimov, Anatoly Mikhailovich

Head of the Administration of Evenky Autonomous *okrug*, Russian Federation.

Born in 1949 in Novosibirsk; member of the CPSU from 1985 to August 1991. After secondary school he entered the Geological Technical College, Novosibirsk and then worked in Kirgizia (Kyrgyzstan). He served in the Soviet Army, and graduated from the institute of the oil chemical and gas industry, Moscow, as an external student. He became acquainted with Krasnoyarsk *krai* for the first time in 1971, and conducted geophysical research along the Podkamennaya, Nizhnyaya Tunguska and Vivi rivers. Then at various times he worked in Dudinka, Igarka, Turukhansk, Eniseisk, Boguchany, Vanavar, Baikit, Osharovo and other places in Krasnoyarsk *krai*. He has been living for the last eight years in the village of Tura where he was assigned to organize a geophysical expedition. Until May 1990 he was head of the Evenky geophysical expedition.

At the first session of the Evenky *okrug* soviet of people's deputies in May 1990 he was elected chairman of the executive committee. At an extraordinary session of the Evenky *okrug* soviet of people's deputies in September 1991 the deputies stated that, although the *okrug* soviet executive committee had not decided to support the actions of the Extraordinary Committee, Yakimov had not yet made clear his position on the attempted coup in August.

On December 18, 1991 he was appointed head of the administration of the Evenky autonomous *okrug* by presidential decree. On assuming office he stated that he viewed the democratic methods of administration as the most reasonable. He welcomed and supported the programme of economic reform adopted by the government, but he saw difficulties in implementing it in the northern territories. The most important reform was work at the local level and he opposed the standardized approach to the regions of the country which all had different conditions. His most important responsibility was to solve the problems of the small nations of the north and to fight for them so as to bring to the native peoples of Evenkia the achievements of culture, education and medicine.

In December 1992 he stated that the VII Congress of People's Deputies was of use only to the opponents of reform and the present government which had broken off half-way through its programme was not in a position to complete its reforms. He believed that neither the people nor the deputies regarded the results of the congress as a way out of the crisis and that failing to extend the President's special powers was premature. It would have been much more appropriate to confirm Egor Gaidar as Prime Minister for a certain period. Yakimov is married and his wife is a geophysicist. They have two children and their daughter is a student in the geophysics department of Novosibirsk State University. He is a keen photographer and likes to read literature.

Yakovlev, Aleksandr Nikolaevich

Co-chairman of the Movement for Democratic Reforms (International).

Born on December 2, 1923 in the village of Korolevo, Yaroslavl *raion*, Yaroslavl *oblast*; Russian; member of the CPSU from 1944 to August 1991. He served in the Soviet Army from 1941 to 1943 and saw action at the front during the Great Fatherland War, but was demobbed after being severely wounded. In 1946 he graduated from the faculty of history, K. D. Ushinsky State Pedagogical Institute, Yaroslavl. He was engaged in the apparatus of the Yaroslavl *oblast* Party committee (*obkom*) (1946-48 and 1950-53), and from 1948 to 1950 he was head of department of the Yaroslavl *oblast* newspaper, *Severny rabochii* (northern worker), senior lecturer in the *oblast* Party school. Between 1953 and 1956 he was an instructor, and head of sector in the apparatus of the Party Central Committee, then from 1957 to 1958 was a student at Columbia University, New York.

In 1960 he graduated from the Academy of Social Sciences of the Party Central Committee, and successfully presented his candidate dissertation in history on American studies (PhD). From 1960 he was in the apparatus of the Party Central Committee and in 1965 became first deputy head of the department of propaganda and agitation for the RSFSR of the Party Central Committee, and later first deputy head of the department of propaganda of the Party Central Committee. In 1967 he successfully presented his doctoral dissertation in history on "The ideology of American imperialism" (DLitt). In the 1960s he published several monographs on the US: *The Poverty of Thought of the Apologists for War* (1961); *The Old Myth about the "New*

World" (1962); *Order to Kill* (1965); *The Ideology of American Imperialism* (1967); *The US: From Greatness to Sickness* (1969); *Pax Americana: Imperialist Ideology: Sources, Doctrines* (1969); *On the Steps of War and Deception* (1971). Between 1971 and 1976 he was elected a member of the Party central revision commission, but fell foul of the Brezhnev administration by being too critical of its weaknesses. The solution adopted was to exile him, and from 1973 to 1983 he was Soviet ambassador to Canada. He met Mikhail Gorbachev during the latter's visit to Canada and made a lasting impression on the future General Secretary.

From 1983 to 1985 he was director of the institute of world economics and international relations, USSR Academy of Sciences. In 1984 he was elected a corresponding member of the USSR Academy of Sciences, and the same year he published *From Truman to Reagan: Doctrines and Realities of the Nuclear Age*. In 1985 he returned to work in the apparatus of the Party Central Committee, accepting Gorbachev's invitation. He was a key figure in the battles in the Party secretariat and Politburo for the implementation of *perestroika* and *glasnost*. From 1985 to 1986 he was head of the department of propaganda and as such was almost always in conflict with Egor Ligachev, who headed the secretariat. Ligachev belonged to the moderate reform wing of the Party while Yakovlev was on the radical wing. Ligachev had grave doubts about the advisability of *glasnost* since he regarded it as providing a licence for malcontents to attack the Party and for nationalists to grind their own anti-Russian axes. In 1986 Yakovlev became a secretary of the Party Central Committee and in 1988 chairman of the Party Central Committee commission on international policy. In 1987 he was elected to the Party Politburo and from 1988 to 1990 was chairman of the Politburo commission on the additional study of materials on the repression which had occurred between 1930 and 1953.

During this period Yakovlev published several books devoted to the problems of renewing the country, its relations with foreign states and the new foreign political thinking: *The Yalta Conference 1945: The Lessons of History* (1985); *Capitalism at the End of the Century* (1987); *Perestroika and the Contemporary World* (1990); *Realism: The Basis for Perestroika* (1990).

In 1989 he was nominated as a USSR people's deputy by the CPSU and elected. At the I Congress of People's Deputies he was elected to the commission on the legal and political evaluation of the German-Soviet treaties of August 1939 and its consequences. At the first meeting of the commission he was elected chairman. In December 1989, at the II Congress of People's Deputies, Yakovlev spoke on the conclusions of the commission and for the first time in the USSR confirmed the existence of the secret protocols to the German-Soviet treaties of August 1939. On the evidence presented, the congress passed a motion condemning the secret agreements between the USSR and Germany. In 1990 Yakovlev became a member of the USSR presidential Council. The same year he was elected an Academician of the USSR Academy of Sciences.

In July 1991 he signed the declaration establishing the movement of democratic reforms for which he was expelled from the CPSU by the committee of Party control in August 1991. He is co-chairman of the movement for democratic reforms (international). During the attempted coup in August 1991 he immediately criticized the Extraordinary Committee and its policies and took part in the defence of the Russian House of Soviets.

In December 1992, by decree of the President of the Russian Federation, he was appointed chairman of the commission for the rehabilitation of the victims of political repression. His latest books have been devoted to rethinking the historical experience of the USSR, *perestroika* and reform in the Soviet Union: *The Torture of Reading About Existence: Perestroika: Hopes and Reality* (1991); *Introduction. Collapse. Epilogue (A Critique of Marxist-Leninist Theory)* (1992). He is married and has grown-up children and grandchildren. He lives in Moscow.

Yakovlev, Egor Vladimirovich

Leading journalist.

Born in 1930 in Moscow. His father was chairman of the Odessa (Odesa) *guberniya* Cheka, later deputy chairman of the all-Ukrainian Cheka and chairman of the timber export company (*eksportles*). His mother was a descendant of the old noble family, Poluboyarinov. He is Russian, and was a member of the CPSU until January 13, 1991. He graduated from the Moscow State Archive Institute in 1954, and was second secretary of the *raion Komsomol* committee, Moscow, editor and correspondent of *Moskovskaya pravda*, and editor-in-chief of *Zhurnalist*, the magazine of the Writers Union (1967). He was appointed to the post by Valentin Falin, then head of the Novosti Press Agency. In the mid-1970s he was an *Izvestiya* correspondent and then their Prague correspondent (1984-85). From 1986 to September 1991 he was editor-in-chief of *Moskovskie novosti* with a brief to publish material that no other newspaper dared to print. He transformed the newspaper which was seen as a propaganda sheet (put out in eight foreign languages) for foreign readers into the most famous voice of *perestroika* and *glasnost*. Its print run reached 1.2 million, and it became enormously popular and prestigious. He was a member of the USSR union of writers, union of cinematographers and union of journalists.

He published books on Richard Sorge, *Comrade Sorge: Documents and Memoirs* (1965) and on the life and times of V. I. Lenin: *Keep your Soul on your Wing* (1977); *Portrait and Time* (1979); *Lenin: Features of a Biography* (1979; *I Hear the Step of the Past* (1985); *The First Third of Life* (1985); *A Difficult Job: Being a Revolutionary* (1986); *Day and Life* (1988); books on the history of the pioneer organization, the *Komsomol*, the revolutionary movement and the Soviet state: *A Tale Written under Duress* (1960); *On Times and One's Self: The First Generation of Communists Speak* (1963); *Drum* (1978); *The Symbols of the Land of Soviets: Coat of Arms, Flag and National Anthem of the USSR* (1984); books of documentary prose: *The Eighth Day* (1963); *I am Going with You* (1965); *Meetings Beyond the Horizon* (1976); *Moscow-Siberia-the Pacific Ocean* (1978); *On Fire and Without it* (1982); *Through Time and Distance* (1984).

He is the co-author of the script of the documentary film, *V. I. Lenin. Pages of His Life*.

In 1989 he was elected a USSR people's deputy as a nominee of the USSR union of cinematographers, and was a member of the interregional group of deputies. In January 1991 he resigned in protest against the use of force in the Baltic states, and in August 1991 he was the journalist behind the publication of *Obshchaya gazeta* (Common newspaper) which appeared only once, on August 21, 1991, consisting of material from 11 newspapers, directed against the Extraordinary Committee.

In August 1991 he became a member of the council of the President of the USSR. On August 27, 1991 he was appointed chairman of the all-Union state television and radio information company (later the inter-state television and radio company, Ostankino), replacing Gorbachev's appointee Kravchenko. On December 27, 1991 the company came under the control of President Yeltsin and the Russian government, and in November 1992, by presidential decree, he was removed because of deficiencies in the presentation of information on events in North Ossetia and Ingushetia, which was under a state of emergency. In December 1992 the decree was amended to read "in connection with his transfer to other work" and then the editors of the 11 newspapers surrendered their rights as founders of *Obshchaya gazeta* and transferred them to Yakovlev. He is chairman of the RTV-press joint stock company.

He is married and his son Vladimir is editor-in-chief of the highly successful business newspaper, *Kommersant*, which also appears in English translation. Yakovlev lives in Moscow.

Yakovlev, Veniamin Fedorovich

Chairman of the Higher Court of Arbitration of the Russian Federation.

Born in 1932 in Petukhovo, Kurgan *oblast*; Russian; member of the CPSU until August 1991. In 1953 he graduated from the R. A. Rudenko Institute of Law, Sverdlovsk (Ekaterinburg). He worked for seven years in Yakutia as a lecturer and director of a law school, Procurator responsible for the supervision of the review of citizens' cases in the courts and senior assistant of the Procurator of the Yakut autonomous republic. From 1960 to 1987 he was in the R. A. Rudenko Institute of Law, Sverdlovsk, where he was a postgraduate student, successfully presenting his candidate dissertation on legal education (LLM). He was head of department, dean of faculty and pro-rector of the institute. He specialized in problems of legal education, civil and family law, housing legislation and the legal aspects of the co-operative movement, and successfully presented his doctoral dissertation (LLD). He is a professor.

From 1987 to 1989 he was director of the all-Union scientific research institute of the Soviet state construction and legislation. He was concerned with problems of the national state structure of the USSR and legal reform and supported those who favoured a law-governed state. In 1989 he was appointed USSR Minister of

Justice, and in 1991 became the chief USSR state arbitrator and simultaneously the chairman of the USSR Higher Arbitration Court, playing a leading role in setting it up.

In January 1992 he was made chairman of the Higher Arbitration Court of the Russian Federation. The main task of the arbitration court is to maintain honest and legal relations in business since the latter is the guarantee of economic reform in Russia. All enterprises, irrespective of types of ownership, can have their cases heard by the court. Precise procedure during sessions has to be agreed, decisions should be collective and a sound legal basis established by the court. The arbitration courts have to ensure that they have the resources to carry out their duties, to train staff and to prevent interference by administrative agencies and those concerned with crime. He lives in Moscow.

Yanaev, Gennady Ivanovich

Member of the Extraordinary Committee.

Born on August 27, 1937 in the village of Perevoz, Perevoz *raion*, Gorky (Nizhny Novgorod) *oblast* into a peasant family; Russian; member of the CPSU from 1962 to August 1991. In 1959 he graduated from Gorky Agricultural Institute and in 1967 from the all-Union extra-mural institute of law. He began working in 1959 in Gorky *oblast* as head of a mechanized group, Rabotinsky Repair Tractor Station, and later became its chief engineer and then head of the Knyaginsky department of Selkhoztekhnika. In 1963 he was elected second and in 1966 first secretary of the Gorky *oblast* committee of the *Komsomol*. In 1968 he became chairman of the committee of youth organizations in the Soviet Union.

In 1980 he was elected deputy chairman of the Presidium of the union of Soviet societies of friendship and cultural links with foreign countries, and in 1986 was elected secretary for international questions of the all-Union central union of trade unions. He worked in the administrative department of the International Labour Organization (ILO). In 1989 he became deputy chairman, and from April to June 1990 chairman of the all-Union central union of trade unions. He was a delegate to the XXIII, XXIV and XXVIII Party congresses. In 1989 he was nominated for election as a USSR people's deputy by the USSR trade unions and was elected to the USSR Supreme Soviet. He worked in the USSR Supreme Soviet committee on international problems. In January 1991 he was elected Vice-President of the USSR, but was not Gorbachev's first choice in this new post. He is the recipient of two orders of the Red Banner of Labour, two orders of the badge of honour and medals.

He was a member of the Extraordinary Committee in August 1991. On August 19 he published a decree stating that he was assuming the responsibilities of President of the USSR and that a state of emergency was being introduced in various regions of the country. He made a poor impression during the first public appearance of the Committee, carried live on TV, when his hands were visibly shaking. He was arrested on August 22, 1991 and during the investigation confined to the *Matrosskaya tishina* isolator. He and the other conspirators were later released. When free Yanaev lost no opportunity to implicate President Gorbachev in the plot, averring that he was party to the deliberations, and took part in various demonstrations. He is married and his wife, Roza Alekseevna, is an agronomist and economist. They have two daughters: Svetlana is a psychologist who works in Moscow and Mariya is a student at the all-Union institute of law. Their grandson Nikolai is 12 years old. Yanaev lives in Moscow.

Yandurin, Dias Khatipovich

Co-Chairman of the Bashkir National Congress, Republic of Bashkortostan, Russian Federation.

Born on January 20, 1940 in the village of Maloyaz, Salavatsky *raion*, Bashkir ASSR, into a peasant family. He has a brother and two sisters. He is a graduate of the faculty of history, Bashkir State University, then became a postgraduate student and in 1973 successfully presented his candidate dissertation in history (specializing in the history of the CPSU) on the activities of the Bashkir Party organization in attracting the working masses to state and economic construction, 1926–32 (PhD). In 1973 he was appointed to the department of the history of the CPSU, Bashkir State University. He is at present assistant professor of the history of the motherland at the university.

He is an active member of the Ural Bashkir National Party and the Bashkir National Congress. In December 1991, at the VI extraordinary all-Bashkir congress, he was elected co-chairman of the Bashkir National Congress. He has published over 30 academic articles and about 10 pieces on public and political themes in the republican mass media. He is a supporter of an independent, democratic Bashkortostan.

He is married. His wife, Tanzilya, is a kindergarten teacher, and a daughter works on a collective farm. They have five children. Another daughter, Gulnara, graduated from the faculty of history, Bashkir State University. The other children are still at school. The eldest son, who was a student in the department of languages at the university, was killed while working in a student construction brigade in 1984. Yandurin's hobby is fishing.

Address: Ufa, ul. M. Gafuri, Dom 27/1, kv. 13.

Yaroshinskaya (Zgerskaya), Alla Aleksandrovna

Member of the Council of the President of the Russian Federation.

Born in 1953; Ukrainian; she was not a member of the CPSU. From 1976, after graduating from university, she worked as a correspondent in the department of industry and capital construction of the *oblast* newspaper, *Radyanska Zhitomirshchina* (Soviet Zhitomir).

In early 1989 she was nominated for election as a USSR people's deputy by the collectives of the *Promavtomatika* production association, the *Elektroizmeritel* production association and the *Avtozapchast* enterprise in the No. 446 Zhitomir territorial district, Ukraine. In the election campaign she supported *perestroika* and the platform of the XIX Party conference and the principles of socialist power to the people. She promised to base herself on the interests of the state, the interests of the electors and the principles of socialist justice. In order to fulfil the housing 2000 programme she proposed the establishment of a group of specialists to examine the situation thoroughly, to make public all the violations of housing legislation and to remove those who were illegally occupying apartments.

She proposed the re-registration of dwelling space, and an inventory of the state and co-operative housing fund and the transfer of the housing administrative offices to social and cultural organizations. She called for the transformation of the agricultural labourer into a full owner of the land, the transfer of land to village residents on advantageous terms and the social re-equipment of the villages. She supported the development of the leasing system, private farming, the rebirth of state-village co-operatives, territorial self-administration, self-provision and self-financing. She called for less food to be delivered to the centre, the end of the secrecy surrounding the *oblast* budget and to keep prices of meat and milk low. In the political sphere she advocated the establishment of a *Rechtsstaat* (law governed state), the reform of the legal system, and the guaranteeing of equality before the law for all.

She called for the abolition of all privileges of those who were in the nomenclature and the end of discrimination against those who were not in the Party and religious believers. She advocated the abolition of the internal passport system, for a free choice as regards place of residence, freedom of expression, the press, association, meetings and demonstrations. She stood for free and equal elections, for smaller armed forces and the provision of social guarantees to those being demobbed and going into the reserve, and for a shortening of national service. There should be a national system of supervision of important decisions and she opposed the subordination of the press in the *oblast* exclusively to the *oblast* party committee. She advocated real press freedom and *glasnost*.

There were five candidates and Yaroshinskaya won in the first round. Her main opponent was F. S. Kulikovich, general director of the *Zhitomirzhelezobeton* production association. Her political activity began in the interregional group of deputies in the USSR parliament and she actively participated in the polemics on the law on the press in the USSR. She fought for more open information about the Chernobyl disaster. She wrote two books on this subject, *Chernobyl and Us* and *Chernobyl. Top Secret* and over a hundred articles. In November 1992, in Stockholm, she received the minor Nobel prize, for a worthy human life. She plans to establish a private international fund and an independent centre for research into the influence of small doses of radiation on humans and the environment with her prize money.

She worked in the Russian Ministry of Press and Information as head of the main administration of the mass media and still combines this activity with her duties in the presidential Council. She regards her main task as helping the press to survive, especially the regional press, and states that even though she is engaged on government work she is still a journalist, working on practical issues. At the end of 1992 she thought the time had arrived to make changes in the Russian government. Gaidar, the outgoing Prime Minister, had done his duty but his potential was not yet exhausted. Mistakes were inevitable but it would have been possible to escape the "extreme shock therapy". She became a member of the presidential Council in February 1993. She lives in Moscow.

Yarov, Yury Fedorovich

Deputy Russian Prime Minister.

Born in 1942 in Leningrad into a Russian family; member of the CPSU until August 1991. He graduated from the Lensovet Leningrad Technological Institute as a chemical engineer, and began work as head of a shift, then later became a design engineer and head of a shop in a Baltic factory. From 1968 to 1976 he worked in the Burevestnik enterprise in Gatchina, Leningrad *oblast* and was elected secretary of the Party committee. Between 1976 and 1978 he was head of the industry and transport department of the Gatchina city Party committee (*gorkom*). In 1978 he was appointed director of the Burevestnik enterprise and in 1985 was elected first secretary of Gatchina Party *gorkom*. He was elected a people's deputy of the Leningrad *oblast* soviet on several occasions.

In June 1987 he became deputy chairman, and in April 1990 chairman, of the Leningrad *oblast* soviet executive committee. In March 1990 he was elected a RSFSR people's deputy in the No. 142 territorial district, Leningrad *oblast* and became a member of the RSFSR Supreme Soviet, but did not join any bloc or faction. In November 1991 he was appointed deputy speaker of the Russian Supreme Soviet, specializing on international relations, and then became the representative of the President of Russia in St Petersburg and Leningrad *oblast*. In the current political climate he is a centrist. He has the reputation of being a politician who takes decisions calmly and after careful consideration. He has received state awards.

In May 1992 Yarov became deputy Russian Prime Minister. He accepted the post since he believed that with the economy in its present state work in the executive was more difficult but it would have been irresponsible to have remained as a deputy. He continued as first deputy Prime Minister in the new Chernomyrdin government in December 1992 and is responsible for socio-economic questions of interregional relations and regional aspects of economic reform. He is married with two grown-up children and grandchildren, and lives in Moscow.

Yaushev, Karim Karamovich

Chairman of the Tatar Public Centre, Republic of Bashkortostan, Russian Federation.

Born on March 2, 1948 in the village of Tukmak-Karan, Tuimazinsky *raion*, Bashkir ASSR. A Tatar. His father, Karam, was a collective farm worker and his mother, Khamida, also worked on a collective farm.

He graduated from the faculty of mathematics, Bashkir State University, as a mathematician and computer scientist. As such he worked in the central statistical administration, Bashkir ASSR. At the first *kurultai* (congress) of the Tatar Public centre of Bashkiria (TPC), in January 1989, he was elected its responsible secretary and at the third *kurultai*, in November 1989, he was elected its chairman.

He often published articles in the republican media on public and political affairs. He advocates equal rights for the Tatar people in the Republic of Bashkortostan, the realization of their national and cultural needs and the raising of the status of the Tatar language to that of a state language alongside Bashkir and Russian. He is a supporter of the resolution, adopted by the TPC of Bashkiria in 1990, to establish a Ufa *oblast* (republic) within the Russian Federation on the territory of the former Ufa *guberniya*. In 1990 he headed a TPC delegation to Moscow which handed over a list of proposals on this question, addressed to President Boris Yeltsin.

He is married to Almira Abdullovna, who is a member of the famous Remeevy gold-mine owning family. They have three children of school age.

Address: Ufa, ul. Blagoev, Dom. 21, kv. 8.

Yavlinsky, Grigory Alekseevich

Chairman of the centre for political and economic research (Epitsentr).

Born in 1952 in Lvov (Lviv). His father was a pupil of the F. E. Dzerzhinsky commune and was head of the reception and distribution centre for children in Lvov. He is Russian, and was a member of the CPSU until August 1991. Grigory only completed nine classes of secondary school before beginning work, but in 1973 he graduated from the G. V. Plekhanov Institute of the National Economy, Moscow. He immediately became a postgraduate student under the supervision of Academician Leonid Abalkin and in 1978 he successfully presented his candidate dissertation in economics on "Perfecting the distribution of the labour of the workers in the chemical industry" (PhD (Econ)).

He worked in the institute for the management of the coal industry, then became head of sector in the scientific research institute of labour. In 1982 he wrote the book *Problems in Perfecting the Economic Mechanism in the USSR*, in which he concluded that the existing economic mechanism in the USSR could not be perfected. The book was taken from the printers, the printed copies destroyed and the manuscript seized. From 1984 to 1985 he was forced to undergo treatment in a closed hospital.

In 1987 he participated in the drafting of the USSR law on state enterprises. Yavlinsky's draft was rejected by the commission, headed by Gaidar Aliev, and the latter ordered an investigation into Yavlinsky's work. After Abalkin was appointed deputy chairman of the USSR Council of Ministers in June 1989, Yavlinsky was invited to head the department of the state commission on economic reform of the USSR Council of Ministers. In 1989 he participated in drafting an economic programme for the government of Ryzhkov and Abalkin, but the material prepared by the group under his direction was not included in the draft.

In early 1990 M. Zadornov, A. Mikhailov, Yavlinsky and others of like mind began drafting a programme for the economic stabilization and radical economic reform in the USSR. After Boris Yeltsin and Ivan Silaev became acquainted with the draft programme Yavlinsky was appointed, on July 14, 1990, deputy chairman of the RSFSR Council of Ministers with instructions to continue working on the programme. The same month an agreement was reached between President Mikhail Gorbachev, Boris Yeltsin, Nikolai Ryzhkov and Ivan Silaev on the drafting of joint measures to promote economic reform. Yavlinsky and Academician S. S. Shatalin were appointed to head the working group. By the middle of August 1990 the draft programme was ready and also about 20 draft laws, and the whole programme became known as the 500-day programme. In September 1990 President Mikhail Gorbachev presented the programme as his proposal for the overcoming of the crisis and the reform of the economy to the USSR Supreme Soviet. However, Prime Minister Nikolai Ryzhkov opposed the plan and countered it by presenting his own "basic directions" and did not exclude the possibility of his resignation if the USSR government's programme was rejected.

The result was a compromise between the 500-day programme and the basic directions, the USSR President's programme, but this did not satisfy Yavlinsky. On October 17, 1990 he resigned as deputy chairman of the RSFSR Council of Ministers and declined President Gorbachev's invitation that he continue working on draft economic reforms in the USSR. In early 1991 the centre for political and economic research (Epitsentr), headed by Yavlinsky, began work. In April 1991 he received an official invitation from the US Department of State to participate in a meeting of the council of the Group of 7. Yavlinsky's speech aroused great interest and served as the basis for a joint programme, and for a chance agreement. Backed by President Gorbachev and Evgeny Primakov, Yavlinsky, in May 1991, at Harvard University, together with a group of Soviet and Western economists drafted a proposal for the transition of the Soviet planned economy to a market economy and its integration into the world economy. This was to be discussed at the Group of 7 meeting in London in July 1991 at which President Mikhail Gorbachev would also be present. Yavlinsky also took part in the meeting.

At the end of August 1991, by decree of the USSR President, Yavlinsky was appointed chairman of the committee on the operational management of the USSR economy, responsible for the drafting and implementation of economic reform. In September 1991 he drafted a treaty on the economic union of the republics, but Yavlinsky's programme, based on the retention of the USSR as a single economic space, became inoperative after the collapse of the USSR in December 1991.

In late 1991 the Epitsentr signed a contract of co-operation with the administration of Nizhny Novgorod *oblast* and from January 1992 became advisers to B. E. Nemtsov, head of administration of the *oblast* on the implementation of economic reform. The timing and means for implementation were different from those prevailing elsewhere in Russia; what was particular about the reforms in Nizhny Novgorod *oblast* was the smoother transition to the liberalization of prices, the provision of social guarantees to the population, the earlier increases in the price of energy and the more rapid implementation of small privatization in association with the European Bank for Reconstruction and Development (EBRD). A branch of Epitsentr began work in Nizhny Novgorod in June 1992.

The experience of the first year's work in the region is presented in the book *Nizhny Novgorod Prologue* by Yavlinsky and other members of Epitsentr in 1993. Yavlinsky is married and has two sons. As a young man he was a boxer. He speaks English and lives in Moscow.

Yavorivsky, Volodymyr Oleksandrovych

Chairman of the Ukrainian Supreme Soviet Committee on Chernobyl; Leader of the Democratic Party of Ukraine.

Born into a Ukrainian peasant's family in the south of what is now Vinnytsia *oblast* in east-central Ukraine in 1942. He was educated at Odesa State University, and thereafter worked as a Ukrainian translator. He is also the author of several well-known works such as *Vichni kortelisy* and *Mariia z ploynom v kintsi stolittia*. With other stalwarts of the Writers' Union of Ukraine, he was one of the main initiators behind the creation of *Rukh* in the winter of 1988-89, serving as the chairman of the original co-ordinating committee that drew up the programme published in February 1989.

In 1989 he was elected a Ukrainian people's deputy to the USSR Congress of People's Deputies and in the 1990 Ukrainian elections was elected to represent

Svitlovodskyi *raion*, Kirovohrad *oblast*, in central Ukraine (on the first round). He also left the Communist Party at the same time as his literary colleagues Ivan Drach and Dmytro Pavlychko in March 1990.

At the founding congress of the Democratic Party of Ukraine in December 1990 he stood for the position of leader, but only received 63 votes against 413 for Yurii Badzio. At first, his connections with the party declined in intensity, but in the long gap before the party's second congress in December 1992 many members grew dissatisfied with Badzio's leadership, and Yavorivskyi duly replaced him at the congress. He then publicly called for a formal union between the two largest nationalist parties, the Democrats and Republicans, but it is doubtful whether he would be prepared to play second fiddle to the better organized Republican Party in such a union.

Yavorivskyi has long campaigned against the authorities' negligence and cover-up of the Chernobyl disaster, and has headed the Supreme Soviet's committee for the clean-up of the disaster since 1990. He has therefore earned a high profile abroad through his campaigning on behalf of the victims of Chernobyl. He also sits on the influential Supreme Soviet Presidium. Critics say that he has been deradicalized by his many foreign trips. Certainly he had increasingly sided with Drach and Pavlychko in their support for Kravchuk.

Home address: Kiev, Vul. Chkalova 52, kv. 84; *telephone*: (home) Kiev 216 8591.

Yazov, Dmitry Timofeevich

Member of the Extraordinary Committee.

Born on November 8, 1923 in the village of Yazovo, Okoneshnikovsky *raion*, Omsk *oblast*; Russian; member of the CPSU from 1944 to August 1991. He entered the Soviet Army in 1941, and in 1942 graduated from the RSFSR Supreme Soviet Infantry Technical School, Moscow. He fought in the Great Fatherland War as a platoon commander and deputy company commander on the Volkhovisk and Leningrad fronts. After the war he was commander of a company, battalion and regiment and had various staff appointments. In 1956 he graduated from the M. V. Frunze Military Academy and in 1967 the Military Academy of the General Staff of the USSR Armed Forces.

In 1967 he was appointed commander of a division, then an army corps and finally an army, and in 1976 became deputy commander of the Far East military district. In 1979 he was appointed commander of the central group of forces; from 1980 to 1984 he was commander of the armies of the Central Asian military district and from 1984 to 1987 of the Far East military district. President Gorbachev met him during a tour of the Far East and this led, in January 1987, to his promotion to deputy USSR Minister of Defence and head of the main administration of cadres. Gorbachev entrusted him with the task of *perestroika* in the officer corps. In May 1987 he became USSR Minister of Defence.

Yazov was a delegate to the XXVI and XXVII Party congresses and the XIX Party conference. Between 1981 and 1987 he was a candidate member and in 1987 a full member of the Party Central Committee. He was a candidate member of the Party Politburo from June 1987 to July 1990. He was elected a USSR people's deputy in 1981 and 1986. He was awarded two orders of Lenin, orders of the Red Banner, the Great Fatherland War, 1st class, and the Red Star for service to the motherland in the USSR Armed Forces, 3rd class, and medals. In May 1987 Gorbachev made him USSR Minister of Defence, succeeding Marshal Sergei Sokolov whose standing had been affected by the flight of Mathias Rust, a German amateur pilot, through Soviet air defences to land near Red Square. On March 24, 1990 Yazov was appointed to the USSR presidential Council. He was promoted to Marshal of the Soviet Union on April 28, 1990.

He was a member of the Emergency Committee and ordered the troops into Moscow. He was arrested on August 21, 1991 and dismissed as USSR Minister of Defence the following day. He was charged with high treason and during the investigation was incarcerated in the *Matrosskaya tishina* isolator. In the immediate post-coup period he was depressed and would not face the TV cameras, but his spirits rose later and he stoutly defended his actions. He and the other conspirators were later released. He participated in demonstrations against the Yeltsin government. He lives in Moscow.

Yeltsin, Boris Nikolaevich

President of Russia.

Born on February 1, 1931 in the village of Butka, Sverdlovsk (Ekaterinburg) *oblast* into a Russian family. His father was a peasant who became a construction worker to escape life under collectivization and when growing up Yeltsin had few comforts, living in workers' huts on construction sites near Perm. As a result he has as an adult never really been at home in hotels and similar establishments. As a young man he was a very keen sportsman, specializing in volleyball and boxing,but later he lost part of his left thumb in a shooting accident. He delighted in exploring the *taiga*, the cold forests of the north, with friends. He entered the Kirov Urals Polytechnical Institute to study construction and graduated in 1955. His examination project was the building of a TV transmission tower. In order to gain practical experience he worked for a short time in each of the building trades, from bricklayer to crane driver.

Between 1955 and 1963 he was a foreman, supervisor, engineer and head of Yuzhgorstroi trust, and became a member of the CPSU in 1961. From 1963 to 1968 he was chief engineer, then head of the Sverdlovsk home construction combine, and in 1968 he transferred to work in the Sverdlovsk Party *oblast* committee (*obkom*). In 1975 he was elected secretary for industry and, in 1976, first secretary, of Sverdlovsk *obkom*. He was elected people's deputy of the USSR Supreme Soviet in 1974. During the night of September 17-18,

1977, under his direction, the house of the merchant Ipatev, a fine example of 19th-century architecture, in which Tsar Nicholas II and his family had been murdered in July 1918, and which was under the protection of the state, was razed to the ground. In his memoirs Yeltsin states that Moscow had instructed him to destroy the house which had become a place of pilgrimage. The site was covered in asphalt and a chapel now stands there. He states that after reading the secret Party files on the murder of the Royal family his heart was heavy. At the XXVI Party congress in 1981 Yeltsin was elected a member of the Central Committee (CC), and he became a popular leader in Sverdlovsk, not least for his energetic style and success in building dwellings for the inhabitants.

During the Great Fatherland War (1941-45) over 500 enterprises had been evacuated to the region and little housing had been built for the workers, who existed only in huts and barracks. The war had transformed Sverdlovsk and it became one of the great industrial centres of the Urals. Yeltsin, like his later adversaries Egor Ligachev and Mikhail Gorbachev, was not tainted with corruption and would have known Gorbachev as a fellow *obkom* first secretary. Between 1984 and 1988 Yeltsin was a member of the Presidium of the USSR Supreme Soviet and when Gorbachev became Party General Secretary in March 1985 he was among the first to be summoned to Moscow to work in Gorbachev's team. He became head of the construction department of the CC secretariat in June 1985. Gorbachev wanted his own man to run the Moscow Party organization (*gorkom*) and he chose Yeltsin, who took over in December 1985. The previous long-term incumbent, Viktor Grishin, a contender for Party leadership in March 1985, had allowed corruption to spread and even boasted that he was untouchable. Yeltsin began a vigorous campaign to clean up the capital and sacked many leading officials.

He was wont to travel to work by bus or underground and became immensely popular with Muscovites, being seen as the people's champion. However, the powerful Moscow *nomenklatura* united against him and he was reported to have put a tail on many of them, which was reminiscent of the bad old Stalinist days and made Yeltsin even more unpopular with the Party élite and officials. He became the target of an orchestrated campaign to denigrate him and all he was striving to do. In his memoirs he points out that he removed over 60% of Party *raion* (*raikom*) first secretaries in Moscow, but Gorbachev cleared out over two thirds of incumbent *obkom* first secretaries around the country. A special target of Yeltsin's ire were Party privileges. He gave up his official car and dacha and expected others to do the same. However he enjoyed the support of Gorbachev, having been made a candidate member of the Politburo at the XXVII Party congress in March 1986.

During the summer of 1987 he forwarded Gorbachev a letter at his summer retreat in the Crimea expressing a wish to resign. Gorbachev persuaded him to rethink but Yeltsin could not curb his tongue and the matter came to a head in October 1987, when Ligachev, the chief accuser, launched into a bitter tirade against Yeltsin at a Politburo meeting. Ligachev was alarmed, among other things, by the damage that Yeltsin's campaign against Party privilege was doing to the Party's authority. He had broken one of the golden rules of Politburo life: never reveal in public the splits which exist in the top Party institution. The vilification of Yeltsin was expressed in language reminiscent of the 1930s, but Gorbachev did not come to his ally's aid. The pressure told on Yeltsin and he suffered a heart attack on November 9, 1987. While recovering he was brought before the Politburo and on November 13 was arraigned before Moscow *gorkom*. Yeltsin's main point was that his detractors were sabotaging *perestroika* and slowing the pace of reform. In no fit state to defend himself, even though his dismissal was a foregone conclusion, Yeltsin appealed for objectivity to be respected when reporting the whole affair. This went unheeded and the press presented him as someone who had abjectly surrendered. To add a touch of irony to the situation, the whole operation of bringing him before the Politburo and Moscow *gorkom* while he was still ill was supervised by General Yury Plekhanov, head of the 9th directorate of the KGB, and this was the same General Plekhanov who arrived at Foros, in the Crimea, on August 18, 1991 to arrest President Mikhail Gorbachev. Yeltsin was not banished from Moscow or political life, but was given a top post in construction which afforded him the rank of minister. In February 1988, the Politburo, at the instigation of Gorbachev, removed him as a candidate member, but, once again, he escaped relatively lightly, being allowed to remain a member of the Party CC. Public disillusionment with the pace of reform reinforced Yeltsin's popularity. Normally excluded from expressing his anti-establishment views in the official Soviet media, he countered by giving interviews to foreign correspondents. These met with a mixed reception in the West which by then was largely on Gorbachev's side. The Western world would have preferred him to desist from criticizing the fine work that Gorbachev was trying to do.

Yeltsin was elected a delegate, for Karelia, to the XIX Party conference in June 1988 despite attempts by the leadership to prevent it. Yeltsin had a feeling for publicity and during President Reagan's visit to Moscow in June 1988, he gave TV interviews to foreign correspondents in which he criticized the opponents of *perestroika*, not omitting a sideswipe at Ligachev personally. The XIX Party conference was carried live on Soviet TV, and on the last day Yeltsin asked for the floor and delivered a detailed apologia of his position, requesting that the Party rehabilitate him completely. He added that he would like this immediately, not posthumously. This was a fine piece of cheek and went down wonderfully well with the population who were able to hear Yeltsin's side of the argument for the first time. Overnight be became the most popular politician in the country. The XIX conference, besides emasculating the CC secretariat and depriving the Party of its co-ordinating role in the country, also agreed to the first nationwide multi-candidate elections since the immediate post-revolutionary years to the USSR Congress of People's Deputies.

On March 27, 1989 Yeltsin won a stunning victory in the Council of Nationalities constituency No. 1 in Moscow. This was the largest constituency in the land and he received 89.6% of the votes, thereby demolishing the official communist candidate. There was little likelihood that the overwhelmingly communist-dominated congress would elect Yeltsin to the Supreme Soviet, the standing parliament. However, the careful work of Gorbachev and the leadership was vitiated by a deputy from Omsk who had been elected to the Supreme Soviet. He proposed that Boris Nikolaevich should replace him and although Gorbachev consulted Lukyanov, a lawyer, they could find no legal objection to the move.

Hence Yeltsin made the Supreme Soviet where he and other leading radicals, such as Academician Andrei Sakharov, had a national platform for the first time to pillory the failings of *perestroika*. Yeltsin was elected chairman of the committee for construction and architecture of the USSR Supreme Soviet and a member of the Presidium of the USSR Supreme Soviet. In July 1989, at the first conference of the interregional group of deputies, he was elected one of the five co-chairmen. Another was Academician Andrei Sakharov. Yeltsin thereby became one of the leaders of the parliamentary opposition in the USSR, and was also active in the Democratic Platform within the CPSU. However as far as the official media were concerned, Yeltsin was *persona non grata*. During a private visit to the US in September 1989, several official newspapers reprinted an article from an Italian newspaper which had written much about Yeltsin's drinking. It was claimed that to him America was one long bar. This produced a howl of protest in Moscow and the official press backtracked.

In March 1990 Yeltsin was elected to the RSFSR Congress of People's Deputies for Sverdlovsk (Ekaterinburg) and on May 25, 1990, despite many manoeuvres inspired by the Kremlin, Speaker. Together with other radicals he walked out of the XXVIII Party congress and resigned from the Party on July 12, 1990. He did not need the Party any more, as for the first time since the 1920s an alternative power base to the Party had opened up. This was the Russian parliament which he used as an instrument to downgrade the authority of the Soviet Union and thereby that of Gorbachev and the CPSU. Many radical politicians came over to Yeltsin, including the pro-market economists, after Gorbachev had turned his back on the 500-day programme in October 1990. Many economists kept a foot in both camps but Yeltsin grasped every opportunity to declare his commitment to the market and democracy. The Russian parliament passed legislation promoting the market and Yeltsin stated that Russia would unilaterally go ahead with radical reforms. This was mainly rhetoric because of the closely-knit Soviet economy, but Russia did dominate economic activity in the USSR.

Gorbachev held a referendum on March 17, 1991 and a majority of the voters accepted the President's concept of a new Union of sovereign states. However, extra questions were added in various republics and Yeltsin grasped the opportunity to ask Russians if they were in favour of a directly elected Russian President. They did and Yeltsin was duly elected on June 12, 1991, choosing Aleksandr Rutskoi as his Vice-President. They trounced the official candidates, Nikolai Ryzhkov and General Boris Gromov, and four other contenders. Yeltsin's hour arrived when the Extraordinary Committee, headed by Vladimir Kryuchkov of the KGB, Marshal Dmitry Yazov, Minister of Defence and Boris Pugo, Minister of the Interior, and fronted by the apparently inebriated and nervous Gennady Yanaev (USSR Vice-President), launched their ill-planned and incompetently implemented attempted coup, at 6 am Moscow time, on August 19, 1991.

Yeltsin made his way to the Russian White House, the seat of the Russian government, daring soldiers to stop him but appealing to them to remain loyal to Gorbachev. He displayed great personal courage and rallied opposition to the putsch. As a democratically elected President he declared that he and Gorbachev were in charge, and demanded the release of Gorbachev from Foros and his return to Moscow. All decrees and orders of the Extraordinary Committee were unilaterally declared null and void. Yeltsin was able to present the attempted coup as an assault on Russia and called on all Russians to defend the country. He was aided by the refusal of leading military and KGB officers to obey instructions and this fatally weakened the putschists. He became an heroic figure in Russia and the world, and outmanoeuvred Kryuchkov by demanding that both fly to the Crimea to see Gorbachev.

It was Rutskoi who flew to the Crimea but Kryuchkov and his associates had left their lair and became vulnerable to arrest, which the Vice-President ordered after his return with Gorbachev to Moscow. Yeltsin had saved Gorbachev but it was only a tactical manoeuvre. When the Soviet President returned to Moscow it had become the capital of Russia. Yeltsin now demonstrated that he was the master and humiliated Gorbachev in the Russian parliament. Gorbachev was now a lame duck President, although he tried everything he knew to bring a new Union of sovereign states into existence. Yeltsin banned the activities of the CPSU and in November banned the Party. (This decision was overturned by the Russian constitutional court in November 1992.) When Gorbachev formally resigned on December 25, 1991 he confirmed that he had handed over control of nuclear weapons to Yeltsin. The hammer and sickle was hauled down and replaced by the Russian tricolour, and Yeltsin remembered it as the most memorable day of his life. With the USSR gone Russia was quick to step into its shoes, taking over Soviet embassies world-wide and the USSR seat on international organizations, including the Soviet Union's seat on the UN Security Council. Yeltsin met the world's leaders and impressed them with his grasp of foreign affairs, but also asked for economic help.

The end of the Soviet Union presented Russia with an identity crisis. Where were the natural frontiers of Russia? In the 1920s Uzbekistan and Turkmenistan had been part of Russia, as had Kazakhstan until the 1930s. Russia had to redefine itself and found it a painful exercise. Is Russia in Europe or Asia or neither? Who is a Russian? Someone who is an ethnic Russian or someone who speaks Russian? What about the 25 million Russians who live outside Russia in the former USSR? Russia was the leading nuclear power but Ukraine, Belarus and Kazakhstan were also nuclear powers. Was the CIS to be a confederation of sovereign states or a vehicle for Russia to dominate the others? Yeltsin was as perplexed as other Russians by these questions and, on reflection, he missed a great opportunity to clarify certain key questions in the immediate post-coup period.

Was Russia to have a presidential or a parliamentary system of government? What was the relationship between President and parliament? Was the government to be subordinate to the President or the parliament? Had a Constituent Assembly been called in late 1991 the elected delegates would have adopted a new constitution which was favourable to the President, but this opportunity was neglected, never to recur, probably because of a lack of understanding of constitutional practice and the importance of political institutions. Valuable time was also squandered on the variant of economic reform to be adopted. The victory of Egor Gaidar meant that Russia would go it alone and stimulate conflict with other states. Liberalization (freeing prices) and stabilization (tight money policy and credit control) were launched in January 1992 and met with mixed fortunes. The government discovered that it did not have control of the money supply since the Central Bank was answerable to the parliament and not the government.

The central statistical office was in the same position, and also CIS members would not agree to a central bank controlling emission of money and credit since each new state had its own central bank and wished to promote its own economic policies. This meant providing vast amounts of credit to their enterprises to acquire goods elsewhere, especially Russia. The government did have some influence over the Central Bank until the summer but the powerful industry lobby, spearheaded by Civic Union in parliament, gradually gained the upper hand. Civic Union argued that a tight credit policy would bankrupt most enterprises and provoke civil war, but Viktor Gerashchenko, formerly head of the USSR State Bank, took over and expanded credit at a stunning rate.

Yeltsin had to pay dearly for not dissolving the Russian Congress of People's Deputies, elected in March 1990 and overwhelmingly conservative. The VI congress in April 1992 was a turning-point, when it was able to force various concessions out of the President. He stood down as Prime Minister and had to accept three new deputy Prime Ministers from the industrial lobby.

Yeltsin appointed Egor Gaidar as acting Prime Minister until the next congress. Another weakness was that support for him in parliament was dwindling as the economy declined and those below the poverty line increased in number. By early 1993 about one third of Muscovites were below the poverty line, and he may have regretted his decision not to found a presidential party to rally support for a move to the market and democracy. The Russian constitution, the 1978 version with over 250 amendments, declared the Congress of People's Deputies to be the supreme legislative body. Over time parliament promulgated laws and decrees but so too did the President. Parliament claimed that presidential laws and decrees were not constitutional and hence need not be implemented, which suited the vast majority of administrators outside Moscow since they were not wedded to either a market economy or democracy.

By late 1992 creeping paralysis was overtaking the government as it found it could not legislate through parliament and presidential power was diminishing fast. Thus Yeltsin decided on drastic action at the VII Congress of People's Deputies in December 1992. He discussed the possibility of disbanding the congress and ruling direct with the military. Reportedly it declined to support him and at the congress it and the militia made plain that they would obey the constitution and would not meddle in politics. At the congress Yeltsin threatened deputies with dissolution unless they compromised with him.

A major reason for the impasse were the skilful tactics of Ruslan Khasbulatov, the Speaker. During the attempted coup he had been a close ally of Yeltsin, but gradually ambition drove a wedge between them and by late 1992 open warfare had broken out between them. A tactic which misfired was to deprive the congress of a quorum, but only about 15% of deputies supported the President. He made concessions in an effort to secure Gaidar's endorsement by the congress but to no avail. With Valery Zorkin, the chairman of the Constitutional Court mediating, it was agreed that congress would then consider three nominations. Gaidar received fewest votes and Yeltsin was obliged to drop him and propose Viktor Chernomyrdin, a representative of Civic Union and the industrial lobby, as his Prime Minister. Yeltsin also called for a referendum on April 11, 1993 to ask the population if it preferred Yeltsin or parliament as ruler and whether it was in favour of private ownership of land. The new government turned out to be pro-reform and Boris Fedorov, the Russian director of the European Bank for Reconstruction and Development in London, who was a strong advocate of the market, took over as deputy Prime Minister for macroeconomic policy. Immediately after the congress Yeltsin flew off to China but cut his visit short when it appeared that Chernomyrdin was going to sack the pro-reform ministers.

Russia's relations with Ukraine provoked much anxiety as Kiev accused Moscow of treating it like a colony and not as an equal sovereign state. Ukraine was economically dependent on Russia, especially for oil, natural gas and timber, and most Ukrainian enterprises obtained their inputs from Russian companies. Rows were frequent and a major one erupted over ownership of the Black Sea Fleet. Both claimed it and eventually an uneasy compromise was reached placing it in joint ownership for three years.

The Crimea, Russian until 1956, was also reclaimed, though never by Yeltsin but by his Vice-President Aleksandr Rutskoi and the Russian parliament. Nuclear weapons were another sore issue, with Ukraine wanting international compensation and guarantees before it handed them over to Russia. During 1992 Russian CIS policy gradually changed. By the end of 1992 the CIS consisted of an inner core, dominated by Russia, and an outer core, led by Ukraine. Russia began to assert its interests as the ruble zone was restricted to those states which would accept Russian leadership in monetary and credit policy. Those which would not accede to Russian requests were told that they would have to pay world market prices for their imports from Russia. Russia's relations with Belarus and Kazakhstan were excellent since these states were accommodating, but Ukraine continued to regard Russia as an imperialist power. The presence of the Russian 14th army in Moldova was resented by the Moldovan government and it intervened to help ethnic Russians during fighting in Pridnestrovie. Yeltsin helped to defuse the situation, but was not completely in control of the Russian military. This also applied to Georgia, where South Ossetia and Abkhazia sought to leave Georgia and Tbilisi accused Russia of aiding the rebels. Yeltsin met Eduard Shevardnadze, the Georgian head of state, several times to stop the fighting. The Chechen-Ingush republic split into two and Russia lost practically all influence in Chechnia.

The treaty formally bringing into existence the Russian Federation was signed by almost all republics and regions on March 31, 1992, but the two important exceptions were Tatarstan and Chechnia, both of which were oil-rich and claimed independence. The oil-producing regions set up their own organization and attempted to retain as much of the oil revenue as possible. This was a major problem for Moscow as regions tried to gain more and more control over their economic activities.

Russia's foreign policy after the attempted coup was dominated by relations with the US and the West. The race to a market economy needed the support and aid of the International Monetary Fund (IMF), the World Bank, the Group of 7 (the most advanced Western states and Japan) and the European Community. The Bush administration promised much and delivered very little, as there were two main schools of thought battling for dominance in Washington. One was that a weak Russia, riven by internal strife, placed the US in a dominant position. The other argued that America should help to bring about the birth of a market economy and democracy in Russia since it would permit lower defence spending and would enhance world security.

The IMF promised US$24 billion but expended little. Organizations always imposed conditions, such as keeping inflation and the budget deficit down, which a Russian government lacks the skill and expertise to implement. In June 1992 Presidents Bush and Yeltsin, in Washington, signed START 2, which foresaw a dramatic reduction in arms arsenals by the end of the century. However START 2 was negotiated only by Russia and America, even though its contents affected Belarus, Kazakhstan and Ukraine. Yeltsin scored a public relations success by promising to find any surviving Americans in the Gulag (the labour camps). He used the archives to denigrate relentlessly the Soviet past, for instance documents on the Katyn murders were handed over to the Poles and it was officially accepted for the first time that they had all been ordered by Stalin. It was revealed that more Soviet soldiers had died at Stalingrad from November 1942 to January 1943 than Germans. The purpose of this was to underline the callous disrespect for human life which was typical of the Soviet era. As living standards tumbled in Russia citizens had to be warned against glorifying the dreadful past. Russian foreign policy gradually changed during 1992.

Yeltsin visited China, South Korea and India to demonstrate that Russia was also an Asian power. He was making concessions to the Eurasian school of thought which emphasized that Russia should have a balanced policy, not favouring either East or West. There were those, especially in Civic Union, who were impressed by the Chinese model, the Korean model and other east Asian approaches to economic plenty. Yeltsin's relations with the military were sometimes strained, as they represented the most powerful, disciplined social force in society. Arms sales to rebel areas and to Serbia took place without Yeltsin's knowledge or permission. Many in the military would have preferred force to be used to dominate the former Soviet Union, especially to support those Russians living outside Russia. They were also unhappy with Russia siding with the US against Serbia, and a majority in the Russian parliament also shared these views as well. Nevertheless Yeltsin could not retreat to the former Soviet Union; his only way was forward to the market and this meant trying to prise money out of the West. His closest ally in Europe was Germany.

Yeltsin appeared to lose self-confidence between December 1992 and April 1993. He did not pursue a consistent line and dismayed radical supporters by seeking compromises with the conservatives. This period of uncertainty ended on April 25, 1993 when Russia's voters gave their verdict on the post-communist record of the President. The referendum posed four questions. Initially parliament had ruled that all four had to receive 50% of the total electorate to be regarded as positive but the Constitutional Court overruled this and stated that on the first two questions, only 50% of those who voted on the day was needed. On the first question, a vote of confidence in the President, Yeltsin polled 58.7%; on the second, about approval of the social and economic record of the government since 1992, 53% voted in favour; on the third questions, on early elections for the presidency, 49.5% were in favour; and on the fourth, on early elections for the parliament, 67.2% were in agreement. The turnout was 64.5%. This was a welcome boost for the President and a defeat for Ruslan Khasbulatov and the parliament who had expected the population to reject the President and his policies. In many cities and regions, more voted for him than in the 1991 presidential election, and these included Moscow and Moscow *oblast*, St Petersburg and Leningrad *oblast*. The President then moved to introduce a new constitution, and parliamentary elections by the autumn of 1993.

Yudin, Nikolai Pavlovich

Acting Head of the Administration of Orlov *oblast*, Russian Federation.

Born in 1938; Russian; member of the CPSU until August 1991. Until 1990 he was director of the SPTU-18 enterprise, Mtsensk, Orlov *oblast*, and in November 1991 he was one of the initiators of the creation in Mtsensk of a branch of the National Party, Free Russia.

In 1990 he was elected a deputy of the Mtsensk city soviet and advocated improving the administrative apparatus and renewing cadres, giving preference to the financing of social programmes, the transfer of power to the soviets, strengthening the agencies of law and order and supervision of co-operatives. In March 1990 he was elected chairman of the Mtsensk village soviet, receiving 68.6% of the votes and thereby defeating his only opponent. He regarded the main functions of the city soviet to be the strengthening of the authority of Soviet power, the expansion of housing, the development of culture and education and the enhancement of law and order.

In August 1991, after failing to receive any instructions from the *oblast* state authorities, he independently established contact with the RSFSR Supreme Soviet and President and declared that only the decrees of the RSFSR President and the decisions of the RSFSR Supreme Soviet were valid on the territory of Orlov *oblast*. On August 31 at a session of the Orlov *oblast* soviet he sharply criticized the lack of activity of the *oblast* soviet and soviet executive committee during the attempted coup.

In November 1991, at a session of the *oblast* soviet, he presented his programme as a candidate for the post of head of the administration of the *oblast*. He regarded the fundamental tasks to be finding a solution to the food problem, increasing the output of consumer goods, developing municipal housing, creating a social base of support for economic reform and restoring state and patriotic ideas. There were two candidates for the post of head of administration, and Yudin received 38 out of 129 votes. The chairman of the Orlov *oblast* soviet executive committee received 86 votes and was proposed to the President for confirmation as head of the administration of Orlov *oblast*, being the only candidate.

However, on October 5, 1991 Yudin was appointed acting head of the administration of Orlov *oblast* by presidential decree. In December 1992, during the VII Congress of People's Deputies, he spoke of the mistakes of the Russian government of Egor Gaidar in implementing economic reforms. The present reforms could not succeed since they were random and did not take objective circumstances into account. The population had to be warned about the effect of reforms and guarantees of social security provided. He lives in Mtsensk, Orlov *oblast*.

Yukhnovskyi, Ihor Rafailovych

First Vice-Prime Minister of Ukraine to March 1993.

Born into a Ukrainian family in 1925 in Kniahynyn in what is now Rivne *oblast*. After service in the Great Fatherland War (1941-45), and a spell working as a miner, he was educated at Lviv State University as a physicist. He successfully presented his candidate dissertation in physical and mathematical sciences (PhD) and his doctoral dissertation (DSc), and was elected a member of the Ukrainian Academy of Sciences. An urbane and popular personality, he was a leading moderating influence and opponent of narrow-minded nationalism in the opposition movement during 1988 to 1990. He was elected people's deputy for Chervonoarmiiskyi *raion*, Lviv *oblast*, on the first ballot in March 1990.

From May 1990 until December 1991 he headed the opposition People's Council faction in the Ukrainian parliament, and also headed the committee on education and science (and was therefore an *ex officio* member of the Presidium). He has remained formally non-party, but his candidature for the Ukrainian presidency in December 1991 was supported by the PDRU, when he came a disappointing fifth (eclipsed by more populist candidates) with 554,719 votes or 1.74% of the total. In 1992 he maintained a loose association with the *New Ukraine* movement.

In March 1992, as part of Kravchuk's general bridge-building to the opposition, Yukhnovskyi was appointed to head the scientific and technical section of the short-lived presidential *Duma*, and in October 1992 was appointed first Vice-Premier (with residual special responsibility for scientific issues) to emphasize the "technocratic" face of Kuchma's new government. In January

1993 he was entrusted with co-ordinating international technical assistance to Ukraine.

He soon found his efforts to root out official corruption (especially in the Ministry of Health) obstructed, however, and he was the target of constant criticism from the neo-socialist left. He also strongly opposed the government's inflationary policies, particularly the granting of huge subsidies to agriculture. An intellectual and polite man, he seemed to find such political struggles faintly sordid, and resigned in protest in March 1993.

Official address: 252008 Kiev, Vul. M. Hrushevskoho 12/2; *telephone*: Kiev 293 7442.

Yuldashev, Shavkat Mukhitdinovich

Speaker (Chairman) of the Supreme Soviet of the Republic of Uzbekistan.

Born on September 20, 1943 in Namangan, Uzbek SSR. He graduated in 1969 from the Institute of Power Engineering, Moscow and in 1980 from the Academy of Social Sciences of the CPSU Central Committee, where he successfully presented his candidate dissertation in economics (PhD (Econ)). He began work in 1961 as a metal worker in the Namangan spinning and weaving factory, Pyatiletka, and then in 1969 and 1970 he was senior engineer in the scientific research institute on electronics, Uzbek Academy of Sciences in Tashkent.

From 1970 to 1974 he was a foreman, senior controller, and senior engineer of the Uzbek Elektroterm production association; head of production, and chief engineer of the electrical engineering workshops; and director of the Namangansvet production enterprise, Namangan. In 1974 he transferred to Party and soviet work in Namangan: as an instructor, deputy head, and head of department, Namangan *oblast* committee, Communist Party of Uzbekistan (CPUzbek); chairman of the Sovetsky *raion* soviet executive committee; deputy chairman of the Namangan *oblast* soviet executive committee; and first secretary of the Namangan city CPUzbek committee.

In 1985 he moved to Moscow as an instructor in the department for the organization of Party work, Central Committee, CPSU, and from 1987 to 1988 he was second secretary of the Syrdarya CPUzbek *obkom*, and then in 1988 he was elected first secretary of the Fergana CPUzbek *obkom*. In March 1990 he became chairman of the Fergana *oblast* soviet executive committee. In June 1991 he was elected Speaker (chairman) of the Supreme Soviet of the Uzbek SSR, and later of the Republic of Uzbekistan. He was also a USSR people's deputy. He is married with three sons and a daughter and lives in Tashkent.

Yunusova, Leila Islam Kyzy

Head of the Centre of Information and Analysis of the Ministry of Defence, Republic of Azerbaijan; deputy Minister of Defence until March 1993.

Born on December 21, 1955 in Baku into an Azeri family. Her father, Islam Veliev, was an engineer and her mother, Zohra Huseinova, born in 1925, and a teacher of English, is now retired.

She entered the faculty of history, Azerbaijani State University in 1973 and graduated in 1978, then becoming a postgraduate student in the Institute of History, Academy of Sciences, Azerbaijan. Her supervisor was Professor F. Aliev and she successfully presented her candidate dissertation in history in 1982 on "Anglo-Russian rivalry in the Caspian Sea and Azerbaijan in the first half of the 18th century" (PhD). She was appointed to the department concerned with links between Azerbaijan and Russia and the peoples of the Caucasus, Institute of History, Academy of Sciences, Azerbaijan, in 1981. Until 1988 she was a junior scientific assistant and from 1988 to 1991 she was a scientific assistant. She was appointed to the Ministry of Defence, Azerbaijan, on May 1, 1992, and remained there until March 1993.

From 1988 she was one of the founders of the Popular Front of Azerbaijan, a co-author of the manifesto and programme of the Popular Front, a member of its executive committee and the only woman among its 15 members. A. Ali-Zade, Z. Ali-Zade and she were among the founders of the social democratic movement in Azerbaijan. On August 20, 1991 the Social Democratic Party of Azerbaijan split into two parts, and Yunusova and her supporters founded the Independent Democratic Party of Azerbaijan. Its constituent conference took place on September 7, 1991 in Baku and its first congress on December 22, 1991. She was elected chairwoman of the party.

She has published over 30 articles and a monograph on the medieval history of Azerbaijan, and has also penned dozens of articles on public and political affairs. She is married. Her husband, Arif Seidgulu Ogly, born on January 12, 1955 in Baku, is an historian, who has successfully presented his candidate dissertation (PhD), and political scientist. Their daughter, Dinara, was born on October 18, 1985, in Baku. Leila's hobbies are travel and collecting art books and she speaks Turkish, Russian and English.

Home address: Baku 370005, ul. Nizami 53, kv. 30; *home telephone*: Baku 94 33 76.

Yushchenko, Viktor Andriiovych

Head of the National Bank of Ukraine since January 1993.

Born in 1954. An economist, Yushchenko rose rapidly inside the ranks of one of the main state agro-industrial banks *Ukraïna* (in which his predecessor as director of the National Bank, Vadym Hetman, had also worked), reaching the position of deputy director by the time he was appointed to head the National Bank of Ukraine on January 26, 1993. Although two of his predecessors (Volodymyr Matvienko in April 1992 and Hetman in November 1992) had been removed for their lax attitude towards monetary control, the new Prime Minister Leonid Kuchma had indicated his desire to exercise tighter control over the Bank's activities.

Yushchenko was soon involved in controversy, however, when he announced 1.23 trillion coupons worth of new agricultural credits in March 1993, causing the Ukrainian coupon to lose half its value against the US dollar overnight (it fell from 2,000 to 3,000 to the dollar). In May 1993 he fought off an attempt by Kuchma to establish direct Prime Ministerial control over the Bank. Hence, despite Yushchenko's relative youth, he has a long way to go in establishing his credentials as a pro-market reformer and supporter of sound money.

Official (Bank) address: 252007 Kiev, Vul. Zhovtnevoï revoliutsi 9; *telephone*: Kiev 226 2914.

Yuzkov, Leonid Petrovych

Head of the Constitutional Court of Ukraine.

Born in 1938 in the village of Novoselytsia in Khmelnytskyi *oblast* in west-central Ukraine. His studies in a pedagological institute were interrupted by national service until 1960, after which he joined the legal department of the Shevchenko State University, Kiev, where he has remained ever since, whilst also working as a lecturer at the Kiev Higher Party School.

In 1990 he was appointed head of the faculty of law at the university, and Yuzkov was also the head of the consultant group of scientific advisers attached to the Ukrainian Supreme Soviet. As part of the agreement that ended the October 1990 student hunger strikes, a Commission to Revise the Ukrainian Constitution was established under Kravchuk and Yuzkov was asked to head its working group. The draft new constitution was published in July 1992.

Although it made detailed promises concerning a limited state, a separation of powers and the defence of human rights, it was much criticized for its creeping presidentialism and catch-all emergency powers provisions. In July 1992, however, Yuzkov was appointed by the Supreme Soviet to head the new Constitutional Court, which the draft constitution envisaged would police the separation of powers and act as guardian of the constitution. At the same time, he helped to organize a Canadian-supported programme to promote the rule of law in Ukraine, which involved retraining of lawyers and practical assistance for measures to promote judicial independence.

It was obvious, however, that Yuzkov faced an uphill struggle to establish a *Rechtsstaat* (law-governed state) in the face of the ingrained habits of the past. In spring 1993 bitter controversy over further appointments to the Supreme Court erupted, when the ex-communist majority in the Ukrainian parliament tried to appoint several notorious hardliners, provoking a walkout by the People's Council faction which temporarily suspended the process.

Official address: 252601 Kiev, Vul. Chekistiv 4; *telephone*: Kiev 226 2304.

Zaiets, Ivan Oleksandrovych

Leading Nationalist Ukrainian Deputy.

Born into a Ukrainian family in Zhytomyr *oblast* in central Ukraine to a family of collective farmers in 1952. He was educated at the Kiev Academy of Agricultural Economics, and then worked in the Ukrainian Academy of Sciences' institute of agrarian research as an economist and mathematician. After becoming people's deputy for Sviatoshynskyi *raion* in Kiev city in March 1990 (on the second round), he continued his studies in the faculty of law, Kiev State University.

In the late 1980s Zaiets had been a prominent Kiev member of *Rukh*, becoming head of its Council of Advisers. In the Supreme Soviet, he is head of the sub-committee on economic reform and economic regulation, and is a hyperactive contributor to all debates, particularly those on economic and foreign affairs. In December 1992 he was chosen to replace Les Taniuk as head of the rump People's Council faction in the Ukrainian Parliament, which now consisted mainly of supporters of the opposition leader Viacheslav Chornovil.

Official address: Kiev, Vul. M. Hrushevskoho 5; *telephone*: Kiev 252 019 (work) or Kiev 444 8585 (home).

Zaitsev, Vitaly Vasilevich

Deputy Commander-in-Chief of the navy for maintenance; head of the chief maintenance administration of the Navy. Admiral since 1990.

Born on January 4, 1932 in the village of Kupalishi, Pestyakovsky *raion*, Ivanovo *oblast*, into a collective farmer's family. Russian. He has been in the military since 1951, and graduated from the Higher Military Engineering Technical School in 1957; the Naval Academy in 1971. He received a higher engineering and technical education and was a member of the CPSU until August 1991.

His career has been in engineering posts in the navy. He was a group commander on a cruiser of the Northern Fleet in 1957/58, group commander, flotilla commander, commander of the electro-mechanical section of a nuclear submarine of the Northern fleet from 1958 to 1968. He participated in several exploratory voyages and has seen much service in the oceans. He was regarded as a highly qualified professional naval engineer. Although Zaitsev occupied technical posts he was obliged by the rules of service in the Soviet navy to take an active part in the work of the Party organization. A technically-minded person, he engrossed himself in finding solutions to applied engineering and technical problems only and did not appear to be interested in political issues.

In 1971, after graduating from the Naval Academy, he was appointed deputy commander for electrotechnical maintenance of a separate subdivision of submarines under repair in the White Sea (Belomorsk) naval base in Severodvinsk. He organized regular repairs of sophisticated matériel and dealt with technical problems, including co-operation with enterprises. In 1974 he was appointed deputy head of technical administration of the Northern Fleet and supervised the combat readiness and maintenance of submarines. From 1978 to 1981 he was head of electromechanical maintenance of a submarine flotilla of the Northern Fleet. He was transferred to Moscow in 1981 to fill the post of head of the ship maintenance administration and deputy head of the chief technical administration of the navy. In 1986 he was appointed deputy Commander-in-Chief of the Navy for maintenance and head of the chief technical administration (renamed chief maintenance administration in 1988). He is exclusively concerned with the problems of the engineering and technical maintenance of the ships and submarines of the navy.

Like almost all Admirals (equivalent to the rank of General in the other armed services) trained under Soviet power, he supports the idea of a strong state domestically and powerful, up-to-date armed forces. He used to be a convinced communist and was very critical towards democratic movements in Russia and the campaign for independence in the non-Russian republics. A conformist, he now supports the new Russian leadership. He is interested in technical questions and in the history of the Russian Navy. He engages in sport. He has been awarded several orders and medals. He is married.

Official address: 103175 Moscow K-175, Bolshoi Komsomolsky pereulok.

Zaitsev, Vladimir Vasilevich

Acting Head of the Administration of Lipetsk *oblast*, Russian Federation.

Born in 1951 in the village of Shakhty No. 17, Kireevsky *raion*, Tula *oblast*, into a civil servant's family; member of the CPSU until August 1991. He graduated from the Tula Polytechnical Institute in 1973 as a mining engineer and economist, and from 1973 to 1979 he worked in the Tulaugol association as an engineer economist, calculator of piece rates, senior engineer in the organization of production and labour, and head of the planning department of the enterprises of the association. From 1980 to 1982 he was senior engineer economist of the scientific economic planning department and management of the general directorate, Kostomukshsky mining combine, Karelian Autonomous Soviet Socialist Republic (ASSR).

From 1982 to 1985 he was a calculator of piece rates in mining, then was elected secretary of the Party committee of the Komsomolskaya mine of the

Vorkutaugol production association, Komi ASSR. In 1985 he moved to Lipetsk and for six years worked at the Novolipetsk metallurgical combine as a senior engineer, head of the bureau of the organization of labour and wages of a steel shop, head of the bureau of shops of the department of the scientific organization of labour and management, and instructor on economics and labour of the trade union committee of the enterprise. In 1991 he was senior lecturer in the department of economics and analysis of production in the Institute of Business and Management, Lipetsk branch.

In January 1992 he was chairman of the commission of economic forecasting and finance, deputy head of the administration of Lipetsk *oblast*. He is the author of various scientific articles on economics and management. On December 23, 1992 he was appointed temporary acting head of the administration of Lipetsk *oblast* by presidential decree.

He states that his democratic will led him to seek high office even though he had been a devoted member of the CPSU for many years. Since August 1991 he does not belong to a political party or participate in any political movement. He does not support extreme measures in politics and belongs neither to the right or the left; he views himself as a centrist. Politicians, in his view, should express the majority view of society.

He is convinced that the market is necessary, but Russia should not leap into it in one jump. A market economy presupposes the existence of various conditions and institutions without which it cannot function. The most important of these are the market, capital and labour and in Russia all are now only at the initial stage. The economy needs to be regulated by strong administrative forms of guidance, which does not mean the return of the old administrative pressures but strong leadership by the government. Economic reforms should be introduced step by step with considerable state control and regulation. Reform needs a base: the establishment of a commercial system, privatization, joint stock enterprises and the development of private farming.

He is married, his wife is a nurse and their daughter is still at school. He lives in Lipetsk.

Zaitsev, Yury Vladimirovich

Chairman of the commission of the Presidium of the Russian Supreme Soviet on citizenship.

Born in 1933; Russian. He was a member of the CPSU until August 1991. He graduated from the V. V. Kuibyshev Construction Engineering Institute, Moscow, and the Diplomatic Academy of the USSR Ministry of Foreign Affairs. He successfully presented his candidate dissertation in technical sciences (PhD) and his doctoral dissertation in technical sciences (DSc). He is a professor, and is an Academician of the Engineering Academy, the Academy of Natural Sciences and the Academy of Technological Sciences of the Russian Federation. He has the rank of an ambassador extraordinary and plenipotentiary, and in 1987 he was rector of the all-Union Extra-mural Polytechnical Institute (now the Moscow State Open University). He was elected an RSFSR people's deputy in 1990; and chairman of the commission of the Presidium of the Supreme Soviet on citizenship in 1991. In 1992 he was also appointed the permanent representative of the Russian Federation at international organizations in Vienna.

Address: 103274 Moscow, K 274, Krasnopresnenskaya nab., d. 2, Dom Sovetov.

Zakharov, Mark Anatolevich

Member of the Council of the President of the Russian Federation.

Born in 1933 in Moscow; member of the CPSU from 1973 to August 1991. He graduated from the faculty of acting, state institute of theatrical art, in 1955, but since he could not get any engagements in Moscow he moved to Perm and took part in student amateur dramatics, becoming producer of the student theatre, Moscow State University. From 1965 he worked in the Moscow theatre of satire and in 1973 became the chief producer of the Lenin *Komsomol* theatre. Among his productions were: *Accessible Place* by A. N. Ostrovsky (1967); *Juno and Perhaps* by A. A. Voznesensky and A. L. Rybnikov (1980); *Rear* by G. I. Gorin after Charles de Coster (1984); *Three Girls in Blue* by L. S. Petrushevsky (1985); *The Dictatorship of the Conscience* by M. F. Shatrov (1986); *Funeral Prayer* by G. I. Gorin after S. N. Sholem-Aleichem, and *The Sage* by A. N. Ostrovsky (1988); *School of Emigrés* by G. I. Gorin (1989); *Sorry* (1991); *The Marriage of Figaro* by G. I. Gorin after de Beaumarchais (1992). He produced many television films: *The Same Münchhausen* (1979); *An Ordinary Miracle* (1981); *The House that Swift Built* (1982); *Formula of Love* (1984); *Kill the Dragon* (1988).

He was secretary of the board of the USSR union of theatre workers, RSFSR people's artist, USSR people's artist and winner of the USSR state prize in 1987. He was the author and head of the popular TV programme *Kinoserpantin* (cinema serpentine) and *The Chauvinism of Mark Zakharov*.

In early 1989 Zakharov was elected a USSR people's deputy as a nominee of the USSR union of theatre workers. He was a member of the USSR Supreme Soviet committee on science, education, culture and training. He became a member of the higher consultative co-ordinating council of the RSFSR Speaker in 1990, then became a member of the presidential consultative Council and is now a member of the presidential Council. He has published articles in the journal *Ogonek* about the defilement of the Kremlin cathedrals and the burial of German soldiers. He has often appeared on the TV programme *Vzglyad* (view) to speak of the need to remove Lenin's body from the mausoleum on Red Square. He regards the mausoleum to be a first class architectural achievement and it should not be turned into a tourist attraction.

He insists that the chief producer is always right. He advocates an authoritarian regime which would protect everyone and the development of a healthy economy with the help of a strong hand. He regards the spreading growth of crime a danger, as is also the thirst to be equal in poverty. The ending of external coercion has produced not democracy in Russia but lack of control and physical and bureaucratic tyranny. He is against Russia having its "own Pinochet" (former dictator in Chile), but the legal and forceful protection of reform is necessary, and he is in favour of entrepreneurial activity. He is proud of having met Academician Andrei Sakharov, S. S. Averintsev and V. I. Ivanov in the USSR Supreme Soviet. The establishment of new institutes and structures for a democratic society are not possible at present without the strong protection of reform by temporary presidential rule. The President needs the trust of the people, and he was in favour of holding the referendum on April 25, 1993.

He is married and has a daughter who is an actress with the Lenin *Komsomol* theatre, Moscow. He lives in Moscow.

Zakharov, Mikhail Lvovich

Chairman of the commission on social policy of the Council of the Republic, Russian Supreme Soviet.

Born on January 22, 1946 in Moscow; Russian. He was a member of the CPSU from 1958 to 1990. He graduated from the Moscow Institute of Law, and in 1970 successfully presented his candidate dissertation in law on "General and specific points in providing workers, employees and collective farm workers with pensions" (LLM). In 1981 he successfully presented his doctoral dissertation in law (LLD), and he is a professor. In 1951 he began working in the USSR Ministry of Social Security; later in the all-Union central council of trades unions; in the USSR Ministry of Finance; and became leading scientific assistant in the all-Union scientific research institute of the Soviet state structure and legislation of the USSR Supreme Soviet (1969-90).

In January 1990 he was nominated for election as an RSFSR people's deputy in the No. 13 Zeleznodorozhny territorial district, Moscow. During the election campaign he advocated changing the role of Russia within the USSR, as he believes that Russia does not need any other kind of Union and must cease being a donor republic as it has been over the previous 70 years. The structures of government have to be changed since their dyed-in-the-wool, dogmatic world outlook lags behind the growth of popular self-awareness. He supported freedom for producers and transfer of land to the peasants, and considered that economic development should be devoted to meeting the needs of the population. There should be a multi-party system with complete ideological freedom of the individual, except the ideology of violence, racism and rebellion. He devoted considerable attention to the solution of legislative problems.

There were seven candidates. In the first round Zakharov polled 25% of the votes and won the second round, polling 48.7% of the votes. His main opponent was V. I. Bystrov, chairman of Moscow city planning organization, first deputy chairman of Moscow city soviet executive committee, who received 18.2% of the votes in the first round and 39% in the second round. During the election campaign Zakharov was supported by the Democratic Russia organization. He was elected a member of the RSFSR Supreme Soviet at the I Congress of People's Deputies (718 voted for, 216 voted against).

He is a member of the Council of the Republic and a member of the Supreme Soviet Presidium. On July 5, 1990 he was elected chairman of the Council of the Republic commission on social policy, on July 4, 1990 he became a member of the Council of the Republic commission on culture, and on July 3, 1990 a member of the constitutional commission. He is a member of the Democratic Russia parliamentary faction, the Russian union group, and the unified parliamentary faction of the social democratic and republican parties of the Russian Federation group. In February 1991 he signed the declaration of the members of the Presidium of the Supreme Soviet defending Boris Yeltsin against the criticisms of S. P. Goryacheva, the Speaker. On October 14, 1991 he became a member of the working group on preparing the ratification of the treaty on the economic commonwealth.

On October 16, 1991 he was elected a member of the working group of members of the Council of the Republic for the drafting of proposals about changes in the structure of the leadership of the Supreme Soviet and on the order of rotation of the members of the Council of the Republic. On November 25, 1991 he became a member of the commission on the legal implementation of the decrees of the Russian President. He was awarded medals, and has published over 200 academic articles. He is married and his wife, Elvira (née Tuchkova), is a lawyer. One daughter, Olga, is a mathematician and the other, Irina, is an economist. Zakharovs hobbies are football and history.

Address: 103274 Moscow, K 274, Krasnopresnenskaya nab., d. 2, Dom Sovetov; *telephone*: Moscow 205 50 26.

Zaveryukha, Aleksandr Kharlampievich

Deputy Russian Prime Minister.

Born on April 30, 1940 in the village of Yasnogorsky, Novosergeevsky *raion*, Orenburg *oblast* into a Ukrainian family; member of the CPSU from 1965 to August 1991. He began work as a tractor driver in 1958, and after military service he entered Orenburg Agricultural Institute where he graduated in 1967. In 1965 he became chief economist in the Elektrozavod state farm, his home farm, and afterwards was elected chairman of the Komsomolsky collective farm in Novosergeevsky *raion*, Orenburg *oblast*. While chairman he successfully presented his candidate dissertation on livestock economics (PhD (Econ)). In 1979 he was appointed deputy, then first deputy head of the administration of agriculture of Orenburg *oblast* soviet executive committee, and later was first deputy chairman of the Orenburg *oblast* agro-industrial complex.

In 1989 after a multi-candidate election he became chairman of the council of agro-industrial complexes of Orenburg *oblast*. He became a member of the all-Russian council of collective farms. As a result he made many foreign visits and studied the organization of agriculture, became convinced of the efficiency of Western agricultural production and began to doubt the viability of state farms. In 1991 he was appointed general director of the all-Russian scientific research institute of meat production in Orenburg. He was elected a deputy of the Orenburg *oblast* soviet of people's deputies.

In the spring of 1990 he was nominated for election as an RSFSR people's deputy in the No. 556 Sol-Iletsky territorial district, Orenburg *oblast*, by the collective of the S. M. Kirov collective farm, Saratashsky *raion*, Orenburg *oblast*. In his election programme he stressed the need to solve a range of village social issues, to establish equal relations between town and country and the reorientation of the economy towards the production of consumer goods. There were five candidates. He polled 38.4% of the votes in the first round and won the second round with 73.1% of the votes. His main opponent, V. N. Lakota, received 20.5% in the second round. He was elected to the Supreme Soviet and joined the agrarian union faction. He was a member of the RSFSR Supreme Soviet committee on the social development of the village, agrarian problems and food and of the commission on deputies' ethics. Awarded the order of the badge of honour and medals.

In January 1993 he was appointed deputy Russian Prime Minister responsible for agricultural affairs. His appointment disappointed the members of the agrarian union faction who had proposed their own leaders for the ministerial post and had counted on a change towards a more conservative agricultural policy. V. Starodubtsev, one of the members of the Extraordinary Committee involved in the attempted putsch of August 1991, even went so far as to express in public great hopes for agriculture now that Zaveryukha was the minister.

He sees his main priority to be the raising of the profile of the villages. In order to achieve this, greater state support for the countryside is needed by concentrating on price and credit policies and considerable attention has to be devoted to rural social problems. The minister is a strong supporter of private family farming and the removal of legal restrictions on the buying and selling of land. As minister he is responsible for all authorities which are concerned with food production and land reform. He lives in Moscow.

Zazulin, Nikolai Afanasevich

Head of Chief Automobile Administration of the Ministry of Defence of the Russian Federation; Colonel-General since 1992.

Born on December 1, 1934 in the village of Sebrovo, Mikhailovsky *raion*, Stalingrad (now Volgograd) *oblast* into a collective farmer's family; Russian. He graduated from the 2nd Military Automobile Technical School with distinction in 1957, and the Military Rear and Transport Academy also with distinction, having received a higher military special education. He was a member of the CPSU until August 1991.

After graduating from technical school he served as a commander of an automobile platoon, and later held all rear officer's posts up to head of automobile and armoured services of the Navy. His record was that of an officer with a talent for organization, capable of pleasing superior officers when it mattered and of guaranteeing the maintenance of official and private automobile transport. He actively participated in the work of local Party agencies, and was elected, on a number of occasions, to Party agencies. He enjoyed the support of the political agencies, something which contributed to his promotion.

Later he was transferred and promoted to the central apparatus of the USSR Ministry of Defence. From 1989 he was the first deputy head of the Chief Automobile Administration. He organized the inspection of plant-produced half-track and full-track automobile *matériel*, its distribution to troops and use by all types of armed forces, the USSR MVD and KGB formations. He was an orthodox communist and opposed democratic movements.

During the anti-constitutional putsch in August 1991 he was not especially active, though he expressed his approval of the Emergency Committee's policy. He carried out the instructions of the General Staff and his immediate superior officers to raise the combat readiness of the troops under his command including the possibility of their use in repressive operations. Like almost all other military leaders he was not held responsible.

In autumn 1991 Lieut.-Gen. N. Zazulin was appointed head of the Chief Automobile Administration of the USSR Ministry of Defence, and from February 1992 head of the Chief Automobile Administration of the unified armed forces of the CIS. He was soon promoted to colonel-general. He was a member of the State Commission for the establishment of the Ministry of Defence, army and navy of the Russian Federation. By President Yeltsin's decree, on August 21, 1992, he was appointed head of the Chief Automobile Administration of the Ministry of Defence of the Russian Federation.

Gen. N. Zazulin supervises the work of all automobile units and services in the various types of armed forces in Russia, organizes orders for industry to produce new *matériel* and its inspection, testing and distribution. It is also he who provides private cars for top military figures, which makes him influential and popular with army generals. Politically he advocates a hard line to retain the supremacy of the state, order and discipline. He is against democratic movements, and like most generals he was brought up to believe in a corporate identity, that the army and its top officers are a special milieu to be treated with respect by the state. He is conformist, ready to support any power which ensures the order he respects and his well-being.

He has no special hobbies, but is interested in sport, hunting and fishing. He does not speak a foreign language and has not been abroad as a member of an official delegation. He has been awarded two orders, and various medals. He is married with a daughter, and has a granddaughter.

Office address: 103175 Moscow K-175, Ministry of Defence of the Russian Federation.

Zbitniev, Yurii Ivanovych

Leader of Social Democratic Party of Ukraine.

Born into a Ukrainian family in 1963 in the town of Smila in Cherkasy *oblast* in central Ukraine. His mother was a doctor, and he was educated at Ivano-Frankivsk State Medical Institute in western Ukraine. From 1987 he worked as a doctor and anaesthetist in a Kiev hospital, but after 1990 became a student in the Kharkiv Academy of Law. Although he had been a candidate member of the Communist Party of Ukraine (CPU) in the 1980s, Zbitniev became active in opposition politics in the late 1980s. He kept his distance from *Rukh*, however, preferring the smaller and less nationalist social democratic movement.

In March 1990 he was elected people's deputy for Gagarinskyi *raion* in Kiev city (on the second round). In the Supreme Soviet he has specialized in youth politics, becoming deputy head of the committee on youth affairs and, in December 1991, the head of the fund for the social adaptation of Ukrainian youth. The Ukrainian Social Democratic movement managed to split in two at its inaugural congress in May 1990. Both factions supported a mixed economy and a federalized Ukraine, opposed national extremism and contained as many Russian as Ukrainian members, but the faction that became the Social Democratic Party of Ukraine (SDPU) supported a sovereign Ukrainian state and favoured a complete break with the ideology of Marxism-Leninism.

Until May 1992, however, the SDPU was headed by the party's other people's deputy, Oleksandr Suhoniako, who opposed efforts to reunite the Social Democratic movement, and was lukewarm concerning co-operation with the *New Ukraine* movement, of which Zbitniev had been an early and enthusiastic member. Zbitniev therefore replaced Suhoniako as leader of the SDPU at the party's third congress in May 1992, and organized a fourth Unity congress aiming at reunion with the United Social Democratic Party of Ukraine in November 1992. The party now claims 1,700 members.

Official address: Kiev, Vul. M. Hrushevskoho 5; *telephone*: Kiev 252 019 or (Kiev) 295 0784.

Zhigulin, Viktor Ivanovich

Deputy Speaker of the Council of the Republic of the Russian Supreme Soviet.

Born on September 13, 1954 in Frunze (Bishkek), Kyrgyzstan; Russian. He was a member of the CPSU until August 1991. He graduated in 1974 from the Novocherkassk Geological Prospecting Technical College, and is a qualified geologist. He worked as a technician, foreman and senior engineer in the Tamvatneisky geological prospecting group of the Anadyr expedition, Magadan *oblast*, then joined the Chukotka department of the north-eastern prospecting association in 1979 and in 1988 became head of the association. In 1989 he enrolled in the all-Union Extra-mural Institute of Law, and in July 1990 he transferred to full-time work in the Russian Supreme Soviet committee on construction. He was elected a deputy of the Anadyr city soviet of people's deputies.

He was nominated for election as an RSFSR people's deputy in the No. 55 Chukotka territorial district, Chukotka autonomous *okrug*. During the election campaign he advocated that the universal declaration on human rights be adopted as the basis of the state system and real power in the country should pass to the soviets; Chukotka autonomous *okrug* should be administratively and economically independent within Russia; freedom to choose the type of economic activity and property relations best suited to the person; Anadyr should be raised to the status of an *okrug*; the annulment of clause 6 of the USSR constitution (on the leading role of the CPSU in society); direct, secret and universal election of chairmen of the presidiums of local soviets, including *oblast* soviets; and longer service in the military to replace conscription. Zhigulin's programme was that of the democratic initiative social organization.

There were 15 candidates. In the first round Zhigulin polled 10.9% of the votes, and he won the second round, polling 41.9% of the votes. His main opponent was B. F. Abakumov, director of the commercial maritime port in Pevek, who received 9.3% of the votes in the first round and 39.7% in the second round. Zhigulin was elected a member of the RSFSR Supreme Soviet at the I Congress of People's Deputies (627 voted for, 295 voted against).

He is a member of the Council of the Republic. On July 1, 1990 he was elected deputy chairman of the Supreme Soviet committee on construction, architecture, housing and municipal services. On October 2, 1991 he became a member of the commission on the observance of banking legislation in the Russian Federation, and the following day he was elected deputy Speaker of the Council of the Republic. He is married with a child.

Address: 103274 Moscow, K 274, Krasnopresnenskaya nab., d. 2, Dom Sovetov; *telephone*: Moscow 205 53 76.

Zhirinovsky, Vladimir Volfovich

Chairman of the Liberal Democratic Party of Russia (LDP).

Born on April 25, 1946 in Alma Ata, Kazakh SSR, into a Russian family. He was the youngest of six children, whose father is a lawyer and whose mother is a housewife. (He is known for the quip: my father is a lawyer but my mother is Russian.) In 1964 at the first attempt he entered the institute of the countries of Asia and Africa, Moscow State University. In 1970 he graduated with distinction and afterwards graduated from the faculty of law, evening department. He also graduated from the faculty of international relations, Marxist-Leninist University, and was then a postgraduate student in Turkey. He speaks English, German, French and Turkish. He served two years in the army in Tbilisi, Georgian SSR.

He worked in the world peace committee, and from 1984 to 1991 he headed the legal service in the Mir publishing house. He began his political activities in 1967 and since 1977 has supported the concept of a multi-party system. His political career dates from May 1988 and he participated in the foundation of the Liberal Democratic Party of the USSR. As leader of the party he visited about 10 countries and established contact with different types of liberal and centrist parties and organizations. His party was not united and split, and a part of it was registered by Zhirinovsky. During the registration he amended the rules and the programme of the central committee. V. Voronin, leader of the centrist bloc, accused him of doing this during the election capmpaign for President of the RSFSR. A group, calling itself the Liberal Democratic party of Russia, broke away from Zhirinovsky, accusing him of harbouring imperialist intentions and displaying a dictatorial manner.

The Liberal Democratic Party of the Soviet Union was registered by the USSR Ministry of Justice and it nominated him for President of the RSFSR. Problems surfaced later over the registration, when the Ministry of Justice of the Russian Federation discovered forgeries and the registration was cancelled. However, the party managed to renew itself by collecting the necessary numbers of signatures and the IV Congress of People's Deputies registered Zhirinovsky as a candidate for President of the RSFSR. About 500 deputies voted for his candidature to be included on the ballot paper. He only needed the support of 20% of the deputies or just over 200 to succeed, but he had failed to collect the requisite number of signatures to support his candidature. Hence the congress had to decide. During his speech to the congress he stated: "Russia is suffering from the Renaissance illness but a good midwife is lacking". He stressed that if he were elected he would end the anti-communist "bacchanalia", would restore order in the country, turn the economy round within two to three years, remove the nationality question from the agenda and refuse the national territorial division of Russia. "It does not matter, there is no other way out". "The USSR is a Russian state". On several occasions he threatened the Baltic republics and Moldova.

He proposed that the resources for reform come from the restructuring of the country's debts, the basing of relations with other countries on mutual advantage, withdrawal from international peacekeeping duties and improvement of relations with the neighbours in the south. He supported all forms of ownership and the removal of all restrictions on the development of enterprises. In the election campaign he advocated a multi-party system, different forms of ownership, the normal development of which should be regulated by taxation, the retention of the USSR, the geopolitical interests of the Soviet Union to be pursued in the world and a professional army.

During the elections he ran with A. Zavidy, president of the Galland concern and a member of the CPSU. The newspaper *Sovetskaya Rossiya* supported them, and Zhirinovsky polled 6,211,007 votes (7.81%) but 71,570,476 voted against (90.03%). Only Boris Yeltsin, elected President, and Nikolai Ryzhkov received more votes. Zhirinovsky got more votes than V. Bakatin, A. Tuleev and A. Makashov.

During the attempted state coup of August 19-21, 1991 he favoured the conspirators. He stated that "on August 19 at 9 am legal power was in the hands of the people, sitting in the Kremlin, therefore we support the programme. . . I underline, programme! However when the President of the USSR returns we shall change our position and support the legal power of the President who has returned to assume his responsibilities". He believed that the democrats had done the dirty work and had saved the Liberal Democratic Party from its main competitor, the ruling Party. As before he thinks that the failure of Yeltsin's policies will in the end bring him, Zhirinovsky, to power, as he is certain that he has the support of about 60 million inhabitants of Russia. He is preparing to establish a new Extraordinary Committee and begin the transformation by closing down newspapers and reforming his party.

Zhirinovsky was critical of President Yeltsin's address to the nation on March 20, 1993 and his intention to introduce a special regime in the country until the crisis had been resolved. On the matter of a strong hand Zhirinovsky stated that Russia really did need strong presidential power "but not you" (Yeltsin). He lives in Moscow.

Zhorzholiani, Timuraz Mikhailovich

Chairman of the Conservative Party of Georgia; Member of Parliament of the Republic of Georgia.

Born on January 28, 1950 in Tbilisi, Georgian SSR. A Georgian. His father, Mikhail Pavlovich, was a teacher of mathematics and his mother, Elena Mikhailovna, was a teacher of Georgian language and literature. His sister, Lamara, is a philologist and chairwoman of a charitable fund.

As a young man Zhorzholiani participated actively in *Komsomol* activities and worked in the agencies of the Ministry of Internal Affairs. He graduated from the faculty of history, Tbilisi State University in 1973. In 1989 after the split in the Party of the Georgian Traditionalists he established the Monarchical Conservative Party. In November 1992 the party changed its name to the Conservative Party of Georgia. He was arrested in October 1991 during the presidency of Zviad Gamsakhurdia, but was freed in December 1991 following the events in Tbilisi. In 1992 he was appointed a member of the State Council. In October 1992 he was elected a member of parliament for the Mshvidoba block.

He has published many articles on historical themes and also on contemporary politics and international relations. He enjoys playing chess. He is married to Nelli Vasilevna, who is a graduate historian and head of department of the state archive of Georgia. They have two sons, both students. Mikhail was born in 1968 and Gocha was born in 1972. There are three daughters; Nino, born in 1982 is at secondary school, Anna was born in 1988 and Teona in 1991.

Home address: Tbilisi, pr. K. Gamsakhurdia, Dom 47, kv. 2; *telephone*: Tbilisi 95 35 44.

Zhukov, Andrei Dmitrievich

Member of the Council of the President of the Russian Federation.

Born in 1948 in Leningrad; Russian. He graduated from the faculty of physics, Moscow State University and worked in the Institute of the World Economy and International Relations, USSR Academy of Sciences. He is a specialist on the strategic problems of political analyses. He is a member of the geopolitics and security section, Russian Academy of Natural Sciences and is an Academician of the Russian Academy of Natural Sciences, Russian Academy of Sciences. He successfully presented his candidate dissertation in history (PhD) and his doctoral dissertation (DLitt). He is first vice-president of the Russian American University Corporation. According to Zhukov the members of the presidential Council, at their meeting on February 11, 1993, did not call for the introduction of presidential rule but for decisive action by the President. Three questions were discussed at the meeting: the interrelationship between the President and the government, the advisability of holding a plebiscite and ways out of the present constitutional crisis. Zhukov said the session was rather like the meeting of an academic council.

He spoke on economic questions. Russia needs to attract the necessary capital funds from the West and not to restrict itself to the Western model. He called for great attention to be paid to production and, for instance, to grant producers tax advantages, but had the impression at the meeting that the President had not yet made up his mind. Zhukov lives in Moscow.

Zhukov, Grigory Semenovich

Chairman of the Russian Supreme Soviet committee on the work of the soviets of people's deputies and development of self-management.

Born on May 9, 1945 in the village of Baturino, Asinovsky *raion*, Tomsk *oblast*; Russian. He was a member of the CPSU from 1974 to August 1991. He graduated in 1967 from the Tomsk Polytechnical Institute as a mining engineer, and after graduating he worked in the enterprises of the *Tomskneftegazgeologiya* association, as head of the central engineering technical service, chief engineer, head of the oil prospecting expedition, and deputy general director of the association. In 1981 he moved into Party work and became deputy head of the oil and gas industrial department, Tomsk Party city committee (1981-82). In 1982 he graduated from the Novosibirsk Higher Party School, becoming first secretary of the Parabelsky Party *raion* committee, Tomsk *oblast* (1982-84); and first secretary of the Kolpashevsky city Party committee (1984-90). He was elected a deputy of the Kolpashevsky city soviet, Parabelsky *raion* soviet, Tomsk *oblast* soviet of people's deputies.

In January 1990 he was nominated for election as an RSFSR people's deputy in the No. 700 Kolpashevsky territorial district, Tomsk *oblast*. During the election campaign he advocated granting Russia the same rights as other Union republics; the same rights for the residents of Siberia as other regions; and the preservation of national traditions, culture and language. Important conditions for the creation of a *Rechtsstaat* (law-governed state) were the reform and democratization of the CPSU. Russia, in order to become prosperous, needed a strong economy based on different types of property ownership, and urgent social problems needing attention were childhood and maternity, youth, veterans and rural life in general. Society should become more committed to *perestroika*; the environment should be cleaned up and put under the supervision of the soviets and the public; and there should be more *glasnost* in local soviet affairs and deputies accountable to the electors.

There were six candidates. In the first round Zhukov polled 26.6% of the votes and won the second round, polling 50.7% of the votes. His main opponent was S. N. Smirnov, first secretary of the Kargasoksky *Komsomol raion* committee, who received 13.8% of the votes in the first round and 36.6% in the second round. Zhukov was elected a member of the Russian Supreme Soviet at the V Congress of People's Deputies, and he is a member of the Council of the Republic. On December 27, 1990 he was elected chairman of the Supreme Soviet committee on questions of the work of the soviets of people's deputies and the development of self-management. He is a member of the Presidium of the Supreme Soviet, and of the Smena (new policy) parliamentary faction.

Address: 103274 Moscow, K 274, Krasnopresnenskaya nab., d. 2, Dom Sovetov; *telephone*: Moscow 205 93 40.

Zhurkin, Vitaly Vladimirovich

Director of the Institute of European Studies, Russian Academy of Sciences; Academician.

Born on January 14, 1928 in Moscow; Russian. He was a member of the CPSU until August 1991. He graduated in 1951 from the Moscow State Institute of International Relations, USSR Ministry of Foreign Affairs, and then began working as a journalist on the USSR Gosteleradio (state television and radio). In 1964 he moved to *Pravda*, and then from 1965 to 1968 he worked in the USSR Ministry of Foreign Affairs. In 1968 he was appointed to the Institute for the Study of the US and Canada, USSR Academy of Sciences and in 1971 became deputy director.

In 1984 he was elected a corresponding member of the USSR Academy of Sciences and in 1990 an Academician. In 1987 he became head of the Institute of European Studies of the academy, and in December 1991 he was elected an Academician of the Russian Academy of Sciences, a member of its Presidium and secretary Academician of its department of world economics and problems of international relations. He also became vice-chairman of the committee on security and co-operation in Europe, vice-president of the Soviet association of political science and chairman of the board of the Russian association of European studies.

He is also a member of the European Academy of Arts and Sciences, Paris, and a member of the scientific council of the International Institute of World Problems, Stockholm. He has published widely and is respected in the international community for his knowledge and expertise. He supported *perestroika* and the new thinking in Soviet foreign policy under Gorbachev and Shevardnadze. His books include: *International Conflicts* (1972); *USSR-USA: the 1970s and 1980s* (1982); *Deterrence: Its Implications for Disarmament, Security and the Arms Race* (1986); *Reasonable Sufficiency and the New Political Thinking* (1989); *The European Dimension in Soviet Foreign Policy* (1989); *The Construction of a Greater Europe* (1990); *Pan-European Architecture* (1990).

He is the recipient of many awards. They include the order of the Red Banner of Labour, the order of the badge of honour, the order of the Friendship of the Peoples, and the USSR state prize in 1990. He speaks English and is married with a son.

Address: 103873 Moscow, Prospekt Marksa 18/3; *telephone*: Moscow 203 7343 (office); 230 0070 (home).

Zlenko, Anatolii Maksymovych

Foreign Minister of Ukraine.

Born into a Ukrainian family in 1938. After finishing his education at Kiev State University in 1967, he spent his whole career in various branches of the Ukrainian diplomatic service. Stalin had secured founder membership for Ukraine (and Belorussia (Belarus)) in the UN and its sister organizations in the late 1940s, but of course all Ukrainian delegations to such institutions were wholly subordinate to Soviet interests until 1990 (when Ukraine began to chart an independent foreign policy after its Declaration of Sovereignty in July of that year).

Zlenko, having worked for many years as a cog in this machine, has nevertheless made the transition to an advocate of Ukrainian national interests with considerable skill. From 1967 to 1973 he worked as an attaché in the department of international organization. In 1973 he moved to UNESCO, becoming the secretary of the Ukrainian SSR commission for UNESCO in 1979. In 1987 he became deputy Ukrainian Minister of Foreign Affairs, first Deputy Minister in 1989, and Minister proper in 1990. He is an *ex officio* member of the Defence and Security Councils established in 1992.

In charting a course for Ukraine's new independent foreign policy, he was considerably hamstrung by the Declaration of Sovereignty's commitments that Ukraine would not "accept, produce or acquire" nuclear weapons, and that it would become a neutral state, standing outside formal blocs and alliances. In practice, Zlenko, pressured from all sides by advocates of a "European orientation" (and closer links with the Visegrad states in particular) and by those who favour concentrating on relations with Russia, has tried to maintain all options at once.

This has preserved tactical flexibility, but has also meant that Ukrainian foreign policy has lacked a coherent thrust (this lack of clarity is also due to rival conceptions of foreign policy emerging from the Foreign and Defence Ministries, and from the President's staff). Zlenko's past experience as a cautious bureaucrat has, however, led him to oppose more extreme nationalist pressures, and to work to maintain relations with Russia on as friendly a basis as possible. Initially seen as a typically faceless national communist, Zlenko managed to cultivate a considerable constituency for himself from 1990 to 1992, and retained his post in the Kuchma government formed in October 1992.

Official (Ministry) address: 252024 Kiev, Vul. Chekistiv 1; *telephone*: Kiev 226 3379.

Zlobin, Konstantin Sergeevich

Press secretary of the Speaker of the Russian Supreme Soviet.

Born on September 27, 1946 in Moscow; Russian. He was a member of the CPSU until August 1991. He graduated from the faculty for translation, Institute of Foreign Languages, Moscow, was a postgraduate student at the Academy of Social Sciences of the Party Central Committee and successfully presented his candidate dissertation in history (PhD). After graduating he joined the USSR state committee for television and radio (Gosteleradio) and rose to become editor-in-chief of the main agency of information on the US and Great Britain. He then moved to Novosti (1969-85); and to the Party journal *Izvestiya TsK, KPSS* (1988-91). In 1991 he was appointed head of the press service of the Supreme Soviet of the Russian Federation and press secretary of the Speaker of the Supreme Soviet of the Russian Federation. He is married with two daughters. He loves reading, especially American literature.

Address: 103274 Moscow, K 274, Krasnopresnenskaya nab., d. 2, Dom Sovetov.

Zorkin, Valery Dmitrievich

Chairman of the Constitutional Court of the Russian Federation.

Born on February 18, 1943 in the village of Konstantinovka, Maritime *krai*, Siberia; Russian; member of the CPSU until August 1991. In 1964 he graduated from the law faculty of Moscow State University, specializing in jurisprudence; he immediately began postgraduate studies there and in 1967 successfully presented his candidate dissertation on "The views of B. N. Chicherin on state and law" (LLM). He then joined the law faculty of Moscow State University as a lecturer, senior lecturer and assistant professor, specializing in the history of legal doctrine, including early Christian doctrine.

In 1978 he successfully presented his doctoral dissertation on "The positivist theory of law in Russia (historical critical research)" (LLD). In 1980 he moved to the Academy of the USSR Ministry of Internal Affairs, where he was professor and head of department of constitutional law and the theory of state and law. In 1991 he was a professor in the faculty of state-legal disciplines of the all-Union extra-mural school of law of the USSR Ministry of Internal Affairs.

From 1990 to 1991 Zorkin headed the group of experts in the RSFSR constitutional commission, and took part in drafting a new RSFSR constitution. On August 19, 1991 he signed the declaration of the group members and experts in the constitutional commission on the anti-constitutional coup being carried out by the Extraordinary Committee.

He has over 200 publications to his name including the book: *On the History of Bourgeois-Liberal Political Thought in Russia in the Second Half of the 19th and Beginning of the 20th Century* (Moscow 1975). His last publications before his election to the Constitutional Court were in specialist periodicals: *Pravovoe gosudarstvo* (*Rechtsstaat*) (1990); *Vlast i pravo* (Power and law) and *Sovety i partii v pravovom gosudarstve* (Soviets and Party in a *Rechtsstaat*) (1991).

He was nominated for election to the Constitutional Court by the deputies' group communists for democracy, and was elected a member on October 29, 1991, at the V Congress of People's Deputies, in the first round of voting. He received 753 votes for and 137 against. At the first meeting of the Constitutional Court in November 1991 he was elected its chairman.

In January 1993 he became the first recipient of the international prize, National Accord, which was awarded for "his civic behaviour on December 9-10, 1992, during the VII Congress of People's Deputies of Russia". The prize includes a cheque for US$5,000.

Zorkin regards the basic duties of the Constitutional Court to be its participation in the construction of a law-governed state (*Rechtsstaat*) in Russia, in helping to overcome the legal nihilism of the authorities and the citizens, the introduction, without any concessions, of the principle of the division of powers into the Russian political system and the defence of the constitutional order of the Russian Federation. In Zorkin's view the Constitutional Court is the natural and necessary implementer of democratic power. He regards himself as outside politics and is guided in his duties only by constitutional norms. The present Russian constitution is an old one but, according to Zorkin, it is better to be under a bad constitution than not having one at all. However, it is necessary to adopt a new constitution as soon as possible and draft a new federal treaty which would transform Russia into a confederation of sovereign states, affording great rights and privileges to the territory of Russia.

Zorkin appeared to be in sympathy with the reform policies of President Yeltsin until the VII Congress of People's Deputies in December 1992. The sharp confrontations between the President and Ruslan Khasbulatov, the Speaker, led to a breakdown in relations. Zorkin brought the two sides together and they all agreed on a compromise. The congress conceded that the President could call a referendum in the spring, but Zorkin later ruled the referendum unconstitutional. The constitution itself was internally inconsistent and conferred supreme power on both the congress and the President. Zorkin chose to interpret the constitution afterwards in favour of the congress.

He played an important role in the events surrounding President Yeltsin's address to the Russian people on March 20, 1993. He was aware beforehand of the contents of the speech and the preparation of a draft decree on introducing a special regime until the crisis of power had been resolved. Zorkin sent the President a letter warning him that the publication of the decree would amount to the suspension of the basic principles of the Russian constitution. It would also push society into a swamp of confrontation and chaos and lead to the collapse of authority. Shortly after the President's speech Zorkin appeared on Russian TV to declare it unconstitutional. However he had forgotten that in Russian law a statement is only unconstitutional when it is published in print.

The Constitutional Court then convened to consider the constitutionality and constitutional responsibility of the President and those who had prepared his address. There were meetings with Sergei Filatov and Sergei Shakhrai in order to clarify the circumstances surrounding the President's statement. Zorkin also saw Viktor Chernomyrdin, Aleksandr Rutskoi, Viktor Barannikov and Pavel Grachev, who reported on the situation and how to stabilize it. In a split decision the Court judged that the President had acted unconstitutionally in some matters but this did not amount to grounds for impeachment. The President removed the term "special regime" when the decree was published. The IX Congress of People's Deputies was immediately convened and Ruslan Khasbulatov, the Speaker, set the tone by launching a vitriolic attack on the President, but those who wanted him impeached were disappointed.

Relations between Zorkin and the Yeltsin camp deteriorated as he was judged to be in Khasbulatov's camp, but this may have been unfair. The President announced a referendum for April 25, 1993 to decide who ruled Russia, the President or the parliament. The latter, in turn, announced its own referendum for April 25 and invited the 106 million voters in the Russian Federation to decide whether they supported the President; whether they supported his economic and social policies since 1992; whether they wanted early presidential elections; and early parliamentary elections. Congress also imposed the condition that in order to win, at least 50% of the electorate had to vote yes.

For a time it looked as if there would be two referenda on April 25. However the President backed down and accepted the parliamentary referendum. His supporters took the issue to the Constitutional Court and it ruled that in order to win, the President only needed 50% of the votes cast on the day on the first two issues but needed 50% of the electorate to win questions three and four. Some observers regarded the Court decision as a compromise and influenced by politics. With a 60% turn out on the day it was virtually impossible for the President to win on the first two issues if the original stipulation of 50% of the electorate had stood. This would then have plunged Russia into a constitutional crisis. The President won a majority on questions one and two and the political situation stabilized. The Constitutional Court takes some of the credit for this.

Zorkin's wife, Tamara, is a specialist in political economy and their daughter is a student in the law faculty of Moscow State University. In his free time Zorkin likes to play the piano and engage in cross-country skiing. He lives in Moscow.

Zotin, Vladislav Maksimovich

President of the Republic of Mari El, Russian Federation.

Born in May 1942 in the village of Kilemary, Mari Autonomous Soviet Socialist Republic (ASSR). He is Mari and a graduate. He is a qualified engineer and began working in 1959 as a mechanic on the M. Gorky collective farm in the former Elasovsky *raion*. From 1960 to 1965 he studied in the institute for engineers in agricultural production, Moscow. After graduating he was chief engineer of the Paranginsky agricultural administration, in 1967 was elected first secretary of the *raion Komsomol* committee, and from 1969 to 1970 he was deputy chairman of the Paranginsky *raion* soviet executive committee. From 1970 to 1974 he was second secretary of the Mari Party *obkom*. From 1974 to 1976 he was a student at the Higher Party School of the Party Central Committee. Afterwards he was appointed an instructor of the Mari Party *obkom* and later the same year elected chairman of the Kuzhenersky *raion* Party committee. In 1985 he was elected first secretary of the Volzhsky city Party committee, and in 1990 was elected first deputy chairman, then Speaker (chairman) of the Supreme Soviet of the Mari ASSR.

Zotin initiated the declaration of the Presidium of the Supreme Soviet of the Mari republic on August 20, 1991 to the citizens of the republic. It stated that "given the lack of sufficient information" it called upon the people to "display calm and restraint" and also referred to the "need to resolve all the problems which had arisen by constitutional means". On December 14, 1991 he was elected President of the Mari El Republic. On December 24, 1991, at the IX session of the Supreme Soviet of the Mari Soviet Socialist Republic, he took the presidential oath.

He observed a neutral position during the VII Congress of People's Deputies and proposed that a balance of forces between the Supreme Soviet and government of the Russian Federation should be reached. He lives in Ioshkar Ola.

Zubov, Valery Mikhailovich

Acting Head of the Administration of Krasnoyarsk *krai*, Russian Federation.

He is Russian and as a young man took part in geological expeditions and served in the Soviet Army. He successfully presented his candidate (PhD (Econ)) and doctoral dissertation in economics (DSc (Econ)). He was dean of the faculty of economics of Krasnoyarsk State University and studied in the US. Recently he was one of the founders of the Troika commodity exchange in Krasnoyarsk.

On January 28, 1993 the resignation of A. F. Veprev, the head of the administration of Krasnoyarsk *krai*, for reasons of ill health, was accepted by presidential decree and Zubov was appointed acting head of the administration. On assuming office Zubov stated that economic reform had to be started immediately since Egor Gaidar had had no other option the previous year. However, many mistakes had been committed in implementing the reforms. He stressed the need to continue the reforms but to regulate the transition to the market by state authorities in a precise manner. He appealed for circumspection in introducing privatization, even to holding it back in 1993, because of the three different forms of land ownership, state, private and collective; and the latter had still not outlived its usefulness.

He advocated state regulation of the economy, a great deal of independence from Moscow and a firm stand against corruption. He regarded the question of a referendum as a dead end which only expressed the serious crisis of power in the country, the opposition of the legislative and executive branches of power. He appealed for everyone to avoid being dragged into political discussions and not to abandon practical matters, and recommended trying to reach an agreement. If this could not be achieved then preparations had to be made to hold a referendum. He lives in Krasnoyarsk.

Zyuganov, Gennady Andreevich

Co-chairman of the political council of the Front of National Salvation, Russia.

Born in 1944 in the village of Mymrino, Khotynetsky *raion*, Orlov *oblast*; Russian. He was a member of the CPSU until August 1991. He graduated from the Orlov State Pedagogical Institute and the Academy of Social Sciences of the Party Central Committee, and successfully presented his candidate dissertation in philosophy (PhD). He began his career in 1961 as a teacher in a village secondary school in Orlov *oblast*, then he served in the Soviet army and in 1967 he moved into trade union, *Komsomol* and Party work.

He taught in a pedagogical institute; was elected first secretary of a Party *raion* committee, Orlov; city *Komsomol* committee, Orlov; was secretary, then second secretary, Orlov city Party committee; head of the department of propaganda and agitation, Orlov Party *obkom* (1974-83); instructor and head of sector, department of propaganda, Party Central Committee, Moscow (1983-89); deputy head of the ideology department, Party Central Committee, Moscow (1989-90); member of the Politburo of the RSFSR Communist Party and also secretary of the Central Committee of the Russian Communist Party; and chairman of the permanent commission of the Central Committee of the Russian Communist Party on humanitarian and ideological problems. In 1992 he was elected chairman of the co-ordinating council of the national patriotic forces of Russia; also in 1992 he was appointed co-chairman of the Duma of the Russian national assembly, and also co-chairman of the political council of the Front of National Salvation, Russia. He is an influential figure in the conservative communist and nationalist opposition to President Yeltsin and the transition to a market economy, as he is a strong opponent of privatization and foreign involvement in the Russian economy. The front has organized demonstrations which have led to clashes with the security forces in Moscow. He lives in Moscow.

Rutskoi, Aleksandr Vladimirovich

Vice-President of Russia.

Born in 1947 in Kursk into a Russian family. His father and grandfather were military officers and his mother is still a barmaid in Kursk. Both his brothers are military officers. Rutskoi graduated from the Air Force higher school in Barnaul, Altai *krai*; from the Air Force Gagarin Academy in Moscow; and from the Academy of the General Staff of the USSR Armed Forces, Moscow, in 1990. In 1964, after leaving school, he became a fitter at an aviation plant, Kursk *oblast*; in 1965 he began his military service in the army and served as a military pilot in the group of Soviet forces in Germany (GDR). From 1985 to 1986 he was commander of an air force regiment, 40th army in Afghanistan; between 1987 and 1988 he was deputy chief of the Air Force pilot combat training centre, Lipetsk; in 1988, as a colonel, he was commander of the Air Force of the 40th army in Afghanistan. He was made a Hero of the Soviet Union. In Afghanistan, he flew 416 combat missions. He was shot down twice and severely wounded and was a prisoner-of-war of the *mujahidin* for six weeks in Pakistan.

During his time at the Academy of the General Staff he began to develop his political activities. He had joined the CPSU in 1970. After returning from Afghanistan he looked around for a political position. In March 1989 he became involved in the Moscow society "Fatherland", and on May 20, 1989, at its founding congress, was elected deputy chairman. The society had about 600 members and included a wide range of views ranging from national bolshevism to supporters of a return of the monarchy. Rutskoi stood as a candidate in the elections to the USSR Congress of People's Deputies in March 1989 but lost, being strongly opposed by the democratic election bloc. He was accused of being a "fascist with bloody hands".

In 1990 he became chief of the Air Force pilot combat centre, Lipetsk. He stood for election to the RSFSR Congress of People's Deputies in March 1990 and was returned for the Kursk constituency. His success was partly the result of the organizational work of the CPSU on his behalf. At the I Congress of People's Deputies he joined the newly-formed faction "Communists of Russia". He was elected to the RSFSR Supreme Soviet and in July 1990 became chairman of the Supreme Soviet committee on invalids, war and labour veterans, social welfare of the military and their families. He was also elected deputy chairman of the Supreme Soviet group of military and KGB officers. The RSFSR Communist Party, led by Ivan Polozkov, a party dominated by conservative apparatchiks, proposed him as a member of its Central Committee, but Rutskoi declined to become involved with the party. This indicated his change of position which was also reflected in the military, where many officers were refusing to obey the reactionary wing of the party and distanced themselves from it. He linked up with Yeltsin at the III RSFSR extraordinary Congress of People's Deputies in March 1991. At the congress the conservatives, primarily the Communists of Russia faction, were trying to overthrow Yeltsin by dismissing him as Speaker of the RSFSR parliament in order to prevent him standing as a candidate for the presidency of the RSFSR. They did not attain their objective, partly because Rutskoi formed his own faction, "Communists for Democracy", which, in alliance with the factions Democratic Russia (DemRossiya) and *Smena* (change), ensured victory for Yeltsin. Rutskoi's faction, Communists for Democracy, attracted 95 people's deputies. He had cleared the way for Yeltsin's presidential ambitions.

Rutskoi became known as an "honest, decent communist". His political views were a mélange of democratic, authoritarian, nationalist and patriotic concepts, and he also proposed reforms within the CPSU and state intervention in the interests of the military-industrial complex. In April 1991 Yeltsin chose him as his Vice-President, and parliament confirmed this move. Tactically Yeltsin was appealing to the military and to moderate, reform-minded communists, especially members of the *nomenklatura*. On June 12, 1991, Yeltsin and Rutskoi, with 57.3% of the votes, topped the poll in the presidential elections. Rutskoi did not want to restrict his initiatives to the Russian parliament and declared the democratization of the CPSU to be a goal. His target was not the democratic forces within the CPSU, but the core around the far right *Soyuz* (union). He regarded the withdrawal of the reform-minded communists (the Democratic Platform) from the CPSU in 1990 as a mistake, and appealed for the establishment of Communists for Democracy cells in all CPSU organizations in order to mobilize all progressive forces in the party. He maintained that the DemRossiya programme and the CPSU election programme agreed on most issues, but that the CPSU had reneged on its more progressive promises. He advocated the formation of a Democratic Party of the Communists of Russia, a party committed to a parliamentary path of development, which would be a counterweight to the Russian Communist Party. Many officers and Afghan veterans were attracted to Rutskoi's ideas and it appeared possible that this new party would come into being during the summer of 1991.

On July 2, 1991 Rutskoi was one of the signatories of an appeal to establish a Movement for Democratic Reform which would bring together all supporters of the concept of a new Soviet democratic federation. Others who signed were Eduard Shevardnadze, Aleksandr Yakovlev, Anatoly Sobchak, the mayor of Leningrad; Gavriil Popov, the mayor of Moscow; the radical economists Stanislav Shatalin and Nikolai Petrakov, and Arkady Volsky. A conference was planned for September 1991 which would bring together parties and movements from all republics to found a democratic party. The Communists for Democracy movement became part of the Movement for Democratic Reform.

During the attempted August 1991 coup Rutskoi never wavered in his support of Yeltsin. On August 19, at 11 pm, he appealed, as an "officer, colonel and hero of the Soviet Union" to "officers, soldiers and sailors" not to act against the people and "not to support the conspirators". The following day, he made a similar appeal to young people. Also on August 20 the executive committee of Rutskoi's party, the Democratic Party of the Communists of Russia, which was in the process of formation, called on communists to leave the CPSU. Rutskoi organized a Russian national guard to defend the White House, composed of Afghan veterans, Cossacks and members of various groups and movements. On August 21 he flew to the Crimea to "liberate" Gorbachev, accompanied him back to Moscow and ordered the arrest of the conspirators. Gorbachev rewarded him by promoting him on August 21 to major-general. After Yeltsin had banned the CPSU on August 23, the proposal to establish a widely-based opposition party collapsed. An added complication was that Eduard Shevardnadze and Aleksandr Yakovlev chose to support the already severely weakened Soviet President Gorbachev. Rutskoi and Arkady Volsky were left as the main proponents of a new movement. However this began to fragment quickly, and in Moscow on September 24, 1991, a group decided to establish the Russian Party of Democratic Transformation. This however remained linked to the Movement for Democratic Reform. Before its founding congress the movement consisted essentially of three parts: the People's Party of Free Russia, the Russian Party of Democratic Transformation, and the Republican Party of the Russian Federation (which still continued to play an active role in DemRossiya). The Movement for Democratic Reform was founded in Moscow on December 14, 1991 as a "free union of political parties, social organizations and individual members" who shared "democratic views" and a market economy. It aimed at providing "constructive support" to President Yeltsin, encouraging moves towards democracy, but opposing a shift to authoritarianism. The movement was later often criticized for being dominated by former party officials and members of the *nomenklatura*. There were also many industrial managers among the membership. It attracted communists after the banning of the CPSU, with the result that there were various groupings within it: industrialists, intellectuals from DemRossiya, conservative communists, and conservative patriots from *Soyuz* with imperial ambitions, who later formed themselves into the Russian All-people's Union. Of the 18 members of the political council of the movement, of which Rutskoi was one, there were seven former members of the Central Committee of the CPSU or the CC secretariat and at the founding congress 16 had occupied leading state positions. The strong personalities and divergent views of the leadership inevitably led to splits within the movement.

On October 26, 1991 the founding congress of the People's Party of Free Russia (PPFR) opened in Moscow. Rutskoi and his supporters thereby removed all references to communists from the title and stated that the new party was not a successor to the CPSU. Nevertheless the PPFR laid claim to some of the property of the CPSU. The programme of the PPFR revealed it as essentially a social democratic party. It opposed the Leninist concept of the *avant garde* party and all social groups should be treated equally. The party advocated a social market economy, a guaranteed minimum wage and the rapid privatization of small enterprises. The 600 delegates, despite the fact that the electoral law forbade independent political activity by the Vice-President, elected Rutskoi chairman. There were few leading personalities in the party. According to the party it had about 100,000 members in 62 regions in January 1992.

After the failed putsch, relations between Yeltsin and Rutskoi became cooler. Originally the Vice-President had, on paper, important responsibilities. However, on November 19, 1991 the President signed an order "on the responsibilities of the Vice-President" which in effect made him the co-ordinator of several low-ranking state committees, and involved him in a wide range of functions from nuclear safety to supervision of economic reform. In order to carry out his duties Rutskoi was provided with his own apparatus, but this only consisted of six persons. He also received the right to attend governmental meetings but was only to play a consultative role. Not surprisingly, Rutskoi felt offended and downgraded. His plans to organize a Russian national guard, to reform the Ministry of the Interior and to promote the conversion of military enterprises were stalled. On December 19, 1991 the President deprived him of some of his functions. In February 1992 the Vice-President was made responsible for agriculture which was a clear demotion. Rutskoi reacted by going over the head of the President and gave critical interviews to many leading newspapers. His views can be summarized as follows: the government's foreign policy is transforming Russia into a "banana republic" and the servant of the West. It is neglecting to defend the interests of Russians outside Russia; domestic policy is promoting the break-up of Russia; there is no real democracy in Russia, only anarchy and the "dictatorship of the street"; the military is disintegrating and is beginning to resemble "village forces"; the government's economic policy is making the population poor; the government is replete with incompetent ministers and officials who are only good at publishing decrees and instructions; the President is surrounded by incompetent people whose style is reminiscent of a "puppet theatre" and who endlessly engage in intrigues. Rutskoi proposed the following solutions: an economic state of emergency; the use of the mailed fist in relations with the successor states to the USSR; and the support of collective and state farms (and in so doing Rutskoi made common cause with the agrarian union parliamentary faction and a part of the Russian Unity bloc, made up of farm managers who opposed privatization of land). The Vice-President also advised regional leaders to stop the dissolution of collective and state farms in their locality. He supported those former party leaders who advocated strict state control of agricultural production through state orders. However, some of his proposals, such as the setting up of a federal centre for agrarian reform and an agricultural bank, received the approval of Yury Chernichenko, leader of the reform-oriented Russian Peasants' Party. In order to promote his ideas he toured the country and established close links with many in the military-industrial complex.

Rutskoi also seized upon another sensitive issue, the plight of the 25 million Russians living outside Russia. During the winter of 1991 to 1992 he visited the Chechen republic and Pridnestrovie many times. In the latter region he appealed for the 14th Russian Army to be deployed in support of "our people — Russians, Russian speakers and Cossacks", but the Russian government turned a deaf ear and Andrei Kozyrev, the Foreign Minister, had his hands full trying to rectify the damage being done to his foreign policy. Rutskoi declared that the Black Sea Fleet and the Crimea belonged to Russia, and this led to his being declared *persona non grata* in Ukraine. Surprisingly, President Yeltsin very seldom reacted to the sentiments of his deputy. However in parliament Rutskoi enjoyed growing support, and this led some observers to the conclusion that Russia was following a dual foreign policy. However he is clear about Russia's role in the world: "Russia is and must remain a great power".

The VI Congress of People's Deputies, in April 1992, was a turning-point in Russian politics. Although the conservative, communist bloc, Russian Unity, failed to overthrow Yeltsin and his reform government, it weakened the latter and succeeded in blocking a decision on privatization. Several significant personnel changes were made.

One of the main reasons for the weakening of the centrist and only mildly opposition forces was the conflict between the Russian Movement for Democratic Reform and the international movement. The latter has almost disappeared from the political stage. The Russian movement itself began to split. Nikolai Travkin's Democratic Party of Russia left; the New Russia bloc of parties (including the People's Party of Russia, the Peasants' Party, and the Social Democratic Party) also withdrew. Konstantin Borovoi founded the Party of Economic Freedom out of frustration at the lack of commitment to economic reform. The setting-up of the Renewal Party soon led to an alliance with *Smena* (change), Rutskoi's party and Travkin's party, and together they established the Civic Union.

The founding congress of the Civic Union began in Moscow on June 21, 1992, and was another attempt, after the failure of the Movement for Democratic Reform, to create a party capable of assuming government. Rutskoi and Arkady Volsky were leading figures, together with Aleksandr Vladislavlev and Sergei Filatov, first Deputy Speaker of the Russian Supreme Soviet. Two significant allies of Rutskoi's PPFR were the Renewal Party and the Democratic Party of Russia. The Renewal Party traced its origins to the scientific and technical union, set up in 1990, by the scientific and technical group in the USSR Supreme Soviet, the association of state enterprises and the united union of co-operatives. Its leadership came mostly from the military-industrial complex. It worked closely with the Central Committee of the CPSU. Rumour had it that the Party laundered money for it. It proved the base for the formation of the Russian Union of Industrialists and Entrepreneurs in January 1992. Volsky became president and Vladislavlev vice-president. It declared its support for the Russian leadership but criticized its economic policy.

The Renewal Party was set up in Moscow on May 30, 1992. Most members were industrial managers from the union of industrialists and entrepreneurs (2,130 large enterprises and 39 companies were registered members), but there were also those from local and city administrations as well as the free trade unions, the successors of the old official Soviet unions. The parliamentary factions *Smena*, the industrial union (a directors' lobby) and *Soglasie* (agreement), were very influential in Renewal. They accounted for about a third of deputies. The party offered Yeltsin qualified support, but its chief goal was Russia's unity and indivisibility. It opposed Gaidar's "shock therapy" and proposed the "soft" approach to the market. It declared its willingness to assume government and remained cool towards Western help. The 52 regional organizations of Renewal were dominated by the former Party *nomenklatura*, enterprise managers and the like. The new members of Yeltsin's government from April 1992 onwards were all members or closely associated with Rutskoi.

At the VII Russian Congress of People's Deputies, in December 1992, about 35% of the deputies were associated with Renewal. To its right were Russian Unity, with 30% of the deputies, and the bloc of Creative Forces with 20%. Only 15% of deputies supported the pro-reform, Yeltsin bloc. Hence Civic Union dominated the Congress and, not surprisingly, Viktor Chernomyrdin came from this bloc. The dismissal of Egor Gaidar, at the Congress, resulted in Civic Union entering into a government coalition with market reformers. However, Civic Union favoured a soft approach to the market; reliance on Russia's own resources and skills; state intervention in the economy so as to ensure the continued viability of enterprises, including providing cheap credit; the territorial integrity of Russia; vigorous defence of the rights of Russians outside Russia; and a minimum of concessions to the West.

Rutskoi enjoyed considerable support among Cossacks who have intervened in Pridnestrovie and South Ossetia. Many of Rutskoi's former associates were involved in the Russian National Assembly, a conservative, nationalist and patriotic association. Aleksandr Sterligov, a former KGB General and adviser in 1991 to Rutskoi, led the assembly. The PPFR and the Democratic Party of Russia were both members of the association of the citizens of the Russian Federation, which was set up on April 5, 1992.

During the tumultuous events of March 1993 when the Congress of People's Deputies attempted to impeach President Yeltsin after he had declared special rule on television, Rutskoi completely identified with Ruslan Khasbulatov, the Speaker, and the conservative communist majority in the Congress. Afterwards President Yeltsin gradually cut away the responsibilities of his number two and in September 1993 he suspended him as Vice-President, ostensibly while charges of corruption against him were investigated.

INDEX

Page numbers in bold indicate main entries in the Directory